# Lecture Notes in Computer Science 5414

Commenced Publication in 1973
Founding and Former Series Editors:
Gerhard Goos, Juris Hartmanis, and Jan van Leeuwen

## Editorial Board

Toshikazu Wada   Fay Huang   Stephen Lin (Eds.)

# Advances in Image and Video Technology

Third Pacific Rim Symposium, PSIVT 2009
Tokyo, Japan, January 13-16, 2009
Proceedings

 Springer

Volume Editors

Toshikazu Wada
Wakayama University, Department of Computer and Communication Sciences
930 Sakaedani, Wakayama-shi, Wakayama, Japan 640 8510
E-mail: twada@ieee.org

Fay Huang
National Ilan University, Institute of Computer Science and Information Engineering
No. 1, Sec. 1, Shen-Lung Rd., Yi-Lan, 26047 Taiwan, ROC
E-mail: fay@niu.edu.tw

Stephen Lin
Microsoft Research Asia, Beijing Sigma Center, 5003
No. 49, Zhichun Road, Beijing 100190, PRC
E-mail: stevelin@microsoft.com

Library of Congress Control Number: 2008942379

CR Subject Classification (1998): H.5.1, H.5, I.4, I.3, H.3-4, E.4

LNCS Sublibrary: SL 6 – Pattern Recognition, Graphics, Image Processing
and Computer Vision

ISSN        0302-9743
ISBN-10     3-540-92956-8 Springer Berlin Heidelberg New York
ISBN-13     978-3-540-92956-7 Springer Berlin Heidelberg New York



Typesetting: Camera-ready by author, data conversion by Scientific Publishing Services, Chennai, India
Printed on acid-free paper        SPIN: 12601424        06/3180        5 4 3 2 1 0

# Preface

We welcome you to the Third Pacific-Rim Symposium on Image and Video Technology (PSIVT 2009), sponsored by the National Institute of Informatics, Microsoft Research, and the Forum for Image Informatics in Japan. PSIVT 2009 was held in Tokyo, Japan, during January 13–16. The main conference comprised eight major themes spanning the field of image and video technology, namely, image sensors and multimedia hardware, graphics and visualization, image and video analysis, recognition and retrieval, multi-view imaging and processing, computer vision applications, video communications and networking, and multimedia processing. To heighten interest and participation, PSIVT also included workshops, tutorials, demonstrations and invited talks, in addition to the traditional technical presentations.

For the technical program of PSIVT 2009, a total of 247 paper submissions underwent a full review process. Each of these submissions was evaluated in a double-blind manner by a minimum of three reviewers. The review assignments were determined by a set of two to four Chairs for each of the eight themes. Final decisions were jointly made by the Theme Chairs, with some adjustments by the Program Chairs in an effort to balance the quality of papers among the themes and to emphasize novelty. Rejected papers with significant discrepancies in review evaluations received consolidation reports explaining the decisions.

In the end, there were 39 papers accepted for oral presentation and 57 for poster presentation. The review process was highly selective, yielding an acceptance rate of less than 40%. Because of the limited size of the symposium and the inevitable variability in the review process, we regret that some worthy papers have likely been excluded. However, we believe that a strong set of papers was identified, and an excellent program was assembled.

We would like to thank the following organizations for their cooperation in administering PSIVT 2009: ACM SIG Multimedia, IEEE Japan Council, IEEE Computer Society Japan Chapter, IPSJ SIG Computer Vision and Image Media, and IEICE TG Pattern Recognition and Media Understanding. We are also grateful to the International Information Science Foundation, the Tateisi Science and Technology Foundation, the Telecommunications Advancement Foundation, and the Tokyo Convention & Visitors Bureau for their generous support. In addition, we wish to acknowledge a number of people for their invaluable help in putting this symposium together. Many thanks to the Organizing Committee for their excellent logistical management, the Theme Chairs for their rigorous evaluation of papers, the reviewers for their considerable time and effort, and the authors for their outstanding contributions. We also wish to acknowledge the following individuals for their tremendous service to the symposium: Ako Maio, Yoko Imagawa, Sakie Suzuki, Reiko Murano, Ayumi Shimizu, and the volunteer students from the University of Tokyo and Chiba University.

We hope that you will find the proceedings enjoyable, enlightening and thought provoking. We wish you a very memorable PSIVT.

January 2009
Toshikazu Wada<br>Fay Huang<br>Stephen Lin

# Organization

## Organizing Committee

### General Chairs

| | |
|---|---|
| Akihiro Sugimoto | National Institute of Informatics, Japan |
| Minoru Etoh | NTT DoCoMo, Japan |
| Domingo Mery | Universidad Católica de Chile, Chile |

### Program Chairs

| | |
|---|---|
| Toshikazu Wada | Wakayama University, Japan |
| Fay Huang | National Ilan University, Taiwan |
| Stephen Lin | Microsoft Research Asia, China |

### Demo/Exhibit Chairs

| | |
|---|---|
| Hideo Saito | Keio University, Japan |
| Kazuhiko Sumi | Mitsubishi Electric Corporation, Japan |

### Workshop/Tutorial Chairs

| | |
|---|---|
| Rin-ichiro Taniguchi | Kyushu University, Japan |
| Noboru Babaguchi | Osaka University, Japan |

### Local Arrangements Chairs

| | |
|---|---|
| Yoichi Sato | The University of Tokyo, Japan |
| Imari Sato | National Institute of Informatics, Japan |

### Finance Chair

| | |
|---|---|
| Yasushi Yagi | Osaka University, Japan |

### Publication Chairs

| | |
|---|---|
| Itaru Kitahara | University of Tsukuba, Japan |
| Atsushi Shimada | Kyushu University, Japan |

### Publicity Chairs

| | |
|---|---|
| Vincent Nozick | Université Paris-Est, France |
| Yo-Sung Ho | Gwangju Institute of Science and Technology, Korea |

## Industrial Liaison Chair

Osamu Yamaguchi        Toshiba Corporation, Japan

## Local Arrangements Committee

Takahiro Okabe         The University of Tokyo, Japan
Hiroshi Mo             National Institute of Informatics, Japan
Mihoko Shimano         JST PRESTO, Japan

## Technical Support Staff

Yoshihiko Mochizuki    Chiba University, Japan
Hiroaki Natsumi        Chiba University, Japan

## Steering Committee

Wen-Nung Lie           National Chung Cheng University, Taiwan
Kap Luk Chan           Nanyang Technological University, Singapore
Yung-Chang Chen        National Tsing Hua University, Taiwan
Yo-Sung Ho             Gwangju Institute of Science and Technology,
                         Korea
Reinhard Klette        The University of Auckland, New Zealand
Mohan M. Tivedi        University of California, San Diego, USA
Domingo Mery           Universidad Católica de Chile, Chile

## Award Panelists

Minoru Etoh            NTT DoCoMo, Japan
Fay Huang              National Ilan University, Taiwan
Katsushi Ikeuchi       The University of Tokyo, Japan
Hong-Yuan Mark Liao    Academia Sinica, Taiwan
Stephen Lin            Microsoft Research Asia, China
Toshikazu Wada         Wakayama University, Japan
Michael S. Brown       National University of Singapore, Singapore

## Theme Chairs

### Image Sensors and Multimedia Hardware

Moshe Ben-Ezra         Microsoft Research Asia, China
Don Murray             Point Grey Research, Canada

### Graphics and Visualization

Brendan McCane         University of Otago, New Zealand
Ping Tan               National University of Singapore, Singapore

## Image and Video Analysis

| | |
|---|---|
| Hidekata Hontani | Nagoya Institute of Technology, Japan |
| Chiou-Ting Candy Hsu | National Tsing Hua University, Taiwan |
| Sang Wook Lee | Sogang University, Korea |
| Yasuyuki Matsushita | Microsoft Research Asia, China |

## Recognition and Retrieval

| | |
|---|---|
| Anton van den Hengel | The University of Adelaide, Australia |
| Shang-Hong Lai | National Tsing Hua University, Taiwan |
| Shuicheng Yan | National University of Singapore, Singapore |

## Multi-view Imaging and Processing

| | |
|---|---|
| Hansung Kim | University of Surrey, UK |
| Takayuki Okatani | Tohoku University, Japan |

## Computer Vision Applications

| | |
|---|---|
| Chu-Song Chen | Academia Sinica, Taiwan |
| Toshio Ueshiba | National Institute of Advanced Industrial Science and Technology, Japan |
| Dong Xu | Nanyang Technological University, Singapore |

## Video Communications and Networking

| | |
|---|---|
| Shueng-Han Gary Chan | Hong Kong University of Science and Technology, Hong Kong |
| Jiro Katto | Waseda University, Japan |
| Jin-Jang Leou | National Chung Cheng University, Taiwan |

## Multimedia Processing

| | |
|---|---|
| Chil-Woo Lee | Chonnam National University, Korea |
| Chia-Wen Lin | National Tsing Hua University, Taiwan |
| Tian-Tsong Ng | Institute for Infocomm Research, Singapore |

# Program Committee

| | |
|---|---|
| Aceves, Mariano | Au, Oscar |
| Ahmad, Imran | Bando, Yukihiro |
| Ahmed, Amr | Barron, John |
| Amano, Toshiyuki | Benes, Bedrich |
| Ariki, Yasuo | Bhatia, Sanjiv K. |
| Arnold, John | Carrasco, Miguel |
| Arns, Laura | Cesar, Roberto Marcondes |

Chan, Kap Luk
Chen, Chia-Yen
Chen, Chi-Fa
Chen, Homer
Chen, Hwann-Tzong
Chen, Jing
Chen, Jing-Fung
Chen, Li
Chen, Mei-Juan
Chen, Yong-Sheng
Cheng, Shyi-Chyi
Chiang, Tihao
Chien, Chang Ee
Chow, Gloria
Dimililer, Kamil
Doretto, Gianfranco
Eng, How-Lung
Escribano, Gerardo F.
Estrada, Giovani Gomez
Favaro, Paolo
Fofi, David
Fookes, Clinton
Frery, Alejandro
Fuh, Chiou-Shann
Fujii, Toshiaki
Fujiki, Jun
Fujimura, Makoto
Fujiyoshi, Hironobu
Fukui, Kazuhiro
Gao, Sheng
Gawley, Darren
Gregor, Jens
Guo, Jiun-In
Guo, Liwei
Haga, Tetsuji
Han, Tony Xu
Hei, Xiaojun
Hernandez, Sergio
Hill, Rhys
Hitschfeld, Nancy
Hlavac, Vaclav
Ho, Yo-Sung
Hoey, Jesse
Hotta, Kazuhiro
Hotta, Seiji

Hou, Ling
Hsieh, Jun-Wei
Hsu, Hui-Huang
Huang, Hui-Yu
Huang, Kaiqi
Huang, Kun
Huang, Yea-shuan
Ide, Ichiro
Iocchi, Luca
Irarrazabal, Pablo
Iwahashi, Masahiro
Iwai, Yoshio
Iwamura, Masakazu
Jeon, Byeungwoo
Jin, Hailin
Jin, Xing
Kakarala, Ramakrishna
Kameda, Yoshinari
Kanbara, Masayuki
Kato, Takekazu
Kawamoto, Kazuhiko
Kawashima, Hiroaki
Kenmochi, Yukiko
Kise, Koichi
Kitamoto, Asanobu
Koch, Reinhard
Kodama, Kazuya
Koeppen, Mario
Koschan, Andreas
Kubota, Akira
Kuo, Tien-Ying
Kurita, Takio
Lee, Gwo Giun
Lee, Yung-Lyul
Li, Fajie
Li, Qiming
Li, Shipeng
Li, Xuelong
Liao, Chia-Te
Lien, Jenn-Jier
Lin, Guo-Shiang
Lin, Huei-Yung
Lin, Wei-Yang
Liu, Damon Shing-Min
Liu, Qingshan

Lopez, Jorge Azorin
Lu, Chun-Shien
Lu, Le
Lu, Yan
Ma, Kai-Kuang
Ma, Mengyao
Masuda, Takeshi
Mei, Tao
Miyazaki, Daisuke
Mukunoki, Masayuki
Muramatsu, Shogo
Naito, Sei
Nakazawa, Atsushi
Narasimhan, Srinivasa
Nasilowski, Simeon
Neumann, Jan
Nobuhara, Shohei
Ogunbona, Philip
Okada, Ryuzo
Omachi, Shinichiro
Palma-Amestoy, Rodrigo
Pang, Henry
Pang, Yanwei
Park, In Kyu
Petkov, Nicolai
Pineda, Javier Vega
Pistori, Hemerson
Pizarro, Luis
Qing, Laiyun
Rivara, Maria Cecilia
Rodriguez, Ramon M.
Romero, Arturo Espinosa
Roy, Sujoy
Rudomin, Isaac
Sakai, Tomoya
Sakano, Hitoshi
Samal, Ashok
Sato, Jun
Satoh, Shin'ichi
Schechner, Yoav
Senda, Shuji
Seo, Yongduek
Shakunaga, Takeshi
Shan, Shiguang
Shen, Day-Fann

Shih, Sheng-Wen
Shimizu, Ikuko
Sim, Dong Gyu
Song, Mingli
Soria-Frisch, Aureli
Sridharan, Mohan
Stolz, Christophe
Su, Po-Chyi
Sugaya, Yasuyuki
Sun, Jian
Swaminathan, Rahul
Tai, Yu-Wing
Takahashi, Keita
Takatsuka, Masahiro
Tamaki, Toru
Tan, Robby
Tang, Chih-Wei
Tat, Ewe Hong
Tavares, Joao Manuel
Tejos, Cristian
Teng, Chin-Hung
Teschner, Matthias
Tourapis, Alexis M.
Tsai, Y. Tim
Uchida, Seiichi
Ukita, Norimichi
Umeda, Kazunorhi
Urahama, Kiichi
Vazquez, Carlos
Verges, Llahi Jaume
Wang, Liang
Wang, Wen-hao
Wang, Ye-Kui
Wei, Li-Yi
Wei, Shou-Der
Wei, Yichen
Wilburn, Bennett
Wilkinson, Michael
Wu, Chuan
Wu, Xiaojun
Wu, Yannan
Xiao, Rong
Yamasaki, Toshihiko
Yanai, Keiji
Yang, Jar-Ferr

Yang, Su
Yang, Yi
Yau, Wei Yun
Yeh, Chia Hung
Yian, Chee Hoo
Zeng, Gang
Zeng, Yi-Chong

Zhang, Li
Zhang, Weiwei
Zheng, Yuanjie
Zhou, Huiyu
Zhu, Yanmin

## Additional Reviewers

Bhotika, Rahul
Blunsden, Scott
Chang, Shih-Hsu
Chang, Ju Yong
Chen, Wen-Jan
Chen, Ying
Chiang, Jui-Chiu
Deng, Cheng
Elinas, Pantelis
Gambini, Juliana
Goncalves, Wesley
Kim, Chang-Su
Latif, Ali
Lee, Donghyuk
Lee, Soochahn
Lin, Guo-Shiang
Lin, Wei-Yang
Munkberg, Jacob

Niu, Zhenxing
Odakura, Valguima
Shen, Li
Souza, Kleber De
Stavrakakis, John
Takahashi, Tomokazu
Takamatsu, Jun
Tan, Evan
Wang, Chieh-Chih
Wang, Meng
Wen, Jing
Wu, Hsien-Huang P.
Wu, Jiunn-Lin
Xiao, Bing
Yang, Mau-Tsuen
Zou, Hua

## Sponsoring Institutions

National Institute of Informatics
Microsoft Research
The Forum for Image Informatics in Japan
ACM SIG Multimedia
IEEE Japan Council
IEEE Computer Society Japan Chapter
IPSJ SIG Computer Vision and Image Media
IEICE TG Pattern Recognition and Media Understanding
The International Information Science Foundation
The Tateisi Science and Technology Foundation
The Telecommunications Advancement Foundation

# Table of Contents

## Faces and Pedestrians



## Panoramic Images



## Local Image Analysis

## Organization and Grouping



## Multiview Geometry



## Detection and Tracking

## Computational Photography and Forgeries



## Coding and Steganography



## Recognition and Search

## Reconstruction and Visualization



## Poster 1

## Poster 2

## Poster 3

# A Self-tuning People Identification System from Split Face Components


Maria De Marsico[2], Michele Nappi[1], and Daniel Riccio[1]

[1] Universitá Degli Studi di Salerno,
via Ponte Don Melillo, 84084, Fisciano, Salerno, Italy
{mnappi,driccio}@unisa.it
[2] Universitá Degli Studi di Roma - La Sapienza,
via Salaria 113, 00198, Roma, Italy
demarsico@di.uniroma1.it



**Abstract.** Multimodal systems can solve a number of problems found in unimodal approaches. We experimented going further along this line, by dividing the face into distinct regions (components) and processing each of them within a single subsystem. Such subsystems are then embedded in a more complex multicomponent architecture. In this way, typical tools of multimodal systems, such as reliability margins or fusion schemes, can be usefully extended to the single face biometry. An additional innovation element in this work is the definition of a global system auto-verification and auto-tuning policy able to produce a significant accuracy enhancement. The paper explores three integration architectures with different subsystem interconnection degree, demonstrating that a tight component interaction increases system accuracy and allows identifying unstable subsystems.


## 1 Introduction

The idea of considering the face as the union of distinct regions is not new in literature, and yet few significant examples exist at present. Poggio and Heisele deal with component-based face recognition [1], focusing on the pose problem. Face is partitioned into regions with limited overlap, each classified using linear operators, e.g. Principal Component Analysis (PCA) or Support Vector Machine (SVM). The superiority over global recognition systems suggests this as a solution for more face recognition problems, e.g. expression, lighting, or occlusions. However, such multicomponent approach inherits issues like normalization, fusion, and reliability of single responses. Most researches stop once regions and fusion modalities have been fixed, merely certifying the superiority of component-based approaches. An exception is [2] by Harandi et al., exploring the hierarchical combination of a global system with a component-based one, which activates when the former cannot return a response with a sufficient score. However, the component-based step is not even started if the first system chooses the wrong class, yet with high confidence. No work in present literature systematically investigates the different possibilities to combine single scores produced


T. Wada, F. Huang, and S. Lin (Eds.): PSIVT 2009, LNCS 5414, pp. 1–12, 2009.

by facial components, in terms of fusion levels, integration schemes, and reliability margins. The main contribution of this paper is therefore the definition of a framework integrating the main concepts of both component-based facial recognition and of multimodal authentication. The proposed system partitions the face image into its constituent regions. Afterwards, each of them is considered as a separate subsystem, which can be integrated with all the others in a multimodal schema. Issues introduced by such new perspective make up further investigation topics in this work. We chose AR-Faces database as a test-bed for our study, as it contains a sufficiently varied set of distortions and a number of subjects suited to the goal. As for the feature extraction process, we chose a fractal-based approach, which is robust to local distortions [3].

## 2   Feature Extraction

The algorithm exploited to extract features from face components is based on the Partitioned Iterated Function Systems (PIFS). In such technique, the original image $I$ is divided into a set $R = r_1, r_2, \ldots, r_{|R|}$ of disjoint square regions, called ranges, which are a covering of $I$. A set of larger regions $D = d_1, d_2, \ldots, d_{|D|}$ called domains, is extracted from $I$. The side length of a domain is twice that of a range. Domains can overlap, and are much more numerous than ranges. The image $I$ is encoded range by range; each range $r$ is approximated by a domain $d$ according to an affine transformation, whose parameters are computed by solving a least square problem. The approximating domain $d$ is chosen so as to minimize the quadratic error with respect to the Euclidean norm. PIFS have been adapted to recognize face [3], by encoding only a selected set of ranges. The original image is divided into interest regions, namely eyes, nose and mouth. Location of regions is performed using an object detector based on Haar features [4], and implemented in the OpenCV library [5] and exploiting data provided in [6], in particular Haar Cascades. A fixed number of entry points are identified on each region. Entry points, for example eye or mouth corners, are in the same positions for every subject. For each entry point in each region, the adopted algorithm extracts the range whose upper left corner corresponds to it, and approximates such range by a domain. In order to make the method robust to image shifts, ranges close to the the entry point are also considered and approximated. In a revised version of the technique, entry points are located on a fixed grid and this change provides better results. The best approximating domains are gradually clustered according to an on-line algorithm. The result obtained at the end of the feature extraction process is a list of centroids, each representing the characterizing element of a cluster of approximating domains. Each centroid $C$ stores three main pieces of information: the $C_x$ and $C_y$ coordinates and the $C_{std}$ variance, computed as the mean value of the corresponding feature of all domains in the cluster. As the algorithm progresses, domains are clustered according to their distance from the present centroids. A list of centroids is obtained for each interest region. For a discussion about algorithm parameters (number of range/domain, clustering options, number of centroids) see [3]). From this point on, we present three possible solutions for the recognition problem.

## 3   The Integration Scheme

Going further along the approach by Heisele and Poggio [1], we propose three architectures with increasing complexity, from a plain component-based method to a component-based self-tuning method). This last architecture, which is significantly different from the state of art in literature, will be presented in the next section. The algorithm implemented by the recognition systems to classify the single components is always the same presented above. Therefore, the reported different performances can be unequivocally ascribed to the peculiar features of the different architectures. This consideration adds value to the experimental results in terms of consistency and readability.

### 3.1   The Plain Component-Based Protocol

In the Plain Component-Based Protocol (PCBP), the lists of centroids obtained through PIFS for the four face interest regions are chained in a single feature vector $V$, characterizing the whole face. We have a single recognition module. Such approach is comparable to component-based methods in literature [1]. A query image undergoes the same process, and the recognition module compares its feature vector with stored ones. The comparison between vectors $V_1$ and $V_2$ exploits an ad hoc distance function. For each centroid $C(x, y) \in V_1$, $V_2$ is searched for the centroid $\bar{C}(x, y)$ that is closest to $C(x, y)$ with respect to Euclidean distance, and the difference $|C_{std} - \bar{C}_{std}|$ is computed to obtain a difference vector $V_{diff}$. The average value $\bar{V}_{diff} = E[V_{diff}]$ of the vector components is computed, and all the values in $V_{diff}$ higher than $\bar{V}_{diff}$ are discarded. In this way, the algorithm is made more robust with respect to occlusions. A detailed discussion about the computed vector distance can be found in [3].

### 3.2   The Parallel Protocol

The first evolution takes to the Parallel Protocol (PP). PIFS are applied to each face region, as in Section 3.1, except that the four feature vectors are not chained. Each one is stored in a distinct database (left eyes, right eyes, etc.). Each component feeds an independent subsystem. In the same way, a query image is divided into the four relevant regions. The four corresponding component subsystems work in parallel and independently, each producing a list of subjects from its specific database; list elements include the ID of a database subject and a numeric score expressing its similarity with the input. Each list is ordered by such similarity, then the four lists are processed by a fusion module to obtain the global response. Such procedure allows further differences from the base schema in Section 3.1, because two elements, which are peculiar of multimodal systems, can be imported here in a component-based system:

- **Reliability Margins:** Subsystems might not be equally reliable, due to the possibly different quality of face regions from time to time. An unreliable response is a valid reason to perform a further check. The definition of a measure for response *reliability* is then a crucial step for fusion. Some solutions use margins, measuring the "risk" associated to a single subsystem response after observing its scores. Poh and Bengio [7] introduce a confidence margin based on False Acceptance Rate (FAR) and False Rejection Rate (FRR). Many responses are marked as reliable, as the margin relies on an estimate of the actual distribution of genuine/impostor subjects' scores. This might be inappropriate when very high security is required. Moreover, frequentist approaches assume that the scores of the testing and development sets always originate from similar distributions. We adopt the new System Response Reliability (SRR) margin [8], based on a system/gallery dependent metric, and measuring the ability of separating genuine subjects from impostors on a single probe basis. Therefore, in our approach, each subsystem $T_k$ produces a *reliability measure* $srr_{k,i}$ for each response $s_{k,i}$. Moreover, each subsystem $T_k$ is characterized by a threshold $th_k$, such that a response $s_{k,i}$ is considered as reliable only if $srr_{k,i} \geq th_k$.
- **Fusion Policies:** Different policies exist for fusion. Veeramachaneni et al [9] investigate decision level fusion in a binary hypotheses-testing problem, and in particular the selection of the best subset from different fusion rules, to optimize FAR or FRR. Apart from the limitations of the approach, the interesting observations are that, for 2 classifiers fusion, AND and OR rules constitute a very important set (out of 16 possible ones), and that, as the number of classifiers increases, the optimal fusion rules are constructed from these two, giving better results than Averaged Sum Rule. This suggests that, despite the variety of fusion policies, we can assume that AND and OR generally represent a suitable choice. In our case, we have a system $S$ composed by 4 subsystems $T_k$, $(k = 1, 2, 3, 4)$, processing right eye, left eye, nose and mouth respectively, each exploiting a gallery $G_k$, $(k = 1, 2, 3, 4)$ of components for the same number of identities. Notice that each identity in the set $H$ of enrolled subjects cane have more than one image in each single gallery. Our fusion rules exploit the above mentioned System Response Reliability (SRR). Each subsystem is able to compute a value $srr_{k,i}$ estimating the reliability associated to its $i$-th response. Such values are normalized in the range $[0, 1]$ for comparability. As discussed above, for each subsystem $T_k$ a threshold $th_k$ is estimated, and possibly updated [8], above which its reliability is satisfactory enough. As for *OR*, the combined response is valid if at least one subsystem response reliability is above the corresponding threshold; the system returns the identity returned by the subsystem with the higher reliability above the corresponding threshold. In *AND* policy, the combined response is valid only if all reliabilities are above the corresponding thresholds; the system returns the identity with the minimum weighted sum of distances from the probe, where weights are the reliability indexes.

We still have to determine the single thresholds $th_k$. They can be fixed in advance, and remain fixed in time, or they can be computed and updated according to obtained responses. A compromise between the number of reliable responses and the system error rate must be obtained. Too high thresholds make the system too restrictive, with a low error rate but also a low number of acceptances, while too low ones risk canceling the advantages of the reliability measure. Assume that $T_k$ has executed $M$ times, producing the set $\{s_{k,1}, \ldots, s_{k,M}\}$ of responses. The corresponding reliability measures are combined in a set $RH = \{srr_{k,1}, \ldots, srr_{k,M}\}$ containing the history of system behaviour (reliability history). The value to assign to $th_k$ is strictly correlated to $RH$ features, in particular to the average and to the variance [8] of its elements. A high $E[RH]$ means that system responses are generally reliable and that the corresponding threshold can be proportionally high. On the other hand, the variance $\sigma[RH]$ measures the stability of $T_k$. The best situation is then when $RH$ elements have a high average and a low variance, so that it is possible to fix a high value for $th_k$. We can summarize the above observations in the formula:

$$th_k = \frac{E[RH]^2 - \sigma[RH]}{E[RH]}, \tag{1}$$

The system, in particular $th_k$ thresholds, has been adjusted according to a set of faces with similar features to those of the set used for identification tests; the two sets are different and disjoint.

## 4    A Self-tuning Architecture: The Supervised Protocol

A further re-examination of the classical component-based schema takes to system self-tuning, with a much more flexible and robust architecture. The main limit of architectures in Section 3 is that they do not seize the main advantage of considering the facial identification system as a multicomponent architecture. Each component works independently and final results give no feedback for the overall system. Formula 1 is good for computing and updating $th_k$ thresholds for single reliability indexes, according to the corresponding subsystem behaviour; however, it only accounts for that subsystem. On the contrary, assume the existence of a *supervisor module* (Supervised Protocol - SP) exploiting single subsystem responses and their reliability to compute the final global response, and using the latter to evaluate the overall system state and update its parameters (Fig. 1). Such module would implement an algorithm to update single thresholds also according to the behavior of the other subsystems, so converging to an optimal configuration independently from the starting $\{th_1, th_2, th_3, th_4\}$ configuration. The algorithm distinguishes two cases:

- No identity is retrieved with more votes than the others, i.e. more identities $I_j, j \in \{1, 2, \ldots, |H|\}$ share the same number of votes. Notice that this case also applies when retrieved identities are all different, with 1 vote each. If at least one $T_k$ in any such group has $SRR_k > th_k$, the response is marked as

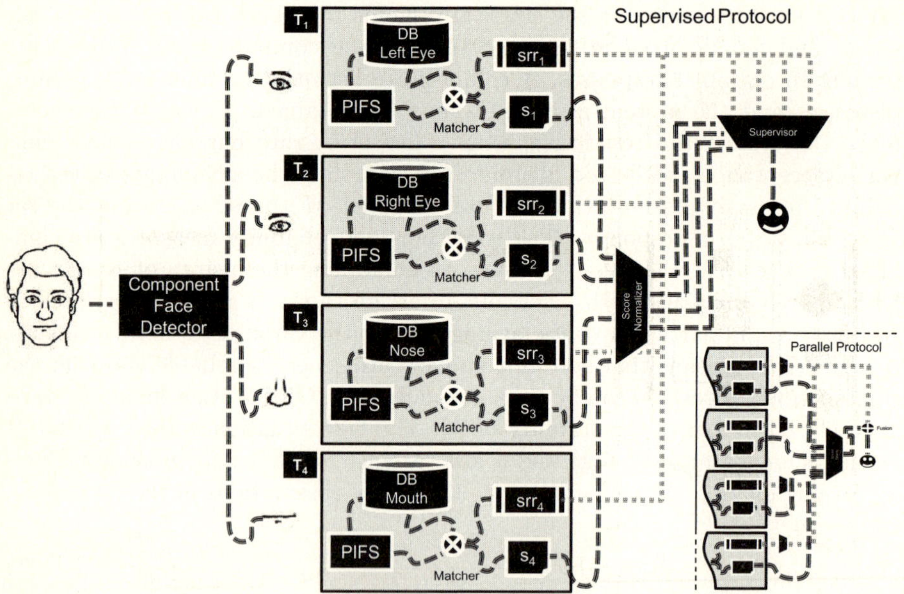


**Fig. 1.** The architecture of the supervised protocol

reliable, and the system returns the identity retrieved by the subsystem with the higher $SRR_k > th_k$, otherwise the response is marked as unreliable.
– One identity $I_j$ gets more votes than the others. $I_j$ is returned and the response is marked as reliable.

In both cases, if the response is reliable, each subsystem $T_k$ voting for the returned identity is rewarded by lowering its threshold $th_k$ by an updating step $us$, unless its current $srr_k$ is already above $th_k$. Each other subsystem $T_k$ is penalized by increasing its threshold $th_k$ by the updating step $us$, unless its current $srr_k$ is already below the respective $th_k$. In this way the supervisor module lowers thresholds of subsystems voting in agreement, considering such behavior a confirmation of reliability, and increases thresholds of discordant ones, compensating possible distortions (local persistent distortions like lighting variations, dirt on lens). Pseudo-code of the resulting supervised face protocol in Fig. 2.

Such an architecture does not need an adjustment phase, since the system can start from a default configuration of its parameters and converge in any case towards an optimal one. The speed to reach such latter configuration is a significant system feature, so that it is important to define how to measure it. As we want to simulate the dynamic behavior of an online identification system, we assume that system time is beaten by performed recognition operations; we define a *probe sequence* $P = \{p_1, p_2, \ldots, p_n\}$ as a series of $n$ probes presented to the system, sharing the same acquisition characteristics (normal conditions, right light, glasses, scarf, dirty lens). A system equilibrium state (*steady state*) is given by the consecutive instants when threshold fluctuations are lower than a

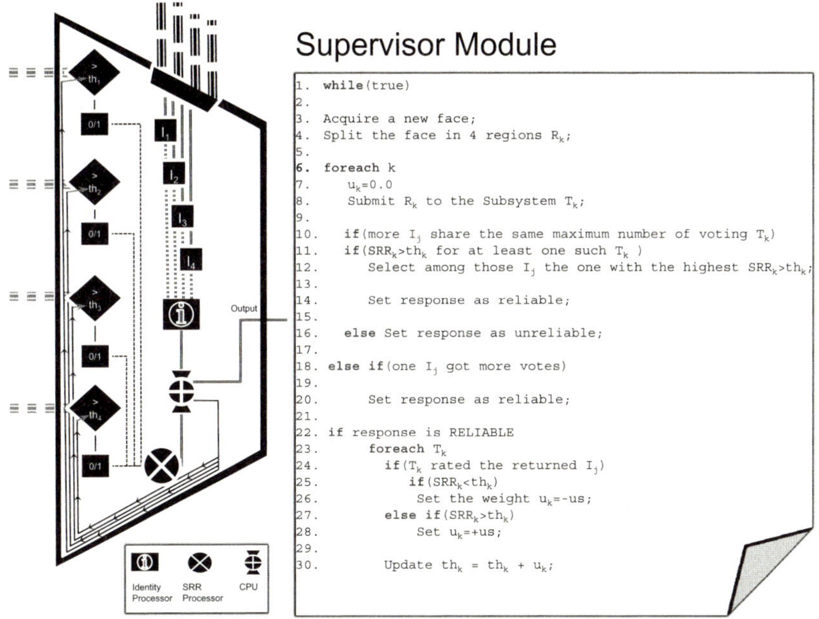


```
1.   while(true)
2.
3.   Acquire a new face;
4.   Split the face in 4 regions R_k;
5.
6.   foreach k
7.       u_k=0.0
8.       Submit R_k to the Subsystem T_k;
9.
10.      if(more I_j share the same maximum number of voting T_k)
11.      if(SRR_k>th_k for at least one such T_k )
12.         Select among those I_j the one with the highest SRR_k>th_k;
13.
14.         Set response as reliable;
15.
16.      else Set response as unreliable;
17.
18.  else if(one I_j got more votes)
19.
20.         Set response as reliable;
21.
22.  if response is RELIABLE
23.         foreach T_k
24.            if(T_k rated the returned I_j)
25.               if(SRR_k<th_k)
26.                  Set the weight u_k=-us;
27.            else if(SRR_k>th_k)
28.                  Set u_k=+us;
29.
30.            Update th_k = th_k + u_k;
```

**Fig. 2.** The pseudo-code of the Supervisor Module

fixed $\mu$, while *convergence speed* of a subsystem $\lambda_k$ is defined as the ratio between the total variation of its threshold and the number of instants needed to obtain such transition. Total system convergence speed is defined as the minimum speed among all its subsystems, i.e. $\lambda = min_k\lambda_k$, $k \in \{1, 2, 3, 4\}$.

## 5   Experimental Results

Our tests exploited AR-Faces database [10]. It consists of 126 persons (70 males and 56 females), each acquired in two different sessions with 13 image sets each. Sets differ in expression (1 neutral, 2 smile, 3 anger, 4 scream), illumination (5 left light, 6 right light, 7 all side light), presence/absence of occlusions (8 sun glasses, 11 scarf), or combinations (9 sun glasses and left light, 10 sun glasses and right light, 12 scarf and left light, 13 scarf and right light). Sets 14 to 26 of second session present the same conditions as 1 to 13. Neutral images from the set 1 have been considered as the system gallery. Seven probe sets (2, 3, 4, 5, 6, 8, 11) have been used for testing. Adopted measures for accuracy are Recognition Rate (RR), Equal Error Rate (EER) and Number of Reliable Responses (NRR).

### 5.1   Comparisons among the Three Architectures

In examining results, bear in mind that we are applying a decomposition to a biometry (the face) which is usually processed as a single overall recognition feature. We chose different test configurations with probe sequences varying in distortion typology. Notice that PCBP was used without SRR support (responses are always considered as reliable), and that PP was augmented with SRR using AND policy as in Section 3.2.

In most cases, PP offers worse performances than PCBP, which is in general robust to occlusions and local distortions. Such result can be ascribed to the fact that single subsystems do not have any information about all the others. In SP, the supervisor module collects information from different subsystems and accordingly changes their parameters, so that they are influenced by what is happening within the global system. Such stronger interconnection among subsystems should increase system accuracy, as confirmed by experimental results.

To clarify the interpretation of the experiments, we notice that each of the selected AR-Faces sets can be considered as a sequence $P$ of test images, sequentially submitted to the system. The initial thresholds configuration is set at $\{th_1 = 0.0,\ th_2 = 0.0,\ th_3 = 0.0,\ th_4 = 0.0\}$, i.e. all responses are initially considered as reliable. The updating step $us$ is fixed at 0.05. Table 1 shows that RR obtained with SP is comparable, or in some cases even better, than with PCBP, also obtaining a lower EER. Notice that the Number of Reliable Responses (NRR) obtained with PCBP is always equal to the total number of responses, as no SRR is used. We focus attention on set 4. In this case the number of reliable responses is quite low, only 50, but such as to guarantee a RR of 0.76, definitely higher than that obtained with the global method. If we consider the sets of equilibrium thresholds (last four columns) reached by the system for sets 2, 3 and 4 , we can see that nose and mouth, as highly unstable regions, often disagreeing with the other subsystems, are penalized with much higher thresholds ($th_3$ and $th_4$) for reliability indexes . The behavior on sets 5 and 6 confirms what stated above, as SP is able to reach higher RR values, yet with a lower EER and a quite high number of reliable responses. The sets of equilibrium thresholds reached by the system perfectly agree with the variations

**Table 1.** Performance comparison on different probes from AR-Faces among the three architectures: Plain Component-Based Protocol (PCBP), Parallel Protocol (PP) and Supervised Protocol (SP)

| SUBSET | | PCBP | PP | EXPRESSION VARIATIONS SP | | | | |
|---|---|---|---|---|---|---|---|---|
| | | | | PERF. | $th_1$ | $th_2$ | $th_3$ | $th_4$ |
| SET 2 | RR | 0.92 | 0.89 | 0.94 | | | | |
| | EER | 0.07 | 0.05 | 0.03 | 0.15 | 0.30 | 0.40 | 0.70 |
| | NRR | 126 | 38 | 120 | | | | |
| SET 3 | RR | 0.95 | 0.98 | 0.94 | | | | |
| | EER | 0.05 | 0.03 | 0.03 | 0.43 | 0.42 | 0.95 | 0.58 |
| | NRR | 126 | 56 | 125 | | | | |
| SET 4 | RR | 0.48 | 0.36 | 0.76 | | | | |
| | EER | 0.15 | 0.29 | 0.12 | 0.1 | 0.40 | 0.73 | 0.72 |
| | NRR | 126 | 33 | 50 | | | | |

| SUBSET | | PCBP | PP | ILLUMINATION VARIATIONS SP | | | | |
|---|---|---|---|---|---|---|---|---|
| | | | | PERF. | $th_1$ | $th_2$ | $th_3$ | $th_4$ |
| SET 5 | RR | 0.92 | 1.00 | 0.96 | | | | |
| | EER | 0.03 | 0.02 | 0.02 | 0.68 | 0.38 | 0.65 | 0.64 |
| | NRR | 126 | 30 | 112 | | | | |
| SET 6 | RR | 0.94 | 0.97 | 0.96 | | | | |
| | EER | 0.05 | 0.07 | 0.03 | 0.35 | 0.75 | 0.62 | 0.75 |
| | NRR | 126 | 37 | 107 | | | | |

| SUBSET | | PCBP | PP | OCCLUSIONS SP | | | | |
|---|---|---|---|---|---|---|---|---|
| | | | | PERF. | $th_1$ | $th_2$ | $th_3$ | $th_4$ |
| SET 8 | RR | 0.71 | 0.25 | 0.98 | | | | |
| | EER | 0.09 | 0.23 | 0.04 | 0.65 | 0.60 | 0.60 | 0.55 |
| | NRR | 126 | 20 | 50 | | | | |
| SET 11 | RR | 0.85 | 0.61 | 0.92 | | | | |
| | EER | 0.09 | 0.19 | 0.02 | 0.45 | 0.40 | 0.84 | 0.90 |
| | NRR | 126 | 23 | 115 | | | | |

introduced by the different sets of face images. Table 1 shows that the number of reliable responses for SP drops to 50 for sun glasses (set 8) and to 115 for scarf (set 11). This agrees with our expectations, as the distortions introduced involve a larger face area. However, out of a lower number of reliable responses, the system is able in both cases to guarantee a significantly higher accuracy than PCBP (RR of 0.98 versus 0.71 and of 0.92 versus 0.85) and lower EER. Even in this case the reached equilibrium thresholds are consistent with variations. As expected, PCBP performances are quite constantly worse than those obtained with SP. We can observe that, even when the accuracy of SP drops slightly below that of PP (sets 5 and 6), this is counterbalanced by a much higher number of reliable responses. As an overall consideration, the increase of accuracy possibly obtained by PP, due to the use of AND fusion policy, is almost always not worth the higher loss of results.

## 5.2   Further Experiments on the Supervised Protocol

The first experiment in this section aims at demonstrating that the behavior of the algorithm for threshold updating is stable. In other words, for different probe sequences $P_j$, all composed by images with the same kind of distortion (smile, right light, sun glasses, dirty lens), the values for the thresholds converge towards the same set, with a small margin of variation. For this experiment, set 1 is used as gallery, while probe sequences are extracted from set 2, 6 and 11. Each probe sequence is built by randomly extracting 1000 times one of the 126 images from the probe set; Fig. 3 shows the results for set 2. We can observe that thresholds $th_1$ and $th_2$ (right and left eye) tend to assume lower values than $th_3$ e $th_4$ (nose and mouth). The latter values show an initial variation, and then stay constant for all the remaining part of the probe sequence. This can be explained by observing that, since images in set 2 belong to smiling subjects, nose and

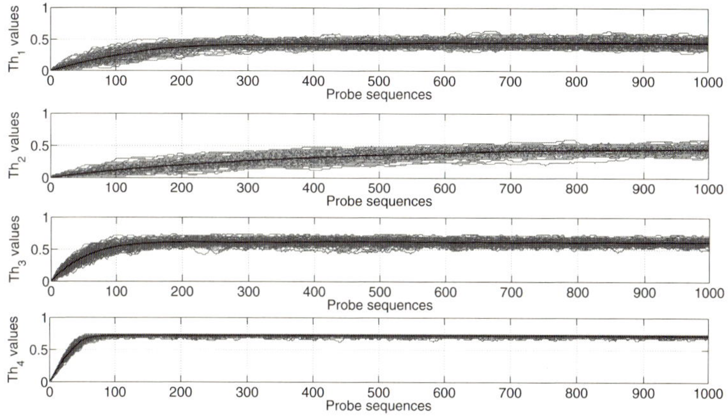

**Fig. 3.** Variation of thresholds of subsystems $T_1$, $T_2$, $T_3$ and $T_4$ for 100 probe sequences of 1000 images of 126 smiling subjects (set 2); the black curve represents the mean trend

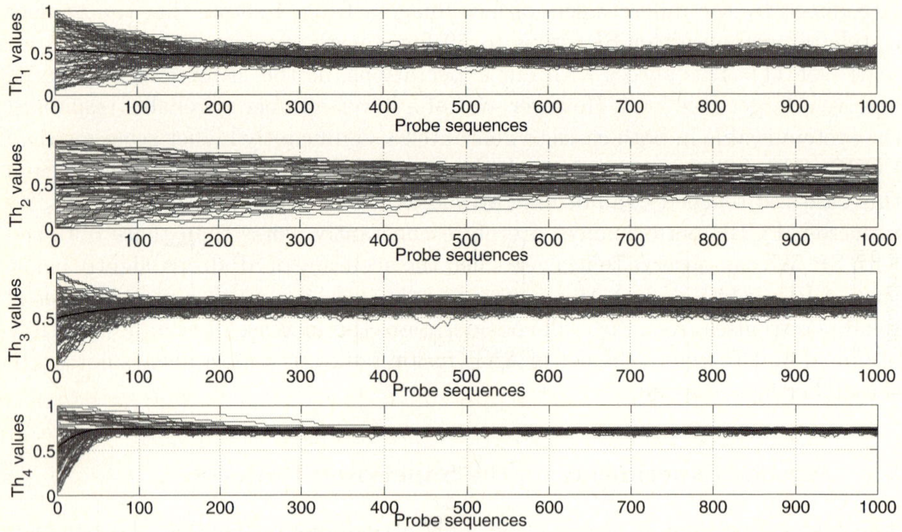

**Fig. 4.** Variation of thresholds of subsystems $T_1$, $T_2$, $T_3$ and $T_4$ for 100 probe sequences of 1000 images of 126 smiling subjects (set 2) according to the initial thresholds configuration ($\{th_1, th_2, th_3, th_4\}$); the black curve represents the mean trend

mouth show an higher variability than eyes, making the corresponding systems $T_3$ e $T_4$ less reliable, and therefore demanding higher values for the respective thresholds. The darker line (in black) in Fig. 3 is the mean value of the 100 computed curves and represents the mean trend for thresholds variation. For each threshold, mean ($\{0.40, 0.32, 0.59, 0.70\}$) and variance ($\{0.10, 0.12, 0.09, 0.09\}$) of the values in the 100 iterations are also computed; the same for the Recognition Rate (mean: 0.94, variance: 0.0072) and the Number of Reliable Responses (mean: 955, variance: 6.2261).

The second experiment aims at highlighting how the threshold configuration towards which the system converges is independent from the starting configuration. Even in this case, we considered 100 probe sequences of 1000 images randomly extracted among the 126 of set 2. For each system run, the initial values for thresholds are randomly chosen (all values are equally probable) in the interval $[0, 1]$. As can be observed from Fig. 4, which reports the results of experiments on set 2 for each threshold, the curves generated by the different probe sequences tend to always concentrate in a relatively small final interval. This confirms the convergence of the updating procedure. As for the preceding experiment, mean ($\{0.45, 0.50, 0.62, 0.72\}$) and variance ($\{0.03, 0.00, 0.02, 0.02\}$) of values in the 100 iterations are computed; the same for the Recognition Rate (mean: 0.94, variance: 0.0072) and the Number of Reliable Responses (mean: 951, variance: 6.7054). We can observe that variance of the single thresholds is lower than in the preceding experiment; this is imputable to the absence of the strong initial variation in the first stretch of the curves in Fig. 3. Fig. 5 shows the thresholds variation over a probe sequence composed of 5 subsequences of

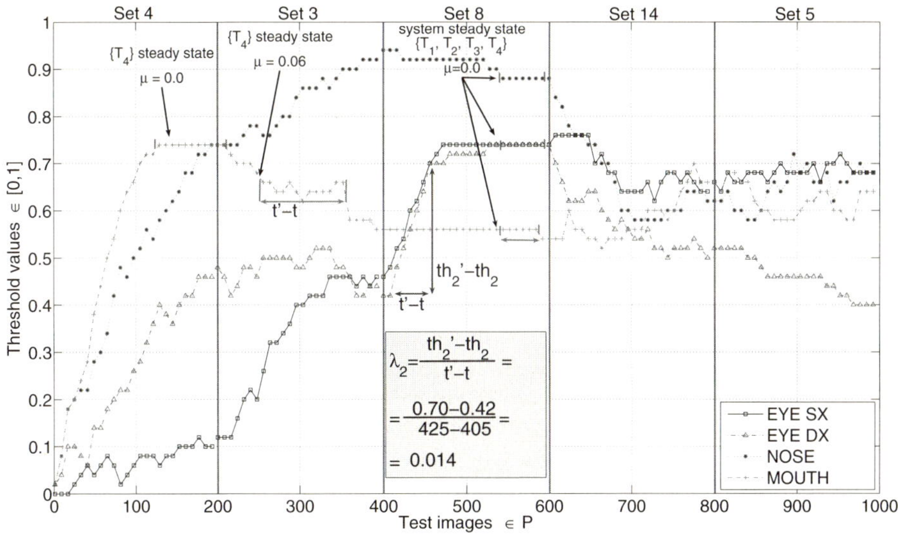


**Fig. 5.** Example of thresholds variation over a probe sequence of 1000 images from set 4 (1 - 200), 3 (201 - 400), 8 (401 - 600), 14 (601 - 800) and 5 (801 - 1000)

200 images each. Each subsequence is composed of randomly extracted images from sets 4, 3, 8, 14 and 5. Notice that for the first sequence the thresholds $th_3$ e $th_4$ reach higher values than the others, consistently with the fact that in images from set 4 mouth presents the higher variability. The configuration undergoes a reversal of trend in the third sequence, corresponding to set 8, where the presence of sun glasses lowers reliability of subsystems $T_1$ and $T_2$. Afterwards it returns to a rather balanced trend on set 14, where no particular expression or lighting variations are present. Lighting variations, and more precisely left light in set 5, lower performances of $T_1$, $T_3$ and $T_4$ subsystems, while the only one to remain more reliable is $T_2$. Fig. 5 shows some examples of the computation of the subsystems convergence speed (for $T_2$) and of the identification of equilibrium states with different values of $\mu$ ($T_4$); it is to also to notice a case when all the subsystems are in equilibrium, so that we can speak about *system equilibrium.*

## 6   Conclusions

We faced the problem of face recognition by a component-based system. Such system integrates peculiar multimodal tools as reliability margins and fusion policies. We discuss three different integration schemes: plain component based protocol, parallel protocol and supervised protocol. They mainly differ for the level of cohesion among subsystems. Experimental results show how a high interconnection degree improves the global system performances in terms of accuracy. Along this line, we can set suitable extensions to properly multimodal systems [11].

# References


1. Heisele, B., Ho, P., Wu, J., Poggio, T.: Face recognition: component-based versus global approaches. Computer Vision and Image Understanding 91, 6–21 (2003)
2. Harandi, M.T., Ahmadabadi, M.N., Araabi, B.N.: A hierarchical face identification system based on facial components. In: Proceedings of the IEEE/ACS International Conference on Computer Systems and Applications, pp. 669–675 (2007)
3. Abate, A.F., Nappi, M., Riccio, D., Tucci, M.: Occluded face recognition by means of the IFS. In: Kamel, M.S., Campilho, A.C. (eds.) ICIAR 2005. LNCS, vol. 3656, pp. 1073–1080. Springer, Heidelberg (2005)
4. Viola, P., Jones, M.: Rapid object detection using a boosted cascade of simple features. In: Proceedings of the IEEE Computer Society Conference on Computer Vision and Pattern Recognition (CVPR), pp. 511–518 (2001)
5. Open Source. Open source computer vision library (2006),
   http://sourceforge.net/projects/opencvlibrary/
6. Bhatti, Z.E.: Face and eyes detection using opencv (2008),
   http://www.codeproject.com/KB/library/eyes.aspx?fid=990485&df=90&
   mpp=25&noise=3&sort=Position&view=Quick&select=2514967&fr=26
7. Poh, N., Bengio, S.: Improving fusion with margin-derived confidence in biometric authentication tasks. In: Kanade, T., Jain, A., Ratha, N.K. (eds.) AVBPA 2005. LNCS, vol. 3546, pp. 474–483. Springer, Heidelberg (2005)
8. Abate, A.F., Nappi, M., Riccio, D., De Marsico, M.: Data normalization and fusion in multibiometric systems. In: Proceedings of the 12th International Conference on Distributed Multimedia Systems (DMS 2007), pp. 87–92 (2007)
9. Veeramachaneni, K., Osadciw, L., Varshney, P.K.: An adaptive multimodal biometric management algorithm. IEEE Transaction on Systems, Man, and Cybernetics-Part C: Applications and Reviews 35, 344–356 (2005)
10. Martinez, A.M.: Recognizing imprecisely localized, partially occluded, and expression variant faces from a single sample per class. IEEE Transaction on Pattern Analisys and Machine Intelligence 24, 748–763 (2002)
11. Abate, A.F., Nappi, M., Riccio, D., De Marsico, M.: Face, ear and fingerprint: Designing multibiometric architectures. In: Proceedings of the 14th International Conference on Image Analysis and Processing (ICIAP 2007), pp. 437–442 (2007)

# Using Face Quality Ratings to Improve Real-Time Face Recognition


Karl Axnick, Ray Jarvis, and Kim C. Ng

Monash University, Wellington Rd, Clayton, VIC, 3800, Australia
{karl.axnick,ray.jarvis,kim.c.ng}@eng.monash.edu.au



**Abstract.** A Face Quality Rating (FQR) is a value derived from a face image that indicates the probability that the face image will be successfully recognized by a specific face recognition method. The FQR can be used as a pre-filter in real-time environments where thousands of face images can be captured every second by multiple surveillance cameras. With so many captured face images, face recognition methods need to strategically decide which face images to attempt recognition on, as it is prohibitively difficult to attempt recognition on all of the images. The FQR pre-filter optimizes processor time utilization resulting in more people being recognized (faster and more accurately) before they leave the surveillance cameras' views. We generate FQR values using Multiple Layered Perceptron (MLP) neural networks. We then use these MLPs in a real-time environment to experimentally prove that FQR pre-filtering improves the speed and accuracy of any real-time face recognition method...


## 1   Introduction

FQR pre-filtering is ideal for real-time face recognition applications [1]. These applications include public environments such as airports, train stations and streets under CCTV surveillance. These are very difficult face recognition environments because there are multiple cameras, multiple entry and exits points, multitudes of targets and vastly varying poses, expressions, occlusions, scales and illumination levels. This is arguably the most difficult environment for face recognition [2]. Systems need to quickly decide which face image to recognize out of thousands, before any number of people leave the scene or enter sensitive areas. The time critical elements, the multitudes of redundant data and the sequence dependent outcomes mean that classical recognition methods [3] are ineffective and readily overwhelmed (refer to Fig. 5).

Face recognition has been an intense and extensive area of research over the past 20 years [4]. Many unique approaches have been adopted outside of the standard "detect a face and recognize it" systems, such as "divide and conquer" strategies [5], cascading filters [6] and pre-recognition normalization [7]. These approaches have enjoyed considerable success in conventional face recognition settings, but they all rapidly fail in difficult real-time environments as the number of people in the scene increases (refer to Fig. 5). This failure can be attributed to


T. Wada, F. Huang, and S. Lin (Eds.): PSIVT 2009, LNCS 5414, pp. 13–24, 2009.

the decision in the approaches that if a face is detected, it must have recognition attempted. Although this decision seems logical given the field, unless the face recognition approach is 100% accurate the decision is going to waste valuable processor time trying to recognize every single face the system detects. FQR pre-filtering enables a system to intelligently allocate recognition cycle times for only those face images that offer the best chance of recognition success. It is important to note that recognition success includes correctly classifying a face as not being present in the database. Without FQR pre-filtering, face recognition methods can repeatedly waste recognition cycles trying to recognize people who simply cannot be recognized because they are not in the database.

FQRs are a probability measure only and other factors besides face quality can affect recognition success. For example, the size, composition, and inter-class variations of the databases play a role in the success of recognition methods that use them. FQR pre-filtering is a powerful tool that is best used in conjunction with other tools that also help increase recognition speed and accuracy such as "divide and conquer" strategies [5].

Xiong [8] improves automatic database image acquisition in unconstrained environments by using Fisher's Linear Discriminant to measure the separability of classes in the database. Whenever the system detects a face, it tries to automatically add this to the database to increase system robustness. If the addition would not increase class seperability or is redundant, then the image is ignored. Subasic [9] helps improve database image acquisition in constrained environments by observing International Civil Aviation Organization (ICAO) rules. ICAO rules are a collection of simple tests such as requiring normalized eye widths from acquired images. These papers are examples of how face/image quality metrics can be used to improve face recognition results by improving database creation. Our FQR method can be used in a similar manner.

It is important to note that during FQR assisted video surveillance all of the people who are detected in the scene have their best images to date stored, and all of the people will eventually be subjected to recognition using their best image, whether or not their best image has a high FQR. We delay using valuable processing time on low FQR images, because on average a better FQR image will eventuate if we wait. In the meantime, that processing time can be more efficiently used on other peoples' more highly ranked FQR images. If a person's best image has a low FQR but must undergo recognition, we increase the required recognition threshold for a match to ensure accurate results from that difficult low FQR image. It should be noted that the detection of a low FQR value for an input face can in effect lead to a decision to classify the input as a possible "reject class". Recognition of reject classes has a long history in pattern recognition [10] and this further validates the FQR pre-filtering approach.

The format of this paper is as follows; Section 2) illustrates our methodology and its advantages; Section 3) explains how an FQR can be learned using an MLP neural network (NN), and proves that the rating can predict the probability of recognition success; Section 4) explains and reports on the experiments that use the MLP NN described in section 3; and finally Section 5) concludes our findings.

## 2  Methodology

A FQR is obtained by using an MLP NN that has been trained with a specific face recognition method and a training database. Training involves exposing a face image to the MLP and using back propagation to reinforce correct predictions of recognition success at the output depending on whether the recognition method correctly classified the face image. This training is time consuming, but it is done off-line and only once for each face recognition method that requires a FQR. The MLP learns how to detect many sub features in the images and uses their presence or absence as recognition predictors. We currently use the MLP FQR pre-filter after the normalization stage and before the face recognition stage in the recognition system (refer to Fig. 1).

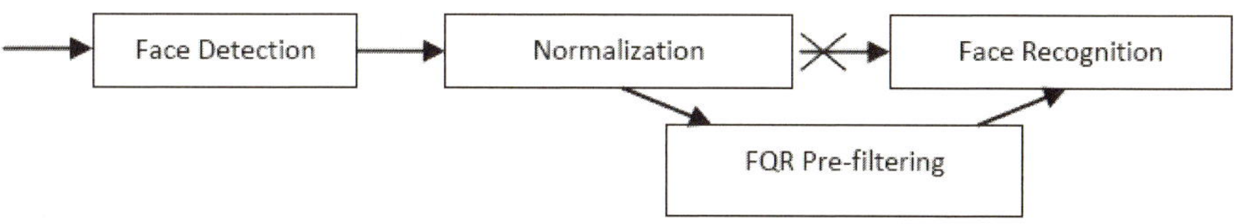


**Fig. 1.** The new face recognition system tests the face quality before recognition is attempted

FQR pre-filtering at this stage offers many advantages over conventional face recognition systems:

1. The final face recognition stage can be avoided for a face image with a low FQR. This saves on the recognition-time expense for an image that is probably unrecognizable.
2. The final face recognition stage can be delayed until a better quality image of that face is captured, thereby improving the probability of success.
3. FQRs could be used to automatically select face recognition thresholds and/or parameters in response to detected FQRs to improve face recognition confidence.
4. While a detected person is still unrecognized, whether in the scene or not, the face recognition system will only need to store a small set of high FQR images for that person (for recognition at a later time). Without FQRs the system would have to store every single image of the person to optimize the chance of recognizing at least one of the input images (an undesired situation especially with many camera's, thousands of frames, and hundreds of people moving quickly through a scene).
5. By attempting to recognize the highest quality faces in a scene first, we quickly remove unrecognized people from the "to do" list of a crowded scene. This makes it less likely that people can leave the scene or enter a sensitive area before having recognition attempted. A person who is difficult to recognize will not "hog" the processor time while many potentially easily recognized people move unrecognized through the scene.

6. Even if face recognition is always attempted regardless of a person's FQR value, the FQR value can: a) generate a confidence value in the match score, b) cause the required threshold for successful matches to be scaled up, and c) help explain if a target's input image fails to be recognized because the target is not in the database or because the target's input image is too poor in face quality to match with the target's database image.

Many face recognition systems rely on face detection [11] as a quality check. However, face detection is not designed to rank face images against each other, nor is face detection designed to detect key features in faces that certain face recognition methods rely on. Face detection methods are "plug and play" in operation for most face recognition methods, whereas FQR pre-filtering is specifically trained for use with the face recognition method for which it is paired.

FQR values are in no way directly related to image quality. An image with blurred lines as well as salt and pepper noise would probably be considered a poor quality image, but if the image clearly shows a sub feature that the utilized face recognition method finds strongly salient, then the low quality image would have a high FQR. Conversely, a well focused high-resolution image that would normally be considered high quality may have a low FQR value if the person in the photo is wearing sunglasses and the utilized face recognition method relies heavily on the eyes for recognition success.

## 2.1   Learning the FQR Value

To learn FQR values for any given face recognition method (and its associated database) a MLP is used. The MLP is trained using back propagation and simulated annealing [12]. The input layer consists of a 1D vector of the normalized grayscale values for the current target image. The desired output from training is a single value predicting whether or not the target image will be successfully recognized. The MLP does not try to recognize the face whilst getting the FQR.

During training the MLP will slowly learn certain image sub features. Unfortunately, due to MLP's being black boxes it is difficult to be aware of the specifics of these sub features so human observations cannot evaluate the use/robustness of these sub features independently from the system results. What can be evaluated however is the fact that the MLP can use the presence or absence of learned image sub features to generate a single value output that gives the likelihood of the current target image being correctly recognized. In other words the MLP can generate the image's FQR value.

The parameters for the MLP were 64 x 64 inputs, 64 x 64 + 64 hidden nodes and 1 output node. However, any NN type, any training method, and any set of parameters could have been used for our purposes as long as a reasonably accurate FQR value for any target image can be learned.

## 2.2   Training Data

The CMU database [13] was used along with our own 3D database [14] (we used the 3D face models to generate multiple 2D face images from many perspectives).

The databases were combined to ensure no bias was found in the results. The individual databases were very effective when used on their own. As well as using real images from the combined database, 10 virtual images of every real image were generated. The virtual images corrupted the originals with various high probability real world degradations such as white noise, occlusions, scale changes, translation changes and pose changes to name a few. These degradations were randomly present or absent in each virtual image. When the images were degraded this was done to a random degree (e.g. anywhere from 20% to 60% of the image pixels could be replaced by salt and pepper noise).

Our training database has 3 images per person: 2 frontal images with different expressions (normal and shocked) and 1 profile image. This gave us a total of 270 real images in the training database. We also used a test set for monitoring the training process. The test set consists of: 1 frontal image (with an angry expression) and 1 profile image (not the same as the one used in the training database), giving us a total of 180 real images in the test set.

Ten virtual images were generated for each of the real images in both sets. This gave us a total of 2970 training images and 1960 test images. We used excessive amounts of virtual images because the random degradations seem to (based on experimentation) more readily expose image sub features to the MLP that are critical for the face recognition being used.

## 2.3   The Training Process

It is necessary to select a face recognition method to train the MLP with. We decided to use a 2D geometric salient feature point (SFP) method [15] and a modified 2D PCA holistic method [16]. We used both holistic and geometric methodologies to prove that FQR pre-filtering can improve the performance of either methodology for face recognition.

FQR pre-filtering will improve real-time performance rates for a face recognition method, no matter how effective that face recognition method is by itself. Any existing face recognition method can be used and improved by our FQR pre-filtering method in both its speed and accuracy for real-time environments. These claims are based on experiments in the next section.

We trained each MLP in parallel with its partnered face recognition method (i.e. one MLP for the SFP method and one for the PCA method). After each face recognition method finished recognizing an input, we used the success of the result to train the MLP which was attempting to predict that success. If the face recognition method succeeded, and the MLP had an output greater than "0.5" then the contributing links would be re-enforced through back propagation. If the MLP instead had a negative prediction (i.e. less than "0.5") then the contributing links would have their weights reduced. This process was re-iterated for all of the training images. After each epoch of training, the error level of the system was evaluated. If the error level was less than 10% we would then test the MLP on the test set without training. If the MLP achieved a success rate greater than 90% on the test set, then training was considered complete. Otherwise a fresh set of virtual training images were generated and the supervised training cycle was repeated.

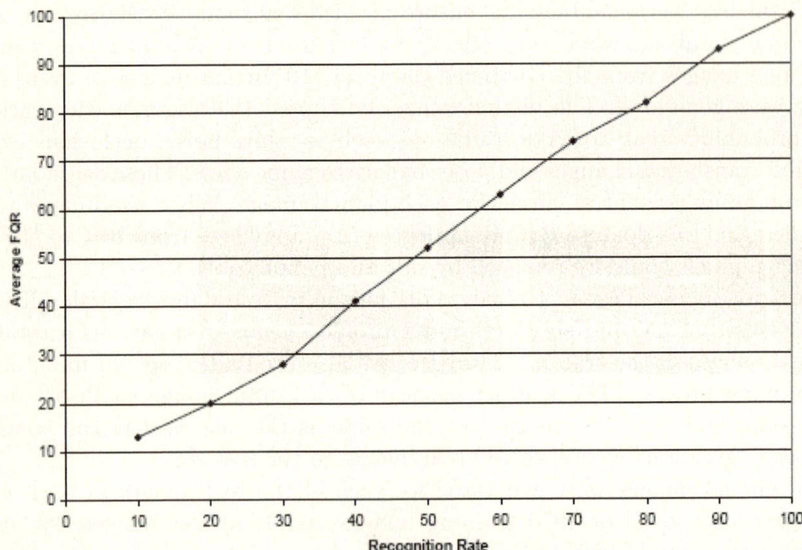


**Fig. 2.** Shows the recognition rate of images at varying FQR levels predicted by the trained MLPs

Once training is completed the MLP can quickly generate FQRs for any input. A system just needs to feed a target image's 64 x 64 1D vector into the trained MLP, and then within 100 ms an output is generated that is the target image's FQR.

Fig. 2 shows a clear linear relationship between FQRs and recognition success. In order to generate this result, two separate tests were combined and averaged. The first test involved creating 10 separate groups of faces with different recognition rates. Each group was labelled with its real recognition rate in terms of what percentage of the group could be recognized by a recognition method. Then for each group of faces the average FQR was found and recorded against the actual recognition rates. This was our first set of data.

The second test used the opposite approach. 10 separate groups of faces were made using only FQR statistics. Each group was then recognized using a face recognition method and the recognition rate versus the average FQR of that group was recorded. This second set of data was combined with the first set to generate Figure 2. The observed linear relationship implies that the FQR value of an image is a very good approximation of the probability that the tested image will be recognized.

## 3   FQR Value Experiments

In order to rigorously evaluate both FQR and noFQR[1] recognition results in real-time environments with unlimited parameter control, we developed a simulation tool (refer to Fig. 3).

---

[1] noFQR is the label used for our 2 face recognition methods when implemented without FQR pre-filtering.

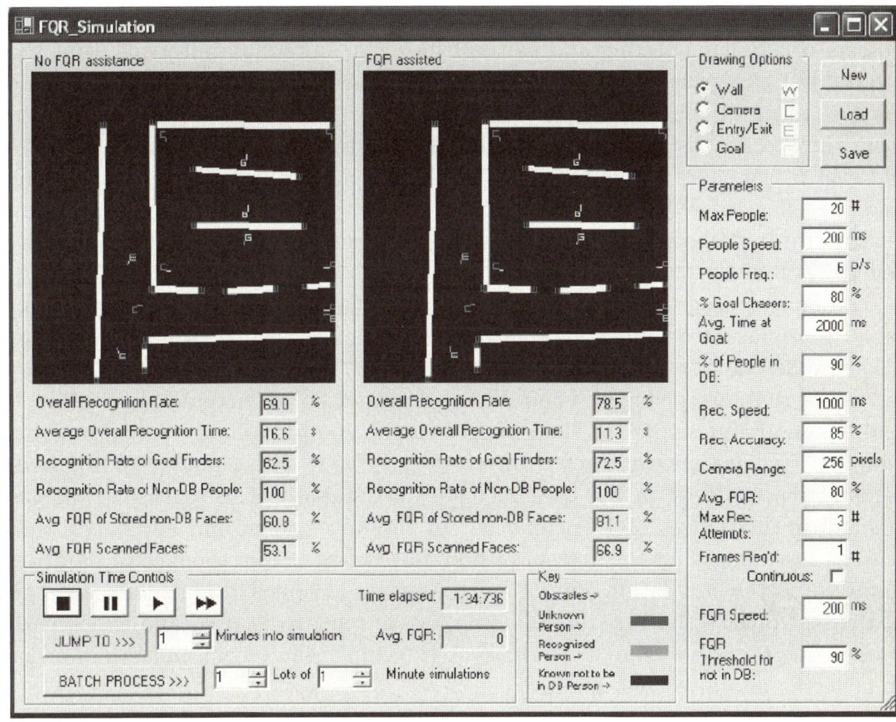

**Fig. 3.** Simulation Tool: Can simulate any environment that comprises of walls/ tables/chairs (obstacles), entries, exits, sensitive equipment (goals) and cameras. A random crowd is then released into this environment and statistics are recorded for both noFQR (left frame) and FQR face recognition (right frame).

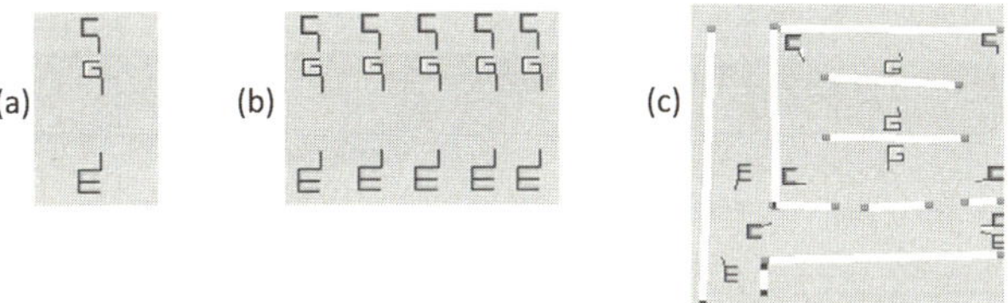

**Fig. 4.** The 3 standard test environments. (a) A simple access control scenario (b) the same as "a" except this is a public gallery example i.e. train station ticket gates (c) a rough model of one of our postgraduate rooms with a public access hallway and 3 entry/exit points. (Code: c= camera, g=goal and e=entry/exit).

The simulation tool lets us create custom environments (refer to Fig. 4) with many restricted areas, cameras, entry and exit points as well as real-time threaded objects representing people in the scene. Whenever a threaded object moves into the field of view of a camera a real image is generated from our test image set (see below) and placed on the "to do" stack for the environment for every single frame the person stays in the camera's field of view. You can expect that with 4 or 5 cameras running at 25 frames per second and hundreds of people objects constantly entering and exiting the scene at random intervals, that the "to do" list can grow extremely rapidly. Only when a person is recognized using our face recognition methods (SFP and PCA), are their image captures removed from the "to do" list. This environment lets us test many hypotheses. Of note however is the effect of changing the maximum population allowed in the scene and the effect of FQR assistance when the recognition methods' speeds were varied. We hypothesize that FQR assisted systems will greatly outperform any noFQR systems.

The images used for these experiments were the same images from the combined database in training except we used 6 images per person and we now also include one of our earlier databases with 120 images of 20 people[14]. This gave us a real-image count of 660. We also generated 10 virtual images of each real-image giving a total of 7260 images in the complete image set. From this complete image set we extracted three real and two virtual images for 100 people and placed these in our face recognition database. The remaining images (including the images of 10 people not in the face recognition database) were used as test images for the system to find matches of within the face recognition database as the simulation environment presented them. During simulations all of the test images (both real and virtual) were repeatedly used and exposed to random degradations, similar to those used to make the virtual images, in order to generate unlimited test inputs.

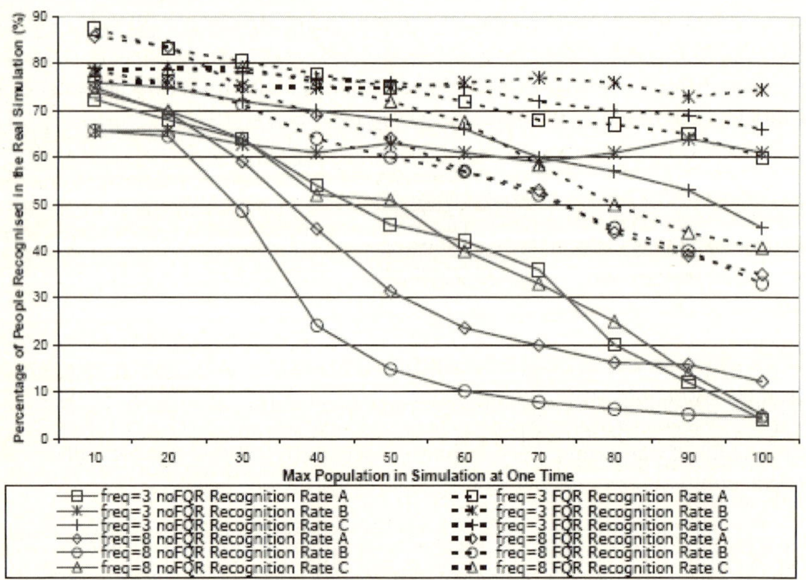


**Fig. 5.** The effect of max population in the environment and the effect of the frequency with which people arrive in the environment on the Face Recognition Rate

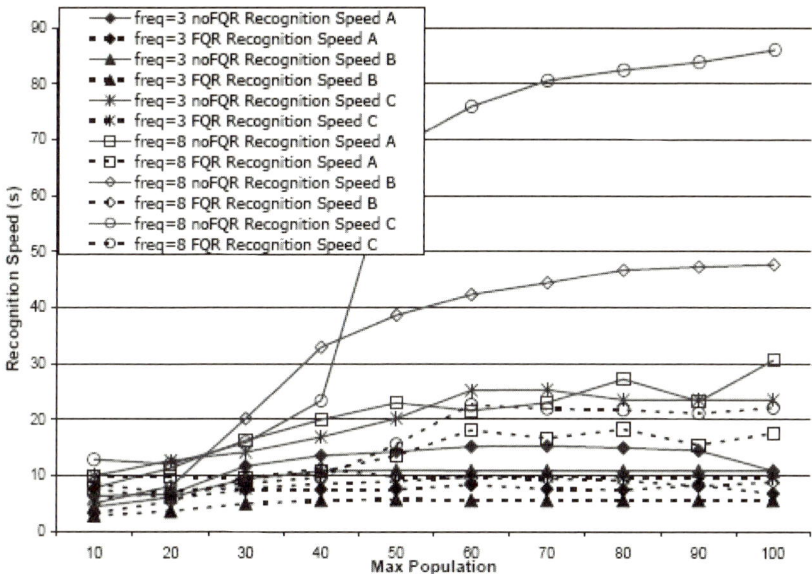


**Fig. 6.** The effect of max population in the environment and the effect of the frequency with which people arrive in the environment on the Face Recognition Speed

The experiments showed conclusively that using FQR pre-filtering with any face recognition system improved the systems' results dramatically and consistently. The data from Fig. 5 and Fig. 6 is the average of both the holistic and the geometric face recognition methods operated in separate tests. The dashed lines representing FQR assisted values show little degradation in performance as the number of people moving through the scene increases, whereas the noFQR methods rapidly degrade. Recognition speed is the average time in seconds it takes to recognize a new arrival in the scene. These graphs show that FQR assistance greatly increases the recognition rate of the face recognition systems. This effect works for both geometric and holistic methods.

It is interesting to note that the noFQR face recognition methods completely fail at relatively small population sizes of 100 people, whereas the FQR methods are almost unaffected. Given that the target applications for FQR assisted methods include airports and train stations where populations sizes will be in the thousands, these initial experiments present a strong case for the FQR tool's inclusion in real-time face recognition approaches.

Fig. 7 and Fig. 8 show that even for very small population sizes of up to 40 people, as soon as a face recognition method's recognition-time approaches a second or more, significant performance degradations are observed. However, when these same systems use FQR pre-filtering the performance is relatively unaffected by recognition-time. This suggests that with the use of FQRs slower but more accurate face recognition methods can be used without effecting overall system speed. This is yet another advantage that FQR pre-filtering can offer.

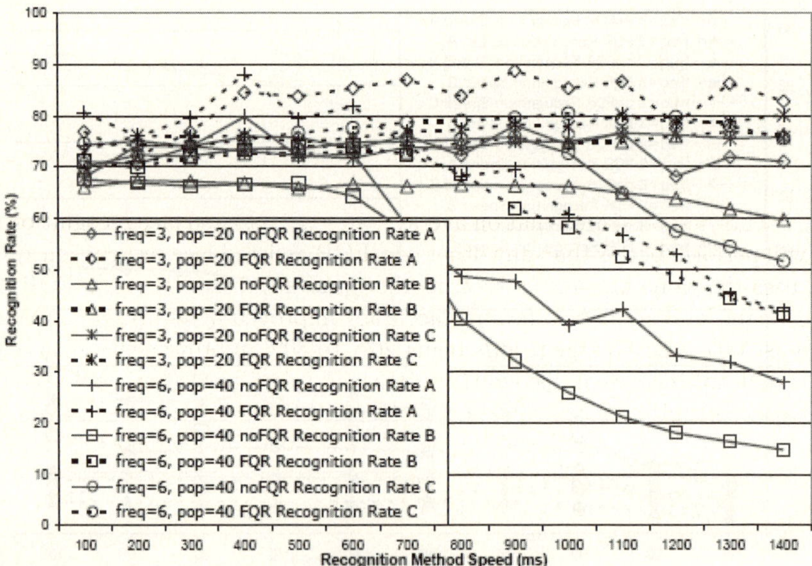


**Fig. 7.** The effect that the speed of the face recognition component of the system has on the overall system's recognition rate

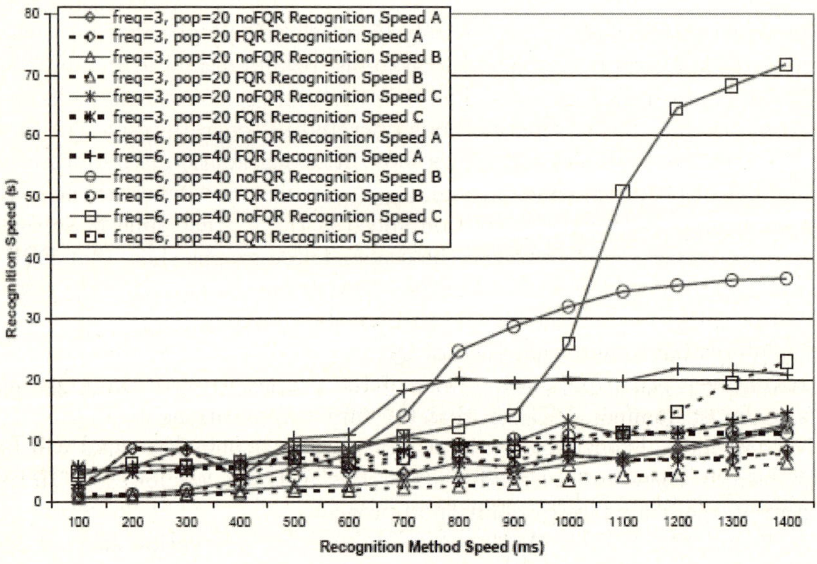


**Fig. 8.** The effect that the speed of the face recognition component of the system has on the overall system's recognition speed

## 4   Conclusion

We developed and tested the use of a novel approach for improving face recognition systems. We proved that by intelligently pre-filtering target images, face recognition systems could become much more efficient. A metric was developed called the face quality rating (FQR) that gave an accurate recognition probability value that could be used as a pre-filter in real-time systems. Real-time face recognition experiments demonstrated that on average, an FQR assisted face recognition system will perform better than any other non-FQR assisted face recognition system that uses the same face recognition method and database. By using FQRs any face recognition method can have its accuracy improved by as little as 5% and as much as 200%, the average results being 20% to 30% improvements. The cost of this significant increase in recognition rates was a significant decrease in the time it takes to recognize unknown parties. The recognition time decreases ranged from 5% to 150% with 50% being the average. As such, there are no negative costs involved with implementing our FQR approach. As long as an FQR value can be learned for a face recognition system (i.e. the linear relationship shown in Fig. 2 can be observed with the FQR prediction and recognition results), then improvements in real-time speed and accuracy will occur. Since our FQR training method is generic and can be applied to any face recognition method we are confident that FQRs can be learned for any method.

Future work would involve testing a face recognition method both with and without FQR assistance in a large high traffic public area, such as a university administration building. We would also like to use many different face recognition methods to prove that an FQR value can be learned for any face recognition method.

## References


1. Nastar, C., Mitschke, M.: Real-time face recognition using feature combination. In: Third IEEE International Conference on Automatic Face and Gesture Recognition. Proceedings, 14-16 April 1998, pp. 312–317 (1998)
2. Gorodnichy, D.O.: Video-based framework for face recognition in video. In: The 2nd Canadian Conference on Computer and Robot Vision. Proceedings, 9-11 May 2005, pp. 330–338 (2005)
3. Donald, T.: The Pattern Recognition Basis of Artificial Intelligence, 388 pages. Wiley-IEEE Computer Society Press (1998)
4. Yongsheng, G., Leung, M.K.H.: Face recognition using line edge map. IEEE Transactions on Pattern Analysis and Machine Intelligence 24(6), 764–779 (2002)
5. Ming, Z., Fulcher, J.: Face recognition using artificial neural network group-based adaptive tolerance (GAT) trees. IEEE Transactions on Neural Networks 7(3), 555–567 (1996)
6. Quan, Y., Thangali, A., Sclaroff, S.: Face Identification by a Cascade of Rejection Classifiers. In: IEEE Computer Society Conference on Computer Vision and Pattern Recognition, 20-26 June, vol. 3, p. 152 (2005)
7. Shan, D., Ward, R.: Wavelet-based illumination normalization for face recognition. In: IEEE International Conference on Image Processing, ICIP 2005, 11-14 September, vol. 2, pp. II 954–II 957 (2005)

to add new keypoints that belong to any new objects appearing in the image. Finally, we obtain trajectories of these keypoints by associating tracked keypoints and newly detected keypoints.

## 2.2   Example of Scale Searching

The value of scale $s$ corresponds to a local region centered on the keypoint for describing SIFT features. Figure 4 shows a tracking example of the location and scale when the image is magnified. White circles in Figure 4(a) show the location of the tracked keypoint, and blue circles show the size of the scale estimated by our proposed method. We can see that the same range of keypoints has been selected automatically, even though the size of the image has changed. Figure 4(b) shows the scaling rate of the image and the rate of the scaling rate estimated using our method. From the graph, we see that the ratio of scale estimated by our proposed method is almost the same as the ratio of image magnification. We used the least-square method to fit the plots, and we obtained a gradient of 0.91, which indicates a high correlation. Our proposed method can calculate the scale and the location of the feature point at the same time because it iterates the mean-shift search in image and in scale space.

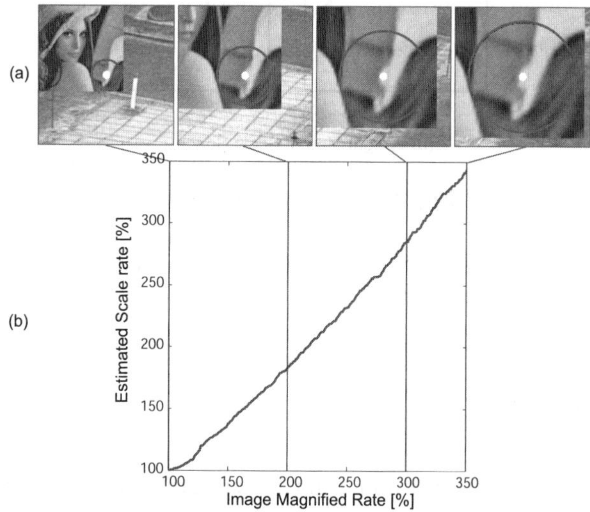

**Fig. 4.** Tracking Example of Location and Scale

## 3   Experimental Results

First, we outline our experimental setup and discuss the issue of generating ground-truth data. Then, this section contains our experimental results obtained using a synthesized image sequence and shows a pedestrian sequence as a tracking example.

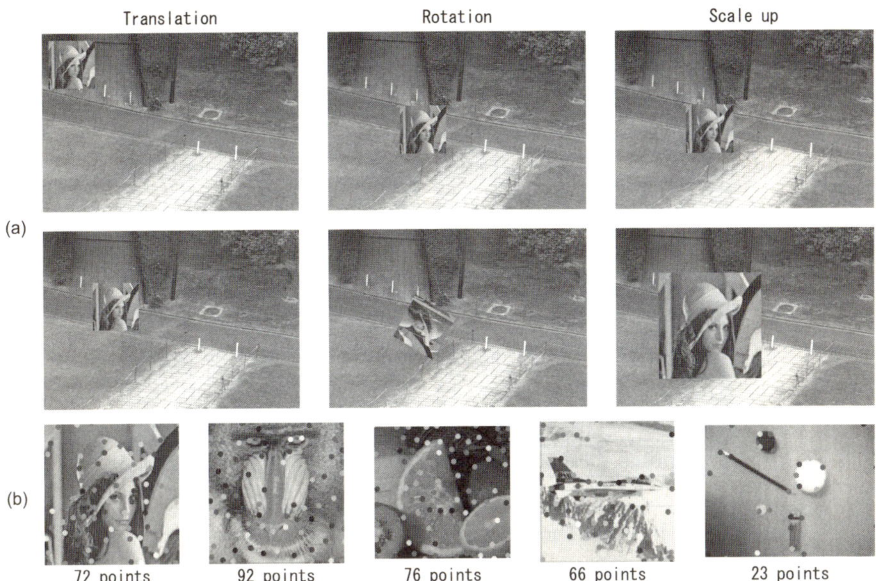


**Fig. 5.** Example of Experimental Image

### 3.1  Experimental Setup

We used synthetic images to quantify our method. We collected a dataset of images and applied the following transformations to each image: (1) translation; (2) rotation; and (3) scaling. To generate an image sequence, we overlapped the transformed image and the background image, as shown in Figure 5(a). For each image, we generated an image sequence of 180 frames par transformation. We investigated the difference in tracking performance between the KLT tracker and our method. To make the difference clear, the same initial keypoints were used in this experiment by both methods for translation and rotation sequences. Figure 5(b) shows examples of initial keypoints for each tracked image.

### 3.2  Ground-Truth Data

The transform (expressed as an affine motion) between two frames in a row is given. Therefore, ground-truth for each frame was made and used for the evaluation. We consider the match to be valid if the keypoint and ground truth are sufficiently close in location. We calculated the Euclidean distance between each tracked keypoint and ground-truth. If the distance was below the threshold, the tracked keypoint was determined to be a successfully tracked point. We then computed a tracking success rate from the total number of successfully tracked points.

### 3.3  Results

Figure 6 shows the tracking success rate calculated from all the frames (180 per frames for each sequence) used in 5 sequences. The horizontal axis represents

**Fig. 9.** Visualization by using Scale Information



**Fig. 10.** Visualization Result

## 4.2   Flow Representation

To express the movement by color information, a color is selected from a hue corresponding to the direction of the movement. The intensity of dense $f_d(\mathbf{x})$ in direction $d$ at the location $\mathbf{x}$ is expressed by the following equation:

$$f_d(\mathbf{x}) = \sum_{t=1}^{T} \sum_{i=1}^{N} \delta(\mathbf{x} - \mathbf{x}_i^t, s_i), \tag{11}$$

$$\delta(\mathbf{x}, s) = \exp\left(\frac{-(x^2 + y^2)}{2s^2}\right), \tag{12}$$

where $T$ is total frames, $N$ is number of tracking points, $\mathbf{x}_i^t$ is a location of the chase point of the number $i$ in frame $t$, and $\delta$ is a Parzen window function, which is based on Gaussian distribution. At this time, scale $s_i$ of the tracking point is used as a standard deviation of Gaussian distribution, as shown in Figure 8. The color intensity corresponding to the direction of the movement will be strongly expressed where the distribution density of a keypoint is high. Figure 9 shows the value of $s$ for a visualization example of pedestrian. Using the location and scale parameter of keypoints, we can obtain a rough silhouette of people, as shown in Figure 9(c).

### 4.3   Visualization Example

Figure 10(a) shows visualization examples of pedestrian flow accumulating tracked points over 1 hour(100,000 frames). The circle in the left a color map of the direction of the movement. From the visualization, we can see that there are a lot of people who were crossing to the left in area A. In area B, we also see that there are two movements in opposite directions. Figure 10(b) shows visualization examples of pedestrian flow for every 2 seconds (60 frames). Since the SIFT feature has a scale parameter, the proposed method can obtain better human shapes than that of the KLT.

## 5   Conclusion

We developed a feature point tracking method that used the mean-shift that of SIFT features. We demonstrated that high accuracy of keypoint tracking was archived for translation and rotation according to the SIFT features. Even if the tracking object was scaled up, it was still possible to track it by updating the scale of the SIFTs adaptively. Moreover, the visualization method of the feature point tracking result was shown as an example of the tracking of a pedestrian. In the future, we intend to develop a method to automatically detect movement in different directions from a regular flow in order to detect unusual events.

## References


1. Lowe, D.G.: Distinctive image features from scale-invariant keypoints. Int. Journal of Computer Vision (2004)
2. Mikolajczyk, K., Schmid, C.: A performance evaluation of local descriptors. In: Proceedings of Computer Vision and Pattern Recognition (2003)
3. Brown, M., Lowe, D.: Recognising panoramas. In: Ninth IEEE International Conference on Computer Vision (2003)

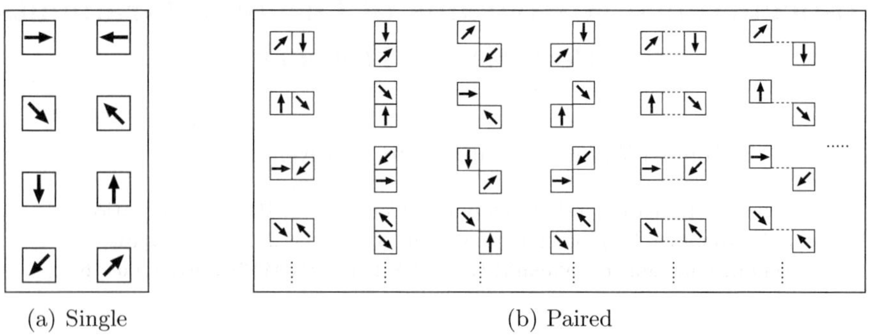

      (a) Single                                          (b) Paired

**Fig. 1.** Vocabulary of gradient orientations. Though (a) a single gradient orientation has only eight varieties, (b) a pair of them has many more varieties than the single one.

Some multiple-edge-based feature descriptors also have been proposed. Wu et al. proposed edgelet feature descriptor which expresses long curves of edges [14]. Sabzmeydani et al. proposed shapelet feature descriptor based on selected edges by AdaBoost [15]. Since shapelets are the combination of edges, they can express more detailed shape information than what SIFT/HOG feature descriptors can.

We propose a multiple-gradient-orientation-based feature descriptor named "Co-occurrence Histograms of Oriented Gradients (CoHOG)". CoHOG is histograms of which a building block is a pair of gradient orientations. Since the pair of gradient orientations has more vocabulary than single one as shown in Fig. 1. CoHOG can express shapes in more detail than HOG, which uses single gradient orientation. Benchmark results on two famous datasets: DaimlerChrysler pedestrian classification benchmark dataset and INRIA person data set, show the effectiveness of our method.

The rest of this paper is organized as follows: Section 2 explains the outline of our pedestrian detection approach; Section 3 briefly explains HOG, and then describes our feature descriptor; Section 4 shows experimental results on two benchmark datasets; The final section is the conclusion.

## 2   Outline of Our Approach

In most pedestrian detection tasks, classification accuracy is the most important requirement. The performance of the system depends on the effectiveness of feature descriptors and the accuracy of classification models.

In this paper, we focus on the feature descriptor. An overview of our pedestrian detection processes is shown in Fig. 2. The first two parts extract feature descriptors from input images, and then the last part classifies and outputs classification results. We propose a high-dimensional feature descriptor in Section 3. Our feature descriptor is effective for classification, because it contains building blocks that have an extensive vocabulary.

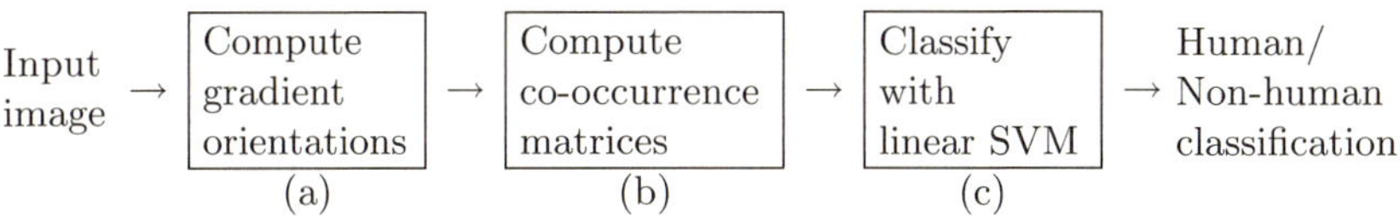


**Fig. 2.** Our classification process. We combine strong feature descriptor CoHOG and a conventional simple classifier. Our classification process consists of three parts: (a) computation of gradient orientations from input images, (b) computation of CoHOG from gradient orientations, and (c) classification with linear SVM classifier which is fast at learning and classification.

If the feature descriptor is informative enough, a simple linear classifier can detect pedestrians accurately. We use a linear classifier obtained by a linear SVM [16] which works fast at learning and classification.

## 3   Gradient Orientation Based Feature Descriptor

### 3.1   Histograms of Oriented Gradients (HOG)

We briefly explain the essence of the HOG calculation process with Fig. 3. In order to extract HOG from an image, firstly gradient orientations at every pixel are calculated (Fig. 3(a)). Secondly a histogram of each orientation in a small rectangular region is calculated (Fig. 3(b)). Finally the HOG feature vector is created by concatenating the histograms of all small regions (Fig. 3(c)).

HOG has two merits for pedestrian detection. One merit is the robustness against illumination variance because gradient orientations are computed from local intensity difference. The other merit is the robustness against deformations because slight shifts and affine deformations make small histogram value changes.

### 3.2   Co-occurrence Histograms of Oriented Gradients (CoHOG)

We propose a high-dimensional feature "Co-occurrence Histograms of Oriented Gradients (CoHOG)". Our feature uses pairs of gradient orientations as units,

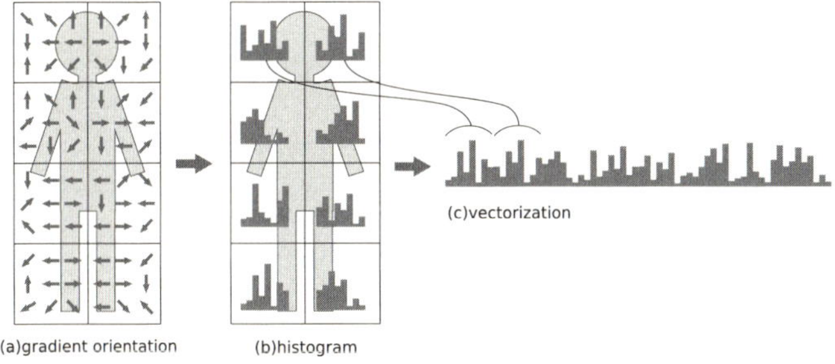


**Fig. 3.** Overview of HOG calculation

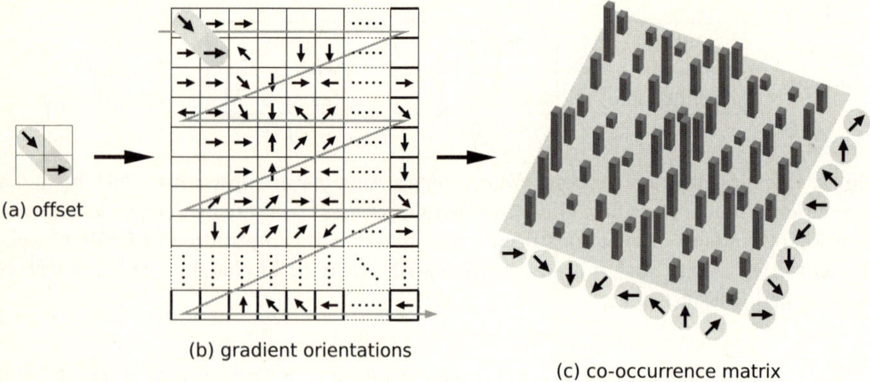


**Fig. 4.** Co-occurrence matrix of gradient orientations. It calculates sums of all pairs of gradient orientations at a given offset.

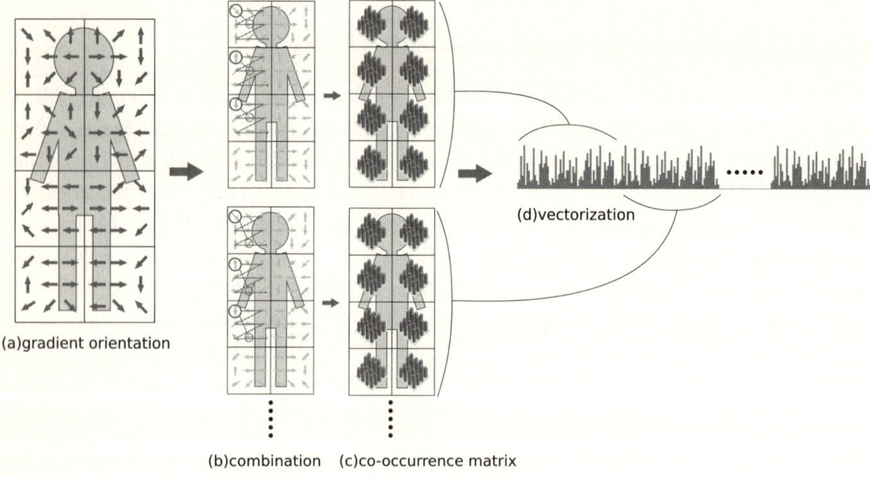


**Fig. 5.** Overview of CoHOG calculation

from which it builds the histograms. The histogram is referred to as the co-occurrence matrix, hereafter. The co-occurrence matrix expresses the distribution of gradient orientations at a given offset over an image as shown in Fig. 4. The combinations of neighbor gradient orientations can express shapes in detail. It is informative for pedestrian classification. Mathematically, a co-occurrence matrix $C$ is defined over an $n \times m$ image $I$, parameterized by an offset $(x, y)$, as:

$$C_{x,y}(i,j) = \sum_{p=1}^{n} \sum_{q=1}^{m} \begin{cases} 1, & \text{if } I(p,q) = i \text{ and } I(p+x, q+y) = j \\ 0, & \text{otherwise.} \end{cases} \tag{1}$$

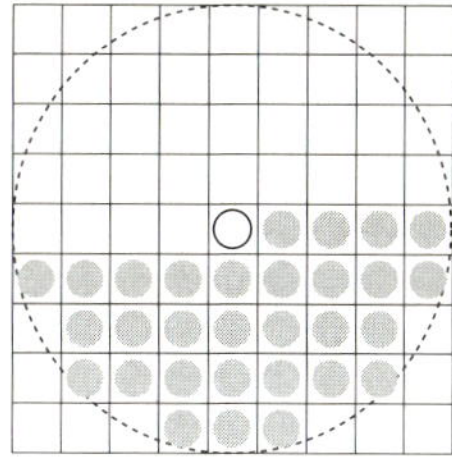

**Fig. 6.** Offsets of co-occurrence matrices. Offsets are smaller than the large dashed-circle. The center small white-circle and the other 30 dark-circles are paired. We calculate 31 Co-occurrence matrices with different offsets including zero offset.

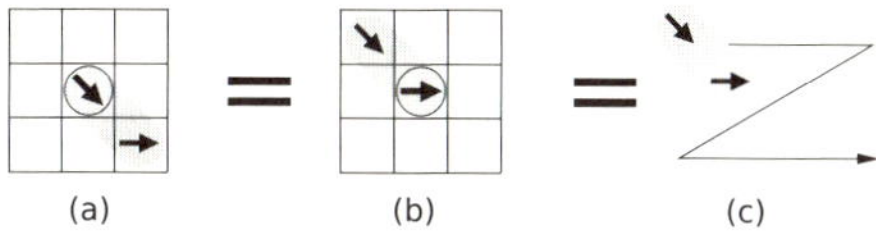



**Fig. 7.** Offset values of (a) $(1, 1)$ and (b) $(-1, -1)$ are different, but they behave as same as the other in the calculation of co-occurrence matrix

```
 1: given I: an image of gradient orientation
 2: initialize H ← 0
 3: for all positions (p, q) inside of the image do
 4:     i ← I(p, q)
 5:     k ← the small region including (p, q)
 6:     for all offsets (x, y) such that corresponds neighbors do
 7:         if (p + x, q + y) is inside of the image then
 8:             j ← I(p + x, q + y)
 9:             H(k, i, j, x, y) ← H(k, i, j, x, y) + 1
10:         end if
11:     end for
12: end for
```

**Fig. 8.** Implementation of CoHOG calculation. The bins of histogram $H$ are initialized to zero before voting. All pixels in the gradient orientation image $I$ are scanned, and bins of $H$ corresponding to pixels are incremented.

CoHOG has robustness against deformation and illumination variance for the same reasons as HOG, because CoHOG is gradient based histogram feature descriptor.

We describe the processes of CoHOG calculation shown in Fig. 5. Firstly, we compute gradient orientations from an image by

$$\theta = \arctan \frac{v}{h}, \tag{2}$$

where $v$ and $h$ are vertical and horizontal gradient respectively calculated by Sobel filter, Roberts filter, etc. We label each pixel with one of eight discrete orientations or as no-gradient (Fig. 5(a)). All $0° - 360°$ orientations are divided into eight orientations per $45°$. No-gradient means $\sqrt{v^2 + h^2}$ is smaller than a threshold. Secondly, we compute co-occurrence matrices by Eq. (1) (Fig. 5(b)). The offsets we used are shown in Fig. 6. By using short-range and long-range offsets, the co-occurrence matrix can express local and global shapes. We do not use half of the offsets, because they behave as same as the others in calculation of co-occurrence matrix as shown in Fig. 7. The dashed-circle is the maximum range of offsets. We can get 31 offsets including a zero offset. The co-occurrence matrices are computed for each small region (Fig. 5(c)). The small rectangular regions are tiled $N \times M$, such as $3 \times 6$ or $6 \times 12$, with no overlapping. Finally, the components of all the co-occurrence matrices are concatenated into a vector (Fig. 5(d)).

Since CoHOG expresses shapes in detail, it is high-dimensional. The dimension is $34,704$, when the small regions are tiled $3 \times 6$. From one small region, CoHOG obtains 31 co-occurrence matrices. A co-occurrence matrix has 64 components (Fig. 4(c)). The co-occurrence matrix calculated with zero offset has only eight effective values because non-diagonal components are zero. Thus CoHOG obtains $(64 \times 30 + 8) \times (3 \times 6) = 34,704$ components from an image. In fact, the effective values are fewer than $34,704$, because co-occurrence matrices have multiple zero valued components. Zero valued components are not used in classification, because their inner product is zero at all times. Nevertheless, CoHOG is a more powerful feature descriptor than HOG.

The implementation of CoHOG is simple. An example of CoHOG implementation is shown in Fig. 8. We can calculate CoHOG by only iterating to increment the components of co-occurrence matrices, whereas HOG calculation includes more procedures, such as orientation weighted voting, histogram normalization, region overlapping, and etc. CoHOG can achieve high performance without those complex procedures.

## 4    Experimental Results

We evaluated the performance of CoHOG by applying our method to two pedestrian image datasets: the DiamlerChrysler dataset [2] and the INRIA dataset [8], which are widely used pedestrian detection benchmark datasets. The DaimlerChrysler dataset contains human images and non-human images cropped into $18 \times 36$ pixels. the INRIA dataset contains human images cropped $64 \times 128$ pixels and non-human images of various sizes. The details of those datasets are shown in Table 1, and some samples of the datasets are shown in Fig. 9.

Because the size of the images are different, in our method we divided the DiamlerChrysler dataset images into $3 \times 6$ small regions, and the INRIA dataset images into $6 \times 12$ small regions. Thus the dimension of our feature is $34,704$ on the DiamlerChrysler dataset, and quadruple that on the INRIA dataset. We used a linear SVM classifier trained with LIBLINEAR [17] which solves linear

**Table 1.** Pedestrian detection benchmark datasets

(a) DaimlerChrysler dataset

| Dataset Name | DaimlerChrysler Pedestrian Classification Benchmark Dataset |
|---|---|
| Distribution site | http://www.science.uva.nl/research/isla/downloads/pedestrians/ |
| Training data | 4,800 $\times$ 3 human images<br>5,000 $\times$ 3 non-human images |
| Test data | 4,800 $\times$ 2 human images<br>5,000 $\times$ 2 non-human images |
| Image size | 18 $\times$ 36 pixels |

(b) INRIA dataset

| Dataset Name | INRIA Person Data Set |
|---|---|
| Distribution site | http://pascal.inrialpes.fr/data/human/ |
| Training data | 2,716 human images<br>1,218 non-human images (10 regions are randomly sampled per an image for training.) |
| Test data | 1,132 human images<br>453 non-human images |
| Image size | Human images are 64 $\times$ 128 pixels<br>Non-human images are various size (214 $\times$ 320 – 648 $\times$ 486 pixels) |

(a) DaimlerChrysler dataset

(b) INRIA dataset

**Fig. 9.** Thumbnails of (a) DaimlerChrysler dataset and (b) INRIA dataset. Upper rows are images of humans and lower rows are images of non-humans in each dataset.

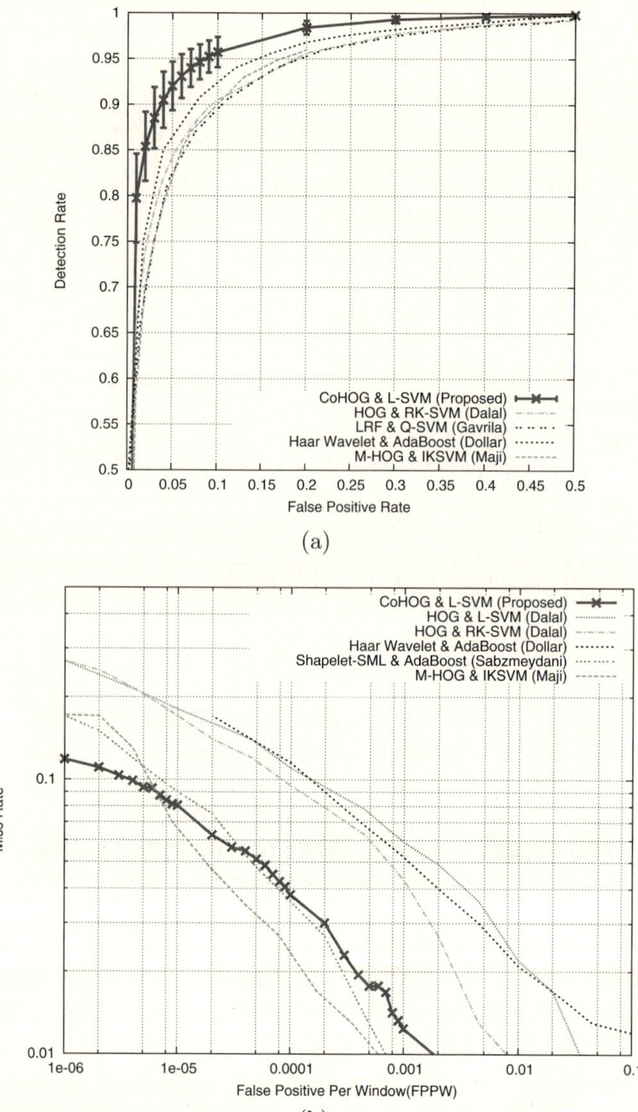


**Fig. 10.** Performance of our methods on (a) DaimlerChrysler dataset and (b) IN-RIA dataset. We compared our method with several previous methods. Our method shows the best performance on the DaimlerChrysler dataset. Miss rate improves more than 40% from that of the state-of-the-art method at a false positive rate of 0.05. On the INRIA dataset, our method decreased miss rate by 30% from that of the state-of-the-art method at a FPPW of $10^{-6}$. Our method reduces miss rate by half compared with HOG on both datasets.

SVM learning problems much faster than previous solvers such as LIBSVM [18] and SVMLight [19].

We compared our method with five previous methods [8], [2], [20], [15], [21]. All the methods use different features and classifiers: Dalal et al. used HOG, and RBF kernel SVM and linear SVM [8]; Gavrila et al. used local receptive fields (LRF) and quadratic SVM [2]; Dollar et al. used Haar wavelet and Ada-Boost [20]; Sabzmeydani et al. used shapelet and AdaBoost [15]; and Maji et al. used multi-level oriented edge energy features and intersection kernel SVM (IKSVM) [21].

The comparison of their performances is shown in Fig. 10. The results of previous methods are traced from the original papers except the performance of HOG on the DaimlerChrysler dataset, because it is not shown by Dalal et al. We show it based on the result of our experiment. The parameters of HOG are as follows: Nine gradient orientations in $0°$–$180°$, cell size of $3 \times 3$ pixels, block size of $2 \times 2$ cells, L2Hys normalized. The classifier is an RBF-kernel SVM. In Fig. 10(a), ROC (Receiver Operating Characteristic) curves on the DaimlerChrysler dataset are shown. An ROC curve further towards the top-left of the diagram means better performance. The results show that our method achieved the best detection rate at every false positive rate. Our method reduced the miss rate ($= 1 -$ detection rate) by about 40% from the state-of-the-art method at a false positive rate of 0.05; the miss rate of our method is 0.08 and that of Dollar et al., the second best, is 0.14.

In Fig. 10(b), DET (Detection Error Tradeoff) curves on the INRIA dataset are shown. A DET curve further towards the bottom-left of the diagram means better performance. The results show that the performance of our method is the best at low FPPW (False Positive Per Window) and comparable to the state-of-the-art method at other FPPW. Our method reduced miss rate by about 30% from the state-of-the-art method at a FPPW of $10^{-6}$; the miss rate of of our method is 0.12 and the that of Maji et al. is 0.17. The performance at low FPPW is important for pedestrian detection, because most of the pedestrian detection systems work at low FPPW to improve usability with few false positives.

The results show that our method is better than the state-of-the-art methods or at least comparable. Furthermore, they show the stability of our method; the performance of the method of Dollar et al. is not good on the INRIA dataset and the method of Maji et al. is not good on the DaimlerChrysler dataset, however, the performance of our method is consistently good on both datasets. Though our method uses a linear classifier which is simpler than an RBF-kernel SVM classifier used with HOG, the miss rate of our method is less than half that of HOG.

## 5 Conclusion

In this paper, we proposed a high-dimensional feature descriptor "Co-occurrence histograms of oriented gradients (CoHOG)" for pedestrian detection. Our feature descriptor uses pairs of gradient orientations as units, from which it builds histograms. Since the building blocks have an extensive vocabulary, our feature descriptor can express local and global shapes in detail. We compared the classification performance of our method and several previous methods on two famous datasets. The experimental results show that the performance of our method is better than that of the state-of-the-art methods or at least comparable, and consistently good on both datasets. The miss rate (i.e. the rate of human images classified as non-human) of our method is less than half that of HOG. Future work involves applying the proposed feature descriptor to other applications.

# References


1. Gavrila, D., Philomin, V.: Real-time object detection for "smart" vehicles. In: The Seventh IEEE International Conference on Computer Vision, vol. 1, pp. 87–93. IEEE Computer Society Press, Los Alamitos (1999)
2. Munder, S., Gavrila, D.M.: An experimental study on pedestrian classification. IEEE Trans. Pattern Anal. Mach. Intell. 28(11), 1863–1868 (2006)
3. Gavrila, D.M., Munder, S.: Multi-cue pedestrian detection and tracking from a moving vehicle. Int. J. Comput. Vision 73(1), 41–59 (2007)
4. Viola, P., Jones, M.J., Snow, D.: Detecting pedestrians using patterns of motion and appearance. In: The Ninth IEEE International Conference on Computer Vision, Washington, DC, USA, pp. 734–741. IEEE Computer Society, Los Alamitos (2003)
5. Mohan, A., Papageorgiou, C., Poggio, T.: Example-based object detection in images by components. IEEE Trans. Pattern Anal. Mach. Intell. 23(4), 349–361 (2001)
6. Papageorgiou, C., Poggio, T.: A trainable system for object detection. Int. J. Comput. Vision 38(1), 15–33 (2000)
7. Lowe, D.G.: Distinctive image features from scale-invariant keypoints. Int. J. Comput. Vision 60(2), 91–110 (2004)
8. Dalal, N., Triggs, B.: Histograms of oriented gradients for human detection. In: IEEE Computer Society Conference on Computer Vision and Pattern Recognition, vol. 1, pp. 886–893 (2005)
9. Mikolajczyk, K., Schmid, C.: A performance evaluation of local descriptors. In: IEEE Computer Society Conference on Computer Vision and Pattern Recognition, pp. 257–263 (2003)
10. Winder, S.A.J., Brown, M.: Learning local image descriptors. In: IEEE Computer Society Conference on Computer Vision and Pattern Recognition, pp. 1–8 (2007)
11. Shashua, A., Gdalyahu, Y., Hayun, G.: Pedestrian detection for driving assistance systems: single-frame classification and system level performance. In: IEEE Intelligent Vehicles Symposium, pp. 1–6 (2004)
12. Mikolajczyk, K., Schmid, C., Zisserman, A.: Human detection based on a probabilistic assembly of robust part detectors. In: Pajdla, T., Matas, J(G.) (eds.) ECCV 2004. LNCS, vol. 3021, pp. 69–82. Springer, Heidelberg (2004)
13. Dalal, N., Triggs, B., Schmid, C.: Human detection using oriented histograms of flow and appearance. In: Leonardis, A., Bischof, H., Pinz, A. (eds.) ECCV 2006. LNCS, vol. 3952, pp. 428–441. Springer, Heidelberg (2006)
14. Wu, B., Nevatia, R.: Detection of multiple, partially occluded humans in a single image by bayesian combination of edgelet part detectors. In: The Tenth IEEE International Conference on Computer Vision, Washington, DC, USA, vol. 1, pp. 90–97. IEEE Computer Society Press, Los Alamitos (2005)

15. Sabzmeydani, P., Mori, G.: Detecting pedestrians by learning shapelet features. In: IEEE Computer Society Conference on Computer Vision and Pattern Recognition, pp. 1–8 (2007)
16. Cortes, C., Vapnik, V.: Support-vector networks. Mach. Learn. 20(3), 273–297 (1995)
17. Hsieh, C., Chang, K., Lin, C., Keerthi, S., Sundararajan, S.: A dual coordinate descent method for large-scale linear svm. In: McCallum, A., Roweis, S. (eds.) The 25th Annual International Conference on Machine Learning, pp. 408–415. Omnipress (2008)
18. Hsu, C.W., Chang, C.C., Lin, C.J.: A practical guide to support vector classification. Technical report, Taipei (2003)
19. Joachims, T.: Training linear svms in linear time. In: The 12th ACM SIGKDD International Conference on Knowledge Discovery and Data Mining, pp. 217–226 (2006)
20. Dollar, P., Tu, Z., Tao, H., Belongie, S.: Feature mining for image classification. In: IEEE Computer Society Conference on Computer Vision and Pattern Recognition, pp. 1–8 (2007)
21. Maji, S., Berg, A.C., Malik, J.: Classification using intersection kernel support vector machines is efficient. In: IEEE Computer Society Conference on Computer Vision and Pattern Recognition (2008)

# Sensor Pose Estimation from Multi-center Cylindrical Panoramas


Fay Huang[1], Reinhard Klette[2], and Yun-Hao Xie[1]

[1] Institute of Computer Science and Information Engineering,
National Ilan University, Taiwan, R.O.C.
`fay@niu.edu.tw`
[2] Department of Computer Science,
The University of Auckland, New Zealand
`r.klette@auckland.ac.nz`



**Abstract.** Cylindrical panoramas can be classified into various types according to their basic scanning properties and mutual spatial alignment, such as single-center (e.g., as in QTVR), concentric, multi-center, symmetric, or (after a transformation onto a cylinder) catadioptric panoramas. This paper deals with a solution of the sensor pose estimation problem using (somehow calculated) corresponding points in the multi-center panoramas. All other types of panoramas are able to be described by this general multi-center model. Due to the non-linearity of the multi-centered projection geometry, the modeling of sensor pose estimation typically results into non-linear and highly complicated forms which incur numerical instability. This paper shows that there exist linear models for sensor pose estimation under minor geometrical constraints, namely symmetric and leveled panoramas. The presented approaches are important for solving the 3D data fusion problem for multiple panoramas; it is also fundamental for an in-depth analysis of multi-view geometry of panoramic images.


## 1  Introduction

Panoramic images have been studied with respect to 3D scene visualization, navigation and reconstruction for more than a decade. Applications include stereoscopic visualization, stereo reconstruction, walkthrough or virtual reality.

Various types of panoramic images are proposed to match particular applications. This paper focuses on those using a cylindrical representation. See Table 1 for a classification of cylindrical panoramas and their applications. A 360° cylindrical panoramic image can be acquired by various means, such as a rotating video or matrix-sensor camera, a catadioptric sensor (with a subsequent mapping onto a cylinder), or a rotating sensor-line camera, as commercially available from various producers since the late 1990s. For simplifying our discussion, we assume a model close to the latter one which has a fixed rotation axis and takes images consecutively at equidistant angles. (Rotating sensor-line cameras allow maximum accuracy, and have been used, e.g., in major architectural photogrammetric projects; see [1]). The projection center of the camera does not have to


T. Wada, F. Huang, and S. Lin (Eds.): PSIVT 2009, LNCS 5414, pp. 48–59, 2009.

**Table 1.** Classification of cylindrical panoramas

| | | |
|---|---|---|
| (A)  Multi-view Panoramas | | Most general case, it is for geometrical studies of finite sets of cylindric panoramas. |
| (B)  Parallel-axis Panoramas<br>(e.g. Leveled Panoramas) | | Virtual Reality Tour Exhibitions<br>Surveillance System |
| (C)  Co-axis Panoramas | | 3D Scene Reconstruction Virtual Reality (a high ceiling environment) |
| (D)  Concentric Panoramas | | Image-Based Rendering |
| (E)  Symmetric Panoramas | | Stereo Visualization 3D Scene Reconstruction |

be on the rotation axis. The major advantage of such off-axis distance is to allow acquiring stereo panoramas that is stereo viewable. The resulting panoramic images in this case, while the off-axis distance is greater than zero, are refereed to as *multi-center* panoramas.

A *multi-view panorama* [2] is a set of multi- or single-center cylindrical panoramas which were recorded at different locations and/or with different capturing parameters. In particular, they might be acquired with respect to different rotation axes. In comparison to a single axial panorama [3,4,5,6,7], the advantages of multi-view panoramas are known to include enlarged visibility and improved stereo reconstruction opportunities; in short, they define multi-view image analysis for the cylindrical panoramic case.

A panoramic image is recorded by a panoramic sensor. Sensor pose estimation deals with recovering the relative pose of two (calibrated) sensors. Compared to planar images or catadioptric images, there is very few literature on sensor pose estimation from cylindrical panoramas.

Ishikuro el at. [8] dealt with a very restricted case of the sensor pose estimation problem, in which the given panoramas are acquired at the same altitude and with parallel rotation axes. Kang and Szeliski [9] discussed the sensor pose estimation problem only for single-center panoramas. Neither generalized multi-view cases (i.e., different intrinsic sensor parameter values and arbitrary sensor poses) nor practically relevant cases (e.g., the multi-view panoramas in [5,7]) of sensor pose estimation have been studied or discussed in the literatures before. This paper provides (for the first time) a cost function whose minimization solves the pose estimation problem for two standard cases of multi-view (and thus also multi-center) cylindrical panoramas.

In the following sections, we first briefly review the chosen basic sensor model and notions used in the paper. Sensor pose estimation from a general multi-view

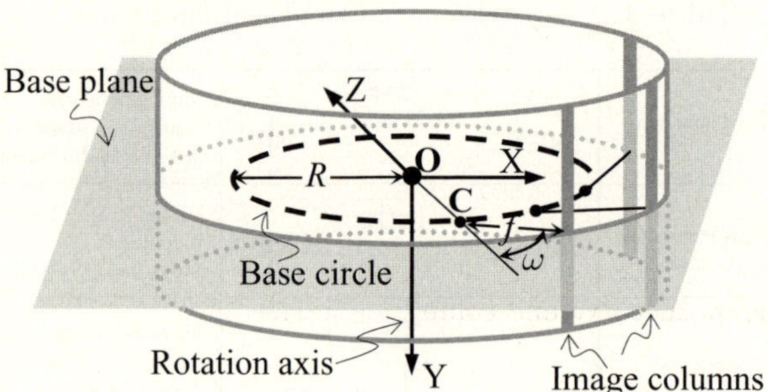


**Fig. 1.** Basic sensor model of multi-center cylindrical panoramas: the origin of the sensor coordinate system is at **O**. Three image columns are shown with their projection centers.

cylindrical panorama is discussed in Section 3. Two general cases of multi-view panoramas are elaborated in Section 4. Section 5 informs about experiments using recorded or synthetic images. There are also concluding remarks.

### 1.1   Sensor Model and Notations

The sensor model used generalizes various panoramic imaging models [3,4,8]. The model consists of multiple projection centers and a cylindrical image surface; see Fig. 1. **C** denotes a projection center. Projection centers are uniformly distributed on the *base circle*. This circle is incident with the *base plane*. **O** denotes the center of the base circle; it is also the origin of the sensor coordinate system. The *off-axis distance* $R$ (radius of the base circle) describes the distance between any projection center and the rotation axis.

A cylindrical panorama is partitioned into *image columns* of equal width which are parallel to the rotation axis. The number of image columns is the *width* $W$ of the panorama. There is a one-to-one ordered mapping between image columns and projection centers. The distance between a projection center and its associated image column is called the *effective focal length*, and is denoted by $f$ (see Fig. 1). The *principal angle* $\omega$ is between a projection ray in the base plane, emitting from **C**, and the normal vector of the base circle at point **C**. The four intrinsic sensor parameters, $R$, $f$, $\omega$, and $W$ characterize how a panoramic image $E_{\mathcal{P}}(R, f, \omega, W)$ is acquired.

Consider two panoramas, $E_{\mathcal{P}_1}$ and $E_{\mathcal{P}_2}$. The geometric relationship between both sensor coordinate systems can be described by a $3 \times 3$ rotation matrix $\mathbf{R}$ and a $3 \times 1$ translation vector $\mathbf{T}$. The rotation matrix is given by three row vectors $[\mathbf{r}_1^T \mathbf{r}_2^T \mathbf{r}_3^T]^T$, and the translation vector equals $(t_x, t_y, t_z)^T$.

## 2   General Multi-view Case

Consider a pair of panoramas, $E_{\mathcal{P}_1}(R_1, f_1, \omega_1, W_1)$ and $E_{\mathcal{P}_2}(R_2, f_2, \omega_2, W_2)$, which are taken at arbitrary poses in 3D space. Let $(x_1, y_1)$ and $(x_2, y_2)$ denote

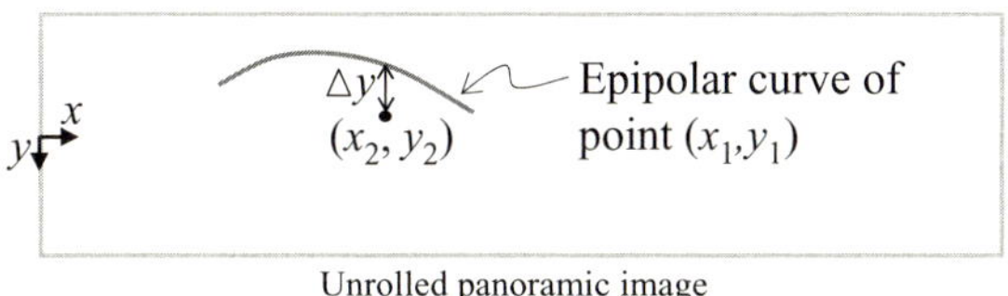


**Fig. 2.** Row difference $\triangle y$ between the actual corresponding image point $(x_2, y_2)$ and the point where epipolar curve and column $x_2$ intersect

the image coordinates of the projection of a 3D point in these two panoramas, respectively. If multiple pairs of corresponding image points are provided, say $(x_{1i}, y_{1i})$ and $(x_{2i}, y_{2i})$, for $i = 1, 2, \ldots, n$, then we are able to estimate sensor poses by minimizing the following cost function,

$$min \sum_{i=1}^{n} \left( y_{2i} - \frac{f_2 \mathbf{r}_2^{\mathrm{T}} \cdot \mathbf{V}}{\sin \delta_{2i} \mathbf{r}_1^{\mathrm{T}} \cdot \mathbf{V} + \cos \delta_{2i} \mathbf{r}_3^{\mathrm{T}} \cdot \mathbf{V} - R_2 \cos \omega_2} \right)^2 \tag{1}$$

where $\alpha_{ki} = \frac{2\pi x_{ki}}{W_k}$, $\delta_{ki} = (\alpha_{ki} + \omega_k)$, $\beta_{ki} = \tan^{-1}\left(\frac{y_{ki}}{f_k}\right)$, and $k = 1$ or 2. Moreover,

$$\mathbf{V} = \mathbf{A} + \frac{R_2 \sin \omega_2 + \cos \delta_{2i} \mathbf{r}_1^{\mathrm{T}} \cdot \mathbf{A} - \sin \delta_{2i} \mathbf{r}_3^{\mathrm{T}} \cdot \mathbf{A}}{\sin \delta_{2i} \mathbf{r}_3^{\mathrm{T}} \cdot \mathbf{B} - \cos \delta_{2i} \mathbf{r}_1^{\mathrm{T}} \cdot \mathbf{B}} \mathbf{B} \tag{2}$$

$$\mathbf{A} = \begin{pmatrix} R_1 \sin \alpha_{1i} - t_x \\ -t_y \\ R_1 \cos \alpha_{1i} - t_z \end{pmatrix} \text{ and } \mathbf{B} = \begin{pmatrix} \sin \delta_{1i} \cos \beta_{1i} \\ \sin \beta_{1i} \\ \cos \delta_{1i} \cos \beta_{1i} \end{pmatrix}$$

The cost function is defined to be the image row difference $\triangle y$, each between the actual corresponding image point in column $x$, and the point where epipolar curve and column $x$ intersect. See Fig. 2 for an unrolled panoramic image. Epipolar curves are calculated based on point coordinates $x_{1i}$, $y_{1i}$ and sensor parameters; see [2]. Note that in our assumed sensor model, the epipolar curve can be considered to be a function $y = G(x)$, which is either monotonically increasing (decreasing), has exactly one turning point (max/min), or is always equals to a constant.

In this general case, the three row vectors of the rotation matrix and the three elements of the translation vector are "distributed" within the given complex cost function. The estimation of sensor poses appears to be rather difficult, if not impossible for the unrestricted case.

## 3   Two Standard Multi-view Cases

However, when using panoramic sensors, such as rotating sensor-line systems, then it is actually standard to aim for a set of leveled panoramas, and for symmetric panoramas if stereo-viewing is also intended; see [1]. (The latter case also simplifies stereo reconstruction.)

## 3.1   Two Symmetric Pairs

$E_{\mathcal{P}_1}(R, f, \omega, W)$ and $E_{\mathcal{P}_2}(R, f, -\omega, W)$ define a symmetric pair of panoramas, both defined on the same sensor coordinate system. (Symmetric pairs can easily be acquired using a single off-shelf camera, e.g., see the approach in [5].) Epipolar curves are in this case lines which may be identified with image rows (see proofs in [2,7,10]). Therefore, dense image correspondences can be calculated by using stereo matching algorithms as developed for stereo pairs of planar images.

If 3D data are collected from multiple pairs of symmetric panoramas, acquired at different locations, then data fusion becomes a challenge, and the registration step requires that the sensor pose estimation problem to be solved in advance.

The basic idea of our sensor pose estimation approach is as follows: first, for each symmetric pair, transform pairs of corresponding image points into directional unit vectors pointing to the reconstructed 3D points; second, establish a geometric relation between these two bunches of unit vectors that are respectively defined in two sensor coordinate systems. The following theorem shows how the directional unit vector of a 3D point (with respect to $\mathbf{O}$) is derived from a pair of corresponding points $(x_1, y)$ and $(x_2, y)$ on symmetric panoramas $E_{\mathcal{P}_1}(R, f, \omega, W)$ and $E_{\mathcal{P}_2}(R, f, -\omega, W)$. Let $\mathbf{u}$ be the directional unit vector of that 3D point which projects into $(x_1, y)$ and $(x_2, y)$.

**Theorem 1.** *This directional vector can be calculated as follows:*

$$u = \frac{\left(\sin\omega\sin\alpha, \, \frac{y}{f}\sin\beta, \, \sin\omega\cos\alpha\right)^T}{\sqrt{\sin^2\omega + \frac{y^2}{f^2}\sin^2\beta}} \tag{3}$$

*where* $\alpha = \frac{(x_1+x_2)\pi}{W}$ *and* $\beta = \frac{(x_2-x_1)\pi}{W}$.

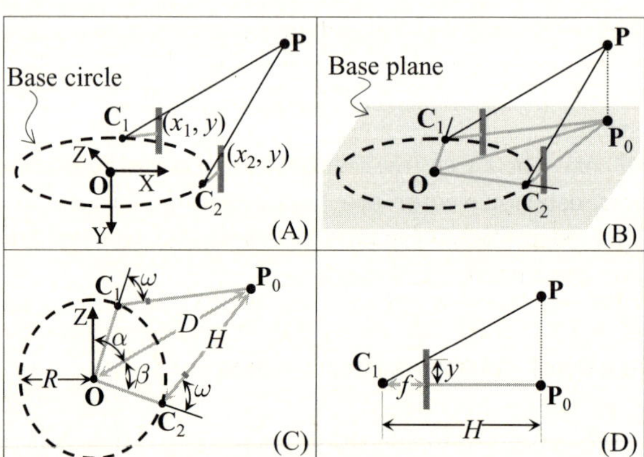


**Fig. 3.** Geometric interpretation of directional unit vector calculation, as described in the proof of Theorem 1

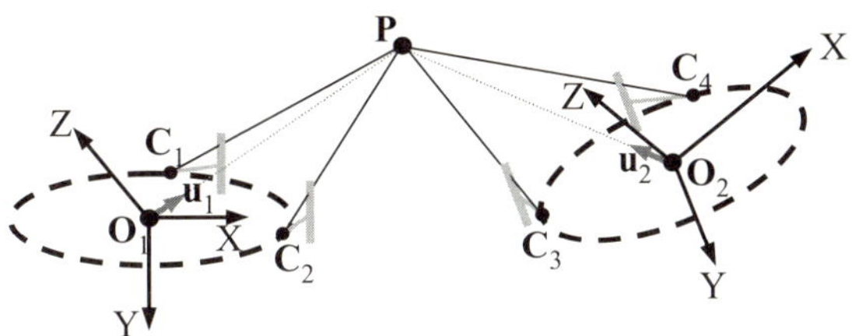

**Fig. 4.** Four corresponding points in two pairs of symmetric panoramas and its pre-image **P** in 3D space. Vectors $\mathbf{u}_1$ and $\mathbf{u}_2$ are two corresponding directional unit vectors of **P** with respect to the sensor coordinate systems $\mathbf{O}_1$ and $\mathbf{O}_2$, respectively.

*Proof.* Let $\mathbf{P}=(P_X, P_Y, P_Z)$ be a 3D point that projects into image points $(x_1, y)$ and $(x_2, y)$ on panoramas $E_{\mathcal{P}_1}$ and $E_{\mathcal{P}_2}$, respectively, see Fig. 3(A). Let $\mathbf{P}_0$ denote the projection of point **P** on the base plane, as illustrated in Fig. 3(B). Define $\alpha$ as the angle between the $Z$-axis and line segment $\overline{\mathbf{OP}_0}$, and $\beta$ be the angle of $\angle \mathbf{P}_0 \mathbf{OC}_1$ (or $\angle \mathbf{P}_0 \mathbf{OC}_2$), see Fig. 3(C). Then we have that $\alpha = \frac{(x_1+x_2)\pi}{W}$ and $\beta = \frac{(x_2-x_1)\pi}{W}$. Moreover, define $H$ to be the length of the line segment $\overline{\mathbf{P}_0 \mathbf{C}_1}$ (or $\overline{\mathbf{P}_0 \mathbf{C}_2}$), and $D$ to be the length of the line segment $\overline{\mathbf{OP}_0}$. We have that $D = \frac{R \sin \omega}{\sin(\omega - \beta)}$. Hence, $P_X = \frac{R \sin \omega \sin \alpha}{\sin(\omega - \beta)}$ and $P_Z = \frac{R \sin \omega \cos \alpha}{\sin(\omega - \beta)}$. Furthermore, we have that $H = \frac{R \sin \beta}{\sin(\omega - \beta)}$, and we know the property $\frac{H}{f} = \frac{\overline{\mathbf{PP}_0}}{y}$ (see Fig. 3(D)), where $\overline{\mathbf{PP}_0} = P_Y$. It follows that $P_Y = \frac{y R \sin \beta}{f \sin(\omega - \beta)}$. After a normalization of vector $(P_X, P_Y, P_Z)$, the directional unit vector **u** of 3D point **P** follows as given in the theorem.

Theorem 1 can directly be applied to approaches in [2] and [5] where angle $\omega$ can take any value. However, for the approach in [7], where the direction of projection is tangential to the base circle (i.e., $\omega = 90°$), the formula in Theorem 1 can even be simplified and is given in the following corollary.

**Corollary 1.** *If $\omega = \frac{\pi}{2}$, then we have that*

$$\boldsymbol{u} = \frac{\left( \sin \alpha, \frac{y}{f} \sin \beta, \cos \alpha \right)^T}{\sqrt{1 + \frac{y^2}{f^2} \sin^2 \beta}} \tag{4}$$

*where $\alpha = \frac{(x_1+x_2)\pi}{W}$ and $\beta = \frac{(x_2-x_1)\pi}{W}$.*

Note that we do not have any dependence of the off-axis distance $R$ in those two formulas, which dramatically simplifies the estimation of sensor poses. For the sensor pose estimation from two arbitrary symmetric pairs (see Fig. 4), we may apply reasoning and results as in [11].

**Theorem 2.** *Given are at least eight pairs of corresponding points in two pairs of symmetric panoramas, where the associated sensor parameters are known except for $R$. The relative sensor poses can then be recovered by the normalized 8-point algorithm up to a scale factor.*

*Proof.* Each pair of corresponding image points in a pair of symmetric panoramas can be transformed into an directional unit vector by Theorem 1. Figure 4 shows a point $\mathbf{P}$ that defines two corresponding directional unit vectors $\mathbf{u}_1$ and $\mathbf{u}_2$ with respect to sensor coordinate systems $\mathbf{O}_1$ and $\mathbf{O}_2$, respectively.

Assume that coordinate system $\mathbf{O}_1$ coincides with the world coordinate system. Let $\mathbf{R}$ and $\mathbf{T}$ describe the orientation and translation of the sensor coordinate system $\mathbf{O}_2$ with respect to the world coordinate system. Since any pair of corresponding directional unit vectors is coplanar in 3D (i.e., epipolar constraint), we have that $\mathbf{u}_1^T(\mathbf{T} \times \mathbf{R}^{-1}\mathbf{u}_2) = 0$. We can rewrite this as $\mathbf{u}_1^T \lfloor \mathbf{T} \rfloor_\times \mathbf{R}^{-1}\mathbf{u}_2 = 0$, where $\lfloor \mathbf{T} \rfloor_\times$ is the skew symmetric matrix of vector $\mathbf{T}$. Then, we have $\mathbf{u}_1^T \mathbf{E}\mathbf{u}_2 = 0$, where $\mathbf{E} = \lfloor \mathbf{T} \rfloor_\times \mathbf{R}^{-1}$. Here, the matrix $\mathbf{E}$ is equivalent to the essential matrix in multiple planar image geometry [11], thus the normalized 8-point algorithm applies to solve the sensor pose estimation problem in this symmetric case.

Hence, we may conclude that eight pairs of corresponding image points are sufficient to determine the relative poses of both sensors up to a scale factor, where the value of sensor parameter $R$ needs not to be known.

Moreover, if all the sensor parameter values (including $R$) are pre-calibrated and given, then the exact sensor pose associated to $\mathbf{O}_2$ can be recovered with respect to the world coordinate system (defined at $\mathbf{O}_1$). This is because those parameter values allow to calculate the exact distance between any two 3D points. Then, these distances can be used as a reference to recover the unknown scale factor in Theorem 2.

### 3.2   One Leveled Pair

In this second common approach for capturing multi-view panoramas, the only constraint is that all associated base planes have to be parallel (say, to the sea level), to be guaranteed by a lever. Figure 5 sketches a leveled pair of panoramas.

Leveled panoramas are common for virtual navigation [12,13] or reconstruction [8,9] of a large scale environments. Leveled panoramas allow large "overlapping" fields of views. The larger the common field of view, the higher the probability that object surfaces are visible in more than one panorama. Hence, this supports more reliable stereo reconstruction and smooth view-transitions between multiple panoramas in a walk-through simulation.

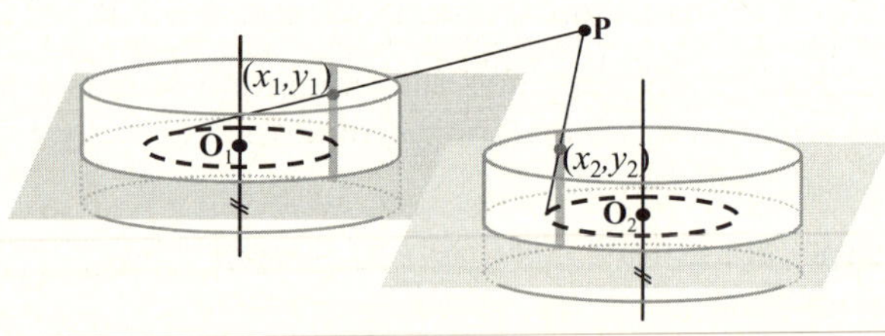


**Fig. 5.** A pair of leveled panoramas and a pair of corresponding image points

The sensor pose estimation criteria of a leveled pair is specified in the following theorem. Two leveled panoramas are acquired by sensors with the same intrinsic parameters, and the sensor poses are related by a single rotation angle $\phi$ with respect to the rotation axis and a translation vector $(t_x, t_y, t_z)^{\mathrm{T}}$. The five variables in this theorem, to be recovered, are $X_1 = \cos\phi$, $X_2 = \sin\phi$, $X_3 = t_x$, $X_4 = t_z$, and $X_5 = t_y$. In the equational system we will also use the following nine coefficients:

$$
\begin{aligned}
c_{1i} &= y_{2i}R\sin(\delta_{1i}-\alpha_{2i}) + y_{1i}R\sin(\delta_{2i}-\alpha_{1i}) \\
c_{2i} &= y_{1i}R\cos(\delta_{2i}-\alpha_{1i}) - y_{2i}R\cos(\delta_{1i}-\alpha_{2i}) \\
c_{3i} &= -y_{2i}\cos\delta_{1i} \qquad c_{4i}=y_{2i}\sin\delta_{1i} \\
c_{5i} &= y_{1i}\cos\delta_{2i} \qquad c_{6i}=-y_{1i}\sin\delta_{2i} \\
c_{7i} &= f\sin(\alpha_{2i}-\alpha_{1i}) \qquad c_{8i}=f\cos(\alpha_{2i}-\alpha_{1i}) \\
c_{9i} &= -(y_{1i}+y_{2i})R\sin\omega
\end{aligned}
$$

where $\alpha_{ki} = \frac{2\pi x_{ki}}{W}$, $\delta_{ki} = (\alpha_{ki}+\omega)$, and $k = 1$ or $2$.

**Theorem 3.** *Given a set of corresponding pairs of points $(x_{1i}, y_{1i})$ and $(x_{2i}, y_{2i})$, where $i = 1, 2, \ldots, n$, the values of $\phi, t_x, t_y$, and $t_z$ can be estimated by minimizing the following sum,*

$$
\sum_{i=1}^{n} (c_{1i}X_1 + c_{2i}X_2 + c_{3i}X_3 + c_{4i}X_4 + c_{5i}X_1 X_3 + c_{6i}X_1 X_4
$$

$$
+ c_{7i}X_1 X_5 + c_{6i}X_2 X_3 - c_{5i}X_2 X_4 + c_{8i}X_2 X_5 + c_{9i})^2
$$

*subjected to the constraints $X_1^2 + X_2^2 = 1$, $X_1^2 \leq 1$, and $X_2^2 \leq 1$.*

*Proof.* Let $(x_1, y_1)$ and $(x_2, y_2)$ be a pair of corresponding image points in a pair of leveled cylindrical panoramas $E_{\mathcal{P}_1}$ and $E_{\mathcal{P}_2}$, respectively. Given $x_1$ and $y_1$, the corresponding epipolar curve in $E_{\mathcal{P}_2}$ can be expressed as follows (see [1]):

$$
\begin{aligned}
&y_2 R\sin(\alpha_1 + \omega - \alpha_2 - \phi) - y_2 R\sin\omega - y_2\cos(\alpha_1 + \omega)t_x \\
&+ y_2\sin(\alpha_1 + \omega)t_z + f\sin(\alpha_2 - \alpha_1 + \phi)t_y - y_1 R\sin\omega \\
&+ y_1 R\sin(\alpha_2 - \alpha_1 + \omega + \phi) + y_1\cos(\alpha_2 + \omega + \phi)t_x \\
&- y_1\sin(\alpha_2 + \omega + \phi)t_z = 0
\end{aligned} \tag{5}
$$

The cost function is defined by the row difference between an actual corresponding image point and the point on the same column incident with the epipolar curve. In short, by algebraic rearrangements of Equation (5), we obtain the second-order algebraic representation for the minimization in this theorem.

## 4   Experiments

Several real-world experiments on estimating sensor poses have been carried out at different places and by using different type of cameras. Camera and sensor

**Fig. 6.** Two symmetric leveled panorama pairs acquired at different locations (top: right panorama of the first pair, bottom: right panorama of the second pair), all marked with 40 corresponding points

**Fig. 7.** Illustration of three epipolar curves calculated based on the pose estimation results

were calibrated separately in advance; thus the camera's intrinsic parameters were known and kept unaltered during image acquisition. Figure 6 illustrate one example of a leveled pair taken by a line-camera at different locations in the same room. Actually, at each location, a pair of stereo panoramas were acquired for experiments, and those shown in Fig. 6 are the "right" panoramas only. In this particular example, we used $R = 100$ mm, $f = 21.7$ mm, and $\omega = \pm 155°$. Each panorama has an image resolution of $324 \times 1,343$. We identified manually in total 40 corresponding points (marked as stars).

The true rotation matrix $\mathbf{R}$ and translation vector $\mathbf{T}$ of these two symmetric panorama pairs were measured with less than $\pm 1\%$ error, and we have $\phi = 50°$ and $(t_x, t_y, t_z) = (-1,000, -45, -1,000)$ in mm. The estimated sensor pose is denoted as $\hat{\mathbf{R}}$ and $\hat{\mathbf{T}}$. The error measurements for rotation and translation are defined as $\arccos\left(\left(tr(\mathbf{R}\hat{\mathbf{R}}^\mathsf{T}) - 1\right)/2\right)$ and $\arccos\left(\mathbf{T} \cdot \hat{\mathbf{T}}/\|\mathbf{T}\|\|\hat{\mathbf{T}}\|\right)$, respectively, both in degrees.

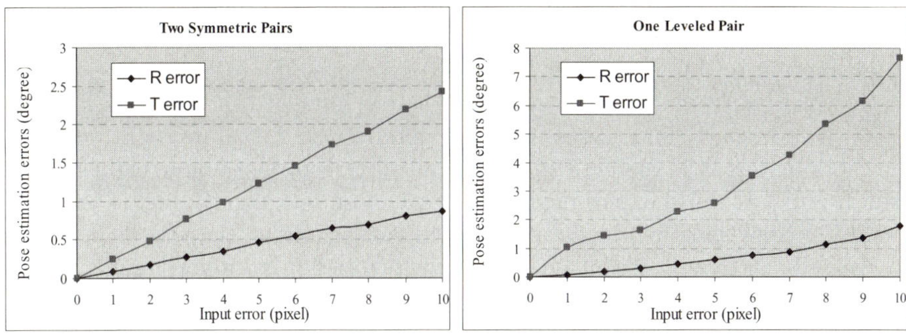

**Fig. 8.** Error sensitivity analysis for the symmetric or leveled case (synthetic images)

We used the SVD method for estimating $\hat{R}$ and $\hat{T}$ when symmetric pairs were used. We obtained 0.54° estimation error for the rotation and 1.85° estimation error for the translation. When only the leveled pair were used, due to the nonlinear constraints, the quadratic programming optimization approach was not directly applicable. Thus, the sequential quadratic programming method was used instead for optimization (i.e., function *fmincon* in MatLab). We obtained 1.22° error in the rotation estimation and 4.65° error in the translation. We show in Fig. 7 three particular epipolar curves calculated based on the erroneous estimations from the leveled case. The average $y$-difference between the identified corresponding points and the calculated epipolar curves is 1.2 pixel. For most points, those pose estimation errors, in this example, cause less than three pixel error in vertical direction while processing stereo matching.

We also conducted an error sensitivity analysis with simulated image data, in analogy to the real-world experiment, for both estimation approaches. Figure 8 plots how errors in detecting corresponding points impact the estimation result. The horizontal axes show various error sizes up to ten pixel. In the analysis, for example, a five-pixel input error means that each pair of corresponding image points was corrupted by errors of max/min five pixel in both $x$- and $y$-values, and the errors are modeled as Gaussian-distributed random numbers.

In the case of symmetric panoramas, the curves (actually, nearly lines) of the estimation errors for rotation and translation show both a monotonic increase measured in the average for 500 runs. For up to ten-pixel input error, the estimation errors of rotation matrix or translation vector are less than one or three degrees, respectively. This analysis suggests that we had input errors of about six to eight pixel in our real-world experiment. However, this conclusion did not match our expectations. Hence, a further error analysis was conducted to test how the sensor calibration errors of $R$ and $\omega$ affect the pose estimation results. In the symmetric case, $R$ is an independent variable; and if $\omega$ has a one-degree error, then it would produce a four-pixel error in the input data. Therefore, the accuracy of sensor calibration, especially for $\omega$, is crucial to the pose estimation result.

For the case of leveled panoramas, the errors for both $\hat{R}$ and $\hat{T}$ are about two point five times the errors in the symmetric-panorama case. It suggests that the quadratic programming approach is more sensitive to input errors than the SVD method. Also, the assignment of initial values has significant impact onto the estimation result. According to our experiments, the estimation result was mostly sensitive to the 'sign' of the initial values but not to their quantities nor inter-ratios. In particular, zeros were not good for an initial guess in our case. The plots in this case indicate that we had input errors of about eight to nine pixel in our real-world experiment, which are close but slightly bigger than the conclusion drawn in the symmetric-panorama case. Error analysis on $R$ and $\omega$ was carried out as well. It concludes that the error of $R$ has a very minor impact on the pose estimation results. Moreover, a $k$-degree error of $\omega$ would cause about a $k$-degree error in the estimated $\hat{\mathbf{T}}$, for any real number $k$, but an error in $\omega$ has very little impact on the estimation of $\mathbf{R}$. The conclusion drawn here is coherent to the symmetric-panorama case.

Finally, more synthetic experiments were designed and performed for different panorama configurations (i.e., different poses, different sensor parameter values, and etc.). They lead to conclusions that the resolution of the input panoramic images, and the distribution of the selected corresponding points are also two critical factors for pose estimation. The panoramic image resolution, especially the width, should be as large as possible. The corresponding points should be distributed uniformly and sparsely on the entire panoramic images. A larger set of corresponding points, say greater than 100, would not guarantee a better estimation result. A much better result can be achieved if image resolution of $1,000 \times 10,000$ is used instead, and the nearest scene point is no less than four meters from both sensors. The estimation errors can be less than 0.5 degrees for both $\mathbf{R}$ and $\mathbf{T}$, allowing for both cases even up to ten-pixel input error.

## 5    Conclusions

This paper presented approaches for pose estimation of multi-view (i.e., also multi-center) cylindrical panoramas. Two geometric constraints were used: one was by coplanarity of corresponding projection rays, and the other was by intersection of corresponding projection rays.

The first constraint was used in the case of two symmetric pairs, and we obtained a "linear" solution for the sensor pose estimation problem. We showed that the (common) normalized 8-point algorithm can be utilized in this case. Experimentally, we found that the normalization step of the normalized 8-point algorithm for improving the accuracy and satiability was ignorable in our case,[1] and this makes a difference to the planar image case. The second constraint was applied to cases of a general pair, or a leveled pair of cylindrical panoramas. Rather poor estimation results were obtained in the case of general pairs, and we did not include those here. In contrast to that, the result for the leveled-panorama case was greatly improved and reasonably stable. The proposed approaches are able to achieve high accuracy of less than 0.5 degree error in general,

---

[1] The corresponding image points on panoramas is likely not as skewed or clustered as in the planar image case.

if high-resolution panoramic images are used and corresponding image points are carefully selected.

According to our error sensitivity analysis, the estimation of $\mathbf{T}$ is generally more sensitive to noise than the estimation of $\mathbf{R}$, and both estimation errors have approximately a linear relation to the input errors (as concluded from extensive simulations). We may also conclude that sensor pose estimation from leveled panoramas is more sensitive to errors than from pairs of symmetric panoramas. Moreover, the sensor calibration results of $R$ and $f$ have very little impact on pose estimation results, while $\omega$'s error has a more serious influence on the accuracy of estimated sensors poses. For future work it is thus of interest to develop an algorithm, or a framework, that takes care of sensor calibration and pose estimation at once, similar to self-calibration for the planar image case.

# References


1. Huang, F., Klette, R., Scheibe, K.: Panoramic Imaging: Sensor-Line Cameras and Laser Range-Finders. Wiley, West Sussex (2008)
2. Huang, F., Wei, S.K., Klette, R.: Geometrical fundamentals of polycentric panoramas. In: Proc. ICCV 2001, Vancouver, Canada, pp. I560–I565 (July 2001)
3. Li, Y., Shum, H.Y., Tang, C.K., Szeliski, R.: Stereo reconstruction from multiperspective panoramas. IEEE Transactions on Pattern Analysis and Machine Intelligence 26(1), 45–62 (2004)
4. Murray, D.: Recovering range using virtual multicamera stereo. CVIU 61(2), 285–291 (1995)
5. Peleg, S., Ben-Ezra, M.: Stereo panorama with a single camera. In: Proc. CVPR 1999, Fort Collins, Colorado, USA, pp. 395–401 (June 1999)
6. Scheibe, K., Suppa, M., Hirschmäller, H., Strackenbrock, B., Huang, F., Liu, R., Hirzinger, G.: Multi-scale 3d-modeling. In: Chang, L.-W., Lie, W.-N. (eds.) PSIVT 2006. LNCS, vol. 4319, pp. 96–107. Springer, Heidelberg (2006)
7. Shum, H.Y., He, L.W.: Rendering with concentric mosaics. In: Proc. SIGGRAPH 1999, Los Angeles, California, USA, pp. 299–306 (August 1999)
8. Ishiguro, H., Yamamoto, M., Tsuji, S.: Omni-directional stereo. PAMI 14(2), 257–262 (1992)
9. Kang, S.B., Szeliski, R.: 3-d scene data recovery using omnidirectional multibaseline stereo. IJCV 25(2), 167–183 (1997)
10. Seitz, S.: The space of all stereo images. In: Proc. ICCV 2001, Vancouver, Canada, pp. 26–33 (July 2001)
11. Hartley, R., Zisserman, A.: Multiple View Geometry in Computer Vision. Cambridge Uni. Press, United Kingdom (2000)
12. Chen, S.E.: QuickTimeVR - an image-based approach to virtual environment navigation. In: Proc. SIGGRAPH 1995, Los Angeles, California, USA, pp. 29–38 (August 1995)
13. Kang, S.B., Desikan, P.: Virtual navigation of complex scenes using clusters of cylindrical panoramic images. In: Graphics Interface, pp. 223–232 (1998)

# Monocular 3D Reconstruction of Objects Based on Cylindrical Panoramas

Ralf Haeusler[1], Reinhard Klette[1], and Fay Huang[2]

[1] The University of Auckland, Computer Science Department, New Zealand
r.haeusler@cs.auckland.ac.nz
[2] CSIE, National Ilan University, Yi-Lan, Taiwan

**Abstract.** This paper discusses ways of using a single panoramic image (captured by a rotating sensor-line camera having very-high spatial resolution) for the geometric shape recovery of a shown object. The objective is to create a sparse polyhedral model, only allowing a few interactive user inputs for a given single panoramic image. The study was motivated by the general question whether a single panoramic image projection allows some kind of 3D shape recovery, possibly benefitting from available monocular approaches for standard (say, pinhole-type) camera models.

**Keywords:** Monocular 3D reconstruction, cylindrical projection, panorama, rotating sensor-line camera.

## 1   Introduction

The computation of 3D structure from stereo images receives increasingly attention due to the enormous progress recently in this area. However, the task of retrieving 3D information from a single image seems to be a rather ill-posed problem, yet scientific interest herein dates back many centuries [2]. In fact, so-called monocular reconstruction cannot work without some kind of a-priori knowledge (i.e., some assumptions about geometric properties or shapes of the shown objects, or about surface reflectance).

Apart from utilizing geometric constraints for specified classes of objects (see, for example, [7,8]), a popular approach to monocular 3D understanding applies the concept of vanishing points (see, for example, [4,5]), as introduced by painters in the renaissance.

Of course, talented artists may often be successful in modelling manually a scene from a single photograph, by using common 3D clues for the human visual system [10].

This paper deals with monocular reconstruction based on images of very high resolution and with a wide field of view. Such images may be recorded with so-called rotating sensor-line cameras [6], and the resulting images are also called *cylindrical panoramas.* The question arises whether such images, projected onto a straight cylinder, provide better opportunities for understanding the 3D structure from only a single image compared to images recorded with a 'normal' (say, *pinhole-type*) camera. [6] uses cylindrical panoramas for 3D modelling of (large)

T. Wada, F. Huang, and S. Lin (Eds.): PSIVT 2009, LNCS 5414, pp. 60–70, 2009.

**Fig. 1.** A 3D model of the throne room in castle Neuschwanstein [6]. Here, multiple laser range-finder scans and multiple cylindrical panoramas have been used. Of course, a single-view panoramic scan cannot provide this complexity of 3D information (not even close to this).

objects such as a castle, by fusion of data of a laser range-finder, yielding visually impressive results, see Figure 1.

However, the 3D information is in this case derived via purpose-designed measuring equipment (laser range-finder) whose application is characterized by difficult and labor-intensive manual handling of the involved equipment.

[3] reports about pioneering work on modeling a 3D scene directly from a panoramic image. However, the presented approach does not yet allow to reconstruct a broad range of objects, and did also not yet cover the recovery of aspect ratios.[1] Aspect ratios of recorded rectangles may be recovered from a single (pinhole-type) image; see [9].

The outline of this paper is as follows: Section 2 provides technical prerequisites related to panoramic imaging when projecting onto a straight cylinder. Section 3 presents a monocular reconstruction method and an example (image with resulting object model). Section 4 is pointing to particularities of cylindrical panoramas concerning monocular reconstructions. Section 5 contains conclusions.

## 2   Cylindrical Panoramas

A common cylindrical panorama results from some kind of image stitching, but to allow for very high-resolution cylindrical panoramas, a rotating sensor-line camera is an appropriate choice. A (typically, CCD) sensor-line and its projection center rotate about a defined axis, describing this way a cylindrical surface

---

[1] When mapping a rectangle into a trapezoid by perspective projection, the ratio of side lengths of the rectangle defines the unknown aspect ratio.

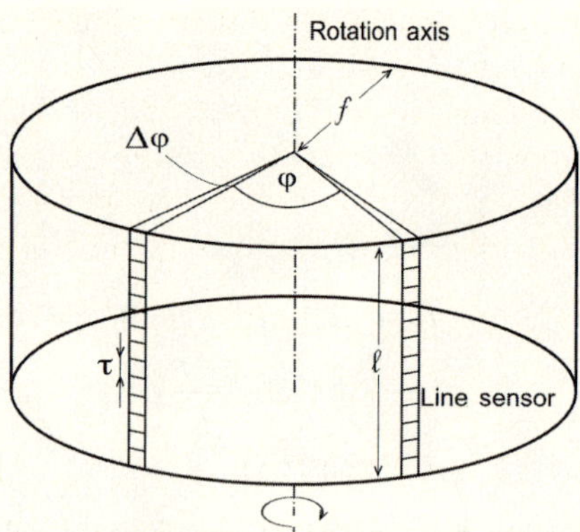


**Fig. 2.** Camera model of a cylindrical projection with a single projection center: $\Delta\varphi$ denotes the angular increment, $f$ the effective focal length of the lens, $\tau$ is the physical size of a pixel on the sensor line (assumed to be constant), and $l$ the total physical length of the sensor line

(with the recorded panorama) and a circular path, respectively. The recorded panorama is composed line by line, after (or during) such a rotation (typically of full 360°).

If the projection centers of all the recorded lines are at the rotation axis, then they all coincide, and the circular path degenerates into a single point. Such a case of a single projection center is illustrated in Figure 2.

The main advantage of such a camera system is its very large spatial resolution. By specifying the number of recorded lines (columns), the wide field of view of the recorded panorama may even extend beyond 360°, by recording into some directions more than once. The data volume of a single 360° panorama is in the range of several gigabytes for contemporary sensor lines of about 10k color pixels. The main disadvantage is the long exposure time, limiting its use for dynamic scenes (but also allowing interesting effects such as having a person repeatedly in a recorded panorama). Some of the intrinsic parameters (such as focal length, angular increment, size of a pixel) are also illustrated in Figure 2.

As it is most appropriate to record images with square pixels,[2] a common target is to specify the number of columns using an angular increase of

$$\Delta\varphi = 2 \cdot \arctan\left(\frac{\frac{1}{2}\tau}{f}\right)$$

for image recording. We assume (and used) a 360° image with pixels known to have square shape, and this specifies the used intrinsic parameters for monocular reconstruction (up to a scaling factor). Of course, this ignores some possible (minor) errors, such as having the projection center always exactly at the rotation axis. We assume a *camera center* **O** which identifies the unique origin of all projection rays.

---

[2] To be precise, these are actually 'cylindrical squares' on a cylindrical surface.

The principal point is defined by the intersection of the optical axis with the sensor line, and the actual position of this point will have no impact on the following discussion. Thus we simply assume that image coordinate $j = 0$ identifies the principal point (i.e., somewhere within this square pixel).

Projection rays, necessary for monocular reconstruction, can be calculated from pixel coordinates $i$ and $j$ in the recorded cylindrical image as follows:

$$t_\varphi = \Delta\varphi * i$$

$$t_\Theta = \arctan(\frac{j \cdot \tau}{f})$$

$$t_\kappa = \cos(t_\Theta)$$

This defines a ray direction $\mathbf{t}$ in spherical coordinates, which is converted into Cartesian coordinates as follows:

$$t_x = t_\kappa \sin t_\Theta \cos t_\varphi$$

$$t_y = t_\kappa \sin t_\Theta \sin t_\varphi$$

$$t_z = t_\kappa \cos t_\Theta$$

A projection ray $\mathbf{r}$ is thus described by $\mathbf{r} = \mathbf{O} + \lambda \cdot \mathbf{t}$, for a real $\lambda$.

## 3  Monocular Reconstruction

*Reconstruction* is the process of determining an approximate geometric surface model of an object and its *pose* or *attitude* (i.e., position and direction) in 3D space.

### 3.1  Proposed Approach

The reconstruction approach based on projection rays, and using only a single image, is as follows: First, some prior knowledge about geometric properties is necessary, usually related to the shape of the shown objects. Then, a selected 3D shape prior has to fit the corresponding family of projection rays such that the image of the object's shape prior matches to the result of the given projection. In the 2D case (pinhole-type images), this was reported in [9] for rectangular objects by calculating a homography such that a given trapezoidal image of a rectangle was actually mapped into a rectangular shape.

We also discuss rectangular geometric primitives here, but apply it to the described cylindrical projection. The diagonals of a rectangle are bisecting each other, say in a 3D point $r_d$. Then we have that

$$r_d = \frac{r_1 + r_3}{2} = \frac{r_2 + r_4}{2}$$

for the four cyclically ordered vertices $r_h$ of the rectangle, with $h \in \{1, 2, 3, 4\}$. As the corresponding projection rays of the image of $r_h$ should be incident with $r_h$, it follows that

$$\lambda_1 \cdot t_1 - \lambda_2 \cdot t_2 + \lambda_3 \cdot t_3 = \lambda_4 \cdot t_4$$

Obviously, from a single image, a reconstruction is only possible up to a scaling factor. Thus, without restriction of the generality, it can be assumed that $\lambda_4 = 1$. This defines a linear equational system

$$
\begin{bmatrix} t_{1x} & -t_{2x} & t_{3x} \\ t_{1y} & -t_{2y} & t_{3y} \\ t_{1z} & -t_{2z} & t_{3z} \end{bmatrix} \cdot \begin{bmatrix} \lambda_1 \\ \lambda_2 \\ \lambda_3 \end{bmatrix} = \begin{bmatrix} t_{4x} \\ t_{4y} \\ t_{4z} \end{bmatrix}
\tag{1}
$$

The unique solution $\lambda_1, \ldots, \lambda_4$ describes the position of those 3D rectangular vertices up to a scale factor $\mu$ as follows: $r_h = \mathbf{O} + \mu \cdot \lambda_h \cdot \mathbf{t_h}$. Scale factor $\mu$ can be determined only if object dimensions are known for real world scenes (e.g., height or width of objects in the real world).

However, applied to an object that is composed of several 'connected' rectangles, a reconstruction result is not satisfactory if every single rectangle is reconstructed separately. The first reason is that every single rectangle would have a different scaling factor $\mu$ as one of the $\lambda_h$ values was set to be equal to one. Adjusting the scale factors $\mu$ over all rectangles based on 'connectedness' (i.e., sharing of edges) properties of faces of the object still does not allow for a closed reconstructed object surface due to unavoidable reconstruction inaccuracies.

The following is now our proposition for solving this problem. From an object consisting of $q$ rectangles with $n$ vertices, a single linear equational system $\mathbf{T} \cdot \lambda = \mathbf{t}$ is derived as follows: An instance of vector $\mathbf{t}$ contains data from the 'first' projection ray to a vertex which may be incident with up to $q$ rectangles. (The component $\lambda_1$ of vector $\lambda$ is set to be equal to one due to scale ambiguity.) Assuming that $q$ is the maximum for all considered rays, we have a matrix $\mathbf{T}$ composed of $n - 1$ columns and $3 \cdot q$ rows. These contain information about all the $n$ projection rays, with up to $q$ rectangles in each case.

All the equations of the derived system are as follows:

$$
\begin{bmatrix}
t_{2x}^1 & -t_{3x}^1 & t_{4x}^1 & \cdots & t_{nx}^1 \\
t_{2y}^1 & -t_{3y}^1 & t_{4y}^1 & \cdots & t_{ny}^1 \\
t_{2z}^1 & -t_{3z}^1 & t_{4z}^1 & \cdots & t_{nz}^1 \\
t_{2x}^2 & -t_{3x}^2 & t_{4x}^2 & \cdots & t_{nx}^2 \\
t_{2y}^2 & -t_{3y}^2 & t_{4y}^2 & \cdots & t_{ny}^2 \\
t_{2z}^2 & -t_{3z}^2 & t_{4z}^2 & \cdots & t_{nz}^2 \\
\vdots & \vdots & \vdots & & \vdots \\
\vdots & \vdots & \vdots & \ddots & \vdots \\
\vdots & \vdots & \vdots & & \vdots \\
t_{2x}^q & -t_{3x}^q & t_{4x}^q & \cdots & t_{nx}^q \\
t_{2y}^q & -t_{3y}^q & t_{4y}^q & \cdots & t_{ny}^q \\
t_{2z}^q & -t_{3z}^q & t_{4z}^q & \cdots & t_{nz}^q
\end{bmatrix}
\cdot
\begin{bmatrix}
\lambda_2 \\ \lambda_3 \\ \vdots \\ \lambda_n
\end{bmatrix}
=
\begin{bmatrix}
t_x^1 \\ t_y^1 \\ t_z^1 \\ t_x^2 \\ t_y^2 \\ t_z^2 \\ \vdots \\ \vdots \\ \vdots \\ t_x^q \\ t_y^q \\ t_z^q
\end{bmatrix}
$$

$\mathbf{T}$ is in general a sparse matrix, as one projection ray is often connected to not more than four rectangles. (For implementation, the `multimap`-datastructure from the Standard Template Library [1] may be recommended.)

In general we have that $3 \cdot q \geq n$, and an overdetermined system needs to be solved, by minimizing the Euclidean norm $\|\mathbf{T} \cdot \lambda - \mathbf{t}\|$. Due to a high sensitivity to outliers, this norm might be unsuitable for some objects, as it may violate our initial assumption of bisecting diagonals of the involved rectangles. Thus, we only use this for an initial solution for a subsequent nonlinear minimization. For this we apply as error metric a function $\Delta$ of the form $\Delta(e) = \log(1 + e^2/c)$ (for some constant $c$) which assigns smaller penalties to larger discrepancies $e$ between vertices of rectangles.

Finally, after having computed a solution vector $\lambda$, the derivation of a list of reconstructed rectangles (from $\mathbf{T}$ and $\mathbf{t}$, using, for example, the `multimap`-datastructure) is kind of straightforward.

### 3.2   An Example

The proposed method can be used for (approximate) reconstructions of various objects defined by multiple rectangles. In the example shown below, a room of an indoor scene is approximated by a cuboid. Corresponding interactive user inputs (for identifying vertices of rectangles) are illustrated in Figure 3. In this case, a user selected eight corners of the room.

The shown arcs demonstrate the complexity of projected edges into such a panorama, basically illustrating that an automated extraction of vertices defines a challenging problem. Note that further rectangles such as windows or doors may be selected as well, leading in general to more robust 3D reconstructions.

Table 1 lists pixel coordinates $(i, j)$ of the illustrated interactive user input and the corresponding coordinates $(x, y, z)$ of reconstructed 3D points.

The maximum angular discrepancy in this example of a reconstructed cuboidal object is 1.4% (assuming right angles as the golden standard). This may be due to reconstruction inaccuracies in our optimization process, errors in the actual imaging process, or even deviations from an ideally cuboidal room in the shown historic architecture itself.

Figure 4 shows the reconstructed cuboidal room together with mapped textures using a projection of the image data available in the original (single) panorama.

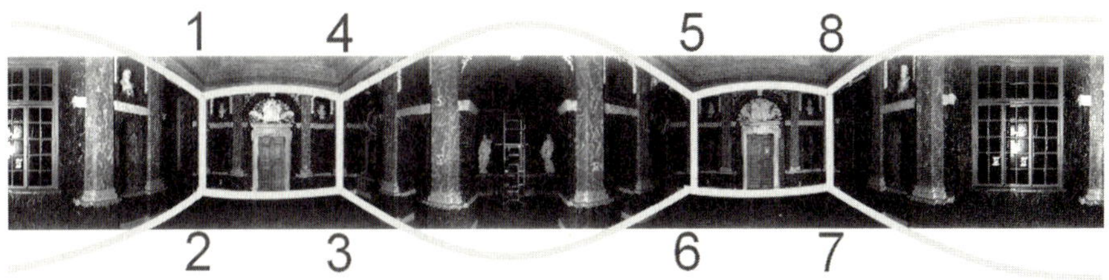


**Fig. 3.** Interactive user input (selection of eight points, or six geometric primitives). The shown arcs only illustrate how straight segments are curved in a cylindrical projection; they are not required for interactive input.

**Table 1.** Image coordinates of pixels selected in Figure 3 together with results of the 3D reconstruction process

| Point | 2D | | 3D | | |
|---|---|---|---|---|---|
| | i | j | x | y | z |
| 1 | 11189 | 2029 | 40.47 | -50.11 | 16.84 |
| 2 | 11191 | 7368 | 40.49 | -50.13 | -21.66 |
| 3 | 18703 | 7414 | -12.09 | -61.76 | -21.83 |
| 4 | 18711 | 2117 | -12.04 | -61.67 | 15.75 |
| 5 | 38702 | 2098 | -36.27 | 51.42 | 15.64 |
| 6 | 38698 | 7409 | -36.17 | 51.39 | -21.83 |
| 7 | 46171 | 7314 | 16.94 | 62.70 | -22.23 |
| 8 | 46171 | 2002 | 16.97 | 62.75 | 16.80 |

**Fig. 4.** Reconstructed cuboidal room with mapped textures. Circular regions on the floor and the ceiling were not recorded by the rotating sensor-line camera, and texture information is thus not available in these areas. (The ceiling is shown to indicate the reconstructed 3D volume.).

## 4   Pinhole-Type versus Cylindrical Camera

The example illustrated that it is possible to generate a full 3D volume model from a single 360° panoramic image, what is, of course, not possible with a single image of a pinhole-type camera. For pointing out whether the cylindrical projection itself is already advantageous compared to the standard pinhole model, we look at panoramic images with a viewing angle less than 360°.

For 360° cylindric images with square pixels, relevant intrinsic camera parameters were assumed to be given in Section 2. However, angular increment and focal length of a rotating line camera may also be estimated based on given (recorded) images.

## 4.1   Estimation of Angular Increment

The most obvious observation (that should be exploited) is that straight lines in the real-world are generally bent under cylindrical projection, in difference to pinhole-type cameras. In the description below we omit lens distortion effects and assume mathematical cylindrical projection.

Keeping in mind that the straightness of line segments is invariant under homographies, it is sufficient to ensure that line segments curved due to cylindrical projection become straight when projected into any plane (e.g., the one shown in Figure 5). A cylinder-to-plane projection involves the sought-after parameter $\Delta\varphi$, and this can be estimated iteratively.

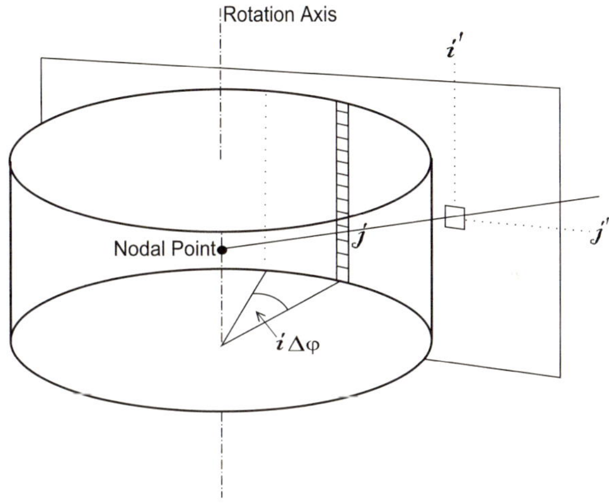


**Fig. 5.** Projection of an image cylinder into a tangential plane

Image coordinates $(i, j)$ of the image cylinder are projected into planar image coordinates $(i', j')$ (on a tangential plane) according to the following equations:

$$i' = f \cdot \tan(i \cdot \Delta\varphi) \cdot \frac{1}{\tau}$$

$$j' = \frac{j}{\cos(i \cdot \Delta\varphi)} \tag{2}$$

The tangential plane coincides with the cylinder surface at $\varphi = 0$.

We refer to this as projection $\Pi$. It is obvious that only image data within a viewing angle of 180° can be projected onto a tangential plane.

Now, for any three points $(i_1, j_1)$, $(i_2, j_2)$ and $(i_3, j_3)$ on a 'curved line' in the cylindrical image, assumed to be a projection of a straight segment, the points $(i'_1, j'_1)$, $(i'_2, j'_2)$ and $(i'_3, j'_3)$, with

$$(i'_1, j'_1) = \Pi((i_1, j_1))$$
$$(i'_2, j'_2) = \Pi((i_2, j_2))$$
$$(i'_3, j'_3) = \Pi((i_3, j_3))$$

have to be collinear. This infers that

$$\frac{j'_3 - j'_1}{i'_3 - i'_1} = \frac{j'_2 - j'_1}{i'_2 - i'_1}$$

Note that for $i'_3 = i'_1$ or $i'_2 = i'_1$, no information about $\Delta\varphi$ can be derived as vertical lines in the world remain straight on the image cylinder provided that the rotation axis is perfectly upright.

We are able to estimate $\Delta\varphi$ numerically by applying interval bisection, with

$$\frac{j'_3 - j'_1}{i'_3 - i'_1} - \frac{j'_2 - j'_1}{i'_2 - i'_1} \leq \epsilon \leq 10^{-5}$$

being the stop criterion.

Note that, although the method is usable for all 'bent straight segments' in the cylindrical image, it yields most accurate results for strongly bended 'horizontal' segments. In this case, precisions of up to 99.8 % were achieved in our experiments.

This is only the most simple method for estimating $\Delta\varphi$. Significant improvements concerning the precision can be made by taking more pixels into account (potentially all available pixels along a bended line segment), and also using more advanced approximation techniques.

## 4.2   Estimation of Focal Length

Concerning the focal length, from Equations (2) we see that parameter $f$ is only a linear coefficient in the projection $\Pi$, and therefore cannot be estimated from curved lines. Normally we also do not know the length $l$ of the sensor line. However, there is anisotropic scaling depending on the focal length, and this allows to estimate the (dimensionless) ratio $l/f$ also using a-priori knowledge about aspect ratios of shown real-world objects (absolute length cannot be estimated in general due to scale ambiguity of the recorded 3D scene).

Given four vertices $r_1, ..., r_4$ of a rectangle and a-priori knowledge about the ratio

$$\Xi = \frac{|k_1|}{|k_2|} = \frac{|r_4 - r_1|}{|r_2 - r_1|}$$

of two of its edges, the ratio $l/f$ can be estimated such that edge ratio $\Xi'$, resulting from the reconstruction of image points of $r_1, ..., r_4$, is equal to $\Xi$. In the reconstruction process of image points of $r_1, ..., r_4$, value $l/f$ is the only unknown as $\Delta\varphi$ was already estimated, independently from $f$, in the previous step. A square-pixel assumption (for the panoramic image) also supports an initialization for a computationally inexpensive iterative search procedure (e. g., interval bisection).

## 4.3   Use of Vanishing Points

Monocular reconstruction for pinhole-type cameras often utilizes vanishing points. Those are also of benefit for cylindrical images. As for pinhole-type camera images, vanishing points allow to estimate object attitudes or the positioning of the camera coordinate system with respect to the scene.

A vanishing point is a point where two lines virtually intersect in an image, for two lines which are actually parallel in the 3D world. These lines (in general) do not project into straight lines in cylindrical panoramas. As a result, one pair of two parallel lines can actually have two vanishing points in the panoramic image.

If line segments are only considered in parts of a cylindrical panorama with a viewing angle less than $180°$, then their vanishing points can be calculated conveniently using the projection $\Pi$ as defined above, as well as its inverse projection $\Pi^{-1}$. Attention must be paid for choosing points in the cylindrical image with $i$-coordinates suitable for $\Pi$, as it is of little use when the calculation of the intersection of two lines (projected into the plane) is numerically unstable (e. g., when they are nearly parallel).

Now assume one line, containing points $p_1$ and $p_2$, and a second parallel line, containing $p_3$ and $p_4$; both vanishing points $v_1$ and $v_2$ are as follows:

$$v_1 = \Pi_{i_1}^{-1}\Psi^{-1}((\Psi\Pi_{i_1}(p_1) \times \Psi\Pi_{i_1}(p_4)) \times (\Psi\Pi_{i_1}(p_2) \times \Psi\Pi_{i_1}(p_3)))$$

$$v_2 = \Pi_{i_2}^{-1}\Psi^{-1}((\Psi\Pi_{i_2}(p_1) \times \Psi\Pi_{i_2}(p_4)) \times (\Psi\Pi_{i_2}(p_2) \times \Psi\Pi_{i_2}(p_3)))$$

where $\Psi$ and $\Psi^{-1}$ denote the transformation from Cartesian to homogeneous coordinates and vice versa, whereas the indices $i_1$ and $i_2$ of $\Pi$ indicate that different cylinder coordinates $i$ have to be used for obtaining both vanishing points.

Points $p_1$ and $p_2$ are unsuitable if the third component of the vanishing point in homogeneous coordinates is close to zero (i.e., parallel lines), and it is also critical if the Euclidean distance between $v_1$ and $v_2$ is very small (i.e., only 'one point'). In any of these cases, some permutation of assigned $i$-values may define a solution.

In case that a pair of bended line segments covers more than $180°$ in the given cylindrical panorama (what occurs, for example, on the ceiling or on the floor of a room), a plane being tangential to the cylinder surface is unsuitable for the considered projection $\Pi$; in this case we would prefer a plane with a normal vector almost parallel to the rotation axis. Apart from projection $\Pi$, the calculation of vanishing points remains the same.

An advantage of panoramic images in comparison to 'normal' images is that panoramas have a wider field of view, such also showing more projected lines, and thus, potentially, more vanishing points.


## 5   Conclusions

In [6] it is discussed how stereo pairs of cylindrical panoramas may be used for 3D reconstruction. In this paper we have specified a way how to use segmentations of 3D shapes into rectangles to ensure approximate 3D reconstruction just based on a single cylindrical panorama. The use of the intersection point of both diagonals of a rectangle proved to be useful for this approach.

The 'bending' of straight lines, as occurring in panoramic images due to cylindrical projection, may be entirely characterized by two pixels on such an arc, the focal length, and the angular increment $\Delta\varphi$. Therefore, it is also possible to apply the concept of vanishing points for 3D reconstruction; see [4,5] for 'normal' images.

Object surfaces different from multiple rectangular faces are also possible for approximate monocular reconstruction; see [8]. These are, for example, spheres, circular discs, cylinders, or some specially shaped room corners (with a-priori knowledge about their geometry). The (manual) reconstruction of freeform shapes, which widely expands the functionality of a system for monocular reconstruction, is demonstrated in [10] and its incorporation for panoramic images was already proposed there.

**Acknowledgments.** The authors thank Karsten Scheibe from DLR (German Aerospace Center) for providing image data for experiments, and source code for efficient I/O operations for panoramic images of very-high spatial resolution.

# References


1. Becker, T.: STL & generic programming: STL containers. C/C++ Users Journal 19 (February 2001)
2. Berkeley, G.: An essay towards a new theory of vision (1709),
   http://www.gutenberg.org/etext/4722
3. Chu, N.S.-H., Tai, C.-L.: Animating Chinese landscape paintings and panorama using multi-perspective modeling. In: Proc. Computer Graphics International, pp. 107–112 (2001)
4. Criminisi, A.: Single-view metrology: Algorithms and applications. In: Van Gool, L. (ed.) DAGM 2002. LNCS, vol. 2449, pp. 224–239. Springer, Heidelberg (2002)
5. Guillou, E., Meneveaux, D., Maisel, E., Bouatouch, K.: Using vanishing points for camera calibration and coarse 3D reconstruction from a single image. The Visual Computer 16, 396–410 (2000)
6. Huang, F., Klette, R., Scheibe, K.: Panoramic Imaging: Laser-Range Finders and Sensor-Line Cameras. Wiley, Chichester (2008)
7. Kanatani, K.: Group Theoretic Methods in Image Understanding. Springer, Berlin (1990)
8. Voss, K., Neubauer, R., Süße, H.: Monokulare Rekonstruktion für Robotvision. Shaker, Aachen (1994)
9. Wang, X., Klette, R., Rosenhahn, B.: Geometric and photometric correction of projected rectangular pictures. In: Proc. Image and Vision Computing, New Zealand, pp. 223–228 (2005)
10. Zhang, L., Dugas-Phocion, G., Samson, J.S., Seitz, S.M.: Single-view modelling of free-form scenes. J. Visualization Computer Animation 13, 225–235 (2002)

# Omnidirectional Image Stabilization
# by Computing Camera Trajectory


Akihiko Torii, Michal Havlena, and Tomáš Pajdla

Center for Machine Perception, Department of Cybernetics,
Faculty of Electrical Engineering, Czech Technical University in Prague,
Karlovo náměstí 13, 121 35 Prague 2, Czech Republic
{torii,havlem1,pajdla}@cmp.felk.cvut.cz
http://cmp.felk.cvut.cz



**Abstract.** In this paper we present a pipeline for camera pose and trajectory estimation, and image stabilization and rectification for dense as well as wide baseline omnidirectional images. The input is a set of images taken by a single hand-held camera. The output is a set of stabilized and rectified images augmented by the computed camera 3D trajectory and reconstruction of feature points facilitating visual object recognition. The paper generalizes previous works on camera trajectory estimation done on perspective images to omnidirectional images and introduces a new technique for omnidirectional image rectification that is suited for recognizing people and cars in images. The performance of the pipeline is demonstrated on a real image sequence acquired in urban as well as natural environments.

**Keywords:** Structure from Motion, Omnidirectional Vision.


## 1 Introduction

Image stabilization and camera trajectory estimation plays an important role in 3D reconstruction [1,2,3], self localization [4], and reducing the number of false alarms in detection and recognition of pedestrians, cars, and other objects in video sequences [5,6,7,8].

Most of the approaches to camera pose and trajectory computation [9,1,2] work with classical perspective cameras because of the simplicity of their projection models and ease of their calibration. However, perspective cameras offer only a limited field of view. Occlusions and sharp camera turns may cause that consecutive frames look completely different when the baseline becomes longer. This makes the image feature matching very difficult (or impossible) and the camera trajectory estimation fails under such conditions. These problems can be avoided if omnidirectional cameras, e.g. a fish-eye lens convertor [10], are used. Large field of view also facilitates the analysis of activities happening in the scene since moving objects can be tracked for longer time periods [7].

In this paper we present a pipeline for camera pose and trajectory estimation, and image stabilization and rectification for dense as well as wide baseline omnidirectional images. The input is a set of images taken by a single hand-held


T. Wada, F. Huang, and S. Lin (Eds.): PSIVT 2009, LNCS 5414, pp. 71–82, 2009.

(a)                                   (b)

**Fig. 1.** (a) Kyocera Finecam M410R camera and Nikon FC-E9 fish-eye lens convertor. (b) The equi-angular projection model. The angle $\theta$ between the casted ray of a 3D point and the optical axis can be computed from the radius $r$ of a circle in the image circular view field.

camera. The output is a set of stabilized and rectified images augmented by the computed camera 3D trajectory and reconstruction of feature points facilitating visual object recognition. We describe the essential issues for a reliable camera trajectory estimation, i.e. the choice of the camera and its geometric projection model, camera calibration, image feature detection and description, robust 3D structure computation, and a suitable omnidirectional image rectification.

The setup used in this work was a combination of Nikon FC-E9, mounted via a mechanical adaptor, and a Kyocera Finecam M410R digital camera (see Figure 1(a)). Nikon FC-E9 is a megapixel omnidirectional add-on convertor with 180° view angle which provides images of photographic quality. Kyocera Finecam M410R delivers 2272×1704 images at 3 frames per second. The resulting combination yields a circular view of diameter 1600 pixels in the image.

## 2   The Pipeline

Next we shall describe our pipeline.

### 2.1   Camera Calibration

The calibration of omnidirectional cameras is non-trivial and is crucial for achieving good accuracy of the resulting 3D reconstruction. Our omnidirectional camera is calibrated off-line using the state-of-the-art technique [11] and Mičušík's two-parameter model [10], that links the radius of the image point $r$ to the angle $\theta$ of its corresponding rays w.r.t. the optical axis (see Figure 1(b)) as

$$\theta = \frac{ar}{1 + br^2}.  \tag{1}$$

After a successful calibration, we know the correspondence of the image points to the 3D optical rays in the coordinate system of the camera. The following steps aim at finding the transformation between the camera and the world coordinate systems, i.e. the pose of the camera in the 3D world, using 2D image matches.

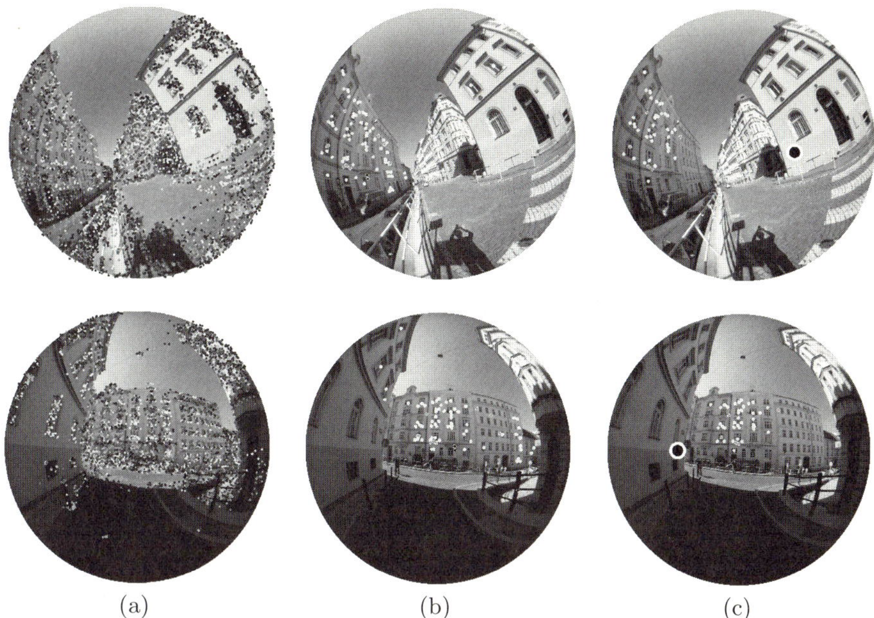

(a)                              (b)                              (c)

**Fig. 2.** Example of the wide baseline image matching. The colors of the dots correspond to the detectors (yellow) MSER-Intensity+, (green) MSER-Intensity−, (cyan) MSER-Saturation+, (blue) MSER-Saturation−, (magenta) Harris Affine, and (red) Hessian Affine. (a) All detected features. (b) Tentative matches constructed by selecting pairs of features which have the mutually closest similarity distance. (c) The epipole (black circle) computed by maximizing the supports. Note that the scene dominated by a single plane does not induce the degeneracy of computing epipolar geometry due to solving the 5-point minimal relative orientation problem.

## 2.2   Detecting Features and Constructing Tentative Matches

For computing 3D structure, we construct a set of tentative matches detecting different affine covariant feature regions including MSER [12], Harris Affine, and Hessian Affine [13] in acquired images. These features are alternative to popular SIFT features [14] and work comparably in our situation. Parameters of the detectors are chosen to limit the number of regions to 1-2 thousands per image. The detected regions are assigned local affine frames (LAF) [15] and transformed into standard positions w.r.t. their LAFs. Discrete Cosine Descriptors [16] are computed for each region in the standard position. Finally, mutual distances of all regions in one image and all regions in the other image are computed as the Euclidean distances of their descriptors and tentative matches are constructed by selecting the mutually closest pairs. Figures 2(a) and (b) show an example of the feature detection and matching for a pair of wide baseline images.

Unlike the methods using short baseline images [2], simpler image features which are not affine covariant cannot be used because the view point can change a lot between consecutive frames. Furthermore, feature matching has to be

(a)          (b)          (c)

**Fig. 3.** Examples of pairs of images (two consecutive frames) from top to bottom in the CITY WALK sequence. Blue circles represent the epipoles and yellow dots are the matches supporting this epipolar geometry. Red dots are the matches feasibly reconstructed as 3D points. (a) contains multiple moving objects and large camera rotation. (b) contains large camera rotation and tentative matches on bushes. (c) contains tentative matches mostly constructed on a complex natural scene.

performed on the whole frame because no assumptions on the proximity of the consecutive projections can be made for wide baseline images. This is making the feature detection, description, and matching much more time-consuming than it is for short baseline images and limits the usage to low frame rate sequences when operating in real-time.

### 2.3  Epipolar Geometry Computation of Pairs of Consecutive Images

Robust 3D structure can be computed by RANSAC [17] which searches for the largest subset of the set of tentative matches which is, within a predefined threshold $\varepsilon$, consistent with an epipolar geometry [3]. We use ordered sampling as suggested in [18] to draw 5-tuples from the list of tentative matches ordered ascendingly by the distance of their descriptors which may help to reduce the number of samples in RANSAC. From each 5-tuple, relative orientation is computed by solving the 5-point minimal relative orientation problem for calibrated cameras [19,20]. Figure 2(c) shows the result of computing the epipolar geometry for a pair of wide baseline images.

Often, there are more models which are supported by a large number of matches. Thus the chance that the correct model, even if it has the largest support, will be found by running a single RANSAC is small. Work [21] suggested to generate models by randomized sampling as in RANSAC but to use soft (kernel) voting for a parameter instead of looking for the maximal support. The best model is then selected as the one with the parameter closest to the maximum in the accumulator space. In our case, we vote in a two-dimensional accumulator for the estimated camera motion direction. However, unlike in [21], we do not cast votes directly by each sampled epipolar geometry but by the best epipolar geometries recovered by ordered sampling of RANSAC [18]. With our technique, we could go up to the 98.5 % contamination of mismatches with comparable effort as simple RANSAC does for the contamination by 84 %. Finally, the relative camera orientation with the motion direction closest to the maximum in the voting space is selected. Figure 3 shows difficult examples of pairs of images to find the correct epipolar geometry.

## 2.4 Chaining Camera Poses for Sequence of Images

Camera poses in a canonical coordinate system are recovered by chaining the epipolar geometries of pairs of consecutive images in a sequence. For the essential matrix $\mathsf{E}_{ij}$ between frames $i$ and $j = i + 1$, the essential matrix $\mathsf{E}_{ij}$ can be decomposed into $\mathsf{E}_{ij} = [\mathbf{e}_{ij}]_{\times}\mathsf{R}_{ij}$. Although there exist four possible decompositions, the right decomposition can be selected to reconstruct all points in front of both cameras [3, $p260$]. Having the normalized camera matrices [3] of the $i$-th frame $\mathsf{P}_i = [\mathsf{R}_i \,|\, \mathbf{T}_i]$, the normalized camera matrix $\mathsf{P}_j$ can be computed by

$$\mathsf{P}_j = [\mathsf{R}_{ij}\mathsf{R}_i \,|\, \mathsf{R}_{ij}\mathbf{T}_i + \alpha\mathbf{e}_{ij}] \tag{2}$$

where $\alpha$ is the scale of the translation in the canonical coordinate system. The scale $\alpha$ can be computed by any 3D point seen in at least three consecutive frames. The best scale is selected to maximize the number of points that pass the feasibility test of $L_1$- or $L_\infty$- triangulation [22,23], i.e., the intersection of pixel-cone rays test. In the final step, we applied the sparse bundle adjustment [24] to refine the structure.

## 2.5 Image Stabilization Using Camera Pose and Trajectory

The recovered camera pose and trajectory can be used to rectify the original images to the stabilized images. If there exists no assumption on the camera motion in a sequence, the simplest way of stabilization is to rectify images w.r.t. the gravity vector in the coordinate system of the first camera and all other images will then be aligned with the first one. This can be achieved by taking the first image with care. When a sequence is captured by walking or driving on the roads, it is possible to stabilize the images w.r.t. the ground plane. For a gravity direction $\mathbf{g}$ and a motion direction $\mathbf{t}$, we compute the normal vector of the ground plane

$$\mathbf{d} = \frac{\mathbf{t} \times (\mathbf{g} \times \mathbf{t})}{|\mathbf{t} \times (\mathbf{g} \times \mathbf{t})|}. \tag{3}$$

## 3    Experimental Results

The experiment with real data demonstrates the use of proposed image stabilization method. Two image sequences of a city scene captured by a single hand-held fish-eye lens camera are used as our input sequences.

The CITY WALK sequence is 190 frames long and the distance between consecutive frames is 1-3 meters. This sequence is challenging for recovering the camera trajectory due to sharp turns, objects moving in the scene, and natural complex environment. The benefit of wide field of view can be seen in Figure 3. The camera motions are reasonably recovered by using the features detected from stational rigid objects. Figure 6(b) shows the camera positions and the world

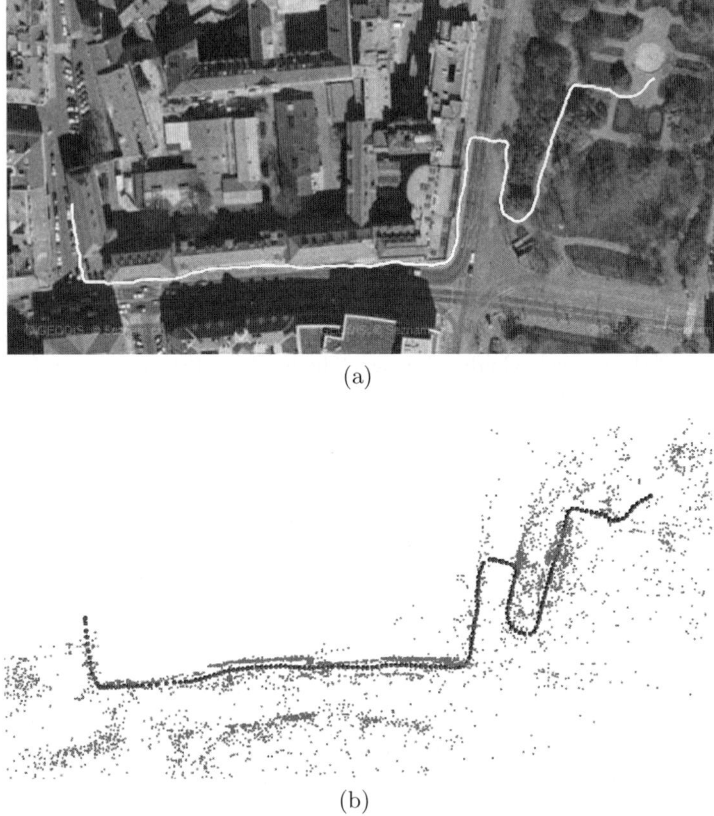

(a)

(b)

**Fig. 6.** Camera trajectory of the CITY WALK sequence. (a) A bird's eye view of the city area used for the acquisition of our test sequence. The trajectory is drawn with a white line. (b) The bird's eye view of the resulting 3D model view. Red dots represent the camera positions recovered by our proposed method. Small gray dots represent the reconstructed world 3D points.

(a) Central projection

(b) Non-central projection

**Fig. 7.** Results of image transformations of frame 67 in the CITY WALK sequence. The images are stabilized w.r.t. the ground plane and panoramic images transformed by (a) central cylindrical projection and (b) non-central cylindrical projection. Note the pedestrians are less deformed on the non-central cylindrical projection while convening larger field of view than the central one.

3D points reconstructed by our structure from motion. The reconstruction is comparable to the walking trajectory shown in Figure 6(a). Since the sequence is captured walking along the planar street, all the images are stabilized using the recovered camera pose and trajectory w.r.t. the ground plane. Figure 7 shows the images generated by using central and non-central cylindrical projections. It can be seen that the non-central cylindrical projection in Figure 7(b) successfully suppresses the deformation at the top and bottom and makes people standing close to the camera looking much more natural.

The FREE MOTION sequence is 187 frames long and the distance between consecutive frames is 0.3-2 meters. This sequence is also challenging for recovering the camera pose and trajectory due to the large view changes by camera rotation and translation. Figure 8(a) shows several frames of the original images in the FREE MOTION sequence. Figure 8(b) shows the panoramic images generated by the non-central cylindrical projection. Since the motion is completely irrelevant w.r.t. the ground plane, all images are stabilized w.r.t. the gravity vector in the coordinate system of the first camera. Figure 8(c) shows the panoramic images stabilized using the recovered camera pose and trajectory. It can be seen clearly from this result that the large image rotation is successfully canceled using the recovered camera pose and trajectory.

**Fig. 2.** Each column represents two images from the same texture (from left to right:D18,D26,D27,D87,D112) but of 4 times scale difference, and you can observe that the texture is entirely different though the upper row is just a 4 up-scaled version of the lower row

two different images of 4 times scale difference, and you can observe that the texture is entirely different though the upper row is just a 4 up-scaled version of the lower row. Hence, in this paper we use the entire Brodatz[1] database with each original texture image rotated by 10 different angles ($0^o$ to $180^o$) with $20^o$ as interval, and scaled with 8 different scales(0.7 to 1.4 with 0.1 intervals). Therefore for each of the 112 texture classes, we create 8 scales($0.7 \sim 1.4$), and for each scale, 10 rotations($0^o \sim 180^o$). Hence we'll have 80 images for each class in which 63 images are concurrently rotated and scaled. Then the center portion of $128 \times 128$ is cropped for each image. Therefore we have $112 \times 8 \times 10 = 8960$ of $128 \times 128$ images created for this database.

## 4.2   Experimental Results

We carried out classification experiments using the database similar to [13] and the Gabor filter based on conventional design which is not invariant. We studied the effects of rotation and scale changes on the method using conventional Gabor filter banks and tunable Gabor filter bank using the large database containing rotated and scaled textures.

Conventional Gabor filter yields the well-known(and probably the best) overall recognition rate of 74.7 percent on the entire 112 texture classes of Brodatz database. However, because of its band directionality and fixed band coverage, it is not rotation and scale invariant in nature. That's the reason why the overall classification rate dropped to an average of around 19 percent when using a large database with rotated and scaled texture images. From Table 1, it is shown that, by using our method, the adaptive Gabor filter's overall classification rate is pushed back by 44.2 percent to show the effectiveness of our method even on our extensive database.

We can see from the result that, for inhomogeneous textures tested on conventional Gabor filters, the rate drop is the lowest when switched to a rotated and scaled dataset, this is because the spectrum of those textures are highly Gaussian and no spectral peak can be located while doing feature extraction. Therefore, the Gabor features between the original and the rotated/scaled are

**Table 1.** Comparison With Respect to Conventional Gabor Implementation(%) Inhomo – Inhomogenous; Rand – Random

| Methods | Datasets | Inhomo. | Periodic | Directional | Rand. | Overall |
|---|---|---|---|---|---|---|
| Conventional | no-rotation/scale | 44.9 | 97.9 | 87.6 | 61.2 | 74.7 |
| Conventional | rotated & scaled | 19.7 | 19.5 | 19.1 | 19.7 | 19.4 |
| Our method | rotated & scaled | 50.2 | 79.7 | 71.7 | 56.7 | 63.7 |
| Rotation/scale effects on conventional | | -25.2 | -78.4 | -68.5 | -40.5 | -55.3 |
| Rate increase due to tuning | | +30.4 | +60 | +51.6 | +37.0 | +44.2 |

not as distinguishable as the ones with high spectral peaks. The corresponding Gabor filter band will still locate similar energy values though not exactly the same while the scale and rotation is small. Whereas for the ones with high spectral peaks, a small change in scale might cause the peak shift to another filter band and the each Gabor filter band could not locate the same amount of energy anymore. In this case, the Gabor filter tuning will be necessary. This is again justified by the column containing periodical textures. The classification rate experience a significant drop by 78.4 percent while the conventional Gabor filter is applied on a rotated and scaled dataset, however, we are able to push the result back by 60 percent to 79.7 on this category by Gabor filter tuning method. Our method improved the result for the directional category by 51.6 percent and random textures by 37 percent, which is in line with our expectation before the experiment, since they've got less significant peaks than the periodical ones.

## 5   Conclusion and Future Work

We address the problem of rotation and scale invariance in texture recognition and propose an tunable Gabor filter approach to achieve concurrent rotation and scale invariant recognition. We carried out experiments on the Brodatz texture with a database whose size is much larger than those presented in any of the existing methods for invariant texture recognition. The performance of our method was tested by a comprehensive experiments across the dataset of the entire brodatz database. The results were carefully analyzed by the grouping based on 2-D Wold-like decomposition. Interesting pattern appears while we compared the performance on the 4 groups side by side with the results of the conventional Gabor filter. Those patterns can be explained by the spectral energy distributions according to the Wold texture model. Our classification result on the entire database($112 \times 80 = 8960$ images) achieves concurrent rotation and scale invariance by 44 percent better accuracy than the well-known method by [13]. Further improvements can be done for estimating rotation and scale change for non-homogenous and random textures which might improve our method further.

## Acknowledgements

This work was supported by project of reference SERC TSRP grant number 062 130 0055 of Agency for Science, Technology and Research (A*STAR), Singapore.

## References

1. Brodatz, P.: Textures: A Photographic Album For Artists and Designers. Dover (1966)
2. Larsen, A., Bundesen, C.: Visual tranformation of size. Journal of Experimental Psychology: Human Perception and Performance 1, 214–220
3. Shepard, R.N., Cooper, L.A.: Mental Images & Their Transformation. MIT Press, Cambridge (1982)
4. Bundesen, L.A.C., Farrell, J.E.: Mental transformations of size and orientation. In: Attention and Performance IX, pp. 279–294. Lawrence Erlbaum, Hillsdale
5. Fountain, S.R., Tan, T.N.: Extraction of noise robust rotation invariant texture features via multichannel filtering. In: Proc. International Conference on Image Processing, October 26–29, vol. 3, pp. 197–200 (1997)
6. Hayley, G.M., Manjunath, B.M.: Rotation invariant texture classification using modified gabor filters. In: Proc. of IEEE ICIP 1995, pp. 262–265 (1994)
7. Ma Ju Han, K.-K.: Rotation-invariant and scale-invariant gabor features for texture image retrieval. Image and Vision Computing 25(9), 1474–1481 (2007)
8. Kashyap, R., Khotanzad, A.: A model based method for rotation invariant texture classification. IEEE Transactions on Pattern Analysis and Machine Intelligence 8(4), 786–804 (1986)
9. Leung, M.M., Peterson, A.M.: Scale and rotation invariant texture classification. In: Conference Record of The Twenty-Sixth Asilomar Conference on Signals, Systems and Computers, vol. 1, pp. 461–465 (1992)
10. Liu, F.: Modeling Spatial and Temporal Textures. PhD thesis, Massachusetts Institute of Technology (September 1997)
11. Madiraju, S.V.R., Liu, C.-C.: Rotation invariant texture classification using covariance. In: Proc. ICIP 1994. IEEE International Conference Image Processing, vol. 2, pp. 655–659 (1994)
12. Mahersia, H., Hamrouni, K.: New rotaion invariant features for texture classification. In: Proc. International Conference on Computer and Communication Engineering ICCCE 2008, pp. 687–690 (2008)
13. Manjunath, B.S., Ma, W.Y.: Texture features for browsing and retrieval of image data. 18(8), 837–842 (1996)
14. Ojala, T., Pietikainen, M., Maenpaa, T.: Multiresolution gray-scale and rotation invariant texture classification with local binary patterns. 24(7), 971–987 (2002)
15. Shepard, R.: The role of transformation in spatial cognition. In: Spatial Cognition, Brain Bases and Development. Lawrence Erlbaum Associates, Mahwah (1988)
16. Greenspan, H., et al.: Rotation invariant texture recognition using a steerable pyramid. In: Proc. of ICPR 1994, pp. 162–167 (1994)
17. Zhang, L., Ma, J., Xu, X., Yuan, B.: Rotation invariant image classification based on mpeg-7 homogeneous texture descriptor. In: Proc. Eighth ACIS International Conference on Software Engineering, Artificial Intelligence, Networking, and Parallel/Distributed Computing SNPD 2007, vol. 3, pp. 798–803 (2007)

18. Jain, A., Mao, J.: Texture classification and segmentation using multiresolution simultaneous autoregressive models. Pattern Recognition 25(2), 173–188 (1992)
19. Pun, C.-M., Lee, M.-C.: Log-polar wavelet energy signatures for rotation and scale invariant texture classification 25(5), 590–603 (2003)
20. Wu, Y., Yoshida, Y.: An efficient method for rotation and scaling invariant texture classification. In: Proc. International Conference on Acoustics, Speech, and Signal Processing ICASSP 1995, May 9–12, 1995, vol. 4, pp. 2519–2522 (1995)
21. Xu, Z., Pietikainen, M., Ojala, T.: Rotation-invariant texture classification using feature distributions. Pattern Recognition 33(2000), 43–52 (2000)
22. Ivry, R., Beck, J., Sutter, A.: Spatial frequency channels and perceptual grouping in texture segmentation. Computer Vision, Graphics, Image Processing 37, 299–325 (1987)
23. Jones, J.P., Palmer, L.A.: An evaluation of the two-dimensional Gabor filter model of simple receptive fields in cat striate cortex. The Journal of Neuroscience 58(6) (1987)
24. Francos, J.M., Meiri, A.Z., Porat, B.: A Wold-Like Decomposition of Two-Dimensional Discrete Homogenous Random Fields. The Annals of Applied Probability 5(1) (1995)

# Local Image Descriptors Using Supervised Kernel ICA

Masaki Yamazaki[1] and Sidney Fels[2]

[1] Faculty of Information Science and Engineering,
Ritsumeikan University, Shiga, Japan
`rs023018@se.ritsumei.ac.jp`
[2] Department of Electrical and Computer Engineering,
University of British Columbia, Vancouver, BC, Canada
`ssfels@ece.ubc.ca`

**Abstract.** PCA-SIFT is an extension to SIFT which aims to reduce SIFT's high dimensionality (128 dimensions) by applying PCA to the gradient image patches. However PCA is not a discriminative representation for recognition due to its global feature nature and unsupervised algorithm. In addition, linear methods such as PCA and ICA can fail in the case of non-linearity. In this paper, we propose a new discriminative method called *Supervised* Kernel ICA (SKICA) that uses a non-linear kernel approach combined with Supervised ICA-based local image descriptors. Our approach blends the advantages of a low dimensionality representation, like PCA-SIFT, with supervised learning based on non-linear properties of kernels to overcome separability limitations of non-linear representations for recognition. Using five different test data sets we show that the SKICA descriptors produce better object recognition performance than other related approaches with the same dimensionality. The SKICA-based representation has local sensitivity, non-linear independence and high class separability providing an effective method for local image descriptors.

## 1 Introduction

Local image descriptors are widely used in many computer vision applications such as object categorization and recognition [1] and image/video retrieval [2]. Probably one of the most popular and widely utilized local feature descriptors is SIFT [3]. SIFT descriptors have good properties including scale and rotation invariance, robustness against changes in viewpoint and illumination. This makes them an effective descriptor for object recognition applications. However, the SIFT descriptor has relatively high dimensionality (128 dimensions), which limits the performance of matching speed. PCA-SIFT [4] is an extension to SIFT which aims to reduce SIFT's high dimensionality by applying Principal Components Analysis (PCA) and yields a 36-dimensional descriptor. PCA is often used for reducing the dimensionality of an input feature space. PCA does not provide a discriminative representation for matching, however it does provide significant improvements in matching speed due to the dimensionality reduction and in reducing the high frequency noise in the descriptors.

T. Wada, F. Huang, and S. Lin (Eds.): PSIVT 2009, LNCS 5414, pp. 94–105, 2009.

Recently, a method closely related to PCA, Independent Component Analysis (ICA) [5], has received high attention. ICA can be viewed as a generalization of PCA, since it is concerned not only with second-order dependencies but also with high-order dependencies. PCA makes the data uncorrelated while ICA makes the data as independent as possible. Applications of ICA to feature extraction from images have been a topic of research interest. It is known that most of the ICA basis images extracted from natural images are sparse and similar to localized and oriented edges[6], which can capture important information for recognition. In addition, using the extracted ICA features for pattern discrimination has been studied for face recognition [7], texture segmentation [8], and object recognition [9][10]. These results indicate the features estimated by ICA are better than the features estimated by PCA with regard to recognition accuracy.

In pattern recognition problems, it is more desirable that extracted pattern features belonging to different classes are mutually separated as much as possible in the feature space. However ICA algorithm is categorized unsupervised learning, class information is not taken into consideration when feature extraction is carried out. Therefore, high separability of extracted features is not always ensured. To overcome this problem, Supervised ICA(SICA) was proposed [11]. The class separability of the SICA features is enhanced by maximizing the Mahalanobis distance between classes. The results suggest that SICA is more efficient than ICA for recognition.

ICA is based on a linear model, so it is inadequate for ICA to describe complex nonlinear variations in pattern recognition due to illumination changes, viewpoint changes and noise. In addition, there are other non-linear factors due to a camera's properties. One approach to solve this problem is kernel-based methods that as they are effective for such non-linearity. Kernel methods allow for the development of a non-linear extension of some linear algorithms, such as PCA and ICA. Recently, Kernel ICA (KICA)[12] was proposed as a nonlinear extension of ICA, which combines the a nonlinear kernel with ICA. KICA can improve the performance of ICA for pattern recognition.

In this paper we propose a supervised Kernel ICA for local image descriptors (SKICA descriptors), which combines nonlinear kernels with SICA. SKICA descriptors accept the input as normalised and gradient patches (the PCA-SIFT descriptor). In natural images, nearby pixels are statistically related and gradients based on edges are important in object recognition. Therefore, the gradient patches is the appropriate input for SKICA descriptors. Our work has two key contributions. First, we propose a novel dimension reduction method for local image descriptors that is a supervised nonlinear method. Second, we show that SKICA descriptors is better than KICA, SICA, ICA and PCA descriptors for object recognition on various sets of natural images.

The paper is organized as follows. Section 2 presents the SKICA Algorithm. Section 3 describes the SKICA-based local image descriptors (SKICA descriptors). Finally, section 4 shows the experimental results and section 5 summaries our conclusion.

We propose Supervised Kernel ICA(SKICA) with a combination of KICA and Kernel Discriminant Analysis(KDA) [14]. As a nonlinear extension of LDA, KDA essentially performs LDA in the feature space $F$. The conventional between-class scatter operator $\mathbf{S}_B^{\Phi}$, within-class scatter operator $\mathbf{S}_W^{\Phi}$ can be expressed as:$\mathbf{S}_B^{\Phi} = \sum_{c=l,m} N_c(\mu_c^{\Phi} - \overline{\mathbf{x}}^{\Phi})(\mu_c^{\Phi} - \overline{\mathbf{x}}^{\Phi})^T$ and $\mathbf{S}_W^{\Phi} = \sum_{c=l,m} \sum_{i\in c}(\mathbf{x}_i^{\Phi} - \mu_c^{\Phi})(\mathbf{x}_i^{\Phi} - \mu_c^{\Phi})^T$, where $\mu_c^{\Phi} = \frac{1}{N_c} \sum_{i\in c} \Phi(\mathbf{x}_i), \overline{\mathbf{x}}^{\Phi} = \frac{1}{C} \sum_i \Phi(\mathbf{x}_i)$. We maximize the Fisher criterion below to obtain the optimal projection directions $\mathbf{w}_i$ in $F$:

$$J_{lm}^{\Phi}(\mathbf{w}_i) = \frac{\mathbf{w}_i^T \mathbf{S}_B^{\Phi} \mathbf{w}_i}{\mathbf{w}_i^T \mathbf{S}_W^{\Phi} \mathbf{w}_i} \ . \tag{10}$$

The weights $1/J_{lm}^{\Phi}{}^2(\mathbf{w}_{i0})$ for the Mahalanobis distance of $J_{lm}^{\Phi}(\mathbf{w}_i)$ are defined as follows:

$$d^{\Phi}(\mathbf{w}_i) = \sum_{l=1}^{c-1} \sum_{m=l+1}^{c} \frac{1}{J_{lm}^{\Phi}{}^2(\mathbf{w}_{i0})} J_{lm}^{\Phi}(\mathbf{w}_i) \ . \tag{11}$$

From this cost function, the following derivative $\psi_i^{\Phi}$ is obtained:

$$\psi_i^{\Phi} = \frac{\partial d^{\Phi}(\mathbf{w}_i)}{\partial \mathbf{w}_i} = \sum_{l=1}^{c-1} \sum_{m=l+1}^{c} \frac{1}{J_{lm}^{\Phi}{}^2(\mathbf{w}_{i0})} \frac{\partial(J_{lm}^{\Phi}(\mathbf{w}_i))}{\partial \mathbf{w}_i} \ . \tag{12}$$

Equation(12) is added to the KICA algorithm, and then the update formula of $\mathbf{W}_{SKICA}^{\Phi}$ in the proposed SKICA is given as follow:

$$\triangle \mathbf{W}_{SKICA}^{\Phi} = (\mathbf{I} + g(\mathbf{Y}^{\Phi})(\mathbf{Y}^{\Phi})^T)\mathbf{W}_{SKICA}^{\Phi} + \alpha\mathbf{\Psi}^{\Phi} \ . \tag{13}$$

where $\mathbf{\Psi}^{\Phi} = [\psi_1^{\Phi}, \psi_2^{\Phi}, \cdots, \psi_N^{\Phi}]^T$ and $\alpha$ is a positive constant.

## 3   Supervised Kernel ICA-Based Local Image Descriptors

SKICA is fundamentally a statistical model for natural images that models images as nonlinear superpositions of basis images, with non-Gaussian, independent weighting coefficients optimized for class separability. Here, we argue that the properties of SKICA applied to the local image descriptors retains the advantages of the reduced dimensionality but improves recognition accuracy due to the nature of the SKICA representation. We call SKICA applied to the local image descriptors, SKICA descriptors. To train SKICA, the image patches at the interest points are collected from a common image database. In this paper, we use the normalised patches and the gradient patches (PCA-SIFT descriptors) as the input data and detect the interest points by Difference-of-Gaussians (SIFT detector). SKICA are applied to the input data and the result is used as the projection matrix for SKICA descriptors. This process is done offline. The Euclidean distance between the feature vectors projected by the projection matrix is used for matching. An important and related advantage of using KPCA is that it reduces the dimensionality of the input data prior to applying SKICA. In

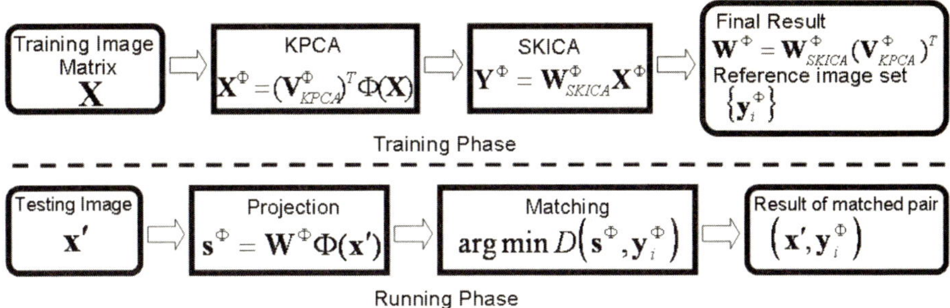


**Fig. 1.** A block diagram for the processing flows in both the learning phase and the running phase of SKICA

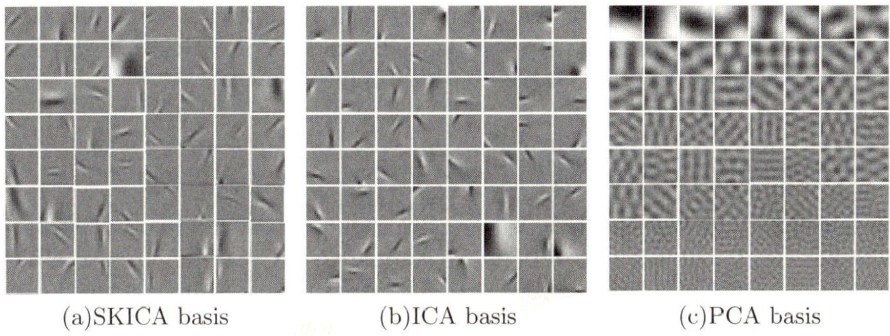


**Fig. 2.** Basis images of natural images

the KPCA-style global filters, noise is automatically associated with the filters with high spatial frequency selectivity whose eigenvectors have small eigenvalues. Thus, KPCA also provides some benefits in reducing the high frequency noise in the descriptors prior to the application of SKICA. A block diagram for the whole process is given in Fig. 1.

In Fig. 2, we show the SKICA basis patches, the ICA basis patches and the PCA basis patches obtained from the normalized image patches in the natural scene data. The PCA-basis consists of global features like 2D Fourier bases. On the other hand, the ICA-basis and the SKICA-basis consist of local features like a sparse coding [15]. Gradient patches are based on the local information such as edges and lines. These edges and lines are both abundant and important in object recognition. Using this information, SKICA can produce nonlinear independent image bases that emphasize important edge information for pattern recognition.

Natural scenes contain many higher-order forms of statistical structure, and they form an extremely non-gaussian distribution that is not at all well captured by orthogonal components. Moreover natural images contain localized, oriented structures with limited phase alignment across spatial frequency. Lines and edges, especially curved and fractal-like edges, cannot be characterized by

**Table 1.** Confusion matrix(%)

| SKICA | Car-side | Car-rear | Motobikes | Airplanes | Face |
|---|---|---|---|---|---|
| Car-side | 88.2 | 0.9 | 4.2 | 3.5 | 3.2 |
| Car-rear | 0.7 | 86.9 | 3.5 | 2 | 6.9 |
| Motobikes | 1.6 | 5.1 | 83.3 | 5.0 | 5.0 |
| Airplanes | 0.4 | 0.7 | 8.0 | 86.6 | 4.3 |
| Face | 0.5 | 3.8 | 8.0 | 2.2 | 85.5 |

| KICA | Car-side | Car-rear | Motobikes | Airplanes | Face |
|---|---|---|---|---|---|
| Car-side | 84.5 | 1.9 | 5.0 | 4.4 | 4.2 |
| Car-rear | 1.5 | 83.2 | 4.5 | 3.0 | 7.8 |
| Motobikes | 2.5 | 6.0 | 79.6 | 6.0 | 5.9 |
| Airplanes | 1.5 | 2.0 | 8.5 | 83.0 | 5.0 |
| Face | 1.5 | 5.0 | 9.0 | 3.2 | 81.3 |

| SICA | Car-side | Car-rear | Motobikes | Airplanes | Face |
|---|---|---|---|---|---|
| Car-side | 83.4 | 2.1 | 5.5 | 4.5 | 4.5 |
| Car-rear | 1.9 | 82.1 | 4.8 | 3.2 | 8.0 |
| Motobikes | 2.9 | 6.3 | 78.5 | 6.2 | 6.1 |
| Airplanes | 1.7 | 2.0 | 9.1 | 81.9 | 5.3 |
| Face | 1.9 | 5.3 | 9.2 | 3.4 | 80.2 |

| ICA | Car-side | Car-rear | Motobikes | Airplanes | Face |
|---|---|---|---|---|---|
| Car-side | 80.2 | 3.1 | 6.1 | 5.4 | 5.2 |
| Car-rear | 2.6 | 79.2 | 5.5 | 4.0 | 8.7 |
| Motobikes | 3.7 | 7.0 | 75.3 | 7.0 | 7.0 |
| Airplanes | 2.5 | 2.8 | 10.0 | 78.6 | 6.1 |
| Face | 2.7 | 6.0 | 10.1 | 4.0 | 77.2 |

| PCA | Car-side | Car-rear | Motobikes | Airplanes | Face |
|---|---|---|---|---|---|
| Car-side | 74.0 | 5.3 | 7.5 | 6.8 | 6.4 |
| Car-rear | 4.0 | 72.8 | 6.7 | 5.3 | 11.2 |
| Motobikes | 6.0 | 8.3 | 69.1 | 8.4 | 8.2 |
| Airplanes | 4.0 | 4.1 | 11.3 | 72.1 | 8.5 |
| Face | 4.0 | 7.2 | 12.5 | 5.4 | 70.9 |

| SIFT | Car-side | Car-rear | Motobikes | Airplanes | Face |
|---|---|---|---|---|---|
| Car-side | 87.7 | 1 | 4.4 | 3.6 | 3.3 |
| Car-rear | 0.8 | 86.4 | 3.7 | 2 | 7.1 |
| Motobikes | 1.7 | 5.2 | 82.8 | 5.1 | 5.2 |
| Airplanes | 0.5 | 0.8 | 8.1 | 86.1 | 4.5 |
| Face | 0.7 | 4 | 8.3 | 2.5 | 84.5 |

different viewpoints. We manually set the thresholds to have each algorithm return 10 matches for comparison. SKICA descriptors correctly match the features near the edges of the motorbike.

**Table 2.** Kurtosis of extracted features for training samples

|       | normalised patches | gradient patches |
|-------|--------------------|------------------|
| SKICA | 32.18              | 38.24            |
| KICA  | 33.87              | 39.65            |
| SICA  | 30.24              | 36.18            |
| ICA   | 31.68              | 37.62            |
| PCA   | 6.82               | 9.51             |

**Table 3.** Class separability of extracted features for training samples

|       | normalised patches | gradient patches |
|-------|--------------------|------------------|
| SKICA | 56.34              | 60.57            |
| KICA  | 53.72              | 56.83            |
| SICA  | 51.41              | 55.04            |
| ICA   | 48.32              | 51.46            |
| PCA   | 44.27              | 49.36            |

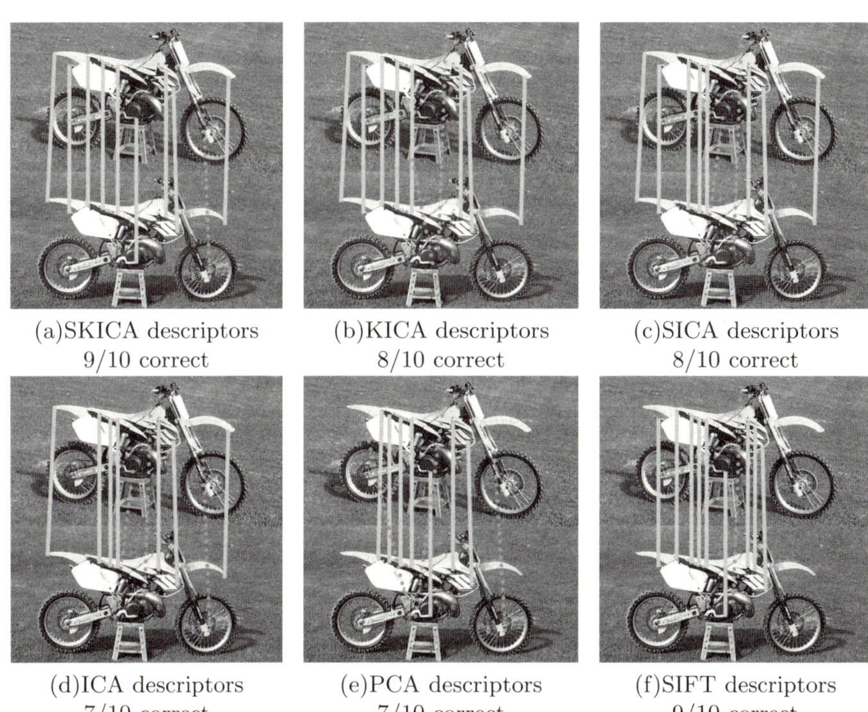

(a)SKICA descriptors
9/10 correct

(b)KICA descriptors
8/10 correct

(c)SICA descriptors
8/10 correct

(d)ICA descriptors
7/10 correct

(e)PCA descriptors
7/10 correct

(f)SIFT descriptors
9/10 correct

**Fig. 4.** The results of matching. The top ten matches are shown for each algorithm: solid lines denote correct matches while dotted lines show incorrect ones.

## 5  Conclusion

We have proposed a new discriminative method for local image descriptors. We have shown that the SKICA descriptors perform better than KICA, SICA, ICA and PCA descriptors for object recognition, since the SKICA-based representation is localised, has non-linear independence and high class separability. However SKICA involves a kernel function selecting problem. Selecting an appropriate kernel function for a particular application area can be difficult and remains largely an unresolved issue. We are conducting further investigations extensions of SKICA-based representation to color image patches and other descriptor algorithms.

## References


1. Fergus, R., Fei-Fei, L., Perona, P., Zisserman, A.: Learning object categories from google's image search. In: Proc. of IEEE International Conference on Computer Vision., vol. 2, pp. 1816–1823 (2005)
2. Sivic, J., Zisserman, A.: Video google: A text retrieval approach to object matching in videos. In: Proc. of IEEE International Conference on Computer Vision., vol. 2, pp. 1470–1477 (2003)
3. Lowe, D.G.: Distinctive image features from scale invariant keypoints. International Journal of Computer Vision 60(2), 91–110 (2004)
4. Ke, Y., Sukthankar, R.: PCA-SIFT: A more distinctive representation for local image descriptors. In: Proc. of IEEE Computer Society Conference on Computer Vision and Pattern Recognition., vol. 2, pp. 506–513 (2004)
5. Hyvarinen, A.: Survey on independent component analysis. Neural Computing Surveys 2, 94–128 (1999)
6. Bell, A.J., Sejnowski, T.J.: The independent components of natural scenes are edge filters. Vision Research 37(23), 3327–3338 (1997)
7. Bartlett, M.S., Movellan, J.R., Sejnowski, T.J.: Face recognition by independent component analysis. IEEE Transactions on Neural Networks 13(6), 1450–1464 (2002)
8. Jenssen, R., Eltoft, T.: Independent component analysis for texture segmentation. Journal of Pattern Recognition Society 36(10), 2301–2315 (2003)
9. Bressan, M., Guillamet, D., Vitria, J.: Using an ICA representation of local color histograms for object recognition. Journal of Pattern Recognition Society 36(3), 691–701 (2003)
10. Sahambi, H.S., Khorasani, K.: A neural-network appearance-based 3-D object recognition using independent component analysis. IEEE Transactions on Neural Networks 14(1), 138–149 (2003)
11. Sakaguchi, Y., Ozawa, S., Kotani, M.: Feature Extraction Using Supervised Independent Component Analysis by Maximizing Class Distance. IEEJ Transactions on Electronics, Information and Systems 124(1), 157–163 (2004) (in Japanese)
12. Liu, Q., Cheng, J., Lu, H., Ma, S.: Modeling Face Appearance With Nonlinear Independent Component Analysis. In: Proc. of IEEE International Conference on Automatic Face and Gesture Recognition, pp. 761–766 (2004)
13. Schalkopf, B., Smola, A., Muller, K.: Nonlinear Component Analysis as a Kernel Eigenvalue Problem. Neural Computation 10(5), 1299–1319 (1998)

14. Baudat, G., Anouar, F.: Generalized discriminant analysis using a kernel approach. Neural Computation 12(10), 2385–2404 (2000)
15. Olshausen, B.A., Field, D.J.: Emergence of simple-cell receptive field properties by learning a sparse code for natural images. Nature 381, 607–609 (1996)
16. van Hateren, J.H., van der Schaaf, A.: Independent component filters of natural images compared with simple cells in primary visual cortex. Proc. of Royal Society London, ser. B. 265, 359–366 (1998)
17. Fei-Fei, L., Fergus, R., Perona, P.: Learning generative visual models from few training examples: an incremental bayesian approach testing on 101 object categories. In: Proc. of IEEE CVPR Workshop of Generative Model Based Vision, pp. 178–187 (2004)

# Fast Simplex Optimization for Active Appearance Model


Yasser Aidarous* and Renaud Séguier

SUPELEC/IETR
Avenue de la Boulaie CS 47601
F-35576 Cesson-Sévigné CEDEX, France
{yasser.aidarous,renaud.seguier}@supelec.fr



**Abstract.** This paper presents a fast optimization method for active appearance model based on Nelder & Mead simplex in the case of mouth alignment under different expressions. This optimization defines a new constraint space. It uses a Gaussian mixture to initialize and constraint the search of an optimal solution. The Gaussian mixture is applied on the dominant eigenvectors representing the reduced data given by Principal Component Analysis. The new algorithm constraints avoid calculating errors of solutions that don't represent researched forms and textures. The constraint operator added to simplex verifies in each iteration that the solution belongs to the space of research. The tests performed in the context of generalization (learning and testing datasets are different) on two datasets show that our method presents a better convergence rate and less computation time compared to the AAM classically optimized.

**Keywords:** Expression analysis, Active Appreance Model, Nelder Mead simplex.


## 1   Introduction

The development of the multifunction mobile technologies (photo, video) and the transmission capacity of the wireless networks claims a fast and reliable communication between the user and the machine. For gestures or motion recognition and users localization, it is necessary to align (find landmarks) objects to be recognized. In our applications in Human Machine Interaction (HMI): animate an avatar to communicate with users depending on their emotion state, we seek to align mouths under different expressions. This application puts several constraints on the choice of the algorithm for several reasons:

- Objects to align are high deformable
- Generalization: the analyzed objects are not belonging to the training dataset (unknown faces and mouths)
- Fast alignment

---


* This work is sponsored by "Région de Bretagne".

T. Wada, F. Huang, and S. Lin (Eds.): PSIVT 2009, LNCS 5414, pp. 106–117, 2009.
© Springer-Verlag Berlin Heidelberg 2009

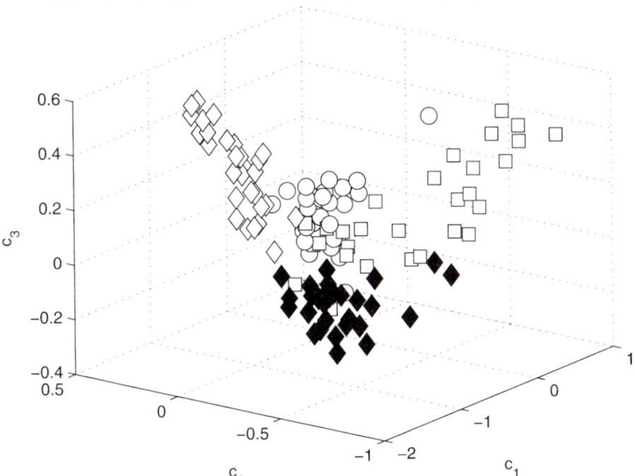


**Fig. 1.** Representation of different mouth expressions. The space formed by first three eigenvectors of the third PCA.

To reach our goal, we opt to use an Active Appearance Models (AAM). The AAM method allows us to model and synthesize object to align by controlling one appearance vector representing form and texture conjointly. In [9] the appearance vector is constrained using the eigenvalue given by the third PCA, this constraints does not take into account the data repartition in reduced dimension. The fig. 1 represents the distribution of mouths images, under different expressions, in the space defined by the first three PCA eigenvectors. We notice the existence of holes in this space where the variables of appearance do not model one of the expressions looked for (and learned). Then, we are faced with a problem of fragmented space. It urges us to redefine our research space in a way that the proposed solutions represent the searched forms.

We add a new "constraints" operator to a simplex optimization applied on appearance vector. This operator will define a relevant space of constraints for the first dominant variables of appearance. We exploit a Gaussian mixture to initialize and model the space of constraints. The new operator will allow to verify the affiliation of the solution in the search space. It will serve to eliminate the solutions presenting different appearances to those searched in the image without error calculation.

The paper is organized as follow. In section 2 we present briefly the AAM and related works for their improvements. In Section 3, which forms the core of the paper, we present an adaptation of the simplex to the AAM, with specific initialization and constraints using Gaussian mixture. Then, in section 4 we present experimental results in the case of fragmented space generalization. Section 5 concludes the paper with advantages supplied by the use of the new optimization.

## 2  Background

### 2.1  Active Appearance Model

AAM [6] uses PCA to encode both shape and texture variation of training dataset. The shape of an object can be represented by vector $s$ and the texture (gray level) by vector $g$. We apply one PCA on shape and another PCA on texture to create the model, given by:

$$s_i = \bar{s} + \Phi_s * b_s$$
$$g_i = \bar{g} + \Phi_g * b_g \tag{1}$$

where $s_i$ and $g_i$ are shape and texture, $\bar{s}$ and $\bar{g}$ are mean shape and mean texture. $\Phi_s$ and $\Phi_g$ are vectors representing variations of orthogonal modes of shape and texture respectively. $b_s$ and $b_g$ are vectors representing parameters of shape and texture. $i$ is the image dataset index. By applying a third PCA on vector $b = \begin{bmatrix} b_s \\ b_g \end{bmatrix}$ we obtain:

$$b = \Phi * c \tag{2}$$

$\phi$ is a matrix of $d_c$ eigenvectors obtained by PCA and $c$ is the appearance parameters vector.

The modifications of c parameters change both shape and texture of the object. Each object is defined by the appearance vector $c$ and pose vector $t$:

$$t = \begin{bmatrix} t_x\ t_y\ \theta\ S \end{bmatrix}^T \tag{3}$$

where $t_x$ and $t_y$ are $x$ and $y$ axis translation, $\theta$ is the angle of orientation and $S$ is Scale.

AAM learns the linear regression models which gives us the predicted modifications of model parameters $\delta c$ and $\delta t$:

$$\delta c = R_c G$$
$$\delta t = R_t G \tag{4}$$

$R_c$ and $R_t$ are the appearance and pose regression matrix respectively. The model search is driven by the residual $G$ of the search image and model reconstruction.

Later in this paper we note Regression Matrix by 'RM'.

### 2.2  Related Works

The segmentation phase proposed by Cootes [6] use an optimization based on multiple linear regression. This optimization have difficulties to align objects which present a fragmented space in reduced dimension (fig. 1). The problem of fragmented space may be treated with a hierarchical method or by executing several AAM (each AAM representing one expressions) but the time consumption must be multiplied by the number of expressions. [1] proposes hierarchical decomposition of the face by several components (eyes, mouths,...), and models the variability of each component. This decomposition is also used in [2] without worrying about the pose parameters to analyze face expressions. In [2] every possible expression of each hierarchical component is modeled by an AAM (for example: two AAM for mouth, one for open mouths and the other for closed mouths). Several AAM was used to overcome the problem of fragmented space. This method was performed in multi view problem in [5] using Direct Appearance Models [3] in which the form is predicted from the texture directly. Several model was created in [4] corresponding to different face expressions and in the search phase it keeps the model which fits the image with minimal error. A Gaussian mixture was used in [8] to make the difference between the different expression classes of the same object modeled by AAM. The mixture is applied on the real learning data images. Each expression class is represented by a Gaussian and defines a model with a specific RM. During the search phase, the number of AAM equals the number of expressions applied. The retained solution generates the minimal error between the generated model and the input image.

[10] suggested, within the framework of fragmented space problem, using an algorithm of optimization based on Simplex to optimize the choice of the vector associating the appearance and the pose. The initialization, of all appearance variables, was made by a Gaussian mixture which allows the simplex to consider all fragments in the search for the optimal solution. The authors use the constraints defined by [9]. However the proposed suffers from an important time execution. In the next section we propose a new initialization and constraints to overcome the fragmented space problem. Unlike in [10] we:

- Apply the Expectation Maximization algorithm on the dominant eigenvectors (defined in the next section) given by PCA to model search space with Gaussian mixture
- Initialize the dominant appearance variables (associated to dominant eigenvectors) using the Gaussian mixture
- Initialize remained variables of appearance vector randomly in the space defined by associated eigenvalues
- Constraint the search of optimal appearance vector using the Gaussian mixture elaborated on the dominant appearance variables. We add new operator to the simplex to verify the affiliation of the proposed solution to the new defined search space
- Constraint remained variables of appearance vector using constraints defined in [9]

This new optimisation reduces the time consuming by avoiding calculating errors of solutions don't belonging to the new search space.

Later in this paper we note our algorithm 'SPGM'.

## 3   Simplex and GM Optimization for AAM

### 3.1   Nelder and Mead Simplex

The simplex Nelder & Mead can find the minimum of a function of $n$ variables iteratively with $n+1$ initial solutions. For two variables, simplex is a triangle. The simplex compares the values of the function on each summit point of triangle. Thus the summit point where the function is the highest is replaced by another which will be calculated based on the existing summits. When we have to align an object (detecting characteristics points and texture) with AAM, we must find a vector $v$ that minimizes the sum of quadratic errors $e^2$ with:

$$v = \begin{bmatrix} c \\ t \end{bmatrix} \quad and: \quad E(v) = \sum_{i=1}^{M} e_i^2 \tag{5}$$

where $c$ is the appearance vector, $M$ is the number of pixels of the model and $e_i$ the error in the pixel $i$.

## 3.2 Simplex and GM

After creating the model, we obtain the appearance vector $c$ representing each image from the learning dataset. We consider that the appearance vector is constituted of two sub-appearance vectors:

$$c = \begin{bmatrix} c_\lambda \\ c_{rand} \end{bmatrix} \tag{6}$$

where $c_\lambda$ is the sub-appearance vector representing the dominant eigenvectors and $c_{rand}$ represents the sub-appearance vector given with the low eigenvectors.

The fig. 2 represents the accumulation percentage of variance of the eigenvectors given by the third PCA (Eq.3). The number of dominant eigenvectors $\lambda$ is the minimal number of eigenvectors that express 80% of data variance. For example in the case of 116 images from France Telecom dataset, According to the accumulative variance represented by eigenvectors given by the third PCA (fig. 2), the number of eigenvectors takes into account is $\lambda = 6$. However, the images form a fragmented space (fig. 1) under the first dominant eigenvectors and uniform space under the other variables. Then we can't consider the variables to optimise with the same importance. This lead us to initialize and constraint the appearance variables using two different manner: Gaussian mixture for the dominant variables and uniform for the other variables. We calculate a Gaussian mixture using Expectation Maximization (EM) [12] algorithm, during the modeling phase, on the sub-appearance vectors $c_\lambda$ given by learning dataset images in the reduced space given by the third PCA:

$$g(c_\lambda, \Theta) = \sum_{k=1}^{N_{gauss}} \pi_k \aleph(\mu_k, \Gamma_k) \tag{7}$$

where $N_{gauss}$ is the number of Gaussians in the mixture, $\pi_k$ is the weights associated to the Gaussian $k$. $\mu_k$ is the mean of the Gaussian $k$, $\Gamma_k$ is the covariance matrix of the Gaussian $k$, $\aleph(\mu_k, \Gamma_k)$ is the normal distribution defined by the mean $\mu_k$ and the covariance matrix $\Gamma_k$, and $\Theta = (\pi_1, ...\pi_k, \mu_1...\mu_{N_{gauss}}, \Gamma_1, ...\Gamma_{N_{gauss}})$ the vector that characterizes the mixture.

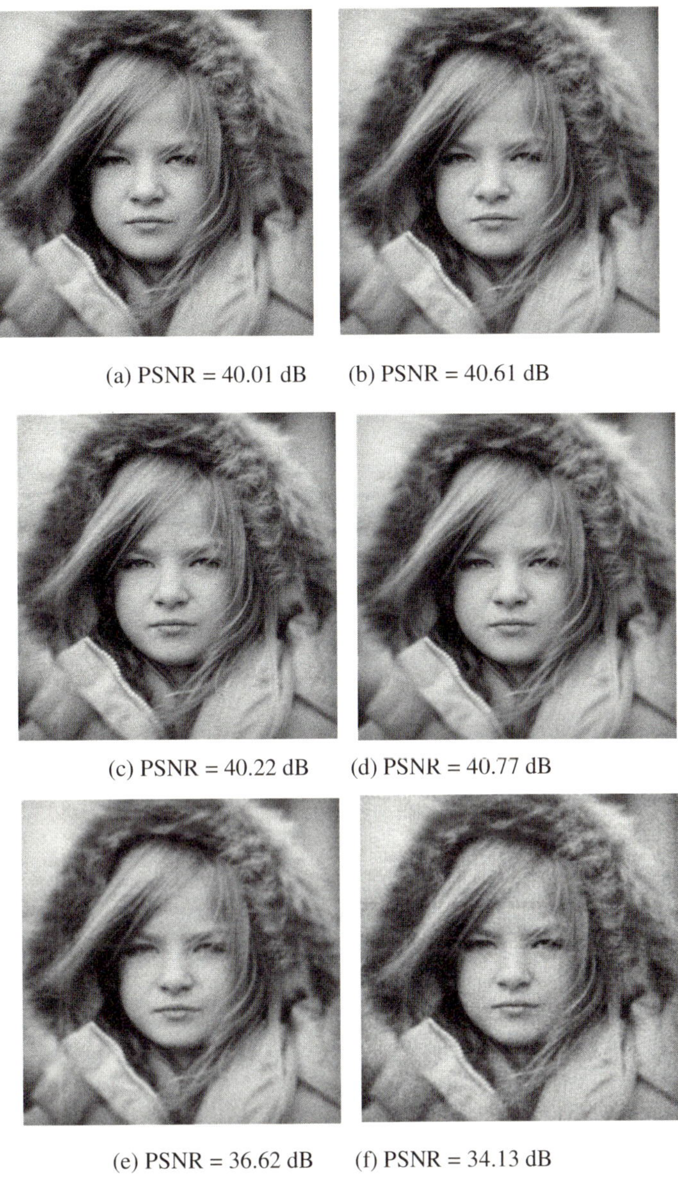

(a) PSNR = 40.01 dB        (b) PSNR = 40.61 dB

(c) PSNR = 40.22 dB        (d) PSNR = 40.77 dB

(e) PSNR = 36.62 dB        (f) PSNR = 34.13 dB

**Fig. 7.** Inverse halftone images using the proposed method with the corresponding optimum support region size. (a) DBS [12] with $L = 9$. (b) EDF [4] with $L = 12$. (c) EDF [5] with $L = 15$. (d) EDF [6] with $L = 16$. (e) DD [2] halfth $L = 26$. (f) DD [3] with class matrix of size 8x8 and $L = 19$, and (g) with class matrix of size 16x16 and $L = 15$. (h) OD [1] Classical-4 cluster-dot dithering with $L = 35$, and (i) Bayer-5 dispersed-dot dithering with $L = 18$. (all printed at 300dpi).

(g) PSNR = 38.07 dB     (h) PSNR = 32.84 dB

(i) PSNR = 33.57 dB

**Fig. 7.** (*continued*)

gray level is 109312. Focus on the range of different support region sizes from 1 to 15 is shown in Fig. 4(b), the memory consumption of Mese-Vaidyanathan's method is superior to the proposed method in range from 1 to 12. However, it cannot provide better inverse halftone image quality for different halftoning techniques with support region size in this small.

Figure 5 shows the comparison of image quality between Mese-Vaidyanathan's method and the proposed method. Among these results, 202 testing images of size 512x512 were used to derive the average PSNR. After which, 9 different halftoning techniques were taken into account, which include Agar-Allebach's DBS [10], error diffusion as Floyd-Steinberg's method [4], Jarvis et al.'s method [5], and Stucki's method [6], dot diffusion as Knuth's method [2] and Mese-Vaidyanathan's method [3], and ordered dithering as Ulichney's Classical-4 clustered-dot and Bayer-5 dispersed-dot [1]. The average PSNRs of Mese-Vaidyanathan's method and proposed method are 33.87 dB and 35.01 dB, respectively.

Figure 6 shows the average PSNR of different kinds of halftoning techniques with different support region sizes using the proposed method. According to these results, the halftoning techniques which can obtain better quality of halftone image have smaller optimal support region size. The region on the tail of curve is flat since the number of representable gray levels is fixed when the support region is increased as shown in Fig. 3. The optimum support region sizes for different halftoning techniques are concentrated in the range from 9 to 35, because the smoothing degree is directly proportional with support region size. Finally, the resulting inverse halftone images obtained by proposed method of different halftoning techniques with corresponding optimum support region size are shown in Fig. 7.

## 5  Conclusions

An inverse halftoning which based on Bayesian theorem is proposed. Two features are taken into account: 1) the probability of black pixel occurrence for each position in the support region, and 2) the probability of mean occurrence which is obtained from all pixels in the support region. Throughout this work, nine different kinds of halftoning were used for evaluating the performance of the proposed method. According to the experimental results, the image quality of proposed method is superior to Mese-Vaidyanathan's inverse halftoning. For Mese-Vaidyanathan's inverse halftoning, when the original halftone images have better image quality, such as error diffusion, DBS, and dot diffusion except Mese-Vaidyanathan's dot diffusion with 8x8 class matrix, the expression on the ramp low frequency part of inverse halftone results is inferior to proposed method. Furthermore, in terms of memory consumption, the proposed method is inferior to Mese-Vaidyanathan's inverse halftoning when the size of support region is from 1 to 12. However, the optimum support region size of all halftoning techniques in experimental results is always bigger than 12 which are except the halftoning technique DBS. In future work, a technique for classifying different kinds of halftoning will be developed.

## References


1. Ulichney, R.: Digital Halftoning. MIT Press, Cambridge (1987)
2. Knuth, D.E.: Digital halftones by dot diffusion. ACM Trans. Graph. 6(4) (October 1987)
3. Mese, M., Vaidyanathan, P.P.: Optimized halftoning using dot diffusion and methods for inverse halftoning. IEEE Trans. on Image Processing 9, 691–709 (2000)
4. Floyd, R.W., Steinberg, L.: An adaptive algorithm for spatial gray scale. In: Proc. SID 75 Digest. Society for information Display, pp. 36–37 (1975)
5. Jarvis, J.F., Judice, C.N., Ninke, W.H.: A survey of techniques for the display of continuous-tone pictures on bilevel displays. Comp. Graph. Image Proc. 5, 13–40 (1976)
6. Stucki, P.: MECCA-A multiple-error correcting computation algorithm for bilevel image hardcopy reproduction. Res. Rep. RZ1060, IBM Res. Lab., Zurich, Switzerland (1981)
7. Ostromoukhov, V.: A simple and efficient error-diffusion algorithm. In: Computer Graphics (Proceedings of SIGGRAPH 2001), pp. 567–572 (2001)
8. Shiau, J.N., Fan, Z.: A set of easily implementable coefficients in error diffusion with reduced worm artifacts. In: SPIE, vol. 2658, pp. 222–225 (1996)

9. Lin, Q., Allebach, J.P.: Color FM screen design using DBS algorithm. In: Proc. SPIE, vol. 3300, pp. 353–361 (1998)
10. Agar, A.U., Allebach, J.P.: Model-based color halftoning using direct binary search. IEEE Trans. on Image Processing 14, 1945–1959 (2005)
11. Chang, P.-C., Yu, C.-S.: Neural net classification and LMS reconstruction to halftone images. In: Proc. SPIE, vol. 3309, pp. 592–602 (1998)
12. Mese, M., Vaidyanathan, P.P.: Look-Up Table (LUT) Method for Inverse Halftoning. IEEE Trans. on Image Processing 10(10), 1566–1578 (2001)

# Live Video Segmentation in Dynamic Backgrounds Using Thermal Vision


Viet-Quoc Pham[1], Keita Takahashi[2], and Takeshi Naemura[1]

[1] Graduate School of Information Science and Technology, The University of Tokyo
[2] IRT Research Initiative, The University of Tokyo
Hongo 7–3–1, Bunkyo-ku, Tokyo, 113–8656 Japan
{viet,keita,naemura}@hc.ic.i.u-tokyo.ac.jp
http://hc.ic.i.u-tokyo.ac.jp



**Abstract.** In this paper we describe a new technique for live video segmentation of human regions from dynamic backgrounds. Correct segmentations are produced in real-time even in severe background changes caused by camera movement and illumination changes. There are three key contributions. The first contribution is the employing of the thermal cue which proves to be very effective when fused with color. Second, we propose a new speed-up GraphCut algorithm by combining with the Bayesian estimation. The third contribution is a novel online learning method using accumulative histograms. The segmentation accuracy and speed are quite capable of the live video segmentation purpose.

**Keywords:** Live video segmentation, infrared image sensors, GraphCut.


## 1   Introduction

This paper addresses the problem of live video segmentation of human regions from dynamic backgrounds. Different from offline video segmentation that can use the whole video as the reference for the segmentation, live video segmentation does not employ future information, so that the estimation should be based only on the past frames. A prime application is live background substitution in broadcasting and teleconferencing. This demands layer separation with high quality and computational efficiency sufficient to attain live streaming speed. Besides, it must deal with dynamic background changes caused by several factors such as camera movement, illumination changes, etc. However, by using only monocular video, even most effective recent researches [1,2] can at most deal with small camera shakes. Therefore, segmentation with more severe background changes like camera movement requires more effective cues besides color and motion.

An impressive decrease in both size and price of thermal vision cameras promises their wide applications in both researches and daily life. Aiming to achieve live video segmentation with higher accuracy, our research group has been developing a unique system named "thermo-key"[3] which combines a color camera and a thermal vision camera. Both cameras share the same optical axis using an IR mirror as shown in Fig. 1, so that each pixel on the combined image


T. Wada, F. Huang, and S. Lin (Eds.): PSIVT 2009, LNCS 5414, pp. 143–154, 2009.

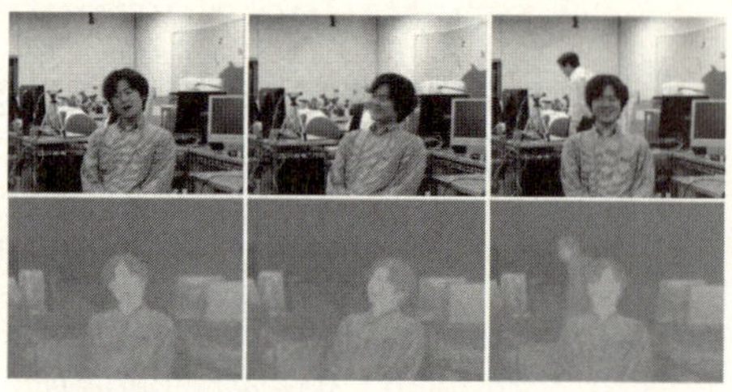

**Fig. 1.** Camera system for thermo-key

**Fig. 2.** Captured sequences from the thermo-key system: first row- color sequence, second row- thermo sequence

has a thermal value as well as a color value. Sample sequences captured from this system are shown in Fig. 2. In this paper, we will prove that by using this thermal cue, we can attain more accurate segmentation results than [1] even when using a simpler probabilistic segmentation model.

We propose three main contributions in this paper. The first one is the employing of the thermal cue which proves to be very effective when fused with color. Second, we propose a new speed-up GraphCut algorithm by combining with the Bayesian estimation. The advantage of GraphCut is that it can simultaneously consider texture (color+thermo) information and edge (contrast) information in its optimization scheme. It has been adopted for interactive image segmentation [4,5] and automatic video segmentation [1,2]. Our method aims to realize accurate human-region segmentation with lower complexity than [1] by combining the Bayesian estimation approach with a GraphCut algorithm. The third contribution is a novel online learning method using accumulative histograms which can be deal with background changes.

In this paper, previous works in video segmentation are described in Section 2. Section 3 introduces our proposed algorithm. Experiments and conclusions are presented in Section 4 and 5.

## 2   Related Works

Classical image segmentation tools use either texture (colour) information, e.g. Magic Wand [6], or edge (contrast) information, e.g. Intelligent Scissors [7]. Recently, an approach based on optimisation by GraphCut has been developed which successfully combines both types of information. Boykov et al. [4] and Rother et al. [5] introduced powerful optimisation techniques using GraphCut for interactive segmentation. Although color/contrast cues have been demonstrated to be very effective for interactive segmentation, they alone are still insufficient for fully automatic segmentation. This suggests a need for a robust approach that fuses a variety of cues, for example depth, motion, and so on.

In [2], segmentation for static background was performed by combining background subtraction with the GraphCut optimization. Criminisi et al. [1] and Kolmogorov et al. [8] described algorithms capable of real-time segmentation of

frame #0   frame #1   frame #2   frame #3

**Fig. 3.** In the segmentation result of the first frame, some errors appear because some parts of the object person have temperatures closed to the background temperature. However, these errors are disappeared in the next frames thanks to our robust segmentation method.

foreground from background layers in video sequences, in which colour, contrast and another key feature were fused to infer layers. The key feature used in [1] was motion, so that their algorithm could be applied to monocular videos, while Kolmogorov et al. [8] employed the depth feature obtained from stereo videos.

As stated before, the above researches can at most deal with small camera shakes. Segmentation with more severe background changes caused by camera movement requires more effective cues besides color and motion. The purpose of this research is to fuse color, contrast with *temperature* to realize the real-time segmentation. Our work is an extension as well as an improvement of the previous work [3] which was based on a simple threshold processing to the thermal images (see Fig. 8).

## 3   Segmentation Algorithm

### 3.1   Assumption

The only constraint for our live video segmentation system is the requiring of the background of the first frame. This simple assumption is reasonable because in most filming works, the background is kept fixed before shooting. This constraint helps us to quickly detect the foreground region from the background for the first frame by a simple background subtraction method. We must notice that the background subtraction is applied for *only* the first frame. After starting capturing, the camera can move freely, making the background changes, and therefore, the background subtraction will be no more in use.

The background subtraction can be performed on both color and thermal channels, however, only thermal channel is enough to produce rather good results. Although it sometimes does not work well due to the closed temperatures in some places between the foreground and the background, but by applying our robust segmentation algorithm, the segmentation errors appeared in the first frame will be removed in the next frames (see Fig. 3).

Some researches like [1] did not require background for the first frame, but they used the motion properties instead. When the object moves while the background is kept static, the moving parts are detected and segmented. Much time was needed until the whole object is segmented (your hand will not be segmented

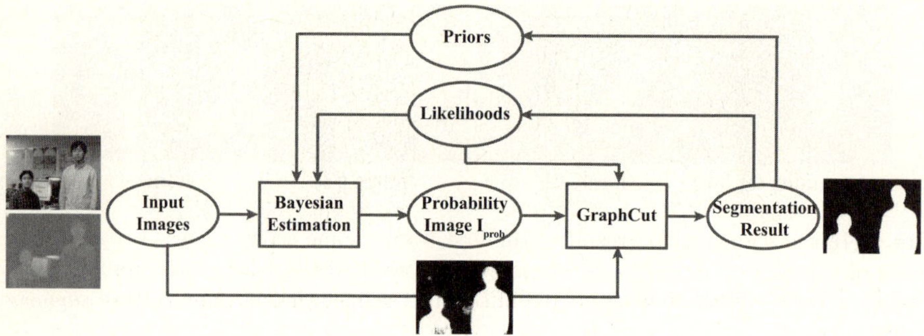


**Fig. 4.** Demonstration for the two-step segmentation algorithm

until you move it). Furthermore, offline learning of motion properties was needed in some cases. For the live video segmentation purpose, it is clearly less practical than our assumption.

The segmentation algorithm for the next frames is stated in the successive sections.

## 3.2 Algorithm Overview

Figure 4 illustrates the entire algorithm. Our algorithm takes the color and thermal images captured by our thermo-key system as the inputs, and outputs the segmentation result (a binary mask) of the foreground region.

The first originality of our algorithm is the employing of the thermal feature combining with the color feature. Second, we propose a probabilistic model combining the Bayesian estimation approach with a GraphCut algorithm. Most GraphCut based segmentation methods including [1] created the graph model for all image pixels. Such methods cost time because the calculation cost of the GraphCut algorithm relies mostly on the number of the graph nodes. Our contribution is that before applying GraphCut, we perform a pre-GraphCut step, or a trimap making step to reduce the unknown region (i.e. the region around the object boundary that is still unknown to be of the background or the foreground class). As a result, we can speed up the GraphCut process. The third originality is a novel online learning method using accumulative histograms which can be deal with background changes. These two steps of segmentation and online learning method are stated in the next sections.

## 3.3 Step 1– Pre-GraphCut Step

The first step calculates the probability of each pixel to be in the foreground based on the Bayesian estimation. This calculation can be performed in the linear time. After that, the results are used to make the trimap.

For details, let $C_i^t$ and $T_i^t$ be the color and thermal values of the $i^{th}$ pixel on the combined image at period $t$ captured by the thermo-key system. Based on the Bayes' formula, the probability of this pixel to be in the foreground is given as

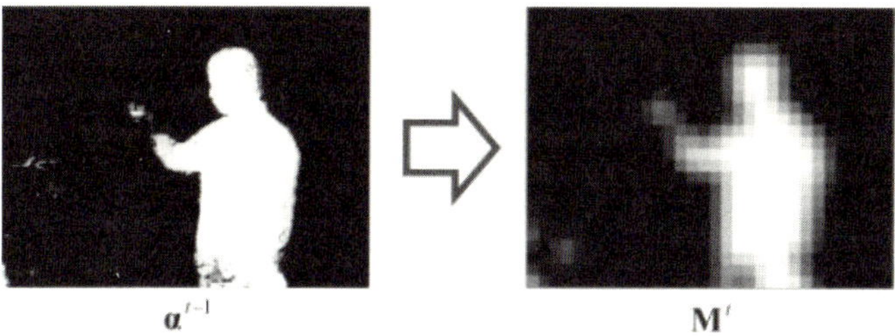


**Fig. 5.** The smoothed map is created from the segmentation result of the previous frame

$$P^t(F|C_i, T_i) = \frac{P^t(C_i, T_i|F)P_i^t(F)}{P^t(C_i, T_i|F)P_i^t(F) + P^t(C_i, T_i|B)P_i^t(B)} \tag{1}$$

where $P(*)$ represents the probability of "$*$". $F$ and $B$ are the foreground and background respectively, into which each pixel should be classified. The posterior probability, $P^t(F|C_i, T_i)$, is represented as the product of the likelihood $P^t(C_i, T_i|F)$, and the prior probability, $P_i^t(F)$. The likelihood is calculated from the histogram which was constructed from previous segmentation results. Since there are some correlations between color and thermal information, we should use a 4-D accumulative histogram, where 3 dimensions are assigned for YUV color channels, and another dimension is for the thermal channel. The meaning of accumulative histogram is explained in section 3.5.

The prior probability is calculated from the previous image frame since successive frames in the temporal domain would have strong correlations. To be more precise, let $\alpha^{t-1}$ be the 2-D mask of the segmentation result (taking 255 for $F$ and 0 for $B$) at period $t-1$, and $M^t$ be the smoothed map of $\alpha^{t-1}$ which is defined as follows

$$M^t = G_{7\times7}(Resize_{\times10}(G_{3\times3}(Resize_{\times1/10}(\alpha^{t-1}))))/255 \tag{2}$$

where $G$ is the Gaussian filter and $Resize$ is the scaling transformation. Then the prior probability $P_i^t(x)$ can be inferred from $M^t$

$$P_i^t(x) = \begin{cases} M_i^t & (x = F) \\ 1 - M_i^t & (x = B) \end{cases} \tag{3}$$

An image of a smoothed map is shown in Fig. 5.

## 3.4   Step 2– GraphCut Optimization

The set of posterior probabilities $P^t(F|C_i, T_i)$ over all image pixels $i$ forms the probability map $I_{prob}$. We create the trimap, $Tr(i)$, which takes one of the three values {F (foreground), B (background), and U (unknown)}, based on the value of $I_{prob}(i)$

$$\begin{cases} if(I_{prob}(i) < \epsilon): & Tr(i) = B \\ if(I_{prob}(i) > 1 - \epsilon): & Tr(i) = F \\ \text{otherwise}: & Tr(i) = U \end{cases}$$

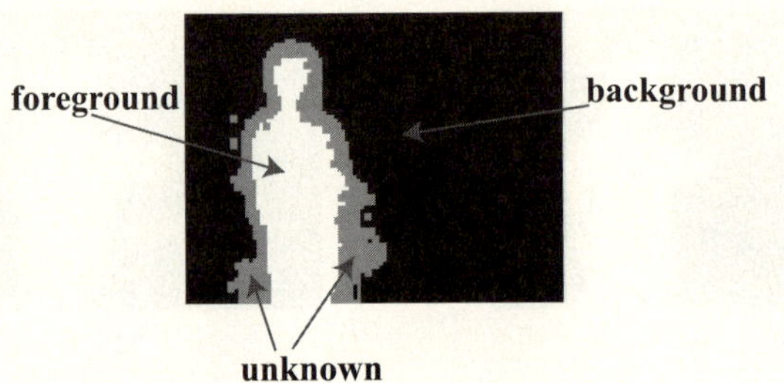


**Fig. 6.** A trimap is a classification of an image into three regions: foreground (white), background (black) and unknown (gray)

where $\epsilon$ is a small real value. Then, a filter is applied to the trimap to remove noises, since clusters of noise pixels seem to be relatively small in size. And this filter operation can be achieved in linear time. An image of a trimap is shown in Fig. 6.

Before getting further into our proposed method, it is better to explain briefly about the GraphCut optimization algorithm [4]. Let $Seg$ be a segmentation of the image where $Seg$(i) takes $F$ (Foreground) or $B$ (Background) for the $i^{th}$ pixel. We define the energy function by

$$\mathrm{E}(Seg) = \mathrm{Data}(Seg) + \lambda\mathrm{Sth}(Seg) \qquad (4)$$

where the data term $\mathrm{Data}(Seg)$ evaluates the pixel-wise costs, and the smoothness term $\mathrm{Sth}(Seg)$ evaluates the inter-pixel costs. $\lambda$ is a weighting coefficient. This function can be minimized by the GraphCut algorithm, and the optimization solution should produce a good segmentation because it keeps the balance between the region property and the boundary property of the segments.

In our method, the above filtered trimap is set as the initial values for the GraphCut optimization. As we can see from Fig. 6, the unknown region is much smaller than the whole image. Because in our proposed algorithm, the GraphCut process is applied only on the unknown region, its calculation speed can increase considerably.

We define the data term as the weighted sum of the likelihood of the color and thermal values $L(C_i, T_i|Seg(i))$, and the probability map given by the first step $I_{prob}(i)$

$$\mathrm{Data}(Seg) = (1 - \mu) \sum_i - \log(L(C_i, T_i|Seg(i)))$$

$$+ \mu \sum_i - \log(I_{prob}(i)) \qquad (5)$$

where the likelihood can be obtained from the accumulative histograms (section 3.5). We employ the probability map $I_{prob}$ here because it is a good estimation which combines both the temporal priors and the likelihoods. This is another different point of our proposed method from the others.

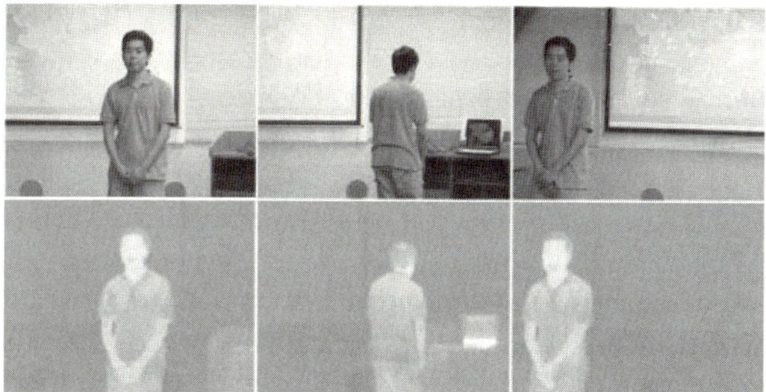

**Fig. 7.** When the camera moves , the textures of the background change noticeably. A new object (a laptop PC) appears in the second image, and the illuminations in the first and third images are clearly different.

To set the smoothness term, we use an ad-hoc function which was used by most other methods

$$\mathrm{Sth}(Seg) = \sum_{(i,j)\in N} [Seg(i) \neq Seg(j)] \frac{e^{-\|C_i - C_j\|^2/(2\sigma^2)}}{\| \operatorname{dist}(i,j) \|} \qquad (6)$$

where $N$ represents all neighborhood pixel pairs, and $\operatorname{dist}(i,j)$ denotes Euclidean distance between $i^{th}$ and $j^{th}$ pixels. $\sigma$ can be estimated as "camera noise". This function imposes larger cost to the discontinuous regions with little color variations. Our implementation of the GraphCut algorithm uses the minimum-cut algorithm from [9].

### 3.5   Accumulative Histogram

The other contribution of our proposed method is the new idea of the accumulative histogram. The main problem of segmentation from dynamic backgrounds is how to deal with the circumstance where the textures of the foreground and background are changing along the time (see Fig. 7). One of the solutions is to update the likelihood, or the 4D histograms of the color and thermal values. Here we creates two accumulative histograms $Hist_F$ and $Hist_B$ for the foreground and background likelihood models, respectively. We update them adaptively over successive frames, based on data from the segmented foreground and background in the previous frame. The new idea of our method is that we do not update all bins of the histograms, but *only the new bins* (a bin is a certain range of 4D vectors expressing the color and thermal values). To be more precise, only bins which have the current values of zeros in the both histograms were updated with the new values learned from the previous segmented image. The reason is that segmentation results always include errors, and if we update all bins, these errors will propagate, and as the sequence, both histograms will converge to each others, making the discrimination between the foreground and background becomes impossible.

## 4   Experimental Results

In our experiment, we captured two video sequences named "Video Chatting" and "Weather Forecast". Each frame in each sequence is a pair of a 24-bit color image and a 8-bit thermal image (both are 320 × 240 pixels). In "Video Chatting", a person who is the segmentation object was talking in front of the camera while the background was changing following the movement of the cameras. In "Weather Forecast", the person was moving backward and forward while making some hand gestures during his presentation. The capturing system was slowly panned during the sequence to track the person's position. Besides, some objects like monitors whose temperatures closed to the body temperature were located in the backgrounds, making the backgrounds more dynamic in both color and thermal channels. Therefore, the segmentation task became so difficult that a simple thresholding method based on the thermal information, which was employed in the earlier implementation of the thermo-key system [3], became inapplicable in such circumstances (see Fig. 8).

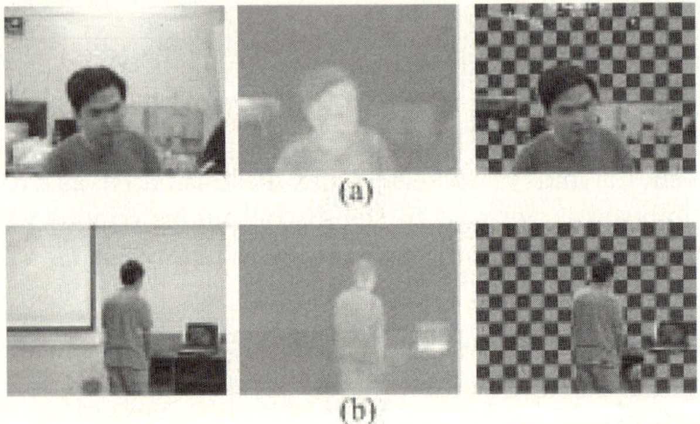

**Fig. 8.** Results from the thresholding method applied to the 100th frame from sequences (a)"Video Chatting" and (b)"Weather Forecast". From left to right: input color images, input thermal images, thresholding results. Some places in the background whose temperatures are closed to the body temperature were misclassified.

Four coefficients $(\epsilon, \lambda, \mu, \sigma)$ in Section 3.4 were set as $(\epsilon = 1/32, \lambda = 20, \mu = 0.75, \sigma = 27)$.

### 4.1   Segmentation Quality

Figure 9 shows the segmentation results for some frames from the two sequences. The first and second rows show the input color and thermal sequences captured from the thermo-key system. The third row shows the segmentation results. On the last row, the segmentation results are superimposed on the corresponding color images. The entire results are available from our web site[1].

---

[1] http://www.hc.ic.i.u-tokyo.ac.jp/~viet/liveseg

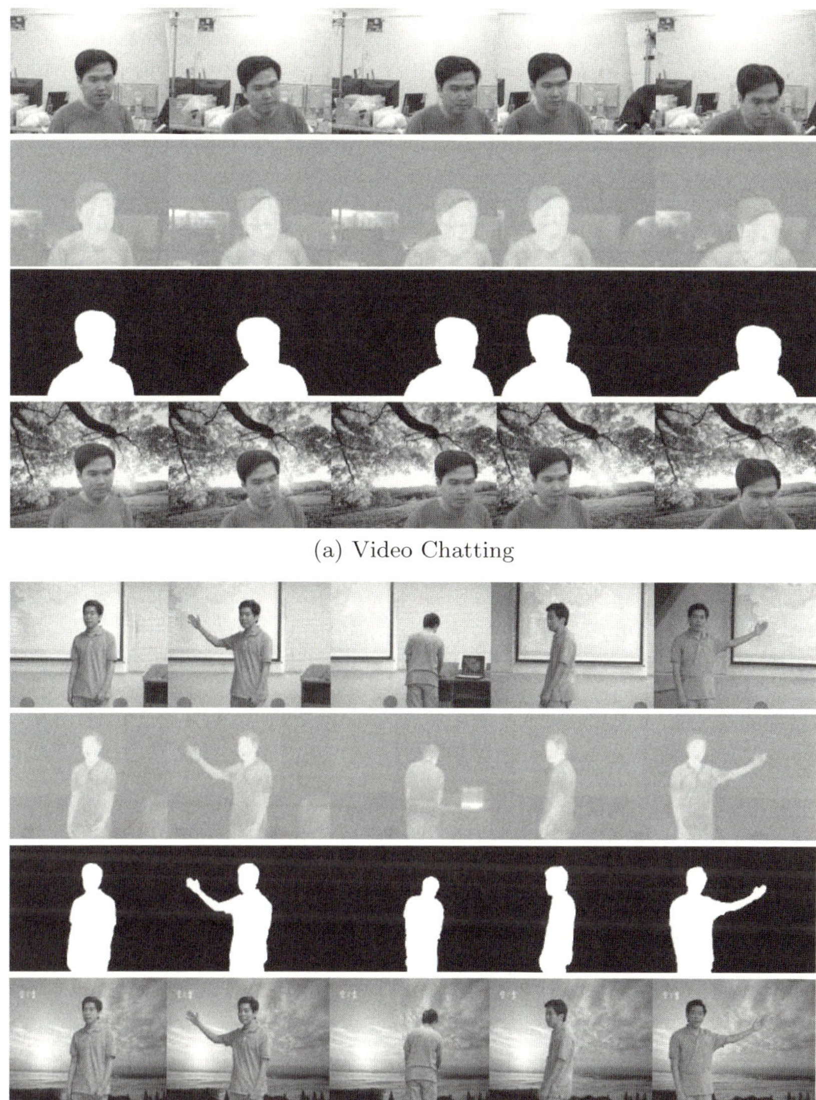

(a) Video Chatting

(b) Weather Forecast

**Fig. 9.** Segmentation results from two sequences (a) "Video Chatting" and (b) "Weather Forecast". First row: input color sequence, second row: input thermal sequence, third row: output segmentation results, last row: background substitution results. Notice that the cameras were panned in both sequences.

To evaluate the results, we first made a comparison between two cases, in which our proposed method was performed with and without using the thermal feature, in order to show the importance of this feature. Second, to prove the effectiveness of our method, we made another comparison between our

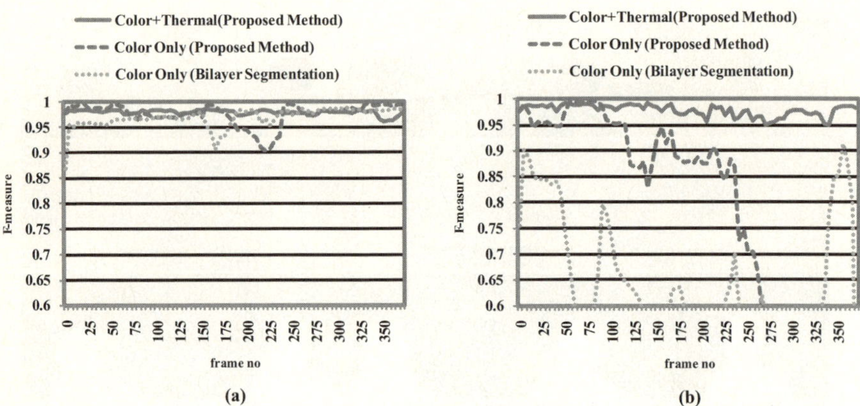


**Fig. 10.** F-measures calculated over 370 frames from two sequences (a) "Video Chatting" and (b) "Weather Forecast"

proposed method with one of the most effective conventional methods- Bilayer Segmentation[1]. This method was implemented from the source code provided in [10]. The temporal prior and the likelihood for motion in this method were learned from the ground truths of the first 100 frames. To evaluate the quality of the segmentation results, we used F-measure which is the harmonic mean of precision and recall

$$F = 2 \cdot (precision \cdot recall)/(precision + recall) \qquad (7)$$

The hand-labeled ground truths were used to calculate the precision and recall. We must notice that these ground truths were only used for the evaluation and *not* employed in our algorithm at all. The graphs of F-measures calculated over 370 frames from the two sequences showed the comparison results (see Fig. 10). In "Video Chatting", where the background textures did not change so much, the differences between the three methods were not so large. However, on an average, our proposed method with using thermal information outperformed the others (its F-measures were always larger than 95%). In "Weather Forecast", where the background changed noticeablely in both its texture and illumination, the differrences between the three methods became more clear. Bilayer Segmentation did not work in this case because its motion model did not adapt to severe changing backgrounds. Besides, because its algorithm needed to be trained by lots of hand-labeled segmentation data to build the temporal prior, color, and motion models, this method was not capable of the live video segmentation purpose. Another thing which can be learned from the graph result is the effectiveness of using the thermal feature. In such case when the color feature are not reliable due to the camera motion and illumination changes, using the thermal feature is a good solution. The F-measures from our proposed method were always over 95%, a value that is quite capable of the live video segmentation purpose.

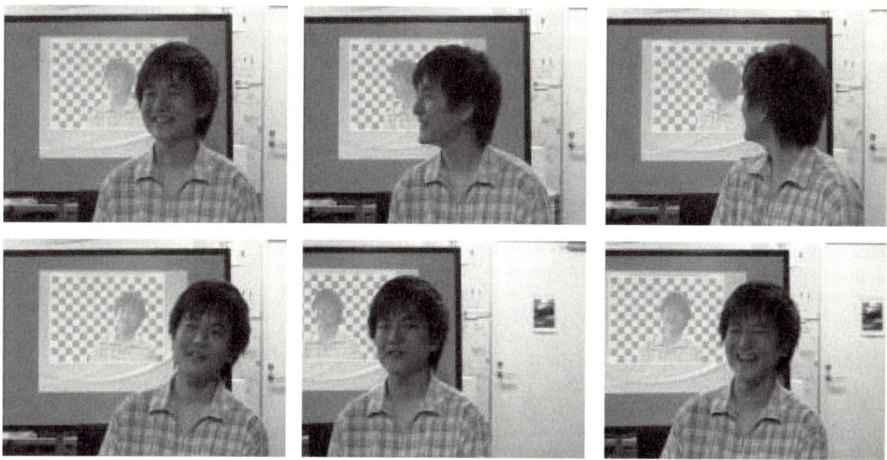

**Fig. 11.** Live video segmentation demonstration. The segmentation results are displayed lively in the behind projector screen.

### 4.2   Calculation Cost

Our experiment was performed on the computer with Intel Core2 Quad CPU, 2.40GHz and 4GB memory. The calculation time was about *90* milliseconds for each frame. To prove the fact that initializing the human and background regions could speed up the GraphCut process, we also measured the calculation time for the case in which the human and background regions were not initialized, i.e. the GraphCut algorithm was applied over the entire image region. This calculation time was about 200-300 milliseconds for each frame which was much slower than the proposed method.

### 4.3   Live Video Segmentation

In the live video segmentation system, the delay times (the waiting time until the result is outputed) must be kept as short as possible. In our implementation, besides employing the speed-up GraphCut algorithm, we also applied parallel processing for the capturing phase and the segmentation processing phase. As a result, the delay time was decreased to less than 200 milliseconds (about two frames' processing time). Fig. 11 shows our live video segmentation demonstration in which the segmentation results are displayed behind the person with a few frames' delay.

## 5   Conclusions

In this paper, we have developed an effective human region segmentation method for the live video segmentation system. The experimental results showed that our method is more effective than conventional methods for segmentation from dynamic backgrounds. There are three key contributions. The first contribution is the employing of the thermal feature. Second, we propose a new speed-up GraphCut algorithm by combining with the Bayesian estimation. The third contribution is a novel online learning method using accumulative histograms. The segmentation accuracy and speed are quite capable of the live video segmentation purpose. Our future work will be focused on further optimization of the algorithm and application of matting methods.

**Acknowledgement:** We express our thanks to Prof. H. Harashima of the University of Tokyo for his discussions.

# References


1. Criminisi, A., Cross, G., Blake, A., Kolmogorov, V.: Bilayer segmentation of live video. In: Computer Vision and Pattern Recognition, vol. 1, pp. 53–60 (2006)
2. Sun, J., Zhang, W., Tang, X., Shum, H.-Y.: Background cut. In: Leonardis, A., Bischof, H., Pinz, A. (eds.) ECCV 2006. LNCS, vol. 3952, pp. 628–641. Springer, Heidelberg (2006)
3. Yasuda, K., Naemura, T., Harashima, H.: Thermo-key: human region segmentation from video. Computer Graphics and Applications, 26–30 (January-February 2004)
4. Boykov, Y., Jolly, M.: Interactive graph cuts for optimal boundary and region segmentation of objects in N-D images. In: IEEE International Conference on Computer Vision, vol. 1, pp. 105–112 (2001)
5. Rother, C., Kolmogorov, V., Blake, A.: Grabcut: interactive foreground extraction using iterated graph cuts. In: SIGGRAPH, vol. 23, pp. 309–314 (2004)
6. Incorp., A.S.: Adobe photoshop user guide (2002)
7. Mortensen, E., Barrett, W.: Intelligent scissors for image composition. In: Computer graphics and interactive techniques, pp. 191–198 (1995)
8. Kolmogorov, V., Criminisi, A., Blake, A., Cross, G., Rother, C.: Bi-layer segmentation of binocular stereo video. In: Computer Vision and Pattern Recognition, pp. 407–414 (2005)
9. Boykov, Y., Kolmogorov, V.: An experimental comparison of min-cut/max-flow algorithms for energy minimization in vision. IEEE Transactions on Pattern Analysis and Machine Intelligence, 1124–1137 (2004)
10. Implementation of Bilayer Segmentation of Live Video, http://vision.caltech.edu/projects/yiw/FgBgSegmentation/

# Image-Based Techniques for Shredded Document Reconstruction


Huei-Yung Lin and Wen-Cheng Fan-Chiang

Department of Electrical Engineering,
National Chung Cheng University,
168 University Rd., Min-Hsiung
Chia-Yi 621, Taiwan, R.O.C
lin@ee.ccu.edu.tw, hdtonestep@yahoo.com.tw



**Abstract.** This paper proposes an image-based technique for shredded document reconstruction. The problem is different from solving jigsaw puzzles since curved boundaries and color information are not available. Currently most research on document recovery focuses on image feature exaction and analysis. In this work, we present a complete procedure which is capable of reconstructing a full page of shredded document. Similarity measure based on shred boundary correlation is defined for pattern matching. A weighted digraph is then used to derive the final shred sorting result. Experiments are presented for both the synthetic and real datasets.


## 1   Introduction

One of the essential problems in digital image processing is the reconstruction of damaged images. In the past few decades, a large number of computational algorithms have been proposed to deal with restoration of degraded images [1,2]. The sources of degradation are commonly modeled by image acquisition noise (e.g., optical defocus and atmospheric turbulence blur), or data transmission noise (e.g., interference between different channels) [3]. In either case, the spatial relationship between pixels in an image is assumed to be available, and most of the existing techniques are focused on the recovery of the photometric aspect of the original image.

There are, however, other classes of image defects which are caused by splitting an image into several pieces. Jigsaw puzzle can be thought as one common example of this type of *damaged* images. The recovery process is usually to assemble the small pieces of a fragmented image based on their contour shapes or contents, such as texture or color information [4,5]. For more general cases, the objective of fragmented image recovery is to find the best subimage arrangement which resembles the original image. Thus, the underlying reconstruction issues are no longer part of the classic image restoration problem, but belong to an object recognition and classification problem. Moreover, the solution to this problem usually involves pattern matching and graph theory.


T. Wada, F. Huang, and S. Lin (Eds.): PSIVT 2009, LNCS 5414, pp. 155–166, 2009.

This paper aims to address the problem of shredded document recovery using image-based techniques. It is not only an interesting research topic, but also has many applications on forensics and investigation science [6]. Although sometimes considered as a special case of jigsaw puzzle [7], this problem actually preserves different characteristics and requires its own solving strategy. In the past few decades, many researchers focused on developing optimal solutions to the jigsaw puzzle problem, but fairly little work has been done for shredded document analysis. Recently, due to the huge demand for document reconstruction, this issue has attracted the attention of government agents and private companies for extensive investigation [8,9,10,11]. However, to the authors' best knowledge, there are still no standard techniques or complete system description available in the literature.

In this work, we present the computational algorithms for shredded document recovery. The boundaries of the shredded document are assumed to be straight and indistinguishable, and only the interiors are used to verify the correctness of the assembled fragments. Moreover, the texture information on the shred boundaries might be lost due to the shredding noise. In our two-stage approach, image-based techniques are first used to evaluate the similarity between any pair of shreds, followed by a graph-based algorithm to derive the best shred sorting result in terms of a locally shortest path. The proposed method using the shred coding scheme and average word length is insensitive to the shredding noise on the image boundaries. Experimental results are presented for both the computer generated and real scanned shredded documents.

## 2   Image-Based Similarity Evaluation

The proposed shredded document reconstruction approach consists of the following five stages: image acquisition and pre-processing, special shred selection, shred coding, similarity measure, and graph-based sorting.

### 2.1   Image Acquisition and Pre-processing

Shred images for reconstruction are acquired by scanning the shredded document placed on a blue background, followed by object segmentation and length normalization in the shredding direction. Although some texture details might be lost during the normalization process, the computational complexity for pattern matching in the subsequent stages is greatly reduced. To remove the saw-tooth shape noise on the boundaries caused by the paper shredder and the shading caused by scanning, a one-dimensional morphological erosion is carried out in the horizontal direction (i.e. orthogonal to the shredding direction). Finally, the resulting shred images are binarized and the image features are extracted for document reconstruction.

One of the important prerequisites for correct pattern matching between the shred images is to align the text lines across all available pieces. This text and non-text region separation is achieved by segmenting the histogram obtained from the horizontal projection of each shred image. Furthermore, the local maxima of the horizontal projection histogram are used to identify the top-lines and base-lines of the text lines [12]. These features will be used later to identify the relationship between the shreds in the shred coding stage.

## 2.2   Special Shred Selection

For a general shredded document there usually exist three types of special pieces, which are different from the majority of the shreds. They are namely the blank (or all-white) shreds, and the leftmost and rightmost shreds containing the text part of the original document.

The blank shreds commonly appear near the borders or on the separation of a multiple column document. Since there is no text information available by definition, they can be freely removed from the document reconstruction process. The leftmost shred is characterized by the one containing no texture near its left border but with texture near or on its right border. Vice versa for the definition of the rightmost shred. It is clear that these two types of shreds can be easily verified by examining the histogram of vertical projections (i.e. along the shredding direction). Thus, they are singled out first and served as the starting and ending vertices in the following graph-based shred sorting stages.

## 2.3   Shred Coding

From the histogram of horizontal projections, each shred image consists of a number of text blocks separated by several disconnected blank blocks. If we compare this binary pattern with the one generated from the original document image, it can be seen that the text blocks of any individual shred is a subset of those in the original document. Furthermore, there might be different text block patterns for different shred images mainly due to the large space introduced by the beginning or ending of a text line. For the shreds with high spatial proximity, however, those patterns can be identical or only differ by a few text blocks.

Based on the above observation, a shred coding scheme is proposed to group the closely related shreds. The idea is to assign similar binary coded patterns to the shreds based on their spatial proximity. This grouping method can significantly reduce the computational complexity, especially for document reconstruction from a large number of shred images. The algorithm consists of first creating a shred model from all of the shred images, followed by binary coding for the individual shreds.

Since the shred model contains all possible text block locations of the individual shred images, it can be constructed by taking the union of the horizontal projections of all shred images. Let the projection distribution of shred $i$ be $p_i(j)$ for $i = 1, 2, \ldots, n$, where $j$ is a variable along the shredding direction, then the shred model is represented by the set

$$M = \{j \mid \sum_{i=1}^{n} p_i(j) > th, 1 \le j \le m\} \tag{1}$$

where $th$ is a threshold and $m$ is the length of the shred images in pixel.

Due to acquisition noise, quantization error, or slight miss alignment between the shreds, the projection histogram might not provide perfectly separable text blocks. Thus, the base-lines of the text regions are further used to robustly indicate the locations of the text blocks. The $k$-th text block of the shred model is then given by

$$B(k) = \{j \mid j \sim b_k, 1 \le j \le m\} \tag{2}$$

where $\sim$ represents the connectivity relation and $b_k$ is the $k$-th base-line from the top.

The binary encoding for each shred is accomplished by comparing its text block or base-line locations with the shred model. Since the text block pattern of an individual shred is merely a subset of the shred model, a "0" or "1" will be assigned depending on whether the text block of a shred is absent or present on the model. More specifically, the $k$-th bit of an $n$-bit binary code $c$ can be written as

$$c_k = \begin{cases} 1, & \text{if } \exists\, j \text{ such that } j \sim b_k \\ 0, & \text{otherwise} \end{cases} \tag{3}$$

where the number of bits $n$ is equal to the number of text block in the shred model.

## 2.4   Similarity Measure

In shredded document reconstruction, a similarity measure is a metric to evaluate the similarity between any two shreds. Higher score on the similarity measure generally means higher correlation between the pair of shreds. Based on this, a probability distribution from the shred permutation can be derived and used to recover the correct shred order in the original document.

In this work, we propose two approaches for the similarity measure computation. One is to use the discrepancy in the shred coding result, and the other is to calculate the correlation between the shreds based on the average word length. It should be noted that, for the shred images from a single-sided document with correct orientation (i.e. all shreds with top-down or bottom-up text), two similarity computations should be carried out between any two shreds since there are two effective boundaries for each of them.[1]

### Shred Coding Discrepancy

The shred coding pattern described in the previous section can be though of as a simplified representation of the document layout. Based on the continuity characteristic of the document content, a negative correlation is assigned to each bit difference between the binary codes. Consequently, there is a negative

---

[1] If the shred images are not oriented, then there will be four and eight similarity computations between any pair of shreds for a single-sided and a double-sided sheet of document, respectively. Moreover, the computational complexity is increased exponentially for multiple-sheet documents. Both cases are not discussed in the current work.

correlation score between any pair of shreds, which serves as one of the similarity measures for sorting shreds to the correct order in the original document.

Different from both-side aligned documents, the space between two words in a text line is constant for general left-aligned or right-aligned documents. As a result, the binary codes for these classes of documents have the property that the shreds with the same code are very likely to belong to the same group in general cases. Furthermore, the smaller bit difference between the binary codes means that the corresponding shreds might be spatially closer to each other. In other words, the shred coding result plays a major role on a coarse level similarity check.

It is clear that the shreds with the same binary code form a unified pattern group, and no further discrepancy exists due to the highest correlation score (i.e. zero) between each other. Thus, a second sorting scheme is required exclusively for each group of the same binary coded shreds. Since this stage is a refinement of the coarse level similarity check, there is usually a limited number of shreds in each group for the similarity measure computation.

**Average Word Length**

The second similarity measure proposed in this work is based on the average word length of a general document. Under the assumption that the length of each word in a document should be as close to the average word length as possible, a negative correlation score can be evaluated using the difference. Although the word lengths are not constant in a document, this similarity measure is valid for a general probability distribution of word length, especially with a large sample size.

For each shred permutation in the same binary coded group, the negative correlation score based on the average word length is defined as the summation of the difference between a word length and the average word length. More

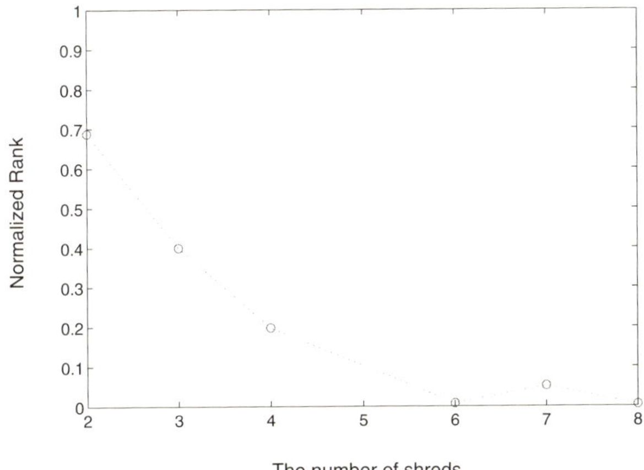

**Fig. 1.** The (normalized) rank of the correct permutation versus the number of shreds in a group for a simulation result. The correct permutations are of relatively high ranks for the groups with a large number of shreds. The result is given by the average of ten computer generated documents.

specifically, suppose the document contains $m$ text lines (which can be identified by the shred model described previously) and there are $n$ shreds in a group, then the similarity measure for a specific shred permutation is given by

$$-\sum_{p=1}^{m}\sum_{q=1}^{\alpha_p}|w_{p,q}-\bar{w}| \qquad (4)$$

where $\bar{w}$ is the average word length, $w_{p,q}$ and $\alpha_p$ the $q$-th word length and the number of words in the $p$-th text line, respectively. The objective is to find the shred permutation, say indexed as $j$, from the $n!$ possible permutations that maximizes the similarity measure, i.e.

$$j = \arg\max_{i} g(i) \qquad (5)$$

where $g(i)$ is the correlation score of the $i$-th shred permutation defined by Eq. (4), and $i = 1, 2, \ldots, n!$. The shred permutation given by Eq. (5) is then used to recover the shred order in the binary coded group.

Ideally, the correlation function $g(i)$ is maximized by the correct permutation of the shreds under the assumption of constant word length. For a general document with variable word lengths, however, high correlation score only implies that the shred permutation result is more reasonable. As an example of the same binary coded group from computer generated documents, Fig. 1 illustrates the statistics of normalized ranks of the correlation scores associated with the correct permutation for various numbers of shreds. Although the correct permutations do not possess the top rank using Eqs. (4) and (5), they are still of relatively high ranks for the groups with a large number of shreds. Thus, the figure indicates that the proposed average word length approach is feasible, especially when the number of shreds increases. By assigning a suitable threshold on the normalized rank, it is guaranteed to cover the correct permutation.

As suggested by the simulation result given in Fig. 1, Table 1 lists the reasonable thresholds versus the number of shreds in a group adopted in the implementation. Note that the threshold is assigned as the rank among all shred permutations instead of the correlation score. It might also be concluded from the table that the rank of $(n-1)!$ is a conservative choice if the number of shreds $n$ in a group is small. This is a good rule of thumb since the shred coding in

**Table 1.** The thresholds versus the number of shreds adopted in the implementation, where $n$ is the number of shreds in a group. The maximum number of $n$ is given by the number of shreds in the document. In this case, only a single binary coded pattern is provided by the shred coding stage.

| Number of shreds | Rank of reasonable threshold |
|---|---|
| $2 \sim 3$ | $n!/2$ |
| 4 | $n!/3$ |
| 5 | $n!/5$ |
| above 6 | $n!/10$ |

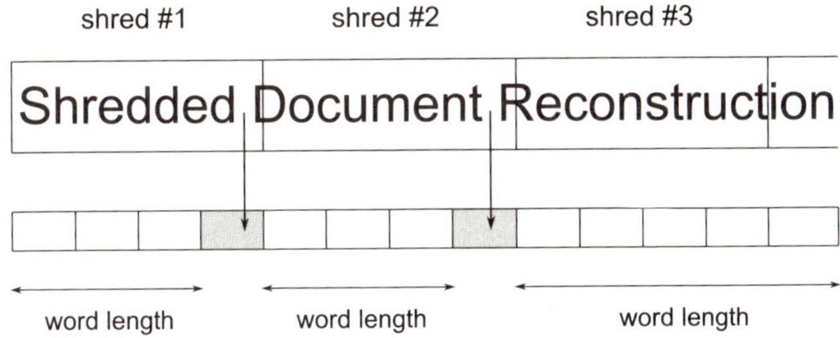



**Fig. 2.** A shred is partitioned to 4 strips and the strip width is used as the unit of word length. Note that the space between two words always occupies one unit strip width.

the coarse level similarity check usually results in a small number of shreds in a group (less than 10 in general).

Since the character size might not be the same for different documents or even varies in a document, it is not suitable to use pixel as the unit of word length. To make the word length distribution less dependent on the metric unit, each shred is further partitioned to several strips and the strip width is set as the unit for correlation score calculation. An example is illustrated in Figure 2, where each shred is further partitioned to four strips. Note that the space between two words always occupies at least one unit strip width, and the word length is rounded to an integer strip width. This quantization process can greatly reduce the computation cost while maintain the correctness of threshold settings.

## 3   Graph-Based Sorting Scheme

The objective of shredded document reconstruction is to sort the unorganized shred images and recover the correct order in the original document. Based on the grouping result from shred coding and the similarity measure, document reconstruction problem is modeled as a weighted digraph (directed graph). More specifically, the shred images are represented by the vertices of the graph, and the correlation scores between the pairs of shred images are assigned as the weighted edges of the graph.

Since each shred image has two boundaries (left and right) when merged with another shred image, directed edges for both the left-right and right-left adjacency relations are assigned to each vertex. Finding the shortest path connecting the starting and ending vertices is then equivalent to selecting the optimal shred permutation (with the fixed leftmost and rightmost ones) for document reconstruction.

### First Stage Sorting
Without any prior knowledge of the shred characteristics, the shredded document reconstruction problem should be modeled as a complete graph since the similarity between any pair of shreds has to be evaluated. The required computation therefore grows exponentially as the number of shreds increases. Because

the improper pairings based on the similarity measure are usually inevitable, the correctness of the reconstruction results will also degrade due to the larger number of inaccurate similarity evaluations.

In this work, a two-stage sorting scheme is proposed to reduced the high computational complexity and mis-pairing rate introduced by a large size complete graph. In the first stage sorting, a simplified digraph is created based on the shred coding result. Each vertex in the graph is modeled as a supernode representing the set of the same binary code. The weighting on the directed edges is defined by the number of bit difference between the pair of binary codes. Since the starting and ending vertices are available from the special shred selection, the shortest path can be easily determined sequentially by the set of minimal weighted edges.

Although rarely happened in practice, there might be a tie on the bit difference between two pairs of binary codes. In this case, the continuity of the bit pattern is further used to determine the best match. Let $s$ be the number of bit pattern change defined as the number of transitions from 0 to 1 or 1 to 0 in a shred image. Suppose $A$ is the set of shred images which have the same number of bit difference when connected to shred $i$ for pairing, then the best match is given by

$$\arg\max_j(s_j - s_i) \tag{6}$$

where $j \in A$. If the ambiguity still cannot be resolved, then the method described in the next stage will be applied on this coarse level sorting.

## Second Stage Sorting

The second stage sorting focuses on finding the shortest path of the digraph associated with the supernode derived from shred coding. Except for the supernodes containing the border shreds (i.e. the leftmost and the rightmost), the starting and ending vertices in the same binary coded set are not available. One simple way to obtain the shortest path is to compute the cost function or the similarity metric exclusively for all possible permutations of the shred images. The computational cost of this brute-force approach is obviously too expensive for a large number of shreds.

In this work, the "shortest" path is generated sequentially by identifying the two adjacent vertices connected by the directed edge with the highest weight in the same coded group. Although the link between any two vertices is bipartite, merging the adjacent vertices using the highest weighted edge will simultaneously removes the possibility of path finding using the other edge. Continue this process of merging the adjacent vertices, the edges for the shortest path is identified and the digraph is shrunk to a single vertex corresponding to the supernode of the coded group. This approach does not guarantee the true shortest path as given by, for example, the Hungarian method used for the assignment model [13]. However, the proposed algorithm is easy to implement and provide the sub-optimal results in most cases.

Note that finding a path using this approach might not result in an ordered set of directed edges during the path creating process. However, the required sorting for the shred images is independent of the edge selection or location orders. More specifically, let $w_{ij}$ represents the weight from vertex $i$ to vertex $j$ where $i \neq j$. Note that $w_{ij}$ is not equal to $w_{ji}$ in general. Then the first edge is given by connecting vertices $p_1$ and $q_1$, where

$$(p_1, q_1) = \arg \max_{i,j,i \neq j} w_{ij} \tag{7}$$

and the $r$-th edge is given by connecting vertices $p_r$ and $q_r$, where

$$(p_r, q_r) = \arg \max_{i,j,i \neq j} \{w_{ij} | i \neq p_1, \ldots, p_{r-1}, j \neq q_1, \ldots, q_{r-1}\} \tag{8}$$

The set of edges $(p_r, q_r)$ for $r = 1, \ldots, n$, where $n$ is the number of shreds in the same coded group, forms a sub-optimal short path.

In the implementation, an $n \times n$ correlation matrix associated with the bipartite graph is created based on the relationship between any pair of shreds in an $n$-shred group. This matrix is not symmetric in general, because there are two possible permutations and therefore two different correlation scores for each pair of shreds. The proposed method can be implemented efficiently as follows:

i) Find the maximum weight, $w_{ij}$, in the matrix. The corresponding directed edge $(i, j)$ is added to the path.
ii) Cross out all entries belonging to the $i$-th row and $j$-th column in the matrix.
iii) Go to Step i) and repeat until $w_{ij}$ is the last entry in the matrix.

The above algorithm automatically set the starting and ending vertices as those connected by the least weighted edge, i.e. the last entry remaining in the matrix.

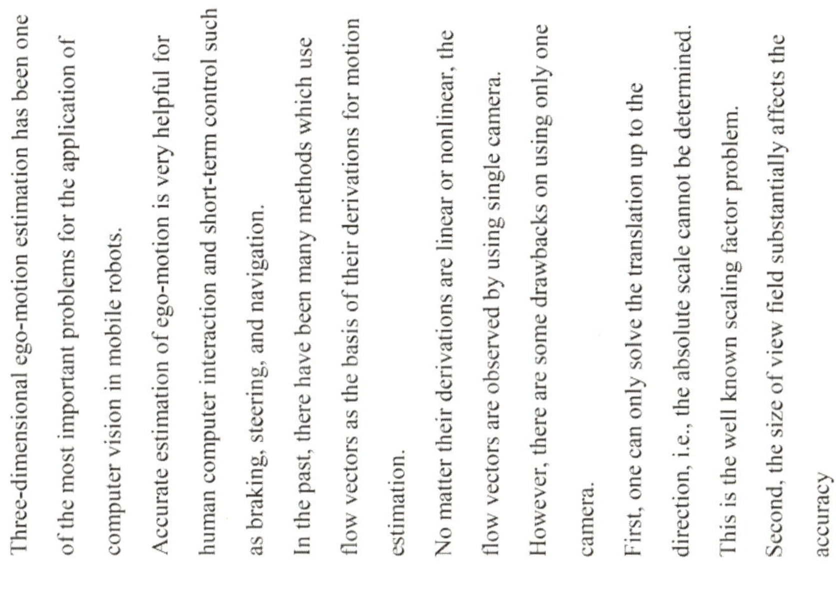

Three-dimensional ego-motion estimation has been one of the most important problems for the application of computer vision in mobile robots. Accurate estimation of ego-motion is very helpful for human computer interaction and short-term control such as braking, steering, and navigation. In the past, there have been many methods which use flow vectors as the basis of their derivations for motion estimation. No matter their derivations are linear or nonlinear, the flow vectors are observed by using single camera. However, there are some drawbacks on using only one camera. First, one can only solve the translation up to the direction, i.e., the absolute scale cannot be determined. This is the well known scaling factor problem. Second, the size of view field substantially affects the accuracy

**Fig. 3.** The document used for reconstruction (Rotated 90° to fit in the page).

## 4   Experiments

A computer generated document image as shown in Fig. 3 is used for the experiments. The unit strip width is set as 1/3 of the average shred width, which is used for the similarity measure based on the average word length. To distinguish two consecutive words by quantized word length as shown in Fig. 2, the word spacing is set as 6 pixels. The average word length is estimated prior to the reconstruction, with 5 and 6 units for the synthetic and real images, respectively.

For the shredded document reconstruction from scanned images, the original document is printed out to an A4 paper and then shredded to 21 pieces (excluding the blank ones) with each 7 mm wide. They are then scanned and normalized

(a)    (b)    (c)    (d)    (e)    (f)    (g)                    (h)

**Fig. 4.** The intermediate image pre-processing results of one scanned shred. The same procedure from (a) to (e) is carried out for all shred images. The histogram of text base-lines (f) from all shreds is then used to create the shred model (g). (h) shows the shredded document reconstruction result using scanned shred images.

to an image with 1000 pixels high. Similar to the synthetic dataset, the shred images are indexed by their original order: $0, 1, 2, \ldots, 20$.

In the image pre-processing stage of the real shreds, the procedure described in Section 2.1 is carried out for feature extraction. Fig. 4 illustrates the intermediate image pre-processing results of one scanned shred. The original shred scan, foreground segmentation, the image after morphological erosion, the histogram of horizontal projections, and the base-line locations of the text lines are shown in Figs. 4(a) – 4(e), respectively.

In the special shred selection, the leftmost border shred is properly identified as shred 0 for this left-aligned document. To generate the shred model for shred coding, the base-line histogram as shown in Fig. 4(f) is obtained by summing the base-line image of each shred. Fig. 4(g) shows the base-lines of the shred model created by taking the local maxima of the base-line projection histogram. Based on the shred coding results, the correct grouping, $\{0, 1, 2\} \rightarrow \{3\} \rightarrow \{4, 5, 6, 7, 8, 9, 10, 11, 12\} \rightarrow \{13\} \rightarrow \{14, 15, 16\} \rightarrow \{17, 18\} \rightarrow \{19\} \rightarrow \{20\}$, is obtained using the first stage sorting.

The similarity measure used for the second stage sorting is calculated with the following settings. Each shred is partitioned to 3 strips, the average word length is set as 6 units in terms of strip width, and the word spacing is set as 6 pixels. The threshold setting for a given number of shreds in a group is based on Table 1. The vertex merging algorithm described in Section 3 is carried out for the second stage sorting, and the final permutation is derived as $0 - 1 - 2 - 3 - 8 - 9 - 12 - 4 - 5 - 6 - 7 - 10 - 11 - 13 - 14 - 16 - 15 - 17 - 18 - 19 - 20$. Fig. 4(h) shows the reconstruction result. The number of discontinuities in this experiment is 8, out of the maximum of 20 possibilities.

## 5   Conclusion

In this work, we have presented an image-based technique for shredded document reconstruction. Several features of shred images are extracted for reconstruction with two similarity measures. The proposed algorithm using the shred coding scheme and average word length is insensitive to the shredding noise on image boundaries. A weighted digraph is then carried out to derive the optimal shred sorting result for document reconstruction in terms of the shortest path. Experiments are presented for both the synthetic and real data sets. The results show that the proposed method have correctly merged the majority of the shredded document.

## Acknowledgment

The support of this work in part by the National Science Council of Taiwan, R.O.C, under Grant NSC-96-2221-E-194-016-MY2 is gratefully acknowledged.

# References


1. Banham, M., Katsaggelos, A.: Digital image restoration. IEEE Signal Processing Magazine 14(2), 24–41 (1997)
2. Loce, R., Dougherty, E.: Enhancement and Restoration of Digital Documents: Statistical Design of Nonlinear Algorithms. In: Society of Photo-Optical Instrumentation Engineers (SPIE), Bellingham, WA, USA (1997)
3. Gonzalez, R., Woods, R.: Digital Image Processing, 2nd edn. Prentice-Hall, Englewood Cliffs (2001)
4. da Gama Leitao, H., Stolfi, J.: A multiscale method for the reassembly of two-dimensional fragmented objects. IEEE Trans. Pattern Analysis and Machine Intelligence 24(9), 1239–1251 (2002)
5. Goldberg, D., Malon, C., Bern, M.: A global approach to automatic solution of jigsaw puzzles. Comput. Geom. 28(2-3), 165–174 (2004)
6. Justino, E., Oliveira, L.S., Freitas, C.: Reconstructing shredded documents through feature matching. Forensic Science International 160(2-3), 140–147 (2006)
7. Zhu, L., Zhou, Z., Hu, D.: Globally consistent reconstruction of ripped-up documents. IEEE Transactions on Pattern Analysis and Machine Intelligence 30(1), 1–13 (2008)
8. Brassil, J.: Tracing the source of a shredded document. In: Petitcolas, F.A.P. (ed.) IH 2002. LNCS, vol. 2578, pp. 387–399. Springer, Heidelberg (2003)
9. Smet, P.D., Bock, J.D., Philips, W.: Semiautomatic reconstruction of strip-shredded documents. In: Said, A., Apostolopoulos, J.G. (eds.) Image and Video Communications and Processing 2005, vol. 5685, pp. 239–248. SPIE (2005)
10. Ukovich, A., Ramponi, G.: Features for the reconstruction of shredded notebook paper. In: International Conference on Image Processing, pp. III: 93–III: 96 (2005)
11. Biswas, A., Bhowmick, P., Bhattacharya, B.: Reconstruction of torn documents using contour maps. In: International Conference on Image Processing, III: 517–III: 520 (2005)
12. Lu, S., Chen, B., Ko, C.: Perspective rectification of document images using fuzzy set and morphological operations. Image and Vision Computing 23(5), 541–553 (2005)
13. Kuhn, H.: The Hungarian method for the assignment problem. Naval Research Logistics 52(1), 7–21 (2005)

# Contour Grouping with Partial Shape Similarity

Chengqian Wu[1], Xiang Bai[1], Quannan Li[1], Xingwei Yang[2], and Wenyu Liu[1]

[1] Dept. of Electronics and Information Engineering,
Huazhong University of Science and Technology, Wuhan, 430074, P.R. China
{angelwuwan,xiang.bai,truthseeker1985}@gmail.com,
liuwy@mail.hust.edu.cn
[2] Dept. of Computer and Information Sciences, Temple University, Philadelphia
xingwei.yang@temple.edu

**Abstract.** In this paper, a novel algorithm is introduced to group contours from clutter images by integrating high-level information (prior of part segments) and low-level information (paths of segmentations of clutter images). The partial shape similarity between these two levels of information is embedded into the particle filter framework, an effective recursively estimating model. The particles in the framework are modeled as the paths on the edges of segmentation results (Normalized Cuts in this paper). At prediction step, the paths extend along the edges of Normalized Cuts; while, at the update step, the weights of particles update according to their partial shape similarity with priors of the trained contour segments. Successful results are achieved against the noise of the testing image, the inaccuracy of the segmentation result as well as the inexactness of the similarity between the contour segment and edges segmentation. The experimental results also demonstrate robust contour grouping performance in the presence of occlusion and large texture variation within the segmented objects.

**Keywords:** Contour grouping, partial shape similarity, particle filter, Normalized Cuts.

## 1 Introduction

Object detection and recognition is a very important issue in computer vision. But due to the high variability of objects and backgrounds in images, it is still an extremely challenging problem. With the progress in shape representation and recognition [1,2,3], researchers start to use shape information to help detecting and recognizing objects in cluttered images [5,6,19]. Different from the methods based on the shape patches [5,6], we detect and group the contour of the object by using shape similarity between edge segments extracted from the image and the learned contour parts.

Although partial shape similarity is not a new topic, only a relatively small number of approaches deal with it. From the viewpoint of human perception, it is enough to use part of an object in order to recognize the whole object. For example, although Fig. 1 only shows several part segments, it is easy for us to

T. Wada, F. Huang, and S. Lin (Eds.): PSIVT 2009, LNCS 5414, pp. 167–178, 2009.

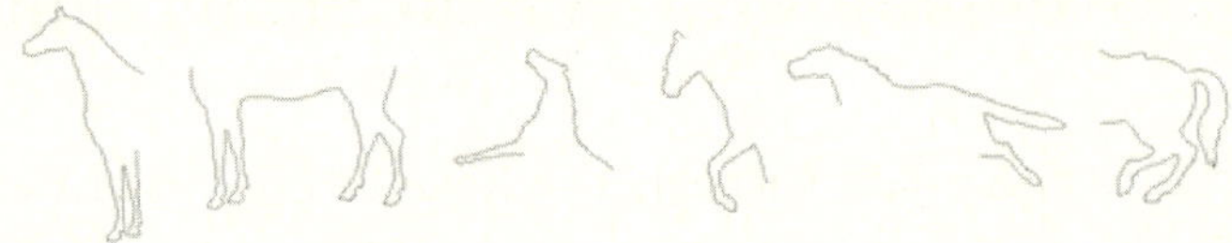

**Fig. 1.** Parts of the horses

recognize that they represent the contour parts of horses. This example motivates our main hypothesis that contour parts of shapes play an essential role in contour grouping. Based on this hypothesis, our approach is able to group contours of the objects with occlusion or missing parts.

Numerous methods have addressed the detection and contour grouping problems by combining information from different visual levels. Borenstein et al. [13] described a frame that integrates top-down with bottom-up segmentation, in which the fragments are detected in image. Borenstein and Malik [5] introduced a Bayesian model to use shape templates to guide the grouping of the homogenous regions. Recently, Srinivasan and Shi [6] used a fixed parse tree to direct the combination. At each level of the parsing process, the combined mask was measured via shape matching with exemplars. Random field (RF) is used in some method. Tu et al. [17] used data-driven Monte-Carlo sampling to guide generative inference. Levin and Weiss [16] have proposed a CRF based segmentation, emphasizing on combining both top-down and bottom-up learning in loop. Ren et al. [7] gave detailed evaluation performance evaluations for integrating low-level, middle-level, high-level cues and a conditional random field formalism is used to combine information. Zheng et al. [8] also combined three levels cues in their method, where classifiers are trained in differently.

Different from the above methods, we learned contour parts instead of shape patches.The partial shape is used as the key information even in the high-level, which is unusual in related works. Besides, we employ particle filtering to integrate the information. As far as we known, it is the very first time that the particle filters is used in such topic.

The first application of particle filter in computer vision is to track the motion boundaries [10]. Particle filters have also been used for contour extraction. Piërez et al. [11] applied a sophisticated version of a particle filters model to accomplish the task of contour detection. The approach in [12] uses local symmetry and continuity to group edges to contour parts. The particle filter is extended so that statistical inference based on a reference shape model is possible.

Now we outline the proposed approach. Firstly, for a testing image, we compute its initial segmentation using Normalized Cuts [4]. Secondly, we learned the training image to build the database. The database consists of part segments which are classified base on their length percentage. Then, the low-level information from the segmentation of testing image and the high-level information from the database are combined by the framework of particle filter.

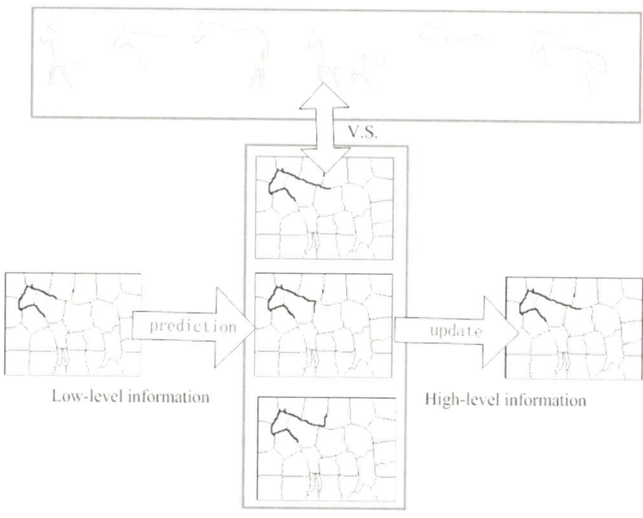


**Fig. 2.** Outline of particle filter

As the essential step of our method, particle filtering is used to group the object's contour, of which the key idea is to recursively estimate the posterior probability density over the state space conditioned on the data collected so far. Fig. 2 gives the illustration of the process of prediction and updating in particle filters. The blue lines in the Normalized Cuts segmentation images are the paths, which are the particles in our method. At the prediction steps, the paths grow along the edges and generate a group of new paths. At the updating steps, the weights of the newly generated paths updates. As the goal is to find the path that follows the true contour of an object, we define the possibilities (weights) of paths as the partial shape similarity between the paths and the known part segments. Therefore, at the updating steps, the newly generated paths are compared to the part segments in the database, and the new paths' weights are updated based on the partial similarity. Accordingly, the path along the object's contour will be assigned with a higher weight and will be more likely to remain after resampling.

The rest of this paper is organized as follows. Section 2 illustrates the extraction of low-level and high-level information. Section 3 gives the main content of the proposed method, how the particle filters model is used to group contours based on partial shape similarity. Section 4 gives the implementation details and the evaluation of our system followed by Section 5 with conclusion.

## 2   Shape Representation

In this section, we discuss the processes of extracting the low-level information and high-level information. The paths and the part segments are the representations of the two levels information respectively. Both of them capture the partial shape of the object, thus the particle filter can combine the two level representations based on the partial similarity.

## 2.1   Extraction of the Paths

The low-level information is obtained from segmentations of the testing image. Normalized Cuts, one of the most popular image segmentation algorithms, is chosen in our method. Fig. 3(b) gives the Normalized Cuts segmentation result of Fig. 3(a).

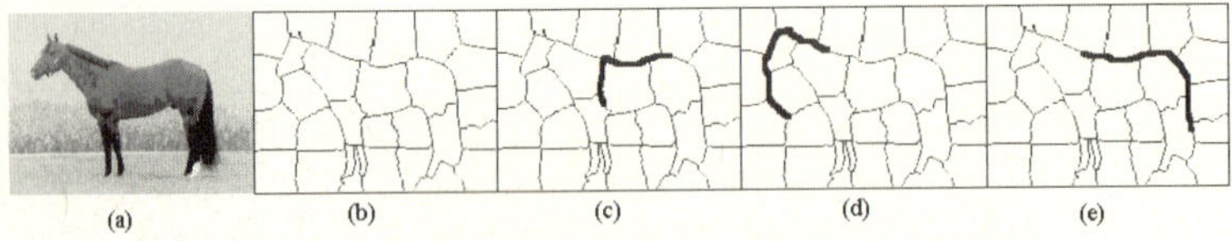



**Fig. 3.** (a) Testing image, (b) Normalized Cuts result, (c)-(e) paths (in blue)

Path, the representation of low-level information, is defined as a piece of connected edges from the Normalized Cuts result. Fig. 3(c)-(e) are examples of paths of the testing image. We can observe that some paths (Fig. 3(e)) are along the object's contour; while some are not (Fig. 3(c),(d)). Therefore, the contour grouping method attempts to assign a higher weight to the "correct" path by the particle filter model, so that the algorithm will converge to the object's contour.

Normalization will be applied to the extracted paths, so the comparison between the paths and the part segments is invariant to the planar transformations. This normalized process is the same to the one applied the part segments, of which will be introduced in section 2.2.

## 2.2   Extraction of the Part Segments

The processes of extraction and description of the high-level information from the training image is illustrated in Fig. 4. Given the contour of the image, firstly, the contour decomposes into a group of part segments, and then a normalization process is applied to the part segments in order to maintain the invariance.

**Extraction:** Assume that there are $M$ training images, $C = (c_1, c_2, ..., c_M)$ denotes the set of contours of the training images. For each contour $c_i (1 \leq i \leq M)$, we sample it into $N$ equidistant points ($N = 100$). The sequence of the sample points of $c_i$ is denoted as $S(c_i) = (s_i^1, s_i^2, ..., s_i^N), (1 \leq i \leq M)$, in which $s_i^j$ means $j^{th}$ sample points on contour $c_i$.

For any pair of sample points $(s_i^k, s_i^l)(1 \leq k, l \leq N; k \neq l)$ on $c_i$, a part segment is obtained by choosing $s_i^k$ as the start point and $s_i^l$ as the end point and traversing from the point $s_i^k$ to the point $s_i^l$ in clockwise along $c_i$. $sp(s_i^k, s_i^l)$

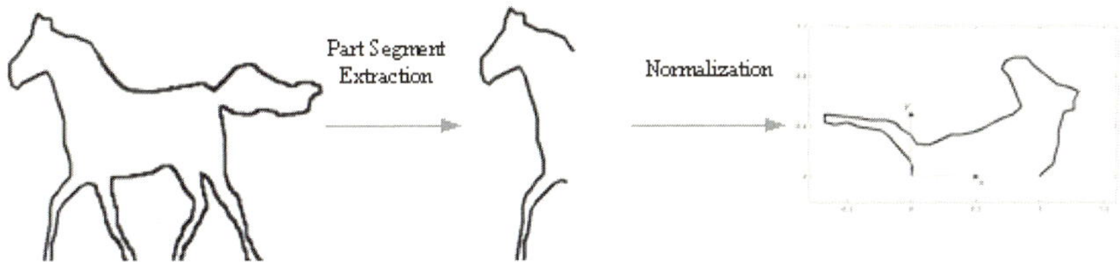


**Fig. 4.** Extraction processes of the part segments

denotes the part segment. In Fig. 4, a piece of part segment is gotten from contour. By selecting different pair of sample points $(s_i^k, s_i^l)(1 \leq k, l \leq N; k \neq l)$, a complete set of part segments of contour $c_i$ is attained. We use $SP_i$ to denote this set of part segments. The part segments set of all the training images is $SP = \{SP_1 \cup SP_2 ... \cup SP_M\}$.

For each part segment, we compute its length percentage $per(sp(s_i^k, s_i^l))$. Let $L(\cdot)$ be the length function for part segment or a closed contour. The length percentage is computed as $per(sp(s_i^k, s_i^l)) = L(sp(s_i^k, s_i^l))/L(c_i) \times 100\%$. The usage of the length percentage will be explained in Section 3.

**Normalization:** To achieve the invariance to planar transformations (2D translations, rotation, and uniform scaling), we use a similar method in [2] to normalize the part segments.

Firstly, each part segment is resampled with n equidistant points ($n = 50$). The resampled part segment is denoted as $sp' = \{x_1, x_2, ..., x_n\}$, in which $x_i$ is a resampled point, $x_i = (x_i, y_i)(1 \leq i \leq n)$. Then, the resample part segment $sp'$ is transformed to the normalized part segment $tp = \{x'_1, x'_2, ..., x'_n\}$. The normalization is realized by mapping $x_1$ to $x'_1 = (0, 0)$, $x_n$ to $x'_n = (1, 0)$ and mapping the remaining points in $sp'$ to $x'_2, ..., x'_{n-1}$ according to the transformation. The normalized part segment $tp$ is invariant to the 2D translation, rotation and uniform scaling in the new reference frame. In Fig. 4, the extracted path transforms into the normalized part segment. The normalized (transformed) part segment set for all the training image is denoted as $TP = \{TP_1 \cup TP_2 ... \cup TP_M\}$. This normalization process is exactly the same to the normalization of paths (Section 2.1).

**Building the database:** Not all the extracted part segments are used to build the database. Firstly, too short and too long part segments are discarded since they carry little valuable information. In our algorithm, only the part segments with a length percentage that is larger than 20% and smaller then 80% are used to build the database. Meanwhile, the part segments that are similar to the linear segment are also abandoned

The part segments in the database are from the same object, horse. We define the classes of the part segments according to the length percentage. $CL_i$ denotes the class of part segments which have the length percentage $pcr$ equals to $i\%$. Therefore, the database updates as $TP = \{CL_{20}, CL_{21}, ..., CL_{80}\}$. The advantage of this classification will be shown in Section 3.

## 3    Particle Filters Based on Partial Shape Similarity

The main idea of our method is to combine different levels information using particle filters and update the weights of particles based on the partial shape similarity.

Particle filters (also known as sequential Monte Carlo method) are sophisticated model estimation techniques based on simulation, which aim to estimate the sequence of hidden states $x_{1:k}$ based on the observed data $z_{1:k}$. The commonly used particle filtering algorithm, *Sampling Important Resampling* (SIR), is chosen in our algorithm, which approximates the filtering distribution $p(x_k|z_{1:k})$ by a weighted set of $N$ particles $\{(x_k^i, w_k^i) : i = 1, 2, ..., N\}$. The main steps for SIR are:

1) **Samples** from the proposal distribution. The current generation of $\{x_k^i\}$ is obtained from the last generation $\{x_{k-1}^i\}$ by sampling from a proposal distribution $\pi(x_k|x_{0:k-1}^i, z_{1:k})$.

$$x_k^i \sim \pi(x_k|x_{0:k-1}^i, z_{1:k}) \tag{1}$$

2) **Importance weights:** An individual importance weight $\widehat{w}_k^i$ is assigned to each newly generated particle with the update of the importance weight.

$$\widehat{w}_k^i \sim w_{k-1}^i \frac{p(z_k^i|x_k^i)p(x_k^i|x_{k-1}^i)}{\pi(x_k^i|x_{0:k-1}^i, z_{1:k})} \tag{2}$$

The weight $\widehat{w}_k^i$ is account for the fact that, generally, the proposal distribution $\pi$ is not equal to the true distribution of successor states.

3) **Resampling:** Particles with a lower importance weight $\widehat{w}_k^i$ are typically replaced by the samples with a higher weight. This step is necessary since only a finite number of particles are used to approximate a continuous distribution. Furthermore, resampling allows application of particle filter in situations in which the true distribution differs from the proposal.

In our application, the state $x_k^i$ is a particle represents a piece of path in the testing image. The observation $z_k^i$ is the likelihood of $x_k^i$ belonging to the "correct" object's contour. The weights of the particles update according to similarity between the newly generated paths and trained part segments. The paths and the part segments are both partial shape information of the object, and they are embedded with low-level and high-level information respectively. The particle filters algorithm combines different levels of information using the partial shape similarity.

In this section, firstly, we give discussion of our application of particle filters, then we introduce the computation of the partial shape similarity in details.

### 3.1    Contour Grouping with Particle Filters

In this section we firstly introduce the model of the particles and then introduce our application of Sampling Important Resampling (SIR) algorithm.

The state $x_k^i = \{xp_k^i, per'(xp_k^i)\}$ is the $i^{th}$ particle at the time step $k$, where $xp_k^i$ denotes the path in the testing image and $per'(xp_k^i)$ denotes the length percentage of path $xp_k^i$. Using $cxp$ denote the object's contour in testing image, the length percentage of path $xp_k^i$ defined as $per'(xp_k^i) = L(xp_k^i)/L(cxp) \times 100\%$, where $L(\cdot)$ is the length function. Length percentage of path $per'(xp_k^i)$ is similar to the length percentage of part segments $per(sp(s_i^k, s_i^l))$. It helps to reduce the computation and control the paths' growth at sampling step. Since $cxp$ is unknown, the above formula is only theoretical one to help understanding. The technical computation of $per'\cdot$ will be discussed later.

***Sampling*** process is to obtain the current generation particles $\{x_k^i\}$ by sampling from the proposal distribution $\pi(x_k|x_{0:k-1}^i, z_{1:k})$. Since the transition prior is easy to draw particles (or samples) and perform subsequent importance weight calculations, it is often used as importance function: $\pi(x_k|x_{0:k}, z_{0:k}) = p(x_k|x_{k-1})$. Technically, the sampling process is modeled as the paths grow along the edges of Normalized Cuts result and the growth is controlled in the same speed for each path at every iterative. The definition of the transition prior is

$$p(x_k^i|x_{k-1}^i) = \begin{cases} \epsilon, & if\ xp_k^i\ forms\ a\ cycle \\ 1 - \epsilon, & L(xp_k^i) = L(xp_{k-1}^i)\frac{per'(xp_{k-1}^i)+\triangle per}{per'(xp_{k-1}^i)} \end{cases} \quad (3)$$

where $\triangle per$ is the parameter controlling the growing speed and $\epsilon$ is a very small positive number. The current particles generate as the last generation path grows by a certain length percentage $\triangle per$. Besides, the estimated length percentage of $xp_k^i$ is $\widehat{per'}(xp_k^i) = per'(xp_{k-1}^i) + \triangle per$. If the path grows through a junction point (see Fig. 5(a), point A) , more than one new paths will generate. In Fig. 5, the path in (a) generates three paths in (b)-(d).

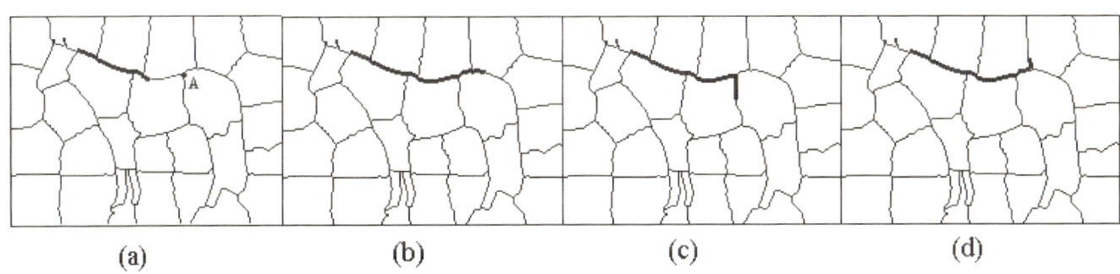

(a)     (b)     (c)     (d)

**Fig. 5.** (a) A path, (b)-(d) are three possible extensions of the path in (a)

At the ***importance weighting*** step, since the transition prior is used as importance function, formula (2) is rewritten as:

$$\widehat{w}_k^i \sim w_{k-1}^i \frac{p(z_k^i|x_k^i)p(x_k^i|x_{k-1}^i)}{\pi(x_k^i|x_{0:k-1}^i, z_{0:k})} = w_{k-1}^i \frac{p(z_k^i|x_k^i)p(x_k^i|x_{k-1}^i)}{p(x_k^i|x_{k-1}^i)} = w_{k-1}^i p(z_k^i|x_k^i)$$

$$(4)$$

We defined the likelihood $p(z_k^i|x_k^i)$ as the similarity between the path $xp_k^i$ and the part segments in training database. It is unnecessary to compare the path with the entire database. So, we only compare with those part segments whose length percentage is close to the path's estimated length percentage $\widehat{per'}(xp_k^i)$. Therefore, the likelihood $p(z_k^i|x_k^i)$ is:

$$p(z_k^i|x_k^i) = p(\cup_{j=\widehat{per'}(xp_k^i)-\omega}^{\widehat{per'}(xp_k^i)+\omega} CL_j|xp_k^i) = \sum_{j=\widehat{per'}(xp_k^i)-\omega}^{\widehat{per'}(xp_k^i)+\omega} p(CL_j|xp_k^i) \qquad (5)$$

where $\omega$ is an integer parameter controlling the length estimation tolerance. $CL_j$ denotes the class of part segments with the length percentage as $j\%$ (Section 2.2). $p(CL_j|xp_k^i)$ is regarded as the similarity between the path and the part segments in $CL_j$.

With the likelihood, the particles' weights update. Besides, the length percentages of the paths update as well. The updated length percentage of the path $xp_k^i$ is computed as:

$$per'(xp_k^i) = argmax_{j=\widehat{per'}(xp_k^i)-\omega,...,\widehat{per'}(xp_k^i)+\omega} p(CL_j|xp_k^i) \qquad (6)$$

At the **resampling** step, particles with a lower importance weight are typically replaced by the samples with a higher weight. In our algorithm, we keep the $N_0$ particles with highest importance weight. The weights are normalized so that the sum of all the particles is 1.

## 3.2   Computation of Partial Shape Similarity

We introduce the computation of partial shape similarity in this section. The posterior probability $p(CL_j|xp_k^i)$, the key item in particle filers, interprets as the similarity between the path $xp_k^i$ and the part segments in $CL_j$.

According to the Bayesian rule, the posterior probability of $p(CL_j|xp_k^i)$ is:

$$p(CL_j|xp_k^i) = \frac{p(xp_k^i|CL_j)p(CL_j)}{p(xp_k^i)} \qquad (7)$$

The probability of path $xp_k^i$ is computed as:

$$p(xp_k^i) = \sum_{j=\widehat{per'}(xp_k^i)-\omega}^{\widehat{per'}(xp_k^i)+\omega} p(xp_k^i|CL_j)p(CL_j) \qquad (8)$$

The class-conditional probability for the path $xp_k^i$ given part segment $tp$ belongs to the class $CL_j$ is

$$p(xp_k^i|CL_j) = \sum_{tp\in CL_j} p(xp_k^i|tp)p(tp|CL_j) \qquad (9)$$

$p(xp_k^i|tp)$ denotes the similarity between the path $xp_k^i$ and the part segment $tp$. We use the function of Gaussian to measure the similarity

$$p(xp_k^i|tp) = \frac{\exp(-\frac{D(xp_k^i,tp)^2}{2\delta^2})}{\sqrt{2\pi\delta}} \qquad (10)$$

where the $D(xp_k^i, tp)$ is the distance between $xp_k^i$ and $tp$, and $\delta$ is experimentally decided. The distance between $xp_k^i$ and $tp$ is

$$D(xp_k^i, tp) = \sum_{j=1}^{n} d(xp_k^i(j), tp(j)) \tag{11}$$

where $n$ is the number of resampled the points after normalization (Section 2.2).

In above formulas, we assume that all classes are equiprobable, i.e. $p(CL_j) = \frac{1}{2\omega}$, since, at each iterative, $2\omega$ classes in the database are used in computation. Also, part segments within a class are equiprobable, i.e. $p(tp|CL_j) = \frac{1}{|CL_j|}$.

## 4 Implementation and Experiments

Now we describe our algorithm with details and then give the experimental results.

### 4.1 Implementation Details

The particle filter is initialized by selecting the paths form Normalized Cuts segmentation results of the testing image. Since object's contour segments are more likely to have a higher magnitude of gradient, the paths with higher mean gradient magnitude value are chosen. Meanwhile, the length percentage of the part segments starts at 20%, therefore we extend the selected paths to a certain length so that they are long enough.

We stop the particle filters when the estimated length percentage of the particle $per'(xp_k^i)$ grows to the threshold $T_P$. Generally, the particle with the highest weight represents a true contour part, but, in experiments, we select the top 10 particles in case of noise.

After we get candidate paths from stop step of particle filters, we apply greedy-search for each path and extend it to form closed contour. All the closed contour are considered as candidate contours. The dissimilarity distances between the candidate contours and the training images are calculated using inner-distance shape context method [3]. The candidate contour with the smallest mean distance is the final result.

In experiments, most results are obtained from Normalized Cuts results with 30 blocks. For images with high texture variation, we use 40 blocks. At every iteration, we resample $n = 50$ particles. When particles reach the length percentage of 70%, we stop the algorithm.

### 4.2 Experiment Results

We use the horse dataset provided by Borenstein et al. [13] with 50 images selected to build the part database TP . The average time for one image (30 blocks) is 3 minutes on a computer with 1.8 GHz CPU and 1.0 GB memory. We can obtain more accurate results on edge images with a large number of regions; however, the processing time will increase significantly.

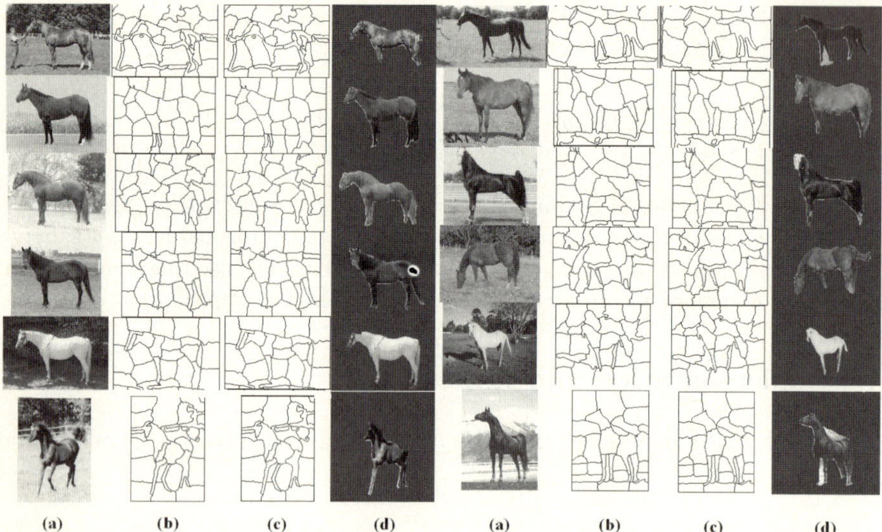

**Fig. 6.** Sample results by our algorithm. (a) are the original input color images, (b) are edge images obtained by Normalized cuts, (c) are the contour grouped (in red) on the edge images(b), and (d) are the detected objects cut from original images.

**Fig. 7.** Sample results on the images with occlusion and large text variation. (a) are the original input images, (b) are edge images obtained by Normalized Cuts, (c) are the contour grouped (in red) on the edge images (b), and (d) are the detected objects.

**Performance:** Fig. 6 shows some results of our method. We can observe that the detections of the horse are generally successful, although the tail or the legs are missing in some images. We provide a failed result last example in Fig.6.

**Experiments on the images with large texture variation or occlusion:** Since our method is based on the shape similarity, it performs very well with the presence of occlusion or large texture variations. The results in Fig. 7 prove that our method can obtain very good performance even in the cases of large texture variation or occlusion. (Some of the test images are obtained from Google.)

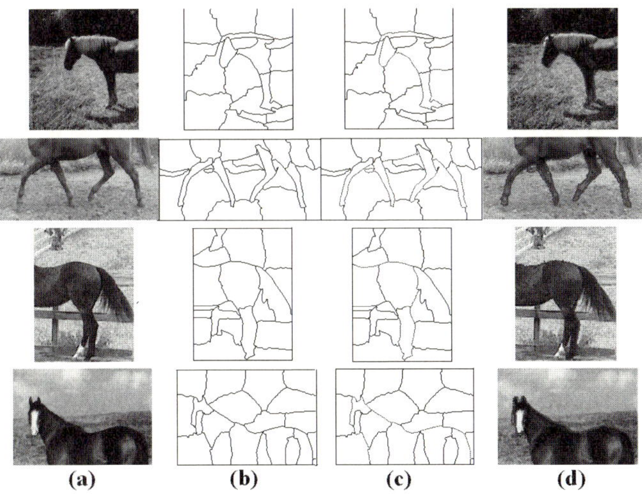

(a)      (b)      (c)      (d)

**Fig. 8.** (a) are the input images, (b) are Normalized Cuts edge images, (c) are the grouped part segments (in red) on (b), and (d) are detected parts on input images

Fig. 8 gives another group of results demonstrate excellent performance of the proposed method against substantial occlusion by cutting the testing images. Although the global shape of the horse is lost, our algorithm still finds the part segment robustly. The methods based the global shape [9,14,15,18] are likely to fail on these images, since global information is no longer preserved here.

## 5   Conclusion and Future Work

We proposed a novel contour grouping method based on partial shape similarity. The partial shape representations, paths and part segments, successfully describe the low-level and high-level information, respectively. With the similarity between the paths and part segments, the particle filters combine the different levels of information and group the contour of object in cluttered images. Our method proves that partial shape can be used as the key element for related research fields. The experimental results demonstrate the impressive performance of the method, especially in the cases of large texture variations or occlusions. In the future, we plan to work on: 1) contour grouping using gradient based edges and 2) contour grouping and detection in the case of multiple classes of known shapes.

## References


1. Belongie, S., Malik, J., Puzicha, J.: Shape Matching and Object Recognition Using Shape Contexts. PAMI (2002)
2. Sun, K., Super, B.J.: Classification of Contour Shapes Using Class Segment Sets. In: CVPR (2005)

3. Ling, H., Jacobs, D.W.: Shape Classification Using the Inner-Distance. PAMI 29(2), 286–299 (2007)
4. Shi, J., Malik, J.: Normalized Cuts and Image Segmentation. In: CVPR (1997)
5. Borenstein, E., Malik, J.: Shape Guided Object Segmentation. In: CVPR (2006)
6. Srinivasan, P., Shi, J.: Bottom-up Recognition and Parsing of the Human Body. In: CVPR (2007)
7. Ren, X., Fowlkes, C., Malik, J.: Cue Integration in Figure/ground Labeling. In: NIPS (2005)
8. Zheng, S., Tu, Z., Yuille, A.: Detecting Object Boundaries Using Low-, Mid-, and High-Level Information. In: CVPR (2007)
9. Kumar, M.P., Torr, P.H.S., Zisserman, A.: OBJ CUT. In: CVPR (2005)
10. Black, M.J., Fleet, D.J.: Probabilistic detection and tracking of motion boundaries. IJCV 38(3), 231–245 (2000)
11. Pérez, P., Blake, A., Gangnet, M.: Jetstream: Probabilistic contour extraction with particles. In: ICCV, pp. 524–531 (2001)
12. Adluru, N., Latecki, L.J., Lakaemper, R., Young, T., Bai, X., Gross, A.: Contour Grouping Based on Local Symmetry. In: ICCV (2007)
13. Borenstein, E., Sharon, E., Ullman, S.: Combining top-down and bottom-up segmentation. In: Proc. IEEE workshop on Perc. Org. in Com. Vis. (2004)
14. McNeill, G., Vijayakumar, S.: Part-based Probabilistic Point Matching Using Equivalence Constraints. In: NIPS (2006)
15. Zöllor, T., Buhumann, J.M.: Robust Image Segmentation Using Resampling and Shape Constraints. PAMI 29(7), 1147–1164 (2007)
16. Levin, A., Weiss, Y.: Learning to combine bottom-up and top-down segmentation. In: Leonardis, A., Bischof, H., Pinz, A. (eds.) ECCV 2006. LNCS, vol. 3954, pp. 581–594. Springer, Heidelberg (2006)
17. Tu, Z., Chen, X., Yuille, A., Zhu, S.C.: Image parsing: unifying segmentation, detection, and object recognition. IJCV (2005)
18. Shotton, J., Blake, A., Cipolla, R.: Contour-Based Learning for Object Detection. In: ICCV (2005)
19. Cremers, D., Kohlberger, T., Schnörr, C.: Shape Statistics in Kernel Space for Variational Image Segmentation. Pattern Recognition 36, 1929–1943 (2003)
20. Tu, Z., Yuille, A.: Shape Matching and Recognition: Using Generative Models and Informative Features. In: Pajdla, T., Matas, J(G.) (eds.) ECCV 2004. LNCS, vol. 3023, pp. 195–209. Springer, Heidelberg (2004)

# Compact Fundamental Matrix Computation

Kenichi Kanatani[1] and Yasuyuki Sugaya[2]

[1] Department of Computer Science, Okayama University, Okayama 700-8530 Japan
[2] Department of Information and Computer Sciences,
Toyohashi University of Technology, Toyohashi, Aichi 441-8580 Japan
`kanatani@suri.cs.okayama-u.ac.jp`, `sugaya@iim.ics.tut.ac.jp`

**Abstract.** A very compact algorithm is presented for fundamental matrix computation from point correspondences over two images. The computation is based on the strict maximum likelihood (ML) principle, minimizing the reprojection error. The rank constraint is incorporated by the EFNS procedure. Although our algorithm produces the same solution as all existing ML-based methods, it is probably the most practical of all, being small and simple. By numerical experiments, we confirm that our algorithm behaves as expected.

## 1  Introduction

Computing the fundamental matrix from point correspondences is the first step of many vision applications including camera calibration, image rectification, structure from motion, and new view generation [6,21]. Although its robustness is critical in practice, procedures for removing outlying matches heavily depend on computation for assumed inliers, e.g., RANSAC-type hypothesis-based computation followed by choosing the solution that has maximum support [6,21]. In this paper, we focus on computation assuming inliers.

Since extracted feature points have uncertainty to some degree, we need statistical optimization, modeling the uncertainty as "noise" obeying a certain probability distribution. The standard model is independent Gaussian noise coupled with maximum likelihood (ML) estimation. This results in the minimization of the "reprojection error", also known as the "Gold Standard" [6].

Although all existing ML-based methods minimizes the same function, vast differences exist in their computational processes. This is mainly due to the fact that the fundamental matrix is constrained to have rank 2. The strategies for incorporating this constraint are roughly classified into three categories:

**A posteriori correction.** The fundamental matrix is first computed without considering the rank constraint and is modified a posteriori so as to satisfy it (Fig. 1(a)). If the rank constraint is not considered, the computation is vastly simplified [6,21]. The crudest method, yet widely used, is to minimize the square sum of the epipolar equation, called *least squares*, *algebraic distance minimization*, or *8-point algorithm* [5]. The *Taubin method* [20] incorporates the data covariance matrices in the simplest way. These two yield

T. Wada, F. Huang, and S. Lin (Eds.): PSIVT 2009, LNCS 5414, pp. 179–190, 2009.

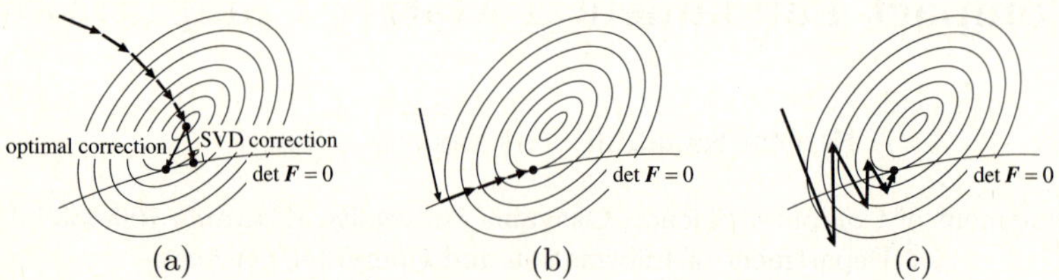


**Fig. 1.** (a) A posteriori correction. (b) Internal access. (c) External access.

the solution with simple algebraic manipulations [12,9]. For incorporating the ML viewpoint, one needs iterations, for which many schemes exist including *FNS* [3], *HEIV* [15,16], and the *projective Gauss-Newton iterations* [10]. For imposing the rank constraint, the most naive method, yet widely used, is to compute the SVD of the computed fundamental matrix and replace the smallest singular value by 0 [5]. A more sophisticated method is the *optimal correction* [8,16]: the computed fundamental matrix is moved in the statistically mostly likely direction until it satisfies the rank constraint (Fig. 1(a)).

**Internal access.** The fundamental matrix is parameterized so that the rank constraint is identically satisfied and is optimized in the ("internal") parameter space (Fig. 1(b)). Many types of such parameterization have been proposed including algebraic elimination of the rank constraint and the expression in terms of epipoles [21,17,22]. Bartoli and Sturm [1] regarded the SVD of the fundamental matrix as its parameterization and do search in an augmented space. Sugaya and Kanatani [18] directly searched a 7-D space by the Levenberg-Marquardt (LM) method.

**External access.** We do iterations in the ("external") 9-D space of the fundamental matrix in such a way that an optimal solution that satisfies the rank constraint automatically results (Fig. 1(c)). This concept was first introduced by Chojnacki et al. [4], who presented a scheme called *CFNS*.

In this paper, we present a new method based on the external access principle. Its description is far more compact than any of existing ML-based methods. Although there is no accuracy gain, since all ML-based methods minimize the same function, the compactness of the algorithm is of great advantage. In fact, the reason why the non-optimal 8-point algorithm [5] is still in wide use is probably for fear of coding a complicated program and uneasiness at relying on "download". One algorithm is simple enough to code oneself[1], consisting only of vector and matrix operations in no higher than 9-D, just like the popular 8-point algorithm, yet producing an optimal solution.

We describe our algorithm in Sec. 2 and give a derivation in Sec. 3. In Sec. 4, we confirm its performance by numerical experiments. We conclude in Sec. 5 that our algorithm best suits practical use because of its compactness and good performance.

---

[1] But one can try ours if one wishes: `http://www.iim.ics.tut.ac.jp/~sugaya/public-e.html`

## 2   Optimal Fundamental Matrix Computation

Given two images of the same scene, suppose a point $(x, y)$ in the first image corresponds to $(x', y')$ in the second. We represent the corresponding points by 3-D vectors

$$
\boldsymbol{x} = \begin{pmatrix} x/f_0 \\ y/f_0 \\ 1 \end{pmatrix}, \qquad \boldsymbol{x}' = \begin{pmatrix} x'/f_0 \\ y'/f_0 \\ 1 \end{pmatrix}, \tag{1}
$$

where $f_0$ is a scaling constant of the order of the image size[2]. As is well known, $\boldsymbol{x}$ and $\boldsymbol{x}'$ satisfy the *epipolar equation*,

$$
(\boldsymbol{x}, \boldsymbol{F}\boldsymbol{x}') = 0, \tag{2}
$$

where and hereafter we denote the inner product of vectors $\boldsymbol{a}$ and $\boldsymbol{b}$ by $(\boldsymbol{a}, \boldsymbol{b})$. The matrix $\boldsymbol{F}$ is of rank 2 and called the *fundamental matrix*. Since its scale is indeterminate, we normalize it to unit Frobenius norm $\|\boldsymbol{F}\| = 1$.

Suppose $N$ correspondence pairs $\{\boldsymbol{x}_\alpha, \boldsymbol{x}'_\alpha\}_{\alpha=1}^N$ are detected. If the noise in their $x$- and $y$-coordinates is assumed to be independent, identical, and Gaussian, maximum likelihood (ML) is equivalent to minimizing the *reprojection error*

$$
E = \sum_{\alpha=1}^N \left( \|\boldsymbol{x}_\alpha - \bar{\boldsymbol{x}}_\alpha\|^2 + \|\boldsymbol{x}'_\alpha - \bar{\boldsymbol{x}}'_\alpha\|^2 \right), \tag{3}
$$

with respect to $\bar{\boldsymbol{x}}_\alpha$, $\bar{\boldsymbol{x}}'_\alpha$, and $\boldsymbol{F}$ subject to

$$
(\bar{\boldsymbol{x}}_\alpha, \boldsymbol{F}\bar{\boldsymbol{x}}'_\alpha) = 0, \qquad \alpha = 1, ..., N. \tag{4}
$$

No simple procedure exists for minimizing (3) subject to (4) and the rank constraint on $\boldsymbol{F}$. Many researchers minimized the "Sampson error" (to be discussed later) that approximates (3) [6,21]. Alternatively, the minimization is done in an "augmented" parameter space, as done by Bartoli and Sturm [1], computing tentative 3-D reconstruction and adjusting the camera positions and the intrinsic parameters so that the resulting projection images are as close to the input images as possible. Such a strategy is called *bundle adjustment*. Search in a high dimensional space, in particular if one wants a globally optimal solution, requires a large amount of computation [7].

We now present a dramatically compact formulation: *we work in 9-D throughout*. Define 9-D vectors

$$
\boldsymbol{u} = \begin{pmatrix} F_{11} \\ F_{12} \\ F_{13} \\ F_{21} \\ F_{22} \\ F_{23} \\ F_{31} \\ F_{32} \\ F_{33} \end{pmatrix}, \qquad \boldsymbol{u}^\dagger \equiv \mathcal{N}\left[ \begin{pmatrix} u_5 u_9 - u_8 u_6 \\ u_6 u_7 - u_9 u_4 \\ u_4 u_8 - u_7 u_5 \\ u_8 u_3 - u_2 u_9 \\ u_9 u_1 - u_3 u_7 \\ u_7 u_2 - u_1 u_8 \\ u_2 u_6 - u_5 u_3 \\ u_3 u_4 - u_6 u_1 \\ u_1 u_5 - u_4 u_2 \end{pmatrix} \right], \tag{5}
$$

---

[2] This is for stabilizing numerical computation [5]. In our experiments, we set $f_0 = 600$ pixels.

where $\mathcal{N}[\,\cdot\,]$ denotes normalization to unit norm. The vector $\boldsymbol{u}$ encodes the nine elements of the fundamental matrix $\boldsymbol{F}$. The normalization $\|\boldsymbol{F}\| = 1$ is equivalent to $\|\boldsymbol{u}\| = 1$. The vector $\boldsymbol{u}^{\dagger}$ encodes the nine elements of the cofactor $\boldsymbol{F}^{\dagger}$ of $\boldsymbol{F}$, so we call $\boldsymbol{u}^{\dagger}$ the "cofactor vector" of $\boldsymbol{u}$. We denote by "det $\boldsymbol{u}$" the determinant of the matrix $\boldsymbol{F}$ corresponding to $\boldsymbol{u}$.

In order to emphasize the compactness of our algorithm, we state it first and then give its derivation, which is straightforward but rather lengthy. The main routine of our algorithm goes as follows:

*main* ________________________________________________

1. Let $\boldsymbol{u}_0 = \boldsymbol{0}$, and initialize $\boldsymbol{u}$.
2. Let $\hat{x}_\alpha = x_\alpha$, $\hat{y}_\alpha = y_\alpha$, $\hat{x}'_\alpha = x'_\alpha$, $\hat{y}'_\alpha = y'_\alpha$, and $\tilde{x}_\alpha = \tilde{y}_\alpha = \tilde{x}'_\alpha = \tilde{y}'_\alpha = 0$.
3. Compute the following 9-D vectors $\boldsymbol{\xi}_\alpha$ and the $9 \times 9$ matrices $V_0[\boldsymbol{\xi}_\alpha]$:

$$
\boldsymbol{\xi}_\alpha = \begin{pmatrix}
\hat{x}_\alpha \hat{x}'_\alpha + \hat{x}'_\alpha \tilde{x}_\alpha + \hat{x}_\alpha \tilde{x}'_\alpha \\
\hat{x}_\alpha \hat{y}'_\alpha + \hat{y}'_\alpha \tilde{x}_\alpha + \hat{x}_\alpha \tilde{y}'_\alpha \\
f_0 (\hat{x}_\alpha + \tilde{x}_\alpha) \\
\hat{y}_\alpha \hat{x}'_\alpha + \hat{x}'_\alpha \tilde{y}_\alpha + \hat{y}_\alpha \tilde{x}'_\alpha \\
\hat{y}_\alpha \hat{y}'_\alpha + \hat{y}'_\alpha \tilde{y}_\alpha + \hat{y}_\alpha \tilde{y}'_\alpha \\
f_0 (\hat{y}_\alpha + \tilde{y}_\alpha) \\
f_0 (\hat{x}'_\alpha + \tilde{x}'_\alpha) \\
f_0 (\hat{y}'_\alpha + \tilde{y}'_\alpha) \\
f_0^2
\end{pmatrix},
\tag{6}
$$

$$
V_0[\boldsymbol{\xi}_\alpha] = \begin{pmatrix}
\hat{x}_\alpha^2 + \hat{x}'^2_\alpha & \hat{x}'_\alpha \hat{y}'_\alpha & f_0 \hat{x}'_\alpha & \hat{x}_\alpha \hat{y}_\alpha & 0 & 0 & f_0 \hat{x}_\alpha & 0 & 0 \\
\hat{x}'_\alpha \hat{y}'_\alpha & \hat{x}_\alpha^2 + \hat{y}'^2_\alpha & f_0 \hat{y}'_\alpha & 0 & \hat{x}_\alpha \hat{y}_\alpha & 0 & 0 & f_0 \hat{x}_\alpha & 0 \\
f_0 \hat{x}'_\alpha & f_0 \hat{y}'_\alpha & f_0^2 & 0 & 0 & 0 & 0 & 0 & 0 \\
\hat{x}_\alpha \hat{y}_\alpha & 0 & 0 & \hat{y}_\alpha^2 + \hat{x}'^2_\alpha & \hat{x}'_\alpha \hat{y}'_\alpha & f_0 \hat{x}'_\alpha & f_0 \hat{y}_\alpha & 0 & 0 \\
0 & \hat{x}_\alpha \hat{y}_\alpha & 0 & \hat{x}'_\alpha \hat{y}'_\alpha & \hat{y}_\alpha^2 + \hat{y}'^2_\alpha & f_0 \hat{y}'_\alpha & 0 & f_0 \hat{y}_\alpha & 0 \\
0 & 0 & 0 & f_0 \hat{x}'_\alpha & f_0 \hat{y}'_\alpha & f_0^2 & 0 & 0 & 0 \\
f_0 \hat{x}_\alpha & 0 & 0 & f_0 \hat{y}_\alpha & 0 & 0 & f_0^2 & 0 & 0 \\
0 & f_0 \hat{x}_\alpha & 0 & 0 & f_0 \hat{y}_\alpha & 0 & 0 & f_0^2 & 0 \\
0 & 0 & 0 & 0 & 0 & 0 & 0 & 0 & 0
\end{pmatrix}.
\tag{7}
$$

4. Call *EFNS* to update $\boldsymbol{u}$.
5. If $\boldsymbol{u} \approx \boldsymbol{u}_0$ up to sign, return $\boldsymbol{u}$ and stop. Else, update $\tilde{x}_\alpha$, $\tilde{y}_\alpha$, $\tilde{x}'_\alpha$, and $\tilde{y}'_\alpha$ by

$$
\begin{pmatrix} \tilde{x}_\alpha \\ \tilde{y}_\alpha \end{pmatrix} \leftarrow \frac{(\boldsymbol{u}, \boldsymbol{\xi}_\alpha)}{(\boldsymbol{u}, V[\hat{\boldsymbol{\xi}}_\alpha]\boldsymbol{u})} \begin{pmatrix} u_1 & u_2 & u_3 \\ u_4 & u_5 & u_6 \end{pmatrix} \begin{pmatrix} \hat{x}'_\alpha \\ \hat{y}'_\alpha \\ f_0 \end{pmatrix},
$$

$$
\begin{pmatrix} \tilde{x}'_\alpha \\ \tilde{y}'_\alpha \end{pmatrix} \leftarrow \frac{(\boldsymbol{u}, \boldsymbol{\xi}_\alpha)}{(\boldsymbol{u}, V[\hat{\boldsymbol{\xi}}_\alpha]\boldsymbol{u})} \begin{pmatrix} u_1 & u_4 & u_7 \\ u_2 & u_5 & u_8 \end{pmatrix} \begin{pmatrix} \hat{x}_\alpha \\ \hat{y}_\alpha \\ f_0 \end{pmatrix}.
\tag{8}
$$

6. Go back to Step 3 after updating $\boldsymbol{u}_0 \leftarrow \boldsymbol{u}$, $\hat{x}_\alpha \leftarrow x_\alpha - \tilde{x}_\alpha$, $\hat{y}_\alpha \leftarrow y_\alpha - \tilde{y}_\alpha$, $\hat{x}'_\alpha \leftarrow x'_\alpha - \tilde{x}'_\alpha$, and $\hat{y}'_\alpha \leftarrow y'_\alpha - \tilde{y}'_\alpha$.

The initialization in Step 1 can be done by the 8-point algorithm [5] or by the Taubin method [20] (also see [12,9]). The EFNS routine in Step 4 goes as follows:

*EFNS* ______________________________________________________________

1. Compute the following $9 \times 9$ matrices $\boldsymbol{M}$ and $\boldsymbol{L}$:

$$M = \sum_{\alpha=1}^{N} \frac{\boldsymbol{\xi}_\alpha \boldsymbol{\xi}_\alpha^\top}{(\boldsymbol{u}, V_0[\boldsymbol{\xi}_\alpha]\boldsymbol{u})}, \qquad L = \sum_{\alpha=1}^{N} \frac{(\boldsymbol{u}, \boldsymbol{\xi}_\alpha)^2 V_0[\boldsymbol{\xi}_\alpha]}{(\boldsymbol{u}, V_0[\boldsymbol{\xi}_\alpha]\boldsymbol{u})^2}. \tag{9}$$

2. Compute the cofactor vector $\boldsymbol{u}^\dagger$ in (5) and the $9 \times 9$ projection matrix

$$\boldsymbol{P_{u^\dagger}} \equiv \boldsymbol{I} - \boldsymbol{u}^\dagger \boldsymbol{u}^{\dagger\top}. \tag{10}$$

3. Compute the following $9 \times 9$ matrices:

$$\boldsymbol{X} = \boldsymbol{M} - \boldsymbol{L}, \qquad \boldsymbol{Y} = \boldsymbol{P_{u^\dagger}} \boldsymbol{X} \boldsymbol{P_{u^\dagger}}. \tag{11}$$

4. Compute the two unit eigenvectors $\boldsymbol{v}_1$ and $\boldsymbol{v}_2$ of $\boldsymbol{Y}$ for the smallest eigenvalues in absolute values, and compute

$$\hat{\boldsymbol{u}} = (\boldsymbol{u}, \boldsymbol{v}_1)\boldsymbol{v}_1 + (\boldsymbol{u}, \boldsymbol{v}_2)\boldsymbol{v}_2. \tag{12}$$

5. Compute

$$\boldsymbol{u}' = \mathcal{N}[\boldsymbol{P_{u^\dagger}}\hat{\boldsymbol{u}}]. \tag{13}$$

6. If $\boldsymbol{u}' \approx \boldsymbol{u}$ up to sign, return $\boldsymbol{u}'$ and stop. Else, let $\boldsymbol{u} \leftarrow \mathcal{N}[\boldsymbol{u} + \boldsymbol{u}']$ and go back to Step 1.

______________________________________________________________

## 3   Derivation

### 3.1   Derivation of the Main Routine

**First Approximation.** We want to compute $\bar{\boldsymbol{x}}_\alpha$ and $\bar{\boldsymbol{x}}'_\alpha$ that minimize (3) subject to (4), but we may alternatively write

$$\bar{\boldsymbol{x}}_\alpha = \boldsymbol{x}_\alpha - \Delta\boldsymbol{x}_\alpha, \qquad \bar{\boldsymbol{x}}'_\alpha = \boldsymbol{x}'_\alpha - \Delta\boldsymbol{x}'_\alpha, \tag{14}$$

and compute the correction terms $\Delta\boldsymbol{x}_\alpha$ and $\Delta\boldsymbol{x}'_\alpha$. Substituting (14) into (4), we have

$$E = \sum_{\alpha=1}^{N} \left( \|\Delta\boldsymbol{x}_\alpha\|^2 + \|\Delta\boldsymbol{x}'_\alpha\|^2 \right). \tag{15}$$

The epipolar equation (4) becomes

$$(\boldsymbol{x}_\alpha - \Delta\boldsymbol{x}_\alpha, \boldsymbol{F}(\boldsymbol{x}'_\alpha - \Delta\boldsymbol{x}'_\alpha)) = 0. \tag{16}$$

Ignoring the second order term in the correction terms, we obtain

$$(\boldsymbol{F}\boldsymbol{x}'_\alpha, \Delta\boldsymbol{x}_\alpha) + (\boldsymbol{F}^\top\boldsymbol{x}_\alpha, \Delta\boldsymbol{x}'_\alpha) = (\boldsymbol{x}_\alpha, \boldsymbol{F}\boldsymbol{x}'_\alpha). \tag{17}$$

Since the correction should be done in the image plane, we have the constraints

$$(\boldsymbol{k}, \Delta\boldsymbol{x}_\alpha) = 0, \qquad (\boldsymbol{k}, \Delta\boldsymbol{x}'_\alpha) = 0, \tag{18}$$

where we define $\boldsymbol{k} \equiv (0,0,1)^\top$. Introducing Lagrange multipliers for (17) and (18), we obtain $\Delta\boldsymbol{x}_\alpha$ and $\Delta\boldsymbol{x}'_\alpha$ that minimize (15) as follows (see [13] for the details):

$$\Delta\boldsymbol{x}_\alpha = \frac{(\boldsymbol{x}_\alpha, \boldsymbol{F}\boldsymbol{x}'_\alpha)\boldsymbol{P}_{\mathbf{k}}\boldsymbol{F}\boldsymbol{x}'_\alpha}{(\boldsymbol{F}\boldsymbol{x}'_\alpha, \boldsymbol{P}_{\mathbf{k}}\boldsymbol{F}\boldsymbol{x}'_\alpha) + (\boldsymbol{F}^\top\boldsymbol{x}_\alpha, \boldsymbol{P}_{\mathbf{k}}\boldsymbol{F}^\top\boldsymbol{x}_\alpha)},$$

$$\Delta\boldsymbol{x}'_\alpha = \frac{(\boldsymbol{x}_\alpha, \boldsymbol{F}\boldsymbol{x}'_\alpha)\boldsymbol{P}_{\mathbf{k}}\boldsymbol{F}^\top\boldsymbol{x}_\alpha}{(\boldsymbol{F}\boldsymbol{x}'_\alpha, \boldsymbol{P}_{\mathbf{k}}\boldsymbol{F}\boldsymbol{x}'_\alpha) + (\boldsymbol{F}^\top\boldsymbol{x}_\alpha, \boldsymbol{P}_{\mathbf{k}}\boldsymbol{F}^\top\boldsymbol{x}_\alpha)}. \tag{19}$$

Here, $\boldsymbol{P}_{\mathbf{k}}$ is the $3 \times 3$ projection matrix along $\boldsymbol{k}$:

$$\boldsymbol{P}_{\mathbf{k}} \equiv \boldsymbol{I} - \boldsymbol{k}\boldsymbol{k}^\top. \tag{20}$$

Substituting (19) into (15), we obtain (see [13] for the details)

$$E = \sum_{\alpha=1}^{N} \frac{(\boldsymbol{x}_\alpha, \boldsymbol{F}\boldsymbol{x}'_\alpha)^2}{(\boldsymbol{F}\boldsymbol{x}'_\alpha, \boldsymbol{P}_{\mathbf{k}}\boldsymbol{F}\boldsymbol{x}'_\alpha) + (\boldsymbol{F}^\top\boldsymbol{x}_\alpha, \boldsymbol{P}_{\mathbf{k}}\boldsymbol{F}^\top\boldsymbol{x}_\alpha)}, \tag{21}$$

which is known as the *Sampson error* [6]. Suppose we have obtained the matrix $\boldsymbol{F}$ that minimizes (21) subject to $\det \boldsymbol{F} = 0$. Writing it as $\hat{\boldsymbol{F}}$ and substituting it into (14), we obtain

$$\hat{\boldsymbol{x}}_\alpha = \boldsymbol{x}_\alpha - \frac{(\boldsymbol{x}_\alpha, \hat{\boldsymbol{F}}\boldsymbol{x}'_\alpha)\boldsymbol{P}_{\mathbf{k}}\hat{\boldsymbol{F}}\boldsymbol{x}'_\alpha}{(\hat{\boldsymbol{F}}\boldsymbol{x}'_\alpha, \boldsymbol{P}_{\mathbf{k}}\hat{\boldsymbol{F}}\boldsymbol{x}'_\alpha) + (\hat{\boldsymbol{F}}^\top\boldsymbol{x}_\alpha, \boldsymbol{P}_{\mathbf{k}}\hat{\boldsymbol{F}}^\top\boldsymbol{x}_\alpha)},$$

$$\hat{\boldsymbol{x}}'_\alpha = \boldsymbol{x}'_\alpha - \frac{(\boldsymbol{x}_\alpha, \hat{\boldsymbol{F}}\boldsymbol{x}'_\alpha)\boldsymbol{P}_{\mathbf{k}}\hat{\boldsymbol{F}}^\top\boldsymbol{x}_\alpha}{(\hat{\boldsymbol{F}}\boldsymbol{x}'_\alpha, \boldsymbol{P}_{\mathbf{k}}\hat{\boldsymbol{F}}\boldsymbol{x}'_\alpha) + (\hat{\boldsymbol{F}}^\top\boldsymbol{x}_\alpha, \boldsymbol{P}_{\mathbf{k}}\hat{\boldsymbol{F}}^\top\boldsymbol{x}_\alpha)}. \tag{22}$$

**Higher Order Correction.** The solution (22) is only a first approximation. So, we estimate the true solution $\bar{\boldsymbol{x}}_\alpha$ and $\bar{\boldsymbol{x}}'_\alpha$ by writing, instead of (14),

$$\bar{\boldsymbol{x}}_\alpha = \hat{\boldsymbol{x}}_\alpha - \Delta\hat{\boldsymbol{x}}_\alpha, \qquad \bar{\boldsymbol{x}}'_\alpha = \hat{\boldsymbol{x}}'_\alpha - \Delta\hat{\boldsymbol{x}}'_\alpha, \tag{23}$$

and computing the correction terms $\Delta\hat{\boldsymbol{x}}_\alpha$ and $\Delta\hat{\boldsymbol{x}}'_\alpha$, which are small quantities of higher order than $\Delta\boldsymbol{x}_\alpha$ and $\Delta\boldsymbol{x}'_\alpha$. Substitution of (23) into (3) yields

$$E = \sum_{\alpha=1}^{N} \left( \|\tilde{\boldsymbol{x}}_\alpha + \Delta\hat{\boldsymbol{x}}_\alpha\|^2 + \|\tilde{\boldsymbol{x}}'_\alpha + \Delta\hat{\boldsymbol{x}}'_\alpha\|^2 \right), \tag{24}$$

where we define

$$\tilde{\boldsymbol{x}}_\alpha = \boldsymbol{x}_\alpha - \hat{\boldsymbol{x}}_\alpha, \qquad \tilde{\boldsymbol{x}}'_\alpha = \boldsymbol{x}'_\alpha - \hat{\boldsymbol{x}}'_\alpha. \tag{25}$$

The epipolar equation (4) now becomes

$$(\hat{\boldsymbol{x}}_\alpha - \varDelta\hat{\boldsymbol{x}}_\alpha, \boldsymbol{F}(\hat{\boldsymbol{x}}'_\alpha - \varDelta\hat{\boldsymbol{x}}'_\alpha)) = 0. \tag{26}$$

Ignoring second order term in $\varDelta\hat{\boldsymbol{x}}_\alpha$ and $\varDelta\hat{\boldsymbol{x}}'_\alpha$, we have

$$(\boldsymbol{F}\hat{\boldsymbol{x}}'_\alpha, \varDelta\hat{\boldsymbol{x}}_\alpha) + (\boldsymbol{F}^\top\hat{\boldsymbol{x}}_\alpha, \varDelta\hat{\boldsymbol{x}}'_\alpha) = (\hat{\boldsymbol{x}}_\alpha, \boldsymbol{F}\hat{\boldsymbol{x}}'_\alpha). \tag{27}$$

This is a higher order approximation of (4) than (17). Introducing Lagrange multipliers to (27) and the constraints

$$(\boldsymbol{k}, \varDelta\hat{\boldsymbol{x}}_\alpha) = 0, \qquad (\boldsymbol{k}, \varDelta\hat{\boldsymbol{x}}'_\alpha) = 0, \tag{28}$$

we obtain $\varDelta\hat{\boldsymbol{x}}_\alpha$ and $\varDelta\hat{\boldsymbol{x}}'_\alpha$ as follows (see [13] for the details):

$$\varDelta\hat{\boldsymbol{x}}_\alpha = \frac{\left((\hat{\boldsymbol{x}}_\alpha, \boldsymbol{F}\hat{\boldsymbol{x}}'_\alpha) + (\boldsymbol{F}\hat{\boldsymbol{x}}'_\alpha, \tilde{\boldsymbol{x}}_\alpha) + (\boldsymbol{F}^\top\hat{\boldsymbol{x}}_\alpha, \tilde{\boldsymbol{x}}'_\alpha)\right)\boldsymbol{P}_{\mathbf{k}}\boldsymbol{F}\hat{\boldsymbol{x}}'_\alpha}{(\boldsymbol{F}\hat{\boldsymbol{x}}'_\alpha, \boldsymbol{P}_{\mathbf{k}}\boldsymbol{F}\hat{\boldsymbol{x}}'_\alpha) + (\boldsymbol{F}^\top\hat{\boldsymbol{x}}_\alpha, \boldsymbol{P}_{\mathbf{k}}\boldsymbol{F}^\top\hat{\boldsymbol{x}}_\alpha)} - \tilde{\boldsymbol{x}}_\alpha,$$

$$\varDelta\hat{\boldsymbol{x}}'_\alpha = \frac{\left((\hat{\boldsymbol{x}}_\alpha, \boldsymbol{F}\hat{\boldsymbol{x}}'_\alpha) + (\boldsymbol{F}\hat{\boldsymbol{x}}'_\alpha, \tilde{\boldsymbol{x}}_\alpha) + (\boldsymbol{F}^\top\hat{\boldsymbol{x}}_\alpha, \tilde{\boldsymbol{x}}'_\alpha)\right)\boldsymbol{P}_{\mathbf{k}}\boldsymbol{F}^\top\hat{\boldsymbol{x}}_\alpha}{(\boldsymbol{F}\hat{\boldsymbol{x}}'_\alpha, \boldsymbol{P}_{\mathbf{k}}\boldsymbol{F}\hat{\boldsymbol{x}}'_\alpha) + (\boldsymbol{F}^\top\hat{\boldsymbol{x}}_\alpha, \boldsymbol{P}_{\mathbf{k}}\boldsymbol{F}^\top\hat{\boldsymbol{x}}_\alpha)} - \tilde{\boldsymbol{x}}'_\alpha. \tag{29}$$

The reprojection error (24) now has the form (see [13] for the details)

$$E = \sum_{\alpha=1}^{N} \frac{\left((\hat{\boldsymbol{x}}_\alpha, \boldsymbol{F}\hat{\boldsymbol{x}}'_\alpha) + (\boldsymbol{F}\hat{\boldsymbol{x}}'_\alpha, \tilde{\boldsymbol{x}}_\alpha) + (\boldsymbol{F}^\top\hat{\boldsymbol{x}}_\alpha, \tilde{\boldsymbol{x}}'_\alpha)\right)^2}{(\boldsymbol{F}\hat{\boldsymbol{x}}'_\alpha, \boldsymbol{P}_{\mathbf{k}}\boldsymbol{F}\hat{\boldsymbol{x}}'_\alpha) + (\boldsymbol{F}^\top\hat{\boldsymbol{x}}_\alpha, \boldsymbol{P}_{\mathbf{k}}\boldsymbol{F}^\top\hat{\boldsymbol{x}}_\alpha)}. \tag{30}$$

Suppose we have obtained the matrix $\boldsymbol{F}$ that minimizes this subject to $\det \boldsymbol{F} = 0$. Writing it as $\hat{\boldsymbol{F}}$ and substituting it into (29), we obtain from (25) the solution

$$\hat{\hat{\boldsymbol{x}}}_\alpha = \boldsymbol{x}_\alpha - \frac{\left((\hat{\boldsymbol{x}}_\alpha, \hat{\boldsymbol{F}}\hat{\boldsymbol{x}}'_\alpha) + (\hat{\boldsymbol{F}}\hat{\boldsymbol{x}}'_\alpha, \tilde{\boldsymbol{x}}_\alpha) + (\hat{\boldsymbol{F}}^\top\hat{\boldsymbol{x}}_\alpha, \tilde{\boldsymbol{x}}'_\alpha)\right)\boldsymbol{P}_{\mathbf{k}}\hat{\boldsymbol{F}}\hat{\boldsymbol{x}}'_\alpha}{(\hat{\boldsymbol{F}}\hat{\boldsymbol{x}}'_\alpha, \boldsymbol{P}_{\mathbf{k}}\hat{\boldsymbol{F}}\hat{\boldsymbol{x}}'_\alpha) + (\hat{\boldsymbol{F}}^\top\hat{\boldsymbol{x}}_\alpha, \boldsymbol{P}_{\mathbf{k}}\hat{\boldsymbol{F}}^\top\hat{\boldsymbol{x}}_\alpha)},$$

$$\hat{\hat{\boldsymbol{x}}}'_\alpha = \boldsymbol{x}'_\alpha - \frac{\left((\hat{\boldsymbol{x}}_\alpha, \hat{\boldsymbol{F}}\hat{\boldsymbol{x}}'_\alpha) + (\hat{\boldsymbol{F}}\hat{\boldsymbol{x}}'_\alpha, \tilde{\boldsymbol{x}}_\alpha) + (\hat{\boldsymbol{F}}^\top\hat{\boldsymbol{x}}_\alpha, \tilde{\boldsymbol{x}}'_\alpha)\right)\boldsymbol{P}_{\mathbf{k}}\hat{\boldsymbol{F}}^\top\hat{\boldsymbol{x}}_\alpha}{(\hat{\boldsymbol{F}}\hat{\boldsymbol{x}}'_\alpha, \boldsymbol{P}_{\mathbf{k}}\hat{\boldsymbol{F}}\hat{\boldsymbol{x}}'_\alpha) + (\hat{\boldsymbol{F}}^\top\hat{\boldsymbol{x}}_\alpha, \boldsymbol{P}_{\mathbf{k}}\hat{\boldsymbol{F}}^\top\hat{\boldsymbol{x}}_\alpha)}. \tag{31}$$

The resulting $\{\hat{\hat{\boldsymbol{x}}}_\alpha, \hat{\hat{\boldsymbol{x}}}'_\alpha\}$ are a better approximation than $\{\hat{\boldsymbol{x}}_\alpha, \hat{\boldsymbol{x}}'_\alpha\}$. Rewriting $\{\hat{\hat{\boldsymbol{x}}}_\alpha, \hat{\hat{\boldsymbol{x}}}'_\alpha\}$ as $\{\hat{\boldsymbol{x}}_\alpha, \hat{\boldsymbol{x}}'_\alpha\}$, we repeat this until the iterations converge. In the end, $\varDelta\hat{\boldsymbol{x}}_\alpha$ and $\varDelta\hat{\boldsymbol{x}}'_\alpha$ in (26) become $\boldsymbol{0}$, and the epipolar equation is exactly satisfied.

**Compact 9-D Description.** The above algorithm is greatly simplified by using the 9-D vector encoding of (5). The definition of $\boldsymbol{\xi}_\alpha$ in (6) and $V_0[\boldsymbol{\xi}_\alpha]$ in (7) implies the following identities:

$$(\hat{\boldsymbol{x}}_\alpha, \hat{\boldsymbol{F}}\hat{\boldsymbol{x}}'_\alpha) + (\hat{\boldsymbol{F}}\hat{\boldsymbol{x}}'_\alpha, \tilde{\boldsymbol{x}}_\alpha) + (\hat{\boldsymbol{F}}^\top\hat{\boldsymbol{x}}_\alpha, \tilde{\boldsymbol{x}}'_\alpha) = \frac{(\boldsymbol{u}, \boldsymbol{\xi}_\alpha)}{f_0^2}, \tag{32}$$

$$(\hat{\boldsymbol{F}}\boldsymbol{x}'_\alpha, \boldsymbol{P_k}\hat{\boldsymbol{F}}\boldsymbol{x}'_\alpha) + (\hat{\boldsymbol{F}}^\top\boldsymbol{x}_\alpha, \boldsymbol{P_k}\hat{\boldsymbol{F}}^\top\boldsymbol{x}_\alpha) = \frac{(\boldsymbol{u}, V_0[\boldsymbol{\xi}_\alpha]\boldsymbol{u})}{f_0^2}. \tag{33}$$

Since we define $\tilde{\boldsymbol{x}}_\alpha$ and $\tilde{\boldsymbol{x}}'_\alpha$ by (25), we obtain from (31) the update form in (8). If we let $\hat{x}_\alpha = x_\alpha$, $\hat{y}_\alpha = y_\alpha$, $\hat{x}'_\alpha = x'_\alpha$, $\hat{y}'_\alpha = y'_\alpha$, and $\tilde{x}_\alpha = \tilde{y}_\alpha = \tilde{x}'_\alpha = \tilde{y}'_\alpha = 0$, as in the Step 2 of the main routine, the update form (8) is equivalent to (22). Thus, the main routine is completed except Step 4, where we need to minimize (21) and (30) subject to $\det \boldsymbol{F} = 0$.

### 3.2   Derivation of EFNS

**Problem.** Using the identities (32) and (33), we can rewrite (30) as

$$E = \frac{1}{f_0^2} \sum_{\alpha=1}^{N} \frac{(\boldsymbol{u}, \boldsymbol{\xi}_\alpha)^2}{(\boldsymbol{u}, V_0[\boldsymbol{\xi}_\alpha]\boldsymbol{u})}. \tag{34}$$

If we let $\hat{x}_\alpha = x_\alpha$, $\hat{y}_\alpha = y_\alpha$, $\hat{x}'_\alpha = x'_\alpha$, $\hat{y}'_\alpha = y'_\alpha$, and $\tilde{x}_\alpha = \tilde{y}_\alpha = \tilde{x}'_\alpha = \tilde{y}'_\alpha = 0$, as in the Step 2 of the main routine, this reduces to the Sampson error in (21). The problem is to minimize (34) subject to $\det \boldsymbol{u} = 0$.

**Geometry.** The necessary and sufficient condition for $E$ to be stationary at a point $\boldsymbol{u}$ on the 8-D unit sphere $\mathcal{S}^8$ in $\mathcal{R}^9$ is that its gradient $\nabla_{\boldsymbol{u}} E$ is orthogonal to the hypersurface defined by $\det \boldsymbol{u} = 0$. Direct manipulation shows

$$\boldsymbol{u}^\dagger = \mathcal{N}[\nabla_{\mathbf{u}} \det \boldsymbol{u}]. \tag{35}$$

In other words, $\boldsymbol{u}^\dagger$ is the unit surface normal to the hypersurface defined by $\det \boldsymbol{u} = 0$. It follows that $\nabla_{\boldsymbol{u}} E$ should be parallel to the cofactor vector $\boldsymbol{u}^\dagger$ at the stationary point. Differentiating (34) with respect to $\boldsymbol{u}$, we see that

$$\nabla_{\mathbf{u}} E = \frac{2}{f_0^2} \boldsymbol{X} \boldsymbol{u}, \tag{36}$$

where $\boldsymbol{X}$ is the matrix in (11). Using the projection matrix $\boldsymbol{P_{u^\dagger}}$ in (10), we can express the parallelism of $\nabla_{\mathbf{u}} E$ and $\boldsymbol{u}^\dagger$ as

$$\boldsymbol{P_{u^\dagger}} \boldsymbol{X} \boldsymbol{u} = \boldsymbol{0}. \tag{37}$$

The rank constraint $\det \boldsymbol{u} = 0$ is equivalently written as

$$(\boldsymbol{u}^\dagger, \boldsymbol{u}) = 0, \tag{38}$$

which is a direct consequence of the identity $\boldsymbol{F}^\dagger \boldsymbol{F} = (\det \boldsymbol{F})\boldsymbol{I}$. In terms of the projection matrix $\boldsymbol{P_{u^\dagger}}$, the rank constraint (38) is equivalently written as

$$\boldsymbol{P_{u^\dagger}} \boldsymbol{u} = \boldsymbol{u}. \tag{39}$$

It follows that the stationarity condition (37) is written as

$$\boldsymbol{Y} \boldsymbol{u} = \boldsymbol{0}, \tag{40}$$

where $\boldsymbol{Y}$ is the matrix defined in (11). Our task is to compute the solution $\boldsymbol{u}$ that satisfies the stationarity condition (40) and the rank constraint (39).

**Justification of the Procedure.** We now show that the desired solution can be obtained by the EFNS routine in Sec. 2. To see this, we show that when the iterations have converged, the eigenvectors $v_1$ and $v_2$ of $Y$ both have eigenvalue 0. From the definition of $Y$ in (11) and $P_{u^\dagger}$ in (10), the cofactor vector $u^\dagger$ is always an eigenvector of $Y$ with eigenvalue 0. This means that either $v_1$ or $v_2$ has eigenvalue 0. Suppose one, say $v_1$, has nonzero eigenvalue $\lambda$ ($\neq 0$). Then, $v_2 = \pm u^\dagger$. By construction, the vector $\hat{u}$ in (12) belongs to the linear span of $v_1$ and $v_2$ ($= \pm u^\dagger$), which are mutually orthogonal, and the vector $u'$ in (13) is a projection of $\hat{u}$ within that linear span onto the direction orthogonal to $u^\dagger$. Hence, $u'$ should coincide with $\pm v_1$. After the iterations have converged, we have $u = u'$ ($= \pm v_1$), so $u$ is an eigenvector of $Y$ with eigenvalue $\lambda$, i.e., $Yu = \lambda u$. Taking the inner product with $u$ on both sides, we have

$$(u, Yu) = \lambda. \tag{41}$$

On the other hand, $u$ ($= \pm v_1$) is orthogonal to the cofactor vector $u^\dagger$ ($= \pm v_2$), so $P_{u^\dagger} u = u$. Hence,

$$(u, Yu) = (u, P_{u^\dagger} X P_{u^\dagger} u) = (u, Xu) = 0, \tag{42}$$

because from the definition of $X$ in (11) we see that $(u, Xu) = 0$ is an identity in $u$. In fact, we can confirm from the definition of $M$ and $L$ in (9) that $(u, Mu) = (u, Lu)$ holds identically in $u$. Since (41) and (42) contradict our assumption that $\lambda \neq 0$, $v_1$ is also an eigenvector of $Y$ with eigenvalue 0. Thus, (39) and (40) both hold, so $u$ is the desired solution.

**Observations.** The EFNS was first introduced by Kanatani and Sugaya [11] as a general constrained parameter estimation in abstract terms. It is a straightforward extension of the *FNS* of Chojnacki et al. [3] to include an arbitrary number of additional constraints. In fact, if we replace $P_{u^\dagger}$ in (11) by the identity $I$, the resulting procedure is identical to FNS. For this reason, Kanatani and Sugaya [11] called it *EFNS* (*Extended FNS*). They applied it to minimization of the Sampson error (21) and pointed out that the CFNS of Chojnacki et al. [4] does not necessarily converge to a correct solution while EFNS does. Our new finding here is that it can also be used for *strict ML* (minimization of the reprojection error) if we introduce the new *intermediate variables* $\xi_\alpha$ and $V_0[\xi_\alpha]$ as in (6) and (7).

The justification described earlier relies on the premise that the iterations converge. As pointed in [11], if we let $u \leftarrow u'$ in the Step 6 of the EFNS routine, the next value of $u'$ computed in Step 5 often reverts to the former value of $u$, falling in infinite looping. So, the "midpoint" $(u' + u)/2$ is normalized to a unit vector $\mathcal{N}[u' + u]$. This greatly improves convergence. In fact, we have confirmed that this technique also improves the convergence of FNS, which sometimes oscillates in the presence of very large noise.

Theoretically speaking, our algorithm may not produce a global minimum of the reprojection error (3). The problem is not the main routine, for which one need not worry about local minima, as argued in the optimal triangulation case [14]. However, the EFNS routine is not theoretically guaranteed to reach the absolute minimum of $E$ in (34), although we have never experienced the contrary in all our experiments.

## 4 Performance Confirmation

Figure 2(a) shows simulated images of two planar grid surfaces. The image size is $600 \times 600$ pixels with 1200 pixel focal length. We added random Gaussian noise of mean 0 and standard deviation $\sigma$ to the $x$- and $y$-coordinates of each grid point independently and from them computed the fundamental matrix.

Since all existing ML-based methods minimize the same reprojection error, their mutual accuracy comparison does not make much sense. Rather, our concern is if our algorithm really converges to a correct solution. To see this, we compare our algorithm with a carefully tuned alternative method. We compute an initial solution by least squares, from which we start the FNS of Chojnacki et al. [3], and the resulting solution is optimally corrected to satisfy the rank constraint. From it, we start a direct 7-D search, using the Levenberg-Marquardt (LM) method [18].

Figure 2(b) plots, for each $\sigma$, the RMS of $\|\boldsymbol{P}_{\mathcal{U}}\hat{\boldsymbol{u}}\|$ for the computed solution $\hat{\boldsymbol{u}}$ over 10,000 independent trials with different noise, where $\boldsymbol{P}_{\mathcal{U}}$ ($\equiv \boldsymbol{I} - \boldsymbol{u}\boldsymbol{u}^\top - \boldsymbol{u}^\dagger\boldsymbol{u}^{\dagger\top}$) denotes projection onto the space of deviations from the true solution $\boldsymbol{u}$ and the rank constraint $\det \boldsymbol{u} = 0$. Our algorithm was initialized by least squares. As a reference, the chained line shows the corresponding result of the 8-point algorithm (least squares followed by SVD rank correction) [5], and the dotted line indicates the theoretical accuracy limit (*KCR lower bound*) [2,8].

From Fig. 2(b), we see that the solid line (our algorithm) and the dashed line (the alternative method) completely coincide, indicating that the same solution is reached although their paths of approach may be very different (Fig. 1). We also see that the accuracy almost coincides with the theoretical limit, so *no further improvement is hoped for*. As predicted, the 8-point algorithm performs poorly. Doing many experiments (not all shown here), we observed the following:

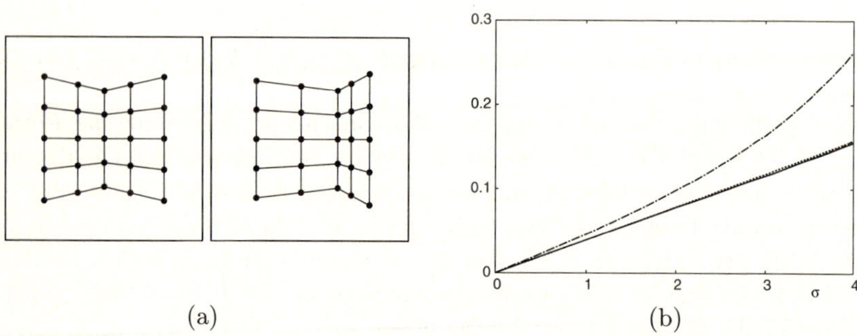

(a)        (b)

**Fig. 2.** (a) Simulated images of planar grid surfaces. (b) The RMS error vs. noise level $\sigma$. Solid line: our algorithm. Dashed line: the alternative method. Chained line: the 8-point algorithm. Dotted line: KCR lower bound.

1. The main routine converges after a few (at most four) iterations.
2. If we stop at Step 4 in the initial round without doing any further iterations, we obtain the Sampson solution. Yet, it coincides with the final (strict ML) solution up to three to four decimal places. The high accuracy of the Sampson solution was also noted by Zhang [21].
3. If initialized by least squares, the 7-D search does not necessarily arrive at the true minimum of the reprojection error, being trapped to local minima, as reported in [19]. After a careful tuning as described above, the solution coincides with our algorithm, which directly arrives at the same solution without any such tuning.

## 5  Concluding Remarks

We have presented a very compact algorithm for computing the fundamental matrix from point correspondences over two images based on the strict ML principle using the EFNS procedure. The computation consists only of vector and matrix operations in no higher than 9-D just like the 8-point algorithm, yet producing an optimal solution. By numerical experiments, we have confirmed that our algorithm behaves satisfactorily. Because of its compactness and good performance, we expect it to be a standard tool for fundamental matrix computation.

## References


1. Bartoli, A., Sturm, P.: Nonlinear estimation of fundamental matrix with minimal parameters. IEEE Trans. Patt. Anal. Mach. Intell. 26(3), 426–432 (2004)
2. Chernov, N., Lesort, C.: Statistical efficiency of curve fitting algorithms. Comp. Stat. Data Anal. 47(4), 713–728 (2004)
3. Chojnacki, W., Brooks, M.J., van den Hengel, A., Gawley, D.: On the fitting of surfaces to data with covariances. IEEE Trans. Patt. Anal. Mach. Intell. 22(11), 1294–1303 (2000)
4. Chojnacki, W., Brooks, M.J., van den Hengel, A., Gawley, D.: A new constrained parameter estimator for computer vision applications. Image Vis. Comput. 22(2), 85–91 (2004)
5. Hartley, R.I.: In defense of the eight-point algorithm. IEEE Trans. Patt. Anal. Mach. Intell. 19(6), 580–593 (1997)
6. Hartley, R., Zisserman, A.: Multiple View Geometry in Computer Vision. Cambridge University Press, Cambridge (2000)
7. Kahl, F., Henrion, D.: Globally optimal estimates for geometric reconstruction problems. Int. J. Comput. Vis. 74(1), 3–15 (2007)
8. Kanatani, K.: Statistical Optimization for Geometric Computation: Theory and Practice. Elsevier, Amsterdam (2005); reprinted. Dover, New York (2005)
9. Kanatani, K.: Statistical optimization for geometric fitting: Theoretical accuracy analysis and high order error analysis. Int. J. Compt. Vis. 80(2), 167–188 (2008)
10. Kanatani, K., Sugaya, Y.: High accuracy fundamental matrix computation and its performance evaluation. IEICE Trans. Information and Systems E90-D(2), 579–585 (2007)

11. Kanatani, K., Sugaya, Y.: Extended FNS for constrained parameter estimation. In: Proc. 10th Meeting Image Recognition Understanding, Hiroshima, Japan, July 2007, pp. 219–226 (2007)
12. Kanatani, K., Sugaya, Y.: Performance evaluation of iterative geometric fitting algorithms, Comp. Stat. Data Anal. 52(2), 1208–1222 (2007)
13. Kanatani, K., Sugaya, Y.: Small algorithm for fundamental matrix computation. In: Proc. Meeting Image Recognition and Understanding, Karuizawa, Japan, July 2008, pp. 947–954 (2008)
14. Kanatani, K., Sugaya, Y., Niitsuma, H.: Triangulation from two views revisited: Hartley-Sturm vs. optimal correction. In: Proc. 19th British Mach. Vis. Conf., September 2008, pp. 173–182 (2008)
15. Leedan, Y., Meer, P.: Heteroscedastic regression in computer vision: Problems with bilinear constraint. Int. J. Comput. Vis. 37(2), 127–150 (2000)
16. Matei, J., Meer, P.: Estimation of nonlinear errors-in-variables models for computer vision applications. IEEE Trans. Patt. Anal. Mach. Intell. 28(10), 1537–1552 (2006)
17. Migita, T., Shakunaga, T.: One-dimensional search for reliable epipole estimation. In: Proc. IEEE Pacific Rim Symp. Image Video Tech., Hsinchu, Taiwan, December 2006, pp. 1215–1224 (2006)
18. Sugaya, Y., Kanatani, K.: High accuracy computation of rank-constrained fundamental matrix. In: Proc. 18th British Mach. Vis. Conf., September 2007, vol. 1, pp. 282–291 (2007)
19. Sugaya, Y., Kanatani, K.: Highest accuracy fundamental matrix computation. In: Proc. 8th Asian Conf. Comput. Vis., Tokyo, Japan, November 2008, vol. 2, pp. 311–321 (2008)
20. Taubin, G.: Estimation of planar curves, surfaces, and non-planar space curves defined by implicit equations with applications to edge and rage image segmentation. IEEE Trans. Patt. Anal. Mach. Intell. 13(11), 1115–1138 (1991)
21. Zhang, Z.: Determining the epipolar geometry and its uncertainty: A review. Int. J. Comput. Vis. 27(2), 161–195 (1998)
22. Zhang, Z., Loop, C.: Estimating the fundamental matrix by transforming image points in projective space. Comput. Vis. Image Understand 82(2), 174–180 (2001)

# Detecting Incorrect Feature Tracking
## by Affine Space Fitting


Chika Takada and Yasuyuki Sugaya

Department of Information and Computer Sciences,
Toyohashi University of Technology, Toyohashi, Aichi, 441-8580, Japan
{takada,sugaya}@iim.ics.tut.ac.jp



**Abstract.** We present a new method for detecting incorrect feature point tracking. In this paper, we detect incorrect feature point tracking by imposing the constraint that under the affine camera model feature trajectories should be in an affine space in the parameter space. Introducing a statistical model of image noise, we test detected partial trajectories are sufficiently reliable. Then we detect incorrect partial trajectories. Using real video images, we demonstrate that our proposed method can detect incorrect feature point tracking fairly well.


## 1   Introduction

Extracting feature points from a video sequence and tracking them is the first step of many computer vision applications including structure from motion [18], and motion segmentation [9,10,11,14,17]. Many authors use the Kanade-Lucas-Tomasi algorithm [19]. However, the resulting trajectories are not always correct. In order to improve the tracking, Ichimura and Ikoma [6] and Ichimura [5] introduced nonlinear filtering. Hyunh and Heyden [4], motivated by 3-D reconstruction applications, showed that outlier trajectories in an image sequence of a static scene taken by a moving camera can be removed by fitting a 4-dimensional subspace to them by LMedS. Sugaya and Kanatani [15] fitted a 4-dimensional subspace to the observed trajectories by RANSAC [2,3] and removed outliers using a $\chi^2$ criterion by observing the error behavior of actual video tracking.

Usually, we simply discard detected outliers. However, outlier trajectories may partially contain correctly tracked data. Fig. 1 shows three examples of such trajectories. In Fig. 1(a), the tracking fails and strays after that. In Fig. 1(b), the tracking returns to a correct path after failing. In Fig. 1(c), the tracking fails and start tracking another path. If we detect incorrect paths from such outlier trajectories, we can estimate their correct paths from correct partial trajectories, and re-use such corrected trajectories as inliers.

Many techniques have proposed in the past for interpolating missing parts of tracking data. Saito and Kamijima [13] projectively reconstructed tentative 3-D positions of the missing points by sampling two frames in which they are visible and then reprojected them onto the frames in which they are invisible. Sugaya and Kanatani [16] extended partial trajectories by imposing the constraint that


T. Wada, F. Huang, and S. Lin (Eds.): PSIVT 2009, LNCS 5414, pp. 191–202, 2009.

## 6  Experiments

We test our method using real video sequences. Fig. 3(a) shows three decimated frames from a 100 frame sequence ($320 \times 240$ pixels) of a static poster scene taken by a moving camera. We detected 200 feature points and tracked them using the Kanade-Lucas-Tomasi algorithm [19]. Among them, 121 feature points are completely tracked over the entire frames, and 6 are regarded as outliers. The symbol □ in Fig. 3 indicates inlier positions, and the symbol × indicates outlier positions.

Fig. 3(b)–(d) show the results of incorrect tracking detection for three outliers. The horizontal and vertical axes show the frame number and the residual for the fitted affine space, respectively. The solid line indicates the residual of the partial trajectory, which is computed by the left hand side of (16). The dotted line indicates the threshold computed by the right hand side of (16). The box marks indicate that the feature points in its frame are correctly tracked. In order to remove outliers and detect incorrect tracking, we need to know the standard deviation of noise $\epsilon$. Theoretically, it can be estimated if the noise in each frame is independent and Gaussian [8]. In reality, however, strong correlations exist over consecutive frames, so that some points are tracked unambiguously throughout the sequence, while others fluctuate from frame to frame [15] as Sugaya and Kanatani [14] pointed out. Considering this, we set the value $\sigma$ to be 0.5 and 0.3, respectively. We visually inspected all the outliers trajectories frame by frame to see if they are really correct and confirmed that our method worked correctly.

We also detected partial trajectories consisting of the points correctly tracked through the longest frame sequence by the method described in Sec. 5. Fig. 3(e)–(g) show the result for the outlier trajectories in Fig. 3(b)–(d). In Fig. 3(e), we visually inspected the result and noticed that some correctly tracked feature points were not detected. However, we confirmed that all the detected feature points were correctly tracked. From the result in Fig. 3(f), we can see that another feature point, not the point extracted from the 1st frame, are correctly tracked from the 3rd frame to the 61st frame. In Fig. 3(g), we also confirm that the same result are given in Fig. 3(d). Using the trajectories obtained in Fig. 3(e)–(g), we estimated the missing parts of the feature trajectories by the method of Sugaya and Kanatani[16]. As we can see in Fig. 3(h), the correct positions are obtained. We also computed the execution time for detecting incorrect tracking. It took about 20 seconds for obtaining each of the results in Fig. 3(b)–(d), and 120 seconds for Fig. 3(e)–(g). We used Intel Core2Duo E6700 2.66 GHz for the CPU and Linux for the OS.

Fig. 4 shows the result of applying the proposed method to a structure from motion. Fig. 4(a) shows three decimated frames from a 150 frame sequence ($640 \times 480$ pixels). We detected 200 feature points and tracked them. Among them, 108 were completely tracked through the sequence. From them, 49 trajectories were regarded as outliers. From these outlier trajectories, we detected longest correct trajectories. Then, we extrapolated them by the method of Sugaya and Kanatani[16]. Fig. 4(b) shows the outlier trajectories. The solid lines indicate corrcct paths. The dotted lines indicate incorrect paths. The dashed lines indicate corrected paths. For details, we picked up one outlier trajectory in Fig. 4(c).

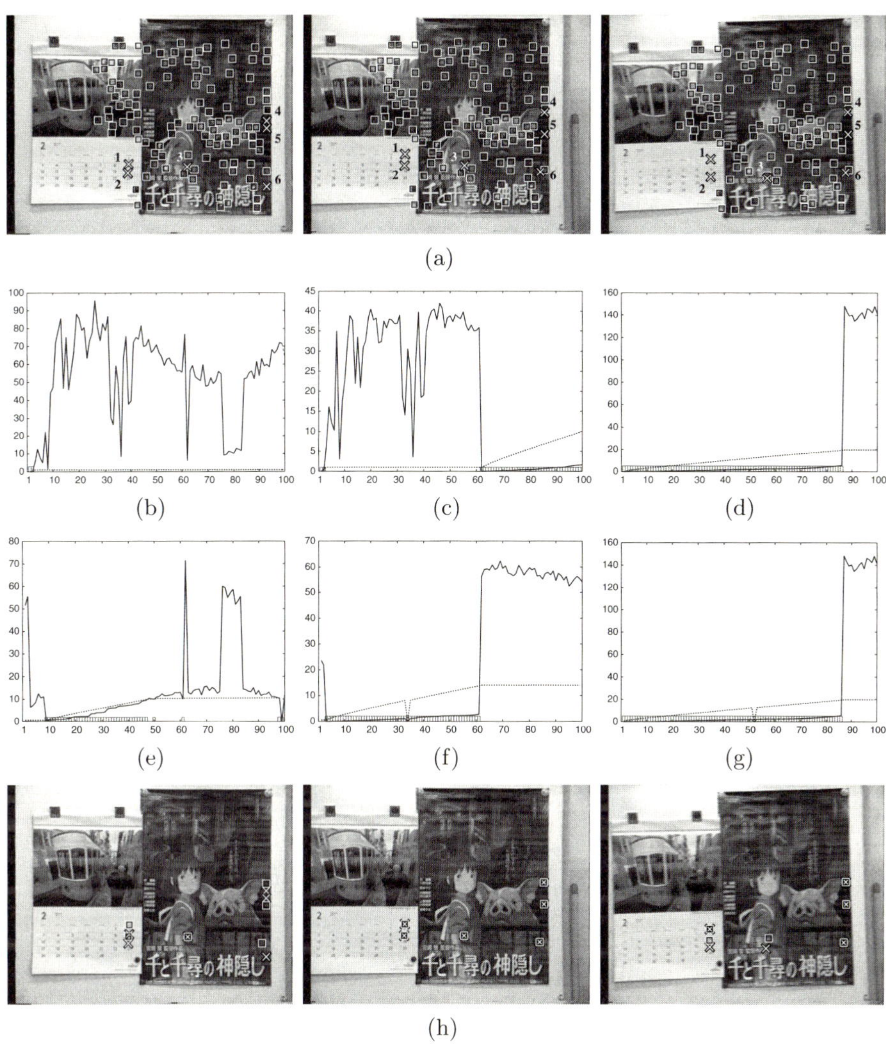

**Fig. 3.** (a) Three decimated frames of a 100 frame image sequence and 121 feature points successfully tracked ($\square$ for inlier positions; $\times$ for outlier positions). (b), (c), (d) The results of detecting incorrect tracking for the feature points starting from the 1st frame (the feature point ID 1, 2, and 3). Solid line is for the residual of the fitted affine space; dotted line is for the threshold; the box marks are for detecting frames for the correctly tracked feature points. (e), (f), (g) The results of detecting the longest tracked feature points (the feature point ID 1, 2, and 3). (h) Estimation of the missing positions for the resulting longest partial trajectories ($\square$ for estimated positions; $\times$ for originally tracked positions).

We reconstructed the 3-D shape by factorization, assuming weak perspective projection. Fig. 4(d) shows the front and the side views of the texture-mapped 3-D shape reconstructed from the original 59 inlier trajectories. Fig. 4(e) shows

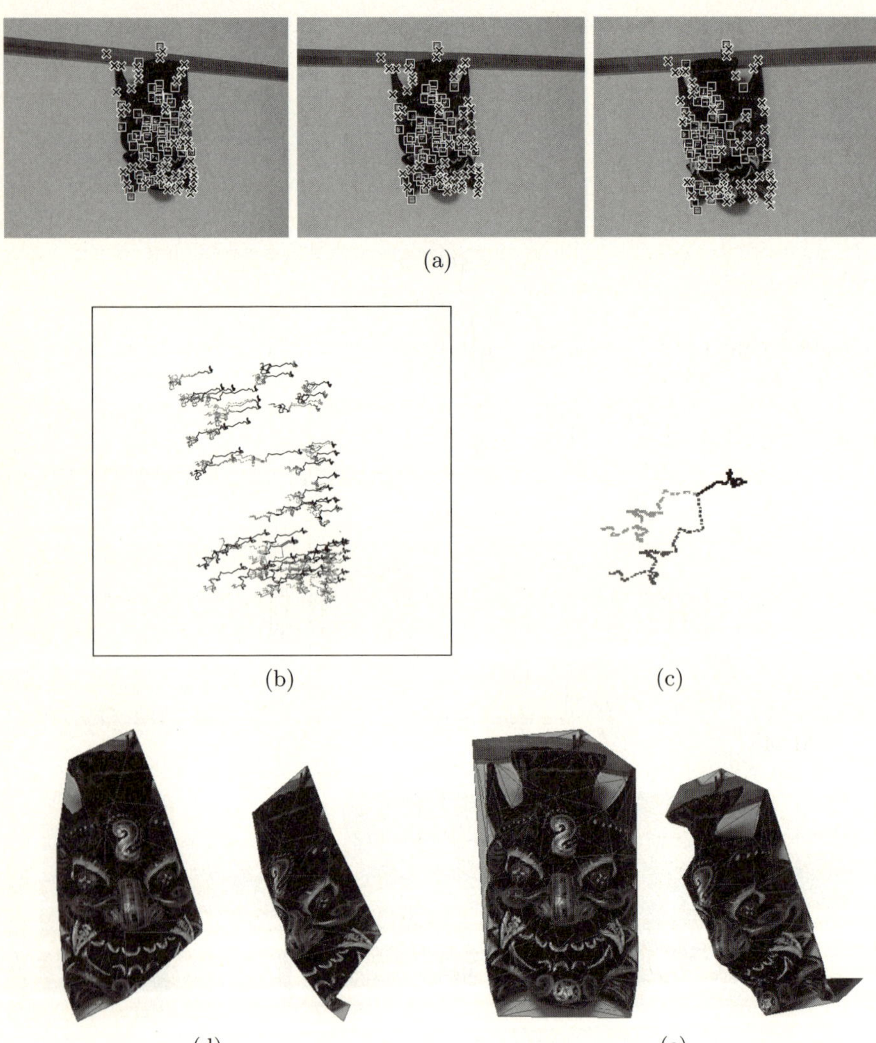

**Fig. 4.** (a) Three decimated frames of a 150 frame age sequence and 108 feature points successfully tracked ($\square$ for inlier positions; $\times$ for outlier positions). (b) Outlier trajectories. Solid lines are for correct paths; dotted lines are for incorrect paths; dashed lines are for corrected paths. (c) One outlier trajectory. (d) The texture-mapped 3-D shape reconstructed from the original 59 inlier trajectories. (e) The texture-mapped 3-D shape reconstructed after adding 49 corrected trajectories.

the front and the side views of the texture-mapped 3-D shape reconstructed after adding 49 corrected trajectories. From these results, we can see that the detailed structure is reconstructed by detecting and correcting incorrect tracking data.

# 7 Concluding Remarks

We have presented a new method for detecting incorrect tracking data in a feature point tracking. We have detected incorrect parts by imposing the constraint that under the affine camera model feature trajectories should be in an affine space in the parameter space. Introducing a statistical model of image noise, we have tested if a partial trajectory is sufficiently reliable. Then we have detected incorrect partial trajectories. Using real video images, we have demonstrated that our proposed method can detect incorrect feature point tracking fairly well.

**Acknowledgments.** This work was partially supported in part by the Ministry of Education, Culture, Sports, Science and Technology, Japan, under the Grant in Aid for Young Scientists (B) (No. 18700181), 2008. The authors thank Kenichi Kanatani of Okayama University, Japan for helpful comments.

# References


1. Brandt, S.: Closed-form solutions for affine reconstruction under missing data. In: Proc. Statistical Methods in Video Processing Workshop, Copenhagen, Denmark, June 2002, pp. 109–114 (2002)
2. Fischler, M.A., Bolles, R.C.: Random sample consensus: A paradigm for model fitting with applications to image analysis and automated cartography. Comm. ACM 24(6), 381–395 (1981)
3. Hartley, R., Horseman, A.: Multiple View Geometry in Computer Vision. Cambridge University Press, Cambridge (2000)
4. Huynh, D.Q., Heyden, A.: Outlier detection in video sequences under affine projection. In: Proc. IEEE Conf. Comput. Vision Pattern Recog., Kauai, HI, U.S.A, December 2001, vol. 2, pp. 695–701 (2001)
5. Ichimura, N.: Stochastic filtering for motion trajectory in image sequences using a Monte Carlo filter with estimation of hyper-parameters. In: Proc. 16th Int. Conf. Pattern Recog., Quebec City, Canada, August 2002, vol. 4, pp. 68–73 (2002)
6. Ichimura, N., Ikoma, N.: Filtering and smoothing for motion trajectory of feature point using non-gaussian state space model. IEICE Trans. Inf. Syst. E84-D(6), 755–759 (2001)
7. Jacobs, D.W.: Linear fitting with missing data for structure-from-motion. Comput. Vision Image Understand. 82(1), 57–81 (2001)
8. Kanatani, K.: Statistical Optimization for Geometric Computation: Theory and Practice. Elsevier Scence, Amsterdam (1996)
9. Kanatani, K.: Motion segmentation by subspace separation and model selection. In: Proc. 8th Int. Conf. Comput. Vision, Vancouver, Canada, vol. 2, pp. 301–306 (2001)
10. Kanatani, K.: Motion segmentation by subspace separation: Model selection and reliability evaluation. Int. J. Image Graphics 2(2), 179–197 (2002)
11. Kanatani, K.: Evaluation and selection of models for motion segmentation. In: Heyden, A., Sparr, G., Nielsen, M., Johansen, P. (eds.) ECCV 2002. LNCS, vol. 2352, pp. 335–349. Springer, Heidelberg (2002)
12. Poelman, C.J., Kanade, T.: A paraperspective factorization method for shape and motion recovery. IEEE Trans. Patt. Anal. Mach. Intell. 19(3), 206–218 (1997)

13. Saito, H., Kamijima, S.: Factorization method using interpolated feature tracking via projective geometry. In: Proc. 14th British Machine Vision Conf., Norwich, UK, vol. 2, pp. 449–458 (September 2003)
14. Sugaya, Y., Kanatani, K.: Automatic camera model selection for multibody motion segmentation. In: Proceedings of the IAPR Workshop on Machine Vision Applications (MVA 2002), Nara, Japan, 11-13 December, pp. 412–415 (2002)
15. Sugaya, Y., Kanatani, K.: Outlier removal for motion tracking by subspace separation. IEICE Trans. Inf. & Syst. E86-D(6), 1095–1102 (2003)
16. Sugaya, Y., Kanatani, K.: Extending interrupted feature point tracking for 3-D affine reconstruction. IEICE Transactions on Information and Systems E87-D(4), 1031–1038 (2004)
17. Sugaya, Y., Kanatani, K.: Multi-stage optimization for multi-body motion segmentation. IEICE Transactions on Information and Systems E87-D(7), 1935–1942 (2004)
18. Tomasi, C., Kanade, T.: Shape and motion from image streams under orthography—A factorization method. Int. J. Comput. Vision 9(2), 137–154 (1992)
19. Tomasi, C., Kanade, T.: Detection and Tracking of Point Features, CMU Tech. Rep. CMU-CS-91-132 (April 1991), http://www.ces.clemson.edu/~stb/klt/

# Outlier Removal by Convex Optimization for L-Infinity Approaches

Yongduek Seo, Hyunjung Lee, and Sang Wook Lee

Department of Media Technology, Sogang University, Korea
{yndk,whitetobi,slee}@sogang.ac.kr

**Abstract.** This paper is about removing outliers without iterations in $L_\infty$ optimization. Existing $L_\infty$ outlier removal method requires iterative removal of the set of measurements with greatest residual during $L_\infty$ minimization. In the method presented in this paper, on the other hand, a threshold is preset once for the maximum residual error in a manner similar to RANSAC, and the measurements yielding greater residuals than the threshold are taken to be outliers. We examine two feasibility test algorithms: 1) one that minimizes the maximum infeasibility and 2) the other that minimizes the sum of infeasibilities (SOI). Both of these can be used for feasibility test in conjunction with the bisection algorithm which attains the $L_\infty$ optimum. We note that the SOI method has an interesting characteristic due to its L1-norm minimization nature. It tries to estimate a robust solution while maximizing the number of feasible constraints. The infeasible constraints are found to be due mostly to outliers. Once we set a threshold, the SOI algorithm sorts out outliers from the data set without any repetition and substantial reduction of computation time can be achieved compared to the iterative method. Experiments with synthetic as well as real objects demonstrate the effectiveness of the SOI method. We suggest that the SOI method precede the outlier-sensitive $L_\infty$ optimization.

## 1 Introduction

The $L_\infty$-norm minimization has recently received a great deal of attention in the area of geometric vision since it yields global optimum because of the quasi-convexity of the L2 re-projection error function [1,2,3]

It can be used to find the global optimum for the problems such as triangulation, inter-image homography, camera resectioning, structure and motion with known rotation or homography. Research topics related to $L_\infty$ optimization include motion estimation [4], robot application [5], non-rigid surface tracking [6], outliers removal [7,8], increasing the speed of computation [9,10], and the pseudo-convexity of the re-projection error function [9].

**Removing outliers.** A major weakness of the $L_\infty$ optimization lies in its susceptibility to outliers since the minimization actually fits the outliers instead of the good data. RANSAC [11] removes most of the outliers during the first stage of computation, but there is still a possibility that some of the outliers remain. Fortunately, one can easily eliminate those remaining outliers by iteratively optimizing and removing the measurements with greatest residual. Sim and Hartley showed that this iterative outlier

T. Wada, F. Huang, and S. Lin (Eds.): PSIVT 2009, LNCS 5414, pp. 203–214, 2009.

elimination is valid for a wide class of $L_\infty$ problems by proving that the set of measurements with greatest residual, called the support set, must contain at least one outlier [7].This iterative scheme has been employed successfully in [6] for 3D deformable surface tracking. The most notable disadvantage of the iterative outlier removal is the long computation time, especially for a problem with a large number of parameters such as the estimation of structure and motion. For such a problem, the computation can easily take much longer than 10 hours with a typical high-performance PC. It may be noted that Li developed a method of removing only outliers rather than the whole support set [8]. Despite its improved efficiency, however, the method still requires a number of tests and considers only the triangulation problem. No framework was provided for applying the method to other problems with larger number of parameters such as homography computation, and motion and structure estimation with known rotation.

**Goal of the presented work.** This paper challenges the problem of computationally efficient outlier removal and suggests an algorithm that does not require iterations for removing outliers. Presented is a one-shot outlier-removal method. We simply specify a maximum threshold for re-projection errors, run a feasibility test algorithm, and regard the infeasible measurements as outliers. Then the $L_\infty$ optimization is carried out once only on the measurements identified as inliers. We experimentally show that this one-shot method reduces the computation time by a factor of $10 \sim 133$ for some typical $L_\infty$ problems compared to the iterative method [7]. The feasibility test is a robust convex optimization algorithm with the second order cone constraints. Like [7], we advocate the use of RANSAC at the initial stage of outlier removal. Our method is intended to get rid of the outliers that may remain even after RANSAC is performed.

**Feasibility problem.** $L_\infty$ optimization is done usually by the bisection method shown in Algorithm 1. Recent study [9] on the pseudo-convexity of the error function opens up a possibility of a new way of fast computation without resorting to the bisection method although a concrete numerical algorithm is yet to be developed for efficient computation. Most of the works on $L_\infty$ minimization heavily rely on the use of a readily available convex solver such as SeDuMi implemented in Matlab [12]. The simplex algorithm can be used for the methods which employ linear programming rather than second-order cone programming (SOCP) [13,10]. In most of these works, the feasibility test problem in Algorithm 1 is not explicitly described. We focus on the feasibility test formulation to find a way to identify outliers. The feasibility problem in Algorithm 1 may be solved numerically by an SOCP formulation which checks the feasibility of the convex constraints and finds a solution. We consider two of such formulations: 1) minimizing the maximum infeasibility and 2) minimizing the sum of the infeasibilities (SOI). The first formulation is appropriate for testing the feasibility of the whole set of constraints. The second allows us to see which are feasible among the constraints and to identify inliers. We call this the SOI method on which our one-shot non-iterative outlier-removal algorithm is based.

Section 2 discusses those two formulations in detail after providing a brief introduction to $L_\infty$ error norm minimization, and our strategy for outlier removal is described. Section 3 shows various experiments with synthetic data to demonstrate the performance of the SOI method for camera resectioning problem. Section 4 presents

---

**Algorithm 1.** Bisection method to minimize $L_\infty$ norm

---

**Input:** initial upper($U$)/lower($L$) bounds, tolerance $\epsilon > 0$.

  **repeat**

    $\gamma := (L + U)/2$

    Solve the feasibility problem (7)

    **if** *feasible* **then** $U := \gamma$ **else** $L := \gamma$

  **until** $U - L \leq \epsilon$

---

our experimental results for the problem of structure and motion with known rotation. Experiments with real data, the well-known dinosaur sequence, are carried out as well as with a set of synthetic data. Concluding remarks are given in Section 5.

## 2   The $L_\infty$ Optimization and Feasibility Test

We take the resectioning problem as a specific example of $L_\infty$ optimization for explaining our approach. Other problems can be formulated in a similar way based on the work shown in [2]. A good introduction to the feasibility problems can be found in [14].

Given a set of $N$ correspondences $\{\mathbf{X}_i, \mathbf{x}_i\}$ of a 3D point $\boldsymbol{X}_i = [X_i, Y_i, Z_i, 1]^\top$ and its noisy image measurement $\boldsymbol{x}_i = [u_i, v_i]^\top$, the resectioning problem is to find the camera matrix P such that

$$[u_i, v_i] = \left[\frac{\boldsymbol{p}_1 \boldsymbol{X}_i}{\boldsymbol{p}_3 \boldsymbol{X}_i}, \quad \frac{\boldsymbol{p}_2 \boldsymbol{X}_i}{\boldsymbol{p}_3 \boldsymbol{X}_i}\right], \quad \forall i \in I = \{1, \ldots, N\}, \tag{1}$$

where $\boldsymbol{p}_k$ is the $k$th row vector of the $3 \times 4$ matrix P. The $L_2$ reprojection error is defined to be

$$e_i = \sqrt{\left(u_i - \frac{\boldsymbol{p}_1 \boldsymbol{X}_i}{\boldsymbol{p}_3 \boldsymbol{X}_i}\right)^2 + \left(v_i - \frac{\boldsymbol{p}_2 \boldsymbol{X}_i}{\boldsymbol{p}_3 \boldsymbol{X}_i}\right)^2} \tag{2}$$

$$= \frac{\left\|[u_i \boldsymbol{p}_3 \boldsymbol{X}_i - \boldsymbol{p}_1 \boldsymbol{X}_i, \quad v_i \boldsymbol{p}_3 \boldsymbol{X}_i - \boldsymbol{p}_2 \boldsymbol{X}_i]\right\|_2}{\boldsymbol{p}_3 \boldsymbol{X}_i} \tag{3}$$

$$= \frac{\left\|\mathsf{A}_i \boldsymbol{\theta} + \boldsymbol{b}_i\right\|_2}{\boldsymbol{c}_i^\top \boldsymbol{\theta} + d_i}, \tag{4}$$

where $\| \cdot \|_2$ is the Euclidean norm, $\boldsymbol{\theta}$ is the vector form of P, and $\mathsf{A}_i$, $\boldsymbol{b}_i$, $\boldsymbol{c}_i$, $d_i$ are appropriate coefficient matrices, vectors and a scalar. The total error is $\boldsymbol{E} = [e_1, \ldots, e_N]$ and the optimum of the reprojection errors in the $L_\infty$ error sense is given by

$$e_\infty = \min_{\boldsymbol{\theta}} \max\{e_1(\boldsymbol{\theta}), \ldots, e_N(\boldsymbol{\theta})\} . \tag{5}$$

Note that finding the optimum can be re-written as

$$\begin{aligned} &\min \quad \gamma \\ &\text{s. t.} \quad \|\mathsf{A}_i \boldsymbol{\theta} + \boldsymbol{b}_i\| \leq \gamma(\boldsymbol{c}_i^\top \boldsymbol{\theta} + d_i) \quad \forall i \in I. \end{aligned} \tag{6}$$

Since the error function in Equation 4 is quasi-convex, the constraints are all convex second order cones for a fixed constant $\gamma$. Therefore, the optimum and the solution $\theta^*$ can be found by the bisection method shown in Algorithm 1, where the following feasibility problem with the constant $\gamma$ should be solved at every iteration:

*Problem 1*

$$\text{find } \boldsymbol{\theta}$$
$$\text{s.t.} \quad \|A_i\boldsymbol{\theta} + \boldsymbol{b}_i\| \leq \gamma(\boldsymbol{c}_i^{\top}\boldsymbol{\theta} + d_i) \quad \forall i \in I. \tag{7}$$

## 2.1 Minimizing the Maximum Infeasibility

Note that the description of Problem 1 neither explicitly specifies how to test the feasibility, nor shows how to find a feasible solution $\boldsymbol{\theta}$ numerically inside the second order cones even when a good convex optimizer is available. A numerically solvable description of the problem can be obtained by introducing a new auxiliary variable $s$ as:

$$\min \ s$$
$$\text{s.t.} \quad \|A_i\boldsymbol{\theta} + \boldsymbol{b}_i\| \leq \gamma(\boldsymbol{c}_i^{\top}\boldsymbol{\theta} + d_i) + s \quad \forall i \in I. \tag{8}$$

By setting $\tilde{\boldsymbol{\theta}} = [\boldsymbol{\theta}; s]$, one may easily see that this formulation is exactly in the form of second order cone programming:

$$\min \ \boldsymbol{f}_0^{\top}\tilde{\boldsymbol{\theta}}$$
$$\text{s.t.} \quad \|\tilde{A}_i\tilde{\boldsymbol{\theta}} + \boldsymbol{b}_i\| \leq (\tilde{\boldsymbol{c}}_i^{\top}\tilde{\boldsymbol{\theta}} + \gamma d_i) \quad \forall i \in I, \tag{9}$$

where $\boldsymbol{f}_0^{\top} = [0; 1]$, and $\tilde{A}_i = [A_i|0]$ and $\tilde{\boldsymbol{c}}_i = [\gamma\boldsymbol{c}_i^{\top}, 1]^{\top}$ are formed by augmenting $A_i$ and $\gamma\boldsymbol{c}_i$ with a column of zeros and a row of one, respectively. The variable $s$ represents the maximum infeasibility for the given constraints, i.e., the whole set of the second order cones. When $s > 0$, the problem is infeasible; otherwise, it is feasible. $L_\infty$ norm minimization can be carried out by minimizing $s$. This minimization based on Equation 9 needs only one extra variable $s$, and thus is simpler to implement than the following alternative feasibility test.

## 2.2 Minimizing the Sum of Infeasibilities (SOI)

To minimize SOI, we use as many variables $s_i$s ($i = 1, \ldots, N$) as the number of measurements (or equivalently second order cones), i.e., we have one $s_i$ per one measurement. The problem description is given as:

$$\min \ s_1 + s_2 + \ldots + s_N$$
$$\text{s.t.} \quad \|A_i\boldsymbol{\theta} + \boldsymbol{b}_i\| \leq \gamma(\boldsymbol{c}_i^{\top}\boldsymbol{\theta} + d_i) + s_i$$
$$s_i \geq 0, \quad \forall i \in I. \tag{10}$$

When the sum of the infeasibilities is found to be zero, the original problem is feasible, i.e., a solution $\boldsymbol{\theta}$ can be found inside the intersection of the second order cones. If any of $s_i$s is not zero, then the original problem is infeasible. It may be noted that the SOI method is $L_1$ minimization of the infeasibility variables. Below, we give a very brief introduction to the $L_1$ norm minimization. Details can be found in [14,15].

### 2.3  $L_1$ Minimization

For the residual vector $r = f(\theta)$ and the parameter vector $\theta$, the $L_1$ norm minimization problem is given by:

$$\min_{\theta} \quad |r_1| + \ldots + |r_N|, \tag{11}$$

where $r = [r_1, \ldots, r_N]^\top$. This is called the sum of (absolute) residuals approximation problem. The $L_1$ norm minimization is robust estimation because it is most robust to outliers among the minimization methods based on convex penalty functions. Its penalty function places relatively large weight on small residuals compared to others such as the quadratic function for least-squares optimization. Therefore, it tends to produce optimal residuals many of which are very small, or even exactly zero. In statistical terms, $L_1$ optimization can be interpreted as the maximum likelihood estimation with a Laplacian noise density function which has larger tails than the Gaussian function.

### 2.4  Outlier Selection with Feasibility Test

Both of the feasibility test algorithms shown above provide an estimate $\theta^*$ whether or not the constraints are found to be feasible. If the constraints are feasible, we can employ the outlier removal scheme shown in [14]. In other words, if the maximum residual $e_\infty$ is larger than a threshold predefined in some way, the support set defined in [14] is discarded and the feasibility test is repeated. Now, here is our question. What if we do not adopt the iterative *optimize-and-discard* strategy and simply run a feasibility test once with a constant (e.g., $\gamma := 3$ pixels) as a threshold for maximum residual?

If we are able to get an estimate $\theta^*$ and identify all the outliers by examining their residuals, we may simply run a feasibility test just once for removing outliers and greatly reduce computation time. The minimization of maximum infeasibility is a useful method that tests the feasibility using $s$ and finds the solution $\theta^*$ inside the intersection of convex constraints. However, it does not provide any clue about the feasibility of each of the constraints when the problem is infeasible due to outliers.

The SOI method, on the other hand, allows us to check the feasibility of individual measurement since its associated variable $s_i$ indicates the infeasibility. If the constraints are all feasible, the objective $\sum_i s_i$ is zero and there are no outliers. If not, the measurements with positive infeasibilities for a given threshold $\gamma$ are considered as outliers and removed. As noted earlier, the SOI method is $L_1$ minimization of the infeasibility variables. Indeed, it has a desirable property that we are looking for. Given a maximum threshold $\gamma$, the SOI method collects as many measurements as possible that satisfy the given constraints to make the objective function as small as possible.

In the following sections, we examine the performance of the SOI method as a global optimizer having the capability of outlier removal.

## 3  Camera Resectioning

We use synthetic data for examining the performance of the feasibility test algorithms: the minimization of maximum infeasibility and the SOI method. We also compare those

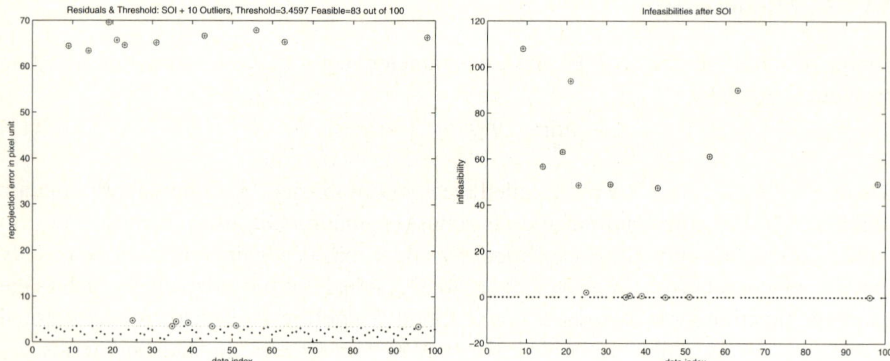

**Fig. 1. Left:** Residuals of the SOI method. Ten percent of the data set is outliers. Seventeen out of a hundred are classified to be outliers which are denoted by red circles. **Right:** Plot of the infeasibilities. True outliers are found to have very large infeasibilities. Green cross inside the red circle denotes a true outlier.

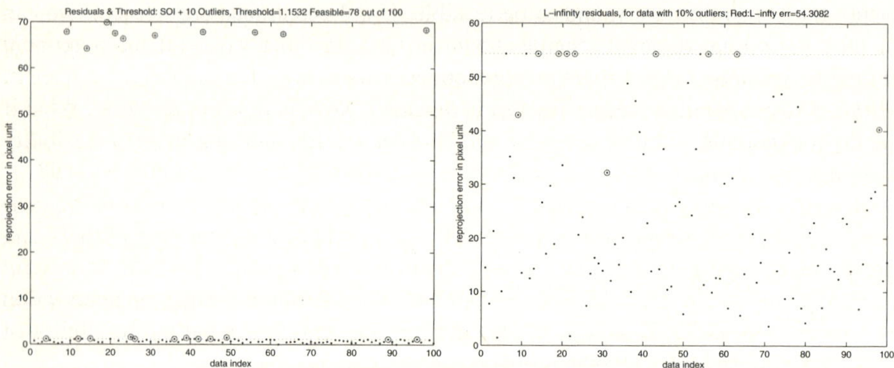

**Fig. 2. Left:** Residuals of the SOI method (10% outliers). Twenty two, denoted by red circles, out of a hundred are greater than the threshold. The separation of outliers and inliers are much more distinct compared to the result of the $L_\infty$ optimization shown below. **Right:** Residual plot of the $L_\infty$ optimization. The support set is composed of true outliers and inliers.

with the iterative outlier-removal algorithm by Sim and Hartley [14]. For the camera re-sectioning problem, 100 synthetic data are generated and corrupted with zero-mean Gaussian noise with standard deviation $\sigma = 0.5$ pixel. For outlier generation, we randomly select some measurements and corrupt it with uniform noise with the range of $\pm[5, 50]$ pixels. For testing our algorithms with this type of synthetic data, we may determine the maximum threshold ($\gamma$) based on the Gaussian noise distribution. It is our rule of thumb to have $\gamma$ three times the standard deviation of residuals. The threshold can also be set arbitrarily, e.g., 3 pixels as was done in [11]. For the experiments shown in this section, the $L_\infty$ optimization is carried out on the outlier-free data to find the maximum reprojection error $e_\infty$, and a multiple of $e_\infty$ is used for $\gamma$.

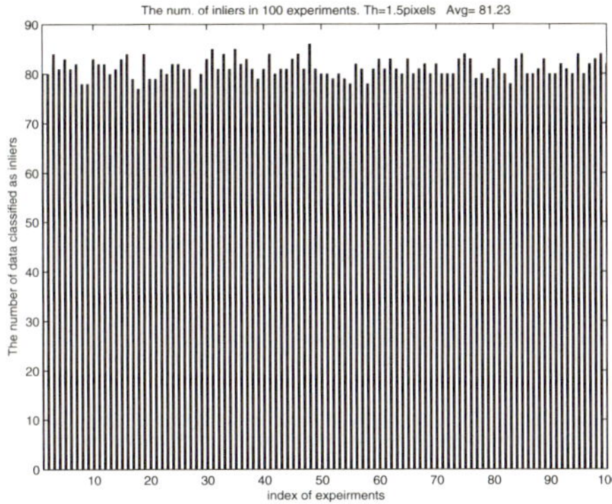

**Fig. 3.** The number of data points classified as inliers through 100 repeated computations of the SOI method

Figure 1 shows an experiment with the SOI method. The population of outliers is 10% of the data. The left plot shows the residuals and the right does the values of the infeasibility variables $s_i$s. The residuals above the threshold and the non-zero $s_i$s are enclosed with red circles, and the true outliers are marked with green cross. Most of the inliers have small residuals and very small values of $s_i$s ($\approx 10^{-12}$) while the data with large residuals or with substantially positive $s_i$s are true outliers. We note that the detected outliers always include the true outliers although the SOI method itself provides no explicit guarantee for such performance.

Figure 2 shows two plots, one from the SOI method and the other from the first iteration of the $L_\infty$ outlier removal method by Sim and Hartley [14]. The data set has 10% outliers (ten out of hundred). It can be easily seen that the separation of outliers and inliers are much more distinct with the SOI method. The SOI method finds twenty two outliers including the ten true outliers. The support set of the $L_\infty$ method has ten elements and seven of them are true outliers. Therefore, iterations are required to find all the outliers. As mentioned earlier, the maximum threshold can be determined arbitrarily and it does not have to rely on $e_\infty$. In this experiment, we set $\gamma$ to the same value as $e_\infty$ for the purpose of comparison with the $L_\infty$ method.

To show the statistical performance, we run the SOI algorithm a hundred times for 100 randomly generated measurements with Gaussian noise ($\sigma = 0.5$) and 10% outliers. The maximum threshold is fixed to $\gamma := 1.5$ pixels. Figure 3 shows the number of data points identified as inliers. On average, 81 inliers are collected. Since the number of true inliers are 90 of 100, approximately $100 \times 81/90 \approx 90\%$ of true inliers are retrieved. In all the 100 experiments, the true outliers are correctly classified. While the set of detected outliers contains some true inliers, the set of identified inliers never includes any true outliers in any experiment.

Finally we compare the computation times for the SOI method and the iterative $L_\infty$ outlier removal method by Sim and Hartley [14]. To examine the number of repetitions of the feasibility test, the iterative $L_\infty$ outlier removal method is applied to 100 synthetically generated data sets with Gaussian noise ($\sigma = 0.5$) and two outliers. Figure 4 shows the result. For the data set we used, the minimum number of repetitions is 22. The

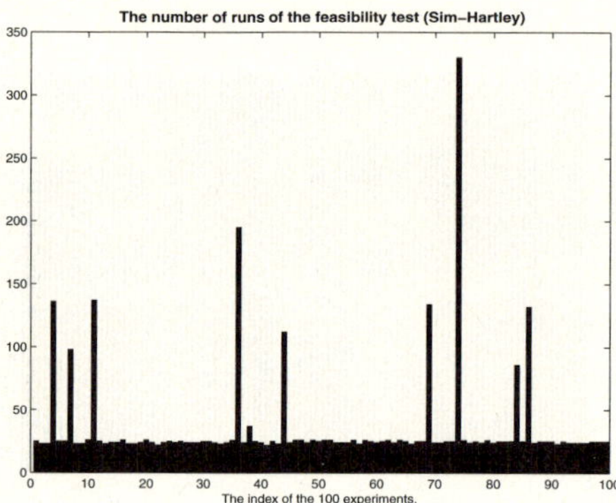


**Fig. 4.** Plotted is the number of runs of the feasibility test for 100 experiments with the method of Sim and Hartley [14]. The number of runs can be very large sometimes and cannot be expected.

bisection algorithm is run twice to have the maximum residual smaller than the threshold of 2 pixels, and the two outliers are eventually eliminated. The computation time for this case of minimum repetition is 2.6 sec and each feasibility test takes $2.6/22 \approx 0.12$ sec. In contrast, the SOI method needs only one feasibility test. It takes 0.25 sec on average and thus it is ten times $(10.1 \approx 2.6/0.25)$ faster than the iterative $L_\infty$ method. In the worst case, the iterative method has 330 repetitions of the feasibility test from 23 runs of the bisection algorithm. It takes 37.8 sec and the computation time is 133 times longer than that of the SOI method.

## 4   Motion and Structure with Known Rotation

### 4.1   Synthetic Data

Synthetic data are generated for three views and each view has one hundred points. The data are contaminated with zero-mean Gaussian noise with standard deviation of 0.5 pixels. The maximum residual $e_\infty$s are found to be in the range of $1.2 \sim 1.8$ pixels after the $L_\infty$ optimization is performed using Kahl's implementation [7]. For generating an outlier, a measurement is randomly selected and the error of $1000e_\infty$ is added to both of the image coordinates. The histogram in Figure 5(Left) shows a result of the SOI method with $\gamma := e_\infty$. To enhance the visibility of the histogram, the residuals $e_i$s are log-normalized by $\gamma$ and the histogram is plotted on $\log(e_i/\gamma)$. The origin (the zero point) in the $x$-axis is the threshold, and all the data located on the left side of the origin are true inliers.

For another experiment, a set of 1000 random data (100 measurements in 10 views) is generated and contaminated with the same Gaussian noise. Then 1% of the data (10 randomly selected data among 1000) are contaminated with random errors of uniform distribution in the range of $[6, 100]$ pixels. The maximum threshold for outliers is set to 2 pixels, i.e., $\gamma := 2$. Figure 5(Right) is the log-residual plot of the result of the SOI method. The detected outliers are 44 and they include all the true outliers. Most of the residuals are on the left side of the origin.

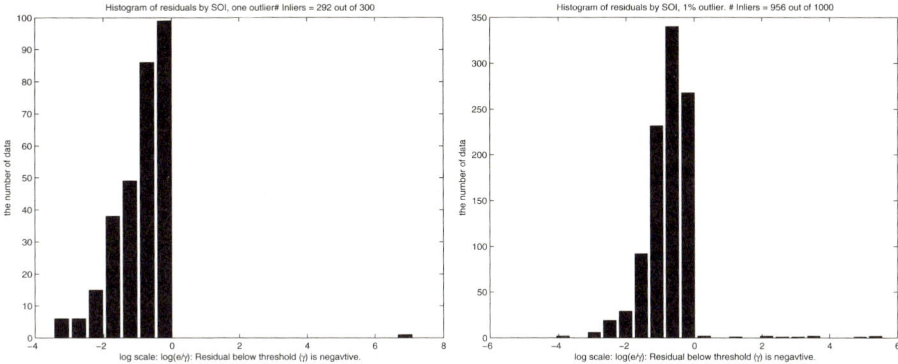

**Fig. 5. Left:** Histogram of the residuals of the SOI method applied to the data set of 299 inliers and one outlier (100 points in three views). The residuals are log-normalized by $\gamma$ and the histogram is plotted on $\log(e_i/\gamma)$. **Right:** Histogram of the residuals when the percentage of outliers are 10% (10 outliers among 1000 measurements in ten views).

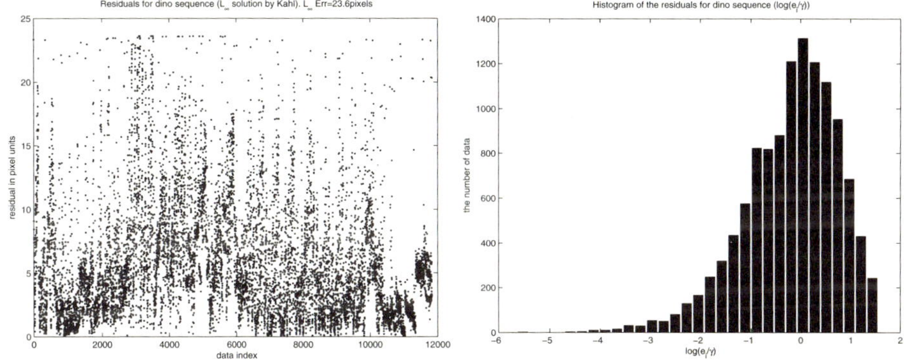

**Fig. 6. Left:** Residuals obtained by the $L_\infty$ optimization with the help of Kahl's program [2]. **Right:** Histogram of the residuals $\log(e_i/\gamma)$.

## 4.2  Real Data

For experiment with real data, we use the dinosaur sequence [1]. The data set provides point correspondences and camera matrices. The $L_\infty$ optimization and the SOI method are used to estimate the 3D structure and the translations of 36 cameras under the assumption of known rotation. The maximum threshold of the SOI method for inlier residuals is taken to be $\gamma := 5$ pixels.

Figure 6 shows the residuals and their histogram after the $L_\infty$ optimization is carried out. The $L_\infty$ error, i.e., the maximum error is 23.6 pixels. The histogram of the log-residuals, $\log(e_i/\gamma)$, is almost symmetrically distributed with respect to the threshold.

---

[1] `www.robots.ox.ac.uk/~vgg/`

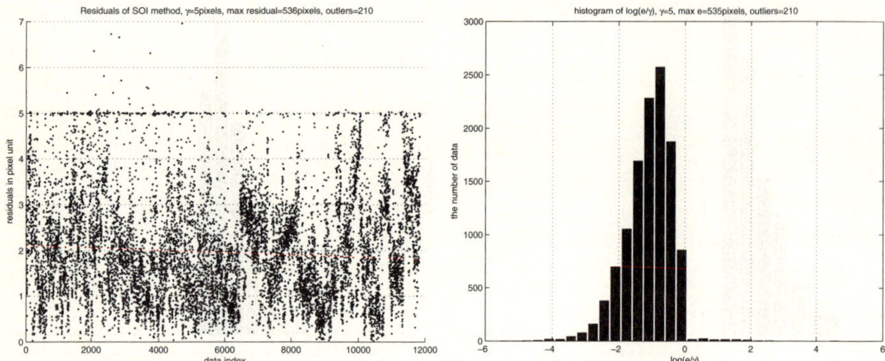

Fig. 7. Left: Residuals obtained by the SOI method ($\gamma := 5$pixels). Right: Histogram of the log-residuals $\log(e_i/\gamma)$.

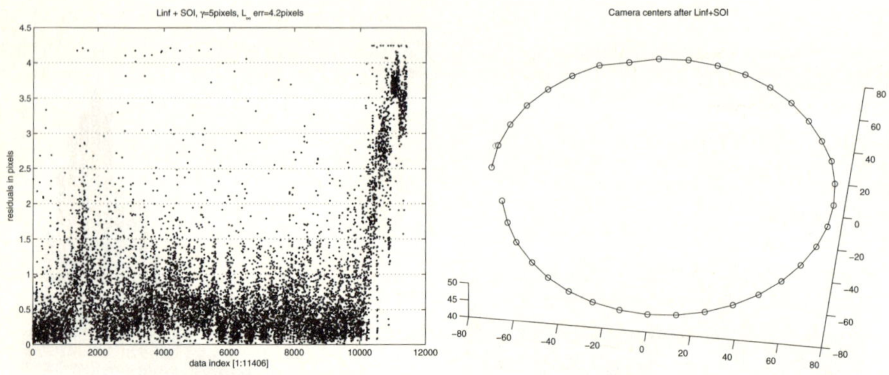

Fig. 8. Left: Residuals of the $L_\infty$ optimization which is preceded by the SOI method. Measurements having residuals larger than $\gamma := 5$ pielxes are all removed by the SOI method. Right: Plot of the camera centers obtained from the $L_\infty$ optimization.

If outliers are mainly responsible for the error, the iterative outlier removal method shown [14] can be used to improve the result.

Figure 7 shows the plot of residuals and the histogram of log-residuals after the SOI method is performed. The maximum residual is as large as 536 pixels, which is not shown in the plot that focuses on the low range of residuals. Notice that most of the residuals are located below the threshold. We remove 210 measurements among 11832 that have larger residuals than the maximum threshold $\gamma := 5$, and their corresponding points in other views. The number of measurements are reduced to 11406, $96.4\%$ of the total measurements. Figure 11 shows the result after the $L_\infty$ optimization is carried out on the inliers. The $L_\infty$ error is decreased to 4.2 pixels. The lower plot shows the 3D locations of the 36 camera centers. We also run the method of Sim and Hartley [14] until the maximum residual become less than the threshold $\gamma := 5$. Our implementation requires 16 iterations of the bisection algorithm to remove the outliers and one more bisection algorithm for the final optimization. It took 66283 seconds in total. Our SOI method and the final optimization took 6131 seconds. Thus, our approach is approximately ten times faster than the iterative $L_\infty$ method for the dino data set. Of course, there will be some ways that help the iterative method do better. The computation result will also be different from one data set to another. However, one cannot expect how long it will take with the iterative $L_\infty$ method. Contrarily, one execution of the SOI method guarantees that the residuals become less than the threshold.

## 5  Conclusion

This paper presented the method of minimizing the sum of infeasibilities (SOI) as a non-iterative outlier removal algorithm. We showed that the SOI method had a very interesting property of collecting inliers as many as possible whereas admitting outliers of large residuals. Therefore, we were able to preset the maximum admissible threshold for the feasibility test to sort out outliers. Experiments with synthetic and real data sets showed the performance of the SOI method. In particular, the experiment with the dinosaur sequence revealed that the algorithm was practically useful in discarding potential outliers and collecting inliers. From the result of this research, we propose that the SOI optimization should precede the $L_\infty$ optimization in order to remove any potential outliers in the data set.

## References


1. Hartley, R., Schaffalitzky, F.: $L_\infty$ minimization in geometric reconstruction problems. In: Proc. IEEE Conf. Computer Vision and Pattern Recognition (2004)
2. Kahl, F.: Multiple view geometry and the $L_\infty$-norm. In: Proc. Int. Conf. on Computer Vision, Beijing, China, pp. 1002–1009 (2005)
3. Ke, Q., Kanade, T.: Quasiconvex optimization for robust geometric reconstruction. In: Proc. Int. Conf. on Computer Vision, Beijing, China (2005)
4. Sim, K., Hartley, R.: Recovering camera motion using $L_\infty$ minimization. In: Proc. IEEE Conf. Computer Vision and Pattern Recognition (2006)
5. Aström, K., Enquist, O., Olsson, C., Kahl, F., Hartley, R.: An L-infinity approach to structure and motion problems for 1d-vision. In: IEEE International Conference on Computer Vision (2007)
6. Salzmann, M., Hartley, R., Fua, P.: Convex optimization for deformable surface 3-d tracking. In: IEEE International Conference on Computer Vision (2007)
7. Sim, K., Hartley, R.: Removing outliers using the $L_\infty$ norm. In: Proc. IEEE Conf. Computer Vision and Pattern Recognition (2006)
8. Li, H.: A practical algorithm for $L_\infty$ triangulation with outliers. In: IEEE Internatonal Conference on Computer Vision and Pattern Recognition (2007)
9. Olsson, C., Eriksson, A.P., Kahl, F.: Efficient optimization for $L_\infty$ problems using pseudo-convexity. In: IEEE International Conference on Computer Vision (2007)
10. Seo, Y., Hartley, R.I.: A fast method to minimize $L_\infty$ error norm for geometric vision problems. In: IEEE International Conference on Computer Vision (2007)
11. Fischler, M.A., Bolles, R.C.: Random sample consensus: A paradigm for model fitting with applications to image analysis and automated cartography. Comm. of the ACM, 381–395 (1981)

12. Sturm, J.: Using SeDuMi 1.02, a Matlab toolbox for optimization over symmetric cones. Optimization Methods and Software 11-12, 625–653 (1999)
13. Hartley, R., Kahl, F.: Global optimization through searching rotation space and optimal estimation of the essential matrix. In: IEEE International Conference on Computer Vision (2007)
14. Boyd, S., Vandenberghe, L.: Convex Optimization. Cambridge University Press, Cambridge (2004)
15. Press, W., Teukolsky, S., Vetterling, W., Flannery, B.: Numerical Recipes in C: The Art of Scientiic Computing. Cambridge University Press, Cambridge (1992)

# The Five Points Pose Problem: A New and Accurate Solution Adapted to Any Geometric Configuration


Mahzad Kalantari[1,2,3], Franck Jung[4], Jean-Pierre Guedon[2,3], and Nicolas Paparoditis[1]

[1] MATIS Laboratory, Institut Geographique National
2, Avenue Pasteur. 94165 Saint-Mandé Cedex, France
[2] Institut Recherche Communications Cybernétique de Nantes (IRCCyN)
UMR CNRS 6597 1, rue de la Noë BP 92101F-44321 Nantes Cedex 03, France
[3] Institut de Recherche sur les Sciences et Techniques de la Ville CNRS FR 2488
[4] DDE - Seine Maritime, France
{mahzad.kalantari,nicolas.paparoditis}@ign.fr,
Franck.Jung@equipement.gouv.fr,
jean-pierre.guedon@polytech.univ-nantes.fr



**Abstract.** The goal of this paper is to estimate directly the rotation and translation between two stereoscopic images with the help of five homologous points. The methodology presented does not mix the rotation and translation parameters, which is comparably an important advantage over the methods using the well-known essential matrix. This results in correct behavior and accuracy for situations otherwise known as quite unfavorable, such as planar scenes, or panoramic sets of images (with a null base length), while providing quite comparable results for more "standard" cases. The resolution of the algebraic polynomials resulting from the modeling of the coplanarity constraint is made with the help of powerful algebraic solver tools (the Gröbner bases and the Rational Univariate Representation).

**Keywords:** Five points pose problem, polynomial direct resolution, Gröbner bases, relative orientation.


## 1   Introduction

The determination of the relative orientation between two cameras with the help of homologous points is the basis of many applications in the domains of photogrammetry and computer vision. The configuration often called "minimal case problem" takes the intrinsic parameters (i. e. the elements of calibration) of the camera as a priori known. Then only five points homologous are necessary to estimate the remaining three unknowns of rotation and two ones of translation (up to a scale factor). This problem has been dealt by many authors, and most of recent methods published provide a resolution based on the properties of the essential matrix. Even if its use simplifies remarkably the problem


T. Wada, F. Huang, and S. Lin (Eds.): PSIVT 2009, LNCS 5414, pp. 215–226, 2009.

of the relative orientation, in some cases, due to the fact that all parameters of rotation and translation are mixed, this is the origin of geometric ambiguousnesses. So as to improve this point, we propose in this article a model that separates completely the rotation and the translation unknowns. We show that the major advantage of this model is that it allows to solve degenerate problems such as pure rotations (null translation). We use an algebraic modeling for the coplanarity constraint, through a system of polynomial equations. We solve them with the help of powerful algebraic solver tools, the Gröbner bases and the Rational Univariate Representation. So as to assess this new approach, three cases have been processed: a classical case, a planar scene, and a case where the base length is close to zero. We will see that the new method is still accurate even for the last two cases - quite unfavorable - configurations. We will also compare with the Stewenius's algorithm and see that in planar scenes the new algorithm is more accurate. An evaluation on real scenes will finally be presented.

## 2    Historical Background of the Five Points Relative Pose Problem

It was for the first time demonstrated by Kruppa [1] in 1913 that the direct resolution of the relative orientation from 5 points in general contained at most 11 solutions. The described method consisted to find all intersections of two curves of degree 6. Unfortunately, one century ago, this method could not lead to a numerical implementation. Lately in [2], [3], [4], [5] it has been demonstrated that the number of solutions is in general equal to 10, including the complex solutions. Triggs [6] has provided a detailed version for a numeric implementation. Philip [7] presented in 1996 a solution using a polynomial of degree 13, and has proposed a numeric method to solve his system. The roots of his polynomial give directly the relative orientation. Philip has exploited the constraints on essential matrix. Philip's ideas have been followed in 2004 by Nister [8] who has refined this algorithm, has obtained a $10^{th}$ order polynomial and has given a numerical resolution using a Gauss-Jordan elimination. Since then, number of papers tried to give some improvements to the method of Nister, notably Stewenius [9] that has provided a polynomial resolution using the Gröbner bases. Many papers have proposed some modifications to the method of Nister in view of a numeric improvement [12], [13], or for a simplification of implementation [10], [11].

## 3    Geometry Review of Relative Orientation

In this section we recall the various ways to present the geometry of relative orientation, that consist in the determination of the translation and the relative rotation between two images of a scene having a common informational part. In general, the position of the first camera is taken as the origin of the system $S_1$ (Fig. 1) and therefore the position of the second camera ($S_2$) is calculated in

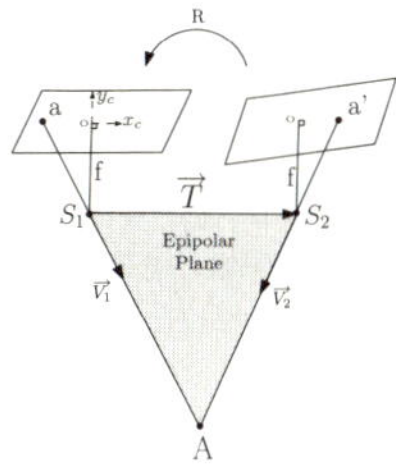


**Fig. 1.** Geometry of relative orientation

relationship to the first one. $O$ named as the principal point of the camera, $f$ is the focal length. $A$ is the world point, and the image projection of A on the left image is $a$ with coordinates $(x_a, y_a, f)^T$, and $a'$ $(x_{a'}, y_{a'}, f)^T$ in the right image. The vector of translation $\overrightarrow{T}$ $(T_x, T_y, T_z)$ is the basis that relies the optic centers of the cameras $(S_1$ and $S_2)$. $R$ is the relative rotation between the two cameras. A way for modelling the relative orientation is known as condition of coplanarity. This constraint has been often used by the community of computer vision since three decades. As pictured in the Fig. 1, the condition of coplanarity between two images expresses the fact that the vector $\overrightarrow{V_1}$, the vector $\overrightarrow{V_2}$(expressed in the reference of $\overrightarrow{V_1}$), and the vector of the translation $\overrightarrow{T}$ are in the same plane, called the epipolar plane. One can translate this condition by a null value for the triple product between these 3 vectors. In other words:

$$\overrightarrow{V_2} \cdot (R\overrightarrow{V_1} \wedge \overrightarrow{T}) = 0 \tag{1}$$

## 4 Algebraic Modelling of the Five-Points Problem

In this section, different ways for algebraic modelling of the relative orientation are recalled. The goal is to obtain a polynomial system, so as to use the powerful mathematical tools developed for solving such systems.

The coplanarity constraint (equation 1) under its algebraic shape is expressed by the equation:

$$\begin{bmatrix} x_{a'} & y_{a'} & f \end{bmatrix} \begin{bmatrix} 0 & T_z & -T_y \\ -T_z & 0 & T_x \\ T_y & -T_x & 0 \end{bmatrix} \begin{bmatrix} r_{11} & r_{12} & r_{13} \\ r_{21} & r_{22} & r_{23} \\ r_{31} & r_{32} & r_{33} \end{bmatrix} \begin{bmatrix} x_a \\ y_a \\ f \end{bmatrix} = 0. \tag{2}$$

In this equation the unknowns are the matrix of rotation $R$ and the translation $T$. Different ways exist to parameter the system so as to obtain polynomials with the rotation and the translation as unknowns. In the present part the main modelling solutions for the rotation and the translation to be used in this research are described.

218    M. Kalantari et al.

### 4.1 Modelling of the Translation

The translation of unity length between the two centres of the cameras may be understood as imaging on the unity sphere its center. The translation has only 2 degree of freedom, and for that reason, with the relative orientation, the scale cannot be determined. The equation of the unity sphere is the following:

$$T_x^2 + T_y^2 + T_z^2 = 1. \tag{3}$$

The advantage of this constraint of normality on the translation is that it is quite possible to work even with a very small translation, allowing to compute precisely the rotation when the translation is null. In this case, as the base $\overrightarrow{T}$ is null, the two homologous vectors $\overrightarrow{V_1}$ and $\overrightarrow{V_2}$ are deduced from each other by a rotation $R$, so that $R\overrightarrow{V_1} \wedge \overrightarrow{V_2} = \overrightarrow{0}$. Thus the triple product $\overrightarrow{T} \cdot (R\overrightarrow{V_1} \wedge \overrightarrow{V_2})$ is null whatever $\overrightarrow{T}$. The fact that we force the translation to be unity prevents that $\overrightarrow{T} = \overrightarrow{0}$ and therefore to suffer numeric instabilities. This implies in turn that the rotation will be correctly estimated in any case.

### 4.2 Modelling of the Rotation in 3D Space

The rotation matrix $(R)$ in the 3D space has 3 degree of freedom. It is thus possible to express it with 3 parameters. However several representations with more than 3 parameters exist. The algebraic model will depend on the chosen representation. In the following part the main models for the coplanarity constraint are described.

**Representation using Thompson rotation.** Another efficient way to represent the rotation with three parameters is given in Thompson's paper [14].

$$\frac{1}{\Delta} \begin{bmatrix} \Delta' & -\nu & \mu \\ \nu & \Delta' & -\lambda \\ -\mu & \lambda & \Delta' \end{bmatrix} + \frac{1}{2\Delta} \begin{bmatrix} \lambda \\ \mu \\ \nu \end{bmatrix} \begin{bmatrix} \lambda & \mu & \nu \end{bmatrix} \tag{4}$$

where $\Delta = 1 + \frac{1}{4}(\lambda^2 + \mu^2 + \nu^2)$ and $\Delta' = 1 - \frac{1}{4}(\lambda^2 + \mu^2 + \nu^2)$. With such a model the number of unknowns for the rotation also resumes to three. Other models of rotation matrix exist, such as the Cayley transfom, often used in robotics or quaternion representation.

### 4.3 Algebraic Modelling of the Coplanarity Constraint

While using the Thompson rotation matrix, the rotation is expressed with 3 parameters. The system will have 6 unknowns, considering the three parameters of translation. The polynomial expressing the coplanarity constraint for a couple of homologous points, taking for model the Thompson rotation, is the following:

$$(xa_i(-4T_z\nu - 2T_z\lambda\mu - 4T_y\mu + 2T_y\lambda\nu) + ya_i(4T_z + T_z\lambda^2 - T_z\mu^2 - T_z\nu^2 +$$
$$4T_x\mu - 2T_x\lambda\nu) + za_i(-4T_y - T_y\lambda^2 + T_y\mu^2 + T_y\nu^2 + 4T_x\nu + 2T_x\lambda\mu))xa'_i +$$
$$(xa_i(-4T_z + T_z\lambda^2 - T_z\mu^2 + T_z\nu^2 + 4T_y\lambda + 2T_y\mu\nu) + ya_i(-4T_z\nu + 2T_z\lambda\mu - 4T_x\lambda -$$
$$2T_x\mu\nu) + za_i(4T_y\nu - 2T_y\lambda\mu + 4T_x - T_x\lambda^2 + T_x\mu^2 - T_x\nu^2))ya'_i + (xa_i(4T_z\lambda - 2T_z\mu\nu$$
$$+ 4T_y - T_y\lambda^2 - T_y\mu^2 + T_y\nu^2) + ya_i(4T_z\mu + 2T_z\lambda\nu - 4T_x + T_x\lambda^2 + T_x\mu^2 - T_x\nu^2) +$$
$$za_i(-4T_y\mu - 2T_y\lambda\nu - 4T_x\lambda + 2T_x\mu\nu))za'_i = 0 \quad (5)$$

The constraint of normality on the translation (equation 3) is added to these 5 equations. So the system has 6 equations and 6 unknowns $[\lambda, \mu, \nu, T_x, T_y, T_z]$.

In conclusion of this section, we have built two polynomial systems, where the translation and rotation parameters are distinct and correspond to separated unknowns. Next, we show how to solve this type of polynomial systems.

## 5    Resolution of the Polynomial Systems

The ways to solve the polynomial systems are widely published [15], [16], and are briefly recalled for the reader not familiar with this topic. The resolution of a polynomial system consists in finding the zeros of an algebraic equation system such as : $P(x) = 0$ with $P = (p_1, p_2, .., p_n)$ where $p_i$ is a $l - variable$ polynomial $x = (x_1, x_2, ..., x_l)$ over the field $\mathbb{C}$ of complex numbers. Differents types of solvers for polynomial equations exist, such as analytic solvers, subdivision solvers, geometric solvers, homotopic solvers and algebraic solvers [17]. In this paper the focus is on algebraic solvers, that exploit the known relationships between the unknowns. They subdivide the problem of the resolution into two steps : the first consists in transforming the system into one or several equivalent systems, but better adapted, and this constitutes what one will call an algebraic solution. The second step consists, in the case where one works in one subfield of the complex field, to calculate the numeric values of the solutions from the algebraic solution. We will see now briefly the principal tools used in this paper for solving polynomial systems. But first, some remainders of geometric algebra are necessary.

### 5.1    Notations

$\mathbb{Q}[X_1, X_2, ..., X_n]$ is the polynomial rings with rational coefficients and unknowns $X_1, X_2, ..., X_n$. $S = P_1, P_2, ...P_s$ is any subset of $\mathbb{Q}[X_1, X_2, ..., X_n]$. A point $x \in \mathbb{C}^n$ is a zero of $S$ if $P_i(x) = 0 \ \forall i = 1, 2, ..., s$. The variety of $P$ is the set of all common complex zeros :

$$\mathcal{V}(P) = \{(a_1, ..., a_n) \in \mathbb{C}^n : p_i(a_1, ..., a_n) = 0 \ for \ all \ 1 \leq i \leq s\}. \quad (6)$$

The ideal $\mathcal{I}$ generated by a finite set of multivariate polynomials $< P_1, P_2, ..., P_s >$ is defined as:

$$\mathcal{I} = \{\sum_{i=1}^{n} h_i P_i | h_i \in \mathbb{Q}[X_1, X_2, ..., X_n]\}. \quad (7)$$

The ideal contains all polynomials which can be generated as an algebraic combination of its generators. An ideal can be generated by many different sets of generators, which all have the same solutions.

## 5.2   Construction of the Algebraic Solver: An Introduction to the Gröbner Bases

A Gröbner basis is a set of multivariate polynomials that has "nice" algorithmic properties. Every set of polynomials can be transformed into a Gröbner basis. This process generalizes three familiar techniques : the Gauss elimination for solving linear systems of equations, the Euclidean algorithm for computing the greatest common divisor of two univariate polynomials, and the Simplex Algorithm for linear programming. The Gröbner bases were developed initially by B. Buchberger in the years 1960 [18]. The first step, when we want to compute a Gröbner basis, is to define an *monomial order*. For polynomial rings with severable variables, there are many possible choices of monomial orders. The following terms and notation are present in the literature of Gröbner bases and will be useful later on. The degree of a polynomial $P$, denoted $DEG(f)$, is the highest degree of the terms in $P$. The leading term of $P$, denoted $LT(P)$, is the term with the highest degree. The leading coefficient of $P$ denoted $LC(P)$ is the coefficient of the leading term in $P$. Finally Gröbner bases can be defined:

**Definition 1.** *Fix a monomial order $>$ on $\mathbb{Q}\,[X_1, X_2, ..., X_n]$, and let $\mathcal{I} \subset \mathbb{Q}\,[X_1, X_2, ..., X_n]$ be an ideal. A Gröbner base for $\mathcal{I}$ (with respect to $>$) is a finite collection of polynomials $G = \{g_1, ..., g_t\} \subset \mathcal{I}$ with the property that for every nonzero $f \in \mathcal{I}$, $LT(f)$ can be divided by $LT(g_i)$ for some $i$.*

Two principal questions immediately arise from this definition:

1. the *existence* of Gröbner bases for any ideal $\mathcal{I}$.
   Hilbert's Basis Theorem says that : Every ideal $\mathcal{I}$ has a Gröbner basis $G$. Furthermore, $\mathcal{I} =< g_1, ..., g_t >$.
2. the issue of *uniqueness* of the Gröbner bases.
   The Buchberger theorem proves that if we fix a term order, then every nonzero ideal $\mathcal{I}$ has an unique *reduced* Gröbner basis with respect to this term order.

There are several possible algorithms to effectively compute Gröbner bases. The traditional one is Buchbergers algorithm, it has several variants and it is implemented in most general computer algebra systems like Maple, Mathematica, Singular [19], Macaulay2 [20], CoCoA [21] and the Salsa Software [22]. In this paper we use the Salsa Software with the F4 algorithm [23]. The Faugère F4 algorithm is based on the intensive use of linear algebra methods.

## 5.3   Application of Gröbner Bases for Systems Solving

Gröbner bases $(G)$ give important informations about the initial system of polynomial equations:

1. *Solvability of the polynomial system.* If $G = \{1\}$, the system has no solution. We check this on our two systems, and we find that: $G \neq \{1\}$. In other terms $\mathcal{V}$ is not empty.

2. *Finite solvability of polynomial equations.* It is easy to see whether the system has a finite number of complex solutions or not : we just check that for each $i$, $1 \leq i \leq n$, there is an $m_i \geq 0$ such that $x_i^{m_i} = LT(g)$ for some $g \in G$. This type of system is called *zero-dimensional system*. In this case, the set of solutions does not depend on the chosen algebraically closed field. If we apply this on two systems, we find that the dimension of the two systems is zero. So the set of solutions is finite.

3. *Counting number of finite solutions of the polynomial system.* One important information is that the Gröbner basis also gives the number of solutions of the system. If we suppose that the system of polynomial equations $P$ has a finite number of solutions, then the number of solutions is equal to the cardinality of the set of monomials that are not multiple of the leading terms of the polynomials in the Gröbner basis (any term ordering may be chosen). This monomials are called *basis monomials* or *standard monomials* ($B$).

Using the system of polynomial equations defined in Section 4.3, the standards bases of this system are the following (in the *DRL order*):

$$B = [1, T_z, T_y, T_x, \nu, \mu, \lambda, T_z^2, T_y T_z, T_y^2, T_x T_z, T_x T_y, \nu T_z, \nu T_y, \nu T_x, \nu^2, \mu T_z,$$

$$\mu T_y, \mu T_x, u\nu, \mu^2, \lambda T_z, \lambda T_y, \lambda T_x, \lambda \nu, \lambda \mu, \lambda^2, T_z^3, T_y T_z^2, T_y^2 T_z, T_x T_z^2,$$

$$T_x T_y T_z, \nu T_z^2, \nu T_y T_z, \nu^2 T_z, \mu T_z^2, \mu T_y T_z, \mu \nu T_z, \lambda T_z^2, \lambda \nu T_z] \quad (8)$$

Which makes a total of 40 bases and therefore 40 solutions. In the present paper the Salsa library has been used.


## 5.4   Finding the Real Roots of the Polynomial Systems

Once the Gröbner basis is calculated, different ways exist to find the roots of the system of polynomial equations, e.g. the method that solves the polynomial systems with the help of elimination and *lex* Gröbner basis. Another most popular way to solve polynomial systems is via eigenvalues and eigenvectors, with the help of *standard monomials* [15]. Here the emphasis is put on the other method, called the Rational Univariate Representation (abbreviated by RUR). Representing the roots of a system of polynomial equations in the RUR was first introduced by Leopold Kronecker [24], but started to be used in computer algebra only recently [25], [27]. The RUR is the simplest way for representing symbolically the roots of a zero-dimensional system without loosing information (multiplicities or real roots) since one can get all the information on the roots of the system by solving univariate polynomials. Let $P(X) = 0$ ($< P_1, P_2, ... P_s >$) where $P_i \in \mathbb{Q}[X_1, X_2, ..., X_n]$ be a zero-dimensional system with its solution set $\mathcal{V} = P^{-1}(0)$, Rational Univariate Representation of $\mathcal{V}$ consists in expressing all the coordinates as functions of the roots of a univariate polynomial such as :

$$f_0(T) = 0, \quad X_1 = \frac{f_1(T)}{q(T)}, X_2 = \frac{f_2(T)}{q(T)}, ...., X_n = \frac{f_n(T)}{q(T)} \quad (9)$$

where $f_0, f_1, f_2, ..., f_n, q \in \mathbb{Q}[T]$ ($T$ is a new variable). Computing a RUR reduces the resolution of a zero-dimensional system to solving one polynomial with one variable ($f_t$) and to evaluate $n$ rational fractions ($\frac{f_i(T)}{q(T)}, i = 1, ..., n$) as its roots. The goal is to compute all the real roots of the system (and only the real roots), providing a numerical approximation with an arbitrary precision (set by the user) of the coordinates. Many efficients algorithms have been implemented to calcultate RUR. More details are easily found in the literature, but a complete explication can be found in [26],[27]. An implementation of the Rouillier algorithm for RUR computation can be found in the SALSA software [22].

# 6    Algorithm Outlines

Now, the different steps of our algorithm for the calculation of the relative orientation are described.

*Step 1*: 5 couples of homologous points are randomly selected with the RANSAC method [28] [29] [30].
*Step 2*: Build the system of polynomial equations.
*Step 3*: Solve polynomials system. In the present paper the Salsa library has been used.
*Step 4*: Identify the solution with a physical sense. The ambiguity resolution may be done through the use of a third image [8], but we prefer to be able to work with only two images. It is important to find the "true" solution in this very large set, and it is necessary to inject information bound to the geometry of the scene. We proceed in this way:

- when intersecting the rays relative to all homologous couples of points, one keeps the solution where the rays cut themselves in front of the image,
- for the 5 randomly selected couples, we calculate the distance to the world points. We keep only the solutions that give a depth superior to the value of the normalised baseline, i. e. 1, the other ones being considered as unrealistic,
- the last step consists in selecting the solution which fits with the highest number of points. This hypothesis requires of course to have more than five points. Other methods exist to find the good solution among all those produced by the direct resolutions, but in general they consist in using a third image [8].

# 7    Results and Evaluation

Here we present the results of an experimentation on both synthetic and real data.

## 7.1    Experimentation on Synthetic Data

To quantify the performances of the presented method, synthetic data have been simulated. The parameters used for the simulations, are the same as Nister's ones. The images size is 352 x 288 pixels (CIF). The field of view is 45 degrees wide. The distance to the scene is equal to 1. Several cases have been treated :

1. Simple configuration : the baseline between the 2 images has a length of 0.3, the depth varies from 0 to 2.
2. Planar Structure and short baseline (0.1) : a degenerate case where all simulated points are on the plane $Z = 2$.
3. Zero translation : the configuration of the points is the same as in the simple configuration, the main difference is that the baseline length is null.

In each configuration a Gaussian noise with a standard deviation varying between 0 and 1 pixel is added. The results are average of 100 times independant experiments. For each situation the minimal case only has been treated, corresponding to the minimum number of points required (5). No least square adjustment has been done. The geometry of the different configurations is illustrated in the Fig. 2.

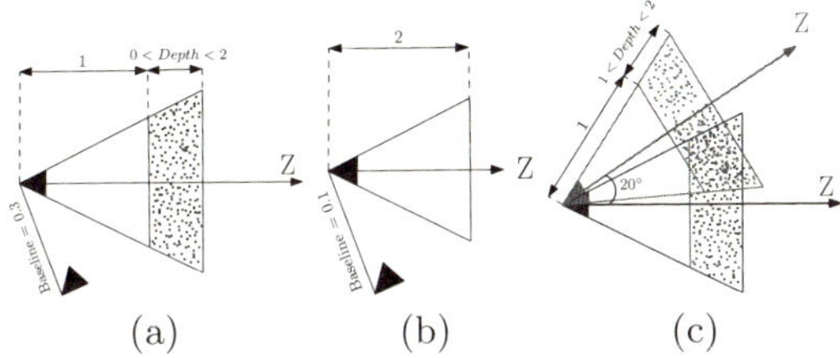


**Fig. 2.** (a) Easy condition (b) Planar Condition (c) Zero translational condition

**Results in the so-called easy configuration.** As a comparison our method has been confronted with Stewenius's one, thanks to the codes that he kindly made downloadable on his website [31]. This allowed us to use it as a reference for the algorithm of 5 points. Two sorts of translations have been treated, one in X (sideway motion) and one in Z (forward motion). Our results are mostly similar, even slightly better. Remark: In these simulations, it is important to specify that the rotation between the two optical axes is always very well determined. The difference between the different methods is the precision of evaluation on the orientation of the base, so this is the assessment that we have used.

**Planar Structure and short base.** Several surfaces are known as "dangerous" [32] the reason of this appellation is due to the fact that if the points chosen for the evaluation of the relative orientation are on this kind of surface, the configuration becomes degenerate. In the following, one of the most unfavorable configurations has been chosen. We note that the method of the 5 points of Stewenius is not robust in the sideways motion case. Besides, Sarkis [13] has shown this weakness of the algorithm, and concluded that it is better in such cases to use an homography. On the other hand, with the method presented here this kind of configuration does not lead to any problem.

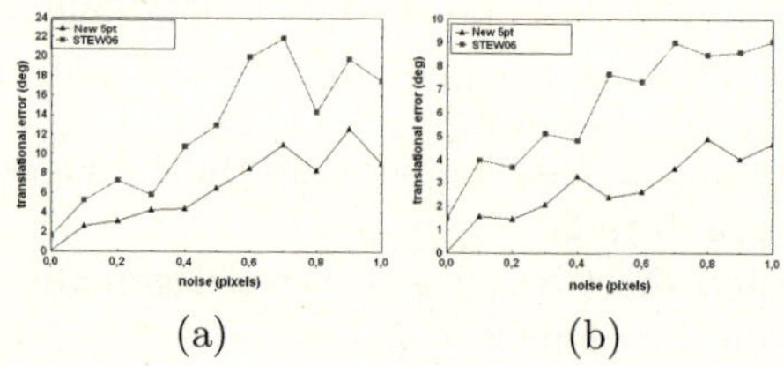

(a)                          (b)

**Fig. 3.** Error on the base orientation (in degree). Easy Case, a) sideway motion. b) forward motion.

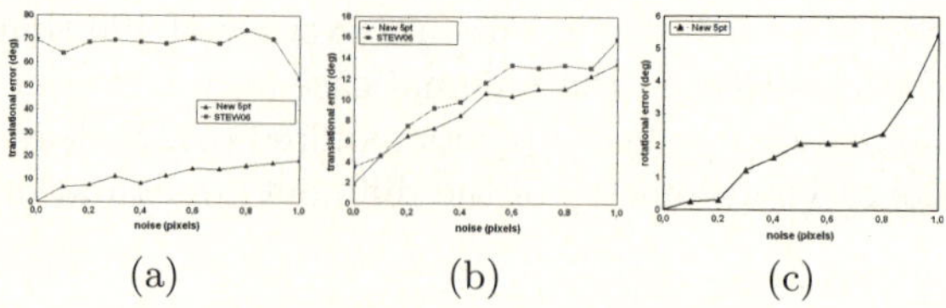

(a)                    (b)                    (c)

**Fig. 4.** a) Error on the base orientation (in degree), planar case, sideway motion b) idem, for a forward motion. c) Error on the relative orientation, non planar case, null base length.

**Results for a null base length.** Even with a null translation, the rotation is very well defined. This is probably due to the fact that the parameters to estimate in our initial equations are completely separated. The rotation is not mixed with the translation. This may explain why a translation of zero length does not affect the results. Fig. 4(c).

## 7.2   Tests on Real Images

So as to test the algorithm presented in section 6, we have used the recently available image base set up by ISPRS [33] for relative orientation tests. We have checked especially our ambiguity resolution so as to find the good physical solution. The mean error on the baseline orientation is equal to $5.25°$ and mean error on the rotation is $1.26°$.

## 8   Conclusion and Future Work

In this paper a new method for the problem of the "five points pose problem" has been described. The main difference with the previous methods is that the rotation and the translation are directly the unknowns of the system. The major advantage, when compared to other methods, is that it works accurately on all cases of plane scenes, or on couples of images with a null base. We work now so as to propose soon in a new paper the codes allowing for a real time process.

## Acknowledgement

We thank Amir Hashemi for his efficient assistance in the use of Salsa library during this work. The work reported in this paper has been performed as part of theCap Digital Business Cluster Terra Numerica project.

## References


1. Kruppa, E.: Zur ermittlung eines objektes aus zwei perspektiven mit innerer orientierung. Other, 1939–1948 (1913)
2. Demazure, M.: Sur deux problemes de reconstruction. Technical Report 882, INRIA (1988)
3. Faugeras, O.: Three-Dimensional Computer Vision: A Geometric Viewpoint. MIT Press, Cambridge (1993)
4. Faugeras, O.D., Maybank, S.: Motion from point matches: multiplicity of solutions. International Journal of Computer Vision 4, 225–246 (1990)
5. Heyden, A., Sparr, G.: Reconstruction from calibrated cameras-a new proof of the kruppa-demazure theorem. Journal of Mathematical Imaging and Vision 10, 123–142 (1999)
6. Triggs, B.: Routines for relative pose of two calibrated cameras from 5 points. Technical report, INRIA (2000)
7. Philip, J.: A non-iterative algorithm for determining all essential matrices corresponding to five point pairs. Photogrammetric Record 15, 589–599 (1996)
8. Nistér, D.: An efficient solution to the five-point relative pose problem. IEEE Transactions on Pattern Analysis and Machine Intelligence 26, 756–777 (2004)
9. Stewénius, H., Engels, C., Nistér, D.: Recent developments on direct relative orientation. ISPRS Journal of Photogrammetry and Remote Sensing 60, 284–294 (2006)
10. Li, H., Hartley, R.: Five-point motion estimation made easy, I: 630–I: 633 (2006)
11. Sarkis, M., Diepold, K., Hüper, K.: A fast and robust solution to the five-point relative pose problem using gauss-newton optimization on a manifold. In: IEEE International Conference on Accoustics, Speech and Signal Processing (ICASSP) (2007)
12. Batra, D., Nabbe, B., Hebert, M.: An alternative formulation for five point relative pose problem, p. 21 (2007)
13. Segvic, M., Schweighofer, G., Pinz, A.: Performance evaluation of the five-point relative pose with emphasis on planar scenes. In: Performance Evaluation for Computer Vision, Austria, Workshop of the Austrian Association for Pattern Recognition, pp. 33–40 (2007)
14. Thompson, E.H.: A rational algebraic formulation of the problem of relative orientation, photogrammetric record. Photogrammetric Record 3, 152–159 (1959)
15. Cox, D., Little, J., O'Shea, D.: Using Algebraic Geometry, 2nd edn. Graduate texts in mathematics. Springer-, Heidelberg (2004)
16. Cox, D., Little, J., O'Shea, D.: Ideals, varieties, and algorithms an introduction to computational algebraic geometry and commutative algebra, 3rd edn. Undergraduate texts in mathematics. Springer, New York (2007)
17. Elkadi, M., Mourrain, B.: Introduction à la résolution des systèmes polynomiaux. Mathématiques et Applications, vol. 57. Springer, Heidelberg (2007)

18. Buchberger, B.: Groebner-Bases: An Algorithmic Method in Polynomial Ideal Theory. In: Bose, N. (ed.) Multidimensional Systems Theory - Progress, Directions and Open Problems in Multidimensional Systems, pp. 184–232. Reidel Publishing Company, Dordrecht (1985)
19. Greuel, G.M., Pfister, G., Schönemann, H.: Singular 3.0. A Computer Algebra System for Polynomial Computations, Centre for Computer Algebra, University of Kaiserslautern (2005), http://www.singular.uni-kl.de
20. Grayson, D.R., Stillman, M.E.: Macaulay 2, a software system for research in algebraic geometry, http://www.math.uiuc.edu/Macaulay2/
21. CoCoATeam: CoCoA: a system for doing Computations in Commutative Algebra, http://cocoa.dima.unige.it
22. SALSA: Solvers for algebraic systems and applications, http://www.inria.fr/recherche/equipes/salsa.en.html
23. Faugère, J.C.: A new efficient algorithm for computing gröbner bases $(f_4)$. Journal of Pure and Applied Algebra 139, 61–88 (1999)
24. Kronecker, L.: Werke. Teubner, Leipzig (1895-1931)
25. Gonzalez-Vega, L.: Implicitization of parametric curves and surfaces by using multidimensional newton formulae. Journal of Symbolic Computation 23, 137–152 (1997)
26. Ouchi, K., Keyser, J., Rojas, J.M.: The exact rational univariate representation and its application. Technical Report 2003-11-1, Department of Computer Science, 3112 Texas A&M University, College Station, TX,77843-3112 (2003)
27. Rouillier, F.: Solving zero-dimensional systems through the rational univariate representation. Journal of Applicable Algebra in Engineering, Communication and Computing 9, 433–461 (1999)
28. Fischler, M., Bolles, R.: Random sample consensus: A paradigm for model fitting with applications to image analysis and automated cartography. Comm. of the ACM 24, 381–395 (1981)
29. Hartley, R.I., Zisserman, A.: Multiple View Geometry in Computer Vision, 2nd edn. Cambridge University Press, Cambridge (2004)
30. Ma, Y., Soatto, S., Kosecka, J., Sastry, S.: An invitation to 3D vision, from images to models. Springer, Heidelberg (2003)
31. Stewenius, H.: Matlab code for the for solving the fivepoint problem, http://vis.uky.edu/~stewe/FIVEPOINT/
32. Philip, J.: Critical point configurations of the 5-, 6-, 7-, and 8-point algorithms for relative orientations. Technical report, TRITA-MAT, KTH,Sweden (1998)
33. Camillo, H.: Test data sets for automatic image orientation (2007), http://www.ipf.tuwien.ac.at/car/isprs/test-data/

# Vehicle Detection from Aerial Images Using Local Shape Information


Jae-Young Choi and Young-Kyu Yang[*]

College of IT, Kyungwon University,
Seongnam, Gyeonggi, 461-701, Republic of Korea
{jychoi,ykyang}@kyungwon.ac.kr



**Abstract.** Detection and extraction of vehicle objects in high resolution satellite imagery are required in many transportation applications. This paper presents an approach to automatic vehicle detection from aerial images. The initial extraction of candidate vehicle is based on Mean-shift algorithm with symmetric character of blob-like car structure. By fusing the density and the symmetry, the method can remove the ambiguous blobs and reduce the cost of the detected ROI processing in the subsequent stage. To verify the blob as a vehicle, log-polar shape descriptor is used for measuring similarity. The edge strengths are obtained and represented as its spatial histogram by the orientation and distance from the center of blob. The proposed algorithm is able to successfully detect the vehicle and very useful for the traffic surveillance system.

**Keywords:** Vehicle detection, Aerial imagery, Traffic monitoring, Mean shift, Shape description, symmetry.


## 1   Introduction

In recent years, analysis of the aerial or satellite imagery play an important role as improving in the performance of equipment and growing the application fields. However, there is not much review on vehicle detection using aerial image. All of them are categorized into a variety of aspects such types of sensors, target vehicle types or types of measurements etc [1].

This paper deals with automatic detection of vehicle in high resolution aerial imagery of approximately 0.25 meter resolution. Mean-shift clustering algorithm extracts the candidate blob with symmetric property of car shape. By using both geometric and radiometric characteristics, the ambiguous blobs are eliminated and the cost of detected ROI processing is reduced in the subsequent step. To verify the blob in the next step, log-polar shape descriptor is used for measuring similarity. The edge strengths are obtained and represented as its spatial histogram by the orientation and distance from the center of blob. The phase symmetry information from above stage helps to compensate the orientation of the shape context. In our last algorithm, the candidate blobs are merged in case that the blobs are extracted from same vehicle.

---


[*] Corresponding author.



T. Wada, F. Huang, and S. Lin (Eds.): PSIVT 2009, LNCS 5414, pp. 227–236, 2009.

The remainder of this paper is organized as follows. We first introduce related work on vehicle detection in Section 2. Section 3 describes the proposed vehicle detection approach. In this section, we present the blob clustering method, measuring phase symmetry of blob, and shape description of detected blob as well as overview of proposed algorithm. Section 4 shows the experiment result and Section 5 contains conclusion.

## 2   Related Works

Detection and segmentation are arguably the most important operations in low-level image processing. Especially, Interesting of the vehicle detection has been increased in the computer vision area because this item is such a significant part of our life.

Several authors suggested the use of feature vectors from image region. Lowe's SIFT algorithm is a popular algorithm for extracting the salient features from object [2]. Invariant features are robust to image scale, rotation, and partially invariant to changing viewpoints, and change in illumination [3]. However, if the object or region is too small to detect, it cannot be known a priori if it will be represented by any key point.

A variety of boosting algorithms have been developed for detecting object by machine learning [4]. After remarkable success of the face detector, boosting method has been widely used for solving recognition problems. The main task of this work is to train a classifier. Therefore, the method depends on the selection and learning of exemplar such as car model or features instead of pixel values. In addition to training, it exhaustively scans the whole image to find the exact object. Some efforts use statistical learning to resolve the variance of appearance, but the complex relationship of the different appearance is difficult to learn.

Neural network or Support Vector Machine algorithm is applied to detect the vehicle from low-resolution image [5]. In this work, they only address detection of cars aligned with road direction. This approach may be sufficient for their data. Generalized Hough Transform is used for extract road side. A certain rectangular band width is examined in search position where GHT response is high. The number of edge pixels inside the search band is taken to be the likelihood of the presence of a vehicle in that area. They use the mask which consists of four elongated operators with first-derivative of Gaussian cross sections in recent work [6,7].

Model based approach is introduced in [8]. The method uses an explicit model that consists mainly of geometric features and radiometric properties. The vehicle is modeled as 3D object by a wire frame representation. They also use vehicle queue model to find stands on a road. In this case, detection relies on matching the model. If there is sufficient support of the model in the image, a vehicle is assumed to be detected.

Above approaches have their advantages and disadvantages. Most of the previous work regards a vehicle as a 2D pattern. Vehicle detection in aerial images is relatively constrained by the resolution. Therefore, we need a variety of information of vehicle in order to extract outstanding characteristics.

## 3   Vehicle Detection Approach

This section describes a proposed approach to detect vehicles. With respect to the detection of a vehicle, we can consider following conditions;

– Vehicle is aligned with road which sides run parallel each other
– Car has symmetric structure as geometric aspect
– Size of car is approximately constant length
– Road surface is almost biggest and homogenous pavement (in case of urban)

To detect a vehicle model, there are two techniques: "top-down" and "bottom-up". The surface of a vehicle is made of pixels. But the vehicles form also very frequently lines themselves settled in meta-lines [9].

Proposed method is intended to use "bottom-up" way that we measure the pixels in an input image, and cluster the pixels which consist of car-structure as a geometric aspect and have a similar value of car as a radiometric point of view. After that, we verify the shape of vehicle using the shape description as shown in Fig. 1.

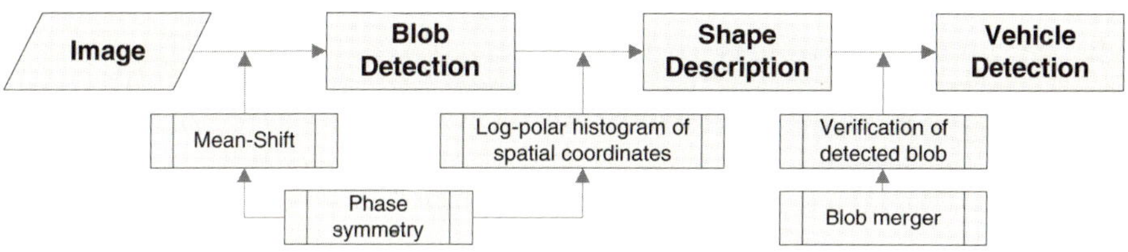


**Fig. 1.** Flow chart of the suggested algorithm

### 3.1   Detection and Clustering of Blob

The mean shift clustering algorithm first applied to image segmentation by Comaniciu and Meer in 1997, whereas the original idea was proposed in 1975 by Fukunaga and Hostetler [10].

This algorithm is designed to find modes, centers of the regions of high concentration, of data represented as arbitrary dimensional vectors. The major steps in the computation of the algorithm as follows [11].

1. Choose the radius r of the search window.
2. Choose the initial location of the window.
3. Compute the mean shift vector and translate the search window by that amount.
4. Repeat till convergence.

The mean shift vector is described in (1).

If $y_j$ is instead of $x$, and $\{y_j\}_{j=1,2,..}$ denotes the sequence of successive locations of the kernel $G(x)$, the equation can be the weighted mean at $y_j$.

$$m(x) = \left[\sum_{i=1}^{n} x_i g\left(\frac{\|x - x_i\|^2}{h}\right)\right] / \left[\sum_{i=1}^{n} g\left(\frac{\|x - x_i\|^2}{h}\right)\right] - x \qquad (1)$$

In case of the color image clustering like our application, the RGB color image is mapped into the $L^*u^*v^*$ color space model. The mean shift method clusters this multi-dimensional data set by associating each point to a peak of the data set's probability density. One of the drawbacks in using mean shift algorithm is choice of the fixed bandwidth. That is, once the kernel bandwidth decided by the size of window, it is invariable in the entire tracking process. Recent method modified the bandwidth in $\pm 10\%$ intervals, the tracks object separately using three different kernel bandwidths in the current frame.

In our approach, we use geometric (symmetry of car shape) property as well as radiometric (intensity of pixel level) characteristics. During the probability density function estimates a density in color space, each point which is peak of data set is examined as local maximum of phase symmetry. The measurement of phase symmetry will be introduced in next section in detail.

The advantage of using above fusion method is that it is able to eliminate the ambiguous blobs. As a result of this, the cost of next step is also reduced because it does not need to check whole detected blobs in order to verify the vehicle.

## 3.2   Symmetric Property of Blob

Symmetry is an important property we identify the structure of objects. In this work, the Wavelet Transform is used to obtain local frequency information. Because we are interested in phase information in signals, the method uses wavelets based on complex valued Gabor functions to modulate sine and cosine waves by Gaussian [12]. Let $I$ denote the signal and $M_n^e$ and $M_n^o$ denote the even-symmetric (cosine) and odd-symmetric (sine) wavelets at a scale $n$, then the responses of each quadrature pair of filters as in (2).

$$[e_n(x), o_n(x)] = [I(x) * M_n^e, I(x) * M_n^o] \tag{2}$$

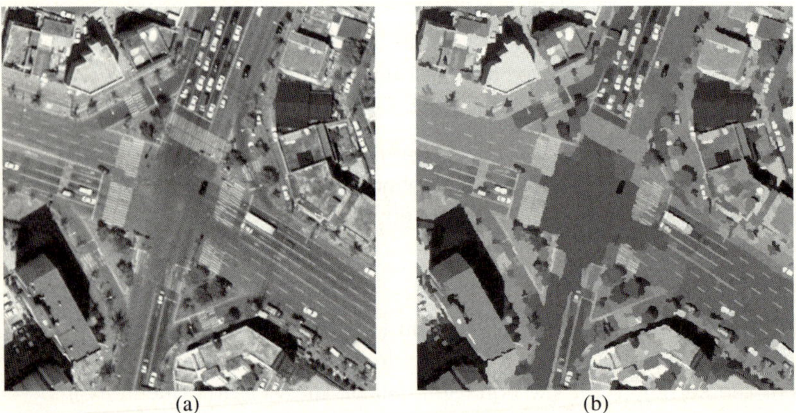

(a)     (b)

**Fig. 2.** Mean-shift clustering. (a) Input aerial image, (b) Clustering of blob using Mean-shift algorithm.

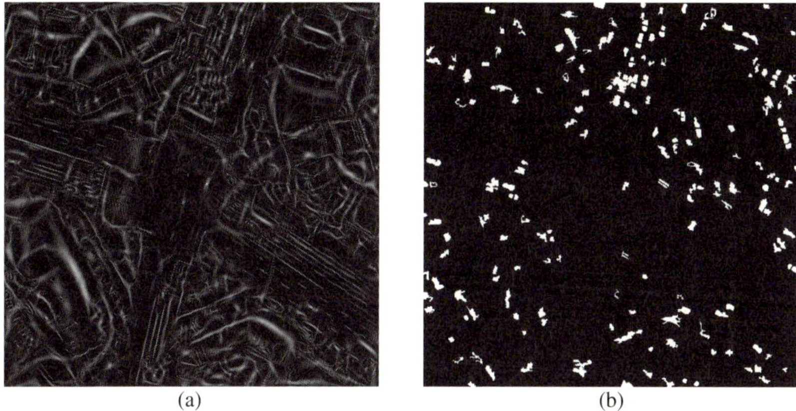

(a)                                              (b)

**Fig. 3.** Results using symmetric property. (a) Phase symmetry output of Fig. 2(a), (b) Blob detection using symmetry information with Mean-shift density.

At each point $x$ in a signal, the response vector for each scale of filter will be obtained. For example, at a point of symmetry, the absolute value of the even-symmetric filter output will be large and another output will be small. This produces a function that varies between $\pm 1$ and varies linearly with phase deviation. In case of multiple scales, the difference of the values of the even and odd filter responses at each scale is weighted by the magnitude of the filter response vector at each scale $n$. This equation is shown in (3). The amplitude of the transform at a given wavelet scale is $A_n(x) = \sqrt{e_n(x)^2 + o_n(x)^2}$ and the phase is $\phi_n(x) = atan2(e_n(x), o_n(x))$.

$$
\begin{aligned}
Sym(x) &= \frac{\sum_n \lfloor A_n(x)[|cos(\phi_n(x))| - |sin(\phi_n(x))|] - T \rfloor}{\sum_n A_n(x) + \varepsilon} \\
&= \frac{\sum_n \lfloor [|e_n(x)| - |o_n(x)|] - T \rfloor}{\sum_n A_n(x) + \varepsilon}
\end{aligned}
\tag{3}
$$

The factor $T$ is a noise compensation term representing the maximum response generated from noise in signal. This 1D equation can extend to 2D by applying the 1D analysis in multiple orientations and forming a weighted sum of the result. This can be used as a line and blob detector. Phase symmetry is an illumination and contrast invariant measure of symmetry in an image.

Fig. 3(a) illustrates phase symmetry measure from the Fig. 2(a). As geometric property of vehicles, there is a bilateral symmetry even though a vehicle has its shadow. Therefore, we calculate the phase symmetry value and apply it to the mean shift process to detect blob which has car-like structure as shown in Fig. 3(b).

### 3.3  Shape Description

In order to verify the detected blob as vehicle, we treat a blob as a point set and assume that the shape of an object is represented by discrete pixel set

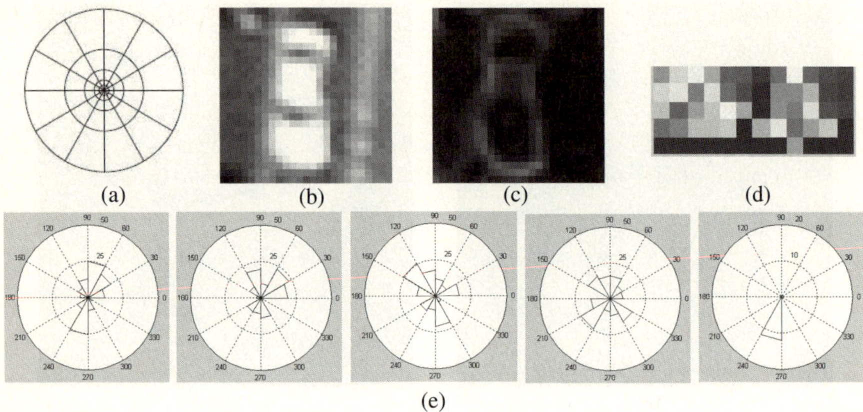

**Fig. 4.** Shape description. (a) Diagram of log-polar histogram, (b) Input region for shape description, (c) Edge image, (d) Shape context represented 5×12 bins, (e) The value of the each shape context bin (from left to right of (e) corresponds to from top row to the bottom row of (d), respectively).

which has the information such as geometric relationship between pixels and the different value among its adjacency pixels. A conventional approach of matching between a given model and target object is an exhaustive search on whole region or histograms for every possible points. In case the search should be done at different orientations, the whole process should be repeated as many times as the number of directions.

In this section, we propose the shape description that is flexible in rotation of object. As mentioned in the beginning of Section 3, the size of a vehicle is approximately constant length and the shape of one is almost uniform. Therefore we can estimate the geometric shape of vehicle by measuring the distance and orientation between the center of blob and its surrounding edges.

Consider an edge of image $I(x, y)$ with a blob and its neighborhood (the size of search mask is 25×25 and the center of mask is a centroid of blob in this experiment), the orientation $\theta$ is defined by $\theta(x, y) = arctan\lfloor d_y(x, y)/d_x(x, y)\rfloor$ where $d_x, d_y$ are the distance from the center of blob. Distance $r$ is also obtained by $r = \sqrt{d_x^2 + d_y^2}$.

We use a log-polar coordinate system which has 5 bins for log $r$ and 12 bins for $\theta$ because the descriptor should be more sensitive to differences in nearby pixels in Cartesian spaces [13]. Fig. 4(a) depicts the diagram of log-polar histogram bins. Each bins of log-polar diagram is represented as a 5×12 array as shown in Fig. 4(b). For normalizing the histogram $H$, each accumulated bin $H(i)$ is divided by the number of detected pixel in each sector.

The direction of blob can be estimated from the phase symmetry information treated in previous section. These directions of interest (DOI) will be used for compensating the orientation of the shape context. In our approach, we rotate the inspect region which contains a blob and its neighborhood by the value of compensated orientation. That is, after the direction of symmetry axis of the inspect region is obtained, its shape context bin is shifted from direction of symmetry to the vertical axis by the difference of orientation.

Reference bins are made by strength of grey level difference along the boundary of general vehicle, assuming that it is approximately a rectangle and ladder. A compensated shape context bins have same direction with reference one, and are matched histogram similarity by Euclidean distance.

## 3.4  Post Processing

As can be seen from Fig. 4(b), the separate detected blob from same vehicle is due to the front and rear windshield of car. For example, in case of a bright car we expect a strong gray value edge since a windshield in usually very dark, while in case of a dark car the gray value edge may disappear completely.

Therefore, the proposed algorithm merges the blobs which are located around and have color constancy between hood(trunk) color and roof color as a radiometric feature.

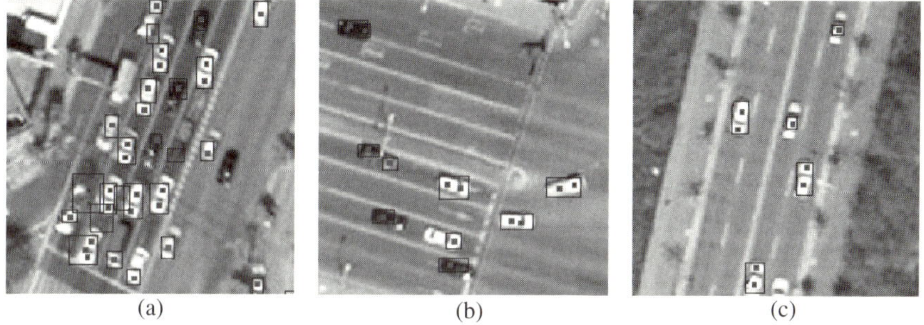

(a)     (b)     (c)

**Fig. 5.** Examples of blob merge (the red dot is a centroid of blob and the blue rectangle is a merged blobs)

Fig. 5 depicts the result of blob merge. The red dot indicates the center of initial blob and the blue rectangle expresses the integration of blobs. Some vehicles such as a truck have a different color of cargo. For this reason, same vehicle is counted as two objects as shown in the center image of Fig. 5.

## 4  Experimental Results

The implemented method is intended to detect vehicles on the aerial images of 0.25 meter resolution and performed on Matlab 7.0 platform. The detector is evaluated on 512×512 sub-images from the whole aerial image. In the test image, a typical vehicle (medium sedan) is around 15 to 25 pixels in length and around 10 to 12 pixels in width.

Some of results show that almost vehicles have been detected by a red rectangle(see Fig. 6). The evaluation does not refer to real ground truth. We marked

 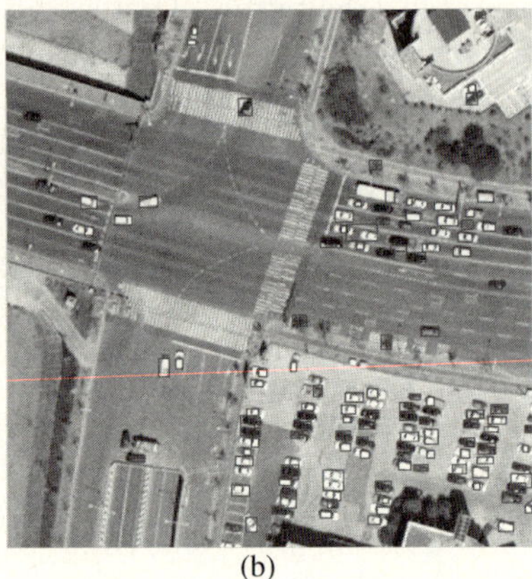

(a)                                    (b)

**Fig. 6.** Results of vehicle detection

**Table 1.** Evaluation of test images

| Evaluation criteria | Left image | Right image |
| --- | --- | --- |
| Number of detection | 63 | 129 |
| False alarms | 5 | 11 |
| False negative alarms | 12 | 16 |
| Detection rate (%) | 84.0 | 88.9 |
| Accuracy rate (%) | 92.1 | 91.5 |

all cars in each sub-images by hand. In both images, the suggested method detected 176 correct vehicles and missed 28 vehicles, hence the detection rate is 87.3% and false alarm rate is 7.8%. There is always a tradeoff between false alarm rate and mis-detection rate. The more detailed descriptions are used, the more number of features and conditions are needed to cover all types of vehicles. Table 1 summarizes the numerical evaluation of the both images in Fig. 6.

In Fig. 6, false negative alarm (missing detection) occurs in regions where the road or parking lot is darkened by building or tree shadows. Large vehicles are also missing because our method focused on the typical vehicles and examined around $25{\times}25$ pixels neighborhood.

In addition to above environment in input image, the detection rate is relative to the setting of parameters during mean-shift algorithm processing. Oversegments cause false negative alarms because the different part of vehicle such as hood, roof, trunk, windshield ,and shadow is not merged. For these reasons, a small blob is eliminated as a noise or an isolated blob. For addressing these problems, the suggested method has to be extended by considering the global information in order not to damage a component of a vehicle structure.

However, the proposed method detects vehicle with higher accuracy rate although there exist many objects in urban scenes with a similar appearance.

## 5  Conclusion

Object detection become challenging due to time-consuming manual detection. We are developing a novel approach for detection of vehicle from aerial image.

In order to extract initial candidate vehicle, Mean-shift clustering algorithm is used for detecting the dense and symmetric blob. Fusing geometric and radiometric characteristics helps to reject ambiguous blobs and save the cost of ROI processing in the subsequent step. To verify the detected blob, we apply the log-polar shape descriptor to measure similarity. It is able to avoid the sensitivity of differences in nearby pixels.

From the phase symmetry information, DOI can be used for compensating the orientation of the shape context to match with reference vehicle. Since the vehicles are represented by a few pixels, their detection is very sensitive to the surrounding context. In post processing step, the candidate blobs are merged in case that the blobs are extracted from same vehicle. Our work will be continued by refining the process and making the robust and flexible shape context bin to verify a variety of vehicles.

We believe that similar approaches can also be useful for other object detection as well as transportation application.

## Acknowledgements

The work presented in this paper was supported by the Ministry of Education, Science and Technology through the Second Stage of BK21(Brain Korea 21).

## References


1. Punvatavungkour, S., Shibasaki, R.: Three Line Scaner Imagery and On-street Packed Vehicle Detection. Int'l Archives of Photogrammetry Remote Sensing and Spatial Information Sciences 35(3), 355–359 (2004)
2. Lowe, D.G.: Distinctive Image Features from Scale-Invariant Keypoints. Int'l J. Computer Vision 60(2), 91–110 (2004)
3. Bay, H., Tuytelaars, T., Van Gool, L.: SURF: Speeded up robust features. In: Leonardis, A., Bischof, H., Pinz, A. (eds.) ECCV 2006. LNCS, vol. 3951, pp. 404–417. Springer, Heidelberg (2006)
4. Viola, P., Jones, M.: Rapid Object Detection using a Boosted Cascade of Simple Features. In: Proc. IEEE Conf. Computer Vision and Pattern Recognition, pp. 511–518 (2001)
5. Zhao, T., Nevatia, R.: Car Detection in Low Resolution Aerial Images. Image and Vision Computing 21, 693–703 (2003)
6. Chellappa, R., Burlina, P., Davis, L.S., Rosenfeld, A.: SAR/EO Vehicular Activity Analysis System Guided by Temporal and Contextual Information. In: Proc. 1994 ARPA Image Understanding Workshop, pp. 615–620 (1998)
7. Moon, H., Chellappa, R., Rosenfeld, A.: Performance Analysis of a Simple Vehicle Detection Algorithm. Image and Vision Computing 20(1), 1–13 (2002)
8. Hinz, S.: Integrating Local and Global Features for Vehicle Detection in High Resolution Aerial Imagery. Photogrammetry Remote Sensing Spatial Information 34(3W/8), 119–124 (2003)

9. Ruskone, R., Guigues, L., Airault, S., Jamet, O.: Vehicle Detection on Aerial Images: A Structural Approach. In: Proc. Int'l Conf. Pattern Recognition, pp. 900–904 (1996)
10. Fukunaga, K., Hostetler, L.D.: The Estimation of the Gradient of a Density Function with Applications in Pattern Recognition. IEEE Trans. Information Theory 21(1), 32–40 (1975)
11. Comaniciu, D., Meer, P.: Robust Analysis of Feature Spaces: Color image Segmentation. In: IEEE Conf. Computer Vision and Pattern Recognition, pp. 750–755 (1997)
12. Kovesi, P.: Symmetry and Asymmetry from Local Phase. In: 10th Australian Joint Conf. on Artificial Intelligence, pp. 185–190 (1997)
13. Belongie, S., Malik, J., Puzicha, J.: Shape Matching and Object Recognition using Shape Contexts. IEEE trans. Pattern Analysis and Machine Intelligence 24(24), 509–522 (2002)

# Estimating 3D Flow
# for Driver Assistance Applications


Jorge A. Sánchez[1], Reinhard Klette[2], and Eduardo Destefanis[1]

[1] Universidad Tecnológica Nacional, Facultad Regional Córdoba
Cordoba, Argentina
{jsanchez,edestefanis}@scdt.frc.utn.edu.ar
[2] The *.enpeda..* Project, The University of Auckland
Auckland, New Zealand
r.klette@auckland.ac.nz



**Abstract.** This paper proposes a technique for estimating 3D flow vectors, by combining a KLT tracker with subsequent scale-space analysis of tracked points. A tracked point defines a 2D vector, which is mapped into 3D space based on ratios of maxima of scale-space characteristics. The approach is tested for night-vision sequences as recorded (at Daimler AG, Germany) for driver assistance projects. Those image sequences (at 25Hz) are characterized by being slightly blurry and of low contrast.

**Keywords:** Motion analysis, motion vector fields, 3D motion, driver assistance.


## 1 Introduction

The estimation of dense motion fields is still a challenging task for vision-based driver assistance systems (DAS), where motion vectors are often relatively long even if sequences are taken at a frame rate of more than 30 Hz. This paper suggests a way to derive 3D directions of observed 2D motion vectors, which allows a more consistent interpretation of motion fields.

Note that a 3D direction of a motion vector is not yet defining its pose, which would also require to identify its position (e.g., via stereo analysis). The 3D pose of projected motion vectors is known as *scene flow*. Scene flow techniques crucially depend on whether a sparse or a dense representation is desired, or whether motion is assumed to be rigid or not.

Sparse representations involve some kind of spatio-temporal feature matching; for the monocular case this is accomplished by methods known from structure-from-motion (SfM), which usually assumes a rigid motion of the whole scene [13]. If there is more than one view available, as in binocular stereo, the computation of scene flow relies on integration of depth and temporal information in some cooperative way [16]. For the case of dense representations, this involves the minimization of energies in a variational framework in order to add some smoothness constraint, needed to deal with the aperture problem [15].


T. Wada, F. Huang, and S. Lin (Eds.): PSIVT 2009, LNCS 5414, pp. 237–248, 2009.
© Springer-Verlag Berlin Heidelberg 2009

Our approach tries to use information provided by observed temporal changes in size (scale) of local image regions if a single camera moves relatively to a scene. (This is known to be a very important source of information for the visual perception of motion.) We use a scale-space representation of consecutive image frames in order to obtain (for each tracked point) a measure for the diameter of image brightness patterns (that surround tracked points), as established by [4,5,6] for automatic scale selection.

The idea is to identify a *characteristic scale* to be the value where a normalized differential entity takes a local extrema. Such scale values are measured in terms of standard deviations of the Gaussian kernel which are used to generate corresponding levels of the scale-space representation.

In [11] it is experimentally shown that the Laplacian of Gaussian (LoG) is the most stable in a considered set of differential normalized operators, possibly used for scale selection. Thus, this operator is selected for the scale selection stage described in Section 4. The remainder of the paper is organized as follows: Section 2 presents equations for analyzing directions of motion; Section 3 describes the used tracking scheme; the complete algorithm is presented in Section 5; finally, Sections 6 and 7 present experimental results and conclusions.

## 2   Estimation of 3D Directions

We consider a 3D point $P$, tracked between frames $I_t$ and $I_{t+1}$, and propose a possible way for calculating the 3D direction of the observed motion.

### 2.1   Update Equation

Consider a disk of radius $\rho$ moving towards an ideal pinhole-type camera of focal length $f$. Without loss of generality, let the radius move parallel to the $Y$-axis of the $XYZ$-camera coordinate system (i.e., $r = Y_c - Y_e$, for center $P_c$ and an edge point $P_e$ of the disk). A 3D point $P = (X, Y, Z)$ in the world (in camera coordinates) projects into a point $p = (x, y, f)$ in the image plane, with $x = f\frac{X}{Z}$ and $y = f\frac{Y}{Z}$. Point $P_c$ projects into $p_c = (x_c, y_c, f)$, and $P_e$ projects into $p_e = (x_e, y_e, f)$. The moving disk is at time $t$ at distance $Z_t$, and projected into image $I_t$ as a disk of radius $r_t$. We obtain the following for the area of this projected disk:

$$A_t = \pi r_t^2 = \pi \left(y_c - y_e\right)^2 = f\frac{\pi}{Z_t^2}\left(Y_c - Y_e\right)^2 = \pi f\frac{\rho^2}{Z^2}$$

Radius $\rho$ of the disk is constant over time, thus, the product $A_t Z_t^2 \sim \rho^2$ will also not change over time.

We consider projections of the disk at times $t$ and $t + 1$. Because the ratio of square roots of areas is proportional to the inverse of the ratio of corresponding $Z$-coordinates of the disk, we are able to define a *z-ratio*

$$\mu_z = \frac{\sqrt{A_t}}{\sqrt{A_{t+1}}} = \frac{Z_{t+1}}{Z_t} \tag{1}$$

either by area or $Z$-values. Such a $z$-ratio can also be defined just for a pair of projected points $P_t = (X_t, Y_t, X_t)$ and $P_{t+1} = (X_{t+1}, Y_{t+1}, Z_{t+1})$ (just by the ratio of $Z$-coordinates).

Using the central projection equations for both projected points, we obtain for their *x-ratio* and *y-ratio* the following:

$$\mu_x = \frac{X_{t+1}}{X_t} = \frac{Z_{t+1}}{Z_t} \cdot \frac{x_{t+1}}{x_t} = \mu_z \frac{x_{t+1}}{x_t} \tag{2}$$

$$\mu_y = \frac{Y_{t+1}}{Y_t} = \frac{Z_{t+1}}{Z_t} \cdot \frac{y_{t+1}}{y_t} = \mu_z \frac{y_{t+1}}{y_t} \tag{3}$$

Altogether, this may also be expressed by the following *update equation*:

$$\begin{pmatrix} X_{t+1} \\ Y_{t+1} \\ Z_{t+1} \end{pmatrix} = \begin{pmatrix} \mu_x & 0 & 0 \\ 0 & \mu_y & 0 \\ 0 & 0 & \mu_z \end{pmatrix} \begin{pmatrix} X_t \\ Y_t \\ Z_t \end{pmatrix} \tag{4}$$

with $\mu_x$, $\mu_y$, and $\mu_z$ as in Equations (2), (3), and (1), respectively. In other words, knowing $\mu_z$ and ratios $\frac{x_{t+1}}{x_t}$ and $\frac{y_{t+1}}{y_t}$ allows to update the position of point $P_t$ into $P_{t+1}$. Assuming that $P_t$ and $P_{t+1}$ are positions of one tracked 3D point $P$, from time $t$ to time $t+1$, we only have to solve two tasks: (1) decide for a technique to track points from $t$ to $t+1$, and (2) estimate $\mu_z$. If an initial position $P_0$ of a tracked point $P$ is known then we may identify its 3D position at subsequent time slots. Without having an initial position, we only have a 3D direction $P_t$ to $P_{t+1}$, but not its 3D position.

## 2.2   3D Direction of Projected Motion

Consider a mobile platform moving on a planar surface, as illustrated in Figure 2. The relative motion of a point in 3D space can be expressed (with respect to the camera coordinate system) by the following increments:

$$\Delta X = X_{t+1} - X_t = (\mu_x - 1)X_t$$
$$\Delta Y = Y_{t+1} - Y_t = (\mu_y - 1)Y_t$$
$$\Delta Z = Z_{t+1} - Z_t = (\mu_z - 1)Z_t$$

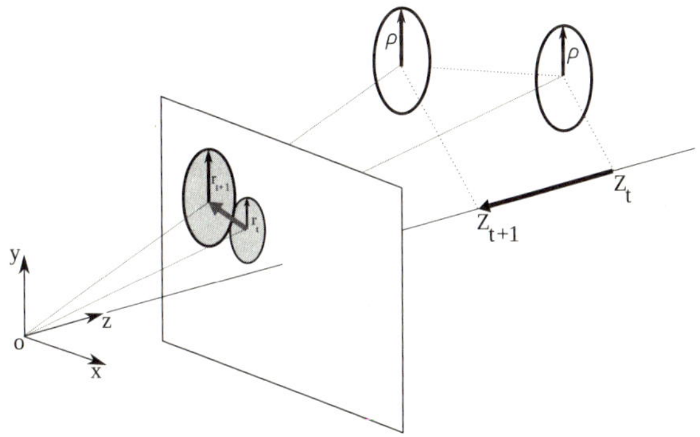


**Fig. 1.** Two projections of a moving disk, at times $t$ and $t+1$

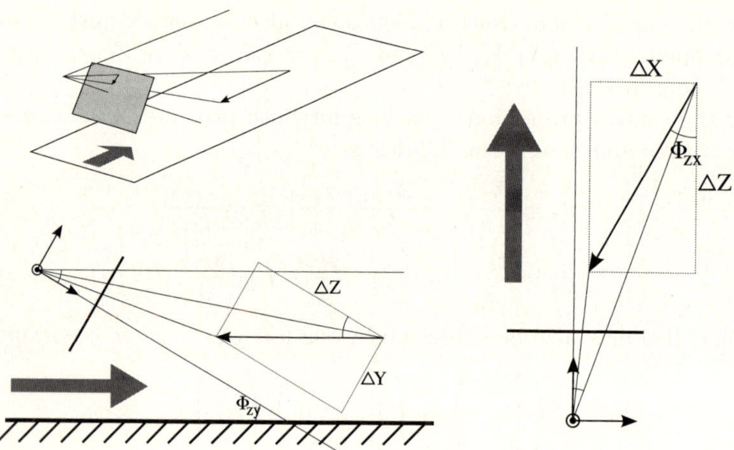


**Fig. 2.** A tilted camera translating along a plane (top left), motion angles on the $ZY$-plane (bottom left), and on the $ZX$-plane (right)

The ratios

$$\frac{\Delta X}{\Delta Z} = \left(\frac{\mu_x - 1}{\mu_z - 1}\right)\frac{X_t}{Z_t} = \left(\frac{\mu_x - 1}{\mu_z - 1}\right)\frac{x_t}{f} \tag{5}$$

$$\frac{\Delta Y}{\Delta Z} = \left(\frac{\mu_y - 1}{\mu_z - 1}\right)\frac{Y_t}{Z_t} = \left(\frac{\mu_y - 1}{\mu_z - 1}\right)\frac{y_t}{f} \tag{6}$$

of those increments are the tangents of the *navigation angles* $\Phi_{zx}$ and $\Phi_{zy}$ (see Figure 2), respectively, that represent the *3D direction of motion* (between two subsequent frames) for a tracked 3D point.

## 3   Feature Tracking and Test Data

The determination of those navigation angles relays on the detected projected motion of tracked points in the image plane. Tracking methods for estimating a dense 2D motion field are known as *optical flow techniques.*

Actually, the used tracking method is not essential for presenting the basic idea of our approach for estimating 3D directions; however, it is, of course, important for obtaining reliable results of the proposed approach.

For this paper we simply used an open implementation [3] of the Lucas-Kanade [9] feature tracker, with initial points selected as in [12].

Regarding test sequences, we decided for Set 1 (seven night vision stereo sequences, provided by Daimler AG) as available on [2]. Those will be called 'Sequence 1', 'Sequence 2', and so forth, as on this website and described in [7]. Additionally, also one 'Desktop sequence' was generated and used for performance analysis. This desktop sequence was generated by translating a calibrated camera along an optical bench, with constant 3D viewing angles relatively to the surface of the desktop.

**Fig. 3.** Optical flow computed for Sequences 1 and 2

**Fig. 4.** Optical flow computed for Sequence 3 and 4

**Fig. 5.** Optical flow computed for Sequence 5 and 6

Figures 3 to 6 illustrate tracking results for Sequences 1 to 7, and the Desktop sequence. By using relatively high thresholds, only relatively sparse motion fields are shown. The used coloring is based on the length of the optic flow vectors.

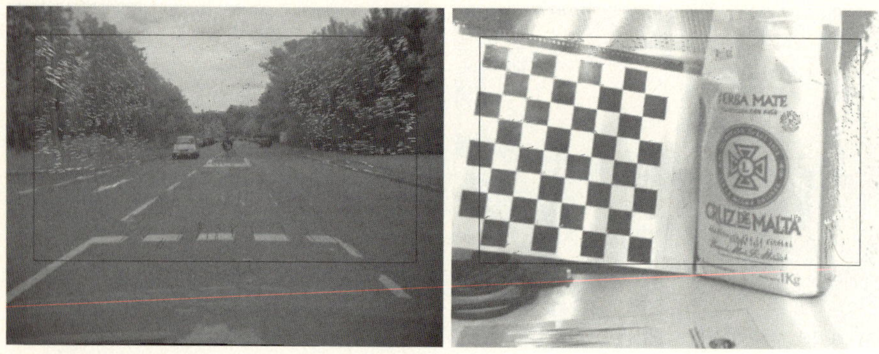

**Fig. 6.** Optical flow computed for Sequence 7 and the Desktop sequence

## 4  Scale Ratio for a Tracked Point

The idea behind the presented approach is as follows: instead of directly tracking image regions (such as disks, as discussed in Section 2), single feature points are tracked, but an 'area of influence' is assigned to such a point, basically taking the role of a tracked disk.

For tracked points, a measure is computed for the 'extension of the local image structure' in a local (or semi-local) neighborhood. Such measures, computed independently for each pair of points (i.e., a 2D flow vector between time $t$ and $t+1$), are then used to determine a scale ratio of associated intensity profiles 'surrounding' those feature points, which is finally used as an estimate of the $z$-ratio $\mu_z$.

The approach for detecting scale-ratios follows *scale space theory* as discussed in [5,6]. Note that this is only one option; similar to the variability when deciding for one optical flow technique, also an alternative method may be used for scale-ratio estimation.

We briefly recall scale space theory. Given an image function $I : \mathbb{R}^2 \to \mathbb{R}$, their scale space representation $L : \mathbb{R}^2 \times \mathbb{R}_+ \to \mathbb{R}$ can be obtained by convolutions

$$L(p, \sigma) = (g_\sigma * I)(p)$$

of image $I$ with a Gauss kernel $g_\sigma$, obtained by the Gauss function $G_\sigma : \mathbb{R}^2 \to \mathbb{R}$,

$$G_\sigma(p) = \frac{1}{2\pi\sigma^2} e^{-\frac{1}{2\sigma^2} p^T p}$$

parameterized by standard deviation $\sigma \geq 1$.

In [6], a method for automatic scale selection is proposed, based on the evolution over scales of (possibly non-linear) combinations of normalized derivatives of $L(p, \sigma)$. The scale level at which such a response takes a local maxima is assumed to reflect the *characteristic diameter* of the surrounding data. The operator used in our experiments for scale selection is the normalized Laplacian, which is defined by

$$\nabla_{norm}L(p,t) = \sigma^2 \left| (D_x^2 L)(p,\sigma) + (D_y^2 L)(p,\sigma) \right| \tag{7}$$

where $D_x^2$ and $D_y^2$ are the second order derivatives of $L$ (at scale level $\sigma$).

We use Figure 7 for visualizing the scale selection principle. In this simple example, the image on the left contains three white disks with center points $p_1$, $p_2$, and $p_3$. On the right, the figure shows the scale evolution of (7) for those three center points. In this example, the ratio between the scales, identified by maxima of the scale characteristics of those three center points, equals the ratio of areas of the corresponding white disks.

Given two consecutive frames $I_t$ and $I_{t+1}$ of a sequence. We calculate their scale space representations $L_t(p,\sigma)$ and $L_{t+1}(p,\sigma)$, for selected scales $\sigma$. For each selected pair of points (as a result of the tracking algorithm), we follow their scale characteristics for the normalized Laplacian of $L_t(p,\sigma)$ and $L_{t+1}(p,\sigma)$, and identify local maxima over the selected scales.

The function

$$c(\sigma) = K\sigma^p e^{-\sigma/\theta}$$

is used in order to obtain sub-scale estimates, where the parameters of this function are directly computed from the local maxima, extracted as an initial estimate, and its both neighboring values $\sigma_1$ and $\sigma_2$. Applying this approach, the maximum (i.e., magnitude)

$$K = c(\sigma_1)\sigma_1^{-a} e^{\sigma_{max}/\theta}$$

is identified at a sub-scale value $\sigma_{max} = a \cdot \theta$ The scale matching process between both projections $p_t$ and $p_{t+1}$ of the tracked point is then based on the magnitude $K$ of the interpolation function at the scale level $\sigma_{max}$.

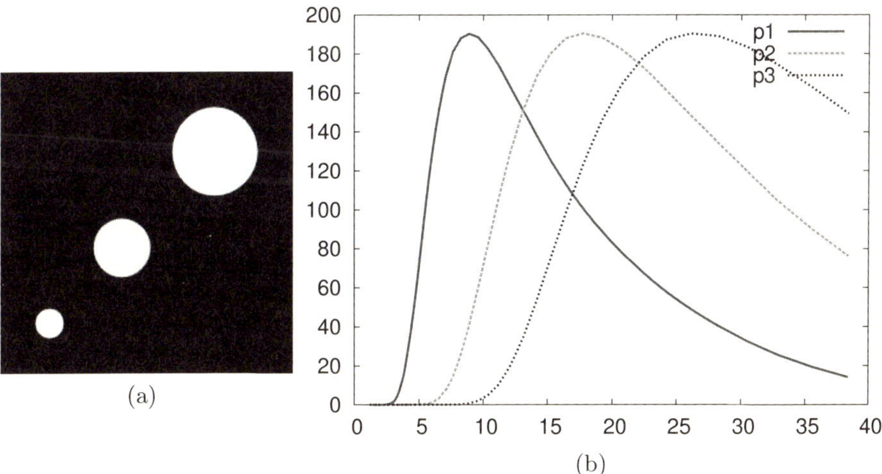


**Fig. 7.** (a) White disks of radius 25, 50 and 75 pixel. (b) Evolution on the Laplacian for center points $p_i$, for $i = 1, 2, 3$.

**Fig. 10.** Optical flow computed for Sequences 3, 7 and for the Desktop sequence

scale ratio $y$ is close to 1, the quotients in Equations 5 and 6 are not well defined, due to noisy measurements. In our computations, points pairs with $|\sigma_{max}/\sigma_{min} - 1| < 10^{-6}$ are discarded, where $\sigma_{max}$ ($\sigma_{min}$) denotes the largest (smallest) detected scale of tracked points. An upper limit to the $\mu_z$'s was also imposed, allowing only values $< 5$.

The Desktop sequence was generated with a calibrated camera, with translational motion on a rail with fixed navigation angles of approximately $\Phi_{zx} = 12°$ and $\Phi_{zy} = -10°$.

In the case of the Desktop sequence, mean and standard deviation of $\Phi_{zx}$ are equal to $13.531°$ and $2.93874°$, respectively. For $\Phi_{zy}$, those values are equal to $-10.3073°$ and $2.93874°$, respectively, taken over the entire sequence. In the case of the Daimler sequences, there was no ground truth available (estimated), and they were only used as a qualitative (visual) reference. For example, for Sequence 7 (see example in Figure 10), estimated directions $\Phi_{zx}$ correspond 'quite well' to the steering of the car over the sequence. Estimated values $\Phi_{zy}$ remain at about $4°$. In Sequence 2 we observed a low frequency oscillation in the value of $\Phi_{zy}$, starting about at frame 180, when the 'squirrel' (actually, a cat) crossed the street and the car made a breaking maneuver.

In all cases, observed noise is mainly due to the scale matching subprocess. As given, for example, projective distortions of local image patches are not taken into account, causing possibly some serious underestimations of scale factors. The proposed (non-run-time-optimized) algorithm runs at approximately 1 fps on a 3.0 GHz Intel© Core 2 Duo CPU.

## 7  Conclusions

A method for the instantaneous (frame to frame) estimation of the 3D direction of motion was proposed and studied, based on the determination of scale ratios between tracked points. The critical issue is the accurate scale estimation step. The MSER region extractor [10] is an alternative (to the presented choice) option and possibly a more robust way for the determination of scales (characteristic diameters), where local image patches can be represented with affine invariance, serving as a first-order approximation for (more general) projective deformations induced by the relative motion of the camera.

Besides some poor estimations for some frames, the proposed method may be recommended as a possible approach for the use of perceptually very important spatio-temporal cues induced on images as an observer moves relatively to the scene. The extracted information has the advantage of being local, and allowing robustness in the case of multiple moving objects. The same principle of scale-ratio estimation could also be used for motion segmentation, or to add new constraints to multiple-view approaches of 3D motion estimation, thus further contributing to the already known coherence between optic flow vectors and image disparities.

The overall run-time of the algorithm can be significantly improved by the use of dedicated hardware (FPGA/ASICs). Here, the bottle-neck remains in the computation of the scale-space representations of the given images. This is done, as mentioned previously, by means of convolution with bi-dimensional Gaussians of variable width. This type of kernels allows for efficient implementations in terms of separable 1D Gaussians (which allow recursive implementations; see [1,14]).

## References


1. Deriche, R.: Recursively implementing the Gaussian and its derivatives. In: Proc. 2nd Int. Conf. on Image Processing, pp. 263–267 (1992)
2. enpeda..Image Sequence Analysis Test Site, http://www.mi.auckland.ac.nz/6D/
3. Intel Open Source Computer Vision Library, http://www.intel.com/research/mrl/research/opencv/
4. Lindeberg, T.: On scale selection for differential operators. In: ISRN KTH/NA/P– 93/12–SE, pp. 857–866 (1993)

5. Lindeberg, T.: Scale-Space Theory in Computer Vision. Kluwer Academic Publishers, Norwell (1994)
6. Lindeberg, T.: Feature detection with automatic scale selection. Int. J. Computer Vision 30, 77–116 (1998)
7. Liu, Z., Klette, R.: Performance evaluation of stereo and motion analysis on rectified image sequences. Technical report, Computer Science Department, The University of Auckland (2007)
8. Lowe, D.G.: Object Recognition from Local Scale-Invariant Features. In: Proc. ICCV, pp. 1150–1157 (1999)
9. Lucas, B., Kanade, T.: An iterative image registration technique with an application to stereo vision. In: Proc. IJCAI, pp. 674–679 (1981)
10. Matas, J., Chum, O., Martin, U., Pajdla, T.: Robust wide baseline stereo from maximally stable extremal regions. In: Proc. British Machine Vision Conference, vol. 1, pp. 384–393 (2002)
11. Mikolajczyk, K.: Detection of local features invariant to affine transformations, PhD hesis, Institut National Polytechnique de Grenoble, France (2002)
12. Shi, J., Tomasi, C.: Good Features to Track. In: Proc. IEEE Conf. Computer Vision Pattern Recognition, pp. 674–679 (1994)
13. Tomasi, C., Kanade, T.: Shape and Motion from Image Streams under Orthography: a Factorization Method. International Journal of Computer Vision 9, 137–154 (1992)
14. van Vliet, L.J., Young, I., Verbeek, P.: Recursive Gaussian derivative filters. In: Proc. Int. Conf. on Pattern Recognition, pp. 509–514 (1998)
15. Vedula, S., Baker, S., Rander, P., Collins, R., Kanade, T.: Three-Dimensional Scene Flow. IEEE Transactions on Pattern Analysis and Machine Intelligence, 475–480 (2005)
16. Wedel, A., Rabe, C., Vaudrey, T., Brox, T., Franke, U., Cremers, R.: Efficient Dense Scene Flow from Sparse or Dense Stereo Data, Technical report, Computer Science Department, The University of Auckland (2008)

# A New Method for Moving Object Extraction and Tracking Based on the Exclusive Block Matching


Zhu Li, Kenichi Yabuta, and Hitoshi Kitazawa

Department of Electrical and Electronic Engineering, Tokyo University of Agriculture
and Technology 2-24-16 Naka-cho, Koganei-shi, Tokyo, 184-8588 Japan
lizhu@m.ieice.org, kyabuta@m.ieice.org, kitazawa@cc.tuat.ac.jp



**Abstract.** Robust object tracking is required by many vision applications, and it will be useful for the motion analysis of moving object if we can not only track the object, but also make clear the corresponding relation of each part between consecutive frames. For this purpose, we propose a new method for moving object extraction and tracking based on the exclusive block matching. We build a cost matrix consisting of the similarities between the current frame's and the previous frame's blocks and obtain the corresponding relation by solving one-to-one matching as linear assignment problem. In addition, we can track the trajectory of occluded blocks by dealing with multi-frames simultaneously.


## 1  Introduction

Tracking objects is an omnipresent elementary task in online and offline image-based applications including traffic surveillance, motion capture, robot vision, etc. After years of researches, many efficient methods have been proposed. However, in order to achieve accurate motion analysis of moving object, it is necessary to obtain the corresponding relation of each part between consecutive frames. Background subtraction[1], which is one of the commonly used techniques for moving object extraction, can not provide the corresponding relation of each part. Mean-Shift[2] and Particle Filter[3][4] which are very popular for object tracking in present research do not obtain it in detail.

On the other hand, optical flow methods estimate pixel motion between two frames. It can obtain the corresponding relations on level of pixel by optical flow method such as Block Matching method, Horn-Schunck[7] method and Lucas-Kanade[8] method. However, aperture problem which is existing in optical flow estimation can give rise to a problem that many blocks match same or neighboring postion in a area covered with uniform color. This problem causes error matching. Moreover, it is impossible to extract feature points in such area that intensity changes smoothly by Lucas-Kanade method.

In order to avoid the situation that destinations of matched blocks are too close or overlap, we assume block matches in such a way that destinations are mutually exclusive and propose a method to obtain the optimal matching using linear assignment. Different from the algorithms base on the graph matching[5][6],


T. Wada, F. Huang, and S. Lin (Eds.): PSIVT 2009, LNCS 5414, pp. 249–260, 2009.

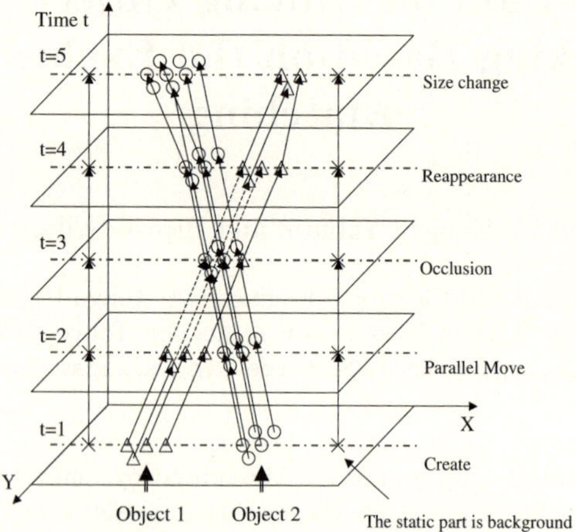


**Fig. 1.** Spatio-temporal tracking

our method simply performs block matching which does not require the graph structures of moving objects. Moreover, compared with the feature of nodes and edges of graph, the features of small blocks shows higher robustness under some situations such as view point change caused by object motion and illumination change. The proposed method aims to achieve spatio-temporal continual object tracking even in the case of occlussion or shape change which is shown in Fig. 1.

## 2    Exclusive Block Matching

### 2.1    The Matching between Current Frame and Previous Frame

This section describes the basic method of block matching. Firstly, we scan the input images by block to convert the images into 1 dimensional data. If we assume that the block size is $n \times n$ pixels, the width and the height of the image are $w$ and $h$, respectively, the number of blocks $N$ is given by the equation $N = w/n \times h/n$ as shown in Fig. 2. We build an $N \times N$ array consisting of the similarities (actually difference measure or distance) between the current frame's (Curr) and the previous frame's (Prev) blocks. It is required to perform all Curr blocks by assigning exactly one Prev block to each Curr block in such a way that the total cost of the assignment is minimized. Then this problem could be solved as a linear assignment problem.

However, it is impossible to archive the one-to-one assigning as long as the object moves in the scene. This is caused by various situations involving hiddenness and reappearance of background, occlusion, creation and vanishment of moving object. Therefore, this problem can not be simply solved as a linear assignment problem.

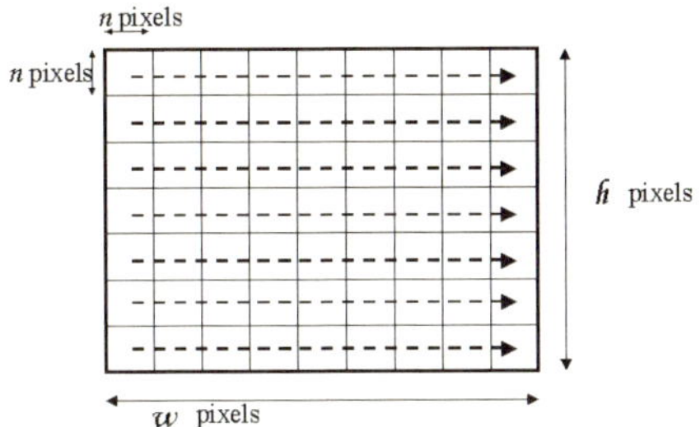


**Fig. 2.** Scan an image into 1 dimensional data

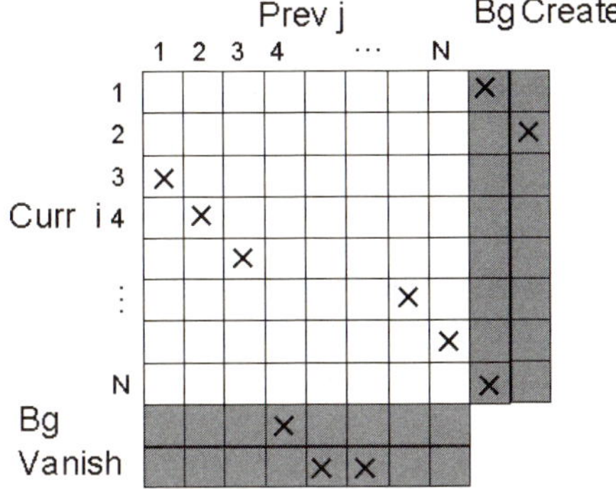


**Fig. 3.** Expand the matrix considering background, occlusion, creation, and vanishment

## 2.2 Expand the Matrix Considering Background, Occlusion, Creation and Vanishment

In order to solve this problem, we expand the basic matrix by adding 2 rows and 2 columns as shown in Fig. 3. The columns correspond to appearance of background and creation of blocks and the rows correspond to hiddenness of background and vanishment of blocks. We calculated the distances between current block and prevous blocks to decide which column's block is the best match. If the distance between current frame's block and background's block is closer than the distance between current frame's and the previous frame's block, this block is matched with the Bg column. If neither previous frame nor Bg column can be matched, this block is matched with the Create column. In the same way, the blocks of previous frame which match neither the current frame's nor the Bg's blocks are matched with the Vanish row. This matching problem becomes the following linear programming problem.

$$Minimize$$

$$z = \sum_{i=1}^{N+2} \sum_{j=1}^{N+2} p_{ij} c_{ij}$$

*Subject   to*

$$\sum_{j=1}^{N+2} p_{ij} = 1 \qquad i = \{1, 2, \ldots, N\}$$

$$\sum_{i=1}^{N+2} p_{ij} = 1 \qquad j = \{1, 2, \ldots, N\}$$

$$p_{ij} = \{0, 1\} \qquad \{i, j\} = \{1, 2, \ldots, N + 2\}$$

$$however, p_{ij} = \{0\} \; \{i, j\} = \{N + 1, N + 2\}$$

$$c_{ij} = \begin{cases} dist\{Curr_i, Prev_j\} & i = \{1, \ldots, N\}, j = \{1, \ldots, N\} \\ dist\{Curr_i, Bg_j\} & i = \{1, \ldots, N\}, j = N + 1 \\ dist\{Bg_i, Prev_j\} & i = N + 1, j = \{1, \ldots, N\} \\ penalty \; for \; creating & i = \{1, \ldots, N\}, j = N + 2 \\ penalty \; for \; vanishing & i = N + 2, j = \{1, \ldots, N\} \end{cases}$$

$dist\{Curr_i, Prev_j\}$ : distance between the current frame's blocks $i$ and the previous frame's blocks $j$.

$dist\{Curr_i, Bg_j\}$ : distance between the current frame's blocks $i$ and the background's blocks $j$.

$dist\{Bg_i, Prev_j\}$ : distance between the background's blocks $i$ and the previous frame's blocks $j$.

*penalty for creating* : fixed value chosen when there is no block similar with it. If this value is chosen, this block is regarded as creating of new block.

*penalty for vanishing* : fixed value chosen when there is no block similar with it. If this value is chosen, this block is regarded as vanishing of block or occlusion.

The part which consists of the $N \times N$ array is an exclusive assignment problem. However, the part which is composed of the Bg row, Bg column, Create row and Vanish column is a partial assignment problem which is likely to be solved out with plural choices. There is no guarantee that such a problem can be solved out in a short time. For this reasaon, we ignore Bg and Vanish row to convert it to the linear assignment problem which is shown in Fig. 4. Only the diagonal elements can be selected in the part of Bg and Create. Since every row is assigned to exactly one column, only $N$ columns are selected. Although the Bg and Vanish row are taken out, the blocks in previous frame which do not match with the blocks in the current frame (shown by $\triangle$ in Fig. 4) are regard as matched with Bg or Vanish.

## 2.3   Multi-frame Expanding

Although we can discern the movement of each block by matching between current frame's and previous frame's blocks, it is still impossible to discern some situations just like occlusion and reappearance. So we expand the matrix again

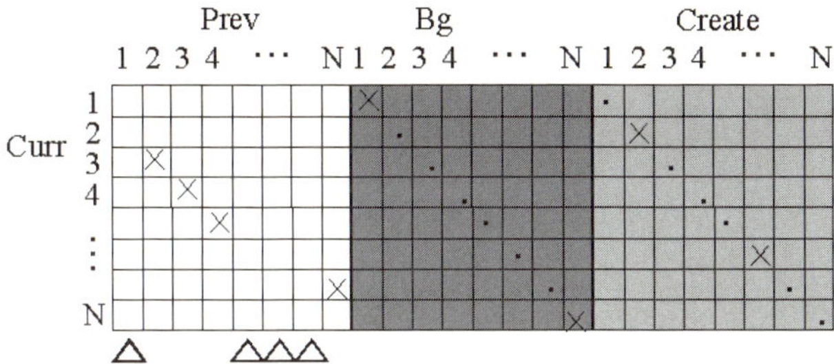


**Fig. 4.** Assignment problem considering background and creation

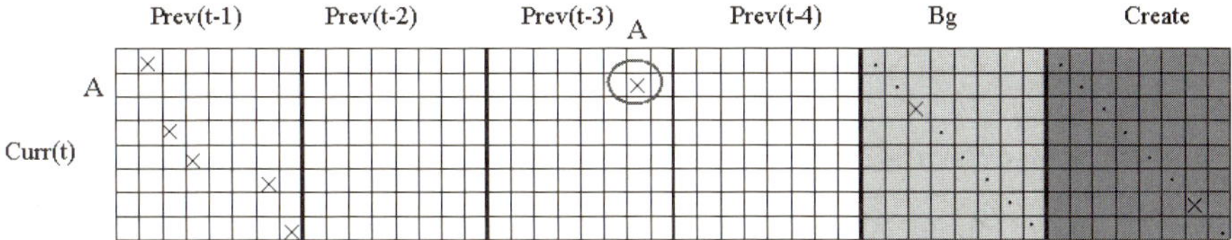


**Fig. 5.** Expand the cost matrix dealing with plural previous frames

by dealing with plural previous frames, as shown in Fig. 5. For example, block
A in the current frame is matched with it in the frame at the moment t-3. The
block A is regarded as occluded at the moment t-1 and t-2. The value in ( )
denotes the time of the frame.

## 2.4   Similarity Measure

Beacuse the capability of matching is depend heavily on the calculation method
of similarity, it is necessary to choose an appropriate measure. Through comparison of various experimental results, we adopt the Bhattacharyya coeffcient[3]
defining a distance on HSV histograms to measure the similarity between 2
blocks. The mathematical formulation of this measure is given by Eq. (1) and
Eq. (2), where $p$ and $q$ represent 2 normalized HSV histogram.

$$\rho[p,q] = \sum_{u=1}^{m} \sqrt{p^{(u)}q^{(u)}} \tag{1}$$

$$d = \sqrt{1 - \rho[p,q]} \tag{2}$$

The HSV histogram is composed of $m = N_h N_s + N_v$ bins and we set $N_h$, $N_s$,
and $N_v$ to 10. So the $m$ becomes 110[3].

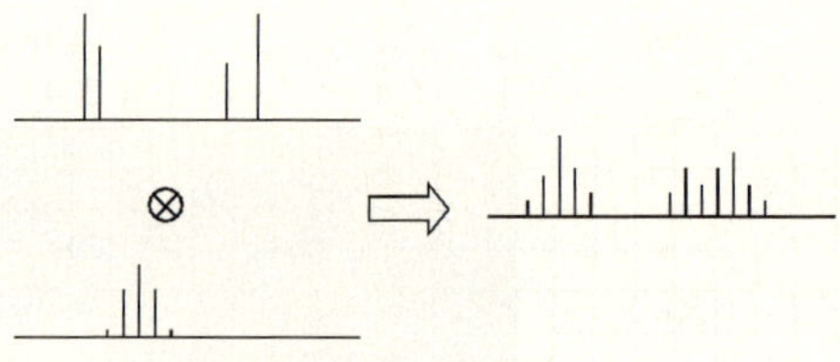

**Fig. 6.** Smooth the histogram

# 3    Enhance Robustness for Real Data

In this section we describe our proposed method to enhance robustness for real data.

## 3.1    Improvement of Similarity Measure

Due to noises, changed illumination environment and the small size of block, a small perturbation of RGB values will cause Bhattacharyya distance great change. As shown in Fig. 6, we calculate a convolution with Gaussian function the mean of which is 0 to smooth the S and V histogram. Considering H is invariant with respect to brightness variations, we do not perform the smooth processing on H. The histogram must be normalized after convolution processing. In addition, we can add some other feature quantities with invariance property in changed illumination environment to improve the robustness under some of the situations such as shadows. Here we use one of the texture features which is statistically represented as variance of color histogram.

Moreover, there is a contradiction between the precision in similarity calculation and the size of blocks. The smaller the block size is, the higher resolution which means more image details of moving object we can get. However, the less pixels each block contains, the lower the precision in similarity calculation becomes. In other words, the amount of blocks with same color information becomes higher. In order to solve this problem in some extent, when we calculate the HSV histogram of a block, not only do we calculate the color information of this block, but also calculate the sum of color informations of the 8 blocks around it for addition. In this method, the HSV histogram will be calculated repeatedly for overlapping blocks.

## 3.2    Restriction of Block State Transition

In our system, each block corresponds to a situation such as moving object, static object, background, etc. We thus consider the state transition of blocks. In section 2.3, a block can become arbitrary state according to the optimal assignment. However, as shown in Fig. 7 state of block changes under some rules. Firstly, states of all blocks are set to Bg (background) by initialization.

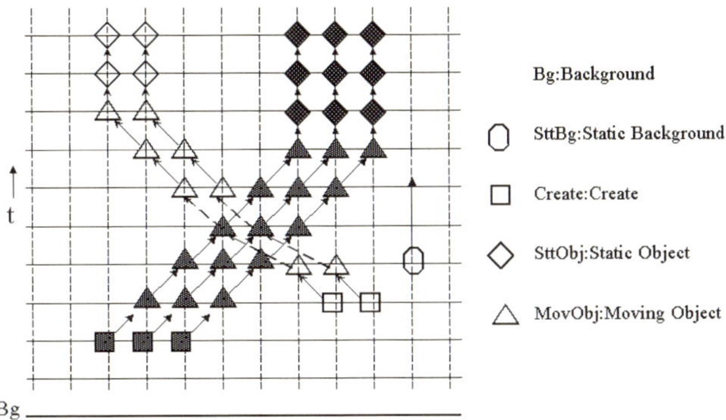


**Fig. 7.** States of blocks

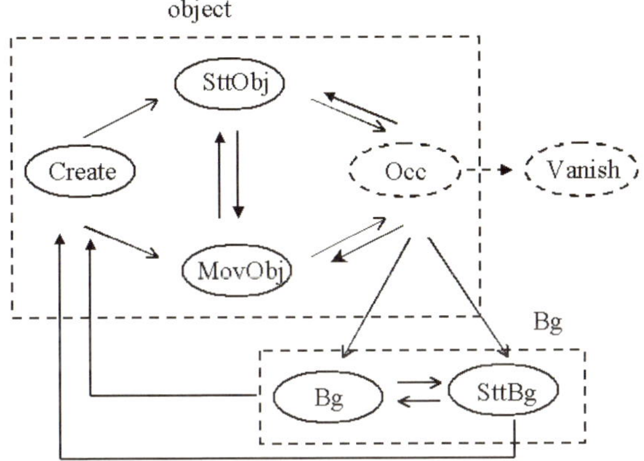


**Fig. 8.** Restriction of block state transition

Now we focus on the state of one block. As the block changes under assignment, if the distance from background is bigger than a pre-assigned threshold, this block's state will be set to Create which means the block belongs to an object. When it is matched with the next frame, if the block moves to another position, the state will be classified as MovObj (moving object). If it is matched with the block which is on the same position, the state is classified as SttObj (static object). Under condition that none of the blocks in the scene are matched with it, the state is set to Occ (occlusion). So long as it can not be matched with MovObj or SttObj again within a pre-assigned number of frames, it is classified as Vanish. Besides, the blocks which are matched with background are classified as Bg. Finally, if the block does not belong to object and matched with the block on same position, it will be classified as SttBg (Static background). Figure 8 shows the diagram of allowed block state transition.

### 3.3   Shape Preserving

Through the proposed method gives the exactly optimal matching, the proper flows what humans see can not always be calculated. It is impossible to track moving object accurately only using color information such as RGB values and HSV histogram. In the Horn-Schunck optical flow calculation method[7], it is assumed that motion vector changes smoothly almost everywhere in a scene. Unfortunally, it is impossible to transform this assumption to the linear assignment problem. We thus assume that the shape of object does not change abruptly and adjust the matching cost matrix. We obtain the mean vector from the initial matching result, then perform matching again with adding a penalty value to each block according to its distance from the mean vector, as shown in Fig. 9.

## 4   Experimental Results

### 4.1   Comparison with Optical Flow Methods

In order to prove the validity of our method, we show the experimental results of CG generated data at first. Two boxes move parallelly and occlusion occurs at the moment of frames 4 and 5. Figure 10 shows the experimental results of our method and 3 kinds of optical flow methods. The optical fow is calculated by OpenCV library[9]. We adjust the values and the numbers of parameters of optical flow methods to obtain the best results we can get. In the experimental results, red line represents the block which matchs with block in previous frame (t-1). Yellow line represents the block matchs with a block in frame (t-2). The green and blue line represent blocks which are matched with a blocks in frame (t-3) and (t-4), respectively. Experiment result indicates that the traditional optical flow methods induce unnatural flows because of pushing and entering of background. On the other hand, our proposed method avoid well this problem, and obtained flows are almost parallel.

### 4.2   Magnification and Rotation

Although we assume blocks match exclusively, our method considering vanishing and creating is applicable for magnification and rotation as well. Figure 11 shows the experimental results of CG data. Accurate tracking was almost realized. As

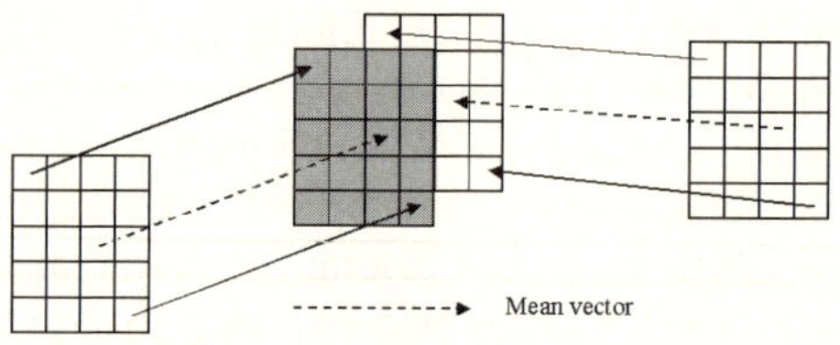


**Fig. 9.** Shape preserving

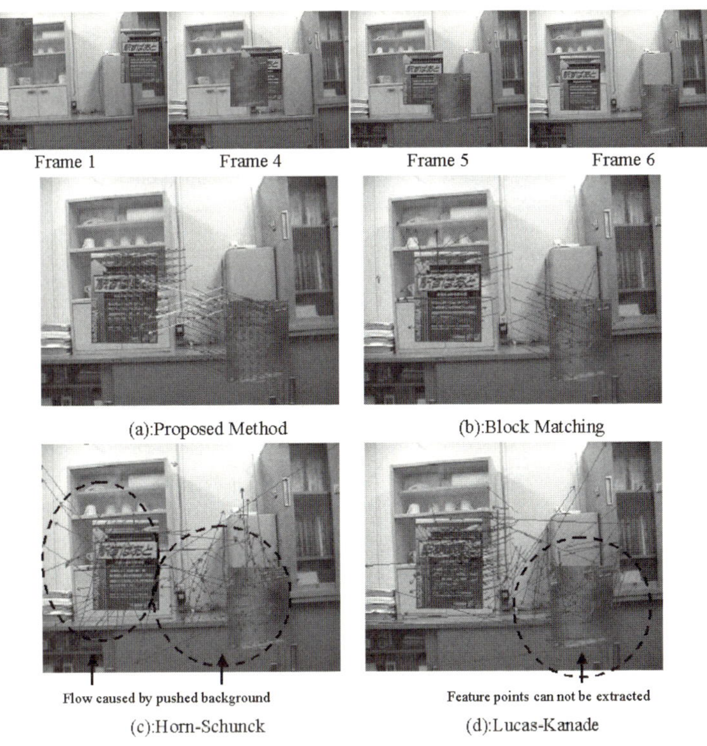



**Fig. 10.** The comparison between proposed method and conventional optical flow methods

the boundaries of blocks change, the similarities between some blocks in current frame and in frame (t-2) become higher than them between blocks in current frame and previous frame (t-1). This causes the error matching represented as yellow flows which appear when occlusion does not occur.

## 4.3   CG Data with Occlusion

The next example shown in Fig. 12(a) is the trajectory of two boxes under occlusion in spatio-temporal space. We use the same data which was used in Fig. 10. The excellent result shows that the continuous tracking is not interrupted even under occlusion. In addition, flows are almost parallel that means the corresponding relation of each part between consecutive frames is obtained accurately.

## 4.4   Real Data

Finally, Fig. 12(b) gives a result of real data with occlusion. Tracking fails after occlusion, flows of blocks on the parts of clothes of which color is very similar

**Fig. 11.** Magnification and Rotation

mixed together. Figure 13 shows another real data with different actions of a person. Althrough there are some inaccurate flows and miss extraction, the obtained flow shows the motion of each part of the person and it will be useful for motion analysis.

## 4.5   Linear Assignment Algorithm and Execution Time

In our experiment, we adopted the Munkres assignment algorithm[10] which is one of the implementations of Hungarian method to solve the linear assignment problem. We also adopted sparse-matrix calculation to improve the processing speed. In addtion, the restriction of state transition aviod a great many unnecessary calculations and greatly improve the processing speed. The image sequences are processed with a Core 2 Duo 3.00 GHz PC under Window XP. The image size is $320 \times 240$ pixels and the block size is $8 \times 8$ pixels. The running time increases with the amount of flows. It is about $0.2sec \sim 3sec$ (averagely $1sec$) per frame. For example, the average processing time of Bhattacharyya calculation and linear assignment for the scenes which are shown in Fig. 13 are $0.38sec$ and $0.47sec$,respectively. The linear assignment is repeaded twice for the shape preserving. This speed is not enough to realize real time processing. However, it is possible to greatly improve the processing speed by various approximate calculations of linear assignment[11] or using hardware to solve it.

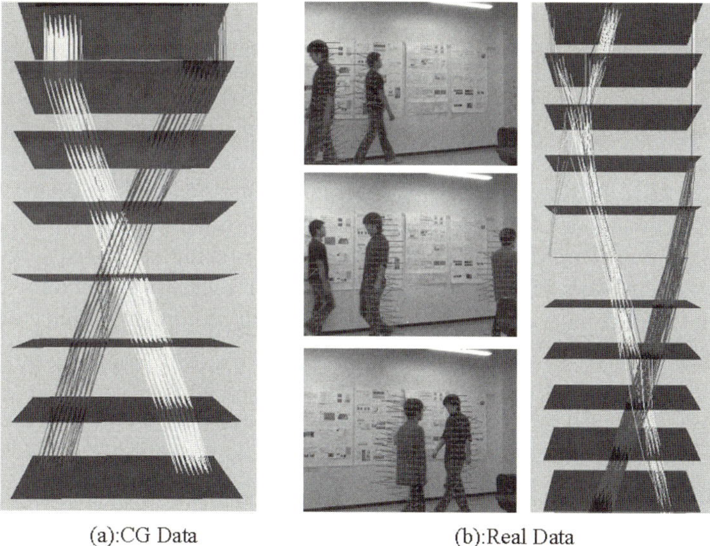

(a):CG Data          (b):Real Data

**Fig. 12.** Spatio-temporal space trajectory of objects when occlussion occur

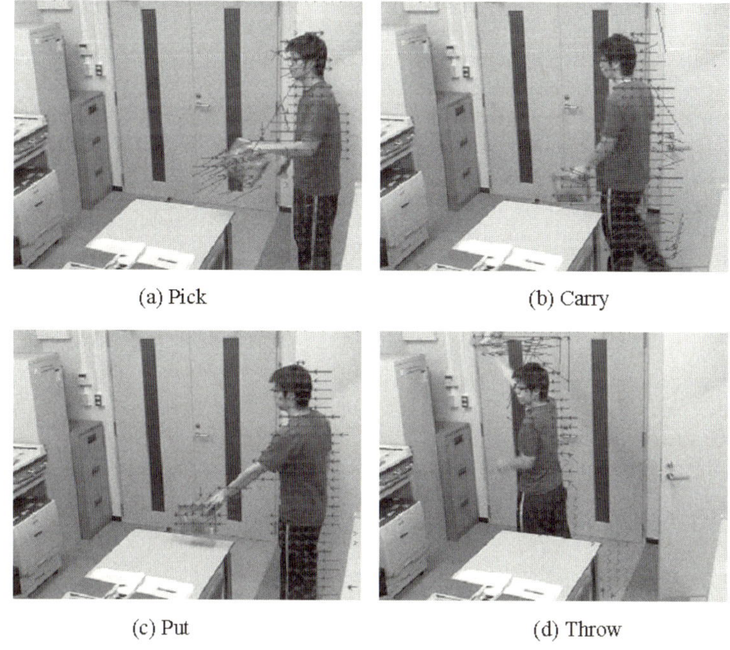

(a) Pick                    (b) Carry

(c) Put                     (d) Throw

**Fig. 13.** Real data with different actions

## 5   Conclusions

This paper has proposed a new method for moving object extraction and tracking based on exclusive block matching. This method has been successfully used to track moving object even in the case of occlusion and provides the corresponding relation of each part between consecutive frames. The assumption that block matches exclusively has improved the error matching caused by aperture problem. But it can not avoid it thoroughly when the colors of blocks are same or very similar. We, therefore, can make clear that tracking is limited if we merely use color information to calculate similarity. Our future work should focus on improving the approach considering shape similarity and connectivity in consecutive blocks.

## References


1. Stauffer, Grimson, W.E.L.: Adaptive background mixture models for real-time tracking. In: CVPR 1999, Fort Colins, CO, p. 2246 (June 1999)
2. Comaniciu, D., Meer, P.: A Robust Approach Toward Feature Space Analysis. IEEE Transactions on Pattern Analysis and Machine Intelligence 24(5), 603–619 (2002)
3. Perez, P., Hue, C., Vermaak, J., Gangnet, M.: Color-Based Probabilistic Tracking. In: Heyden, A., Sparr, G., Nielsen, M., Johansen, P. (eds.) ECCV 2002. LNCS, vol. 2350, pp. 661–675. Springer, Heidelberg (2002)
4. Nummiaro, K., Koller-Meierand, E., Van Gool, L.: A Color-based Particle Filter. Image and Vision Computing (2002)
5. Caetano, T.S., Cheng, L., Le, Q.V., Smola, A.J.: Learning Graph Matching. In: IEEE 11th International Conference on Computer Vision, ICCV 2007, 14-21 October 2007, pp. 1–8 (2007)
6. Jiang, H., Drew, M.S., Li, Z.-N.: Linear Programming Matching and Appearance-Adaptive Object Tracking. In: Rangarajan, A., Vemuri, B.C., Yuille, A.L. (eds.) EMMCVPR 2005. LNCS, vol. 3757, pp. 203–219. Springer, Heidelberg (2005)
7. Berthold, K., Horn, P., Schunck, B.G.: Determining Optical Flow. Artificial Intelligence 17, 185–203 (1981)
8. Bouguet, J.-Y.: Pyramidal Implementation of the Lucas Kanade Feature Tracker. The paper is included into OpenCV distribution
9. OpenCV, http://opencv.jp/document/opencvref_cv.html
10. Munkres assignment algorithm,
    http://csclab.murraystate.edu/bob.pilgrim/445/munkres.html
11. Trick, M.A.: A Linear Relaxation Heuristic For The Generalized Assignment Problem. Naval Research Logistics 39, 137–152 (1992)

# Visual Tracking Using Particle Filters with Gaussian Process Regression

Hongwei Li, Yi Wu, and Hanqing Lu

National Laboratory of Pattern Recognition, Institute of Automation, Chinese
Academy of Sciences, Beijing, China
{hwli,ywu,luhq}@nlpr.ia.ac.cn

**Abstract.** Particle degeneracy is one of the main problems when particle filters are applied to visual tracking. The effective solution methods on the degeneracy phenomenon include good choice of proposal distribution and use of resampling. In this paper, we propose a novel visual-tracking algorithm using particle filters with Gaussian process regression and resampling techniques, which effectively abate the influence of particle degeneracy and improve the robustness of visual tracking. The main characteristic of the proposed algorithm is that we incorporate particle filters with Gaussian process regression which can learn highly effective proposal distributions for particle filters to track the visual objects. Experimental results in challenging sequences demonstrate the effectiveness and robustness of the proposed method.

**Keywords:** Gaussian Processes, Particle Filter, Particle Degeneracy, Visual Tracking.

## 1   Introduction

Visual tracking is currently one of the most actively researched areas of computer vision and pattern recognition. During many practical applications such as surveillance and human-computer interfaces, visual tracking is a challenging task owing to the difficulties arising from illumination changes, occlusions, diverse appearance of objects, low-image resolution and noises etc.

Tracking algorithms generally involve two basic procedures: object observation (the object representation and similarity measurement) and object tracking control. Based on the nature of object tracking control, tracking algorithms can be roughly classified into two categories: deterministic methods and stochastic methods. In deterministic methods, the object is tracked by implementing an iterative search for the local maximum of a similarity cost function between the target image and the candidate images. These algorithms, such as the Mean Shift algorithm [1], are fast and efficient, but can not recover from the temporary tracking failures because of being sensitive to occlusion and clutter. In stochastic methods, the object is tracked by estimating the probability distribution and maintain multiple hypotheses in the state space. These algorithms, such as Particle Filter algorithm [2,3,4,5], can achieve more robustness and have the capability to recover from the temporary tracking failures.

T. Wada, F. Huang, and S. Lin (Eds.): PSIVT 2009, LNCS 5414, pp. 261–270, 2009.

The Particle Filter is a mainstream algorithm for online nonlinear/non-Gaussian Bayesian tracking, which is convenient to handle multivariate and nonlinear processes in contrast to traditional time-series techniques. The Particle Filter has been widely applied in many fields, such as visual tracking, video surveillance, mobile robot localization and failure detection etc. But Particle degeneracy, where all but one particle will have negligible weight after a few iterations [2], blocks the further development of algorithms, which means a large computational effort is devoted to updating particles whose contribution is almost zero. The degeneracy problem can be effectively mitigated by choosing better proposal distribution and using resampling techniques.

The main idea of resampling techniques is to reduce the influence of particles with small weights and to focus on particles with large weights. In this paper, we use resampling techniques whenever a significant degeneracy is observed. Better proposal distributions can minimize the variance of the true weights. For example, Freitas [6] introduced Extended Kalman Filtering into the particle filter algorithm. Eric A. Wan [7] presented unscented Particle Filter by incorporating the unscented Kalman Filtering. In this paper, we can learn effective proposal distributions for particle filters by incorporating Gaussian process regression, which can provide full predictive distributions modeling predictive uncertainties and choose the particles with the highest likelihood. In the following sections, the key steps of proposed algorithm are described in detail.

The organization of the paper is as follows: Section 2 briefly reviews the algorithm of Particle Filters. Gaussian process regression and the proposed algorithm with Gaussian process proposals are presented in Section 3. Experimental Results and Analysis are discussed in Section 4. The conclusions and possible extension are given in Section 5.

## 2   Particle Filters

In this section, we briefly review some basic notions of particle filter algorithm. Particle filters, known as sequential Monte Carlo method, are based on the point mass representations of probability densities. Through using the Bayesian inference framework, the particle filter algorithm is developed for visual tracking problem viewed as a state-space estimation problem. These state-space methods focus attention on the state vector( feature vector) of dynamic system, which is convenient to handle multivariate data and contains the correlative information (features) describing this dynamic system. For the sake of making a better state estimation of tracked objects, the importance sampling technique is employed on particle filters to obtain the samples of random variable generated from other distribution, called proposal distribution, which is easy to be sampled from.

### 2.1   A Brief Review of Particle Filters

Let $X = \{x_t, t \in \mathbb{N}\}$ denote the state sequence and $Y = \{y_t, t \in \mathbb{N}\}$ the corresponding observation sequence respectively. The objective of tracking is to recursively estimate the state $\{x_t\}$ of tracked objects from the observation $\{y_t\}$:

$$y_t = f_t(x_t, n_t), t \in \mathbb{N} \tag{1}$$

where $n_t$ denotes an i.i.d observation noise at time $t$.

Based on the Bayesian rule and conditional independence properties, the posterior distribution of the state variable $\{x_t\}$ can be formulated as follows:

$$p(x_t|y_{1:t}) \propto p(y_t|x_t) \int p(x_t|x_{t-1})p(x_{t-1}|y_{1:t-1})dx_{t-1} \tag{2}$$

The function $f$ in Equation (1) is generally nonlinear/non-Gaussian that makes the posterior distribution $p(x_t|y_{1:t})$ analytically intractable, so generating samples from this posterior distribution is usually not possible and the analytic approximations of integrals are needed.

In view of visual tracking problems, the true posterior distribution $p(x_t|y_{1:t})$ can be approximated by a weighted particle set $\{x_t^i, w_t^i\}_{i=1}^{N_s}$, where $N_s$ is the number of particles and the weights are normalized by $\sum_{i=1}^{N_s} w_t^i = 1$. All the particles are directly generated from an approximation distribution $q(x_t|x_{t-1}, y_t)$, called proposal distribution, which is easy to be sampled from. Then the Particle filter algorithm proceeds with two key steps:

(1) The updated weights. Drawing $N_s$ particles from the proposal density, each particle is assigned by appropriate importance weights:

$$w_t^i \propto w_{t-1}^i \frac{p(y_t|x_t^i)p(x_t^i|x_{t-1}^i)}{q(x_t^i|x_{t-1}^i, y_t)} \tag{3}$$

(2) The predictive distribution. By introduced by the modified weights $w_t^i$, the predictive posterior distribution can be approximated as:

$$p(x_t|y_{1:t}) \propto \sum_{i=1}^{N_s} w_t^i \delta(x_t - x_t^i) \tag{4}$$

where the function $\delta(\cdot)$ is the Dirac delta measure.

Note that the proposal distribution $q(x_t|x_{t-1}, y_t)$ is significant for any Monte Carlo method and should be properly approximated. In this paper, we propose Gaussian Processes as the proposal distribution, which incorporates arbitrary features into the covariance matrix modeling the uncertainties and provides a transition probability needed for the weight updating. Furthermore, Gaussian process proposal distribution, described in the following section, can choose the particles with highest likelihood by the optimal algorithm.

## 3   Gaussian Processes

Gaussian processes (GP) [8] [9] can facilitate modeling the uncertainty of complex data sets, and provides a completely theoretical framework for model selection and probability prediction simultaneously. Gaussian processes is a generalization of a multivariate Gaussian distribution and has the marginalization property. GP controls the properties of random data $x$ by a random process $f(x)$ and synchronously describes this random process by a probability distribution. GP describes a distribution over function and is fully specified by the mean function $m(x) = E[f(x)]$ and the covariance function (kernel function) $K(x, x') = E[(f(x) - m(x))(f(x') - m(x'))]$ of this random process $f(x)$:

$$f(x) \sim GP(m(x), K(x, x'))  \tag{5}$$

where the kernel $K(x, x')$ is usually chose as the form of Mercer kernel. For example, the Radial Basis Function (RBF) kernel function has the following form:

$$K(x, x') = \theta_1 \exp\left(-\frac{(x - x')^T (x - x')}{2\theta_2^2}\right)  \tag{6}$$

where $\theta_1$ and $\theta_2$ are the hyperparameters of the RBF kernel, which are generally selected by maximizing the marginal likelihood (evidence).

### 3.1   Gaussian Process Regression

We assume we are given a dataset (input vectors) $X = \{x_i\}_{i=1}^N$ and the corresponding target values $Y = \{y_i\}_{i=1}^N$. The graphical representation of Gaussian process regression [10] [11] is shown in Figure 1: The nodes are shaded to represent different treatments. White shaded nodes are unobserved variables (the latent function $f_i = f(x_i)$ ), grey shaded nodes are observed variables (input vectors $X$ and target values $Y$) and black shaded nodes are optimized (hyperparameters $\theta$ of kernel function $K$).

The main idea of Gaussian process regression is to assume that there is an unobservable latent function $f(x)$ which is imposed on a Gaussian process prior $f(X, \theta) \sim GP(0, K)$ , and the latent function preserves the mapping relationships between input vectors $X$ and target values $Y$: $Y = f(X) + \varepsilon$, where $\varepsilon \sim \mathcal{N}(0, \sigma^2)$ is an i.i.d Gaussian noise. Based on the Bayesian theorem, the posterior probability of the latent function $f$ given the input vectors $X$ can be written as:

$$p(f|y, X, \theta) = \frac{p(y|f)p(f|X, \theta)}{p(y|X, \theta)}  \tag{7}$$

where $p(y|f)$ is a Gaussian likelihood function, $p(f|X, \theta)$ is a Gaussian process prior and $p(y|X, \theta)$ is the normalization factor known as the evidence for the hyperparameters.

Based on the marginalization (consistency) property of Gaussian processes, the mean $\mu$ and the variance $\Sigma$ of the predictive distribution is obtained as following:

$$\mu = k_*^T (K + \sigma^2 I)^{-1} y  \tag{8}$$

$$\Sigma = k(x_*, x_*) - k_*^T (K + \sigma^2 I)^{-1} k_*  \tag{9}$$

where $k_* = k(x, x_*)$ is the covariance matrix between the known target value $x$ and the new target $x_*$.

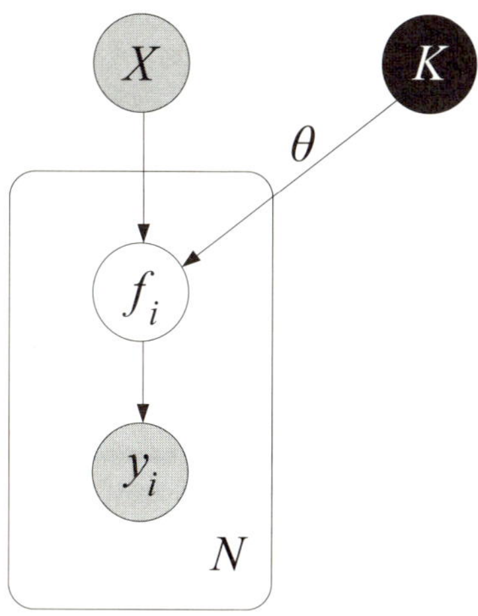

**Fig. 1.** The graphical representation of Gaussian Process Regression

## 3.2   Particle Filters with Gaussian Process Proposal

Based on the ideas of the previous sections, we propose the algorithm of particle filters with Gaussian process proposal as following:

- 1. At each time $t - 1$, we obtain $N_s$ particles (i.e., target candidates) and extract the feature vectors $X_{t-1} = \{x_{t-1}^i\}_{i=1}^{N_s}$ for each particle;
- 2. Then we calculate the similarity (distance) between the target and target candidate: $Y_{t-1} = \{y_{t-1}^i\}_{i=1}^{N_s} = \{w_{t-1}^i\}_{i=1}^{N_s}$;
- 3. Given the feature vectors $X_{t-1}$ and the similarity measurement $Y_{t-1}$, we learn the Gaussian process regression model (hyperparameters $\theta$ of the covariance function $K$) by maximizing the marginal likelihood as following:

$$p(y|X,\theta) = \int p(y|f)p(f|X,\theta)df \qquad (10)$$

and the covariance function $K$ has a squared-exponential form in this paper:

$$K(x,x') = \theta_1 \exp\left(-\frac{(x - x')^T(x - x')}{2\theta_2^2}\right) + \sigma^2 \delta_{xx'} \qquad (11)$$

where the optimal hyperparameters $\theta^* = (\theta_1^*, \theta_2^*, \sigma^*)$ is needed to be learned in this step;

- 4. At each time $t$, we sample $n$ times and draw $N_s$ particles each time from Gaussian process proposal as the following formula:

$$\{x_t^i\}_{i=1}^{N_s} = m + chol(K^*)u \qquad (12)$$

where $chol(K^*)$ is the Cholesky decomposition of covariance matrix $K^*$ with the optimal hyperparameters $\theta^*$, $m$ is the mean and $u \sim \mathcal{N}(0,I)$. Then we choose one $N_s$ particles set from $n$ sets, which can maximize the marginal likelihood in Equation (10), namely, this selected set particles with highest likelihood can maximize the item $p(y_t|x_t^i)$ in Equation (3);

- 5. Assign the weight $w_t^i$ to each particle according to Equation (3);
- 6. Resampling technique is applied to decrease the number of low weighted particles and to increase the ones with high weighted particles.

To sum up the ideas described above, a pseudo code description of this proposed algorithm is given as following:

---

**Algorithm 1.** Particle Filters with Gaussian Process Proposal (PFGP)

---

$[\{x_t^i, w_t^i\}_{i=1}^{N_s}] = PFGP[\{x_{t-1}^i, w_{t-1}^i\}_{i=1}^{N_s}, y_t]$

- Extract the feature vectors: $X_{t-1} = \{x_{t-1}^i\}_{i=1}^{N_s}$

- Calculate the similarity: $Y_{t-1} = \{y_{t-1}^i\}_{i=1}^{N_s} = \{w_{t-1}^i\}_{i=1}^{N_s}$

- Learn the optimal hyperparameters $\theta^*$ of the covariance function $K$

**for** $j = 1 : n$ **do**
- Draw $N_s^j$ particles from GP proposal according to Equation (12)
- Choose one $N_s$ particles set with highest likelihood in Equation (10)

**end**

**for** $i = 1 : N_s$ **do**
- Assign the weight $w_t^i$ to each particle according to Equation (3)

**end**

- Calculate total weight: $sum = \sum_{i=1}^{N_s} w_t^i$

**for** $i = 1 : N_s$ **do**
- Normalize: $w_t^i = sum^{-1} w_t^i$

**end**

- Evaluate the Particle Degeneracy by a certain rule: $N_e$

**if** $N_e$ *below threshold* $N_T$ **then**
- Resampling
- the weights are reset to $w_t^i = 1/N_s$

**end**

---

## 4   Experiments

To order to evaluate the effectiveness and robustness of the particle filters with Gaussian process proposal algorithm, we have experimented with jogging sequences (200 frames) and person-car sequence (120 frames) respectively under the different experimental conditions. The number of particles is set to 100 in the each experiment. We have also tried to compare the results of our proposed algorithm to the results of standard Particle Filters algorithm.

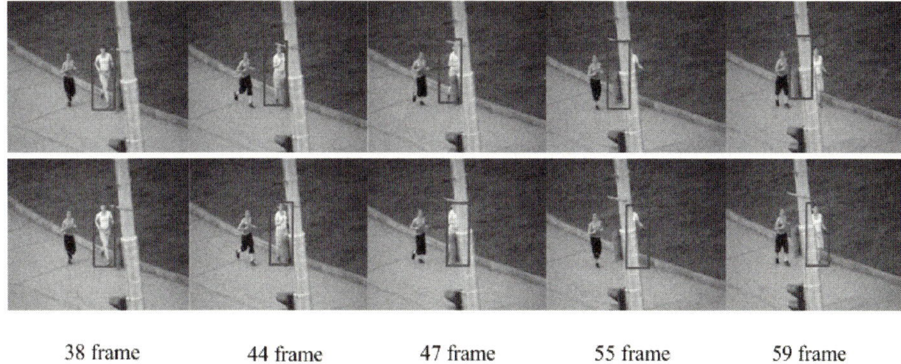

38 frame        44 frame        47 frame        55 frame        59 frame

**Fig. 2.** Tracking results of jogging sequence employing color histogram as features. Standard Particle Filter tracker(the first row). Our proposed tracker (the second row).

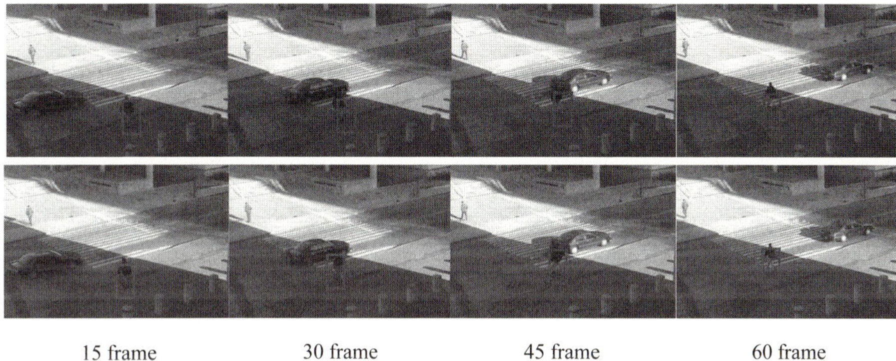

15 frame        30 frame        45 frame        60 frame

**Fig. 3.** Tracking results of person-car sequence employing color histogram as features. Standard Particle Filter tracker(the first row). Our proposed tracker (the second row).

## 4.1   Experiment 1

In experiment 1, for the purpose of demonstrating the effectiveness of proposed algorithm, we employ the simplest features, the normalized 8-bin color histogram, describing the target and candidate regions for each particle. For the similarity measure, we apply the Bhattacharyya distance [12], as the following equation, to measure the distance between the normalized color histograms of two regions.

$$B(h_t, h_c) = \sum_{i=1}^{m} \sqrt{h_t^i h_c^i} \tag{13}$$

where $h_t$ and $h_c$ respectively denote the $m$-bin normalized color histograms of target and candidate.

In Figure 2 and Figure 3, we demonstrate the tracking results of jogging sequence and person-car sequence respectively. The first row of each figure corresponds to the standard particle filter tracker, and the second rows to the results of our method. We can notice that the jogger is occluded from 44 frame to 59 frame and the color of clutters is similar to the target in the jogging sequence. Also in the person-car sequence, the color of the shadow and the car is similar to the walker. As a result, the standard Particle Filters method fails to track the target in the occlusion, while our proposed method better deals with the occlusion case with weak features exactly demonstrating the effectiveness of our algorithm.

## 4.2 Experiment 2

In experiment 2, we employ the stronger features, 7-dimentional feature[13], describing the target and candidate regions for each particle:

$$F(x,y) = (x, y, \Delta_x(x,y), \Delta_y(x,y), R(x,y), G(x,y), B(x,y)) \tag{14}$$

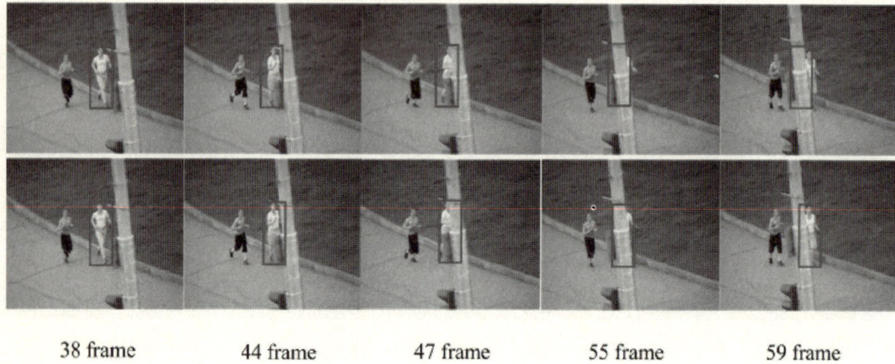


**Fig. 4.** Tracking results of jogging sequence employing 7-dimentional features. Standard Particle Filter tracker(the first row). Our proposed tracker (the second row).

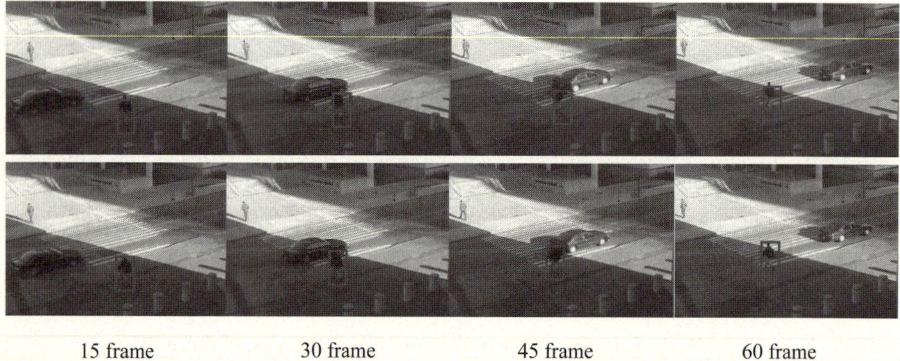


**Fig. 5.** Tracking results of person-car sequence employing 7-dimentional features. Standard Particle Filter tracker(the first row). Our proposed tracker (the second row).

where $x$ and $y$ are are pixel location, $\Delta_x$ and $\Delta_y$ denote the intensity derivatives, $R$, $G$ and $B$ are RGB color values.

As the results shown in Figure 4 and Figure 5, we note that the standard Particle Filter tracker and our proposed tracker also improve the performance over the occlusion with the stronger features, simultaneously our proposed method obtains the optimal tracking results that further demonstrate the effectiveness and robustness of our proposed algorithm.

## 5   Conclusion

In this paper we have presented an algorithm that applies Gaussian process regression as the proposal distribution of Particle filters, which can choose the particles with the highest likelihood for particle filters, and improve the robustness and ability of the standard particle filter tracker, even obtain better performance in the occlusion case. As future work, we plan to extend the approach in order to be able to track multiple objects with occlusions and improve the multi-object tracking performance.

**Acknowledgments.** The work is supported by National Natural Science Foundation of China (Grant No.60605004), Key Project of National Natural Science Foundation of China (Grant No.60833006) and National High-Tech Research and Development Plan of China (863) (Grant No.2006AA01Z117).

## References


1. Comaniciu, D., Ramesh, V., Meer, P.: Kernel-based Object Tracking. IEEE Trans. Pattern Analysis and Machine Intelligence 25(5), 564–577 (2003)
2. Arulampalam, M.S., Maskell, S., Gordon, N., Clapp, T.: A Tutorial on Particle Filters for Online Nonlinear/Non-Gaussian Bayesian Tracking. IEEE Transactions On Signal Processing 50(2) (2002)
3. Pérez, P., Hue, C., Vermaak, J., Gangnet, M.: Color-Based Probabilistic Tracking. In: Heyden, A., Sparr, G., Nielsen, M., Johansen, P. (eds.) ECCV 2002. LNCS, vol. 2350, pp. 661–675. Springer, Heidelberg (2002)
4. Okuma, K., Taleghani, A., de Freitas, N., Little, J.J., Lowe, D.G.: A boosted particle filter: Multitarget detection and tracking. In: Pajdla, T., Matas, J(G.) (eds.) ECCV 2004. LNCS, vol. 3021, pp. 28–39. Springer, Heidelberg (2004)
5. Jin, Y., Mokhtarian, F.: Variational Particle Filter for Multi-Object Tracking. In: International Conference on Computer Vision (2007)
6. De Freitas: Sequential Monte Carlo methods to train neural network models. Neural Computation 12(4), 955–993 (2000)
7. Wan, E.A., van der Merwe, R.: The Unscented Kalman Filter for Nonlinear Estimation. Adaptive Systems for Signal Processing, Communications, and Control Symposium (2000)
8. Rasmussen, C.E., Williams, C.K.I.: Gaussian Processes for Machine Learning. MIT Press, Cambridge (2006)

9. Rasmussen, C.E.: Advances in Gaussian Processes. Advances in Neural Information Processing Systems (2006)
10. Williams, C.K.I.: Prediction with Gaussian processes:from the linear regression to linear prediction and beyond. Learning and Inference in Graphical Models (1998)
11. Csato, L., Opper, M.: Sparse online Gaussian processes. Neural Computation (2002)
12. Nummiaroa, K., Koller-Meierb, E., Gool, L.V.: An Adaptive Color-Based Particle Filter. Image and Vision Computing 21, 99–110 (2003)
13. Wu, Y., Wu, B., Liu, J., Lu, H.: Probabilistic Tracking on Riemannian Manifolds. In: The 19th International Conference on Pattern Recognition (2008)

# Image Inpainting Considering Brightness Change and Spatial Locality of Textures and Its Evaluation


Norihiko Kawai, Tomokazu Sato, and Naokazu Yokoya

Graduate School of Information Science, Nara Institute of Science and Technology
8916-5 Takayama, Ikoma, Nara 630-0192, Japan
{norihi-k,tomoka-s,yokoya}@is.naist.jp
http://yokoya.naist.jp/



**Abstract.** Image inpainting techniques have been widely investigated to remove undesired objects in an image. Conventionally, missing parts in an image are completed by optimizing the objective function using pattern similarity. However, unnatural textures are easily generated due to two factors: (1) available samples in the image are quite limited, and (2) pattern similarity is one of the required conditions but is not sufficient for reproducing natural textures. In this paper, we propose a new energy function based on the pattern similarity considering brightness changes of sample textures (for (1)) and introducing spatial locality as an additional constraint (for (2)). The effectiveness of the proposed method is successfully demonstrated by qualitative and quantitative evaluation. Furthermore, the evaluation methods used in much inpainting research are discussed.

**Keywords:** Image Inpainting, Energy Minimization, Evaluation Method.


## 1   Introduction

Image inpainting methods have been widely investigated to remove undesired visual objects in an image. These methods can be classified into two categories. One is a non-exemplar-based method and the other is an exemplar-based method. The non-exemplar-based methods [1,2,3,4,5,6,7,8,9,10,11] are based on pixel interpolation considering the continuity of pixel intensity. These methods are effective for small image gaps like scratches in a photograph. However, the resultant image easily becomes unclear when the missing region is large. Therefore, recently many exemplar-based inpainting methods have been intensively developed because they can synthesize complex textures in the missing region.

Exemplar-based methods basically synthesize textures for the missing region based on pattern similarity that is defined between the missing region and the rest of the image (data region). Some of the exemplar-based methods use the distance in the feature space as a similarity measure. As the feature space, Fourier space, wavelet domain and eigenspace have been used [12,13,14]. Most of the other exemplar-based methods simply employ SSD (Sum of Squared Differences)-based pattern similarity measures [15,16,17,18,19,20,21,22,23,24]. Efros et al. [15] have proposed a method that successively copies the most similar


T. Wada, F. Huang, and S. Lin (Eds.): PSIVT 2009, LNCS 5414, pp. 271–282, 2009.

pattern from the data region to the missing region. Although this method can generate complex textures, the quality of resultant images is severely affected by the order of texture copy. To obtain good results with successive texture copy, confidence maps such as the number of fixed pixels in a window, strength of isophotes around the missing regions and pattern similarity have been used to determine the order of texture copy [16,17,18]. Although the duplication of similar textures preserves the local texture continuity in these methods, discontinuous textures are easily synthesized in the completed image. To avoid the ordering problem, recent inpainting methods employ the iterative global optimization approach [19,20,21]. In these methods, the objective functions that evaluate the pattern similarity are defined and optimized by using EM algorithm, Belief Propagation approach and graph cut approach.

Although the global optimization methods have obtained good results for many images, unnatural images are still generated due to two factors: (1) available samples in the data region are quite limited, and (2) pattern similarity is one of the required conditions but is not sufficient for reproducing natural textures. Thus, in order to improve the image quality, these two factors should be considered. There have already been some attempts at this. For (1), the scale and orientation of textures have been considered to obtain effective samples [22]. For (2), Sun et al. [23] and Jia et al. [24] have proposed techniques that use explicit constraints for texture boundaries. These methods synthesize textures preserving the edges or boundaries of the texture. However, automatic and effective determination of these explicit constraints is still difficult.

In this paper, we propose a new approach that is different from conventional ones. For (1), brightness change of sample textures that has not been considered in the literature is allowed to obtain effective samples. For (2), the spatial locality of texture pattern is considered as an implicit constraint that is usually satisfied in a lot of real scenes. In this study, these ideas are implemented with the framework of energy minimization. The effectiveness of our method is demonstrated with subjective and objective evaluation. In addition, in this paper, the validity of evaluation methods for image inpainting which has not been well discussed is analyzed. Furthermore, the problems of qualitative and quantitative evaluation methods that have been used in the literature are clearly demonstrated.

## 2    Image Inpainting Based on Energy Minimization

In the proposed method, after initial values are given to missing regions, the target regions are completed by minimizing an energy function. In the following sections, the definition of an energy function and the minimization method of the energy function are described.

### 2.1    Energy Function Considering Brightness Change and Spatial Locality

As illustrated in Figure 1, an image is divided into region $\Omega'$ including the missing region $\Omega$ and the data region $\Phi$, which is the rest of the image. The plausibility

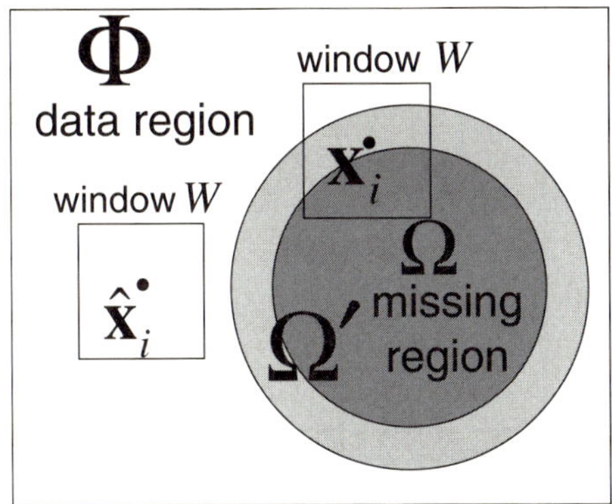


**Fig. 1.** Data and missing regions in an image

in the missing region $\Omega$ is defined by using image patterns in the data region $\Phi$. Here, $\Omega'$ is the expanded area of the missing region $\Omega$. $\Omega'$ has a central pixel $\mathbf{x}_i$ of a square window $W$ overlapping the region $\Omega$. The energy function is defined as the weighed sum of $SSD'$ representing the pattern similarity considering brightness change and $SD$ representing the spatial locality as follows:

$$E = \sum_{\mathbf{x}_i \in \Omega'} w_{\mathbf{x}_i} \left\{ SSD'(\mathbf{x}_i, \hat{\mathbf{x}}_i) + w_{dis} SD(\mathbf{x}_i, \hat{\mathbf{x}}_i) \right\}, \tag{1}$$

where $\mathbf{x}_i$ is the pixel in the region $\Omega'$, $\hat{\mathbf{x}}_i$ is the corresponding pixel in the data region $\Phi$ and $w_{dis}$ is the weight for the spatial locality. Here, $w_{\mathbf{x}_i}$ is the weight for pixel $\mathbf{x}_i$ and is set as 1 if $\mathbf{x}_i$ is inside of the region $\Omega' \cap \overline{\Omega}$ because pixel values in this region are fixed: otherwise $w_{\mathbf{x}_i}$ is set as $c^{-d}$ ($d$ is the distance from the boundary of $\Omega$ and $c$ is a constant) because pixel values around the boundary have higher confidence than those in the center of the missing region. In the following, definitions of $SSD'(\mathbf{x}_i, \hat{\mathbf{x}}_i)$ and $SD(\mathbf{x}_i, \hat{\mathbf{x}}_i)$ are described.

**Similarity considering brightness change**

The similarity measure $SSD'$ is defined as:

$$SSD'(\mathbf{x}_i, \hat{\mathbf{x}}_i) = \sum_{\mathbf{p} \in W} \left\{ I(\mathbf{x}_i + \mathbf{p}) - \alpha_{\mathbf{x}_i \hat{\mathbf{x}}_i} I(\hat{\mathbf{x}}_i + \mathbf{p}) \right\}^2, \tag{2}$$

where $I(\mathbf{x})$ represents the intensity of pixel $\mathbf{x}$. $\alpha_{\mathbf{x}_i \hat{\mathbf{x}}_i}$ is the intensity modification coefficient. By using this coefficient, the brightness of the texture in the data region is adjusted to that in the missing region so as to prevent unnatural brightness changes. In this paper, we employ the ratio of average pixel values around the pixels $\mathbf{x}_i$ and $\hat{\mathbf{x}}_i$ as the coefficient $\alpha_{\mathbf{x}_i \hat{\mathbf{x}}_i}$.

$$\alpha_{\mathbf{x}_i \hat{\mathbf{x}}_i} = \frac{\sqrt{\sum_{\mathbf{q} \in W} I(\mathbf{x}_i + \mathbf{q})^2}}{\sqrt{\sum_{\mathbf{q} \in W} I(\hat{\mathbf{x}}_i + \mathbf{q})^2}}. \tag{3}$$

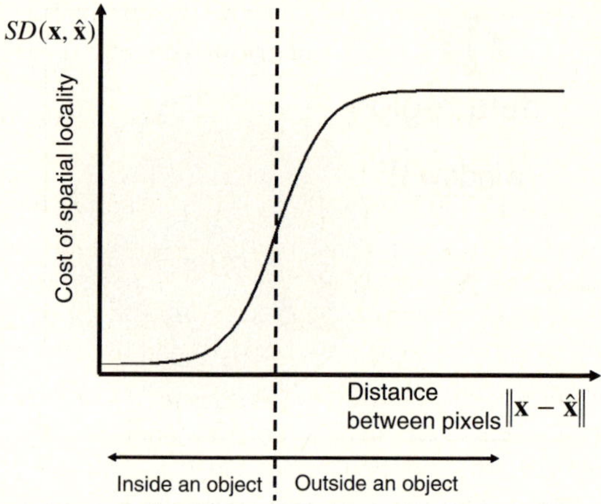


**Fig. 2.** Sigmoid function for cost of spatial locality

However, an unnatural image is easily generated if large brightness change is approximated by linear transformation. Therefore, we limit the range of the value $\alpha_{\mathbf{x}_i \hat{\mathbf{x}}_i}$.

**Spatial locality of texture**

Cost term $SD$ for spatial locality of a texture pattern is defined by using a sigmoid function:

$$SD(\mathbf{x}_i, \hat{\mathbf{x}}_i) = \frac{\| W \|}{1 + e^{\{-K(\|\mathbf{x}_i - \hat{\mathbf{x}}_i\| - X_0)\}}}, \tag{4}$$

where $K$ and $X_0$ are constant and $\| W \|$ is the number of pixels in a window. As illustrated in Fiture 2, this cost term is based on the assumption that the probability of similar texture existence for a certain pixel is uniformly high (cost is uniformly low) in the object region which the pixel belongs to. On the other hand, outside the object region, the probability can be assumed to be uniformly low (cost is uniformly high). By adding the constraint of spatial locality, even when the deformation of texture pattern exists around the missing region, appropriate textures that exist near the missing region are preferentially selected.

## 2.2 Energy Minimization

The energy function $E$ in Eq. (1) is minimized by using a framework of greedy algorithm. In our definition of the energy $E$, the energy for each pixel can be treated independently if pattern pairs $(\mathbf{x}_i, \hat{\mathbf{x}}_i)$ can be fixed and the change of the coefficient $\alpha_{\mathbf{x}_i \hat{\mathbf{x}}_i}$ in iteration is very small. Thus, we repeat the following two processes until the energy converges: (i) update of pairs of windows keeping pixel values fixed, and (ii) parallel update of all the pixel values keeping pairs of windows fixed.

In process (i), the update of the pair of windows is performed by calculating $\hat{\mathbf{x}}_i$ keeping the pixel values $I(\mathbf{x}_i)$ fixed. $\hat{\mathbf{x}}_i$ is determined as follows:

$$\hat{\mathbf{x}}_i = f(\mathbf{x}_i) = \underset{\mathbf{x} \in \Phi}{\operatorname{argmin}}(SSD'(\mathbf{x}_i, \mathbf{x}) + w_{dis}SD(\mathbf{x}_i, \mathbf{x})). \tag{5}$$

In process (ii), all the pixel values $I(\mathbf{x}_i)$ are updated in parallel so as to minimize the energy keeping the similar pairs of windows fixed. In the following, the method for calculating the pixel values $I(\mathbf{x}_i)$ is described. First, the energy $E$ is resolved into the element energy $E(\mathbf{x}_i)$ for each pixel in the missing region.

As shown in Figure 3, the target pixel to be updated is $\mathbf{x}_i$, and the pixel position inside a window can be expressed as $\mathbf{x}_i + \mathbf{p}$ ($\mathbf{p} \in W$) and is corresponded to $f(\mathbf{x}_i + \mathbf{p})$ by Eq. (5). Thus, the position of the pixel corresponding to the pixel $\mathbf{x}_i$ is $f(\mathbf{x}_i + \mathbf{p}) - \mathbf{p}$. Now, the element energy $E(\mathbf{x}_i)$ can be expressed in terms of the pixel values of $\mathbf{x}_i$ and $f(\mathbf{x}_i + \mathbf{p}) - \mathbf{p}$, the coefficient $\alpha$ and the Euclid distance between $\mathbf{x}_i$ and $f(\mathbf{x}_i)$ as follows:

$$E(\mathbf{x}_i) = \sum_{\mathbf{p} \in W} w_{(\mathbf{x}_i + \mathbf{p})} \{ I(\mathbf{x}_i) - \alpha_{(\mathbf{x}_i + \mathbf{p})f(\mathbf{x}_i + \mathbf{p})} I(f(\mathbf{x}_i + \mathbf{p}) - \mathbf{p}) \}^2$$

$$+ w_{dis} \frac{\| W \|}{1 + e^{\{-K(\|\mathbf{x}_i - f(\mathbf{x}_i)\| - X_0)\}}}. \tag{6}$$

The relationship between the energy $E$ for all of the missing region and the element energy $E(\mathbf{x}_i)$ for each pixel can be written as follows:

$$E = \sum_{\mathbf{x}_i \in \Omega} E(\mathbf{x}_i) + C. \tag{7}$$

$C$ is the energy of pixels in the region $\overline{\Omega} \cap \Omega'$, and is treated as a constant because pixel intensities in the region and all pairs of windows are fixed here. Therefore, by minimizing the element energy $E(\mathbf{x})$ respectively, the total energy $E$ can be minimized. Here, if it is assumed that the change of $\alpha_{\mathbf{x}_i f(\mathbf{x}_i)}$ is smaller than that of the pixel intensity $I(\mathbf{x}_i)$, by differentiating $E(\mathbf{x}_i)$ with respect to $I(\mathbf{x}_i)$, each pixel value $I(\mathbf{x}_i)$ in the missing region can be calculated in parallel as follows:

$$I(\mathbf{x}_i) = \frac{\sum_{\mathbf{p} \in W} w_{(\mathbf{x}_i + \mathbf{p})} \alpha_{(\mathbf{x}_i + \mathbf{p})f(\mathbf{x}_i + \mathbf{p})} I(f(\mathbf{x}_i + \mathbf{p}) - \mathbf{p})}{\sum_{\mathbf{p} \in W} w_{(\mathbf{x}_i + \mathbf{p})}}. \tag{8}$$

Additionally, in order to avoid local minima efficiently, a coarse-to-fine approach is also employed for energy minimization. Specifically, an image pyramid is generated and the energy minimization processes (i) and (ii) are repeated from higher-level to lower-level layers successively using a certain size of window. Good initial values are given to the lower layer by projecting results from the higher layer. This makes it possible to decrease computational cost and avoid local minima. In the lowest layer (original size), the energy minimization process is repeated while reducing the size of the window, and it enables reproduction of more detailed textures.

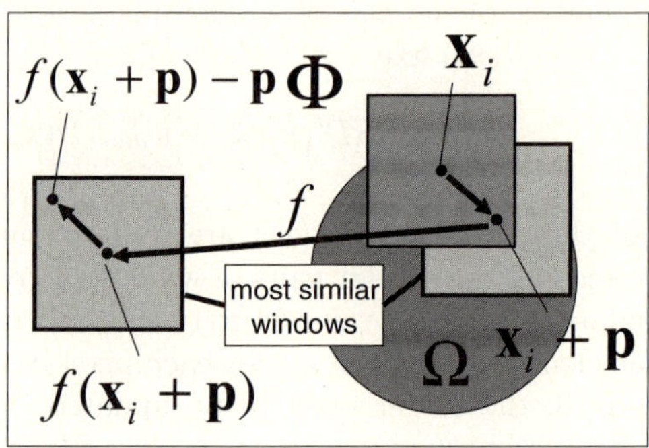


**Fig. 3.** Relationship between pixels in energy calculation

## 3    Experiments

In experiments, we have compared the proposed method with conventional ones using 100 images. The methods are our implemented Criminisi's method (Method A) [17], our implemented Wexler's method (Method B) [20] and the proposed method (Method E). To confirm the effectiveness of considering the brightness change and spatial locality, respectively, the proposed method allowing only brightness change (Method C) and the proposed method considering only spatial locality (Method D) were also evaluated. In these experiments, each parameter in the energy function was set as shown in Table 1 for all the images. Here, the missing region was manually specified, and the average pixel value of the boundary of the missing region was given as an initial value in the missing region.

### 3.1    Qualitative Evaluation

All the completed images by 5 methods were subjectively evaluated by 37 subjects. The subjects were requested to access the web page for questionnaire evaluation and evaluate the resultant images arranged in random order by giving a score of 1(bad) to 5 (good).

**Table 1.** Parameters in experiments

| Window size | $N_w$ | max 9×9 |
|---|---|---|
| | | min 3×3 |
| Weight for distance | $w_{dis}$ | 120 |
| Parameter in sigmoid function | $K$ | 0.4 |
| | $X_0$ | 20 |
| Range of coefficient $\alpha$ | $D$ | 0.1 |

The average scores of the 100 resultant images are shown in Table 2 for each method.[1] Table 2 shows that the average score by the proposed method (method E) is higher than the scores by the conventional methods (methods A and B). In this experiment, scores of the proposed method (method E) and the conventional methods (methods A and B) were compared by using the t-test with a 5% significant level. Resultingly, significant difference was observed between these scores. In addition, both methods C and D obtained higher scores than methods A and B and significant differences were also observed by using the t-test with a 5% significant level. Therefore, the proposed method can be statistically verified to be better than the conventional methods A and B, and considering brightness change and spatial locality is respectively effective. Figure 4 shows example images for which the proposed method had better scores. The proposed method has generated better results for the images in which brightness change and deformation of texture patterns exist around the missing regions due to the illumination change and the perspective projection effect.

## 3.2   Quantitative Evaluation

In this experiment, RMSE was computed for 29 images whose missing regions were specified regardless of the object regions, and we did not use the remaining 71 images because the missing regions of the 71 images are specified so as to remove certain objects. Table 3 shows the average RMSE. From the results, the proposed method is the best of all 5 the methods and significant differences between the proposed (E) and conventional methods (A and B) were observed by using the t-test with a 5% significant level.

## 3.3   Discussion of Evaluation Methods

Although some evaluation have been done in the literature of image inpainting, the validity of evaluation methods has not been well discussed. In this section, qualitative and quantitative evaluation methods are analyzed using our results and their problems are clarified.

**Table 2.** Average score from 100 images

| Method | A | B | C | D | E |
|---|---|---|---|---|---|
| Average score | 2.21 | 3.24 | 3.39 | 3.42 | 3.60 |

**Table 3.** Average RMSE from 29 images

| Method | A | B | C | D | E |
|---|---|---|---|---|---|
| RMSE | 42.95 | 28.40 | 27.83 | 28.36 | 27.44 |

---

[1] One hundred input and resultant images are shown on the web page [http://yokoya.naist.jp/research/inpainting/].

(a) Input images with a missing region.

(b) Results by Wexler's method [20].

(c) Results by the proposed method.

**Fig. 4.** Example images providing the proposed method with better scores

## Reliability of qualitative evaluation

The evaluation using a few images and a few subjects may not be able to validate
the effectiveness of inpainting methods due to the bias of images and subjects.
In this section, the reliability of the result when the images and subjects are

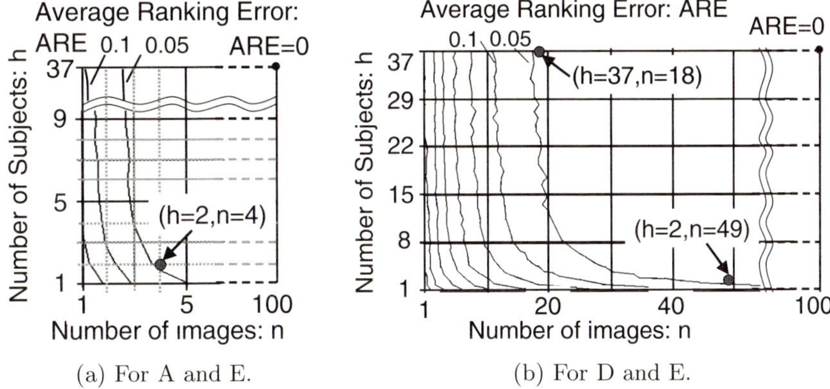


(a) For A and E.                    (b) For D and E.

**Fig. 5.** Relationships among ARE and the number of images and subjects

decreased in a questionnaire is analyzed in simulation. Here, the ranking of the methods decided by the average of scores given by 37 subjects in the questionnaire using 100 images were used as the ground truth.

In this paper, as the reliability measure of evaluation results, RE (Ranking Error) is defined as:

$$RE(n,h) = \begin{cases} 0 & (\forall i, g(i,100,37) - g(i,n,h) = 0) \\ 1 & (otherwise), \end{cases} \tag{9}$$

where $g(i,n,h)$ represents the rank order of the method $i$ determined by $n$ images and $h$ subjects. In this study, we compute $RE(n,h)$ with respect to random selection of $n$ images and $h$ subjects from 100 images and 37 subjects. $ARE(n,h)$ is the average score of $RE(n,h)$ by 10,000 times selection.

Figure 5 shows the relationship among ARE and the number of images and subjects. In this figure, (a) and (b) illustrate isolines of ARE for the methods A and E, and D and E, respectively. In this figure, isolines are drawn every 0.05.

The scores of the methods A and E are significantly and largely different. From Figure 5(a), when $h=2$, the ranking corresponds to the ground truth more than 95% of the time ($ARE=0.05$) if $n>3$. Therefore, for methods that generate significantly different results, the ranking is usually equivalent to the ground truth even if the numbers of subjects and images are small. On the other hand, the scores of the methods D and E are significantly but a little different. From Figure 5(b), in order for the ranking to correspond to the ground truth more than 95% of the time, more than 49 images are needed if $h=2$. Even if $h=37$, at least 18 images are needed. Therefore, if the numbers of subjects and images are small, the ranking may not correspond to the ground truth and the result of subjective evaluation is not reliable. Therefore, to evaluate image inpainting methods persuasively, many images and subjects (for example, 40 images and 5 subjects) are needed.

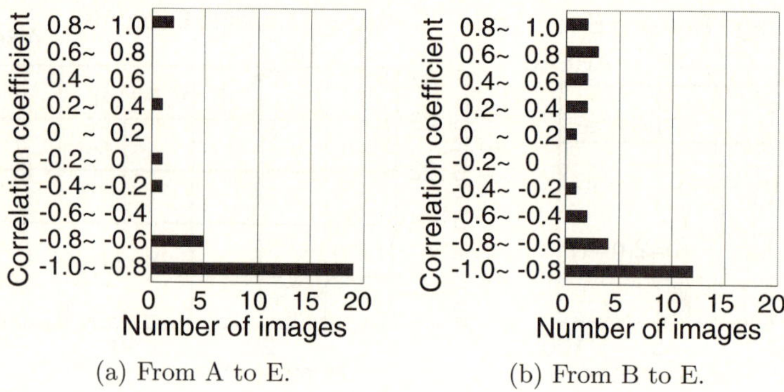

(a) From A to E.                    (b) From B to E.

**Fig. 6.** Correlation coefficient between RMSE and subjective score

**Fig. 7.** Images with inverse correlation between RMSE and subjective evaluations

## Relationship between quantitative and qualitative evaluation

In the literature on image inpainting, as the quantitative evaluation, MSE (Mean Squared Error), RMSE (Root Mean Squared Error) and PSNR (Peak Signal-to-Noise Ratio), which are based on computing pixel-wise differences between original and inpainted images, have been often used. In this evaluation, RMSE is computed for each image, and the relationship between RMSE and scores given by subjects is discussed.

Figure 6 illustrates the distribution of the correlation coefficient between RMSE and the subjective score for 29 images: (a) is by 5 methods, (b) is by 4 methods except for method A [17]. Correlation coefficient $Cc$ is computed as follows:

$$Cc = \frac{N_m \Sigma_i^{N_m} R_i S_i - \Sigma_i^{N_m} R_i \Sigma_i^{N_m} S_i}{\sqrt{N_m \Sigma_i^{N_m} R_i^2 - (\Sigma_i^{N_m} R_i)^2} \sqrt{N_m \Sigma_i^{N_m} S_i^2 - (\Sigma_i^{N_m} S_i)^2}}, \quad (10)$$

where $N_m$ is the number of methods, $R_i$ is RMSE and $S_i$ is the average score by subjects. From Table 3 and Figure 6(a), there is a clear negative correlation between RMSE and subjective score. From this, although the evaluation result by RMSE may correspond to the ground truth, there also exist three images (Figure 7) where positive correlation exists. As shown in Figure 7, these images have very high-frequency components. It is well known that pixel correlation-based similarity measures including RMSE are sensitive to pixel phase shift for a high frequency component. However, such a pixel phase shift does not always affect the naturality of images. Thus, RMSE cannot appropriately evaluate the images with a high frequency component. Figure 6(b) illustrates the distribution of the correlation coefficient by the 4 methods except for method A, whose score is extremely low. In Figure 6(b), one third of the coefficients indicate positive correlation. This means that the small difference in RMSE does not always represent that of image naturality. Therefore, RMSE cannot be used as an absolute criterion of image naturality but can be used for a rough evaluation.

## 4   Conclusion

In this paper, the new energy function for image inpainting has been proposed. To obtain good results for many images, two factors were considered: (1) brightness change of sample textures was allowed, (2) spatial locality was introduced as a new constraint. By considering these two factors, the missing region was completed successfully for many images. In experiments, we have demonstrated the effectiveness of our method by qualitative and quantitative evaluation. we have also discussed the validity of evaluation methods for image inpainting. In future work, we should establish a method to decide optimum parameters automatically by analyzing an image.

**Acknowledgments.** This research was partially supported by the Ministry of Education, Culture, Sports, Science and Technology, Grant-in-Aid for Scientific Research (A), 19200016.

## References


1. Levin, A., Zomet, A., Weiss, Y.: Learning How to Inpaint from Global Image Statistics. In: Proc. ICCV, vol. 1, pp. 305–312 (2003)
2. Ballester, C., Bertalmio, M., Sapiro, V., Verdera, J.: Filling-In by Joint Interpolation of Vector Fields and Gray Levels. Trans. on Image Processing 10(8), 1200–1211 (2001)
3. Ballester, C., Caselles, V., Verdera, J., Bertalmio, M., Sapiro, G.: A Variational Model for Filling-In Gray Level and Color Images. In: Proc. ICCV, pp. 10–16 (2001)
4. Tschumperlé, D.: Curvature-preserving regularization of multi-valued images using pDE's. In: Leonardis, A., Bischof, H., Pinz, A. (eds.) ECCV 2006. LNCS, vol. 3952, pp. 295–307. Springer, Heidelberg (2006)
5. Villéger, E., Aubert, G., Blanc-Féraud, L.: Image Disocclusion Using a Probabilistic Gradient Orientation. In: Proc. ICPR, vol. 2, pp. 52–55 (2004)
6. Bertalmio, M., Bertozzi, A.L., Sapiro, G.: Navier-Stokes, Fluid Dynamics, and Image and Video Inpainting. In: Proc. CVPR, pp. 355–362 (2001)

7. Bertalmio, M., Sapiro, G., Caselles, V., Ballester, C.: Image Inpainting. In: Proc. SIGGRAPH 2000, pp. 417–424 (2000)
8. Esedoglu, S., Shen, J.: Digital Inpainting Based on the Mumford-shah-euler Image Model. European J. of Applied Mathematics 13, 353–370 (2003)
9. Masnou, S., Morel, J.M.: Level Lines Based Disocclusion. In: Proc. ICIP, vol. 3, pp. 259–263 (1998)
10. Chan, T., Shen, J.: Non-texture Inpainting by Curvature-Driven Diffusions (CDD). J. of Visual Communication and Image Representation 12(4), 436–449 (2001)
11. Chan, T., Kang, S., Shen, J., Osher, S.: Euler's Elastica and Curvature Based Inpaintings. SIAM J. of Applied Mathematics 63(2), 564–592 (2002)
12. Hirani, A.N., Totsuka, T.: Combining Frequency and Spatial Domain Information for Fast Interactive Image Noise Removal. In: Proc. SIGGRAPH 1996, pp. 269–276 (1996)
13. Rane, S.D., Remus, J., Sapiro, G.: Wavelet-Domain Reconstruction of Lost Blocks in Wireless Image Transmission and Packet-Switched. In: Proc. ICIP, vol. 1, pp. 309–312 (2002)
14. Amano, T.: Image Interpolation by High Dimensional Projection Based on Subspace Method. In: Proc. ICPR, vol. 4, pp. 665–668 (2004)
15. Efros, A.A., Leung, T.K.: Texture Synthesis by Non-parametric Sampling. In: Proc. ICCV, pp. 1033–1038 (1999)
16. Bornard, R., Lecan, E., Laborelli, L., Chenot, J.: Missing Data Correction in Still Images and Image Sequences. In: Proc. ACM Int. Conf. on Multimedia, pp. 355–361 (2002)
17. Criminisi, A., Pérez, P., Toyama, K.: Region Filling and Object Removal by Exemplar-Based Image Inpainting. Trans. on Image Processing 13(9), 1200–1212 (2004)
18. Li, B., Qi, Y., Shen, X.: An Image Inpainting Method. In: Proc. IEEE Int. Conf. on Computer Aided Design and Computer Graphics, pp. 531–536 (2005)
19. Allène, C., Paragios, N.: Image Renaissance Using Discrete Optimization. In: Proc. ICPR, pp. 631–634 (2006)
20. Wexler, Y., Shechtman, E., Irani, M.: Space-Time Completion of Video. Trans. on PAMI 29(3), 463–476 (2007)
21. Komodakis, N., Tziritas, G.: Image Completion Using Global Optimization. In: Proc. CVPR, pp. 442–452 (2006)
22. Drori, I., Cohen-Or, D., Yeshurun, H.: Fragment-Based Image Completion. In: Proc. SIGGRAPH 2003, pp. 303–312 (2003)
23. Sun, J., Yuan, L., Jia, J., Shum, H.: Image Completion with Structure Propagation. In: Proc. SIGGRAPH 2005, pp. 861–868 (2005)
24. Jia, J., Tang, C.: Image Repairing: Robust Image Synthesis by Adaptive ND Tensor Voting. In: Proc. CVPR, pp. 643–650 (2003)

# A Digital Image Denoising Method with Edge Preservation Using Dyadic Lifting Schemes


Teruya Minamoto and Satoshi Fujii

Saga University, Saga, Japan
{minamoto,fujii}@ma.is.saga-u.ac.jp



**Abstract.** In this paper we proposed a new wavelet denoising method for digital images with edge preservation. Briefly stated, our method consists of a combination of the dyadic lifting schemes with the edge-preserving wavelet thresholding. The dyadic lifting schemes have free parameters which enable us to construct the filters having important image features. We describe how to determine these parameters and the denoising algorithm with edge preservation in detail. Some numerical experiments are presented, and we show that these parameters play an important role to denoise.


## 1 Introduction

Digital imaging has seen a huge progress over the last decade through the broad availability of digital cameras including web cameras and mobile phones. Since these digital images are often taken in poor conditions (e.g., photographing in a dark place), many images are corrupted by noise of several types. Therefore, the efficient image restoration methods are needed.

There are already commonly used spatial domain filters such as the weighted mean and median which can reduce corruption within images. In particular, PDE-based methods have been widely used for image denoising with edge preservation over the past few decades. These methods are either based on the nonlinear diffusions, or on the variational approach of energy functional minimization [1]. There are also an optimal Bayesian minimum mean square estimation (MMSE) based method to denoise [5]. An alternative approach would be to use the frequency domains. Especially, wavelet transforms have been successfully employed in image processing. Donoho proposed the soft-threshold method in which the wavelet coefficients are below a certain threshold value reduced gradually to zero [2]. This method based on down-sampling type of wavelet transform. However down-sampling wavelet is not shift-invariant, thus it tends to fail to carry out edge detection, feature extraction, and denoising. On the other hand, dyadic wavelet transform is shift-invariant as compared to discrete down-sampling type wavelet transform. Mallat has performed edge detection using discrete dyadic wavelet transform with quadratic spline dyadic wavelets [3,4].

In general, denoising algorithms have to balance the trade-off between denoising and preservation of structure. To overcome such a difficulty, there has


T. Wada, F. Huang, and S. Lin (Eds.): PSIVT 2009, LNCS 5414, pp. 283–294, 2009.

been a lot of work in the recent years on edge preserving algorithms. Standard algorithms are based on non-linear diffusion, or wavelets [1,8]. Unfortunately, in spite of the sophistication of the recently proposed methods, most algorithms have not yet attained a desirable level of applicability. The study for efficient image denoising methods still is a valid challenge.

Very recently, the dyadic lifting schemes which extend Sweldens lifting schemes [7] is proposed in [6]. This dyadic lifting schemes have free parameters and two construction methods for custom-design of dyadic wavelets having desirable number of vanishing moments are also proposed in [6]. The authors designed spline dyadic wavelet filters with higher numbers of vanishing moments for denoising digital images and show its effectiveness in [6]. But the authors do not touch on the topic of edge-preserving, explicitly.

The purpose of this paper is to develop a new wavelet denoising method that exploit the dyadic lifting schemes and edge-preserving denoising method proposed in [8]. Differently from [6], we do not use their construction methods. We propose a new way to determine the free parameters in the dyadic lifting schemes which is suited to maintaining important image features instead.

This paper is organized as follows: in Section 2, we briefly introduce the dyadic lifting schemes which have the free parameters. The learning method to determine these free parameters is presented in Section 3. We describe the edge preserving method in Section 4 and the denoising algorithm in Section 5. Simulation results are demonstrated in Section 6, and Section 7 conclude this paper.

## 2   Dyadic Lifting Schemes

The arguments outlined in this section are very similar to those given in Refs.[3,4,6]. We include this outline to make the present paper self-contained.

Let $L^2(\mathbb{R})$ be the space of square integrable functions on real line $\mathbb{R}$. We define the Fourier transform of the function $\psi \in L^2(\mathbb{R})$ by $\hat{\psi}(\omega) = \int_{-\infty}^{\infty} \psi(t)e^{-i\omega t}dt$. If there exist $A > 0$ and $B$ such that

$$A \leq \sum_{j=-\infty}^{\infty} |\hat{\psi}(2^j\omega)|^2 \leq B, \tag{1}$$

then $\psi(t)$ is called dyadic wavelet function. It follows from (1) that $\hat{\psi}(0) = 0$, i.e., $\int_{-\infty}^{\infty} \psi(t)dt = 0$. Dyadic wavelet transform of $f(t)$ with the dyadic wavelet function $\psi(t)$ is defined by

$$Wf(u, 2^j) = \int_{-\infty}^{\infty} f(t)\frac{1}{\sqrt{2^j}}\psi\left(\frac{t-u}{2^j}\right)dt. \tag{2}$$

To construct the dyadic wavelet function, we need a scaling function $\phi(t)$ satisfying a two-scale relation

$$\phi(t) = \sum_{k} h[k]\sqrt{2}\phi(2t - k). \tag{3}$$

The scaling function $\phi(t)$ is usually normalized as $\int_{-\infty}^{\infty} \phi(t)dt = 1$.

The Fourier transform of the scaling function (3) yields

$$\hat{\phi}(\omega) = \frac{1}{\sqrt{2}}\hat{h}\left(\frac{\omega}{2}\right)\hat{\phi}\left(\frac{\omega}{2}\right),\qquad(4)$$

where $\hat{h}(\omega)$ denotes a discrete Fourier transform

$$\hat{h}(\omega) = \sum_k h[k]e^{-i\omega k}.\qquad(5)$$

Since $\hat{\phi}(0) = 1$ we can apply (4) and (5) to obtain $\hat{h}(0) = \sqrt{2}$ or $\sum_k h[k] = \sqrt{2}$. Using the scaling function $\phi(t)$ and the wavelet filter $g[k]$, a dyadic wavelet function is defined by $\psi(t) = \sum_k g[k]\sqrt{2}\phi(2t - k)$. The expansion of any $f \in L^2(\mathbb{R})$ by dyadic wavelet basis can be reconstructed under the reconstruction condition which is described in [4]. To derive the reconstruction condition, a dual scaling function and a dual wavelet function are required. The dual scaling function $\tilde{\phi}(t)$ is defined by $\tilde{\phi}(t) = \sum_k \tilde{h}[k]\sqrt{2}\tilde{\phi}(2t - k)$, and the dual wavelet function $\tilde{\psi}(t)$ is given by $\tilde{\psi}(t) = \sum_k \tilde{g}[k]\sqrt{2}(2t - k)$.

Let us denote the discrete Fourier transforms of the filters $h[k], g[k], \tilde{h}[k], \tilde{g}[k]$ by $\hat{h}(\omega), \hat{g}(\omega), \hat{\tilde{h}}(\omega), \hat{\tilde{g}}(\omega)$, respectively. Then the reconstruction condition are described as

$$\hat{\tilde{h}}(\omega)\hat{h}^*(\omega) + \hat{\tilde{g}}(\omega)\hat{g}^*(\omega) = 2, \quad \omega \in [-\pi, \pi],\qquad(6)$$

where the symbol $*$ denotes complex conjugation. The reconstruction condition (6) plays an important role in constructing lifting dyadic wavelet filters.

**Proposition 1 (Ref.[6]).** *Suppose the discrete Fourier transforms $\hat{h}^o(\omega)$, $\hat{g}^o(\omega)$, $\hat{\tilde{h}}^o(\omega)$, and $\hat{\tilde{g}}^o(\omega)$ of the initial filters $h^o[k]$, $g^o[k]$, $\tilde{h}^o[k]$ and $\tilde{g}^o[k]$, respectively, satisfy the reconstruction condition (6). Then, the Fourier transforms $\hat{h}(\omega)$, $\hat{g}(\omega)$, $\hat{\tilde{h}}(\omega)$, and $\hat{\tilde{g}}(\omega)$ of dual lifting dyadic wavelet filters defined by*

$$\begin{aligned}
h[k] &= h^o[k],\\
\tilde{h}[k] &= \tilde{h}^o[k] + \sum_m s[-m]\tilde{g}^o[k - m],\\
g[k] &= g^o[k] - \sum_m s[m]h^o[k - m],\\
\tilde{g}[k] &= \tilde{g}^o[k]
\end{aligned}\qquad(7)$$

*satisfy the reconstruction condition (6). Here $s[m]$ are free parameters.*

To compute the dyadic wavelet transform and its inverse, the following proposition is very useful.

**Proposition 2 (Ref.[4]).** *Under the condition (6), the relations*

$$a_{j+1}[n] = \sum_k h[k]a_j[n + 2^j k], \quad j = 0, 1, \ldots,\qquad(8)$$

$$d_{j+1}[n] = \sum_k g[k]a_j[n + 2^j k], \quad j = 0, 1, \ldots,\qquad(9)$$

*and*

$$a_j[n] = \frac{1}{2} \sum_k \left( \tilde{h}[k]a_{j+1}[n - 2^j k] + \tilde{g}[k]d_{j+1}[n - 2^j k] \right), \quad j = 0, 1, \ldots \quad (10)$$

*hold. Here $a_0[n]$ is given by $a_0[n] = \int_{-\infty}^{\infty} f(t)\phi(t - n)dt$.*

In the case of images, these formulas are applied in each direction, that is, the horizontal and vertical direction. To describe more precisely, let $C^j[n, m]$, $D_1^j[n, m]$, $D_2^j[n, m]$, and $D_3^j[n, m]$ indicate low frequency components, high frequency components in horizontal, in vertical, and in diagonal directions, respectively. The indices $n$ and $m$ are the locations in vertical and horizontal directions, respectively. At first, we apply (8) to $C^j[n, m]$ in the vertical direction to construct $D_1^{j+1}[n, m]$, and we put

$$C^{j,row}[n, m] = \sum_k h[k]C^j[n, m + 2^j k].$$

Then, applying (9) to $C^{j,row}[n, m]$ in the horizontal direction, we obtain

$$D_1^{j+1}[n, m] = \sum_l g[l]C^{j,row}[n + 2^j l, m]. \quad (11)$$

Similarly, applying (8) to $C^j[n, m]$ in the horizontal direction, and we set

$$C^{j,col}[n, m] = \sum_k h[k]C^j[n + 2^j k, m].$$

Using this relation and (9), we get

$$D_2^{j+1}[n, m] = \sum_l g[l]C^{j,col}[n, m + 2^j l]. \quad (12)$$

Applying (9) twice in each direction, we can obtain $D_3^j[n, m]$.

## 3   Learning Method

In this section, we describe how to determine free parameters $s[m]$ in (7). To distinguish free parameter of the filters in vertical and horizontal direction, we use the symbols $g_d[k]$ and $g_e[k]$ corresponding to vertical and horizontal directions, respectively. Then, by Proposition 1, we can obtain

$$g_d[k] = g^o[k] - \sum_m s_d[m]h^o[k - m] \quad (13)$$

$$g_e[k] = g^o[k] - \sum_m s_e[m]h^o[k - m], \quad (14)$$

where $s_d$ and $s_e$ are free parameters.

Substituting (13) and (14) for (11) and (12), we obtain the following relations.

$$D_1^{j+1}[n,m] = \sum_k g_d[k] C^{j,col}[n, m + 2^j k]$$

$$= \sum_k g^o[k] C^{j,col}[n, m + 2^j k] - \sum_l s_d[l] \sum_k h^o[k - l] C^{j,col}[n, m + 2^j k]$$

$$= \hat{D}_1^{j+1}[n,m] - \sum_l s_d[l] \hat{C}^{j+1}[n,m]$$

$$D_2^{j+1}[n,m] = \sum_k g_e[k] C^{j,row}[n + 2^j k, m]$$

$$= \sum_k g^o[k] C^{j,row}[n + 2^j k, m] - \sum_l s_e[l] \sum_k h^o[k-l] C^{j,row}[n + 2^j k, m]$$

$$= \hat{D}_2^{j+1}[n,m] - \sum_l s_e[l] \hat{C}^{j+1}[n,m],$$

where we put $\hat{D}_1^{j+1}[n,m] = g^o[k] C^{j,col}[n, m + 2^j k]$ $\hat{D}_2^{j+1}[n,m] = \sum_k g^o[k] C^{j,row}[n + 2^j k, m]$ and $\hat{C}^{j+1}[n,m] = C^{j,row}[n + 2^j k, m] = C^{j,col}[n, m + 2^j k]$.

To simplify the onward discussion, we discuss only wavelet decomposition from level 0 to 1. Let $C^0[n,m]$ be an noisy image, then $\hat{D}_1^1[n,m]$ and $\hat{D}_2^1[n,m]$ are high frequency components of $C^0[n,m]$. Since the high frequency components of the noisy image contain the information of noise in general, we determine free parameters $s_d$ and $s_e$ so as to vanish the high frequency components $D_1^1[n,m]$ and $D_2^1[n,m]$ as follows:

$$D_1^1[n,m] = \hat{D}_1^1[n,m] - \sum_{l'} s_d[l'] \hat{C}^1[n,m] = 0$$

$$D_2^1[n,m] = \hat{D}_2^1[n,m] - \sum_{k'} s_e[k'] \hat{C}^1[n,m] = 0.$$

Since $D_1^1[n,m]$ and $D_2^1[n,m]$ contain several free parameters $s_d$ and $s_e$, we prepare $2N$ exactly similar images $\hat{C}^{1,\nu}(\mu = 1, 2, \ldots, 2N)$ as training patterns ,and impose on them the following conditions:

$$\hat{D}_1^{1,\nu}[n,m] - \sum_{l'=m-N}^{m+N} s_d[l'] \hat{C}^{1,\nu}[n,m] = 0 \quad \nu = 1, 2, \cdots, 2N \qquad (15)$$

$$\hat{D}_2^{1,\nu}[n,m] - \sum_{k'=n-N}^{n+N} s_e[k'] \hat{C}^{1,\nu}[n,m] = 0 \quad \nu = 1, 2, \cdots, 2N, \qquad (16)$$

where $\hat{D}_1^{1,\nu}[n,m]$ and $\hat{D}_2^{1,\nu}[n,m]$ are the frequency components $\hat{C}^{1,\nu}[n,m]$ is the low frequency component based on the initial initial filters.

The number of $s_d$ and $s_e$ is $2N + 1$, but the number of equations (15) and (16) is $2N$, respectively. We need one more condition for each of $s_d$ and $s_e$

to determine uniquely. Since $g_d$ and $g_e$ are highpass filters, these filters should satisfy

$$\sum_k g_d[k] = \sum_k \left( g^o[k] - \sum_{l'=m-N}^{m+N} s_d[l']h^o[k-l'] \right) = 0,$$

$$\sum_k g_e[k] = \sum_k \left( g^o[k] - \sum_{k'=n-N}^{n+N} s_e[k']h^o[k-k'] \right) = 0.$$

Therefore

$$\sum_{l'=m-N}^{m+N} s_d[l'] = 0 \quad \text{and} \quad \sum_{k'=n-N}^{n+N} s_e[k'] = 0 \tag{17}$$

hold, because $\sum_k g^o[k] = 0$ and $\sum_k h^o[k]$ is constant. Then we can obtain $s_d$ by solving the linear equation (15) and (17) using a certain numerical method, for example, the Gaussian elimination method. Similarly, solving the linear equation (16) and (17), we can get $s_e$.

## 4    Edge Preserving Wavelet Thresholding

In general, denoising algorithms remove not only noise but also important image features. To improve the the image quality as possible, we employ the modified version of the edge-preserving wavelet thresholding proposed in [8] for preserving image features.

Let $\bar{C}[n,m] = C[n,m] + E[n,m]$ be a noisy image , and $C[n,m]$ and $E[n,m]$ correspond to the original image and noise, respectively. We consider the following minimization problems which find $\dot{D}_r^1$ as the minimizer of a penalized least-square functionals $F_p(D_r^1)$.

$$\dot{D}_r^1 = \text{argmin}F_p(D_r^1) = \text{argmin}(||\bar{D}_r^1 - D_r^1||_2^2 + \lambda p(D_r^1)), \quad r = 1,2,3, \tag{18}$$

where $p(D_r^1)$ is a given penalty function and $\lambda$ is a positive parameter which balances the effect of the data fidelity and the penalization terms, $\bar{D}_r^1$ and $D_r^1$ are the high frequency components in each direction corresponding to $\bar{C}$ and $C$, respectively.

We represent the strength of edges as

$$M[n,m] = \sqrt{|(D_1^1[n,m])|^2 + |(D_2^1[n,m])|^2 + |(D_3^1[n,m])|^2},$$

and use as penalty term the following expression:

$$p(D) = \sum_{n,m} \varphi(M[n,m])$$

to preserve the value of $M[n,m]$ as possible. Here $\varphi$ is chosen to be one of the most used potential function of nonlinear diffusion filtering method. In our method, we set

$$\varphi(M[n,m]) = \mu \left( \sqrt{\mu^2 + M[n,m]^2} - \mu \right)$$

which is one of functions presented in [8], and the parameter $\mu$ plays the role of a scale-dependent contrast parameter representing the threshold between edge and not-an-edge. We set

$$\mu = 1.4826 \cdot \left( \sum_{r=1}^{3} \text{MAD} \left[ (\bar{D}_r[n,m])^2 \right]_{n,m=1}^{N^2} \right).$$

This value comes from the classical tools in the robust statistics, and MAD denotes the median absolute deviation. Then, according to [8], the denoising algorithm is reduced to the solving of non-linear equations

$$\dot{D}_r^1[n,m] + \frac{\lambda}{2}\varphi' \left( \dot{M}[n,m] \right) = |\bar{D}_r^1[n,m]| \quad r = 1,2,3 \tag{19}$$

Using a certain iterative approach, we can obtain approximate solutions of (19).

## 5  Denoising Algorithm

We describe the our denoising algorithm based on the arguments in previous sections.

Since the number of $s_d$ and $s_e$ is equal to the one of $h[k]$ and $g[k]$, we have to decompose the original image into sub-images depending on the number of these parameters, and then apply the dyadic lifting schemes to each sub-images. If the support length is $\alpha$, the size of each sub-images is $\alpha \times \alpha$. Let us denote the each sub-images as $C_i^0 (1 \leq i \leq M)$, and we decompose $C_i^0 (1 \leq i \leq M)$ into the frequency components $C_i^1[n,m]$, $D_{1,i}^1[n,m]$, $D_{2,i}^1[n,m]$, and $D_{3,i}^1[n,m]$ by using $g_d^i[k]$ and $g_e^i[k]$ described in Sections 3. Then, we solve the equation (19) at each sub-image using iterative method as follows:

1. Set the initial values $(D_1)_0, (D_2)_0, (D_3)_0$ and $\tau = 0$. Here $\tau$ stands for the iteration number.
2. Compute $M_\tau = \sqrt{(D_1)_\tau^2 + (D_2)_\tau^2 + (D_3)_\tau^2}$ and

$$y_{\tau+1}^r = \varphi'(M_\tau)/(2(D_r)_\tau)$$
$$(D_r)_{\tau+1} = |D_{r,i}^1|/(1 + \lambda y_{\tau+1}^r), \quad r = 1,2,3.$$

3. If $(D_r)_\tau$ converge when $\tau = \hat{\tau}$, then stop and move to the next step. If not, set $\tau \leftarrow \tau + 1$ and return to step 2.
4. Using $(D_r)_{\hat{\tau}}$, compute

$$\dot{D}_r^1[n,m] = (D_r)_{\hat{\tau}}[n,m] \cdot \text{sign}(D_r^1[n,m]), \quad r = 1,2,3.$$

5. Using $C^1[n,m]$, $\dot{D}_1^1[n,m]$, $\dot{D}_2^1[n,m]$, $\dot{D}_3^1[n,m]$ and the initial filters, reconstruct the image.

Fig.1 shows our denoising process.

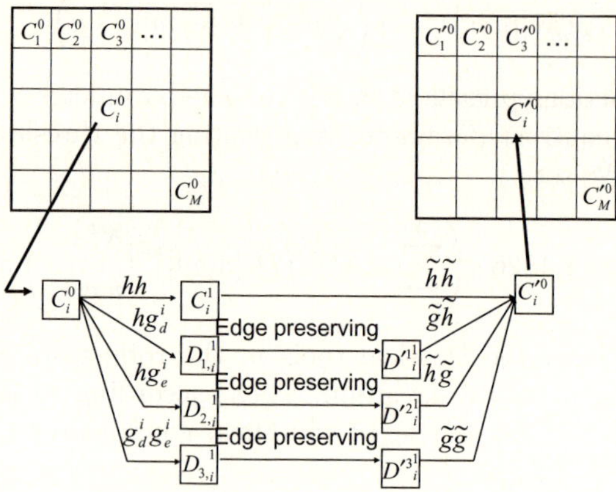

**Fig. 1.** Denoising algorithm

# 6    Numerical Results

We employ the well-known Lenna, Boat and Title grayscale images each of size $256 \times 256$ as benchmarks, shown in Fig.3. The noisy images corrupted by adding white Gaussian noise are shown in Fig.4. We have used the $64 \times 64$ pixel fragment of "Title" to highlight the edge preservation properties in Fig.8. The performance of the estimators was measured by the usual peak signal to ratio(PSNR). In this simulation, we employ the spline dyadic wavelet filters as initial filters shown in Table.1

**Table 1.** Initial filter

| n | $h^o[n]/\sqrt{2}$ | $g^o[n]/\sqrt{2}$ | $\tilde{h}^o[n]/\sqrt{2}$ | $\tilde{g}^o[n]/\sqrt{2}$ |
|---|---|---|---|---|
| -2 | | | | -0.03125 |
| -1 | 0.125 | | 0.125 | -0.21875 |
| 0 | 0.375 | -0.5 | 0.375 | -0.6875 |
| 1 | 0.375 | 0.5 | 0.375 | 0.6875 |
| 2 | 0.125 | | 0.125 | 0.21875 |
| 3 | | | | 0.03125 |

Table 2 lists the value of PSNR for various version of the benchmarks recovered from their noisy versions using median filter and our method. In Proposed method 1, we determine the free parameters using the method described in section 3. On the other hand, we determine the free parameters so as to preserve the features of initial filters and adjust the peak based on our experiences. The shape of the initial filter and the determined filter in Proposed method 2 is showed in Fig.2.

Therefore Proposed method 2 is not theoretical but intuitive, however, Table 2 shows that Proposed method 2 is superior to Proposed method 1 in

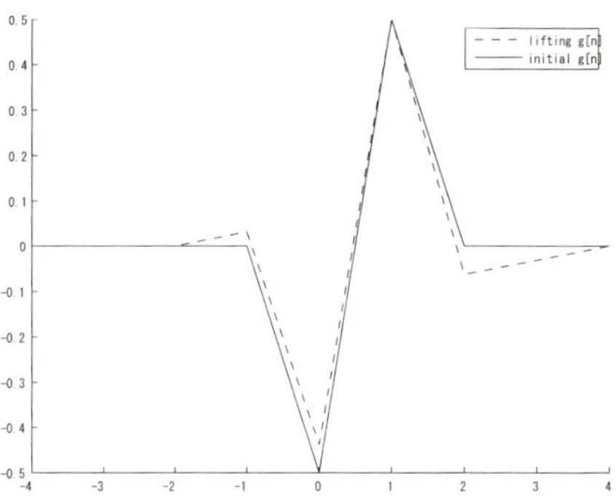

**Fig. 2.**

**Table 2.** PSNR

|      |       |        | Noisy | Median | Proposed method1 | Proposed method2 |
|------|-------|--------|--------|--------|------------------|------------------|
| PSNR | Lenna |        | 16.1335 | 22.5340 | 23.1725 | 25.0105 |
|      |       |        | 18.0880 | 24.1028 | 24.6104 | 26.0055 |
|      |       |        | 20.0476 | 25.6968 | 25.8689 | 26.7741 |
|      | Boat  |        | 16.0252 | 22.5085 | 23.2077 | 25.2972 |
|      |       |        | 18.0034 | 24.1800 | 24.8185 | 26.4044 |
|      |       |        | 20.0137 | 25.5941 | 26.1401 | 27.1942 |
|      | Title |        | 11.7421 | 12.9030 | 14.0684 | 14.0713 |

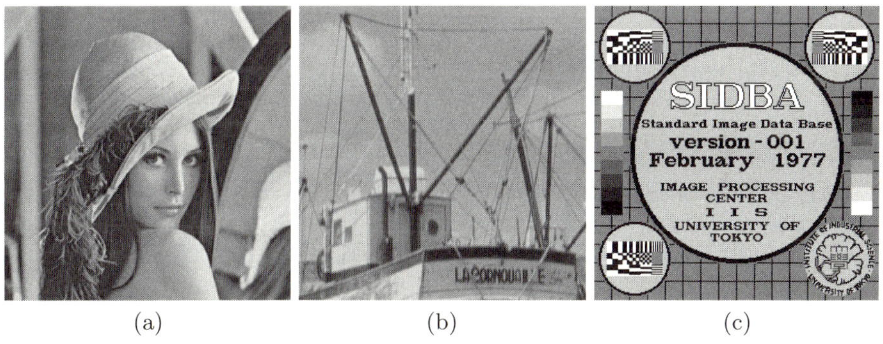


(a)                          (b)                          (c)

**Fig. 3.** (a) Lenna image.    (b) Boat image.    (c) Title image.

many cases. Reversely, Figs.5-8 demonstrate that Proposed method 1 preserves the edges in comparison with other methods. This means that the choice of the free parameters is very important for denoising. Anyway, both Proposed method 1 and 2 are superior to median filter.

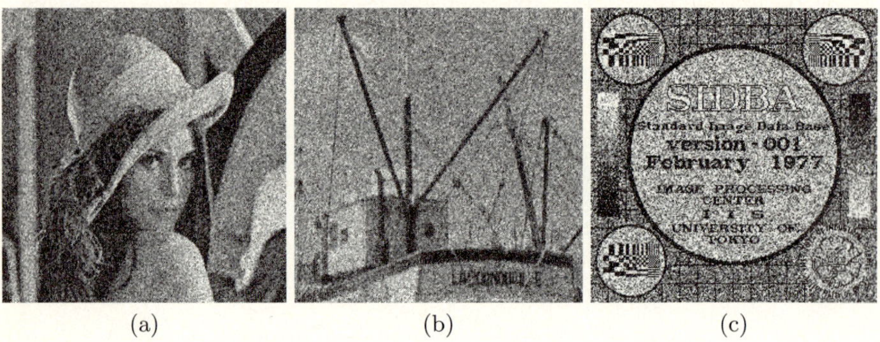

**Fig. 4.** (a) Noisy Lenna(PSNR= 16.1355).    (b) Noisy Boat(PSNR= 16.0252).    (c) Noisy Title(PSNR= 11.7421).

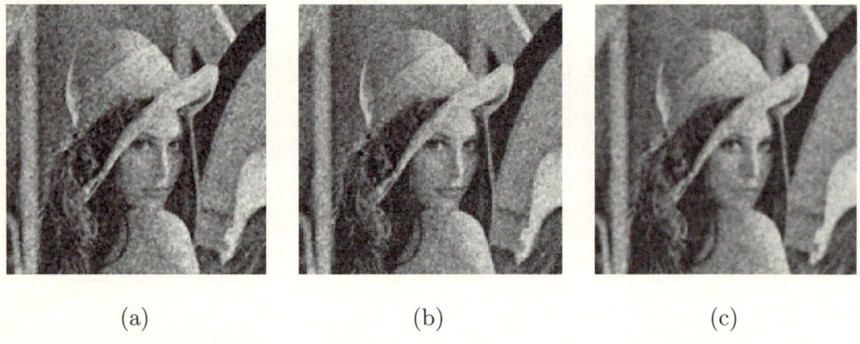

**Fig. 5.** (a) Median(PSNR= 22.5340).    (b) Proposed method1(PSNR= 23.1725).    (c) Proposed method2(PSNR= 25.0105).

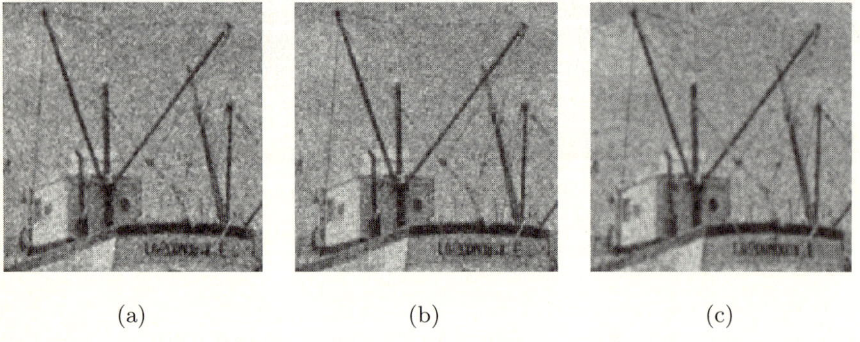

**Fig. 6.** (a) Median(PSNR= 22.5085).    (b) Proposed method1(PSNR= 23.2077).    (c) Proposed method2(PSNR= 25.2972).

Fig. 7. (a) Median(PSNR= 12.9030).    (b) Proposed method1(PSNR= 14.0684).    (c) Proposed method2(PSNR= 14.0713).

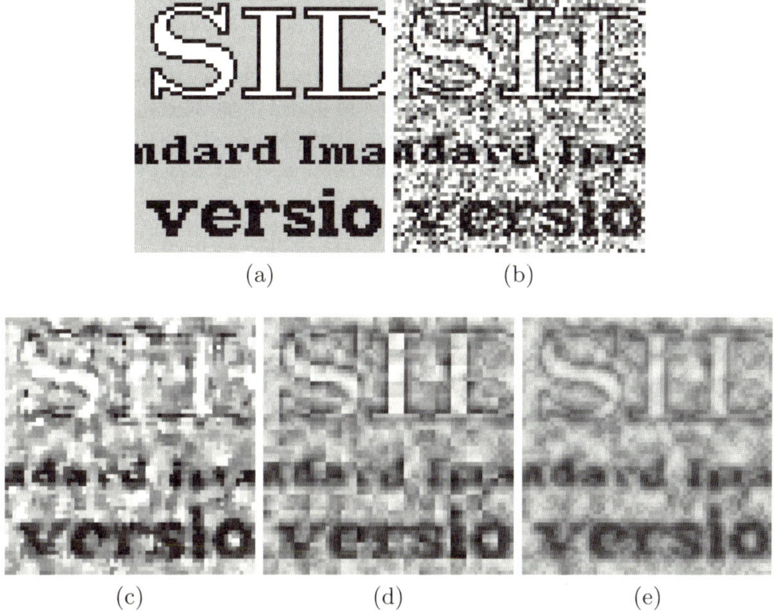

Fig. 8. (a) Original image.    (b) Noisy image.    (c) Median.    (d) Proposed method1. (e) Proposed method2.

## 7    Conclusion

We proposed a new wavelet denoising method for digital images with edge preservation. Once we give the initial filter, our denoising method is carried out automatically thanks to the learning method. The performance of our method is compared to that of median filters in numerical experiments. Our numerical results show that our methods work well in comparison with median filter. Since the free parameters appearing in the dyadic lifting schemes play an important role to denoise, the development of new learning methods to determine the best parameters remains as a future work.

# References


1. Aubert, G., Kornprobst, P.: Mathematical problems in image processing, 2nd edn. Partial differential equations and the calculus of variations. Springer, Heidelberg (2006)
2. Donoho, D.L.: De-noising by soft-thresholding. IEEE Trans. Inform. Theory 41(3), 613–627 (1995)
3. Mallat, S., Zhong, S.: Characterization of signals from multiscale edges. IEEE trans. pattern anal. mach. intell. 14(7), 710–732 (1992)
4. Mallat, S.: A wavelet tour of signal processing. Academic press, London (1998)
5. Papari, G., Campisi, P., Petkov, N., Neri, A.: Contour detection by multiresolution surround inhibition. In: Proc. Int. Conf. on Image Processing ICIP 2006, Atlanta, GA, October 8-11, pp. 749–752 (2006)
6. Türüki, T.A., Hussain, M., Niijima, K., Takano, S.: The dyadic lifting schemes and the denoising of digital images. International Journal of Wavelets, Multiresolution and Information Processing 6(3), 331–351 (2008)
7. Sweldens, W.: The lifting scheme:A construction of second generation wavelets. SIAM J. Math. Anal. 29(2), 511–546 (1997)
8. Lazzaro, D., Montefusco, L.B.: Edge-preserving wavelet thresholding for image denoising. J. Comput. Appl. Math. 210, 222–231 (2007)

# A Self-governing Hybrid Model for Noise Removal


Mohammad Reza Hajiaboli

Department of Electrical and Computer Engineering
Concordia University, Montreal, Canada
mohammad.hajiaboli@ieee.org



**Abstract.** Denoising methods based on using fourth-order partial deferential equations (PDEs) are providing a good combination of the noise smoothing and the edge preservation without creating blocky effects on the smooth regions of the image. However, finding an optimal choice of model parameters for numerical solver of these techniques is a challenging problem and generally, these model parameters are image-content dependent. In this paper, a hybrid fourth-order PDE-based filter is proposed so that it does not need a manual adjustment of the model parameters. It is shown that by setting the numerical solver of proposed filter for operation at a minor time step-size derived under a data-independent stability condition, the filter can still provide a significantly fast convergence rate. Therefore, the model parameters are reduced to one parameter estimated by using a well-studied mechanism applying in the second-order nonlinear diffusion denoising techniques. Simulation results show that the proposed method can provide a denoised image with higher quality in comparison with that of the existing methods.

**Keywords:** Denoising, Diffusion, Laplacian, Gradient, Convergence.


## 1   Introduction

In the last two decades, the use of partial differential equations (PDEs) in image processing has significantly grown. This paper is mainly focused on a class of PDE-based denoising methods known as nonlinear/anisotropic diffusion denoising techniques. The first kind of these methods is introduced by Perona and Malik [1] in 1990 in which the denoised image is the solution of a nonlinear second-order PDE. Since then, there has been a great deal of research in this field which led to the introduction of a variety of nonlinear diffusion denoising techniques (see [2], [3] as a few examples). Although the method proposed by Perona and Malik and its variants are known as good edge preservation denoising methods, these methods tend to produce blocky effects in the images [4].

An effective solution to this problem has been introduced by You and Kaveh [4] in which a fourth-order PDE is used for image noise removal. A significant improvement in the ramp edge preservation and a dramatic reduction of blocky effects are the result of using this fourth-order diffusion denoising scheme. However, the fourth-order diffusion dampens high spatial frequency components (i.e.


T. Wada, F. Huang, and S. Lin (Eds.): PSIVT 2009, LNCS 5414, pp. 295–305, 2009.

noise and step edges) much faster than second-order diffusion [5]. This feature might result in the edge distortion during the evolutionary process of the image denoising especially when smoothing strength of the filter for the detected edges is not effectively reduced by a diffusivity function. The diffusivity function in the fourth-order PDE filters is a function of absolute value of Laplacian of the evolved image and it is more sensitive to the noise compared to the diffusivity function of the second- order nonlinear diffusion filters where the diffusivity is a function of the modulus of the gradient of the evolved image. Moreover, the well-established techniques for estimation of the model parameters in second-order nonlinear diffusion filters are not directly applicable in the fourth-order filters. Therefore, fourth-order denoising filters including the recently developed ones such as [5], [6], and [7] are mainly known as a manual or a man-operated noise removal technique. Due to severe nonlinearity of the fourth-order dynamic flow and strong smoothing property of the Laplacian filter embedded in the structure of these filters, finding the optimal parameters setting is very crucial and these optimal parameters are very image-content-dependent. On the other hand, an optimal parameters selection for these filters usually results in a very slow convergence rate as it has been reported in [4] and [5].

In this paper, a new fourth-order PDE-based denoising method is introduced in which the model parameters is reduced to only one parameter that can be estimated. The simulation results show that the proposed method can outperform the other techniques in terms of the quality of the denoised image. The other significance of the proposed method is its fast convergence rate which is been compared with that of the other techniques as well.

## 2    Theoretical Background

The basic diffusion equation of Perona and Malik [1] is given by

$$\partial u/\partial t = div. \left(c\left(\|\nabla u\|\right)\nabla u\right) , \tag{1}$$

where $u$ is image intensity function, $c(.)$ is diffusivity function by which the diffusion coefficient is calculated and $t$ is time. Symbols of $div.$ and $\|.\|$ are used for mathematical notation of Euclidian norm and divergence respectively. The diffusivity function is a positive and none increasing function of $\|\nabla u\|$. One of these diffusivity functions defined by Perona and Malik is given by

$$c\left(\|\nabla u\|\right) = k^2/\left(k^2 + \|\nabla u\|^2\right) , \tag{2}$$

where $k$ is the so-called contrast parameter. There are some effective automatic mechanism for estimation of the contrast parameter such as the schemes introduced in [1] and [3].

In [8], You and his colleagues carried out a detailed analysis to show that the solution of (1) is equal to minimization of an energy functional. If the diffusivity function of (2) is used then the energy functional is

$$R\left(u\right) = \int_{\Omega} \frac{k^2}{2} \ln\left(k^2 + \|\nabla u\|^2\right) dxdy , \tag{3}$$

where $\Omega$ is region of support of $u$. $R(u)$ is minimized when $\|\nabla u\|^2$ is minimum, which leads to a piecewise constant approximation of $u$. Therefore, formation of staircase artifacts on the ramp edges is unavoidable. In order to resolve this problem, You et al. [4] introduce a new fourth-order PDE-based denoising method in which the denoised image is obtained by minimization of the potential function given by

$$E(u) = \int_\Omega f\left(|\nabla^2 u|\right) dxdy , \tag{4}$$

where $f'(s) = sc(s)$. Minimization of (4), after using Euler equation, can be solved by the following gradient descent procedure:

$$\partial u/\partial t = -\nabla^2 \left(c\left(|\nabla^2 u|\right)\nabla^2 u\right) , \tag{5}$$

with the noisy image as the initial condition. By the forward Euler approximation of the $\partial u/\partial t$ , the numerical solver of (5) is given by

$$u^{n+1} = u^n - dt \times \nabla^2 \left(c\left(|\nabla^2 u^n|\right)\nabla^2 u^n\right) ,$$
$$u^0 = u_0 \quad \text{and} \quad n = 0, 1, \cdots, N , \tag{6}$$

where $n$ is number of iterations, $dt$ is time step-size and $u_0$ is a noisy image. This process is an iterative process. In order to protect the edges from over-smoothing, the process needs to be stopped at a certain number of iterations denoted by $N$.

Apart from a significant advancement in reduction of blocky effect on the de-noised image using (5), the optimal parameter setting for the numerical solver of (6) leads to very slow convergence rate especially, when the level of conta-minating noise is moderately high. A recently developed technique known as hybrid model of fourth-order PDE [6] tries to address this problem and by using a relaxed median filter [9] tends to improve the quality of denoised image, when the image is highly noisy. The numerical model of this filter is given by

$$u^{n+1} = RM_{\alpha\omega}\left(u^n - dt \times \nabla^2 \left(c\left(|\nabla^2 u^n|\right)\nabla^2 u^n\right)\right) , \tag{7}$$

where RM denotes the relaxed median filter with lower bound $\alpha$ and upper bound $\omega$. This filtering process needs a lower number of iterations to give an estimation of denoised image. On the other hand, computational burden per iteration for this filtering scheme is dramatically higher than that of the You et al. filter.

However, both of these techniques are still suffering from lack of parame-ter estimation mechanisms particularly for the contrast parameter and the time step-size. As mentioned earlier, the performance of these filters strongly depends on the selection of these parameters and unfortunately, the optimal parameters selection is image-content-dependent. In the following section, a new filtering scheme is introduced by which the contrast parameter is estimated based on the modulus of the gradient of the evolved image.

## 3   The Proposed Method

### 3.1   The Proposed Partial Differential Equation

The ability of edge preservation in the fourth order PDE-based denoising method strongly depends on the extent by which the diffusivity function, $c(.)$, can detect the edges and reduce the strength of the smoothness of the filter for these detected edges. However, when the diffusivity function is a function of the absolute value of the Laplacian of the image, the probability of a false edge-detection in Laplacian map of the image is significantly higher comparing to the case that the diffusivity function is a function of the modulus of the gradient. In fact, as much as the order of the derivative of the image is higher, the sensitivity to the noise is higher [10]. Therefore, the new PDE for denoising is introduced in which the diffusivity function is a function of the gradient modulus of the evolved image in form of

$$u^{n+1} = u^n - dt \times \nabla^2 \left( c\left(\|\nabla u^n\|\right) \nabla^2 u^n \right) ,$$
$$u^0 = u_0 \quad \text{and} \quad n = 0, 1, \cdots, N , \tag{8}$$

In this case, the optimal contrast parameter, $k$, in the diffusivity function, $c(.)$, is proportionally related to the noise level [11] and can be estimated by Canny noise-estimation technique [12] as following:

*A histogram of the magnitude values of the gradient throughout the image is computed and* k *is set to the 80%-90% value of its integral at each iteration.*

As the results in the next section show, this simple change can lead to significant improvement in the quality of the denoised image, while the fundamental relation between (8) and its associated potential function need to be explored by conducting a further research. However, it can be shown that the proposed method does not introduce any blocky effect on the image (as it is seen in the second-order nonlinear diffusion filter). The results demonstrated in Fig. 1 give a compression between the performance of the proposed filter and Perona and Malik filter, where the signal shown in Fig. 1-(a) is been filtered for $t=150$. The diffusivity function for the proposed filter and Perona and Malik filter is chosen to be (2) and contrast parameter estimation is based on the Canny noise estimation mechanism mentioned earlier. While the result obtained by Perona and Malik filter shown in Fig. 1-(b) apparently suffers from formation of Blocky effect, the results of the proposed method in Fig. 1-(c) have no sign of formation of staircase artifacts.

The other important aspect of fourth-order PDE-based denoising techniques is the stability of the numerical solver in order to guarantee the convergence of the solution. Setting a small time step-size, $dt$, in (8), can guarantee the stability of the dynamic flow, however if $dt$ is too small, it results in numerous number of iterations. Finding an optimal time step-size is a challenging task knowing

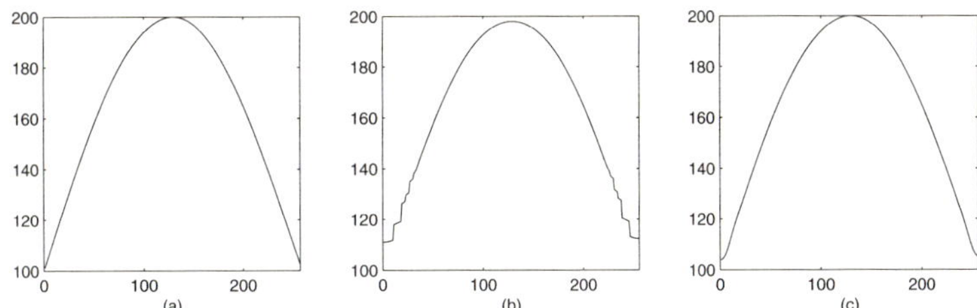

**Fig. 1.** Comparing the result of the proposed method with the result obtaied by Perona Malik filter in term of formation of artifacts. Fig. 1-(a) is the original image, Fig. 1-(b) is the result of Perona-malik filter ($t=150$ ) and Fig. 1-(c) is the result obtained by the proposed method ($t=150$).

that this optimal value is normally image-data-dependent. On the other hand, if the diffusivity function can distinguish between noise and edge with high degree of certainty, the convergence rate of the PDE-based denoising method can be dramatically increased. Comparing the diffusion coefficient map of noisy image of *"Lena"* at the fifth iteration for the You et al. filter with the one that is obtained by proposed method shows that in the proposed method, the wider regions of the image can be detected as smooth regions, therefore noise reduction is significantly faster than that of (6). Thus, finding a constant $dt$ as a data-independent stability condition for (8) (i.e. very smaller than the optimal time step-size) and setting the numerical solver of (8) so that it operates with this time step-size make the proposed filter applicable to a wide category of images without any stability concern and yet deliver a good convergence rate.

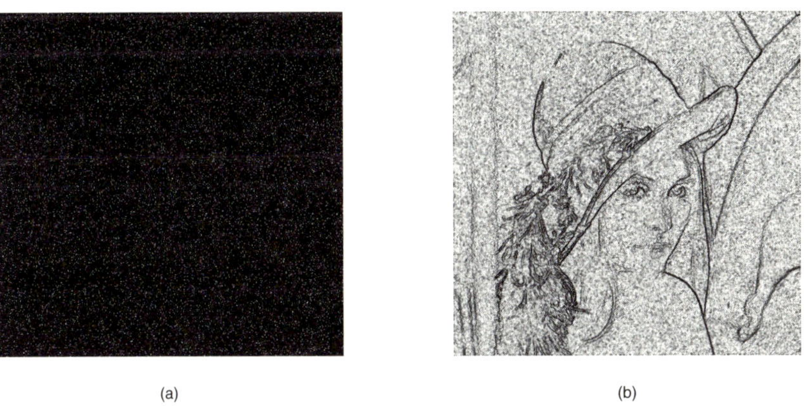

**Fig. 2.** Comparing the map of $c\left(|\nabla^2 u|\right)$ in You et al. filter, (a), with the map of $c\left(\|\nabla u\|^2\right)$ in the proposed filter, (b), for test image "Lena" degraded by additive white Gaussian noise with standard deviation of 15. The bright regions in the both maps indicate the regions in which a strong diffusion is carried out.

## 3.2   Data-Independent Stability Condition

The purpose of this subsection is to find a time step-size, $dt$, for numerical solver of (8) so that the numerical solver is always convergent to the steady state value. In the other word, for stability of (8), it is needed to show that $\partial u/\partial t \to 0$ when $t \to \infty$. If $c\left(\|\nabla u\|^2\right) \approx 0$ the changes in $u$ is almost zero and $\partial u/\partial t \approx 0$. Therefore, the worst condition for stability is when $c\left(\|\nabla u\|^2\right) = 1$ . Note that $c\left(\|\nabla u\|^2\right)$ is bounded in $(0, 1]$. For $c\left(\|\nabla u\|^2\right) = 1$, the numerical solver of (8) can be written in form of

$$u^{n+1} = u^n - dt \times ((L * L) * u^n) , \tag{9}$$

where $L$ is a small Laplacian kernel and symbol of $*$ denotes the convolution operation. If $u$ is arranged in column-wise order, the linear system in (9) can be written as a system of state equations given by

$$u^{n+1} = (I + S) \times u^n , \tag{10}$$

where $(I+S)$ is the state matrix of (9) in which $S$ is an sparse matrix representing the convolution of $u$ with the small convolution kernel of $-dt \times (L * L)$ and $I$ is the identity matrix. When $L$ is a standard Laplacian kernel given by

$$\begin{bmatrix} 0 & 1 & 0 \\ 1 & -4 & 1 \\ 0 & 1 & 0 \end{bmatrix} \tag{11}$$

then $-dt \times (L * L)$ is

$$- dt \times (L * L) = dt \times \begin{bmatrix} 0 & 0 & -1 & 0 & 0 \\ 0 & -2 & 8 & -2 & 0 \\ -1 & 8 & -20 & 8 & -1 \\ 0 & 0 & -1 & 0 & 0 \\ 0 & -2 & 8 & -2 & 0 \end{bmatrix} , \tag{12}$$

which means that $S$ is a sparse matrix that in each row the nonzero matrix values are in the following order:

$$dt \times \begin{bmatrix} -1 & -2 & 8 & -2 & -1 & 8 & -20 & 8 & -1 & -2 & 8 & -2 & -1 \end{bmatrix} \tag{13}$$

while -20 is always in the main diagonal of $S$.

For stability of state system in (10) the spectral radius, $SP$, of $(I + S)$ should be less than one and the same value of dt led to stability of (10) results to stability of

$$u^{n+1} = - (I + S) \times u^n , \tag{14}$$

However, the state system in (14) can be written in standard form of Jacobi solver in form of

$$u^{n+1} + ((2I + S) - I) u^n = 0 , \tag{15}$$

Stability of the Jacobi solver in (15) can be obtained if matrix $(2I - S)$ is strictly row-wise diagonally dominant (see [13] page 626 for proof). By definition, the matrix $A_{ij}$ is strictly row-wise diagonally dominant if

$$|a_{rr}| > \sum_{j \neq r} |a_{rj}| \ \text{ for } \ r = 1, 2, \cdots, n \ . \tag{16}$$

This condition for $(2I - S)$ means that $2 - 20dt > 44dt$ needs to be satisfied. In the other word, when the time step-size is $dt < 0.0313$, the proposed method using $L$ as discrete approximation of Laplacian is data-independently stable.

In general, for using different Laplacian kernels in implementation of (8), with the same presented argument, one can conclude that the data-independent stability condition for dt is

$$dt < 2 \left( \sum |data \ mask \ of \ (L * L)\,| \right)^{-1} . \tag{17}$$

## 4   Comparative Results

In this section, we are presenting the comparative results of the proposed method with two other Fourth-order PDEs: 1) the equation of (6) introduced by You et al. [4]. 2) the PDE introduced in [6] known as relaxed median regularized filter. The proposed method does not need to be operated manually, however for the other methods, the suggestive parameters are set to maximize the performance of the filters. For You et al. filter time step size is $dt=0.25$ and $k=0.75$ and the parameters of relaxed median regularized filter are chosen to be $dt=0.1$, $k=3$, as they were suggested in [6].

Three test images of *"Pepper"*, *"Cameraman"* and *"House"* have been corrupted by white additive Gaussian noise with standard deviation of 15. In Table 1, an objective comparison between the performances of these filters in terms of signal-to-noise ratio (SNR) of the denoised image and their computational complexity are presented.

**Table 1.**  Objective Comparison Results

| Test Images | Noisy Image SNR(dB) | Method | Denoised Image SNR(dB) | Num. of Iter. | CPU/Iter. |
|---|---|---|---|---|---|
| | | Proposed | 17.31 | 15 | 0.08 |
| *Pepper* | 11.03 | (6) | 15.86 | 3450 | 0.03 |
| | | (7) | 15.10 | 3 | 0.15 |
| | | Proposed | 16.89 | 7 | 0.08 |
| *Cameraman* | 12.37 | (6) | 16.61 | 3288 | 0.03 |
| | | (7) | 13.60 | 2 | 0.16 |
| | | Proposed | 17.17 | 35 | 0.08 |
| *House* | 9.76 | (6) | 15.91 | 3904 | 0.03 |
| | | (7) | 15.38 | 3 | 0.16 |

The results show that the proposed method constantly produces the denoised image with higher SNR. It is important to note that the results are obtained at the optimal number of iterations in which the maximum SNR in evolutionary process of the filters are achieved. If the iterative filtering process is continued after the optimal number of iterations, the SNR of denoised image is reduced due to over-smoothness of edges. The other important feature in the proposed method is its fast convergence rate. As it is shown in Fig. 3, for *"Pepper"* test image, the convergence rate in the proposed method is much higher than filter of You et al. The computational burden of the filters is measured as CPU time of each iterations provided that they are filtering the same image on the same computer. Thus, the total time for filtering process is a multiplication of CPU/iteration by number of iterations. The relaxed median regularized filter converges faster than the proposed method, however the maximum SNR is significantly lower than that of other methods, and the decay rate of SNR due to over-smoothness of the edges is also very fast. Moreover, the higher computational cost of this filter compared to the proposed filter increases the overall process time due to high computational complexity associated with each iteration of this filtering process.

In Fig. 4, the perceptual quality of the denoised image by the proposed method is compared with that of the other methods. In the first row, the whole image and in the second row, a magnified portion of the image are shown. Each pair of the images is labeled from (a)-(e). The first two images (a) and (b) are the noiseless and the noisy images. In Fig. 4-(c), the denoised image by You et al. filter is shown in which formation of some speckle noise is visible. This drawback

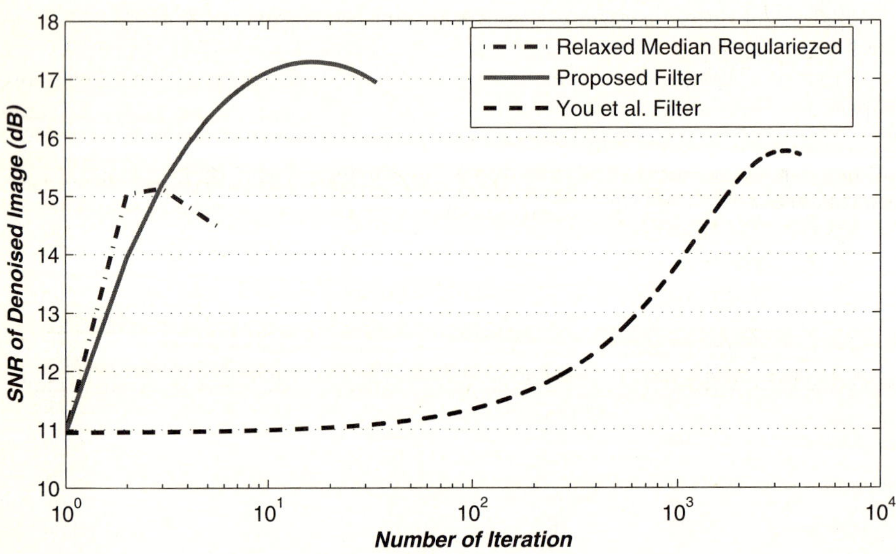


**Fig. 3.** Comparing the convergence rate of the filters for denoising of test image *"Pepper"*

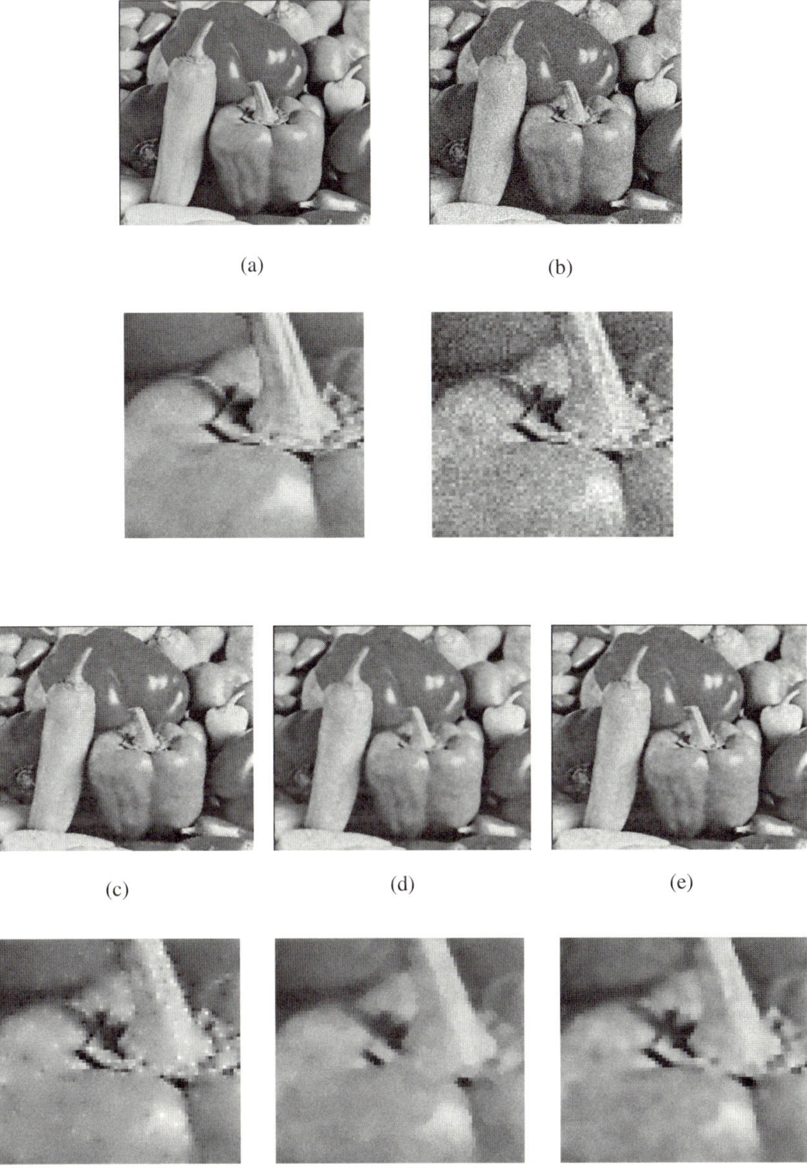

**Fig. 4.** Comparing the perceptual quality of the results. The pair of images labaled (a) to (e) are as the following: (a) noiseless image, (b) noisy image, (c) denoise image using (6), (d) denoised image using (7) and (e) the proposed method.

is known and addressed by You et al. in [4] and it is as a result of choosing small value for $k$ in diffusivity function, however this setting of $k$ is necessary to protect the edges from over-smoothing. In the Fig. 4-(d), the denoised image by the relaxed median regularized filter using (7) is shown. This denoised image is blurred and some staircase artifacts on smooth regions of the image are formed. The last image, shown in Fig.4-(e) is the result of the proposed method in which the extent of denoising and edge preservation is noticeably better than that of the other methods.

## 5   Conclusion

A method for noise removal based on using the fourth-order PDE has been proposed. A theoretical background of the fourth-order denoising methods has been presented with highlighting the major challenges of parameters estimation and slow convergence rate of these techniques. To resolve these drawbacks, in the proposed method, the diffusion coefficient is calculated using a diffusivity function as a function of modulus of the gradient of the evolved image while, in the existing fourth-order PDE-based filters, the diffusivity function is a function of absolute value of Laplacian of the image. The simulation results show that the proposed method can provide a high SNR and a tangible improvement of perceptual quality of the denoised images in comparison with that of the other techniques. The fast convergence obtained by the proposed method pave the road toward its utilization in real time applications.

## References


1. Perona, P., Malik, J.: Scale-space and edge detection using anisotropic diffusion. IEEE Transactions on Pattern Analysis and Machine Intelligence 12(7), 629–639 (1990)
2. Catte, F., et al.: Image selective smoothing and edge detection by nonlinear diffusion. SIAM J. Numer. Anal. 29(1), 182–193 (1992)
3. Black, M.J., et al.: Robust anisotropic diffusion. IEEE Transactions on Image Processing 7(3), 421–432 (1998)
4. You, Y.L., Kaveh, M.: Fourth-order partial differential equations for noise removal. IEEE Transactions on Image Processing 9(10), 1723–1730 (2000)
5. Lysaker, M., Lundervold, A., Tai, X.-C.: Noise removal using fourth-order partial differential equation with applications to medical magnetic resonance images in space and time. IEEE Tran. on Image Processing 12(12), 1579–1590 (2003)
6. Rajan, J., Kannan, K., Kaimal, M.R.: An Improved hybrid model for molecular image denoising. Journal of Mathematical Imaging and Vision 31, 73–79 (2008)
7. Li, F., et al.: Image restoration combining a total variational filter and a fourth-order filter. Journal of Visual Communication and Image Representation 18, 322–330 (2007)
8. You, Y.-L., et al.: Behavioral analysis of anisotropic diffusion in image processing. IEEE Trans. Image Processing 5, 1539–1553 (1996)
9. Hamza, A.B., et al.: Removing noise and preserving details with relaxed median filters. Journal of Mathematical Imaging and Vision 11(2), 161–177 (1999)

10. Nixon, M., Aguado, A.: Feature Extraction and Image Processing. Oxford, Newnes (2002)
11. Guido, G., et al.: Nonlinear anisotropic filtering of MRI data. IEEE Transactions on Medical Imaging 11(2), 221–232 (1992)
12. Canny, J.F.: A computational approach to edge detection. IEEE Transactions on Pattern Analysis and Machine Intelligence 8(6), 679–698 (1986)
13. Stoer, J., Bulirsch, R.: Introduction to Numerical Analysis. Texts in Applied Mathematics 12. Springer, New York (2002)

# Detecting Video Forgeries Based on Noise Characteristics

Michihiro Kobayashi, Takahiro Okabe, and Yoichi Sato

Institute of Industrial Science, The University of Tokyo
{michi,takahiro,ysato}@iis.u-tokyo.ac.jp

**Abstract.** The recent development of video editing techniques enables us to create realistic synthesized videos. Therefore using video data as evidence in places such as a court of law requires a method to detect forged videos. In this paper we propose an approach to detect suspicious regions in video recorded from a static scene by using noise characteristics. The image signal contains irradiance-dependent noise where the relation between irradiance and noise depends on some parameters; they include inherent parameters of a camera such as quantum efficiency and a response function, and recording parameters such as exposure and electric gain. Forged regions from another video camera taken under different conditions can be differentiated when the noise characteristics of the regions are inconsistent with the rest of the video.

## 1 Introduction

In the last decade digital cameras have become so popular that enormous numbers of photographs and videos are taken by amateur photographers. On the other hand, the recent development of digital editing techniques can be used to synthesize realistic images and videos that could also be used in courts of law. Unfortunately, photographs taken by amateur photographers are not protected from tampering. So if these photographs are used as testimony in courts of law, how is it possible to distinguish true evidence from false one?

In the early days of the Internet, *digital watermarking* was the main countermeasure against illegal use of digital contents [6]. However, most images and videos do not have an embedded digital watermark. Once images or videos without watermarks are uploaded to the Internet, digital watermarks are ineffective even if they are embedded afterwards because the contents may have already been tampered with by someone. Therefore digital watermarking is found to be limited in its ability to assure authenticity.

Recently a number of forgery detecting techniques for images without watermarking have been studied [14]. These techniques exploit inconsistencies or unnaturally high coherence observed in an image. Jonson and Farid used inconsistencies in lighting [4] and chromatic aberration [5]. Lin et al. estimated camera response function and verified its uniformity across an image [7]. Lukáš et al. extracted fixed pattern noise from an image and compared it with a reference pattern [10]. Fridrich et al. computed correlation between segments in an image

T. Wada, F. Huang, and S. Lin (Eds.): PSIVT 2009, LNCS 5414, pp. 306–317, 2009.

and detected cloned regions [2]. Ye et al. used an estimated JPEG quantization table and evaluated its consistency [17]. The different digital image forensic methods mentioned above help us to aggressively estimate the authenticity of digital images. In contrast, research for digital video forensics is just getting started, and the development of forgery detecting techniques for video is in high demand.

One of the most frequent digital evidence declared invalid in a court of law is a video recorded by a fixed surveillance camera. Tampering methods for a scene that contains a static background can be classified into two approaches. One is replacing regions or frames with duplicates from the same video sequence: forgers can hide unfavorable objects in a scene by overwriting these with the background. The other is clipping objects from other images or video segments and superimposing them on the desired regions in the video. This type of forgery aims to show objects that are advantageous for false evidence.

The method for detecting replacement or duplication has been studied by Wang and Farid [16]. Duplication yields high correlation between original frames or regions and cloned ones. Detecting unnaturally high coherence is useful for discovering copy-paste tampering. It has been demonstrated in the research that we can find substitutions from another frame in the same video sequence. However, their proposed method has a serious limitation in that it can only detect copy-paste tampering from the same video sequence. It cannot be used to detect superimposition, i.e., inserting objects from other video segments. In contrast, our aim is to propose a method that can detect superimposition.

The basic idea of our proposed method is to use noise inconsistencies between the original video and superimposed segments to detect forgeries. We exploit the *photon shot noise* in a digital camera as a clue to tampering. Photon shot noise results from the quantum nature of photons and follows a Poisson distribution, where the variance of the number of photons equals the mean. This dependency on the irradiance of photon shot noise gives us a clue to inconsistencies in the video. A CCD camera converts photons into electrons and finally into bits; therefore, the relation between the variance and the mean of the number of photons is converted into that between the variance and the mean of the observed value. This relation is formulated as the *noise level function* (NLF) by Liu et al [8]. The NLF depends on such parameters as inherent parameters of the camera and recording parameters. Consequently, by comparing the relation of the variance and the mean in a video clip, we can detect forged regions clipped from another video.

Specifically, given input video, we first analyze the noise characteristics at each pixel. Fig.1 shows a diagram of the noise characteristics. The solid line is the NLF of this distribution. Points in the figure represent the noise characteristic computed from each pixel. Once we obtain the per-pixel noise characteristics, NLF is fitted to the points using the least squares method. In this paper, we assume a linear *camera response function* (CRF). Since it is known that the linear CRF yields a linear NLF [13], the problem of estimating the NLF of the original video results in the problem of fitting a linear function to the data. We adopt

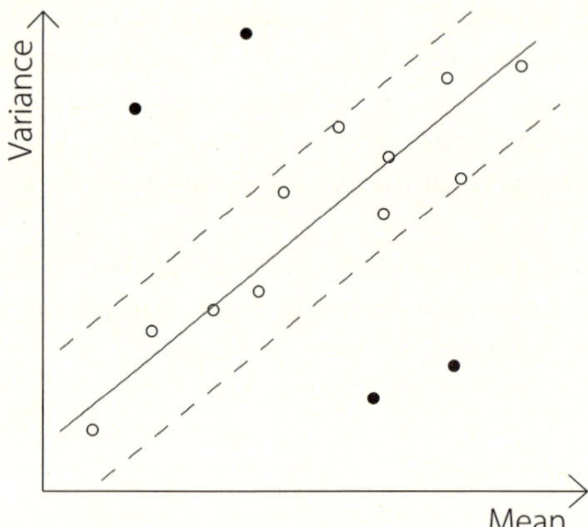


**Fig. 1.** Diagram of noise characteristics. Solid line is the estimated noise level function. Points inside the dashed lines (open circles) are regarded to be authentic. Closed circles are regarded to be from forged pixels.

the simplest metrics for the forgery measure, i.e., a point whose distance from the estimated function is greater than a threshold is from a forged pixel. The dashed lines in Fig.1 are the thresholds that separate the noise characteristic points into authentic (open circle) pixels and forged (closed circle) pixels. By evaluated every pixel in this way, we can detect per-pixel forgery in the given video.

We recorded some real videos for experiments and demonstrated that different recording parameters resulted in different noise characteristics. Then we applied the proposed method to the tampered video, we found that our method could properly detect the forged region.

## 2　Related Work

### 2.1　Forgery Detection Methods for Images and Video

The area of digital image forensics has progressed so markedly in the last few years that several approaches have been developed to detect forgeries in a digital image. Image tampering methods can be classified into two approaches. One is replacing regions with others in the same image and the other is superimposing regions clipped from other images.

The first attempt of forgery detection was proposed by Fridrich et al [2]. This method targets the copy-move method of attack, which yields unnaturally high correlation between duplicated regions. The researchers introduced a detection method based on robust block matching, which was carried out by using Discrete Cosine Transform (DCT) coefficients in order to deal with lossy JPEG compression.

Subsequent approaches target the superimposition-based forgeries, which verify the uniformity of characteristics in an image; therefore objects clipped from other images could be detected. Jonson and Farid proposed methods based on optical clues. They estimated the light source directions from some contours in an image and checked the consistency of estimated light source directions [4]. This technique showed so accurate estimation of light source directions for outdoor scenes that it could differentiate tampered objects in the image. Jonson and Farid also developed a method for detecting forgeries based on lateral chromatic aberration [5]: a spatial shift of light passing through the optical system due to the difference of refraction between wavelengths. Global model parameters that determine the displacement vector at each pixel in an image were estimated, and the degree of tampering was evaluated by calculating the average angular error between the displacement vector determined by global parameters and the actual local vector.

Lin et al. checked for the consistency of the camera response function estimated by analyzing the edges [7]. The irradiance on an edge should be a linear combination of those from objects at both sides of the edge, but a nonlinear camera response skews the linearity of signal processing. This approach estimates the nonlinear inverse response functions that convert a nonlinear relation of observed pixel values on the edge into a linear relation. If the function estimated from an edge does not conform to the rest of the image, the edge is marked as a sign of tampering.

JPEG is a compression technique for images; different manufacturers design different quantization tables used in a compression process. Ye et al. proposed a method to detect inconsistencies in an image based on the blocking artifact measure [17]. If blocks compressed with different quantization tables are combined in an image, the blocking artifact measure of forged blocks is much larger than that of an authentic block. They estimated the quantization table from the histogram of DCT coefficients and evaluated the blocking artifact measure of each block.

Compared to the image forensic techniques mentioned above, only a few techniques have been developed for video. Wang and Farid proposed forgery detecting methods based on video duplication and a deinterlacing algorithm [15,16]. The first approach that detect duplication is similar to the correlation-based detection proposed by Fridrich et al., extended so that it could detect duplicated regions across frames. They combined spatial and temporal correlation for detecting duplicated frames as well. On the other hand, the deinterlacing algorithm is a technique of converting interlaced video into a non-interlaced form. Due to the half resolution of interlaced video, the deinterlacing algorithm makes full use of insertion, duplication, and interpolation of frames to create full-resolution video. Parameters in the interpolation and the posterior probability of forgery are estimated by using the Expectation Maximization (EM) algorithm. Wang and Farid referred to forgery detection for interlaced videos in the same paper. They suggested that the motion between fields of a frame is closely related to that across fields in interlaced videos. Evaluating the interference to this relation by tampering, they detect the forgeries in the given interlaced video.

The methods proposed by Wang and Farid are interesting attempts for digital video forensics. It should be pointed out, however, that these methods have limitations for forgery detection. The first forensic technique based on correlation assumes that forged regions are duplicated from the same video sequence. As a result, this method has the same limitation for forgery detection as the method proposed by Fridrich et al., that it cannot detect superimposed regions from other videos. The second method targeting deinterlaced and interlaced videos can detect superimposing from other video sequences, but it limits the form of the video to deinterlaced or interlaced form.

Our proposed method is based on the inconsistencies of the noise characteristics in the given video. Forged regions brought from other video clips can be effectively detected by our method. In addition, our method exploits the characteristic of camera noise. Noise is a stable clue for forensics because it is an inevitable phenomenon in signal processing. Therefore our method is applicable to a wide range of videos.

## 2.2   Effective Use of Noise in Digital Data

Since the early period of digital camera, various reports have been given on the study of noise in signal processing. The main purpose of this field of research is to remove noise in images. Many denoising techniques have been developed and systematically classified [12].

On the other hand, some researchers have recently introduced interesting attempts to make effective use of noise, rather than trying to remove it from images and videos. Matsushita and Lin exploited the distribution of noise intensity for each scene irradiance to estimate the *camera response functions* (CRFs) [11]. Noise distribution is by nature shown to be symmetric, but it is skewed by nonlinear CRFs. Conversely, the inverse CRF can be estimated by evaluating the degree of symmetry of back-projected irradiance distribution. Using the noise in an image, the detection ability of the method is not degraded by noise and thus the method can be used under conditions of high-level noise.

Liu et al. estimated the *noise level function* (NLF) from a single image, which relates the noise intensity with the image intensity [8]. The spatial variance in an image contains the variance resulted in object's texture as well as the intensity of the noise. Obtaining the component of the real noise from NLF, we can disassociate the component of texture from the variance of the observation. They utilized the function not only for denoising but also for adaptive bilateral filtering and edge detection.

Noise information is available for camera identification and forgery detection as well. Due to the sensor imperfections developed in a manufacturing process, the CCD camera contains pixels with different sensitivity to light. This spatial variation of sensitivity is temporally fixed and known as *fixed pattern noise*. Since this non-uniformity is inherent in a camera, we can exploit it as a fingerprint. Lukáš et al. determined the reference noise pattern of a camera by averaging the noise extracted from several images [9]. They extracted fixed pattern noise from a given image using a smoothing filter and identified the camera that took the image. The authors also proposed a method for detecting forgeries in an image using the same approach [10].

This paper introduces a video forensic method by checking for inconsistency of the noise characteristics, which has never been proposed among the forensic methods for videos. Since the proposed method aggressively exploits noise, it is effective also for a video contaminated by significant noise. Other approaches are not able to handle high levels of noise.

## 3   Proposal Method

In this section, we propose a forgery detecting method using a noise characteristics model. In this paper, we will consider the inconsistencies of the characteristics of the noise mixed in the signal to be a clue to tampering. We first introduce a noise characteristic model in Section 3.1. As stated before, we focus in particular on *photon shot noise* for detecting forgeries in the given video. This is because the variance of observed intensity caused by photon shot noise is closely related to its mean. The relationship between the variance and mean of observed intensity is formulated as the *noise level function* (NLF), which is the clue to tampering. In Section 3.2, we propose a method to estimate NLF and detect forgeries by using the estimated NLF.

### 3.1   Noise Level Function of Video

A CCD digital camera converts photons into electrons and finally into bits. This signal processing has been studied for a long time [3,13]. In the signal process of a digital camera, several noise sources corrupt the signal such as *photon shot noise, dark current noise, thermal noise, read-out noise* and *quantization noise*. We focus on photon shot noise among these noise sources because of the following two reasons: (1) photon shot noise is dominant noise in a scene except in an extremely dark environment, and (2) the relation between the brightness and the noise intensity is useful for forgery detection.

The number of photons that enters a CCD element has temporal fluctuation and thus this variation behaves as noise. Since this fluctuation follows a Poisson distribution, the noise intensity depends on its mean – the noiseless irradiance. Unfortunately, we cannot measure the distribution of photons directly because photons are converted into electrons, electric voltage, and finally bit chains. However, we can instead compute the relation between the mean and the variance of the observed pixel value. We consider their relation as a measure of tampering.

Let $\hat{O}$ be the noiseless observed intensity. Due to the effect of noise, the real observation has fluctuation and thus we obtain a random variable of observation $O$. Let $\mu_{\hat{O}}$ and $\sigma_{\hat{O}}^2$ be the mean and the variance of the observed pixel intensity $O$, respectively, when the noiseless observation is $\hat{O}$. Following the formulation described in [8], we introduce NLF $\tau(\mu_{\hat{O}})$ as

$$\tau(\mu_{\hat{O}}) = \mathrm{E}[(O - \mu_{\hat{O}})^2]. \tag{1}$$

Unlike the equation in [8], we do NOT calculate the square root of Mean Square Error. This function represents how the variance changes with respect to the mean of the observed pixel value. When we obtain the mean observation $\mu_{\hat{O}}$, the variance is described by a function with respect to the mean as

$$\sigma_{\hat{O}}^2 = \tau(\mu_{\hat{O}}). \tag{2}$$

NLF depends on such parameters as inherent parameters of the camera and recording circumstance; they include inherent parameters of a camera such as quantum efficiency and the response function, and recording parameters such as exposure and electric gain.

For the sake of simplicity, we make two assumptions regarding the input video. The first assumption is that the distribution of the noise is zero-mean, and therefore we can obtain noiseless observed intensity of each pixel by averaging. Since this assumption suggests that the mean of observed intensity equals the noiseless intensity, we rewrite $\mu_{\hat{O}}$ as simply $\mu$. Second, we assume a linear camera response function (CRF). Former research on noise in a CCD camera [13] implies that a linear CRF yields a linear NLF. Therefore we simply apply linear least squares method to the calculated points.

## 3.2   Detection of Forged Pixels

Based on the theoretical background described in the previous section, we analyze the noise characteristics and detect forgeries of the given video by the following process. First, the mean and the variance of the pixel value are calculated at each pixel. Next, the NLF is estimated by fitting a function to the noise characteristic points. Finally, each pixel is evaluated based on its distance from the estimated NLF. We describe each step in detail in the following.

**Calculation of noise characteristics.**   If we have an image or a single frame of video sequence, NLF can be obtained by calculating spatial mean and variance. This approach, however, requires an assumption of the local uniformity of the object's reflectance and shading. If there is a textured object in a scene, we cannot obtain the noise component independently from the total variance because the spatial variation is mixed in the signal. The proposed method proves its merits in this case. As mentioned in the introduction, we deal with a static scene where the camera and the objects are fixed during recording. Therefore a conclusion is drawn that the temporal variation of each pixel value results entirely from noise. Operating statistical analysis along a time-line to the given video, we obtain the relation between $\mu$ and $\sigma_{\hat{O}}^2$ at each pixel.

**NLF estimation.**   Analyzing observed intensity along a time-line, we obtain a dense set of points, as many as the resolution of the video. Then we fit a linear NLF $\tau(\mu)$ to the points using linear least squares method as

$$\tau(\mu) = \alpha\mu + \beta, \tag{3}$$

where $\alpha$ and $\beta$ are the estimated parameters. In order to eliminate the effect of the scale factor between the mean and the variance, they are normalized before estimation.

**Fig. 2.** Example of the recorded video

**Table 1.** Recording parameters

| No. | Shutter time[ms] | Gain[dB] |
|-----|------------------|----------|
| (a) | 19.79 | 0.00 |
| (b) | 11.22 | 4.99 |
| (c) | 6.60 | 9.90 |
| (d) | 3.85 | 15.08 |
| (e) | 2.29 | 20.04 |
| (f) | 1.25 | 24.96 |

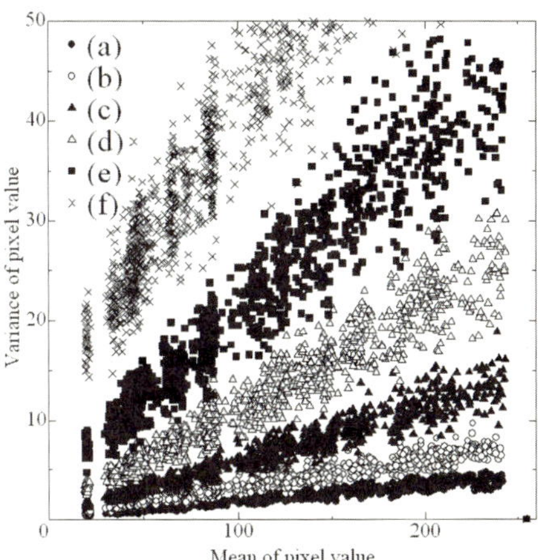


**Fig. 3.** Noise characteristics with different gain. Data points are thinned out for display. Shutter times and gain of data sets are shown in Table 1.

Because the noise intensity of the video created from an authentic process is uniquely determined by the estimated NLF, every pixel value converted from the same irradiance should yield the same noise intensity. Consequently, inconsistencies of the relation between the mean and the variance can be a clue to the forgery. Therefore we can claim pixels whose noise characteristic is far from NLF to be from a tampering process.

In this paper we use RANSAC [1] so that the NLF is estimated robust to the outliers calculated from the forged regions. The closed circles in Fig.1 are the outliers. Although we need to set a threshold manually, RANSAC is relatively robust to outliers, considering its ease of implementation.

**Evaluation of pixels.** Once we obtain the NLF $\tau(\mu)$, the authenticity of each pixel in the video is evaluated based on the distance from the estimated NLF according to (2). The evaluation of the pixel $N$ located at the position $r$ is determined as follows.

$$N(\boldsymbol{r}) = \begin{cases} \text{forged} & \text{if } \left|\sigma_{\hat{O}}^2(\boldsymbol{r}) - \tau(\mu(\boldsymbol{r}))\right| > \varepsilon \\ \text{authentic} & \text{otherwise,} \end{cases} \tag{4}$$

where $\varepsilon$ is the constant threshold.

Note that near the maximum pixel value (Here we consider 8-bit depth, hence the maximum is 255), the observed values are saturated and their apparent variances are smaller than real ones, which causes degradation of the detection quality. Therefore we set an upper limit $T$ for the mean value to omit evaluation of the pixels with the mean larger than $T$.

## 4   Experimental Results

All the experiments were done on video recorded on a PointGrey Flea digital camera. 128 grayscale frames are recorded at 30 fps for the 640 × 480-resolution compressed by Huffyuv, lossless compression Codec. We chose a Macbeth Color Checker Board under sunlight as the object. Fig. 2 shows an example of the recorded video.

### 4.1   Noise Characteristics with Various Parameters

We first showed how the noise characteristics change based on the recording parameters. Fig.3 shows the comparison of the noise characteristics with various electric gain. The shutter times and the gain of the data sets are shown in Table 1. Note that the horizontal and vertical axes indicate absolute, not normalized, values. The data points of each set distribute on a line that rises steeply corresponding to the gain. In the range of upper limit, the variances fall rapidly to zero, which results from the saturation in the quantization process.

### 4.2   Forgery Detection Using Noise Characteristics

We conducted another experiment of forgery detection. We created forged video clips as follows from 6 video sources analyzed above. At first a pair of videos taken under different parameters was chosen from the sources: they are a pair of the original and the replaced video clips. A forged region of 100 × 100-dimension was randomly located, and the position was kept as the ground truth. The pixel values in the located region over all frames in the original video were overwritten by those in the replaced video. An example of a frame in the forged video is shown in Fig.5 (Left). The white box in the image indicates the forged region.

The noise characteristics of the forged video were calculated as described in the previous section. Fig.4(A) shows the noise characteristics of the forged video created by replacing a part of the video of parameter (a) with that of parameter (c) in Table 1. Note that the means and the variances are normalized in this figure. Using RANSAC, we fitted a linear NLF to the calculated points. The threshold parameter of RANSAC was empirically set to 0.1 in the normalized noise characteristics space. There are two clusters: a dense cluster projected from the region of parameter (a) and a sparse cluster from the region of parameter (c). The solid line in the figure is the estimated NLF. Due to RANSAC, the linear NLF is properly estimated robust to the outliers.

Next, we assessed the pixels based on (4) and the estimated NLF. The boundary of forgery $\varepsilon$ is set to 0.1, which is equal to the threshold of inliers on RANSAC. The upper limit of the mean value for evaluation $T$ is empirically set to 0.9.

Fig.5 (Right) shows the detection result for the test data shown in Fig.5 (Left). The highlighted pixels in the figure represent the pixels determined to be forged. The proposed method detects most of the forged pixels in the color patches, while some pixels in the border are accepted. This is because the noise characteristic in the dark border is not sufficiently distinctive from that of the pixels in the authentic region to differentiate between them.

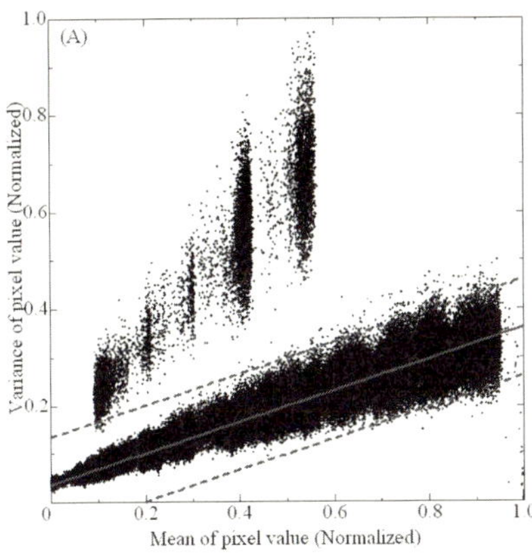
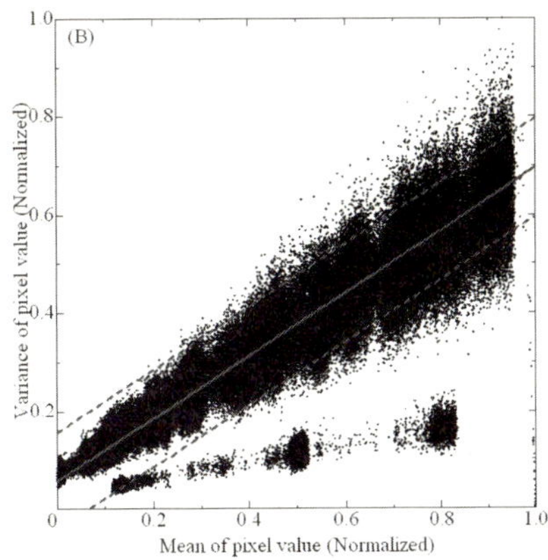

**Fig. 4.** Noise characteristics of a mixture video containing parameter (a) for the original and (c) for the replaced region (A) and vice versa (B). The solid line is the estimated NLF by using RANSAC and the dashed lines are the boundaries of forgery.

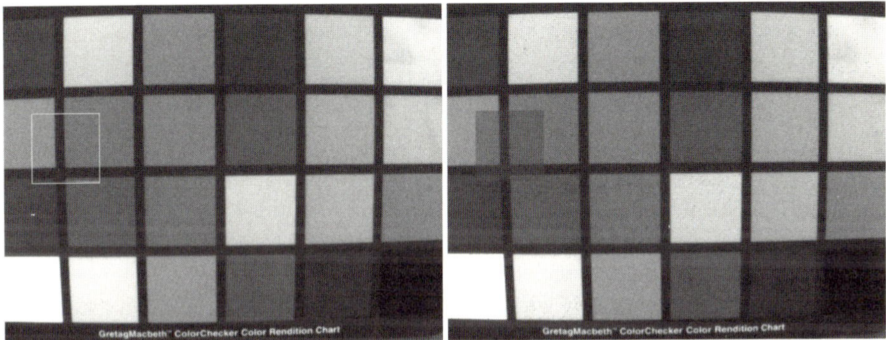


**Fig. 5.** Left: Example of the forged video. White box indicates the forged region. Right: Detection result for the video shown in the left figure. Highlighted pixels are determined to be forged.

To evaluate our method, we calculated the recall and the precision rates for every combination of the video clips. For one set of the recording parameters, we averaged over 30 random trials. The parameters in the fitting and the detection process were constant over this evaluation. The experimental result is shown in Table 2. We found that the proposed method can differentiate the forged pixels when the noise characteristics in the forged region are sufficiently isolated from the rest of the video.

However, the proposed method does not evaluate the authenticity of the pixels brighter than the upper limit $T$, which may cause degradation of detection. Even in the case that the noise characteristics are well separated, recall becomes worse if the forged region is located on a bright color patch. In addition, we should take notice of the low precision rate in the lower triangular portion of the table. The

**Table 2.** Evaluation result (Top: Recall [%], Bottom: Precision [%])

| Original Video | Replaced Video | | | | | |
|---|---|---|---|---|---|---|
| | (a) | (b) | (c) | (d) | (e) | (f) |
| (a) | - | 80.6 | 95.1 | 95.1 | 95.3 | 96.2 |
| (b) | 52.8 | - | 82.2 | 95.1 | 95.3 | 96.2 |
| (c) | 95.8 | 74.3 | - | 88.6 | 95.3 | 96.2 |
| (d) | 95.8 | 96.1 | 85.8 | - | 90.1 | 96.2 |
| (e) | 95.8 | 96.1 | 95.3 | 88.9 | - | 94.9 |
| (f) | 95.8 | 96.4 | 95.3 | 95.1 | 94.8 | - |

| Original Video | Replaced Video | | | | | |
|---|---|---|---|---|---|---|
| | (a) | (b) | (c) | (d) | (e) | (f) |
| (a) | - | 71.4 | 94.5 | 99.7 | 99.9 | 100.0 |
| (b) | 61.0 | - | 76.2 | 91.9 | 98.3 | 99.7 |
| (c) | 70.7 | 64.9 | - | 81.6 | 96.7 | 99.8 |
| (d) | 72.5 | 72.6 | 70.1 | - | 82.6 | 97.8 |
| (e) | 69.9 | 70.0 | 69.7 | 68.2 | - | 84.3 |
| (f) | 66.6 | 66.7 | 66.4 | 66.3 | 66.3 | - |

characteristic points of the original video in these conditions spread broad in spite of the constant boundary of forgery (See Fig.4(B) for an example). That is why there occurred many false-positives and the quality of the detection is degraded.

It should be noted that the threshold for outliers in RANSAC is empirically adjusted and constant with the gain. Nevertheless, the proposed method achieves robust fitting for all combinations of the recording parameters because of the benefit of robust fitting. It is interesting that the parameters can be fixed because we can easily detect forgeries properly without a probabilistic model or adaptive learning.

## 5   Conclusions and Future Work

In this paper we introduce a noise level function of a video clip and propose a digital video forensic technique based on the noise characteristics. The proposed method calculates the noise characteristic of each pixel by using temporal averaging, and achieves per-pixel evaluation of the authenticity with a high degree of accuracy by using a fitting method robust to outliers.

The following considerations will provide work for the future. First, in this paper we deal only with the videos recorded from a static scene, but in the future we will definitely have to consider working with persons and moving objects. In addition, the spatial relation of pixels is not used in this paper, but it will be useful for locating objects to integrate information of neighboring pixels. Also, combined with image segmentation techniques, it is expected that the method will reveal suspicious regions in the given video. Second, nonlinear CRFs are not considered in this report. In order to apply our method to a variety of cameras, we should expand it to generalized NLFs.

# References


1. Fischler, M.A., Bolles, R.C.: Random sample consensus: a paradigm for model fitting with applications to image analysis and automated cartography 24(6), 381–395 (1981)
2. Fridrich, J., Soukal, D., Lukáš, J.: Detection of copy-move forgery in digital images. In: Proc. of Digital Forensic Research Workshop (2003)
3. Healey, G.E., Kondepudy, R.: Radiometric ccd camera calibration and noise estimation. IEEE Transactions on Pattern Analysis and Machine Intelligence 16(3), 267–276 (1994)
4. Johnson, M.K., Farid, H.: Exposing digital forgeries by detecting inconsistencies in lighting. In: Proc. of Workshop on Multimedia and security (2005)
5. Johnson, M.K., Farid, H.: Exposing digital forgeries through chromatic aberration. In: Proc. of International Multimedia Conference, pp. 48–55 (2006)
6. Lee, S.-J., Jung, S.-H.: A survey of watermarking techniques applied to multimedia. In: Proc. of IEEE International Symposium on Industrial Electronics, vol. 1, pp. 272–277 (2001)
7. Lin, Z., Wang, R., Tang, X., Shum, H.-Y.: Detecting doctored images using camera response normality and consistency. In: Proc. of IEEE Computer Society Conference on Computer Vision and Pattern Recognition, vol. 1, pp. 1087–1092 (2005)
8. Liu, C., Szeliski, R., Kang, S.B., Lawrence Zitnick, C., Freeman, W.T.: Automatic estimation and removal of noise from a single image. Technical Report MSR-TR-2006-180, Microsoft Research (December 2006)
9. Lukáš, J., Fridrich, J., Goljan, M.: Determining digital image origin using sensor imperfections. In: Proc. of Society of Photo-Optical Instrumentation Engineers Conference, vol. 5685, pp. 249–260 (2005)
10. Lukáš, J., Fridrich, J., Goljan, M.: Detecting digital image forgeries using sensor pattern noise. In: Proc. of Society of Photo-Optical Instrumentation Engineers Conference, vol. 6072, pp. 362–372 (2006)
11. Matsushita, Y., Lin, S.: Radiometric calibration from noise distributions. In: Proc. of IEEE Computer Society Conference on Computer Vision and Pattern Recognition, pp. 1–8 (2007)
12. Motwani, M.C., Gadiya, M.C., Motwani, R.C., Harris Jr., F.C.: Survey of image denoising techniques. In: Proc. of Global Signal Processing Expo. and Conference (2004)
13. Tsin, Y., Ramesh, V., Kanade, T.: Statistical calibration of ccd imaging process. In: Proc. of IEEE International Conference on Computer Vision, vol. 1, pp. 480–487 (2001)
14. Van Lanh, T., Chong, K.-S., Emmanuel, S., Kankanhalli, M.S.: A survey on digital camera image forensic methods. In: Proc. of IEEE International Conference on Multimedia and Expo., pp. 16–19 (2007)
15. Wang, W., Farid, H.: Exposing digital forgeries in interlaced and deinterlaced video. IEEE Transactions on Information Forensics and Security 2(3), 438–449 (2007)
16. Wang, W., Farid, H.: Exposing digital forgeries in video by detecting duplication. In: Proc. of Workshop on Multimedia & security in International Multimedia Conference, pp. 35–42 (2007)
17. Ye, S., Sun, Q., Chang, E.-C.: Detecting digital image forgeries by measuring inconsistencies of blocking artifact. In: Proc. of IEEE International Conference on Multimedia and Expo., pp. 12–15 (2007)

# An Approach to Trajectory Estimation of Moving Objects in the H.264 Compressed Domain

Christian Käs and Henri Nicolas

LaBRI, University of Bordeaux,
351, cours de la libération, 33405 Talence, France
{kaes,nicolas}@labri.fr
http://www.labri.fr

**Abstract.** This paper presents a simple and fast method for unsupervised trajectory estimation of multiple moving objects within a video scene. It is entirely based on the motion vectors that are present in compressed H.264/AVC or SVC video streams. We extract these motion vectors, perform robust frame-wise global motion estimation and use these estimates to form outlier masks. Motion segmentation on the spatio-temporally filtered outlier masks is performed to detect moving regions in the scene, which are analyzed over time in order to identify similar objects in adjacent frames. The construction of so-called Object History Images (OHIs) is proposed to stabilize the trajectories, which are finally interpolated with X-splines. The system enables real-time analysis with standard hardware.

**Keywords:** Scene Analysis, Trajectory estimation, H.264-AVC/SVC compressed domain.

## 1 Introduction

The detection and tracking of moving objects in video scenes is an interesting and challenging research topic. Possible applications of such algorithms include video surveillance, retrieval tasks and scene analysis. Video processing tasks working at pixel level are usually computationally very expensive.

We aim at providing a method for efficient and fully automatic trajectory estimation of multiple objects, that is applicable to scalable state-of-the-art streams encoded by H.264/SVC, without implying any constraints on the nature of the moving objects. We assume that we have separated video scenes without any cuts or transitions. This can be achieved by first applying a compressed domain shot boundary detector, one of which was proposed by Bruyne [1] specifically for H.264 streams.

In general, object tracking in the pixel domain is more robust and performs better than compressed domain methods, since more and more precise information is available. Nevertheless, the motivation for compressed domain analysis

T. Wada, F. Huang, and S. Lin (Eds.): PSIVT 2009, LNCS 5414, pp. 318–329, 2009.

remains and is driven by fast processing speed and the fact that videos are primarily stored in compressed form. Faster processing becomes possible due to the fact that motion information is already present in the stream. Decreased robustness of motion-based, compressed domain approaches usually results from the noisy nature of the motion vectors, which are optimized in terms of coding efficiency and represent a sparse and noisy version of the real optical flow.

## 2   Related Work

A large number of compressed domain object segmentation and tracking algorithms appeared over the years. Some publications concerning pure object *segmentation* in the MPEG domain include [2,3,4,5,6].
Babu et al. [2,3] proposed an accumulation of motion vectors (MVs) over time, followed by a K-Means clustering to determine the number of objects in the scene and the EM algorithm for object segmentation. Zeng et al. [4] employ a block-based Markov Random Field (MRF) model to segment moving objects from the sparse MV field, which is extracted from H.264 compressed streams. The proposed method is limited to static cameras.

The proposed tracking approaches in the compressed domain rely either on MVs, residual information, or both. A lot of these works exploit the information found in MPEG-1/2 streams, where MVs and DCT coefficients are easily accessible. Hesseler et al. [7] perform the tracking initialization on decoded I-frames and use histograms of MVs of the MPEG-2 stream to perform tracking. The method does not support rotating objects and changes in size. Lie et al. [8] proposed a system that tracks single macro-blocks (MBs) under consideration of residual information. Trajectories are afterwards merged to obtain a moving object segmentation. Other MPEG-2 based methods have been proposed in [9,10,11,12,13,14,15].

Though most of the mentioned work can generally be ported to the H.264-AVC/SVC domain, some basic assumptions are no longer valid. The often used AC and DC coefficients (e.g., [9,13,14,15]) of intra-coded blocks in H.264/AVC are transformed from spatially intra-predicted values instead of the original pixel values, so full decoding is necessary. Concerning our goal of unsupervised, compressed domain scene analysis, other shortcomings of former approaches include manual tracking initialization (e.g., [12,15]), no support for camera motion (e.g., [11,15]) and no support for multiple, occluding objects (e.g., [10]).

A few approaches specific to MPEG-4 and H.264-AVC/SVC have been proposed in the literature. Sutter et al. [16] presented a lightweight tracking algorithm for MPEG-4/FGS. No indication for the performance in the case of multiple occluding objects are given and the system has to be initialized by the user. You et al. [17] perform tracking of feature points selected by the user. The matching of these points uses the dissimilarity energies related to texture, form, and motion. Therefore, they partially decode the stream around the Region-of-Interest (ROI) back to pixel level and fully decode I-frames.

## 3   Compressed Domain Trajectory Estimation

The presented approach consists of the stages depicted in Fig. 1. We extract the
MVs from the compressed stream, perform global motion estimation (GME),
filter the outliers and perform object detection on the resulting masks. A simple
matching algorithm is then applied to solve object correspondence. We introduce
Object History Images (OHIs) as a tool to stabilize the trajectories. Finally, the
center of gravity-based trajectories are represented by smooth splines. In the
following, we further explain each of these steps. Our method does not imply
constraints on the nature of the objects and can cope with moving cameras.
However, as also stated in [7], object detection and tracking that relies solely on
block-based MVs implies some requirements on the video scene. Our method is
subject to the following limitations:

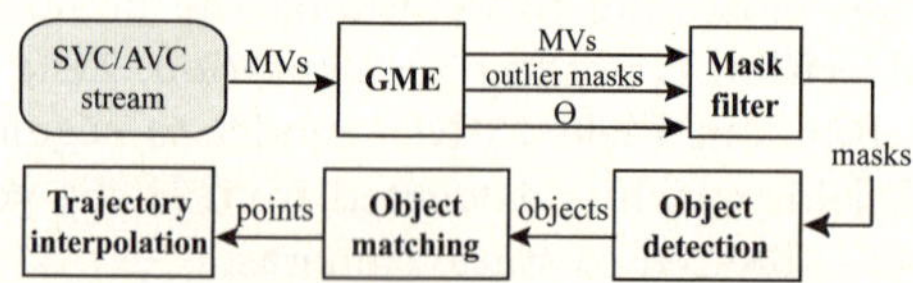

**Fig. 1.** Overview of trajectory estimation steps

- The scene background should be largely static in itself. Problematic areas
  are water or trees in the wind. In the case of present camera motion, the
  background should be well textured to limit the impact of noisy MV fields.
- Moving objects should neither be too numerous nor should they occupy the
  whole viewable image area.

If these constraints are met, the global motion estimation will deliver valid and
reliable results, which builds the basis for further processing.

### 3.1   H.264 AVC/SVC Test Sequences

H.264/AVC (MPEG-4/Part 10) is the successor of MPEG-2 and gains more and
more popularity due to its superior performance and efficiency. H.264/SVC [18]
is the scalable extension to AVC. Figure 3a shows an example of the macroblock partitions and MVs of a B-slice of the AVC-compatible base layer with a
resolution of 480x272 pixels, extracted from a SVC stream with Full-HD (1080p)
resolution at top level. Except for *Hall Monitor* and *Surveillance*, all of our test
sequences are encoded in this format. *Hall Monitor* and *Surveillance* are single-
layer streams with 352x288 pixels and 480x360 pixels, respectively.

We used the SVC reference software JSVM [19] in version 9.8 for our experiments. In case of High-Definition (HD) streams with spatial scalability, we only
process the AVC-compatible base layer to save computing time. We encoded all
streams with temporal scalability, enabled by the *hierarchical B-picture prediction* of SVC, with a Group-of-Picture (GOP) size of 8.

### 3.2  Global Motion Estimation (GME)

We adopted a similar robust motion estimation algorithm as proposed in [20] and [21], which proved to deliver good results. It basically consists of an iterative re-weighted least squares estimation of the well known 2-D 6-parameter affine model and is followed by a camera motion characterization. We estimate the global motion for each video frame.

In order to obtain the MV values in quarter-pel precision, the entropy coding of H.264 has to be reversed as the only decoding step. For each B-frame MB, depending on the prediction mode (LIST_0, LIST_1, direct or bi-prediction), we get a MV from LIST_0 and one from LIST_1. The choice between LIST_0 or LIST_1 MVs as active estimation support has shown to be arbitrary, since the distance to the reference frames in both temporal directions is the same (*hierarchical prediction structure* of SVC). We further process only forward-predicted LIST_1 MVs. To obtain uniform results, we scale all MVs by the distance to its respective reference picture. To obtain an estimate for I-frames, we take the mirrored LIST_0 vectors from the subsequent B-frame in display order as an estimation basis. MBs in *skip*-mode are excluded from the estimation support.

The 2-D 6-parameter affine motion model is given by

$$d_x = a_1 + a_2(x - x_0) + a_3(y - y_0)$$
$$d_y = a_4 + a_5(x - x_0) + a_6(y - y_0), \tag{1}$$

where $(x_0, y_0)^T$ denotes the reference point in the image (e.g., the image center) and $(x, y)^T$ the MB center. We estimate the model in the weighted least squares sense with a Gaussian weighting function. The process is repeated iteratively and outliers are discarded after each iteration. It showed that convergence is reached after approximately 4 iterations. The result of the GME process is the vector $\theta = (pan, tilt, zoom, rot)$, containing the frame-wise camera operation parameters. A mapping from the parameters $a_1..a_6$ to $pan..rot$ is performed according to [21].

### 3.3  Outlier Masks

The outlier masks which are output of the GME process contain noise (see Fig. 2) due to the block-based estimation process. Spatio-temporal filtering of the raw outlier masks is performed to alleviate the influence of miss-detected MVs. The temporal filtering window is set to the intra-period of the coded video, which is 8 frames in our experiments. Within this window, outlier MBs are median-filtered along their motion trajectories, followed by morphological filters to fill small holes in object masks and to remove background-noise.

### 3.4  Object Detection

The filtered outlier masks represent silhouette images and give a rough separation of the scene in background and foreground objects. We split the masks into

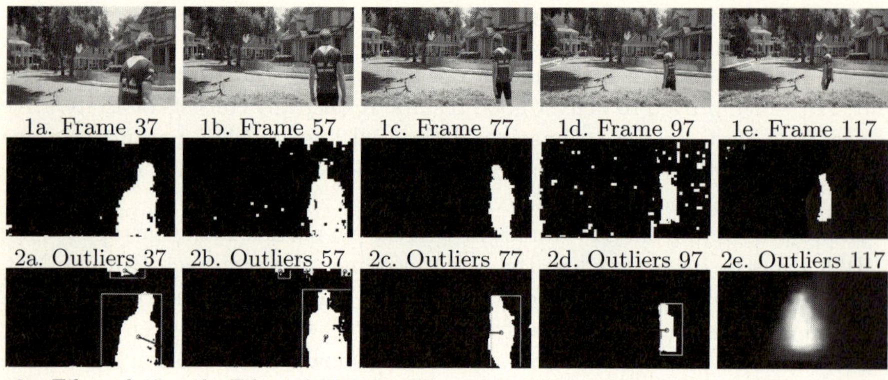

1a. Frame 37      1b. Frame 57      1c. Frame 77      1d. Frame 97      1e. Frame 117

2a. Outliers 37   2b. Outliers 57   2c. Outliers 77   2d. Outliers 97   2e. Outliers 117

3a. Filtered 37   3b. Filtered 57   3c. Filtered 77   3d. Filtered 97   3e. OHI of object

**Fig. 2.** Example of raw and filtered outlier masks. 3a-d) detected objects. Local object motion is represented by a vector leaving the centroid, which is represented by a circle. 3e) OHI of main object. Sequence *street with trees and bicycle* ©*Warner Bros. Advanced Media Services Inc.*

single moving objects by using a simple motion segmentation algorithm similar to the approach of timed *Motion History Images* (MHI) from Bradski and Davis [22].

Motion history images store the motion history for multiple frames in one single channel image. The MHI is updated by setting the corresponding mask pixels in the MHI to the current time stamp. Figure 3b shows an example of a MHI for the *street* sequence. Each connected region in the MHI sharing the most recent time stamp is considered as one independent object. All regions smaller than a minimal, pre-defined threshold-size $MIN_SIZE$ are discarded. We set $MIN_SIZE$ to a region height or width smaller than 3% of the image height or width, respectively. Each detected object is labeled and a some object properties are calculated and stored for further processing: i) The object mask, defined by the connected region in the tMHI; ii) The centroid; iii) The size, i.e., the number of pixels in the mask and iv) the object motion parameters (*pan..rot*).

The object motion parameters are estimated similarly to the global motion (see Sec. 3.2), using all MVs covered by the mask. Global motion is compensated

a. MV field

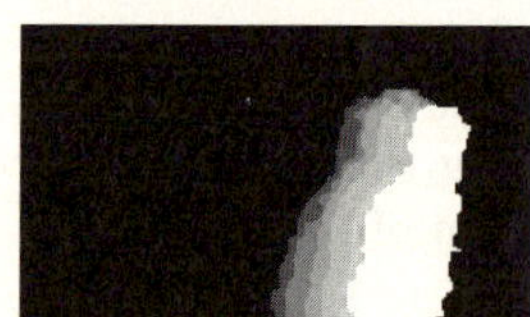

b. Motion history image

**Fig. 3.** Example of MVs (a) and a MHI (b) of the sequence *street_with_trees_and_bicycle*. Image (a) was magnified and cropped for better visibility.

before the estimation and the reference point is set to the center of gravity of the mask. The quality of these parameters depends on the number of MVs covered by the object, indicated by the object size. The two translational parameters $a_1 \stackrel{\wedge}{=} pan$ and $a_4 \stackrel{\wedge}{=} tilt$ are robust to small estimation supports, whereas the significance of the parameters *zoom* and *rot* decreases.

Examples showing the temporal evolution of the local object motion are given in Fig. 4 for the man in the *street* sequence and for the pedestrian in *parkrun* (see Fig. 6 for screenshots). The small estimation support in the latter case leads to very noisy results for zoom and rotation. For the *street* sequence, the estimation reflects well the real object motion. The indicated zoom-in and zoom-out around frames 15-50 and 120-170 represents the objects' motion towards and away from the camera. In both figures, the curves for *zoom* and *rot* have been scaled for the sake of better comparability to *pan* and *tilt*.

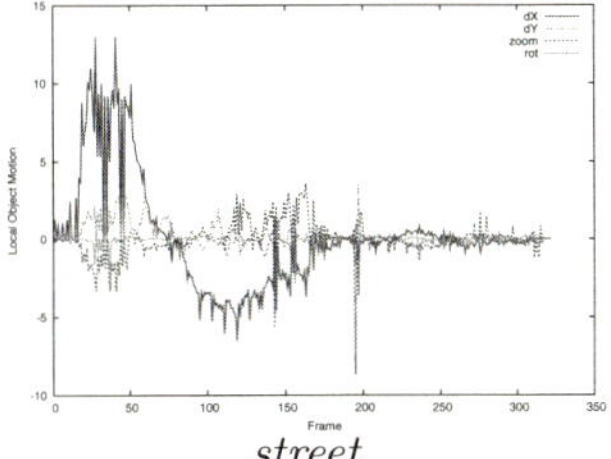

*street*

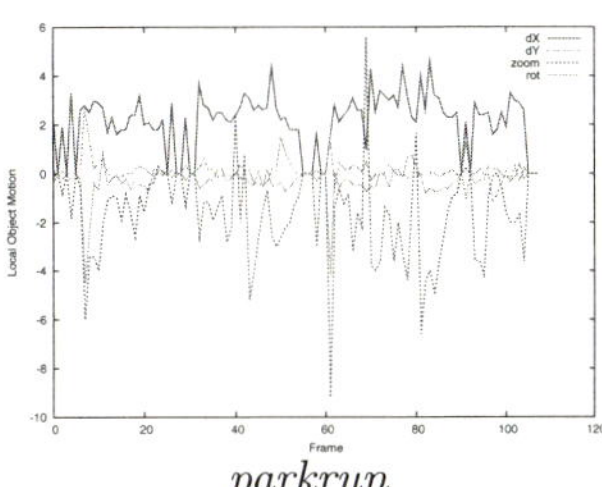

*parkrun*

**Fig. 4.** Local object motion for sequences *parkrun* and *street_with_trees_and_bicycle*. The parameter *zoom* is very noisy for the pedestrian in *parkrun*, because only a very small number of MBs is covered by the mask.


## 3.5   Object Matching

At this stage, we have the frame-wise, independent object detection results as described above. The most important step in the trajectory estimation process is to track the detected objects over time, i.e., to identify similar objects in adjacent frames and to define a reference point within the object that represents its current position. We treat these problems separately in the following.

A temporal analysis of the calculated object properties (see Sec. 3.4 ) allows to draw certain conclusions about what is happening in the scene:

▷ **mask:** Represents regions in motion. Its position gives an indication if the object enters or leaves the scene.

▷ **size:** Continuous changes in size are usually caused either by objects leaving or entering the scene, by changes of the visible object surface (occlusions), by changes of the distance to the camera or by a non-rigid object that partially stops or resumes moving. Rapid, significant changes in the object size indicate split-and-merge situations.

▷ **centroid:** Center of gravity of moving region. Rapid changes of position also indicate split-and-merge situations.

▷ **motion:** The translational motion parameters *pan* and *tilt* indicate the moving direction and predict the position in the next frame (relative to the camera position). If the estimation support is sufficiently large, *zoom* may give an indication if the object approaches or moves away from the camera.

**Object Correspondence.** The initialization takes place when the first objects are detected at time $t_i$. Each object is assigned with a unique label and is kept in memory along with its properties. The expected position in the following frame is estimated using the translational motion parameters. At time $t_i + 1$, the algorithm searches a limited area of 20 pixels around the predicted position for new input objects. If an object with similar size and moving direction is found in the search area, we assign the same label to it. Otherwise we mark the object as *inactive*.

If an object of significantly larger size is found in the search area, we check if that new object coincides with the predicted position of another object. If this is true, the objects "merged" and we assign both labels to that joint object. Otherwise we check for inactive objects that have been lastly detected at this position (with compensated global motion). If there seems to be no such explanation for the abrupt change in size, we however copy the same object label to it and set a flag of uncertainty. Possible other explanations include fast objects re-appearing behind occluding obstacles, or a merging with another previously static object (e.g., a pedestrian takes a bike and rides away).

"Split" situations, where multiple smaller objects replace a big one, are treated similarly. If a crossing of multiple objects occurs (merge-split), we assume the objects' moving directions are hardly affected, so after the split we re-assign the labels according to the closest match to the motion parameters before the merging. This may lead to a false label switching in certain scenarios.

If at a given moment, a new object appears "out of nowhere", i.e., one that is neither entering nor leaving the scene, we search for *inactive* objects in that region to reactivate them. If none is found, we assign a new label to the appearing object.

## 3.6   Reference Point

At this stage, we have identified similar objects over time. Moving objects are often occluded by obstacles like cars or tables and we look for a reference point within the object that remains as stable as possible. We therefore chose the center of gravity. Problematic are non-rigid objects and occlusions. To give an example, the waiter in the sequence shown in Fig. 5 moves from one table to the next, stops to clean them and is often partially occluded. While wiping the table, the centroid of the mask moves away from the original one, which was located around the waistline. In order to stabilize the reference point over time, we propose the construction of so-called *Object History Images* (OHI). We extended the idea from global MHIs [22] to object silhouette construction. The goal is to create a more stable representation of an object than the quickly fluctuating object mask.

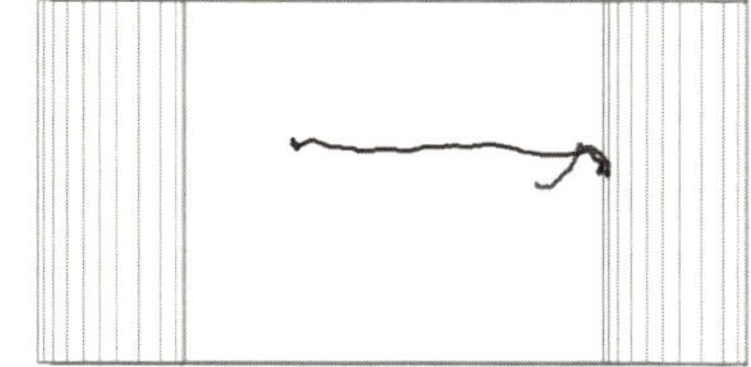

**Fig. 5.** Left: Exemplary deformations of the same moving object at different moments in time. Red circle is centroid of mask. Middle: OHI of object. Right: Trajectory. Sequence *man_in_restaurant* ©*Warner Bros. Advanced Media Services Inc.*

At the first occurrence of an objet, we initialize the OHI with the first object mask. Each time a previously present object is detected in the current frame, we project the OHI to the position predicted by $\hat{a}_1$ and $\hat{a}_4$. We superimpose it with the new mask image and increment the value of the OHI at positions where mask pixels are set. If the new mask does not entirely fit into the projected OHI, we enlarge it.

We keep one "long-term" OHI for each detected object and continuously update as long as the object is visible and moving. The OHI represents a silhouette image of the object, where the most rigid regions appear brighter than parts like legs or arms. As the reference point, we compute the center of gravity, which assigns more importance to higher values. Darker zones in the OHI, like moving hands or shadows, only cause slight fluctuations. Examples of OHIs are given in Fig. 5 and Fig. 2.

The most problematic cases regarding the objects' reference points are merged object masks. When we detect a merging situation, we only update the intersection between the past OHI at its predicted position and the merged mask. This way

If the system gets initialized with merged objects that split later on, we only know after the split that the area contained more than one object. We then reset the merged OHI and re-initialize a new OHI for each object.

### 3.7 Trajectory Construction

We draw the trajectories in the image plane seen by the camera. The trajectories, represented by the centre of gravity of the OHIs over time, are smoothed using X-splines [23] as a final step. X-splines combine the properties of Catmull-Rom splines and cubic B-splines in one curve, adding the feature of sharp bends at abrupt turns. To achieve that, each control point is parameterized by a factor $k \in [-1; 1]$, where $k = -1$ gives Catmull-Rom like behavior (interpolation), $k = +1$ leads to B-spline like behavior (approximation) and $k = 0$ gives a sharp bend at the control point.

For each control point, we assign $k$ as a function of the object size in relation to the size of the OHI. If the mask size is below 30% of the OHIs' size, we assign $k = +1$, otherwise $k = -1$. That means that small masks are considered to be less reliable and their centroids are approximated rather than crossed by the spline. Control points at moments of merged masks with multiple objects are also weighted with $k = +1$, because the position estimation is less reliable due to likely inter-object occlusions.

## 4   Results

Figure 6 shows the estimated trajectories for some test sequences. Each trajectory plot shows the position of the visible image area over time, represented by one rectangle for every 20th image, and the global camera motion over time, represented by purple curves connecting the rectangle corners. The trajectories are drawn as thick colored lines, and the brightness of the color corresponds to the moment in time. The brightest point denotes the position in the beginning of the sequence, the darkest one the position at the end. Each detected object is represented by a different color. The most-right plots in Fig. 6 show the trajectories obtained manually by users, who we demanded to click on the estimated center of gravity of all relevant objects in each frame.

The two short lines in the top left corner of the *street* sequence trajectory plot (Fig. 6a) are caused by moving branches of a tree. By comparing the main trajectory with the camera motion, it can be noticed that the camera is following the object. This can also be noticed in the *parkrun* sequence, where a pedestrian is walking along the river and is followed by the camera. He always appears in the center of the image. The trajectory of the waiter in the *restaurant* sequence is shown in Fig. 6f. The fluctuations of the most right part of the trajectory are caused by a long period where he stands still while cleaning a table.

Figure 6e shows the results for the well-known *Hall_Monitor* sequence. Both objects are detected and tracked over time, where the jitter in the middle of the left trajectory results from the man stopping at the small table for about 50 frames. To provide an example of two crossing objects, we show the results for a surveillance video showing two pedestrians with opposed trajectories in Fig. 6c.

The largest differences between the estimated and the manually determined trajectories are observed in the *Kung Fu* sequence (Fig. 6d). The system did not recognize that one fighter over-jumped the other, which ducked down, and could not exactly follow during the vigorous fight. However, the object did not get lost and the trajectories reflect well both positions.

Table 1 summarizes the results of the object *detection* stage for the given test sequences. We counted the total number of object occurrences in all frames and provide results for the number of correctly detected objects, the missed detections and false positives. The high numbers of missed objects in the sequences *Hall Monitor* and *Man in Restaurant* appear because objects stop moving for several frames and we detect only objects in motion. The trajectories are hardly affected of this detection loss, because the objects are correctly re-identified after they continue moving. The false positives in the *Street* sequence represent moving branches of a tree, which we consider as background.

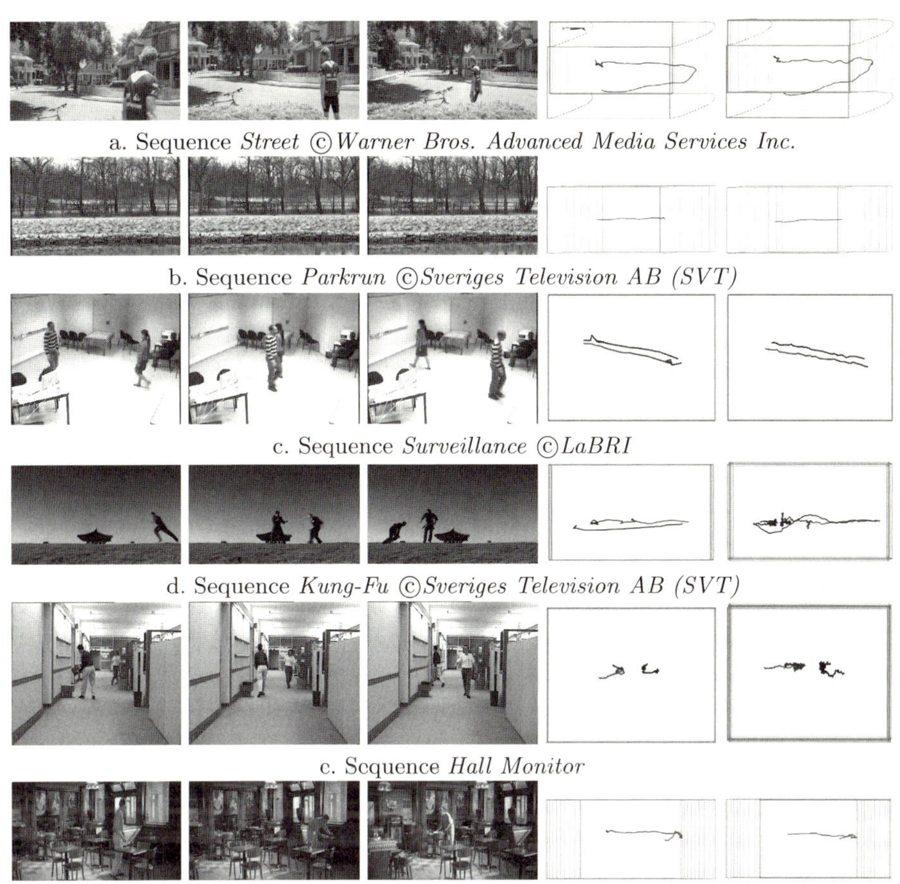

a. Sequence *Street* ©*Warner Bros. Advanced Media Services Inc.*

b. Sequence *Parkrun* ©*Sveriges Television AB (SVT)*

c. Sequence *Surveillance* ©*LaBRI*

d. Sequence *Kung-Fu* ©*Sveriges Television AB (SVT)*

e. Sequence *Hall Monitor*

f. Sequence *Man in Restaurant* ©*Warner Bros. Advanced Media Services Inc.*

**Fig. 6.** Results for some test sequences. From left to right: 1-3) Screenshots 4) Estimated trajectory 5) Manually obtained trajectories

**Table 1.** Object Detection Results

| Sequence | Duration in frames (sec) | Corr. detected objects | Missed objects | False positives | Processing time in sec (fps) |
|---|---|---|---|---|---|
| *street* | 270 (10.8s) | 268/270 (99%) | 2/270 | 22 | 10.1s (26.7 fps) |
| *parkrun* | 100 (4.0s) | 95/100 (95%) | 5/100 | 3 | 3.5s (28.5 fps) |
| *surveillance* | 118 (4.7s) | 224/236 (95%) | 12/236 | 3 | 4.32s (27.3 fps) |
| *kung fu* | 180 (7.2s) | 291/303 (96%) | 14/303 | 0 | 6.7s (26.8 fps) |
| *hall monitor* | 300 (12.0s) | 404/455 (89%) | 51/455 | 0 | 11.3s (26.5 fps) |
| *man in restaurant* | 310 (12.4s) | 288/310 (93%) | 22/310 | 7 | 10.9s (28.4 fps) |

The processing times given in Tab. 1 were measured on a 2.16 GHz Intel Core2Duo with 2 GB of RAM. The simplicity of the algorithm allows real-time processing.

## 5  Conclusions

We presented an approach to estimating the trajectories of moving objects in the H.264 compressed domain. The method is completely unsupervised and is entirely based on the motion vectors present in the compressed stream. It is able to detect and track multiple objects of any kind, given that they also appear clearly geometrically separated at some moments in time. Our method is computationally efficient and can cope with complex camera motion. An inconvenience is the dependency on reliable global motion estimation results. We will further evaluate and improve our algorithm for different types of videos and applications.

## Acknowledgments

This work has been carried out in the context of the french national project ICOS-HD (ANR-06-MDCA-010-03) funded by the ANR (Agence Nationale de la Recherche).

## References

1. De Bruyne, S., De Neve, W., De Schrijver, D., Lambert, P., Verhoeve, P., Van de Walle, R.: Shot boundary detection for H.264/AVC bitstreams with frames containing multiple types of slices. In: Ip, H.H.-S., Au, O.C., Leung, H., Sun, M.-T., Ma, W.-Y., Hu, S.-M. (eds.) PCM 2007. LNCS, vol. 4810, pp. 177–186. Springer, Heidelberg (2007)
2. Babu, R.V., Ramakrishnan, K.: Content-based video retrieval using motion descriptors extracted from compressed domain. In: IEEE International Symposium on Circuits and Systems (ISCAS 2002), Phoenix, USA, vol. 4, pp. 141–144 (2002)
3. Babu, R.V., Ramakrishnan, K., Srinivasan, S.: Video object segmentation: a compressed domain approach. IEEE Transactions on Circuits Systems for Video Technology 14(4), 462–474 (2004)
4. Zeng, W., Du, J., Gao, W., Huang, Q.: Robust moving object segmentation on h.264/avc compressed video using the block-based mrf model. Real-Time Imaging 11(4), 290–299 (2005)
5. Sukmarg, O., Rao, K.: Fast object detection and segmentation in mpeg compressed domain. In: 10th IEEE Region Annual International Conference, Kuala Lumpur, Malaysia, vol. 3, pp. 364–368 (September 2000)
6. Mezaris, V., Kompatsiaris, I., Boulgouris, N.V., Strintzis, M.G.: Real-time compressed-domain spatiotemporal segmentation and ontologies for video indexing and retrieval. IEEE Transactions on Circuits and Systems for Video Technology 14, 606–621 (2004)
7. Hesseler, W., Eickeler, S.: Mpeg-2 compressed-domain algorithms for video analysis. EURASIP Journal on Applied Signal Processing 2, 1–11 (2006)

8. Lie, W.N., Hsiao, W.C.: Content-based video retrieval based on object motion trajectory. In: IEEE Workshop on Multimedia Signal Processing, pp. 237–240 (December 2002)

9. Radhakrishna, A., Kankanhalli, M., Mulhem, P.: Compressed domain object tracking for automatic indexing of objects in mpeg home video. In: IEEE International Conference in Multimedia and Expo (ICME 2002), Lausanne, Switzerland (August 2002)

10. Park, S.M., Lee, J.: Compressed domain object tracking for automatic indexing of objects in mpeg home video. In: 4th Pacific Rim Conference on Multimedia, Singapore, vol. 2, pp. 748–752 (December 2003)

11. Lie, W.N., Chen, R.L.: Tracking moving objects in mpeg-compressed videos. In: IEEE International Conference on Multimedia and Expo. (ICME 2001), vol. 2001, p. 245 (2001)

12. Favalli, L., Mecocci, A., Moschetti, F.: Object tracking for retrieval applications in mpeg-2. IEEE Transactions on Circuits and Systems for Video Technology 10, 427–432 (2000)

13. Chen, H., Zhan, Y., Qi, F.: Rapid object tracking on compressed video. In: Shum, H.-Y., Liao, M., Chang, S.-F. (eds.) PCM 2001. LNCS, vol. 2195, pp. 1066–1071. Springer, Heidelberg (2001)

14. Manerba, F., Benois-Pineau, J., Leonardi, R., Mansencal, B.: Multiple moving object detection for fast video content description in compressed domain. EURASIP J. Adv. Signal Process 2008(1), 1–13 (2008)

15. Aggarwal, A., Biswas, S., Singh, S., Sural, S., Majumdar, A.: Object tracking using background subtraction and motion estimation in MPEG videos. In: Narayanan, P.J., Nayar, S.K., Shum, H.-Y. (eds.) ACCV 2006. LNCS, vol. 3852, pp. 121–130. Springer, Heidelberg (2006)

16. Sutter, R.D., DeWolf, K., Lerouge, S., de Walle, R.V.: Lightweight object tracking in compressed video streams demonstrated in region-of-interest coding. EURASIP J. Appl. Signal Process 2007(1), 59 (2007)

17. You, W., Sabirin, M., Kim, M.: Moving object tracking in H.264/AVC bitstream. In: Sebe, N., Liu, Y., Zhuang, Y.-t., Huang, T.S. (eds.) MCAM 2007. LNCS, vol. 4577, pp. 483–492. Springer, Heidelberg (2007)

18. Schwarz, H., Marpe, D., Wiegand, T.: Overview of the scalable h.264/mpeg4-avc extension. In: IEEE International Conference on Image Processing (ICIP 2006), Atlanta, USA, October 2006, pp. 161–164 (2006)

19. Software, J.R.: Reference software for h.264/svc,
http://ftp3.itu.ch/av-arch/jvt-site/

20. Bouthemy, P., Gelgon, M., Ganansia, F.: A unified approach to shot change detection and camera motion characterization  9, 1030 (1999)

21. Durik, M., Benois-Pineau, J.: Robust motion characterisation for video indexing based on mpeg2 optical flow. In: Proceedings of International Workshop on Content-Based Multimedia Indexing (CBMI 2001), Brescia, Italy, pp. 57–64 (September 2001)

22. Bradski, G.R., Davis, J.W.: Motion segmentation and pose recognition with motion history gradients. Mach. Vision Appl. 13(3), 174–184 (2002)

23. Blanc, C., Schlick, C.: X-splines: a spline model designed for the end-user. In: SIGGRAPH 1995: Proceedings of the 22nd annual conference on Computer graphics and interactive techniques, pp. 377–386. ACM Press, New York (1995)

# Enhanced Side Information Generator with Accurate Evaluations in Block-Based Wyner-Ziv Video Coding


Chang-Ming Lee[1,2], Jui-Chiu Chiang[1,2], Zhi-Heng Chiang[2], Kuan-Liang Chen[1], and Wen-Nung Lie[1,2]

[1] Department of Electrical Engineering
[2] Department of Communication Engineering
National Chung Cheng University, Chia-Yi, 621, Taiwan, ROC
{changminglee,rachel}@ee.ccu.edu.tw, a1010820a2002@hotmail.com,
{klchen@samlab.ee,wnlie@}ccu.edu.tw



**Abstract.** Wyner-Ziv coding (WZC) has received a lot of attention lately. Based on the block unit for WZ-/intra-coding and the temporal distance between two consecutive key blocks, two techniques are proposed to improve the performance of block-based distributed video coding. Depending on the spatio-temporal analysis, the first method adjusts the mode assignment to a more precise generation of side information. In addition, the second method carries out the correlation calculation in the encoder side to ensure a better statistical estimation between the side information frame and the original frame. Thus, the more accurate side information combined with the more reliable statistical parameters results in an improved coding efficiency. The simulation results show that the compound of these two proposed methods has an improvement up to 2.7 dB with respect to the previous work in block-based WZC.

**Keywords:** Wyner-Ziv coding, distributed video coding.


## 1 Introduction

Today's video coding standards, such as MPEG-X, H.26X, etc., are based on predictive coding techniques which use motion estimation (ME) to eliminate the temporal redundancy. The complexity of this kind of video codec is high due to ME process. These techniques are practical for applications where information is encoded only once and decoded many times. However, some applications require low complexity at the encoder side, and possibly disregard high complexity at the decoder side, such as wireless sensor networks. Slepian-Wolf theorem [1] and Wyner-Ziv (WZ) theorem [2] indicate a possibility to design coding schemes to fit the above requirements: The Slepian-Wolf theorem illustrates that given two correlated sources, the rate of independent and lossless encoding is greater than or equal to the rate of joint encoding, which means that the coding efficiency of the joint encoding technique is higher. On the other hand, the WZ theorem is a lossy version of the Slepian-Wolf theorem, exhibiting the rate region for encoding one source without any knowledge of the second source, and decoding this source with side information generated from the second one.


T. Wada, F. Huang, and S. Lin (Eds.): PSIVT 2009, LNCS 5414, pp. 330–339, 2009.

When the above two algorithms are adopted in video coding, it is usually called distributed video coding (DVC). The pixel-domain DVC has been proposed in [3]. The conventional DVC architecture is based on a predefined group of picture (GOP). Frames in a video are organized as I-WZ-I-WZ…, where the GOP size is 2. Usually, I frames are recognized as key frames and are intra-coded, which are responsible for generating the side information for WZ frames at the decoder side. With more accurate side information, the bitrate required for WZ frames reconstruction in the decoder could be reduced and the coding efficiency will be better. Therefore, some researchers focused on the side information estimation improving [4-6].

Recently, due to the complicated implementation for WZ frames reconstruction, fast algorithms were proposed to speed up the process of WZ frames reconstruction. A parallelized DVC scheme [7] with an effective estimation is proposed to manage the decoding of subsequent bitplanes. Another issue in WZ video coding is the improvement of channel coding. Brites et al. [8] proposed a method to estimate the channel model parameter more accurately, which is then capable of providing a more reliable initial probability for turbo decoding. The channel model parameter is estimated at frame, block, or pixel level, for different granulations. Varodayan et al. [9] modified the LDPC codec such that it is rate-adaptive in contrast to the traditional fixed-length LDPC codec. Some researches considered parts of transmission as a virtual channel [10]. This virtual channel was analyzed and modeled. For example, they brought in the relation between the video compression ratio and the sensitivity of the estimated channel model parameter at the decoder side.

However, the temporal correlation between consecutive frames is not stationary and thus the fixed GOP structure will not be efficient enough. Therefore, a method to overcome the shortcoming of the traditional scheme was presented in [11] where the idea of a dynamic temporal distance (called temporal group of blocks (TGOBs)) between two consecutive key blocks was proposed. In attempt to improve the side information accuracy and also ease the design of the decoder, we propose two techniques in this paper where the key/WZ block decision rule is modified and the estimate of the noise model is performed in the encoder side rather than in the decoder side.

## 2 Key-Block-Based Wyner-Ziv Coding

In [12], the I-WZ-I-WZ… coding structure is maintained, but some blocks in the WZ frames may be changed into intra-coding, meaning that the WZ frames may be encoded in mixed modes. On the other hand, blocks of the key frames are all intra-coded. The gain of this coding-mode change for WZ frames is not high enough. On the other hand, Ascenso et al. [13] made the GOP size (i.e., the distance between two consecutive key frames) adjustable, according to the motion activity along the temporal domain within the sequence. However, these two techniques did not consider the tiny content variations in both the spatial and the temporal directions.

These issues motivate us to explore the spatial and temporal correlation in a finer granularity. In the spatial direction, a block is adopted as intra- or WZ encoding after block-mode decision. In the temporal direction, the GOP structure/length is dynamic, depending on the variations of temporal correlation in the video contents.

# 3  Detials of the Proposed Scheme

## 3.1  Block-Based Wyner-Ziv Coding with Modified TGOB Structure

For the proposed scheme, the temporal distance TGOB between consecutive key blocks is determined by the block-mode-decision unit and is limited by an upper bound $U$. An intra-coding mode (key block) is determined when the current block has a low correlation with the prior key block (often, the motion between them is significant), or the temporal distance from the prior key block equals to the maximum delay ($U$). However, interpolating two key blocks in distance will not guarantee a reliable estimation for WZ block. For the scenario in high quality requirement, more key blocks can support an accurate generation of side information. Therefore, the performance of reconstruction of WZ block would be enhanced.

For high-quality applications, we need to modify the rule of block mode decision mentioned in Section 2.1. The revised coding structure will be in a form of "IB-WZB...WZB-IB-IB-WZB... ZB-IB-IB-....". In this way, two consecutive and non-adjacent key blocks will have high correlation, and then more accurate side information and a higher PSNR can be ensured. To cope with coding efficiency at the same time, one more rule is introduced in the block-mode decision unit as follows.

1. If TGOB is less then $U$: two intra blocks are inserted (the identified current block and its co-located block in the previous frame).
2. ELSE: only one intra block is inserted; it implies the co-located MB is identified as a key block.

For example, Fig. 2 shows that the TGOB size varies in the order of 3, 4 and 1, for the $Block_{0,\,1}$ with $U$ (the upper bound of TGOB size) equals 4. After adapting the proposed block-mode decision rule, Fig.3 presents the new block mode distribution.

In Fig.3, the block in red circle in the left side is decided as key block according to the first condition, while the one in the right side is unchanged and marked as WZ mode followed by one key block according to the second condition. Although more blocks are intra-coded, WZC is more efficient in precisely generating side information and therefore reducing the parity bits required to reconstruct the WZ frames. To implement this modified scheme, an additional frame delay at encoder side is demanded. However, we can achieve a higher PSNR with this modified scheme as indicated by experimental results.

## 3.2  Correlation Calculator Relocation

Normally, the side information generator among the DVC decoder in Fig.1 usually involves the correlation calculator and MCI (motion compensation interpolation for the frame-based WZC structure). In Fig.4, the module of the correlation calculator is realized in the encoder. The estimate of the noise model between the block $WZB^{i,\,j,\,t}$ and the side information would be carried out by using the original WZ block and the estimated one by interpolating associated original key blocks. The calculation of the

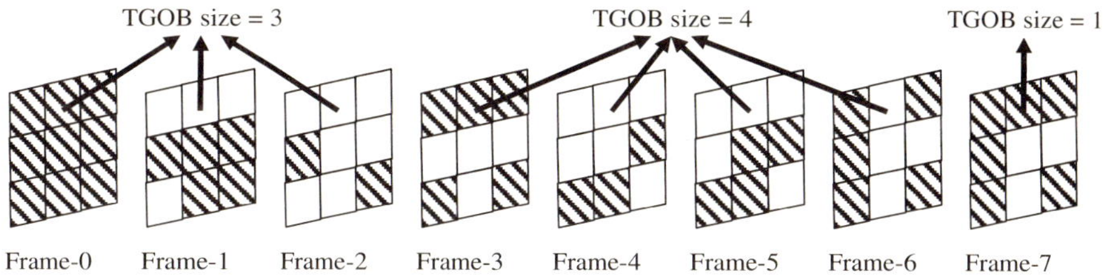



**Fig. 2.** The concept of dynamic TGOB with $U = 4$, where the shaded blocks represent the key blocks and the others are WZ blocks

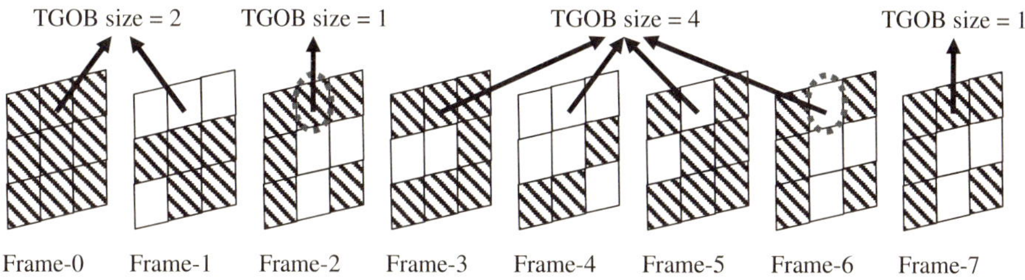



**Fig. 3.** The modified block-mode map according to highly correlated key blocks, with $U = 4$

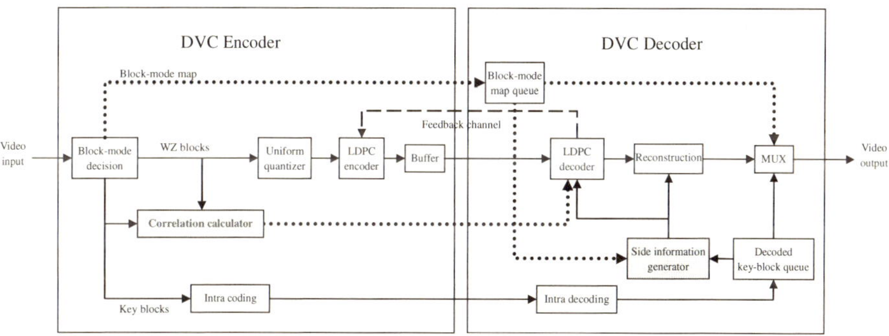



**Fig. 4.** Key-block-based Wyner-Ziv coding architecture with Correlation calculator in the DVC encoder

block variance $\sigma^2_{i,j,t}$ and the Laplacian distribution parameter $\alpha$ is similar to formulas in Section 2.2.

Consequently, this novel technique would cause a complexity shift from the decoder to the encoder. According to the block-based architecture, linear interpolation is used in the DVC, instead of MCI (motion compensation interpolation). Besides, the sample size for the corresponding analysis ($\alpha$) is 16 x 16. Thus, the complexity to construct $WZB^{i,j,t}$ and obtain the related information in DVC encoder is still light. In addition, a buffer is required to preserve the content of key blocks decided by the block-mode decision.

The proposed codec is compared to two schemes in [3] and [11]. The first is a traditional LDPC-based DVC scheme adopting the frame-based "I-WZ-I-WZ…" coding structure (i.e., GOP size = 2) and a weighted-average interpolation, similar to (3), for side information generation. The other is block-based Wyner-Ziv coding, mentioned in Section 2.

Fig.5 shows the histogram of the TGOB size for sequences "Salesman" and "Akiyo" with $U = 10$. For the conventional WZ codec [3], the GOP size is 2, which is similar to the coding with TGOB = 2, $L = 2$ and $U = 2$. This is not efficient for videos with stationary contents. A codec capable of adaptation to dynamic video contents will be desired. Ideally, a smaller TGOB size should be chosen for MBs with low temporal correlation, while a larger TGOB size is suitable for MBs with high temporal correlation. Compared to our previous work [11], there are 22% and 15% increase for TGOB = 1 in the process of "Salesman" and "Akiyo", respectively. This is due to the fact that we enforce some MBs to be intra-coded if they satisfy the conditions mentioned in Section 3.1.

Fig. 6 shows the rate-distortion performance of the proposed coding scheme where the bitrates and PSNRs are averaged over the whole sequence (291 frames). Fig. 6(b) reveals that the block-based WZC scheme in [11] has a PSNR gain up to 7.8 dB compared to [3] at the same bit-rate. This gain is even up to 11.8 dB, compared to the H.264 intra coding (GOP=1). Moreover, the proposed new paradigm outperforms our previous work [11] and could achieve an improvement about 0.8, 0.7 and 2.7 dB in average for "Salesman", "Akiyo" and "Tennis", respectively. Besides, the proposed scheme also guarantees good performance in low quality/rate scenario. This achievement shows the proposed scheme has the ability to resist the instability of the channel coding.

## 5  Conclusion

In this paper, two approaches are proposed to increase the coding efficiency for block-based DVC scheme. First, more precise side information could be generated with an accurate evaluation by increasing the density of key blocks.  Then, a more accurate noise model between the original WZ block and the associated side information is evaluated in the DVC encoder side. These two strategies aim at providing the LDPC decoder with more accurate information and less parity bit are required consequently. In particular, for the high bitrate, the improvement is obvious due to more key blocks. Furthermore, the correlation calculator in the encoder can still ensure satisfactory performance for the scenario of low bitrate. It reveals that the proposed DVC system is flexible in numerous applications.

## Acknowledgement

This paper was supported by National Science Council of Taiwan (NSC 96-2221-E-194-013-MY2).

# References


1. Slepian, D., Wolf, J.K.: Noiseless coding of correlated information sources. IEEE Trans. on Information Theory 19(4), 471–480 (1973)
2. Wyner, D., Ziv, J.: The rate-distortion function for source coding with side information at the decoder. IEEE Trans. on Information Theory 22, 1–10 (1976)
3. Aaron, A., Zhang, R., Girod, B.: Wyner-Ziv Coding of Motion Video. In: 36th Asilomar Conference on Signals, Systems and Computer, Pacific Grove, USA (November 2002)
4. Ascenso, J., Brites, C., Pereira, F.: Motion Compensated Refinement for Low Complexity Pixel Based Distributed Video Coding. In: IEEE Int'l Conf. on Advanced Video and Signal-Based Surveillance, Como, Italy (September 2005)
5. Kubasov, D., Guillemot, C.: Mesh-based motion compensated interpolation for side information extraction in distributed video coding. In: IEEE Int'l Conf. on Image Processing (ICIP), Atlanta, USA, October 8-11 (2006)
6. Ascenso, J., Brites, C., Pereira, F.: Improving frame interpolation with spatial motion smoothing for pixel domain distributed video coding. In: 5th EURASIP Conference on Speech and Image Processing, Multimedia Communications and Services, Slovak Republic, June 29 - July 2 (2005)
7. Tonomura, Y., Nakachi, T., Fujii, T.: Efficient index assignment by improved bit probability estimation for parallel processing of distributed video coding. In: IEEE Int'l Conf. on Acoustics, Speech and Signal Processing (ICASSP), USA, March 31 - April 4 (2008)
8. Brites, C., Ascenso, J., Pereira, F.: Studying temporal correlation noise modeling for pixel based Wyner-Ziv video coding. In: Proc. of IEEE Int'l Conf. on Image Processing (ICIP), Atlanta, USA, October 8-11 (2006)
9. Varodayan, D., Aaron, A., Girod, B.: Rate-adaptive codes for distributed source coding. EURASIP Signal Processing 86, 3123–3130 (2006)
10. Westerlaken, R.P., Borchert, S., Gunnewiek, R.K., Lagendijk, R.L.: Dependency channel modelling for a LDPC-based Wyner-Ziv video compression scheme. In: Proc. of IEEE Int'l Conf. on Image Processing (ICIP), Atlanta, USA (October 2006)
11. Tsai, D.-C., Lee, C.-M., Lie, W.-N.: Dynamic key block decision with spatio-temporal analysis for Wyner-Ziv video coding. In: IEEE Int'l Conf. on Image Processing (ICIP), USA, September 16 - October 19 (2007)
12. Tagliasacchi, M., Trapanese, A., Tubaro, S., Ascenso, J., Brites, C., Pereira, F.: Intra mode decision based on spatio-temporal cues in pixel domain Wyner-Ziv video coding. In: IEEE Int'l Conf. on Acoustics, Speech, and Signal Processing (ICASSP), Toulouse, France, May 14-19 (2006)
13. Ascenso, J., Brites, C., Pereira, F.: Content adaptive Wyner-Ziv video coding driven by motion activity. In: IEEE Int'l Conf. on Image Processing (ICIP), USA, October 8-11 (2006)

# Watermarking of Raw Digital Images in Camera Firmware: Embedding and Detection


Peter Meerwald and Andreas Uhl

University of Salzburg, Dept. of Computer Sciences,
Jakob-Haringer-Str. 2, A-5020 Salzburg, Austria
{pmeerw,uhl}@cosy.sbg.ac.at



**Abstract.** In this paper we investigate 'real-time' watermarking of single-sensor digital camera images (often called 'raw' images) and blind watermark detection in demosaicked images. We describe the software-only implementation of simple additive spread-spectrum embedding in the firmware of a digital camera. For blind watermark detection, we develop a scheme which adaptively combines the polyphase components of the demosaicked image, taking advantage of the interpolated image structure. Experimental results show the benefits of the novel detection approach for several demosaicking techniques.

**Keywords:** Watermarking, demosaicking, signal detection, firmware.


## 1 Introduction

Digital cameras are in ubiquitous use. Most popular digital cameras use a single, monochrome image sensor with a color filter array (CFA) on top, often arranged in the Bayer pattern, see Figure 1. In order to provide a full-resolution RGB image, the sensor data has to be interpolated – a process called demosaicking – as well as color, gamma and white point corrected. Different demosaicking techniques exist, e.g. [1,2], yet the basic processing steps are shared by most camera implementations.

The digital nature of the recorded images which allows for easy duplication and manipulation, poses challenges when these images are to be used as evidence in court or when resolving ownership claims. Active techniques, such as watermarking [3], as well as passive or forensic approaches have been suggested to address image integrity verification, camera identification and ownership resolution. Many different forensic techniques have been proposed to detect image forgeries. For example, Chen et al. [4] exploit the inherent Photo-Response Non-Uniformity (PRNU) noise of the image sensor for camera identification and image integrity verification. Interpolation artefacts due to demosaicking are used by Popescu et al. [5] to verify the integrity of the image. Passive techniques have the disadvantage that camera characteristics such as PRNU have to be estimated before use.

Blythe et al. [6] propose a secure digital camera which uses lossless watermarking to embed a biometric identifier of the photographer together with a cryptographic hash of the image data. Their embedding method efficiently changes


T. Wada, F. Huang, and S. Lin (Eds.): PSIVT 2009, LNCS 5414, pp. 340–348, 2009.

the JPEG quantization tables and DCT coefficients but precludes watermarking of raw images. Tian et al. [7] propose a combined semi-fragile and robust watermarking for joint image authentication and copyright protection during the image capture process. However, the employed wavelet transform is computationally expensive. The image data volume and constrained power resources of digital cameras demand efficient processing. Mohanty et al. [8] describe a hardware implementation for combined robust and fragile watermarking. Few authors have considered watermark protection of the raw images, although the raw data is probably the most valuable asset. Nelson et al. [9] propose an image sensor with watermarking capabilities that adds pseudo-random noise. Lukac et al. [10] introduce a visible watermark embossed in sensor data.

In this paper, we propose a simple, additive spread-spectrum watermarking scheme for 'real-time' watermarking of single-sensor image data ('raw' images) and describe its software-only implementation in the firmware of a digital camera in section 2. For blind watermark detection in demosaicked images, we propose a scheme that adaptively combines the polyphase components of the demosaicked image in section 3, taking advantage of the interpolated image structure [11]. In section 4, we demonstrate the firmware implementation of the watermark embedding and analyze the performance of the novel detection approach after JPEG compression. Concluding remarks are offered in section 5.

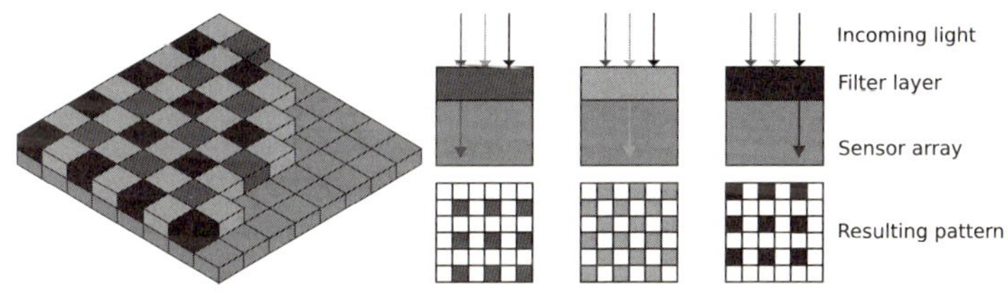


**Fig. 1.** Color filter array (CFA) arranged in the popular Bayer pattern

## 2  Watermark Embedding in Camera Firmware

Watermarking in digital cameras has not yet gained wide acceptance, although Kodak and Epson both have manufactured cameras with digital watermarking capabilities [6]. For this paper, we build on the CHDK project[1], which provides an open-source firmware add-on for Canon consumer cameras, based on the DIGIC II and III image processors – essentially a 32-bit ARM9 architecture processor, augmented with custom hardware functionality for JPEG coding, scaling, color conversion, etc. CHDK provides a Linux-hosted cross-compilation environment to build a firmware loader that partially replaces the original Canon firmware and hooks into the image processing pipeline as illustrated in Figure 2. This way, we gain access to the memory buffer holding the raw single-sensor image data after image acquisition.

---

[1] Available at `http://chdk.wikia.com`. We are using SVN revision 470.

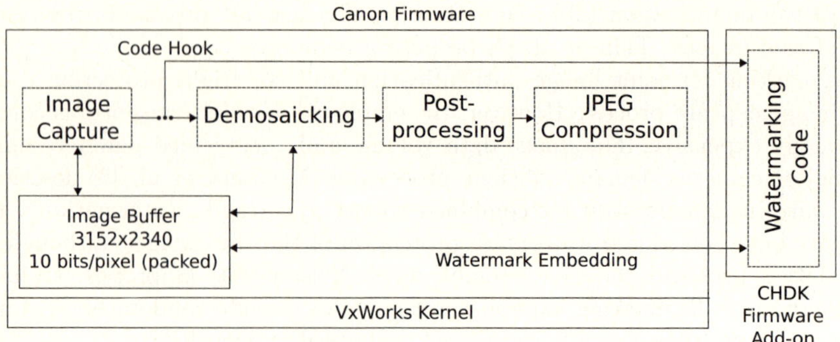

**Fig. 2.** Architecture of the watermarking firmware add-on

For watermark embedded in camera firmware, we opt for a simple, additive spread-spectrum watermark design to meet the runtime requirement. Note that Nelson et al. [9] essentially perform the same embedding operation, but in the image sensor hardware. Furthermore, the choice to watermark only the perceptually least significant blue color channel helps to reduce the data volume.

The raw image data is represented with 10 bits/pixel in packed format in the camera's memory buffer, hence the individual pixels must be shifted into place before further processing. Care must be taken not to watermark dead pixels due to sensor imperfections and to properly clip the pixel values to 10 bits, otherwise visible distortion results. Initially, the pixels were addressed and processed individually consuming approximately 40 seconds to watermark the raw data ($3112 \times 2328$ pixels, 9.2 MB, in case of the Canon IXUS 70 camera). Memory throughput is about 45 MB/second, but performance was constrained mainly by the repetitive address computation for unaligned byte memory accesses. Optimized loop unrolling and the implicit arithmetic bit shift option of the load/store instructions in the ARM instruction set help to achieve close to 'real-time' performance with a delay of less that one second[2]. Algorithm 1 shows the watermark embedding implementation and the resulting annotated optimized ARM assembler code produced by the GCC 4.3.0 compiler. Note that the implementation is plain C source code. Use of SIMD assembler instructions or hardware assistance may further improve performance.

After embedding, the watermarked raw image can be stored at this point for later post-processing with third party software or, alternatively, the data is upsampled in the demosaicking stage of the camera and the image is compressed and stored in JPEG format. Watermarking the raw image data has the advantage that copyright protection is incorporated at an early point in the image life cycle. The most valuable original sensor data as well as all derived images are protected by the same watermark. On the downside, the watermarked raw images has to withstand many processing steps. We provide first results on the impact of demosaicking on an additive watermark in section 4.

---

[2] The firmware source based on CHDK is available at `http://wavelab.at/sources`

**Algorithm 1.** Processing the first two pixels of a packed image buffer row

...

```
prow_out = prow_in = (uint16 *) &rowbuf[PIXTOBYTES(RAW_LEFT_MARGIN+4)];
bit_buf = *prow_in++;                        // LDRH R7, [SL], #2
out_bit_buf = bit_buf >> 6;                  // MOV R6, R7, ASR #6
bit_buf = (bit_buf << 16) + *prow_in++;      // LDRH R3, [SL], #2
                                             // ADD R7, R3, R7, ASL #16
pixel = bit_buf >> 12 & 0x3ff;               // MOV R3, R7, ASR #12
                                             // MOV R4, R3, ASL #22
                                             // MOV R4, R4, LSR #22
out_bit_buf = WATERMARK(pixel)                  // R2 = WATERMARK(R4)
      + (out_bit_buf << 10);                 // ADD R6, R2, R6 ASL #10
*prow_out++ = out_bit_buf >> 4;              // MOV R3, R6, ASR #4
                                             // STRH R3, [R8], #2
out_bit_buf = (bit_buf >> 2 & 0x3ff)         // MOV R2, R7, ASR #2
      + (out_bit_buf << 10);                 // MOV R4, R2, ASL #22
                                             // ADD R6, R4, R6, ASL #10
```

...

The actual camera implementation of the demosaicking, post-processing and compression stage is unknown. However, we can make assumptions on the interpolation and demosaicking step. In the next section, we utilize the interpolated structure of the demosaicked image for efficient watermark detection.

## 3   Watermark Detection from the Demosaicked Image

Figure 3 depicts the intercalated watermark embedding stage and the following demosaicking, post-processing and JPEG compression stages. In the embedding stage, a pseudo-random bipolar spread-spectrum watermark $w$ generated from a secret seed value $k$ identifying the copyright owner is added to the blue color component of the sensor data: $x_w[\mathbf{m}] = x[\mathbf{m}] + \alpha \cdot w[\mathbf{m}]$ where $\mathbf{m}$ denotes pixel indices and $\alpha > 0$ controls the embedding strength.

The watermark detector does not know which demosaicking algorithm and post-processing operations have been applied on the watermarked raw image. Nevertheless, we can approximate the effect of the demosaicking step on the watermarked blue color component pixels with an expansion of the data with a matrix $M = [2\ 0; 0\ 2]$ which yields an image $x_e$ twice the size in each dimension and interpolation with a low-pass filter $h_I = [1/4\ 1/2\ 1/4; 1/2\ 1\ 1/2; 1/4\ 1/2\ 1/4]$ resulting in an upsampled image $\tilde{x}$. Finally, we roughly model the impact of the post-processing and JPEG compression stage as an additive noise source $n$.

Relying on these assumptions, we can adapt the watermark detection strategy proposed by Giannoula et al. [11] for interpolated, noisy images. While the watermark is embedded in the low-resolution raw data, watermark detection takes place using the high-resolution blue channel of the demosaicked and compressed image, exploiting the watermark information spread out due to interpolation. The received demosaicked image $s$ is split into its noisy polyphase components $s_i$ where $0 \leq i \leq 3$ refers to one of our four components [12]. Figure 4 illustrates

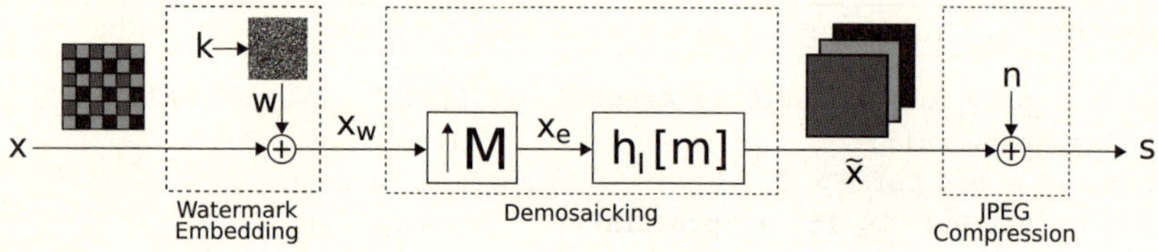


**Fig. 3.** Watermarking embedding and image processing pipeline

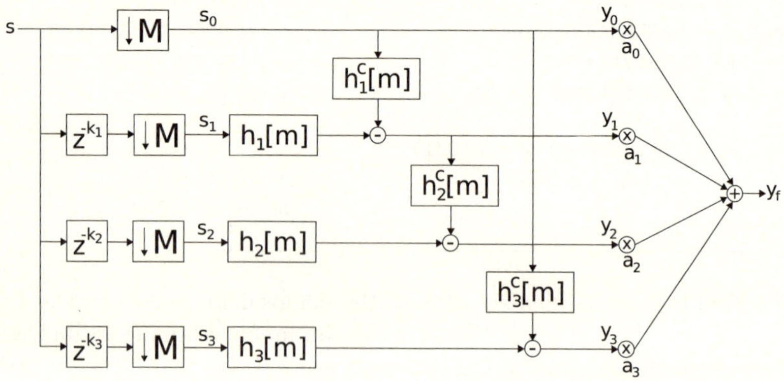


**Fig. 4.** Polyphase component fusion of the received image

this process. $s_0$ represents the low-resolution watermarked data, corrupted by a noise component $n_0$, $y_0[\mathbf{m}] = s_0[\mathbf{m}] = x_w[\mathbf{m}] + n_0[\mathbf{m}]$. With the help of two linear filters for estimation and interference cancellation,

$$h_i[\mathbf{m}] = b \cdot h_I[\mathbf{m}] \quad \text{and} \quad h_i^c[\mathbf{m}] = b \cdot h_I[\mathbf{m}] * h_I[\mathbf{m}] - \delta[\mathbf{m}], \tag{1}$$

respectively, further noisy estimates of $x_w$ are computed, such that

$$y_i[\mathbf{m}] = x_w[\mathbf{m}] + n_i[\mathbf{m}] = h_i[\mathbf{m}] * s_i[\mathbf{m}] - h_i^c[\mathbf{m}] * s_0[\mathbf{m}]. \tag{2}$$

The scaling factor $b$ is adjusted such that $h_i^c[0] = 0$ for $1 \leq i \leq 3$ and $\delta[\mathbf{m}]$ is the Kronecker delta. Finally, the components $y_i$ are *fused* according to optimal weight factors $a_i \in [0,1]$, $\sum_i a_i = 1$, depending on the estimated noise variance $\sigma_{n_i}^2$ of each component,

$$y_f[\mathbf{m}] = \sum_i a_i \cdot y_i[\mathbf{m}] \quad \text{where} \quad (a_0, ..., a_3) = \left( \frac{1}{\sigma_{n_0}^2 \sum_i \frac{1}{\sigma_{n_i}^2}}, ..., \frac{1}{\sigma_{n_3}^2 \sum_i \frac{1}{\sigma_{n_i}^2}} \right). \tag{3}$$

Giannoula et al. [11] suggest to estimate the noise variance $\sigma_{n_i}^2$ by filtering the initial component samples $s_0$ and subtracting the result form $s_i$, i.e.

$$\hat{\sigma}_{n_i}^2 = \text{var}\left(s_i[\mathbf{m}] - h_I[\mathbf{m}] * s_0[\mathbf{m}]\right). \tag{4}$$

We apply a linear correlation detector on the *fused* image. See [11] for a detailed analysis of the detector.

# 4   Results

We have implemented watermark embedding in firmware using CHDK for the Canon IXUS 70 and PowerShot A720, 7 and 8 Megapixel cameras, respectively. CHDK adds approximately 150 KB new firmware code to the 3.5 MB Canon firmware image. About 3 KB of code and data is occupied by watermarking functionality, leaving roughly 880 KB free memory available. The watermark embedding stage consumes less than one second, about the same time as storing the raw image data to disk. The experiments in [9] confirm that watermark embedding in sensor data with strength $\alpha = 4$ is imperceptible.

In Figure 5, we present nine test images taken with the Canon IXUS 70 camera and corresponding detection results. A watermark is embedded in the blue channel (embedding strength $\alpha = 4$) of the raw image. Watermark detection is performed on the demosaicked image obtained with the default Adaptive Homogeneity-Directed (AHD) method [1] of the `dcraw`[3] program and after JPEG compression with quality factors ranging from 100 to 30. Note that `dcraw` also performs white-balance adjustment and color conversion in addition to demosaicking. The plots show the probability of missing the watermark estimated from 1000 test runs with four different detectors: the proposed *fused* detector, *direct* correlation of the watermark with the $y_0$ component, and the reference methods (upsampling the watermark to match the received image dimensions and downsampling the image to match the size of the watermark). The probability of false-alarm $(P_{fa})$ is set to $10^{-6}$. The $y_0$ component simply corresponds to the originally watermarked pixels and does not contain interpolated pixel data. Clearly, the proposed detector delivers best performance for all images. Similar results were obtained with raw images taken by other digital cameras.

In Table 1 we compare the impact of different demosaicking methods as implemented by `dcraw` on watermark detection performance. For a false-alarm rate of $10^{-6}$, we compare the probability of missing the watermark for our nine test images with the *direct* and *fused* detector after demosaicking the raw images with the AHD [1], threshold-based Variable Number of Gradients (VNG) [2] and Patterned Pixel Grouping (PPG)[4] algorithm. We found that VNG demosaicking allows for the best watermark detection, followed by the AHD and PPG method. With moderate JPEG compression $(Q = 70)$, the *fused* detector shows best performance for all images, followed by the *direct* approach. The other two detectors always perform worse and results are omitted.

The impact of the image processing pipeline of the Canon IXUS 70 camera on the watermark is explored in Table 2. The raw data of the first test image (depicted in Figure 5) is watermarked $(\alpha = 4)$ and then processed by the camera into a JPEG image with varying image quality and resolution settings. Note that the camera stores a slightly cropped version of the raw image ($3072 \times 2304$

---

[3]  `dcraw` is available at `http://www.cybercom.net/~dcoffin/dcraw/`. Version 8.86 was used for the experiments.

[4]  By Chuan-kai Lin, described at `http://web.cecs.pdx.edu/~cklin/demosaic/`

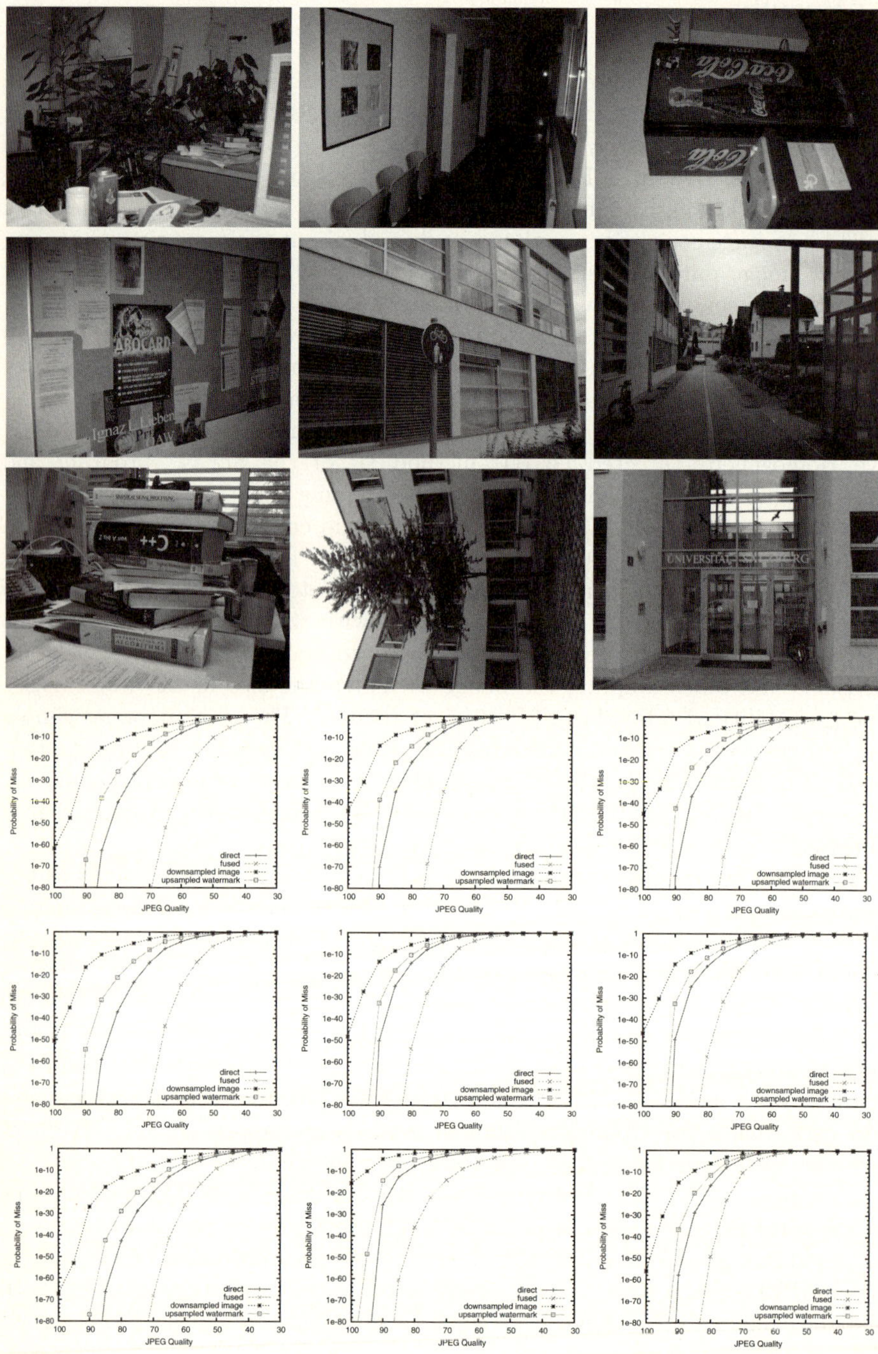

**Fig. 5.** Test images ($3112 \times 2328$ pixels) and simulated watermark detection results after AHD demosaicking and JPEG compression; $P_{fa} = 10^{-6}$

**Table 1.** Probability of missing the watermark for the demosaicking methods AHD, VNG, PPG and after JPEG compression ($Q = 70$); $P_{fa} = 10^{-6}$

| Image | AHD | | VNG | | PPG | |
|---|---|---|---|---|---|---|
| | Direct | Fused | Direct | Fused | Direct | Fused |
| #1 | $9.9 \cdot 10^{-20}$ | $1.8 \cdot 10^{-84}$ | $6.2 \cdot 10^{-43}$ | $3.4 \cdot 10^{-294}$ | $6.1 \cdot 10^{-12}$ | $2.3 \cdot 10^{-29}$ |
| #2 | $9.9 \cdot 10^{-08}$ | $1.1 \cdot 10^{-35}$ | $1.2 \cdot 10^{-21}$ | $3.3 \cdot 10^{-160}$ | $7.5 \cdot 10^{-6}$ | $1.2 \cdot 10^{-13}$ |
| #3 | $4.0 \cdot 10^{-10}$ | $3.2 \cdot 10^{-38}$ | $2.2 \cdot 10^{-23}$ | $2.6 \cdot 10^{-145}$ | $9.2 \cdot 10^{-7}$ | $7.9 \cdot 10^{-16}$ |
| #4 | $5.3 \cdot 10^{-15}$ | $5.7 \cdot 10^{-80}$ | $6.5 \cdot 10^{-42}$ | $0.0$ | $6.1 \cdot 10^{-9}$ | $4.8 \cdot 10^{-19}$ |
| #5 | $6.9 \cdot 10^{-5}$ | $1.2 \cdot 10^{-15}$ | $5.8 \cdot 10^{-19}$ | $1.9 \cdot 10^{-116}$ | $4.8 \cdot 10^{-4}$ | $5.1 \cdot 10^{-7}$ |
| #6 | $7.3 \cdot 10^{-6}$ | $3.6 \cdot 10^{-18}$ | $2.5 \cdot 10^{-16}$ | $2.3 \cdot 10^{-102}$ | $2.1 \cdot 10^{-4}$ | $3.2 \cdot 10^{-9}$ |
| #7 | $6.6 \cdot 10^{-21}$ | $6.4 \cdot 10^{-69}$ | $3.0 \cdot 10^{-53}$ | $3.9 \cdot 10^{-289}$ | $1.0 \cdot 10^{-14}$ | $3.3 \cdot 10^{-29}$ |
| #8 | $1.5 \cdot 10^{-3}$ | $8.5 \cdot 10^{-15}$ | $8.9 \cdot 10^{-10}$ | $5.7 \cdot 10^{-69}$ | $1.3 \cdot 10^{-2}$ | $1.3 \cdot 10^{-6}$ |
| #9 | $2.5 \cdot 10^{-4}$ | $5.3 \cdot 10^{-11}$ | $8.5 \cdot 10^{-15}$ | $9.4 \cdot 10^{-77}$ | $4.5 \cdot 10^{-3}$ | $1.8 \cdot 10^{-4}$ |

**Table 2.** Probability of missing the watermark for different resolution and JPEG quality settings (Canon IXUS 70), first test image; $P_{fa} = 10^{-6}$

| Resolution | Quality | Direct | Fused | Downsampled Image | Upsampled Watermark |
|---|---|---|---|---|---|
| $3072 \times 2304$ | SuperFine | $2.4 \cdot 10^{-161}$ | $0.0$ | $2.4 \cdot 10^{-15}$ | $2.5 \cdot 10^{-100}$ |
| $3072 \times 2304$ | Fine | $3.0 \cdot 10^{-125}$ | $0.0$ | $2.2 \cdot 10^{-15}$ | $2.8 \cdot 10^{-83}$ |
| $3072 \times 2304$ | Normal | $5.1 \cdot 10^{-88}$ | $0.0$ | $1.2 \cdot 10^{-14}$ | $1.9 \cdot 10^{-63}$ |
| $2592 \times 1944$ | SuperFine | $4.0 \cdot 10^{-68}$ | $0.0$ | $3.4 \cdot 10^{-14}$ | $1.1 \cdot 10^{-50}$ |
| $2048 \times 1536$ | SuperFine | $3.3 \cdot 10^{-60}$ | $4.4 \cdot 10^{-223}$ | $1.7 \cdot 10^{-16}$ | $4.5 \cdot 10^{-46}$ |
| $1600 \times 1200$ | SuperFine | $2.4 \cdot 10^{-38}$ | $2.9 \cdot 10^{-117}$ | $1.2 \cdot 10^{-8}$ | $6.8 \cdot 10^{-29}$ |

pixels). The smaller resolution images are upsampled to $3072 \times 2304$ pixels using a bilinear filter before watermark detection. The experiment is repeated 100 times for each setting using the scripting capabilities of the CHDK firmware. We estimate the probability of missing the watermark for each of our four detectors. The *fused* detectors is least likely to miss the watermark in all cases. Repeating the experiment with other test images shows consistent results.

## 5   Conclusion

Digital watermarking has to be applied close to the image acquisition stage in order to protect the copyright of both, the raw and compressed image. Hence, we have implemented additive spread-spectrum watermark embedding of the raw image data in digital camera firmware building on the CHDK firmware add-on for Canon digital cameras.

A framework for blind watermark detection in noisy, interpolated images has been successfully applied to demosaicked images, irrespective of a particular interpolation technique. We evaluated the impact of different demosaicking methods on watermark detection performance, including the particular Canon implementation.

## Acknowledgments

Supported by Austrian Science Fund project FWF-P19159-N13. Thanks to Colin M. L. Burnett for the graphics used in Figure 1.

## References


1. Hirakawa, K., Parks, T.W.: Adaptive homogeneity-directed demosaicing algorithm. IEEE Transactions on Image Processing 14(3), 360–369 (2005)
2. Chang, E., Cheung, S., Pan, D.Y.: Color filter array recovery using a threshold-based variable number of gradients. In: Proceedings of SPIE, Sensors, Cameras, and Applications for Digital Photography, San Jose, CA, USA, January 1999, vol. 3650, pp. 36–43 (1999)
3. Cox, I.J., Miller, M.L., Bloom, J.A., Fridrich, J., Kalker, T.: Digital Watermarking and Steganography. Morgan Kaufmann, San Francisco (2007)
4. Chen, M., Fridrich, J., Goljan, M., Lukas, J.: Determining image origin and integrity using sensor noise. IEEE Transactions on Information Security and Forensics 3(1), 74–90 (2008)
5. Popescu, A.C., Farid, H.: Exposing digital forgeries in color filter array interpolated images. IEEE Transactions on Signal Processing 53(10), 3948–3959 (2005)
6. Blythe, P., Fridrich, J.: Secure digital camera. In: Digital Forensic Research Workshop, Baltimore, MD, USA (August 2004)
7. Tian, L., Tai, H.M.: Secure images captured by digital camera. In: International Conference on Consumer Electronics, Digest of Technical Papers, ICCE 2006, pp. 341–342. IEEE, Los Alamitos (2006)
8. Mohanty, S.P., Kougianos, E., Ranganathan, N.: VLSI architecture and chip for combined invisible robust and fragile watermarking. IET Computers & Digital Techniques 1(5), 600–611 (2007)
9. Nelson, G.R., Julien, G.A., Yadid-Pecht, O.: CMOS image sensor with watermarking capabilities. In: Proceedings of the IEEE International Symposium on Circuits and Systems, ISCAS 2005, vol. 5, pp. 5326–5329. IEEE, Los Alamitos (2005)
10. Lukac, R., Plataniotis, K.K.: Camera image watermark transfer by demosaicking. In: Proceedings of the 48th International Symposium ELMAR 2006, Multimedia Signal Processing and Communication, Zadar, Croatia, pp. 9–12 (June 2006)
11. Giannoula, A., Boulgouris, N.V., Hatzinakos, D., Plataniotis, K.N.: Watermark detection for noisy interpolated images. IEEE Transactions on Circuits and Systems 53(5), 359–363 (2006)
12. Vaidyanathan, P.P.: Multirate digital filters, filter banks, polyphase networks, and applications: a tutorial. Proceedings of the IEEE 78(1), 56–93 (1990)

# An Advanced Least-Significant-Bit Embedding Scheme for Steganographic Encoding

Yeuan-Kuen Lee[1], Graeme Bell[2], Shih-Yu Huang[1], Ran-Zan Wang[3],
and Shyong-Jian Shyu[1]

[1] Computer Science and Information Engineering, Ming Chuan University, Taiwan
[2] International College, Ming Chuan University, Taiwan
[3] Computer Science and Engineering, Yuan Ze University, Taiwan
{yklee,gbb,syhuang,sjshyu}@mail.mcu.edu.tw, rzwang@saturn.yzu.edu.tw

**Abstract.** The advantages of Least-Significant-Bit (LSB) steganographic data embedding are that it is simple to understand, easy to implement, and it results in stego-images that contain hidden data yet appear to be of high visual fidelity. However, it can be shown that under certain conditions, LSB embedding is not secure at all. The fatal drawback of LSB embedding is the existence of detectable artifacts in the form of pairs of values (PoVs). The goals of this paper are to present a theoretic analysis of PoVs and to propose an advanced LSB embedding scheme that possesses the advantages of LSB embedding suggested above, but which also provides an additional level of communication security. The proposed scheme breaks the regular pattern of PoVs in the histogram domain, increasing the difficulty of steganalysis and thereby raising the level of security. The experimental results show that both the Chi-square index and RS index are less than 0.1, i.e., the hidden message is undetectable by the well-known Chi-square and RS steganalysis attacks.

**Keywords:** Steganography, steganalysis, LSB embedding.

## 1 Introduction

Both steganography and cryptography may be used to protect secret messages in order to achieve private communication. Steganography not only hides the meaning but also the existence of the hidden message. Ideally, only the intended receiver can extract the message, as other people viewing the carrier medium are unaware of the existence of the hidden message. Steganographic techniques can therefore protect not only the secret message but also the sender and the receiver. In the field, cryptographic techniques are typically sufficient to protect secret data. However, users such as informers may need steganographic techniques to protect themselves and their whole organization [1].

In recent years, many discreet methods for hiding encrypted messages within digital 'carrier' media have become conveniently available. One such approach is the LSB embedding approach, which simply replaces the least significant bit of

T. Wada, F. Huang, and S. Lin (Eds.): PSIVT 2009, LNCS 5414, pp. 349–360, 2009.

each carrier data value with the message-bit. This approach is simple to understand and easy to implement, and the resulting 'stego-media' containing hidden messages appear to be of high visual fidelity. Consequently, the LSB embedding approach has become the basis of many techniques that hide messages within multimedia carrier data. LSB embedding may even be applied in particular data domains - for example, embedding a hidden message into the color values of RGB bitmap data, or into the frequency coefficients of a JPEG image. LSB embedding can also be applied to a variety of data formats and types [2]. Therefore, LSB embedding is one of the most important steganographic techniques in use today.

Since LSB embedding is one of the simplest effective data hiding techniques, it has long been a focus for researchers proposing steganalytic attack methods. The Chi-square attack was the first statistical test that could detect hidden messages automatically [3]. Two values whose binary representations differ only in the LSB are called a pair of values (PoV). For example, $68(01000100)_2$ and $69(01000101)_2$ are a PoV. If the numbers of 1s and 0s are equal and distributed randomly in the secret message that is to be embedded steganographically, the frequency of two values in each PoV will be equal after message embedding. This regular equality pattern, called the PoVs artifact, is an unusual characteristic in the histogram domain. If the PoVs artifact can be found in a digital media, there is a high probability that a hidden message is embedded in the media. The Chi-square attack is a very effective technique against LSB embedding systems. A known counter-technique to avoid exposing hidden messages to this attack involves decreasing the embedding capacity of the carrier medium. If less than 50% of the maximum capacity of the carrier medium is used, the risk of detection drops accordingly.

For detecting messages embedded in 24-bit color images, Fridrich et al. proposed the RPQ (Raw Quick Pairs) steganalysis system in 2000 [4]. However, the technique was shown to be unreliable for digital camera images that are stored in an uncompressed format, where a large number of unique color values may exist. In 2001, Fridrich et al. proposed a more reliable attack on LSB embedding called RS steganalysis [5]. Fridrich et al. estimate that messages hidden within high quality images using an embedding rate of more than 0.005 bits per pixel are detectable by RS steganalysis.

F5 is a steganographic algorithm proposed in 2001 for JPEG images [6]. In the F5 algorithm, statistical properties in the histogram of quantized DCT coefficients are preserved and a matrix encoding [7] is implemented. Matrix encoding decreases the number of changes needed, in order to improve the embedding efficiency. In IHW 2002, Fridrich et al. proposed a steganalytic method for breaking the F5 algorithm [8]. The key element of this attack comes from the estimation of the cover-image histogram from the stego-image. Experimental results have shown that modifications of as few as 10% of the usable capacity of the DCT coefficients, can be reliably detected.

Recently, many steganographic methods based upon LSB embedding have attracted statistical attacks, and experimental results have shown that this approach is generally not secure at all. T. Sharp proposed an implementation, called '*Hide*', of key-based image steganography in 2001 [9]. *Hide* uses a modified LSB method for embedding messages. The LSBs are not simply replaced; instead the data value is incremented or decremented if the LSB differs from the message-bit. *Hide* uses a pseudorandom sequence generator to determine whether to increment or decrement the data value.

In this paper, we first present a theoretic analysis of the LSB embedding approach and then propose an advanced LSB embedding scheme. The sample value that will be incremented or decremented depends on a series of predefined thresholds that are generated by the user-specified stego-key. The new sample value not only depends on the generated pseudorandom number but also depends on the original sample value. Experimental results show that both of the well-known Chi-square and RS steganalysis attacks are unable to detect the existence of secret messages embedded with the new system. Using the proposed scheme is therefore more secure than using traditional LSB embedding techniques.

The rest of this paper is organized as follows. In Section 2, a theoretic analysis of the weakness of the LSB embedding approach is presented. An advanced LSB embedding scheme is proposed in Section 3. The experimental results are discussed in Section 4. Finally, the paper is concluded in Section 5.

## 2   Analysis of LSB Embedding

LSB embedding involves replacing the least significant bit of the original data value with the secret message-bit directly. For a grayscale image, the intensity values range from 0 to 255. These can be grouped into 128 PoVs, i.e., $(2k, 2k + 1), k = 0, 1, \ldots, 127$. Applying the LSB embedding operation cannot change a value so that it corresponds to another, different PoV. Thus, the operation of LSB embedding on a PoV satisfies the closure property, i.e., no matter whether the embedded message-bit is 1 or 0, the result will continue to belong to the same PoV.

Let $I$ denote an original grayscale cover-image and $I'$ denote the created stego-image in which the secret message is embedded. Let $H_I$ denote the histogram of a grayscale image $I$. Let $H_I(i)$ denote the frequency of gray value $i$, and let $HP_I(k)$ denote the frequency of values in the k-th PoV in $I$. Then,

$$HP_I(k) = H_I(2k) + H_I(2k + 1), \tag{1}$$

$$HP_{I'}(k) = H_{I'}(2k) + H_{I'}(2k + 1). \tag{2}$$

The closure property ensures that summing the histogram values for each value in the PoV, produces a total that will be unchanged by LSB modification. Thus,

$$HP_I(k) = HP_{I'}(k) \tag{3}$$

Let $T$ denote the embedding rate, that is,

$$T = t/N, \tag{4}$$

$0 \leq T \leq 1$, where $t$ is the length of secret message and $N$ is the total number of pixels in the image $I$. A total of $t$ pixels are selected randomly for embedding $t$ bits of secret message. In general, the secret message that is being embedded is always compressed and encrypted before embedding. The number of '1' and '0' in the hidden message can therefore reasonably be assumed to be equal. Thus, among the selected pixels, half of the pixels with even values $(2k)$ will not change when the embedded message-bit is 0, and half of the pixels with odd values $(2k+1)$ will change into $2k$ when the embedded message-bit is 0. Similarly, among the unselected pixels, the number of pixels with value $2k$ is $H_I(2k)(1-T)$. Thus, the number of pixels with value $2k$ can be derived as follows.

$$H_{I'}(2k) = H_I(2k)(1 - T) + H_I(2k)(T/2) + H_I(2k + 1)(T/2)$$
$$= H_I(2k)(1 - T) + [(H_I(2k) + H_I(2k + 1)](T/2)$$
$$= H_I(2k)(1 - T) + HP_I(k)(T/2), \tag{5}$$

Similarly, the frequency of the other value in the same PoV can be derived as follows.

$$H_{I'}(2k + 1) = H_I(2k + 1)(1 - T) + H_I(2k + 1)(T/2) + H_I(2k)(T/2)$$
$$= H_I(2k + 1)(1 - T) + [(H_I(2k + 1) + H_I(2k)](T/2)$$
$$= H_I(2k + 1)(1 - T) + HP_I(k)(T/2), \tag{6}$$

Let $DP_I(k)$ denote the difference between the frequencies of values in the k-th PoV in the cover-image $I$. Thus,

$$DP_I(k) = |H_I(2k) - H_I(2k + 1)|, \tag{7}$$

From Eqs. (5) and (6), when the embedding rate is $T$, the difference between the frequencies of values in the k-th PoV in the stego-image $I'$ can be derived as follows.

$$DP_{I'}(k) = |H_{I'}(2k) - H_{I'}(2k + 1)|$$
$$= |H_I(2k)(1 - T) - H_I(2k + 1)(1 - T)|$$
$$= |[H_I(2k) - H_I(2k + 1)]|(1 - T)$$
$$= DP_I(k)(1 - T). \tag{8}$$

So, the difference between the frequencies of values in the same PoV will become $(1 - T)$ times after LSB embedding. When $T = 0$, there is no secret message embedded in the image. Thus,

$$H_{I'}(2k) = H_I(2k), \tag{9}$$

$$H_{I'}(2k + 1) = H_I(2k + 1), \tag{10}$$

$$DP_{I'}(k) = |H_{I'}(2k) - H_{I'}(2k + 1)|$$
$$= |H_I(2k) - H_I(2k + 1)|$$
$$= DP_I(k). \tag{11}$$

So, the closure property of LSB embedding is obvious. When $T = 1$, all pixels will used to embed the secret message. From Eqs. (5), (6) and (8),

$$H_{I'}(2k) = HP_I(k)/2, \tag{12}$$

$$H_{I'}(2k+1) = HP_I(k)/2, \tag{13}$$

$$DP_{I'}(k) = 0. \tag{14}$$

From Eqs. (12) and (13), when $T = 1$, then

$$H_{I'}(2k) = H_{I'}(2k+1) = HP_I(k)/2. \tag{15}$$

The regular equality pattern of PoVs in the histogram domain has been proven.

Fig. 1 is an example of the PoVs artifact caused by LSB embedding in the histogram domain. Figs. 1(a) and 1(b) show the original cover-image entitled Waterlily and its corresponding stego-image with full capacity of binary random data, respectively. The peak signal-to-noise ratio (PSNR) of Fig. 1(b) is $51.1409db$. Figs. 1(c) and 1(d) are the histograms of Figs. 1(a) and 1(b), respectively. Figs. 1(e) and 1(f) show the enlarged histograms between values from 130 to 139 of Figs. 1(c) and 1(d). Note that the PoVs artifact appears in Fig. 1(f), and that the differences decrease within the 5 PoVs from $(130, 131)$ to $(138, 139)$.

## 3  Proposed Scheme and Discussion

The PoVs artifact exposes the existence of a hidden message. One obvious way to decrease the risk of message exposure resulting from the PoVs artifact is to decrease the embedding capacity. This paper proposes a second way to raise the security level, in which the embedding capacity is not reduced, while the fidelity of the stego-image is maintained.

The idea behind the proposed scheme is direct. PoVs will be disturbed in the embedding process. For any integer $q$, there are two neighbors with the same LSB, i.e., $q-1, q+1$. The PoVs artifact is caused by having a fixed choice of neighbor value to replace the original value, that is, a 'pair value'. Yet, two possible neighbors of equal difference to the integer $q$ exist. Further, no matter which neighbor is selected, the fidelity of the resulting stego-image will be as good as that created by a traditional LSB embedding approach.

Two data embedding models, a basic model and an advanced model that are both based upon this idea of alternative neighbours, are included in the proposed scheme. Basically, the basic model is similar to the method used in [9]. Note that the message extraction process for both of these new models is almost identical to the traditional LSB embedding method. The embedding process will now be described in detail.

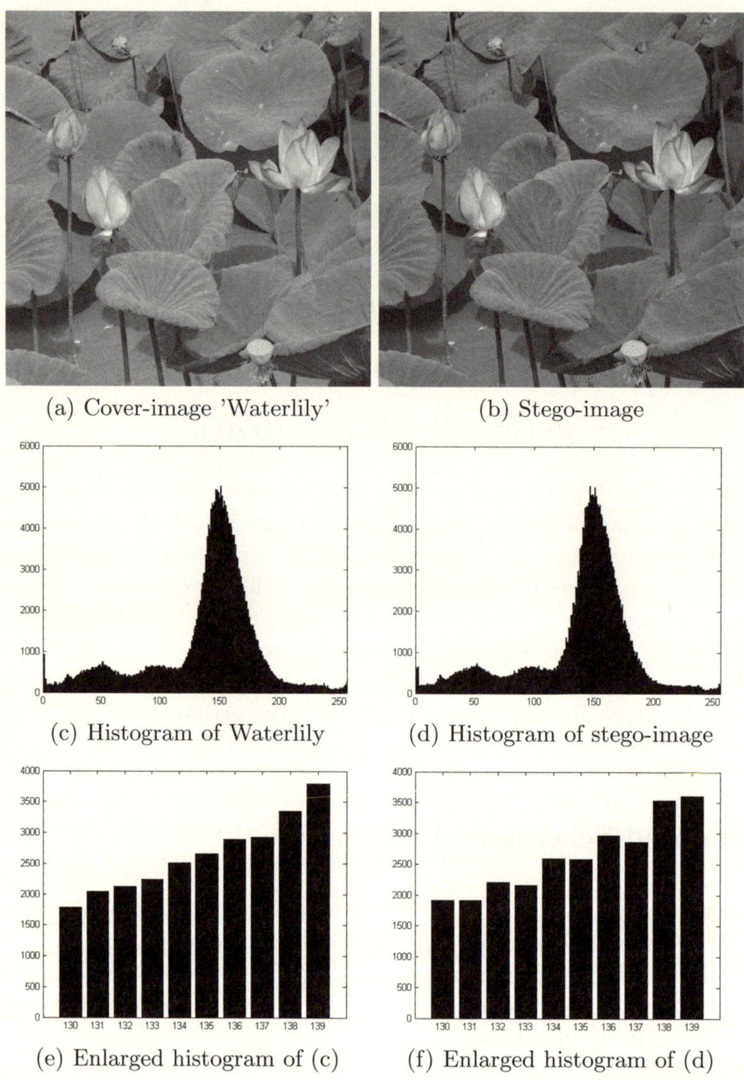

(a) Cover-image 'Waterlily'          (b) Stego-image

(c) Histogram of Waterlily          (d) Histogram of stego-image

(e) Enlarged histogram of (c)          (f) Enlarged histogram of (d)

**Fig. 1.** PoVs artifact exists in the histogram after applying LSB embedding

### 3.1   Basic Model

A pseudorandom number generator (PRNG) seeded with a value known to both sender and receiver, is used to randomly select one of two neighbors, i.e., $q - 1$ or $q + 1$, where $q$ is the original value. Let $M$ denote a binary secret message sequence, $M = \{m_i | m_i \in \{0, 1\}, i = 0, 1, \ldots, t - 1\}$, where $t$ is the message length. Let $f_I(x, y)$ denote the grayscale value at $(x, y)$ in cover-image $I$, and let $LSB_I(x, y)$ denote the LSB of the grayscale value at $(x, y)$. The embedding algorithm is as follows.

**Embedding algorithm of basic model:** $E_B$
**Input**: cover-image $I$, binary message sequence $M$.
**Output**: stego-image $I'$.

**Step 1**:
  Set $I' = I$.
**Step 2**:
  Use a PRNG to randomly select $t$ pixels from $I'$.
  Let $(x_i, y_i)$ denote the coordinate of the selected pixel. $i = 0, 1, \ldots, t-1$.
**Step 3**:
  Let $q_i = f_I(x_i, y_i)$ denote the grayscale value of pixel $(x_i, y_i)$.
  Let $m_i$ denote the message-bit to be embedded in pixel $(x_i, y_i)$.
  For all pixels $(x_i, y_i)$,
      if $LSB_{I'}(x_i, y_i) = m_i$,
          do nothing;
      if $LSB_{I'}(x_i, y_i) \neq m_i$,
          use a PRNG to generate a random number $\gamma$, $0 \leq \gamma \leq 1$,
          if $\gamma > 0.5$,
              set $f_{I'}(x_i, y_i) = q_i + 1$;
          if $\gamma \leq 0.5$,
              set $f_{I'}(x_i, y_i) = q_i - 1$;
**Step 4**:
  Output $I'$

So, in short, we choose pseudorandomly (but in a manner predictable to both sender and receiver) one of the two possible neighboring values, whenever it is necessary to perturb the pixel value to encode a message bit. The receiver can reconstruct the message by revisiting the pseudorandomly selected pixels and extracting the LSBs of pixel values directly.

Fig. 2 illustrates how the LSB embedding and the basic model perform message embedding under the condition where the value is an even number $2k$. Thus, $LSB_{I'}(x_i, y_i) = 0$. The probability that message bit $m_i = 1$ is $1/2$, hence half of the pixel values will change to $2k + 1$ by using the LSB embedding. However, in the embedding process of the basic model only a quarter of the pixel values will change to $2k + 1$, and the other quarter of the pixel values will change to $2k - 1$. Therefore, there is no fixed pair of values in the histogram of stego-image $I'$. The frequency of pixel value q can be derived as:

$$H_{I'}(q) = H_I(q - 1)(T/4) + H_I(q)(1 - T/2) + H_I(q + 1)(T/4). \qquad (16)$$

Since the frequency of pixel value $q$ in the stego-image $I'$ is contributed towards from the frequencies of $q - 1, q$ and $q + 1$ in the cover-image $I$, there is no PoVs artifact.

Fig. 3 gives a sample of experimental results examining the behavior of the basic model. Both the cover-image and the secret message are the same as those used in Fig. 1. Figs. 3(a) and 3(b) show the created stego-image and its corresponding histogram, respectively. The PSNR of Fig. 3(b) is $51.1409db$, which is

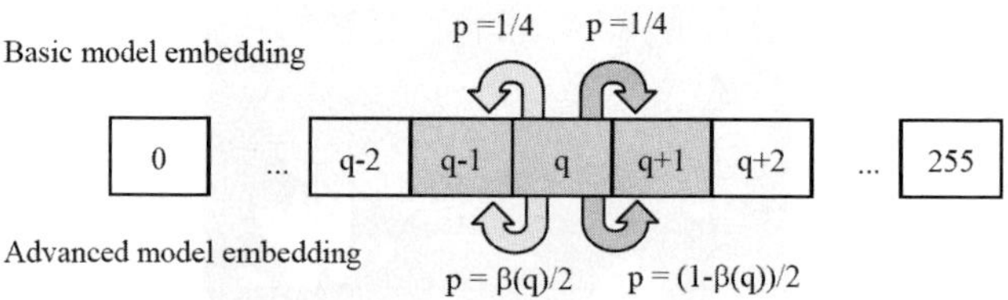



**Fig. 4.** Comparison between two proposed models

$$H_{I'}(q) = H_I(q-1)(T)(1-\beta(q-1))/2 + H_I(q)(1-T/2) + H_I(q+1)(T)(\beta(q+1)/2). \tag{17}$$

Obviously, Eq. (17) is more complex than Eq. (16). In addition to the embedding rate $T$, another (unpredictable) value $\beta(q)$ has been added to the right side of Eq. (17). Thus, the security level has been elevated further in the advanced model.

## 4   Experimental Results

To verify the undetectability of the proposed modified LSB embedding scheme, two statistical attacks are used, the Chi-square attack and RS steganalysis. These two attacks generally perform very well at detecting hidden messages embedded by LSB embedding techniques.

The test set contains 150 original images - including 8 standard images downloaded from the USC-SIPI image database [10], 75 images downloaded from the photoSIG [11], and 67 images obtained from a Panasonic Lumix FX7 digital camera. A PRNG was used to generate simulated encrypted secret messages. This is reasonable because encrypted message binary data would be indistinguishable from pseudo random binary data.

For every image, pseudorandom data was embedded using LSB embedding, basic model embedding and advanced model embedding, respectively. Varied embedding rates (from 5% to 100%) were also tested to measure the risk of exposure of the hidden message.

Fig. 5 shows the average experimental result for 150 stego-images with the same embedding rate. The x-axis shows the embedding rate from 5% to 100%. The y-axis is the Chi-square index which estimates the probability of a hidden message existing in the picture. In Fig. 5, using LSB embedding, the average Chi-square index is larger than 0.5 when the embedding rate is over 80%. Using the basic model to embed a message, the average Chi-square index is always below 0.1, no matter what embedding rate is chosen. Using the advanced model, all of the average Chi-square index values are near 0 - that is, lower than the value of original cover-image.

Fig. 6 shows the average experimental result of RS steganalysis. The x-axis shows the actual embedding rate and the y-axis is the estimated embedding rate using RS steganalysis. In Fig. 6, we can observe clearly that the embedding rate of traditional LSB embedding can be estimated precisely with RS steganalysis.

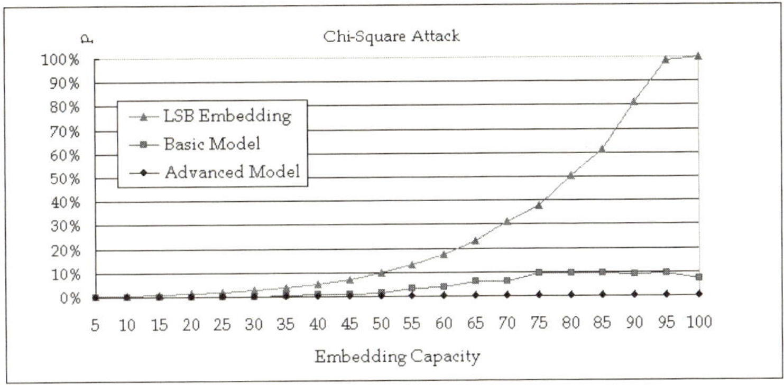


**Fig. 5.** Average experimental result of Chi-Square attack

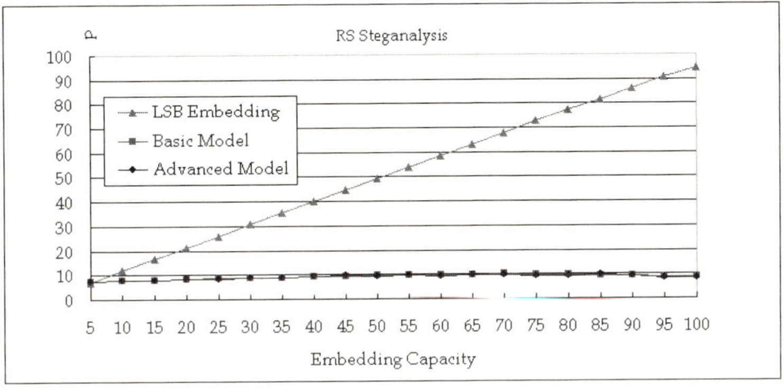


**Fig. 6.** Average experimental result of RS steganalysis

In contrast, when using either the basic model or the advanced model to embed the secret message, all the embedding rates estimated by RS steganalysis fall in the range 7% to 10%. This experimental result demonstrates that the proposed scheme is essentially undetectable when attacked by RS steganalysis.

## 5   Conclusion

The PoVs artifact caused by traditional LSB embedding exposes the existence of a hidden message. In order to raise the security level of covert communication, the weakness of the LSB embedding system has been theoretically analyzed here and a two-variant modified LSB embedding scheme has been proposed. There are three important features within the modified scheme. Firstly, the extraction process used in the proposed scheme is almost identical to the one used in traditional LSB embedding. Secondly, from a PSNR point of view, the fidelity of the stego-images resulting from the proposed scheme is as good as those created by traditional LSB embedding. Finally and most importantly, the PoVs artifact is removed from the stego-images. Experimental results show that both of the well-known Chi-square and RS steganalysis attacks are unable to detect the existence of secret messages embedded with the new system. Using the proposed scheme is therefore more secure than using traditional LSB embedding techniques.

# References


[1] Kahn, D.: The Codebreakers - the Comprehensive History of Secret Communication from Ancient Times to the Internet. Scribner, New York (1996)

[2] Johnson, N., Jajodia, S.: Exploring Steganography: Seeing the Unseen. IEEE Computer, 26–34 (February 1998)

[3] Westfeld, A., Pfitzmann, A.: Attacks on Steganographic Systems. In: Pfitzmann, A. (ed.) IH 1999. LNCS, vol. 1768, pp. 61–76. Springer, Heidelberg (2000)

[4] Fridrich, J., Du, R., Meng, L.: Steganalysis of LSB Encoding in Color Images. In: IEEE International Conference on Multimedia and Expo., pp. 1279–1282 (2000)

[5] Fridrich, J., Goljan, M., Du, R.: Detecting LSB Steganography in Color and Gray Images. Magazine of IEEE Multimedia (Special Issue on Security), 22–28 (October-November 2001)

[6] Westfeld, A.: F5 - A Steganographic Algorithm High Capacity Despite Better Steganalysis. In: Moskowitz, I.S. (ed.) IH 2001. LNCS, vol. 2137, pp. 289–302. Springer, Heidelberg (2001)

[7] Crandall, R.: Some Notes on Steganography. Posted on Steganography Mailing List (1998), http://os.inf.tu-dresden.de/~westfeld/crandall.pdf

[8] Fridrich, J., Goljan, M., Hogea, D.: Steganalysis of JPEG Images: Breaking the F5 Algorithm. In: Petitcolas, F.A.P. (ed.) IH 2002. LNCS, vol. 2578, pp. 310–323. Springer, Heidelberg (2003)

[9] Sharp, T.: An Implementation of Key-Based Digital Signal Steganography. In: Moskowitz, I.S. (ed.) IH 2001. LNCS, vol. 2137, pp. 13–26. Springer, Heidelberg (2001)

[10] USC-SIPI image database (accessed 12th August 2008), http://sipi.usc.edu/database/

[11] photoSIG (accessed 12th August 2008), http://www.photosig.com

# Can Geotags Help Image Recognition?

Keita Yaegashi and Keiji Yanai

Department of Computer Science,
The University of Electro-Communications
1–5–1 Chofugaoka, Chofu-shi, Tokyo, 182–8585 Japan
{yaegas-k,yanai}@mm.cs.uec.ac.jp

**Abstract.** In this paper, we propose to exploit geotags as additional information for visual recognition of consumer photos to improve its performance. Geotags, which represent places where the photos were taken, for photos can be obtained automatically by carrying a portable small GPS device with digital cameras. Geotags have potential to improve performance of visual image recognition, since recognition targets are unevenly distributed. For example, "beach" photos can be taken near the sea and "lion" photos can be taken only in a zoo except Africa.

To integrate geotag information into visual image recognition, we adopt two types of geographical information, raw values of latitude and longitude, and visual feature of aerial photos around the location the geotag represents. As classifiers, we use both a discriminative method and a generative method in the experiments.

The objective of this paper is to examine if geotags can help category-level image recognition. Note that we define an image recognition problem as deciding if an image is associated with a certain given concept such as "mountain" and "beach" in this paper. We propose a novel method to carry out geotagged image recognition in this paper. The experimental results demonstrate effectiveness of usage of geographical information for recognition of consumer photos.

## 1   Introduction

Due to the spread of consumer digital cameras and camera-equipped cell phones, we can easily take a large number of digital photos, while managing them is a troublesome job. To manage a large number of photos, word-tagging is one of popular methods, which enables us to search our personal photo storages with words. However, word-tagging by hand for a lots of photos is too boring and time-consuming task for many people. Therefore, automatic word-tagging is desirable.

In fact, in the research community of image recognition, visual recognition of generic consumer photos taken by people with usual digital cameras is one of hot topics. Recent progress on image representation [2,7], machine learning and computation power of computers have made visual recognition of consumer photos possible. Actually, 101 kinds of photo images can be classified automatically with the 87.8% classification rate by the state-of-the-art method [12]. However, since we have several thousands of kinds of targets to be recognized, visual image

T. Wada, F. Huang, and S. Lin (Eds.): PSIVT 2009, LNCS 5414, pp. 361–373, 2009.

recognition for consumer photos in which targets are not restricted is still far from practical use.

In this paper, we propose to exploit geotags as additional information for visual recognition of consumer photos to improve its performance. Geotags for photos can be obtained automatically by carrying a portable small GPS device with digital cameras. Geotags have potential to improve performance of visual image recognition, since recognition targets are unevenly distributed in the real world. For example, "beach" photos can be taken near the sea and "lion" photos can be taken only in a zoo except Africa. In this way, geotags can restrict concepts to be recognized for images, so that we expect geotags can help visual image recognition. In this paper, we examine if geotags can help visual recognition of consumer photos by experiments.

To utilize geotags in visual image recognition, we propose two methods: (1) combine values of latitude and longitude with visual feature extracted from a photo image. (2) combine visual feature extracted from aerial photo images with visual feature extracted from a photo image. The former method is relatively straightforward way, and it is expected to improve recognition performance for concepts associated with specific places such as "Disneyland" and "Mt. Fuji". On the other hand, in the latter method we utilize aerial photo images around the place where a photo was taken as information regarding that place. This will help more generic concepts such as "sea" and "mountain". Since "sea" and "mountain" are distributed all over the world, it is difficult to associate values of latitude and longitude with such generic concepts directly. Then, we regard aerial photo images around the place where the photo is taken as the information expressing the condition of the place, and utilize visual feature extracted from aerial images as yet another geographical information associated with geotags of photos. Especially, for geographical concepts such as "sea" and "mountain", using feature extracted from aerial photos is expected to be more effective than using values of latitude and longitude directly.

To collect geotagged images for experiments, we use Flickr. After Flickr launched an online geotagging interface in 2006, it became the largest geotagged photo database in the world. Flickr online geotagging system allows us to indicate the place where photos are taken by clicking the online map. In general, most of photos on the Web have no geospatial information, and photos in which GPS-based location information is embedded as the Exif data are very rare on the Web, People who like to add geotags their photos with GPS devices and upload them to the Web are very limited. Therefore, it was very difficult to collect large amount of geotagged images for research purpose so far. However, Flickr has changed this situation. They have a large number of images geotagged by Flickr's online geotagging system, and provide API to search Flickr photo databases for geotagged images. Everyone can access geotagged images on the Flickr very easily. From another point of view, in this paper, we propose to learn geotagged images from Flickr for visual recognition of consumer photos.

As related work related to geotagged photos, Kennedy et al. [5] proposed to select representative images by clustering based on visual feature regarding a specific place. They used geottaged image collected from Flickr, and used geotags and word-tags to associate photos with a specific place. Snavely et al. [11] proposed to collect images associated with a specific place by sending the name of the place to Web image search engines and to estimate relative positions among the collected images by computer vision technique. They provided a new interface which enables us to see the given place from any direction of view.

Regarding recognition of aerial photo, it has been researched as "remote sensing" for more than thirty years [6]. To examine condition of the grounds effectively, aerial or satellite photos are analyzed with image recognition technique. Geographical features of the land such as the sea, rivers, mountains, city areas, islands and deserts in the photos are recognized. Therefore, in terms of recognition of aerial images, our work is related to remote sensing. The difference is that remote sensing aims at recognizing geographical features which appear in aerial photos directly, while the objective of our work is recognizing various kinds of concepts for consumer photos taken on the ground taking advantage of features which appear in aerial photos in addition to image features extracted from photos themselves. Since the concepts we intend to recognize are generic, that is, not restricted to geographical concepts such as rivers and roads, they do not always appear in aerial photos directly. For example, "flowers" do not appear in aerial photos directly in general. However, the places where "flower" photos are taken might have causal relationship to geographical features which appear directly in aerial photos. The places where "flower" photos are taken are unevenly distributed, and are usually not commercial areas or mountainous areas, but parks, farming areas or residential areas. We expect that this goes for many non-geographical concepts other than flowers. Then, in this paper, we take advantage of this indirect causal relation for geotagged image recognition.

The main objective of this paper is to examine if geotags can help image recognition by exploiting causal relation between aerial photos and concepts to be recognized. In this paper, we define an image recognition problem as judging if an image is associated with a certain given concept such as "mountain" and "beach". We propose a novel method to carry out geotagged image recognition in this paper, and we show the experimental results, which demonstrate effectiveness of usage of geographical information for recognition of consumer photos.

The rest of this paper is organized as follows: Section 2 describes basic idea of geotagged image recognition. Section 3 explains the procedure of geotagged image recognition for the experiments. Section 4 shows the experimental results and discusses them, and we conclude this paper in Section 5.

## 2 Geotagged Image Recognition

The objective of this paper is to examine if geotags can help image recognition. There are several types of image recognition. In this paper, we assume that image recognition means judging if an image is associated with a certain given concept such as "mountain" and "beach", which can be regarded as a photo detector for a specific given concept. By combining many detectors, we can add many kinds of words as word-tags to images automatically.

As mentioned in the previous section, to integrate geotag information into visual image recognition, we adopt two types of geographical information, raw values of latitude and longitude, and visual feature of aerial photos around the geotagged location. To carry out experiments on the proposed geotagged image recognition, we need aerial photos corresponding to the geotags in addition to geotagged photos. We collect them from Flickr and an online aerial photo map site.

To perform geotagged image recognition, we need to extract feature vectors from images and geotags. As a representation of photo images, we adopt the bag-of-visual-words representation [2], which attracts much attention recently as a state-of-the-art method in the research community of image recognition. It has been proved that it has excellent ability to represent image concepts in the context of visual image recognition in spite of its simplicity. In the bag-of-visual-words method, an image is expressed by a high dimensional vector in the same way as a text document is expressed by a high dimensional bag-of-words vector. As a representation of geotags, we also adopt the bag-of-visual-words representation of aerial photos around the geotagged location in addition to raw values of latitude and longitude. After converting images and geotags into feature vectors, in this paper we adopt concatenation strategy, that is, combine them into one vector for each image.

After obtaining features vectors into which both visual and geographical information are mixed, we carry out two-class classification with two kinds of methods: a discriminative method and a generative method. As the discriminative method, we use Support Vector Machine (SVM), which is known as its excellent performance. As the generative methods, we use probabilistic latent topic mixture models [9]. In this paper, we use Probabilistic Latent Semantic Analysis (PLSA) [4] and Latent Dirichlet Allocation (LDA) [1] as latent topic models, while in [9] they used only PLSA.


# 3    Methods

In this section, we describe how to recognize images with visual features and geotags. First of all, we need to decide several concepts for the experiments. In this paper, we selected ten concepts for the experiments. Ideally, thousands kinds of concepts should be treated with as future work.


## 3.1    Data Collection

In this paper, we obtain geotagged images for the experiments from Flickr by searching for images which have Flickr tags corresponding to the given concept. Since the raw images fetched from Flickr include some noise images which are irrelevant to the given concepts, we select only relevant images by hand. In the experiments, relevant images are used as positive samples, while randomly-sampled images from all the geotagged images fetched from Flickr are used as

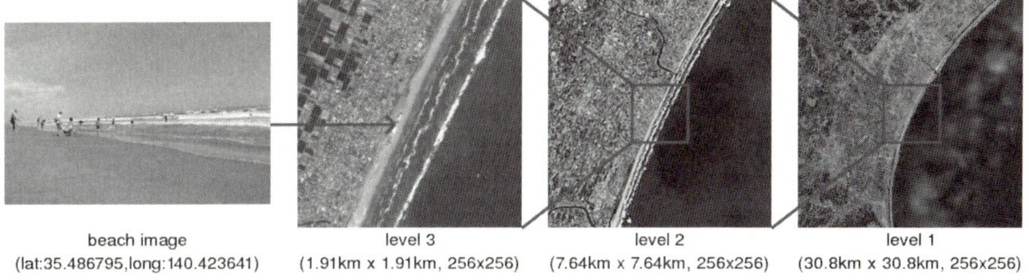



**Fig. 1.** Correspondence between a geotagged photo and aerial images

negative samples. We select 100 positive samples and 100 negative samples for each concept.

After obtaining geotagged images, we collect aerial photos around the points corresponding to the geotags of the collected geotagged image with several scales from an online aerial map site by screen-capturing so that the geotagged point is located at the center of an aerial photo. In the experiments, we collect $256 \times 256$ aerial photos in three different kinds of scales for one Flickr photo as shown in Figure 1. The larger-scale one (level 3) corresponds to an area of 1.91 kilometers square, the middle one (level 2) corresponds to a 7.64 kilometer-square area, and the smaller-scale one (level 1) corresponds to a 30.8 kilometer-square area. The level-1 and level-2 images are 16 times as large as the level-2 and level-3 images in terms of their size, respectively.

### 3.2    Extraction of Visual Features

To extract visual feature vectors from photos, we use the bag-of-visual-words method [2]. The main idea of the bag-of-visual-words is representing images as collections of independent local patches, and vector-quantizing them as histogram vectors. Note that the processing described below is carried out independently for each given concept.

The main steps to build a bag-of-visual-words vector are as follows:

1. Sample many patches from all the images. In the experiment, we sample patches on a regular grid with every 10 pixels.
2. Generate local feature vectors for the sampled patches by the SIFT descriptor [7] with four different scales.
3. Construct a codebook with $k$-means clustering over extracted feature vectors. A codebook is constructed for each concept independently. We set the size of the codebook $k$ as 300 in the experiments.
4. Assign all feature vectors to the nearest codeword (visual word) of the codebook, and convert a set of feature vectors for each image into one $k$-bin histogram vector regarding assigned codewords.

**SIFT Descriptors.** Scale Invariant Feature Transform (SIFT) proposed by D. Lowe [7] provides a multi-scale representation of an image neighborhood. They are Gaussian derivatives computed at 8 orientation planes over a $4 \times 4$ grid of spatial location, giving 128-dimension vector. The biggest advantage of SIFT descriptor is invariant to rotation. It has been shown that the SIFT descriptor is the best local patch descriptor for object recognition [8]. We compute SIFT vectors with the following four kinds of scales for regular grid points with every 10 pixels with the following four different scales: 4, 8, 12, and 16.

**Generation of Codebook and Quantization.** We obtain a collection of 128-dimension vectors for each image after the previous steps. Then, we apply vector quantization for them. Firstly, we compute a codebook by applying $k$-means clustering for all or randomly-sampled extracted SIFT vectors over both the positive training samples and negative training samples. In the experiment, we set the size of a codebook $k$ as 300. Secondly, we assign all the SIFT vectors to the nearest codewords, which is sometimes called "visual words". This is the same as nearest neighbor search. Finally, we convert a set of the SIFT vectors for each image into one $k$-bin histogram of assigned codewords. Each histogram is represented by a $k$-dimension vector, so we have converted one image into one $k$-dimension feature vector based on the bag-of-visual-words representation.

### 3.3   Extraction of Geographical Features

As described before, we use visual features of aerial images around the point corresponding to the geotag, and raw values of latitude and longitude as geographical information.

Since a pair of latitude and longitude can be treated as a two-dimensional vector as it is, we need no conversion. On the other hand, since aerial photos are images, they should be converted into feature vectors. To do that, we adopt the bag-of-visual-words representation in the same way as extraction of visual features from photos. $256 \times 256$ aerial images the center of which correspond to the geotagged locations are converted into the bag-of-visual-words vectors. Note that the visual codebook for aerial images is constructed based of a set of SIFT vectors extracted from all the collected aerial images.

After converting both images and geotags into feature vectors, we combine them into one vector for each image by concatenating them.

### 3.4   Image Classification

After obtaining features vectors into which both visual and geographical information are mixed, we carry out two-class classification with two kinds of methods: a discriminative method and a generative method. As the discriminative method, we use Support Vector Machine (SVM). As the generative method, we use probabilistic latent topic mixture models [9].

**Image Classification with SVM.** As the first method, we use a Support Vector Machine (SVM) classifier with the RBF kernel. We train an SVM classifier with positive and negative training samples. Next, we classify test samples with the trained SVM one by one.

**Image Classification with Latent Topic Mixture Models.** As the generative method, we use probabilistic latent topic mixture models [9]. In this paper, we use Probabilistic Latent Semantic Analysis (PLSA) [4] and Latent Dirichlet Allocation (LDA) [1] as latent topic models, while in [9] they used only PLSA.

Recently, PLSA and LDA were applied to object recognition task as probabilistic generative models [10,3,9]. Since latent topic models such as PLSA and LDA were originally proposed for analyzing documents represented by bag-of-words, the mixture models of topics obtained by PLSA or LDA is more appropriate for classifying images represented by bag-of-visual-words than the Gaussian mixture model (GMM) which was commonly used as a probabilistic generative model before the bag-of-visual-words methods was proposed.

The main idea is that we apply probabilistic latent models to all the training samples to get latent topics, and decide "positive topics" and "negative topics" using the positive and negative training images.

The main steps are as follows:

1. Apply the latent topic method such as PLSA or LDA with the given number of topics to the bag-of-visual-words vectors of all the positive and negative training images, and get $P(z|d)$ where $z \in Z = (z_1, .., z_k)$ is the latent topic variable, and $d \in D = (d_1, ..., d_N)$ is an image.
2. Calculate the probability of being positive or negative over each topic, $P(pos|z)$ and $P(neg|z)$ using the pseudo-training images which are automatically selected in the collection stage.
3. Calculate $P(pos|d) = \sum_{z \in Z} P(pos|z)P(z|d)$, and evaluate relevancy of each image to the given keywords.

**PLSA:** The PLSA model is represented as the generative model of each word $w$ in a document $d$:

$$P(w, d) = P(d) \sum_{z \in Z} P(w|z)P(z|d) \tag{1}$$

where $z \in Z = (z_1, .., z_k)$ is a latent topic variable, $k$ is the number of topics, $d \in D = (d_1, ..., d_N)$ is an image expressed by bag-of-visual-words, and $w \in W = (w_1, ..., w_M)$ is a visual word. The joint probability of the observed variables, $w$ and $d$, is the marginalization over the $k$ latent topics $Z$. The parameters are estimated by the EM algorithm. For full explanation of the PLSA model refer to [4].

**LDA:** Latent Dirichlet Allocation (LDA) by Blei et al. [1] is also a probabilistic model to detect latent topics from text documents represented by bag-of-words. It was proposed as a method to resolve a drawback of PLSA that the number of parameters in the models grows linearly with the size of the data which leads to serious overfitting. LDA models each image as a mixture over topic, where each vector of mixture proportions is assumed to have been drawn from a Dirichlet distribution. The parameters are estimated by the variational EM algorithm. We also obtain $P(z|d)$ by applying LDA. For the detail refer to [1].

Next we estimate "positive topics" and "negative topics". A "positive topic" means that the latent topic is associated with images relevant to the given concept, and "negative topic" means that the latent topic is associated with irrelevant images. The probability of being positive and negative over a topic is calculated as follows:

$$p_0 = \frac{1}{|D_{pos}|} \sum_{d \in D_{pos}} P(d|z) \tag{2}$$

$$p_1 = \frac{1}{|D_{neg}|} \sum_{d \in D_{neg}} P(d|z) \tag{3}$$

$$P(pos|z) = p_0/(p_0 + p_1) \tag{4}$$

$$P(neg|z) = p_1/(p_0 + p_1), \tag{5}$$

where

$$P(d|z) = \frac{P(z|d)P(d)}{\sum_{d \in D} P(z|d)P(d)} \tag{6}$$

and, $D_{pos}$ and $D_{neg}$ are positive and negative samples, respectively.

Finally, we can calculate the probability of being positive over each image $P(pos|d)$ by marginalization over topics:

$$P(pos|d) = \sum_{z \in Z} P(pos|z)P(z|d) \tag{7}$$

We can rank all the candidate images based on this probability, $P(pos|d)$, and obtain the final result.

## 4  Experimental Results

### 4.1  Settings of the Experiments

We prepared the ten concepts shown in Table 1. The first two concepts, "mountain" and "beach" in Table 1 are geographical concepts which can be recognized in aerial images directly. The third and forth concepts, "road" and "train", are concepts related to social infrastructure which also is likely to be recognized in aerial photos. The fifth, "landscape", is relatively an abstract concept, which might corresponds to a broad area. The sixth, "shrine", is a concept related to architectures or religious places. The seventh concept, "flower", is an object concept, which is difficult to be recognized in aerial photos but existence of causal relation to geographical features is expected. The next one, "Chinese noodle", is a food concept. We do not know causal relation between it and aerial images. The last two concepts, "Disneyland" and "Tokyo Tower", represents specific places. For them, raw values of latitude and longitude are expected to be effective as an additional feature for image recognition. Note that we restricted the area of geotags attached to Flickr photos within Japan in the experiments.

**Table 1.** Ten concepts for the experiments

|    | concept | definition is this pape |
|----|---------|-------------------------|
| 1  | mountain | a mountain landscape photo including mountain peaks |
| 2  | beach | a beach photo |
| 3  | road | a photo including roads clearly |
| 4  | train | a photo containing train vehicles |
| 5  | landscape | a landscape photo with no obstacles |
| 6  | shrine | architectures related to shrines |
| 7  | flower | a close-up photo for flowers or a photo mostly occupied with flowers |
| 8  | Chinese noodle | Chinese noodle with ready-to-east condition |
| 9  | Disneyland | photos taken inside the Disneyland |
| 10 | Tokyo Tower | The Tokyo Tower (in downtown Tokyo) |

We collected geotagged images corresponding to the ten concepts from Flickr, and select 100 positive samples by hand. Table 1 shows the standard to select positive sample images by hand. Basically, we selected obvious positive images so that everyone agrees that selected images belong to the given concept. In addition, we prepare 100 randomly-sampled images as negative samples. After that, we collect three-different-scale aerial images of the places associated to all the positive and negative images.

In the experiments, we tried nine different combinations of visual feature of photos (V), raw values of latitude and longitude (R), and visual feature of aerial photos in three different level (L1, L2, L3). V can be regarded as a baseline. All the results were ranked by the output value of SVM or P(pos—d) computed by the probabilistic methods, and were evaluated by the average precision (AP) based on the following formula:

$$AP = \frac{1}{N} \sum_{i=1}^{N} Prec(i), \qquad (8)$$

where $Prec(i)$ is the precision rate of the top $i$ images which is defined as (number of positive images within the top $i$ images)$/i$ and $N$ is the number of test images for each fold.

We evaluate experimental results with five-fold cross validation, which means that all the data regarding one given concept are divided into five groups, four of them are used as training samples and the rest of them are used as to-be-recognized test samples. We perform classification and evaluate results repeatedly five times by exchanging test samples with the average precision. Finally we average the average precisions for five folds, and obtain the average precision for the given concept.

**Table 2.** Experimental results by SVM for nine combinations of visual feature of photos (V), raw values of latitude and longitude (R), and visual feature of aerial photos in three different level (L1, L2, L3). The red-colored bold value in each row represents the best result for each concept.

| concept | V | V+L1 | V+L2 | V+L3 | V+R | L1 | L2 | L3 | R | diff |
|---|---|---|---|---|---|---|---|---|---|---|
| mountain | 87.25 | 91.24 | 90.37 | 89.81 | **91.84** | 87.21 | 78.86 | 80.53 | 86.54 | **+4.59** |
| beach | 90.02 | 91.37 | 91.93 | **93.32** | 83.68 | 79.16 | 76.63 | 85.14 | 82.08 | **+3.30** |
| road | 71.27 | 72.11 | 73.08 | **75.63** | 69.28 | 62.71 | 65.85 | 59.09 | 69.62 | **+4.36** |
| train | 72.83 | 76.31 | **77.38** | 77.02 | 71.05 | 64.54 | 65.97 | 62.52 | 69.26 | **+4.55** |
| landscape | 77.16 | 79.16 | **80.98** | 80.98 | 77.75 | 64.52 | 65.30 | 67.35 | 66.04 | **+3.82** |
| shrine | 67.88 | 72.28 | 69.80 | 72.20 | **72.89** | 70.12 | 61.85 | 62.44 | 71.64 | **+5.01** |
| flower | 79.38 | 85.43 | 85.00 | **86.63** | 68.95 | 78.19 | 77.62 | 78.64 | 64.13 | **+7.25** |
| Chinese noodle | 86.49 | 87.31 | **89.67** | 87.71 | 86.65 | 68.01 | 73.13 | 68.29 | 82.28 | **+3.18** |
| Disneyland | 67.70 | 95.83 | 89.90 | 92.67 | 86.37 | **98.56** | 94.43 | 93.65 | 86.38 | **+30.86** |
| Tokyo Tower | 85.80 | 90.73 | 91.06 | 88.94 | 85.16 | 91.21 | 72.42 | **91.70** | 66.93 | **+5.90** |
| AVG. | 78.58 | 84.18 | 83.92 | 84.49 | 79.36 | 76.42 | 73.21 | 74.93 | 74.49 | **+7.28** |

## 4.2  Results

Table 2 shows the average precisions of the experimental results of visual image classification employing SVM on the given ten concepts regarding the following nine different combinations of features: V, V+L1, V+L2, V+L3, V+R, L1, L2, L3, and R. V represents the baseline with only visual features of images, while V+L1, V+L2, and V+L3 represent the combination of visual features of images and visual features of aerial images. V+R means the combination of visual features of images and the raw values, L1, L2, L3 and R represents only geographical features without visual features of the images. "Diff" in the table represents the difference on AP between the baseline and the best result incorporated with geospatial information.

Similarly, table 3 and Table 4 show the results in case of using the PLSA-based latent topic mixture and the LDA-based latent topic mixture, respectively. We set the number of topics as 20, which is selected from 10, 20 and 30 based on the preliminary experiments. Note that raw value of latitude and longitude cannot be incorporated with feature vectors in case of using probabilistic methods with PLSA or LDA, since LDA and PLSA assume that input vectors are represented by the bag-of-words representation. Therefore, results on V+R and R were omitted in Table 3 and Table 4.

## 4.3  Discussions

In case of PLSA, the average of APs over ten concepts are were degraded compared to the results by SVM and LDA. This is likely to come from the overfitting problem, which may also cause irregularly-biased results from concept to concept. On average, SVM outperformed PLSA and LDA for all kinds of the combinations of features except the baseline (V). Therefore, in this subsection, we discuss about the SVM results mainly.

**Table 3.** Experimental results by the PLSA mixture model

| concept | V | V+L1 | V+L2 | V+L3 | L1 | L2 | L3 | diff |
|---|---|---|---|---|---|---|---|---|
| mountain | 85.65 | 86.40 | 85.27 | **87.50** | 81.18 | 79.22 | 63.61 | **+1.85** |
| beach | 89.58 | 89.03 | **90.03** | 88.49 | 69.17 | 66.40 | 72.58 | **+0.45** |
| road | 62.22 | **78.86** | 67.56 | 63.13 | 61.30 | 61.91 | 48.84 | **+16.64** |
| train | **71.07** | 67.07 | 64.22 | 66.39 | 53.46 | 64.23 | 52.97 | **+0.00** |
| landscape | **77.90** | 72.43 | 73.76 | 76.82 | 48.57 | 60.85 | 59.60 | **+0.00** |
| shrine | 62.02 | **77.13** | 60.77 | 67.96 | 65.83 | 53.45 | 56.12 | **+15.11** |
| flower | 77.01 | **86.79** | 81.85 | 85.70 | 73.69 | 72.35 | 77.11 | **+9.78** |
| Chinese noodle | 75.76 | 74.02 | 73.60 | **75.84** | 50.70 | 55.01 | 62.23 | **+0.08** |
| Disneyland | 62.33 | 83.28 | **90.81** | 80.72 | 64.56 | 83.14 | 83.05 | **+28.48** |
| Tokyo Tower | 83.25 | 88.37 | **91.63** | 86.74 | 69.73 | 67.10 | 71.53 | **+8.38** |
| AVG. | 74.68 | 80.34 | 77.95 | 77.93 | 63.82 | 66.36 | 64.76 | **+8.08** |

**Table 4.** Experimental results by the LDA mixture model

| concept | V | V+L1 | V+L2 | V+L3 | L1 | L2 | L3 | diff |
|---|---|---|---|---|---|---|---|---|
| mountain | 86.64 | **89.52** | 88.24 | 88.72 | 84.60 | 79.98 | 83.10 | **+2.88** |
| beach | 89.93 | 90.48 | 91.13 | **92.12** | 79.01 | 76.53 | 76.87 | **+2.19** |
| road | **71.70** | 69.60 | 70.12 | 68.05 | 58.59 | 61.55 | 59.27 | **+0.00** |
| train | 74.87 | **76.59** | 74.34 | 74.30 | 66.69 | 64.64 | 58.50 | **+1.72** |
| landscape | 83.51 | 83.55 | 83.29 | **86.13** | 62.58 | 61.17 | 67.72 | **+2.62** |
| shrine | 66.13 | **70.29** | 68.93 | 68.76 | 68.76 | 62.81 | 56.45 | **+4.16** |
| flower | 80.08 | **88.50** | 85.69 | 87.60 | 76.87 | 76.24 | 78.79 | **+8.42** |
| Chinese noodle | 85.85 | **89.25** | 85.83 | 82.89 | 72.05 | 63.91 | 65.38 | **+3.40** |
| Disneyland | 64.80 | 86.11 | 92.02 | 92.60 | **98.82** | 94.96 | 97.05 | **+34.02** |
| Tokyo Tower | 85.28 | 91.04 | 91.43 | 87.59 | 96.00 | 70.91 | **96.28** | **+11.01** |
| AVG. | 78.88 | 83.49 | 83.10 | 82.88 | 76.40 | 71.27 | 73.94 | **+7.04** |

In case of SVM as a classifier, for all the ten concepts, the best results among eight combinations including geospatial features were superior to the baseline. Basically this is because the places where positive sample photos were taken are unevenly distributed, while the places where negative sample photos were taken are randomly distributed. Especially, all the SVM results by the combination of visual features of images and aerial photos (V+L1/L2/L3) outperformed the baseline results. This shows that incorporating visual features extracted from aerial photos with visual features extracted from images are effective and promising for image recognition.

The APs by SVM were improved by about 3% to 5% except for "Disneyland". For "Disneyland" which is a specific place name, geotags boosted the results greatly, and with only aerial photos and no visual information of the images the 98.56% average precision was obtained. From this result, to discriminate images associated with specific place names from randomly-sampled negative images, only geospatial information is enough. As we expected, for "Tokyo Tower", the

**Fig. 2.** Positive sample photos of ten categories: Disneyland, flower, landscape, mountain, Chinese noodle, road, beach, shrine, Tokyo Tower, and train

similar tendency was observed. However, the improvement is not as large as "Disneyland", since "Tokyo Tower" which is a 333 meter-high architecture can be seen from the relatively broad area of downtown Tokyo and the geotagged places are not as well-concentrated as "Disneyland".

Among concepts other than two specific location concepts, the result on "flower" were improved most. For "flower", while the result by visual features and raw coordinate values (V+R) was inferior to the baseline result (V), the results by the combinations of visual features and aerial photo features (V+L1/L2/L3) was much superior to the baseline (V). This shows "indirect causal relation" between "flower" concept and visual features extracted from aerial photos helped recognition of "flower" images.

From these results, we can conclude that geographical information has ability to help visual image recognition by using visual features of aerial images as additional features, although further experiments which should be more extensive are needed to examine effectiveness of this novel idea in detail.

## 5   Conclusions

In this paper, we proposed a novel method for "geotagged image recognition", which exploits aerial photos corresponding to the geotagged point as additional features for image classification. We made experiments so as to examine if geotags can help image recognition. The experimental results demonstrated effectiveness of usage of geographical information for recognition of consumer photos. We believe this is the first attempt to utilize aerial photos where a photo was taken as additional features for image recognition.

In this paper, although we showed novel results that geotags helped performance of visual image recognition, the number of concepts examined in the experiments were limited. For future work, we plan to make more comprehensive experiments with several thousands of concepts and we also study more sophisticated method to integrate visual features of photos, visual features of aerial photos and raw values of latitude and longitude. In addition, it also should be investigated how to use aerial photos regarding levels and a range. Although we made the experiments on nine combinations of features in this paper, appropriate combinations for each concept should be selected automatically. Using several levels of aerial images at the same times will be possible. The final objective of this research project is to identify concepts for which geographical information helps image recognition effectively by examining several thousands of concepts.

# References


1. Blei, D., Ng, A., Jordan, M.: Latent dirichlet allocation. Journal of Machine Learning Research 3, 993–1022 (2003)
2. Csurka, G., Bray, C., Dance, C., Fan, L.: Visual categorization with bags of keypoints. In: Proc. of ECCV Workshop on Statistical Learning in Computer Vision, pp. 59–74 (2004)
3. Fei-Fei, L., Perona, P.: A bayesian hierarchical model for learning natural scene categories. In: Proc. of IEEE Computer Vision and Pattern Recognition, pp. 524–531 (2005)
4. Hofmann, T.: Unsupervised learning by probabilistic latent semantic analysis. Machine Learning 43, 177–196 (2001)
5. Kennedy, L., Naaman, M.: Generating diverse and representative image search results for landmarks. In: Proc. of the International World Wide Web Conference, pp. 297–306 (2008)
6. Lillesand, T.M., Kiefer, R.W., Chipman, J.W.: Remote sensing and image interpretation. John Wiley, Chichester (2004)
7. Lowe, D.G.: Distinctive image features from scale-invariant keypoints. International Journal of Computer Vision 60(2), 91–110 (2004)
8. Mikolajczyk, K., Schmid, C.: A performance evaluation of local descriptors. IEEE Transactions on Pattern Analysis and Machine Intelligence 27(10), 1615–1630 (2005)
9. Monay, F., Gatica-Perez, D.: Modeling semantic aspects for cross-media image retrieval. IEEE Transactions on Pattern Analysis and Machine Intelligence 29(10), 1802–1817 (2007)
10. Sivic, J., Russell, B.C., Efros, A.A., Zisserman, A., Freeman, W.T.: Discovering objects and their localization in images. In: Proc. of IEEE International Conference on Computer Vision, pp. 370–377 (2005)
11. Snavely, N., Seitz, S., Szeliski, R.: Photo tourism: exploring photo collections in 3d. ACM Transactions on Graphics (TOG) 25(3), 835–846 (2006)
12. Varma, M., Ray, D.: Learning the discriminative power-invariance trade-off. In: Proc. of IEEE International Conference on Computer Vision, pp. 1150–1157 (2007)

# Principal Component Hashing:
# An Accelerated Approximate Nearest Neighbor Search

Yusuke Matsushita and Toshikazu Wada

Graduate School of Systems Engineering, Wakayama University
930 Sakaedani, Wakayama, 640-8510, Japan
`{ymatsushita,twada}@vrl.sys.wakayama-u.ac.jp`

**Abstract.** Nearest Neighbor (NN) search is a basic algorithm for data mining and machine learning applications. However, its acceleration in high dimensional space is a difficult problem. For solving this problem, approximate NN search algorithms have been investigated. Especially, LSH is getting highlighted recently, because it has a clear relationship between relative error ratio and the computational complexity. However, the p-stable LSH computes hash values independent of the data distributions, and hence, sometimes the search fails or consumes considerably long time. For solving this problem, we propose Principal Component Hashing (PCH), which exploits the distribution of the stored data. Through experiments, we confirmed that PCH is faster than ANN and LSH at the same accuracy.

**Keywords:** Approximate Nearest Neighbor Search, High dimensional space, p-stable Locality Sensitive Hashing.

## 1 Introduction

Nearest neighbor (NN) search algorithm finds the nearest data to a query from stored data. This algorithm plays important roles in wide varieties of applications, e.g., NN classification [1], stitching geometric objects [2], and so on. For avoiding time consuming exhaustive search, many accelerated algorithms have been proposed, which works well on low dimensional distributions. However, most of them lose effect on high dimensional data distributions, i.e., the computational efficiency decreases almost comparably as the exhaustive search.

For solving this problem, approximated NN search algorithms have been proposed. Approximate Nearest Neighbor (ANN [4, 5]) and Locality Sensitive Hashing (LSH [6, 7]) are the typical examples.

ANN is the k-d tree [3] based search algorithm which first finds an NN candidate by binary tree search and checks other possibilities in the following procedure. This procedure is called priority search. The binary tree corresponds to a box decomposition of the search space, where each box involves a single vector. In the priority search, the algorithm checks the boxes intersecting the hyper sphere whose center is at the query vector and the NN candidate is on its surface. The approximation is reducing the radius of this sphere. Let feasible error and radius $\varepsilon$ and $r$, respectively.

T. Wada, F. Huang, and S. Lin (Eds.): PSIVT 2009, LNCS 5414, pp. 374–385, 2009.

Then the approximation is reducing the radius $r$ to $r/(1+\varepsilon)$. This reduction decreases the number of boxes checked in the priority search, but increases the chance of inaccurate NN search. Of course, $\varepsilon = 0$ corresponds to exact NN search with no errors.

On the other hand, LSH is the hash based approximation of NN search, which has a clear relationship between error ratio and the computational complexity, where

$$ErrorRatio = \frac{\text{distance between query and its approximate NN}}{\text{distance between query and its true NN}} .$$

The basic LSH decomposes the search space into buckets (hash bins), each of which has the same hash value. This algorithm first computes the hash value of the query and finds the NN candidates in the bucket having the same hash value. Finally, it finds approximate NN vector from the candidates. Therefore, a few candidates are preferable for fast search but are not preferable for accurate search.

In the basic LSH [6] and p-stable LSH [7], the hash function is determined without referring the distribution of stored vectors. This causes the following problems:

**P1.**  When the query is given at low density area, the search may fail, because no bucket may have the same hash value with the query.
**P2.**  When the query is given at high density area, the search time may increase, because those buckets usually include more data than low density area.

For solving this problem, we propose Principal Component Hashing (PCH), which exploits the distribution of stored vectors for computing hash function. This NN search algorithm has the following advantages.

- PCH decomposes whole search space into finite buckets involving the same expected number of vectors. This guarantees constant search time independent of query vectors. Also, PCH can find NN candidates for any query vector.
- PCH finds the NN vector from the NN candidates by efficient distance computation on the principal components.

PCH assumes that data distribution obeys Gaussian distribution. However, most practical data distribution does not. Hence, we further extend it to NN search algorithm for general distributions while guaranteeing the above advantages. We call it Adaptive PCH (A-PCH).


## 2  Approximate Nearest Neighbor Search

Many researches on accelerating NN search have been done before. Through those researches, most algorithms use the following two techniques.

**[Reducing the number of distance computation].** The NN candidates for distance computation are narrowed based on the triangular inequality [8, 9, 10] or the space decomposition [4, 11, 12].

**[Pruning of distance computation].** The pruning stops distance computation when halfway distance exceeds given tentative distance [4].

This research field has been regarded matured, because many researchers spent long time and some accelerated search algorithms have been produced. However, their computational efficiency decreases almost comparably as the exhaustive search.

For solving this problem, approximated NN search algorithms, e.g., ANN and LSH, have been proposed. Especially, LSH is getting highlighted recently, because it has a clear relationship between relative error ratio and the computational complexity.

## 2.1  $(R,c)$ − Nearest Neighbor Problem

Suppose $X$ is a metric space and $x_1, x_2 \in X$. Let $D(x_1, x_2)$ be the distance between $x_1$ and $x_2$, $S\, (\subset X)$ be the stored vector set, $q$ be a query, and $NN(q) \in S$ be the nearest vector to $q$ within $S$. Then, $(R,c)$-NN problem is to find an approximate nearest neighbor vector $NN'(q)$ satisfying

$$D(q, NN'(q)) \le cD(q, NN(q)),\tag{1}$$

where $c(\ge 1)$ is called error ratio.

For solving this problem, we define the following hash function:

**Definition 1.** *Let $U$ be a set of hash values, $h(x): X \to U$ be the hash function, locality-sensitive hash function satisfies the conditions below:*

- *if $D(v,q) \le r_1$ then $\Pr[h(q) = h(v)] \ge p_1$,*
- *if $D(v,q) > r_2$ then $\Pr[h(q) = h(v)] < p_2$,*

*where $p_2 \le p_1$ and $r_2 = cr_1$.*

By using those hash functions satisfying this definition, we can realize $(R,c)$-NN search based on the following theorem:

**Theorem 1.** *Let $h_1, h_2, \cdots$ be hash functions, $n$ be the number of vectors in the dataset, and $\rho(c) = \ln p_1 / \ln p_2$. Then, it is possible to find $NN'(q)$ satisfying Equation (1) by $L = n^{\rho(c)}$ times bucket search with constant probability.*

LSH is an approximate NN search algorithm based on this theorem, whose efficiency is characterized by $\rho(c)$. For realizing better search algorithm, which finds approximate NN vector with high accuracy ($|c-1|$ is small) within short time ($\rho(c)$ is small), $\rho(c)$ should decrease quickly. Various researches are being conducted about what kind of hash function brings good $\rho(c)$.

## 2.2  P-Stable LSH

P-stable LSH is an example of practical LSH, which finds approximate NN vector in Euclidean distance. Suppose $q$ is a query, $a$ is a vector, $b$ and $\omega$ are constants. Then the p-stable hash function is defined by the following formula.

$$h_{a,b}(\boldsymbol{q}) = \left\lfloor \frac{\boldsymbol{a} \cdot \boldsymbol{q} + b}{\omega} \right\rfloor, \tag{2}$$

where $\lfloor . \rfloor$ is floor function.

This hash function projects vectors onto the vector $\boldsymbol{a}$ and quantize the axis with the interval $\omega$, which is decided based on the distribution width of the inner product $\boldsymbol{a} \cdot \boldsymbol{q}$. In this sense, the parameter $b$ can be regarded as adjusting the bias, which is chosen uniformly from the range $[0, \omega]$. $\boldsymbol{a}$ is sampled from a p-stable distribution, for example, isotropic Gaussian. Depending on the property of p-stable distribution, it can be proven that the hash function achieves $\rho(c) \leq 1/c$ [6].

Recently, [8] claims that $\rho(c) = 1/c^2$ can be achieved by using Voronoi decomposition of search space. However, this is impractical in high dimensional space, because the computational complexity of the Voronoi decomposition over $n$ samples in $d$ dimensional space is $O(n^{\lfloor d/2 \rfloor})$.

## 3  Principal Component Hashing

Here we describe the algorithm of PCH. This algorithm performs 1) hash value computation, 2) NN candidate generation, 3) refinement of NN candidate to find approximate NN. We will explain these three processes and some tips for improving the performance.

### 3.1  Hash Functions

In the p-stable LSH, parameters of the hash function are determined independent of the data distribution. However, the accuracy and the efficiency can vary depending on the data distribution. For example, we can easily generate the data distribution and query that causes problems P.1 and P.2 described in section 1. This means $\rho(c)$ does not guarantee the actual performance but just illustrates the trend of accuracy versus speed independent of the data distribution.

Our basic idea is to use the data distribution for designing the hash function. In practice, we use the principal components of the distribution instead of $\boldsymbol{a}$. This is because the standard deviation of the projected vectors is maximized when vectors are projected to the principal component. This implies projected vectors are widely distributed on the principal component.

Once vectors are projected, we have to segment the projection axis into buckets. Of course, optimally segmented buckets should involve the same number of vectors. If we know the probabilistic data distribution $p(x)$ on the projection axis, we can compute cumulative probability distribution $P(x)$ as

$$P(x) = \int_{-\infty}^{x} p(\xi) d\xi . \tag{3}$$

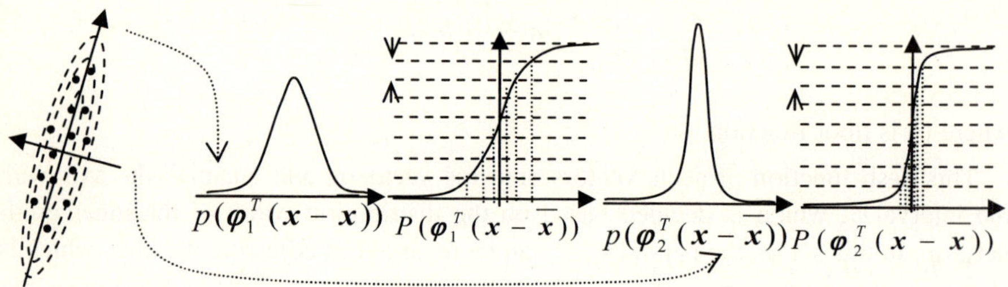



**Fig. 1.** The hash function and bucket division **in PCH**

$P(x)$ is monotonically increasing. Also, its domain and the range are $(-\infty, +\infty)$ and $[0,1]$, respectively. This implies that there is an inverse mapping $P^{-1}:[0,1] \mapsto (-\infty, +\infty)$.

Hence, by dividing the range of $P(x)$ into $n+1$ uniform intervals $[0,\Delta]$, $(\Delta, 2\Delta], \cdots, (n\Delta, 1]$, the whole projection axis can be decomposed into $n+1$ disjoint buckets: $(-\infty, P^{-1}(\Delta)]$, $(P^{-1}(\Delta), P^{-1}(2\Delta)], \cdots, (P^{-1}(n\Delta), +\infty)$ as shown in Fig. 1. This disjoint decomposition guarantees

- Every query must fall into a bucket.
- Every bucket involves the same expected number of vectors.

These facts are most suitable for approximate NN search. In p-stable LSH, queries provided at low density area can easily fail, but PCH never fails without adding exception handling code. Also, expected number of vectors contained by a bucket directly influences the efficiency of the search. Then, equal expected number implies constant search time.

For the realization of this idea, we introduce an assumption:

**Assumption 1.** *The distribution of the stored vector is Gaussian.*

Assuming this, we can say that the projected vectors to a principal component also obey Gaussian distribution. Then we can fit Gaussian $p(x)$ to the projected vectors.

In practice, Equation (3) should not be computed when performing search, because it consumes considerably long time. In this research, since $p(x)$ is a Gaussian distribution, Equation (3) is approximated by the sigmoid function shown below.

$$P(x) \cong P_s(x) = 1/(1 + e^{-x/\sigma}) \, . \tag{4}$$

This approximation is for designing a fast hash function. When the $i$-th principal component $\varphi_i$ is used, the hash function is expressed as

$$h_i(x) = \left\lfloor P_s(\varphi_i^T(x - \bar{x}))/\Delta \right\rfloor , \tag{5}$$

where $\Delta$ is the interval.

The series of independent hash functions can casily be created by using orthonormal bases $\varphi_i$ $(i = 1, \cdots, M)$ obtained by performing PCA on the given dataset. These hash functions corresponds to a lattice decomposition of the whole search space.

By using above hash functions, each bucket on an axis $i$ has a single hash value $H$. Hereafter, we denote this bucket $B_{iH}$. That is,

$$B_{iH} = \{x \mid x \in S, h_i(x) = H\}, \tag{6}$$

where $S$ represents the search space.

## 3.2  Generation of NN Candidates

According to the discussion above, when the hash values of a query $q$ are $h_i(q)$ $(i = 1, \cdots, m)$, we should find the candidates in $\bigcap_{i=1}^{m} B_{ih_i(q)}$. This strategy drastically reduces the number of NN candidates, however, it may produce empty set of candidates and may produce erroneous search results when the query is located near the boundary between buckets.

Hence, the candidates should be in those buckets which have at least one hash value $h_i(q)$. This means initial estimate of candidate set $C_0(q)$ for query $q$ should be the union of $B_{ih_i(q)}$:

$$C_0(q) = \bigcup_{i=1}^{m} B_{ih_i(q)}. \tag{7}$$

The problem remaining here is the candidates in $C_0(q)$ are still too many for distance computation. For reducing the number of candidates, PCH performs "refinement of candidates".

## 3.3  Refinement of NN Candidates

When performing the hashing, we can count the frequency of hits for each stored vector $x$, i.e., how many times hash values match. We represent this frequency $w(x)$. According to this value, we can select a tentative NN vector $NN^0(q)$:

$$NN^0(q) = \arg\max_{x \in C_0(q)} w(x). \tag{8}$$

Then the tentative distance $z$ can be expressed as

$$z = D(q, NN^0(q)). \tag{9}$$

This tentative distance is used for pruning the distance computation, i.e., while computing the distance between $q$ and a stored vector $x$, whenever the halfway distance grows bigger than $z$, the distance computation can be terminated.

This type of pruning is also employed in ANN [4], however, the pruning in PCH is much more efficient. This is because the distance computation can be done on the principal axes.

In the PCH, we first apply PCA to stored vectors and all vectors are projected onto the principal axes $\varphi_i$ $(i = 1, \cdots, M)$, i.e., orthonormal bases. In this case, $L_p$ distance $D(x_1, x_2)$ between $x_1$ and $x_2$ can be expressed as

$$D(\boldsymbol{x}_1, \boldsymbol{x}_2) = \sqrt[p]{\sum_{i=1}^{M} |x_{1i} - x_{2i}|^p} = \sqrt[p]{\sum_{i=1}^{M} |\varphi_i^T (\boldsymbol{x}_1 - \boldsymbol{x}_2)|^p} \, . \tag{10}$$

This is based on the Parseval's identity.

If $\varphi_i$ is sorted in descent order of eigen values, projection to $\varphi_1$ has the biggest deviation. This implies that many candidates can be pruned only by comparing $|\varphi_1^T \boldsymbol{q} - \varphi_1^T \boldsymbol{x}|$ with $z$, i.e., if $|\varphi_1^T \boldsymbol{q} - \varphi_1^T \boldsymbol{x}|$ is bigger than $z$ then $\boldsymbol{x}$ can not be a candidate of $NN'(\boldsymbol{q})$. This pruning can be generalized using multiple bases as below.

Suppose $m \leq M$ and $\boldsymbol{x} \in C_0(\boldsymbol{q})$, if the following inequality is satisfied, $\boldsymbol{x}$ cannot be a candidate of $NN'(\boldsymbol{q})$.

$$D^P(\boldsymbol{q}, \boldsymbol{x}) = \sum_{i=1}^{m} |\varphi_i^T \boldsymbol{q} - \varphi_i^T \boldsymbol{x}|^p > z^p \, . \tag{11}$$

In practice, this pruning does not require special computation. For computing hash function $h_i(\boldsymbol{q})$, $\varphi_i^T \boldsymbol{x}$ is also obtained. Just by using this value, we can prune the distance computation and refine the candidate based on the inequality (11). This is because $\varphi_i^T \boldsymbol{x}$ is already computed when vectors are stored. We show an algorithm of "refinement the NN candidates" below.

This algorithm computes $\sum_{i=1}^{A} |\varphi_i^T \boldsymbol{q} - \varphi_i^T \boldsymbol{x}|^p$ and check the inequality (11) within a range $1 \leq i \leq A(<< m)$. If the inequality (11) is not satisfied with $i = A$, compute actual distance $D(\boldsymbol{x}, \boldsymbol{q})$ and compare $D(\boldsymbol{x}, \boldsymbol{q})$ with $z$. If $D(\boldsymbol{x}, \boldsymbol{q}) < z$ then $z$ is updated, otherwise $\boldsymbol{x}$ is excluded from the candidates. We perform this processing for all NN candidates in $C_0(\boldsymbol{q})$.

This algorithm directly finds NN vector from $C_0(\boldsymbol{q})$ without generating series of candidates and decreases the chances of actual distance computations by updating of $z$ accelerates the pruning of distance computation. Since the performance depends on the parameter $A$, we have to find the best parameter for each problem.

## 3.4  Tips for Improving the Performance

In this section, we describe two tips for improving the performance of PCH to achieve higher accuracy and faster speed for practical use.

### 3.4.1  Bucket Overlapping

It is important for accurate search to select buckets including true NN $NN(\boldsymbol{q})$. However, when the query is given near the boundary between buckets, $NN(\boldsymbol{q})$ may not be in the bucket. The essential problem is not the size but the disjoint arrangement of the buckets. Then, we introduce the overlapped arrangement of buckets as follows.

$$B_{iH}^{\delta} = \{\boldsymbol{x} \mid \boldsymbol{x} \in S, H - \delta \leq h_i(\boldsymbol{x}) \leq H + \delta\} \, . \tag{12}$$

By employing this arrangement, $\Pr[NN(q) \in B_{iH}^{\delta}] \geq \Pr[NN(q) \in B_{iH}]$ holds. $\delta$ is called a margin. Bigger $\delta$ produces more accurate search results.

### 3.4.2  Cutoff the NN Candidates

When we employ the bucket overlapping, the number of candidates will increase. In spite of the efficient pruning of the distance computation, too many candidates slow down the search speed. In such cases, we can reduce the number of candidates while keeping the accuracy according to the hit frequency $w(x)$, because the data having bigger $w(x)$ can have bigger chance to become $NN(q)$. In practice, candidates $C_0(q)$ are sorted in the descent order of $w(x)$, and top $b$ % of sorted candidates are extracted as reduced NN candidates $C_0'(q)$. This $b$ is named *cutoff ratio*.

## 3.5  Extension of PCH to General Distribution

For constructing the basic PCH algorithm, we introduced **ASSUMPTION 1** that stored data obeys Gaussian distribution. From this distribution model, cumulative distribution model is approximated by the sigmoid function, and by segmenting the cumulative probability (vertical axis) uniformly, we get non-uniform buckets on the projection axis. However, once we get this non-uniform bucket decomposition, it can be stored in a tree structure, which can be utilized in the search process. This implies we don't have to rely on the **ASSUMPTION 1.**

In this section, we extend the PCH to Adaptive PCH (A-PCH), which can be applied to general distributions.

### 3.5.1  A-PCH: Extension to General Distributions

In the data storing stage, all vectors are projected on a principal axis. Then, we can generate cumulative histogram $H(x)$. By scanning this histogram, the domain can be decomposed into non-uniform buckets involving the same number of projected vectors. Suppose that the intervals $(-\infty, H^{-1}(\Delta)]$, $(H^{-1}(\Delta), H^{-1}(2\Delta)], \cdots, (H^{-1}(n\Delta), +\infty)$ represent the bucket decomposition, then the tree structure can be constructed as below.

The root node of the tree has a threshold $I(\lfloor (n+1)/2 \rfloor) = H^{-1}(\lfloor \Delta(n+1)/2 \rfloor)$. The left descendant node has $I(\lfloor (n+1)/4 \rfloor)$ and right node has $I(\lfloor 3(n+1)/4 \rfloor)$. By recursively applying this rule, we can generate a balanced binary search tree.

In the search stage, A-PCH performs binary search using this tree structure for finding the bucket where the query falls in. The rest of the process is the same as PCH.

## 4  Experiments

For evaluating PCH and A-PCH, we conducted the following experiments:

4.1 Performance comparison among A-PCH, ANN and p-stable LSH.
4.2 Performance comparison between PCH and A-PCH.

The specification of the platform PC is: CPU (Intel Xeon 3.72GHz x 2), Memory (32 GB), OS (x86_64 Linux Kernel Version 2.6.20), Compiler (gcc 4.1.2-13 built for x86_64).

For the fair evaluation, we have to take account of the balance between the accuracy and the speed. Then, we employ "time versus error ratio curve". Curves passing closer to left-bottom corner have better performance.

## 4.1  Comparison among A-PCH, ANN, and LSH

The purpose of this experiment is to compare the properties of A-PCH, LSH, and ANN under special and realistic conditions.

As for the special condition, we use the following dataset and queries:

> Dataset: 5000 vectors sampled from 3000-dimensional isotropic Gaussian distribution. Queries: 1000 uniformly distributed queries within a hyper cube $(-3\sigma, 3\sigma)^{3000}$.

This is the most difficult dataset for A-PCH, because the distribution essentially has no principal component, and hence, PCA does not play important role. One may think that a priori knowledge on the distribution is useless in this case.

For the realistic condition, we use the following dataset and queries:

> Dataset: 10000 vectors sampled from 4096-dimensional (64x64) monochrome images (CASPEAL). Queries: 1000 images independent of stored images.

This is a suitable dataset for A-PCH, because the distribution may be biased, and hence, the knowledge on the distribution can be utilized for generating hash functions and pruning the candidates.

For both datasets, all parameters in each NN search algorithm are changed as possible as we can:

- ANN: Feasible error $\varepsilon$ is changed within the range $[1,100]$.
- LSH: Number of projections per hash value $k$ is changed within the range $[2,40]$. Number of hash tables $L$ within the range $[3,171]$.
- A-PCH: Number of a principal axis $A$ within the range $[5,100]$, Number of buckets on an axis $1/\Delta$ within the range $[5,100]$, Bucket overlapping $\delta$ within the range $[0,2]$, Cutoff ratio $b$ within the range $[20,80]$.

Fig. 2 and 3 show the "time versus error ratio curves" using simulated data and CASPEAL image dataset, respectively. In these graphs, horizontal axis represents time [s] and vertical axis is error ratio. P-stable LSH can generate "search failures", which means no NN vector is found. In this case, the graph is plotted using successful search results. ANN and A-PCH do not generate any search failure. This means the plot of p-stable LSH overestimates its performance.

For the simulated data, the performance seems almost the same, but p-stable LSH generates a lot of search failures (from 0 to 997 failures per 1000 queries). The maximum number of failures are observed at K=40 and L=3, which is plotted at (0.000379[s], 1.0298 error ratio). This implies the leftmost area of p-stable LSH

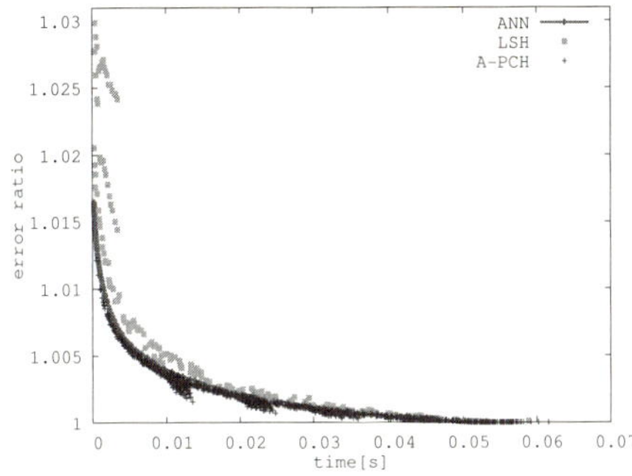

**Fig. 2.** Isotropic Gaussian

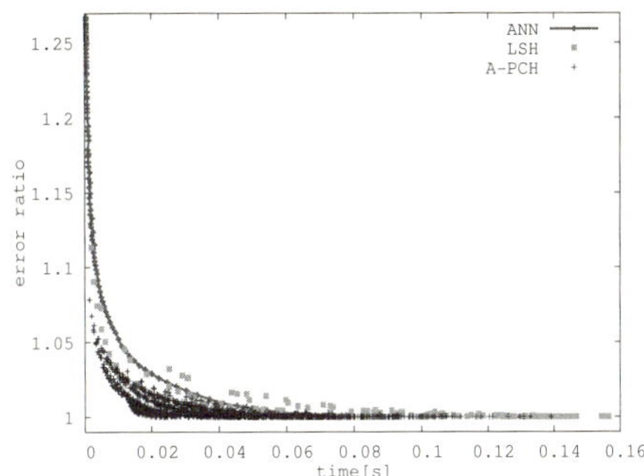

**Fig. 3.** CAS-PEAL image database

plotting is not reliable. ANN performs better than p-stable LSH, because p-stable LSH does not make initial guess but ANN makes initial guess by k-d tree search and approximated priority search accelerates the search keeping the accuracy. In spite that this is the most difficult case for A-PCH, it performs better than others. This is because the initial guess using the hit frequency and the pruning work better than ANN.

For the real data, LSH produces less search failures (from 0 to 42 failures per 1000 queries) than the simulated data and seems better than ANN. Comparing with them, A-PCH outperforms. This is because the performance of A-PCH mainly depends on the dimensionality of the data distribution, however, others depends on the dimensionalities of search space as well as distribution.

### 4.2   Comparison between PCH and A-PCH

The purpose of this experiment is to compare A-PCH with PCH, for clarifying the effect of the extension described in section 3.5.

PCH cannot guarantee "each bucket includes the same expected number of vectors" when data distribution does not obey Gaussian. But, A-PCH can guarantee that in every case. This may make some differences.

Also, we will not use empty buckets for avoiding search failure in PCH and A-PCH. Then, the maximum number of buckets along each projection axis in PCH is less than that of A-PCH. This also makes some differences.

We conducted comparative experiments with PCH and A-PCH. In the experiment, we applied them to the data used in section 4.1 and the following additional data:

> Dataset: 10000 data sampled from mixture of two isotropic 3000-dimensional Gaussians $2\sigma$ apart each other, where $\sigma$ represents the standard deviation of each Gaussian. Query: Sampled data from this distribution but independent of the stored vectors.

This data is for simulating non-Gaussian distribution.

The parameter ranges of PCH and A-PCH are same as that of A-PCH in section 4.1 except the number of buckets is limited not to produce empty buckets.

Fig. 4, 5, and 6 shows the comparison experiment result of A-PCH and PCH using the isotropic distribution, CASPEAL image dataset, and the data sampled from a

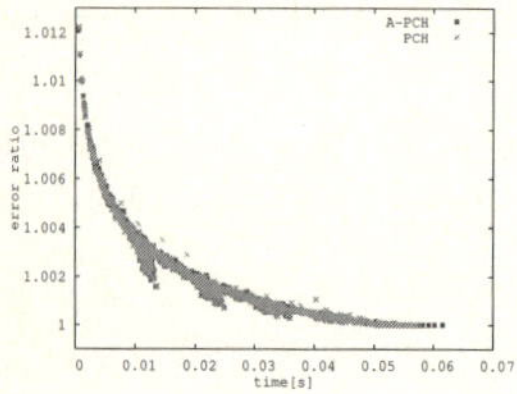

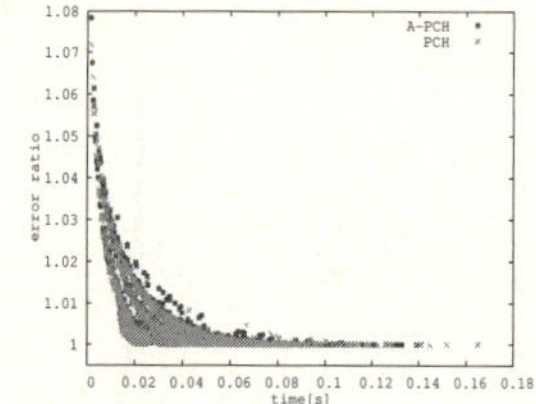

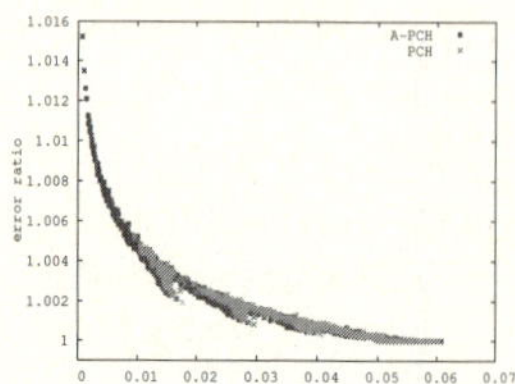

**Fig. 4.** Isotropic Gaussian: A-PCH vs. PCH.

**Fig. 5.** CASPEAL Image database: A-PCH vs. PCH.

**Fig. 6.** Mixture of Gaussians: A-PCH vs. PCH.

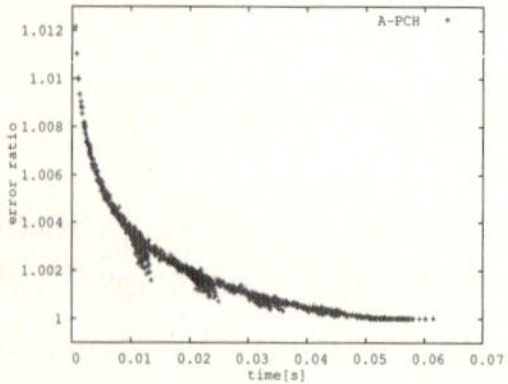

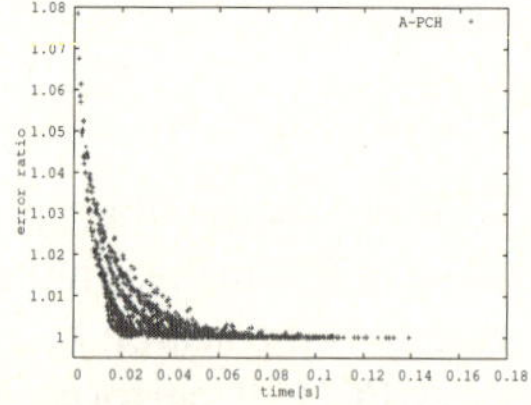

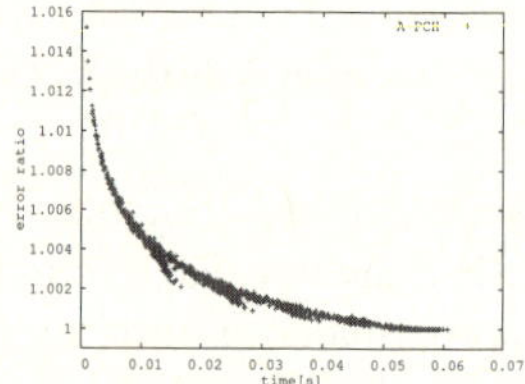

**Fig. 7.** Isotropic Gaussian. Result of A-PCH.

**Fig. 8.** CASPEAL Image database. Result of A-PCH.

**Fig. 9.** Mixture of Gaussians. Result of A-PCH.

mixture of Gaussians, respectively. The experiment result of A-PCH is hidden behind that of PCH. So it is shown in Fig. 7, 8, and 9 independently.

In Fig. 4, the performances seem almost the same between PCH and A-PCH. This is because the data distribution in Fig. 4 is a perfect Gaussian. In Fig. 5, the performances seem slight difference but the best performances between PCH and A-PCH are almost the same.

In Fig. 6, the best performance of A-PCH is slightly better than PCH. This trend can be observed from 0.01[s] to 0.035[s] in search time. This is because the non-uniform numbers of vectors involved in buckets.

Also, in this figure, in the very short time area less than 0.008[s] no PCH plot can be found. This is because the maximum bucket number of A-PCH is bigger than PCH for avoiding the search failures.

## 5    Conclusions

This paper presents Principal Component Hashing (PCH) and its extension Adaptive PCH (A-PCH). Both of them exploit the properties of distributions of stored data. PCH projects data to principal axes, where each axis is decomposed into disjoint buckets involving the same number of stored data. This disjoint decomposition guarantees 1) no search failure and 2) constant search time. In the search stage, a NN candidate set is extracted using hash functions and the hit frequency of hash values is utilized for making initial guess of the tentative NN candidate. By using this initial guess and NN candidates, we can efficiently pick up the approximate NN by pruning the distance computations. PCH assumes that the stored data obey a Gaussian distribution. For removing this assumption, we extended PCH to A-PCH, which can be applied to dataset obeying wide varieties of distributions.

Through extensive experiments, we confirmed that PCH and A-PCH perform better than ANN and standard p-stable LSH without producing search failures. Also A-PCH performs better than PCH for non-Gaussian distributions.

# References


1. Cover, T.M., Hart, P.E.: Nearest neighbor pattern classification. IEEE Transactions on Information Theory IT-13(1), 21–27 (1967)
2. Zhang, Z.: Iterative Point Matching for Registration of Free-Form Curves and Surfaces. Tech. Report INRIA, No 1658 (1992)
3. Bentley, J.L.: Multidimensional binary search trees used for associative searching. Commun. ACM 18(9), 509–517 (1975)
4. Arya, S., Mount, D.M., Netanyahu, N.S., Silverman, R., Wu, A.Y.: An optimal algorithm for approximate nearest neighbor searching. Journal of the ACM 45, 891–923 (1998)
5. ANN: Library for Approximate Nearest Neighbor Searching,
   `http://www.cs.umd.edu/~mount/ANN/`
6. Indyk, P., Motwani, R.: Approximate Nearest Neighbors: Towards Removing the Curse of Dimensionality. In: Proceedings of the 30th ACM Symposium on Theory of Computing (STOC 1998), pp. 604–613 (May 1998)
7. Datar, M., Indyk, P., Immorlica, N., Mirrokni, V.: Locality-Sensitive Hashing Scheme Based on p-Stable Distributions. In: Proceedings of the 20th Annual Symposium on Computational Geometry (SCG 2004) (June 2004)
8. Andoni, A., Indyk, P.: Near-Optimal Hashing Algorithms for Approximate Nearest Neighbor in High Dimensions. In: Proc. of FOCS 2006, pp. 459–468 (2006)
9. Vidal, R.: An algorithm for finding nearest neighbor in (approximately) constant average time. Pattern Recognition Letters 4, 145–158 (1986)
10. Mico, L., Oncina, J., Vidal, E.: A new version of the nearest-neighbor approximating and eliminating search algorithm (AESA) with linear preprocessing time and memory requirements. Pattern Recognition Letters 15, 9–17 (1994)
11. Brin, S.: Near neighbor search in large metric spaces. In: Proc. of 21st Conf. on very large database (VLDB), Zurich, Switzerland, pp. 574–584 (1995)
12. Yianilos, P.Y.: Data structures and algorithms for nearest neighbor search in general metric spaces. In: Proc. of the Fourth Annual ACM-SIAM Symp. on Discrete Algorithms, Austin, TX, pp. 311–321 (1993)

# Novel Approaches for Exclusive and Continuous Fingerprint Classification


Javier A. Montoya-Zegarra[1,2], João P. Papa[2], Neucimar J. Leite[2],
Ricardo da Silva Torres[2], and Alexandre X. Falcão[2]

[1] Computer Engineering Department, Faculty of Engineering, San Pablo Catholic University,
Av. Salaverry 301, Vallecito, Arequipa, Peru
[2] Institute of Computing, State University of Campinas,
Av. Albert Einstein 1216, Campinas, São Paulo, Brazil
{jmontoyaz,papa.joaopaulo}@gmail.com



**Abstract.** This paper proposes novel exclusive and continuous approaches to
guide the search and the retrieval in fingerprint image databases. Both approaches
are useful to perform a coarse level classification of fingerprint images before
fingerprint authentication tasks. Our approaches are characterized by: (1) texture
image descriptors based on pairs of multi-resolution decomposition methods that
encode effectively global and local fingerprint information, with similarity measures used for fingerprint matching purposes, and (2) a novel multi-class object
recognition method based on the Optimum Path Forest classifier. Experiments
were carried out on the standard NIST-4 dataset aiming to study the discriminative and scalability capabilities of our approaches. The high classification rates
allow us demonstrate the feasibility and validity of our approaches for character-
izing fingerprint images accurately.


## 1   Introduction

Fingerprints are considered nowadays one of the most reliable biometric characteristic
for human recognition due to their individuality and persistence [1]. Traditionally, a
fingerprint-recognition system may operate in two distinct modes [2]: verification and
identification. In *verification mode*, the system determines whether an input fingerprint
corresponds to a claimed identity by performing *one-to-one* comparisons. Because of
the discriminating power needs for establishing the subjects identity, local fingerprint
information such as minutiae and, more recently, pores are used for that purposes (they
are believed to be unique across individuals and across fingers of the same individual) [3]. In *identification mode*, the system identifies which database images resemble
best an input fingerprint image without having any kind of a-priori knowledge. To accomplish this task, the system performs *one-to-many* comparisons and uses typically
the global information of fingerprints contained in their central region (ridge and valley
structures).

While systems operating in verification mode establish the identity of an individual,
systems in identification mode are useful to reduce search spaces during the matching phase and therefore play an important role during the recognition process. Despite
the concerted efforts of researchers in fingerprint identification, this objective remains


T. Wada, F. Huang, and S. Lin (Eds.): PSIVT 2009, LNCS 5414, pp. 386–397, 2009.

open [4]. In fact, the popularity of fingerprint-based recognition has led to large-scale databases. While the large size of these collections compromise the retrieval speed, the presence of noise and distortions in fingerprint images may reduce the overall retrieval accuracy. Therefore, both retrieval accuracy and speed are key factors during the fingerprint recognition process.

Roughly speaking, there are two kinds of approaches that can be used to reduce the retrieval space during fingerprint matching, they are namely the exclusive-, and the continuous-fingerprint classification [5]. The former uses some high-level characteristics to partitionate the fingerprint database into mutual exclusive bins. Once the fingerprint query image is classified, it will be searched only in its corresponding bin. In the latter, the fingerprint images are not represented by a single class, but by feature vectors spread over a feature space. Hence, database images that fall within a given radius to the query fingerprints are considered as valid matches. The objective of both approaches is to characterize the fingerprint images by some global information for indexing purposes, instead of offering some kind of discriminatory information for recognition.

In this context, we propose novel exclusive and continuous approaches to guide the search and the retrieval in fingerprint image databases. More specifically, they are used to perform a coarse level classification of fingerprint images before fingerprint recognition tasks. Our approaches are characterized by: (1) texture image descriptors based on multi-resolution decomposition methods that encode effectively global and local fingerprint information, and (2) a novel multi-class object recognition method based on the Optimum Path Forest classifier [6], which models the pattern recognition problem as a optimum partition of the feature space according to some criterion optimality. Since in identification tasks, the similarity measures play also an important role, we show how, in combination, with our fingerprint representation methods, the accuracy of our systems is improved.

The outline of this paper is as follows. In the next section, we introduce the architecture of our system, whilst Section 3 describes how the fingerprint images are represented as feature vectors. Section 4 introduces the Optimum Path Forest classifier method, which is the basis of our exclusive classification method. The experimental setup conducted in our study is presented in Section 5. In section 6, experimental results on the standard Nist4 databse are given and are used to show the high accuracy of our approaches. Finally, some conclusions are drawn in Section 7.

## 2   System Overview

The architecture of our proposed approach, presented in Figure 1, can be divided into two main subsystems, namely, the enrollment- and the query-subsystem. The enrollment-subsystem acquires the information that will be stored in the database for later use. On the other side, the query subsystem is responsible for retrieving similar fingerprints from the database according to the user's fingerprint query image. Our system operates as follows:

1. Enrollment-subsystem: several fingerprint images are first captured (arrow labeled 1 in Figure 1) and a Region of Interest (ROI) within the fingerprint is marked (module 1, arrow 2) by a center point area detection module. The fingerprint ROI is represented by the central part of the fingerprint images, since most of the category

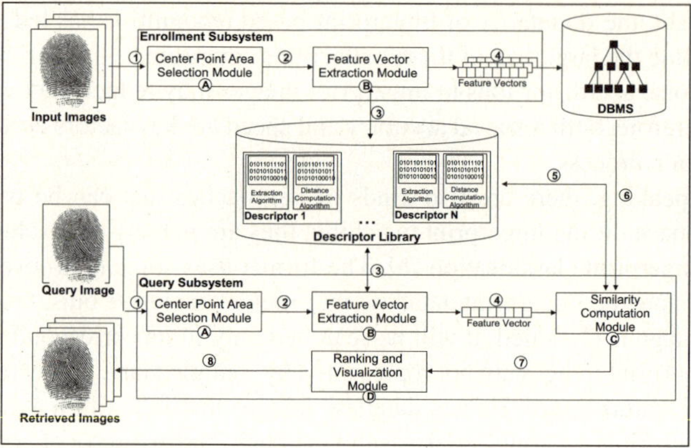

**Fig. 1.** Architecture of the proposed system

information is contained in it. The feature extraction algorithms contained in the descriptor library (module B, arrow 3) are used by the feature extraction module to generate the features (arrow 4) that are stored for later use.

2. Query-subsystem: a fingerprint query image is received as input (arrow 1). Once, the fingerprint ROI is detected (module A, arrow 2) the feature extraction algorithms contained in the descriptor library are used to extract the feature vectors from the query image (module B with arrows 3 and 4, respectively). The query image feature vector is used to rank the database images according to their similarity to the query image (module C). For that purposes, a distance computation algorithm is first selected from the descriptor library (arrow 5), and a subset of feature vectors are retrieved from the database by considering their distance to the query image feature vector (arrow 6). Finally, the most similar database images are ranked (arrow 7) and returned to the user (arrow 8).

## 3 Wavelet-Based Feature Extraction

In our approach, three main steps are needed to compute the feature vectors: (1) construct a circular tesellation around a reference point, (2) decompose the fingerprint images into a set of scale and orientation tunnable components, (3) compute the average absolute deviation ($AAD$) from the tesellated sectors of the decomposed images.

### 3.1 Fingerprint Image Tesellation

To compute the multi-resolution and multi-orientation feature vector, a region of interest (ROI) represented by a circular tesellation around a reference point is used. Let $I(x, y)$ be the gray level image value at pixel $(x, y)$ of a fingerprint of size $M \times N$, and $(x_r, y_r)$ be the location of the reference point, the circular tesellation of radius $r$ is composed by a set of independent sectors $S_{i,j}$ at different bands $j$ defined as [7]:

$$S_{i,j} = \{(x, y)|(i - 1) \cdot b + b_o \leq r < i \cdot b + b_o,$$
$$\theta_j \leq \theta < \theta_{j+1}, 1 \leq x \leq M, 1 \leq y \leq N\} \tag{1}$$

where $\theta_j = (i \bmod k) \cdot (2\pi/k)$, $b$ denotes the bandwidth and $b_o$ is the width of the most inner band around the reference point, and $j = 0 \ldots B \times k - 1$, where $B$, and $k$ represent the number of cocentric bands, and the number of sectors in each band, respectively. Considering that the images we used for test purposes were scanned at 500 dpi, we considered $B = 5$ bands, each of 20 pixels wide, and a total number of $k = 16$ sectors.

### 3.2   Fingerprint Image Decomposition

We exploit the capability of two effective bandpass multiresolution techniques for capturing useful fingerprint information at different scales and orientations. These techniques, include Gabor-, and Steerable-Wavelets [8,9]. Moreover, the use of these image decomposition approaches is motivated by the following reasons: (1) they integrate both multiresolution, and space-frequency properties naturally, therefore both global and local fingerprint information can be captured, (2) their tunable components make them flexible to different computation and recognition needs, and finally (3) they have demonstrated high accuracy in texture analysis applications [8]. The fingerprint $ROI$ is decomposed into a set of orientation, and scale components by using the mentioned image transforms.

### 3.3   Feature Vector Extraction

To generate feature vectors, statistical measures are applied. More precisely, we use the average absolute deviation of the mean value at each sector of the decomposed images. The feature value $F_{i\theta s}$ is computed as follows [7]:

$$
F_{i\theta s} = \frac{1}{K_{i\theta s}} \left( \sum_{(x,y) \in S_{i\theta s}} |S_{i\theta s}(x,y) - S_{i\theta s}^{-}(x,y)| \right) \tag{2}
$$

where $S_{i\theta s}$ represents the sector at position $i$ in the decomposed image at orientation $\theta$, and at scale $s$. $K_{i\theta s}$ is the number of pixels in sector $S_{i\theta s}$, and $S_{i\theta s}^{-}$ represents the mean value of pixels in sector $S_{i\theta s}$. The feature vectors of an input fingerprint image are represented in Figure 2 by using tesellated images with five bands and sixteen sectors.

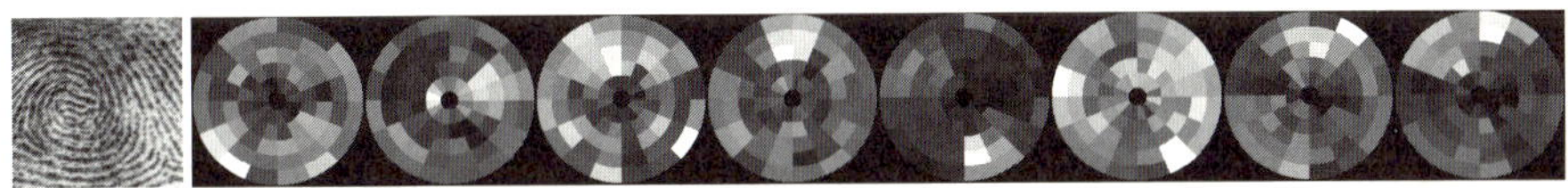

**Fig. 2.** Feature vector representation of a fingerprint image

## 4   Fingerprint Feature Classification

This section aims to present the new approach for pattern recognition called OPF (Optimum-Path Forest). It demonstrated to be generally more efficient than Artificial Neural Networks and Support Vector Machines in some applications [6]. The OPF approach works by modeling the patterns as being nodes of a graph in the feature space, where every pair of nodes is connected by an arc (complete graph). This classifier creates a discrete optimal partition of the feature space such that any unknown sample can be classified according to this partition. This partition is an optimum path forest computed in $\Re^n$ by the image foresting transform (IFT) algorithm [10].

Let $Z_1$ and $Z_2$ be training and test sets with $|Z_1|$ and $|Z_2|$ samples such as feature vectors. Let $\lambda(s)$ be the function that assigns the correct label $i$, $i = 1, 2, \ldots, c$, from class $i$ to any sample $s \in Z_1 \cup Z_2$. Let $S \subset Z_1$ be a set of prototypes of all classes (i.e., key samples that best represent the classes). Let $v$ be an algorithm which extracts $n$ attributes (texture properties) from any sample $s \in Z_1 \cup Z_2$ and returns a vector $v(s) \in \Re^n$. The distance $d(s,t)$ between two samples, $s$ and $t$, is the one between their feature vectors $v(s)$ and $v(t)$ (Figure 3a) (e.g., Euclidean or any valid metric).

Let $(Z_1, A)$ be a complete graph whose the nodes are the samples in $Z_1$. We define a path as being a sequence of distinct samples $\pi = \langle s_1, s_2, \ldots, s_k \rangle$, where $(s_i, s_{i+1}) \in A$ for $1 \leq i \leq k - 1$. A path is said *trivial* if $\pi = \langle s_1 \rangle$. We assign to each path $\pi$ a cost $f(\pi)$ given by a path-cost function $f$. A path $\pi$ is said optimum if $f(\pi) \leq f(\pi')$ for any other path $\pi'$, where $\pi$ and $\pi'$ end at a same sample $s_k$. We also denote by $\pi \cdot \langle s, t \rangle$ the concatenation of a path $\pi$ with terminus at $s$ and an arc $(s, t)$. The OPF algorithm uses the path-cost function $f_{max}$, because of its theoretical properties for estimating optimum prototypes:

$$f_{max}(\langle s \rangle) = \begin{cases} 0 & \text{if } s \in S, \\ +\infty & \text{otherwise} \end{cases}$$

$$f_{max}(\pi \cdot \langle s, t \rangle) = \max\{f_{max}(\pi), d(s, t)\} \tag{3}$$

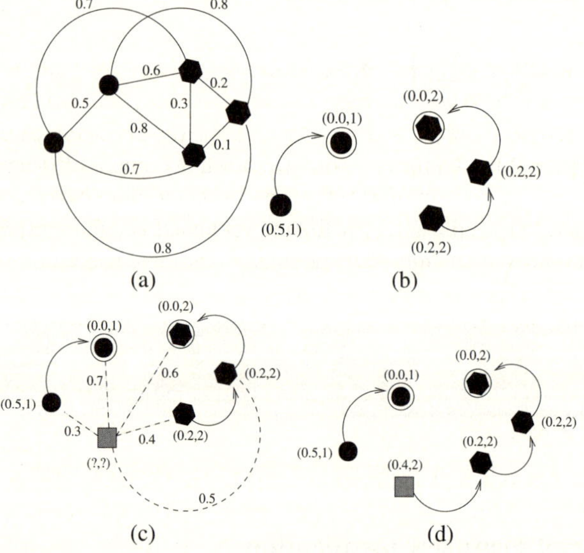

(a)        (b)

(c)        (d)

**Fig. 3.** (a) Complete weighted graph for a simple training set. (b) Resulting optimum-path forest for $f_{max}$ and two given prototypes (circled nodes). The entries $(x, y)$ over the nodes are, respectively, the cost and the label of the samples. The directed arcs indicate the predecessor nodes in the optimum path. (c) Test sample (gray square) and its connections (dashed lines) with the training nodes. (d) The optimum path from the most strongly connected prototype, its label 2, and classification cost 0.4 are assigned to the test sample.

We can observe that $f_{max}(\pi)$ computes the maximum distance between adjacent samples in $\pi$, when $\pi$ is not a trivial path.

The OPF algorithm assigns one optimum path $P^*(s)$ from $S$ to every sample $s \in Z_1$, forming an optimum path forest $P$ (a function with no cycles which assigns to each $s \in Z_1 \backslash S$ its predecessor $P(s)$ in $P^*(s)$ or a marker $nil$ when $s \in S$ (Figure 3b). Let $R(s) \in S$ be the root of $P^*(s)$ which can be reached from $P(s)$. The OPF algorithm computes for each $s \in Z_1$, the cost $C(s)$ of $P^*(s)$, the label $L(s) = \lambda(R(s))$, and the predecessor $P(s)$, as follows.

**Algorithm 1** – OPF ALGORITHM

INPUT:	A $\lambda$-labeled training set $Z_1$, prototypes $S \subset Z_1$ and the pair $(v, d)$ for feature vector and distance computations.

OUTPUT:	Optimum path forest $P$, cost map $C$ and label map $L$.

AUXILIARY: Priority queue $Q$ and cost variable $cst$.

1.	*For each $s \in Z_1 \backslash S$, set $C(s) \leftarrow +\infty$.*
2.	*For each $s \in S$, do*
3.	  └ *$C(s) \leftarrow 0$, $P(s) \leftarrow nil$, $L(s) \leftarrow \lambda(s)$, and insert $s$ in $Q$.*
4.	*While $Q$ is not empty, do*
5.	  *Remove from $Q$ a sample $s$ such that $C(s)$ is minimum.*
6.	  *For each $t \in Z_1$ such that $t \neq s$ and $C(t) > C(s)$, do*
7.	    *Compute $cst \leftarrow \max\{C(s), d(s, t)\}$.*
8.	    *If $cst < C(t)$, then*
9.	      *If $t \in Q$, then remove $t$ from $Q$.*
10.	      └ *$P(t) \leftarrow s$, $L(t) \leftarrow L(s)$, $C(t) \leftarrow cst$, and insert $t$ in $Q$.*

Lines $1 - 3$ initialize maps and insert prototypes in $Q$. The main loop computes an optimum path from $S$ to every sample $s$ in a non-decreasing order of cost (Lines $4 - 10$). At each iteration, a path of minimum cost $C(s)$ is obtained in $P$ when we remove its last node $s$ from $Q$ (Line 5). Lines $8 - 10$ evaluate if the path that reaches an adjacent node $t$ through $s$ is cheaper than the current path with terminus $t$ and update the position of $t$ in $Q$, $C(t)$, $L(t)$ and $P(t)$ accordingly. The label $L(s)$ may be different from $\lambda(s)$, leading to classification errors in $Z_1$. The training finds prototypes with minimum classification errors in $Z_1$. The OPF algorithm works with two phases: training and classification (test), as follows. The prototypes set S are found in the training phase, as described below.

### 4.1  Training Phase

We say that $S^*$ is an optimum set of prototypes when Algorithm 1 minimizes the classification errors for every $s \in Z_1$. Set $S^*$ can be found by exploiting the theoretical relation between *Minimum Spanning Tree* (MST) [11] and optimum path tree for $f_{max}$. The training essentially consists of finding $S^*$ and an OPF classifier rooted at $S^*$.

By computing an MST in the complete graph $(Z_1, A)$, we obtain a connected acyclic graph whose nodes are all samples in $Z_1$ and the arcs are undirected and weighted by the distance $d$ between the adjacent sample feature vectors. This spanning tree is optimum in the sense that the sum of its arc weights is minimum as compared to any other spanning tree in the complete graph. In the MST, every pair of samples is connected by a single path which is optimum according to $f_{max}$. That is, for any given sample $s \in Z_1$, it is possible to direct the arcs of the MST such that the result will be an optimum path tree $P$ for $f_{max}$ rooted at $s$. The optimum prototypes are the closest elements in the MST with different labels in $Z_1$. By removing the arcs between different classes, their adjacent samples become prototypes in $S^*$ and Algorithm 1 can compute an optimum-path forest with high accuracy in $Z_1$ [12].

On the other side, we are currently working with different approaches to choose the prototypes set [13], leading to different accuracies, depending on the application. In all of these approaches, one interesting point is that the number of prototypes encodes how much a feature space is overlapped. If we have a high number of prototypes, this means that, for MST approach, for instance, we have a lot of samples from different classes in the decision region, leading to a high number of misclassifications in the test phase, or even so in the training phase for other classifiers. In the OPF version presente here, a high number of these problematic samples will be prototypes, and can not be misclassified.

### 4.2   Classification

For any sample $t \in Z_2$, the OPF consider all arcs connecting $t$ with samples $s \in Z_1$, as though $t$ were part of the graph (Figure 3c). Considering all possible paths from $S^*$ to $t$, we wish to find the optimum path $P^*(t)$ from $S^*$ and label $t$ with the class $\lambda(R(t))$ of its most strongly connected prototype $R(t) \in S^*$ (Figure 3d). This path can be identified incrementally, by evaluating the optimum cost $C(t)$ as

$$C(t) = \min\{\max\{C(s), d(s,t)\}\}, \ \forall s \in Z_1. \tag{4}$$

Let the node $s^* \in Z_1$ be the one that satisfies the above equation (i.e., the predecessor $P(t)$ in the optimum path $P^*(t)$). Given that $L(s^*) = \lambda(R(t))$, the classification simply assigns $L(s^*)$ as the class of $t$. An error occurs when $L(s^*) \neq \lambda(t)$.

## 5   Experimental Setup

To test our approach, we used the NIST special database 4 (NIST-4) [14]. It comprises 2000 pairs of fingerprint images. The size of each image is $480 \times 512$ pixels with a resolution of 500 DPI. Each fingerprint is assigned into one of the following five classes: Whorl (W), Right Loop (R), Left Loop (L), Arch (A), and Tented Arch (T). To resemble a real distribution of fingerprint classes, the cardinality of the five classes was adapted, leading to a database of 1024 pairs of images (W=27.9%, R=31.7%,L=33.8%,A=3.7%,T=2.9%). The first fingerprint instances are used as image databases, whereas the second ones as query fingerprints.

## 6   Experimental Results

To demonstrate the discriminating power of our classification methods, we conducted two series of experiments. In the first series of experiments (Subsection 6.1), we evaluated the recognition accuracy of the proposed exclusive classification approach, whilst the second series of experiments (Subsection 6.2), are used to evaluate the effectiveness of the continuous classification method.

In both series of experiments, we used different multi-resolution parameters for the Gabor and Steerable Decomposition methods. Our experiments agree with [15] in that, the most relevant textural information in images is contained in the first two levels of decomposition, since little recognition improvement is achieved by varying the number of scales during image decomposition. Therefore, we focus our discussions on image decompositions having ($S = 2$) scales at several orientations ($K = 4, 5, 6, 7, 8$).

The dimensionality of the feature vectors depends on four parameters: the number of scales ($S$) and the number of orientations ($O$) considered during multi-resolution image decomposition, as well as the number of bands ($B$) and sectors ($k$) during fingerprint image tesellation. Thus, the total length of the feature vectors is computed as follows: $O \times S \times B \times k$. An important motivation in our study was to study the impact of different multi-resolution settings in the recognition accuracies of our approaches. By doing this, different computational needs may be attended.

## 6.1  Exclusive Classification Approach

In our experiments, the accuracy is measured by taking into account that the classes may have different sizes in $Z_2$ [6]. In all experiments, the NIST-4 dataset was divided into two parts: a training set $Z_1$ with 50% of the samples and a test set $Z_2$ with also 50% of the samples. These samples were randomly selected and each experiment was repeated 10 times with different sets $Z_1$ and $Z_2$ to compute the mean accuracy.

The accuracy of our exclusive classification approach is summarized in Table 1. It compares the recognition accuracy obtained by the Gabor and Steerable Wavelets using ($S = 2$) scales with different orientations ($K = 4, 5, 6, 7, 8$). Furthermore, for each different pair of parameter combinations, we also computed the recognition accuracy using the following similarity measures: Bray Curtis, Canberra, Euclidean, Manhattan, Square Chord, and Square Chi-Squared distances. The referred Table reveals some relevant information:

1. First, by comparing the recognition accuracies of the Gabor Wavelets and the Steerable Wavelets, one can observe that regardless of the parameter settings, the Steerable Wavelets achieve higher recognition rates.
2. Second, for the different Gabor and Steerable decompositions, the higher recognition accuracies were achieved by using either the Euclidean or the Manhattan distances. This observation is relevant since it allow us, on the one hand, to demonstrate the stability of our image descriptors across the different parameter configurations, on the other, it help us to decide which similarity measure will perform better in most of the cases.
3. Finally, higher recognition rates are obtained by using more number of orientations. These results make intuitive sense since by using more orientations, more information is captured at different angles. However, as one can see, the difference of recognition rates across the different orientations is slight.

By considering the achieved classification rates described in Table 1, we selected the image descriptor with highest recognition rates to display the resultant confusion matrix

**Table 1.** Classification accuracy summarization using the OPF classifier obtained in the NIST-4 database using ($S = 2$) scales with ($K = 4, 5, 6, 7, 8$) orientations for Gabor and Steerable Wavelets

| Metric | S=2,K=4 | | S=2,K=5 | | S=2,K=6 | | S=2,K=7 | | S=2,K=8 | |
|---|---|---|---|---|---|---|---|---|---|---|
| | Gabor | Steer | Gabor | Steer | Gabor | Steer | Gabor | Steer | Gabor | Steer |
| Bray Curtis | 85.83 | **86.73** | 86.13 | **86.99** | 86.57 | **87.34** | 86.31 | **87.09** | 86.01 | **86.98** |
| Canberra | 86.51 | **87.14** | 86.30 | **87.10** | 85.83 | **86.82** | 85.68 | **87.04** | 85.21 | **86.71** |
| Euclidean | 85.45 | **88.61** | 86.92 | **88.03** | 86.19 | **88.76** | 86.17 | **88.51** | 86.07 | **89.64** |
| Manhattan | 85.58 | **87.56** | 87.19 | **88.20** | 85.96 | **88.89** | 87.44 | **89.29** | 86.68 | **89.40** |
| Square Chord | 85.80 | **87.64** | 85.61 | **87.52** | 85.28 | **88.81** | 85.28 | **87.62** | 84.44 | **87.69** |
| Square Chi-Squared | 85.42 | **86.92** | 84.89 | **88.09** | 85.08 | **87.91** | 84.85 | **88.39** | 84.85 | **88.65** |

**Table 2.** (a) Confusion matrix for Steerable Wavelets ($S = 2, K = 8$) with Euclidean distance. (b) Confusion matrix for Gabor Wavelets ($S = 2, K = 8$) with Euclidean distance. (c) Classification results summarization of our approach against the method of Yao et al [16].

(a)

| | W | R | A | L | T |
|---|---|---|---|---|---|
| W | **250** | 10 | 0 | 26 | 0 |
| R | 16 | **293** | 6 | 4 | 6 |
| A | 0 | 4 | **29** | 0 | 4 |
| L | 8 | 18 | 4 | **315** | 2 |
| T | 2 | 6 | 2 | 0 | **19** |

(b)

| | W | R | A | L | T |
|---|---|---|---|---|---|
| W | **242** | 16 | 0 | 26 | 2 |
| R | 0 | **301** | 2 | 16 | 6 |
| A | 0 | 2 | **21** | 14 | 0 |
| L | 2 | 22 | 4 | **315** | 4 |
| T | 0 | 4 | 2 | 8 | **15** |

(c)

| Method | Accuracy |
|---|---|
| RNN [16] | 71.5% |
| SVM [16] | 89.1% |
| SVM+RNN [16] | 90.0% |
| Our approach | 89.64% |

for the five fingerprint classes. This image descriptor corresponds to the combination of Steerable Wavelets for feature extraction with the Euclidean distance for similarity measurement. Tables 2(a) and 2(b) show how Steerable Wavelets outperform Gabor Wavelets on the five fingerprint classes.

We also compared the accuracy of our method against an approach that uses texture information for fingerprint characterization and combines two well known approaches to increase fingerprint classification rates, those approaches are namely support vector machines (SVM) and recursive neural networks (RNN) [16] (See Table 2(c)). From the results, we can see that our method obtains high classification rates without the need of combining two classifiers for achieving higher classification rates.[1]

## 6.2   Continuous Classification Analysis

The accuracy of our continuous classification approach was evaluated by using the *retrieval-accuracy* vs. *penetration-rate* curves [17]. The *retrieval-accuracy* is defined as the average number of correctly retrieved fingerprints, whereas the *penetration-rate* represents the number of images in the database. The search is said to be successful, if one of the retrieved images belongs to the same finger as the query.

---

[1] Note that, the OPF classifier has proven to be at least 10 times faster than the SVM classifier in most of the cases [6].

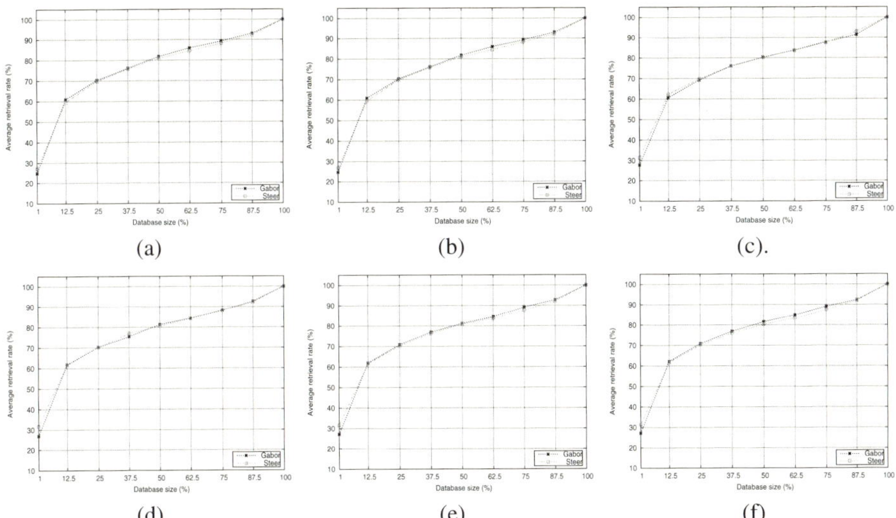

**Fig. 4.** Effectiveness of our various image descriptors. Each subfigure represents the higher retrieval accuracies obtained for each different similarity measure. Average retrieval rates using: (a) Bray Curtis distance. (b) Canberra distance. (c) Euclidean distance. (d) Manhattan distance. (e) Square Chi-Squared distance. (f) Square Chord distance.

In these series of experiments, we wanted to know how well our image descriptors performed in the context of continuous classification schemes, e.g., no a priori information is given about the fingerprint classes, and thus no classifier should be used for recognition purposes. The fingerprints are just represented by feature vectors spread over a feature space. Ideally, feature vectors corresponding to related fingerprints will be close to each other. The accuracy of our continuous classssification approach is ilustrated in Figure 4. Since an image descriptor consists of a pair of feature extraction method with a similarity measure, we show the best combination of similarity measure with parameter settings for both Gabor and Steerable Wavelets.

In our experiments, we varied the size of the fingerprint database by considering different numbers of top retrieved images (*x-axis*). For each different database size, we computed the relevant retrieval average of both feature extraction methods (*y-axis*). In the ideal case, a perfect retrieval accuracy is said to be achieved, if the average retrieval rate is equal to $100\%$ by considering just $1\%$ of the database size.

From the set of Figures, one can see that both feature extraction methods performs almost the same. However, Steerable Wavelets perform better than Gabor Wavelets for almost each different similarity measure. As in the exclusive classification approach, the higher accuracies were achieved by using the Euclidean distance. This means that our image descriptors perform well for both exclusive and continuous applications. Furthermore, as it can be noticed, by just using $12.5\%$ of the images during the retrieval phase, our descriptors are able to identificate more than $60\%$ of the fingerprint images. At the same time, an accuracy of almost $80\%$ is achicved by considering just $37.5\%$ of the database size. These results are very promising and demonstrate the effectiveness of our approach.

## 7    Conclusions

In this paper a new scheme for fingerprint classification was proposed, that is suitable for both exclusive and continuous classification domains. Its main features include: (1) a set of texture-based image descriptors composed by feature extraction methods and similariy measures, and (2) a novel multi-class recognition method based on Optimum Path Forest.

The feature representation methods exploit the discriminability properties of two multi-resolution approaches to capture relevant fingerprint texture information. Furthermore, an importat key characteristic of our representation methods is that they enconde both global and local fingerprint information into a single feature vector. The global information of fingerprint images is captured by a set of image representations located at different scales and orientations, whilst the local information is captured in each decomposed image by a tesellation grid. By doing this, reliable and discriminant fingerprint characteristics are captured. Since similarity measurement for feature representations plays also an important role in the recognition rates, we evaluated how different combinations of feature representations with similarity measures affect the classification rates. From our results, we conclude that our feature representation methods are benefited by using the Euclidean or Manhattan distances for similarity measurement purposes.

In addition, our system adopted a novel approach for pattern classification based on Optimum Path Forest, which finds prototypes with minimum classification errors in the training set. By combining the discriminating power of our image descriptors and classifier, our approaches achieved high classification rates.

## Acknowledgments

This work was partially supported by CAPES, FAPESP, CNPQ, and Microsoft Research.

## References

1. Pankanti, S., Prabhakar, S., Jain, A.K.: On the individuality of fingerprints. IEEE Transactions on Pattern Analysus and Machine Intelligence 24, 1010–1025 (2002)
2. Jain, A.K., Ross, A., Pankanti, S.: Biometrics: A tool for information security. IEEE Transactions on Information Forensics and Security 1, 125–143 (2006)
3. Jain, A.K., Chen, Y., Demirkus, M.: Pores and ridges: High-resolution fingerprint matching using level 3 features. IEEE Transactions on PAMI 29, 15–27 (2007)
4. Yager, N., Amin, A.: Fingerprint classification: a review. Pattern Anal. Appl. 7, 77–93 (2004)
5. Lumini, A., Maio, D., Maltoni, D.: Continuous versus exclusive classification for fingerprint retrieval. Pattern Recognition Letters 18, 1027–1034 (1997)
6. Papa, J., Falcão, A., Suzuki, C., Mascarenhas, N.: A discrete approach for supervised pattern recognition. In: Brimkov, V.E., Barneva, R.P., Hauptman, H.A. (eds.) IWCIA 2008. LNCS, vol. 4958, pp. 136–147. Springer, Heidelberg (2008)
7. Jain, A.K., Prabhakar, S., Hong, L., Pankanti, S.: Filterbank-based fingerprint matching. IEEE Transactions on Image Processing 9, 846–859 (2000)
8. Manjunath, B.S., Ma, W.Y.: Texture features for browsing and retrieval of image data. IEEE Transactions on Pattern Analysis and Machine Intelligence 18, 837–842 (1996)

9. Portilla, J., Simoncelli, E.P.: A parametric texture model based on joint statistics of complex wavelet coefficients. International Journal of Computer Vision 40, 49–70 (2000)

10. Falcão, A., Stolfi, J., Lotufo, R.: The image foresting transform: theory, algorithms, and applications. IEEE Trans. Pattern Anal. Mach. Intell. 26, 19–29 (2004)

11. Cormen, T., Leiserson, C., Rivest, R.: Introduction to Algorithms. MIT Press, Cambridge (1990)

12. Cousty, J., Bertrand, G., Najman, L., Couprie, M.: Watersheds, minimum spanning forests, and the drop of water principle, École Supérieure d'Ingénieurs (2007)

13. Papa, J., Falcão, A.: A new variant of the optimum-path forest classifier. In: 4th International Symposium on Visual Computing (accepted, 2008)

14. Watson, C., Wilson, C.: Nist special database 4, fingerprint database. U.S. National Institute of Standards and Technology (1992)

15. Do, M.N., Vetterli, M.: Wavelet-based texture retrieval using generalized gaussian density and kullback-leibler distance. IEEE Transactions on Image Processing 11, 146–158 (2002)

16. Yao, Y., Marcialis, G.L., Pontil, M., Frasconi, P., Roli, F.: Combining flat and structured representations for fingerprint classification with recursive neural networks and support vector machines. Pattern Recognition 36, 397–406 (2003)

17. Cappelli, R., Lumini, A., Maio, D., Maltoni, D.: Fingerprint classification by directional image partitioning. IEEE Trans. Pattern Anal. Mach. Intell. 21, 402–421 (1999)

# A Novel Visual Speech Representation and HMM Classification for Visual Speech Recognition


Dahai Yu, Ovidiu Ghita, Alistair Sutherland[*], and Paul F. Whelan

Vision Systems Group, School of Electronic Engineering and Computing
Dublin City University, Dublin, Ireland
dahai.yu2@mail.dcu.ie



**Abstract.** This paper presents the development of a novel visual speech recognition (VSR) system based on a new representation that extends the standard viseme concept (that is referred in this paper to as Visual Speech Unit (VSU)) and Hidden Markov Models (HMM). The visemes have been regarded as the smallest visual speech elements in the visual domain and they have been widely applied to model the visual speech, but it is worth noting that they are problematic when applied to the continuous visual speech recognition. To circumvent the problems associated with standard visemes, we propose a new visual speech representation that includes not only the data associated with the articulation of the visemes but also the transitory information between consecutive visemes. To fully evaluate the appropriateness of the proposed visual speech representation, in this paper an extensive set of experiments have been conducted to analyse the performance of the visual speech units when compared with that offered by the standard MPEG-4 visemes. The experimental results indicate that the developed VSR application achieved up to 90% correct recognition when the system has been applied to the identification of 60 classes of VSUs, while the recognition rate for the standard set of MPEG-4 visemes was only in the range 62-72%.

**Keywords:** Visual Speech Recognition, Visual Speech Unit, Viseme, EMPCA, HMM, Dynamic Time Warping.


## 1 Introduction

Automatic Visual Speech Recognition (VSR) plays an important role in the development of many multimedia systems such as audio-visual speech recognition (AVSR) [1], mobile phone applications, human-computer interaction and sign language recognition [2]. Visual speech recognition involves the process of interpreting the visual information contained in a visual speech sequence in order to extract the information necessary to establish the communication at perceptual level between humans and computers. The availability of a system that is able to interpret the visual speech is opportune since it can improve the overall accuracy of audio or hand recognition systems when they are used in noisy environments.

---

[*] Corresponding author.


T. Wada, F. Huang, and S. Lin (Eds.): PSIVT 2009, LNCS 5414, pp. 398–409, 2009.

The task of solving visual speech recognition using computers proved to be more complex than initially envisioned. Since the first automatic visual speech recognition system was reported by Petajan [7] in 1984, abundant VSR approaches have been reported in the computer vision literature over the last two decades. While the systems reported in the literature have been in general concerned with advancing theoretical solutions to various subtasks associated with the development of VSR systems, this makes their categorization difficult. However, the major trends in the development of VSR can be divided into three distinct categories: feature extraction, visual speech representation and classification. In this regard, the feature extraction techniques that have been applied in the development of VSR systems can be divided into two main categories, shape-based and intensity based. In general, the shape-based feature extraction techniques attempt to identify the lips in the image based either on geometrical templates that encode a standard set of mouth shapes [17] or on the application of active contours [3]. Since these approaches require extensive training to sample the spectrum of mouth shapes, recently the feature extraction has been carried out in the intensity domain. Using this approach, the lips are extracted in each frame based on the colour information and the identified image sub-domain detailing the lips is compressed to obtain a low-dimensional representation.

A detailed review on the research on VSR indicates that numerous methods have been proposed to address the problems of feature extraction and visual speech classification, but very limited research has been devoted to the identification of the most discriminative visual speech elements that are able to model the speech process in the continuous visual domain. Thus, most works on VSR focused on the identification of visemes, but the visemes identification in continuous visual speech proved problematic since visemes have a limited visual support when analysed for continuous lip motions. Consequently, different visemes may overlap in the feature space, a fact that makes their recognition difficult.

To address the problems associated with the standard viseme recognition approach a new set of visual speech elements for VSR, referred to as Visual Speech Units (VSU), is proposed in this paper. This new visual speech representation has been included in the development of a VSR system that consists of four major components:

- Intensity-based lip segmentation.
- Feature extraction using Expectation Maximization PCA (EM-PCA).
- Visual Speech Units speech modelling.
- Visual Speech Units registration and HMM classification.

The main objective of this paper is to demonstrate that the inclusion of this new visual speech representation in the development of VSR leads to improved performance when compared with the performance offered by the standard set of MPEG-4 visemes.

## 2 Lip Segmentation and EM-PCA Manifold Representation

### 2.1 Lip Segmentation

To enhance the presence of the skin in the image, the pseudo-hue [5] component is calculated from the RGB representation for each frame in the video sequence. The

# Shape Reconstruction by Combination of Structured-Light Projection and Photometric Stereo Using a Projector-Camera System

## High Quality Reproduction of a Virtual Reflectance Property on a Real Object Surface


Tomoya Okazaki, Takayuki Okatani, and Koichiro Deguchi

Graduate School of Information Sciences, Tohoku University
6-6-01 Aza Aoba, Aramaki, Aoba-ku, Sendai, Japan
{okazaki,okatani,kodeg}@fractal.is.tohoku.ac.jp
http://www.fractal.is.tohoku.ac.jp



**Abstract.** In this paper, we present a method for synthesizing virtual appearance of an object by projecting images onto the surface of the object using projectors. The object surface is assumed to have a known diffuse reflectance property; its shape is allowed to have an arbitrary shape. Using a system consisting of multiple projectors and a camera, the method first estimates their internal and external parameters as well as the object surface based on the projection of structured patterns, and then measures surface normals by the method of photometric stereo that uses the same projectors as point sources of illumination. By enabling highly accurate calibration of the projectors as well as reconstruction of the object shape and also by reducing the random errors in surface normals that significantly affect final appearance, it is made possible to synthesize high-quality appearance associated with an arbitrary virtual reflectance property.

**Keywords:** Projector-camera, autocalibration, photometric stereo, augmented reality.


## 1  Introduction

There are several studies of the methods for realizing various visual effects by projecting images onto the surfaces of real-world objects using image projectors[1,2]. Their potential applications include virtual museums, industrial designs, and entertainment uses. Suppose as an example their applications to the design of products such as automobiles and mobile phones; these products have curved surfaces with complicated surface reflectance (e.g., metallic color coating of automobiles). Currently, the designing process of these products usually requires trial productions; it is inevitable to examine how the designed product actually looks in the real world. Even if state-of-the-art CG rendering algorithms are used, the trial productions are necessary because of the limitation of the quality


T. Wada, F. Huang, and S. Lin (Eds.): PSIVT 2009, LNCS 5414, pp. 410–422, 2009.

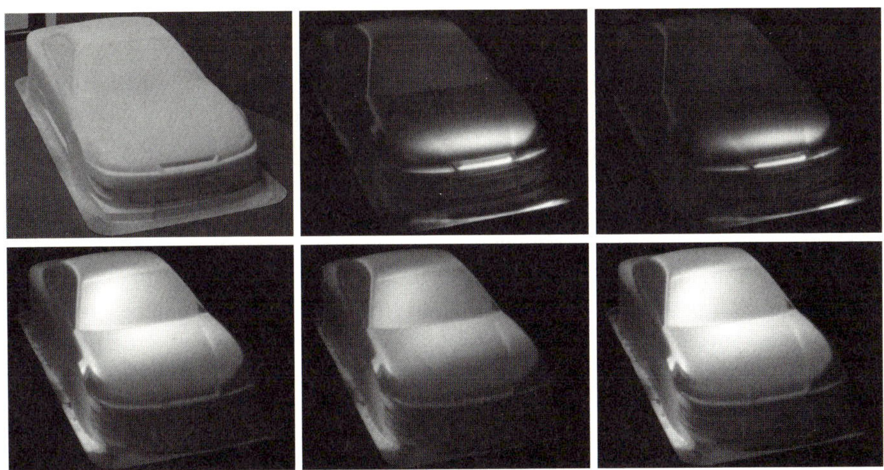

**Fig. 1.** A projector-camera system virtually reproduces arbitrary reflectance properties on a real-world object

of CG images and/or two-dimensional image displays. Therefore, it could drastically reduce the labor and time required if a projector-based system enables the designers to see the precise appearance of the product being designed in front of them; for example, it can immediately reflects the designer's choice of surface reflectance.

As mentioned earlier, there are similar methods that alter the appearance of real objects by using projectors. Raskar et al. present a method for visually reproducing apparent motion of a target object by changing the projected pattern[3]. Grossberg et al. and Fujii et al. present methods for realizing a desired appearance for a textured object by photometric compensation[4,5]. Yamamoto et al. present a method for reproducing an appearance of a real object that is the same as a reference object by image projection[6]. The purpose of this study is to highly accurately reproduce any virtual reflectance property on a real object surface that have an arbitrary shape by image projection.

In this paper, we consider a system consisting of multiple projectors and one and more cameras. We then assume dedicated objects for appearance synthesis, such that their surface has a simple reflectance property dominated by diffuse reflectance. As its realistic application, we consider a system for assisting a purchaser of an automobile in selecting a color out of a number of candidates. By using a scaled model of the automobile, the system synthesizes its appearance in a more realistic manner than the conventional presentation methods (e.g., photographs in brochures) so that the viewer can experience the real appearance(Fig.1).

In order to synthesize a desired appearance by our system, besides the virtual reflectance property to be realized (which is given by a BRDF), it is necessary to acquire 1) the three dimensional shape of the object, 2) the relative poses of the projectors, and 3) the real reflectance property of the object surface. It is especially important to acquire precise information as to (1) and (2). For this purpose, as was done in some of the previous studies, it makes sense to use the same projectors used for the appearance synthesis also for measuring the object shape; the projectors project structured light (e.g. stripe patterns) onto the object surface and then its shape is reconstructed based on stereo in combination with a camera.

In this paper, using the same system configuration, we propose a systematic method of acquiring precise information on (1) and (2); its purpose is to maximize the visual quality of the synthesized appearance. Considering the above applications, the visual quality must be the main concern. (In our opinion, it seems to have been loosely considered in previous studies.) Toward this end, we propose a) to perform the autocalibration of the projector-camera system that can accurately reconstruct the object shape as well as the poses of the projectors and cameras, and b) to use the method of photometric stereo [7], along with the stereo-based shape reconstruction by structured light projection, to obtain accurate normals of the object surface. The method makes full use of the fact that the system has multiple projectors. The existence of multiple projectors is inevitable to eliminate or minimize the shadowed areas on the object surface in the appearance synthesis.

Since the object shape is already reconstructed by the stereo-based method that uses structured light projection, it might appear awkward to further use photometric stereo to compute the surface normals. The necessity for photometric stereo stems from the fact that when using the surface normals computed from the reconstructed shape, it is quite difficult to synthesize high-quality appearance. There are two reasons for the difficulty. One is that since the surface normal is the derivative of the surface shape, only a slight error of the reconstructed shape results in a relatively large error in the surface normal. The other is that the errors in the surface normals affect the synthesized appearance to a great extent. This is significant especially when the desired virtual reflectance includes specular components (this is almost always the case). More specifically, the highlights of the synthesized appearance will have distorted erroneous shapes in the presence of small random errors of the surface normals. On the other hand, photometric stereo directly computes the surface normals from image brightness; differentiation is not necessary. Since the estimated surface normals have direct relation to the appearance of the object, it is more appropriate to synthesize virtual appearance. Combining depths and normals for better shape reconstruction has been proposed by Nehab et al.[8]. In their method, there is a risk that small shapes are lost since it smooths the reconstructed shape to remove a slight error. In contrast, the shape is not smoothed in our method, since the surface normals are connected based on the nature of the reconstructed shapes that their errors are random. Therefore, small shapes can be maintained. Details are described in Sec.2.5.

# 2  Method for Acquiring Necessary Information for Appearance Synthesis

## 2.1  Problem Formulation

The system consists of three and more projectors and one camera. We assume the external parameters of the projectors and the camera to be unknown and their internal parameters to be known except for their focal lengths. As in the case of multi-camera systems, this setting is based on the fact that the focal lengths will vary whenever reconfiguring the system, whereas the other internal parameters are assumed to be constant (therefore it is sufficient to calibrate once).

## 2.2  Establishing Point Correspondences by the Phase Shifting Method

The method starts with establishing the point correspondences between each projector image and the associated camera image using the phase shifting method [9]. While a projector projects sinusoidal brightness pattern onto the object surface, the camera captures its image, from which the phase of the initial sinusoidal pattern is calculated. In order to stably perform the phase unwrapping, the object shape is roughly estimated by projecting binary patterns onto the surface. This process is performed in turn for each of the projectors.

## 2.3  Autocalibration-Based Shape Reconstruction

If the internal and external parameters of the projectors and the camera are *all* unknown, it is only possible to obtain the projective reconstruction from the point correspondences. However, since the focal lengths are only unknown internal parameters, the projective ambiguity can be removed, as is well known for multi-camera systems [10].

To be specific, we first estimate the fundamental matrix between each projector and the camera from a decimated set of the point correspondences obtained above. Then, applying the method of [11], the fundamental matrix is decomposed, and the focal lengths of the projectors and the camera are calculated. From this, the external parameters of the projector relative to the camera are determined.

Using these estimates as initial values, the method of bundle adjustment is performed. Since the corresponding points in the projector image are not measurements but true values, we minimize the sum of the squared distance between the measurements and their estimates with respect to the corresponding points in the camera images. The parameters to be determined in the optimization are the focal lengths and the external parameters of the projectors and the camera and the depths of the points. The overall scaling ambiguity of the system is constrained by setting the distance from the first projector to the camera to be 1.

Finally, using the estimated poses of the projectors and the camera, the object shape is reconstructed in a dense manner from the all point correspondences. The estimated object shape and projector poses are represented in a single common Euclidean coordinate system.

## 2.4  Recovering the Surface Normals by Photometric Stereo

Then, using the same projectors as simple illumination sources, the method of photometric stereo is applied. Photometric stereo [7] estimates the normal of an object surface from its multiple images taken under different illuminations, and it assumes the illuminant directions to be known. In our case, we have obtained the projector poses relative to the object surface as above and use them here. When projecting an uni-colored pattern onto the object surface from a projector, we assume it to be a point source of illumination; the position of the point source coincides with the projector position. Although the projectors have projection optics, this is a good approximation when the projectors are distant from the object surface.

The same camera captures three and more shaded images for different illuminant directions by projecting an uni-colored pattern in turn from each projector. Let $b_{pi}$ be the image brightness of image point $i$ under the illuminant direction $p$. Assuming the surface reflectance of the object to be Lambertian, we have $b_{pi} = \rho_i \mathbf{n}_i^\top \mathbf{l}_p$, where $\rho_i$ is the albedo, $\mathbf{n}_i$ is the surface normal, and $\mathbf{l}_p$ is the orientation of the projector $p$ from the surface point of interest multiplied by the strength of the illumination. The brightness $b_{1i}, \ldots, b_{mi}^\top$ for $m$ different illuminant directions $(p = 1, \ldots, m)$ are given by

$$\begin{bmatrix} b_{1i} \\ \vdots \\ b_{mi} \end{bmatrix} = \begin{bmatrix} \mathbf{l}_1^\top \\ \vdots \\ \mathbf{l}_m^\top \end{bmatrix} (\rho_i \mathbf{n}_i). \tag{1}$$

The relative strengths of the projector light sources are calibrated in advance. Then, $[\mathbf{l}_1, \cdots, \mathbf{l}_m]^\top$ can be calculated using also the estimated projector poses relative to the object surface. Solving Eq.(1) in a least squares sense with respect to the unknown $\rho_i \mathbf{n}_i$, the surface normal $\mathbf{n}_i$ and the albedo $\rho_i$ are determined. When the surface reflectance is not Lambertian but it is known, these can be determined by performing nonlinear optimization.

As will be observed later, as compared with those computed from the surface shape by difference approximation, the surface normals thus obtained tend to have much smaller random errors between neighboring surface points. This local accuracy of the estimation is the main reason that we employ here the method of photometric stereo. On the other hand, it is unavoidable that the estimated surface normals have systematic biases due to the modeling errors of the real reflectance property of the object and interreflections, which is a well known limitation of photometric stereo. In the next subsection, we present a method for correcting such systematic biases by estimating the real reflectance property.

## 2.5    Correction of Surface Normals Based on Recovered 3D Shape

As described above, the surface normals obtained from photometric stereo will have small random errors but large systematic errors. The main source of the systematic errors is the modeling error of the real reflectance property of the object. Thus, the systematic errors can be mitigated by estimating the real reflectance property from the measured data.

Since we wish to obtain accurate surface normal after all, instead of estimating the reflectance property itself, we estimate here nonlinear transform from the normal $\mathbf{n}$ that has been obtained by assuming Lambertian reflectance to the normal $\tilde{\mathbf{n}}$ that would be obtained by assuming true reflectance. Namely, $\tilde{\mathbf{n}} = F(\mathbf{n})$. We then represent $F$ by $k$-th order polynomial as

$$\tilde{n}_x = F_x(\mathbf{n}) = \sum_{\alpha=0}^{k}\sum_{\beta=0}^{k}\sum_{\gamma=0}^{k} a_{\alpha\beta\gamma} n_x^{\alpha} n_y^{\beta} n_z^{\gamma}, \tag{2a}$$

$$\tilde{n}_y = F_y(\mathbf{n}) = \sum_{\alpha=0}^{k}\sum_{\beta=0}^{k}\sum_{\gamma=0}^{k} b_{\alpha\beta\gamma} n_x^{\alpha} n_y^{\beta} n_z^{\gamma}, \tag{2b}$$

$$\tilde{n}_z = F_z(\mathbf{n}) = \sum_{\alpha=0}^{k}\sum_{\beta=0}^{k}\sum_{\gamma=0}^{k} c_{\alpha\beta\gamma} n_x^{\alpha} n_y^{\beta} n_z^{\gamma}. \tag{2c}$$

Then, we estimate the coefficients $a_{\alpha\beta\gamma}$, $b_{\alpha\beta\gamma}$, and $c_{\alpha\beta\gamma}$ for.

In order to estimate these parameters, the correct surface normal $\tilde{\mathbf{n}} = [\tilde{x}, \tilde{y}, \tilde{z}]^{\top}$ is necessary. We use the surface normals obtained by differentiating the recovered 3D shape. As mentioned earlier, these normals have large random errors, whereas they have only small systematic errors. Then, we estimate the parameter by minimizing the sum of the Euclidean distance between $\mathbf{n}$ and $\tilde{\mathbf{n}}$ (i.e. the normals obtained from the 3D shape) over the entire object surface:

$$(\tilde{n}_x - n_x)^2 + (\tilde{n}_y - n_y)^2 + (\tilde{n}_z - n_z)^2. \tag{3}$$

Since the number of data participating in this minimization is much larger than the degrees of freedom of the parameters to be estimated, this minimization is expected to yield good parameter estimates. The parameter estimates are obtained by a linear least squares method.

## 2.6    On the Calibration of Projector Image Center

We assume for both the camera and the projectors that the internal parameters but the focal length are all known. Thus, it is necessary to estimate them in advance. For the camera, it is possible to use the existing calibration tools such as Camera Calibration Toolkit for Matlab. For the projectors, we employ the following calibration procedures.

First, the aspect ratio of an image pixel is determined from the factory sheet of the imaging engine of the projector. We then assume the skew to be 0. With respect to the principal point, it has usually a vertical offset for ordinary projectors such as PC projectors. Thus, a special care is necessary to determine it. In our experience, it is easy and accurate to use the focus-of-expansion (FOE) of the projected image when manually varying the zoom value of the projector. The FOE of the projected image gives the projection of the image point that is on the optical axis of the projector lens. Since this image point coincides with the principal point, by identifying the projection of this image point and transferring this to the projector image, we obtain the principal point. The transfer (i.e., back-projection) is given by a 2D projective transformation (or a planar homography), which can be estimated by using a stationary camera. The identification of the FOE is also possible by using the same camera.

## 3   Computation of Projector Images

A virtual appearance is reproduced by projecting images from the projectors onto the surface of the real object. The images that are input to the projectors are computed in the following manner.

Figure 2 shows the geometry of a projector and the object surface. Suppose a particular image pixel of the projector and its corresponding point (i.e., its projection) on the object surface. Let $L_p$ be the radiance of this projector pixel in the direction of the projector lens and $E_o$ be the irradiance of the surface point. (We assume here there is no (real) ambient illumination in space.)

Further let $I_p$ be the image brightness of this projector pixel. The optical system of a projector is usually designed so that when an image is projected onto a fronto-parallel screen, the irradiance ($E'_o$) of the screen is proportional to $I_p$. By assuming the distance to the screen to be $r_0$, we have

$$I_p(\propto E'_o) \propto L_p \left( \frac{\pi d^2}{4 r_0^2} \right) \cos^4 \theta. \tag{4}$$

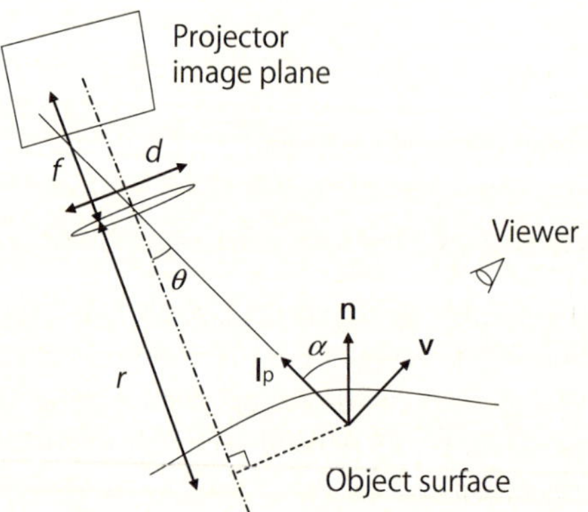


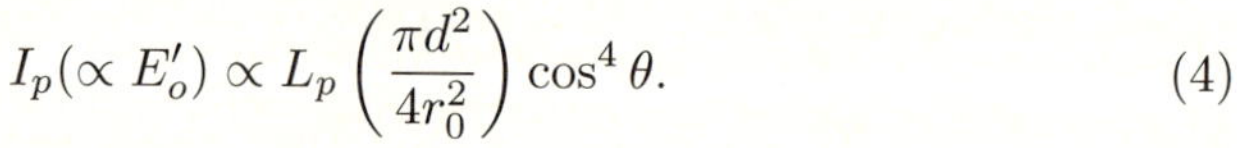
**Fig. 2.** Geometry of a projector and the object surface

The cosine fourth law may, in reality, not be accurate considering the optical construction of projectors. In that case, we will need to photometrically calibrate the projectors.

Let $\mathbf{X}_v$ be the spatial position of the viewer eye that we want to present the virtual appearance. We denote the true BRDF of the object surface by $f_o(\tilde{\mathbf{v}}; \tilde{\mathbf{l}}_p)$, where $\tilde{\mathbf{v}}$ and $\tilde{\mathbf{l}}_p$ indicate the direction of the viewer $\mathbf{X}_v$ and the projector lens, respectively, in the local surface coordinates of the surface point of interest. When the incident light from the projector to the surface point reflects in the direction of $\tilde{\mathbf{v}}$, the corresponding radiance $L_o$ can be written as $L_o = f_o(\tilde{\mathbf{v}}; \tilde{\mathbf{l}}_p)E_o$. Therefore, by combining this with Eq.(4), the brightness of the projector pixel to realize the desired radiance $\hat{L}_o$ in the direction of the viewer $\mathbf{X}_v$ is given by

$$I_p \propto \frac{\hat{L}_o r^2 \cos\theta}{f_o(\tilde{\mathbf{v}}; \tilde{\mathbf{l}}_p) \cos\alpha}. \tag{5}$$

The projector image that realizes a desired appearance of the object is computed in the following steps. First, virtual illumination and virtual BRDF of the object are selected. The directions of the virtual illumination and viewer position at each surface point are computed using the recovered 3D shape of the object. In order to convert these directions to the representation in the surface local coordinates, the surface normals estimated by the proposed method are used. Then, the desired radiance $\hat{L}_o$ that we wish to present to the viewer is determined. This is substituted into Eq.(5), where $r$ and $\theta$ are computed from the 3D shape, and $\alpha$ is computed from the surface normal. With respect to the real reflectance $f_o(\tilde{\mathbf{v}}; \tilde{\mathbf{l}}_p) = 1$, we use a mathematical model in the experiments shown in the next section, which approximates the reflectance of the object surface material. It could be possible to derive the reflectance from the estimated nonlinear transform $F$ in the method presented in 2.5 and to use it as $f_o(\tilde{\mathbf{v}}; \tilde{\mathbf{l}}_p) = 1$ here.

Following these steps, the brightness $I_p$ of the image that is input to the projector is determined. Note that when the projector and the object surface is sufficiently distant, it is a good approximation to assume the projector to be a point light source. We assumed so in the experiments in what follows.

## 4   Experimental Results

We conducted experiments to test the efficacy of the proposed method. Fig.3 shows the overview of the experimental setup. The system consists of four NEC VT595 projectors and one DELL 3400 MP projector (all have $1024 \times 768$ pixels) and a Point Grey Research Frea2 camera ($1024 \times 768$ pixels) with a Fujinon HF12.5SA-1 lens. We used several objects that have diffuse reflectance properties; they are assumed to be Lambertian.

The proposed method starts with the pattern projection shown in Fig.3 to obtain the point correspondences. Then, the focal lengths as well as the external parameters of the projectors and the camera is estimated; the result is shown in Fig.4. Using these parameters, the shape of the object is reconstructed. Next,

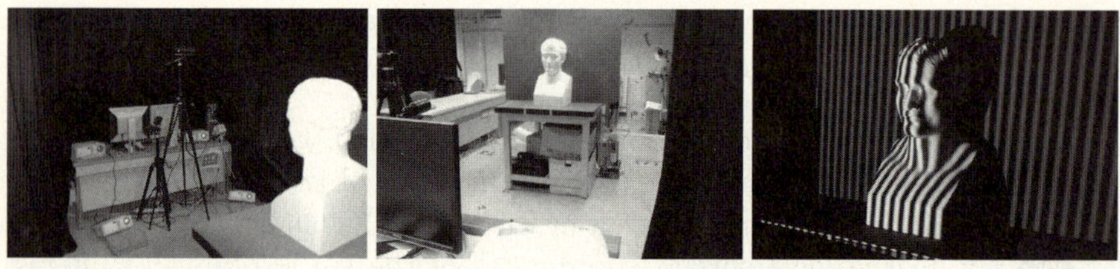

**Fig. 3.** The experimental setup (left and middle) and the structured pattern projection (right)

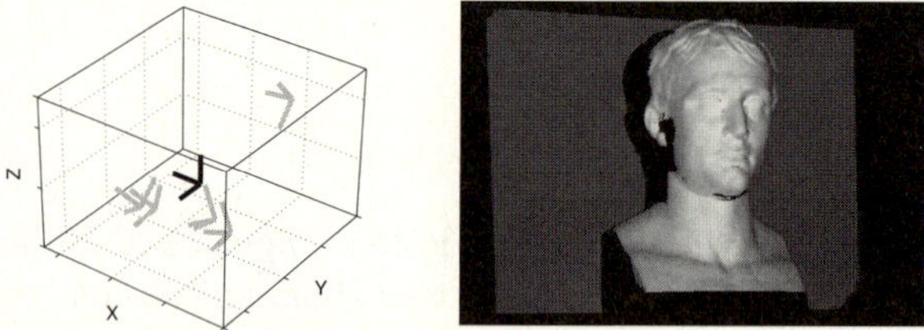

**Fig. 4.** A result of the autocalibration-based shape reconstruction. Left: Estimated poses of the projectors and the camera. Right: Reconstructed shape.

the surface normals are computed by the photometric stereo method. While the five projectors project a uni-colored pattern in turn, the camera captures the images, as shown in Fig.5.

In order to demonstrate the efficacy of using photometric stereo in combination with the (geometric) stereo-based shape reconstruction, we show in Fig.6 the surface normals computed from the reconstructed shape by difference approximation and those obtained by the proposed method. In the images, the $x$ components of the surface normals are represented as brightness. They are mostly identical when globally comparing the two images. However, when comparing in a finer scale, it is observed that they are considerably different. There exist several artifacts in the surface normals obtained from the reconstructed shape The possible causes for the artifacts are the errors of the phase estimation in the phase shifting method, aliasing due to the quantization of the projector and the camera images, etc. They are not easy to eliminate by, for example, spatially smoothing the surface normals, as will be demonstrated below.

Using the surface shape along with precise normals thus obtained, arbitrary surface reflectance can be virtually reproduced on the object surface; the images to be projected are synthesized according to the physics-based model [2] between a projector image and the projected image on the object. In the experiments, we reproduced several reflectance properties based on the dichromatic reflectance model, where the diffuse component is given by the Lambertian model and the specular component is given by Phong or Torrance-Sparrow models; their model parameters were changed within certain ranges. When synthesizing the appearance, arbitrary virtual illumination can be used.

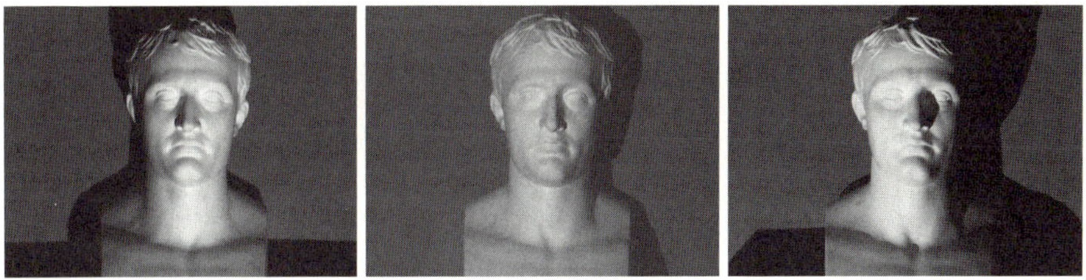

**Fig. 5.** Selected three images used for photometric stereo

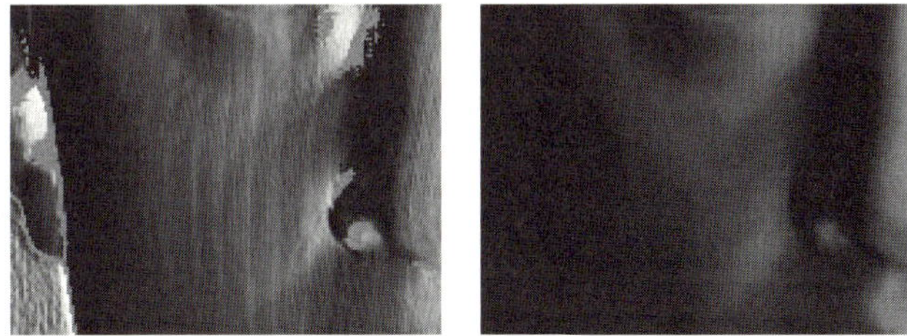

**Fig. 6.** Visualized surface normals. Left: When computed from the shape. Right: Proposed method.

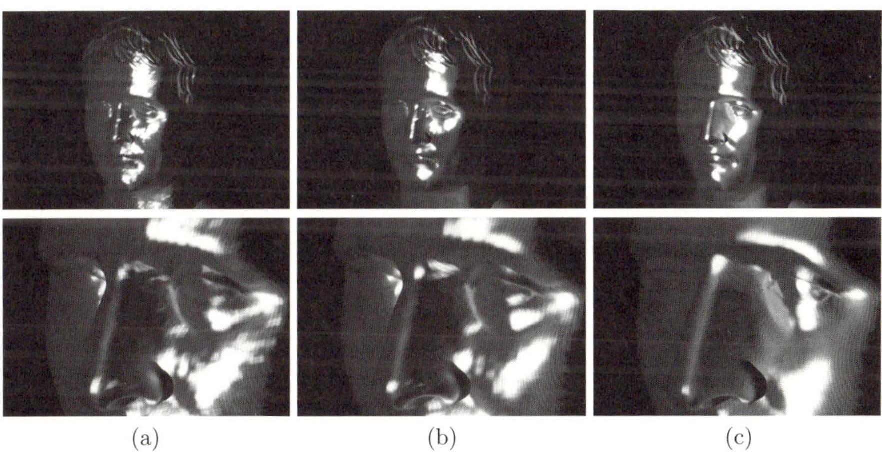

(a)        (b)        (c)

**Fig. 7.** Comparison of the synthesized appearances. (a) 3x3 filter. (b) 5x5 filter. (c) Proposed method.

Again, in order to demonstrate the efficacy of the proposed method, we show in Fig.7 the synthesized appearances between the case where the surface normal is computed from the reconstructed shape and the case where they are estimated by the proposed method. The images in column (a) and (b) show the results when the surface normals are computed from the reconstructed shape and then

**Fig. 8.** Left: An overview of a working system of the virtual reflectance reproduction. A camera and two projectors were used in the calibration stage, and they are removed in the stage of virtual appearance display. Right: Image-based head tracking is now incorporated into the system to enable the appearance change in response to viewer head motion.

smoothed by $3 \times 3$ and $5 \times 5$ pixel filters, respectively. Those in the column (c) show the results of the proposed method. It is observed that the highlights are randomly distorted in (a) and (b), whereas they are smooth in (c). Note that the object surface is in reality smooth and does not have the undulations that yield those highlight distortions seen in (a) and (b).

By using the proposed method, it is possible to easily acquire the surface shape information that enables natural appearance simulating any arbitrary reflectance property.

Fig.9 shows several results; also see Fig.1. It is observed that high-quality appearance is realized; glosses of metallic surfaces are reproduced that are completely different from the real reflectance of the objects, and they precisely reflects the delicate undulations of the object surface shape.

## 5   Summary

In this paper, we present a method for synthesizing a high-quality virtual appearance of an object when assuming an arbitrary reflectance property on the object surface. Using a system of multiple projectors and a camera, the method first estimates the surface shape as well as the internal and external parameters of the projectors and the camera based on structured light projection. Based on the estimation, it then performs photometric stereo using the same projectors as simple illuminations to measure the normals of the object surface. As is shown in the experimental results, when the surface normals are computed from the reconstructed surface by difference approximation, they will have random errors between neighboring surface points, which considerably deteriorates the visual quality of the synthesized appearance. The proposed method resolve this problem. Along with the accurate (auto)calibration of the projector-camera system as well as the accurate shape reconstruction, it enables the reproduction of any virtual reflectance property with high visual quality.

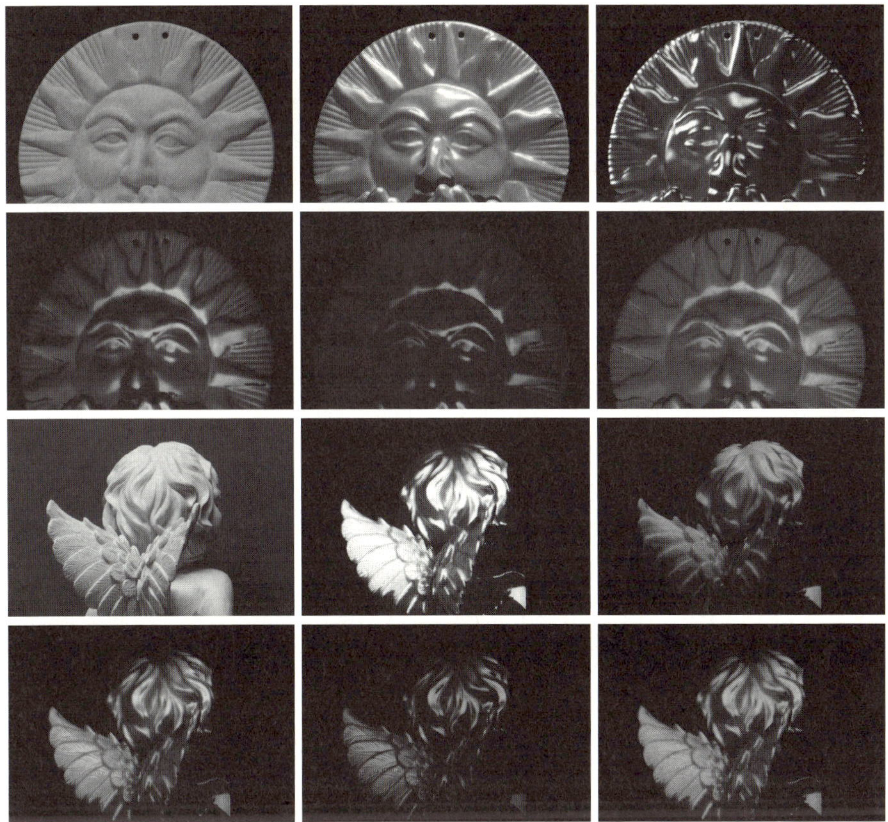

**Fig. 9.** Examples of the appearance synthesis when assuming various virtual reflectance properties

In this paper, assuming fixed viewer position, we have not considered the case where the viewer moves. However, the appearance of an object will depend on the viewer position, and therefore it is necessary to consider viewer movement. In fact, we have implemented a method that tracks the viewer head motion with a 6D sensor and/or cameras, and uses it to synthesis viewer-dependent appearance of objects(Fig.8).

## References

1. Raskar, R., Welch, G., Low, K., Bandyopadhyay, D.: Shader Lamps: Animating Real Objects With Image-Based Illumination. In: Eurographics Rendering Workshop 2001 (2001)
2. Raskar, R., van Baar, J., Beardsley, P., Willwacher, T., Rao, S.: Geometrically aware and self-configuring projectors. In: Proceedings of SIGGRAPH 2003 (2003)
3. Raskar, R., Ziegler, R., Willwacher, T.: Cartoon dioramas in motion. In: Proceedings of International Symposium on Non-Photorealistic Animation and Rendering (2002)

4. Grossberg, M.D., Peri, H., Nayar, S.K., Belhumeur, P.N.: Making one object look like another: Controlling appearance using a projector-camera system. In: Proc. CVPR 2004, pp. 452–459 (2004)
5. Fujii, K., Grossberg, M.D., Nayar, S.K.: A projector-camera system with real-time photometric adaptation for dynamic environments. In: Proc. CVPR 2005, pp. 814–821 (2005)
6. Yamamoto, S., Tsurase, M., Ueda, K., Tsumura, N., Nakaguchi, T., Miyake, Y.: Reproducing an appearance of the objects using high bright projector. In: AIC 2005 Annual Conference, pp. 1043–1046 (2005)
7. Woodham, R.J.: Photometric method for determining surface orientation from multiple images. Optical Engineering 19(1), 139–144 (1980)
8. Nehab, D., Rusinkiewicz, S., Davis, J., Ramamoorthi, R.: Efficiently combining positions and normals for precise 3d geometry. In: SIGGRAPH 2005: ACM SIGGRAPH 2005 Papers, pp. 536–543 (2005)
9. Surrel, Y.: Design of algorithms for phase measurements by the use of phase-stepping. Applied Optics 35, 51–60 (1996)
10. Pollefeys, M., Koch, R., Gool, L.V.: Self-calibration and metric reconstruction inspite of varying and unknown intrinsic camera parameters. International Journal of Computer Vision 32(1), 7–25 (1999)
11. Kanatani, K.: Gauge-based reliability analysis of 3-d reconstruction from two uncalibrated perspective views. In: Proc. ICPR 2000, vol. I, pp. 76–79 (2000)

# Image-Based Rendering by Virtual 1D Cameras


Naoyuki Ichimura

National Institute of Advanced Industrial Science and Technology (AIST)
1-1-1, Umezono, Tsukuba, Ibaraki 305-8568, Japan
`nic@ni.aist.go.jp`
`http://staff.aist.go.jp/naoyuki.ichimura/`



**Abstract.** Image-based rendering (IBR) has been used to synthesize images corresponding to a new view point from stored images. Rendering methods based on a three-dimensional plenoptic function are attractive due to the simplicity of image capture. Only a few specific discussions, however, have been done for the scaling problem to correct aspect ratio distortion, which heavily affects the quality of a synthesized image. This paper presents a rendering algorithm with a scaling scheme, which is general in that it can handle arbitrary camera paths. We model a virtual camera by a set of one-dimensional (1D) cameras. The ray representation of the 1D camera enables us to devise a rendering algorithm for the cases where the camera paths to create ray databases are arbitrary curves. We conclude with experimental results that demonstrate the usefulness of the proposed algorithm.


## 1   Introduction

Image-based rendering (IBR) has been used to synthesize images corresponding to a new view point from stored images [1]. Figure 1 shows an example of IBR. A scene is captured by multiple cameras set on a linear camera path as shown in Fig. 1 (a). A set of images captured by the cameras is called a ray database, because storing the images is equivalent to storing the rays associated with the cameras. A new view is generated by properly extracting the rays in the database, which correspond to the rays of a virtual camera. Figure 1 (b) shows a new view obtained by placing a virtual camera at the back of the camera path.

Making a ray database is interpreted as sampling the plenoptic function [2] shown in Fig. 2 (a). Due to the high dimensionality of the plenoptic function $P(\mathrm{x}, \mathrm{y}, \mathrm{z}, \theta, \phi, \lambda, t)$, which has 7 dimensions of positions, directions, wavelength and time, sampling the function by arranging cameras in space is extremely difficult. Practical IBR algorithms have been developed using a 4- or 3-dimensional (4D or 3D) plenoptic function by providing constraints for the arrangement of cameras, wavelength and time. Typical algorithms using a 4D function $P(\mathrm{x}, \mathrm{y}, \theta, \phi)$ are light field rendering [3] and lumigraph [4], in which cameras are arranged on the vertical plane defined by the $\boldsymbol{X}_{\mathrm{w}}$ and $\boldsymbol{Y}_{\mathrm{w}}$ axes in Fig. 2 (a). Cameras are arranged on the horizontal plane defined by the $\boldsymbol{X}_{\mathrm{w}}$ and $\boldsymbol{Z}_{\mathrm{w}}$ axes in concentric mosaics [5], bi-centric camera [6,7] and cross-slits projection [8,9,10]; this enables us to use a 3D function $P(x, z, \phi)$.


T. Wada, F. Huang, and S. Lin (Eds.): PSIVT 2009, LNCS 5414, pp. 423–435, 2009.

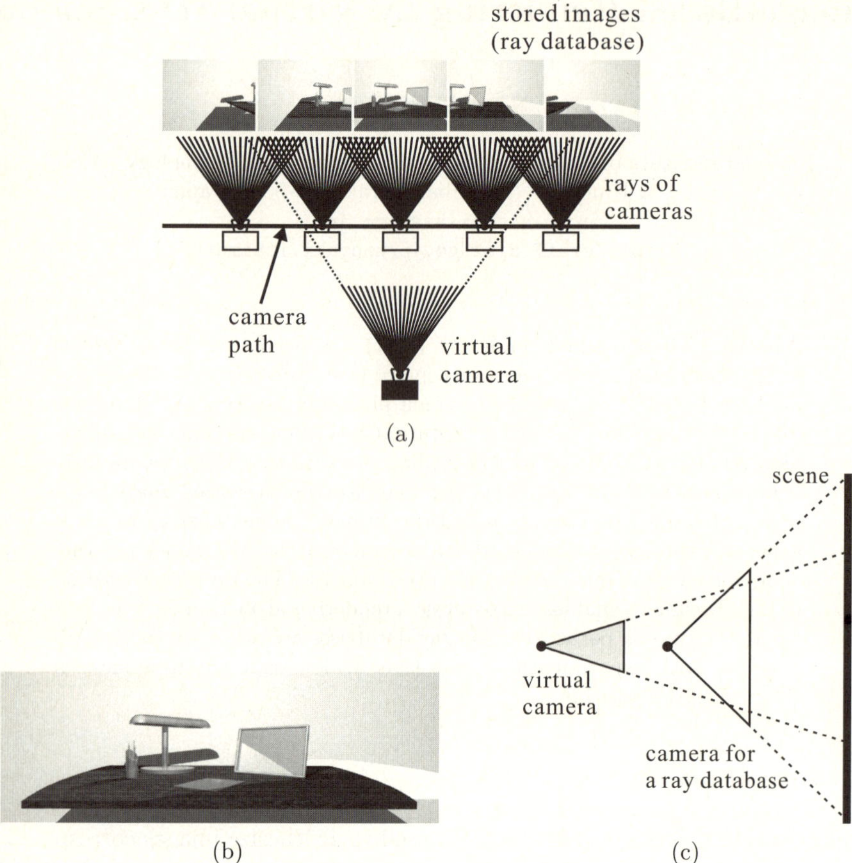


**Fig. 1.** An example of image-based rendering (IBR). (a) A ray database and a virtual camera. (b) A new view from the virtual camera. Note that the image shows an entire scene. (c) The difference between the vertical fields of views of a camera used for a ray database and a virtual camera. The difference is the source of aspect ratio distortion which would appear in a new view.

Since no cameras are required for the vertical direction, there are two advantages of IBR with a 3D plenoptic function. The first advantage is ease of image capture. The second one is that new view generation can be simply performed by mosaicing, where columns (or vertical strips) of pixels of images in a ray database are concatenated [5,6,7,8,9,10]. On the other hand, there is a serious drawback as well; the aspect ratio of a new view is changed depending on the difference between the vertical fields of views of cameras used for a ray database and the vertical field of view of a virtual camera. Figure 1 (c) shows an example of the difference. Since we can determine the position and focal length of a virtual camera arbitrary, the extent of the scene captured by a virtual camera could be smaller or larger than that captured by cameras for a ray database. If a new view is generated by concatenating columns of pixels of images in a ray database without taking the difference of the fields of views into account, the aspect ratio of the new view is changed because we only have images captured from the positions of cameras for a ray database. Thus the distortion due to the change in the aspect ratio would appear in the new view. This distortion is called aspect ratio distortion or vertical distortion [5,8], and badly affects the quality of a synthesized image, especially when forward/backward motions of a virtual camera are simulated.

In order to remove this distortion, we need to find an appropriate factor for scaling columns of pixels used in mosaicing to compensate for the difference between the vertical fields of views. Without any scaling, a virtual camera has to have the same vertical field of view as cameras for a ray database have. This is unacceptable for practical new view generation, because the position and focal length of a virtual camera are strictly restricted. The derivation of the scaling factor has been discussed only for the cases where the camera paths for ray databases are linear and circular [5,6,7,8,9,10]. The limitation on the camera paths should be removed to take full advantage of a 3D plenoptic function. The unstructured Lumigraph rendering [11] which allows an arbitrary configuration of a set of cameras for a 4D plenoptic function may be used with a 3D plenoptic function. No explanation for distortion correction, however, has been presented. To the best of our knowledge, no complete consideration of the scaling factor exist for the cases where the camera paths are arbitrary curves.

This paper presents a rendering algorithm with a scaling scheme, which is general in that it can handle arbitrary camera paths. First, we model a virtual camera by a set of one-dimensional (1D) cameras. Then, we present a rendering algorithm for the cases where the camera paths to create ray databases are arbitrary curves. We conclude with experimental results that demonstrate the usefulness of the proposed algorithm.

## 2   Modeling Virtual Camera

In this section, we first explain how the rays of a virtual camera are represented by view planes of 1D cameras. Then, we derive the equation for the view plane.

### 2.1   Representing Rays of Virtual Camera

In IBR based on a 3D plenoptic function, a new view is generated by concatenating columns of pixels corresponding to the rays of a virtual camera [5,6,7,8,9,10] (Fig. 2 (b)). Since a single column of pixels serves as the building block for a new view, we can bundle the rays of each column to represent a virtual camera by a set of 1D cameras corresponding to the columns of pixels. Using 1D cameras, we can model a virtual camera in which all the rays pass through a view point, i.e., a central camera, as shown in Fig. 2 (b).

We call the plane containing the rays of a 1D camera a *view plane*. The position and direction of a view plane determine which a column of pixels needs to be extracted from a ray database. We derive the equation representing the position and direction of a view plane in the next section.

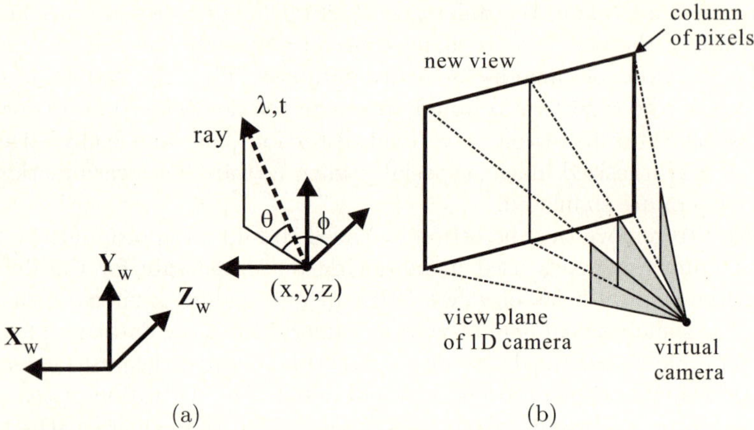


**Fig. 2.** The plenoptic function and a virtual camera. (a) The plenoptic function in the world coordinate system defined by the $X_w$, $Y_w$, and $Z_w$ axes. Rays are represented by the 7 dimensional plenoptic function with positions $(x, y, z)$, directions $(\theta, \phi)$, wavelength $\lambda$ and time $t$. To generate new views by extracting rays sampled as a ray database, we represent a virtual camera by a set of 1D cameras. (b) The 1D cameras emulate a central camera in which all rays pass through a view point.

## 2.2   Deriving View Plane Equation

Figure 2.2 depicts the imaging geometry of a 1D camera. The world coordinate system is denoted by $X_w$, $Y_w$ and $Z_w$. The index of the position of a camera is represented by $k$. The motion of the $k$-th camera is represented by the rotation matrix $R_k$ and translation vector $t_k$, which define the camera coordinate system given by $X_k$, $Y_k$ and $Z_k$. The 1D detector of the camera lies on the $Y_k$–$Z_k$ plane and it produces a 1D image.

We denote the world and camera coordinates of a 3D point P as $p_w = (x_w, y_w, z_w)^t$ and $p_k = (x_k, y_k, z_k)^t$, respectively. We know that the camera and world coordinates are related to each other as follows:

$$p_k = \left( R_k^t \,|\, - R_k^t t_k \right) \begin{pmatrix} p_w \\ 1 \end{pmatrix} , \tag{1}$$

where,

$$R_k^t = \left( i_k, j_k, k_k \right)^t , \quad t_k = \left( t_{xk}, t_{yk}, t_{zk} \right)^t . \tag{2}$$

The rows of the rotation matrix, $i_k$, $j_k$ and $k_k$, define the directions of the axes of the camera coordinate system, $X_k$, $Y_k$ and $Z_k$.

We can express the camera coordinate $x_k$ by expanding Eq. (1) as follows:

$$x_k = i_k \cdot p_w - i_k \cdot t_k . \tag{3}$$

Note that, since the view plane (1D detector) lies on the $Y_k$–$Z_k$ plane, we have $x_k = 0$. Therefore, we have:

$$i_k \cdot p_w = i_k \cdot t_k . \tag{4}$$

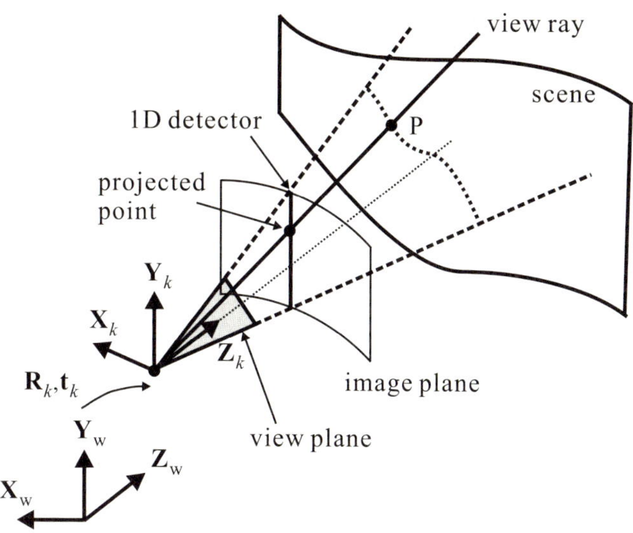


**Fig. 3.** Imaging geometry of a 1D camera. The world coordinate system is denoted by the $X_w$, $Y_w$ and $Z_w$ axes. The camera coordinate system for the $k$-th camera is denoted by the $X_k$, $Y_k$ and $Z_k$ axes. The relationship between the world and camera coordinate systems is given by the rotation matrix $R_k$ and translation vector $t_k$. The world and camera coordinates of a 3D point P are $p_w = (x_w, y_w, z_w)^t$ and $p_k = (x_k, y_k, z_k)^t$, respectively. The 1D detector (and hence the view plane) lies on the $Y_k$–$Z_k$ plane.

The above expression, which represents the view plane of a 1D camera with the position $t_k$ and direction $R_k$ passing through the 3D point, is called the *view plane equation*.

The rotation of a 1D camera is only along the horizontal direction, i.e., around the $Y_k$ axis, for a 3D plenoptic function $P(x, z, \phi)$. The vertical component of the translation is zero because the camera is on the $X_w$–$Z_w$ plane. These facts lead to the following camera motion:

$$
R_k^t = \begin{pmatrix} \cos\phi_k & 0 & -\sin\phi_k \\ 0 & 1 & 0 \\ \sin\phi_k & 0 & \cos\phi_k \end{pmatrix}, \quad t_k = (t_{xk}, 0, t_{zk})^t . \tag{5}
$$

where, $\phi_k$ is the rotation angle around the $Y_k$ axis of the $k$-th camera. Using the camera motion, we have the following equations from Eq. (1):

$$
x_k = x_w \cos\phi_k - z_w \sin\phi_k - t_{xk} \cos\phi_k + t_{zk} \sin\phi_k , \tag{6}
$$

$$
y_k = y_w , \tag{7}
$$

$$
z_k = x_w \sin\phi_k + z_w \cos\phi_k - t_{xk} \sin\phi_k - t_{zk} \cos\phi_k . \tag{8}
$$

Then we have the view plane equation for a 3D plenoptic function $P(x, z, \phi)$:

$$
x_w \cos\phi_k - z_w \sin\phi_k = t_{xk} \cos\phi_k - t_{zk} \sin\phi_k . \tag{9}
$$

In the next section, we present an IBR algorithm with a general scaling factor using Eq. (6), (7), (8) and (9).

# 3   IBR with General Scaling Factor

We propose an IBR algorithm with a general scaling factor in this section. First, we present the algorithm and then derive the scaling factor.

## 3.1   IBR Algorithm

The overview of the proposed algorithm is shown in Fig. 4. There are 3 curves in the figure, i.e., a camera path, a focal surface and a geometric proxy. Cameras for a ray database are arranged on the camera path. The focal surface denotes the positions where a virtual camera adjusts its focus [12]. The geometric proxy is used as an approximated shape of a scene. All the curves are represented by polygons whose vertexes are given by the sets of vectors: $\{c_l\}_{l=1}^{L}$, $\{f_m\}_{m=1}^{M}$ and $\{g_n\}_{n=1}^{N}$, respectively. Each vector has the position of a vertex as well as additional information such as the direction of the camera for a ray database.

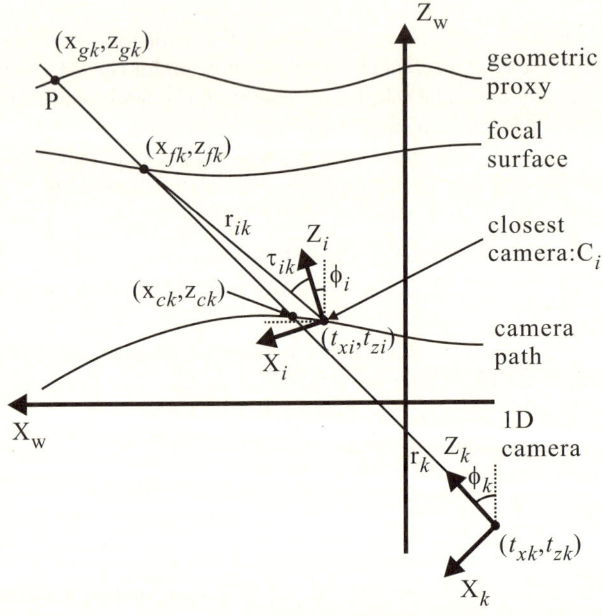


**Fig. 4.** The overview of the proposed IBR algorithm. The ray associated with the 1D camera with the position $(t_{xk}, t_{zk})$ and direction $\phi_k$ is $r_k$. The camera $C_i$, which is closest to the point of intersection of $r_k$ and the camera path, $(x_{ck}, z_{ck})$, is found from a ray database to know its position $(t_{xi}, t_{zi})$ and direction $\phi_i$. Then the point of intersection of $r_k$ and the focal surface, $(x_{fk}, z_{fk})$, is computed. The angle of the ray $r_{ik}$, $\tau_{ik}$, is obtained by the intersection point and the position of $C_i$. The position of a column of pixels corresponding to $r_{ik}$ is calculated. After extracting the column at the position, the column is scaled based on the distances from the point of intersection of $r_k$ and the geometric proxy, $(x_{gk}, z_{gk})$, to the 1D camera and the closest camera $C_i$.

The proposed IBR algorithm is summarized as follows:

[Step 1: Setting a view point] The position $(t_{xk}, t_{zk})$ and direction $\phi_k$ of a 1D camera are given based on a user request. The ray of the camera is expressed as $r_k$.

[Step 2: Finding the closest camera] The point of intersection of the ray $r_k$ and the camera path is computed. This computation is performed by intersection check between the view plane of $r_k$ obtained by Eq. (9) and the polygons $\{c_l\}_{l=1}^{L}$. The vertex $c_i$, which is closest to the point of intersection $(x_{ck}, z_{ck})$, is found and the camera at the vertex is regarded as the closest camera $C_i$. The vertex has the position and direction of $C_i$, and these are denoted as $c_i = (t_{xi}, t_{zi}, \phi_i)^t$.

[Step 3: Finding the intersection point with the focal surface] The point of intersection between the ray $r_k$ and the focal surface is computed. This computation is done by intersection check between the view plane of $r_k$ and the polygons $\{f_m\}_{m=1}^{M}$. The point of intersection is shown as $(x_{fk}, z_{fk})$.

[Step 4: Computing the angle of the ray] The ray of $C_i$ passing through the point $(x_{fk}, z_{fk})$, i.e., $r_{ik}$ shown in Fig. 4, corresponds to the column of pixels required for generating a new view. The view plane of $r_{ik}$ is obtained by Eq. (9) as follows:

$$x_{fk} \cos(\phi_i + \tau_{ik}) - z_{fk} \sin(\phi_i + \tau_{ik})$$
$$= t_{xi} \cos(\phi_i + \tau_{ik}) - t_{zi} \sin(\phi_i + \tau_{ik}). \tag{10}$$

where, $\tau_{ik}$ is the angle of $r_{ik}$, which is needed to extract the required column of pixels. This angle is expressed as:

$$\tau_{ik} = \mathrm{Tan}^{-1}\left(\frac{a - \tan\phi_i}{1 + a \tan\phi_i}\right), \quad a = \frac{x_{fk} - t_{xi}}{z_{fk} - t_{zi}}. \tag{11}$$

[Step 5: Finding the position of the column of pixels] The position of the column of pixels for mosaicing, $d_{ik}$, is obtained as follows:

$$d_{ik} = f_i \tan \tau_{ik}. \tag{12}$$

where, $f_i$ is the focal length of $C_i$.

[Step 6: Finding the intersection point with the proxy] The point of intersection P between the ray $r_k$ and the geometric proxy is computed. This computation is performed by intersection check between the view plane of $r_k$ and the polygons $\{g_n\}_{n=1}^{N}$. The point of intersection is shown as $(x_{gk}, z_{gk})$.

[Step 7: Scaling the column of pixels] The column of pixels at the position $d_{ik}$ is scaled using the scaling factor $s_k$.

$$s_k = \frac{f_k}{f_i} \frac{z_{ik}}{z_k}, \tag{13}$$

where,

$$z_{ik} = x_{gk} \sin\phi_i' + z_{gk} \cos\phi_i' - t_{xi} \sin\phi_i' - t_{zi} \cos\phi_i', \tag{14}$$
$$\phi_i' = \phi_i + \tau_{ik}', \tag{15}$$

$$\tau'_{ik} = \mathrm{Tan}^{-1}\left(\frac{a' - \tan\phi_i}{1 + a'\tan\phi_i}\right), \quad a' = \frac{x_{gk} - t_{xi}}{z_{gk} - t_{zi}}, \tag{16}$$

$$z_k = x_{gk}\sin\phi_k + z_{gk}\cos\phi_k - t_{xk}\sin\phi_k - t_{zk}\cos\phi_k, \tag{17}$$

$f_k$ is the focal length of the 1D camera and $\tau'_{ik}$ is the angle of the ray connecting the position of the closest camera and the intersection point P. The use of the angle implies that the scaling factor is determined by the position of the geometric proxy; the position of the focal surface is ignored in scaling.

[Step 8: Averaging the columns of pixels] Step1 to Step7 are applied not only to the closest camera but also to multiple cameras near the intersection point $(x_{ck}, z_{ck})$. Then the weighted average of the scaled columns of pixels is calculated. The number of cameras that plays the role of the aperture of a virtual camera [12] is 3 for this algorithm. The weights for averaging are given by the Gaussian distribution $N(0, 4)$.

[Step 9: Mosaicing] Step1 to Step 8 are applied to all 1D cameras in a virtual camera. By concatenating the averaged columns of pixels, we can generate a new view.

The scaling factor $s_k$ of Eq. (13) is derived in the next section.


## 3.2   Deriving Scaling Factor

Assume that a 1D camera and the closest camera $C_i$ observe the same point P on a geometric proxy with the coordinates $(x_{gk}, z_{gk})$. The points projected on the cameras are denoted by $v$ and $v'$, respectively. The ratio between $v$ and $v'$ is the required scaling factor. Using the perspective projection of the cameras, we can express the ratio as follows:

$$\frac{v}{v'} = \frac{f_k y_k}{z_k}\frac{z_{ik}}{f_i y_{ik}}. \tag{18}$$

where, $y_k$, $z_k$ and $y_{ik}$, $z_{ik}$ are the camera coordinates of P for a 1D camera and $C_i$, respectively.

From Eq. (7), we know that $y_k = y_{ik} = y_w$. Thus, Eq. (18) is equivalent to Eq. (13). We can represent $z_{ik}$ and $z_k$ as shown in Eq. (14) to (17) using Eq. (8), (11). Therefore, the scaling factor represented by Eq. (13) to (17) is obtained.

The scaling factor for polar coordinates is useful for the IBR algorithm using the circular camera path for a ray database [5,7,8,9,10]. The scaling factor is derived in Appendix A.

It is important to note that no assumption is imposed on the shape of the camera path in the above derivation. The derived scaling factor is, therefore, general in that it can be applied to the cases where camera paths are arbitrary curves.

## 4   Experimental Results

In this section, we show experimental results of the proposed algorithm. The main purpose of the experiments was to confirm the effect of the proposed scaling scheme.

Figure 5 shows a ray database created by using 3D rendering software, POV-Ray [13]. We rendered 900 frames including the 3 frames in the figure. Note that the camera path for the database was a sine curve, which leads to the changes in the depths between the cameras and the scene. The virtual camera was the central one, as shown in Fig. 2 (b). Since the distance between the virtual camera

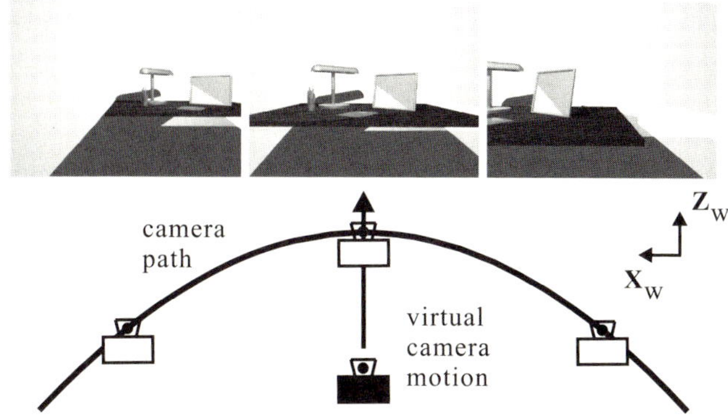


**Fig. 5.** The ray database obtained by POV-Ray [13]. The camera path was a sine curve. The virtual camera was the central one, as shown in Fig. 2 (a), and it was moved forward.

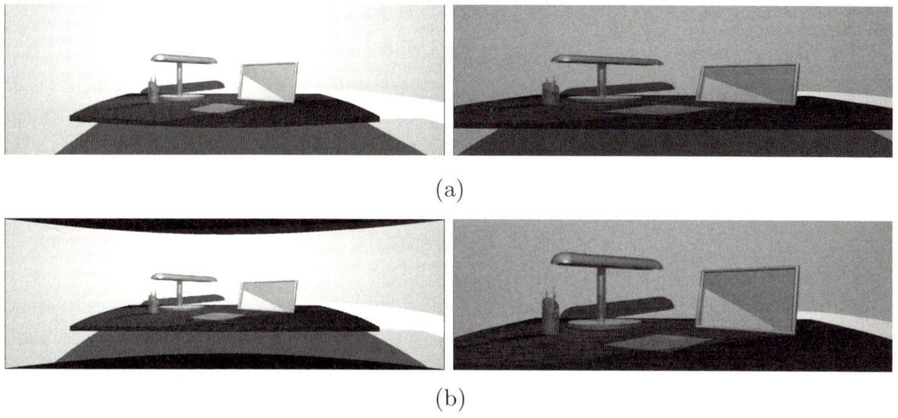


**Fig. 6.** The new views obtained from the virtual camera with the motion shown in Fig. 5. (a) without scaling. (b) with scaling. Left,Right: the new views corresponding to the different positions of the virtual camera. Note the changes in the aspect ratios of the objects in (a). The deformation of the left image in (b) demonstrates the compensation of the change in depth of the camera path in Fig. 5 by the scaling factor.

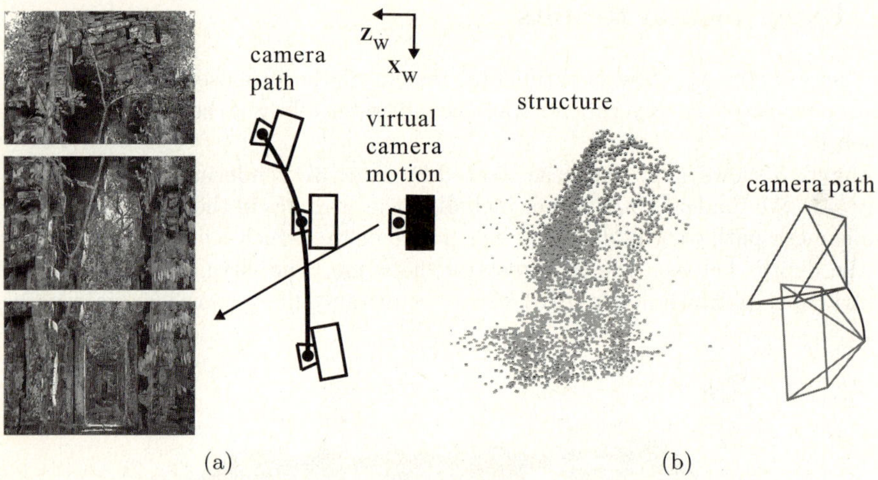


**Fig. 7.** The ray database for a remain in the Kingdom of Cambodia. (a) The virtual camera was the central one and it was moved downward from the center of the scene. (b) The camera path and the rough structure of the scene were estimated by using Voodoo Camera Tracker [14]. Note that the rough structure is enough for a geometric proxy.

and the scene has to be changed significantly in order to confirm the usefulness of the scaling factor, the virtual camera was moved forward.

The focal surface and geometric proxy were planes and these were placed at the same position as the average depth of the scene. The focal lengths of the cameras for the ray database and the virtual camera were $f_i = 480$ and $f_k = 960$[pixel], respectively. The change in the depth of the camera path, the position of a virtual camera and the difference between the focal lengths yielded the aspect ratio distortion.

The new views are shown in Fig. 6. Figure 6 (a) is the result obtained without scaling and Fig. 6 (b) is the result obtained with scaling. The left and right images of the figures correspond to the different positions of the virtual camera. Without scaling, the aspect ratios of the objects were changed as the virtual camera was moved. On the other hand, the aspect ratio distortion was corrected by scaling. The deformation of the left image in Fig. 6 (b) demonstrates that the scaling of the columns of pixels compensated for the change in the depth of the camera path.

We now present the results for IBR using real images. Figure 7 (a) shows the ray database using the images of a remain in the Kingdom of Cambodia. We used 330 frames, including the 3 frames in the figure. The positions and directions of the cameras for the frames were estimated by using Voodoo Camera Tracker [14], software for a structure from motion algorithm, as shown in Fig. 7 (b). Since the camera motion was controlled by a dolly, the camera moved on a plane. This fact enables us to use the 3D plenoptic function. The virtual camera was the central one and it was moved downward from the center of the scene as depicted in Fig. 7 (a).

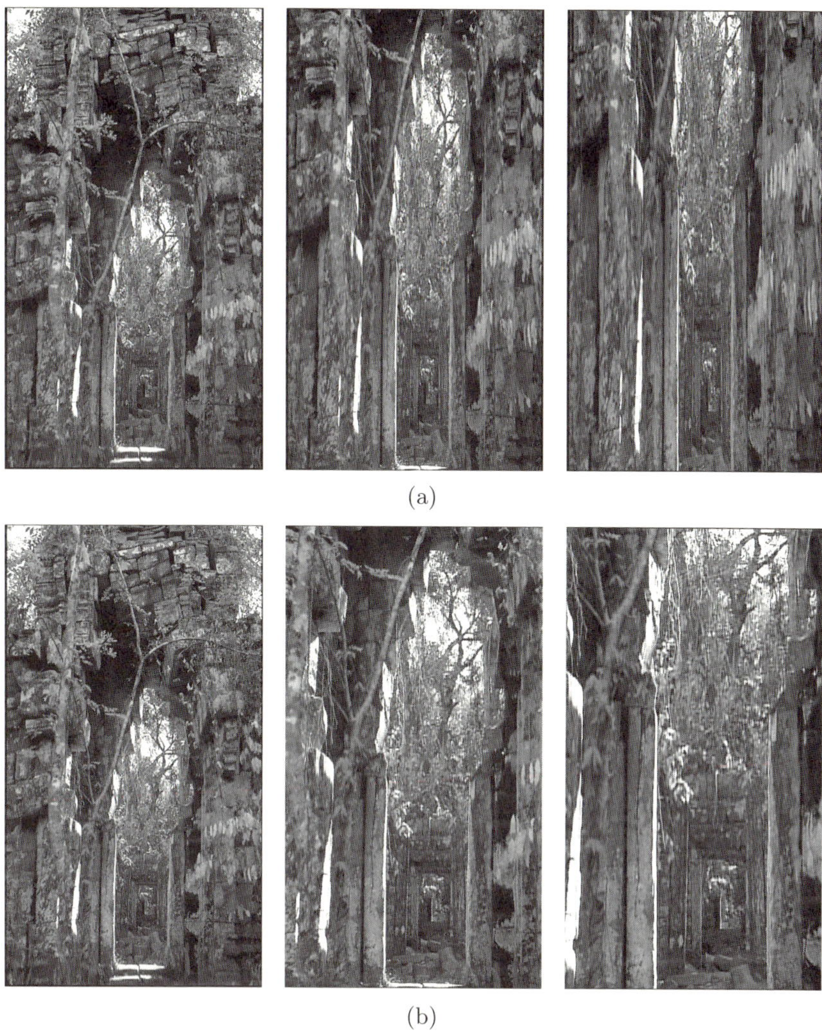

Fig. 8. The new views obtained from the virtual camera with the motion shown in Fig. 7. (a) without distortion correction. (b) with distortion correction. Note the serious aspect ratio distortions in the new views of (a).

The fixed focal length of the camera for the ray database and the 3D structure of the scene were also estimated by the software. The focal surface and geometric proxy were planes and these were placed at the same position as the average depth of the scene. The focal lengths of the cameras for the ray database and the virtual camera were $f_i = 46$ and $f_k = 91$[pixel], respectively. The focal length $f_k$ was determined to cover the entire scene at the initial position of the virtual camera.

Figure 8 shows the new views. Since no aspect ratio correction was done in Fig. 8 (a), the new views had the serious aspect ratio distortion which deteriorated the quality of the new views. For example, the width of the gate in the scene did not change although the virtual camera was moved. In Fig. 8 (b) using the proposed scaling scheme, the width of the gate gradually changed as the virtual camera was moved owing to the compensation of the aspect ratio. The quality of the new views was sufficient to emulate the virtually generated camera motion.

In summary, the experimental results with large changes in the distances between the virtual cameras and the scenes demonstrate that our algorithm can correct aspect ratio distortions.

## 5   Summary

We have proposed an IBR algorithm with a scaling scheme based on the modeling of a virtual camera using 1D cameras. The scaling scheme is general in that it can handle arbitrary camera paths. We demonstrated the usefulness of the proposed IBR algorithm by the experiments in which new views were generated using several ray databases. We believe that the scaling scheme presented here will facilitate the use of IBR based on a 3D plenoptic function.

## References


1. Shum, H.Y., Chan, S.C., Kang, S.B.: Image-Based Rendering. Springer, Heidelberg (2007)
2. Adelson, E.H., Bergen, J.R.: The Plenoptic Function and the Elements of Early Vision, pp. 3–20. MIT Press, Cambridge (1991)
3. Levoy, M., Hanrahan, P.: Light field rendering. In: Proc. SIGGRAPH 1996, pp. 31–42 (1996)
4. Gortler, S.J., Grzeszczuk, R., Szeliski, R., Cohen, M.F.: The lumigraph. In: Proc. SIGGRAPH 1996, pp. 43–54 (1996)
5. Shum, H.Y., He, L.W.: Rendering with concentric mosaics. In: Proc. SIGGRAPH 1999, pp. 299–306 (1999)
6. Weinshall, D., Lee, M.S., Brodsky, T., Trajkovic, M.: New view generation with a bi-centric camera. In: Heyden, A., Sparr, G., Nielsen, M., Johansen, P. (eds.) ECCV 2002. LNCS, vol. 2350, pp. 614–628. Springer, Heidelberg (2002)
7. Bakstein, H., Pajdla, T., Vecerka, D.: Rendering almost perspective views from a sparse set of omnidirectional images. In: Proc. BMVC, pp. 241–250 (2003)
8. Zomet, A., Feldman, D., Peleg, S., Weinshall, D.: Mosaicing new views: The cross-slits projection. IEEE Trans. PAMI 25(6), 741–753 (2003)
9. Bakstein, H., Pajdla, T.: Rendering novel views from a set of omnidirectoinal mosaic images. In: Proc. IEEE Conf. on Computer Vision and Pattern Recognition Workshop (CVPRW 2003), pp. 74–79 (2003)
10. Bakstein, H., Pajdla, T.: Omnidirectional image-based rendering. In: Proc. Computer Vision Winter Workshop (CVWW 2006), pp. 99–104 (2006)
11. Buehler, C., Bosse, M., McMillan, L., Gortler, S., Cohen, M.: Unstructured lumigraph rendering. In: Proc. SIGGRAPH 2001, pp. 425–432 (2001)
12. Isaksen, A., McMillan, L., Gortler, S.J.: Dynamically reparameterized light fields. In: Proc. SIGGRAPH 2000, pp. 297–306 (2000)
13. http://www.povray.org/
14. http://www.digilab.uni-hannover.de/docs/manual.html

# A    Scaling Factor for Polar Coordinate System

The camera coordinates $z_{ik}$ and $z_k$ of Eq. (14) and (17) are expressed as follows:

$$z_{ik} = d_k \sqrt{1 - \left\{ \frac{R_i}{d_k} \sin \left( \xi_i - \phi_i' \right) \right\}^2} - R_i \cos \left( \xi_i - \phi_i' \right), \tag{19}$$

$$z_k = d_k \sqrt{1 - \left\{ \frac{R_k}{d_k} \sin \left( \beta_k - \phi_k \right) \right\}^2} - R_k \cos \left( \beta_k - \phi_k \right), \tag{20}$$

where,

$$d_k = \sqrt{x_{gk}^2 + z_{gk}^2}, \tag{21}$$

$$R_i = \sqrt{t_{xi}^2 + t_{zi}^2}, \quad \tan \xi_i = t_{xi}/t_{zi}, \tag{22}$$

$$R_k = \sqrt{t_{xk}^2 + t_{zk}^2}, \quad \tan \beta_k = t_{xk}/t_{zk}. \tag{23}$$

Using the expression, we can derive the scaling factor of Eq. (13). This scaling factor is useful for the IBR algorithms using the polar coordinate system to represent the rotation of cameras for a ray database [5,7,8,9,10]. For example, if the camera path is circular, $R_i$ in Eq. (22) is the radius of the circle and $\xi_i$ the angle of the closest camera $C_i$.

We show the derivation of Eq. (19) as follows. Equation (14) is denoted as:

$$z_{ik} = d_k \left( \sin \alpha_k \sin \phi_i' + \cos \alpha_k \cos \phi_i' \right) - R_i \left( \sin \xi_i \sin \phi_i' + \cos \xi_i \cos \phi_i' \right),$$

$$= d_k \sqrt{1 - \sin \left( \alpha_k - \phi_i' \right)^2} - R_i \cos \left( \xi_i - \phi_i' \right). \tag{24}$$

where, $\phi_i'$, $d_k$ and $R_i$ are given by Eq. (15), (21) and (22), and $\tan \alpha_k = x_{gk}/z_{gk}$. The view plane of the ray of $C_i$ passing through the coordinates $(x_{gk}, z_{gk})$ is given by Eq. (9):

$$x_{gk} \cos \phi_i' - z_{gk} \sin \phi_i' = t_{xi} \cos \phi_i' - t_{zi} \sin \phi_i'. \tag{25}$$

From the expression, we have:

$$\sin \left( \alpha_k - \phi_i' \right) = \frac{R_i}{d_k} \sin \left( \xi_i - \phi_i' \right). \tag{26}$$

Substituting Eq. (26) in Eq. (24), we obtain Eq. (19).

We can obtain Eq. (20) for the camera coordinate $z_k$ by applying the same procedure as that used for Eq. (19).

# Implicit Surface Reconstruction with an Analogy of Polar Field Model


Yuxu Lin[1], Chun Chen[1], Mingli Song[1,*], Jiajun Bu[1], and Zicheng Liu[2]

[1] College of Computer Science, Zhejiang University
linyuxu@zju.edu.cn,
chenc@zju.edu.cn,
brooksong@ieee.org,
bjj@zju.edu.cn
[2] Microsoft Research Redmond
zliu@microsoft.com



**Abstract.** Implicit surface reconstruction has been a challenging work for decades. In this paper, motivated by the concept of classic physical polar field model and off-set points strategy, we present a new approach, called Field Fitting. In this approach, we express a 3D surface as an equipotential surface of scalar polar field which is produced by a number of paired field generating primitives, then a surface reconstruction process is cast as a primitives localization process, and finally, we solve this problem with a greedy method. Experimental results demonstrate that the proposed method outperforms the previous by providing better surface reconstruction results.

**Keywords:** Surface fitting, reconstruction, polar field, implicit surface, Field Fitting.


## 1 Introduction

Implicit Surface [1] is widely used for a compact representation of surface, which can produce higher resolution surfaces by sampling on predefined implicit function. Typically, an implicit surface reconstruction problem can be described as: given a point cloud along the surface, to find an implicit function $F(\boldsymbol{x})$ whose zero-sets approximate the original surface as accurate as possible. However, a 3D surface usually exhibits not only the smooth plane, but also the subtle and sharp details caused by corners, deformations etc. Due to such complexity of 3D surface, robust and accurate surface fitting is still a challenging work for computer graphics and geometric modeling researchers.

There have been a lot of approaches in surface fitting in the past decades. It is virtually impossible to enumerate all of them. The book written by Dierckx [2] and the review by Floater et al. [3] provided excellent surveys. Here we would like to review some representative implicit surface reconstruction approaches presented very recently.

---


* Corresponding author.



T. Wada, F. Huang, and S. Lin (Eds.): PSIVT 2009, LNCS 5414, pp. 436–448, 2009.

The first group is global fitting method, which commonly define one global function to express the surface, such as polynomial surface [4] and radius basis functions(RBFs) [5,6]. The most popular global fitting method is RBFs which have been proved extremely effective to construct implicit surface from points and widely used, however, the solving process of ideal RBFs involve a large solution matrix which is rather time consuming, a practical solution (FastRBF) on large data sets involves adaptive RBF center reduction and fast multipole method[5].

The second group is local fitting method, which generates implicit function for each local patches. In [7], the implicit function was defined as the signed distance to the tangent plane of the closest point, and in [8,9], a moving least squares (MLS) projection was performed to find local function, and in [10], a technique named Multi-level Partition of Unity Implicits(MPU) was developed to reconstruct implicit surface as the blending of local implicit functions, MPU performs efficient on large scale data sets.

Very recently, a novel "Poisson Surface Reconstruction" was introduced in [11] which treated the surface reconstruction process as a spatial Poisson problem, and the experiments showed that it was also an effective way.

In this paper, inspired by the concept of classic physical polar field model and off-set points strategy in 3L algorithm [4], we propose a new implicit surface reconstruction approach called Field Fitting. By making an analogy between the fitting surface and the equipotential surface yielded by paired primitives, the implicit surface fitting is treated as a process of estimating the paired primitives' distribution. Then, the implicit surface fitting is formulated into an energy minimization problem. A greedy strategy is used to solve this problem iteratively. Moreover, multi-scaling strategy is adopted to overcome the unwanted holes on the surface. The experimental results demonstrate that the proposed Field Fitting approach outperforms previous ones by providing better surface fitting result on different 3D models.

This paper introduces the following key-contributions:

i) A novel implicit surface fitting approach is presented to carry out the reconstruction in a simple and effective way by analogy of a physical polar field model.

ii) The implicit surface fitting is formulated into an energy minimization problem. And,

iii) a greedy method is introduced to solve the energy minimization problem, which is more effective than conventional solving strategy.

The paper is organized as follows. Firstly, in section 2, we briefly describe the original physical polar field model and the off-set points' strategy in implicit surface reconstruction. Then, we describe our surface reconstruction approach in section 3. In section 4 and section 5, we explain how to extract isosurface and evaluate the proposed approach respectively. Finally, we conclude in section 6.

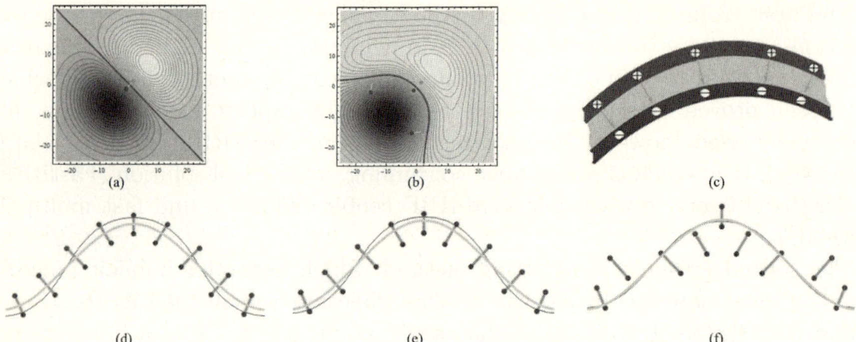

**Fig. 1.** From top to bottom and from left to right, (a): the equipotential curves yielded by a paired primitives with opposite polarity, the red line denote the zero potential curve, green point denote positive primitive and red point denote negative primitive; (b): the equipotential curves yielded by three paired primitives with opposite polarity, the zero potential curve does not go through the middle of all three paired primitives;(c): a typical profile of The Parallel-Plate Capacitor model, the red and blue stripe are paralleled conductor plates which carry equal quantity but opposite positive/negative primitives, and the yellow part in the middle is the insulator which separates the two paralleled conductors; (d): the zero potential curve(blue curve) for Parallel-Plate Capacitor; (e): the zero potential curve after adjusting positive/negative primitives for 10 times with Quasi-Newton method; (f): the zero potential curve after 120 rounds positive/negative primitives adjustments

## 2   Preliminary

### 2.1   Physical Polar Field Model

In physics world, there are two types of fields, the first type is nonpolar fields, such as gravity field and temperature field, the second type is polar fields, such as magnetic field and electric field which can be yield by two types of primitives with opposite polarity. For a field, given the location of primitives and the potential function, there will be an equipotential surface in field. Such characteristic motivates us greatly for a better fitting of implicit surfaces. If we regard the surface as an equipotential surface to be reconstructed, and the fitting points as the sampling of the surface, a surface reconstruction problem can be transformed to a procedure of estimating the primitives' distribution.

Considering a pair of primitives with same strength but opposite polar (we name them as positive and negative primitive), they set up field across the space and their corresponding equipotential curves in a plane are shown in Figure 1 (a), the red line denote the zero potential curve, the green point denote the positive primitive and the red point denote the negative primitive, for a single paired primitives, the zero potential curve go through the middle of two primitives. In Figure 1 (b), the equipotential curves governed by three paired primitives are plotted, and it is noticeable that the zero potential curve does not go through the middle of all three paired primitives. The potential function of a single positive/negative primitives is described as:

$$w^+(\boldsymbol{r}) = \psi(|r|), \qquad w^-(\boldsymbol{r}) = -\psi(|r|) \tag{1}$$

where $|\boldsymbol{r}|$ is the 3D distance from the positive/negative primitive. $\psi$ is a monotonic decreasing function according to $|r|$.

Making an extension of the simple polar field model with a few positive/ negative primitives mentioned above, a model named Parallel-Plate Capacitor with a pair of paralleled conductors (red and blue part in Figure 1 (c)) (only a patch is plotted) has plenty of primitives (Figure 1 (c)) which have equal strength but opposite polarity (positive/negative) primitives. Besides, there is an insulator in the middle of the capacitor (yellow part in Figure 1 (c), it intend to be infinite thin, and we thicken it for easily observation) which separates the two paralleled conductors. We plot the zero potential curve for Parallel-Plate Capacitor (blue line in Figure 1 (d)), it is noticeable that the zero potential curve (blue line) is close to the insulator(yellow line), by adjusting the position of primitives (with Quasi-Newton method[12], discussed in section 3) several times (10 times in Figure 1 (e) and 120 times in Figure 1 (f)), the zero potential curve can fit the insulator. In other words, by adjusting the position of positive/negative primitives, the insulator can be defined as a zero set of the following implicit function:

$$f(\boldsymbol{p}) = \sum_{i=1}^{n} w_i^+(\boldsymbol{p} - \boldsymbol{L}_i^+) + \sum_{i=1}^{n} w_i^-(\boldsymbol{p} - \boldsymbol{L}_i^-) \tag{2}$$

where $n$ stands for the number of positive/negative primitives, $\boldsymbol{L}_i^+/\boldsymbol{L}_i^-$ is the position of $i$_th positive/negative primitives. $f(\boldsymbol{p})$ denotes the potential yield by all the primitives at point $\boldsymbol{p}$.

## 2.2  Off-Set Points Strategy

In 3L algorithm [4], given a points set $P = \{\boldsymbol{p}_i\}$ and its corresponding normal set $N = \{\boldsymbol{n}_i\}$ on a surface, we can approximate the surface with an implicit function $f$ in terms of an off-set points strategy. $f$ satisfies $f(\boldsymbol{p}_i) = 0$. In addition, $f(\boldsymbol{p}_{i+}) > 0$ and $f(\boldsymbol{p}_{i-}) < 0$ where $\boldsymbol{p}_i^+ = \boldsymbol{p}_i + \lambda \cdot \boldsymbol{n}_i$, $\boldsymbol{p}_i^- = \boldsymbol{p}_i - \lambda \cdot \boldsymbol{n}_i$, $\lambda > 0$, it means that given points which are in the zero-set of the implicit surface, we can infer that the implicit function value of a point will be positive when it moves forwards along the normal and negative when it moves backwards along the normal.

This property is usually utilized for constructing implicit surface as follows:

$$\begin{aligned} f(\boldsymbol{p}_i^-) &= -c \\ f(\boldsymbol{p}_i) &= 0 \quad where \quad c > 0 \\ f(\boldsymbol{p}_i^+) &= c \end{aligned}$$

The extra equations $f(\boldsymbol{p}_i^-) = -c$ and $f(\boldsymbol{p}_i^+) = c$ are used to enhance the stability of reconstruction process. And in our Field Fitting approach, we utilize the off-set points to generate the positive and negative primitives (in analogy of $\boldsymbol{p}_i^+$

and $p_i^-$ ) from the sampled points (in analogy of $p_i$ on the insulator) in the Parallel-Plate Capacitor model. In other words, once the locations of positive and negative primitives are deduced, the insulator between them can be located as the zero set of implicit function shown in Eq. (2) correspondingly.

## 3   Field Fitting

In this section, we introduce our Field Fitting approach by the analogy between surface reconstruction and the primitives' distributions estimation of Parallel-Plate Capacitor model.

Given an original 3D scattered point cloud, which can be treated as a coarse discrete representation of the insulator, we can estimate the initial locations of the positive/negative primitives with the guidance of the Parallel-Plate Capacitor model. Then the surface fitting can be carried out by reconstructing of continuous insulator based on the estimated location of primitives.

### 3.1   The Analogy of Parallel-Plate Capacitor Model

As mentioned before, we use $P = \{p_i\}$ to denote points sampled from the original surface (the insulator), and $N = \{n_i\}$ are the corresponding normal values. The normal values can be captured by 3D scanner or computed by methods like [13], in our approach, the normals of input points are precalculated by the method proposed in[13].

Similar to the off-set points strategy, we can infer the off-set points $P^+ = \{p_i^+\}$ and $P^- = \{p_i^-\}$ shown in Figure 2(a). With the analogy of the Parallel-Plate Capacitor, $P^+$ and $P^-$ are regarded as subsets of positive/negative primitives of the parallel conductors. As mentioned before, We can estimate the global potential based on the distribution of the primitives on both sides of capacitor. However, the distribution of all primitives are still unknown.

Taking a positive primitive $p_i^+$ for example, to compute the primitives' distribution in its neighborhood, we define a local coordinate whose origin is at

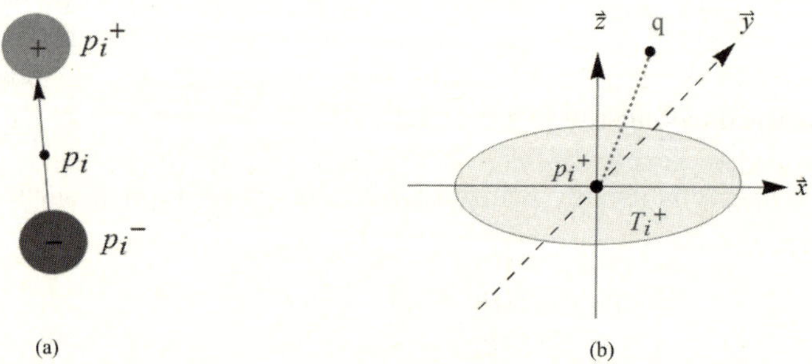



**Fig. 2.** From left to right, (a): given a point $p_i$ on the surface, we can infer a paired primitives $p_i^+$ and $p_i^-$ whose middle is at $p$; (b): the distribution of primitives near $p_i^+$

$p_i^+$, and direction of local $z$ axis is the same as $n_i$, as shown in Figure 2(b). $T_i^+$ is the tangent plane corresponding to $p_i^+$. $N(p_i^+)$ includes $p_i^+$'s neighboring primitives in $P^+$. Thus the distribution of primitives on the $T_i^+$ in the capacitor can be described by the probability below:

$$h\left(t\right) = \frac{1}{2\pi|\Sigma|^{\frac{1}{2}}} \cdot e^{-t^T \Sigma^{-1} t} \tag{3}$$

where $t = \begin{pmatrix} x \\ y \end{pmatrix}$ and $\Sigma$ is covariance of the Gaussian distribution. That is, we suppose the primitives are distributed on a local tangent plane and $h(t)$ defines the probability of those primitives in local tangent plane whose distance from $p_i^+$ are $t$. The covariance $\Sigma$ can be estimated by the neighboring primitives $N(p_i^+)$ as below:

$$\Sigma = \frac{1}{k} \sum^{j} \left(\left(x_j - p_i^+\right) \perp T_i^+\right) \cdot \left(\left(x_j - p_i^+\right) \perp T_i^+\right)^T \tag{4}$$

where $k = \left|N\left(p_i^+\right)\right|$, $x_j \in N\left(p_i^+\right)$ and $\perp$ denote the projection operator. Eq. (4) means that $\Sigma$ can be achieved by the neighboring primitives' projection points on tangent plane. Note that $\Sigma$ can be decomposed through Singular Value Decomposition (SVD) as below:

$$\Sigma = \begin{bmatrix} u & v \end{bmatrix} \begin{bmatrix} a^2 & 0 \\ 0 & b^2 \end{bmatrix} \begin{bmatrix} u^T \\ v^T \end{bmatrix} \tag{5}$$

Then the expected local potential at location $q$ yielded by primitives on plane $T_i^+$ can be computed as:

$$W_{T_i^+}\left(q\right) = \int_{-\infty}^{+\infty} \int_{-\infty}^{+\infty} h\left(t\right) \cdot w_i^+\left(r\right) dx\, dy \tag{6}$$

where $t = \begin{pmatrix} x \\ y \end{pmatrix}$, $r = q - \begin{pmatrix} x \\ y \\ 0 \end{pmatrix}$ and $w_i^+(r)$ is the potential function for one positive primitive in $T_i^+$, in our approach we express $w_i^+(r)$ as a Gaussian function due to its natural smooth blending characteristics. In other words, $w_i^+\left(r\right) = e^{-\frac{|r|^2}{2m^2}}$. Eq. (6) means the local potential value around $p_i^+$ is yielded by all the primitives on its tangent plane $T_i^+$ with probability $h\left(t\right)$.

Substituting Eq. (3) into Eq. (6), we have:

$$W_{T_i^+}\left(q\right) = C_i^+ \cdot e^{-\frac{1}{2}\left(q'^T \cdot \Sigma_g^{-1} \cdot q'\right)} \tag{7}$$

$$C_i^+ = \frac{2\pi}{\sqrt{\frac{1}{a^2} + \frac{1}{m^2}} \sqrt{\frac{1}{b^2} + \frac{1}{m^2}}}$$

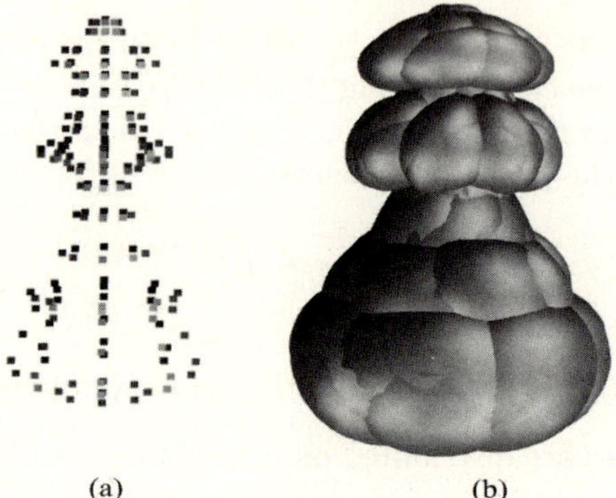

(a)                          (b)

**Fig. 3.** From left to right, (a): the original point cloud sampled from a chess; (b): the ellipsoids which stand for the support regions of all $W_{T_i^+}/W_{T_i^-}$

$$\Sigma_g = \begin{bmatrix} a^2 + m^2 & 0 & 0 \\ 0 & b^2 + m^2 & 0 \\ 0 & 0 & m^2 \end{bmatrix}$$

where $q'$ is the local coordinate of $q$ corresponding to point $\boldsymbol{p}_i^+$ and

$$\boldsymbol{q}' = (\boldsymbol{u}, \boldsymbol{v}, \boldsymbol{n}_i)^T \cdot \left(\boldsymbol{q} - \boldsymbol{p}_i^+\right) \tag{8}$$

Note that the local potential function $W_{T_i^+}$ in Eq. (7) is a Gaussian function whose covariance is $\Sigma_g$. As Gaussian function is a compact support function, whose support region is an ellipsoid defined by $e^{-\frac{1}{2}\left(\boldsymbol{q}'^T \cdot \Sigma_g \cdot \boldsymbol{q}'\right)} \leq dmin$ where $dmin$ is the minimal value according to the computer's precision limitation. Figure 3(b) shows the support regions of all $W_{T_i^+}$ and $W_{T_i^-}$ for a 3D chess model. The parameter $m$ in Eq. (7) controls the thickness of support regions along the direction of $n_i$ (shaped like a cake) in Figure 3(b), in our approach, the parameter $m$ in $W_{T_i^+}$ is estimated by:

$$m = \sqrt{\frac{1}{k} \sum_{\boldsymbol{x} \in N\left(\boldsymbol{p}_i^+\right)} \left((\boldsymbol{x} - \boldsymbol{p}_i^+) \cdot \boldsymbol{n}_i\right)^2} \tag{9}$$

where $k = \left|N\left(\boldsymbol{p}_i^+\right)\right|$ is the number of neighboring positive primitive of $\boldsymbol{p}_i^+$. Eq. (9) means that we get the thickness of the support regions along the direction of $\boldsymbol{n}_i$ through stat the variance of neighboring primitives' projection points on $\boldsymbol{p}_i^+$'s normal direction $\boldsymbol{n}_i$. And it's the same for negative primitives.

## 3.2   Field Fitting Model Construction

As we explained in section 2.1, the zero equipotential surface does not necessarily appear in the middle of the capacitor(the insulator) which goes through $P = \{\boldsymbol{p}_i\}$. The positions of positive/negative primitives need to be adjusted to fit the insulator. And in our approach, moving tangent planes $T_i^+/T_i^-$ are equivalent to moving primitives near $p_i^+/p_i^-$ (because it is supposed that the neighboring primitives of $p_i^+/p_i^-$ are distributed in $T_i^+/T_i^-$ with some probabilities in section 2.1).

Therefore, the local potential function (Eq. (7)) is reformulate as:

$$W_{T_i^+}(d_i, \boldsymbol{q}) = C_i^+ \cdot e^{-\frac{1}{2}\left(\boldsymbol{q}''^T \cdot \Sigma_g^{-1} \cdot \boldsymbol{q}''\right)} \tag{10}$$

where $\boldsymbol{q}'' = (\boldsymbol{u}, \boldsymbol{v}, \boldsymbol{n_i})^T \cdot \left(\boldsymbol{q} - \left(\boldsymbol{p_i^+} + d_i \cdot n_i\right)\right)$. Note that this is the same for negative primitives.

The global potential at $q$ can be inferred to be a combination of all local potentials:

$$F(D, \boldsymbol{q}) = \sum_i W_{T_i^+}(d_i, \boldsymbol{q}) + \sum_i W_{T_i^-}(d_i, \boldsymbol{q}) \tag{11}$$

where $F(D, \boldsymbol{q})$ denotes the global potential value after doing movement $D = \{d_i\}$. $W_{T_i^+}(d_i, \boldsymbol{q})$ and $W_{T_i^-}(d_i, \boldsymbol{q})$ compute the local potential function after doing $d_i$ movement respectively.

Given an ideal local tangent plane movement set $D_0 = \{d_{i0}\}$, we have a zero potential surface defined by $F(D_0, \boldsymbol{p_i}) = 0$. Therefore, the energy function $J$ measuring the distance between the potential function $F$ and the exact surface can be defined as below:

$$J(D) = \sum_{\boldsymbol{p_i} \in P} F(D, \boldsymbol{p_i})^2 - \sum_{\boldsymbol{p_i} \in P} F(D_0, \boldsymbol{p_i})^2 = \sum_{\boldsymbol{p_i} \in P} F(D, \boldsymbol{p_i})^2 \tag{12}$$

From the definition of $J$, it is easy to infer that all we need is to find $D_0 = \{d_{i0}\}$, which can generate the minimum energy $J$.

However, solving the minimization of Eq. (12) with conventional Broyden's method [12] is too slow to be acceptable. In our approach, we introduce a greedy method which is more efficient according to empirical studies. The greedy method estimates each $d_i$ through a local potential function. For each paired plane $T_i^+$ and $T_i^-$, we use $S_{pi}(S_{pi} \subset P)$ to denote the points which are in the support region of $W_{T_i^+}$ or $W_{T_i^-}$. Then the local energy function $J_i$ can be rewrited as:

$$J_i(d_i) = \sum_{\boldsymbol{x} \in S_{p_i}} F(D, \boldsymbol{x})^2 = \sum_{\boldsymbol{x} \in S_{p_i}} (A(\boldsymbol{x}) + B(\boldsymbol{x}))^2 \tag{13}$$

where

$$A(\boldsymbol{x}) = \sum_{\boldsymbol{T_j^+} \in R_i^+} W_{\boldsymbol{T_j^+}}(d_j, \boldsymbol{x}) + \sum_{\boldsymbol{T_j^-} \in R_i^-} W_{\boldsymbol{T_j^-}}(d_j, \boldsymbol{x})$$

$$B(\boldsymbol{x}) = W_{T_i^+}(d_i, \boldsymbol{x}) + W_{T_i^-}(d_i, \boldsymbol{x})$$

where $R_i^+ = T^+ - \{\boldsymbol{T_i^+}\}$, $R_i^- = T^- - \{\boldsymbol{T_i^-}\}$, so $A(\boldsymbol{x})$ is the potential yield by primitives other than $W_{T_i^+}$, and $B(\boldsymbol{x})$ denote the potential yield by $W_{T_i^+}$. Then $d_{i0}$ can be achieved by solving:

$$d_{i0} = \arg\min_{d_i} J_i(d_i) \tag{14}$$

**Table 1.** Algorithm to obtain the potential function

<table>
<tr><td>

**Input**: Unorganized points $P = \{p_i\}$ equipped with normals $N = \{n_i\}$
**Output**: The potential function $\mathbf{F}$
**Initialization**:
Obtain the off-set points $P^+ = \{p_i^+\}$ and $P^- = \{p_i^-\}$ by
$p_i^+ = p_i + \lambda \cdot n_i,\ p_i^- = p_i - \lambda \cdot n_i$
**For** each pair of primitives $p_i^+/p_i^-$ do
    Get the local potential function through formula (7)
**end**
Calculate the initial energy $J^0$ by minimize (12)
**Do**
    Update each $d_i$ by solving (14)
    Calculate the new energy function $J^t$
**While** $(J^t - J^{t-1} < \epsilon)$, usually, we set $\epsilon$ to $J^0 * 0.001$
Estimate $\mathbf{F}$ through (11)

</td></tr>
</table>

Note that we split the energy function into two parts, the part of $A(\boldsymbol{x})$ is a constant value independent of $d_i$, and $B(\boldsymbol{x})$ is dependent of $d_i$. Therefore solving Eq. (14) with Quasi-Newton method [12] is much simpler than that of Eq. (12). Table 1 lists the proposed algorithm to obtain the potential function $F$.

### 3.3   Multi-scaling Strategy

Due to inevitable scanning errors, the input point cloud often has some unsampled regions which introduce holes on the surface. To fix these holes, we utilize the multi-scaling strategy in our Field fitting method which is widely used by the previous surface reconstruction approaches [10,14,15].

Point cloud thinning method [15] is employed to sample the multi-resolution point clouds from $P$, which down samples the point cloud through picking out the points with the minimum distance to their nearest neighbor. For each level of point cloud $L^i$, we can use the algorithm described in table 1 to estimate its corresponding $i$th-level global potential function $F^i$, and the overall global potential function F can be simply expressed as the sum of $F^i$. In our approach, we only use a very small number of levels, usually 2 or 3 and the down sampling ratio is set to be 0.1 for adjacent level. We apply Field Fitting to a incomplete bunny model (Figure 4 (a)), the reconstruction result by 1 level Field Fitting is shown in Figure 4(b), and the reconstruction result by multi levels (2 levels) Field Fitting is shown in Figure 4(c), it is noticeable that multi-scaling strategy can effectively fix holes which are introduced by unsampled regions.

## 4   Visualization

Polygonization [16], ray tracing [17] as well as point based rendering [9] can be used to visualize the surface fitting result. We employ the point based rendering method in our approach.

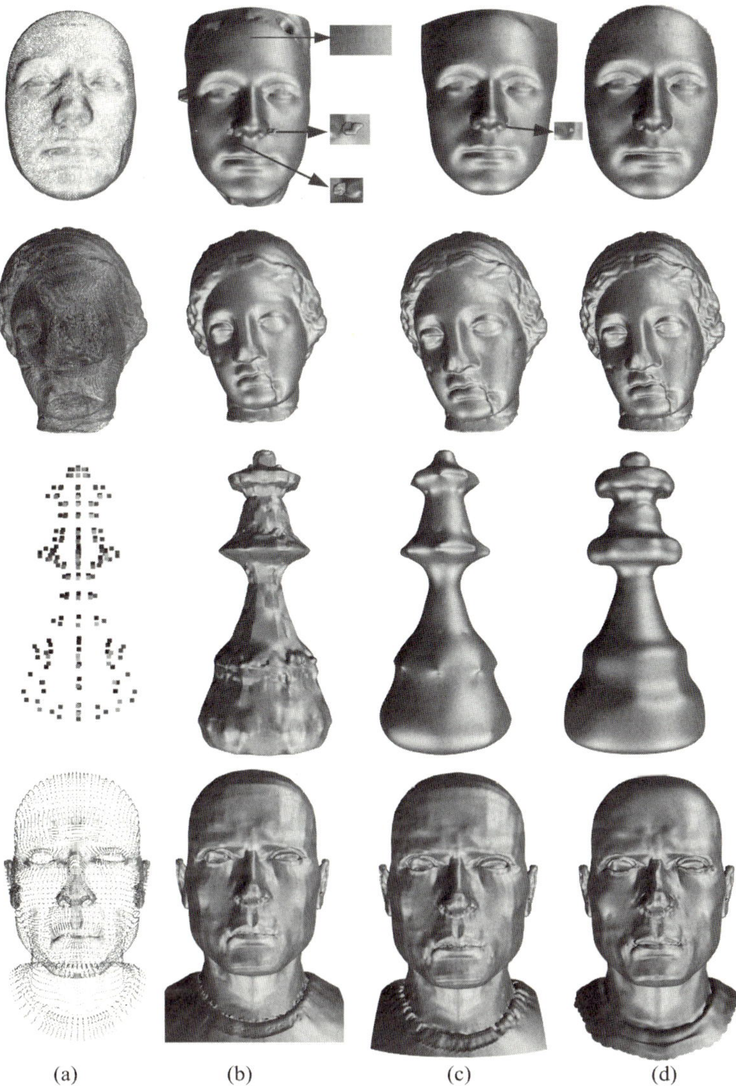

(a)      (b)      (c)      (d)

**Fig. 4.** The testing models and the reconstruction results. From left to right, the original models; MPU reconstruction results; Fast RBF reconstruction results; Field Fitting reconstruction results. From top to bottom, frontal face model (33,053 points), 'igea' (134,345 points), chess model (186 points), head model (15,941 points).

After obtaining the global potential function, a tracking process is carried out to obtain the zero level set points of the global potential function. This tracking process is very similar to the implicit surface polygonizing process [16], the only difference is that we do not polygonize the tracked cubes which are intersected with implicit surface, but only mark the centers of these cubes as the coarse zero level set points and by using binary search, a precisely locations the zero level set points can be found.

**Table 2.** Time, memory and triangles/points generated by different method, note that MPU and fRBF(denote Fast RBF) approach generate triangles while Our Field Fitting approach generate points

| Model | Approach | Fitting time | Isosurface extraction | Memory | Tris/Points |
|---|---|---|---|---|---|
| Frontal Face | MPU | 1.1s | 20.2s | 325M | 1,603K |
| | fRBF | 203.4s | 123.9s | 105M | 643K |
| | Ours | 36.6s | 183.3s | 850M | 1,037K |
| Igea | MPU | 4.6s | 20.1s | 320M | 1,253K |
| | fRBF | 105.6s | 396.3s | 162M | 1,042K |
| | Ours | 141.1s | 297.6s | 1500M | 2,128K |
| Chess | MPU | 0.23s | 22.1s | 180M | 2,092K |
| | fRBF | 0.14s | 7.3s | 73M | 393K |
| | Ours | 0.23s | 45.4s | 600M | 981K |
| Head | MPU | 17.2s | 28.4s | 374M | 1,929K |
| | fRBF | 1051.6s | 396.0s | 460M | 910K |
| | Ours | 17.4s | 199.0s | 720M | 1,649K |

## 5  Experiments

The experiments are performed on an Intel Core2 Q6600 with 2GBytes ram running windows server 2003. We make comparison between the proposed approach and two representative existing methods, namely, MPU[10], and FastRBF[5], to perform evaluation.

We firstly test a frontal face which has 33053 points, as shown in the first row of Figure 4. It is noticeable that there are some extra artifacts near the nose in the result by MPU because the inherent limitation of the quadric function for local domain operation and there are also artifacts near nose in RBF's result. Moreover, the narrow scar on the forehead is smoothed off by MPU due to the quadric function's strong smoothing effect. RBF can produce more reasonable and competitive result (first row third column). But some subtle details in the face are missed. Fortunately, it is noticeable that more subtle details (the scar on forehead) are preserved naturally in result of Field Fitting(the forth column) than that of MPU and RBF, i.e. in the result of our Field Fitting approach, the scar on forehead is clearly to be seen, but in MPU's result, the scar is smooth off and in RBF's result the scar is not so clearly as ours. Further, for a head model in forth row, there are many strange stripes in the result of RBF and MPU, Field Fitting outperforms RBF and MPU by giving natural and realistic surface reconstruction with better global stability and local details' preservation.

We also perform test on the model with very sparse point cloud. As shown in third row of Figure 4, neither MPU nor RBF produces qualified result because of some unnatural distortion and artifacts. The proposed Field Fitting method works well on this sparse model (forth column). This demonstrates that the proposed method outperforms both the two previous methods for its higher robustness.

We also compare the time consumption, memory and triangles/points generated by different methods in Table 2. Although in this table, our approach is neither fastest nor most memory saving (due to the deep space splits for isosurface extraction), it is noticeable that our approach generate a smooth and detail reserved surfaces which have nicer appearance than MPU and FastRBF.

## 6   Conclusion

In this paper, we present a novel implicit surface reconstruction approach by an analogy of classic physical polar field model. The experimental results show that the proposed Field Fitting approach outperforms the previous methods by generating results with more subtle details while keeping global smoothness. Moreover, it is noticeable that the proposed approach keeps robust to sparse input point cloud.

Though the proposed method provides a better solution on implicit surface fitting, we notice that there are still several problems with it. For example, the proposed approach needs larger memory to extract isosurfaces than the representative existing approaches. And, the efficiency still needs improved. In our future work, we will pay more attention to the reduction of memory requirement and try to explore a more efficient fitting strategy to strengthen the method's usability.

**Acknowledgments.** This paper is supported by National Science Foundation of China (Grant No. 60873124), and thanks to FarField Technology Ltd who provide us a demonstration license of FastRBF Toolkit with a capability of 1000k input points.

## References


1. Bloomenthal, J., Bajaj, C.: Introduction to Implicit Surfaces. Morgan Kaufmann, San Francisco (1997)
2. Dierckx, P.: Curve and Surface Fitting with Splines. Oxford University Press, Oxford (1993)
3. Floater, M., Hormann, K.: Surface Parameterization: a Tutorial and Survey. Advances In Multiresolution For Geometric Modelling (2005)
4. Blane, M., Lei, Z., Çivi, H., Cooper, D.: The 3L Algorithm for Fitting Implicit Polynomial Curves and Surfaces to Data. IEEE Transactions on Pattern Analysis and Machine Intelligence, 298–313 (2000)
5. Carr, J., Beatson, R., Cherrie, J., Mitchell, T., Fright, W., McCallum, B., Evans, T.: Reconstruction and representation of 3D objects with radial basis functions. In: Proceedings of the 28th annual conference on Computer graphics and interactive techniques, pp. 67–76 (2001)
6. Carr, J., Beatson, R., McCallum, B., Fright, W., McLennan, T., Mitchell, T.: Smooth surface reconstruction from noisy range data. ACM GRAPHITE 3, 119–126 (2003)
7. Hoppe, H., DeRose, T., Duchamp, T., McDonald, J., Stuetzle, W.: Surface reconstruction from unorganized points. In: Proceedings of the 19th annual conference on Computer graphics and interactive techniques, pp. 71–78 (1992)

8. Alexa, M., Behr, J., Cohen-Or, D., Fleishman, S., Levin, D., Silva, C.: Point set surfaces. In: Proceedings of the conference on Visualization 2001, pp. 21–28 (2001)
9. Alexa, M., Behr, J., Cohen-Or, D., Fleishman, S., Levin, D., Silva, C.T.: Computing and Rendering Point Set Surfaces. Computing 9(1), 3–15 (2003)
10. Ohtake, Y., Belyaev, A., Alexa, M., Turk, G., Seidel, H.: Multi-level partition of unity implicits. In: International Conference on Computer Graphics and Interactive Techniques, pp. 463–470 (2003)
11. Kazhdan, M., Bolitho, M., Hoppe, H.: Poisson Surface Reconstruction. Indicator 1(1) (2006)
12. Press, W., Teukolsky, S., Vetterling, W., Flannery, B.: Numerical Recipes in C++. Cambridge Univ. Press, Cambridge (2002)
13. Mitra, N., Nguyen, A.: Estimating surface normals in noisy point cloud data. In: Proceedings of the nineteenth annual symposium on Computational geometry, pp. 322–328 (2003)
14. Ohtake, Y., Belyaev, A., Seidel, H.: A multi-scale approach to 3D scattered data interpolation with compactly supported basis functions. In: Shape Modeling International 2003, pp. 153–161 (2003)
15. Tobor, I., Reuter, P., Schlick, C.: Multi-scale reconstruction of implicit surfaces with attributes from large unorganized point sets. In: Proceedings of Shape Modeling Applications, pp. 19–30 (2004)
16. Bloomenthal, J.: An implicit surface polygonizer. Graphics Gems IV 349 (1994)
17. Hart, J.: Sphere tracing: a geometric method for the antialiased ray tracing of implicit surfaces. The Visual Computer 12(10), 527–545 (1996)

# Dense Stereo Correspondence with Contrast Context Histogram, Segmentation-Based Two-Pass Aggregation and Occlusion Handling


Tianliang Liu, Pinzheng Zhang, and Limin Luo

Lab of Image Science and Technology (LIST), Southeast University
No.2 Sipailou, Nanjing, 210096, China
{ltl315,luckzpz,luo.list}@seu.edu.cn



**Abstract.** In a local and perceptual organization framework, a novel stereo correspondence algorithm is proposed to provide dense and accurate disparity maps under point ambiguity. First, the initial matching technique is based on raw matching cost obtained from local descriptor with contrast context histogram and two-pass cost aggregation via segmentation-based adaptive support weight. Second, the disparity estimation procedure consists sequentially of two steps: namely, a narrow occlusion handling and a multi-directional weighted least square (WLS) fitting for large occlusion. The experiment results indicate that our algorithm can increase robustness against outliers, and then obtain comparable and accurate disparity than other local stereo methods effectively, and it is even better than some algorithms using advanced and offline but computationally complicated global optimization based algorithms.

**Keywords:** Stereo vision, stereo matching, local descriptor, segmentation, parallel computing, weighted least square, large occlusion.


## 1   Introduction

Accurate dense stereo matching is a fundamental and crucial problem in computer vision. A comparison of current stereo matching algorithms is given on the Middlebury Stereo Pages [1]. In general, stereo vision algorithms can be classified into local and global methods [1]. In local method, an area-based cost function is carefully selected and aggregated within a certain neighborhood to obtain resulting disparity with winner-takes-all (WTA) optimization [2,3,4,5,6,7,8,9,10]. To provide a robust result in stereo matching, the family of global algorithms seeks a disparity surface minimizing a global cost function defined by making an explicit smoothness assumption [12,13,14,15,16,17]. Recently there also exists trade-off between local and global methods, such as semi-global matching [18].The latter two families usually have high matching accuracy. But most of them are computationally expensive and need many parameters that are hard to be set. However, the local methods are generally outperformed by the global and semi-global ones in higher speed.


T. Wada, F. Huang, and S. Lin (Eds.): PSIVT 2009, LNCS 5414, pp. 449–461, 2009.
© Springer-Verlag Berlin Heidelberg 2009

To resolve the point ambiguity problem in image matching, many methods have been proposed for decades. Feature-based methods match only a few points proper for matching [20,21] while filtering out ambiguous points. In general, the idea is to detect the invariant local properties of salient image corners under a class of transformations, and then establish discriminating descriptors for these corners. As a result, feature-based methods yield sparse disparity maps. This approach is comparatively robust to the point ambiguity and produces accurate results rapidly in general. However, an efficient discriminating local descriptor, which is called contrast context histogram (CCH) and adopted previously for object recognition and image matching [20], is now proposed to extract local feature from image pairs to be constructed raw and robust matching cost for dense disparity map in local stereo correspondence in our work.

The local techniques typically use some kinds of statistical correlation among color or intensity patterns in local support windows in cost aggregation step [2,5,6]. In this approach, it is implicitly assumed that all points in a support window are from the same disparity in the scene. The variable support strategies with or without segmentation information in a specific support window are proposed to compute matching costs for the state-of-art local stereo methods [2,5]. But these variable support strategies with large window size have much high computational complexity because of symmetry (left-and-right) and traverse (pixel-by-pixel).

Recently a new post-processing technique has been studied to improve stereo matching performance [23]. This approach was presented to address the disparity discontinuity problem in narrow occluded regions when the better initial disparity maps were obtained from global method (such as graph cut). It consists of two parts; namely, a greedy disparity filling and a least-squared-errors (LSE) fitting. However, if the initial results with worse quality were gotten from a simple and efficient local method other than good global method, this approach can not effectively improve the resulting disparity maps. The latter one should be modified a bit to solve new problem.

This paper proposes a novel local stereo method which employs segmentation cue and can be divided into two steps: initial matching and disparity estimation. The initial matching is on the basis of raw matching cost with the CCH descriptor and two-pass cost aggregation with segmentation-based adaptive support weight (SASW). The disparity estimation in turn consists of two parts: narrow occlusion handling and multi-directional weighted least square (WLS) fitting for the broad or large occlusion areas. By means of experimental results we demonstrate that our approach can obtain the comparable disparity maps with high quality compared to some other traditional stereo algorithms.

The remainder of this paper is organized as follows. In Section 2, the CCH-based initial matching algorithm with segmentation information is discussed. The disparity estimation is addressed as a post-processing module for some unreliable disparities in Section 3. Experimental results are shown in Section 4. At last, conclusion and our future work are given in Section 5.

## 2   Initial Matching

### 2.1   The CCH-Based Cost Initialization and Color Segmentation

The dissimilarity measure is a crucial part of the stereo correspondence in a local perspective. In this paper, before computing pixel-wise matching cost, we select a local discriminating CCH descriptor to capture the feature for each pixel robustly and efficiently [20]. The local descriptor is a histogram of the contrast values inside the local region, which features log-polar mapping. The use of log-polar transformation is introduced as a preprocessing module to recover large scale changes and arbitrary rotations, which is a nonlinear and non-uniform sampling of spatial domain. Meanwhile, the histogram of the contrast values, comparing with other dissimilarity measures, are more insensitive to image noise and intensity difference of stereo pairs.

In general, how to construct the CCH descriptors for each pixel can be described as follows: firstly, to define a specified Log-polar mask $M$ of the CCH descriptors, which is divided into several non-overlapping regions, $R_1, R_2, \ldots, R_t$, by quantizing the radius and the direction in a $n \times n$ local region $\mathbf{R}$, as illustrated in Fig. 1. The current point $p_c$ lies in the center of the coordinate. Then, according to the mask $M$ with several sub-regions, we traverse each pixel $p_c$ ignoring image borders to compute statistically positive and negative contrast histogram for each sub-region $R_i$. For each $p$ in $R_i$, we can in turn define the two contrast histogram bins with respect to $p_c$ as

$$H_{R_i^+} = \frac{\sum \{Diff \mid p \in R_i \ and \ Diff \geq 0\}}{\#R_i^+} \tag{1}$$

$$H_{R_i^-} = \frac{\sum \{Diff \mid p \in R_i \ and \ Diff < 0\}}{\#R_i^-} \tag{2}$$

where $Diff$ is the center-based intensity difference between $p$ and $p_c$, $\#R_i^+$ and $\#R_i^-$ are the number of the positive and negative contrast values in the $i^{th}$ region $R_i$, respectively. And then, by concatenating the values of all the contrast histogram entries from all the sub-regions into a single vector, the CCH descriptor of $p_c$ in correspondence with its local region can be defined as follows:

$$CCH(p_c) = \{H_{R_1^+}, H_{R_1^-}, H_{R_2^+}, H_{R_2^-}, \ldots, H_{R_t^+}, H_{R_t^-}\} \tag{3}$$

which can be considered as robust measurement of local intensity variations. The vector length $T$ of this descriptor accords with the number of histogram bins.

The cost initialization module computes the initial matching cost $C(p_b, q_{m,d})$ (or $C(p_{bx}, p_{by}, d)$) between points $p_b \in I_b$ and $q_{m,d} \in I_m$ for assigning disparity hypothesis $d$ to each pixel $p_b$ in which the coordinates of $p_b$ and $q_{m,d}$ are $(p_{bx}, p_{by})$ and $(p_{bx} - d, p_{by})$. To deal with linear lighting change and make the best use of the range that a single byte offers similarly to [6], the CCH descriptor can be normalized to a unit vector and scaled with 255. As the computed CCH descriptors are distributions represented as histograms, it is natural to calculate the correspondence scores using $\chi^2$ distance [21]:

$$C(p_b, q_{m,d}) = \frac{1}{2} \sum_{k=1}^{T} \frac{(h_k(p_b) - h_k(q_{m,d}))^2}{h_k(p_b) + h_k(q_{m,d})} \tag{4}$$

where $h_k(p_b)$ and $h_k(q_{m,d})$ denote the $k$-bin normalized and scaled histogram at $p_b$ and $q_{m,d}$, respectively. This matching will result in close distributions because this distance measures how unlikely it is that one distribution is drawn from the population represented by the other.

And then, we adopt color segmentation and then assume that pixels in the each segment should have similar disparity values. In our implementation, the Mean Shift algorithm [22] is used for color segmentation in CIELab space. The difference between pixel colors is measured in the CIELab color space because it provides three-dimensional representation for the perception of color stimuli similar to human color discrimination performance in short Euclidean distances [2].

## 2.2 The SASW-Based Two-Pass Cost Aggregation and Disparity Selection

The robust and fast support aggregation stage is also an important part in the local stereo matching. In order to reduce false matches owing to the point ambiguity and preserve efficient computation, we adopt a two-pass weighted cost aggregation with color segmentation cue. This SASW-based two-pass aggregation is inspired by the work of [5,19] and [6]. To construct the matching cost between two points $p_b$ and $q_{m,d}$, a specific support weight, which is determined by color proximity from $p_b$ as well as on segmentation information in monocular cue, is first assigned during the aggregation step to each point of $I_b$. In particular, weight $w_b(p_i, p_b)$ for point $p_i$ belonging to $I_b$ and close to $p_b$ is defined as:

$$w_b(p_i, p_b) = \begin{cases} 1.0 & p_i \in S_b \\ \exp(-\frac{d_c(I_b(p_i), I_b(p_b))}{\gamma_c}) & otherwise \end{cases} \tag{5}$$

with $S_b$ being the segment on which $p_b$ lies, $d_c$ being the Euclidean distance between two RGB triplets and the constant $\gamma_c$ being an experimental parameter of the algorithm. Instead, the use of segmentation plays the role of an intelligent proximity criterion. It is a weight with zero value that is assigned to those points of $I_b$ which lie too far from $p_b$, i.e. whose distance in the horizontal or vertical direction exceeds a certain length. As the use of segmentation in CIELab color space implies adding robustness to the support, we operate the RGB space for its convenience outside of segment in order to enforce smoothness over textured planes as well as to increase the accuracy of depth borders localization.

When aggregating matching costs, the original segmentation-based adaptive-weight approach computes the weighted average of adjacent matching costs, with the weights generated using both stereo images [5,19]. A similar approach is adopted to assign a weight $w_m(q_i, q_{m,d})$ to each point $q_i \in I_m$. The strategy of SASW is similar to that of traditional adaptive weight approach [2]. Under the left-and-right stereo setting with the weights being calculated, the matching cost for correspondence $(p_b, q_{m,d})$ depends on summing over the image area the product of such weights with the above point-wise matching score normalized by the weight sum:

$$C_{osaw}(p_b, q_{m,d}) = \frac{\displaystyle\sum_{p_i \in N_{p_b}, q_i \in N_{qm}} w_b(p_i, p_b) \cdot w_m(q_i, q_{m,d}) \cdot C(p_i, q_i)}{\displaystyle\sum_{p_i \in N_{p_b}, q_i \in N_{qm}} w_b(p_i, p_b) \cdot w_m(q_i, q_{m,d})} \tag{6}$$

where $N_{p_b}$ and $N_{qm}$ are respectively support neighbor window around $p_b$ in base image and that of $q_{m,d}$ with respect to a disparity value $d$ in matching image.

In this paper, we present two simplifications to the original segmentation-based algorithm with high computational complexity for achieving better performance in computational time similar to [6]. The first one is to ignore the weight term obtained from the matching image and its monocular segmentation cue. Therefore, to make it possible to compute the aggregated matching costs for different disparity hypotheses in parallel, the same weight is imposed to the same pixel when handling different disparity hypotheses. The second simplification is to approximate the weighted average of matching costs in the 2D rectangle window (i.e. $r \times r$) using a two-pass technique, in which the first pass computes the weighted average along the horizontal scanline while the second pass computing along the vertical scanline. This can further decrease the computational complexity of the aggregation approach from $O(r^2)$ to $O(r)$, which depends strongly on the window size used. Two additional steps are used to calculate the weighted averages being splitted in two separate components (horizontal and vertical). As a result, the aggregated costs are calculated in the simplified version using:

$$T^r(p_{bx}, p_{by}, d) = \frac{\sum_{u=-r}^{r} w(p_{bx}, p_{by}, u, 0) \cdot C(p_{bx} + u, p_{by}, d)}{\sum_{u=-r}^{r} w(p_{bx}, p_{by}, u, 0)} \tag{7}$$

$$C_{sasw}^r(p_{bx}, p_{by}, d) = \frac{\sum_{v=-r}^{r} w(p_{bx}, p_{by}, 0, v) \cdot T^r(p_{bx}, p_{by} + v, d)}{\sum_{v=-r}^{r} w(p_{bx}, p_{by}, 0, v)} \tag{8}$$

This cost aggregation with SASW mentioned above is a good technique for strengthening dissimilarity measure in itself. It is possible to get accurate dense matching results by performing a simple and local WTA optimization at each pixel with the proposed SASW without any complicated processes. The WTA method for the disparity of $p_b$ in the base image can be formally defined as:

$$D_{init}(p_b) = \arg\min_{d \in R_d} C_{sasw}^r(p_{bx}, p_{by}, d) \tag{9}$$

with $R_d = [d_{min}, d_{max}]$ being the predefined range of all possible disparities. A similar approach can be adopted for the matching image $I_m$. After the WTA-based local optimization, coarse outliers are filtered using a $3 \times 3$ median filter.

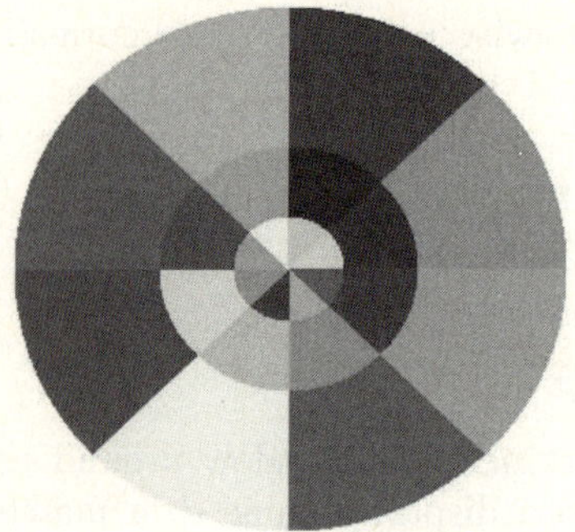

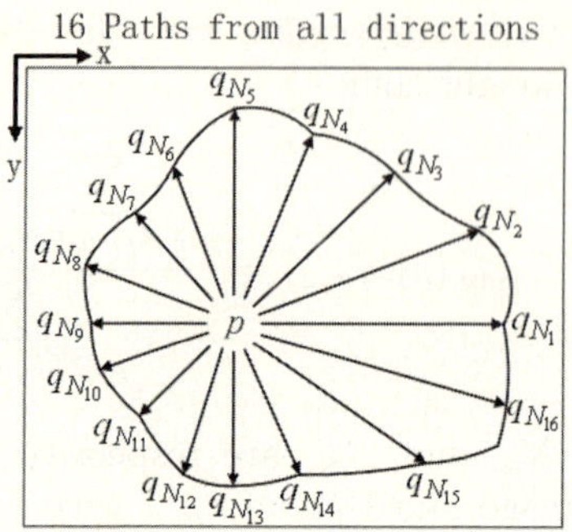


**Fig. 1.** Log-polar mask for the CCH    **Fig. 2.** WLS fitting paths in all directions

## 3   Disparity Estimation

### 3.1   Narrow Occlusion Handling

Firstly, unreliable disparities should be detected in this phase before addressing occluded regions which are small or narrow. To filter out these more erroneous matches, we apply the left-right consistency check symmetrically from stereo itself [19,23]. A threshold $T_{occ}$ can be used for uniqueness constraint in our implementation. As mentioned above, color segmentation algorithm [22] is firstly employed for the selected base or matching image in CIELab color space in the implementation. It is more suitable for detecting outlier in segmented patch with small enough area and similar color if the segmentation is strong over-segmented.

After that, outlier removal is used to cluster reliable disparities in the same color segment into groups in an iterative framework, and identify unreliable disparity based on two measurements proposed in [26]. And then, greedy disparity filling is deployed to address the unreliable disparity when the occlusion region is small or narrow. The basic assumption for the disparity filling scheme is that the disparity of an unreliable pixel is the same as that of one of its neighbors in the same color segment by using the greedy-based strategy. The algorithm can be represented in details in [23]. The binocular and the monocular image data are used sequentially. There exists a threshold $s$ as an appropriate constraint for both image cues to fill the unreliable disparities from neighboring reliable pixels.

### 3.2   Large Occlusion Handling

After the narrow occlusion handling procedure, it is possible that the disparity map still has unreliable pixels which do not have a disparity value. To resolve this issue more efficiently in purely local stereo correspondence perspective, the multi-directional WLS technique is proposed in this paper.

We assume that pixels which do not have a disparity up to now are justly resolved by the WLS scheme. In a known epipolar geometry, least-square-errors (LSE) fitting [23] with only intensity cue along the corresponding horizontal scanline is naturally selected while ignoring the boundaries of color segmentation. However, to resolve still existed larger and more unreliable disparities, we do not have to enforce only the one or two ordering direction constraint in the horizontal scanline in LSE , and should exploit sufficiently monocular cues (intensity, color and shape etc.) in all directions to pursuit perfect disparity filling.

This leads to a new idea of greedy filling unreliable disparities by means of adaptive weight WLS fitting in 1D from all directions, while looking like semi-global cost aggregation step radially and equally for each path [18]. Each 1D measured path is started from an unreliable disparity pixel $p$ and ended in first existed disparity pixel $q_{Nk}$ encountered in the given radial direction. This can be explained by Fig. 2. The pixels outside of a convex hull in Fig. 2 represent pixels that have a disparity while the pixels inside of the hull have no disparity. The pixels of the hull itself also represent existed disparities passed a chain of procedures above. We assume that the disparity of the pixels inside the hull varies from the range of the existed disparities on the convex hull in this example.

These are the closest disparity values that can be obtained using the greedy disparity filling scheme when being approached from not only the left and the right directions, but multi-directions in a 2D image space. Considering computation complexity, we can assume that the number of all directions with WLS is in practice not arbitrarily large, but finite positive integer $K$ (such as, $2 < K \leq 36$). The weight in this phase can be determined similarly by adaptive support weight [2]. The reason for the weight used in the disparity filling is that the smaller the distance between them in image spatial domain is, the higher the priority of filling candidate is; while the reason for color contribution is similar.

The WLS is calculated as a function of intensity variations along specific directional paths equally, which can be defined as minimizing the total weighted intensity variations along each 1D measured path from all 1D intensity variation paths with unreliable disparity pixels. We can get

$$q_{k_i}^* = \underset{k=1,\ldots,K}{\arg\min} \{ f_1(q_{N1}), \cdots, f_k(q_{Nk}), \cdots, f_K(q_{NK}) \} \tag{10}$$

where

$$f_k(q_{Nk}) = \frac{\sum_{i=0}^{M_k} w(p, q_{k_i}) \cdot (I_{L_k}(q_{k_i}) - Mean(p, k))^2}{\sum_{i=0}^{M_k} w(p, q_{k_i})} \tag{11}$$

$$Mean(p, k) = \frac{1}{M_k} \sum_{i=0}^{M_k} I_{L_k}(q_{k_i}) \tag{12}$$

with $I_{L_k}(q_{k_i})$ being the intensity of pixel $q_{k_i}$ in the $k^{th}$ radial direction path $L_k$, $M_k$ being the length of the given $k^{th}$ path $L_k$ and $q_{k_i}$ denoting the $i^{th}$ pixel close to the current unreliable disparity pixel $p$ in the path $L_k$. $w(p, q_{k_i})$ indicates the support weight between $p$ and $q_{k_i}$ using color similarity and spatial proximity [2]. $f_k(q_{Nk})$ represents the perceptual distance between unreliable disparity pixel $p$ and nearest disparity existed pixel $q_{k_i}$ in the path $L_k$, which is weighted and normalized from three monocular cues: intensity, color and spatial distance etc.

Then, we assign reliable and closest disparity value $q_{Nk}$ to unreliable pixels $q_{k_i}$ when satisfying the criteria function (10). Finally, median filter can be adopted to remove remaining irregularities and smooth the last disparity map.

## 4    Experiment Results

### 4.1    Experiment Setup on Middlebury Stereo Pairs

To verify the effectiveness of our method at present, we computed the dense disparity maps while exploiting color segmentation in local technique for the Tsukuba, Venus, Teddy and Cones from the Middlebury 's second version stereo evaluation data set [1]. The parameters were kept constant for all stereo pairs.

In the CCH descriptor, we adopt three levels in the quantization of the distance and eight intervals in the quantization of the orientation under the log-polar coordinate system to generate the mask $M$ with $3 \times 8 = 24$ non-overlapping regions, as shown in Fig. 1. Hence, the dimensions of the CCH descriptor $T$ are $2 \times 3 \times 8 = 48$. And the definition of the distance and orientation is similar to that of them in the paper [20]. The color segmentation is obtained by running the Mean Shift algorithm using high speed version in CIELab space with a constant set of parameters (spatial radius $\delta S = 3$, range radius $\delta R = 3$, minimum region size $minR = 35$). For what means the variable support for the base image

**Table 1.** Quantitative evaluation of the proposed algorithm, comparing the percentage of "bad pixels" in non-occluded regions ($R_{O-}$), all regions except for unknown pixels ($R_A$), and regions near depth discontinuities ($R_D$). In each column, our result and some best of them are in bold and italic print, respectively. The overall performance measure is displayed in the $2^{th}$ column, in which the average rank are over all latter 12 columns while subscript numbers being the relative ranks similar to the website [1].

| Algorithm | Rank | Tsukuba | | | Venus | | | Teddy | | | Cones | | |
|---|---|---|---|---|---|---|---|---|---|---|---|---|---|
| | | $R_{O-}$ | $R_A$ | $R_D$ | $R_{O-}$ | $R_A$ | $R_D$ | $R_{O-}$ | $R_A$ | $R_D$ | $R_{O-}$ | $R_A$ | $R_D$ |
| CooptRegion [16] | $3.3_1$ | *0.87* | *1.16* | *4.6* | 0.11 | 0.21 | 1.54 | 5.16 | 8.31 | 13.0 | 2.79 | *7.18* | 8.01 |
| AdaptingBP [13] | $3.5_2$ | 1.11 | 1.37 | 5.79 | *0.10* | 0.21 | *1.44* | 4.22 | 7.06 | 11.8 | *2.48* | 7.92 | 7.32 |
| AdaptOvrSegBP [14] | $11.6_7$ | 1.69 | 2.04 | 5.64 | 0.14 | *0.20* | 1.47 | 7.04 | 11.1 | 16.4 | 3.60 | 8.96 | 8.84 |
| AdaptDispCalib [4] | $13.8_{10}$ | 1.19 | 1.42 | 6.15 | 0.23 | 0.34 | 2.50 | 7.80 | 13.6 | 17.3 | 3.62 | 9.33 | 9.72 |
| C-SemiGlob [18] | $15.0_{12}$ | 2.61 | 3.29 | 9.89 | 0.25 | 0.57 | 3.24 | 5.14 | 11.8 | 13.0 | 2.77 | 8.35 | 8.20 |
| SO+borders [19] | $15.0_{13}$ | 1.29 | 1.71 | 6.83 | 0.25 | 0.53 | 2.26 | 7.02 | 12.2 | 16.3 | 3.90 | 9.85 | 10.2 |
| CostAggr+occ [3] | $17.2_{16}$ | 1.38 | 1.96 | 7.14 | 0.44 | 1.13 | 4.87 | 6.80 | 11.9 | 17.3 | 3.60 | 8.57 | 9.36 |
| SegmentSupport [5] | $17.3_{17}$ | 1.25 | 1.62 | 6.68 | 0.25 | 0.64 | 2.59 | 8.43 | 14.2 | 18.2 | 3.77 | 9.87 | 9.77 |
| AdaptWeight [2] | $20.7_{20}$ | 1.38 | 1.85 | 6.90 | 0.71 | 1.19 | 6.13 | 7.88 | 13.3 | 18.6 | 3.97 | 9.79 | 8.26 |
| 2OP+occ [17] | $26.8_{27}$ | 2.91 | 3.56 | 7.33 | 0.24 | 0.49 | 2.76 | 10.9 | 15.4 | 20.6 | 5.42 | 10.8 | 12.5 |
| **Our method** | $27.6_{28}$ | **1.74** | **2.11** | **9.23** | **0.41** | **0.94** | **3.97** | **8.08** | **14.3** | **19.8** | **7.07** | **12.9** | **16.3** |
| FastAggreg [8] | $28.0_{29}$ | 1.16 | 2.11 | 6.06 | 4.03 | 4.75 | 6.43 | 9.04 | 15.2 | 20.2 | 5.37 | 12.6 | 11.9 |
| GC+occ [12] | $28.2_{30}$ | 1.19 | 2.01 | 6.24 | 1.64 | 2.19 | 6.75 | 11.2 | 17.4 | 19.8 | 5.36 | 12.4 | 13.0 |
| AdaptPolygon [10] | $30.6_{33}$ | 2.29 | 2.88 | 8.94 | 0.80 | 1.11 | 3.41 | 10.5 | 15.9 | 21.3 | 6.13 | 13.2 | 13.3 |
| TensorVoting [11] | $32.4_{35}$ | 3.79 | 4.79 | 8.86 | 1.23 | 1.88 | 11.5 | 9.76 | 17.0 | 24.0 | 4.38 | 11.4 | 12.2 |
| RealTimeGPU [6] | $32.8_{36}$ | 2.05 | 4.22 | 10.6 | 1.92 | 2.98 | 20.3 | 7.23 | 14.4 | 17.6 | 6.41 | 13.7 | 16.5 |
| CostRelax [9] | $33.7_{37}$ | 4.76 | 6.08 | 20.3 | 1.41 | 2.48 | 18.5 | 8.18 | 15.9 | 23.8 | 3.91 | 10.2 | 11.8 |
| TreeDP [15] | $36.7_{39}$ | 1.99 | 2.84 | 9.96 | 1.41 | 2.10 | 7.74 | 15.9 | 23.9 | 27.1 | 10.0 | 18.3 | 18.9 |

**Fig. 3.** Dense disparity results for the Tsukuba, Venus, Teddy and Cones stereo pairs: base images (first column), ground truth (second column), our results (third column) and bad pixels (last column)

in stereo pairs, the size of support window $r$ is set to 51; and the parameter $\gamma_c$ is equal to 15 in the two-pass cost aggregation stage.

For parameters in Section 3, the parameter $T_{occ}$ in the symmetrical occlusion detection module is set to 2 in order to consider appropriately for part slanted object surfaces. In outlier removing [23], the first criterion (i.e., the ratio of occlusion in the segment) is set to be $O/S \geq 0.75$, where $O$ and $S$ are the numbers of pixels without disparity values and the area of the segment. The second criterion is chosen to be "if the percentage of the same disparity is smaller than 0.05%", pixels with a disparity value are still set to unreliable pixels. Meanwhile the threshold $s$ is set to 5 for greedy disparity filling. $K$ is equal to 36 and the parameters for the adaptive weight in WLS fitting are set by default values [2].

## 4.2   Quantitative and Qualitative Evaluation

The comparative results measured for each pair are summarized in Table 1 in terms of the percentage of bad matching pixels with the error tolerance $\delta = 1.0$. The Middlebury's second version stereo evaluation is measured based on known ground truth data. We cannot list total 49 algorithms including ours (as of July 2008) for lacking enough space; some other details can be found in the website [1].

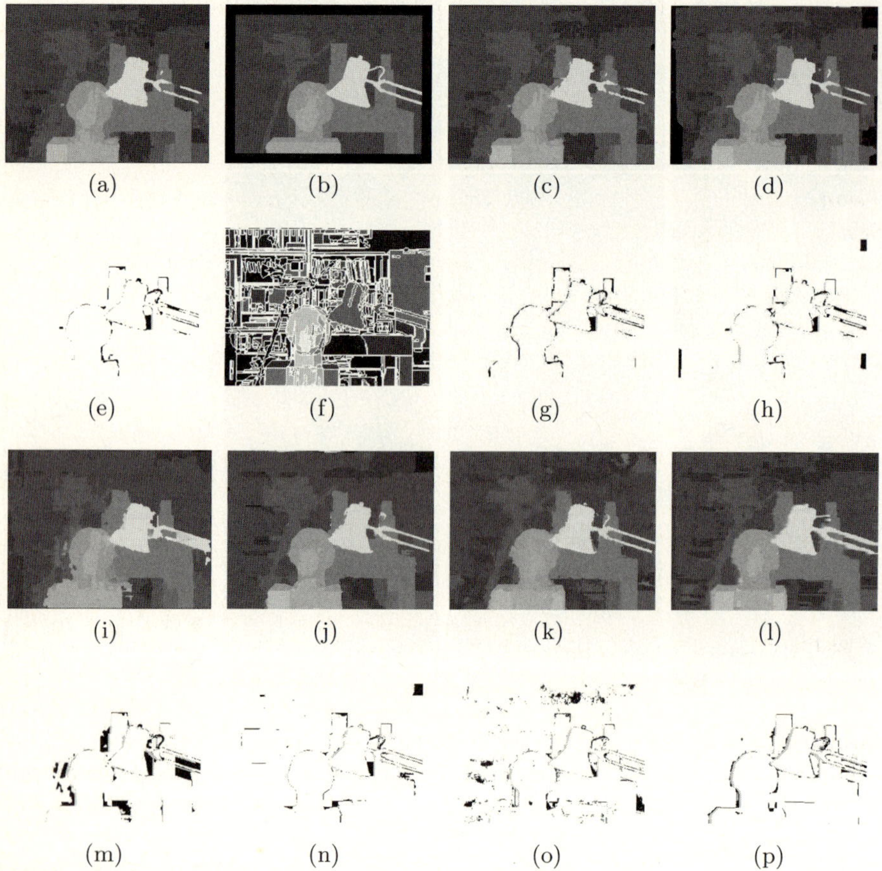

**Fig. 4.** Some parts of our algorithm contribute to the robustness of the disparity maps while comparing with several well-known local algorithms on the famous Tsukuba stereo image pair. (a and e) our final result and its bad pixels, (b and f) ground truth and segmentation result, (c and g) the result and its bad pixels replacing our disparity estimation by the default disparity estimation [23], (d and h) our initial result and its bad pixels, (i and m) the result and its bad pixels replacing our raw CCH-based matching cost by non-truncated SSD, (j and n) the result and its bad pixels via AdaptPolygon [10], (k and o) the result and its bad pixels via TensorVoting [11], (l and p) the result and its bad pixels via RealTimeGPU [6].

As it is clear from the Table 1 and the website, the rank of our algorithm with low computation cost is currently the $28^{th}$ top of overall 49 algorithms in the evaluation. Our overall results in matching precision are apparently improved on the whole than some local methods, such as FastAggreg [10], TensorVoting [11], RealTimeGPU [6] and CostRelax [9] et al., and some advanced global ones such as GC+occ [12] and TreeDP [15] et al. However, our results are a bit worse than the other state-of-the-art methods in overall performance measure, such as CooptRegion [16], AdaptingBP [13], AdaptDispCalib [4], C-SemiGlob [18],

SO+borders [19], SegmSupport [5] and 2OP+occ [17] et al. As can be seen from the table, the proposed approach is comparably good among the purely local methods on standard stereo benchmarks.

Meanwhile, the proposed method is less expensive than other local methods in computational complexity. For some state-of-art local methods, such as Adapt-DispCalib, AdaptWeight, SO+borders and SegmSupport, the support window selected with too large value in cost aggregation will introduce very expensive complexity being the dominant processing time in the overall computation time; however, our method with parallel computing ability can generate efficiently comparative or equivalent result. But the complexity in two other modules will be increased a bit in computation time. The reasons may be listed as follows. Firstly, the Log-polar transformation should be run on several non-uniform sampling sub-regions to retrieval the local feature in the raw matching cost. Secondly, the disparity maps for both views should be doubly obtained from initial matching to check left-right consistency symmetrically in the narrow occlusion handling. Finally, the WLS fitting with $K$ directions should be deployed to each unreliable disparity pixel in the large occlusion area. Fortunately, comparing with the obvious increase of matching precision, the little additional computational cost is negligible.

To compare visually and understand clearly our discussed algorithm, Fig. 3 shows the actual dense disparity results in our experiment. As can be seen clearly from the figure, the proposed approach can produce dense and accurate piecewise smooth disparity maps. Fig. 4 shows the disparity maps from some parts of our algorithm replaced by other traditional and similar module, while comparing with several previously known local algorithms, to illustrate how they complement each other to achieve robust disparity estimation. Especially, our algorithm can handle large occlusion effectively while comparing our results (a and e) with the results (c and g) by the default disparity estimation [23] without multi-directional weighted large occlusion handling in Fig. 4.


## 5   Conclusion

This paper presents a new and simple stereo approach with the CCH descriptor, SASW-based two-pass cost aggregation and multi-directional WLS fitting in a local perspective to generate more reliable and accurate disparity maps under point ambiguity effectively and efficiently. The stereo correspondence roughly consists of two steps sequentially: initial matching and disparity estimation. The CCH descriptor in the cost initialization, color segmentation and variable support weight in the two-pass cost aggregation are combined to obtain reliable and initial disparity maps; and then disparity estimation via narrow occlusion handling and multi-directional WLS fitting is designed to improve the stereo matching performance.

The advantages and shortcomings of the underlying design mechanisms in our method are discussed and analyzed through experimental evaluations conducted for the Middlebury data sets quantitatively and qualitatively. The experimental results show that the proposed algorithm has higher matching precision and better robustness when compared with some part of standard stereo benchmarks.

In our future, we plan to observe this technique with more robust and other dissimilarity measure as raw pixel-wise matching cost, resegment strategy for large segments and more robust post-processing with reduced border errors while preserving higher processing speed.

# References


1. Scharstein, D., Szeliski, R.: A taxonomy and evaluation of dense two-frame stereo correspondence algorithms. Int. Jour. Computer Vision (IJCV) 47(1/2/3), 7–42 (2002), http://vision.middlebury.edu/stereo/
2. Yoon, K.J., Kweon, I.S.: Adaptive support-weight approach for correspondence search. IEEE Trans. PAMI 28, 650–656 (2006)
3. Min, D.B., Sohn, K.: Cost aggregation and occlusion handling with WLS in stereo matching. IEEE Trans. IP 17(8), 1431–1442 (2008)
4. Gu, Z., Su, X.Y., Liu, Y.K., Zhang, Q.C.: Local stereo matching with adaptive support-weight, rank transform and disparity calibration. Pattern Recognition Letters (PRL 2008) 29, 1230–1235 (2008)
5. Tombari, F., Mattoccia, S., Di Stefano, L.: Segmentation-based adaptive support for accurate stereo correspondence. In: Mery, D., Rueda, L. (eds.) PSIVT 2007. LNCS, vol. 4872, pp. 427–438. Springer, Heidelberg (2007)
6. Gong, M.L., Yang, R.G., Wang, L., Gong, M.W.: A performance study on different cost aggregation approaches used in real-time stereo matching. Int. Jour. Computer Vision (IJCV) 75(2), 283–296 (2007)
7. Yoon, K.J., Kweon, I.S.: Stereo matching with the distinctive similarity measure. In: Proc. Int. Conf. on Computer Vision (ICCV 2007), pp. 1–7 (2007)
8. Tombari, F., Mattoccia, S., Di Stefano, L., Addimanda, E.: Near real-time stereo based on effective cost aggregation. In: Proc. Int. Conf. on Pattern Recognition (ICPR 2008) (2008)
9. Brockers, R., Hund, M., Mertsching, B.: Stereo vision using cost-relaxation with 3D support regions. In: Image and Vision Computing New Zealand (IVCNZ 2005) (2005)
10. Lu, J.B., Lafruit, G., Catthoor, F.: Anisotropic local high-confidence voting for accurate stereo correspondence. In: Proc. SPIE, vol. 6812 (2008)
11. Mordohai, P., Medioni, G.: Stereo using monocular cues within the tensor voting framework. IEEE Trans. PAMI 28(6), 968–982 (2006)
12. Kolmogorov, V., Zabih, R.: Computing visual correspondence with occlusions using graph cuts. In: Proc. Int. Conf. on Computer Vision (ICCV 2001), pp. 508–515 (2001)
13. Klaus, A., Sormann, M., Karner, K.: Segment-based stereo matching using belief propagation and a self-adapting dissimilarity measure. In: Proc. Int. Conf. on Pattern Recognition (ICPR 2006), vol. 3, pp. 15–18 (2006)
14. Taguchi, Y., Wilburn, B., Zitnick, C.L.: Stereo reconstruction with mixed pixels using adaptive over-segmentation. In: Proc. Int. Conf. on Computer Vision and Pattern Recognition (CVPR 2008), pp. 2720–2727 (2008)
15. Veksler, O.: Stereo correspondence by dynamic programming on a tree. In: Proc. Int. Conf. on Computer Vision and Pattern Recognition (CVPR 2005), pp. 384–390 (2005)

16. Wang, Z.F., Zheng, Z.G.: A region based stereo matching algorithm using cooperative optimization. In: Proc. Int. Conf. on Computer Vision and Pattern Recognition (CVPR 2008), pp. 887–894 (2008)
17. Woodford, O.J., Torr, P.H.S., Reid, I.D., Fitzgibbon, A.W.: Global stereo reconstruction under second order smoothness priors. In: Proc. Int. Conf. on Computer Vision and Pattern Recognition (CVPR 2008), pp. 2570–2577 (2008)
18. Hirschmuller, H.: Stereo processing by semiglobal matching and mutual information. IEEE Trans. PAMI 30(2), 328–341 (2008)
19. Mattoccia, S., Tombari, F., Di Stefano, L.: Stereo vision enabling precise border localization within a scanline optimization framework. In: Yagi, Y., Kang, S.B., Kweon, I.S., Zha, H. (eds.) ACCV 2007, Part II. LNCS, vol. 4844, pp. 517–527. Springer, Heidelberg (2007)
20. Huang, C.R., Chen, C.S., Chung, P.C.: Contrast context histogram–an efficient discriminating local descriptor for object recognition and image matching. Pattern Recognition (PR 2008) 41(10), 3071–3077 (2008)
21. Belongie, S., Malik, J., Puzicha, J.: Shape matching and object recognition using shape contexts. IEEE Trans. PAMI 24(4), 509–522 (2002)
22. Comaniciu, D., Meer, P.: Mean shift: A robust approach toward feature space analysis. IEEE Trans. PAMI 24(5), 603–619 (2002)
23. Oh, J.D., Ma, S.W., Kuo, C.-C.J.: Stereo matching via disparity estimation and surface modeling. In: Proc. Int. Conf. on Computer Vision and Pattern Recognition (CVPR 2007), pp. 1696–1703 (2007)

# SUBSMELL: Multimedia with a Simple Olfactory Display


Chomtip Pornpanomchai, Arinchaya Threekhunprapa, Krit Pongrasamiroj, and Phichate Sukklay

Mahidol University, Department of Computer Science, Faculty of Science, Rama 6 Road, Rajchatavee, Bangkok 10400, Thailand
`{cccpp,u4788241,u4788324,ccpsk}@mahidol.ac.th`



**Abstract.** The idea of adding the SubSmell logo to the movie for describing the scent of each event in the movie has been proposed to improve the current way of seeing movies, which can perceive only pictures and sound. Using the SubSmell, the audience can smell the movie. The audiences need a SubSmell application to read a SubSmell and an olfactory display in order to release scent.

There are two main parts in SubSmell system, which are an olfactory display and a SubSmell application. An olfactory display consists of a control box and four smell boxes with four fans. Fans will be turned on and release scents when receiving the signal from a SubSmell application. A SubSmell application is designed to read a SubSmell in the movie and decide to send signals to an olfactory display. A SubSmell application consists of four major components: 1) Movie Controlling, 2) SubSmell Reading, 3) Scent Releasing and 4) Olfactory Display Monitoring. We use Microsoft Visual Basic 6.0 to develop the user interface and the SubSmell components.

The experiment was done in order to assess the following qualities: 1) Usability: to prove that the system can read a SubSmell in the movie and release scent. 2) Efficiency: to show that the system can work with high accuracy.


## 1 Introduction

Nowadays, we can enjoy movies only by watching motion-pictures and listening to the sound which accompanies the movies. We use only two senses out of the five senses; which are sight and hearing. Movie makers try to improve the audience's feelings more by several ways. Regarding sight, they have studied optical nerves and how human eyes can receive color and pictures and how humans could feel distance of the objects. They have invented and developed many new technologies to capture and keep the best quality of images to make everything in the movies look more real so that the audience can feel it. One of those developed technologies was three-dimension imagining (3-D). The same way in hearing, they also studied the physical auditory nerve and also researched the way of how to keep the best sound quality for playing back to the audience.


T. Wada, F. Huang, and S. Lin (Eds.): PSIVT 2009, LNCS 5414, pp. 462–472, 2009.

# 4   Testing and Evaluation

In this part, we test the system with various conditions in various cases to measure its efficiency and effectiveness. After that we evaluate the system so that it can be used in the real world.

This part presents experimentation on the SubSmell system, which is developed and based on the concepts and the design mentioned in the previous section. In this system, the experiments were focused on its usability and effectiveness.

Usability testing was to prove whether the system was capable of performing the proposed functions as we had mentioned earlier. The effectiveness test determined the correctness of the system and whether the system results could be used in real life.

## 4.1   Usability

The first thing was to use the SubSmell system to open and play the movie. We tested this function by selecting many kinds of movies that were encoded by .AVI code. We had known that the limitation of the SubSmell system was its ability to open and play only .AVI files. When users used Adobe Premiere or any other video editing program to make SubSmell Movie, they should export by using only "Microsoft AVI" to open the file. All of the data tested were selected and played until the end. The testing results are shown in Table 1.

**Table 1.** Testing Data Details

| Title | Type | Length | Use n scent(s) | Play result |
|---|---|---|---|---|
| Perfume | Movie | 13 mins 31 secs | 5 | Great |
| Saying you love me | Music video | 4 mins 2 secs | 5 | Great |
| Eu: cologne | Advertisement | 33 secs | 5 | Great |

The second thing we had checked was the readability of the SubSmell system and how well it could read each pixel in each frame, and what value of each color it got. We had tested the system to read each SubSmell color in the specified position and corrected the number that the System read.

## 4.2   Effectiveness

To measure how well the SubSmell system could release scent, we had tested the system by using the SubSmell movie and observed at the olfactory display port. The olfactory display had four fans, out of three fans were used to blow out the scent and the other one to blow into the clear scent. Table 2 shows all SubSmell colors with control port number and event of a fan.

**Table 2.** Color and Port Information

| Color | Port number | Event |
|---|---|---|
| Red | Port1 (&H8) | Blow out |
| Green | Port2 (&H4) | Blow out |
| Blue | Port3 (&H2) | Blow out |
| White | Port4 (&H1) | Blow in |
| Black | Port0 (&H0) | Idle |

## 5   Conclusion

The SubSmell system has been proved to be usable and effective as we have described in the testing and evaluation section. We may conclude that the SubSmell system supports the following. 1) the movies audiences can view the pictures with aesthetic quality, which means they can see the scenes and smell the scents simultaneously, and 2) the audiences get more detail of the movie, either scene, sound or smell, which makes it more entertaining and interactive.

## References


[1]   Chen, Y.: Olfactory display: development and application in virtual reality therapy. In: Pan, Z., Cheok, D.A.D., Haller, M., Lau, R., Saito, H., Liang, R. (eds.) ICAT 2006. LNCS, vol. 4282. Springer, Heidelberg (2006)

[2]   Washburn, D.A., Jones, L.M.: Could olfactory displays improve data visualization? Computer in Science & Engineering (November/December 2004)

[3]   Tan, E.C., Wahab, A., Goh, G.H., Wong, S.H.: PC-Controlled Scent System. IEEE transactions on Consumer Electronics (December 1998)

[4]   Nakamoto, T., Otaguro, S., Kinoshita, M., Nakamaha, M., Ohinishi, K., Ishida, T.: Cooking up an Interactive Olfactory Game Display. IEEE Transactions on Computer Graphics and Applications (January/February 2008)

[5]   Project Scent Projector – ATR MIS (accessed date: April 25, 2008), `http://www.mis.atr.jp/past/sem/scent.html`

[6]   Kim, D.W., Nishimoto, K., Kunifuji, S.: An Editing and Displaying System of Olfactory Information for the Home Video. Springer, Heidelberg (2006)

[7]   Smell-O-Vision (creation date: unknown, last modified date: unknown accessed date: January 20, 2007), `http://en.wikipedia.org/wiki/Smell-o-vision`

[8]   Odorama (creation date: unknown, last modified date: unknown, accessed date: January 20, 2007), `http://en.wikipedia.org/wiki/Odorama`

[9]   iSmell (creation date: unknown, last modified date: unknown, accessed date: January 20, 2007), `http://en.wikipedia.org/wiki/ISmell`

[10]  Sensoroma (creation date: unknown, last modified date: unknown, accessed date: January 20, 2007), `http://www.sensomatic.com/sensorama/.`

[11]  Kaori Web (creation date: unknown, last modified date: unknown, accessed date: January 20, 2007), `http://gizmodo.com/archives/kaori-web-internet-smellovision-018646.php`

[12]  Digital Scentware? (creation date: unknown, last modified date: unknown, accessed date: January 20, 2007), `http://findarticles.com/p/articles/mi_pwwi/is_200005/-ai_mark15009826`

[13]  Scentware (creation date: unknown, last modified date: unknown, accessed date: January 20, 2007), `http://www.ediblecomputer.com/040802.html`

# Fixed-Coefficient Iterative Bilateral Filters for Graph-Based Image Processing

Chang Jian, Kohei Inoue, Kenji Hara, and Kiichi Urahama

Kyushu University, Fukuoka 815-8540, Japan
{jian,k-inoue,hara,urahama}@design.kyushu-u.ac.jp

**Abstract.** We present a graph-based image processing algorithm using fast iterative bilateral filters. The computation of bilateral filters is accelerated with fixation of the coefficients during iterations and their approximate decomposition further speeds up the computation. We show that this fixed-coefficient iterative bilateral filter is an alternative solver for optimization problems in graph-based data analyses and apply its fast algorithm to graph-based image processing tasks. Performance of the present algorithm is demonstrated with experiments of contrast enhancement and smoothing of images using cross bilateral filters, in addition to semi-supervised image segmentation and colorization of monochromatic images.

## 1 Introduction

Graph-based learning algorithms and multivariate data analysis techniques[1] have become widely used in the fields of pattern recognition and computer vision[2]. Graph-based techniques are usually formulated by optimization problems of which iterative solution generally demands long computational time. Images and videos are typical examples of such large scale data.

In image processing, many iterative algorithms for solving optimization problems have also been used for various tasks such as segmentation and noise reduction by anisotropic diffusion[3]. The bilateral filter[4] has been developed for a one-step filtering without iterations for smoothing of images. In practice, however, it is applied to an image repeatedly if one-step smoothing is insufficient.

Though these graph-based algorithms and iterated filters have similar forms, they have been developed almost independently in different fields, therefore their relationship has not been noticed explicitly.

In this paper, we fix the weighting coefficients in the bilateral filter in order to accelerate its computational speed and show it is another iterative algorithm in addition to a graph-based algorithm for solving the common optimization problem. From this observation, we present a fast algorithm for graph-based image processing using an iterative filter with approximately decomposed weighting coefficients.

T. Wada, F. Huang, and S. Lin (Eds.): PSIVT 2009, LNCS 5414, pp. 473–484, 2009.

## 2    Graph-Based Data Analysis

A graph is composed of nodes linked with edges. We deal with only undirected graphs with symmetric edges in this paper. In this section, we review a principal graph-based technique for analyzing graphs with weighted edges and extend it to the graphs in which nodes are also weighted.

### 2.1    Laplacian Eigenmaps

Let there be given a set of $n$ data between which the similarity is denoted by $s_{ij}$ which is usually expressed by $s_{ij} = e^{-\alpha\|d_i - d_j\|^2}$ where $d_i$ is the feature vector of datum $i$. Such a dataset is called the similarity data and represented by an undirected graph in which the edge weight is $s_{ij}$. A fundamental procedure in graph-based approaches is embedding of data into a low dimensional space. In order to preserve the topology of data, mutually similar data are mapped to mutually close places of which coordinate $x_i$ is given by

$$\min \quad \sum_{i=1}^{n}\sum_{j=1}^{n} s_{ij}(x_i - x_j)^2 \tag{1}$$

of which optimal solution is computed with an iterative algorithm:

$$x_i^{(\xi+1)} = \sum_{j=1,\neq i}^{n} s_{ij}x_j^{(\xi)} / \sum_{j=1,\neq i}^{n} s_{ij} \tag{2}$$

where $\xi$ is an iteration counter. Notice that $i$ is excluded from $\sum_j$. This iteartive algorithm is the Jacobi method for solving the system of linear equations $(D' - S')x = 0$ where $S' = [s'_{ij}]$; $s'_{ii} = 0, s'_{ij} = s_{ij}$ $(i \neq j)$, $D' = \mathrm{diag}(d'_1, ..., d'_n)$; $d'_i = \sum_j s'_{ij}$. This algorithm is also the power method for computing the eigenvector of the stochastic matrix $(D')^{-1}S'$ where $x^{(\xi)}$ converges to a constant vector $[c, ..., c]^T$ which is the eigenvector of $(D')^{-1}S'$ with the maximal eigenvalue 1. This vector coincides with the eigenvector of the Laplacian matrix $L' = D' - S'$ with the minimal eigenvalue 0.

Whereas this principal eigenvector is discarded in the Laplacian eigenmaps[5] because the constant vector contains no information for discriminating data, this vector gives us useful information in the midway of the iteration before its convergence. As will be described below in this paper, the principal eigenvector on the midway of the iteration is outputted as a smoothed result in the iterated filtering of images.

### 2.2    Semi-supervised Clustering

The spectral clustering method[1] is an unsupervised learning algorithm where data are partitioned into several clusters in the low dimensional space mapped with the Laplacian eigenmap described above.

Let us next consider semi-supervised clustering methods where the membership is known for some data in advance of the learning. We deal here with the simplest case of bi-partitioning, i.e. partitioning data into two clusters. Its extension to multiple clusters is straightforward. Let $(x_i + 1)/2$ represent the membership in the first cluster, that is, if $x_i = 1$ datum $i$ belongs to the first cluster, conversely if $x_i = -1$ it belongs to the second cluster. Some data $i \in T_1$ are known to belong to the first cluster and data $i \in T_2$ belong to the second cluster. Based on this knowledge, we estimate $x_i$ of the remaining data $i \notin \{T_1, T_2\}$. A popular algorithm for this task is the semi-supervised learning by label propagation[6] of which iterative algorithm is eq.(2). The value of $x_i$ for $i \in \{T_1, T_2\})$ is fixed throughout the iteration.

## 2.3   Graph with Weighted Nodes

In the graph treated above, only the edges are weighted, while nodes are weightless, i.e. every node has weight 1. If nodes have weights $w_i$ in addition to edges, eq.(1) becomes

$$\min \quad \sum_{i=1}^{n} \sum_{j=1}^{n} w_i w_j s_{ij} (x_i - x_j)^2 \tag{3}$$

of which solution can be computed with the iterative algorithm similar to eq.(2):

$$x_i^{(\xi+1)} = \sum_{j=1,\neq i}^{n} w_j s_{ij} x_j^{(\xi)} \Big/ \sum_{j=1,\neq i}^{n} w_j s_{ij} \tag{4}$$

which is also used for the label propagation in the graphs with weighted nodes and edges.

## 3   Bilateral Filter

The bilateral filter (hereinafter abbreviated as BF) has been widely used for image smoothing such as abstract stylization and noise reduction. We deal with grayscale images for simplicity. Let the graylevel of pixel $(i, j)$ be $d_{ij}$. The output of BF with the window $[-p, p] \times [-p, p]$ is given by

$$f_{ij} = \sum_{k=-p}^{p} \sum_{l=-p}^{p} s_{ijkl} d_{i+k,j+l} \Big/ \sum_{k=-p}^{p} \sum_{l=-p}^{p} s_{ijkl} \tag{5}$$

where $s_{ijkl} = e^{-\alpha(k^2+l^2)-\beta(d_{ij}-d_{i+k,j+l})^2}$ which has the same expression as the similarity in the above graph-based data analyses. In practice, however, only one-step filtering of an image with BF often results in insufficient smoothing. For such cases, BF is applied repeatedly as

$$f_{ij}^{(\xi+1)} = \sum_{k=-p}^{p} \sum_{l=-p}^{p} s_{ijkl}^{(\xi)} f_{i+k,j+l}^{(\xi)} \Big/ \sum_{k=-p}^{p} \sum_{l=-p}^{p} s_{ijkl}^{(\xi)} \tag{6}$$

where $s_{ijkl}^{(\xi)} = e^{-\alpha(k^2+l^2)-\beta(f_{ij}^{(\xi)}-f_{i+k,j+l}^{(\xi)})^2}$. The initial value of $f_{ij}$ is set to the graylevel in the input image as $f_{ij}^{(0)} = d_{ij}$. The following proposition holds for this iterated BF:

[Proposition 1] Eq.(6) is an iterative solution algorithm for the optimization problem

$$\max \quad \sum_{i,j} \sum_{k=-p}^{p} \sum_{l=-p}^{p} e^{-\alpha(k^2+l^2)-\beta(f_{ij}-f_{i+k,j+l})^2} \tag{7}$$

with a decelerated Jacobi method.

Since we do not experiment this iterated BF in this paper, the proof of this proposition is omitted. Also the proof of the monotonic increase in the objective function in eq.(7) through the iteration is omitted.

## 3.1   Fixed-Coefficient Iterative BF

This iterated BF takes long computational time because $s_{ijkl}^{(\xi)}$ must be updated at every iteration step. To alleviate this computational cost, we fix $s_{ijkl}^{(\xi)}$ to its initial value $s_{ijkl} = e^{-\alpha(k^2+l^2)-\beta(d_{ij}-d_{i+k,j+l})^2}$, then eq.(6) becomes

$$f_{ij}^{(\xi+1)} = \sum_{k=-p}^{p} \sum_{l=-p}^{p} s_{ijkl} f_{i+k,j+l}^{(\xi)} \Big/ \sum_{k=-p}^{p} \sum_{l=-p}^{p} s_{ijkl} \tag{8}$$

We call this algorithm the fixed-coefficient iterative BF (FCIBF). This algorithm can be implemented faster than the iterated BF by computing and saving $s_{ijkl}$ before starting the iteration and using it during the iteration. For instance, this FCIBF is about 5-times faster than the iterated BF in their 20 iterations for a $500 \times 500$ image.

This FCIBF resembles eq.(2), that is, we denote every pixel by nodes and link the nodes $(i,j)$ and $(i+k,j+l)$ in the window with an edge of the weight $s_{ijkl}$, then we can manipulate the FCIBF graph-theoretically. In the Markov random field (MRF), only 4 or 8 nearest-neighbor pixels are linked together, whereas edges are drawn between every pair of pixels in the window $\{(k+i,j+l);\ -p \leq k \leq p, -p \leq l \leq p\}$ in the FCIBF. Slight difference between eq.(2) and eq.(8) is that the righthand-side in eq.(8) includes $f_{ij}^{(\xi)}$ but eq.(2) does not. This difference is stated as eq.(2) is the Jacobi method while eq.(8) is a decelerated Jacobi method:

[Proposition 2] Eq.(8) is an iterative solution algorithm for eq.(8) for the optimization problem

$$\min \quad \sum_{i,j} \sum_{k=-p}^{p} \sum_{l=-p}^{p} s_{ijkl}(f_{ij} - f_{i+k,j+l})^2 \tag{9}$$

with a decelerated Jacobi method.

(Proof) The iterant in the Jacobi method for eq.(9) is

$$\tilde{f}_{ij}^{(\xi+1)} = \sum_{k,l}{}' s_{ijkl} f_{i+k,j+l}^{(\xi)} / \sum_{k,l}{}' s_{ijkl} \tag{10}$$

where $\sum_{k,l}{}'$ denotes the summation excluding $\{k=0, l=0\}$ from $\sum_{k=-p}^{p}\sum_{l=-p}^{p}$. Eq.(10) coincides with eq.(2). By denoting $\mu_{ij} = \sum_{k,l}{}' s_{ijkl} / \sum_{k=-p}^{p}\sum_{l=-p}^{p} s_{ijkl}$, we can express the relationship between $f_{ij}^{(\xi+1)}$ in eq.(8) and $\tilde{f}_{ij}^{(\xi+1)}$ in eq.(10) as

$$f_{ij}^{(\xi+1)} = \mu_{ij} \tilde{f}_{ij}^{(\xi+1)} + (1 - \mu_{ij}) f_{ij}^{(\xi)} \tag{11}$$

which states that $f_{ij}^{(\xi+1)}$ is an interior division between $f_{ij}^{(\xi)}$ and $\tilde{f}_{ij}^{(\xi+1)}$ and is a point pulled back from the Jacobi iterant $\tilde{f}_{ij}^{(\xi+1)}$ directed to the previous iterant $f_{ij}^{(\xi)}$. Thus eq.(8) is a decelerated Jacobi method.      (Q.E.D.)

The convergence of eq.(8) is therefore slower than the Jacobi method of eq.(10). The distance of pulling back of $\tilde{f}_{ij}^{(\xi+1)}$ is however short, hence $\mu_{ij} \cong 1$ and the difference between their convergence rates is small. We verify this observation with a $500 \times 500$ image in Fig.1 where the original image is shown on the left and it added with Gaussian noises of standard deviation 40 is shown on the right.

Firstly the variation in the value of eq.(9) for Fig.1(a) is shown in Fig.2 where the solid line denotes the FCIBF of eq.(8) and the dotted line is the Jacobi method (JM) of eq.(10). We set $\alpha = 0.001, \beta = 0.01$ and $p = 2$. The value of $E$ in the FCIBF is slightly larger than that of JM, that is, the convergence of FCIBF is slightly slower than JM. As is expected, however, this difference can be observed only when the window is narrow and becomes negligible for the window of $p$ larger than 5. The convergence is theoretically ensured for eq.(8) and eq.(10) since both the matrices $D^{-1}S$ and $(D')^{-1}S'$ are irreducively diagonal dominant.

Nextly, the PSNR(Peak Signal-to-Noise Ratio) between the iterated outputs of iterative filtering of Fig.1(b) and the noise-free Fig.1(a) is shown in Fig.3. The PSNR of FCIBF is slightly greater than JM, that is, the noise reduction

(a) original image                    (b) image with noise

**Fig. 1.** Input image

capability of FCIBF is slightly higher than JM. This superiority of FCIBF may be attributed to that FCIBF is the average of more pixels than JM because FCIBF includes the central pixel of the window while JM does not.

The concave variation in the PSNR in Fig.3 is commonly observed. In the early steps in the iteration, the PSNR increases because added noises are reduced by smoothing and the PSNR reaches its maximum after which it turns to decrease by over-smoothing of the original image components in addition to noises. It is the best to stop the iteration at the peak of the PSNR, but the automatic determination of the stopping time is difficult and beyond the scope of this paper.

Notice furthermore that eq.(8) is also an adaptive steepest descent method besides the decelerated Jacobi method. Since the derivative of the function $E$ in eq.(9) is $\partial E/\partial f_{ij} = \sum_{k,l}{}' s_{ijkl}(f_{ij} - f_{i+k,j+l})$, the steepset descent iteration $f_{ij}^{(\xi+1)} = f_{ij}^{(\xi)} - h_{ij}\partial E/\partial f_{ij}^{(\xi)}$ reduces to eq.(8) by setting the step-length as $h_{ij} = 1/\sum_{k=-p}^{p}\sum_{l=-p}^{p} s_{ijkl}$.

Consequently, though there is slight difference between eq.(8) and eq.(10), they are alternative algorithms for solving the same optimization problem. Therefore the iterated filter of eq.(8) can be applied to the graph-based data analysis in section 2. This exploitation of eq.(8) for graph-based image processing is beneficial since eq.(8) can be executed fast using an approximated algorithm as will be described below.

### 3.2    Fixed-Coefficient Iterative Cross BF

In the above BF, the input is a single image and the coefficient $s_{ij}$ is calculated from the input image itself. On the other hand in the graph-based method in section 2, the edge weight $s_{ij}$ is calculated from the feature vector $d_i$ different from the variable $x_i$ which is the target of processing of the algorithms.

The same situation also appears in BF where the coefficient $s_{ij}$ is calculated from an augmented image different from an input image which is the target of processing. This BF utilizing an augmented image is called the cross BF[7]. The

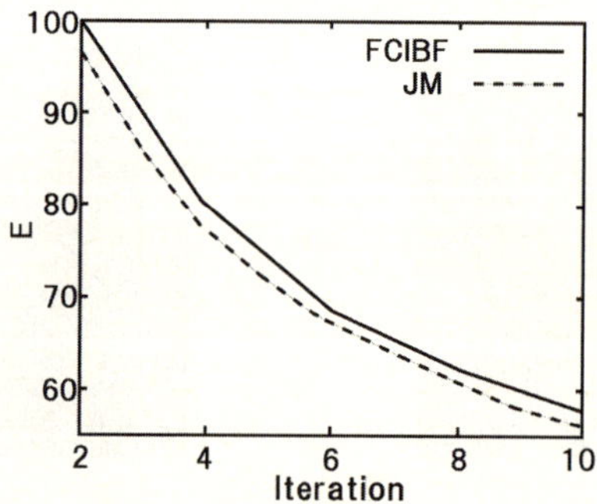


Fig. 2. Variantion in the objective function $E$ in eq.(9)

above trick of fixing the filter coefficients during the iteration is also available in the cross BF leading to the fixed-coefficient iterative cross BF (FCICBF) where the coefficient in eq.(8) is calculated from the pixel value $e_{ij}$ in an augmented image as $s_{ij} = e^{-\alpha(k^2+l^2)-\beta(e_{ij}-e_{i+k,j+l})^2}$.

## 3.3 Fast Algorithm with Approximated Decomposition of Coefficients

By approximately decomposing the coefficient $s_{ijkl}$ in eq.(8) into the product of the component along the $k$ direction and that along the $l$ direction as $e^{-\alpha k^2-\beta(d_{ij}-d_{i+k,j})^2}e^{-\alpha l^2-\beta(d_{i+k,j}-d_{i+k,j+l})^2}$, we can implement a fast procedure for the FCIBF in eq.(8) (its detailed derivation is omitted) as:

[Construction of arrays]
Step 1) We calculate $u_{ijk} = e^{-\alpha k^2-\beta(d_{ij}-d_{i+k,j})^2}$ for every $i, j, k$, and also $v_{ijl} = e^{-\alpha l^2-\beta(d_{ij}-d_{i,j+l})^2}$ for all $i, j, l$, and save them in 3-dimensional arrays.

Step 2) We calculate $b_{ij} = \sum_{l=-p}^{p} v_{ijl}$ for all $i, j$.

Step 3) We calculate $t_{ij} = \sum_{k=-p}^{p} u_{ijk} b_{i+k,j}$ for all $i, j$ and save it in a 2-dimensional array.

[Iteration of Filter]
Step 4) For all $i, j$, we calculate

$$a_{ij} = \sum_{l=-p}^{p} v_{ijl} f^{(\xi)}_{i,j+l}, \quad s_{ij} = \sum_{k=-p}^{p} u_{ijk} a_{i+k,j} \tag{12}$$

from which we compute $f^{(\xi+1)}_{ij} = s_{ij}/t_{ij}$ and repeat this computation.

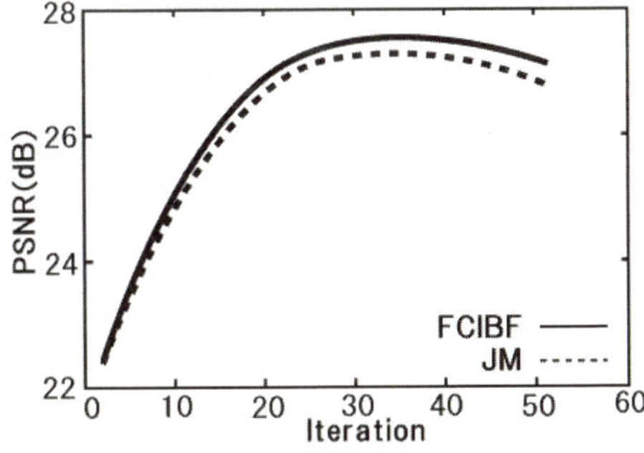



Fig. 3. Variation in PSNR

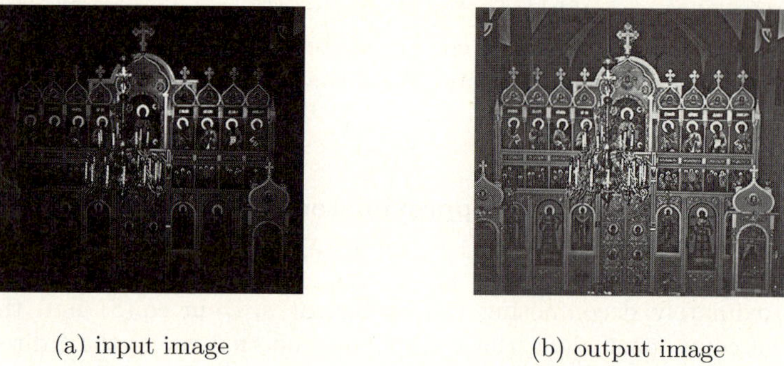

(a) input image                    (b) output image

**Fig. 4.** Contrast enhancement of under-exposed image

(a) photograph without flash        (b) photograph with flash

(c) result of FCIBF                 (d) result of FCICBF

**Fig. 5.** Example of cross BF

For instance, this algorithm is about 6-times faster than the FCIBF in eq.(8) in its 20 iterations for a $500 \times 500$ image. We use this fast algorithm in the following experiments.

The first experiment is an application of the FCIBF to the enhancement of the contrast of an under-exposed image in Fig.4(a) of the size $319 \times 284$ of which pixel value is denoted as $d_{ij}$. We set $p = 5, \alpha = 0.01, \beta = 0.025$ and extract the pixel value $e_{ij}$ of the second output of the FCIBF, 30-th output $f_{ij}$, and 100-th output $g_{ij}$. By combining these outputs as $h_{ij} = w_1 g_{ij} + w_2(f_{ij} - g_{ij}) + w_3(e_{ij} - f_{ij}) + w_4(d_{ij} - e_{ij})$, we obtain a contrast-enhanced image by normalizing $h_{ij}$ to [0,255]. The resultant image is shown in Fig.4(b) where we set $w_1 = 0.2, w_2 = 0.2, w_3 = 0.2, w_4 = 0.4$. The dark areas in Fig.4(a) where detail textures cannot be discriminated become visible more clearly in Fig.4(b). The computational time is 29.5 seconds for the FCIBF in eq.(8) which is reduced to 7.0 seconds using the fast algorithm described above.

Next experiment is an application of the FCICBF in section 3.2. We smooth the image in Fig.5(a) using an augmented image in Fig.5(b) for computing the filter coefficients. The size of both images is $400 \times 365$. Fig.5(a) is an ordinary photograph without flash lighting where the color of objects is faithfully captured but is dark and noisy. Contrastively object edges are clear and noise level is low in the photograph with flash in Fig.5(b) where, however, the color of every object is whitened. We set $p = 5, \alpha = 0.1, \beta = 0.02$ and iterate the filters 10 times. Fig.5(c) is a result of the fast FCIBF applied to Fig.5(a) solely. Noises are remained in Fig.5(c). Next Fig.5(d) is a result of the fast FCICBF where major edges are preserved and noises are satisfactorily reduced. Their computational time is 8.8 seconds for the naive FCIBF and is 4.3 seconds with the fast FCIBF.

## 4   Semi-supervised Image Processing

All of the above experiments are the examples of unsupervised image processing. We turn into the semi-supervised image processing in this section.

### 4.1   Semi-supervised Segmentation

We apply the semi-supervised clustering method in section 2.2 to image segmentation in this section. We compute the edge weight $s_{ijkl}$ from the pixel values in an input image and attach the label $x_{ij} = 1$ and $x_{ij} = -1$ to some pixels. We then propagate these labels to the remaining pixels in the image.

This semi-supervised label propagation can be equivalently reformulated by an unsupervised iterative filter for a graph with weighted nodes as follows.

When each pixel $(i, j)$ has a weight $w_{ij}$, eq.(8) becomes

$$f_{ij}^{(\xi+1)} = \sum_{k=-p}^{p} \sum_{l=-p}^{p} s_{ijkl} w_{i+k,j+l} f_{i+k,j+l}^{(\xi)} / \sum_{k=-p}^{p} \sum_{l=-p}^{p} s_{ijkl} w_{i+k,j+l} \tag{13}$$

which is an unsupervised iterative filter. In this weighted filter, if we set $w_{ij} = 1$ at labeled pixels and set $w_{ij}$ sufficiently small at the remaining unlabeled pixels, $x_{ij}$ of the labeled pixels does not vary from its initial value throughout the iteration and they propagate to their surrounding unlabeled pixels. Thus we can perform the semi-supervised clustering in section 2.2 using this weighted unsupervised filtering scheme.

482    C. Jian et al.

The above fast algorithm for eq.(8) becomes for eq.(13):

[Construction of arrays]
Step 1) We calculate $u_{ijk} = e^{-\alpha k^2 - \beta(d_{ij} - d_{i+k,j})^2}$ for all $i, j, k$, and calculate $v_{ijl} = e^{-\alpha l^2 - \beta(d_{ij} - d_{i,j+l})^2}$ for all $i, j, l$, and we save them into 3-dimensional arrays.

Step 2) We calculate $b_{ij} = \sum_{l=-p}^{p} v_{ijl} w_{i,j+l}$ for all $i, j$.

Step 3) We calculate $t_{ij} = \sum_{k=-p}^{p} u_{ijk} b_{i+k,j}$ for all $i, j$ and save it in a 2-dimensional array.

[Iteration of Filter]
Step 4) For all $i, j$, we calculate

$$a_{ij} = \sum_{l=-p}^{p} v_{ijl} w_{i,j+l} f_{i,j+l}^{(\xi)}, \quad s_{ij} = \sum_{k=-p}^{p} u_{ijk} a_{i+k,j} \tag{14}$$

from which we calculate $f_{ij}^{(\xi+1)} = s_{ij}/t_{ij}$ and repeat this computation.

We experiment this algorithm for an image of blood vessels in Fig.6(a) of size $295 \times 175$. We attach labels to 10 pixels shown in Fig.6(b) where labeled pixels are shown with disks. We set $x_{ij} = 1$ at the pixels of the center of 5 white disks and $x_{ij} = -1$ at the center pixels of 5 black disks for their initial values in the iterations. We set $p = 5, \alpha = 0.001, \beta = 0.01$ and iterate the filter 2000 times starting with the initial value $x_{ij} = 0$ for all the remaining unlabeled pixels. We set the weight of pixels as $w_{ij} = 1$ at 10 labeled pixels and $w_{ij} = 0.001$ at the unlabeled pixels. The value of $(x_{ij} + 1)/2$ after the 2000 iterations is shown in Fig.6(c) where major streams of blood vessels are extracted. Computational times are 286.6 seconds for FCIBF and 74.9 seconds with the fast FCIBF algorithm. This long computational time is due to many iterations of the filter needed for propagation of labels attached to a few pixels to the whole image. Full convergence is the reason for many iterations of 2000 times extremely longer than the optimal 30 times in Fig.3 for noise reduction which does not need the convergence of iterations. The convergence time can be decreased if labels are attached to more pixels.

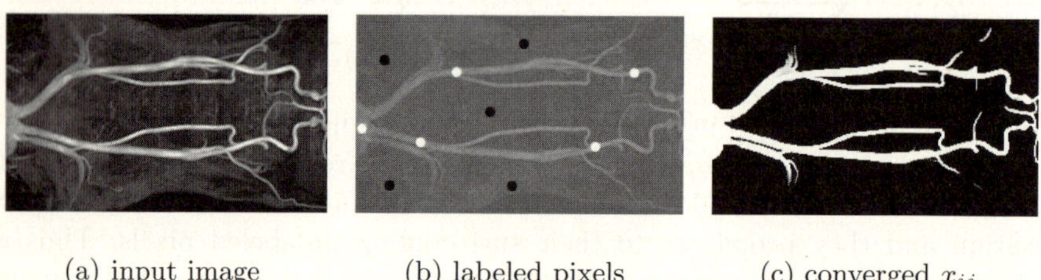

(a) input image   (b) labeled pixels   (c) converged $x_{ij}$

**Fig. 6.** Semi-supervised image segmentation

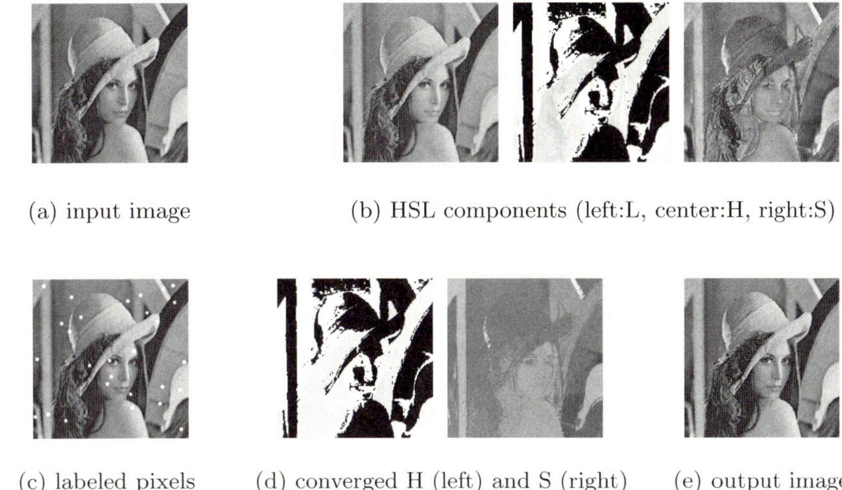

(a) input image        (b) HSL components (left:L, center:H, right:S)

(c) labeled pixels    (d) converged H (left) and S (right)      (e) output image

**Fig. 7.** Semi-supervised colorization of image

Object extraction scheme in the image matting task[8] is the same procedure as this semi-supervised image segmentation and the present algorithm is also useful for fast extraction of objects from photographs or videos with the aid of scribbles drawn by users.

## 4.2  Semi-supervised Colorization of Image

As a final experiment, we apply the above algorithm for semi-supervised label propagation to the colorization of monochromatic images. We compute the edge weight $s_{ijkl}$ between pixels from the pixel values in an input monochromatic image and teach the correct color at some pixels.

The color of the remaining monochromatic pixels is estimated by propagating the colors attached to these labeled pixels. We decompose the color values into HSL components in which the luminance is given as the input monochromatic image and we propagate the hue and saturate components from the labeled pixels to their surroundings.

We experiment with a color image in Fig.7(a) whose HSL components are shown in Fig.7(b) where the left is the luminance which is the input image, the center is the hue and the right is the saturation.

We give the correct color values at 28 pixels shown in Fig.7(c). We set $p = 10, \alpha = 0.01, \beta = 0.1$ and iterate the filter 2000 times. We set the node weights as $w_{ij} = 1$ at labeled pixels and $w_{ij} = 0.001$ for the remaining unlabeled pixels. The initial values of the hue and the saturation are set 127.5 at every unlabeled pixels. The hue after 2000 iterations of the filter is shown on the left in Fig.7(d) and the saturation on the right. Recombination of these hue and saturation with the luminance on the left in Fig.7(b) yields the color image shown in Fig.7(e) which reproduces Fig.7(a) well. The computational times are 228.3 seconds for the FCIBF and 60.6 seconds with the fast FCIBF. This experiment also demands many iterations due to the color inputs at only a few pixels. The convergence becomes faster if the color is given at more pixels.

## 5    Conclusion

We have shown that the fixed-coefficient iterative bilateral filter is an equivalent solver for an optimization problem for a graph-based data analysis technique. Based on this equivalence, we have proposed a fast algorithm for the graph-based image processing using an iterated filter accelerated with decomposition of its coefficients. We have applied this algorithm to semi-supervised image segmentation and semi-supervised colorization of monochromatic images. Owing to its iterative nature of solution, our algorithm is suitable for interactive image processing with incremental labeling of pixels.

## References


1. von Luxburg, U.: A tutorial on spectral clustering. Stat. Comput. 17(4), 395–416 (2007)
2. Shi, J., Malik, J.: Normalized cuts and image segmentation. IEEE Trans. Patt. Anal. Mach. Intell. 22(8), 888–905 (2000)
3. Perona, P., Malik, J.: Scale-space and edge detection using anisotropic diffusion. IEEE Trans. Patt. Anal. Mach. Intell. 12(7), 629–639 (1990)
4. Tomasi, C., Manduchi, R.: Bilateral filtering for gray and color images. In: Proc. ICCV, pp. 839–846 (1998)
5. Belkin, P.M., Niyogi, P.: Laplacian eigenmaps and spectral techniques for embedding and clustering. In: Proc. NIPS, pp. 585–591 (2001)
6. Wang, F., Zhang, C.: Label propagation through linear neighborhoods. In: Proc. ICML, pp. 985–992 (2006)
7. Eisemann, E., Durand, F.: Flash photography enhancement via intrinsic relighting. ACM Trans. Graph. 23(3), 673–678 (2004)
8. Levin, A., Rav-Acha, A., Lischinski, D.: Spectral matting. In: Proc. CVPR, pp. 1–8 (2007)

# Texture Retrieval Effectiveness Improvement Using Multiple Representations Fusion


Noureddine Abbadeni

Al-Ain University of Science and Technology
College of Engineering and IT
Al-Ain, UAE
`noureddine.abbadeni@usherbrooke.ca`



**Abstract.** We propose a multiple representations approach to tackle the problem of content-based image retrieval effectiveness. Multiple representations is based on the use of multiple models or representations and make them cooperate to improve search effectiveness. We consider the case of homogeneous textures. Texture is represented using two different models: the well-known autoregressive model and a perceptual model based on perceptual features such as coarseness and directionality. In the case of the perceptual model, two viewpoints are considered: perceptual features are computed on original images and on the autocovariance function corresponding to original images. Thus, we use a total of three representations (models and viewpoints) to represent texture content. Simple results fusion models are used to merge search results returned by each of the three representations. Benchmarking carried out on the well-known Brodatz database using the recall graph is presented. Retrieval relevance (effectiveness) is improved in a very appreciable way with the fused model.


## 1   Introduction

Content-based image and multimedia retrieval has became one of the most active research areas in the last two decades and many approaches have been proposed and various results and systems have been carried out since then [5], [8]. In the first years of such Systems, content representation and similarity matching were considered as fundamental issues. More recently, researchers have paid more attention to other approaches including relevance feedback-based image retrieval ([27], [22]) and semantics-based image retrieval ([18], [23]). These approaches allow generally an interesting improvement in search relevance even if they can be criticized at least on the fact that an important effort is asked to users to give relevance judgments or to perform annotations on images.

One approach, which still in the visual CBIR approach, and does not necessarily require the intervention of users, has not received enough attention in our opinion. This approach is Data fusion. Data fusion has been extensively used in the traditional text information retrieval (IR) field, and particularly in distributed IR (DIR) [9], [16], [26]. Data fusion, within DIR, recover three parts:


T. Wada, F. Huang, and S. Lin (Eds.): PSIVT 2009, LNCS 5414, pp. 485–496, 2009.

collection description, collection selection and results fusion. Collection description consists in acquisition of information related to the different (distributed) collections of data used to search information. Collection selection consists to choose which are the most relevant data collections to the user's needs and the queries submission to the corresponding systems. Results fusion, finally, consists in merging returned by different systems (from different selected collections) using appropriate results fusion models.

In content-based image retrieval, among the rare works dealing with data fusion, we cite [10], [14], and [1]. In [10], a data fusion model working on distributed collections of images is proposed based on a normalization procedure of similarities among the various image collections. In [14], a results fusion model working on a centralized image collection is proposed based on multiple representations, called viewpoints or channels, of both the query and the images in the database. They used four channels: the original color images, their corresponding grey-level images and their negatives. Results merging coming from different channels is shown to improve performance in a very important way. In [1], a results fusion approach based on multiple queries was used to tackle the problem of invariant image retrieval.

The work presented in this paper explores the idea of results fusion and applies it in the case of texture retrieval. Texture content is represent by two different models: the autoregressive model and a perceptual model based on a set of perceptual features such as coarseness and contrast. The perceptual model is considered in two viewpoints: the original images viewpoint and the autocovariance function viewpoint. Computational measures are based on these two viewpoints. So we have a total of three models/viewpoints (called representations). Benchmarking presented at the end of the paper show how a multiple representations and results fusion approach to CBIR can improve, in an incredible way, the search effectiveness (relevance) without, necessarily, altering, in an important way, search efficiency.

The rest of this paper is organized as follows: In section 2, we present the multiple representation models considered in this paper and we discuss briefly their capacity to model textures; We also show the benefits from using multiple representations and present the results fusion models used to fuse results returned by different representations; In section 3, benchmarking over the well-known Brodatz database using the recall graph is presented and discussed, and comparison to related works is given; And finally, in section 4, a conclusion is given and further investigations related to this work are briefly depicted.

## 2    Multiple Representations, Similarity Matching, and Results Fusion

### 2.1    Multiple Representations

To represent content of textures, we use two different models, the autoregressive model and a perceptual model based on a set of perceptual features[7]. The autoregressive (AR) model used is a causal simultaneous AR model with a non-symmetric half-plan (NSHP) neighborhood with four neighbors. The perceptual model is considered with two viewpoints: the original images viewpoint and the autocovariance function (associated to original images) viewpoint. Each of the viewpoints of the perceptual model used is based on four perceptual features, namely coarseness, directionality, contrast and busyness. So we have a total of three content representations, each having a parameter vector of size four for a total of twelve parameters.

The autoregressive model is characterized, in particular, by a forecasting property that allows to predict the grey-level value of a pixel of interest in an image by using the grey-level values of pixels in its neighborhood. The autoregressive model, when used to model a textured image, allow to estimate a set of parameters (their number corresponds to the number of neighbors considered), each one corresponds to the contribution of its corresponding pixel in the forecasting of the pixel of interest (the total of contributions of all pixels in an image is close to 100%).

The perceptual model, which is perceptual by construction, is based on a set of four computational measures that simulate four perceptual features mentioned above. Briefly, coarseness was estimated as an average of the number of extrema; Contrast was estimated as a combination of the average amplitude of the gradient, the percentage of pixels having the amplitude superior to a certain threshold and coarseness itself; Directionality was estimated as the average number of pixels having the dominant orientation(s); And finally, busyness was estimated based on coarseness since the two features are related to each other. The computational measures proposed for each perceptual textural feature were evaluated by conducting a set of experimentations taking into account human judgments and using a psychometric method. Thirty human subjects were asked to rank a set of textures according to each perceptual feature. Then, for each perceptual feature, we consolidate the different human rankings into one human ranking using the sum of rank values. For each feature, the consolidated human ranking obtained was compared to the ranking given by the corresponding computational measure using the Spearman coefficient of rank-correlation.

Experimental results showed very strong correspondence between the proposed computational measures and human rankings. Values of Spearman coefficient of rank-correlation $r_s$ found are as follows: for coarseness, $r_s = 0.913$; for directionality, $r_s = 0.841$; for contrast, $r_s = 0.755$; and finally, for busyness, $r_s = 0.774$. Comparatively to related works, our results were found better. [7].

The set of features of the perceptual model have a perceptual meaning by construction. The set of features derived from the autoregressive model have no perceptual meaning by construction, however we have proposed in [3] a perceptual interpretation of the set of features derived from the autoregressive model. This perceptual interpretation consists in considering those features as a measure of the randomness/regularity of the texture. For more details on the perceptual model, refer to [7] and for more details on the autoregressive model, refer to [3], [2].

## 2.2  Similarity Matching

The similarity measure used is based on the Gower coefficient of similarity we have developed in our earlier work [6]. The non-weighted similarity measure, denoted $GS$, can be defined as follows:

$$GS_{ij} = \frac{\sum_{k=1}^{n} S_{ij}^{(k)}}{\sum_{k=1}^{n} \delta_{ij}^{(k)}} \tag{1}$$

Where $S_{ij}^{(k)}$ is the partial similarity between images $i$ and $j$ according to feature $k$, $\delta_{ij}^{(k)}$ represents the ability to compare two images $i$ and $j$ on feature $k$ ($\delta_{ij}^{(k)} = 1$ if images $i$ and $j$ can be compared on feature $k$ and $\delta_{ij}^{(k)} = 0$ if not. $\sum_{k=1}^{n} \delta_{ij}^{(k)} = n$ if images $i$ and $j$ can be compared on all features $k, k = 1..n.$).

Quantity $S_{ij}^{(k)}$ is defined as follows:

$$S_{ij}^{(k)} = 1 - \frac{|x_{ik} - x_{jk}|}{R_k} \tag{2}$$

Where $R_k$ represents a normalization factor. $R_k$ is computed on the database considered for experimentations and is defined as follows:

$$R_k = Max(x_{ik}) - Min(x_{ik}) \tag{3}$$

The weighed version of the similarity measure can be defined as follows:

$$GS_{ij} = \frac{\sum_{k=1}^{n} w_k S_{ij}^{(k)}}{\sum_{k=1}^{n} w_k \delta_{ij}^{(k)}} \tag{4}$$

Where $w_k$ corresponds to the weight associated with feature $k$. As mentioned, $w_k$ can be either the inverse of variance of feature $k$ or the Spearman coefficient of rank-correlation. For more details on the similarity measure, please refer to [6].

## 2.3  Multiple Representations Fusion Benefits

Different representations of the same query or the images in the database, or different search strategies for the same query, etc. return normally different search results. Results fusion is then the merging of the different lists of results returned by the different models, representations, or queries to form a unique fused (merged) list which is, hopefully, more effective (relevant) than the separated lists [9], [16]. Given several list results returned by different representations, there are three important phenomena that can be observed [25], [16]:

- Skimming effect: Each model retrieve a subset of the relevant images and intersection between them is rather low. A relevant image is retrieved, often, by only one model. In this case, results fusion must consider images that are ranked in top positions in different lists.

- Chorus effect: Different models retrieve approximately the same results but with different ranks and similarity values. In this case, a relevant image is ranked by several models in top positions (not necessarily the same position). The fact that several models retrieve an image is a more convincing evidence or proof that this image is relevant to the query compared to the case where this image is retrieved by only one representation. Results fusion, in this case, must take in consideration all the representations used.
- Dark horse effect: Exceptionally, even a good model can return some irrelevant images for a given query. Generally, different models did not return the same irrelevant images. Results fusion, in this case, must consider all the representations and use appropriate techniques to eliminate irrelevant images.

Another important point in image retrieval is retrieval efficiency, which is closely related to the size of feature vectors used to represent the content of images. In fact, the more the size of feature vectors is large, the less the retrieval efficiency is good. Efficiency of fusion-based approaches is quite equivalent to traditional approaches since they use models separately in the matching and retrieval step, which means a reduced size of feature vectors compared to traditional approaches, even if they need to add a fusion step at the end. In general the fusion step is less costly than the matching and retrieval step.

## 2.4   Results Fusion Models

In literature on results fusion, in particular in the DIR field, many fusion models were presented and experimented including the use of maximum function, average function and other linear combination models [16], [26]. Generally, the proposed models are simple and, even though, they allow sometimes a drastic improvement in retrieval relevance. Results fusion, in our case, is the fusion of results returned by each of the three representations used to represent texture content. Results returned for a query contain mainly two pieces of information that can be used: similarity values (scores) and ranks. Any results fusion model may make use of one or both of these two pieces of information. We have used and experimented three basic results fusion models that are denoted FusMAX (or MAX), FusCL (or CL) and FusComb (or Comb) defined respectively as follows:

$$FusMAX_{ij} = MAX(GS_{M_{ij}^k})$$

(5)

$$FusCL_{ij} = \frac{\sum_{k=1}^{K} GS_{M_{ij}^k}}{K}$$

(6)

$$FusComb_{ij} = \Pi_{k=1}^{K} GS_{M_{ij}^k}$$

(7)

where $M^k$ represents model/viewpoint $k$, $K$ represents the number of models/viewpoints used, $i$ represents a given query, $j$ represents images that are found similar to query $i$ according to model $M^k$ and $GS_{M_{ij}^k}$ is the similarity value between query $i$ and image $j$ when using model/viewpoint $M^k$. These fusion models use only the values of the similarity function returned by the considered model/viewpoint. Ranks can be also used. We have used them as weights. In fact, more an image is ranked at top positions, more is its weight in the fusion models. Thus, we can define a weighted version for each of the FusCL, FusMAX and FusComb model. In such weighted models, each image $j$ is weighted with its rank in the list of results returned for query $i$ using model $M^k$.

Fusion models FusCL and FusComb, both non-weighted and weighted, exploit the chorus effect since these models give more importance to images that are retrieved and ranked in top positions by different models/viewpoints. They also exploit the dark horse effect since an irrelevant image that is ranked in top positions by one model/viewpoint is not ranked at top positions in the fused list given that this irrelevant image is not ranked at top positions by the other models/viewpoints. The FusMAX model exploits the skimming effect, until some degree, since this model takes images that are classified in top positions in different results lists but it re-ranks them according to similarity values. Generally, when the chorus effect exists in an important way between different lists, the gain that we can obtain by exploiting the skimming effect becomes low and *vice-versa* [25].

## 3    Experimental Results and Benchmarking

### 3.1    Experimental Results

We have conducted a large experimentation on Brodatz database [12] [1]. This database contains originally 112 images. We have divided each of the 112 images in 9 tiles to obtain a total of 1008 128x128 images (112 images x 9 tiles per image). Among the 112 original images of Brodatz database, we have counted 29 highly non-homogeneous images. Creating a class of images from an original image by dividing it into tiles and considering them as similar is a questionable procedure. In fact, when the original image is highly non-homogeneous, the resulting tiles are not visually similar. Considering such images can be misleading. For this reason, and for benchmarking purposes, we consider only 83 queries (by excluding the 29 highly non-homogeneous images), each from a different class (we have taken the first image of each class corresponding to the top left corner tile).

Experimental results show that: 1. The autoregressive model in its non-weighted NSHP version perform better that the other versions of the autoregressive model; 2. The weighted version, using Spearman coefficients of rank-correlation, of the perceptual model based on original images performs better than the other versions of this model; 3. And, finally, the weighted version, using the inverse of variances, of the perceptual model based on the autocovariance function performs better than the other versions of this model. For results merging, the FusCL model gives the best results compared to the FusMAX model and gives similar results compared to FusComb model. So, in the following, we will show results for only these best models. Here is the list of notations used to name different models:

---

[1] We used the version available at http://www.ux.his.no/ tranden/brodatz.html

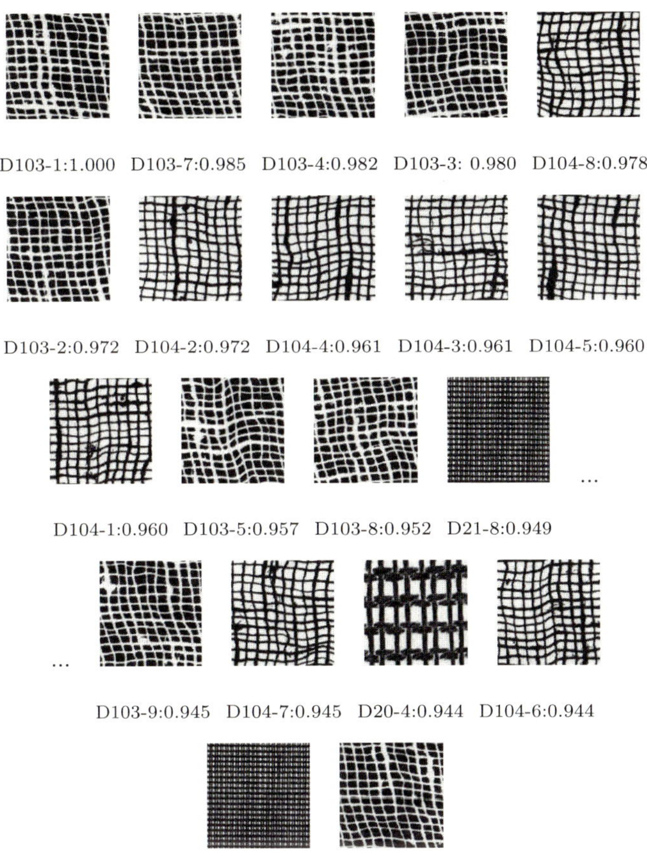

D103-1:1.000  D103-7:0.985  D103-4:0.982  D103-3: 0.980  D104-8:0.978

D103-2:0.972  D104-2:0.972  D104-4:0.961  D104-3:0.961  D104-5:0.960

D104-1:0.960  D103-5:0.957  D103-8:0.952  D21-8:0.949

D103-9:0.945  D104-7:0.945  D20-4:0.944  D104-6:0.944

D21-2:0.943  D103-6:0.943

**Fig. 1.** Results returned for query image D103-1 using the PCP-COV-V model: images and similarities (scores). The results are quite good even if we used only one model (this is not the case always).

- **AR**: The autoregressive model with NSHP neighborhood.
- **PCP-COV-V**: Weighted combination, using the inverse of each feature variance, of the four perceptual features computed on the autocovariance function.
- **PCP-S**: Weighted combination, using the Spearman rank-correlation coefficients, of the four perceptual features computed on original images.
- **CL**: Fusion of **PCP-V**, **PCP-COV-V** and **AR** two by two or all of the three using the **FusCL** data fusion model.

The following figure (Fig. 1) shows an example of results obtained with the $PCP - COV - V$ model taken separately without fusion with other models. The results are quite good even if we used only one model (no fusion here).

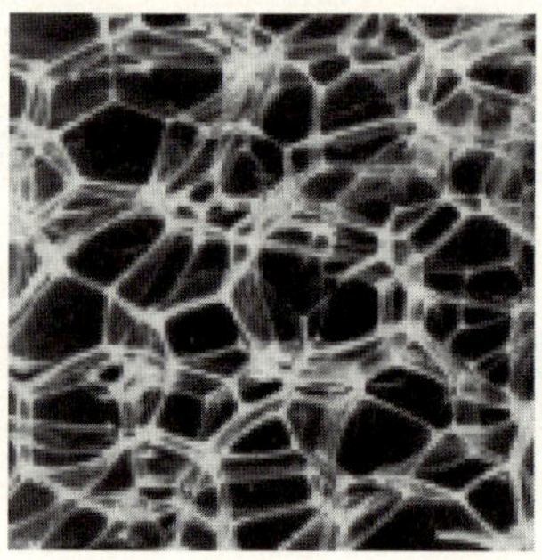

D111-1

**Fig. 2.** Retrieval rate for image query when using separate models is respectively 0.33 with the PCP-S model or the PCP-COV-V model and 0.22 with the AR model. With the fused model, the retrieval rate reaches 0.88.

Of course, this is not the case always and most of retrieval cases will require fusion of multiple models to obtain acceptable results. For example, for image D111-1 (Fig. 2), we found a retrieval rate of 0.33 with the PCP-S model or the PCP-COV-V model and a retrieval rate of 0.22 with the AR model while the retrieval rate for image D111-1 when we fused all these 3 models was improved in an important way and reaches 0.88.

## 3.2   Recall Graph

Recall is quite a standard technique used to benchmark search relevance (effectiveness) in information retrieval systems in general. Recall, which can be defined as the number of relevant and retrieved images divided by the number of relevant images in the database for the considered query, measures the ability of a model to retrieve all relevant images. Recall is computed for each query at each position. Then, average recall is computed as an average across a set of representative queries.

Figure 3 shows the recall graph. From this figure, we can point out that the overall performance of the different models is as follows (in a decreasing order): **CL, AR + PCP-S, AR + PC-COV-V, PCP-S + PCP-COV-V, AR, PCP-S** and **PCP-COV-V**. The fused model CL (using all of the three basic representations) gives the best results. The fusion two by two also gives better results than the separated models. The perceptual model using the original images viewpoint (**PCP-S**) performs better than the perceptual model using the auto-covariance function viewpoint (**PCP-COV-V**), but when these two viewpoints are fused, the resulting model (**PCP-S + PCP-COV-V** performs better than each of them taken separately. The autoregressive model (**AR**) performs better than the perceptual model (**PCP-COV-V**) based on the autocovariance function viewpoint and have a quite similar performance compared to the perceptual model based on the original images viewpoints (**PCP-S**).

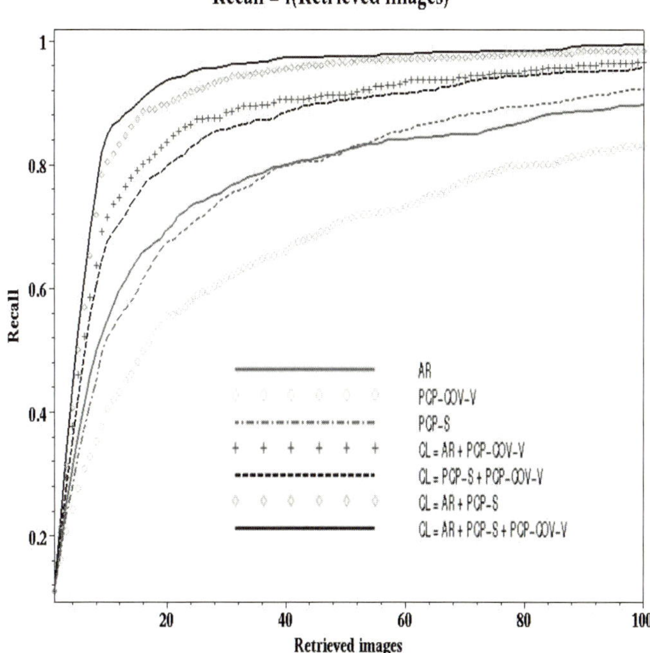


**Fig. 3.** Recall graph (Recall = f(Retrieved images)) for different separate models as well as Fused models. We can see that fusion of multiple representations, in particular the fusion of all three representation models (AR, PCP-S, and PCP-COV-V), outperforms all the other models.

## 3.3   Comparison to Related Works

When comparing retrieval performance in terms of recall rate with other works, we can point out the following remarks (see table 1):

**Table 1.** Average recall rate for different models. We used the rates given by authors of the corresponding model.

| Model | Recall rate |
|---|---|
| FusCL (112 classes) | .687 |
| FusCL (83 classes) | .819 |
| MRSAR | .74 |
| Gabor | .74 |
| WOLD | .75 |
| RBF | .737 |
| MARS | .671 |

- If we consider only 83 classes, our fused model performs better than most of the known works including pure CBIR approaches such as Gabor filters [19], MRSAR [19], [17] and Wold model [17], and relevance feedback-based approaches such as MARS [22] and RBF-based retrieval [20]. Note that for table 1, we give the retrieval rate at the position that corresponds to the number of relevant images for each class. Note that in our approach no relevance feedback from users is used.
- If we consider all of the 112 classes, including highly non-homogeneous images, our model performs better than some and less than some other models. We must mention again that considering the 29 highly non-homogeneous classes may lead to incorrect conclusions since these classes contain images that are not visually similar.

## 4    Conclusion

An approach to CBIR based on multiple representations and results fusion has been presented in this paper. To demonstrate the power of such an approach, we have considered the case of textures. Texture content are represented by two different content representation models: the autoregressive model and a perceptual model based on a set of perceptual features such as coarseness, directionality, contrast, etc. Two viewpoints were considered in the case of the perceptual models: the original images and the autocovariance function. The similarity model used was based on Gower's coefficient of similarity. Experimental results and benchmarking against the well-known Brodatz database of textures was presented using the recall graph. The fused model is shown to improve in a very appreciable way retrieval performance compared to different single representations.

Extended research related to the work presented in this paper can be done through different directions, in particular the investigation of the possibility to define more representations as well as the possibility to use more complex fusion models.

## References


1. Abbadeni, N., Alhichri, H.: Low-level invariant image retrieval based on results fusion. In: Proceedings of the IEEE ICME, Hannover-Germany (June 2008)
2. Abbadeni, N.: Texture Representation and Retrieval Using the Causal Autoregressive Model. In: Qiu, G., Leung, C., Xue, X.-Y., Laurini, R. (eds.) VISUAL 2007. LNCS, vol. 4781, pp. 559–569. Springer, Heidelberg (2007)
3. Abbadeni, N.: Perceptual meaning of the estimated parameters of the autoregressive Model. In: Proceedings of the International Conference of Image Processing, Genova-Italy, pp. 1164–1167. IEEE, Los Alamitos (2005)
4. Abbadeni, N.: Multiple representations, similarity matching, and results fusion for CBIR. Multimedia Systems Journal 10(5), 444–456 (2005)
5. Datta, R., Joshi, D., Li, J., Wang, J.Z.: Image Retrieval: Ideas, Influences, and Trends of the New Age. ACM Transactions on Computing Surveys 40(2), 60 (2008)

6. Abbadeni, N.: A new similarity matching measure: application to texture-based image retrieval. In: Proceedings of the $3^{rd}$ International Workshop on Texture Analysis and Synthesis. IEEE, Nice-France (2003)

7. Abbadeni, N., Ziou, D., Wang, S.: Computational measures corresponding to perceptual textural features. In: Proceedings of the $15^{th}$ International Conference on Pattern Recognition, Barcelona-Spain, pp. 3913–3916. IEEE, Los Alamitos (2000)

8. Lew, M., Sebe, N., Djeraba, C., Jain, R.: Content-Based Multimedia Information Retrieval: State of the art and challenges. ACM Transactions on Multimedia Computing, Communications, and Applications 26 (2006)

9. Belkin, N.J., Cool, C., Croft, W.B., Callan, J.P.: The effect of multiple query representation on information retrieval performance. In: Proceedings of the 16th International ACM SIGIR Conference, pp. 339–346 (1993)

10. Berretti, S., Del Bimbo, A., Pala, P.: Merging results for distributed content-based image retrieval. Multimedia Tools and Applications 24, 215–232 (2004)

11. Del Bimbo, A.: Visual information retrieval. Morgan Kaufmann Publishers, San Francisco (1999)

12. Brodatz, P.: Textures: A Photographic Album for Artists and Designers. Dover, New York (1966)

13. Dunlop, M.D.: Time, relevance and interaction modeling for information retrieval. In: Proceedings of the International ACM SIGIR Conference, Philadelphia, USA, pp. 206–213 (1997)

14. French, J.C., Chapin, A.C., Martin, W.N.: An application of multiple viewpoints to content-based image retrieval. In: Proceeding of the ACM/IEEE Joint Conference on Digital Libraries, pp. 128–130 (May 2003)

15. Gower, J.C.: A general coefficient of similarity and some of its properties. Biometrics Journal 27, 857–874 (1971)

16. Lee, J.H.: Analysis of multiple evidence combination. In: Proceedings of the ACM SIGIR Conference, Philadelphia, PA, USA, pp. 267–276 (1997)

17. Liu, F., Picard, R.W.: Periodicity, directionality and randomness: Wold features for image modeling and retrieval. IEEE Transactions on Pattern Analysis and Machine Intelligence 18(7), 722–733 (1996)

18. Lu, Y., Hu, C., Zhu, X., Zhang, H., Yang, Q.: A unified framework for semantics and feature based relevance feedback in image retrieval systems. In: Proceedings of the $8^{th}$ ACM International Conference on Multimedia, Marina Del Rey, CA, pp. 31–37 (2000)

19. Manjunath, B.S., Ma, W.Y.: Texture features for browsing and retrieval of image data. IEEE Transactions on Pattern Analysis and Machine Intelligence, special issue on Digital Libraries 18(8), 837–842 (1996)

20. Muneesawang, P., Guan, L.: An interactive approach for CBIR using a network of radial basis functions. IEEE Transactions on Multimedia 6(5), 703–716 (2004)

21. Payne, J.S., Hepplewhite, L., Stonham, T.J.: Texture, human perception, and information retrieval measures. In: Proceedings of the ACM SIGIR MF/IR Workshop (July 2000)

22. Rui, Y., Huang, T.S., Mehrota, S.: A Relevance feedback architecture for multimedia information retrieval systems. In: IEEE Workshop on Content-based Access of Image and Video Libraries, pp. 82–89 (1997)

23. Sun, Y., Ozawa, S.: Semantic-meaningful content-based image retrieval in wavelet domain. In: Proceedings of the $5^{th}$ ACM International Workshop on Multimedia Information Retrieval (held in conjunction with ACM Multimedia), Berkeley, CA, pp. 122–129 (November 2003)

24. Tamura, H., Mori, S., Yamawaki, T.: Textural features corresponding to visual perception. IEEE Transactions on Systems, Man and Cybernetics 8(6), 460–472 (1978)
25. Vogt, C.C., Cottrell, G.W.: Fusion via a linear combination of scores. Information Retrieval Journal 1, 151–173 (1999)
26. Wu, S., Crestani, F.: Data Fusion with Estimated Weights. In: Proceedings of the International ACM Conference on Knowledge and Information Management (CKIM), McLean, Virginie, USA, November 4-9, pp. 648–651 (2002)
27. Zhou, X.S., Huang, T.S.: Relevance feedback for image retrieval: a comprehensive review. ACM Multimedia Systems Journal 8(6), 536–544 (2003)

# Recognizing Multiple Objects via Regression Incorporating the Co-occurrence of Categories

Takahiro Okabe[1], Yuhi Kondo[1,2], Kris M. Kitani[1,3], and Yoichi Sato[1]

[1] Institute of Industrial Science, The University of Tokyo
[2] Sony Corporation
[3] Graduate School of Information Systems,
The University of Electro-Communications
takahiro@iis.u-tokyo.ac.jp, ykondo@iis.u-tokyo.ac.jp,
kitani@is.uec.ac.jp, ysato@iis.u-tokyo.ac.jp

**Abstract.** Most previous methods for generic object recognition explicitly or implicitly assume that an image contains objects from a single category, although objects from multiple categories often appear together in an image. In this paper, we present a novel method for object recognition that explicitly deals with objects of multiple categories coexisting in an image. Furthermore, our proposed method aims to recognize objects by taking advantage of a scene's context represented by the co-occurrence relationship between object categories. Specifically, our method estimates the mixture ratios of multiple categories in an image via MAP regression, where the likelihood is computed based on the linear combination model of frequency distributions of local features, and the prior probability is computed from the co-occurrence relation. We conducted a number of experiments using the PASCAL dataset, and obtained the results that lend support to the effectiveness of the proposed method.

## 1 Introduction

With the proliferation of digital cameras, enormous numbers of digital images have been accumulated on the Internet. Since manually processing such a huge amount of data is almost impossible, automatic image classification and retrieval are research areas of increasing importance. Thus, a research topic called *generic object recognition* has recently been brought back into the spotlight in the computer vision community. In this study, we focus on the problem of object categorization among various tasks of generic object recognition.

It is generally recognized that object categorization is a very difficult task due to the following two reasons. First, objects of the same category differ in both color and shape, that is, intra-category variation. Second, the appearance of an object varies drastically depending on imaging conditions such as camera viewpoints, the object's pose, and illumination. To cope with these difficulties, previous work mainly studies feature detection[8,14], object and category representation[4,2,11], or classifiers[5,14] robust against appearance changes due to intra-category variation and variable imaging conditions.

T. Wada, F. Huang, and S. Lin (Eds.): PSIVT 2009, LNCS 5414, pp. 497–508, 2009.

The previous studies however share a common limitation. That is, most previous methods explicitly or implicitly assume that an image contains objects from a single category, and evaluate whether objects of each category are present or not, independent of the presence or absence of objects of the other categories. Therefore, they are not well suited for recognizing objects of various categories coexisting in an image and do not consider the fact that certain combinations of categories are more likely to appear together than others. For example, given an image of a street, it is highly probable that a "car" will coexist with a "motorbike", while it is very unlikely that a "car" and a "cow" will appear together.

Accordingly, we present a novel method for object recognition that explicitly deals with objects of multiple categories coexisting in an image. Furthermore, our proposed method aims to recognize objects by taking advantage of a *scene's context* represented by the co-occurrence relationship between object categories. The use of such contextual cues makes it possible to classify objects of different categories but with similar appearance.

In order to achieve our objective, we chose to use the bag-of-features (BoF) paradigm[2], which is now known as one of the most promising paradigms for generic object recognition. In particuloar, our proposed method estimates the mixture ratios of multiple categories in an image via maximum *a posteriori* (MAP) regression, where the likelihood is computed based on the linear combination model of frequency distributions (*i.e.* histograms) of local features, and the prior probability is computed from the co-occurrence relation. We conducted a number of experiments using the PASCAL dataset, and obtained the results that give support to the effectiveness of the proposed method.

The rest of this paper is organized as follows. We briefly summarize related work in Section 2. We describe our proposed method in Section 3, and report the experimental results in Section 4. Finally, in Section 5, we present concluding remarks.

## 2   Related Work

We briefly summarize previous studies relating to the basic idea of our proposed method from two distinct points of view; *multiple categories* and *context*.

### Multiple Categories

In order to recognize objects of various categories coexisting in an image, a segmentation-based approach and a regression-based approach have been developed. The former approach segments an image into regions so that each segmented region contains objects of a single category, and then conducts object categorization for each region[10]. However, segmenting images of complex scenes is not necessarily an easy task, and the accuracy of classification depends on that of image segmentation.

The latter approach estimates the mixture ratios of multiple categories in an image via regression, where the mixture ratio is defined based on the number of feature points arising from each category in the BoF paradigm (see Section 3.1). For example, Sivic *et al.*[12] estimate the mixture ratios of various categories in an individual image by applying probabilistic Latent Semantic Analysis (pLSA) to a set of unlabeled images. Their regression-based method is similar to ours in the sense that the frequency distribution of feature points in an image is modeled by the linear combination of frequency distributions of feature points arising from various categories. However, their method finds the mixture ratios based on the framework of maximum likelihood (ML) estimation, and the prior information other than images that can be inferred from scene's context is not taken into account. Consequently, it is difficult to classify objects of different categories but with similar appearance.

**Context**

Obviously the context of the scene is one of the most important clues for understanding images and has in fact been utilized in the field of generic object recognition[1,7]. However, the co-occurrence relation of object categories has received little attention compared with other contextual information such as size and position[10].

Recently, Rabinovich *et al.*[10] proposed a method for object categorization incorporating the co-occurrence relation of object categories, and Galleguillos *et al.*[6] extended their method by incorporating the spatial context with respect to the relative location of objects. First, they segment an image into regions, and then tentatively estimate a category label and its confidence for each segmented region based on the BoF paradigm. Finally, they revise the label based on the confidence of the tentative label and the co-occurrence relation. As we described before, however, image segmentation itself is a potential limitation for images with complex scenes. In addition, our method differs from their segmentation-based method with respect to the manner in which we describe the co-occurrence relationship between object categories. They model the co-occurrence relation based on the presence of objects in terms of *frequencies*, that is, the number of times that certain combinations of categories appear together. In contrast, we model the co-occurrence relation in terms of *mixture ratios* based on the number of feature points arising from each category (see Sections 3.3 and 4.1 for details). The co-occurrence in terms of mixture ratios can capture contextual information such as an object's size, beyond the presence of objects.

From the viewpoint of co-occurrence, the method for image categorization proposed by Qi *et al.*[9] is related to our study. They also segment an image into regions, and represent each region by a set of low-level features such as color and size, and then classify the image based on the co-occurrence of the low-level features. Their co-occurrence describes the relationship among features arising from *a single* category, and is effective for classifying an image into *one* of given categories. On the other hand, our co-occurrence that describes the relationship between *multiple* categories is essential for estimating mixture ratios of *multiple* categories in an image.

As described above, our proposed method is differentiated from related work by the following: (i) our method is a regression-based approach and avoids troublesome segmentation for images with complex scenes, and (ii) our method

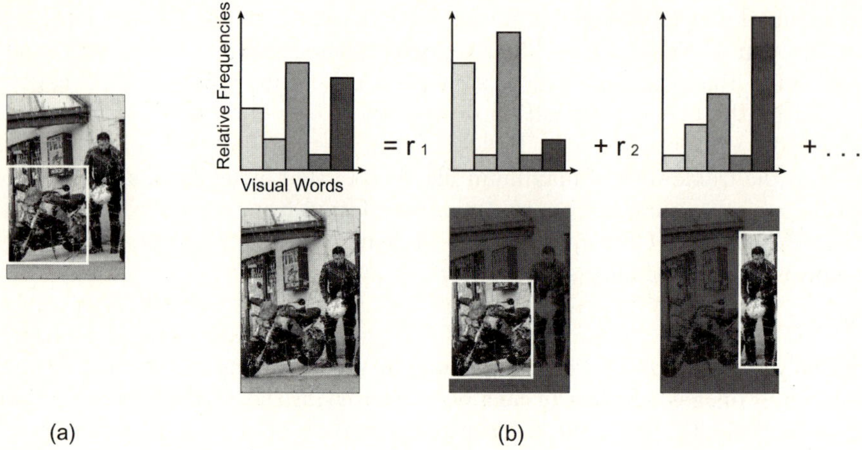


**Fig. 1.** (a) The mixture ratio of a "motorbike" is defined by the ratio between the number of feature points detected within the bounding box and the total number of feature points. (b) The histogram of an entire image is described by the linear combination of a motorbike's histogram, a person's histogram, *etc.*

takes account of the co-occurrence relation of object categories in terms of mixture ratios, which captures more contextual information than that in terms of frequencies.

## 3    Proposed Method

### 3.1    Overview

We represent an image as a set of local features such as SIFT[8] based on the BoF paradigm. Let us denote the label of a category by $c$ ($c = 1, 2, 3, ..., C$), and define the mixture ratio $r_c$ of the category in an image as the ratio between the number of feature points arising from the category $c$ and the total number of feature points as shown in Fig.1(a). Here, $C$ is the total number of categories and $\sum_{c=1}^{C} r_c = 1$ by definition. We concatenate $r_c$ into a vector and denote the mixture ratios of all categories in the image by $\boldsymbol{r} = (r_1, r_2, r_3, \cdots, r_C)^T$.

We compress the local features via vector quantization (see Section 4.1), and call the quantized features visual words. Let us denote the label of a visual word by $w$ ($w = 1, 2, 3, ..., W$), and the relative frequency of the visual word $w$ arising from an image by $h_w$. Here, $W$ is the total number of visual words and $\sum_{w=1}^{W} h_w = 1$ by definition. We concatenate $h_w$ into a vector and denote the relative frequency distribution of the visual words arising from the image by $\boldsymbol{h} = (h_1, h_2, h_3, ..., h_W)^T$. Hereafter, we often call the relative frequency distribution of visual words the histogram in short.

Our proposed method finds the mixture ratios $\boldsymbol{r}$ from the histogram $\boldsymbol{h}$ of a given image based on the framework of MAP estimation. The posterior probability $p(\boldsymbol{r}|\boldsymbol{h})$ is given by the Bayes' rule as

$$p(\boldsymbol{r}|\boldsymbol{h}) \propto p(\boldsymbol{h}|\boldsymbol{r})p(\boldsymbol{r}). \tag{1}$$

Here, as described in Sections 3.2 and 3.3, the likelihood $p(\boldsymbol{h}|\boldsymbol{r})$ is derived from the relative frequency distribution of visual words, and the prior probability $p(\boldsymbol{r})$ is derived from the co-occurrence relation of object categories.

### 3.2   Likelihood

As shown in Fig.1(b), the histogram of an image which includes a motorbike and a person is represented by the linear combination of a motorbike's histogram, a person's histogram, *etc.* Therefore, it is clear that the relative frequency distribution $\boldsymbol{h}$ arising from the entire image is described by the linear combination of relative frequency distributions $\boldsymbol{h}_c$ arising from various categories in the image:

$$\boldsymbol{h} = \sum_{c=1}^{C} r_c \boldsymbol{h}_c, \tag{2}$$

where the mixture ratios are the coefficients of the linear combination.

Assuming that the relative frequency of each visual word is independent of those of the other visual words, the likelihood $p(\boldsymbol{h}|\boldsymbol{r})$ is represented by the product of individual likelihoods $p(h_w|\boldsymbol{r})$ as

$$p(\boldsymbol{h}|\boldsymbol{r}) = \prod_{w=1}^{W} p(h_w|\boldsymbol{r}). \tag{3}$$

In addition, let us assume that each component $h_{cw}$ of $\boldsymbol{h}_c$ obeys a normal distribution $\mathcal{N}(\mu_{cw}, \sigma_{cw}^2)$ with the mean $\mu_{cw}$ and the variance $\sigma_{cw}^2$. Then, the linear combination of relative frequency $h_w = \sum_{c=1}^{C} r_c h_{cw}$ also obeys the normal distribution $\mathcal{N}(\sum_{c=1}^{C} r_c \mu_{cw}, \sum_{c=1}^{C} r_c^2 \sigma_{cw}^2)$ due to the reproductive property of the normal distribution. Hence, the likelihood is given by

$$p(\boldsymbol{h}|\boldsymbol{r}) = \prod_{w=1}^{W} \frac{1}{\sqrt{2\pi \sum_{c=1}^{C} r_c^2 \sigma_{cw}^2}} \exp\left[ -\frac{(h_w - \sum_{c=1}^{C} r_c \mu_{cw})^2}{2 \sum_{c=1}^{C} r_c^2 \sigma_{cw}^2} \right]. \tag{4}$$

For the sake of simplicity in the following discussion, we define $\mathcal{E}_{\text{like}}$ as

$$\mathcal{E}_{\text{like}} = -\ln p(\boldsymbol{h}|\boldsymbol{r}) \simeq \sum_{w=1}^{W} \left[ \frac{(h_w - \sum_{c=1}^{C} r_c \mu_{cw})^2}{\sum_{c=1}^{C} r_c^2 \sigma_{cw}^2} + \ln\left( \sum_{c=1}^{C} r_c^2 \sigma_{cw}^2 \right) \right]. \tag{5}$$

Here, we omit constants for estimation.

### 3.3   Prior Probability

We address the co-occurrence relationship between two object categories. Specifically, we assume that the mixture ratios obey a $C$-dimensional normal distribution $\mathcal{N}_C(\boldsymbol{\nu}, \Sigma)$ with the mean vector $\boldsymbol{\nu}$ and the covariance matrix $\Sigma$. In the similar way to the above, we define $\mathcal{E}_{\text{pri}}$ as

$$\mathcal{E}_{\text{pri}} = -\ln p(\boldsymbol{r}) \simeq (\boldsymbol{r} - \boldsymbol{\nu})^T \Sigma^{-1} (\boldsymbol{r} - \boldsymbol{\nu}). \tag{6}$$

### 3.4   Cost Function

Substituting (5) and (6) into the negative logarithm of (1) and introducing a parameter $\lambda$, we define the empirical cost function $\mathcal{E}_{\mathrm{pos}}$ as

$$\mathcal{E}_{\mathrm{pos}} = \mathcal{E}_{\mathrm{like}} + \lambda \mathcal{E}_{\mathrm{pri}}. \tag{7}$$

Our proposed method estimates the mixture ratios of multiple categories in an image by minimizing this empirical cost function. Because the mixture ratios are non-negative and their summation is equal to 1, our method results in a nonlinear minimization problem with the following constraints:

$$\begin{aligned} \text{minimize} \quad & \mathcal{E}_{\mathrm{pos}} \\ \text{subject to} \quad & r_c \geq 0 \ (c = 1, 2, 3, ..., C) \\ & \sum_{c=1}^{C} r_c = 1. \end{aligned} \tag{8}$$

The parameter $\lambda$ is a relative weight between $\mathcal{E}_{\mathrm{like}}$, which represents the degree by which the linear combination of histograms fits the data, and $\mathcal{E}_{\mathrm{pri}}$, which represents the statistical constraints enforced by the co-occurrence relationship between object categories. The ML estimation (*i.e.* without the prior probability) corresponds to the case when $\lambda = 0$.

We note here that the solution of the optimization problem is influenced by the initializing values. Our current implementation finds the initial values by minimizing $\sum_{w=1}^{W}(h_w - \sum_{c=1}^{C} r_c \mu_{cw})^2$ under the constraints $r_c \geq 0$ ($c = 1, 2, 3, ..., C$) and $\sum_{c=1}^{C} r_c = 1$. Then, we optimize the exact cost function by using *fmincon* in the MATLAB toolbox.

## 4   Experiments

### 4.1   Procedures

**Dataset**

We used the PASCAL2006 dataset[3] for evaluating the performance of our proposed method. This dataset contains objects of ten categories; "bicycle", "bus", "car", "cat", "cow", "dog", "horse", "motorbike", "person", and "sheep". The dataset consists of a set of data for training and another set for test. In addition, the annotations describing the labels and bounding boxes of those objects are given for all images.

**Bag of Features**

We used SIFT [8] for detecting and describing local features in images, and k-means clustering for vector quantization. Although other detectors, descriptors [14], and quantization algorithms [13] could be used as well, we implemented the above standard BoF since the main purpose of our experiments is to confirm the advantage of incorporating the co-occurrence relation into generic object recognition.

First, we prepared 50 images for each category from the training data by cropping regions inside the bounding boxes. Then, local features were detected and vector-quantized via k-means algorithm. The number of visual words $W$ are $32, 64, 128, 256, 512,$ and $1024$. We computed the histograms of those 500 images and finally obtained the means $\mu_{cw}$ and variances $\sigma^2_{cw}$ of relative frequencies for describing the likelihood in (5).

So far, we implicitly assume that images contain objects of only given categories. However, objects of other categories generally appear in images. Accordingly, we consider those objects as backgrounds, and investigate the effects of adding background categories to the ten object categories. We manually classified backgrounds into two categories: one contains artificial materials such as buildings and the other contains natural objects such as grass. Then, we selected 50 images for each background category and detected local features from the outside of the bounding boxes. The calculating statistics of the histograms is straightforward.

## Co-occurrence of Categories

We acquired the following two co-occurrence relations of object categories from 2618 images in the training data. The first type of co-occurrence relation is described in Section 3.3. Because the labels and bounding boxes are given, calculating the mixture ratio of each category is straightforward. We denote the mean vector and the covariance matrix of the mixture ratios by $\boldsymbol{\nu}_r$ and $\Sigma_r$.

The second type of co-occurrence relation is used for (partially) comparing our proposed method with the method proposed by Rabinovich[10]. Specifically, we confirm the advantage of the co-occurrence relation in terms of mixture ratios over that in terms of frequencies. We calculate the mean vector $\boldsymbol{\nu}_f$ and covariance matrix $\Sigma_f$ based on the presence of objects: $r_c = 1$ if objects of the category $c$ are present and $r_c = 0$ otherwise.

Fig.2 shows the two covariance matrices $\Sigma_r$ and $\Sigma_f$ (we show only the lower left values due to symmetry). The combinations of categories with positive covariance tend to appear together, but those with negative covariance have a tendency not to appear at the same time. For example, a "person" often appears with a "motorbike" and a "horse", but a "cat" rarely appears with a "dog". Interestingly, we observe that the sign of covariance differ between $\Sigma_r$ and $\Sigma_f$ for a few combinations of categories.

## Measure for Quantitative Evaluation

We used all of 2686 images from the test data. For quantitative evaluation, we use a measure known as the Area Under Curve (AUC), *i.e.* the area under the Receiver Operating Characteristic (ROC) curve, which is commonly used in the field of generic object recognition. Specifically, we consider the estimated *mixture ratio* of a given category as the *probability* that objects of that category are present in an image. Namely, we consider objects of the category $c$ to be present if $r_c$ is greater than a threshold, and draw the ROC curve by varying the threshold.

| | bicycle | bus | car | cat | cow | dog | horse | motorbike | person | sheep |
|---|---|---|---|---|---|---|---|---|---|---|
| bicycle | +3.4 | | | | | | | | | |
| bus | -0.2 | +1.9 | | | | | | | | |
| car | -0.3 | -0.2 | +2.8 | | | | | | | |
| cat | -0.5 | -0.3 | -0.6 | +5.9 | | | | | | |
| cow | -0.2 | -0.1 | -0.2 | -0.3 | +2.0 | | | | | |
| dog | -0.4 | -0.2 | -0.5 | -0.6 | -0.3 | +4.5 | | | | |
| horse | -0.2 | -0.1 | -0.2 | -0.3 | -0.1 | -0.3 | +1.9 | | | |
| motorbike | -0.2 | -0.1 | -0.2 | -0.4 | -0.2 | -0.3 | -0.2 | +2.7 | | |
| person | -0.2 | -0.1 | -0.4 | -0.5 | -0.2 | -0.3 | **+0.0** | **+0.1** | +2.3 | |
| sheep | -0.2 | -0.1 | -0.3 | -0.3 | -0.1 | -0.3 | -0.1 | -0.2 | -0.2 | +2.0 |

| | bicycle | bus | car | cat | cow | dog | horse | motorbike | person | sheep |
|---|---|---|---|---|---|---|---|---|---|---|
| bicycle | +9.2 | | | | | | | | | |
| bus | -0.6 | +6.2 | | | | | | | | |
| car | -1.0 | **+1.4** | +16.7 | | | | | | | |
| cat | -1.5 | -1.0 | -3.1 | +12.6 | | | | | | |
| cow | -0.8 | -0.5 | -1.6 | -1.1 | +7.2 | | | | | |
| dog | -1.4 | -0.9 | -2.7 | -1.8 | -1.1 | +12.0 | | | | |
| horse | -0.9 | -0.6 | -1.7 | -1.4 | -0.7 | -1.2 | +8.5 | | | |
| motorbike | -0.7 | -0.4 | -0.3 | -1.3 | -0.7 | -1.2 | -0.8 | +8.2 | | |
| person | **+0.5** | **+1.1** | -1.2 | -3.3 | -1.4 | -1.4 | **+2.6** | **+3.0** | +19.0 | |
| sheep | -1.0 | -0.6 | -1.9 | -1.4 | -0.7 | -1.2 | -0.9 | -0.9 | -1.8 | +8.7 |

**Fig. 2.** The covariance matrices in terms of mixture ratios (top) and frequencies (bottom). The numerical values are multiplied by 100 for display purpose.

In general, performance is considered to be better as the AUC grows closer to one. However, the way of evaluation that regards the ratio as the probability has some limitations. For example, an object with a small mixture ratio will be considered to be a false negative even though its mixture ratio is accurately estimated by our method, and as a result would degrade the AUC. We note that because our method characterizes the mixture ratios of multiple categories (*i.e.* not the presence and absence of objects), the AUC may not provide a holistic measure.

## 4.2   Results

### Effects of the Co-occurrence Relation in terms of Mixture Ratios

First, we examined the effects of incorporating the co-occurrence relation in terms of mixture ratios $(\nu_r, \Sigma_r)$ into generic object recognition. Fig. 3 (left) shows the average of AUCs with respect to the ten object categories for various combinations of the weight $\lambda$ and the number of visual words $W$. We can find that

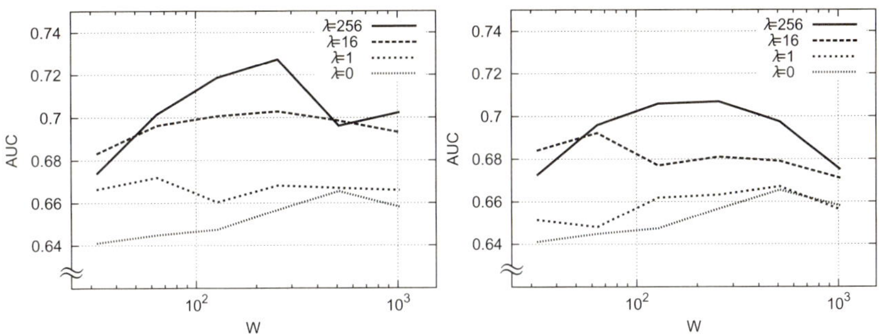

**Fig. 3.** AUCs: incorporating the co-occurrence relation in terms of mixture ratios (left) and frequencies (right)

| | ML | MAP: freq | MAP: ratio | ground truth | ML | MAP: freq | MAP: ratio | ground truth | ML | MAP: freq | MAP: ratio | ground truth |
|---|---|---|---|---|---|---|---|---|---|---|---|---|
| bicycle | 0 | 0 | 0 | 0 | 0 | 0 | 0 | 0 | 0 | 0 | 0 | 0 |
| bus | 0 | 0 | 0 | 0 | 0.09 | 0.03 | 0.01 | 0 | 0 | 0 | 0.01 | 0 |
| car | 0 | 0.14 | 0 | 0 | 0 | 0 | 0 | 0 | 0 | 0 | 0 | 0 |
| cat | 0 | 0 | 0 | 0 | 0 | 0 | 0 | 0 | 0.51 | 0.50 | 0.52 | 0.82 |
| cow | 0 | 0 | 0 | 0 | 0 | 0 | 0 | 0 | 0 | 0 | 0.03 | 0 |
| dog | 0 | 0 | 0 | 0 | 0 | 0 | 0 | 0 | 0.40 | 0.36 | 0.28 | 0 |
| horse | 0 | 0 | 0 | 0 | 0.70 | 0.60 | 0.41 | 0.38 | 0 | 0.02 | 0.05 | 0 |
| motorbike | 1.00 | 0.86 | 0.63 | 0.61 | 0 | 0 | 0.19 | 0 | 0 | 0 | 0.02 | 0 |
| person | 0 | 0 | 0.37 | 0.28 | 0 | 0.11 | 0.35 | 0.31 | 0 | 0 | 0.04 | 0 |
| sheep | 0 | 0 | 0 | 0 | 0.20 | 0.27 | 0.05 | 0 | 0.09 | 0.12 | 0.05 | 0 |

**Fig. 4.** Mixture ratios found via ML estimation (ML), via MAP estimation using the co-occurrence relation in terms of frequencies (MAP: freq)/mixture ratios (MAP: ratio), and ground truth

the results using the prior probability are better than those of ML estimation ($\lambda = 0$). Our proposed method and ML estimation achieve maximum AUCs of 0.73 and 0.66 respectively. Thus, we can say that the co-occurrence relation in terms of mixture ratios works well for recognizing multiple objects.

In Fig.4, we show the estimated mixture ratios and the ground truth for some images. For example, the ML estimation (ML) yields the result of "motorbike"

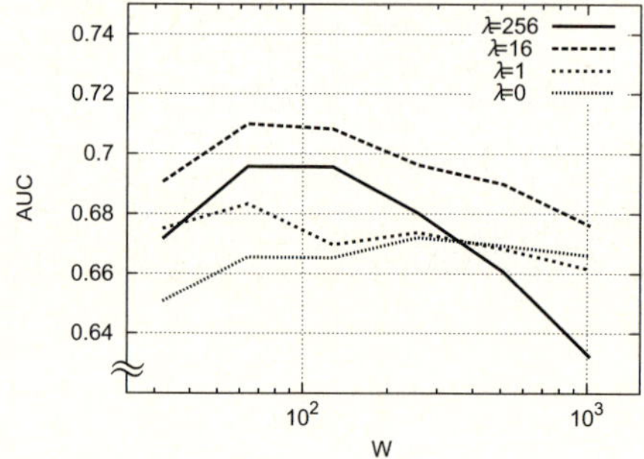



**Fig. 5.** AUCs: adding background categories

for the left image. On the other hand, our method based on MAP estimation (MAP: ratio) yields the result of "motorbike" and "person", which is consistent with the ground truth. These results also support the effectiveness of the proposed method.

### Effects of the Co-occurrence Relation in terms of Frequencies

Second, we examined the effects of the co-occurrence relation in terms of frequencies $(\boldsymbol{\nu}_f, \Sigma_f)$. In the similar manner to the above, we show the average of AUCs in Fig. 3 (right). Also in this case, the results that make use of the prior probability are better than those of ML estimation in most combinations. However, the performance of the method using the co-occurrence relation in terms of frequencies is worse than that using the relation in terms of ratios. Therefore, one can conclude that the co-occurrence relation in terms of frequencies (*i.e.* based only on the presence of categories) is also effective for object recognition, but the relation considering mixture ratios works better. We show the estimated mixture ratios (MAP: freq) in Fig.4.

### Effects of Background Categories

Finally, we examined the effects of adding background categories to the ten object categories. Fig. 5 shows the results obtained by using the co-occurrence relation $(\boldsymbol{\nu}_r, \Sigma_r)$. Although the results are similar to the previous experiments in the sense that the co-occurrence relation works well, the performance becomes slightly worse than the case without background categories. As described in Section 4.1, this is because the background categories lower the mixture ratios of the object categories, and therefore increase the number of false negatives.

We show the estimated mixture ratios and the ground truth in Fig.6. Here, "bg" stands for the summation of the mixture ratios of two background categories. When we ignore the background categories (C=10), the estimated ratios are significantly different from the ground truth, because the histogram of visual words arising from backgrounds is forced to be described by those arising from the object categories. On the other hand, when the background categories are combined (C=12), the mixture ratios of the backgrounds have larger values, and

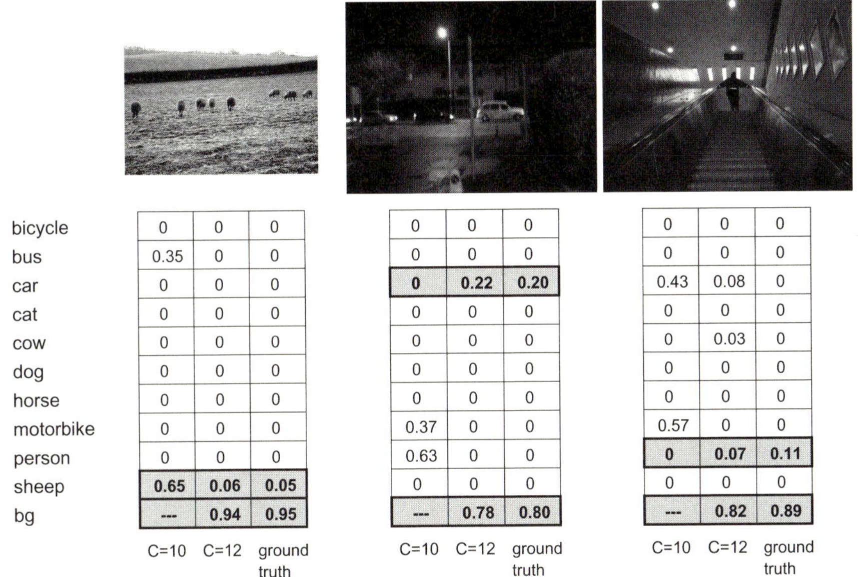

**Image 1 (sheep)**

| | C=10 | C=12 | ground truth |
|---|---|---|---|
| bicycle | 0 | 0 | 0 |
| bus | 0.35 | 0 | 0 |
| car | 0 | 0 | 0 |
| cat | 0 | 0 | 0 |
| cow | 0 | 0 | 0 |
| dog | 0 | 0 | 0 |
| horse | 0 | 0 | 0 |
| motorbike | 0 | 0 | 0 |
| person | 0 | 0 | 0 |
| sheep | 0.65 | 0.06 | 0.05 |
| bg | --- | 0.94 | 0.95 |

**Image 2 (car)**

| | C=10 | C=12 | ground truth |
|---|---|---|---|
| bicycle | 0 | 0 | 0 |
| bus | 0 | 0 | 0 |
| car | 0 | 0.22 | 0.20 |
| cat | 0 | 0 | 0 |
| cow | 0 | 0 | 0 |
| dog | 0 | 0 | 0 |
| horse | 0 | 0 | 0 |
| motorbike | 0.37 | 0 | 0 |
| person | 0.63 | 0 | 0 |
| sheep | 0 | 0 | 0 |
| bg | --- | 0.78 | 0.80 |

**Image 3 (escalator)**

| | C=10 | C=12 | ground truth |
|---|---|---|---|
| bicycle | 0 | 0 | 0 |
| bus | 0 | 0 | 0 |
| car | 0.43 | 0.08 | 0 |
| cat | 0 | 0 | 0 |
| cow | 0 | 0.03 | 0 |
| dog | 0 | 0 | 0 |
| horse | 0 | 0 | 0 |
| motorbike | 0.57 | 0 | 0 |
| person | 0 | 0.07 | 0.11 |
| sheep | 0 | 0 | 0 |
| bg | --- | 0.82 | 0.89 |

**Fig. 6.** Mixture ratios found via MAP estimation without (C=10)/with (C=12) background categories, and ground truth

those of the object categories come closer to the ground truth. These results imply the effectiveness of the background categories for recognizing images with large background area.

## 5 Conclusions and Future Work

In this paper, we proposed a novel method for recognizing objects of multiple categories coexisting in an image. In particular, our proposed method estimates the mixture ratios of multiple categories in an image via regression by incorporating the co-occurrence relationship between object categories. We implemented a prototype system of our method, and confirmed its effectiveness through experiments using the PASCAL dataset.

Future directions of this study include incorporating the co-occurrence relationship among more than three categories and modeling background categories via unsupervised learning. In addition, individual elements of BoF such as feature detection, description, and vector quantization should be improved.

**Acknowledgement.** A part of this work was supported by Grants-in-Aid for Scientific Research from the Ministry of Education, Culture, Sports, Science and Technology of Japan (No. 20700153).

# References


1. Biederman, I., Mezzanotte, R., Rabinowitz, J.: Scene perception: detecting and judging objects undergoing relational violations. Cognitive Psychology 14(2), 143–177 (1982)
2. Csurka, G., Dance, C., Fan, L., Willamowski, J., Bray, C.: Visual categorization with bags of keypoints. In: Proc. ECCV 2004 Workshop on Statistical Learning in Computer Vision, pp. 1–22 (2004)
3. Everingham, M., Zisserman, A., Williams, C., Van Gool, L.: The 2006 PASCAL Visual Object Classes Challenge (VOC 2006) Results,
   http://www.pascal-network.org/challenges/VOC/voc2006/results.pdf
4. Fergus, R., Perona, P., Zisserman, A.: Object class recognition by unsupervised scale-invariant learning. In: Proc. IEEE CS Conf. Computer Vision and Pattern Recognition (CVPR 2003), pp. II-264–II-271 (2003)
5. Frome, A., Singer, Y., Sha, F., Malik, J.: Learning globally-consistent local distance functions for shape-based image retrieval and classification. In: Proc. IEEE Int'l Conf. Computer Vision (ICCV 2007), pp. 1–8 (2007)
6. Galleguillos, C., Rabinovich, A., Belongie, S.: Object categorization using co-occurrence, location and appearance. In: Proc. IEEE CS Conf. Computer Vision and Pattern Recognition (CVPR 2008), pp. 1–8 (2008)
7. Hoiem, D., Efros, A., Hebert, M.: Putting objects in perspective. In: Proc. IEEE CS Conf. Computer Vision and Pattern Recognition (CVPR 2006), pp. 2137–2144 (2006)
8. Lowe, D.: Distinctive image features from scale-invariant keypoints. Int'l Journal of Compute Vision 60(2), 91–110 (2004)
9. Qi, G.-J., Hua, X.-S., Rui, Y., Mei, T., Tang, J., Zhang, H.-J.: Concurrent multiple instance learning for image categorization. In: Proc. IEEE CS Conf. Computer Vision and Pattern Recognition (CVPR 2007), pp. 1–8 (2007)
10. Rabinovich, A., Vedaldi, A., Galleguillos, C., Wiewiora, E., Belongie, S.: Objects in context. In: Proc. IEEE Int'l Conf. Computer Vision (ICCV 2007), pp. 1–8 (2007)
11. Savarese, S., Fei-Fei, L.: 3D generic object categorization, localization and pose estimation. In: Proc. IEEE Int'l Conf. Computer Vision (ICCV 2007), pp. 1–8 (2007)
12. Sivic, J., Russell, B., Efros, A., Zisserman, A., Freeman, W.: Discovering objects and their location in images. In: Proc. IEEE Int'l Conf. Computer Vision (ICCV 2005), pp. 370–377 (2005)
13. Yang, L., Jin, R., Sukthankar, R., Jurie, F.: Unifying discriminative visual codebook generation with classifier training for object category recognition. In: Proc. IEEE CS Conf. Computer Vision and Pattern Recognition (CVPR 2008), pp. 1–8 (2008)
14. Zhang, J., Marszalek, M., Lazebnik, S., Schmid, C.: Local features and kernels for classification of texture and object categories: a comprehensive study. Int'l Journal of Computer Vision 73(2), 213–238 (2007)

# An Adaptive and Efficient Selective Multiple Reference Frames Motion Estimation for H.264 Video Coding[*]

Yu-Ming Lee, Yong-Fu Wang, Jia-Ren Wang, and Yinyi Lin

Department of Communication Engineering,
National Central University, Taiwan 32054
{yuming0727,cyee01,kevinwang72326}@gmail.com,
yilin@ce.ncu.edu.tw

**Abstract.** In the popular video coding standard H.264/AVC, many advanced techniques are employed. One important technique is the use of multiple reference frames motion estimation. However, the computational load increases with the number of references frames. In this paper, we suggest a selective multiple reference frames motion estimation (SMRFME) architecture which takes use of the information of the $1^{st}$ reference frame to determine whether it is necessary to search remaining reference frames. In addition, three early termination schemes are applied to the remaining reference frames of the candidate modes. The simulation results demonstrate that the proposed algorithm can achieve up to 77% of time saving compared to the multiple reference frames full search algorithm, while maintaining a high coding performance.

**Keywords:** H.264, multiple reference frames, selective multiple reference frames motion estimation (SMRFME), early termination, AZB, region based.

## 1 Introduction

The international video coding standard H.264/AVC has been approved by ITU-T as recommendation H.264 and by ISO/IEC as international standard MPEG-4 part 10 advanced video coding (AVC) [1]. The state-of-art H.264/AVC achieves significantly better performance in both PSNR and video quality at the same bit-rate compared with prior video coding standards. The improvement is typically 2-3 dB in PSNR, or equivalently 40%-60% in bit-rate reduction. One important technique is the use of multiple reference frames motion estimation (ME), and the computational complexity of H.264/AVC increases with the number of reference frames employed. The full selection procedure provides the best coding efficiency, but the five-fold increase in computation load is unbearable.

Many fast and efficient multi-frames ME algorithms have been investigated in recent years to reduce the computation cost and maintain coding performance. Some algorithms attempt to use context-based or histogram-similarity based method to

[*] This work was supported by the National Science Council, R.O.C. under Grant Number NSC 96-2221-E-008-013-MY2.

T. Wada, F. Huang, and S. Lin (Eds.): PSIVT 2009, LNCS 5414, pp. 509–518, 2009.

speed up the multiple reference frames ME [2]. Some other algorithms attempt to reduce the computation using various prediction methods for selecting the initial search point [3]-[4]. In most of researches investigated perform the multiple reference frames ME mode by mode and select the best macroblock (MB) mode by considering the rate-distortion (RD) optimization technique. It is observed that most of the MB modes are finally predicted using the first reference frames, and just few of them are predicted with other reference frames. Another observation is that if the MB mode predicted using the $1^{st}$ frame has a bad motion cost (*MCOST* is shown in equation 1), it is then less likely to be the best mode predicted from its other reference frames. In this paper, based on these observations we propose a selective multiple reference frames ME (SMRFME) scheme which performs the $1^{st}$ reference frame ME first and performs remaining reference frames only for those modes with good *MCOST* predicted using the $1^{st}$ reference frame.

$$MCOST(s,c) = SAD(s,c) + \lambda_{MOTION} \cdot Bit(\Delta MV) \tag{1}$$

where $SAD(s,c)$ is the sum of absolute differences between original block $s$ and candidate matching block $c$. $\lambda_{MOTION}$ is the Lagrange multiplier for ME. $\Delta MV$ is the difference between the predicted MV and the actual MV. $Bit(\Delta MV)$ is the number of bits representing the $\Delta MV$.

## 2   Statistical Analysis of Multi-Reference Frames ME (MRFME)

In the inter mode decision, 7 different block-size modes, varying among $16x16(m_1)$, $16x8(m_2)$, $8x16(m_3)$, $8x8(m_4)$, $8x4(m_5)$, $4x8(m_6)$ and $4x4(m_7)$, are performed in each MB to achieve the best coding efficiency, in addition to the skip mode $(m_0)$. These modes form a two-level hierarchy inside a MB. The first level L1 includes modes of 16x16, 16x8, 8x16, while the second level L2 includes modes of 8x8, 8x4, 4x8 and 4x4. In the H.264/AVC reference software baseline encoder, the multiple reference frames ME is conventionally performed mode by mode with full search of five reference frames, as illustrated in Fig. 1.

In most video sequences lots of background or motionless MBs are finally determined as a skip mode or L1 modes after computationally expensive rate distortion optimization. The MBs belonging to a high detail or fast motion area must be further split into L2 modes to get the best coding efficiency. In addition, most of MB modes end up with being predicted using the $1^{st}$ reference frame. An intensive experiment was conducted on many CIF and QCIF video sequences, to evaluate the distribution of best reference frame in each sequence.

The results conducted on 10 test video sequences are displayed in Table 1 for QP=28. As shown, most of MBs are predicted from $1^{st}$ reference frame (78%). We have observed that the MB mode, with a bad *MCOST* on the $1^{st}$ frame prediction, is then less likely to be the best MB mode predicted from its other reference frames.

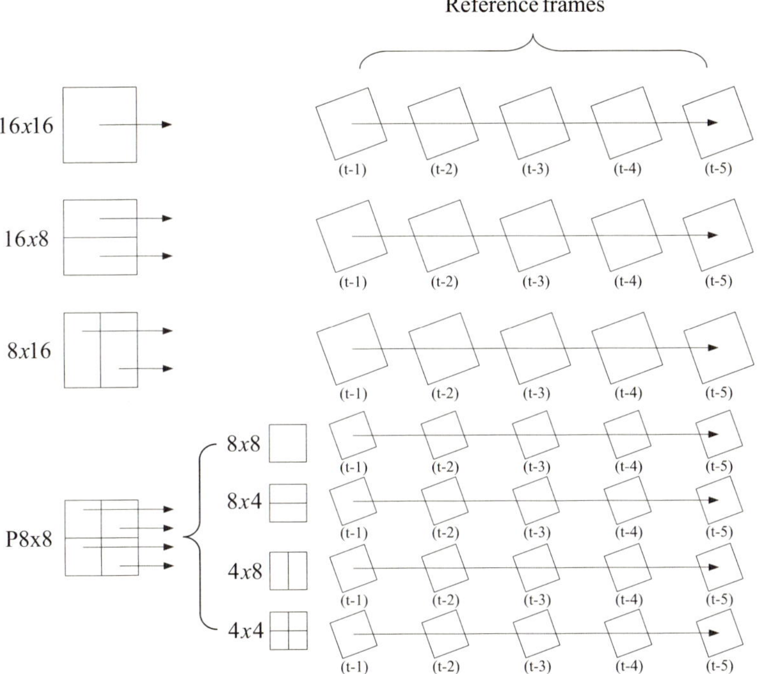



**Fig. 1.** Conventional Multi-Reference Frames Motion Estimation

**Table 1.** The distribution of the best reference frame

| QP=28 | | Distribution of the best reference frame | | | | |
|---|---|---|---|---|---|---|
| sequence | | t-1 | t-2 | t-3 | t-4 | t-5 |
| QCIF | claire | 96.70 | 1.18 | 1.10 | 0.35 | 0.68 |
| | grandma | 96.32 | 1.46 | 1.34 | 0.35 | 0.53 |
| | foreman | 73.50 | 11.68 | 8.72 | 3.32 | 2.77 |
| | football | 78.52 | 8.95 | 6.28 | 3.14 | 3.12 |
| | carphone | 75.66 | 8.75 | 8.41 | 3.54 | 3.65 |
| CIF | container | 91.68 | 3.69 | 2.07 | 1.40 | 1.17 |
| | tempete | 54.74 | 14.55 | 16.17 | 7.69 | 6.84 |
| | mobile | 46.87 | 16.14 | 16.86 | 10.32 | 9.81 |
| | paris | 93.13 | 3.51 | 2.01 | 0.78 | 0.57 |
| | stefan | 72.36 | 10.79 | 9.51 | 3.89 | 3.46 |
| Avg. | | 77.95 | 8.07 | 7.25 | 3.48 | 3.26 |

## 3 Proposed Fast MRFME Algorithm

Based on the analysis above, we propose a fast MRFME algorithm which takes use of
the characteristics of the video sequences.

### 3.1 Selective MRFME Scheme (SMRFME)

From the statistical analysis described previously, the conventional multiple reference
frames ME proposed in the reference software encoder, checking all reference frames

equally likely for each mode, might not be an efficient scheme. To reduce the computation cost and maintain coding performance several fast and efficient multiple reference frames ME algorithms have been investigated in recent years. In [2], the context-based method was proposed to speed up the multiple reference frames ME. In [2], after the 1st frame for all seven modes are performed, several context-based adaptive criteria are used to determine whether it is necessary to search the next reference frames. The procedure repeats until all 5 reference frames have been checked. The algorithm shows more efficient than the conventional one due to that most of best MB modes have been obtained in the 1st reference frame prediction (as can be seen in Table 1), and the prediction in all other reference frames can be skipped with negligible degradation.

The algorithm proposed in [2], to whatever extent it occurs, doesn't consider that the probability is very low for a MB mode with a bad *MCOST* predicted in the 1st frame, which becomes the final best MB mode predicted from its other reference frames. To improve the computation efficiency, in this section we propose a selective multiple reference frames ME algorithm. The SMRFME scheme is illustrated in Fig. 2. The SMRFME scheme is briefly summarized as follows:

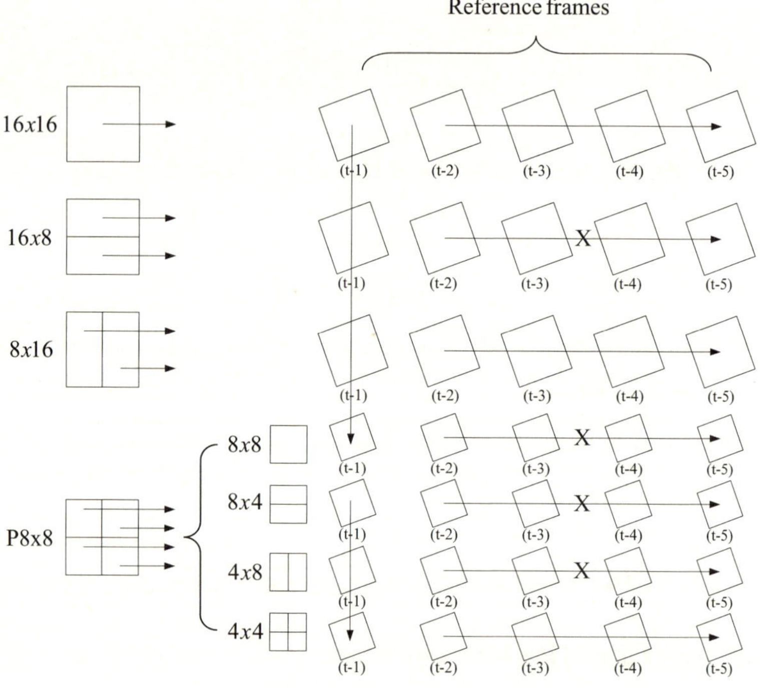


**Fig. 2.** Selective Multi-Reference Frames Motion Estimation

Assume $MCOST_{1,best}$ as the best *MCOST* predicted in the 1[st] reference frame among all MB modes, which is given by

$$MCOST_{1,best} = \min\{MCOST_{1,i}, i = 0,1,2,3,4,5,6,7\} \qquad (2)$$

where $MCOST_{1,i}$ represents the $MCOST$ in mode $i$. Define the ratio of the $MCOST$, $\beta_{MCOST,i}$, as

$$\beta_{MCOST,i} = \frac{MCOST_{1,i}}{MCOST_{1,best}} \tag{3}$$

To speed up the multiple reference frames decision process, after the $1^{st}$ reference frame prediction only the modes with $\beta_{MCOST,i}$ less than a threshold $\beta$ are still performed ME for other reference frames. To determine the threshold $\beta$ for SMRFME, we examine the cumulative distribution function (CDF) of the best modes finally predicted from other reference frames that still can be acquired with this criterion, as a function of $\beta$ for several test sequences. The results are demonstrated in Fig. 3. As shown, a very large number of the best modes can be identified when $\beta = 1.2$, i.e., the mode with $MCOST$ value $MCOST_{1,i} \geq 1.2 MCOST_{1,best}$ are unlikely to obtain the best reference frame in its remaining reference frames.

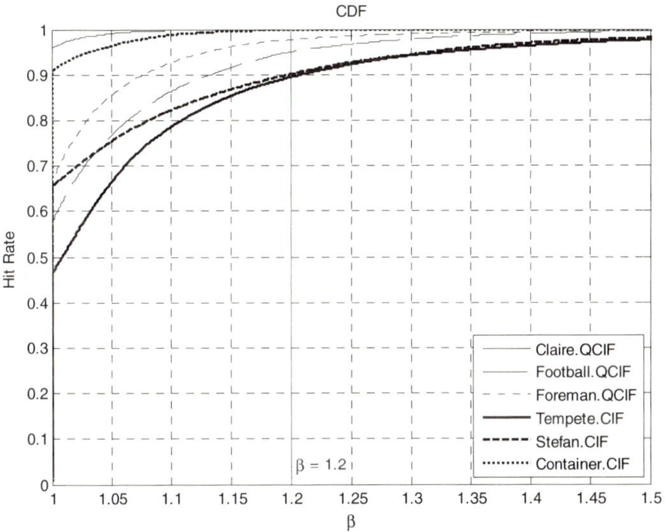


**Fig. 3.** CDF of the hit rate as a function of factor ($\beta$)

## 3.2  Early Termination Algorithms for Remaining Reference Frames

Though the SMRFME scheme can bring out good coding performance, it achieves 41% of computation reduction on average. Although the remaining reference frames of least possible modes are discarded, five reference frames of the candidate modes are still performed. In this section, three early termination algorithms are proposed to further quicken the process of searching reference frames.

### 3.2.1  Region Based Algorithm (Denoted as Region Based)

Generally, the correlation between the adjacent frames is very strong. Our investigation revealed that the continuity of the motion can be explored in order to simplify the multi-reference frames selection. Assume an object is moving in a video sequence and keeps the similar appearance in adjacent frames. The best reference frame of previous frame can be used as the maximum reference frame of current frame. An example is given in Fig. 4, which illustrates the best reference frame for each macroblock in two successive encoded frames of Foreman, where 0 to 4 are the best reference index (ref_idx). It is clearly shown that the MB in frame$_{(t)}$ are highly correlated with their co-located or surrounding MB in the frame$_{(t-1)}$. Fig. 5 shows the MB in current and its co-located and neighbouring MBs in reference frame, where co-located (E') and surrounding (A-I) MBs form a region. For the frame$_{(t)}$, we first check the ref_idx of the region in previously encoded frame$_{(t-1)}$. To avoid additional computation complexity, we just find out the maximum ref_idx in the region. We use the maximum ref_idx to determine the maximum searched frame for the frame$_{(t)}$. The maximum searched frame is defined as

$$Maximum\ searched\ frame = \max\{ref_idx_A, ref_idx_B, ..., ref_idx_I\} \qquad (4)$$

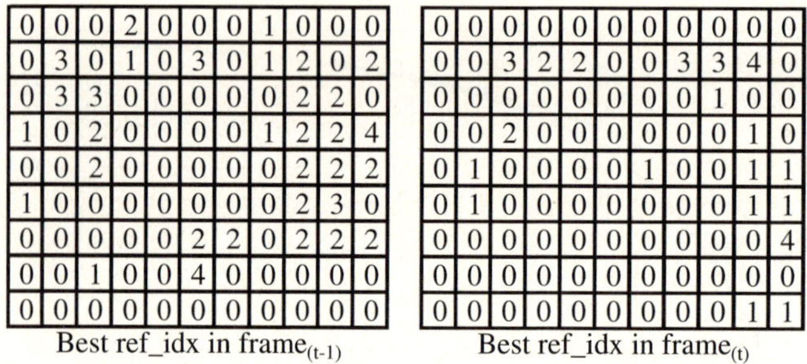

<table>
<tr><td>0</td><td>0</td><td>0</td><td>2</td><td>0</td><td>0</td><td>0</td><td>1</td><td>0</td><td>0</td><td>0</td></tr>
<tr><td>0</td><td>3</td><td>0</td><td>1</td><td>0</td><td>3</td><td>0</td><td>1</td><td>2</td><td>0</td><td>2</td></tr>
<tr><td>0</td><td>3</td><td>3</td><td>0</td><td>0</td><td>0</td><td>0</td><td>0</td><td>2</td><td>2</td><td>0</td></tr>
<tr><td>1</td><td>0</td><td>2</td><td>0</td><td>0</td><td>0</td><td>0</td><td>1</td><td>2</td><td>2</td><td>4</td></tr>
<tr><td>0</td><td>0</td><td>2</td><td>0</td><td>0</td><td>0</td><td>0</td><td>0</td><td>2</td><td>2</td><td>2</td></tr>
<tr><td>1</td><td>0</td><td>0</td><td>0</td><td>0</td><td>0</td><td>0</td><td>0</td><td>2</td><td>3</td><td>0</td></tr>
<tr><td>0</td><td>0</td><td>0</td><td>0</td><td>0</td><td>2</td><td>2</td><td>0</td><td>2</td><td>2</td><td>2</td></tr>
<tr><td>0</td><td>0</td><td>1</td><td>0</td><td>0</td><td>4</td><td>0</td><td>0</td><td>0</td><td>0</td><td>0</td></tr>
<tr><td>0</td><td>0</td><td>0</td><td>0</td><td>0</td><td>0</td><td>0</td><td>0</td><td>0</td><td>0</td><td>0</td></tr>
</table>

Best ref_idx in frame$_{(t-1)}$

<table>
<tr><td>0</td><td>0</td><td>0</td><td>0</td><td>0</td><td>0</td><td>0</td><td>0</td><td>0</td><td>0</td><td>0</td></tr>
<tr><td>0</td><td>0</td><td>3</td><td>2</td><td>2</td><td>0</td><td>0</td><td>3</td><td>3</td><td>4</td><td>0</td></tr>
<tr><td>0</td><td>0</td><td>0</td><td>0</td><td>0</td><td>0</td><td>0</td><td>0</td><td>1</td><td>0</td><td>0</td></tr>
<tr><td>0</td><td>0</td><td>2</td><td>0</td><td>0</td><td>0</td><td>0</td><td>0</td><td>0</td><td>1</td><td>0</td></tr>
<tr><td>0</td><td>1</td><td>0</td><td>0</td><td>0</td><td>0</td><td>1</td><td>0</td><td>0</td><td>1</td><td>1</td></tr>
<tr><td>0</td><td>1</td><td>0</td><td>0</td><td>0</td><td>0</td><td>0</td><td>0</td><td>0</td><td>1</td><td>1</td></tr>
<tr><td>0</td><td>0</td><td>0</td><td>0</td><td>0</td><td>0</td><td>0</td><td>0</td><td>0</td><td>0</td><td>4</td></tr>
<tr><td>0</td><td>0</td><td>0</td><td>0</td><td>0</td><td>0</td><td>0</td><td>0</td><td>0</td><td>0</td><td>0</td></tr>
<tr><td>0</td><td>0</td><td>0</td><td>0</td><td>0</td><td>0</td><td>0</td><td>0</td><td>0</td><td>1</td><td>1</td></tr>
</table>

Best ref_idx in frame$_{(t)}$

**Fig. 4.** The ref_idx of the two adjacent frames in Foreman

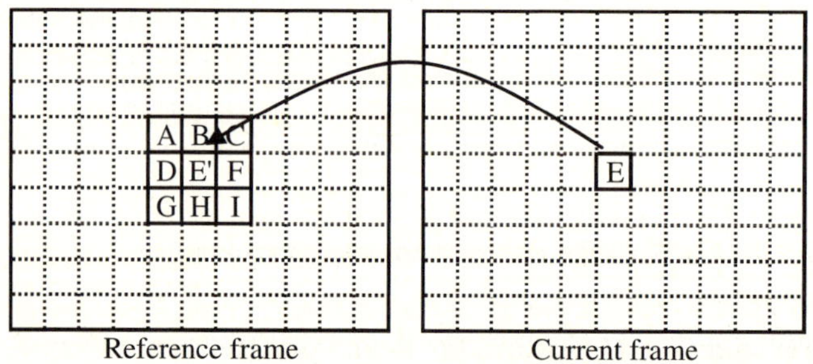


**Fig. 5.** Region based macroblocks

### 3.2.2  Detection of All Zero Coefficients Algorithm (Denoted as AZB)

In motion estimation process, the SAD between the current block and its best matching block can be used to detect all zero blocks. If it is detected that the transformed and quantized coefficients are very close to zero, the remaining reference frames can be terminated. In order to save the DCT and quantization, a nearly sufficient condition for early zero-block detection is derived [5]. If all the SAD blocks are smaller than threshold ($3.5 \cdot Q_{step}$), the ME process of the remaining reference frames is terminated immediately.

### 3.2.3  Detection of Monotonic Increment Algorithm (Denoted as Monotonic)

We can see form Table 1 that the probability that $ref_{t-1}$, $ref_{t-2}$ and $ref_{t-3}$ are selected as the best reference frame is very high, more than 93% on average. Thus, the *MCOST*s of $ref_{t-1}$, $ref_{t-2}$ and $ref_{t-3}$ can also be used to determine whether or not search $ref_{t-4}$ and $ref_{t-5}$. When the *MCOST* of $ref_{t-3}$ is largest among the first three reference frames, these three *MCOST*s will most likely be monotonic increment. The probability that $ref_{t-4}$ and $ref_{t-5}$ selected as the best reference frame is very little. For this condition, the ME procedure of the $ref_{t-4}$ and $ref_{t-5}$ is omitted.

### 3.2.4  Analysis of Our Proposed Early Termination Algorithms

The hit rate analysis of these three algorithms is shown in Table 3. It can be seen that the average hit rate of these three algorithms reaches 95%, 89% and 97%, respectively. Thus, we can get the good coding performance in simulation.

**Table 3.** The hit rate analysis

| Sequence | | Region based | AZB | Monotonic |
|---|---|---|---|---|
| QCIF | football | 94.51% | 92.89% | 95.24% |
| | coastguard | 94.01% | 91.98% | 98.37% |
| | trevor | 95.69% | 93.19% | 99.28% |
| | claire | 97.58% | 98.03% | 99.42% |
| | foreman | 92.49% | 83.60% | 96.58% |
| | tennis | 96.04% | 90.09% | 97.73% |
| CIF | bus | 94.42% | 88.56% | 97.30% |
| | dancer | 94.31% | 91.32% | 98.69% |
| | waterfall | 93.00% | 89.59% | 97.14% |
| | news | 97.16% | 96.52% | 99.39% |
| | stefan | 93.27% | 84.88% | 96.18% |
| | mobile | 97.18% | 72.23% | 89.01% |
| AVG. | | 94.97% | 89.41% | 97.03% |

## 4  Experimental Results

To evaluate the performance of the efficient selective multiple reference frames ME algorithm, our proposed algorithms were implemented in H.264 reference encoder JM12.2. The proposed algorithms were tested on 4 QCIF (176x144) and CIF (352x288) sequences which represent different motion activities. The test conditions for simulation are given as follows:

**Table 4.** Simulation condition

| # of coded frames | 100 | GOP structure | IPPP... |
|---|---|---|---|
| # of reference frames | 5 | Search range | ±16 |
| RDO | on | QP | 20, 24, 28, 32, 36 |
| Entropy coding | CAVLC | Resolution | 1/4 pixel |
| Intra mode | on | Inter mode | on |

**Table 5.** Performance comparison for QP=28

(a) PSNR comparison

| QP=28 | | Orig. | SMRFME | Rgeion based | AZB | Monotonic | Proposed |
|---|---|---|---|---|---|---|---|
| Sequence | | PSNR comparison (dB, $\triangle$(dB)) | | | | | |
| QCIF | football | 34.547 | -0.011 | -0.028 | -0.009 | -0.018 | -0.023 |
| | coastguard | 34.682 | -0.013 | -0.025 | 0.006 | -0.017 | -0.035 |
| | trevor | 36.912 | 0.003 | -0.008 | -0.023 | 0.000 | -0.016 |
| | claire | 39.823 | 0.061 | 0.004 | 0.008 | 0.007 | -0.015 |
| CIF | bus | 35.718 | -0.017 | -0.020 | -0.005 | -0.006 | -0.037 |
| | dancer | 40.609 | -0.001 | -0.003 | -0.017 | -0.001 | -0.025 |
| | waterfall | 35.454 | -0.004 | -0.036 | 0.004 | -0.029 | -0.052 |
| | news | 38.585 | -0.013 | -0.020 | -0.016 | -0.016 | -0.033 |
| Avg. | | | 0.001 | -0.017 | -0.006 | -0.010 | -0.030 |

(b) Bit-rate comparison

| QP=28 | | Orig. | SMRFME | Rgeion based | AZB | Monotonic | Proposed |
|---|---|---|---|---|---|---|---|
| Sequence | | Bit rate comparison (bps, $\triangle$(%)) | | | | | |
| QCIF | football | 1060999 | 0.41 | 0.08 | -0.03 | 0.03 | 0.59 |
| | coastguard | 279156 | 0.37 | 0.55 | 0.46 | 0.00 | 0.58 |
| | trevor | 142279 | 0.12 | 0.02 | -0.18 | -0.37 | 0.07 |
| | claire | 32599 | -0.39 | 1.71 | -0.46 | -0.04 | 0.10 |
| CIF | bus | 1328657 | 1.05 | 0.08 | -0.08 | 0.04 | 1.50 |
| | dancer | 608738 | 0.11 | -0.15 | 0.10 | -0.05 | 0.39 |
| | waterfall | 324540 | -0.08 | 0.51 | 0.18 | 0.48 | 0.64 |
| | news | 227602 | -0.01 | 0.01 | 0.00 | 0.10 | 0.40 |
| Avg. | | | 0.20 | 0.35 | 0.00 | 0.02 | 0.53 |

(c) Time comparison

| QP=28 | | Orig. | SMRFME | Rgeion based | AZB | Monotonic | Proposed |
|---|---|---|---|---|---|---|---|
| Sequence | | Time comparison (ms, $\triangle$(%)) | | | | | |
| QCIF | football | 137340 | -43.37 | -15.89 | -5.11 | -25.60 | -60.36 |
| | coastguard | 108387 | -41.77 | -44.09 | -10.60 | -32.52 | -65.41 |
| | trevor | 76118 | -39.52 | -42.04 | -20.13 | -31.95 | -67.74 |
| | claire | 49666 | -48.18 | -47.68 | -29.38 | -31.71 | -71.20 |
| CIF | bus | 468038 | -44.60 | -26.50 | -13.13 | -27.86 | -64.85 |
| | dancer | 380253 | -41.18 | -46.70 | -38.39 | -36.97 | -77.81 |
| | waterfall | 347551 | -38.85 | -22.42 | -15.15 | -21.72 | -56.07 |
| | news | 237827 | -35.68 | -46.11 | -27.84 | -31.42 | -68.91 |
| Avg. | | | -41.64 | -36.43 | -19.97 | -29.97 | -66.54 |

The simulation results of PSNR gain, bit-rate increment and coding time compared to multiple reference frames full search algorithm (denoted as Orig.) are shown in Table 5. The algorithm which combines SMRFME algorithm with all early termination algorithms is denoted as proposed algorithm. The simulation results show that our proposed algorithm achieves 66% coding time on average. Meanwhile the performance of our proposed algorithm is almost the same as the Orig., with negligible loss in PSNR (0.03 dB loss) and bit-rate (0.53% bit-rate increment).

Fig. 6 depicts the rate-distortion (RD) performance of sequence football and Stefan. Compared with Orig. and our proposed algorithm, the average PSNR drop of our algorithm is negligible. Therefore, the rate-distortion curve of our proposed algorithm and the Orig. algorithm are hardly distinguishable. Table 6 shows that the complexity reduction of our proposed algorithm in various bit-rate. Results also show that our proposed algorithm can reduce computation load efficiently, while keeping good coding performance.

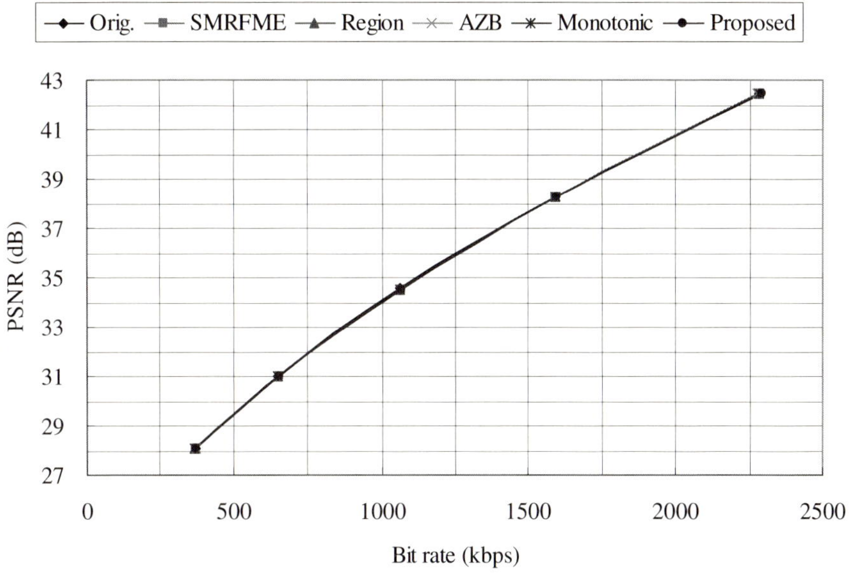



(a) Football.QCIF

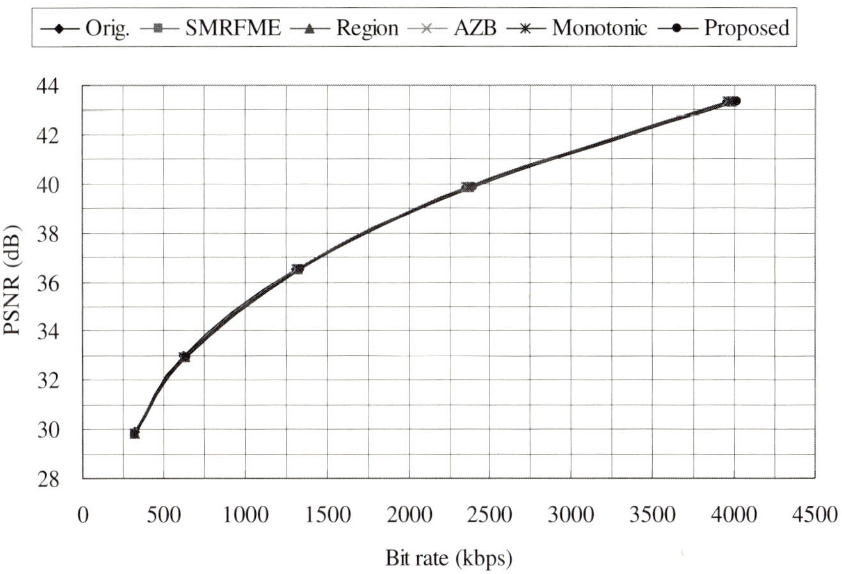



(b) Stefan.CIF

**Fig. 6.** Rate-distortion performance comparison

**Table 6.** Coding efficiency comparison

(a) Football.QCIF

| Football.QCIF | Time comparison (ms, $\triangle(\%)$) | | | | | |
|---|---|---|---|---|---|---|
| QP | Orig. | SMRFME | Rgeion based | AZB | Monotonic | Proposed |
| 20 | 146613 | -44.17 | -15.25 | -0.27 | -24.73 | -60.89 |
| 24 | 142596 | -44.30 | -14.87 | -1.60 | -25.31 | -61.04 |
| 28 | 136813 | -43.34 | -15.94 | -4.96 | -25.42 | -60.74 |
| 32 | 129417 | -40.96 | -18.16 | -11.51 | -25.88 | -60.32 |
| 36 | 118116 | -37.66 | -24.48 | -16.71 | -26.86 | -62.59 |

(b) Stefan.CIF

| Stefan.CIF | Time comparison (ms, $\triangle(\%)$) | | | | | |
|---|---|---|---|---|---|---|
| QP | Orig. | SMRFME | Rgeion based | AZB | Monotonic | Proposed |
| 20 | 443593 | -41.67 | -17.66 | -8.93 | -22.51 | -60.72 |
| 24 | 416228 | -41.67 | -22.16 | -12.09 | -23.30 | -62.92 |
| 28 | 389335 | -42.63 | -25.80 | -13.74 | -24.40 | -64.41 |
| 32 | 363736 | -44.18 | -31.59 | -16.63 | -26.50 | -66.16 |
| 36 | 339981 | -43.76 | -41.35 | -20.99 | -29.31 | -68.86 |

# 6   Conclusion

In this paper we present a fast algorithm for multiple reference frames motion estimation in H.264/AVC to reduce the computation. To skip unnecessary reference frames motion estimation, the proposed algorithm uses information of the previous search reference frames and the correlation among the neighboring blocks. Experimental results show that the proposed algorithm reduces the coding complexity notably while achieves similar gain as the multiple reference frames full search algorithm.

# References


1. Wiegand, T., Sullivan, G.J., Bjontegaard, G., Luthra, A.: Overview of the H.264/AVC video coding standard. IEEE Trans. Circuits Syst. Video Technol. 13(7), 560–576 (2003)
2. Huang, Y.W., Hsieh, B.Y., Chien, S.Y., Ma, S.Y., Chen, L.G.: Analysis and Complexity Reduction of Multiple Reference Frames Motion Estimation in H.264/AVC. IEEE Trans. Circuits Syst. Video Technol. 16(7), 507–522 (2006)
3. Su, Y., Sun, M.T.: Fast multiple reference frame motion estimation for H.264/AVC. IEEE Trans. Circuits Syst. Video Technol. 16, 447–452 (2006)
4. Chen, M.J., Chiang, Y.Y., Li, H.J., Chi, M.C.: Efficient multi-frame motion estimation algorithm for MPEG-4 AVC/JVT/H.264. In: Proc. IEEE ISCAS, pp. III-737-III-740 (May 2004)
5. Lee, Y.M., Lin, Y.: An improved zero-block mode decision algorithm for H.264/AVC. In: Proc. IEEE ICIP, vol. 5, pp. V-293–V-296 (September 2007)

# A Framework for Suspicious Action Detection with Mixture Distributions of Action Primitives

Yoshio Iwai

Graduate School of Engineering Science, Osaka University
1-3 Machikaneyama, Toyonaka, Osaka 560-8531, Japan
`iwai@sys.es.osaka-u.ac.jp`

**Abstract.** In this paper, we propose a generic framework for detecting suspicious actions with mixture distributions of action primitives, of which collection represents human actions. The framework is based on Bayesian approach and the calculation is performed by Sequential Monte Carlo method, also known as Particle filter. Sequential Monte Carlo is used to approximate the distributions for fast calculation, but it tends to converge one local minimum. We solve that problem by using mixture distributions of action primitives. By this approach, the system can recognize people's actions as whether suspicious actions or not.

## 1 Introduction

In recent years, the social environment has become more complex and people's personal lives have become more varied, so the development of security systems that detect hazards and allow us to avoid these has become necessary for us to be safe and secure. However, it is too heavy work for administrators to monitor the environment in 24 hours because they are tied on monitor TVs, and such heavy work causes a mistake. Therefore, a system would need facilities to detect unusual situations automatically and inform system administrators of unusual situations by sensing and recognizing our environment. Such a system would reduce surveillance load, because administrators only pay attention when the system warns.

To detect suspicious actions, the system needs to detect and track people surreptitiously. Cameras have usually been utilized as environmental sensors because they do not make us feel uncomfortable. People are detected and tracked through input images by image processing, and our purpose is to do this and to recognize their actions by using trajectories of movement.

Numerous methods using various features for specific purposes have been proposed to recognize human actions. In general, a system to recognize human actions is consists of two parts: tracking module and recognition module. In tracking people, a human detector is made by Boosting method from the action database[1] or Bayesian approach[2]. Many methods for tracking people have been proposed, but any method is applicable because tracking module and recognition module can be designed separately, so we focused on recognition of human actions and detection of suspicious actions in this paper.

T. Wada, F. Huang, and S. Lin (Eds.): PSIVT 2009, LNCS 5414, pp. 519–530, 2009.
© Springer-Verlag Berlin Heidelberg 2009

To recognize human actions, many probabilistic approaches have been proposed. Models of action are mainly classified into two models: the first is used to construct continuous human actions and the other is used to define human actions as discrete state transition. Hidden Markov Model (HMM) have frequently been used to model human actions as discrete state transition[3]. To recognize continuous actions, stochastic methods have frequently been used recently, such as the CONDENSATION algorithm[4] and particle filters[5]. These methods require non-linear and non-Gaussian models to distinguish them from methods using a linear model like the Kalman filter. We call these methods Monte Calro method because these methods use Monte Carlo approximation to calculate marginal probability used for Bayesian estimation. Monte Carlo method can recursively calculate the marginal probability at each time step in real time and can calculate the expectation value of the probability distribution by using sample points.

One approach using Monte Carlo method has been proposed[6]. However, there is a problem that they assume that the distribution of human action state would be uniform. In this paper, we reformulate human actions by the posterior probability different from the method proposed by [6], and approximate it by the Monte Calro method. By this reformulation, we can treat human actions within the Monte Calro approximation theory, and also solve the local minimum problem of sequential Monte Calro method described in 3.2.

In this paper, we describe an overview of the proposed system for detecting suspicious actions in the next section, and then we explain the action model and detection method in Sec. 3. In Sec. 4, we describe the implementation of the system, the probability and the likelihood, and we show experimental results in Sec. 5, and summaries in Sec. 6.

## 2   Action Model

### 2.1   Representation of Action Models

Human action can be considered as the trajectories of movement in the observation space as shown in Fig. 1. In this work, human actions can be classified into sub trajectories, called action primitive, in the feature space extracted from the observation sensor. Human actions can be modeled by discrete states considered as action primitives $m$ and its transition as shown in Fig. 2. Action primitive $m$ has a trajectory $z = m(f)$ in the feature space, where $z$ is an observation feature and $f$ is a "frame" parameter of trajectory.

A state of action at time $t$ is denoted by $\boldsymbol{x}_t$. We assume that the transition of action state $\boldsymbol{x}$ is a Markov chain that the transition only depends on the previous state. In short, the following equation is satisfied:

$$p(\boldsymbol{x}_t|\boldsymbol{x}_{t-k:t-1}) = p(\boldsymbol{x}_t|\boldsymbol{x}_{t-1}), \tag{1}$$

where $\boldsymbol{x}_{t-k:t}$ is a state sequence from time 0 to time $t$. In the implementation, $\boldsymbol{x}_t$ consists of

1. action primitive at time $t$: $m_t$,
2. frame position of action primitive: $f_t$,
3. velocity of action: $v_t$.

We denote that $\boldsymbol{x}_t = (m_t, f_t, v_t)$. At this time, we can rewrite:

$$p(\boldsymbol{x}_t|\boldsymbol{x}_{t-1}) = p(m_t, f_t, v_t|\boldsymbol{x}_{t-1}) = p(v_t, f_t|m_t, \boldsymbol{x}_{t-1})p(m_t|\boldsymbol{x}_{t-1}). \tag{2}$$

Especially, we assume that $f_t$ and $v_t$ is independent, and $v_t$ is only dependent on $v_{t-1}$, we get

$$p(\boldsymbol{x}_t|\boldsymbol{x}_{t-1}) = p(v_t|v_{t-1})p(f_t|m_t, \boldsymbol{x}_{t-1})p(m_t|\boldsymbol{x}_{t-1}). \tag{3}$$

From the above equation, we can obtain probability distributions of each parameters. This equation is used for Monte Carlo approximation to get sample points. The detail method is described in Section 4.3.

## 2.2 Detecting Action Primitives and Learning Action Models

Before performing the recognition process, action models must be learned from the action database. First, input trajectories of human actions in the feature space are automatically divided into segments separated at stationary points, and the separated segments are candidates as action primitives, but short segments are removed from the candidate set. Next, if a segment in the candidate set have a similar part of a segment in the action database, a similar part is automatically removed from the candidate segment, and the rest of the segment is automatically added to the candidate set. The above process is done until no similar part exists in the action database. After the process ends, if the candidate set is not empty, all segments in the candidate set is added to the action database. At this time, the transition probability of action primitives $p(m_i|m_j)$ is also updated by counting the number of transition in the action database.

Comparison a segment in the candidate set with an action primitive $m_i$ in the action database is automatically performed as follows:

1. Find the nearest points $p_s, p_e$ in a segment to the first and the last frame points in an action primitives $m_i$.
2. Accumulate the distances between the points on a part of the segment $[p_s, p_e]$ and the corresponding frame points in an action primitive $m_i$.
3. If the accumulated distance is less than a certain threshold value, we determine that a part of the segment $[p_s, p_e]$ is similar to an action primitive $m_i$.

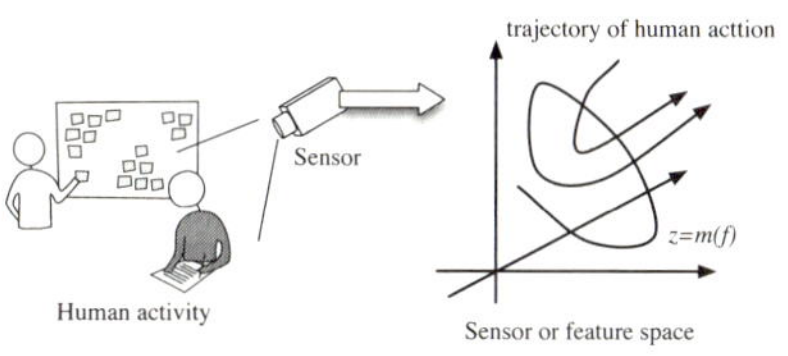


**Fig. 1.** Trajectories represent human activities

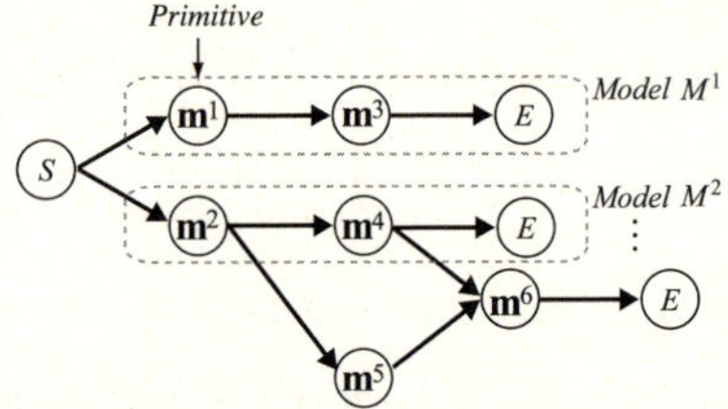


**Fig. 2.** Action model and action primitive

# 3　Framework for Action Recognition and Suspicious Action Detection

## 3.1　Action Recognition

The action recognition is performed by MAP estimation using the posterior probability, $p(M_t|\boldsymbol{z}_{t-k:t})$, of action model $M_t$ at time $t$ given the observation sequence $\boldsymbol{z}_{t-k:t}$, where $k$ is a number of observation frames. The action recognition is formulated by the following equation:

$$M_s = \arg\max_{M_t} p(M_t|\boldsymbol{z}_{t-k:t}). \tag{4}$$

To calculate the posterior probability $p(M_t|\boldsymbol{z}_{t-k:t})$, we use a state of action $\boldsymbol{x}$ as follows:

$$p(M_t|\boldsymbol{z}_{t-k:t}) = \int p(M_t|\boldsymbol{x}_{t-k:t})p(\boldsymbol{x}_{t-k:t}|\boldsymbol{z}_{t-k:t})d\boldsymbol{x}_{t-k:t}, \tag{5}$$

where $\boldsymbol{x}_{t-k:t}$ is a state sequence from time 0 to time $t$. Assuming that state $\boldsymbol{x}_t$ is conditionally independent from the observation sequence and is not affected by future observation, we get

$$p(M_t|\boldsymbol{z}_{t-k:t}) = \int p(M_t|\boldsymbol{x}_{t-k:t}) \prod_{s=t-k}^{t} p(\boldsymbol{x}_s|\boldsymbol{z}_{t-k:s})d\boldsymbol{x}_{t-k:t}. \tag{6}$$

Because of the assumption of Markovian process of state transition, the probability of states, $p(\boldsymbol{x}_t|\boldsymbol{z}_{t-k:t})$, is calculated recursively by the following equations:

$$p(\boldsymbol{x}_t|\boldsymbol{z}_{t-k:t-1}) = \int p(\boldsymbol{x}_t|\boldsymbol{x}_{t-1})p(\boldsymbol{x}_{t-1}|\boldsymbol{z}_{t-k:t-1})\,d\boldsymbol{x}_{t-1}, \tag{7}$$

$$p(\boldsymbol{x}_t|\boldsymbol{z}_{t-k:t}) = \frac{1}{p(\boldsymbol{z}_t|\boldsymbol{z}_{t-k:t-1})}p(\boldsymbol{z}_t|\boldsymbol{x}_t)p(\boldsymbol{x}_t|\boldsymbol{z}_{t-k:t-1}). \tag{8}$$

Action recognition is performed by iteratively calculating the posterior probability by using Eqs. 7, 8, and 6 as $p(\boldsymbol{x}_{t-1}|\boldsymbol{z}_{t-k:t-1})$ is known. This calculation can be performed recursively because $p(\boldsymbol{x}_t|\boldsymbol{z}_{t-k:t})$ is obtained from Eq. 8. The integrals in the above equations are approximated by Monte Carlo method by sampling of a state $\boldsymbol{x}^{(i)}$ from the action state space $\boldsymbol{x}$. The likelihood $p(\boldsymbol{z}_t|\boldsymbol{x}_t)$ is

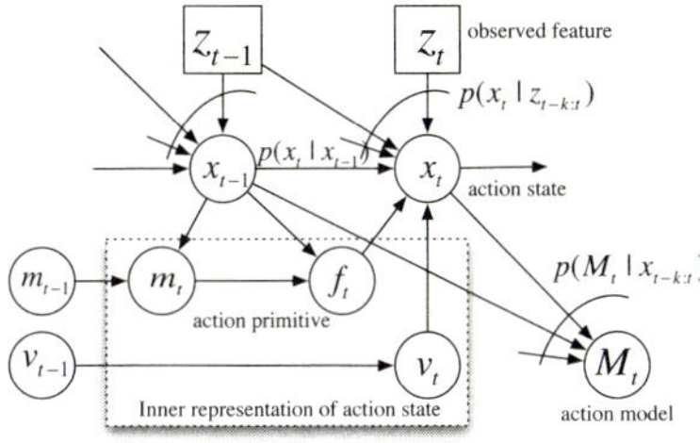



**Fig. 3.** Probability structure of the proposed framework

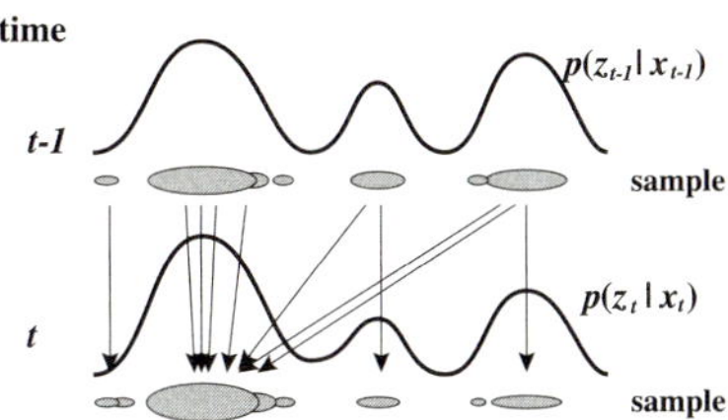



**Fig. 4.** Convergence to the local minimum

designed to be suit for a given problem. We note that the probability $p(z_t|z_{t-k:t-1})$ in Eq. 8 can be treated as a normalize constant when the probability is calculated by Monte Carlo method, therefore, we do not need the concrete shape of the distribution. Figure 3 shows the probability structure of the proposed framework.

## 3.2   Resolving Multi-peak Problem

When the above equations are approximated by Monte Carlo method, The samples of states are updated by the probability, $p(\boldsymbol{x}_t|\boldsymbol{x}_{t-1})$, in Eq. 7. In short, the states are updated by $\boldsymbol{x}_{t-1}$ without observations $\boldsymbol{z}_t$, and during sampling, samples are biased by $p(\boldsymbol{x}_t|\boldsymbol{x}_{t-1})$, and then the accuracy of approximation becomes worse. Therefore, new samples of states are made from the old sample sets by weighted resampling to be ubiquity. The method for determining the weight for resampling has been proposed that uses the likelihood[9]. In that case, sampling points have a tendency to converge one local minimum as shown in Fig. 4.

To avoid a local minimum, one solution is that we increase the number of sampling points to approximate the probability distribution accurately, but the computation time would increase. Dispersing Deterministic Crowdings (DDC) method[10] has been proposed to avoid a local minimum in Genetic Algorithm research field, and a method using DDC is applied for Monte Carlo approximation[6]. However, the method does not suit for Monte Carlo approximation because it changes the distribution of weights during resampling. On the other hand, the method using a mixture distribution for modeling the distribution of states[11] has been proposed as follows:

$$p\left(\boldsymbol{x}_t|\boldsymbol{z}_{t-k:t}\right) \stackrel{\text{def}}{=} \sum_{m=1}^{N_m} \pi_{m,t} p_m\left(\boldsymbol{x}_t|\boldsymbol{z}_{t-k:t}\right), \quad \sum_{m=1}^{N_m} \pi_{m,t} = 1, \tag{9}$$

where $N_m$ is the number of local distribution, $\pi_{m,t}$ is the weight for the local distribution $p_m$ at time $t$.

In this paper, by substituting the above equations for Eq. 7 and 8, we obtain the update equation of $\pi_{m,t}$ and $p_m\left(\boldsymbol{x}_t|\boldsymbol{z}_{t-k:t}\right)$ as follows:

$$p_m\left(\boldsymbol{x}_t|\boldsymbol{z}_{t-k:t-1}\right) = \int p\left(\boldsymbol{x}_t|\boldsymbol{x}_{t-1}\right) p_m\left(\boldsymbol{x}_{t-1}|\boldsymbol{z}_{t-k:t-1}\right) d\boldsymbol{x}_{t-1}, \tag{10}$$

$$p_m\left(\boldsymbol{x}_t|\boldsymbol{z}_{t-k:t}\right) = \frac{p\left(\boldsymbol{z}_t|\boldsymbol{x}_t\right) p_m\left(\boldsymbol{x}_t|\boldsymbol{z}_{t-k:t-1}\right)}{p_m\left(\boldsymbol{z}_t|\boldsymbol{z}_{t-k:t-1}\right)}, \tag{11}$$

$$\pi_{m,t} = \frac{\pi_{m,t-1} p_m\left(\boldsymbol{z}_t|\boldsymbol{z}_{t-k:t-1}\right)}{\sum_{m=1}^{N_m} \pi_{m,t-1} p_m\left(\boldsymbol{z}_t|\boldsymbol{z}_{t-k:t-1}\right)}. \tag{12}$$

By using the above equation, we can use the weights of local distributions as the weights of samples in the framework of Monte Carlo approximation, and we can also approximate the distribution having local minima by the Monte Carlo method. In this paper, the local distribution $p_m$ is the probability distribution of action primitives. This approach naturally introduces the method[11] in the framework of Monte Carlo approximation.

## 3.3    Approximation by Sequential Monte Carlo Method

In this section, we describe the resampling method for approximating Eq. 6. An $i$-th sample of state at time $t$ is denoted by $\boldsymbol{x}_t^{(i)} = (m_t^{(i)}, f_t^{(i)}, v_t^{(i)})$. $\boldsymbol{x}_t^{(i)}$ is generated from probability distribution $p(\boldsymbol{x}_t|\boldsymbol{x}_{t-1})$. $w_t^{(i)}$ is the weight of a sample and $\pi_{m,t}$ is the weight of a local distribution $p_m$.

First, we obtain the sample set $\mathcal{X}_{t-1} = \{\boldsymbol{x}_{t-1}^{(i)}|i = 1...N\}$ and the distribution of weights $W_{t-1} = \{w_{t-1}^{(i)}|i = 1...N\}$ at time $t-1$ in advance. The next sample is generated by the following equation:

$$\boldsymbol{x}_t^{(i)} \sim p(\boldsymbol{x}_t|\boldsymbol{x}_{t-1}^{(i)}), \tag{13}$$

however, to avoid a bias, we must resample them before it. As a resampling, we determine the sample points by the distribution of weights $W_{t-1}$:

$$\boldsymbol{x}_*^{(i)} \sim W_{t-1}, \tag{14}$$

and then, we update the state:

$$\boldsymbol{x}_t^{(i)} \sim p(\boldsymbol{x}_t|\boldsymbol{x}_*^{(i)}). \tag{15}$$

The details of update will be described in Section 4.3. We note that Vermaak's method[11] requires a clustering process to determine which local distribution the state $\boldsymbol{x}_t^{(i)}$ belongs to, but the proposed method implicitly includes such a clustering process because the state has an information which cluster the state belongs to, i.e., action primitive $m_t$.

Next, we determine the weights of samples and local distributions by the following equations:

$$w_*^{(i)} = \frac{\tilde{w}_t^{(i)}}{\tilde{w}_{m_{t-1}^{(i)},*}}, \quad \pi_{m,*} = \frac{\tilde{w}_{m,*}}{\sum_{n=1}^{N_m} \tilde{w}_{n,*}}, \tag{16}$$

where

$$\tilde{w}_t^{(i)} = p(\boldsymbol{z}_t|\boldsymbol{x}_t^{(i)}), \quad \tilde{w}_{m,*} = \sum_{\forall j \ \text{s.t.} \ m_{t-1}^{(j)}=m} \tilde{w}_t^{(j)}. \tag{17}$$

These equations approximates Eqs. 11 and 12, but resampling and reclustering are performed, so we calculate the weights as follows:

$$\pi_{m,t} = \sum_{\forall j \ \text{s.t.} \ m_t^{(j)}=m} \pi_{m_{t-1}^{(j)},*} w_*^{(j)}, \quad w_t^{(i)} = \frac{\pi_{m_{t-1}^{(i)},*} \, w_*^{(i)}}{\pi_{m_t^{(i)},t}}. \tag{18}$$

Finally, Eq. 9 is approximated by the following equation:

$$p(\boldsymbol{x}_t|\boldsymbol{z}_{t-k:t}) = \sum_{j=1}^{N} \pi_{m_t^{(j)},t} w_t^{(j)} \delta(\boldsymbol{x}_t, \boldsymbol{x}_t^{(i)}), \tag{19}$$

where $N$ is the total number of samples, and $\delta$ is the Kronecker delta function. After all, we get the following equation and we can perform action recognition by the following equation:

$$p(M_t|\boldsymbol{z}_{t-k:t}) = \sum_{i=1}^{N} p(M_t|\boldsymbol{x}_{t-k:t}^{(i)}) \prod_{s=t-k}^{t} p(x_s^{(i)}|\boldsymbol{z}_{t-k:s}), \tag{20}$$

where $\boldsymbol{x}_{t-k:t}$ is a transition path of $i$-th particle from time $t-k$ to time $t$. Particle $x_t^{(i)}$ is resampled by the distribution $p(x_t^{(i)}|x_{t-1}^{(i)})$, and weight $w_t^{(i)}$ is calculated as follows:

$$\tilde{w}_t^{(i)} = w_{t-1}^{(i)} p(\boldsymbol{z}_t|x_t^{(i)}), w_t^{(i)} = \frac{\tilde{w}_t^{(i)}}{\sum_{j \in \mathcal{I}_m} \tilde{w}_t^{(j)}}, \tag{21}$$

where $\mathcal{I}_m$ is the particle set whose member has the same action primitive as $m_t^{(i)}$ of particle $x_t^{(i)}$.

### 3.4   Initialization of Sample Set

The initial sample set $\mathcal{X}_{t=0}$ must be given in advance because sample $\boldsymbol{x}_t^{(i)}$ is generated from probability distributions $p(\boldsymbol{x}_t|\boldsymbol{x}_{t-1}^{(i)})$. Initial sample $\boldsymbol{x}_{t=0}^{(i)} =$

$(m_{t=0}^{(i)}, f_{t=0}^{(i)}, v_{t=0}^{(i)})$ is determined randomly like that; action primitive $m_{t=0}^{(i)}$ is randomly determined at first, and then frame position $f_{t=0}^{(i)}$ is randomly selected from the several first frames of learning data of $m_{t=0}^{(i)}$. Movement velocity $v_{t=0}^{(i)}$ is randomly chosen between the range $[v_{\min}, v_{\max}]$.

### 3.5    Suspicious Action Detection

We consider an action not in the action database as a suspicious action. However, all sample points are generated from the action database and no sample points are generated from a suspicious actions. Therefore, we need some criteria to detect suspicious actions. In this research we use the probability $p(z_t|x_t)$ that means the accuracy of the prediction of actions in the action database, and we determined an action as a suspicious action when all likelihood $p(z_t|x_t^{(i)})$ of all samples $x_t^{(i)}$ becomes less than a certain threshold value $\varepsilon_L$ as follows:

$$\forall i \ \ p(z_t|x_t^{(i)}) < \varepsilon_L, \tag{22}$$

which means all samples fail to predict the next position of the action.

In addition, when a suspicious action is detected, all samples are discarded and then all samples are initialized by the method describe in the above section for further detection process.

## 4    Design of Probability and Likelihood

### 4.1    State of Actions

State of action $x_t$ expresses a point in the action space spanned by the state trajectories. We use center points $(X_{x_t}, Y_{x_t})$ of human regions in input images as feature vectors in this paper. Therefore, human actions are modeled by trajectories $\{(X_{x_t}, Y_{x_t})\}_{t=0}$ of center points and action primitives are modeled by segments of the trajectories. State of action $x_t^{(i)}$ indicates a center point $(X_{x_t}, Y_{x_t})$ determined by its action primitive $m_t^{(i)}$ and its frame position $f_t^{(i)}$. We denotes the center point $(X_{x_t}, Y_{x_t})$ indicated by $x_t^{(i)}$ as follows:

$$\left( X_{x_t^{(i)}}, Y_{x_t^{(i)}} \right) = (X_\tau^m, Y_\tau^m). \tag{23}$$

### 4.2    Likelihood

Likelihood of a sample $p(z_t|x_t^{(i)})$ is calculated from the Mahalanobis distance between a center position indicated by a sample and observation $z_t = (X_t^z, Y_t^z)$ as follows:

$$p(z_t|x_t^{(i)}) \propto \exp \left( -\frac{1}{2} \frac{\sum_{l=-L/2}^{L/2} D_{t+l,\tau+\kappa l}}{L+1} \right), \tag{24}$$

where

$$D_{t,\tau} = \sqrt{S_{t,\tau}^T \Sigma^{-1} S_{t,\tau}}, \quad S_{t,\tau} = \begin{bmatrix} X_t^z - X_\tau^m \\ Y_t^z - Y_\tau^m \end{bmatrix}, \quad \Sigma = \begin{bmatrix} \sigma_X^2 & 0 \\ 0 & \sigma_Y^2 \end{bmatrix}, \qquad (25)$$

and $\sigma_X^2 \sigma_Y^2$ are scaling parameters.

The proposed framework uses the Monte Carlo approximation. The accuracy of approximation increases in proportion to the number of particles and reaches the upper limit when the number of particles is infinity. In a real system it is impossible to prepare infinite particles, therefore prior knowledge of the target is incorporated into the likelihood for better calculation using finite particles.

### 4.3   State Transition

State transition formula, Eq. 15 is calculated by using Eq. 3. First, an action primitive is selected according to $p(m_t|\boldsymbol{x}_{t-1})$. This can be done by using the transition probability of action primitives expressed by the following equation:

$$p(m_t|\boldsymbol{x}_{t-1}) = r(x_{t-1})p(m_t|m_{t-1}) + (1 - r(x_{t-1}))\delta(m_t, m_{t-1}), \qquad (26)$$

where $\delta(m_t, m_{t-1})$ is the Kronecker delta function that becomes 1 when $m_t = m_{t-1}$, otherwise 0, and $r(\boldsymbol{x}_t)$ is a transition probability that the transition of action primitives occurs or not. In this paper, $r(\boldsymbol{x}_t)$ is defined as follows:

$$r(\boldsymbol{x}_t) = \begin{cases} 1 - \varepsilon & f_{m_t} < f_t + v_t, \\ 0 & \text{no transition exists in the action database,} \\ \varepsilon & \text{otherwise,} \end{cases} \qquad (27)$$

where $f_{m_t}$ is the end frame of action model $m_t$.

Next, frame position $f_t$ is updated. If $m_t = m_{t-1}$, the frame position $f_t$ is updated as follows:

$$f_t = f_{t-1} + v_{t-1} + \mathcal{N}(0, \Sigma_f), \qquad (28)$$

where $v_{t-1}$ is velocity of state $\boldsymbol{x}_{t-1}$, and $\mathcal{N}(0, \Sigma_f)$ is an system noise assumed to be a Gaussian noise. Otherwise, it means that action primitive is changed, therefore $f_t$ is chosen from several first frames of action primitive $m_t$. Finally, velocity $v_t$ is updated by the following equation:

$$v_t = v_{t-1} + \mathcal{N}(0, \Sigma_v), \qquad (29)$$

where $\mathcal{N}(0, \Sigma_v)$ is also a system noise assumed to be a Gaussian noise.

### 4.4   Transition Probability of Action Primitives

The transition probability of action primitives varies a frame position $f_t$ of action state $\boldsymbol{x}_t$ because transition probability would increase when a frame position $f_t$ draw near the last frame of a action primitive. Therefore, the transition probability of action primitive must be calculated from the current action state $\boldsymbol{x}_t$.

In this research, we calculate the transition probability $,r(\boldsymbol{x}_t) = r(m_t, v_t, f_t)$, for simplicity by the following equation:

$$r(m_t, v_t, f_t) = \begin{cases} \varepsilon_r & f_m - f_t + v_t > \varepsilon_f \\ 1 - \varepsilon_r & \text{otherwise} \end{cases} , \tag{30}$$

where $f_m$ is number of frames of action primitive $m_t$ indicated by action state $\boldsymbol{x}_t$. $f_t$ and $v_t$ are a frame position and velocity of action primitive $m_t$ indicated by action state $\boldsymbol{x}_t$, respectively. $\varepsilon_r$ and $\varepsilon_f$ are small positive constants. The above equation expresses that the transition might not occur until one action primitive would finish.

## 5   Experiments

50 indoor scenes captured with an omnidirectional image sensor[7] were used to test the proposed method. The size of images was $512 \times 440$ pixels and the depth of images was 8 bits gray. The room was $7 \times 7$ m. The camera was fixed at the center of the room at height of 140 cm. Trajectories of human movement extracted with a tracking module were shown in Fig. 5. We use 5 routes of trajectories and 10 trajectories of each route, and total 50 trajectories were used in the experiments. Each route is shown in Table 1.

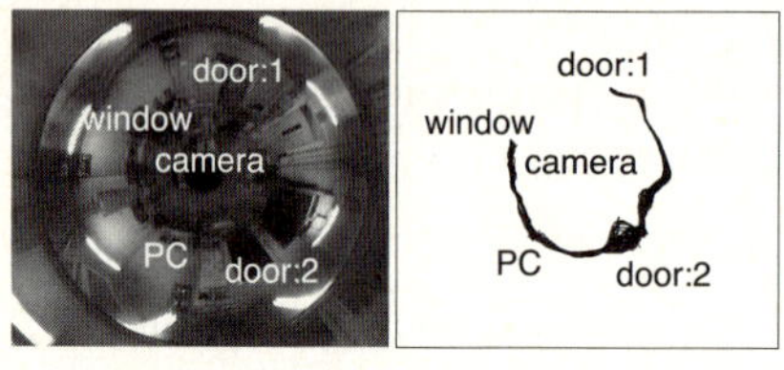


**Fig. 5.** Input image and trajectories

**Table 1.** Routes

| Route | Trajectory |
|---|---|
| 1 | door:1 $\rightarrow$ door:2 |
| 2 | door:2 $\rightarrow$ door:1 |
| 3 | door:1 $\rightarrow$ PC $\rightarrow$ door:1 |
| 4 | door:2 $\rightarrow$ window $\rightarrow$ door:2 |
| 5 | door:2 $\rightarrow$ PC $\rightarrow$ door:2 |

### 5.1   Suspicious Action Detection

Detection rate is affected by parameters such as a threshold value and number of sampling points. Therefore, we examine the detection rate by fixing one parameter and changing another parameter. Experiment is performed by the jackknife test.

Figure 6 (a) shows the detection rate that the threshold value is fixed at $1.0 \times 10^{-4}$ and Fig. 6 (b) shows the detection rate that the number of sample points is fixed at 1000. From Fig. 6 (a), the accuracy of approximation becomes better when the number of samples is increased, therefore, false rejection rate (FRR) becomes smaller, but it takes much time that all samples are below the threshold and false accept rate (FAR) becomes worse. In the range of number of samples, $600 \sim 1000$, the both error are equal. The system performs detection process in 60 fps when the system uses 1000 samples. From Fig. 6 (b), when the

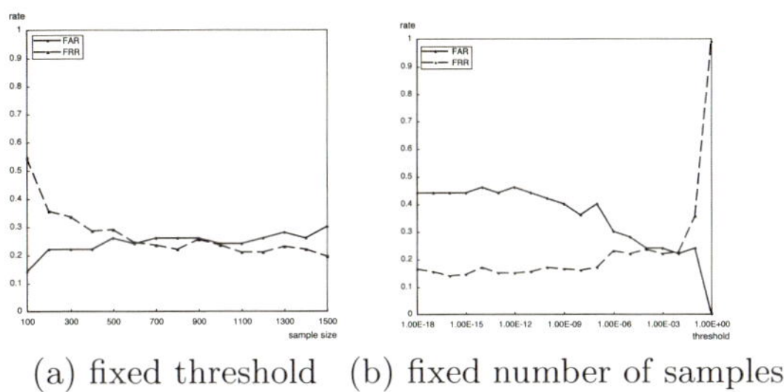

(a) fixed threshold    (b) fixed number of samples

**Fig. 6.** Detection rate of suspicious action

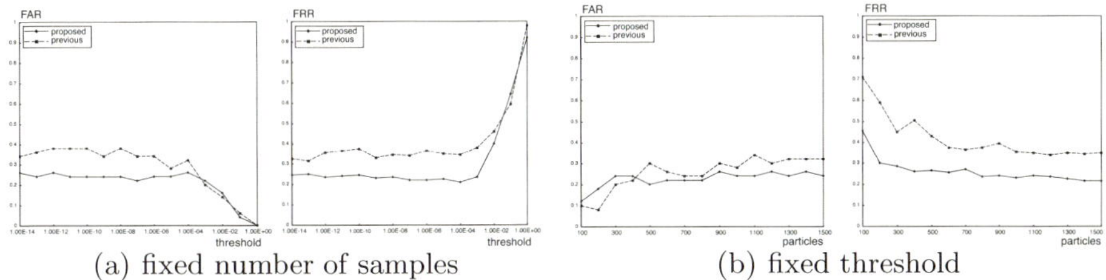

(a) fixed number of samples                    (b) fixed threshold

**Fig. 7.** Comparative experiment: detection rate

threshold value becomes larger, normal actions are misclassified to suspicious actions, so FRR becomes worse, vice versa, when the threshold value becomes smaller, suspicious actions are accepted as normal actions, and FAR becomes worse. As a result, we must carefully choose the threshold value and the number of samples. In this experiment, if these parameters are selected carefully, equal error rate (ERR) is about 20%. In future work, we will improve the detection rate.

We also conducted a comparative experiments with the proposed method and the previous method[6]. Figure 7(a) shows the detection rate that the number of sample points is fixed at 1000, and Fig. 7(b) show the detection rate that the threshold value is fixed at $1.0 \times 10^{-4}$. The left column in the both figure shows FAR and the other side shows FRR. The proposed and previous method have the same tendency, but the FAR and FRR in the proposed method are better than those of the previous method.

## 6   Conclusions and Future Work

We have proposed a generic framework for detecting suspicious actions with mixture distributions of action primitives, of which collection represents human actions. We used an Bayesian approach to recognize human actions and approximate the probability by the Monte Carlo method. We also applied Sequential Monte Calro method for fast calculation. Sequential Monte Calro has the disadvantage that it converges one local minimum. We have solved that problem by using mixture distributions of action primitives. The EER of the proposed method is 20 % and 80 % of suspicious actions are successfully detected in the experiment. In addition, it is clarified that the number of samples for Monte Carlo approximation and the threshold value for detection of suspicious actions must carefully be selected. In future work, we will investigate the effects of these parameters and improve the recognition rate.

# References


1. Viola, P., Jones, M.: Rapid object detection using a boosted cascade of simple features. In: IEEE Computer Society Conference on Computer Vision and Pattern Recognition (CVPR 2001), vol. 1, pp. 511–518 (2001)
2. Pérez, P., Hue, C., Vermaak, J., Gangnet, M.: Color-based probabilistic tracking. In: Heyden, A., Sparr, G., Nielsen, M., Johansen, P. (eds.) ECCV 2002. LNCS, vol. 2350, pp. 661–675. Springer, Heidelberg (2002)
3. Oliver, N.M., Rosario, B., Pentland, A.P.: A Bayesian computer vision system for modeling human interactions. IEEE Trans. on PAMI 22(8), 831–843 (2000)
4. Isard, M., Blake, A.: Condensation - conditional density propagation for visual tracking. IJCV 29, 5–28 (1998)
5. Sidenbladh, H., Black, M.J., Sigal, L.: Implicit probabilistic models of human motion for synthesis and tracking. In: Heyden, A., Sparr, G., Nielsen, M., Johansen, P. (eds.) ECCV 2002. LNCS, vol. 2350, pp. 784–800. Springer, Heidelberg (2002)
6. Matsumura, A., Iwai, Y., Yachida, M.: Stochastic action recognition from omnidirectional images. In: Proc. of Asian Conf. on Computer Vision, vol. 1, pp. 120–125 (2004)
7. Yamazawa, K., Yagi, Y., Yachida, M.: Omnidirectional imaging with hyperboloidal projection. In: Proc. of the Int. Conf. on Intelligent Robots and Systems(IROS 1993), vol. 2, pp. 1029–1034 (1993)
8. Mituyoshi, T., Yagi, Y., Yachida, M.: Real-time human feature acquisition and human tracking by omnidirectional image sensor. In: Proc. IEEE Conf. on Multisensor Fusion and Integration for Intelligent Systems, pp. 258–263 (2003)
9. Black, M.J., Jepson, A.D.: A probabilistic framework for matching temporal trajectories: CONDENSATION-based recognition of gestures and expressions. In: Burkhardt, H.-J., Neumann, B. (eds.) ECCV 1998. LNCS, vol. 1406, pp. 909–924. Springer, Heidelberg (1998)
10. Himeno, M., Himeno, R.: The effect of crossover and mutation to DC in early generations for multimodal function optimization. IEICE (D-I) J85-D-I(11), 1015–1027 (2002)
11. Vermaak, J., Doucet, A., Pérez, P.: Maintaining multi-modality through mixture tracking. In: Proc. 9th ICCV, vol. 2, pp. 1110–1116 (2003)

# Framework for Illumination Invariant Vehicular Traffic Density Estimation


Pranam Janney and Glenn Geers

Dept of Computer Science and Engineering,
University of New South Wales, Australia
and
National ICT Australia (NICTA)[*]
Sydney, Australia
{pranam.janney,glenn.geers}@nicta.com.au



**Abstract.** CCTV cameras are becoming a common fixture at the roadside. Their use varies from traffic monitoring to security surveillance. In this paper a novel technique, using Invariant Features of Local Textures (IFLT) & Support Vector Machine (SVM), for estimating vehicular traffic density on a road segment is presented. The proposed approach is computationally efficient and robust to varying illumination. Experimental results have shown that the proposed framework can achieve high performance than extant state-of-the-art techniques in varying illumination conditions.

**Keywords:** Intelligent Transport Systems (ITS), Invariant Features of Local Textures (IFLT), Support Vector Machines (SVM), density estimation, traffic information, parameters, illumination invariance.


## 1   Introduction

Intelligent Transportation Systems (ITS) are used in many cities to provide information about traffic conditions on the road network and as an aid to streamlining vehicular traffic flow in an effort to reduce traffic congestion. An ITS typically uses various kinds of sensors, such as video cameras and inductive loop detectors to measure the significant properties of vehicular traffic flow. Traffic density is a useful property that an ITS can use to perform *higher level* functions such as traffic light sequencing.

Video monitoring systems promise many advantages over the now-dominant inductive loop detectors which are point detectors that sense the vehicles passing over them [1]. Cameras are cost effective and easier to maintain than other road-mounted sensors. They also offer the potential of providing a much richer data stream than the simple loop.

Vehicle tracking is a popular technique for traffic density estimation [5,13,4]. Vehicle tracking algorithms are generally flexible enough to determine almost any type of traffic


---

[*] NICTA is funded by the Australian Federal Government as represented by the Department of Broadband, Communications and the Digital Economy, the NSW Department of State and Regional Development, the ACT Government and the Australian Research Council through the ICT Centre of Excellence Program.



T. Wada, F. Huang, and S. Lin (Eds.): PSIVT 2009, LNCS 5414, pp. 531–541, 2009.

information. But in terms of just determining the traffic density, the performance of vehicle tracking algorithms tends to degrade in heavy traffic situations due to occlusion, cluttering and false background estimation.

Porikli and Li published two closely related papers [6,10] that used the learning from low-level features technique. Their main idea is to extract low-level features from traffic video and learn the traffic density state *a priori*. In [12] it has been rightly pointed out that the drawback of this technique is that the motion information used in their implementation is produced by the video encoder, and this does not represent true motion but the best match with respect to some dissimilarity measure (e.g. Sum of Absolute Differences). Also, Gaussian Mixture Hidden Markov Models (GMHMM) are used in their implementation but the number of Gaussians used per state is unknown while the structure of the Hidden Markov Model (HMM) is determined empirically in [10] and *a priori* in [6].

In [12], a technique similar to that described above is proposed. Low-level features are directly extracted from the traffic video. The number of Gaussians and HMM structure is determined from information provided by an unsupervised learning scheme called AutoClass [2]. The features used are a combination of different types of texture statistics and Edge Histogram Descriptors (EHID) proposed for MPEG-7 [14]. Even though the framework uses very simple low-level features, classification using an HMM and Autoclass is computationally inefficient. Also, using edge features could prove problematic in varying illumination conditions as varying illumination changes the appearances of edges thereby leading to confusing feature sets. There is a need to develop systems that can analyze surveillance footage especially in the field of vehicular traffic analysis in varying illumination conditions.

In this paper, we propose a novel varying illumination resilient technique for estimating traffic density which uses Invariant Features of Local Textures' descriptors [3] and Support Vector Machines (SVM) [11]. For the purpose of this paper *traffic density* is defined as the percentage of the Region-of-Interest (ROI—usually a lane segment) occupied by vehicles. The system framework and detailed description is presented in Section 2 and preliminary experimental results and analysis are provided in Section 3.

## 2    Traffic Lane Density Estimation

We consider an ROI within which we need to estimate the traffic density. Invariant Features of Local Textures (IFLT) [3] are used to generate local texture descriptors to represent the ROI.

For every input frame, IFLT descriptors of the ROI are generated and assembled into a feature vector. The feature vectors are input to an SVM in order to,classify the traffic density of the particular traffic lane into one of four states:

1. *Empty:* less than 5% of the lane is occupied by vehicles.
2. *Low:* 5–30% of the lane is occupied by vehicles.
3. *High:* 30–90% of the lane is occupied by vehicles.
4. *Full:* more than 90% of thc lane is occupied by vehicles.

Manually labelled video sequences were used for training the SVM.

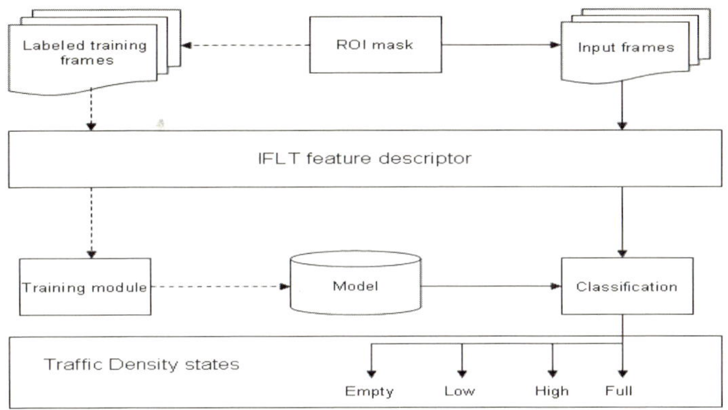


**Fig. 1.** Framework for Traffic lane density estimation using IFLT descriptors

The architecture of the traffic lane density estimation system described in this paper is shown schematically in Figure 1.

Sample frames from video sequence captured by traffic cameras on Anzac Parade/ Barker Street junction with ROI lane which denotes the four different density states are shown in Figure 2.

**Fig. 2.** *Empty*, *Low*, *High* and *Full* states of a lane of traffic at the Anzac Parade/Barker street junction. (the circular reflection is that of the camera lens onto the window of the camera housing).

Traffic density is being estimated for a ROI covering one traffic lane. We use IFLT to generate feature descriptors. IFLT is a texture descriptor that is scale, rotation and (essentially) illumination invariant [3]. The density of local textures will provide an approximate of the coverage of traffic lane. Experimental results have demonstrated that the IFLT descriptors exceeds performance of previously published state of the art local texture algorithms at a significantly lower computational cost [3]. Traffic surveillance cameras are subjected to varying illumination due to changes in sunlight. IFLT descriptors are very robust towards illumination variation and are, therefore, eminently suited for traffic density estimation.

A detailed explanation of IFLT descriptors [3], dimension selection process and a brief explanation regarding the usage of Support Vector Machine is provided in the sections below.

## 2.1   Invariant Features of Local Textures (IFLT)

Consider a $3 \times 3$ neighbourhood of pixels. True circular symmetry around $X_c$ can be achieved by recalculating pixel intensities at the co-ordinates given by,

$$X_i = \left( R\cos\frac{2\pi i}{p}, \; R\sin\frac{2\pi i}{p} \right) \tag{1}$$

where $X_i$ is the equivalent position of the $i^{th}$ of $p - 1$ pixels in circular symmetry around $X_c$ with radius $R$. In the work that follows $R$ is set to unity.

The gray values of neighbors which do not fall exactly on integral pixels are estimated by interpolation. With $I_c$ as the intensity of the centre pixel, the gradient of intensity in all directions with reference to the centre pixel are computed.

The gradient intensities around a centre pixel can be re-written as a one-dimensional vector, $\mathbf{I}$, as shown in Equation 2,

$$\mathbf{I} = [\mathbf{I_c} - \mathbf{I_0}, ..., \mathbf{I_c} - \mathbf{I_7}] \tag{2}$$

where $I_c$ is the intensity of the centre pixel and $I_{(0..7)}$ are the intensities of the neighbouring pixels.

This one-dimensional vector is further normalised.

$$\mathbf{I_{norm}} = \frac{\mathbf{I}}{\max(\mathbf{I})} \tag{3}$$

The discrete wavelet transform (DWT) of the signal $I_{norm}$ is calculated by passing it through a series of filters [7]. In this work Haar wavelets were used because of their computational efficiency. The required filter coefficients are given in Equation 4.

$$h = \left[ \frac{1}{\sqrt{2}}, \frac{-1}{\sqrt{2}} \right], \; g = \left[ \frac{1}{\sqrt{2}}, \frac{1}{\sqrt{2}} \right] \tag{4}$$

The signal is decomposed simultaneously using a high-pass filter $h$ and a low-pass filter $g$. The outputs of the high pass filter and low pass filter are known as the *detail* and *approximate* coefficients respectively.

Noting that the wavelet transform operation corresponds to a convolution followed by downsampling by 2 allows the filter outputs to be written more concisely as,

$$y_{\text{low}} = (I_{\text{norm}} * g) \downarrow 2, \; y_{\text{high}} = (I_{\text{norm}} * h) \downarrow 2 \tag{5}$$

where $\downarrow$ is used to denote the Downsampling Operator.

The detail and approximate coefficients have shift invariant energy distributions. As shown above, rotations in image space have been transformed into linear shifts in transform space and so the energy distribution of the detail and approximate coefficients are also rotation invariant. In the experiments described below the mean and standard deviation of the high pass and the low pass filter outputs generated by one step of the wavelet transform of Equation 2 are used as the texture features. These features are inherently intensity and rotation invariant for a small $3 \times 3$ neighborhood of pixels.

A histogram is built from the extracted local texture features in the texture patch. This involves partitioning the 4-dimensions of texture features (mean and the standard deviation of the energy distributions of the high pass and the low pass wavelet bands) into a number of bins and calculating the number of occurrence of local texture feature values in those bins. In our current set-up we use 32-bin histogram.

## 2.2  Dimension Selection

We have used 32-bin histograms, thus our feature vector has minimum 32 dimensions. Figure 3 shows a representative plot of average of features of each state in each dimension for a video sequence (*Anzac Parade/Barker Street Jtn -1*). It is clearly evident that features from some of the dimensions were not distinctive enough to discriminate between the four density states.

Consider, $e_{N,D}$ where $e_{N,D}$ is a matrix of $N$ samples representing *Empty* state with $D$ dimensions. Similarly, we have, $l_{N,D}$, $h_{N,D}$ and $f_{N,D}$ corresponding to *Low*, *High* and *Full* states.

Considering $e_{N,D}$ we have,

$$\bar{e}_j = \frac{1}{N} \sum_{i=1}^{N} e_{i,j} \tag{6}$$

$$\sigma_{e_j} = \sqrt{\frac{1}{N} \sum_{i=1}^{N} (e_{i,j} - \bar{e}_j)^2} \tag{7}$$

where $j = 1, ..., D$; and $\bar{e}_j$ and $\sigma_{e_j}$ are the average and standard deviation models of the 'empty' state respectively. $[\bar{l}_j, \sigma_{l_j}]$ , $[\bar{h}_j, \sigma_{h_j}]$ and $[\bar{f}_j, \sigma_{f_j}]$ corresponding to 'low', 'high' and 'stop' states are calculated similarly.

Next, the contribution of each dimension in one state towards distinguishing that particular state from the other three states is determined as follows:

Consider the 'empty' state model (i.e. $[\bar{e}, \sigma_e]$) and the 'low' state model (i.e. $[\bar{l}, \sigma_l]$),

1. The distance between the two states is given by

$$\text{dist}_{e \to l, j} = |(\bar{e}_j - \bar{l}_j)| + |(\sigma_{e_j} - \sigma_{l_j})| \tag{8}$$

   where, $j = 1, ..., D$ and $\text{dist}_{e \to l}$ is a vector in which the $j^{\text{th}}$ element represents the distance between the corresponding states with respect to the $j^{\text{th}}$ dimension.

2. Calculate a threshold using Equation 9, which can be used to eliminate dimensions that do not particularly help in distinguishing between the two states.

$$T = \frac{1}{D} \sum_{j=1}^{D} \text{dist}_{e \to l, j} \tag{9}$$

3. Select dimensions by comparing the distance generated by each dimension with the threshold, $T$.

$$p_{e \to l, j} = \{j | (\text{dist}_{e \to l, j} \geq T)\} \tag{10}$$

   where, $j = 1, .., D$ and $p_{e \to l}$ is a set of dimensions.

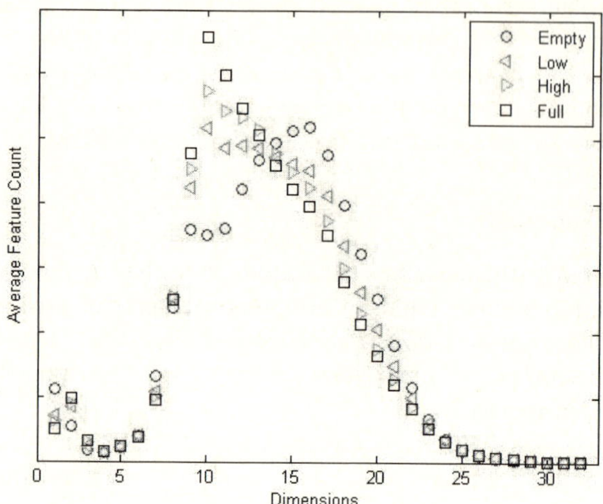


**Fig. 3.** Average of features for each dimension of each state clearly showing the dimensions that help in discriminating between four density states

Repeat steps 1 through to 3, for all combinations of states i.e $e \rightarrow h, e \rightarrow s, l \rightarrow h, l \rightarrow f, h \rightarrow f$.

Hence, the dimensions, $P$, which are best suited to distinguish states from one another are given by,

$$P = \{p_{e \rightarrow l} \cup p_{e \rightarrow h} \cup p_{e \rightarrow s} \cup p_{l \rightarrow h} \cup p_{l \rightarrow s} \cup p_{h \rightarrow s}\} - \{0\} \qquad (11)$$

In our tests, features from 19 dimensions out of the available 32 could clearly discriminate between all the different states and these 19 dimensions are used as our feature descriptors.

## 2.3   Support Vector Machine

SVM has extraordinary generalisation capacity and is also one of the popular large margin classifiers [11]. An SVM constructs a binary classifier from a set of labeled patterns called *training samples*. Let $(x_i, y_i) \in \mathbb{R}^N \times \{\pm 1\}, i = 1, ..., l$ be such a set of *training samples*. The purpose is to select the function $f_\alpha : \mathbb{R}^N \longrightarrow \{\pm 1\}$ from a given class of functions $\{f_\alpha : \alpha \in \Lambda\}$ such that $f$ will correctly classify test examples $(x, y)$. The reader is referred to [11] for details.

We use three different types of kernels in our experiments.

1. Linear kernel: $K(x, y) = (x.y)$
2. Polynomial kernel: $K(x, y) = (x.y)^p$, where $p = 2$
3. Gaussian kernel: $K(x, y) = exp(-\frac{1}{2\sigma^2}|x - y|^2)$, where $\sigma = 0.70$ ($\sigma$ is optimised via cross-validation)

## 3   Experimental Setup

In our experiments we have used video sequences from a busy intersection located just outside the Sydney CBD (Anzac Parade/ Barker Street Junction). All video sequences used for this experiment were captured during daytime and exhibit the expected range of natural lighting variation. Each video sequence is of 6 minutes—9000 frames—duration. Resolution of each frame is $320 \times 240$. In our experiments we have used only one lane as the ROI. Figure 2 shows four sample frames (with ROI shown in red) that are representative of the *Empty*, *Low*, *High* and *Full* traffic density states used in this paper. Table 1 details the illumination effects present in each of the video sequences.

**Table 1.** Illumination effects present in each of the video sequences used for testing. All these video sequences were captured by traffic cameras installed by the Roads and Traffic Authority of New South Wales, Australia.

| Sequence | Effect of Illumination |
|---|---|
| Anzac Parade/Barker Street Jtn. − 1 | Bright/Sunny |
| Anzac Parade/Barker Street Jtn. − 2 | Raining |
| Anzac Parade/Barker Street Jtn. − 3 | Cloudy |
| Anzac Parade/Barker Street Jtn. − 4 | Sun-glare |

### 3.1   Experiment-I

For Experiment-I we implemented the method described in [12] and reproduced the reported results. We tested our algorithm on video sequences containing both cloudy and sunny conditions captured during the daytime. The test as described in [12] comprises of training a model using 70% of samples from a particular sequence and testing the model with the remaining 30% of samples from the same sequence.

**Table 2.** Comparison of performance results of framework in [12] and the proposed framework

| Illumination | Framework [12],(AutoClass/Kmeans) | | Proposed Framework | |
|---|---|---|---|---|
| | Training Accuracy | Testing Accuracy | Training Accuracy | Testing Accuracy |
| Sunny only | 98.9 / 98.8 | 95.4 / 96.9 | 99 | 98.1 |
| Cloudy only | 99.5 / 99.3 | 97.8 / 98.3 | 99.2 | 97.9 |
| Sunny and cloudy | 99.8 / 99.2 | 94.4 / 83.3 | 99.8 | 97 |

Table 2 shows the comparison of performance results for the framework in [12] and the proposed framework (using SVM with gaussian kernel, $\sigma = 0.7$ ). Under conditions of uniform illumination both methods have comparable performance. However, the current technique achieves (as expected) better results under conditions of varying illumination. It is also interesting to note that the performance results of the proposed approach is very consistent for all tests. We also used SVM with linear/polynomial kernels but for this experimental setup, the results were inferior compared to that of SVM with gaussian kernel. Hence, those results have been omitted from this paper.

Computation time required for the framework of [12] is very high. Using the proposed framework, we were able to process 1-2 frames per second using unoptimized Matlab implementations of the methods , running on a PC with Pentium 3.2GHz processor. It seems likely that the proposed framework will be capable of running in real-time when implemented in C or C++.

We feel that experimental set-up in [12] is a very lenient test for illumination invariant traffic density estimation. Primary reason being that the illumination variations included only sunny and cloudy sequences. And the second but very important reason is that for a particular test sequence, 70% of frames are used for training and the remaining 30% is used for testing. So, considering "Sunny" sequence, model is trained using 70% of frames from this sequence and the rest 30% of the frames from the same sequence is used for testing. Trained model is being tested with samples/frames with illumination effect, which the model has already learnt. Many of the parameters required in [12] are *ad hoc*, which again is not feasible for real world applications.

Thus, we feel this experimental setup is not a valid test for illumination invariant traffic density estimation.

### 3.2   Experiment-II

This set of experiments were conducted on all combinations of sequences listed in Table 1. Sequences used to train the model and then to test it have different illumination effects.

The results presented are average of classification accuracies for a sequence, when tested on a model that is trained by a sequence other than itself.

**Table 3.** 4-State classification accuracy for the proposed framework where testing sequence and training sequence have different illumination effect. (%) denoting the percentage of correct classifications.

| Sequence | Linear kernel (%) | Polynomial kernel (%) | Gaussian kernel(%) |
|---|---|---|---|
| Anzac Parade/Barker Street Jtn. − 1 | 81.3 | 80.2 | 80.2 |
| Anzac Parade/Barker Street Jtn. − 2 | 78.7 | 79.1 | 77.1 |
| Anzac Parade/Barker Street Jtn. − 3 | 77.1 | 76.5 | 75.4 |
| Anzac Parade/Barker Street Jtn. − 4 | 79.1 | 78.2 | 76.8 |

As seen from Table 3, the proposed framework shows consistent classification accuracy for all sequences when the testing and training sequences have different illumination effects. Previously, The difference in performance between linear, polynomial and gaussian kernels is negligible.

The results for the proposed framework presented in Table  2 was achieved using SVM with gaussian kernel (sigma =0.7). Comparing performance of the proposed framework from Tables  2 and  3, it is evident that SVM with a gaussian kernel does not outperform SVM with a linear kernel when testing sequence has a different illumination effect than that of the training sequence. This could be an effect of noisy data or may be a consequence of the illumination invariant nature of IFLT. During the course

**Table 4.** Comparison of average classification accuracies between IFLT,Texture statistics,EHID [12] and LBP [9] using different classification algorithms, when testing and training sequences have different illumination effect. $l - SVM, p - SVM, g - SVM$ denotes SVM with Linear, Polynomial and Gaussian kernels respectively. AP/BS = Anzac Parade/Barker Street.

| Sequence | Texture Statistics,EHID [12] | | | LBP [9] | | | IFLT | | |
|---|---|---|---|---|---|---|---|---|---|
| | l-SVM | p-SVM | g-SVM | l-SVM | p-SVM | g-SVM | l-SVM | p-SVM | g-SVM |
| AP/BS Jtn. − 1 | 48.2 | 51.8 | 51.9 | 73.1 | 71.2 | 72.8 | 81.3 | 80.2 | 80.2 |
| AP/BS Jtn. − 2 | 40.1 | 41.1 | 41.1 | 73.5 | 73.2 | 69.1 | 78.7 | 79.1 | 77.1 |
| AP/BS Jtn. − 3 | 48.2 | 48.2 | 47.9 | 72.9 | 71.1 | 70.9 | 77.1 | 76.5 | 75.4 |
| AP/BS Jtn. − 4 | 45.1 | 42.9 | 42.8 | 70.4 | 71 | 70.1 | 79.1 | 78.2 | 76.8 |

of our initial experiments we noticed that it is difficult to reduce the error rate of *High* states being misclassified mostly as *Full* or sometimes as *Low*. Looking at frames of our annotated training sequence, we realised that annotation of frames whose density state is in-between two states is very subjective to the person annotating the sequence. Especially if the density state of frames lie in-between *High* and *Full* then it is hard, even for the person annotating the sequence, to arrive at a decision as to whether the frame has to be annotated as *High* or *Full*. Hence, subjective annotation is a major contributor to noisy data.

Table 4 shows the performance comparison between IFLT feature descriptors , texture statistics features [12] and Linear Binary Patterns (LBP) [9] in the proposed framework. Texture statistics features used in [12] are a combination of first & second order texture statistics and Edge Histogram Descriptors (EHID) proposed for MPEG-7 [14]. Linear Binary Patterns are state-of-the-art local texture descriptors proposed by [9]. A detailed description of LBP can be found in [8]. IFLT features have very high classification accuracy when compared to that of texture statistics proposed in [12] and LBP [9] for illumination invariant traffic density estimation.

Results from Tables 3 and 4, indicate that a SVM with a linear kernel is the best option for classification because it provides good classification accuracy and is computationally less intense. Hence, IFLT descriptors are the best descriptors for use in illumination invariant traffic density estimation.

Considering noisy data due to subjective annotation, we conducted tests where *High* and *Full* were merged as one state i.e.*High* state. We also divided the ROI into $N$ regions, using IFLT descriptors for each region. Using $N$ regions would provide us with more local information thus improving the performance. In our experiments we have used 8-regions.

Table 5 shows that merging two states, i.e. reducing a 4-state classification problem to 3-state classification problem, we can achieve higher performance. This also supports the fact that subjective annotation is a major contributor for noise in 4-state classification problem. It is interesting to note that dividing ROI into 8-regions did not improve performance by a big margin. However, by close observation of prediction outputs we realised that output predictions for 8-regions based approach were complimenting the errors of output predictions from the 1-region based approach. Table 5 presents results for $combination(1, 8)$ based approach where in we can achieve classification accuracies in excess of $90\%$ irrespective of varying illuminations. Thus, we were able to

**Table 5.** Comparison of average classification accuracies between 4-state and 3-state classification with 1-region/8-regions using SVM linear kernel for classification. Testing and training sequence had different illumination effects. AP/BS = Anzac Parade/Barker Street.

| Sequence | 4-States | | | 3-States | | |
|---|---|---|---|---|---|---|
| | 1-region | 8-regions | Combination(1,8) | 1-region | 8-regions | Combination(1,8) |
| AP/BS Jtn. − 1 | 81.3 | 82.2 | 85.1 | 84.7 | 87.4 | 92.4 |
| AP/BS Jtn. − 2 | 78.7 | 79.5 | 83.2 | 83.6 | 86.9 | 91.1 |
| AP/BS Jtn. − 3 | 76.5 | 76.1 | 83 | 82.9 | 83.1 | 89.9 |
| AP/BS Jtn. − 4 | 79.1 | 77.2 | 83.1 | 83.5 | 84.8 | 90.8 |

achieve higher performance by combining global and local information available from the ROI.

# 4  Conclusion

In this paper, we have presented a new framework for vehicular traffic density estimation using IFLT descriptors and SVMs. The framework uses illumination invariant feature descriptors in conjunction with an SVM with a linear kernel, for classification. Both algorithms are computationally efficient. Although we were only able to process 1–2 frames per second in Matlab on a Pentium 3.2GHz class machine, our technique should be capable of working in real-time when coded in C or C++. We were able to achieve in excess of 90% correct classification of vehicle density states in varying illumination conditions.

The authors would like to take this opportunity to point out the need for an annotated traffic video database, which could be used as ground truth for research in this area. Such databases are widely available in other image processing specialities (such as face recognition) but are sadly lacking in others, making performance comparison difficult. In due course, we hope to make our data publicly available.

## Acknowledgments

The assistance of the Roads and Traffic Authority of New South Wales in obtaining the video sequences is gratefully appreciated.

The authors would also like to thank Dr Jing Chen and Mr Sakrapee Paisitkriangkrai for useful discussions during the preparation of this paper.

## References

1. Beymer, D., McLauchlan, P., Coifman, B., Malik, J.: A real-time computer vision system for measuring traffic parameters. In: IEEE Conference on Computer Vision and Pattern Recognition (CVPR), pp. 495–501 (1997)
2. Cheeseman, P., Stutz, J.: Bayesian classification (autoclass): Theory and results. In: Advances in Knowledge Discovery and Data Mining, pp. 153–180 (1996)

3. Janney, P., Yu, Z.: Invariant features of local textures - a rotation invariant local texture descriptor. In: IEEE conference on Computer Vision and Pattern Recognition (CVPR) (BP-Workshop) (June 2007)

4. Kamijo, S., Matsushita, Y., Ikeuchi, K., Sakauchi, M.: Traffic monitoring and accident detection at intersections. In: IEEE Trans. on ITS, vol. 1 (June 2000)

5. Koller, D., Weber, J., Huang, T., Malik, J., Ogasawara, G., Rao, B., Russell, S.: Towards robust automatic traffic scene analysis in real-time. In: Proceedings of the International Conference on Pattern Recognition, Israel (1994)

6. Li, X., Porikli, F.M.: A hidden markov model framework for traffic event detection using video features. In: Proceedings of International Conference on Image Processing (ICIP) (2004)

7. Mallat, S.: A Wavelet Tour of Signal Processing, 2nd edn. (Wavelet Analysis & Its Applications). Academic Press, London (1999)

8. Ojala, T., Pietikainen, M., Maenpaa, T.: Multiresolution gray-scale and rotation invariant texture classification with local binary patterns. IEEE Transactions on Pattern Analysis and Machine Intelligence (PAMI) 24(7), 971–987 (2002)

9. Ojala, T., Pietikinen, M., Mäenpää, T.: Gray scale and rotation invariant texture classification with local binary patterns. In: Vernon, D. (ed.) ECCV 2000. LNCS, vol. 1842, pp. 404–420. Springer, Heidelberg (2000)

10. Porikli, F., Li, X.: Traffic congestion estimation using hmm models without vehicle tracking. In: IEEE Intelligent Vehicles Symposium, pp. 188–193 (June 2004)

11. Shawe-Taylor, J., Cristianini, N.: Support Vector Machines and other kernel-based learning methods. Cambridge University Press, Cambridge (2000)

12. Tan, E., Chen, J.: Vehicular traffic density estimation via statistical methods with automated state learning. In: IEEE Conference on Advanced Video and Signal Based Surveillance (AVSS) (September 2007)

13. Tseng, B., Lin, C.-Y., Smith, J.: Real-time video surveillance for traffic monitoring using virtual line analysis. In: Proceedings of IEEE International Conference on Multimedia and Expo. (ICME), vol. 2, pp. 541–544 (August 2002)

14. Won, C.S., Park, D.K., Park, S.-J.: Efficient use of mpeg-7 edge histogram descriptor. ETRI Journal 24(1) (February 2002)

# Robust Facial Feature Location on Gray Intensity Face

Qiong Wang, Chunxia Zhao, and Jingyu Yang

School of Computer Science and Technology
Nanjing University of Science and Technology, Nanjing, China
`nustdaisy@gmail.com`

**Abstract.** In this paper, we propose an efficient algorithm for facial feature location on gray intensity face. Complex regions in a face image, such as the eye, exhibit unpredictable local intensity and hence high entropy. We use this characteristic to obtain eye candidates, and then these candidates are sent to a classifier to get real eyes. According to the geometry relationship of human face, mouth search region is specified by the coordinates of the left eye and the right eye. And then precise mouth detection is done. Experimental results demonstrate the effectiveness of the proposed method.

**Keywords:** Facial feature location, image entropy, SVM classifier, maximum-minimum filter.

## 1 Introduction

This paper addresses the problem of locating facial features (eyes, nose, mouth corners and so on) in images of frontal faces. Locating such features is an important stage in many facial image interpretation tasks (such as face verification, face tracking or face expression recognition).Generally, there are two types of information available for facial feature detection [1]: (1) local texture around a given feature, for example, the pixel values in a small region around an eye, and (2) the geometric configuration of a given set of facial features, e.g. both eyes, nose, mouth and etc. Many different methods for modeling these types of information have been proposed. In Ref. [1] a method for facial feature detection was proposed which utilizes the Viola and Jones face detection method [2], combined with the statistical shape models of Dryden and Mardia [3]. In Ref. [4] an efficient method was proposed for eye detection that used iris geometries to determine the region candidates which possibly contain the eye, and then the symmetry, for selecting the couple of eyes. In Ref. [5], Gabor feature is used to extract eyes. The EOF (entropy of likelihood) feature points are found to do feature selection and correspondence for face images in Ref. [6].

In this paper, we propose an efficient approach combining image entropy and classifier to precisely extract the eyes and locate the mouth with the coordinate information of eyes. We address the problem of facial feature detection, so our research work is based on face detection. The rest of this paper is organized as follows. In Section 2, the eye candidates extraction method will be introduced. Eyes verification will be presented in Section 3. In Section 4, mouth location algorithm will be introduced. Some experimental results will be demonstrated in Section 5 to corroborate the proposed approach. Section 6 concludes the paper.

T. Wada, F. Huang, and S. Lin (Eds.): PSIVT 2009, LNCS 5414, pp. 542–549, 2009.

## 2  Eye Candidates Extraction

Complex regions in a face image, such as the eyes, exhibit unpredictable local intensity and hence have higher entropy than skin region, as illustrated in Fig. 1. This fact leads us to use entropy as a measure for uncertainty and unpredictability. We use this characteristic to obtain eye candidates.

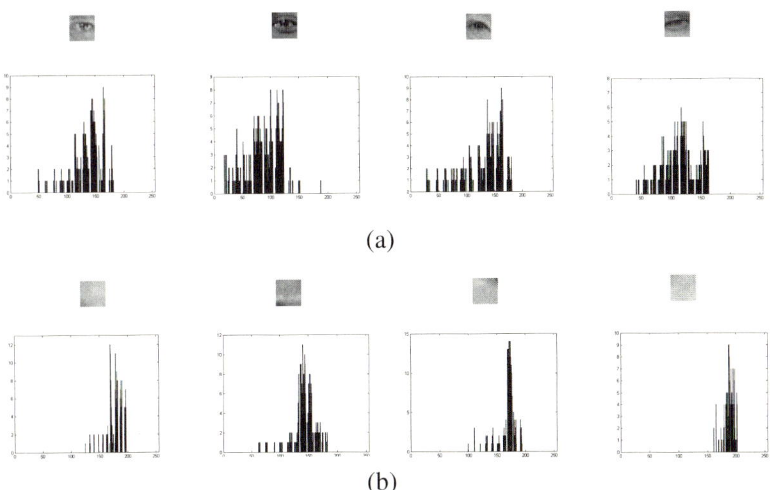

(a)

(b)

**Fig. 1.** Entropy comparison between eye region and skin region. (a) entropy of eye region is higher. (b) entropy of skin region is lower.

### 2.1  Image Entropy

The basic concept of entropy in information theory has to do with how much randomness there is in a signal or random event. An alternative way to look at this is to talk about how much information is carried by the signal.

Claude E. Shannon [7] defines entropy in terms of a discrete random event $x$, with possible states (or outcomes) $1...n$ as:

$$H(x) = \sum_{i=1}^{n} p(i) \log_2 \left( \frac{1}{p(i)} \right) = -\sum_{i=1}^{n} p(i) \log_2 p(i) \tag{1}$$

Conversion from probability $p(i)$ to entropy $h(i)$ is illustrated in Fig. 2, and shows that probabilities close to zero or one produce low entropy and intermediate values produce entropies near 0.5.

Shannon shows that any definition of entropy satisfying his assumptions will be of the form:

$$-K \sum_{i=1}^{n} p(i) \log p(i) \tag{2}$$

where $K$ is a constant (and is really just a choice of measurement units).

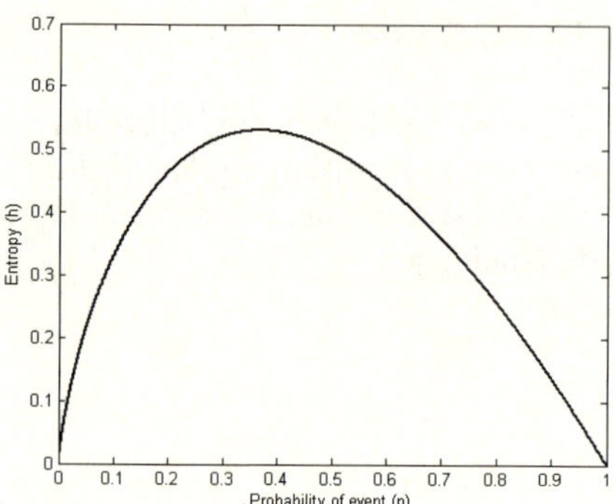

**Fig. 2.** Conversion from probability pi to entropy hi

The texture of the input image can be characterized by using the entropy which is a statistical measure of randomness.

For an image $x$, quantised to $M$ levels, the entropy $H_x$ is defined as:

$$H_x = \sum_{i=0}^{M-1} \left( p_i \log_2 \left( \frac{1}{p_i} \right) \right) = -\left( \sum_{i=0}^{M-1} (p_i \log_2 p_i) \right) \qquad (3)$$

where $p_i$ ( $i = 0 ... M - 1$ ) is the probability of the $i^{th}$ quantiser level being used (often obtained from a histogram of the pixel intensities). For grey image, the value of $M$ is 256.

## 2.2 Eye Candidates Extraction

Our work is focus on facial feature location, so face area is detected by using upright frontal face detector [2]. Then eye candidates are extracted on the detected face area.

A square window moves on the upper part of detected face to extract eye candidates by calculating the entropy value in each window. The size of moving window is calculated according to the face size, Eq. (4) gives the relationship.

$$win_eye = win_face / 4.6 \qquad (4)$$

where $win_eye$ is the slide length of moving square window; $win_face$ is the slide length of detected face region.

The areas where their local entropy is above average are considered as eye candidates and sent to the eye verifier. Examples of eye candidates extraction are shown in Fig. 3.

In order to detect faces in different scales, the facial image is repeatedly scaled by a factor of 1.2. In each scale, all eye pair candidates are extracted and verified by the eyes verifier which will be described in the next section. Consequently, all the faces in one image can be detected.

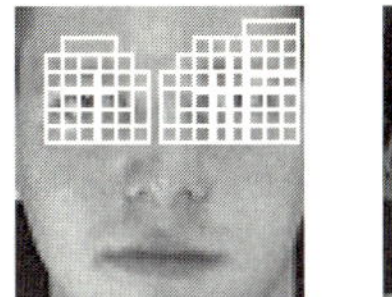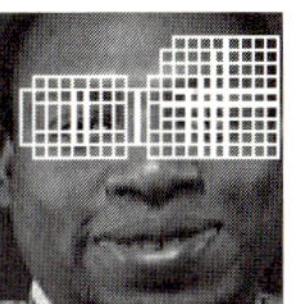

**Fig. 3.** Examples of eye candidates extraction

# 3  Eye Verification

After eye candidates are extracted by calculating entropy, an eye verifier is applied to obtain real eyes. We train a SVM classifier to do eye verification.

## 3.1  Support Vector Machine

In this paper, we choose the SVM as the classifying function. One distinctive advantage this type of classifier has over traditional neural networks is that SVMs achieve better generalization performance.

SVM is a patter classification algorithm developed by V. Vapnik and his team [8]. It is a binary classification method that finds the optimal linear decision surface based on the concept of structural risk minimization. Given a set of N examples:

$$(x_1,y_1), ...(x_i,y_i), ...(x_N,y_N) \quad x_i \in \mathbf{R}^N, y_i \in \{-1,1\}$$

In case of linear separable data, maximum margin classification aims to separate two classes with hyperplane that maximizes distance of supports vectors. This Optimal Separating Hyperplane can be expressed as following formula:

$$f(x) = \sum_{i=1}^{N} \alpha_i y_i (x_i^T x) + b \tag{5}$$

This solution is defined in terms of subset of training samples (supports vectors) whose $\alpha_i$ is non- zero.

In the case of linearly non-separable patterns, SVM is to perform non-linear mapping of input vector into high dimensional dot product space $F$ . In general, however, the dimension of the feature space is very large, so we have the technical problem of computing high dimensional spaces. Kernel method gives the solution to this problem. In Eq. (5), substituting $x_i^T x$ to $\varphi^T(x_i)\varphi(x)$ leads to the following formula:

$$f(x) = \mathrm{sgn}[\sum_{i=1}^{N} y_i \alpha_i \varphi^T(x_i)\varphi(x) + b] \tag{6}$$

This kernel method is backed up by Mercer's theorem. Thus the formula for non-linear SVM with kernel is

$$f(x) = \sum_{i=1}^{N} \alpha_i y_i k(x_i, x) + b \tag{7}$$

The requirement on the kernel $k(x_i, x)$ is to satisfy Mercer's theorem. Within this requirement there are some possible inner product kernels. There are Gaussian Radial Basis Functions, polynomial functions, and sigmoid polynomials whose decision surfaces are known to have good approximation properties. In this paper, we choose Gaussian radial basis function as the kernel function.

### 3.2  Eye Verifier

We apply SVM classifier to verify the eye candidates. The training data used for generating eye verification SVM consists of 600 images of each class (eye and non-eye). Selection of proper non-eye images is very important to train SVM because performance of SVM is influenced by what kind of non-eye images is used. In the initial stage of training SVM, we use non-eye images similar to eyes such as eyebrows, nostrils and other eye-like patches. And we generate non-eye images using bootstrapping method [9].

## 4  Mouth Location

Mouth location is also an important part in facial expression recognition and face states recognition. After the real eyes are obtained, mouth is located sequentially. Firstly, mouth region is calculated according to the coordinates of left eye and right eye so that the searching region for mouth location is effectively reduced. On this basis, precise mouth location is done.

### 4.1  Mouth Search Region Calculation

A mouth search region is specified by the positions of the detected eyes regarding the geometric information of a face. That is, the eyes and mouth are located statistically [10].

The mouth search region is represented with two coordinates $(M_{left}, M_{top})$ and $(M_{right}, M_{bottom})$ by equation (8).

$$
\begin{bmatrix}
M_{left} \\
M_{right} \\
M_{top} \\
M_{bottom}
\end{bmatrix}
=
\begin{bmatrix}
0.965x_{left} + 0.035x_{right} \\
0.035x_{left} + 0.965x_{right} \\
y_{eye} + 0.64(x_{right} - x_{left}) \\
y_{eye} + 1.44(x_{right} - x_{left})
\end{bmatrix}
\tag{8}
$$

where $(x_{left}, y_{left})$ and $(x_{right}, y_{right})$ are the coordinates of left eye center and right

eye center respectively, and $y_{eye} = \dfrac{y_{left} + y_{right}}{2}$.

In Fig. 4, each white rectangle windows on the mouth is the mouth region calculated by two eyes coordinates.

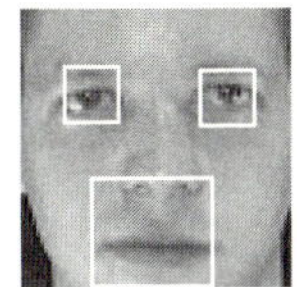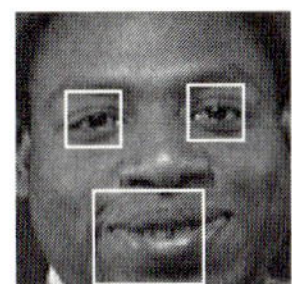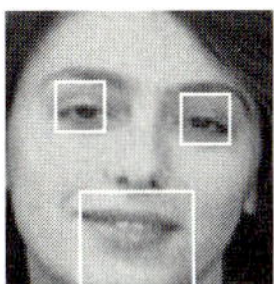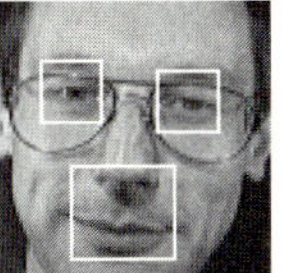

**Fig. 4.** Mouth region extraction

## 4.2 Precise Mouth Location

Once the mouth search region is extracted, precise mouth location can be done by further image processing. Because mouth has lower pixel value in mouth search region, using binary image to segment mouth is feasible. Maximum filter and Minimum filter are applied to the mouth region image as in Eq. (9).

$$f' = MinFilter(MaxFilter(f)) - f \qquad (9)$$

where $f$ is original image and $f'$ is differential image.

Then thresholding and close operation is applied to the differential image and mouth can be segmented, as shown in Fig. 5(a). Mouth center will be located by calculating gravity center of connected component. Fig. 5(b) shows some mouth location results.

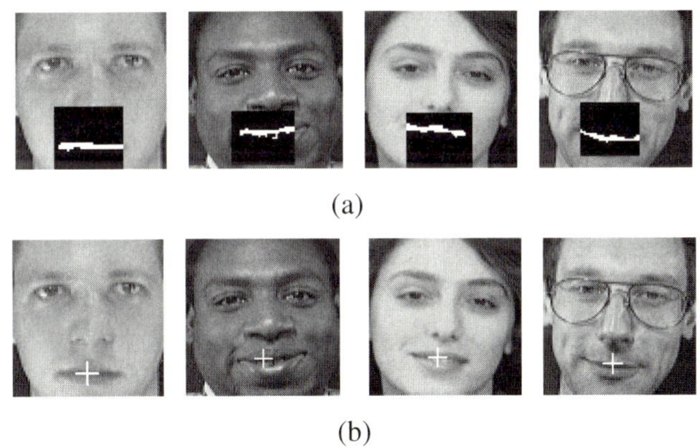

(a)

(b)

**Fig. 5.** Mouth Location. (a) mouth segmentation. (b) precise mouth location.

## 5 Experimental Results

The proposed approach was tested on the JAFFE face database and ORL face database. The JAFFE database consists of 213 frontal face images. The ORL database consists of 400 frontal face images from 40 individuals. Face is firstly detected, and then eyes and mouth are detected.

To evaluate the precision of eye localization, a scale independent localization criterion [11] is used. This relative error measure compares the automatic location result with the manually marked locations of each eye. Let $C_l$ and $C_r$ be the manually extracted left and right eye positions, $C_l'$ and $C_r'$ be the detected positions, $d_l$ be the Euclidean distance between $C_l'$ and $C_l$, $d_r$ be the Euclidean distance between $C_r'$ and $C_r$, $d_{lr}$ be the Euclidean distance between the ground truth eye centers. Then the relative error of this detection is defined as follows:

$$err = \frac{\max(d_l, d_r)}{d_{lr}} \tag{10}$$

JAFFE contains only female faces and there is no mustache occlusion, the mouth detection rate is high. When $err < 0.1$, the eye detection rate is 99.13%, the mouth detection rate is 99.32% based on eye detection. Our algorithm outperforms the Ref. [12] and Ref. [13]. Some detection results are shown in Fig. 6 (a). However, some faces in ORL dataset contain glasses and mustache. When the glisten of glasses is too strong, the eye detection will fail, also when the occlusion on mouth is heavy, the mouth detection will fail. When $err < 0.1$, the eye detection rate is 90.67%, the mouth detection rate is 97.76% based on eye detection. Fig. 6 (b) shows some detection results.

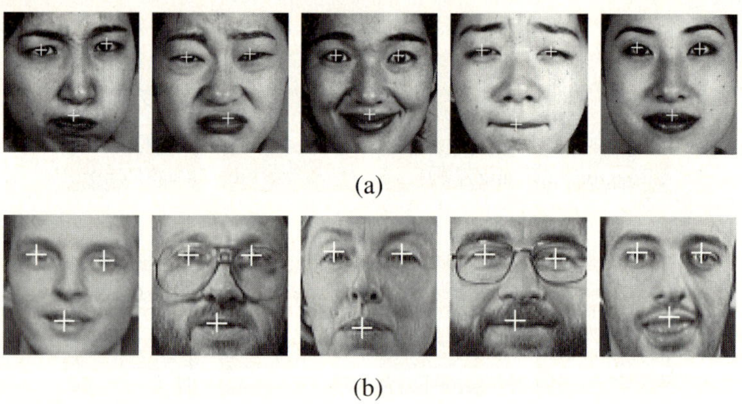

(a)

(b)

**Fig. 6.** Some location results. (a) results on JAFFE database. (b) results on ORL database.

## 6  Conclusions and Future Research

In this paper, an efficient facial features location method for gray intensity face is presented. Experimental results show that entropy measure can extract eye candidates effectively. Based on the precise eye location, mouth search region can be calculated by the coordinates of two eyes. This makes mouth location much easier. The experimental results demonstrate its efficiency. Future work will focus on resolving the occlusion on faces and the influence of face pose to improve the algorithm performance.

## Acknowledgment

This work was supported by National Natural Science Foundation of China (Grant No. 60503026, 60632050), and the Project of Science and Technology Plan of Jiangsu Province (Grant No. BG2005008).

## References

1. Cristinacce, D., Cootes, T.: Facial Feature Detection Using AdaBoost with Shape Constraints. In: Proceedings of British Machine Vision Conference, pp. 231–240 (2003)
2. Viola, P., Jones, M.: Rapid Object Detection Using a Boosted Cascade of Simple Features. In: Proceedings of Computer Vision and Pattern Recognition Conference, vol. 1, pp. 511–518 (2001)
3. Dryden, I., Mardia, K.V.: The Statistical Analysis of Shape. Wiley, London (1998)
4. D'Orazio, T., Leo, M., Cicirelli, G., Distante, A.: An Algorithm for Real Time Eye Detection in Face Images. In: Proceedings of 17th International Conference on Pattern Recognition, vol. 3, pp. 278–281 (2004)
5. Du, S., Ward, R.: A Robust Approach for Eye Localization Under Variable Illuminations. In: Proceedings of International Conference on Image Processing, vol. 1, pp. 377–380 (2007)
6. Toews, M., Arbel, T.: Entropy-of-likelihood Feature Selection for Image Correspondence. In: Proceedings of 9th International Conference on Computer Vision, vol. 2, pp. 1041–1047 (2003)
7. Shannon, C.E., Waver, W.: A Mathematical Theory of Communication. Bell System Technical Journal 27, 379–423 (1948)
8. Vapnik, V.: The Nature of Statistical Learning Theory. Springer, New York (1995)
9. Sung, K.K., Poggio, T.: Example-based Learning for View-based Human Face Detection. IEEE Trans. Pattern Anal. Mach. Intell. 20(1), 39–51 (1998)
10. Oh, J.-S., Kim, D.-W., Kim, J.-T., Yoon, Y.-I., Choi, J.-S.: Facial component detection for efficient facial characteristic point extraction. In: Kamel, M.S., Campilho, A.C. (eds.) ICIAR 2005. LNCS, vol. 3656, pp. 1125–1132. Springer, Heidelberg (2005)
11. Jesorsky, O., Kirchberg, K.J., Frischholz, R.W.: Robust face detection using the hausdorff distance. In: Bigun, J., Smeraldi, F. (eds.) AVBPA 2001. LNCS, vol. 2091, pp. 90–95. Springer, Heidelberg (2001)
12. Zhou, Z.H., Geng, X.: Projection Functions for Eye Detection. Pattern Recognition 37, 1049–1056 (2004)
13. Ma, Y., Ding, X.Q., et al.: Robust Precise Eye Location under Probabilistic Framework. In: Proceedings of FGR, pp. 339–344 (2004)

# Error-Diffused Image Security Improving Using Overall Minimal-Error Searching


Jing-Ming Guo[*] and Yun-Fu Liu

Department of Electrical Engineering,
National Taiwan University of Science and Technology
Taipei, Taiwan
jmguo@seed.net.tw, yunfuliu@gmail.com



**Abstract.** This study presents a high capacity data hiding method for generating high quality watermarked halftone images. The embedded watermarks can be distributed into single or multiple halftone images with the proposed Overall Minimal-Error Searching (OMES). The proposed method modifies the halftone values at same position of all host images with the trained Substitution Table (S-Table). The S-Table makes the original combination of these halftone values as another meaningful combination for embedded watermark, which is the key part in determining the image quality. Hence, an optimization procedure is proposed to achieve the optimized S-Table. As demonstrated in the experimental results, the proposed approach provides good image quality and is able to guard against some frequent happened attacks in printing applications.

**Keywords:** Digital watermarking, digital halftoning, error diffusion, iteration-based halftoning, ordered dithering, overall minimal-error searching.


## 1  Introduction

Digital halftoning [1] is a technique for changing grayscale images into two-tone halftone images, which include Ordered Dithering (OD) [1], Error Diffusion (EDF) [2], and Dot Diffusion (DDF) [3]. Among these, error diffusion offers good visual quality and reasonable computational complexity.

Digital watermarks have many usages, including protecting ownership of an image, preventing the illegal use of an image without permission, and authenticating an image to verify that it has not been altered. Currently, many methods that use halftones to embed watermarks have been studied. These techniques can be used for printing security documents such as an ID cards, currency, and confidential documents, and prevent illegal duplication and forgery by further scanning these documents to digital forms.

The watermark which is embedded in halftone images can be retrieved by scanning and applying some extraction algorithms. These methods include using a number of different dither cells to create a threshold pattern in the halftoning process [4]; using Smart Pair-Toggling (DHSPT) to embed data into error-diffused images [5];

---


[*] Member IEEE.



T. Wada, F. Huang, and S. Lin (Eds.): PSIVT 2009, LNCS 5414, pp. 550–561, 2009.

coordinating the BCH error-correcting code with data-hiding techniques [6]; authentication based on halftoning and coordinate projection [7], and data hiding in several halftone images or color planes using Minimal-Error Bit Searching (MEBS) [8]. The MEBS preserves excellent image quality when embedded capacity is as high as 33.33%. However, the quality degrades significantly when capacity increases up to 50%. This study presents an Overall Minimal-Error Searching (OMES) to improve the image quality when the data capacity is 50%.

## 2  Performance Evaluations

In this section, the performance evaluations, Peak Signal-to-Noise Ratio (PSNR) and Correct Decoding Rate (CDR), employed in this work are defined. Suppose the host image is of size $P \times Q$. The quality evaluation of Watermarked Halftone image ($WH$) is defined as follows,

$$PSNR = 10log_{10} \frac{P \times Q \times 255^2}{\sum_{i=1}^{P}\sum_{j=1}^{Q}[\sum_{m,n\in R}\sum c_{m,n}(ori_{i+m,j+n} - wh_{i+m,j+n})]^2}, \qquad (1)$$

where the variables $ori_{i,j}$ and $wh_{i,j}$ denote the grayscale value and watermarked halftone value at position $(i,j)$, respectively. The variable $c_{m,n}$ denotes the Least-Mean-Square (LMS) trained filter ($R$) coefficient at position $(m,n)$. In this work, the size of the support region $R$ is fixed at $7 \times 7$. The LMS-trained filter can be obtained by psychophysical experiments [9]. The other way to derive the filter can use a training set of both pairs of grayscale images and good halftone results of them, such as using error diffusion or ordered dithering to produce the set. The LMS is described as follows,

$$\hat{h}_{i,j} = \sum_{m,n\in R}\sum c_{m,n}h_{i+m,j+n}, \qquad (2)$$

$$e_{i,j}^2 = (ori_{i,j} - \hat{h}_{i,j})^2, \qquad (3)$$

$$\frac{\partial e_{i,j}^2}{\partial c_{m,n}} = -2e_{i,j}h_{i+m,j+n}, \qquad (4)$$

$$\begin{cases} c_{m,n} \text{ should be decreased, if } c_{m,n} > c_{m,n,opt} \\ c_{m,n} \text{ should be increased, if } c_{m,n} < c_{m,n,opt} \end{cases}, \qquad (5)$$

$$c_{m,n}^{(k+1)} = c_{m,n}^k + \mu e_{i+m,j+n}h_{i+m,j+n}, \qquad (6)$$

where the variable $h_{i,j}$ denotes the halftone value at position $(i,j)$ of a halftone image ($H$); variable $e_{i,j}^2$ denotes the Mean-Square Error (MSE) between $ori_{i,j}$ and $\hat{h}_{i,j}$; variable $c_{i,j,opt}$ denotes the coefficient of the optimized LMS-trained filter ($C_{opt}$), and $\mu$ denotes the adjusting parameter used to control the convergent speed of the LMS optimization procedure. In this work, the variable $\mu$ is set to $10^{-5}$. Some other quality evaluation methods can be found in [10]-[11].

The other performance evaluation is the CDR, which determines the similarity between the original binary watermarks ($W$) and corresponding decoded watermarks ($DW$). The CDR is based on the concept of Hamming distance as defined below,

$$CDR = \frac{\sum_{i=1}^{P}\sum_{j=1}^{Q}\left(\overline{w_{i,j} \oplus dw_{i,j}}\right)}{P \times Q} \times 100\%, \tag{7}$$

where the size of watermarks is $P \times Q$, which is same as original grayscale images. The variables $w_{i,j}$ and $dw_{i,j}$ denote the original watermark ($W$) and corresponding decoded watermarks ($DW$), respectively, and the notation $\oplus$ denotes the XOR operation.

## 3  Data Hiding with Overall Minimal-Error Searching

This section describes the proposed OMES encoding scheme, which embeds watermark information into multiple halftone images. The concept is similar to the Secret Sharing Scheme (SSS) [12], and the algorithm is depicted in Fig. 1.

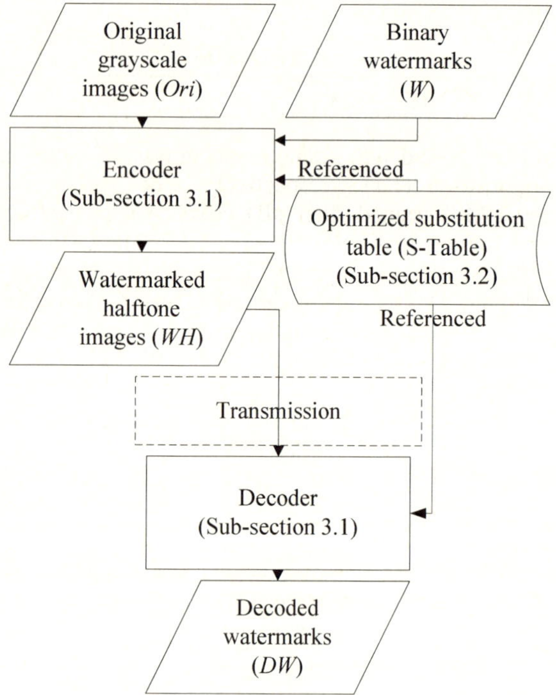


**Fig. 1.** Flow chat of the proposed algorithm

### 3.1  Encoder

The proposed OMES encoder is illustrated in Fig. 2. The variable $ori_{i,j}^{n}$ denotes the grayscale value at current processing position $(i,j)$ of the $n$th original grayscale image. The variables $h_{i,j}^{n}$ and $wh_{i,j}^{n}$ denote the temporary halftone output $H$ and final watermarked halftone output $WH$ at current processing position $(i,j)$. The blocks with name "Halftoning" represent the typical error diffusion. The function $N(\cdot)$ of $Ori$ denotes

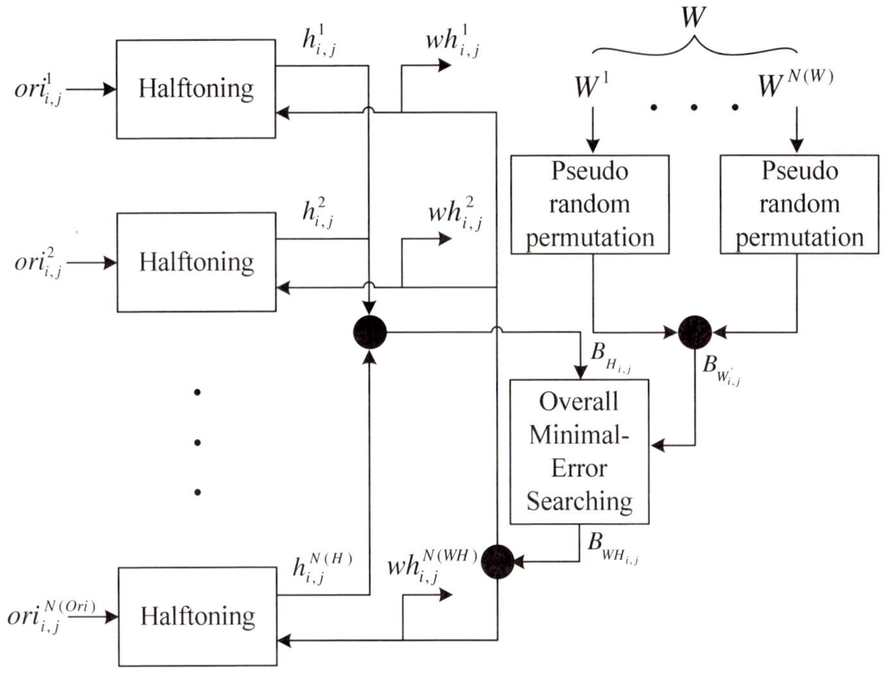

**Fig. 2.** Proposed Overall Minimal-Error Searching (OMES) encoder algorithm

the number of original grayscale images. In this work, $N(Ori) = N(H) = N(WH)$. The variable $W$ denotes watermark set for embedding, and $W^n$ denotes the $n$th watermark. After the pre-processing "pseudo random permutation", the new set of watermarks $W'$ can be obtained. The variables $B_{H_{i,j}}$, $B_{WH_{i,j}}$ and $B_{W'_{i,j}}$ denote the vector of values $H$, $WH$, and $W'$ at position $(i, j)$, which are with the form of $\{h^1_{i,j}, h^2_{i,j}, \cdots, h^n_{i,j}\}$, $\{wh^1_{i,j}, wh^2_{i,j}, \cdots, wh^n_{i,j}\}$, and $\{w'^1_{i,j}, w'^2_{i,j}, \cdots, w'^n_{i,j}\}$.

The OMES observes the temporary halftone output vector and the corresponding permutated halftone values of watermark at same position, and then modifies the output vector according to the S-Table, which will be introduced later. The quantized errors are feedback-diffused to the neighboring pixels of the temporary halftone images (host images) to reduce the damage caused by the binary outputs modification. The $B_{H_{i,j}}$ has many configurations: Assume the number of host images is 2, the corresponding combinations are given in Table I. The number of configurations is $2^{N(H)}$, where $N(H) = 2$ in this case. The variable $N(W)$ denotes the number of watermarks, and the number of groups is $2^{N(W)}$. Hence, the Table I(a) can be expressed as Table I(b), where each row represents a group. This table is called the Substitution Table (S-Table), and each number in S-Table is called a state.

Given a specific order of host images, the corresponding $B_{H_{i,j}}$ is first transformed to a decimal value, then this value maps to a corresponding group in S-Table. The mapped group is called original group ($G_O$). Meanwhile, the vector $B_{W'_{i,j}}$ of the watermarks with

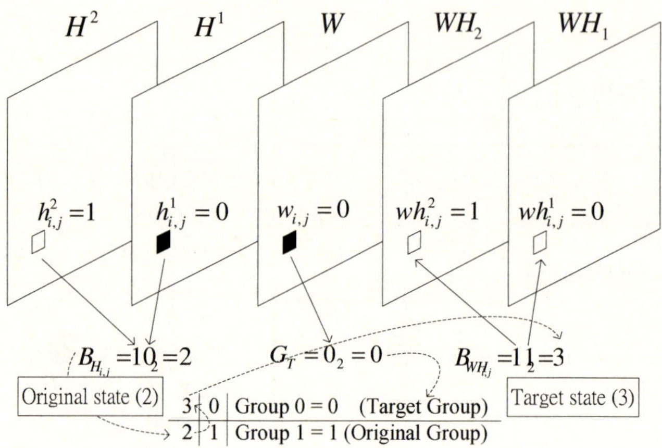


**Fig. 3.** Example of the $G_0$ and $G_T$ with two host images and one embedded halftone watermark

the same position as host images is transformed to decimal value, then this value also maps to a corresponding group in S-Table. The watermark mapped group is called the target group ($G_T$). When $G_O = G_T$, then let $B_{H_{i,j}} = B_{WH_{i,j}}$; When $G_O \neq G_T$, then all the states in $G_T$ should be used for testing which state causes minimal overall error. Herein, the overall error is defined as the overall quantized error caused by the tested state. The one with the minimal overall error is employed to replace the original state. An example is illustrated in Fig. 3. The procedure of the proposed OMES is organized as below:

$$\mathbb{S}_{GT} = \left\{ s^a_{GT} \mid a = 1,2,\cdots,2^{N(H)-N(W)} \right\}, \text{ where } 0 \leq s < 2^{N(H)}, \tag{8}$$

$$s^a_{GT} = \left\{ h^1_{a,i,j}, h^2_{a,i,j}, \cdots, h^{N(H)}_{a,i,j} \right\}, \text{ where } h = \{0,1\}, \tag{9}$$

$$e^a_{i,j} = \sum_{n=1}^{N(H)} \left| v^n_{i,j} - h^n_{a,i,j} \right|, \tag{10}$$

$$e^k_{i,j,min} = min\left( e^a_{i,j} \mid a = 1,2,\cdots,2^{N(H)-N(W)} \right), \tag{11}$$

where the vector $\mathbb{S}_{GT}$ denotes the set of states of $G_T$ in S-Table, and variable $s$ denotes the state. The variable $a$ denotes the state number in $G_T$, and the variable $n$ denotes the host image number. The variable $v^n_{i,j}$ denotes the modified grayscale output of the $n$th host image, and the variable $e^a_{i,j}$ denotes the difference between the modified grayscale output $v^n_{i,j}$ and $a$th halftone output $h^n_{a,i,j}$ in $G_T$. The target state $s^k_{GT}$ ($k$th state) is obtained with the steps given in Eqs. (8)-(11), which is able to minimize the overall error and hence maintains the image quality.

However, when the capacity is as high as 50%, a large amount of outputs $wh_{i,j}$ with high quantization error $e_{i,j}$ are forced to be used, which then degrades the image quality. For this, a pre-defined error threshold $e_{th}$ is set to overcome this problem. The feedback error denotes as following,

$$e_{i,j}^n = \begin{cases} e_{th}, & \text{if } v_{i,j}^n - h_{k,i,j}^n > e_{th} \\ -e_{th}, & \text{if } v_{i,j}^n - h_{k,i,j}^n < -e_{th}, \\ v_{i,j}^n - h_{k,i,j}^n, & \text{Otherwise} \end{cases} \tag{12}$$

In this work $e_{th} = 127$. In the decoder, we simply need to collect the corresponding halftone values in these watermarked halftone images and form into the decoded vector sets, and then look up the S-Table for decoding.

## 3.2  Optimization Procedure for Achieving a Substitution Table (S-Table)

The watermarked halftone image quality obtained by OMES is determined by the quantity of alternations of halftone value from original state to target state. Theoretically, the halftones created by original state have the best image quality compared to the halftones created by other target states. Nonetheless, the quality between halftones created by target state and original state are demanded to be similar to achieve good embedded image quality. However, when the differences between target and original states have too much discrepancies, the image quality will significant degrade. Based on this, we develop an optimized procedure of constructing S-Table as below.

The 18 different natural grayscale images are employed in the optimization training procedure of S-Table. To generate the training watermarks, a uniform distributed image with grayscale value 128 is adopted to perform three different halftoning approaches: Classical-4 clustered-dot dithering [1], Bayer-5 dispersed-dot dithering [1], and Mese's dot diffusion with class matrix of size 8x8 [3]. To evaluate the quality of the obtained watermarked halftone image, the average PSNR is calculated. The following steps are developed to provide a fair PSNR distribution across multiple embedded watermarks.

$$\mathbb{P} = \{PSNR_n | n = 1, 2, \cdots, N(WH)\}, \tag{13}$$

$$Var(\mathbb{P}) = \sum_{n=1}^{N(I)} \left(PSNR_n - Average(\mathbb{P})\right)^2 p(PSNR_n), \tag{14}$$

$$Cost = \begin{cases} \sum_{n=1}^{N(I)} PSNR_n p(PSNR_n), & \text{if } Var(\mathbb{P}) < 0.4 \\ 0, & \text{Otherwise} \end{cases} \tag{15}$$

where the vector $\mathbb{P}$ denotes the set of PSNRs of the watermarked halftone images; the variable $n$ denotes the $n$th watermarked halftone image, and $Var(\mathbb{P})$ denotes the discrepancies between PSNRs. In this study, the upper bound of $Var(\mathbb{P})$ is set at 0.4. The S-Table which achieves the highest cost is employed for applications. The steps of the optimization procedure are organized as below,

Step 1. Given an initial S-Table ($S$).

Step 2. Suppose the states within S-Table are rearranged as 1-D sequence. Each states $s_i$ in the S-Table is successively swapped with one of the other $2^{N(H)}$ states $s_j$, where $i \neq j$.

Step 3. Evaluating the cost of the set of watermarked halftone images using the S-Table obtained from Step 2.

Step 4. The swapped S-table leads to the highest cost, $maxCost(S, swapped\ S)$, is taken as a new S-Table. Otherwise, the swapped states within S-Table are recovered to their original positions.

Step 5. Another states $s_i$ in the S-Table is selected, and then performs Steps 3 and 4.

Step 6. If any swapping cannot improve the cost of the set of watermarked halftone images, the optimization procedure is terminated. Otherwise, Steps 2 to 5 are repeated.

Notably, in order to provide good initial S-Table candidates, 5000 random-generated S-Tables are tested, and the one achieves the highest cost is adopted. Table II shows the final convergent S-Tables for different numbers of host images, which include three configurations: One watermark embedded into two host images, two watermarks embedded into four host images, three watermarks embedded into six host images. All of the configurations can achieve capacity 50%. In this study, no more than eight host images are explored, since it is impractical in applications.

## 4   Experimental Result

Figures 4(d)-(e) show the watermarked halftone images using MEBS [8] with capacity 50%, and Figs. 4(f)-(q) show the watermarked halftone images with the proposed OMES under the same capacity 50%. It is clear that the OMES yields better average image quality than MEBS whether in subjective or objective quality criterion.

An interesting phenomenon is explored as below: When the number of host images is few, such as two, one host image with explicit edge structure or a cluster of bright or dark area, the other watermarked halftone image will suffer from serious interference and then degrades in quality. This problem is raised because there are few selectable states ($2^{N(H)-N(W)}$) in target group. To solve this problem, the difference between $N(H)$ and $N(W)$ should be increased. Notably, the ratio between $N(H)$ and $N(W)$ has to be maintained to keep it in the same capacity. For example, $N(H)$ and $N(W)$ are increased from 2 and 1 to 4 and 2, respectively.

The performance comparisons among the various watermarking approaches using 12 test images are depicted in Fig. 5, which include MEBS [8], OMES with two host images and one watermark (EDF 1H2), OMES with four host images and two watermarks (EDF 2H4), OMES with six host images and three watermarks (EDF 3H6), The results consist with the discussions given above. The results show the image quality is improved when the difference between $N(H)$ and $N(W)$ is increased.

Two of the most frequent happened attacks, cropping (tampering) and print-and-scan, are involved in the experiments to analyze the robustness performance. The cropping (tampering) rates range from 5% to 40%. To avoid the cluster losing of information by cropping, the watermark is pseudo-permutated before being embedded.

**Fig. 4.** Watermarked halftone images with the MEBS [8] and proposed OMES, where the S-Table as shown in Table II. (a)-(c) Halftone watermarks. (d)-(e) Two $WH$s which hide $W$ (a) (MEBS). (f)-(g) Two $WH$s which hide $W$ (a) (OMES). (h)-(k) Four $WH$s which hide $W$s (a) and (b) (OMES). (l)-(q) Six $WH$s which hide $W$s (a), (b), and (c) (OMES). (all printed at 450 dpi).

(l) PSNR=28.1 dB     (m) PSNR=27.7 dB     (n) PSNR=28.6 dB

(o) PSNR=28.6 dB     (p) PSNR=28.2 dB     (q) PSNR=27.7 dB

**Fig. 4.** (*continued*)

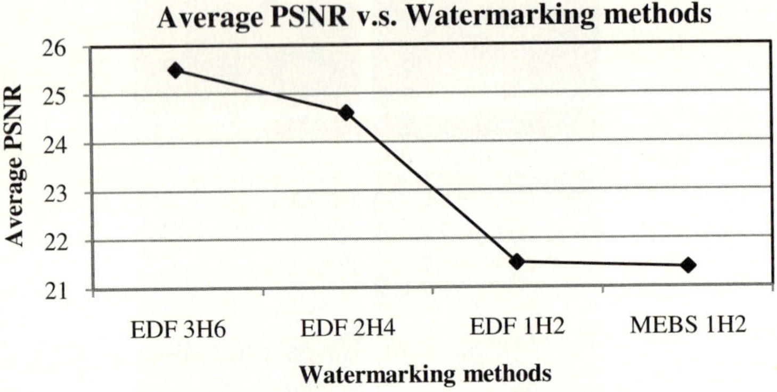



**Fig. 5.** Performance comparisons between OMES and MEBS [8] watermarking

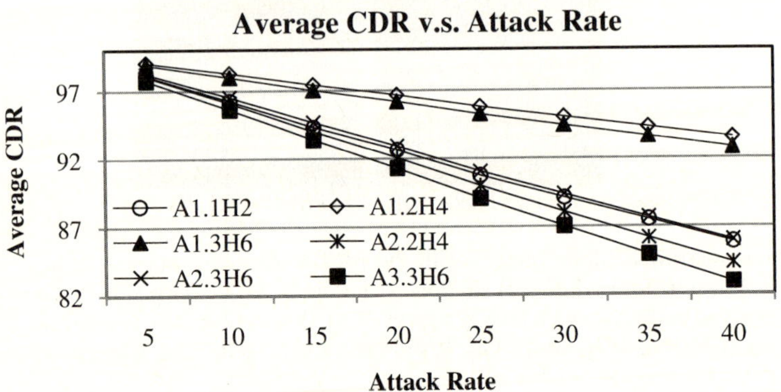



**Fig. 6.** Cropping attack with cropping rates range from 5% to 40%

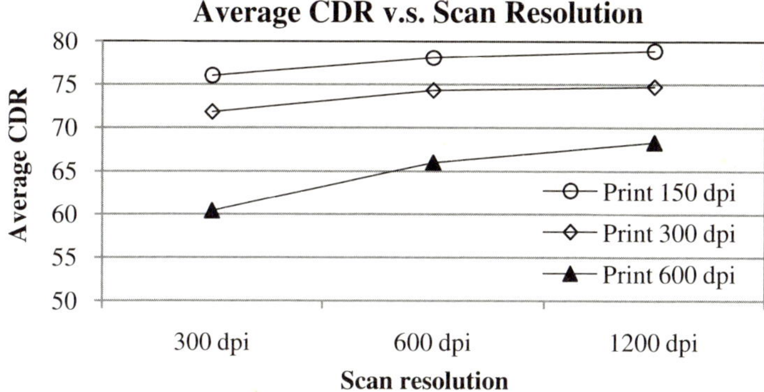

**Fig. 7.** Print-and-Scan attack with different configurations of print-and-scan resolutions

**Table 1.** Substitution table (S-Table): relationships between watermark and the corresponding vector

| Group # (Watermark Information bit) | Group 0 (black) | Group 1 (white) | Group 1 (white) | Group 0 (black) | ... |
|---|---|---|---|---|---|
| Corresponding decimal value | 0 | 1 | 2 | 3 | ... |
| Input Image #1 | 0 | 1 | 0 | 1 | ... |
| Input Image #2 | 0 | 0 | 1 | 1 | ... |
| Input Image #n | ⋮ | ⋮ | ⋮ | ⋮ | ⋱ |

(a)

| States | | Group # |
|---|---|---|
| 3 | 0 | Group 0 |
| 2 | 1 | Group 1 |

(b)

**Table 2.** Substitution table trained for 2, 4 and 6 host images with capacity 50%

| States | | Group # |
|---|---|---|
| 3 | 0 | Group 0 |
| 2 | 1 | Group 1 |

(a) For one watermark hiding in two images.

| States | | | | Group # |
|---|---|---|---|---|
| 11 | 9 | 4 | 2 | Group 0 |
| 14 | 5 | 15 | 0 | Group 1 |
| 3 | 13 | 8 | 6 | Group 2 |
| 1 | 12 | 10 | 7 | Group 3 |

(b) For two watermarks hiding in four images.

| States | | | | | | | | Group # |
|---|---|---|---|---|---|---|---|---|
| 19 | 36 | 55 | 15 | 13 | 34 | 41 | 24 | Group 0 |
| 60 | 17 | 10 | 54 | 33 | 4 | 59 | 30 | Group 1 |
| 38 | 50 | 12 | 45 | 7 | 53 | 27 | 16 | Group 2 |
| 20 | 62 | 49 | 8 | 56 | 3 | 43 | 29 | Group 3 |
| 39 | 25 | 23 | 18 | 32 | 5 | 61 | 14 | Group 4 |
| 21 | 26 | 6 | 35 | 63 | 40 | 48 | 9 | Group 5 |
| 37 | 46 | 31 | 58 | 44 | 0 | 11 | 22 | Group 6 |
| 51 | 42 | 1 | 2 | 28 | 52 | 47 | 57 | Group 7 |

(c) For three watermarks hiding in six images.

The embedded images are re-permutated before the decoding is performed. Figure 6 shows the decoded results, where the "A#" represents the number of attacked watermarked halftone images, and the "types" represents the different host image and watermark configurations with capacity 50%. Notably, the CDRs are the averaged results of the 12 test images. Finally, multiple configurations of print-and-scan attacks are involved in the experiments, namely printing at 150, 300, and 600 dpi, and scanning at 300, 600, and 1200 dpi. Here the RGB color image of size $P \times Q$ is used, which is divided into several cells of size $M \times N$. An information bit is embedded in a cell, which means that every vector in cell has to embed the same information bit. The average CDRs with the 12 test images are organized in Fig. 7.

## 5  Conclusions

This work presents a high payload watermarking in multiple halftone images using Overall Minimal-Error Searching (OMES). Employing the concept that a vector can be used to represent an information bit of watermark, the proposed OMES effectively shares a watermark into two halftone images with data capacity 50%. The image quality can be further improved when the difference between $N(H)$ and $N(W)$ is increased, since more potential selectable state are available. As documented in the experimental results, the image quality of the proposed OMES is significantly superior to the pervious Minimal-Error Bit Searching (MEBS) under the same embedded capacity. Moreover, it can guard against most frequent happened cropping and print-and-scan attacks. Due to the high capacity nature of the proposed method, it is also applicable to secret communication application.

## References


1. Ulichney, R.: Digital Halftoning. MIT Press, Cambridge (1987)
2. Floyd, R.W., Steinberg, L.: An adaptive algorithm for spatial gray scale. In: Proc. SID 75 Dig.: Society for information Display, pp. 36–37 (1975)
3. Mese, M., Vaidyanathan, P.P.: Optimized halftoning using dot diffusion and methods for inverse halftoning. IEEE Trans. Image Processing 9, 691–709 (2000)
4. Hel-Or, H.Z.: Watermarking and copyright labeling of printed images. J. Electron. Imaging 10(3), 794–803 (2001)
5. Fu, M.S., Au, O.C.: Data hiding by smart pair toggling for halftone images. In: Proc. IEEE Int. Conf. Acoustics, Speech and Signal Processing, vol. 4, pp. 2318–2321 (June 2000)
6. Fu, M.S., Au, O.C.: Data hiding watermarking for halftone images. IEEE Trans. Image Processing 11, 477–484 (2002)
7. Wu, C.W.: Multimedia data hiding and authentication via halftoning and coordinate projection. Eurasip J. Appl. Signal Processing 2002(2), 143–151 (2002)
8. Pei, S.C., Guo, J.M.: High-capacity data hiding in halftone images using minimal-error bit searching and least-mean square filter. IEEE Trans. Image Processing 15, 1665–1679 (2006)

9. Mannos, J., Sakrison, D.: The effects of a visual fidelity criterion on the encoding of images. IEEE Trans. Inform. Theory 20, 526–536 (1974)
10. Wang, Z., Bovik, A.C.: A Universal Image quality Index. IEEE Signal Processing Letters 9(3), 81–84 (2002)
11. Damera-Venkata, N., Kite, T.D., Geisler, W.S., Evans, B.L., Bovik, A.C.: Image Quality Assessment Based on a Degradation Model. IEEE Transactions on Image Processing 9(4), 636–650 (2000)
12. Shamir, A.: How to share a secret. Commun. ACM 22, 612–613 (1979)

# Automatic Segmentation of Non-rigid Objects in Image Sequences Using Spatiotemporal Information


Cheolkon Jung and Joongkyu Kim

School of Information and Communication Engineering, Sungkyunkwan University,
Suwon 440-746, Republic of Korea
ckjung@ece.skku.ac.kr, jkkim@skku.edu



**Abstract.** This paper provides an automatic segmentation method of non-rigid objects in image sequences. The non-rigid objects have fuzzy, blurred, and indefinite boundaries such as smoke and clouds, and are random and unpredictable in spatial and temporal domains. To segment the non-rigid objects, a new segmentation approach considering random and unpredictable characteristics of the non-rigid objects is needed. In this paper, we propose a new segmentation method of the non-rigid objects in image sequences using spatiotemporal information. The procedure toward complete segmentation consists of three steps: spatial segmentation, temporal segmentation, and fusion of the spatial and temporal segmentation results. By means of experiments on various test sequences, we demonstrate that the performance of our method is quite impressive from the viewpoints of the segmentation accuracy.


## 1  Introduction

Recent advances in the internet, high-speed computing, and storage systems have resulted in tremendous interest in digitizing large archives of video data and providing users with interactive access. Due to the shear volume of video data, all these capabilities require an efficient video analysis algorithm that can automatically segment the video objects and index video data. The development of a powerful moving object segmentation algorithm is an important requirement for many computer vision and ubiquitous systems. In video surveillance applications, motion detection can be used to determine the presence of people, vehicles, or other unexpected objects. This initiates more complex activity recognition steps. Segmentation of moving objects in the observed scenes is an important issue in order to solve traffic flow measurements or for behavior detection during sports activities [1-5].

Up to the present, many significant achievements have been made by researchers in the field of the moving object segmentation. Arch and Kaup presented a moving object segmentation method using a statistical approach for video analysis [6]. They modeled the characteristics of pixel difference for background between two consecutive frames, as a Gaussian distribution. For a given level of significance, the resulting threshold value was theoretically obtained and a threshold level was set for the frame difference image, so as to yield a change detection mask (CDM). The CDM was a binary image in which pixel differences exceeding the threshold value were declared


T. Wada, F. Huang, and S. Lin (Eds.): PSIVT 2009, LNCS 5414, pp. 562–573, 2009.

as being of changed intensity and, otherwise, as being intensity-invariant. Meier and Ngan presented an automatic segmentation method for moving objects using a binary image model to track a moving object [7]. The binary model was derived from an edge image and updated every frame to keep the moving object undergoing changes in its shape and spatial location at a certain instance of time. Detection of a moving object was made based on binary model matching between two consecutive frames using Hausdorff distance. The localization of a moving object relies on binary image matching; temporal coherence of the object is preserved even in the case of discontinuous object motion. Kim et al. presented an automatic segmentation method for moving objects based on spatiotemporal information [8]. The method utilized temporal information for localizing the moving objects and spatial information for the acquisition of precise object boundaries and semantic region partition. A combination method for spatiotemporal segmentation improves segmentation accuracy and temporal coherence of moving object boundaries. This method has been adopted as an automatic segmentation tool as informative in MPEG-4. In addition, there have been edge-based methods, feature-based methods, semiautomatic segmentation methods, and so on [4, 9-11, 23].

However, these methods do not consider random and unpredictable characteristics of non-rigid objects with large deformation rates over time. A non-rigid object has fuzzy, blurred, and indefinite boundaries such as smoke and clouds, and is random and unpredictable in both spatial and temporal domains as shown in Fig. 1. Therefore, a new approach for the non-rigid object segmentation should be needed.

(a)                (b)

**Fig. 1.** Representative non-rigid objects with large deformation rates over time. (a) *Cloud.* (b) *Smoke.*

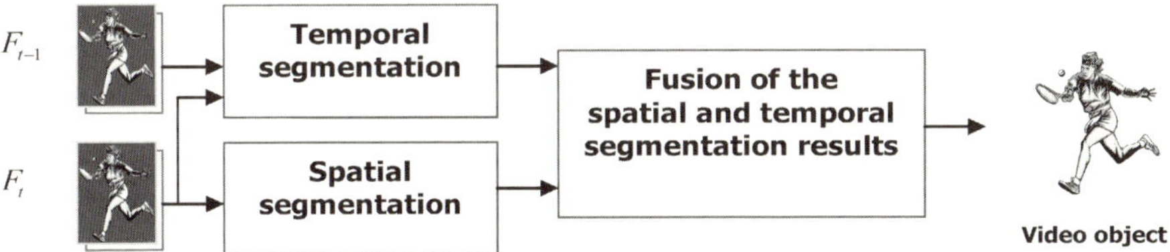


**Fig. 2.** Flow chart of the proposed algorithm

In this paper, we present an automatic segmentation algorithm of the non-rigid objects with large deformation rates. Due to the randomness and unpredictability of the non-rigid objects, we make use of a Markov random field (MRF) model in both spatial and temporal domains. The segmentation flow of the presented scheme is shown in Fig. 2, where $F_{t-1}$ and $F_t$ are previous and current frames, respectively. The scheme consists of three procedures: 'spatial segmentation', 'temporal segmentation', and 'fusion of the spatial and temporal segmentation results'. The spatial segmentation procedure divides the image into semantic regions with precise object boundaries using a MRF model. The temporal segmentation procedure localizes moving regions of objects in the image. Then, the fusion of the spatial and temporal segmentation results produces accurate segmentation results for moving objects. Experimental results show that the presented algorithm achieves for the accurate non-rigid object segmentation.

This paper is organized as follows. Spatial and temporal segmentation are addressed in Sections 2 and 3, respectively. In Section 4, the fusion of the spatial and temporal segmentation results is explained. Section 5 presents experimental results, and we conclude this paper in Section 6.

## 2  Spatial Segmentation

We have used a MRF model for the spatial segmentation. In order to model the intensity of an image as MRF, the correct number of clusters should be determined. If $z(x,y)$ is the intensity of a pixel $(x,y)$, the distribution of $z$ is represented as the sum of $K$ probability density functions (PDFs) in Fig. 3. Assuming these PDFs are Gaussian, the mixture density model takes the equation (1) [12, 24].

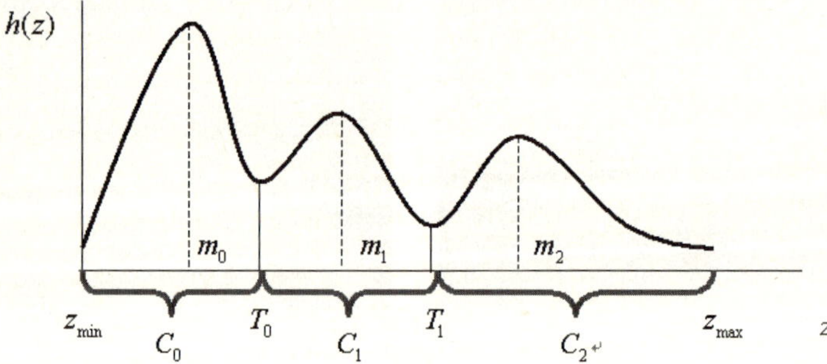

Fig. 3. Distribution of $z$

$$h(z) = \sum_{l=0}^{K-1} \frac{P_l}{\sigma_l \sqrt{2\pi}} \exp\left[ -\frac{1}{2}\left( \frac{z - m_l}{\sigma_l} \right)^2 \right] \tag{1}$$

where $P_l$ denotes the *a priori* probability of the particular mode such that $\Sigma P_l = 1$, and $m_l$ and $\sigma_l$ denote the mean and the standard deviation of each mode, respectively. Since the number of PDFs is equal to the number of clusters, we have used the cluster validity measure presented by Rose to determine the number of clusters, $K$. The idea of this method is that optimal $K$ minimizes within-cluster scatter and maximizes the between-cluster separation [13]. The improved cluster validity measure *validity* is defined as

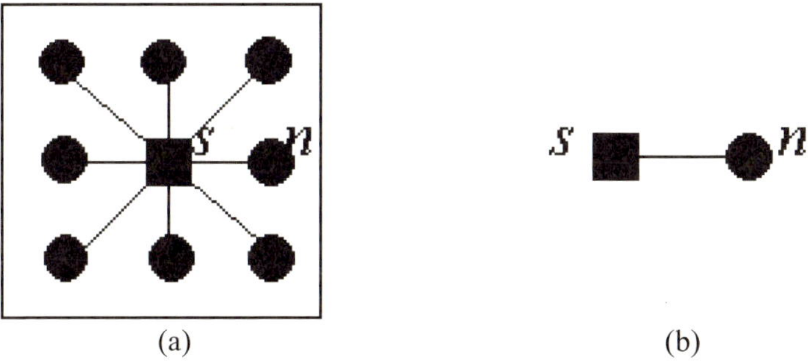

<table>
<tr><td align="center">(a)</td><td align="center">(b)</td></tr>
</table>

**Fig. 4.** (a) Neighborhood system. (b) A binary click.

$$validity = w \cdot \frac{\dfrac{1}{N} \displaystyle\sum_{l=0}^{K-1} \sum_{z \in C_l} |z - m_l|}{\dfrac{1}{K-1} \displaystyle\sum_{l=1}^{K-1} |m_l - m_{l-1}|}. \tag{2}$$

where $w$ is weighted constants, $N$ is the number of pixels in the image, and $C_l$ is the $l$'th cluster ($l=0,1,...,K-1$). The optimal $K$ is the value which minimizes the *validity*. To find the cluster of a pixel, we should determine the optimal threshold value $T_n$. If we assume that $\sigma = \sigma_0 = \cdots = \sigma_{K-1}$, the optimal threshold value $T_n$ is given in [14]

$$T_n = \frac{m_n + m_{n+1}}{2} + \frac{\sigma^2}{m_n - m_{n+1}} \ln \frac{P_{n+1}}{P_n}. \tag{3}$$

If $P_n$ is equal to $P_{n+1}$, the optimal threshold is simply the average of the two class means. By equation (3), we can assign the cluster label to each pixel. If the label field of each pixel is $L(x,y)$, the label $l$ is equal to the index of cluster $C_l$ as follows.

$$L(x, y) = l, \quad z(x, y) \in C_l \tag{4}$$

Since the initial label $l$ is determined by equation (4), we can merge regions with spatial homogeneity using the MRF model. Neighborhood system $N$ and binary cliques at each pixel $(x,y)$ are defined as shown in Fig. 4. If we regard a random field $z$ as MRF, the probability of $z$ is given by a Gibbs distribution that has the following form according to the Hammersley-Clifford theorem [10, 15].

$$P(z) = Q^{-1} \times e^{-U(z)} \tag{5}$$

566     C. Jung and J. Kim

where $Q$ is a constant called the partition function, and $U(z)$ is the energy function. We can find the label $l^*$ that the posteriori probability $P(l|z)$ is maximal. By using the maximum *a posteriori* criterion (MAP), the label $l^*$ is obtained by equation (6).

$$l^* = \arg \max_l P(l \mid z) . \tag{6}$$

By Bayes' rule, the relationship between $z$ and $l$ is expressed as

$$P(l \mid z) \propto P(z \mid l) P(l) . \tag{7}$$

where $P(l|z)$ is a conditional probability of $l$ in dependence on $z$, and $P(l)$ is *a priori* probability of $l$. Therefore, we can express equation (6) as the following form.

$$l^* = \arg \max_l (P(z \mid l) \cdot P(l)) \tag{8}$$

From equation (5), we get:

$$\max_l (P(l \mid z)) = \min_l (U(l \mid z)) \tag{9}$$

Then, the maximization of the *a posteriori* probability is equivalent to the minimization of the energy function $U$. The energy function is classically the sum of two terms (corresponding to data-link and prior knowledge, respectively) [10]:

$$U(l \mid z) = U_a(z \mid l) + U_m(l) \tag{10}$$

The link-to-data energy $U_a(z|l)$ (attachment energy) is expressed as

$$U_a(z \mid l) = \frac{1}{2\sigma^2} \sum_{(x,y)} [z - m_l]^2 . \tag{11}$$

where $\sigma^2$ is the observation variance.

The model energy $U_m(l)$ is a regularization term, and puts *a priori* constraints on the masks of moving objects, erasing isolated points due to noise. Its expression is given by

$$U_m(l) = \sum_c V_c(l_s, l_n) \tag{12}$$

where $c$, $s$, and $n$ denote a binary clique, a current pixel, and pixel of a neighbor, respectively. $l_s$ is a label of $s$, $l_n$ is a label of $n$, and $V_c(l_s,l_n)$ is a potential function associated with a binary clique, $c=(s,n)$. To put homogeneity constraints into the model, it is defined as:

$$V_c(l_s, l_n) = \begin{cases} -\beta, & \text{if } l_s = l_n \\ +\beta, & \text{if } l_s \neq l_n \end{cases} \tag{13}$$

where the positive parameter $\beta$ depends on the nature of the clique.

In order to find the minimum of the energy function, ICM (iterated conditional modes) is used [16]. For each pixel $s$ of the current image, the labels from 0 to $K$-$1$ are tested, and the label that induces the minimum local energy in the neighborhood is kept. The process iterates over the image until convergence. Suppose the label of a current pixel in iteration $k$ is denoted as $l^k$ and a prescribed small number is $\varepsilon$. The fixed label of each pixel is achieved if the following condition is satisfied [17]:

$$\sum_{(x,y)} | l^k - l^{k-1} | < \varepsilon \tag{14}$$

## 3  Temporal Segmentation

In the temporal segmentation procedure, moving parts of objects are localized in sequential images. Using the temporal segmentation procedure, we can find mobile regions in spatially segmented regions. Optical flow is the distribution of apparent velocities of movement of brightness patterns in an image. Let $I$ be the intensity of a pixel $(x,y)$ of an image in time $t$. The optical flow constraint equation can be expressed as [12, 18, 22]:

$$I_x u + I_y v + I_t = 0. \tag{15}$$

where $u$ and $v$ are two components of the velocity vector, and $I_x$, $I_y$, $I_t$ are partial derivatives about $x$, $y$, $t$, respectively. To compute $u$ and $v$, we use the method presented by Lucas and Kanade [12]. This approach assumes that the motion vector remains unchanged over a particular block of pixels denoted by $B$. Under this assumption, the velocity vector is computed as follows:

$$\begin{bmatrix} u \\ v \end{bmatrix} = \begin{bmatrix} \sum_{X \in B} I_x I_x & \sum_{X \in B} I_x I_y \\ \sum_{X \in B} I_x I_y & \sum_{X \in B} I_y I_y \end{bmatrix}^{-1} \begin{bmatrix} -\sum_{X \in B} I_x I_t \\ -\sum_{X \in B} I_y I_t \end{bmatrix}. \tag{16}$$

The output of each pixel in images is binary: the motion exists or does not. The situation where motion exists is denoted as $s_1$, and the opposite, stationary, situation is denoted as $s_0$ [19]. Let random variable $r$ be the magnitude of the velocity vector. Then, $r$ is defined as:

$$r = \sqrt{u^2 + v^2}. \tag{17}$$

We have modeled $r$ as a Gaussian random variable. If $a_0$ is the mean of $r$ when motion does not exist and $a_1$ is the mean when motion exists, the random variable, $r$, has the two conditional probability density functions (PDFs), $p(r|s_0)$, $p(r|s_1)$, with mean value of $a_0$ and $a_1$, respectively, as shown in Fig. 5.

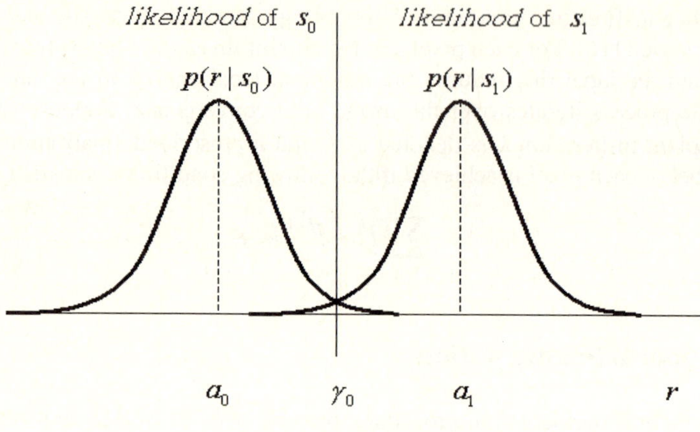



**Fig. 5.** Conditional probability density function: $p(r|s_0)$, $p(r|s_1)$

These PDFs are represented as [20]:

$$p(r \mid s_0) = \frac{1}{\sigma\sqrt{2\pi}} \exp\left[-\frac{1}{2}\left(\frac{r-a_0}{\sigma}\right)^2\right] \tag{18}$$

$$p(r \mid s_1) = \frac{1}{\sigma\sqrt{2\pi}} \exp\left[-\frac{1}{2}\left(\frac{r-a_1}{\sigma}\right)^2\right] \tag{19}$$

where, $\sigma^2$ is a variance of noise.

In order to optimize the binary decision threshold for deciding motion existence, we use the *minimum error* criterion for equally likely binary signals corrupted by Gaussian noise. The threshold level, $r_0$, is represented by $(a_0+a_1)/2$. Using the threshold level, we can assign a label $l$ to each pixel. We assign the label 1 to a pixel where motion exists and the label 0 to a pixel where it does not. The label is obtained as follows:

$$l = \begin{cases} 1, & r \geq \gamma_0 \\ 0, & r < \gamma_0 \end{cases}. \tag{20}$$

When we decide the presence of motion by $r_0$, two types of errors occur. The first type is that we make a decision on motion, when motion does not exist, and this error is called the false alarm. The second type is that we make a decision on non-motion, when motion actually exists, and this error is called the miss. We make use of the MRF model based on Bayes' rule to resolve these two types of errors [10, 15].

## 4  Fusion of the Spatial and Temporal Segmentation Results

By using the fusion module that combines the spatial segmentation result and temporal segmentation result, moving regions are discriminated from background regions. Through connected component labeling, we assign the proper label to each spatially segmented region [21]. Then, $R_{i,t}^{\text{proj}}$ is projected region on top of the spatially segmented region $R_{i,t}$ by the temporal mask $TM_t$ obtained from temporal segmentation between the previous frame $F_{t-1}$ and the current frame $F_t$. Let $N(R_{i,t}^{\text{proj}} \cap R_{i,t})$ be the number of pixels within the intersection $R_{i,t}^{\text{proj}} \cap R_{i,t}$ of the two regions $R_{i,t}^{\text{proj}}$ and $R_{i,t}$. A decision rule whether or not $R_{i,t}$ is a moving region is defined as:

$$P = \frac{N(R_{i,t}^{\text{proj}} \cap R_{i,t})}{N(R_{i,t})} \begin{cases} \geq \tau : & \text{moving region} \\ < \tau : & \text{background region} \end{cases} . \tag{21}$$

where $N(R_{i,t})$ is the number of pixels in $R_{i,t}$. If the value of $P$ is greater than or equal to a given threshold $\tau$, the whole region $R_{i,t}$ is considered as a moving region; otherwise a background region [8]. Here, the value $\tau$ was determined by experiments.

## 5  Experimental Results

The proposed segmentation algorithm has been experimentally investigated by means of computer simulations. First, four test sequences, *Table tennis*, *Foreman*, *Street*, and *Smoke* with the QCIF format (176×144), were used in the experiment (Fig. 6). *Table tennis* and *Foreman* sequences have non-rigid objects with small deformation rates, and *Street* and *Smoke* sequences with large deformation rates.

In the spatial segmentation procedure, the intensity field in an image is regarded as MRF, and segmented by energy minimization. We should determine the number of clusters before energy minimization. Table 1 shows the *validity* for each $K$. The optimal number $K$ is 9 for the *Table tennis* sequence, 10 for the *Foreman* sequence, 6 for the *Street* sequence, and 7 for the *Smoke* sequence. By using the optimal $K$, we can find averages and thresholds for labeling at each point in the image. Then, we can segment an image by energy minimization. Fig. 7 shows the results of the spatial segmentation.

(a)       (b)       (c)       (d)

**Fig. 6.** Original images. (a) *Table tennis*. (b) *Foreman*. (c) *Street*. (d) *Smoke*.

**Table 1.** *Validity*

| K | Table tennis | Foreman | Street | Smoke |
|---|---|---|---|---|
| 2 | 0.04232 | 0.06757 | 0.07306 | 0.02579 |
| 3 | 0.01685 | 0.03920 | 0.04285 | 0.01956 |
| 4 | 0.01880 | 0.02463 | 0.04593 | 0.01784 |
| 5 | 0.01393 | 0.01694 | 0.02706 | 0.02286 |
| 6 | 0.00854 | 0.02188 | **0.01908** | 0.02060 |
| 7 | 0.00777 | 0.02499 | 0.02095 | **0.00583** |
| 8 | 0.00650 | 0.02541 | 0.02345 | 0.00591 |
| 9 | **0.00535** | 0.01831 | 0.02160 | 0.00773 |
| 10 | 0.21581 | **0.01618** | 0.02150 | 0.00890 |

While the spatial segmentation procedure proceeds, the temporal segmentation procedure is performed on consecutive frames. In the temporal segmentation procedure, the velocity vector is computed at each pixel by optical flow analysis, and then the existence of motion is determined by the velocity vector. The size of a particular block $B$ is 3x3, $\varepsilon$ is 1, and $\sigma$ is 100. The iteration number $k$ varies from 5~15. Fig. 8 shows the results of the temporal segmentation. As shown in this figure, black and white pixels are non-motion and motion pixels, respectively. Here, the label where motion exists is assigned 1, and the label where motion does not exist is assigned 0.

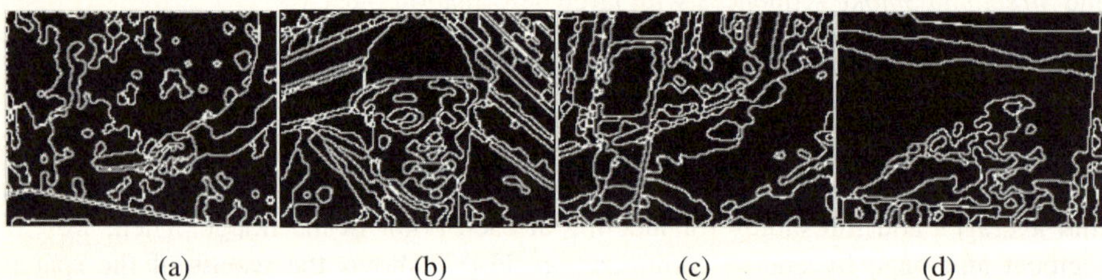

(a)          (b)          (c)          (d)

**Fig. 7.** Spatial segmentation results. (a) *Table tennis.* (b) *Foreman.* (c) *Street.* (d) *Smoke.*

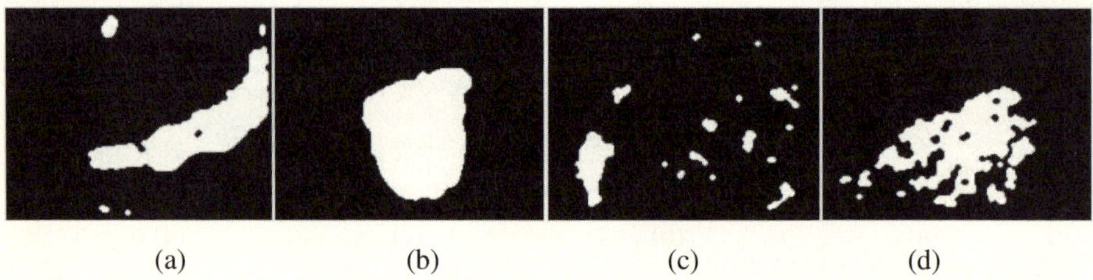

(a)          (b)          (c)          (d)

**Fig. 8.** Temporal segmentation results. (a) *Table tennis.* (b) *Foreman.* (c) *Street.* (d) *Smoke.*

After the spatial and temporal segmentation procedures are performed, both segmentation results are combined to yield final segmentation results. Fig. 9 shows the final segmentation results. Moving objects are captured by the temporal segmentation procedure and the spatial segmentation results precisely represent the object boundaries. These results show that the presented algorithm has good performance in automatic segmentation of the non-rigid objects.

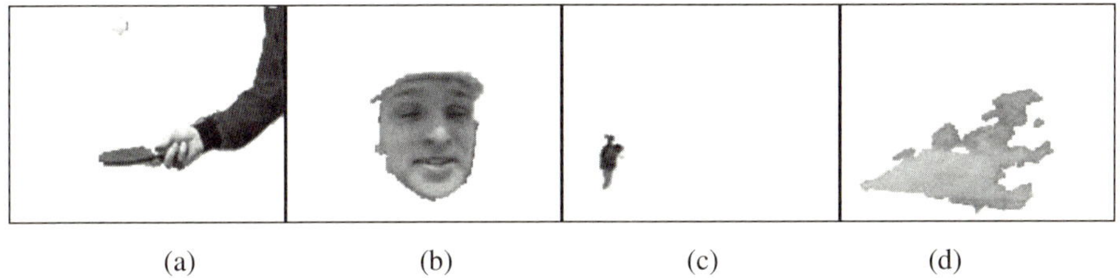

(a)                    (b)                    (c)                    (d)

**Fig. 9.** Final segmentation results. (a) *Table tennis*. (b) *Foreman*. (c) *Street*. (d) *Smoke*.

(a)                                        (b)

**Fig. 10.** Some other non-rigid objects. (a) *Diffusion*. (b) *Cloud*.

(a)                                        (b)

**Fig. 11.** Final segmentation results of the *Diffusion* sequence. (a) $450^{th}$ frame. (b) $465^{th}$ frame. (c) $480^{th}$ frame. (d) $495^{th}$ frame.

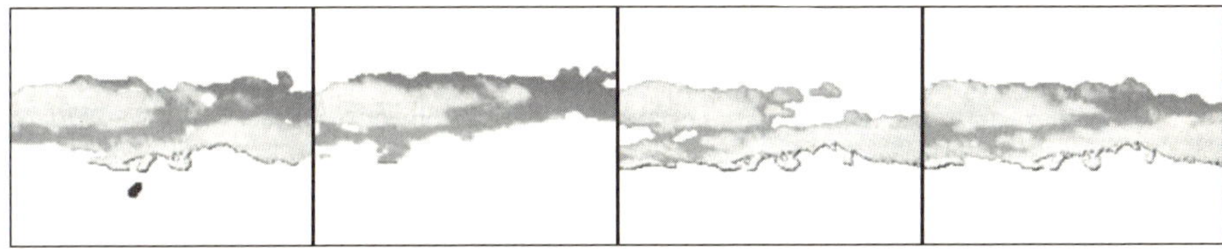

**Fig. 12.** Final segmentation results of the *Cloud* sequence. (a) $7^{th}$ frame. (b) $8^{th}$ frame. (c) $9^{th}$ frame. (d) $10^{th}$ frame.

Experiments are performed on some other non-rigid objects: cloud (*Cloud*) and diffusing dye (*Diffusion*) as shown in Fig. 10. In the *Diffusion* sequence, the water –soluble dye diffuses in water. We have captured 30 frames per second using a digital camcorder (Sony DCR-TRV20). Since the diffusing dye is the object with a fuzzy, blurred, and indefinite boundary, it would be considered as a non-rigid object. In the *Cloud* sequence, the cloud floats around a mountain; this object is also a non-rigid object because the shape changes much over time. 6 frames per hour are captured in this sequence since cloud movement is slow. Figs. 11 and 12 show the segmentation results for the *Diffusion* and *Cloud* sequences, respectively. The diffusing dye in Fig. 11 is well segmented even though the object shape deforms over time. Also, segmented results for the cloud (Fig. 12) satisfactorily track its deforming shape over time.

## 6  Conclusions

In this paper, we present an automatic segmentation algorithm of moving non-rigid objects in image sequences. The segmentation of foreground moving objects from the background is very useful in many contexts. These include domains such as video surveillance, traffic flow measurements, behavior detection, and object based video coding. We designed a robust algorithm for foreground segmentation that combines temporal segmentation using optical flow analysis. We considered random and unpredictable characteristics of the non-rigid objects using a MRF model in both spatial and temporal domains. We carried out various experiments of non-rigid objects, such as smoke, clouds, and diffusing dye. Experimental results show that the presented algorithm performs well in segmenting the non-rigid objects with large deformation rates over time.

Practical applications of the proposed segmentation algorithm would be observation part of the weather forecast using satellite scenes, medical part of the diagnosis of a skin disease, defense part of the watching system using infrared scenes, chemical part of the flow measurement of a gas or bubbles, and environmental part of the analysis of environmental pollution.

## Acknowledgement

An initial version of this paper appeared in the International Conference on Signal Processing (ICSP) [25]. The authors would like to thank the anonymous ICSP and PSIVT reviewers for their valuable comments and suggestions.

## References

1. Spagnolo, P., Orazio, T.D., Leo, M., Distante, A.: Moving object segmentation by background substraction and temporal analysis. Image and Vision Computing 24, 411–423 (2006)
2. Kuo, M., Hsieh, C.H., Huang, Y.R.: Automatic extraction of moving objects for head-shoulder video sequences. Journal of Visual Communication and Image Representation 16, 68–92 (2005)
3. Dimitrova, N., Zhang, H.J., Shahraray, B., Sezan, I., Zakhor, A., Huang, T.: Applications of video content analysis and retrieval. IEEE Multimedia 9, 43–55 (2002)

4. Fan, J., Yu, J., Fujita, G., Onoye, T., Wu, L., Shirakawa, I.: Spatiotemporal segmentation for compact video representation. Signal Processing: Image Communication 16, 553–566 (2001)

5. Kim, M.C., Jeon, J.G., Kwak, J.S., Lee, M.H., Ahn, C.: Moving object segmentation in video sequences by user interaction and automatic object tracking. Image and Vision Computing 19, 245–260 (2001)

6. Aach, T., Kaup, A.: Bayesian algorithms for adaptive change detection in image sequences using Markov random fields. Signal Processing: Image Communication 7, 147–160 (1995)

7. Meier, K., Ngan, N.: Automatic segmentation of moving objects for video object plane generation. IEEE trans. Circuits and Systems for Video Technology 8(5), 525–538 (1998)

8. Kim, M.C., Choi, J.G., Kim, D., Lee, H., Lee, M.H., Ahn, C., Ho, Y.S.: A VOP generation tool: automatic segmentation of moving objects in image sequences based on spatio-temporal information. IEEE Trans. Circuits and Systems for Video Technology 9 (1999)

9. Jung, C., Kim, K.S., Kim, J.K.: Automatic moving object segmentation using automatic region growing algorithm. Journal of Korea Information and Communications Society 26, 187–193 (2001)

10. Luthon, F., Caplier, A., Lievin, M.: Spatiotemporal MRF approach to video segmentation: Application to motion detection and lip segmentation. Signal Processing 76, 61–80 (1999)

11. Grinias, I., Tziritas, G.: A semi-automatic seeded region growing algorithm for video object localization and tracking. Signal Processing: Image Communication 16, 977–986 (2001)

12. Tekalp, A.M.: Digital video processing. Prentice Hall, Englewood Cliffs (1995)

13. Ray, S., Turi, R.H.: Determination of number clusters in K-means clustering and application in colour image segmentation. In: Proc. of ICAPRDT 1999, pp. 137–143 (1999)

14. Gonzalez, R.C., Woods, R.E.: Digital image processing, pp. 443–458. Addison Wesley, Reading (1992)

15. Zimanyi, M.: Reconstruction of tomographic data by Markov random fields. In: Proc. of Central European Seminar on Computer Graphics (1998)

16. Dubes, R.C., Jain, A.K., Nadabar, S.G., Chen, C.C.: MRF model-based algorithms for image segmentation. In: Proc. of ICPR (10 th International Conference on Pattern Recognition), vol. 1, pp. 808–814 (1990)

17. Wei, J., Li, Z.: An efficient two-pass MAP-MRF algorithm for motion estimation based on mean field theory. IEEE Trans. on Circuits and Systems for Video Technology 9, 960–972 (1999)

18. Horn, B.K.P., Schunck, B.G.: Determining optical flow. Artificial Intelligence 17, 185–203 (1981)

19. Barkat, M.: Signal detection & estimation, pp. 115–174. Artech House (1991)

20. Sklar, B.: Digital commnication, pp. 132–138. Prentice Hall, Englewood Cliffs (1988)

21. Jain, R., Kasturi, R., Schunck, B.G.: Machine vision, pp. 25–72. McGraw-Hill, New York (1995)

22. Jung, C., Kim, J.K.: Motion segmentation using Markov random field model for accurate moving object segmentation. In: Proc. of ACM ICUIMC 2008, pp. 414–418 (2008)

23. Zitnick, L., Jojic, N., Kang, S.B.: Consistent segmentation for optical flow estimation. In: Proc. ICCV 2005, pp. 1308–1315 (2005)

24. Chen, J., Tang, C.K.: Spatio-temporal markov random field for video denosing. In: Proc. of IEEE CVPR 2007, pp. 1–8 (2007)

25. Jung, C., Kim, J.K.: Non-rigid object segmentation in video sequences using Markov random field. In: Proc. of ICSP 2002 (6th International Conference on Signal Processing), vol. 1, pp. 624–627 (2002)

# Robust Simultaneous Low Rank Approximation of Tensors


Kohei Inoue, Kenji Hara, and Kiichi Urahama

Kyushu University, Fukuoka 815-8540, Japan
{k-inoue,hara,urahama}@design.kyushu-u.ac.jp



**Abstract.** We propose simultaneous low rank approximation of tensors (SLRAT) for the dimensionality reduction of tensors and modify it to the robust one, i.e., the robust SLRAT. For both the SLRAT and the robust SLRAT, we propose iterative algorithms for solving them. It is experimentally shown that the robust SLRAT achieves lower reconstruction error than the SLRAT when a dataset contains noise data. We also propose a method for classifying sets of tensors and call it the subspace matching, where both training data and testing data are represented by their subspaces, and each testing datum is classified on the basis of the similarity between subspaces. It is experimentally verified that the robust SLRAT achieves higher recognition rate than the SLRAT when the testing data contain noise data.


## 1  Introduction

Dimensionality reduction is an important topic in image processing, pattern recognition, computer vision and data mining researches. Recently, Yang et al. [1] presented two-dimensional principal component analysis (2DPCA) for reducing the dimensions of matrices. In the 2DPCA, each matrix does not need to be transformed into a vector prior to the dimensionality reduction. However, the 2DPCA is approximately equivalent to the traditional PCA operated on the row vectors of matrices [2,3,4]. Ye [5] proposed generalized low rank approximation of matrices (GLRAM). Different from the 2DPCA, the GLRAM reduces the dimensions of both rows and columns of matrices. Inoue and Urahama [6] showed a relationship between the GLRAM and the other non-iterative algorithms. Ding et al. [7] provided the error analysis of these methods and derived error bounds similar to Eckart-Young theorem which plays critical role in the development and application of singular value decomposition (SVD). Lu et al. [8] proposed a multilinear PCA (MPCA) for tensor object feature extraction and discussed the issues of initialization, convergence and subspace dimensionality determination. Huang and Ding [9] proposed robust tensor factorization using $R_1$ norm, i.e., rotationally invariant $L_1$ norm.

In this paper, we propose simultaneous low rank approximation of tensors (SLRAT) which is an extension of the GLRAM to higher-order tensors, and then we modify the SLRAT to its robust version. We also propose a method for classifying sets of tensors, which we call the subspace matching. The proposed


T. Wada, F. Huang, and S. Lin (Eds.): PSIVT 2009, LNCS 5414, pp. 574–584, 2009.

subspace matching method calculates the similarity between subspaces of sets of tensors and classifies each set of tensors on the basis of the similarity. Therefore, using the subspace matching, we can calculate the similarity between two sets of different cardinalities. Experimental results on the ORL face image database, which is a widely used face image database, show the effectiveness of the proposed methods.

The rest of this paper is organized as follows: In Section 2, we propose the SLRAT and derive an iterative solution algorithm. In Section 3, we modify the SLRAT to its robust version and derive an iterative solution algorithm. In Section 4, we propose the subspace matching method for classifying sets of tensors. Experimental results are shown in Section 5, where examples of image reconstruction and face recognition are shown. Section 6 summarizes the main results of this paper.

## 2 Simultaneous Low Rank Approximation of Tensors

In this section, we propose simultaneous low rank approximation of tensors (SLRAT). The notations used in this paper follow De Lathauwer et al. [10,11] and Bader and Kolda [12] mainly.

Let $\mathcal{A}_i = [a_{i_1 \ldots i_N i}] \in \mathbb{R}^{I_1 \times \cdots \times I_N}$ for $i = 1, \ldots, M$, where $a_{i_1 \ldots i_N i}$ is the $(i_1, \ldots, i_N)$ element of $\mathcal{A}_i$ and $\mathbb{R}^{I_1 \times \cdots \times I_N}$ denotes an $(I_1 \times \cdots \times I_N)$-dimensional real space. Then the simultaneous low rank approximation of tensors (SLRAT) is formulated as follows:

$$\min_{U, \{\mathcal{B}_i\}_{i=1}^M} \sum_{i=1}^M \|\mathcal{A}_i - \mathcal{B}_i \times \{U\}\|_F^2 \tag{1}$$

$$\text{subj.to} \quad U^{(n)^T} U^{(n)} = I_{R_n}, \quad n = 1, ..., N, \tag{2}$$

where $U = \{U^{(1)}, ..., U^{(N)}\}$ is a set of $U^{(n)} = [u_{i_n i'_n}^{(n)}] \in \mathbb{R}^{I_n \times R_n}$ for $i_n = 1, \ldots, I_n$, $i'_n = 1, \ldots, R_n$ and $n = 1, ..., N$, and $\mathcal{B}_i \times \{U\} = \mathcal{B}_i \times_1 U^{(1)} \cdots \times_N U^{(N)}$ [12], where $\mathcal{B}_i = [b_{i'_1 \ldots i'_N i}] \in \mathbb{R}^{R_1 \times \cdots \times R_N}$ and $\mathcal{B}_i \times_n U^{(n)} = [\sum_{i'_n=1}^{R_n} b_{i'_1 \ldots i'_n \ldots i'_N i} u_{i_n i'_n}^{(n)}] \in \mathbb{R}^{R_1 \times \cdots \times R_{n-1} \times I_n \times R_{n+1} \times \cdots \times R_N}$ is the $n$-mode product of $\mathcal{B}_i$ and $U^{(n)}$ [10,11]. $\| \cdot \|_F$ denotes the Frobenius norm and $I_{R_n}$ is the $R_n \times R_n$ identity matrix. We assume that $R_n \leq I_n$ for $n = 1, ..., N$. Let $E(U, \{\mathcal{B}\})$ be the objective function in Eq. (1). Then it follows from $\partial E / \partial \mathcal{B}_i = 0$ that

$$\mathcal{B}_i = \mathcal{A}_i \times \{U^T\}, \quad i = 1, ..., M, \tag{3}$$

where $U^T = \{U^{(1)^T}, ..., U^{(M)^T}\}$. By substituting Eq. (3) into $E$ we find that

$$E(U) = \sum_{i=1}^M \|\mathcal{A}_i\|_F^2 - \tilde{E}(U), \tag{4}$$

where

$$\tilde{E}(U) = \sum_{i=1}^M \|\mathcal{A}_i \times \{U^T\}\|_F^2. \tag{5}$$

Since $\sum_{i=1}^{M} \|\mathcal{A}_i\|_F^2$ is a constant, we may rewrite Eq. (1) as follows:

$$\max_{U} \quad \tilde{E}(U). \tag{6}$$

$\tilde{E}(U)$ can be written in the form

$$\tilde{E}(U) = \sum_{i=1}^{M} \left\| \left(\mathcal{A}_i \times_{-n} \{U^T\}\right) \times_n U^{(n)^T} \right\|_F^2 \tag{7}$$

$$= \sum_{i=1}^{M} \left\| U^{(n)^T} \tilde{A}_{i(n)} \right\|_F^2 \tag{8}$$

$$= \mathrm{tr}\left( U^{(n)^T} \tilde{A}_{(n)} U^{(n)} \right), \tag{9}$$

where tr denotes the matrix trace and $\tilde{A}_{(n)} = \sum_{i=1}^{M} \tilde{A}_{i(n)} \tilde{A}_{i(n)}^T$ where $\tilde{A}_{i(n)}$ is the mode-$n$ matricizing [12] or the matrix unfolding [10,11] of

$$\mathcal{A}_i \times_{-n} \{U^T\} = \mathcal{A}_i \times_1 U^{(n)^T} \cdots \times_{n-1} U^{(n-1)^T} \times_{n+1} U^{(n+1)^T} \cdots \times_N U^{(N)^T}. \tag{10}$$

Thus, from Eq. (9), we see that if $U^{(1)}, ..., U^{(n-1)}, U^{(n+1)}, ..., U^{(N)}$ are fixed, then the optimal $U^{(n)}$ is a matrix whose columns are the principal eigenvectors of $\tilde{A}_{(n)}$. Consequently, we obtain an iterative algorithm as follows:

**[SLRAT]**

**Step 0 (Initialization):** Initialize $U^{(n)}$ for $n = 1, \ldots, n$ as $U^{(n,0)} = [v_1^{(n)}, \ldots, v_{R_n}^{(n)}]$ where $v_1^{(n)}, \ldots, v_{R_n}^{(n)}$ are the eigenvectors of $\sum_{i=1}^{M} A_{i(n)} A_{i(n)}^T$ corresponding to the largest $R_n$ eigenvalues, where $A_{i(n)}$ is the mode-$n$ matricizing [12] or the matrix unfolding [10,11] of $\mathcal{A}_i$. Initialize the iteration counter $t$ as $t = 0$. Initialize the root mean squared error (RMSE) at $t = 0$ as $\mathrm{RMSE}^{(0)} = \sqrt{\frac{1}{M} \sum_{i=1}^{M} \|\mathcal{A}_i\|_F^2}$.

**Step 1:** For $n = 1, ..., N$, compute the eigenvectors $u_1^{(n,t+1)}, ..., u_{R_n}^{(n,t+1)}$ of $\sum_{i=1}^{M} \tilde{A}_{i(n,t)} \tilde{A}_{i(n,t)}^T$ corresponding to the largest $R_n$ eigenvalues and form $U^{(n,t+1)} = [u_1^{(n,t+1)}, ..., u_{R_n}^{(n,t+1)}]$, where $\tilde{A}_{i(n,t)}$ is the mode-$n$ matricizing [12] or the matrix unfolding [10,11] of $\mathcal{A}_i \times_{-n} \{U_n^{(t)}\}$ for $U_n^{(t)} = \{U^{(1,t+1)}, ..., U^{(n-1,t+1)}, U^{(n,t)}, ..., U^{(N,t)}\}$.

**Step 2:** Compute the RMSE as

$$\mathrm{RMSE}^{(t+1)} = \sqrt{\frac{1}{M} \sum_{i=1}^{M} \left\| \mathcal{A}_i - \tilde{\mathcal{A}}_i^{(t+1)} \right\|_F^2}, \tag{11}$$

where $\tilde{\mathcal{A}}_i^{(t+1)} = \mathcal{B}_i^{(t+1)} \times \{U^{(t+1)}\}$ for $\mathcal{B}_i^{(t+1)} = \mathcal{A}_i \times \{U^{(t+1)^T}\}$ and $U^{(t+1)} = \{U^{(1,t+1)}, ..., U^{(N,t+1)}\}$. If $(\mathrm{RMSE}^{(t)} - \mathrm{RMSE}^{(t+1)})/\mathrm{RMSE}^{(t)} < \epsilon$ for $\epsilon > 0$ then proceed to the next step, otherwise increase $t$ by 1 and go to Step 1.

**Step 3:** Output $U^* = U_{t+1}$ and $\mathcal{B}_i^* = \mathcal{A}_i \times \{U^{*T}\}$ for $i = 1, ..., M$.

Note that the SLRAT is reduced to the generalized low rank approximation of matrices (GLRAM) presented by Ye [5] when $N = 2$, i.e., the objective function in Eq. (1) is reduced to

$$\sum_{i=1}^{M} \left\| A_i - B_i \times_1 U^{(1)} \times_2 U^{(2)} \right\|_F^2 = \sum_{i=1}^{M} \left\| A_i - U^{(1)} B_i U^{(2)^T} \right\|_F^2, \tag{12}$$

where $A_i \in \mathbb{R}^{I_1 \times I_2}$ and $B_i \in \mathbb{R}^{R_1 \times R_2}$ are the second-order tensors or the matrices. The right hand side of Eq. (12) coincides with the objective function of the GLRAM.

## 3  Robust Simultaneous Low Rank Approximation of Tensors

The SLRAT described in the previous section is formulated as a minimization of the sum of the Frobenius norm. Therefore, The SLRAT is not robust to noise data. In this section, we modify Eq. (1) as follows:

$$\min_{U, \{\mathcal{B}_i\}_{i=1}^{M}} \sum_{i=1}^{M} \rho \left( \|\mathcal{A}_i - \mathcal{B}_i \times \{U\}\|_F \right), \tag{13}$$

where $\rho(x)$ is the Welsch's function commonly used in robust statistics [13]:

$$\rho(x) = 1 - e^{-\alpha x^2}, \tag{14}$$

where $\alpha > 0$. Let $F(U, \{\mathcal{B}_i\})$ be the objective function in Eq. (13). Then we have

$$F(U, \{\mathcal{B}_i\}) = M - \sum_{i=1}^{M} e^{-\alpha \|\mathcal{A}_i - \mathcal{B}_i \times \{U\}\|_F^2}. \tag{15}$$

Since $M$ is a constant, we may rewrite Eq. (13) as follows:

$$\max_{U, \{\mathcal{B}_i\}_{i=1}^{M}} \tilde{F}(U, \{\mathcal{B}_i\}), \tag{16}$$

where

$$\tilde{F}(U, \{\mathcal{B}_i\}) = M - F(U, \{\mathcal{B}_i\}) = \sum_{i=1}^{M} e^{-\alpha \|\mathcal{A}_i - \mathcal{B}_i \times \{U\}\|_F^2}. \tag{17}$$

Then it follows from $\partial \tilde{F} / \partial \mathcal{B}_i = 0$ that

$$\mathcal{B}_i = \mathcal{A}_i \times \{U^T\}, \quad i = 1, \ldots, M, \tag{18}$$

where $U^T = \{U^{(1)^T}, \dots, U^{(N)^T}\}$. Also, we have

$$\frac{\partial \tilde{F}}{\partial U^{(n)}} = 2\alpha \sum_{i=1}^{M} \left( A_{i(n)} - U^{(n)} \tilde{B}_{i(n)} \right) \tilde{B}_{i(n)}^T e^{-\alpha \|\mathcal{A}_i - \mathcal{B}_i \times \{U\}\|_F^2}, \qquad (19)$$

where $A_{i(n)}$ and $\tilde{B}_{i(n)}$ are the mode-$n$ matricizing [12] or the matrix unfolding [10,11] of $\mathcal{A}_i$ and $\mathcal{B}_i \times_{-n} \{U\} = \mathcal{B}_i \times_1 U^{(1)} \cdots \times_{n-1} U^{(n-1)} \times_{n+1} U^{(n+1)} \cdots \times_N U^{(N)}$, respectively. From $\partial \tilde{F}/\partial U^{(n)} = 0$, we have

$$U^{(n)} = \sum_{i=1}^{M} A_{i(n)} \tilde{B}_{i(n)}^T e^{-\alpha \|\mathcal{A}_i - \mathcal{B}_i \times \{U\}\|_F^2} \left( \sum_{i=1}^{M} \tilde{B}_{i(n)} \tilde{B}_{i(n)}^T e^{-\alpha \|\mathcal{A}_i - \mathcal{B}_i \times \{U\}\|_F^2} \right)^{-1}.$$

$$(20)$$

Since the right hand side of Eq. (20) contains $U^{(n)}$ in $\{U\}$, we cannot solve Eq. (20) with respect to $U^{(n)}$ analytically. Instead, we solve Eq. (20) by an iterative algorithm. First, we initialize $U^{(n)}$ as $U^{(n,0)} = [v_1^{(n)}, \dots, v_{R_n}^{(n)}]$ where $v_1^{(n)}, \dots, v_{R_n}^{(n)}$ are the eigenvectors of $\sum_{i=1}^{M} A_{i(n)} A_{i(n)}^T$ corresponding to the largest $R_n$ eigenvalues. Next, we update $U^{(n)}$ as

$$\tilde{U}^{(n,t+1)} = \sum_{i=1}^{M} A_{i(n)} \tilde{B}_{i(n,t)}^T e^{-\alpha \left\| \mathcal{A}_i - \tilde{\mathcal{A}}_i^{(t)} \right\|_F^2} \left( \sum_{i=1}^{M} \tilde{B}_{i(n,t)} \tilde{B}_{i(n,t)}^T e^{-\alpha \left\| \mathcal{A}_i - \tilde{\mathcal{A}}_i^{(t)} \right\|_F^2} \right)^{-1},$$

$$(21)$$

where $t$ is the number of iterations, $\tilde{\mathcal{A}}_i^{(t)} = \mathcal{B}_i^{(t)} \times \{U^{(t)}\}$ for $\mathcal{B}_i^{(t)} = \mathcal{A}_i \times \{U^{(t)^T}\}$ and $U^{(t)} = \{U^{(1,t)}, \dots, U^{(N,t)}\}$, and $\tilde{B}_{i(n,t)}$ is the mode-$n$ matricizing [12] or the matrix unfolding [10,11] of $\mathcal{B}_i^{(t)} \times_{-n} \{U^{(t)}\}$. Since Eq. (21) can be written as

$$\tilde{U}^{(n,t+1)} = U^{(n,t)} + \frac{1}{2\alpha} \frac{\partial \tilde{F}^{(t)}}{\partial U^{(n,t)}} \left( \sum_{i=1}^{M} \tilde{B}_{i(n,t)} \tilde{B}_{i(n,t)}^T e^{-\alpha \left\| \mathcal{A}_i - \tilde{\mathcal{A}}_i^{(t)} \right\|_F^2} \right)^{-1}, \qquad (22)$$

this iterative algorithm can be interpreted as a gradient method [14]. Lastly, we orthogonalize $\tilde{U}^{(n,t+1)}$ as $U^{(n,t+1)} = \mathrm{orth}(\tilde{U}^{(n,t+1)})$, where $\mathrm{orth}(\cdot)$ is an orthogonalization function, in order to satisfy the constraints in Eq. (2). The above procedure is repeated until it converges. The proposed iterative algorithm is summarized as follows:

**[Robust SLRAT]**

**Step 0 (Initialization):** Initialize $U^{(n)}$ for $n = 1, \dots, n$ as $U^{(n,0)} = [v_1^{(n)}, \dots, v_{R_n}^{(n)}]$ where $v_1^{(n)}, \dots, v_{R_n}^{(n)}$ are the eigenvectors of $\sum_{i=1}^{M} A_{i(n)} A_{i(n)}^T$ corresponding to the largest $R_n$ eigenvalues. Initialize the iteration counter $t$ as $t = 0$. Initialize the root mean squared error (RMSE) at $t = 0$ as $\mathrm{RMSE}^{(0)} = \sqrt{\frac{1}{M} \sum_{i=1}^{M} \|\mathcal{A}_i\|_F^2}$.

**Step 1:** Compute $\tilde{U}^{(n,t+1)}$ for $n = 1, \dots, n$ using Eq. (21).

**Step 2:** Orthogonalize $\tilde{U}^{(n,t+1)}$ for $n = 1,\ldots,N$ as $U^{(n,t+1)} = \mathrm{orth}(\tilde{U}^{(n,t+1)})$.
Compute $\mathcal{B}_i^{(t+1)} = \mathcal{A}_i \times \{U^{(t+1)^T}\}$ for $i = 1,\ldots,M$.
**Step 3:** Compute the RMSE as

$$\mathrm{RMSE}^{(t+1)} = \sqrt{\frac{1}{M}\sum_{i=1}^{M}\left\|\mathcal{A}_i - \tilde{\mathcal{A}}_i^{(t+1)}\right\|_F^2}. \tag{23}$$

If $(\mathrm{RMSE}^{(t)} - \mathrm{RMSE}^{(t+1)})/\mathrm{RMSE}^{(t)} < \epsilon$ for $\epsilon > 0$ then proceed to the next
step, otherwise increase $t$ by 1 and go to Step 1.
**Step 4:** Output $U^* = U^{(t+1)}$ and $\mathcal{B}_i^* = \mathcal{B}_i^{(t+1)}$ for $i = 1,\ldots,M$.

In our implementation, we used MATLAB orth function in Step 2 of the above
procedure.


## 4    Subspace Matching for Classifying Sets of Tensors

In this section, we propose a method for classifying sets of tensors.

Let $\mathcal{A}_{i_c} \in \mathbb{R}^{I_1 \times \cdots \times I_N}$ for $i_c = 1,\ldots,M_c$ and $c = 1,\ldots,C$ be a set of tensors
for training, where $C$ is the number of classes. Then, for each class $c$, we solve
the following optimization problem:

$$\min_{U_c,\,\{\mathcal{B}_{ic}\}_{i=1}^{M_c}} \sum_{i_c=1}^{M_c} \rho\left(\left\|\mathcal{A}_{i_c} - \mathcal{B}_{i_c} \times \{U_c\}\right\|_F\right) \tag{24}$$

$$\mathrm{subj.to} \quad U_c^{(n)^T} U_c^{(n)} = I_{R_n}, \quad n = 1,...,N, \tag{25}$$

where $U_c = \{U_c^{(1)},\ldots,U_c^{(N)}\}$ is a set of $U_c^{(n)} \in \mathbb{R}^{I_n \times R_n}$ for $n = 1,\ldots,N$, and
$\mathcal{B}_{i_c} \in \mathbb{R}^{R_1 \times \cdots \times R_N}$. Let $U_c^* = \{U_{c*}^{(1)},\ldots,U_{c*}^{(N)}\}$ be the solution of Eq. (24) with
(25). Then we store $U_c^*$ for $c = 1,\ldots,C$ and use them for classifying test sets of
tensors to be classified.

Let $\mathcal{A}_i \in \mathbb{R}^{I_1 \times \cdots \times I_N}$ for $i = 1,\ldots,M$ be a set of tensors to be classified.
Then we solve the optimization problem in Eq. (13) with Eq. (2). Let $U^* = \{U_*^{(1)},\ldots,U_*^{(N)}\}$ be the solution of the optimization problem. Then we classify
the set of tensors into the $c^*$th class selected by the following rule:

$$c^* = \arg\max_{c\in\{1,...,C\}} S(U_c^*, U^*), \tag{26}$$

where $S(U_c^*, U^*)$ is a similarity between $U_c^*$ and $U^*$, and is defined as follows:

$$S(U_c^*, U^*) = \max_{\{x_{i_n}\},\{y_{i_n}\}} \sum_{n=1}^{N}\sum_{i_n=1}^{R_n} x_{i_n}^T \left|U_{c*}^{(n)^T} U_*^{(n)}\right|_{\mathrm{abs}} y_{i_n} \tag{27}$$

$$\mathrm{subj.to} \quad x_{i_n}^T x_{i_n'} = \delta_{i_n i_n'}, \quad y_{i_n}^T y_{i_n'} = \delta_{i_n i_n'}, \tag{28}$$

$$x_{i_n j_n} \in \{0,1\}, \quad y_{i_n j_n} \in \{0,1\}, \tag{29}$$

where $x_{i_n} = [x_{i_n j_n}] \in \mathbb{R}^{R_n}$ and $y_{i_n} = [y_{i_n j_n}] \in \mathbb{R}^{R_n}$ for $j_n = 1, \ldots, R_n$, $\delta$ is the Kronecker delta, and $|A|_{\mathrm{abs}}$ denotes the absolute value of a matrix $A$ [15]. The optimization problem in Eq. (27), (28) and (29) is no less than the assignment problem. We compute the optimal solution using Munkres algorithm [16].

An advantage of the proposed classification method is that the proposed method can accept various numbers of tensors in each set for training or testing, because the sizes of $U_c$ and $U$ are independent of $M_c$ and $M$, respectively.

## 5    Experimental Results

In this section, we experimentally evaluate the performance of the robust SLRAT on the ORL face image database. The ORL database [17] contains face images of 40 persons. For each person, there are 10 different images. That is, the total number of the images in the database is 400. The size of each image is $112 \times 92$ pixels, i.e., $I_1 = 112$, $I_2 = 92$.

The reconstruction errors for $R_1 = R_2 = 20$, $R_1 = R_2 = 30$ and $R_1 = R_2 = 40$ are shown in Fig. 2(a), (b) and (c), respectively.

### 5.1    Image Reconstruction

We first demonstrate the robustness of the proposed robust SLRAT using the ORL face images. Some example images are shown in Fig. 1, where the first three persons in the database are selected and presented in Fig. 1(a), (b) and (c), respectively. For each person, the original images are shown in the first row, in which a noise image is added (the rightmost image). The reconstructed images with the conventional and the robust SLRATs for $R_1 = R_2 = 30$ are shown in the second and the third rows for each person in Fig. 1(a), (b) and (c), respectively. The reconstructed images with the conventional SLRAT (the second rows) are disturbed by the added noise images. On the other hand, the reconstructed images with the robust SLRAT (the third rows) are less sensitive to the noise images than that of the conventional SLRAT.

We set $\alpha = 10^{-6}$ for the robust SLRAT and $\epsilon = 10^{-6}$ for both the conventional and the robust SLRATs.

The errors are measured by the RMSE for the face images except the noise images. In each figure, the horizontal axis denotes the number of noise images per person, and the vertical axis denotes the RMSE. The robust and the conventional SLRATs are denoted by solid lines with "+" marks and broken lines with "$\times$" marks, respectively. The RMSEs for the robust SLRAT are lower than that for the conventional SLRAT. Although the RMSEs for the conventional SLRAT increase with the number of noise images, the RMSEs for the robust SLRAT are almost constant.

### 5.2    Face Recognition

We next show the experimental results of face recognition by the subspace matching method described in Sec. 4. From the ORL database [17], we select the first

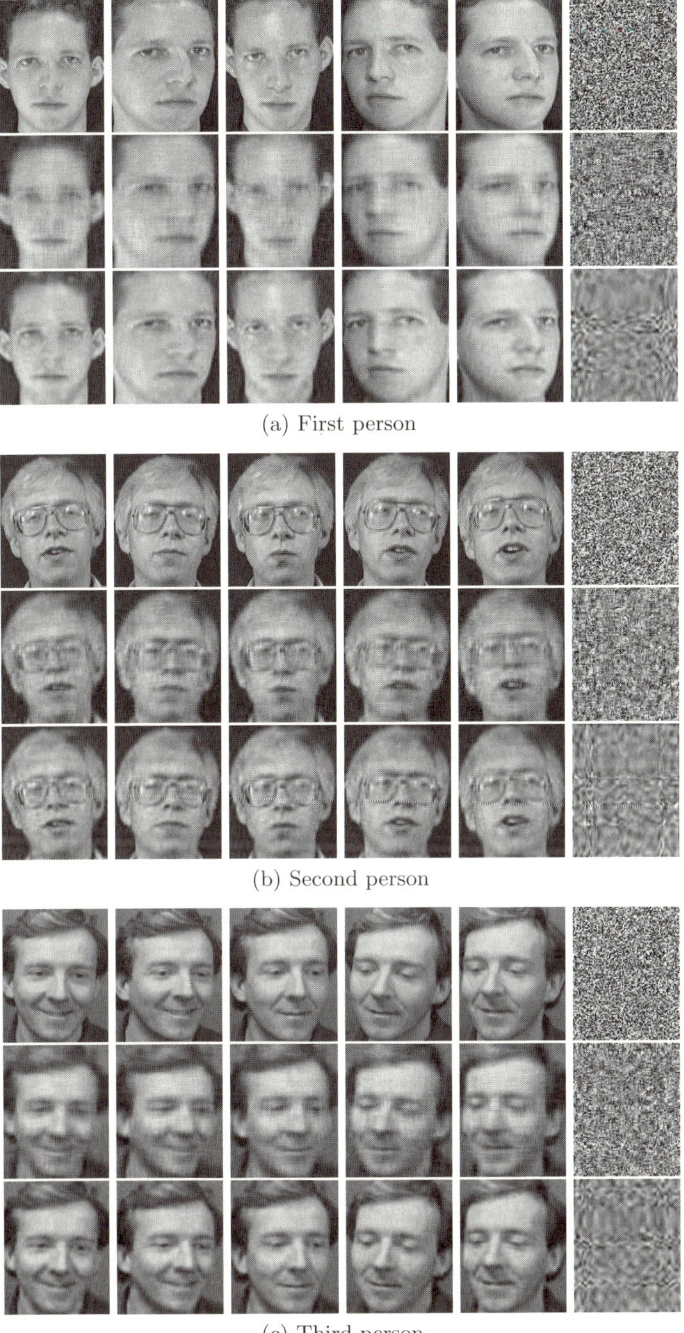



(a) First person

(b) Second person

(c) Third person

**Fig. 1.** Example images: for each person, input images, reconstructed images with the conventional and the robust SLRATs are shown in the top, middle and bottom rows, respectively

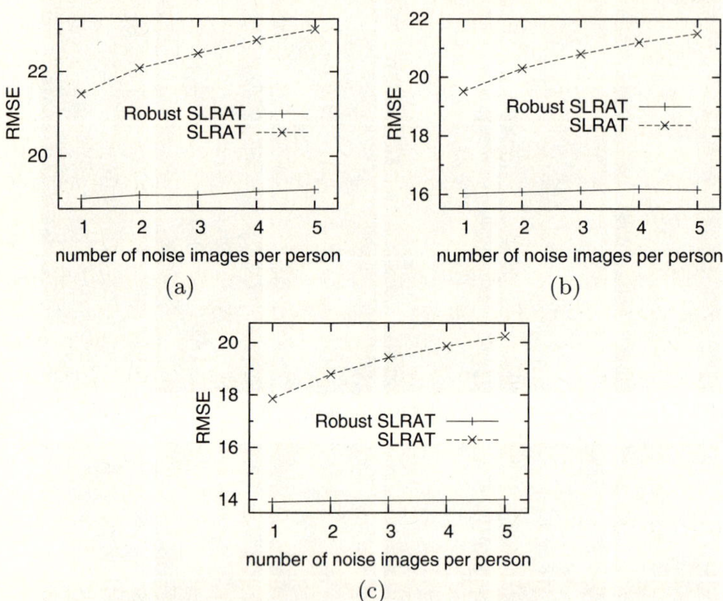

**Fig. 2.** Reconstruction errors: (a) $R_1 = R_2 = 20$, (b) $R_1 = R_2 = 30$, (c) $R_1 = R_2 = 40$

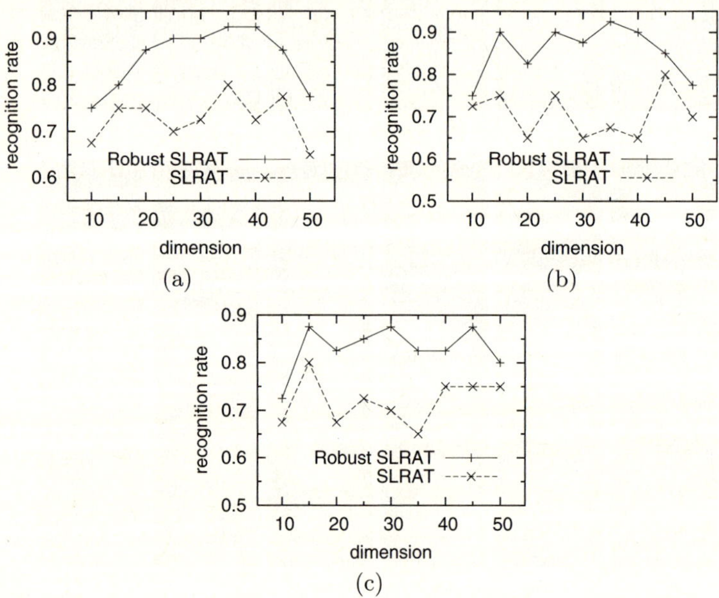

**Fig. 3.** Recognition rates: (a) $K = 1$, (b) $K = 2$, (c) $K = 3$

five images per person for training, and the remaining five images for testing. The number of classes coincides with that of persons in the database, i.e., $C = 40$. In the training phase, for each class $c$, we compute $U_c^*$ for $c = 1, \ldots, C$ and store them. In the testing phase, in order to verify the robustness of the proposed robust SLRAT, we include noise images in the set of test images. For each person, we add $K = 1, 2, 3$ noise images and then compute $U^*$. Each set of test images with several noise images is classified on the basis of the classification rule described in Eq. (26).

The recognition rates for $K = 1, 2$ and 3 are shown in Fig. 3(a), (b) and (c), respectively. In each figure, the horizontal axis denotes the reduced dimension $R$ of each mode. We set $R_1$ and $R_2$ as $R_1 = R_2 = R$ for simplifying our experiments. The vertical axis denotes the recognition rate. The robust and the conventional SLRATs are denoted by solid lines with "+" marks and broken lines with "×" marks, respectively. The recognition rates for the robust SLRAT are higher than that for the conventional SLRAT.


## 6    Conclusion

In this paper, we have formulated simultaneous low rank approximation of tensors (SLRAT) as an optimization problem and modified it to the robust one. For both the SLRAT and the robust SLRAT, we proposed iterative algorithms for solving them. It is experimentally shown that the robust SLRAT achieves lower reconstruction errors than the conventional SLRAT. We also proposed a method for classifying sets of tensors, the subspace matching, where both training data and testing data are represented by their subspaces. The similarity between two subspaces are calculated by using Munkres algorithm [16] for assignment problems. The proposed classification method is applied to the example of face recognition on the ORL database [17]. It is experimentally verified that the robust SLRAT achieves higher recognition rates than the conventional SLRAT.


## Acknowledgment

This work was partially supported by Grant-in-Aid for Young Scientists (B) No. 20700165.


## References

1. Yang, J., Zhang, D., Frangi, A.F., Yang, J.: Two-dimensional PCA: A new approach to appearance-based face representation and recognition. IEEE Trans. Pattern Anal. Mach. Intell. 26, 131–137 (2004)
2. Wang, L., Wang, X., Zhang, X., Feng, J.: The equivalence of two-dimensional PCA to line-based PCA. Pattern Recognition Letters 26, 57–60 (2005)
3. Gao, Q.: Is two-dimensional PCA equivalent to a special case of modular PCA? Pattern Recognition Letters 28, 1250–1251 (2007)

4. Zhang, D., Chen, S., Liu, J.: Representing image matrices: Eigenimages versus eigenvectors. In: Wang, J., Liao, X.-F., Yi, Z. (eds.) ISNN 2005. LNCS, vol. 3497, pp. 659–664. Springer, Heidelberg (2005)
5. Ye, J.: Generalized low rank approximations of matrices. Machine Learning 61, 167–191 (2005)
6. Inoue, K., Urahama, K.: Equivalence of non-iterative algorithms for simultaneous low rank approximations of matrices. In: IEEE Proc. CVPR, pp. 154–159 (2006)
7. Ding, C., Huang, H., Luo, D.: Tensor Reduction Error Analysis – Applications to Video Compression and Classification. In: Proc. CVPR (2008)
8. Lu, H., Plataniotis, K.N., Venetsanopoulos, A.N.: MPCA: Multilinear principal component analysis of tensor objects. IEEE Trans. Pattern Anal. Mach. Intell. 19, 18–39 (2008)
9. Huang, H., Ding, C.: Robust Tensor Factorization Using R1-Norm. In: Proc. CVPR (2008)
10. De Lathauwer, L., De Moor, B., Vandewalle, J.: A multilinear singular value decomposition. SIAM J. Matrix Anal. Appl. 21, 1253–1278 (2000)
11. De Lathauwer, L., De Moor, B., Vandewalle, J.:On the best rank-1 and rank-$(R_1, R_2, ..., R_N)$ approximation of higher-order tensors. SIAM J. Matrix Anal. Appl. 21, 1324–1342 (2000)
12. Bader, B.W., Kolda, T.G.: Algorithm 862: MATLAB tensor classes for fast algorithm prototyping. ACM Trans. Math. Software 32, 635–653 (2006)
13. Huber, P.J.: Robust Statistics. Wiley, Chichester (1981)
14. Ortega, J.M., Rheinboldt, W.G.: Iterative Solution of Nonlinear Equations in Several Variables. Academic Press, NY (1970)
15. Lütkepohl, H.: Handbook of Matrices. John Wiley & Sons, Chichester (1996)
16. Munkres, J.: Algorithms for the Assignment and Transportation Problems. Journal of the Society of Industrial and Applied Mathematics 5, 32–38 (1957)
17. Samaria, F., Harter, A.: Parameterisation of a stochastic model for human face identification. In: Proc. 2nd IEEE Workshop on Appl. Comput. Vision (1994)

# Video-Based Modeling of Dynamic Hair

Tatsuhisa Yamaguchi[1,*], Bennett Wilburn[2], and Eyal Ofek[3]

[1] Kyoto University
`yamaguti@vision.kuee.kyoto-u.ac.jp`
[2] Microsoft Research Asia
`bennett.wilburn@microsoft.com`
[3] Microsoft Corporation
`eyalofek@microsoft.com`

**Abstract.** We present a method for creating realistic hair animation models based on videos of real hair in motion. We use an array of synchronized cameras to capture dynamic hairstyles. The hair structure and motion is modeled using an algorithm that grows each hair in segments from the root to the tip. Our algorithm generates hairs that are consistent with hair orientations observed in the input images and also enforces temporal smoothness constraints on the shape of the hair from frame to frame. Examples of synthesized hair models show the effectiveness of the method.

## 1  Introduction

As computer graphics technologies for rendering human skin and hair improve, accurately modeling the structure and motion of realistic hairstyles is becoming one limiting factor for creating lifelike renderings of people. Modeling hair is difficult because there are typically over 100,000 hairs on a human head, the hairs themselves are very thin, and the interactions can be complex. Moreover, there is currently no standard physically-based model for the mechanics of hair [1]. One approach to creating realistic dynamic hair motions, or studying the properties of hair to create a physically-based model, would be to capture the structure and motion of real, moving hair styles. The number of hairs and their fine structure make this quite challenging. The texture of hair is very self-similar, making it difficult to compute its three-dimensional structure or to track individual hairs from frame to frame.

We present a system for creating dynamic hair models by capturing the approximate structure and motion of real, moving hairstyles. Our system has two main components. The first is a set of cameras that record synchronized videos of moving hair. To prevent motion blur, we use strobe lights to capture images with a very short effective exposure time. The second component of the system is an algorithm that generates hair positions that are consistent with the input images. We strive to ensure that the hairs lie within the hair volume computed for each frame in the input videos, that their orientations are consistent with the two-dimensional orientations measured in the input views, and that their shapes do not change drastically from one time instant to the next. To our knowledge, our system is the first for automatically capturing dynamic hair styles.

---

* This work was done while the author was visiting Microsoft Research Asia.

T. Wada, F. Huang, and S. Lin (Eds.): PSIVT 2009, LNCS 5414, pp. 585–596, 2009.

In the next section, we discuss prior art for capturing static hair models. Section 3 describes our approach to capturing and modeling moving hair, and Section 4 details our specific implementation. In Section 5, we present experimental results. Finally, we close with a discussion of the limitations of our method and avenues for future work.

## 2  Related Work

For an excellent survey of hair modeling, simulation and rendering, we refer the reader to Ward et al. [1]. Several methods are capable of modeling static hairstyles from real images. Some use constraints provided by varying illumination [2,3], while others use multiple view geometry [4,5]. Wei et al. [5] capture many images of a static hairstyle from different viewpoints and measure 2D hair orientations in the images to determine 3D hair orientations. Their algorithm attempts to grow hairs, starting from the scalp, in such a way that the hair orientations match the input views. Paris et al. [6] recently demonstrated a system for capturing the shape and appearance of real hairstyles. They capture images from multiple viewpoints under multiple illumination conditions to create very high-quality hair shape and appearance models. They create geometric models using a plane sweep of light from video projectors and require images taken under different lighting conditions, so the method does not extend to moving hair.

## 3  Image-Based Dynamic Hair Modeling

We model hair using a hair-growing approach based on orientation information from multiple images, similar to Wei et al. [5]. To handle moving hair, though, we use a synchronized video camera array to simultaneously film the hair from many different viewpoints. We model each hair as a piecewise linear curve with equal length segments, and compute the 3D line segment positions for every frame in the input video. In this paper, "viewpoints" and "frames" refer to the spatial positions and the times at which we record the hair, respectively. Our cameras are synchronized such that at every frame, we simultaneously capture an image from every camera.

Applying Wei et al.'s algorithm independently to each frame in the multi-view video would not guarantee temporal consistency of the recovered hair geometry. The main contribution of this work is a hair growth algorithm that includes constraints for temporal continuity. Starting from the root for a given hair, the algorithm adds each new hair segment in parallel across all the frames of the video. Thus, starting from the root of a specific hair, we compute the endpoints of the first segment for that hair in all frames of the video, then the endpoints of the second segment for that hair in all frames of the video, and so on. For each segment, we optimize so that the hair growth direction at each frame is as consistent with the input images as possible, and so that the hair shape and motion varies smoothly from frame to frame.

In the next subsection, we describe the capture and preprocessing of multi-view videos of moving hair. The preprocessing includes generating visual hulls for the hair volume at each frame in the video and computing the two-dimensional hair orientation in the input images. Section 3.2 describes how we use this data to compute estimates of the 3D hair orientation, based on the input images, for any given point in the hair volume. In section 3.3 we explain how we use those estimates along with smoothness constraints for the hair shape and motion to create a temporally consistent model of the moving hairstyle.

## 3.1  Capture and Preprocessing

*Multi-viewpoint video capture.*  We assume that $N_f$ frames have been captured by $N_c$ video cameras, meaning a total of $N_f N_c$ images are the input to the system. Hair often moves rapidly enough to cause motion blur in videos, which makes it much more difficult to estimate hair orientation and segment the hair from the background. We use a set of strobe lights synchronized to the cameras to create a very short effective exposure time. There are no other light sources in our system, and the strobe flash is intense but very brief, so the cameras capture blur-free, bright images regardless of their minimum exposure time.

*Image segmentation.*  For every input image, we generate a pair of binary mask images that represent two different image segmentations. The first one is a silhouette mask which identifies the non-background region, including the subject's hair and skin. The second one is a hair mask which only segments the visible hair. We use the silhouette masks to create a visual hull [7] of the subject. The hair masks are used to limit the possible locations for hair roots and to restrict hair growth to regions where hair is present in the images.

*Modeling the hair volume and scalp.*  Our hair growth algorithm requires a model of the hair volume for each frame in order to compute which cameras view a given hair tip and to know when the modeled hair grows out of the observed hair volume. We bound the hair volume by an inner scalp surface and an outer hair surface. We denote the hair surface in frame $k$ as $S_{\mathtt{hair}}^{k}$ and the scalp surface as $S_{\mathtt{scalp}}^{k}$. $S_{\mathtt{hair}}^{k}$ is approximated using the visual hull reconstructed from the silhouette masks at each frame. The scalp surface, $S_{\mathtt{scalp}}^{k}$, is approximated by fitting a generic head model to the video and the reconstructed visual hull. For a moving head, one must manually or automatically track the head motion. For simplicity, we do not attempt to track head pose in this work. Instead we capture moving hair on a still head, allowing us to focus purely on hair modeling.

*Hair root generation.*  Our hair growth algorithm requires initial locations for the hair roots. We evenly distribute root positions over the scalp surface $S_{\mathtt{scalp}}^{k}$ wherever the hair masks show hair. We assume that the root positions are fixed relative to the scalp model and generate them using the model from the first frame.

*2D hair orientation.*  As we explain later, our hair growth algorithm estimates the observed three-dimensional growth direction at the tip of each growing hair. To do this, we must first compute the two-dimensional orientation of the local texture at each hair pixel, for every frame in all of the input videos. We adapted the filtering method developed by Paris et al[3] to compute hair orientation. Their method applies oriented edge detection filters at many angles, computes a filter response curve, and then selects the orientation at which the filter response is strongest. They produce a pair of values per pixel: a line orientation angle and a variance. The line orientation is an angle in $[0, \pi)$ that encodes the line direction in the image. The variance is a positive real value whose inverse represents the edge intensity and the certainty at each pixel.

## 3.2   Static Three Dimensional Hair Orientation

As our hair modeling algorithm grows a single hair, it estimates the observed three dimensional hair orientation at the tips of the hair in every frame. This observed direction is computed independently for each frame, based solely on the input images from that frame, in a manner very similar to that of Wei et al. [5]. We briefly describe the method here, and refer the reader to their paper for more details.

We define a vector function for each frame $k$ that maps a point $P$ to its estimated orientation $D_k(P)$:

$$D_k(P) = o, D_k : \mathbf{R}^3 \rightarrow \{o|o \in \mathbf{R}^3, ||o|| = 1\} \cup \{\phi\} \tag{1}$$

Here, $\phi$ indicates that too few cameras viewed $p$, and thus we cannot estimate the hair orientation. The direction, $o$, is a three-dimensional vector of unit length. For each hair tip position and frame, we compute which cameras view that point, then triangulate the observed two-dimensional orientations to produce the estimated three-dimensional orientation.

*Computing hair visibility.* Given a hair tip at position $P$, we first compute which cameras view that point. For points on the hair surface, we can use the hair surface to determine visibility. The visibility at the surface can be computed once for each frame and stored. The visibility for points within the hair volume is defined to be the same as that of the closest point $P'$ on $S_{\text{hair}}^k$. For such points, the projection point of $P$ on each image does not truly reflect the 3D orientation of the hair fiber at $P$, but we assume that the orientations at the surface are similar to the orientation within the volume. When we compute the 3D orientation of $P$, we average the orientation over the image area corresponding to the projection of a sphere that is centered at $P$ with radius $\overline{PP'}$. This is a heuristic to obtain smoother orientations inside the hair volume.

*Orientation triangulation.* For each camera that views the hair tip, the computed 2D image orientation at the projection of $P$ defines a line in the image. The camera center and this line define a plane with unit normal $n$ in 3D world coordinates. If the 3D hair orientation $o$ matches the observed orientation in the image, the hair must grow along this plane, meaning that $(n \cdot o) = 0$. Each camera $j$ that views the hair tip yields a normal $n_j$, and thus one linear homogeneous equation $(n_j \cdot o) = 0$. If at least two camera views are available, and barring degenerate cases, we can solve for the 3D hair direction. If more are available, we compute an estimate of the true 3D hair direction based on the observed orientations and accounting for the confidence in the observations. We solve for the orientation $o$ by minimizing

$$\Sigma_j \frac{1}{\sigma_j^2} (n_j \cdot o)^2, \text{subject to} ||o|| = 1, \tag{2}$$

where $\sigma_j$ is the variance of the orientation filter response curve at that position. Eq.2 is a linear optimization problem that is efficiently solved by singular value decomposition. The direction for $o$ is ambiguous; if $o$ is a solution, $-o$ is, too. This ambiguity is resolved by choosing the direction that forms the largest angle with the computed hair growth direction of the previous segment.

## 3.3 Temporally Consistent Hair Models

Once we have the hair volume model, 2D orientation information for the input images, and the initial hair root locations and growth directions, we can begin to grow hair segments from the roots. We add segments one by one to each hair and determine the growth direction of each new segment in all frames by optimizing an energy function that has terms for data consistency and smoothness. Figure 1 shows an example of the known and unknown quantities during the optimization for segment $l$ on a hair. The position of the current hair tip is known for all frames (shown as $P_k^{l-1}, P_{k+1}^{l-1}, P_{k+2}^{l-1}, ...$) as well as the previous growth directions $d_k^{l-1}$ for all $k$. These quantities are expressed in world coordinates. As described in the previous subsection, we can compute an estimate of the observed 3D hair orientation for each frame, shown as $o_k^l, o_{k+1}^l, o_{k+2}^l, ....$. To add a new hair segment to the hair, we simultaneously solve for the growth direction of the segment in all frames, i.e. $d_k^l$ for all $k$. Because the segment length is fixed, this also determines the new hair tip positions, $P_k^l$ for all $k$. Not shown in the figure are $P_k^0$ and $d_k^0$, the root position and the initial growth direction for the hair, and $L_s$, the length of each hair segment (a user-specified parameter for the algorithm).

Algorithm 1 summarizes our method in pseudocode. Each hair is grown independently from the others. We attempt to ensure that each new hair segment's 3D orientations in each frame are consistent with the observed 2D orientations in the videos, that the hair stays within the observed hair volume, and that the hair shape varies smoothly from frame to frame. We formulate these constraints as minimizing an energy with terms for orientation consistency, shape smoothness, motion smoothness, curvature and surface potential (described below) as follows:

$$E(\{d_k^l\}_{k=0,1,...,N_f-1}) = E_o + \alpha_1 E_s + \alpha_2 E_{ss} + \alpha_3 E_c + \alpha_4 E_B \qquad (3)$$

Here, $\alpha_1, \alpha_2, \alpha_3, \alpha_4 \in \mathbf{R}$ are manually specified weights for each term.

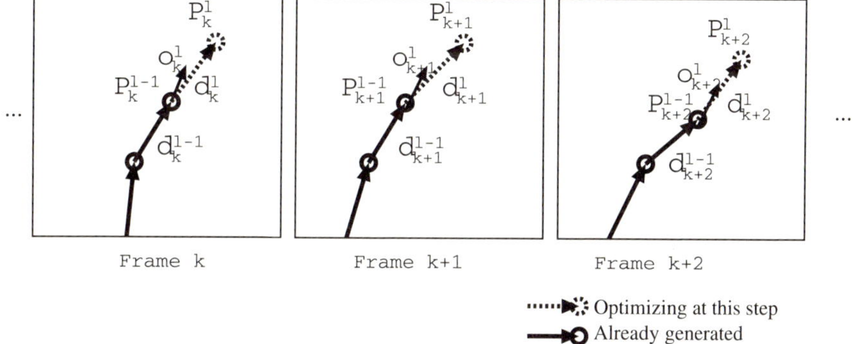


**Fig. 1.** Notation for the hair growing algorithm. See the text for details.

---

**Algorithm 1.** HAIR GROWTH ALGORITHM

---

Capture synchronized, multi-viewpoint videos of a moving hair style.
**for all** input images **do**
    Compute silhouette and hair masks.
    Compute 2D hair orientation at each pixel.
**end for**
Fit scalp model $S^k_{\mathrm{scalp}}$ to first frame of input videos.
**for all** frames **do**
    Compute subject's visual hull, $S^k_{\mathrm{hair}}$
**end for**
Compute initial hair root positions and growth directions.
**for all** hairs **do**
    Initialize hair root position and growth direction, $P^0_0$ and $d^0_0$
    $l \leftarrow 0$
    **repeat**
        $l \leftarrow l + 1$
        Add a new hair segment, computing $P^l_k$ and $d^l_k$ for that segment in each frame $k$ as follows:
        **for all** time frames $k = \{0, 1, \ldots, N_f - 1\}$ **do**
            Independently compute observed 3D hair orientations $o^l_k$ at hair tips $P^{l-1}_k$ as described in section 3.2
        **end for**
        Jointly compute $\{d^l_k\}_{k=0,1,\ldots,N_f-1}$, the growth directions for this segment in all frames, using the optimization described in section 3.3.
        **for all** time frames $k = \{0, 1, \ldots, N_f - 1\}$ **do**
            Compute new hair tip points $P^l_k = P^{l-1}_k + L_s d^l_k$.
        **end for**
    **until** $P^l_k$ is outside the hair volume, for any $k$
**end for**

---

$E_o$ measures the consistency of the 3D hair growth direction with the orientation estimated from the images:

$$E_o = \sum_{k=0}^{N_f-1} \mathtt{dist}(d^l_k, o^l_k), \tag{4}$$

Here, $\mathtt{dist}(a, b) = (1 - a \cdot b)^2$ is a distance function for a pair of unit vectors which is always non-negative. The value of this function is defined as 0 when either $a$ or $b$ is $\phi$, i.e. when the orientations $o^l_k$ are not available. This occurs, for example, when too few cameras view the hair tip. In this case, we set Eq.4 to a constant value (for some frames $k$), and the growth directions are optimized based only on the remaining terms.

$E_s$ is a motion smoothness term that represents the difference in growth direction from frame to frame:

$$E_s = W(l) \sum_{k=1}^{N_f-1} \mathtt{dist}(d^l_k, d^l_{k-1}) \tag{5}$$

where $W(l)$ is positive and non-increasing function of $l$. This ensures that growth directions are similar near the root, but can vary more and more towards the end of the hair.

$E_{\mathrm{SS}}$ ensures that the hair shape is similar from frame to frame:

$$E_{\mathrm{SS}} = \sum_{k=1}^{N_{\mathrm{f}}-1} \mathtt{dist}(d_k^l - d_k^{l-1}, d_{k-1}^l - d_{k-1}^{l-1}) \qquad (6)$$

To ensure that hairs do not double back on themselves and that the shape is realistic, we discourage highly curved hair with a curvature cost:

$$E_{\mathrm{C}} = \sum_{k=0}^{N_{\mathrm{f}}-1} \left( \frac{R_0 \mathtt{arg}(d_k^l, d_k^{l-1})}{L_{\mathrm{s}}} \right)^4 \qquad (7)$$

$R_0$ is the threshold curvature expressed as a radius, typically 20mm, and $\mathtt{arg}(d_k^l, d_k^{l-1})$ is the angle between the two vectors, in radians. The curvature cost approximates the fourth power of the sine of the angular difference in hair directions from segment to segment. Thus, it is small in areas of low curvature but grows rapidly as the curvature increases.

The final term, $E_{\mathrm{B}}$, is a surface potential which prevents hairs from leaving the hair volume:

$$E_{\mathrm{B}} = E_{\mathrm{B}}^{\mathrm{S}}(l_d(P_k^{l-1} + L_{\mathrm{s}}d_k^l)) + E_{\mathrm{B}}^{\mathrm{H}}(l_h(P_k^{l-1} + L_{\mathrm{s}}d_k^l)) \qquad (8)$$

In this equation, $l_{\mathrm{d}}(P)$ is the "depth" inside the hair surface, meaning the distance from $P$ to the nearest point on $S_{\mathtt{hair}}^k$. It is negative if the point is outside the hair surface. $l_{\mathrm{h}}(P)$ is the "height" from scalp surface, i.e. the distance from $P$ to $S_{\mathtt{scalp}}^k$. It is negative if the point is inside the scalp surface. The surface potential functions, $E_{\mathrm{B}}^{\mathrm{S}}$ and $E_{\mathrm{B}}^{\mathrm{H}}$ are ramp functions. This surface potential curve is shown graphically in Figure 2.

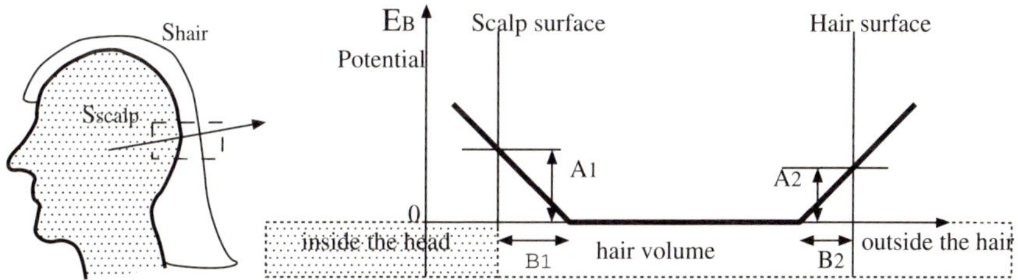


**Fig. 2.** The surface potential function that encourages hairs to grow only within the hair volume. The potential is a function of the distances from a point P to the nearest points on the hair and scalp surfaces, $S_{\mathtt{hair}}^k$ and $S_{\mathtt{scalp}}^k$. $A_1$, $A_2$, $B_1$, and $B_2$ specify the potential ramp functions.

## 4   Implementation

*Multiple-viewpoint video capture.* We use twelve synchronized PointGrey Research Dragonfly cameras to capture our videos. The cameras are on a hexagonal frame with a two meter diameter, shown in Figure 3. The subject is set in the center of the frame. Due to the limited number of cameras, we can only observe one side of the subject with enough cameras to accurately estimate hair orientations. Thus, for our experiments we reconstruct only one side of the hair volume. The videos are VGA (640x480 pixel) resolution at 30 frames per second. For illumination, we use six SHIMPO DT-311A stroboscopes synchronized to the cameras. The walls and floor of the camera frame are covered with green fabric so we can use green screen matting to segment the subject in the images. The cameras are geometrically calibrated using Zhang's method[8].

*2D orientation map computation.* To compute the orientation at each pixel in each image, we apply two Canny-like first derivative of Gaussian filters with different wavelengths ($\lambda = 2$ and $\lambda = 4$) and apply them at discrete angles for each pixel. The angle at which the filter gives the highest response is the orientation for that pixel. We use the inverse of the variance of the filter response versus angle as a confidence measure for the orientation.

*Image segmentation.* We use very simple chroma keying in the HSV color space for foreground/background and skin/hair segmentation. We manually select the foreground hue mean and threshold values. All pixels whose hue is within the threshold of the mean are labeled foreground. Very dark pixels are also assumed to be foreground. We create the visual hulls at each frame using the method of Franco and Boyer [9]. To create scalp models, we manually fit a generic model to the first frame of the input data. For experiments using a mannequin head and wig, we use images without the wig to make a visual hull for the scalp model. When we do not use a wig, we manually fit a generic scalp model to the subject.

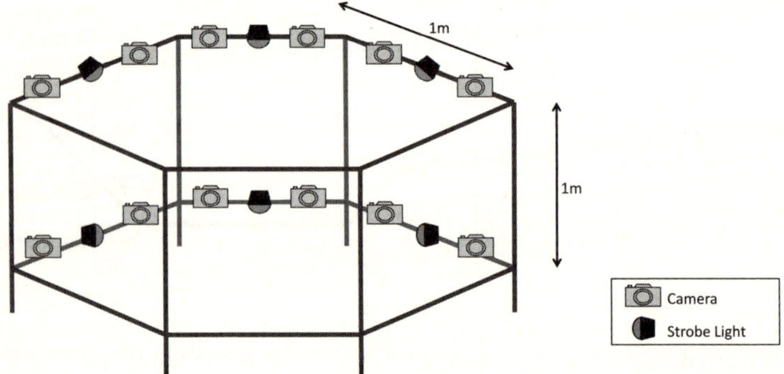


**Fig. 3.** Our camera array setup. Twelve cameras on one side of a hexagonal frame film the subject. Ideally, we would use more cameras to fully surround the subject. Strobe lights synchronized to the cameras provide intense, brief flashes of light, leading to images with negligible motion blur.

*Hair root formation.* We generate hair roots on the scalp surface as follows. First, we use Saff and Kuijlaar's algorithm [10] to generate evenly distributed samples on a unit sphere. These unit vectors can be considered sampled directions from the origin. We place this origin roughly in the center of $S^k_{\text{scalp}}$ for the first frame of the video, cast rays from the origin in each sampled direction, and compute where they intersect $S^k_{\text{scalp}}$. We check the projection of each intersection point into the hair mask from the most fronto-parallel camera view. If the projection lies on a pixel for which the mask indicates hair, we use the intersection point as a hair root position.

We must also set an initial hair growth direction, $d^0_0$, for each root. We use a heuristic to set this properly so hairs grow down the head, not up. As just described, each root corresponds to a sample point (or direction) $P$ on the unit sphere. Let $P = (x, y, z)$, with the positive $z$ axis pointing up vertically. For hair roots corresponding to $z < 0$, $d^0_0$ is set to $(0, 0, -1)$. Otherwise, $d^0_0$ is the unit vector in the plane orthogonal to $P$ with the most negative z component.

*Hair shape reconstruction.* We found that choosing $L_{\text{s}} = 0.8\text{mm}$ generates visually smooth hairs with reasonable computation time. For each new hair segment, we solve the minimization problem in Section 3.3 using the Levenberg-Marquardt algorithm [11,12]. The initial value for each segment is set as follows:

$$\text{init} d^l_k = \begin{cases} o^l_k & (\text{if } o^l_k \neq \phi) \\ \text{init} d^l_{k-1} & (\text{if } o^l_k = \phi \text{ and k>0}) \\ d^{l-1}_k & (\text{otherwise}) \end{cases} \tag{9}$$

$$(k = 0, 1, \ldots, N_{\text{f}} - 1)$$

*Noisy hair removal.* Our algorithm occasionally produces hairs whose shape and motion are noisy. We remove them based on the following noise measure:

$$E_{\text{N}} = \Sigma^{L-1}_{l=0} \frac{1}{L_{\text{s}}(l+1)} \Sigma^{N_{\text{f}}-3}_{k=0} || - P^l_k + 2P^l_{k+1} - P^l_{k+2}||, \tag{10}$$

where $L$ is the number of segments in the hair. $E_{\text{N}}$ is the sum of the second derivatives of the hair segment endpoints. Intuitively, it measures the total energy required to realize the hair motion. This measure tends to be large for hairs that vibrate vigorously due to noise. Hairs with noise measures above a threshold value are eliminated. Once the hair model has been generated, the noise energy threshold can be adjusted interactively to produce visually pleasing results.

## 5   Results

We captured videos of an artificial hairstyle using a wig on a mannequin head, with a fan to make the hair move. In this way, we could concentrate solely on hair modeling. Because of our limited number of viewpoints, we reconstruct only the right side of the hairstyle. Figure 4 shows example input images and the resulting hair motion model for videos of a wig with short, multi-colored hair. The execution time for this result was nearly a day. This is more than a factor of $N_f$ increase over the static hair execution

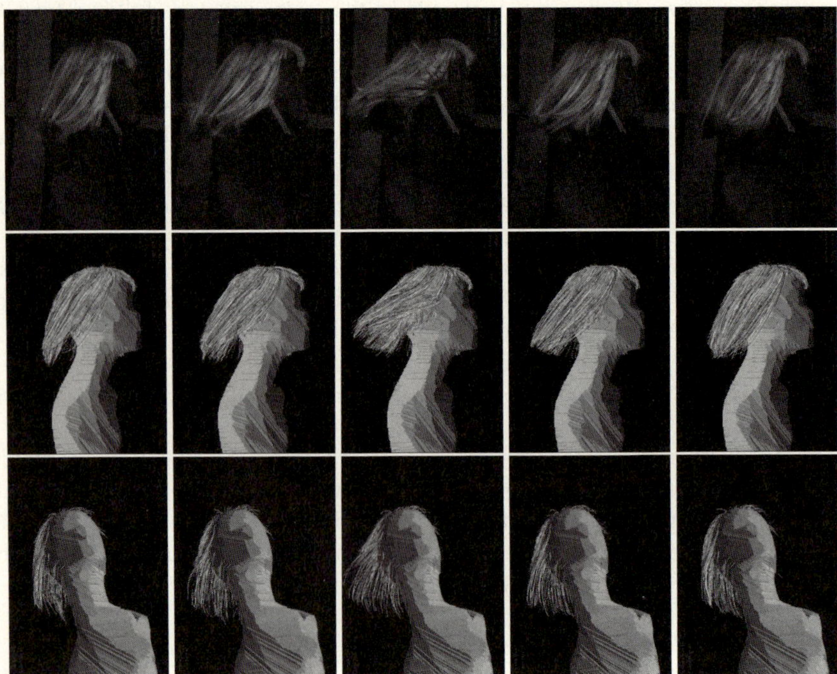

**Fig. 4.** Modeling result for artificial hair on a mannequin head. These images show every sixth frames from a thirty frame sequence. Top row: real images from one camera view. Middle row: reconstructed hair rendered from the same view point and camera parameters show motion similar to the original images. The hair fibers are colored with the same value in all images for easier identification. Bottom row: Rendering the hair from a new viewpoint shows that we have recovered the three dimensional structure and motion of the hair. Some fibers were not drawn to make the visualization clearer.

time because of the Levenberg-Marquardt optimization for each hair segment. About 5000 hair fibers were generated for the 30-frame sequence. The results show that the recovered hair shape and motion is similar to the actual hair behavior.

One limitation we found on datasets with more complicated hairstyles and motions is that clumps of long hairs spread out in some frames, increasing the probability that the modeled hair strands will grow out of the hair volume. When this happens, the hair growth is terminated prematurely, and the modeled hairs are shorter than the real ones. This is a limitation of our method; as the hair shape or motion gets more complex, the chance of modeled hairs growing out of the hair volume increases.

## 6    Conclusions and Future Work

In the near future, we would like to address some of the resource limitations of our system. Adding more cameras would enable us to observe and model all of the hair on the subjects, and would also increase the robustness of our orientation data. We would also like to incorporate head tracking to capture real human subjects.

One fundamental limitation of our approach is that it cannot recover from early errors estimating hair growth directions. Wei et al.'s method also suffers from this drawback, but for static hairstyles, the resulting hair model is often plausible. For a dynamic hairstyle, however, early errors in the hair growth directions for different frames increase the chance that the hair will not resemble any of the actual filmed hairs. Such incorrectly modeled hairs leave the hair volume prematurely in some frames or simply do not match the input data. Ideally, we would iteratively refine the entire length of each modeled hair instead of simply growing the hair from the tip, but this would dramatically increase the time required to create the model.

We have presented the first system for automatically creating models of moving hair from multiple viewpoint video of real, dynamic hairstyles. Our method has produced compelling results for simple hairstyles and motions, and we hope to see others build on this work. Creating more accurate models, and modeling more complicated hairstyles and motions, would have many benefits beyond simply capturing and reproducing existing hair motions. We anticipate capturing hair motions in order to infer physical models for the dynamic behavior of real hairstyles. This would not only deepen our understanding of how hair behaves, but also lead to easily controllable, realistic, dynamic hair models.

## Acknowledgements

The authors would like to thank Sing Bing Kang and YiChen Wei for helpful discussions, and YeBin Liu for assistance with our capture system.

## References


1. Ward, K., Bertails, F., Kim, T., Marschner, S., Cani, M., Lin, M.: A survey on hair modeling: Styling, simulation, and rendering. IEEE Transactions on Visualization and Computer Graphics 13(2), 213–234 (2007)
2. Grabli, S., Sillion, F., Marschner, S., Lengyel, J.: Image-based hair capture by inverse lighting. In: Proc. Graphics Interface, pp. 51–58 (May 2002)
3. Paris, S., Briceno, H.M., Sillion, F.X.: Capture of hair geometry from multiple images. ACM Transactions on Graphics 23(3), 712–719 (2004)
4. Kong, W., Takahashi, H., Nakajima, M.: Generation of 3d hair model from multiple pictures. In: Proc. Multimedia Modeling, pp. 183–196 (1997)
5. Wei, Y., Ofek, E., Quan, L., Shum, H.: Modeling hair from multiple views. ACM Transactions on Graphics 24(3), 816–820 (2005)
6. Paris, S., Chang, W., Jarosz, W., Kozhushnyan, O., Matusik, W., Zwicker, M., Durand, F.: Hair photobooth: Geometric and photometric acquisition of real hairstyles. ACM Trans. on Graphics 27(3) (2008)
7. Laurentini, A.: The visual hull concept for silhouette based image understanding. IEEE Trans. on Pattern Analysis and Machine Intelligence 2(16), 150–162 (1994)
8. Zhang, Z.: A flexible new technique for camera calibration. IEEE Transactions on Pattern Analysis and Machine Intelligence 22(11), 1330–1334 (2000)

9. Franco, J., Boyer, E.: Exact polyhedral visual hulls. In: Proceedings of the Fourteenth British Machine Vision Conference, Norwich, UK, pp. 329–338 (September 2003)
10. Saff, E.B., Kuijlaars, A.: Distributing many points on a sphere. Mathematical Intelligencer 19(1), 5–11 (1997)
11. Levenberg, K.: A method for the solution of certain non-linear problems in least squares. The Quarterly of Applied Mathematics 2, 164–168 (1944)
12. Marquardt, D.: An algorithm for least-squares estimation of nonlinear parameters. SIAM Journal on Applied Mathematics 11, 431–441 (1963)

# Optimal Pixel Matching between Images

Yuichi Yaguchi, Kenta Iseki, and Ryuichi Oka

The University of Aizu
Tsuruga, Ikkimachi, Aizuwakamatsu, Fukushima, Japan
{d8101109,m5111118,oka}@u-aizu.ac.jp
http://iplpcx1.u-aizu.ac.jp

**Abstract.** A two-dimensional continuous dynamic programming (2DCDP) method is proposed for two-dimensional spotting recognition of images. Spotting recognition is simultaneous segmentation and recognition of an image by optimal pixel matching between a reference and an input image. The proposed method performs optimal pixel-wise image matching and two-dimensional pixel alignment, which are not available in conventional algorithms. Experimental results show that 2DCDP precisely matches the pixels of non-linearly deformed images.

**Keywords:** Optimal Pixel Matching, DP, Spotting, Image Registration, Segmentation.

## 1 Introduction

Optimal pixel matching between images is widely used in image processing [1] for such tasks as recognition [2], retrieval [3], registration [4,5], and three-dimensional reconstruction from stereoscopic and/or time series images [6,7,8]. Image registration is done by using feature point matching [9,10], histogram matching [11], or based-on-correlation template matching [12]. Matching methods are usually divided into two categories: linear and non-linear. Feature point matching is non-linear, and histogram matching and based-on-correlation template matching are linear. Feature point matching using scale invariant feature transformation (SIFT) [10] is robust against variations in pixel shift and non-linear translation of feature points because it takes the advantages of point-to-point matching algorithm. Three-dimensional shape reconstruction using SIFT requires the use of a tracking procedure like Kanade-Lucas-Tomasi tracker [9]. We propose another non-linear approach to three-dimensional shape reconstruction without using a tracking procedure.

Unlike the images in the previous works that are assumed as linear-transformed or affine-transformed, most real-world images are non-linearly deformed compared with ones captured in a different time or from a different viewpoint. Additionally, for the strict matching, image registration can be made more precise and accurate if we match the images at the pixel level rather than at the feature point level. Segmentation, in the other hand, is a big challenging problem which also needs to be solved. Our objective is to develop a method which is able to solve both above mentioned problems: non-linear deformation and segmentation. Moreover, we aim to

T. Wada, F. Huang, and S. Lin (Eds.): PSIVT 2009, LNCS 5414, pp. 597–610, 2009.

enhance this method in order to obtain optimal pixel correspondence by aligning the non-linear deformation of pixels between images. Our approach is based on the previous studies on the two-dimensional extension of dynamic programming (DP) matching [13,14]. There have been several studies on applying DP-based matching to two-dimensional data, such as real-world images. DP-based matching was originally developed for one-dimensional data sequences. Myers and Rabiner introduced dynamic time warping (DTW) [15] for connected word recognition. Uchida and Sakoe developed two-dimensional time warping (2DTW) by extending one-dimensional DTW [16]. They argued that 2DTW has a pattern combination problem in the vertical and horizontal correlation [13], so its calculating time becomes nondeterministic polynomial-time hard (NP-Hard). Furthermore, 2DTW requires the pre-segmentation of images for identifying the matching area because it needs fixed start and end points as its input. Continuous DP (CDP) [17], a well-known spotting method, uses simultaneous recognition and segmentation, so there is no need to segment the input time sequence to be matched in advance. CDP has been applied to continuous sound [17,18] and gesture recognition [19]. It is superior to conventional DTW because it does not require pre-segmentation. Thus, a two-dimensional extension of CDP is able to overcome the problems of 2DTW matching. The first two-dimensional CDP (2DCDP), proposed by Nishimura et al. [14], applies CDP two times: the first one is used to calculate the difference of pixel intensity between input and reference images, and then accumulate series of that results for each row in the input image on row direction, the second one is used to accumulate the results for all rows that align on column direction. Therefore, this method is not considered as a fully two-dimensional extension of CDP. It was extended by Suto et al. for arbitrary shaped queries [20]. Iwasa et al. proposed a modification of Suto's method to enable continuous and monotonic pixel alignment [21]. However, these three methods still suffer pixel alignment errors because of the separation of column and row directions when accumulating the local distances between pixels in the two images. Moreover, Iwasa's method tends to miss matching pixels between images derived from a kind of post-processing. To dispose of the problems of all these methods, Yaguchi et al. [22] proposed a accumulation and back tracking methods to create a fully two-dimensional extension of CDP.

Based on Yaguchi's approach, the method is developed for simultaneous accumulation of local distances in both the row and column directions. It optimally accumulates distances between corresponding pixels in two images, starting with the pixels in one corner of the reference image and moving toward those in the opposite corner. Because the pixels used in the reference image are positioned obliquely to each other, the total distances of pixels from the starting to the ending points can be obtained by simply adding up the distances by the row and column directions. Each pixel location in the input image is assumed to be the end point for the corresponding accumulation of local distances, and the optimal accumulation value is stored at that location. The location of the pixel in the local area of the input image which has the local minimum optimal accumulation value will be selected for spotting point of the reference image. A segmented area of the input image is then extracted using back tracking of matching paths which are construct of a mesh plane. This method is completely two-dimensional CDP. It ensures the completely two-dimensional alignment of the pixels in the input image by matching to all pixels in the reference image. In addition, 2DCDP attains the spotting recognition by extracting pixel correspondence between input and reference images, and recognizing labeled information of reference image through the pixel correspondence of the two images. The remainder of this paper is divided into three sections as follows: Section 2 describes the algorithm of our optimal pixel matching method. Section 3 describes our spotting recognition experiments and the results. Finally, section 4 summarizes the key points and mentions some future works.

## 2   2DCDP: An Optimal Pixel Matching Method

### 2.1   The Road Map of DP Algorithm

DP algorithm is designed to solve sequential decision problems. Such problems are usually expressed as an automaton or a tree structure. DTW algorithm [15] is used to accumulate the minimum amount of errors from the start to the end point under the principle of optimality. For large-scale input data, DTW needs to extract short segment for matching. Then, if DTW processes the large-scale input data, it will set many start and end points in the input sequence, and will duplicate many processes to calculate the accumulation values. CDP is able to reduce the calculation time of duplicated processes in DTW, and enables start-point-free non-linear sequential data matching [17].

In image processing, spotting recognition is used to identify segmentation and non-linear pixel movement by using a reference image. The conventional 2DTW method [13] is unable to segment into an input image because it requires pre-segmentation for matching like DTW. In this paper, we introduce a method which is able to perform spotting recognition, and we developed a two-dimensional extension derived from CDP for spotting recognition.

### 2.2   Definition of 2DCDP Algorithm

2DCDP supports full-pixel matching and it is extended from CDP into two-dimensional correlation. The pixel coordinates of input image $S$ and reference image $R$ are defined by:

$$S \triangleq \{(i,j)|1 \le i \le I, 1 \le j \le J\} \tag{1}$$

$$R \triangleq \{(m,n)|1 \le m \le M, 1 \le n \le N\}. \tag{2}$$

The pixel value at location $(i,j)$ of an input image $Sp$ is $Sp(i,j) = \{r,g,b\}$, and the pixel value at location $(m,n)$ of an reference image $Rp$ is $Rp(m,n) = \{r,g,b\}$. Values r, g and b express red, green and blue respectively, and each value has the range $(0 \le \{r,g,b\} \le 1)$. We define the mapping $R \to S$, $(m,n) \in R$ and $(\xi(m,n),\eta(m,n)) \in S$ by:

$$(m,n) \Longrightarrow (\xi(m,n),\eta(m,n)), \tag{3}$$

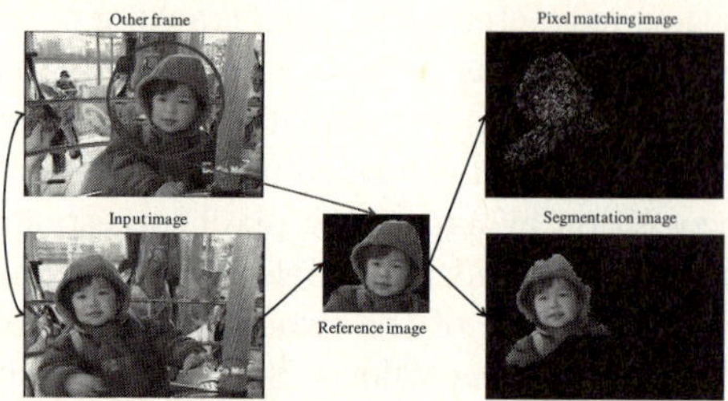


**Fig. 1.** Image spotting: recognize input image using reference image and simultaneous optimal pixel matching and segmentation. There is no limit to number of matching segments.

and we set the end location of pixel matching as

$$\xi(M, N) = i, \quad \eta(M, N) = j. \tag{4}$$

Next, we set local distance $d(i, j, m, n)$ as the different value between $Sp(i, j)$ and $Rp(m, n)$, and $w(i, j, m, n)$ as the weighted value of each local calculation. Accumulated local minimum $D(i, j, m, n)$, defined as follows, is used to evaluate the decision sequence.

$$D(i, j, m, n) = \frac{1}{W} \min_{\xi, \eta} \{ \sum_{m=1}^{M} \sum_{n=1}^{N} w(\xi(m,n), \eta(m,n), m, n) d(\xi(m,n), \eta(m,n), m, n) \} \tag{5}$$

Then, $\xi^*(m, n)$ and $\eta^*(m, n)$ are used to represent the optimal solution in $\xi(m, n)$ and $\eta(m, n)$ respectively, where $W$ is the optimal accumulated weight:

$$W = \sum_{m,n} w(\xi^*(m, n), \eta^*(m, n), m, n). \tag{6}$$

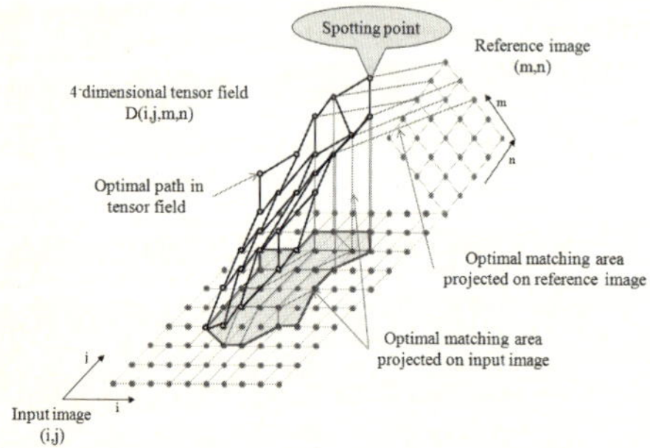


**Fig. 2.** Relation of accumulation, spotting point and projecting spotting area

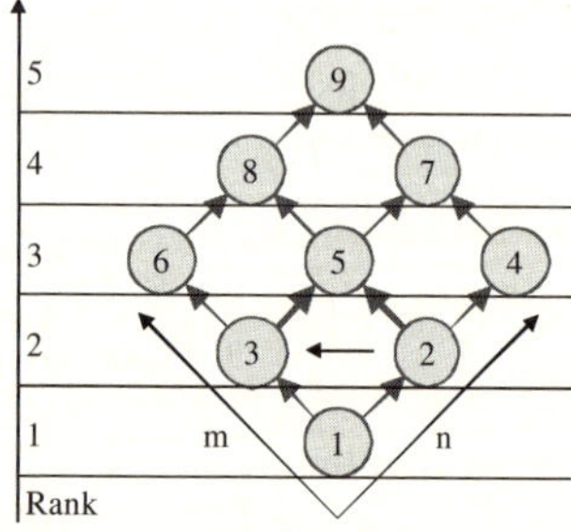


**Fig. 3.** Definition of rank in accumulation and computation sequences

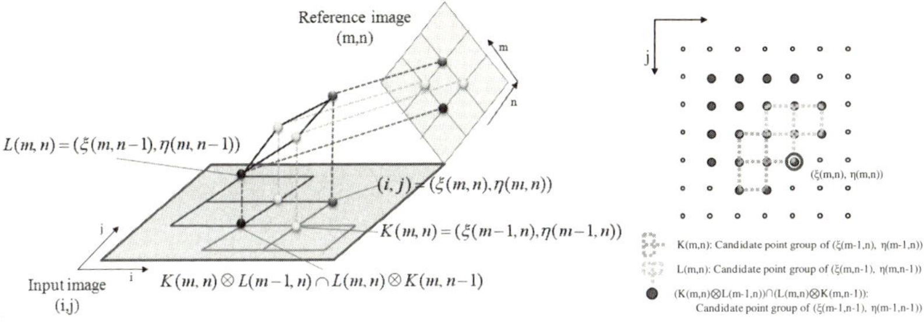

**Fig. 4.** Constraint of pixel connection: each $i$ and $j$ direction can connects 7 candidate pixels

To ensure continuity and monotonicity, $K(m,n) = \{\xi(m-1,n), \eta(m-1,n)\}$ and $L(m,n) = \{\xi(m,n-1), \eta(m,n-1)\}$ are used to define the sets of points in the input image that are movable in the $m$ and $n$ directions from the reference image. The following relationship is required for point $(m-1,n-1)$ corresponding to $(m,n)$ (see Figure 2 and Figure 4).

$$(\xi(m-1,n-1), \eta(m-1,n-1)) \in K(m,n) \otimes L(m-1,n) \cap L(m,n) \otimes K(m,n-1) \quad (7)$$

The operator $\otimes$ represents the connection between a set of points on the left and a set of points on the right.

To calculate accumulated local distance, each accumulated local minimum $D(i,j,m,n)$ is derived from two previous accumulated local minimums $D(i',j', m-1,n)$ and $D(i'',j'',m,n-1)$. Thus, we define rank $l = m+n$ as shown in Figure 3 in order to smoothly calculate the accumulated local minimum.

### 2.3   Inplementation of Local Distance

The accumulation of the local distance in optimal pixel matching requires simultaneous accumulation in m and n directions for each pixel. In the accumulation

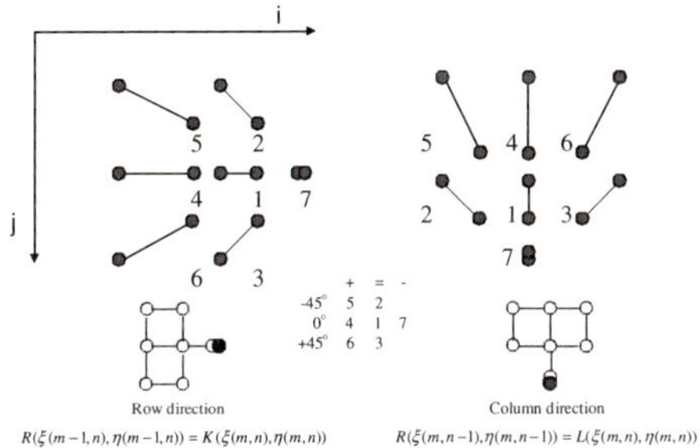

**Fig. 5.** Local path direction: seven candidate paths at 45-degree left and right rotations; doubled path expansion and shrinkage for each m and n direction

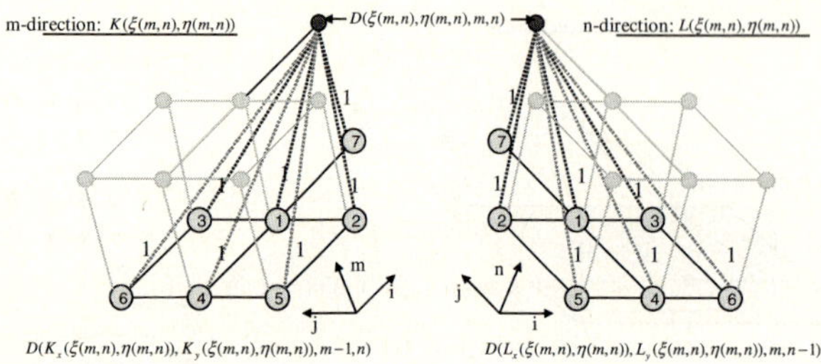

**Fig. 6.** Definition of local path weight: all paths determined as path weight becomes 3 in each m and n value increment

calculation, the accumulated values are optimally selected by two directions. However, there is no difference in the pixel distance between m and n directions because the data consists of only the distance values of a corresponding pixel.

In our experimental implementation, the pixel distance is as follows:

$$d(i, j, m, n) = \frac{1}{3} \sum_{k=1}^{3} |Sp_k(i, j) - Rp_k(m, n)|, \qquad (8)$$

when the variable k is k-th element of $Sp(i, j)$ and $Rp(m, n)$. Then, variance range of d(i,j,m,n) is set as $0 \le d(i, j, m, n) \le 1$.

## 2.4   Algorithm for Optimal Local Distance Accumulation

2DCDP selects two local paths that need to check the connection of the four points $(m, n)$, $(m-1, n)$, $(m, n-1)$ and $(m-1, n-1)$ that become a quadrangle

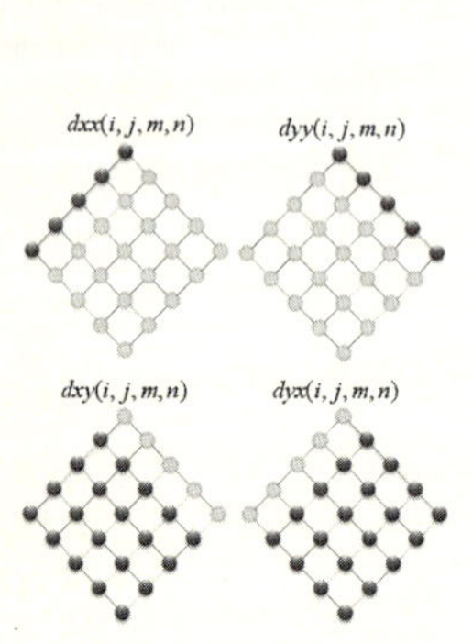

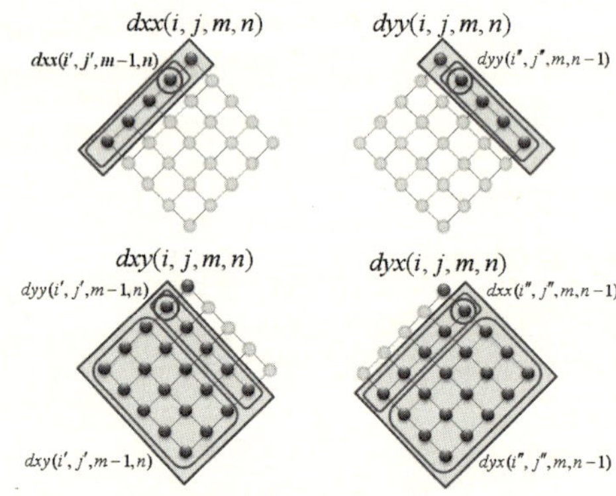

**Fig. 7.** Definition of four accumulated values of accumulating combination

**Fig. 8.** Definition of accumulation calculation of $D(i,j,m,n)$

(Figure 7). 2DCDP defines seven paths for each m and n direction for the local accumulation paths, as shown in Figure 5: (1) same size, (2) same size and a minus 45-degree rotation, (3) same size and a plus a 45-degree rotation, (4) doubled, (5) doubled and minus a 45-degree rotation, (6) doubled and plus a 45-degree rotation, and (7) a shrinking path, and each accumulation point has four values as shown in Figure 7 and  8. If these four-point $(m,n)$, $(m-1,n)$, $(m,n-1)$ and $(m-1,n-1)$ make a quadrangle like Figure 4, we need to check 165 patterns that are derived from local accumulation paths above. This checking procedure takes long time because of the recalculating operations. Therefore, we set four values for accumulating calculation $dxx$, $dxy$, $dyx$ and $dyy$ as Figure 8 to overload low-level accumulation results and keep the path constraints. Next, we set the path weight as Figure 5 to simplify the algorithm. Then, any path weight value will be set as $w(i,j,m,n) = 1$.

The algorithm for accumulation local minimum is shown as following equations:

**For** $l = m + n, 2 \leq l \leq M + N,\ l = l + 1$
**For** $m = 1$ and $n = l$, $1 \leq m \leq M$ and $1 \leq n \leq N$, $m = m + 1$ and $n = n - 1$
**Path selection:**

$$(i',j',m-1,n) \triangleq arg\min \left\{ \begin{array}{c} D(i-1,j,m-1,n) - dyx(i-1,j,m-1,n) \\ D(i-1,j-1,m-1,n) - dyx(i-1,j-1,m-1,n) \\ D(i-1,j+1,m-1,n) - dyx(i-1,j+1,m-1,n) \\ D(i-2,j,m-1,n) - dyx(i-2,j,m-1,n) \\ D(i-2,j-1,m-1,n) - dyx(i-2,j-1,m-1,n) \\ D(i-2,j+1,m-1,n) - dyx(i-2,j+1,m-1,n) \\ D(i,j,m-1,n) - dyx(i,j,m-1,n) \end{array} \right\}, \quad (9)$$

$$(i'',j'',m,n-1) \triangleq arg\min \left\{ \begin{array}{c} D(i,j-1,m,n-1) - dxy(i,j-1,m,n-1) \\ D(i-1,j-1,m,n-1) - dxy(i-1,j-1,m,n-1) \\ D(i+1,j-1,m,n-1) - dxy(i+1,j-1,m,n-1) \\ D(i,j-2,m,n-1) - dxy(i,j-2,m,n-1) \\ D(i-1,j-2,m,n-1) - dxy(i-1,j-2,m,n-1) \\ D(i+1,j-2,m,n-1) - dxy(i+1,j-2,m,n-1) \\ D(i,j,m,n-1) - dxy(i,j,m,n-1) \end{array} \right\}, \quad (10)$$

**Accumulation four values:**

$$dxx(i,j,m,n) \triangleq d(i,j,m,n) + dxx(i',j',m-1,n) \quad (11)$$
$$dxy(i,j,m,n) \triangleq dxy(i',j',m-1,n) + dyy(i',j',m-1,n) \quad (12)$$
$$dyx(i,j,m,n) \triangleq dyx(i'',j'',m,n-1) + dxx(i'',j'',m,n-1) \quad (13)$$
$$dyy(i,j,m,n) \triangleq d(i,j,m,n) + dyy(i'',j'',m,n-1), \quad (14)$$

**Accumulation local minimum value:**

$$D(i,j,m,n) \triangleq dxx(i,j,m,n) + dxy(i,j,m,n) + dyx(i,j,m,n) + dyy(i,j,m,n) \quad (15)$$

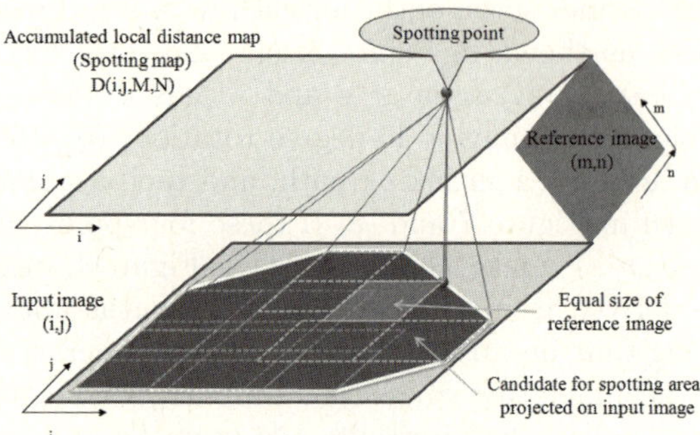


**Fig. 9.** Spotting point and spotting area candidate: Candidate spotting area in input image is about 12 times larger than reference image

The equations (9)-(15) imply that an accumulated value $D(i, j, m, n)$ is recursively calculated by $D(i', j', m - 1, n)$ and $D(i'', j'', m, n - 1)$ as a result of the application of DP The path configuration in Figure 5 enables infinite path shrinking. Therefore, in our experiment, we counted the number of times of shrinking and set the limitation for the consecutive times of shrinking.

Finally, the optimal spotting point corresponding to pixel $(i, j)$ in the input image is given by:

$$D(i, j, m, n) = \min_{\xi, \eta} \{ \sum_{m=1}^{M} \sum_{n=1}^{N} dxx(\xi(m,n), \eta(m,n), m, n) + dxy(\xi(m,n), \eta(m,n), m, n)$$
$$+ dyx(\xi(m,n), \eta(m,n), m, n) + dyy(\xi(m,n), \eta(m,n), m, n) \}$$
$$= \min_{\xi, \eta} \{ \sum_{m=1}^{M} \sum_{n=1}^{N} 2d(\xi(m, n), \eta(m, n), m, n) \}$$
$$= 2 \min_{\xi, \eta} \{ \sum_{m=1}^{M} \sum_{n=1}^{N} d(\xi(m, n), \eta(m, n), m, n) \}. \tag{16}$$

This equation follows the equation (5).

### 2.5   Correction of Mesh Structure Using Back Tracking

After the spotting point has been determined, we need to extract spotting area from four-dimensional accumulated local minimum space. The back tracking is used to optimally accumulate the local distance. The back tracking in CDP traces only the connected path. However, the connected path in 2DCDP sometimes twists between m and n directions. Therefore, each matching point $D(i, j, m, n)$ has an optimal accumulated value from start to that point. Thus, the algorithm for finding the optimal path from two points is expressed as following equation:

$$(i^*, j^*) \in K(\xi^*(m + 1, n), \eta^*(m + 1, n)) \otimes L(\xi^*(m, n + 1), \eta^*(m, n + 1)) \tag{17}$$
$$(\xi^*(m, n), \eta^*(m, n)) = \min_{i^*, j^*} \{ D(i^*, j^*, m, n) \}. \tag{18}$$

Candidate spotting area in input image is about 12 times larger than reference image (Figure 9) because of the implementation allows 45-digrees rotation and doubled size each connected paths. The problem of the back tracking is: it is able to unlimitedly select a shrinking path that can cause over-shrinking spotting area. Then, we implement a control variable to limit the consecutive times of shrinking.

Finally, set $P$, containing segments is defined as:

$$P \subset \{(\xi^*(m,n), \eta^*(m,n))|1 \le m \le M, 1 \le n \le N\}. \tag{19}$$

In addition, when recognizing multiple segments, back tracking from the minimum order of spotting points, and sometimes skipping the trial if the trial contains the element of earlier segments, is exclusive.

## 2.6   Arbitrary Shape of Reference Image

When the value of local distance of pixels in discarded area is set to maximum value, the local distance value of pixels in background will have the same value. Therefore, the arbitrary shape can be cut off from the reference image as shown in Figure 10. In our experiment, local distance is set to 1.

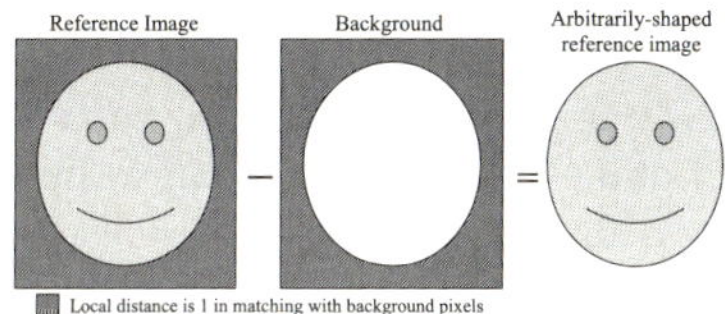


**Fig. 10.** Image of arbitrary reference image matching

## 2.7   Calculation Time and Memory Amount

2DCDP takes one time to calculate local distance and accumulation at every element in four-dimensional tensor field. Thus, the time needed 2DCDP calculation is $O(N^4)$ because the amount of element in the tensor field is $I \times J \times M \times N$. In this algorithm, back tracking needs each value of accumulated local minimum $D(i,j,m,n)$. Therefore, the amount of memory size is also $O(N^4)$.

# 3   Spotting Recognition Experiments

## 3.1   Methods and Materials

To experimentally evaluate our optimal pixel matching method, we used only a single OS-implemented thread (MacOS X running on an Xserve with a dual 2.8-GHz Xeon processor 4-cores and 32-GB SDRAM). In the first experiment, spotting recognition was done using an arbitrary shaped query extracted from the original image (image on the top of Figure 11). In the second experiment, multi-answer spotting recognition was done using real world data. The third experiment is used to apply 2DCDP for nature images.

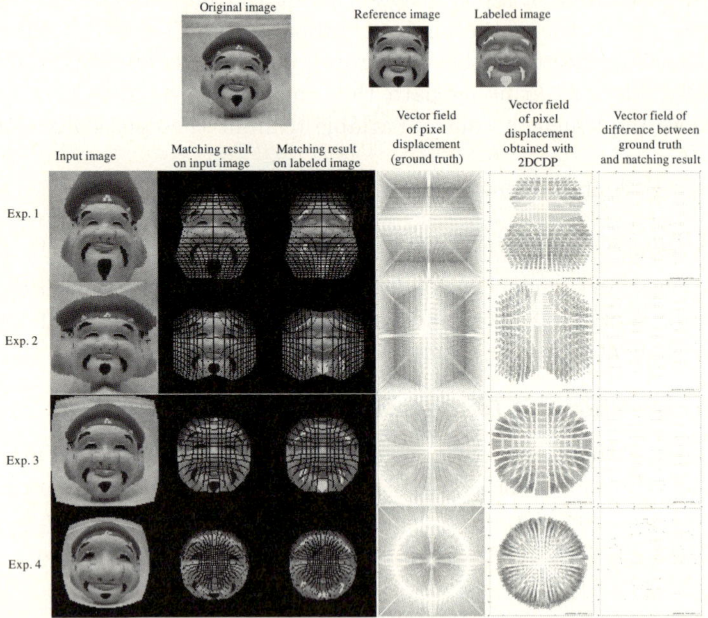


**Fig. 11.** Experimental result of 2DCDP; Exp. 1: vertically divided affine image. Exp. 5: horizontally divided affine image. Exp. 3: thick lens distortion; applied transform $a_1 r - a_2 r^3$, $a_1 = 0.3, a_2 = 0.0001$. Exp. 4: thick lens distortion; applied transform $a_1 r - a_2 r^3$, $a_1 = 0.6, a_2 = 0.0005$.

**Exp. 1:** Spotting recognition used four input images (Figure 11) as follows:

Input 1: Spotting recognition is done by using affine transformed image in top and bottom halves of image extracted from original image.

Input 2: Spotting recognition is done by using affine transformed image in left and right halves of image extracted from original image.

Input 3: Spotting recognition is done by using a distorted image such as one captured through a thick lens, as expressed by $a_1 r - a_2 r^3, a_1 = 0.3, a_2 = 0.0001$, extracted from original image.

Input 4: Spotting recognition is done by using a distorted image such as one captured through a thick lens, as expressed by $a_1 r - a_2 r^3, a_1 = 0.6, a_2 = 0.0005$, extracted from original image.

**Exp. 2:** Spotting recognition is done by using input image constructed by several images picked up from a movie and another picture($I = 320, J = 240$) and reference image bring another frame into the movie($M = 63, N = 61$).

**Exp. 3:** Some nature image spotting using 2DCDP as Figure 13 and Figure 14.

In experiments 1, we used $100 \times 100$ pixels image for input and $55 \times 55$ pixels image for reference. In experiment 2, we used several frames from a video database [23] and cut and pasted other face-image frames that had several margins. In these experiments, the limitation of shrinking was set to 2.

## 3.2 Experimental Results

For experiments 1, Figure 11 shows the ground truth (labeled as "Vector field of pixel displacement (ground truth)"), the pixel movement (labeled as "Vector field of pixel displacement obtained by 2DCDP"), and the difference between the ground truth and the pixel movement (labeled as "Vector field of difference between ground truth and matching result"). The accuracy rate results are shown in Table 1. Input 4 showed that, although some pixel movements exceeded the limited path constraint in the ground truth, this method was still effective because it is a method for finding global optimality. Experiment 2 showed that, for several extracted facial areas, it was able to find multiple candidates for each

**Table 1.** Performance in Experiment 1: Accuracy rate of pixel movement was calculated to be less than $\sqrt{2}$ of pixel movement error

|  | Input 1 | Input 2 | Input 3 | Input 4 |
|---|---|---|---|---|
| No. of corresponding pixels | 2741 | 2741 | 2724 | 1820 |
| No. of corresponding errors | 1 | 0 | 3 | 20 |
| Accuracy rate of pixel movement | 99.963% | 100.00 % | 99.890 % | 98.901 % |
| Calculation time (sec) | 4.931 | 4.954 | 4.954 | 4.855 |

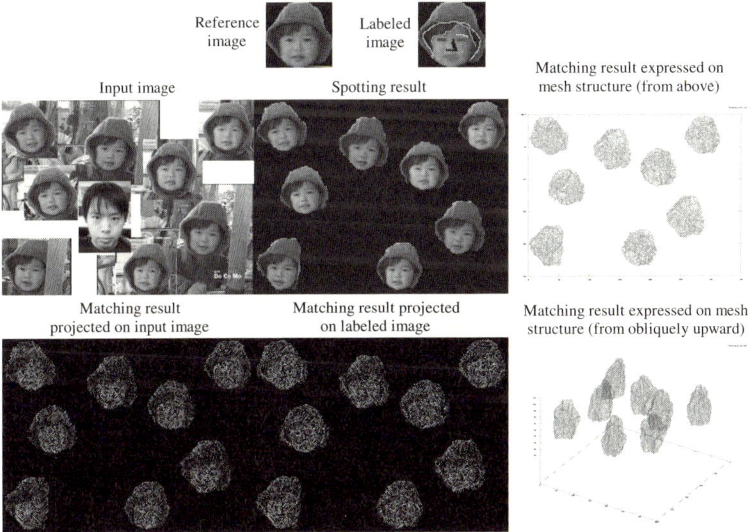


**Fig. 12.** Exp. 2: multi-extraction using face query. Eight objects extract from input image. Each face pick up from other frame into a movie. Reference image is also pickup from other frame into same movie.

**Table 2.** Performance in Experiments 2,3: Calculation time and memory size increase $O(N^4)$ order

|  | Fig. 12 | Fig. 13 Ref. 1 | Fig. 13 - Ref. 2 | Fig 14 Average |
|---|---|---|---|---|
| Input image size | $320 \times 240$ | $416 \times 339$ | $416 \times 339$ | $300 \times 199$ |
| Reference image size | $63 \times 61$ | $96 \times 98$ | $90 \times 96$ | $219 \times 63$ |
| Calculation time (sec) | 59.823 | 235.000 | 261.478 | 159.500 |
| Memory usage (GByte) | 5.3 | 23.9 | 21.9 | 14.8 |

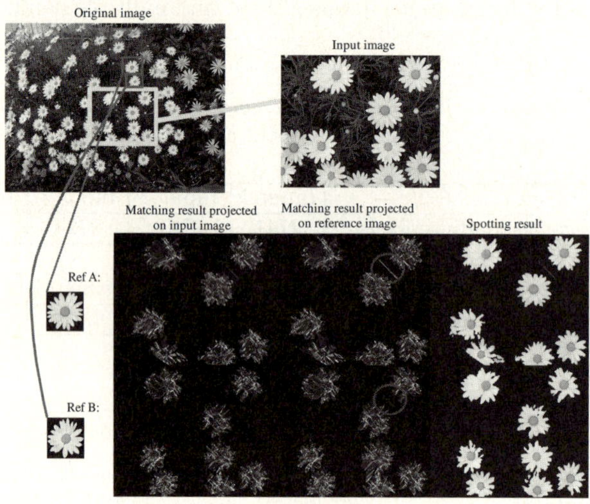


**Fig. 13.** Multi-object extraction using flower query: Program tries to extract 9 objects. Two different query can spotting 7 or 8 objects because of color difference between references. Red circle pointed area of matching miss.

area and that each area had a pixel-to-pixel relationship between the subject and reference images. Figure 12 shows that every result was success to indicate the borderline between hair, face, eyes, nose and mouth. The calculation time and memory usage is shown in Table 2. In the experiment 3, Figure 13 also shows that 2DCDP is able to extract multiple spotting area and capture different results using two different reference images because these two reference images have difference in color and shape. In the Figure 13, we obtain 9 objects in each trial and some spotting errors are indicated in red circle in the figure. Figure 14 indicates that 2DCDP is able to extract the object which has perspective transformation. This is a special feature for image based modeling because this full-pixel matching easily allows the reconstruction of 3D shape from two or more images.

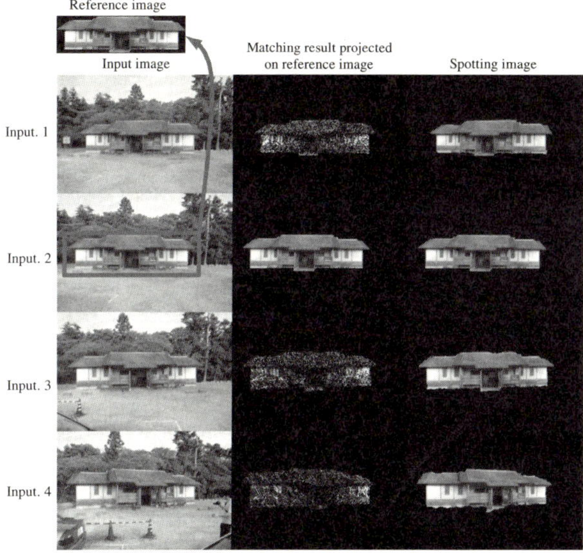


**Fig. 14.** Extracting building from different frame into motion picture

## 4    Conclusion

We developed and tested a two-dimensional continuous dynamic programming (2DCDP) method for spotting recognition of images. It achieves simultaneous segmentation and image recognition due to continuous and monotonic pixel-to-pixel matching. Our testing demonstrated that it is robust against non-linear deformation of images. Our future work would enable this method to use other indicators instead of only RGB in above experiments. We also includes investigating applications of 2DCDP such as finding errors in medical images from non-linear image registration, three-dimensional reconstruction, and recognition of facial expressions in our future plan.

## References


1. Forsyth, D., Ponce, J.: Computer Vision: A Modern Approach. Prentice Hall Professional Technical Reference, Englewood Cliffs (2002)
2. Brunelli, R., Poggio, T.: Face recognition: features versus templates. IEEE Trans. on PAMI 15(10), 1042–1052 (1993)
3. Geiger, D., Gupta, A., Costa, L., Vlontzos, J.: Dynamic programming for detecting, tracking, and matching deformable contours. IEEE Trans. on PAMI 17(3), 294–302 (1995)
4. Zitová, B., Flusser, J.: Image registration methods: a survey. Image and Vision Computing 21(11), 977–1000 (2003)
5. Pluim, J., Maintz, J., Viergever, M.: Mutual-information-based registration of medical images: a survey. IEEE Trans. on Medical Imaging 22(8), 986–1004 (2003)

6. Ohta, Y., Kanade, T.: Stereo by intra-and inter-scanline search. IEEE Trans. on PAMI 7(2), 139–154 (1985)
7. Okutomi, M., Kanade, T.: A multiple-baseline stereo. IEEE Trans. on PAMI 15(4), 353–363 (1993)
8. Tomasi, C., Kanade, T.: Shape and motion from image streams under orthography: a factorization method. IJCV 9(2), 137–154 (1992)
9. Tomasi, C., Kanade, T.: Detection and tracking of point features. School Comput. Sci., Carnegie Mellon Univ., Pittsburgh, PA, Tech. Rep. CMU-CS-91-132 (1991)
10. Lowe, D.: Distinctive Image Features from Scale-Invariant Keypoints. IJCV 60(2), 91–110 (2004)
11. Hashizume, C.: Vinod, V.V., Murase, H.: Robust object extraction from color images under illumination changes. Technical report of IEICE. PRMU 97(325), 33–40 (1997)
12. Pereira, S., Pun, T.: Robust template matching for affine resistant image watermarks. IEEE Trans. on Image Processing 9(6), 1123–1129 (2000)
13. Uchida, S.: Dp matching: Fundamentals and application. Technical report of IEICE. PRMU, pp. 31–36 (December 2006)
14. Nishimura, T., Oka, R.: Spotting Image Recognition using Two-Dimensional Continuous Dynamic Programming. Technical Report of IEICE. PRMU, 1–7 (July 1997)
15. Myers, C., Rabiner, L., Rosenberg, A.: Performance tradeoffs in dynamic time warping algorithms for isolated word recognition. IEEE Trans. on ASSP 28(6), 623–635 (1980)
16. Uchida, S., Sakoe, H.: Piecewise linear two-dimensional warping. Systems and Computers in Japan 32(12), 1–9 (2001)
17. Oka, R.: Spotting method for classification of real world data. The Computer Journal 41(8), 559–565 (1998)
18. Yaguchi, Y., Watanabe, Y., Naruse, K., Oka, R.: Speech and Song Search on the Web: System Design and Implementation. In: CIT 2007, pp. 270–278 (2007)
19. Oka, R., Nishimura, T., Yabe, H.: On Spotting Recognition of Gesture Motion from Time-varying Image. Trans. of IPSJ 43, 54–68 (2002)
20. Suto, N., Nishimura, T., Fujii, R.H., Oka, R.: Spotting Recognition of Concave and Convex Reference Image with Pixel-wise Correspondence using Two-dimensional Continuous Dynamic Programming. In: Technical report of IEICE. PRMU (July 2003)
21. Iwasa, Y., Oka, R.: Algorithm for Guaranteeing Monotonuous Contiguity of Pixel Correspondence in Spotting Recognition of Image. In: MIRU 2005, pp. 997–1004 (July 2005)
22. Yaguchi, Y., Iseki, K., Oka, R.: Two-dimensional Continuous Dynamic Programming for Spotting Recognition of Image. In: MIRU 2008, pp. 708–714 (July 2008)
23. Babaguchi, N., Etoh, M., Satoh, S., Adachi, J., Akutsu, A., Ariki, Y., Echigo, T., Shibata, M., Zen, H., Nakamura, Y., Minoh, M.: Video Database for Evaluating Video Processing. In: Technical Report of IEICE. PRMU (June 2002)

# Moving Object Segmentation Using Optical Flow and Depth Information

Jens Klappstein[1], Tobi Vaudrey[2], Clemens Rabe[1],
Andreas Wedel[1], and Reinhard Klette[2]

[1] Environment Perception Group, Daimler AG, Sindelfingen, Germany
[2] *.enpeda..* Project, The University of Auckland, New Zealand
jens.klappstein@daimler.com, t.vaudrey@auckland.ac.nz,
clemens.rabe@daimler.com, andreas.wedel@daimler.com

**Abstract.** This paper discusses the detection of moving objects (being a crucial part of driver assistance systems) using monocular or stereo-scopic computer vision. In both cases, object detection is based on motion analysis of individually tracked image points (optical flow), providing a motion metric which corresponds to the likelihood that the tracked point is moving. Based on this metric, points are segmented into objects by employing a globally optimal graph-cut algorithm. Both approaches are comparatively evaluated using real-world vehicle image sequences.

**Keywords:** Motion detection, optical flow, stereo, segmentation.

## 1   Introduction

Kinesthesia, the sensation or perception of motion, is an important part of human perception. It encompasses both the perception of motion of one's own body and a spectators perception of the motion of a scene. In vehicle applications these two steps refer to ego-motion and the detection of other moving traffic participants. Visual kinesthesia is done by using the sense of sight to observe the effect of scene motion. In this paper, we model such perception of motion using computer vision.

Detecting moving objects is a major issue for driver assistance and road safety. The detection of moving traffic participants is an important step toward attention-based environment perception. In this paper, we investigate methods and limitations of both monocular and binocular camera systems for motion detectability. It is evident that a monocular system is cheaper, uses less installa-tion space, and suffers less decalibration issues, compared to the stereo system. However, a stereo system yields direct range measurement estimates, but the orientation between the two cameras needs to be known accurately, and decal-ibration can cause major issues. This paper provides insight into the difference between monocular and stereo camera performance.

The key idea behind our approach of detecting independently moving objects is to distinguish between motion in the images caused by the ego-motion of the ego-vehicle (static objects) and motion caused by dynamic objects in the scene.

T. Wada, F. Huang, and S. Lin (Eds.): PSIVT 2009, LNCS 5414, pp. 611–623, 2009.

The motion of the ego-vehicle greatly complicates the problem of motion detection because simple background subtraction of successive images yields no result. This paper presents and investigates techniques to distinguish between stationary and non-stationary points. They are based on tracking feature points in sequential images. As a result, feature points on independently moving objects are detected as moving. These features, however, are sparse and do not characterize the whole image. In a second step, moving objects are segmented in the images using these sparse features as seeds for segmentation. We make use of the globally optimal graph-cut segmentation algorithm [6] to reject outliers and to find image regions with an accumulation of image features lying on moving objects. The proposed algorithm is able to find both rigid objects such as cars and non-rigid objects such as moving pedestrians.

The paper is organized as follows. Section 2 investigates the motion analysis techniques. Section 3 deals with the segmentation of the objects. In the result of Section 4 different scenarios are presented, confirming the practicality of computer vision for the sensation and perception of motion. Differences between monocular and binocular motion detection are discussed and segmentation results for moving objects are presented. A concluding section on future work and obtained insights closes this paper.

## 2   Motion Analysis

The detection of moving objects is based on motion analysis of individual tracked image features, using the KLT tracker [20]. Tracked features are then reconstructed into 3D coordinates. The stereoscopic approach accomplishes this using a pair of stereo images by estimating the disparity and using triangulation, where as the monocular approach accomplishes this using sequential images and evaluating the optical flow. The monocular approach additionally requires the knowledge about the ego-motion of the camera which can be obtained either by an inertial measurement unit (IMU) [7] or based on optical flow [2,14].

There is a fundamental difference between the monocular and the stereoscopic reconstruction. Moving points cannot be correctly reconstructed by monocular vision, except in special situations, such as using trajectory triangulation [3]. The erroneous reconstruction of moving points can be identified as erroneous if the constraints for a static 3D point are violated. The monocular detection of moving points relies on this fact. In Section 2.2 the constraints for static 3D points are defined and an algorithm, evaluating them, is discussed.

In the case of stereoscopic vision, moving points are reconstructed correctly for every stereo pair using [4,19], by considering reconstructed 3D points over time and integrating the results. This allows to calculate 3D velocity as well, referred to as 6D-Vision in [9]. (The 3D velocity of a point indicates whether the point is moving or not.) The 6D-Vision approach is discussed further in Section 2.1.

Both approaches, monocular and stereoscopic, provide a motion metric which is correlated to the likelihood that the point is moving. This motion metric serves as input for the segmentation. See Figure 1.

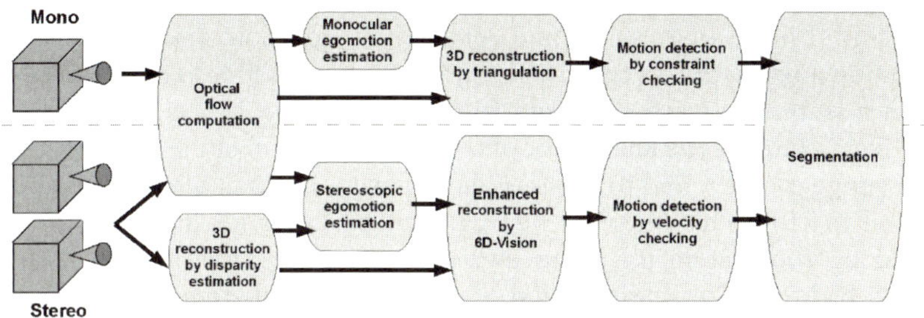


**Fig. 1.** Work flow for monocular or binocular motion segmentation

## 2.1   Stereo Vision

We start with the stereo case. The displacement of image features between the left and the right image (the disparity) is inversely related to the depth of the corresponding 3D point. This information is accumulated in an evidence-grid, similar to approaches such as in [18]. We refer to it as the *bird-view map*. This map is usually segmented, and detected objects are tracked over time in order to obtain their motion. The major disadvantage of this standard approach is that the performance of the detection depends highly on the correctness of the segmentation. Especially moving objects in front of stationary ones are often merged and therefore not detected. This causes dangerous misinterpretations and requires more powerful solutions.

In order to obtain motion information directly from the images, the optical flow has to be analysed. It gives the displacement of image features in two consecutive images of one camera, and depends on the motion of the observer as well as the motion of the corresponding 3D point. By combining the left and right optical flow fields [22], or the optical flow field of one camera with the stereo information [1,13], the 3D scene motion relative to the observer is reconstructed. Inconsistencies in scene motion fields are then detected as independently moving objects.

Direct optical flow analysis provides fast detection results, but is limited with respect to robustness and accuracy due to the immanent measurement noise. To get more reliable results, an integration of the observations over time is necessary. The Kalman filter solves this in an elegant manner. Each measurement is used to improve the current estimate of the systems state. In addition, the Kalman filter propagates the covariances of the estimated state over time, which allows the application of stochastical methods.

The core algorithm of the stereo vision system presented here follows the principle of fusing optical flow and stereo information given in [9]. The basic idea is to track points with depth estimated from stereo vision over two or more consecutive frames and to fuse the spatial and temporal information using Kalman filters. The result is an improved accuracy of the 3D-position and an estimation of the 3D-motion of the considered point at the same time. Taking into account the motion information, the above mentioned segmentation problem can be solved much more easily and robustly. In addition, using the 3D-motion information a prediction of the objects movement is possible. This allows a driver assistance system to warn and react to potential collisions in time.

The fusion implies the knowledge of the ego-motion. In our system we compute it from image points found to be stationary using a Kalman filter based approach described in [19]. This allows a fast calculation using all information already acquired by the system including inertial sensor data. We briefly discuss the proposed Kalman filter-based fusion of optical flow and stereo information.

**System Model.** We use a left handed coordinate system with the origin on the road. This coordinate system is fixed to the car, so that all estimated positions are given in the coordinate system of the moving observer. The lateral $x$-axis points to the left, the height axis $y$ points upwards and the $z$-axis represents the distance of a point straight ahead. The camera is at $(x, y, z)^T = (0, height, 0)^T$ looking along the positive $z$-direction.

Let $\mathbf{p}_k = (x, y, z)^T$ be an observed 3D point and $\mathbf{v}_k = (\dot{x}, \dot{y}, \dot{z})^T$ its associated velocity vector at the time step $k$. Assuming a constant motion during the time interval $\Delta t$ the 3D position at the time step $k + 1$ is given by

$$\mathbf{p}_{k+1} = \mathbf{R}\mathbf{p}_k + \mathbf{t} + \Delta t \mathbf{R}\mathbf{v}_k \tag{1}$$

Here the rotation matrix $\mathbf{R}$ and the translation vector $\mathbf{t}$ give the motion of the scene, that is the inverse ego-motion. The new velocity vector of the observed point is described by

$$\mathbf{v}_{k+1} = \mathbf{R}\mathbf{v}_k \tag{2}$$

Combining the location $\mathbf{p}_k$ and the velocity $\mathbf{v}_k$ in the 6D state vector $\mathbf{s}_k = (x, y, z, \dot{x}, \dot{y}, \dot{z})^T$, the time-discrete linear system model is given by

$$\mathbf{s}_k = \mathbf{A}_k \mathbf{s}_{k-1} + \mathbf{b}_k + \omega \tag{3}$$

with state transition matrix

$$\mathbf{A}_k = \begin{bmatrix} \mathbf{R}_k & \mathbf{R}_k \Delta t \\ 0 & \mathbf{R}_k \end{bmatrix} \tag{4}$$

control vector $\mathbf{b}_k = [\mathbf{t}_k , 0 , 0 , 0]^\top$ and noise term $\omega$ (assumed to be Gaussian white noise with covariance matrix $\mathbf{Q}$).

**Measurement Model.** We measure image coordinates $u$ and $v$ of a tracked feature and the disparity $d$ delivered by stereo vision, working on rectified images.

**Fig. 2.** Monocular (left) and stereo (right) motion analysis for a moving pedestrian appearing behind a stationary vehicle

Assuming a pinhole-type camera, the non-linear measurement equation for a point given in the camera coordinate system is as follows:

$$\mathbf{z} = \begin{bmatrix} u \\ v \\ d \end{bmatrix} = \frac{1}{z} \begin{bmatrix} x f_u \\ y f_v \\ b f_u \end{bmatrix} + \nu \tag{5}$$

with focal lengths $f_u$ and $f_v$ (in pixels), and baseline $b$ (in metres). The noise term $\nu$ is assumed to be Gaussian white noise with covariance matrix $\mathbf{S}$.

As the measurement equations are non-linear, we have to apply the Extended Kalman Filter (EKF), which is known to be sensitive to wrong initializations. To improve the Kalman filter's rate of convergence, a multi-filter system is used. It consists of multiple differently initialized and parameterized Kalman filters running in parallel. By analysing the innovation of each filter the best matching estimation is chosen. A detailed description of this approach is given in [9].

The result of a 6D-vision algorithm is illustrated in Figure 2. Images are taken from a moving vehicle, driving at about 30 km/h. We see that, 160 ms after the pedestrian's head was first visible, an estimation of its motion is already available, which allows analysis for the risk of collision. [The colour encoding on the left corresponds to the motion metric (blue: 0 px, red: 2 px); the arrows in the 6-D vision image on the right point to the estimated 3D position in 0.5 s, reprojected into the current image, where the colour encoding corresponds to estimated depth (close = red, far = green).]

**Scalar Motion Metric for Moving Object Detection.** The monocular or binocular algorithm estimates the position and velocity of independent image features. Due to systematical measurement errors, induced for example by occlusion effects or repetitive patterns, single points may be incorrect and a driver assistance system has to deal with them accordingly. This is accomplished by combining the estimates of multiple image features belonging to the same object, which in turn requires an object segmentation.

In order to obtain the boundaries of all moving objects, we are first interested in the question whether a 3D point is static or moving. As 6D vision estimates the 3D velocity vector, we reduce this information to absolute velocity.

## 2.2   Monocular Vision

In this case we forbear from the usage of the second camera. This affects the approach for the detection of moving points, since moving 3D points cannot be reconstructed with one camera only. A reconstruction of a moving 3D point is erroneous. The point is detected as moving if its reconstruction is identified as erroneous. To this end, one checks whether the reconstructed 3D point fulfills the constraints of a static 3D point. These constraints are as follows:

*Epipolar Constraint:* This constraint expresses that viewing rays of a static 3D point (lines joining projection centres and the 3D point) must meet. A moving 3D point in general induces skew viewing rays violating the constraint.

*Positive Depth Constraint:* The fact that all points seen by the camera must lie in front of it is known as the positive depth constraint. It is also called *cheirality constraint.* If viewing rays intersect behind the camera the actual 3D point must be moving.

*Positive Height Constraint:* All 3D points must lie above the road plane. If viewing rays intersect underneath the road the actual 3D point must be moving. This constraint requires knowledge about normal vectors of the road surface and the camera distance to the road surface. These entities are estimated exploiting the optical flow on the road [16].

*Trifocal Constraint:* A triangulated 3D point utilizing the first two views must triangulate to the same 3D point when the third view comes into consideration. This constraint is also called *trilinear constraint.*

Existing motion detection schemes exploit a subset of the above constraints either directly or indirectly. A popular scheme is the angle criterion [8,24] which uses the direction of optical flow vectors. When moving purely translational toward the scene, all flow vectors are parallel to the corresponding epipolar lines and point away from the epipole (focus of expansion). This holds true for the entire static scene. If a measured optical flow vector deviate from this expected flow direction (i.e., if the angle between measured and expected direction is not zero), the corresponding 3D point is moving. This angle criterion indirectly exploits the epipolar and the positive depth constraint.

Another popular scheme is the planar motion parallax. It is defined as the deviation of the measured optical flow from the expected flow on the road plane. For correspondences violating the positive height constraint, the parallax vector points toward the epipole since the measured flow is shorter than expected. [5,10] evaluate the planar motion parallax. A scheme exploiting the trifocal constraint is presented in [11]. It not only detects moving points but also clusters them. However, the computational burden is high.

We now develop an algorithm evaluating all available constraints quantitatively. In the work flow diagram (Figure 1), reconstruction and detection are shown as two separate steps. However, the actual algorithm avoids the explicit reconstruction in favour of a reduced computational complexity and a better statistical manageability.

The algorithm provides a motion metric measuring to which extent the constraints are violated. It is correlated to the likelihood that the point is moving (i.e., higher values indicate a higher probability).

The motion metric is developed in two steps. First, the two-view constraints are evaluated taking view one and two into account. Afterward, the trifocal constraint is evaluated using the third view.

**Two-View Constraints.** A motion metric combining the two-view constraints has been introduced in [15]. It measures the distance of a given image point in the first view to the closest point fulfilling all constraints (epipolar, positive depth, and positive height constraint). For the ease of computational complexity image points in the second view are considered noise free. We use this metric but swap the roles of the views [i.e., we compute the error (distance) in the second view].

This is illustrated in Figure 3. We first consider the correspondence $\mathbf{x}_1 \leftrightarrow \mathbf{x}_2$ in views one and two. The closest point to $\mathbf{x}_2$, fulfilling the two-view constraints, is $\mathbf{x}_{f2}$. It lies on the epipolar line $\mathbf{l}_2 = \mathbf{F}\mathbf{x}_1$ with $\mathbf{F}$ as the fundamental matrix. Note that the vector from $\mathbf{x}_{f2}$ to $\mathbf{x}_2$ is not necessarily perpendicular to $\mathbf{l}_2$. The distance $d_2$ between $\mathbf{x}_{f2}$ and $\mathbf{x}_2$ is the error arising from the first two views. For the computation of $d_2$ see [15].

**Three-View Constraint.** We now add the third view and consider the correspondence $\mathbf{x}_1 \leftrightarrow \mathbf{x}_2 \leftrightarrow \mathbf{x}_3$. As the point $\mathbf{x}_{f2}$ is defined such that it fulfills the two-view constraints, the reconstructed 3D point, arising from the triangulation of the points $\mathbf{F}\mathbf{x}_1$ and $\mathbf{x}_{f2}$, constitutes a valid 3D point. This 3D point is projected into the third view, yielding $\mathbf{x}_{f3}$. The measured image point $\mathbf{x}_3$ will coincide with $\mathbf{x}_{f3}$ if the observed 3D point is actually static. Otherwise there

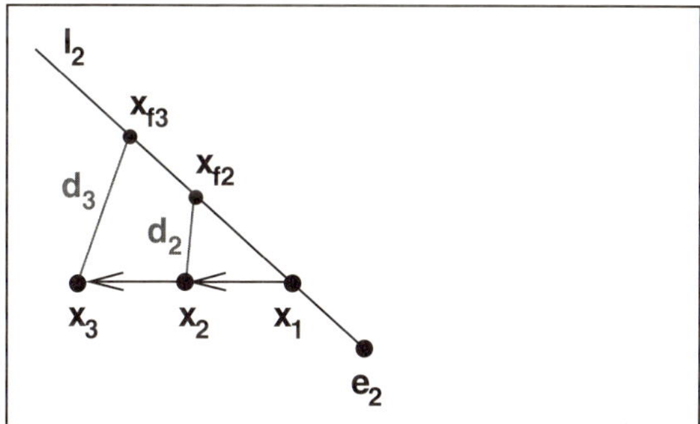


**Fig. 3.** Monocular motion metric. The image of the second view is shown. The camera moves along its optical axis observing a lateral moving point $\mathbf{x}_1 \leftrightarrow \mathbf{x}_2 \leftrightarrow \mathbf{x}_3$. The closest point to $\mathbf{x}_2$ fulfilling the two-view constraints is $\mathbf{x}_{f2}$. The error arising from two-views is the distance $d_2$. Transferring the points $\mathbf{x}_1$ and $\mathbf{x}_{f2}$ into the third view yields $\mathbf{x}_{f3}$. If the observed 3D point was actually static, $\mathbf{x}_3$ would coincide with $\mathbf{x}_{f3}$. However, the 3D point is moving which causes the trifocal error $d_3$. The overall error is $d = d_2 + d_3$. Note: in general, $\mathbf{x}_1$ and $\mathbf{x}_{f3}$ do not lie on the epipolar line $\mathbf{l}_2$.

is a distance $d_3$ (Figure 3) between them which we call *trifocal error*. $\mathbf{x}_{f3}$ is computed via the point-point-point transfer using the trifocal tensor [12]. This approach avoids the explicit triangulation of image points $\mathbf{F}\mathbf{x}_1$ and $\mathbf{x}_2$.

The final motion metric, combining the two-view constraints and the three-view constraint, is $d = d_2 + d_3$. It measures the minimal required displacement in pixel necessary to change a given correspondence into a correspondence belonging to a valid static 3D point. See Figure 3 for an example of the final motion metric. To be exact, $d$ is a pseudo-metric only since we may have $d_2\left(\mathbf{x}_2, \mathbf{x}_{f2}\right) = 0$ for distinct points $\mathbf{x}_2 \neq \mathbf{x}_{f2}$.

## 3  Segmentation

In order to derive objects from individual tracked image features, the features have to be clustered into coherent objects. Image features are usually sparse and appropriate for ego-motion estimation, however, they are not sufficient to describe whole objects or object boundaries. Objects could be found by calculating a dense flow field in which each image pixel yields an error value. A subsequent connected components analysis yields objects. Such dense flow calculation is computationally expensive and the result needs to be post-processed to distinguish between noise and moving objects.

We therefore find objects by segmenting the image into foreground (moving objects) and background (stationary world) taking the motion metric values as probabilities for the tracked image features. Image features with values above a noise threshold vote for foreground, all other features below the threshold vote for background. The noise in the motion metric is mainly due to the tracking and disparity measuring inaccuracies. For monocular motion analysis we assume an inaccuracy of $\sigma = 0.1$ px, for the stereo approach the threshold is set at $1.0$ m/s. Accumulations of such foreground seeds denote an object. Single features with a high error metric value need to be rejected as outliers. We define an energy which penalizes boundary length of object segments. The energy is then minimized using a global optimal graph-cut algorithm [6]. Further speed up techniques for flow vector segmentation can be achieved using a Multi-Resolution Graph Cut [21].

In a first step, every image pixel $\mathbf{x}$ corresponds to a node in a graph with a source node $s$ representing the background and a sink node $t$ for the foreground. Pixels voting for background are connected via an (undirected) edge to the source node, those voting for foreground to the sink node vice versa. The cost of an edge is defined as

$$d(\mathbf{x}) < \sigma \Rightarrow e(s, \mathbf{x}) = \sigma - d(\mathbf{x}) \tag{6}$$

$$d(\mathbf{x}) > \sigma \Rightarrow e(\mathbf{x}, t) = \min(d(\mathbf{x}) - \sigma, C_{max}) \ . \tag{7}$$

where $C_{max}$ is a threshold to limit outliers. The minimum function is necessary to limit the influence of wrong tracks (outliers) on the result. Additionally, adjacent image pixels (here only 4-adjacency is taken into account) are connected by

**Fig. 4.** The images on the left show the segmentation for a moving pedestrian appearing behind a stationary vehicle. Outliers are rejected and the segmentation border is accurate. The four images on the right show the influence of the edge costs on the segmentation result (later in the sequence). While small edge costs result in segments with only a few pixels (left), high edge costs result in small regions (such that the number of cut edges is minimized, right). From left to right: $C_e = \{1.5, 50, 500, 1000\}$.

edges. The costs of these edges depend on the grey-value difference of its two end points. The cost values are defined by

$$e(\mathbf{x}, \mathbf{y}) = \frac{C_e}{\|I(\mathbf{x}) - I(\mathbf{y})\| + \varepsilon} \tag{8}$$

where $C_e$ is a constant scaling factor, used to regularize the influence of edge costs (boundary length), and $\varepsilon$ is a small value to prevent numerical instability. $I(\mathbf{x})$ is the grey value of $\mathbf{x}$, in our case a scalar value between 0 and 4095, as we use 12 bit images. Equation (8) is designed such that segmentation boundaries along high image gradients are more likely than in homogeneous regions.

Clearly, the result depends on the costs of the edges, especially on the constant $C_e$. If $C_e$ is too low, the segmentation only contains single pixels whereas a high value of $C_e$ results in only one small segment (or no segment at all) because removing edges to the source or the sink becomes less costly than removing those edges connecting image pixels. Both situations can be seen in Figure 4. If the sum of all edges of a pixel is larger than $C_{max}$, the pixel will not be cut. Therefore we set $e(\mathbf{x}, \mathbf{y}) = 0.5\, C_{max}$ , for all tracked points $\mathbf{x}$.

To regularize the size of the segments, especially in low-contrast regions such as the road surface, the number of foreground pixels is penalized. This is done by adding additional edges with constant cost $e(s, \mathbf{x}) = C_{BG}$, from every node $\mathbf{x}$ to the source $s$.

This is equivalent to adding a background prior for every pixel in the image. In the following results section we use constant values for the determinable parameters of the algorithm, demonstrating the adaptability of the algorithm for different scenarios:

$$C_{max} = 6 \qquad C_e = 150 \qquad C_{BG} = 0.01 \ .$$

This is a usual mapping of image pixels onto a graph representation as done in [6,23]. A cut in a graph is found by removing edges such that no more connections between source and sink exist. The cost of a cut is the sum of its comprised edges.

The minimal cut is defined as the cut with the minimal cost out of all possible cuts in the graph; see, for example, [21] for a diagram.

## 4    Experimental Results

This section applies our motion analysis and segmentation to real imagery. We use the same set of features for monocular and binocular motion analysis. The first example in Figure 4 (left) shows the segmentation of the pedestrian appearing behind a stationary vehicle. The segmentation boundary proves to be accurate keeping in mind that features are sparse in the image (compared with Figure 2, right and left). The monocular and the stereo approach yield exactly the same segmentation result for the lateral moving pedestrian.

Figure 5 shows a traffic scene with a crossing car and a preceding car in 31 m distance. The speed of both cars is approximately 36 km/h. Both approaches, monocular and stereo motion analysis, yield similar segmentation results. Looking at the motion metric values, which are the driving energies for the graph-cut segmentation, the difference between both approaches becomes visible. In the monocular case, the energy values of features located on the preceding car are small. This is due to the fact that the car moves longitudinal at a high distance and the corresponding flow vectors do not differ much from those generated by stationary objects. On the other hand, most flow vectors induced by the crossing car deviate from any flow vectors of stationary objects, which fulfill the monocular motion constraints. However, the flow vectors in the vicinity of the horizon are similar to those generated by stationary objects. The segmentation result still is accurate and both moving vehicles are detected. For a more detailed investigation of these phenomena, see [17].

The stereo approach measures the absolute 3D velocities of tracked features. The preceding car is moving at a relatively high speed of 36 km/h while the crossing car is moving at lower speed. This is clearly represented by the motion metric. In contrast to the monocular approach, all features on both cars yield correct results as the stereo approach does not suffer from the motion

(a)       (b)       (c)       (d)

**Fig. 5.** Detection and segmentation results of a crossing and a preceding object. Monocular vision (a,b) performs similar to stereoscopic vision (c,d). Tracked image features are shown on the left of each pair; they are color encoded according to the corresponding motion metric. For monocular vision (a), the range is from 0 px (blue) to 7 px (red); for stereoscopic vision (b), the range is from 0 m/s (blue) to 7 m/s (red).

(a)        (b)        (c)        (d)

**Fig. 6.** Detection and segmentation results of preceding and oncoming objects. Monocular vision (a,b) is only able to detect the lower parts of the preceding objects; the oncoming object is not detected at all. Stereoscopic vision (c,d) does not suffer from these limitations. (Color encoding as in Figure 5.)

ambiguity between features on moving and stationary objects. The preceding car is therefore fully segmented.

This situation becomes even more evident when looking at the autobahn sequence in Figure 6. The vehicles move with a speed of 84 km/h. The monocular approach is able to detect the car driving ahead, and the truck, being overtaken, on the right side. But only the lower parts of the vehicles are detected, resulting in an incomplete segmentation of the vehicles. The stereo approach not only detects the vehicles completely, it is also able to detect oncoming traffic.

## 5   Conclusion

This paper investigates a monocular and a stereo approach to perceive motion in image sequences. For each approach a motion metric was introduced measuring the likelihood that a tracked image feature corresponds to a moving 3D point. We applied motion metrics to traffic scenes captured by a camera installed in a vehicle. Using image segmentation based on the investigated motion metrics we were able to detect and segment other moving traffic participants. On average, the stereo approach outperforms the monocular approach in terms of accuracy. However, there is a higher computational cost for the computation of both stereo and KLT tracks. Image sequences on highways and urban scenarios using the same parameter sets demonstrate the practicality of this novel approach to machine sensing of motion.

Future work in this area may consist of integrating the tracking of features in the monocular approach for a temporal integration of information. Also, the extension of the segmentation algorithm. to distinguish between different motion directions, is in the scope of future work, to be able to determine different objects and obstacles.

## References


1. Argyros, A.A., Lourakis, M.I., Trahanias, P.E., Orphanoudakis, S.C.: Qualitative detection of 3d motion discontinuities. In: Proc. IEEE/RSJ Int. Conf. Intelligent Robots Systems, vol. 3, pp. 1630–1637 (1996)

2. Armangué, X., Araújo, H., Salvi, J.: Differential epipolar constraint in mobile robot egomotion estimation. In: Proc. IEEE Int. Conf. Pattern Recognition, pp. 599–602 (2002)
3. Avidan, S., Shashua, A.: Trajectory triangulation: 3d reconstruction of moving points from a monocular image sequence. IEEE Trans. Pattern Analysis Machine Intelligence 22, 348–357 (2000)
4. Badino, H.: A robust approach for ego-motion estimation using a mobile stereo platform. In: Proc. Int. Workshop Complex Motion (2004)
5. Baehring, D., Simon, S., Niehsen, W., Stiller, C.: Detection of close cut-in and overtaking vehicles for driver assistance based on planar parallax. In: Proc. IEEE Intelligent Vehicles Symposium (2005)
6. Boykov, Y., Kolmogorov, V.: An experimental comparison of min-cut/Max-flow algorithms for energy minimization in vision. In: Figueiredo, M., Zerubia, J., Jain, A.K. (eds.) EMMCVPR 2001. LNCS, vol. 2134, pp. 359–374. Springer, Heidelberg (2001)
7. Chalimbaud, P., Berry, F., Marmoiton, F., Alizon, S.: Design of a hybrid visuo-inertial smart sensor. In: Proc. Workshop Integration Vision Inertial Sensors (in conjunction with IEEE Int. Conf. Robotics Automation) (2005)
8. Clauss, M., Bayerl, P., Neumann, H.: Segmentation of independently moving objects using a maximum-likelihood principle. In: Proc. Autonome Mobile Systeme (2005)
9. Franke, U., Rabe, C., Badino, H., Gehrig, S.: 6D-vision: Fusion of stereo and motion for robust environment perception. In: Kropatsch, W.G., Sablatnig, R., Hanbury, A. (eds.) DAGM 2005. LNCS, vol. 3663, pp. 216–223. Springer, Heidelberg (2005)
10. Giachetti, A., Campani, M., Torre, V.: The use of optical flow for road navigation. IEEE Trans. Robotics and Automation 14, 34–48 (1998)
11. Hartley, R., Vidal, R.: The multibody trifocal tensor: Motion segmentation from 3 perspective views. In: Proc. IEEE Int. Conf. Computer Vision Pattern Recognition (2004)
12. Hartley, R., Zisserman, A.: Multiple View Geometry in Computer Vision, 2nd edn. Cambridge University Press, Cambridge (2003)
13. Heinrich, S.: Fast obstacle detection using flow/depth constraint. In: Proc. IEEE Intelligent Vehicles Symposium, vol. 2, pp. 658–665 (2002)
14. Ke, Q., Kanade, T.: Transforming camera geometry to a virtual downward-looking camera: Robust ego-motion estimation and ground-layer detection. In: IEEE International Conference on Computer Vision and Pattern Recognition (CVPR), pp. I–390– I–397 (2003)
15. Klappstein, J., Stein, F., Franke, U.: Monocular motion detection using spatial constraints in a unified manner. In: IEEE Intelligent Vehicles Symposium, IV (2006)
16. Klappstein, J., Stein, F., Franke, U.: Applying Kalman filtering to road homography estimation. In: Proc. Workshop Planning Perception Navigation Intelligent Vehicles (in conjunction with IEEE Int. Conf. Robotics Automation) (2007)
17. Klappstein, J., Stein, F., Franke, U.: Detectability of moving objects using correspondences over two and three frames. In: Hamprecht, F.A., Schnörr, C., Jähne, B. (eds.) DAGM 2007. LNCS, vol. 4713, pp. 112–121. Springer, Heidelberg (2007)
18. Martin, M.C., Moravec, H.: Robot evidence grids. Technical Report CMU-RI-TR-96-06, Robotics Institute, Carnegie Mellon University (1996)
19. Rabe, C., Franke, U., Gehrig, S.: Fast detection of moving objects in complex scenarios. In: Proc. IEEE Intelligent Vehicles Symposium, pp. 398–403 (2007)
20. Tomasi, C., Kanade, T.: Detection and tracking of point features. Carnegie Mellon University, Technical Report CMU-CS-91-132 (1991)

21. Vaudrey, T., Gruber, D., Wedel, A., Klappstein, J.: Space-time multi-resolution banded graph-cut for fast segmentation. In: Rigoll, G. (ed.) DAGM 2008. LNCS, vol. 5096, pp. 203–213. Springer, Heidelberg (2008)
22. Waxman, A.M., Duncan, J.H.: Binocular image flows: steps toward stereo-motion fusion. IEEE Trans. Pattern Analysis Machine Intelligence 8, 715–729 (1986)
23. Wedel, A., Schoenemann, T., Brox, T., Cremers, D.: Warpcut - fast obstacle segmentation in monocular video. In: Hamprecht, F.A., Schnörr, C., Jähne, B. (eds.) DAGM 2007. LNCS, vol. 4713, pp. 264–273. Springer, Heidelberg (2007)
24. Woelk, F., Koch, R.: Fast monocular bayesian detection of independently moving objects by a moving observer. In: Rasmussen, C.E., Bülthoff, H.H., Schölkopf, B., Giese, M.A. (eds.) DAGM 2004. LNCS, vol. 3175, pp. 27–35. Springer, Heidelberg (2004)

# Usefulness of Retina Codes in Biometrics*

Thomas Fuhrmann, Jutta Hämmerle-Uhl, and Andreas Uhl

Department of Computer Sciences, Salzburg University, Austria
uhl@cosy.sbg.ac.at

**Abstract.** We discuss methods for generating retina codes from retinal images for biometric user authentication. Starting from the optical disc, concentric circles are placed over the binary vessel image for data sampling and different variants of retina code are generated after transformation to polar coordinates. The methods inter personal variability and robustness is evaluated on the publicly available DRIVE database. Results indicate a low inter personal variability questioning the usefulness of retina codes in sensible authentication systems.

## 1   Introduction

With the increasing usage of biometric systems the interest in not-yet widely accepted modalities rises. Retina features are among these potentially promising but not mainstream techniques. Being transparent, the retina is situated in the innermost part of the ocular fundus, retinal features mainly consist of blood vessels originating from the entry point of the optic nerve and spreading across the ocular fundus (see Fig. 1.a for an example). The pattern of these vessels is said to be unique for each individual person and might therefore be used for biometric recognition systems. However, the scanning operation is required to be much more intrusive and controlled as compared to e.g. iris-based systems due to the location in the inner parts of the eye and user acceptance of such conditions is generally low. Therefore, the primary application context of this modality will be in high security environments like military or governmental agencies.

According to literature [4, p.106ff], retina-scan based biometric systems exhibit the following strengths: high spoofing resistance, high stability in the sense of time-invariance, and high recognition accuracy.

In fact, due to their location at the background of the eye, retinal features can hardly be replaced or modified, also sensors capturing the respective images can hardly by fooled. On the other hand, the stability of retinal vessels is questionable since many eye diseases include some blood vessel pathology as found e.g. in proliferative diabetic retinopathy [3], which is characterized by new vessel growth especially near the optical disk. The possible impact of such diseases on retina feature based biometric systems has to be seriously considered and investigated before a sensible deployment should take place.

---

* This work has been partially supported by the Austrian Science Fund, project no. L554-N15.

T. Wada, F. Huang, and S. Lin (Eds.): PSIVT 2009, LNCS 5414, pp. 624–632, 2009.
© Springer-Verlag Berlin Heidelberg 2009

Eye-based biometric modalities in general are believed to be highly secure due to the well investigated low FAR of some popular iris recognition systems [5]. However, also in iris recognition several techniques exist which exhibit significantly inferior recognition performance (e.g., based on histograms [6]). Obviously, it is not only the potential distinctiveness of the physiological trait that determines the recognition accuracy but of course the type of extracted template data plays an at least equally important role as well.

There is not much work available on using retinal features for biometric purposes. Most of the literature on retinal features is found in ophthalmology where retinal vessels are used in diagnosis or as landmarks for image registration (see e.g. [7]). Strengths and weaknesses of retina-scan based biometrics are discussed in [4], but no concrete feature extraction technique or template data structure is described. Crossings of retinal vessels are suggested to be used as biometric features in [8,9] and good accuracy is reported. Retica Systems Inc.[1] offers a different (commercial) solution based on a "retina code" (inspired by Daugmans' "iris code" principle [5]).

In this work we discuss the use of retina codes for biometric recognition as inspired by the solution sketched by Retica Systems Inc. Section 2 discusses feature extraction techniques for subsequent retina code generation which include optical disc segmentation and retinal vessel extraction. Section 3 describes several variants of retina code generation and Section 4 is devoted to experimental testing with emphasis on the overall code variation within a population and FMR under signal distortion. Section 5 concludes the paper.

## 2   Feature Extraction

Retina-based methods use ocular fundus images as a source for extracting biometric features for user authentication. Extracting usable feature sets for retina code generation from these images requires a combination of two different preprocessing methods.

### 2.1   Optical Disc Segmentation

For retina code generation a reference point has to be defined (analogous to the center of the pupil with iris recognition). Here the optical disc (where the optical nerve leaves the retina) seems suitable. In the retinal images the optical disc appears as a bright circular shaped object partly covered with vessels that has a higher background luminance and higher local variance as the rest of the retina. So the center of the optical disc can be used as a reference point for developing a retina template out of a segmented vessel feature image.

Detection of the optical disc has been largely covered in literature and numerous methods have been developed. Many applications choose a method that uses circular Hough transform on an thresholded edge image of the retinal surface as in Barret et al. [10]. In our context this method sometimes yields poor

---

[1] `www.retica.com`

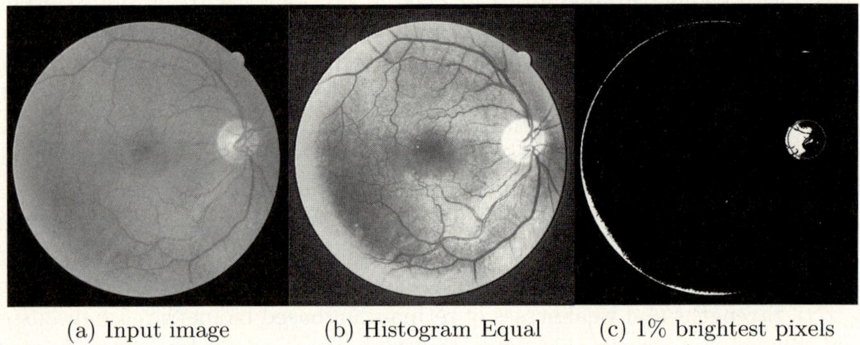

(a) Input image          (b) Histogram Equal          (c) 1% brightest pixels

**Fig. 1.** Finding the optical disc

results both in accuracy and detection time especially when testing robustness. In this case only few edges of the optical disc are detected making it often even impossible to locate it with the Hough transform.

So we adapted this technique by taking into account the fact that the optical disc is usually an object with the highest luminance values in the image. Another possible criterion suggested in literature is highest variance [11]. In order to use a global threshold $t$ for all possible input images (and also distorted versions) we first apply a histogram equalization to the image. Using the highest 1 percent of the intensity image pixels ($t = 0.99$) a binary image is created that predominantly contains pixels of the optical disc (see Fig. 1.c). For finding the center of the circle that encloses the majority of pixels concentrated in a small region finally the Hough transform is applied locally. Fig. 1 displays the steps for finding the optical disc.

## 2.2   Vessel Extraction

Different approaches for automatic vessel segmentation have been proposed in literature (e.g. [7]). We have chosen to adapt the MATLAB software package `mlvessel`[2] based on the wavelet-domain method described in [3] since it yields good results in enhancing vessel contrast while filtering out noise. First the retinal image is pre-processed by artificially extending the border that is defined by the camera's aperture in order to remove the strong contrast between the optical fundus and the image mask. Realizing that the wavelet transform is able to filter locally makes it effective for detecting local properties such as blood vessels. The continuous wavelet transform of a signal $f(x)$ is defined

$$W_\psi(b, a) = \frac{1}{\sqrt{a}} \int f(x)\psi^* \left( \frac{x - b}{a} \right) d^2x \qquad (1)$$

---

[2] `http://www.retina.iv.fapesp.br`

with $\psi^*$ denoting the complex conjugate of the 2-D Morlet wavelet $\psi$ defined by [3] as:

$$\psi(x) = e^{ik_0 x} e^{-\frac{1}{2}|Ax|^2} \tag{2}$$

where $A = diag[\sqrt{\epsilon}, 1], \epsilon \geq 1$ is a 2 x 2 diagonal matrix defining the anisotropy of the filter. We only use the results produced by the Morlet wavelet with parameters $a = 2$, $k_0 = [0, 3]$ and $\epsilon = 4$ since this yields the best resolution of vessels. So for the scale value $a = 2$ maximum response over all possible angles of the Morlet wavelet starting from 0 up to 170 degrees in steps of 10 is being calculated.

The resulting feature image is used for creating a binary vessel segmentation image by thresholding. Simple thresholding is the method of first choice because of its speed. However using a global threshold results in very different binary images concerning the number of vessels thus it is not very suitable for creating a retina template and matching. In order to achieve a well-balanced number of vessels in the binary images we first statistically determine the mean value of vessel pixels in a set of typical images suited for matching. For the data base used in our experiments (see Section 4.1) this gave us a mean value of vessel pixels of 8.5 % and a standard deviation of 1,5 %. Starting from a standard threshold we slightly adjust the threshold up or down until the number of vessel pixels meets our above criteria. In order to get rid of unconnected vessels resulting from our thresholding process all connected objects that have fewer than a certain number of pixels are removed (see Fig. 2).

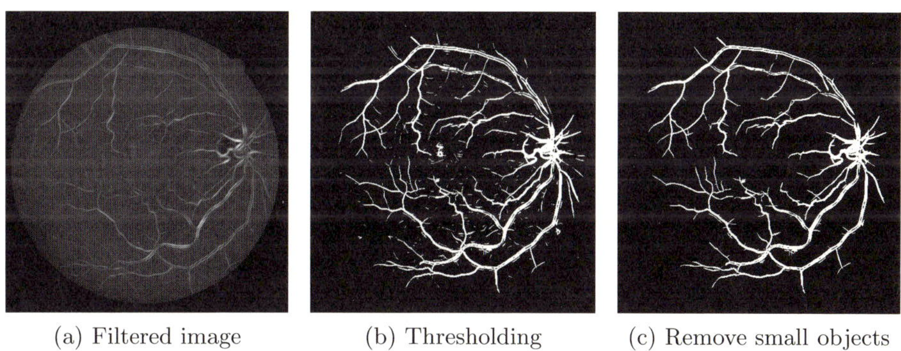

(a) Filtered image      (b) Thresholding      (c) Remove small objects

**Fig. 2.** Vessel Segmentation

## 3   Retina Code Generation

Starting from the center of the optical disc we use concentric circles for taking samples from the binary vessel images. For construction of these circles we have implemented Bresenham's circle drawing algorithm [1]. For every circle pixel its value is set according to the underlying vessel or non-vessel pixel. Then the values of $n_{avg}$ neighbouring circles are averaged and transformed to polar coordinates

**Table 1.** Sampling settings

| Name | $N_{circ}$ | $n_{step}$ | $n_{avg}$ | $r_0$ |
| --- | --- | --- | --- | --- |
| **L1** | 15 | 3 | 3 | 5 |
| **L2** | 30 | 3 | 3 | 5 |
| **H1** | 60 | 5 | 3 | 5 |

in steps of 1°. It is important to mention that outer circles usually degrade to circular arcs since the optical disc is mostly located at the left or right border of the retinal surface. This results in lower information density concerning the whole retina code which is further decreased by the higher arc length of the circles when using steps of 1° and the fact that the density of the vessels is usually higher around the optical disc. Thus hitting an underlying vessel pixel becomes more unlikely for bigger (outer) circles. This is confirmed also in the example in Fig. 3.c. So we see that it is vital for our method to set the right parameters for the sampling procedure i.e., the number of samples (circles) $N_{circ}$, the averaging value $n_{avg}$ (i.e. how many neighbouring circles are used for producing a single bit value), and the radius of the first circle $r_0$.

We investigate different retina code variants as shown in the settings of Table 1 in order to see how the sampling parameters affect the matching performance. The resulting retina codes are of sizes 360x5 (225 Byte), 360x10 (450 Byte) and 360x20 (900 Byte). These templates can be further compressed by using Run-Length Encoding since there are usually long sequences of non-vessel pixels within each code. Retica Systems Inc. provide the information of using 50-100 or even 20-50 bytes for their templates, but this could refer to encoded data.

Setting L1 only samples around the optical disc (mostly resulting in entire circles), L2 is the same as L1 but with increased $N_{circ}$ and H1 also includes degraded circles due to the increased sampling area. Examples for the resulting retina codes from this sampling process are shown in Fig. 3.

(a) Setting L1                (b) Setting L2                (c) Setting H1

**Fig. 3.** Retina Codes

## 4    Experiments

### 4.1    Experimental Settings

We tested and evaluated our methods on a publicly available database of non-mydriatic images and corresponding manual vessel segmentations: the DRIVE[3]

---

[3] www.isi.uu.nl/Research/Databases/DRIVE/

**Table 2.** Robustness Tests

| Test | Settings |
| --- | --- |
| **JPEG** | Quality 10% |
| **JPEG2000** | Compression ratio 100:1 |
| **Rotation** | $90°, -90°$ and $180°$ |
| **Sharpening** | r=1 pixel, $\sigma$=1, amount=500% |
| **Hist. Equal.** | Standard flat histogram |

database [2]. The DRIVE database consists of 40 images that were captured in digital form from a Canon CR5 non-mydriatic 3CCD camera at 45 field of view (FOV). The images are stored in TIFF format of size 565 x 584 with 8 bits per color channel. Since the DRIVE database only contains images of different persons our experiments are limited to examining the inter person variability and FMR under image distortions. The green channel of the non-mydriatic images shows the best contrast so we chose it for optical disc detection as well as for vessel extraction (and subsequent code generation).

Matching between two distinct retina codes is done by calculating their Hamming distance. In order to compensate for rotated versions of the images the two retina patterns are shifted against each other and the minimum of all Hamming distances is calculated. For each image to be tested the Hamming distance with each of the remaining templates in the database is determined ("leave one out" strategy). A pair having Hamming distance below a decision threshold $T$ indicates a positive match.

For testing the robustness and the performance of our approach we generate several distorted versions of our input images by using the open-source tool `Imagemagick` (see Tab. 2 for the specifications) and matching the resulting templates with the images in the database.

### 4.2 Experimental Results

The first step in testing our method is matching all retina codes against each other (for each of the settings shown in Tab.1) to see how the scores are distributed and if the codes are sufficiently discriminative. The mean relative Hamming distances $\bar{h}$, their standard deviations $s_h$, and the maximum and minimum Hamming distances $h_{max}$ and $h_{min}$ for this test are shown in Tab. 3. Assuming uncorrelated templates from different persons an average close to 0.5 in terms of Hamming distance is expected. In fact, the mean Hamming distances $\bar{h}$ are much smaller ($0.123 \leq \bar{h} \leq 0.216$). In addition to that, the range of obtained Hamming distances $[h_{min}, h_{max}]$ is very small and covers only 7-8% of the overall possible range.

Setting L2 shows the best results with respect to highest average Hamming distance values and standard deviation. The low values for H1 may be explained when taking Fig.3.c as example: of course, the large black areas – stemming from the circular arcs without any vessels close to the images' edges – in the

**Table 3.** Score distribution

|  | $\bar{h}$ | $s_h$ | $h_{max}$ | $h_{min}$ |
|---|---|---|---|---|
| **L1** | 0.206 | 0.022 | 0.236 | 0.165 |
| **L2** | 0.216 | 0.028 | 0.250 | 0.172 |
| **H1** | 0.123 | 0.027 | 0.172 | 0.079 |

**Table 4.** Results of Robustness Tests

|  | L1 | | | L2 | | | H1 | | |
|---|---|---|---|---|---|---|---|---|---|
|  | $h_{max}$ | $h_{min}$ | $FMR$ | $h_{max}$ | $h_{min}$ | $FMR$ | $h_{max}$ | $h_{min}$ | $FMR$ |
| **JPEG** | 0.115 | 0.053 | 0 % | 0.107 | 0.064 | 0 % | 0.074 | 0.032 | 0 % |
| **JPEG2000** | 0.108 | 0.065 | 0 % | 0.109 | 0.057 | 0 % | 0.104 | 0.037 | 25 % |
| **Rotation** | 0.151 | 0.073 | 0 % | 0.115 | 0.081 | 0 % | 0.095 | 0.039 | 25 % |
| **Hist. Equal.** | 0.172 | 0.097 | 17.5 % | 0.187 | 0.119 | 5 % | 0.118 | 0.055 | 17.5 % |
| **Sharpening** | 0.181 | 0.121 | 2.5 % | 0.158 | 0.124 | 0 % | 0.103 | 0.06 | 30 % |

code result in low Hamming distances. This is also true (in less pronounced manner) for the other settings where we also find an imbalance between black (non-vessel) and white (vessel) areas causing low differences in general. These results indicate a very low inter personal variability of the generated code which makes the occurrence of false positive matches highly probable. While actual matching performance can not be derived directly from these values since intra personal variability can not be assessed at present state (due to the lack of corresponding data in the DRIVE database), low inter personal variability suggests the approach not to be suited for larger populations at least. The retina code example given by Retica Systems Inc. ("Multi-Radius Digital Pattern"[4]) seems to indicate even smaller potential for high variability (since the generation is not explained in detail, a reliable statement on this issue is not possible of course). Recall that Retica Systems Inc. claims a template size of 20 - 100 bytes whereas the smallest template investigated here has 225 byte. This of course worsens the situation for the commercial system. Also, the comparison to an iris code[5] suggests the retina code to be of significantly lower variability potential.

The results of the robustness test are shown in Tab. 4. Again, $h_{max}$ denotes the highest relative Hamming distance of all matches, $h_{min}$ the lowest value and $FMR$ indicates the FMR ratio (ratio of false positive matches and the number of tests performed). The decision threshold $T$ for computing FMR was derived from the score distribution test and is set to $T = h_{min}$ for all subsequent robustness and sampling tests (see Tab. 3).

Setting L2 performs best of all having only minor problems when the image is histogram-equalized. This is usually a problem with vessel segmentation yielding

---

[4] http://www.retica.com/site/images/howitworks.pdf
[5] http://www.retica.com/site/technology/irisretina.html

to many vessels and sometimes distorting the code too much. Both Settings L1 and L2 show very good robustness against false positive matches even under severe compression. This confirms previous results on lossy compression of biometric sample data not to effect FAR as long as applied in sensible ranges. Also rotation and sharpening does not lead to false positives in case of L2. A severe problem occurs with lowpass filtering. Here the vessels lying over the optical disc cannot be clearly distinguished any more, resulting in corrupted codes for all settings (since sampling near the optical disc is most crucial for our templates). Thus Lowpass filtering is omitted in Tab. 4. H1 shows very poor results with respect to robustness. Even rotation leads to 25% FMR although rotation is compensated in the matching stage. It is also remarkable that the higher sampling rate of H1 does not at all improve accuracy when using distorted images. Overall, it gets clear that the sampling strategy for H1 is not at all suited for generating sensible retina codes.

## 5   Conclusion and Future Work

The methods considered for generating retina codes from retinal images have exhibited very low inter personal variability – given the fact that retina based biometrics are probably restricted to high security environments due to the inconvenient data acquisition process, the real-life applicability of these techniques as a stand-alone technique is as least questionable (as long as the encoding of the data is not adapted properly). Good robustness against JPEG and JPEG2000 compression not leading to false positives at low bitrates has been observed. Note that all those findings only apply to retina code templates but not for retina-scan based biometrics in general.

Future work will involve a cooperation with the Department of Ophthalmology at the local hospital to get access to data allowing the determination of intra personal variability and to study the effects of eye diseases on a retina code based recognition scheme. Additionally, we will study the effect of using run-length encoding of the retina codes on the resulting Hamming distances.

## References


1. Bresenham, J.: A linear algorithm for incremental display of circular arcs. Communications of the ACM 20(2), 100–106 (1977)
2. Staal, J., Abramoff, M., Niemeijer, M., Viergever, M., van Ginneken, B.: Ridge based vessel segmentation in color images of the retina. IEEE Transactions on Medical Imaging 23(4), 501–509 (2004)
3. Soares, J.V.B., Leandro, J.J.G., Cesar Jr., R.M., Jelinek, H.F., Cree, M.J.: Retinal vessel segmentation using the 2-d gabor wavelet and supervised classification. IEEE Transactions on Medical Imaging 25(9), 1214–1222 (2006)
4. Nanavati, S., Thieme, M., Nanavati, R.: Biometrics – Identity verification in a networked world. Wiley Computer Publishing, Chichester (2002)
5. Daugman, J.: How iris recognition works. IEEE Transactions on Circiuts and Systems for Video Technology 14(1), 21–30 (2004)

6. Ives, R., Guidry, A., Etter, D.: Iris recognition using histogram analysis. In: Conference Record of the 38th Asilomar Conference on Signals, Systems, and Computers, vol. 1, pp. 562–566. IEEE Signal Processing Society, Los Alamitos (2004)
7. Vermeer, K., Vos, F., Lemij, H., Vossepoel, A.: A model based method for retinal blood vessel detection. Computers in Biology and Medicine 34, 209–219 (2004)
8. Lin, T., Zheng, Y.: Node-matching-based pattern recognition method for retinal blood vessel images. Optical Engineering 42(11), 3302–3306 (2003)
9. Xu, Z., Guo, X., Hu, X., Chen, X., Wang, Z.: The identification and recognition based on point for blood vessel of ocular fundus. In: Zhang, D., Jain, A.K. (eds.) ICB 2005. LNCS, vol. 3832, pp. 770–776. Springer, Heidelberg (2005)
10. Barrett, S.F., Naess, E., Molvik, T.: Employing the hough transform to locate the optic disk. Biomedical Sciences Instrumentation 37, 81–86 (2001)
11. Sinthanayothin, C., Boyce, J., Cook, H., Williamson, T.: Automated localisation of the optic disc, fovea, and retinal blood vessels from digital colour fundus images. British Journal of Ophthalmology 83, 902–910 (1999)

# Inclusion of a Second-Order Prior
# into Semi-Global Matching


Simon Hermann[1], Reinhard Klette[1], and Eduardo Destefanis[2]

[1] The *.enpeda..* Project, The University of Auckland, New Zealand
s.hermann@cs.auckland.ac.nz
[2] Universidad Tecnológica Nacional, Facultad Regional Córdoba, Argentina



**Abstract.** Today's stereo vision algorithms and computing technology
allow real-time 3D data analysis, for example for driver assistance
systems. A recently developed Semi-Global Matching (SGM) approach
by H. Hirschmüller became a popular choice due to performance and
robustness. This paper evaluates different parameter settings for SGM,
and its main contribution consists in suggesting to include a second order
prior into the smoothness term of the energy function. It also proposes
and tests a new cost function for SGM. Furthermore, some preprocessing
(edge images) proved to be of great value for improving SGM stereo
results on real-world sequences, as previously already shown by S. Guan
and R. Klette for belief propagation. There is also a performance gain for
engineered stereo data (e.g.) as currently used on the Middlebury stereo
website. However, the fact that results are not as impressive as on the
*.enpeda..* sequences indicates that optimizing for engineered data does
not neccessarily improve real world stereo data analysis.


## 1   Introduction

Stereo algorithms are currently evaluated either on selected images with
calculated ground truth, or on real-world stereo sequences, such as typical
for driver assistance systems (DAS). Interestingly, evaluation results differ; for
example, algorithms performing well on engineered image examples may fail on
real-world sequences [7].

This paper evaluates variants of the SGM algorithm of [5] both on stereo
images of the Middlebury stereo website[1] as well as on real-world image
sequences of the *.enpeda..* test image website.[2] It discusses various parameter
settings and possible preprocessing steps.

### 1.1   Semi-Global Matching

The SGM algorithm approximates the minimum of a 2D energy function by
minimizing multiple 1D energies, employing a dynamic programming scheme.
The energy function consists of a data term and two smoothness terms. The first

---

[1] *vision.middlebury.edu/stereo/*
[2] *www.mi.auckland.ac.nz*, and follow the data link.


T. Wada, F. Huang, and S. Lin (Eds.): PSIVT 2009, LNCS 5414, pp. 633–644, 2009.

smoothness term penalizes small disparity changes of neighboring pixels with a rather low penalty $c_1$ to allow slanted surfaces. The second term penalizes larger disparity changes with a higher penalty $c_2$. This second penalty is independent of the actual disparity change in order to preserve depth discontinuities. The previously mentioned 1D energies are defined as minimum cost paths $L_\mathbf{a}$ that start at each border pixel of the image and are traversed in direction $\mathbf{a}$.

A direction is basically a digitized line, and all digital lines of identical slopes are considered to be equivalent. Usually eight directions are sufficient in SGM to obtain high-quality results. For a digital line in direction $\mathbf{a}$, processed between image border and pixel $p$, we only consider the segment $p_0 p_1 \ldots p_n$ of that digital line, with $p_0$ on the image border, and $p_n = p$. The cost at pixel position $p$ (for a disparity $d$) on the path $L_\mathbf{a}$ is recursively defined as follows (for $i = 1, 2, \ldots, n$):

$$
\begin{aligned}
L_\mathbf{a}(p_i, d) = \ &C(p_i, d) + \min\big[L_\mathbf{a}(p_{i-1}, d), \\
&L_\mathbf{a}(p_{i-1}, d-1) + c_1, L_\mathbf{a}(p_{i-1}, d+1) + c_1, \\
&\min_\Delta L_\mathbf{a}(p_{i-1}, \Delta) + c_2\big] - \min_\Delta L_\mathbf{a}(p_{i-1}, \Delta)
\end{aligned}
$$

where $C(p, d)$ corresponds to the data term and is the similarity cost of pixel $p$ for disparity $d$. The costs of paths $L_\mathbf{a}$, for all (say, eight) directions $\mathbf{a}$, are accumulated at a pixel $p$, for all disparities $d$ with $0 \leq d \leq d_{max}$, and the disparity $d_{opt}$ with the lowest cost is finally selected.

To achieve subpixel accuracy it is proposed to fit a parabolic curve through costs of disparities $d_{opt} - 1$, $d_{opt}$, and $d_{opt} + 1$, and to take the position of the minimum. Outliers may be filtered by applying a small median filter. For a given stereo pair of images, one image serves as base, and the other one is matched against the base image.

To enforce the uniqueness of a disparity map (for a given stereo pair), roles of base and match images are swapped, which allows to calculate a second disparity image. In a final consistency check, a pixel is labeled valid if the difference of corresponding disparities (in both disparity maps) does not exceed 1; otherwise the pixel is labeled invalid.

[6] identifies invalid disparities either as occlusions or mismatches. For subsequent validation of those, a discontinuity preserving interpolation method is proposed in which valid disparities are propagated into adjacent invalid disparities. This propagation uses, similar to the SGM step, a number of (say, eight) directions, and generates possible values, one for each direction. The original paper suggests to treat mismatches and occlusions differently, by choosing the second lowest value for occlusions (since this value would rather come from the background), and to use the median value as a fair representative for a mismatch. For further details of the algorithm and instructions for implementation, see [5,6].

## 1.2   Experimental Setup

We classify potential parameters of an SGM algorithm into primary and secondary parameters.

**Table 1.** Errors in % for the reference configuration of secondary parameters

|  | Mean 1/4 | Mean 1/2 | Mean | Median | Min | Max |
|---|---|---|---|---|---|---|
| Reference parameter | **13.1** | **13.5** | **19.3** | **14.3 / (40,125)** | **12.8 / (20,125)** | **90.1 / (0,0)** |

**Primary and Secondary Parameters.** Penalties $c_1$ and $c_2$ are primary parameters of the cost accumulation step of the algorithm. Hirschmüller suggested to adjust $c_2$ to the magnitude of the local intensity gradient. As a simple approximation, $c_2$ is divided by the intensity difference of the current and the previous pixel. If, after such an adjustment, $c_2 \leq c_1$, we set $c_2 = c_1 + 1$.

Any other parameter is considered in this paper to be secondary. The objective now is to derive normative statements about secondary parameters. For that we define a reference configuration of secondary parameters, and evaluate image pairs based on ground truth, for all the possible combinations of $c_1$ and $c_2$, with $c_1 = 0, ..., 50$ and $c_1$ incremented in steps of 5, and $c_2 = 0, ..., 250$ and $c_2$ incremented in steps of 25.

We then change only one secondary parameter, evaluate for all combinations of $c_1$ and $c_2$, and compare the results with the reference configuration. For our reference configuration we implemented the algorithm as described in the previous section but without subpixel accuracy. Also for simplicity reasons we treated occlusions and mismatches equally by simply choosing the lowest valid value of propagated disparities.

Costs are computed using Birchfield and Tomasi's similarity measure [2]. A $3 \times 3$ median filter is used for eliminating outliers, and the described consistency check ensures the uniqueness of the solution. No smoothing of the input images is done prior to this processing, and parameter $c_2$ is adjusted by intensity differences.

For our experiments we decided for the Tsukuba sequence from the Middlebury stereo website, taking image *scene1.row3.col2.ppm* to be the left and *scene1.row3.col3.ppm* to be the right input image. The disparity range was chosen to be limited by $d_{max} = 18$.

We evaluate the error at all pixels, and consider a disparity to be false if it differs from the ground truth. Results (i.e., percentage of bad pixels) are shown in Table 1. The 'Mean 1/4' error value is calculated by taking the mean of the best 25% of the error results, and the 'Mean 1/2' by taking the mean of the best 50%. Numbers in brackets (after median, minimum and maximum values) specify the corresponding $(c_1, c_2)$ configuration. We now describe changes of parameters and present obtained results.

**Table 2.** Results for different smoothing filters

|  | Mean 1/4 | Mean 1/2 | Mean | Median | Min | Max |
|---|---|---|---|---|---|---|
| Reference parameter | 13.1 | 13.5 | 19.3 | 14.3 / (40,125) | 12.8 / (20,125) | 90.1 / (0,0) |
| Smooth 3x3 | **11.4** | **11.9** | **17.7** | **12.9 / (30,125)** | **10.4 / (10,0)** | **86.0 / (0,0)** |
| Smooth 5x5 | 13.5 | 14.2 | 19.8 | 15.2 / (35,150) | 12.4 / (10,0) | 86.3 / (0,0) |

**Table 3.** Results for different median filters

|  | Mean 1/4 | Mean 1/2 | Mean | Median | Min | Max |
|---|---|---|---|---|---|---|
| Reference parameter | 13.1 | **13.5** | 19.3 | 14.3 / (40,125) | 12.8 / (20,125) | 90.1 / (0,0) |
| Median 5x5 | **12.9** | **13.5** | 18.8 | **14.3 / (40,125)** | **12.6 / (20,125)** | 88.6 / (0,0) |
| Median 7x7 | 13.1 | 13.7 | **18.7** | 14.5 / (40,100) | 12.7 / (20,125) | **88.4 / (0,0)** |

**Use of Smoothing or Median Filters.** We applied either a $3 \times 3$ or a $5 \times 5$ smoothing filter on the input images prior to processing them with the SGM algorithm:

$$\frac{1}{16} \cdot \begin{bmatrix} 1 & 2 & 1 \\ 2 & 4 & 2 \\ 1 & 2 & 1 \end{bmatrix} \qquad \text{or} \qquad \frac{1}{100} \cdot \begin{bmatrix} 1 & 2 & 4 & 2 & 1 \\ 2 & 4 & 8 & 4 & 2 \\ 4 & 8 & 16 & 8 & 4 \\ 2 & 4 & 8 & 4 & 2 \\ 1 & 2 & 4 & 2 & 1 \end{bmatrix}$$

Minimum error values are printed in bold in Table 2. This experiment indicates that using a small $3 \times 3$ smoothing kernel generally improves the results of SGM, independent of the setting of $c_1$ and $c_2$. A larger kernel seems to have a negative influence on results.

Now, a $3 \times 3$ median filter is used as part of the reference configuration. We extend the window size of the median filter to $5 \times 5$ and $7 \times 7$ while leaving the rest of the reference configuration unchanged; see Table 3.

Best results are typically obtained when using the $5 \times 5$ median. In cases of the overall mean and the maximum value, smaller error values are obtained for the $7 \times 7$ median. In general it seems that a $5 \times 5$ median performs better than a $3 \times 3$ median, for any configuration $(c_1, c_2)$. However, the improvement seems to be minor.

**Use of Different Numbers of Paths.** Hirschmüller suggested in his paper [5] that "the number of paths must be at least 8 and should be 16 for providing a good coverage"; results in Table 4 confirm his statement.

Eight paths lead to better results than four paths. Improvements are about 1% by comparison. Also, choosing 16 paths results in lower errors. However, improvements in this experiment are around 0.1 %. In practical applications like DAS, where real time performance is crucial, such a marginal quality gain would not justify any increase in computational time.

**Table 4.** Results for different median filters

|  | Mean 1/4 | Mean 1/2 | Mean | Median | Min | Max |
|---|---|---|---|---|---|---|
| Reference parameter | 13.1 | **13.5** | 19.3 | **14.3 / (40,125)** | 12.8 / (20,125) | **90.1 / (0,0)** |
| Path 4 | 14.3 | 14.5 | 21.3 | 14.9 / (50,75) | 14.0 / (30,25) | **90.1 / (0,0)** |
| Path 16 | **13.0** | **13.5** | **19.0** | 14.5 / (40,100) | **12.7 / (20,175)** | **90.1 / (0,0)** |

## 2  Use of Second Order Prior and New Cost Function

We suggest a possible improvement of SGM results by adding an additional penalty during the cost accumulation process, based on a second order prior. The idea is that a configuration of disparities should be favored for which the second order derivative at $p_i$ is small. This should equalize the high penalty $c_2$ which is added regardless of the discontinuity.

### 2.1  New Smoothness Term

Consider three consecutive pixel positions along a path $L_{\mathbf{a}}$, say $p_{i-1}$, $p_i$, and $p_{i+1}$, with disparities $d_{i-1}$, $d_i$ and $d_{i+1}$, respectively. This defines a triangle in 3D space, with disparities being the third coordinate. The angle $\alpha$ at $(p_i, d_i)$ can easily be computed using the formula

$$\alpha = \arccos\left(\frac{a^2 + b^2 - c^2}{2ab}\right)$$

(see Figure 1) with

$$a = ||(p_{i-1}, d_{i-1}), (p_i, d_i)||_2$$
$$b = ||(p_i, d_i), (p_{i+1}, d_{i+1})||_2$$
$$c = ||(p_{i-1}, d_{i-1}), (p_{i+1}, d_{i+1})||_2$$

$|| \cdot ||_2$ is the Euclidean distance. The goal is to favor smooth transitions (i.e., we need a function that increases the penalty when the angle gets smaller, and decreases when the angle gets larger). Since the maximum possible angle is $\pi$, we choose

$$c_3 = (\frac{\pi}{\alpha} - 1.0) \cdot \tau$$

as a function of $\alpha$ and of an external scalar $\tau$. Positions $p_{i-1}$ and $p_{i+1}$ are determined by pixel position $p_i$ and direction $\mathbf{a}$. Thus, $c_3$ is basically a function

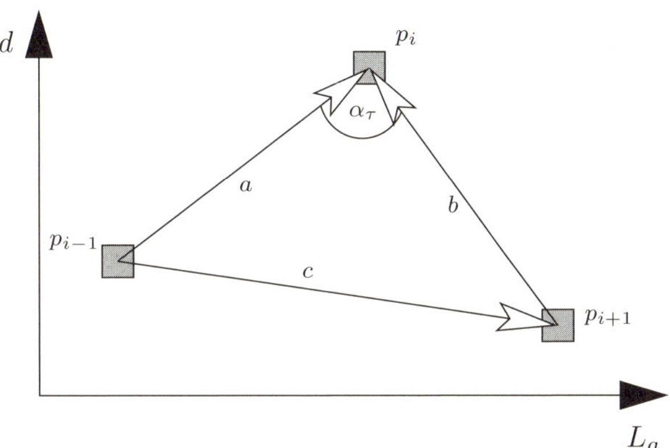


**Fig. 1.** Estimation of second order prior

of disparities $d_{i-1}$, $d_i$, and $d_{i+1}$ (and of $\tau$). We now need to compute $c_3$ at every $p_i$, for every $d$ during the accumulation. Thus, when computing the penalty we already know the disparity at $p_i$. We have to select an a-priori disparity $d_{mx}$ with the most likely minimum cost at $p_{i+1}$ (i.e., most likely to be selected as $d_{opt}$). We select

$$d_{mx} = \min_{\Delta} C(p_{i+1}, \Delta)$$

to be a 'good guess'. Now we may write $c_3$ as a function of the disparity only, chosen for the previous position $(p_{i-1})$ (i.e., $c_3(d_{prev})$). Define

$$d_{mp} = \min_{\Delta} L_{\mathbf{a}}(p_{i-1}, \Delta)$$

which is the disparity with the current minimum cost on the path at the previous position. Also define the cost at pixel $p$ for disparity $d$ on the path $L_{\mathbf{a}}$ as follows:

$$\begin{aligned} L_{\mathbf{a}}(p, d) = \ & C(p, d) + \ \min\big[ L_{\mathbf{a}}(p_{i-1}, d), L_{\mathbf{a}}(p_{i-1}, d-1) + c_1 + c_3(d-1), \\ & L_{\mathbf{a}}(p_{i-1}, d+1) + c_1 + c_3(d+1), \min_{\Delta} L_{\mathbf{a}}(p_{i-1}, \Delta) + c_2 + c_3(d_{mp}) \big] \\ & - \min_{\Delta} L_{\mathbf{a}}(p_{i-1}, \Delta) \end{aligned}$$

For results of this approximation, see Table 5. With the exception of the overall mean, the errors tend to be slightly reduced when using a second order prior. The constant $\tau$ was set to be $\frac{3}{2}$. However, this is just an initial experience with including a second order prior. More experiments and modified approaches (say, with other parameter settings for $\tau$ or function $c_3$) should be performed in future; this may just define a new direction of research.

**Table 5.** Results for 2nd Order Prior

|  | Mean 1/4 | Mean 1/2 | Mean | Median | Min | Max |
|---|---|---|---|---|---|---|
| Reference parameter | 13.1 | 13.5 | **19.3** | 14.3 / (40,125) | 12.8 / (20,125) | 90.1 / (0,0) |
| 2nd Order Prior | **12.8** | **13.2** | 19.5 | **14.0 / (40,25)** | **12.2 / (20,200)** | **76.6 / (0,0)** |

## 2.2   New Cost Function Based on Signal Deviation

The reference configuration of the SGM algorithm uses the BT cost function [2]. This function computes the cost at pixel $p_i$ as follows: Let $I_{p_i}$ be the intensity value of pixel $p_i$ in the base image and $I_{q_i}$ the intensity for the corresponding pixel in the match image, for disparity $d$. Intensities in both images are interpolated using intensities of previous or subsequent pixels along the epipolar line. For example, let $I_{p_{i-1/2}} = \frac{1}{2} \cdot I_{p_i} + \frac{1}{2} \cdot I_{p_{i-1}}$ be an interpolated value at $p_i$, just using the previous pixel. The absolute difference of $\min(I_{p_{i-1/2}}, I_{p_i}, I_{p_{i+1/2}})$ and $\min(I_{q_{i-1/2}}, I_{q_i}, I_{q_{1+1/2}})$ is then used for the final matching cost.

This new scheme for cost calculations considers a 1D window around pixels $p_i$ and $q_i$. Usually, this window should have a size of $\omega = 5$ or $\omega = 7$. We take the mean of the sum of absolute intensity differences,

$$\frac{1}{\omega} \cdot \sum_{j=i-\frac{\omega}{2}}^{i+\frac{\omega}{2}} \delta_j$$

with three options for $\delta_j$. This value is one of the following:

(1) $\delta_j = \left| I_{p_j} - I_{q_j} + (I_{q_i} - I_{p_i}) \right|$
(2) $\delta_j = \left| I_{p_j} - I_{q_j} \right|$
(3) $\delta_j = \left| I_{p_j} - I_{q_j} \right| - \left| I_{p_i} - I_{q_i} \right|$

The first two options can be interpreted as a mean deviation from the intensity signal of the match image compared to the signal of the base image. Thus, this similarity is not only (as in BT) based on intensity differences at pixel locations, but also on the 'structure' of the signal. See Table 6.

For option (1), by shifting the intensities by offset $(I_{q_i} - I_{p_i})$, the difference of intensities at $j = i$ becomes zero. See, for example Figure 2. The intensity signal around $q_i$ is shifted, and differences are taken at new positions. This option emphasizes almost completely the structure of the signal, and not so much intensity differences. This might be of value if changes in lighting occur between both images of a stereo pair. However, results are similar to the reference configuration if input images do not show such changes in lighting.

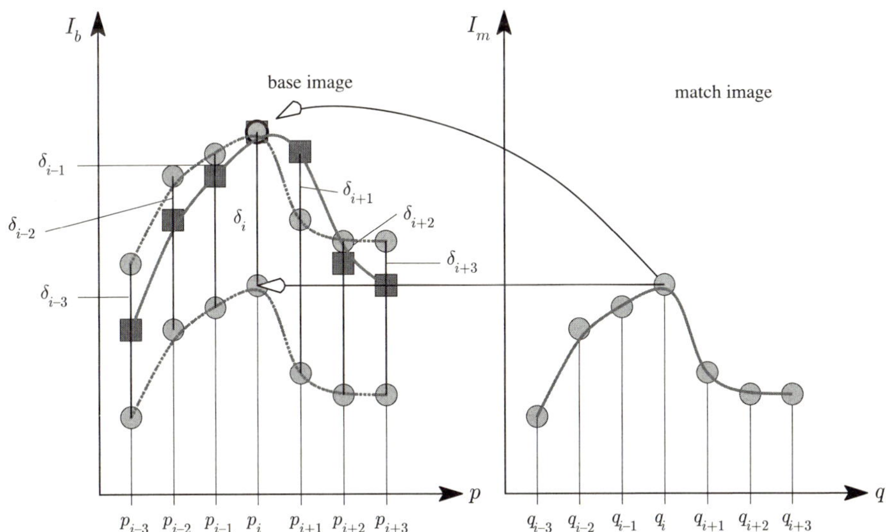


**Fig. 2.** The cost function and the structure of the signal: the intensity value of $q_i$ is shifted such that we have $I_{p_i} - I_{q_i} = 0$. The cost at $p_i$ is the mean of all absolute differences within the selected neighborhood.

**Table 6.** Results for different window sizes for new cost function

|  | Mean 1/4 | Mean 1/2 | Mean | Median | Min | Max |
|---|---|---|---|---|---|---|
| Reference parameter | 13.1 | 13.5 | 19.3 | 14.3 / (40,125) | 12.8 / (20,125) | 90.1 / (0,0) |
| Cost opt.1 w=5 | 13.1 | 13.3 | 16.5 | 13.8 / (50,200) | 12.9 / (35,25) | 52.1 / (0,0) |
| Cost opt.1 w=7 | 14.1 | 14.3 | 18.0 | 15.0 / (25,175) | 14.0 / (45,50) | 46.4 / (0,0) |
| Cost opt.2 w=5 | 12.4 | 12.6 | 16.3 | 13.0 / (25,225) | 12.1 / (35,50) | 44.8 / (0,0) |
| Cost opt.2 w=7 | 12.7 | 12.9 | 16.2 | 13.3 / (25,100) | 12.6 / (30,25) | **41.8 / (0,0)** |
| Cost opt.3 w=5 | **11.3** | **11.7** | **14.6** | **12.4 / (35,125)** | **10.9 / (35,50)** | 52.6 / (0,0) |
| Cost opt.3 w=7 | **11.3** | **11.7** | **14.6** | 12.7 / (10,50) | 11.0 / (20,75) | 47.2 / (0,0) |

Option (2) leaves intensity values unshifted, and simply computes the mean of the sum of differences. This option emphasizes intensity differences as well as the structure of the signal. See the lower signal of the match image in Figure 2. Results are about 1% better than for the reference configuration.

Option (3) improves results by about 2% compared to the reference configuration, which is certainly very good! The difference to option (i) is that we subtract the absolute value of the offset. A geometric interpretation of (iii) is still missing.

## 2.3 Best Configuration

Finally we choose a best configuration by picking from every analyzed secondary parameter the, to our opinion, best option (i.e., we choose eight paths for the

**Table 7.** Results for the best configuration

|  | Mean 1/4 | Mean 1/2 | Mean | Median | Min | Max |
|---|---|---|---|---|---|---|
| Reference parameter | 13.1 | 13.5 | 19.3 | 14.3 / (40,125) | 12.8 / (20,125) | 90.1 / (0,0) |
| Best parameter | **9.9** | **10.2** | **12.6** | **10.8 / (40,50)** | **9.1 / (15,0)** | **32.5 / (0,0)** |

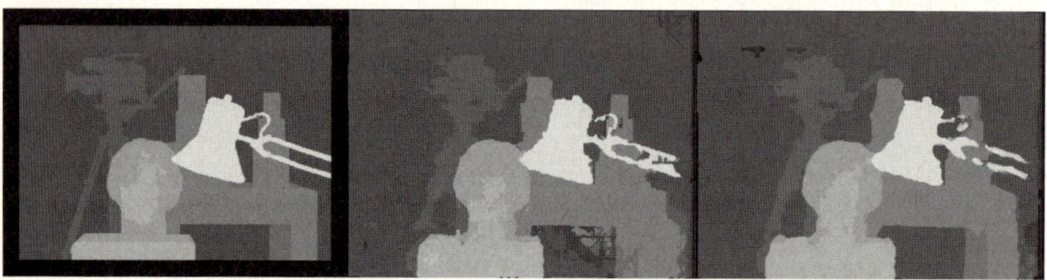

**Fig. 3.** Left: ground truth of Tsukuba. Middle: result of SGM using the reference configuration. Right: result of SGM using the best configuration.

accumulation, also considering the computational cost, use a $5 \times 5$ median filter for outliers, a $3 \times 3$ smoothing kernel, and option (2) for the cost function because we have a geometrical motivation and improvement).

The second order prior is included into the cost accumulation step. Results outperform, as expected, any result obtained for modifying just a single parameter; see Table 7.

Figure 3 shows the Tsukuba ground truth on the left. The image in the middle shows the obtained result when using the reference parametrization, and the image on the right the resulting disparity map for our identified 'optimum configuration'. Obviously, there are some major improvements.

## 3 Application to *.enpeda..* Sequences

We also applied the discussed versions of the SGM algorithm to the sequences of Set 1 of the *.enpeda..* test image website. Our experiments confirmed that Sobel preprocessing for those sequences is beneficial, as already shown for belief propagation [4]; see Table 8 for edge results on Tsukuba image sequence.

Figure 4 illustrates results for frame 106 of the *construction site* sequence (not using the original depth of 12 bits but scaled to 8 bits).

The image in the upper row, left, shows the right input image of the stereo pair, and in upper row, right, its Sobel edge image. The depth maps in this figure have value $200 - d_{opt} \cdot 5$ if $d_{opt}$ is calculated at that pixel, with $d_{max} = 40$.

The images in the middle row shows the result of applying SGM to the original image data using the reference configuration with $c_1 = 20$ and $c_2 = 125$, which was the suggested primary parameter setting (left: original input, right: Sobel images as input).

Resulting depth maps appear to be, obviously, more accurate in general with Sobel preprocessing. (Studies for approximated ground truth are a subject for future work.)

The images in the bottom row are results for our 'optimum configuration' as described above (also with $c_1 = 20$ and $c_2 = 125$), again either on the original data (left) or on Sobel image pairs (right).

In our experiments, we processed the sequences of Set 1 (Daimler sequences) of the *.enpeda..* test image website, using throughout our 'optimum configuration' on the Sobel input data. Figure 5 illustrates examples; each row has an original image on the left and our optimized SGM result on the right. From top to

**Table 8.** Results for edge preprocessing on Tsukuba images

|  | Mean 1/4 | Mean 1/2 | Mean | Median | Min | Max |
|---|---|---|---|---|---|---|
| Reference parameter | 13.1 | 13.5 | 19.3 | 14.3 / (40,125) | 12.8 / (20,125) | **90.1 / (0,0)** |
| Sobel Preprocessing | **12.5** | **12.8** | **18.5** | **13.3 / (35,50)** | **12.2 / (20,75)** | 94.7 / (0,0) |

bottom, the rows are showing the *intern on bike, save turn, dancing light,* and *squirrel* sequences, in this order.

The *squirrel sequence* was taken at night which possibly contributes to the difficulty here. The daylight sequences seem to perform reasonably well. Improvements from the reference to the optimized configuration are obvious especially on Sobel preprocessed images.

**Fig. 4.** Top: image of original input sequence (left) and its Sobel image (right). Middle: results of SGM (reference configuration) on original image pair (left) and on Sobel image pair (right). Bottom: results of SGM (using our optimized configuration f) on original image pair (left) and on Sobel image pair (right).

**Fig. 5.** Left: example of a right input image of the processed sequence. Right; depth maps, after Sobel preprocessing, and using SGM with the optimized configuration.

## 4 Conclusions

This paper proposes a new cost function and tested it with the SGM algorithm. It also contributes by presenting a first attempt to include an additional penalty to the accumulation step, based on a second order prior. Results indicate that there is a potential for performance gain and justifies more experiments for this subject in future.

We also tested SGM on Sobel images of the Tsukuba image sequence on the Middlebury stereo page. Results indicate that edge preoprocessing can improve the quality of the algorithm (see Table 8). Especially the outcome of our experiments on real-world sequences suggest that processing SGM on edge images can also result in a big performance gain.

Obviously, the discussed options of variations in primary and secondary SGM parameters allow for many more optimization experiments, also with respect to possible preprocessing. However, [7] indicates that the Sobel operator compares well against other edge operators (Canny, Kovesi-Owens) in case when using belief propagation for disparity calculation. However, performance gains are much better on real world sequences than on engineered data. Therefore it would be interesting to quantify how much real world stereo analysis really benefit from optimizating for engineered data.

## Acknowledgement

The authors would like to thank Thomas Pock for the idea to include a second order prior into the cost accumulation step of the algorithm.

## References

1. Badino, H.: A robust approach for ego-motion estimation using a mobile stereo platform. In: Jähne, B., Mester, R., Barth, E., Scharr, H. (eds.) IWCM 2004. LNCS, vol. 3417, pp. 198–208. Springer, Heidelberg (2007)
2. Birchfield, S., Tomasi, C.: Birchfield and C. Tomasi. Depth discontinuities by pixel-to-pixel stereo. Int. J. Computer Vision 35, 269–293 (1999)
3. Gehrig, S., Franke, U.: Improving stereo sub-pixel accuracy for long range stereo. Daimler A.G., Internal Report, Sindelfingen (2007)
4. Guan, S., Klette, R.: Belief-propagation on edge images for stereo analysis of image sequences. In: Sommer, G., Klette, R. (eds.) RobVis 2008. LNCS, vol. 4931, pp. 291–302. Springer, Heidelberg (2008)
5. Hirschmüller, H.: Accurate and efficient stereo processing by semi-global matching and mutual information. In: IEEE Conf. Computer Vision Pattern Recognition, vol. 2, pp. 807–814 (2005)
6. Hirschmüller, H.: Stereo vision in structured environments by consistent semi-global matching. In: IEEE Conf. Computer Vision Pattern Recognition, vol. 2, pp. 2386–2393 (2006)
7. Klette, R.: Evaluation of stereo and motion techniques on real-world video sequences. Dagstuhl seminar Statistical and Geometrical Approaches to Visual Motion Analysis (2008), http://kathrin.dagstuhl.de/08291/Materials2/

# Object Detection under Varying Illumination Based on Adaptive Background Modeling Considering Spatial Locality


Tatsuya Tanaka[1], Atsushi Shimada[1], Daisaku Arita[1,2],
and Rin-ichiro Taniguchi[1]

[1] Department of Intelligent Systems Kyushu University, Japan
`{tatsuya,atsushi,rin}@limu.is.kyushu-u.ac.jp`
[2] Institute of Systems, Information Technologies and Nanotechnologies, Japan
`arita@isit.or.jp`



**Abstract.** We propose a new method for background modeling. Our method is based on the two complementary approaches. One uses the probability density function(PDF) to approximate background model. The PDF is estimated non-parametrically by using Parzen density estimation. And foreground object is detected based on the estimated PDF. The other method is based on the evaluation of the local texture at pixel-level resolution while reducing the effects of variations in lighting. Fusing their approach realize robust object detection under varying illumination. Several experiments show the effectiveness of our approach.

**Keywords:** Object detection, Adaptive background model, Illumination change, Parzen density estimation, Radial Reach Filter.


## 1 Introduction

Background subtraction technique has been traditionally applied to detection of objects in image. Without prior information about the objects, we can get object regions by subtracting a background image from an observed image. However, when simple background subtraction technique is applied to video-based surveillance which usually captures outdoor scenes, it often detects not only objects but also a lot of noise regions. This is because it is quite sensitive to small illumination changes caused by moving clouds, swaying tree leaves, etc.

There are many approaches to handle these background changes [1,2,3,4,5, 6,7,8,9]. Shimada et al. proposed a background estimation method, in which mixture-of-Gaussians is used to approximate background model, and the number of Gaussians is changed dynamically to adapt to the change of the lighting condition. However, in principle, Gaussian Mixture Model (GMM) can not make a well-suited background model and can not detect foreground objects accurately when the intensity of the background changes frequently. Especially when the intensity distribution of the background is very wide, it is not easy to represent the distribution with a set of Gaussians. In addition, if the number of Gaussians


T. Wada, F. Huang, and S. Lin (Eds.): PSIVT 2009, LNCS 5414, pp. 645–656, 2009.

is increased, the computation time to estimate the background model is also increased. Thus, GMM is not powerful enough to represent the various changes of the lighting condition.

To solve the problem, Elgammal et al employed non-parametric representation of the background intensity distribution, and estimated the distribution by Parzen density estimation [1]. However, in their approach, the computation cost of the estimation is quite high, and it is not easy to apply it to real-time processing. Tanaka et al proposed its fast algorithm to estimate the background intensity distribution [9]. In this approach, the computational cost is greatly reduced by efficient updating algorithm of probability distribution function.

Though these methods previously described are effective against gradual or periodical change of background, they can not handle sudden illumination changes because the background model is established based on statistical characteristics of observed pixel values in a certain duration. To solve such a problem, it is effective to fuse a background model which can adapt to sudden illumination changes with the background model established according to the observation in the past. Then, in this paper, we propose an enhanced background modeling method under varying illumination with a "long-term model" and a "short-term model". The long-term model approximates the change of the pixel value such as gradual or periodical change of background, which is acquired by a long-term observation, and it is represented in a probability density function. The short-term model, on the other hand, approximates the sudden background change such as a illumination change based on Radial Reach Filter which is known as a robust background model against varying illumination [4].

## 2   Long-Term Model

In this section, we describe about the long-term model. The LTM represents the background in a certain duration. We use the fast algorithm to estimate the background intensity distribution [9].

### 2.1   Basic Algorithm

At first, we describe basic background model estimation and object detection process. The background model is established to represent recent pixel information of an input image sequence, reflecting the change of intensity, or pixel-value, distribution as quickly as possible.

We consider values of a particular pixel $(x, y)$ over time as a "pixel process", which is a time series of pixel values, e.g. scalars for gray values and vectors for color images. Each pixel is judged to be either a foreground pixel or a background pixel by observing the pixel process. In Parzen density estimation, or the kernel density estimation, the probability density function (PDF) of a pixel value is estimated referring to the latest pixel process, and, here, we assume that a pixel process consists of the latest $N$ pixel values. Let $\boldsymbol{X}$ be a pixel value observed at pixel $(x, y)$, and $\{\boldsymbol{X}_1, \cdots, \boldsymbol{X}_N\}$ be the latest pixel process. The PDF of the pixel value is estimated with the kernel estimator $K$ as follows

$$P(\boldsymbol{X}) = \frac{1}{N} \sum_{i=1}^{N} K(\boldsymbol{X} - \boldsymbol{X}_i) \tag{1}$$

Usually a Gaussian distribution function $N(\boldsymbol{0}, \Sigma)$ is adopted for the estimator $K$[1]. In this case the equation (1) is reduced into the following formula:

$$P(\boldsymbol{X}) = \frac{1}{N} \sum_{i=1}^{N} \frac{1}{(2\pi)^{\frac{d}{2}} |\boldsymbol{\Sigma}|^{\frac{1}{2}}} \exp\left( -\frac{1}{2} (\boldsymbol{X} - \boldsymbol{X}_i)^T \boldsymbol{\Sigma}^{-1} (\boldsymbol{X} - \boldsymbol{X}_i) \right) \tag{2}$$

where $d$ is the dimension of the distribution (for example, $d = 3$ in color image pixels).

To reduce the computation cost, the covariance matrix in equation (2) is often approximated as follows.

$$\boldsymbol{\Sigma} = \boldsymbol{\sigma} \boldsymbol{I} \tag{3}$$

This means that each dimension of the distribution is independent from one another. By this approximation, equation (2) is reduced into the following.

$$P(\boldsymbol{X}) = \frac{1}{N} \sum_{i=1}^{N} \prod_{j=1}^{d} \frac{1}{(2\pi [\boldsymbol{\sigma}]_j^2)^{\frac{1}{2}}} \exp\left( -\frac{1}{2} \frac{([\boldsymbol{X}]_j - [\boldsymbol{X}_i]_j)^2}{[\boldsymbol{\sigma}]_j^2} \right) \tag{4}$$

This approximation might make the density estimation error a little bigger, but the computation is considerably reduced.

The detailed algorithm of background model construction and foreground object detection is summarized as follows:

1. When a new pixel value $\boldsymbol{X}_{N+1}$ is observed, $P(\boldsymbol{X}_{N+1})$, the probability that $\boldsymbol{X}_{N+1}$ occurs is estimated by equation (4).
2. If $P(\boldsymbol{X}_{N+1})$ is greater than a given threshold, the pixel is judged to be a background pixel. Otherwise, it is judged to be a foreground pixel.
3. The newly observed pixel value $\boldsymbol{X}_{N+1}$ is kept in the "pixel process," while the oldest pixel value $\boldsymbol{X}_1$ is removed from the pixel process.

Applying the above calculation to every pixel, the background model is generated and distinction between a background pixel and a foreground pixel is accomplished.

## 2.2    Fast Algorithm

When we estimate the generation probability of pixel value $\boldsymbol{X}$ in every frame using equation (4) and estimate the background model, its computation cost becomes quite large. To solve this problem, at first, a kernel with rectangular shape,

---

[1] Here, $\Sigma$ works as the smoothing parameter.

or hypercube, is used instead of Gaussian distribution function. For example, in 1-dimensional case, the kernel is represented as follows.

$$K(u) = \begin{cases} \frac{1}{h} & \text{if } -\frac{h}{2} \leq u \leq \frac{h}{2} \\ 0 & \text{otherwise} \end{cases} \tag{5}$$

where $h$ is a parameter representing the width of the kernel.

Using this kernel, equation (1) is represented as follows:

$$P(\boldsymbol{X}) = \frac{1}{N} \sum_{i=1}^{N} \frac{1}{h^d} \psi \left( \frac{\|\boldsymbol{X} - \boldsymbol{X}_i\|}{h} \right) \tag{6}$$

where, $\|\boldsymbol{X} - \boldsymbol{X}_i\|$ means the chess-board distance in d-dimensional space, and $\psi(u)$ is calculated by the following formula.

$$\psi(u) = \begin{cases} 1 & \text{if } u \leq \|\frac{1}{2}\| \\ 0 & \text{otherwise} \end{cases} \tag{7}$$

When an observed pixel value is inside of the kernel located at $\boldsymbol{X}$, $\psi(u)$ is 1; otherwise $\psi(u)$ is 0.

Thus, we estimate the PDF based on equation (6), and $P(\boldsymbol{X})$ is calculated by enumerating pixels in the latest pixel process whose values are inside of the kernel located at $\boldsymbol{X}$. However, if we calculate the PDF, in a naive way, by enumerating pixels in the latest pixel process whose values are inside of the kernel located at $\boldsymbol{X}$, the computational time is proportional to $N$. Instead, Tanaka et al have proposed a fast algorithm to compute the PDF, whose computation cost does not depend on $N$.

In background modeling we estimate $P(\boldsymbol{X})$ referring to the latest pixel process consisting of pixel values of the latest $N$ frames. Let us suppose that at time $t$ we have a new pixel value $\boldsymbol{X}_{N+1}$, and that we estimate an updated PDF $\boldsymbol{P}_t(\boldsymbol{X})$ referring to the new $\boldsymbol{X}_{N+1}$. Basically, the essence of PDF estimation is accumulation of the kernel estimator, and, when a new value, $\boldsymbol{X}_{N+1}$, is acquired the kernel estimator corresponding to $\boldsymbol{X}_{N+1}$ should be accumulated. At the same time, the oldest one, i.e., the kernel estimator at $N$ frames earlier, should be discarded, since the length of the pixel process is constant, $N$. This idea leads to reduction of the PDF computation into the following incremental computation:

$$P_t(\boldsymbol{X}) = P_{t-1}(\boldsymbol{X}) + \frac{1}{Nh^d} \psi \left( \frac{\|\boldsymbol{X} - \boldsymbol{X}_t\|}{h} \right) - \frac{1}{Nh^d} \psi \left( \frac{\|\boldsymbol{X} - \boldsymbol{X}_{t-N}\|}{h} \right) \tag{8}$$

where $P_{t-1}$ is the PDF estimated at the previous frame.

The above equation means that the PDF when a new pixel value is observed can be acquired by:

- increasing the probabilities of pixel values which are inside of the kernel located at the new pixel value $\boldsymbol{X}_t$ by $\frac{1}{Nh^d}$
- decreasing those which are inside of the kernel located at the oldest pixel value, a pixel value at $N$ frames earlier, $\boldsymbol{X}_{t-N}$ by $\frac{1}{Nh^d}$.

In other words, the new PDF is acquired by local operation of the previous PDF, assuming the latest $N$ pixel values are stored in the memory, which achieves quite fast computation of PDF estimation.

## 3   Short Term Model

In this section, we describe the short-term model (STM). STM handles short-term changes of pixel values and detects foreground objects using Radial Reach Filter, which is known as robust background subtraction method under varying illumination [4].

### 3.1   Radial Reach Filter (RRF)

RRF judges each pixel as either the foreground or the background based on Radial Reach Correlation (RRC), which is defined to evaluate local texture similarity at pixel-level resolution without suffering from the effects of variation in brightness.

RRC is calculated for each pixel $(x, y)$. At first, pixels whose brightness differences to $f(x, y)$, the brightness of the pixel $(x, y)$, exceed a threshold are searched for in every radial extension reach in 8 directions around the pixel $(x, y)$. Then, the signs of brightness differences (positive difference or negagive difference) of the 8 pairs, each of which is a pair of one of eight found pixels and the center pixel $(x, y)$, are represented in a binary code. The correlation value of the codes between the input image pixel and the background image pixel is regarded as a representation of their similarity.

The position of pixel $(x, y)$ in the image is represented as the vector $\boldsymbol{p} = (x, y)$, and the directional vector $\boldsymbol{b}_k (k = 0, 1, \ldots, 7)$ is defined as follows. $\boldsymbol{d}_0 = (1, 0)^T$ C $\boldsymbol{d}_1 = (1, 1)^T$ $\boldsymbol{d}_2 = (0, 1)^T$ C $\boldsymbol{d}_3 = (-1, 1)^T$ C $\boldsymbol{d}_4 = (-1, 0)^T$ C $\boldsymbol{d}_5 = (-1, -1)^T$ $\boldsymbol{d}_6 = (0, -1)^T$ C and $\boldsymbol{d}_7 = (1, -1)^T$. Then the reach $\{r_k\}_{k=0}^{7}$ for these directions are defined as follows:

$$r_k = \min\{r \mid \ |f(\boldsymbol{p} + r\boldsymbol{d}_k) - f(\boldsymbol{p})| \geq T_P\} \tag{9}$$

where $f(\boldsymbol{p})$ represents the pixel value of the position of $\boldsymbol{p}$ in the image, and $T_P$ represents the threshold value of brightness difference.

Based on the brightness difference between the center pixel and the pixels selected by the reach group (defined by equation (9)), the coefficients of incremental encoding, or polarity encoding, of the brightness distribution around a pixel in the reference image $f$ is given by the following formula:

$$b_k(\boldsymbol{p}) = \begin{cases} 1 & \text{if } f(\boldsymbol{p} + r_k \boldsymbol{d}_k) \geq f(\boldsymbol{p}) \\ 0 & \text{otherwise} \end{cases} \tag{10}$$

where $k = 0, 1, \ldots, 7$. In the same manner, the incremental encoding string is calculated for the input image $g$. Here, please note that the reach group $\{r_k\}_{k=0}^{7}$ is defined based on the reference image $f$.

$$b_k{}'(\boldsymbol{p}) = \begin{cases} 1 & \text{if } g(\boldsymbol{p} + r_k \boldsymbol{d}_k) \geq g(\boldsymbol{p}) \\ 0 & \text{otherwise} \end{cases} \tag{11}$$

650     T. Tanaka et al.

Based on the obtained $b_k(\boldsymbol{p})$, $b_k'(\boldsymbol{p})$, the number of matches (correlation), $B(\boldsymbol{p})$ between the two incremental encodings is calculated as follows.

$$B(\boldsymbol{p}) = \sum_{k=0}^{7} \{ b_k(\boldsymbol{p}) \cdot b_k'(\boldsymbol{p}) + \overline{b_k(\boldsymbol{p})} \cdot \overline{b_k'(\boldsymbol{p})} \} \tag{12}$$

where $\overline{x} = 1 - x$ represents the inversion of a bit. $B(\boldsymbol{p})$ represents the similarity, or correlation value, of the brightness distribution around the pixel $\boldsymbol{p}$ in the two images, and it is called Radial Reach Correlation (RRC).

Since RRC of the input image pixels and the background image pixels represents their similarities, it can be used as a measure to detect foreground pixels. In other words, pixels whose RRC is smaller than a certain threshold $T_B$ can be judged as foreground pixels. In the following formula, the foreground detection result is represented in $C(\boldsymbol{p})$, and it is called RRC image.

$$C(\boldsymbol{p}) = \begin{cases} 1 & \text{if } B(\boldsymbol{p}) < T_B \\ 0 & \text{otherwise} \end{cases} \tag{13}$$

### 3.2   Construction of Background Model and Foreground Detection

In RRC, the similarity between incremental encoding of the background image and the input image is calculated referring to the reach group defined in the background image $f$, and foreground is detected based on the similarity. In principle, it is possible that a fixed background image can be prepared in advance, if the background does not change. However, if the background often changes, using such fixed background image does not produce an accurate result. Rather, we should update the background image properly. In STM, sudden changes of background should be reflected and the background model is constructed based on the observation of pixel values in very recent frames. In our approach, the change of the background is represented in a single Gaussian distribution at every pixel. Then, the average and the variance of the distribution are used to represent the background image $f$, and RRC is calculated referring to $f$.

Again, we represent the pixel value of pixel $(x, y)$ at time $t$ as $d$ dimensional vector $\boldsymbol{X}_t$. Then, the average $\boldsymbol{\mu}_t$ and the variance $\boldsymbol{\sigma}_t^2$ of Gaussian distribution are updated as follows:

$$\boldsymbol{\mu}_t = (1 - \rho)\boldsymbol{\mu}_{t-1} + \rho \boldsymbol{X}_t \tag{14}$$

$$\boldsymbol{\sigma}_t^2 = (1 - \rho)\boldsymbol{\sigma}_{t-1}^2 + \rho(\boldsymbol{X}_t - \boldsymbol{\mu}_{t-1})^T(\boldsymbol{X}_t - \boldsymbol{\mu}_{t-1}) \tag{15}$$

Where $\rho$ is the learning rate, which is represented in the following formula:

$$\rho = \frac{\alpha}{(2\pi)^{\frac{n}{2}} |\boldsymbol{\Sigma}|^{\frac{1}{2}}} \exp\left( -\frac{1}{2}(\boldsymbol{X}_t - \boldsymbol{\mu}_t)^T \boldsymbol{\Sigma}^{-1}(\boldsymbol{X}_t - \boldsymbol{\mu}_t) \right) \tag{16}$$

$\alpha$ is a constant parameter, or an internal learning rate, and it is possible to adapt to a sudden background change by enlarging $\alpha$. Applying the above calculation to every pixel, the parameters of Gaussian distribution are updated.

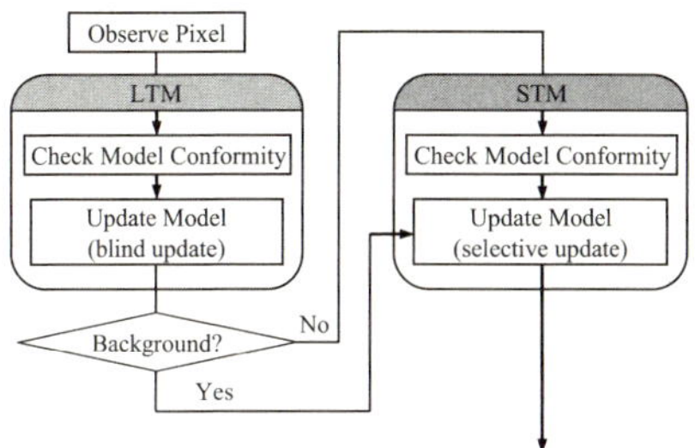

**Fig. 1.** Flowchart

**Table 1.** Fusion rule and selective update of STM

| LTM | STM | Fused Result | Update(STM) |
|-----|-----|--------------|-------------|
| BG | — | BG | ◯ |
| BG | — | BG | ◯ |
| FG | BG | BG | ◯ |
| FG | FG | FG | ✕ |

The detailed algorithm of background model construction and foreground detection in STM is summarized as follows:

**Step 1:** The background image $f$ is created from the mean value of Gaussian distribution in each pixel.

**Step 2:** RRC is constructed based on the background image $f$ in Step1, and each pixel of the input image is judged as either the foreground or the background. Here, we set the threshold $T_P$ is $2.5\sigma$.

**Step 3:** The parameters of Gaussian distribution are updated by equation $(14)\sim(16)$, if the conditions for model update in STM is satisfied. In the other cases, the parameters are not updated. (The condition for model update in STM will be described in section4.)

## 4   Fusion of LTM and STM

In this section, we describe the fusion rule of LTM and STM. The processing flow is shown in figure 1. First of all, background subtraction is done according to the long-term model. Then if a pixel is labeled as foreground, the pixel is examined whether it is the foreground or the background referring to the short-term model. Finally, the pixel is regarded as foreground by the rule described in table 1.

Next, we describe how to update the background model. In general, there are two methods to update background models. The one is selective update, which updates the model only when the pixel is labeled as background. The other is blind update, which adds every new sample to the model. The selective update enhances detection accuracy of the foreground, because foreground pixels are not added to the model. However, for instance, if the background changes while the object has been detected, regions which should be regarded as the background keep being detected as the foreground. The blind update, on the other hand, allows foreground objects to be added to the background model. In case of the long-term model, this drawback is not significant since LTM is created by observing the pixel value for a long time. Therefore, we have decided to use the blind update for the long-term model. On the other hand, the blind update is not suitable for the short-term model since it is very sensitive for the changes of the pixel values. Considering these effects, we use the selective update for the short-term model. In particular, only when the observed pixel value is finally judged as the background, the short-term model is updated.

## 5    Experimental Results

### 5.1    Computational Cost

To evaluate the computational time to process one image frame, we have used data set of PETS(PETS2001)[2] after the image resolution was reduced into $320 \times 240$ pixels. The data set includes images in which people are passing through streets, tree leaves are flickering, and the illumination condition are varying rapidly. For the evaluation of computation speed, we have used a PC with a Pentium IV 3.2GHz and 2.0GB memory.

Figure 2 shows the processing speed of the proposed method. Where, for the parameters of LTM, we have used $N = 500$, $h = 9$. For the parameters of STM, we have used $T_B = 6$ and $T_P = 2.5\sigma$. The horizontal axis shows the frame number. The left vertical axis shows the computational time and the right one shows the number of pixels labeled as foreground by LTM.

The computation cost to maintain LTM is 23msec/frame in average, and it does not change largely. On the other hand, the computation cost in STM varies according to the number of pixels labeled as foreground by LTM. This is because STM was only applied to pixels judged as foreground by the LTM. The total computational time was about 60msec, and this is enough to achieve object detection in real-time.

### 5.2    Comparison of Characteristics between LTM and STM

We have verified the characteristics of LTM and STM. To compare the characteristics of each model, we have conducted experiments of object detection by LTM, STM and their fused model. The data set includes images in which tree leaves are flickering, and the illumination condition are varying rapidly.

Figure 3 shows results of the experiment. Figure 3(a), 3(b), 3(c) and 3(d) show the input image sequence, the object areas detected by LTM, ones by STM and ones by the fused model, respectively.

First, figure 3(b) shows LTM could adapt the background changes such as flickering tree leaves. However, ground and the roof were mis-detected, because it could not adapt sudden illumination changes. Thus though stochastic adaptive background model is effective against gradual or periodical change of background, it can not handle sudden illumination changes because the background model is established based on statistical characteristics of observed pixel values in a certain duration. On the other hand, STM could adapt the sudden illumination changes. However, it could not handle a background changes such as ones caused by flickering of tree leaves. Because STM is based on the evaluation of

---

[2] Benchmark data of International Workshop on Performance Evaluation of Tracking and Surveillance. From ftp://pets.rdg.ac.uk/PETS2001/ available

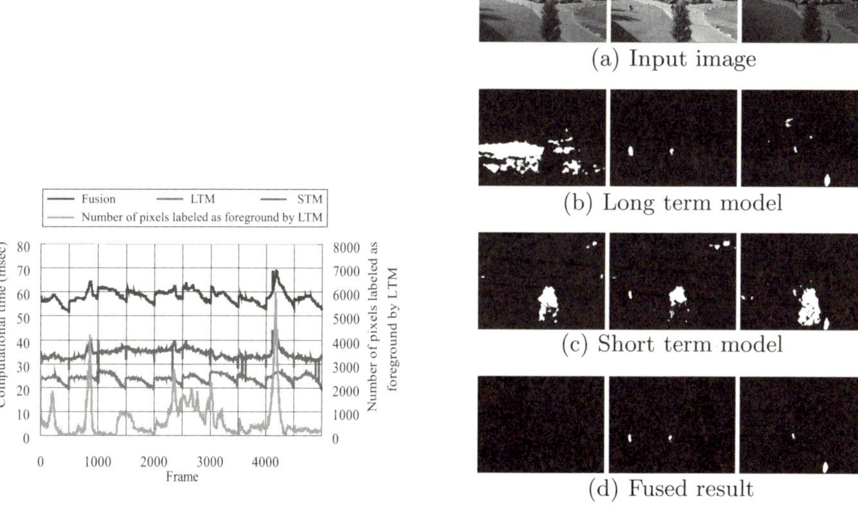

(a) Input image

(b) Long term model

(c) Short term model

(d) Fused result

**Fig. 2.** Computational time of proposed method

**Fig. 3.** Performance comparison between LTM and STM

the local texture, though it is effective against sudden illumination changes, it can not handle such the background changes. As shown Figure 3(d), fusing these approaches realizes robust object detection under varying illumination condition.

## 5.3   Object Detection Accuracy

To evaluate the object detection accuracy, we have used two scenes shown in Figure 4. One of them is an outdoor scene(PETS2001) which was used in Section 5.1. And the other is an indoor scene, which we took a rate of 15fps. The image resolution is $320 \times 240$ pixes. The indoor scene includes sudden illumination changes caused by turning off and on the light. Using these data sets, we have examined precision and recall of object detection on the basis of ground truth[3].

Precision and recall are respectively defined as follows:

$$\text{precision} = \frac{\# \text{ correctly detected pixels}}{\# \text{ of detected pixels}} \tag{17}$$

$$\text{recall} = \frac{\# \text{ of correctly detected pixels}}{\# \text{ of pixels which should be detected}} \tag{18}$$

Outdoor scene and indoor scene were composed of about 5000 frames and about 3000 frames respectively, and their first 500 frames are used for initialization.

---

[3] Several kinds of ground truth have been opened to the public through the web, http://limu.is.kyushu-u.ac.jp/dataset

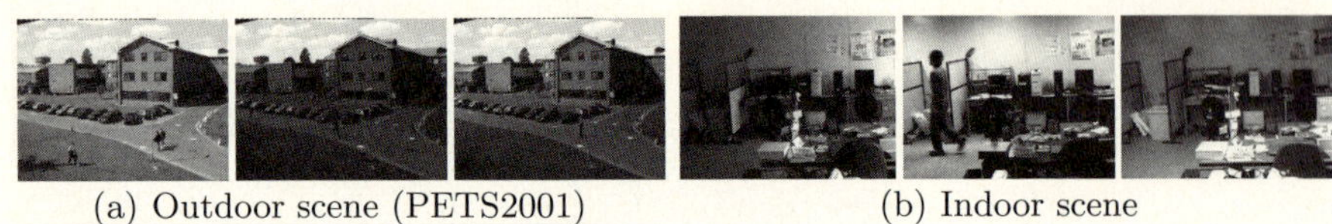

(a) Outdoor scene (PETS2001)          (b) Indoor scene

**Fig. 4.** Experimental data

**Table 2.** Object detection accuracy

|  | Outdoor scene | | Indoor scene | |
|---|---|---|---|---|
|  | Recall | Precision | Recall | Precision |
| **Proposed method** | **71.6%** | **72.6%** | **52.1%** | **60.0%** |
| Radial Reach Filter | 37.5% | 22.4% | 26.9% | 24.9% |
| Gaussian Mixture Model | 61.3% | 58.2% | 35.6% | 46.1% |
| Parzen density estimation | 56.3% | 51.6% | 37.8% | 58.5% |

The recall and the precision were evaluated in the rest of the data. Ground truth represents regions that should be detected as object regions. Test data are extracted in every 15 frames and their ground truth is added manually.

Table 2 shows the average accuracy of the proposed method, RRF [4], Gaussian Mixture Model [8] and adaptive background model based on Parzen density estimation [9]. This table also shows the proposed method outperformed the other methods.

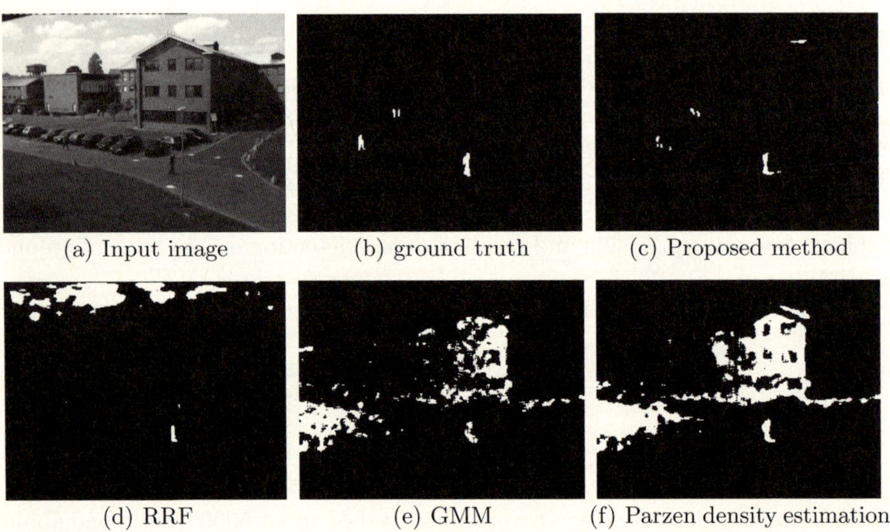

(a) Input image          (b) ground truth          (c) Proposed method

(d) RRF          (e) GMM          (f) Parzen density estimation

**Fig. 5.** Object detection by the proposed method, Radial Reach Filter, Gaussian Mixture Model and Adaptive background model based on Parzen density estimation

Figure 5 shows results of object detection by the proposed method. Figure 5(a) $\sim$ 5(f) show the input image , ground truth, the object areas detected by our approach, the result in case of RRF, the one of Gaussian Mixture Model and the one of adaptive background model based on Parzen density estimation, respectively. For the proposed method, we have used $N = 500$, $h = 9$, $T_B = 6$, $T_P = 2.5\sigma$. Where, an initial frame was used as a background image $f$ in RRF. This result shows that, RRF can not handle the background change such as movements of cloud since the background model was created at the first frame and was not updated in the later process. As a result, some non-object region had been mis-detected. On the other hand, though Gaussian Mixture Model and the adaptive background model based on Parzen density estimation could handle those background changes, the ground and the wall of building had been mis-detected because they were not possible to adapt sudden illumination changes. Our method, which combines two complementary approaches properly, could detect object regions robustly compared with the other methods.

## 6   Conclusion

In this paper, we have proposed a new method for background modeling based on the combination of non-parametric background model using Parzen density estimation and Radial Reach Filter, which is known as a robust background subtraction method under varying illumination. In our experiment, we have got a good result that the computational time was 60msec (about 15fps) and the precision ratio and recall ratio were superior to the traditional approaches under varying illumination.

Future works are summarized as follows:

- **Stabilization of computational time**
  When a sudden background change takes place or when the proportion of the area to be detected on the image becomes large, the computation cost becomes large. In other words, the computational time varies largely. This is because if the pixels are labeled as foreground by LTM, they should be further examined, by STM, whether it is weather foreground or background. It is not a good characteristic for real-time processing and, therefore, we should develop a mechanism to stabilize the computation cost.
- **Cooperation between Long-term model and Short-term model**
  Our combination rule of LTM and STM is rather simple and straightforward, i.e., logical AND of the results acquired by LTM and STM. Therefore, it is necessary to establish more sophisticated combination mechanism to make better use of the characteristics of the both models.

## References

1. Elgammal, A., Harwood, D., Davis, L.: Non-parametric Model for Background Subtraction. In: Vernon, D. (ed.) ECCV 2000. LNCS, vol. 1843, pp. 751–767. Springer, Heidelberg (2000)

2. Toyama, K., Krumm, J., Brumitt, B., Meyers, B.: Wallflower: Principle and Practice of Background Maintenance. In: International Conference on Computer Vision, pp. 255–261 (1999)
3. Li, L., Huang, W., Gu, I.Y.H., Tian, Q.: Statistical Modeling of Complex Background for Foreground Object Detection. IEEE Transactions on Image Processing 13(11), 1459–1472 (2004)
4. Satoh, Y., Kaneko, S., Niwa, Y., Yamamoto, K.: Robust object detection using a Radial Reach Filter (RRF). Systems and Computers in Japan 35(10), 63–73 (2004)
5. Monari, E., Pasqual, C.: Fusion of Background Estimation Approaches for Motion Detection in Non-static Backgrounds. In: CD-ROM Proceedings of IEEE International Conference on Advanced Video and Signal Based Surveillance (2007)
6. Ukita, N.: Target-color learning and its detection for non-stationary scenes by nearest neighbor classification in the spatio-color space. In: Proceedings of IEEE International Conference on Advanced Video and Signal based Surveillance, pp. 394–399 (2005)
7. Stauffer, C., Grimson, W.: Adaptive background mixture models for real-time tracking. In: IEEE International Conference on Computer Vision and Pattern Recognition (CVPR), vol. 2, pp. 246–252 (1999)
8. Shimada, A., Arita, D., Ichiro Taniguchi, R.: Dynamic Control of Adaptive Mixture-of-Gaussians Background Model. In: CD-ROM Proceedings of IEEE International Conference on Advanced Video and Signal Based Surveillance (2006)
9. Tanaka, T., Shimada, A., Arita, D., Ichiro Taniguchi, R.: A Fast Algorithm for Adaptive Background Model Construction Using Parzen Density Estimation. In: CD-ROM Proceedings of IEEE International Conference on Advanced Video and Signal Based Surveillance (2007)

# Accelerating Face Detection by Using Depth Information


Haiyuan Wu, Kazumasa Suzuki, Toshikazu Wada, and Qian Chen

Faculty of Systems Engineering, Wakayama University 930 Sakaedani,
Wakayama-city, Wakayama, 640-8510 Japan
{wuhy,twada,chen}@sys.wakayama-u.ac.jp,
suzuki@vrl.sys.wakayama-u.ac.jp



**Abstract.** In the case that the sizes of faces are not available, all possible sizes of faces have to be assumed and a face detector has to classify many (often ten or more) sub-image regions everywhere in an image. This makes the face detection slow and the high false positive rate. This paper explores the usage of depth information for accelerating the face detection and reducing the false positive rate at the same time. In detail, we use the depth information to determine the size of the sub-image region that needs to be classified for each pixel. This will reduce the number of sub-image regions that need to be classified from many to one for one position (pixel) in an image. Since most unnecessary classifications are effectively avoided, both the processing time for face detection and the possibility of false positive can be reduced greatly. We also propose a fast algorithm for estimating the depth information that is used to determine the size of sub-image regions to be classified.

**Keywords:** Face detection, Face size, Depth information, Stereo, Video rate.


## 1   Introduction

Face detection is a time consuming job[4][5]. This is not only because of the difficulty of classifying a sub-image region into "face" or "non-face" class, but also because of the huge number of sub-image regions to be classified. There are two possible approaches to make face detection fast. The first one is to reduce the processing time for classifying a sub-image region. The second one is to reduce the number of sub-image regions to be classified in an image.

Many methods about the first approach have been proposed, among them there is the Viola's one. They used *Integral Image* to computer the Haar-Like features quickly, and selected a small number of critical visual features by AdaBoost. They also combined classifiers in a *cascade* to discarded the background regions quickly.

In the job of face detection where the sizes and the positions of faces are not available, sub-image regions of all possible sizes at any position have to classify. Therefore, the number of sub-image regions to be classified is so many that makes the face detection slow even with a very efficient face detection algorithm.

In an experiment of detecting faces in images of $320 \times 240$ pixels using the Viola's algorithm[1] implemented in OpenCV[2], the processing time was about 70 milliseconds on a 3.0 GHz Pentium 4 PC. In this experiment, the size of sub-image regions (windows) for detecting faces starts from $20 \times 20$ pixels and is enlarged by 1.25 time in


T. Wada, F. Huang, and S. Lin (Eds.): PSIVT 2009, LNCS 5414, pp. 657–667, 2009.

each step until it covers the whole image. In this case, the number of sub-image regions to be classified at the same position is

$$N_{classification} = \frac{\log(Biggest) - \log(Smallest)}{\log(Scale\ facteor)}$$
$$= \frac{\log 240 - \log 20}{\log 1.25} = 11.$$

This indicates that the famous approach only cannot make face detection fast enough. Another problem is the difficulty of telling a real face from a face in a photograph (See figure 1).

Another necessary approach to make face detection fast is to reduce the number of sub-image regions to be classified in an image. In this paper, we describe a new method for reducing the sub-image regions to be classified for face detection. We estimate the size of face that may exist at each position in an image from the depth information. In this way we can determine the size of sub-image regions that need to be classified. Therefore the number of sub-image regions to be classified at each position can be reduced from several (often ten or more) to one. The depth information is obtained from a stereo camera while the faces are detected from one image of the stereo image pair.

Assuming the 3D size of human's heads is constant and the images are taken by a calibrated camera, the size of a face in an image can be calculated from the depth information. For each pixel in an image, if we assume that a face exists there, we can determine the size of the face from the depth at that pixel. Thus for that pixel we only need to check if the sub-image region of that size really contains a face or not.

Since most unnecessary classifications can be effectively avoided with our method, both the processing time for face detection and the possibility of false positive can be reduced greatly. We also propose a fast algorithm for estimating the depth information that is used to determine the size of sub-image regions to be classified.

Several researches related to face detection using stereo cameras have been reported. All of them are different from our method.

Darrell et al. [6] used stereo vision, color and pattern recognition to track a head. In this research, they segmented the range data into several connected regions. If a face detected with pattern recognition or by skin color detection overlaps with one of the segmented region, they say that region indicates a human body.

There are some researches about head tracking (not detecting) that *only use range images*. Yang et al. [7] presented a model-based stereo head tracking system. The processing is purely performed on range image; the color/grey camera images were not used. Seven landmark points on each face in the first image frame have to be selected manually for estimating the initial 3D head pose. N. Jojic[8]'s method requires manual initialization. B. Deniel[9]'s method requires that the background is modeled and can be updated.

Luo et al [10] used stereo camera to detect heads by subtracting the background, which requires the prior knowledge of background. Wang et al [11] detected heads in range image by using morphological watersheds. They separated the nearest face from other objects by analysis of the disparity histogram. They only track the face nearest to the camera.

**Fig. 1.** An pattern recognition based face detection method can not distinguish a real face and the face in a photograph

This paper describes an efficient approach that enables video rate face detection by using depth information. We use a commercial stereo camera and the software for estimating range data provided by the camera maker. In order to complete the depth estimation within 10 millisecond, we propose a new adaptive sparse sampling method optimized for determining the size of sub-image regions to be classified called *important sampling*. The classifier for detecting a face in a sub-image region is the one of Viola et al[1].

## 2   Video-Rate Face Detection with Stereo-Camera

### 2.1   Stereo Depth Estimation[3]

We use the Triclops library, which is provided with the Bumblebee stereo camera made by the Point Grey Research Inc., to estimate the depth information. The correspondence between two images, which is necessary for calculating the disparity, is established with the SAD (Sum of Absolute Differences) correlation algorithm. Given a pixel $(x, y)$ in the right image, its corresponding pixel $(x + d, y)$ in the left image is determined by finding a $d_c$ that minimizes the $F(x, y, d)$ as follows.

$$d_c = \underset{d_{min} \leq d \leq d_{max}}{\mathrm{argmin}} F(x, y, z),$$

where,

$$F(x, y, d) = \sum_{i=-m/2}^{m/2} \sum_{j=-m/2}^{m/2} |I_R(x + i, y + j) - I_L(x + i + d, y + j)|, \quad (1)$$

$m$ is the mask size, $d_{min}$ and $d_{max}$ arc the minimum and maximum disparities. $I_R$ and $I_L$ are the right and left images.

In this research, the window size we used for stereo correlation is $9 \times 9$ pixels ($m = 8$), and the surface validation filter and the edge filter are used in the depth estimation.

## 2.2   Accelerating Depth Estimation by Important Sampling

Estimating dense (pixel by pixel) depth information from stereo image pairs is computationally expensive and is difficult to be performed at video rate. In this research, since the depth information is used for predicting the sizes of faces appeared in the image, one depth is enough for one region which containing a face. Therefore, the required depth information is sparse so that the time for depth estimation can be greatly reduced.

In this paper, we propose a novel method for adjusting the sampling interval adaptively for face detection so that the required depth information can be estimated within 10 millisecond for stereo images of $320 \times 240$ pixels.

**Sparse Depth Estimation.**  Since the smallest detectable face is $20 \times 20$ pixels, we let the sampling interval be 20 pixels as shown in Figure 2 so that there will be at least one sample point on any detectable faces. However, the sample points are still too many for the computer to process within 10 milliseconds. In order to solve this problem, we divide the sample points into two groups (the red and blue group in Figure 2), and estimate the depths of each group alternately. This ensures that the depth of any sample point will be estimated for every two frames.

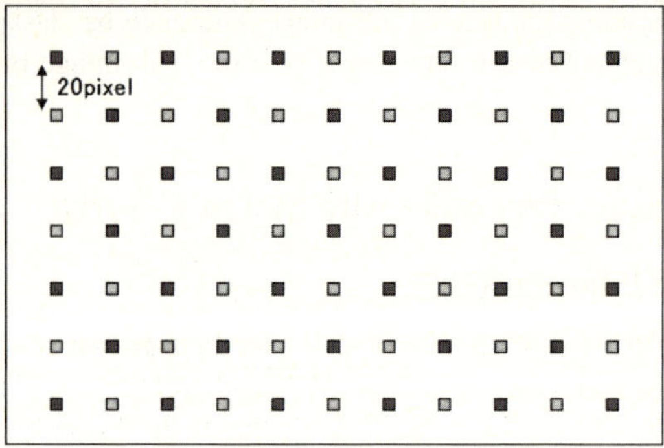


**Fig. 2.** Arrangement of sample points

There are two problems in this sampling method. For small faces, since the depths of the red sample points and blue sample points are estimated alternately, the depth information may not be available for every frame. And for big faces, multiple depth information will be estimated for a face which is redundancy.

**Important Sampling.**  Since faces in video sequences move continuously, if they have been detected in an image frame, in the next frame they should be near where they have been detected. According to this fact, for each face detected in the previous frame, we set $4 \times 4$ sample points on a double sized square centered at the center of this ensures that

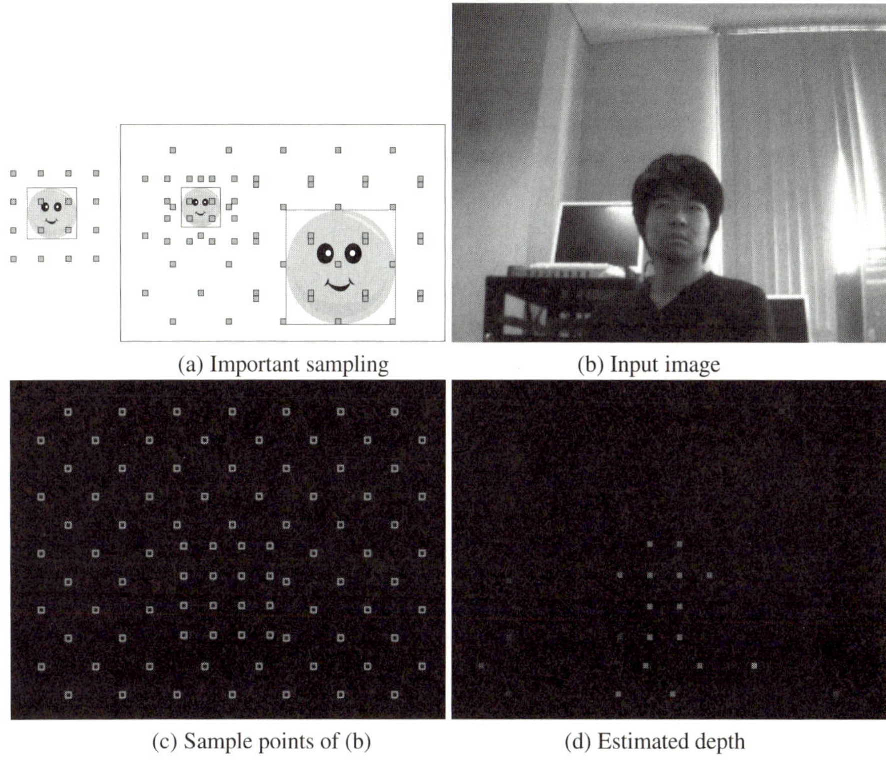

(a) Important sampling                    (b) Input image

(c) Sample points of (b)                  (d) Estimated depth

**Fig. 3.** Important sampling

the depth information of previously detected faces will be available for every frame and the sampling interval is adjusted adaptively. We call this sampling strategy as *important sampling*. Figure 3(b) shows an input image, and Figure 3(c) shows the arrangement of sample points for the input image. Figure 3(d) shows the estimated depths where the brightness of green dots indicates the depth (the near the brighter), while the sample points where the estimated face sizes that are too big or too small are not shown.

### 2.3 Depth Based Classification Reduction

The relation between the distance from a face to a camera (the depth $Z$), the width of the face in the image ($I_{size}$) and the diameter of the face ($W_{size}$) can be described (see figure 4) as follows.

$$I_{size} = f \frac{W_{size}}{Z},\tag{2}$$

where $f$ is the focal length of the camera. Since the size of human head is almost the same, if a sample point is on a face in the image, the face width can be calculated from the depth with eq.(2). This indicates that we only need to check if the sub-image region of the estimated face size contains a face.

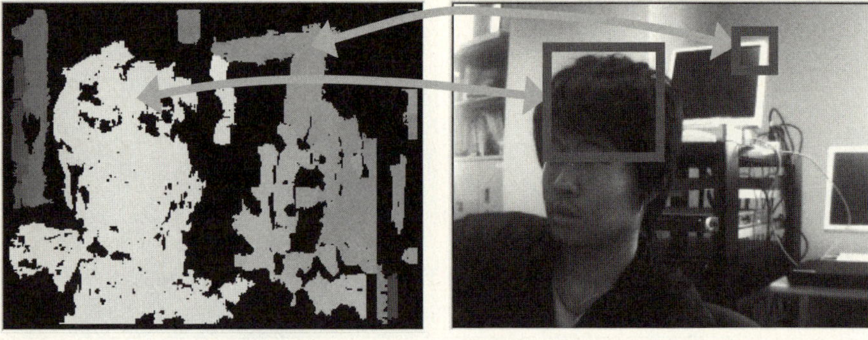

**Fig. 4.** Estimating the face width in image using depth information

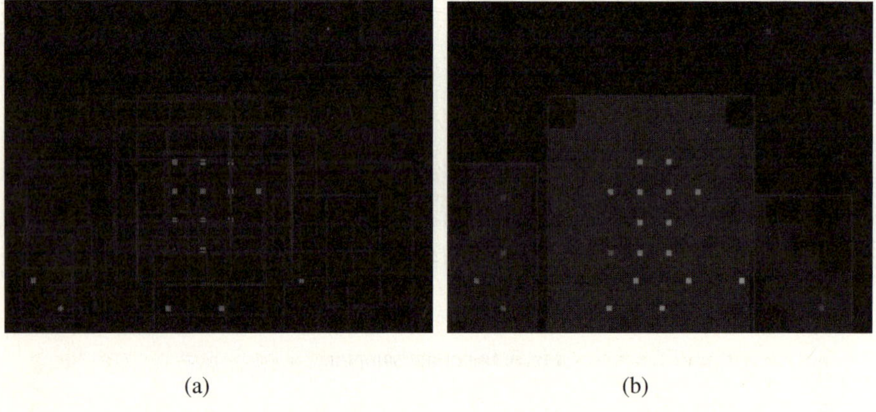

(a)          (b)

**Fig. 5.** Integration of overlapped image regions for face detection

If a sample point is on a face, the image region where the face may exist will be a square centered at the sample point and is double width of the estimated face width. Since the width of the square is much longer than the interval between two sample points, there may be many image regions that overlap each other. The multiple classifications for those overlapped regions are a waste of time thus should be avoided. For this purpose, we integrate the overlapped image regions where the estimated face sizes are almost same into one big rectangular image region. The face classifier is applied to that image region by using the estimated face width as the window size. Figure 5(a) and (b) shows an example of determined image regions for face detection from all sample points and the ones after the integration.

## 3   Experimentation [12]

### 3.1   Experimental Environment

We used a PC with a 3.0GHz Pentium 4(R) CPU, a Bumblebee Stereo Vision Camera made by Point Grey Research Inc. and its supported software in the experiments. We set

$W_{size}$ in eq.(2) to 14cm. Since the diameter of a head is not exactly same for different person and the estimated depth may contain some error, we tolerant the restriction of face size by using two different window size simultaneously: $I_{size}$ and $1.25 I_{size}$.

## 3.2   Comparison of Processing Speed

We applied our method and Viola's algorithm[1] to two stereo image sequences (320 × 240 pixels). In sequence 1 there is one person and in the sequence 2 there are two persons. Each of them contains about 100 frames.

Figure 6 and figure 7 show the processing time of our method for sequence 1 and 2, respectively. The horizontal and vertical axis indicates the frame number and the processing time in millisecond, respectively. The green, orange and blue curve show the face classification time, the depth estimation time, and the sum time of our method, respectively.

Comparing figure 6 and figure 7, we noticed that the time for depth estimation (orange curve) was almost constant, while the total processing time (blue curve) for sequence 2 was longer than the one for sequence 1. The reason is that since there are two faces in sequence 2, the image regions that need to be classified are bigger than the ones for sequence 1. In both cases the face detection for one frame was finished in 33 milliseconds.

We also tested our method with various image sequences and confirmed that the average processing time was about 25 milliseconds for one frame. On the other hand, Viola's algorithm[1] needed about 70 milliseconds for one frame of image.

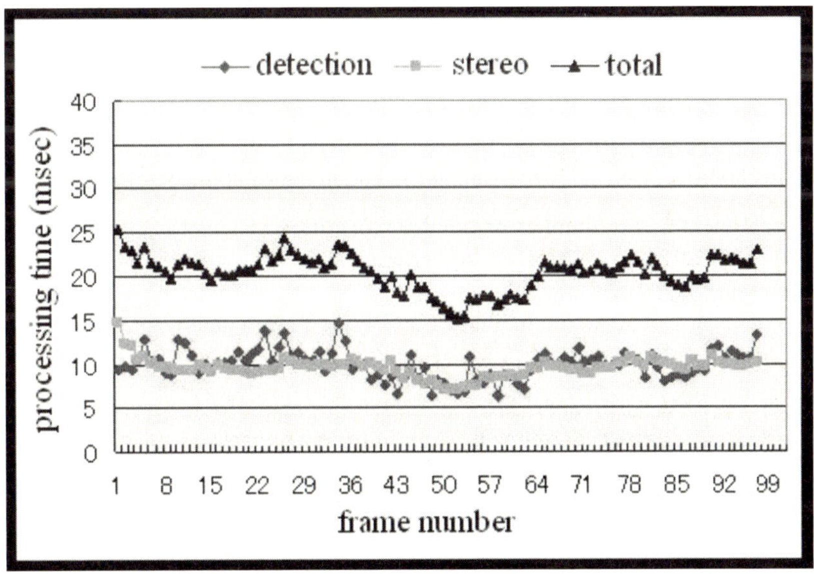


**Fig. 6.** The processing time of our method for sequence 1 using our method

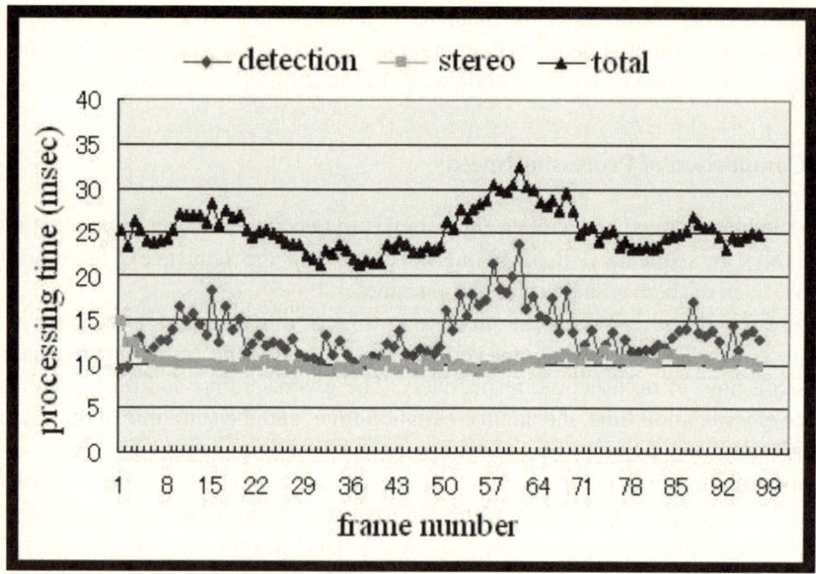



**Fig. 7.** The processing time of our method for sequence 2 using our method

## 3.3   Comparison of Detection Accuracy

In order to confirm the detection accuracy of the proposal method, three stereo image sequences containing 101 frames ($320 \times 240$ pixels) were prepared. There is one face in the sequences 1 and 2, and are two faces in sequence 3, while the face in sequence 2 moves faster.

For each sequence we conducted two different experiments as follows.

- **Experiment 1:** Detect faces with Viola's algorithm[1] for monocular images (using the right image of a stereo pair)
- **Experiment 2:** Detect faces with our method in the right image of a stereo pair.

In experiment 1, the number of windows of different size for classification was $(\log 240 - \log 20)/\log 1.25 = 11$. In experiment 2, we used two window sizes for classification: $Isize$ and $1.25 Isize$.

The results are summarized in Table 1 and Table 2. In sequence 3, the results were showed separately in 3a and 3b for each face.

**Table 1.** The experimental results of face detection. The numbers show the total frames where the faces were successfully detected.

| Series No. | 1 | 2 | 3a | 3b |
|---|---|---|---|---|
| Experiment 1 | 82 | 52 | 54 | 83 |
| Experiment 2 | 87 | 77 | 55 | 92 |

**Table 2.** The experimental results of false positive. The numbers are false detection in the total frames.

| Series No. | 1 | 2 | 3a | 3b |
| --- | --- | --- | --- | --- |
| Experiment 1 | 8 | 20 | 22 | 22 |
| Experiment 2 | 2 | 7 | 2 | 2 |

From table 1, comparing the results of experiment 1 and 2, we noticed that the detection rate of our method was higher than Viola's algorithm. One considerable reason is that the window size in our method was fine fitting to the actual face, thus more reliable results can be obtained.

From table 2, we confirmed our method had much less false positive than Viola's algorithm[1].

### 3.4   Other Detection Results

**Detecting Real Human Face.**   An example frame in a video sequence is shown in Figure 8. There is a real human face and a photograph of a face in the input image. As shown in Figure 8(a), both the real human face and the face in the photograph were detected by the viola's method. As shown in Figure 8(b), only the real human face was detected by our method. This is because our method estimates the window size of a face in input image from the stereo depth information. If the size of a face appeared in an image is much different from the size estimated from the depth information, it will not be considered as a real human face.

**Detecting Rotated Faces.**  Since the time for face detection can be significantly reduced by using the proposed method, we can use the saved time to rotate the image so that the faces with rotation in the image plane will also become detectable.

We performed several experiments where we rotated the input images to left and right by 30 degrees, then we applied the our method to detect face in the original image and

(a) Viola's method;                              (b) Our method.

**Fig. 8.** A example result of detecting real human face

**Fig. 9.** A example result of detecting a face with rotation

the two rotated images. An example of the face detection result is shown in Figure 9. The processing time of these experiments was about 40-50 milliseconds per frame.

## 4  Conclusion

In this paper, we have proposed a novel method for accelerating face detection by reducing the number of sub-image regions that need to be classified. This is carried out by estimating the possible face size from the depth information obtained from a stereo camera. This has the significant effects of reducing the number of classification and suppressing the false positive rate. Moreover, we have proposed a novel method for estimating the depth information efficiently for face detection called *important sampling*.

Extensive experiments using various real image sequences showed that the processing time was short enough for video rate face detection. Also we have confirmed that our method can improve the detection accuracy and can decrease the false positive compared with the conventional algorithm[1].

## References


1. Viola, P., Jones, M.: Robust Real-Time Face Detection. IJCV 57(2), 137–154 (2004)
2. OpenCV, `http://www.intel.com/technology/computing/opencv`
3. StereoVisionProducts,
   `http://www.ptgrey.com/products/triclopsSDK/index.asp`
4. Hjelmas, E.: Face detection: A survey. Computer Vision and Image Understanding 83, 236–274 (2001)
5. Yang, M.-H., Kriegman, D.J., Ahuja, N.: Detecting faces in images: a survey. PAMI 24(1), 34–58 (2002)
6. Damell, T., Gordon, G., Woodfill, J., Harville, M.: Integrated person tracking using stereo, color and pattern detection. IJCV, 175–185 (2000)

7. Yang, R., Zhang, Z.: Model-based head tracking with stereo vision, FG, pp. 255-260 (2002)
8. Jojic, N., Turk, M., Huang, T.: Tracking self occlude articulated objects in dense disparity maps. ICCV, 123–130 (1999)
9. Deniel, B., Herman, M.: Head tracking using stereo. Machine Vision and Applications 13, 164–173 (2002)
10. Luo, R., Guo, Y.: Real-time stereo tracking of multiple moving heads. In: Proceedings of International Workshop on Recognition, Analysis and Tracking of Faces and Gestures in Real-time Systems, pp. 62–67 (2001)
11. Wang, J., Lim, E., Venkateswarlu, R.: Stereo Head/Face Detection and Tracking. ICIP, 605–608 (2004)
12. Suzuki, K., Oike, H., Wu, H., Wada, T.: Video-rate face detection and tracking using active stereo-camera. In: PSIVT 2009 Demo (2009)

# Rotated Image Based Photomosaic Using Combination of Principal Component Hashing

Hideaki Uchiyama and Hideo Saito

Keio University, 3-14-1 Hiyoshi, Kohoku-ku 223-8522, Japan
{uchiyama,saito}@ozawa.ics.keio.ac.jp

**Abstract.** This paper introduces a new method of Photomosaic. In this method, we propose to use tiled images that can be rotated in a restricted range. The tiled images are selected from a database. The selection of an image is done by a hashing method based on principal component analysis of a database. After computing the principal components of the database, various kinds of hash tables based on the linear combination of the principal component are prepared beforehand. Using our hashing method, we can reduce the computation time for selecting the tiled images based on the approximated nearest neighbor searching in consideration of a distribution of data in a database. We demonstrate the effectiveness of our hashing method by using a huge number of data in high dimensional space and better looking results of our tiling in experimental results.

## 1   Introduction

Mosaic is one of the traditional arts in which a large image is generated by tiling small pieces of colored glass, stone and so on. The tiling ways are determined depending on a shape and a texture of the image and pieces. Recently, computer-generated mosaics are studied as a non-photorealistic rendering [1,2].

Photomosaic is an image that has packed with many smaller images called tiles by using a reference image [3]. In a Photomosaic image, pixel colors are replaced with small tiled images that approximate pixel colors in local regions in the reference image. Then small tiled images can be seen by observing in close-up, while the approximated reference image can be seen by observing from the distance. The applications of Photomosaic have already been available in [4,5].

In Photomosaic, research topics can be divided into two aspects as follows:

- To find optimized arrangement of tiled images that provides better approximation of the reference image
- To select tiled images that represent local regions in a good approximation from a database of tiled images

In the first research topic, previous tiling methods replace a pixel or local square region in a reference image with an image without overlapping and rotating [3,4,5]. As a result, some parts of the Photomosaic image are not matched

T. Wada, F. Huang, and S. Lin (Eds.): PSIVT 2009, LNCS 5414, pp. 668–679, 2009.

with the reference image because the color of the image in a database is not always matched with the color of the local region in the reference image.

In the second research topic, the selection of tiled images from a database is addressed as an approximate nearest neighbor searching problem. Previous researches described the method for evaluating color difference between a square region in a reference image and every image in a database to find the best matching image. However, the searching problem is also very important in Photomosaic for reducing the computation for generating a Photomosaic image.

As an extended approach of Photomosaic, Videomosaic which generates a video composed of many smaller videos has been proposed [6]. A method called Jigsaw Image Mosaics (JIM) is another tiling method by using an arbitrary shape image. The images can be deformed for packing into an arbitrary area [7]. Puzzle Image Mosaics (PIM) is an improved method of JIM for reducing the computation cost and generating better result visually by enhancing edges of shapes [8]. However, JIM and PIM are applied to only less textured images. In addition, the small pieces cannot be sometimes observed in close-up because they may be deformed and upside down [7,8].

In this paper, we propose a Photomosaic method with two following contributions:

- Tiling method using rotated images
- Approximate nearest neighbor searching method based on hashing by combinations of principal components

In our tiling method, images for tiling are not deformed because deformed images cannot be sometimes recognized as a small image due to loss of the original appearance. Instead of deforming, our method allows images to be rotated and overlapped. The use of rotated images increases the possibility of a region in a reference image to match with an image in a database. Our method has templates for several rotated images beforehand. In a local region, the best template matched with the region is selected. As a result, a Photomosaic image with tiled images is generated.

Approximate nearest neighbor searching is one of the important techniques for example based pattern recognition. In Photomosaic, the searching tiled images from a database needs much computation cost. As mentioned above, the quick searching is important. Many works discussed in Section 2 have already proposed for reducing computation cost. However there is still a problem for accelerating the search of nearest data from huge number of data in high dimensional space. We adopt a hashing method based on principal component analysis for considering the distribution of data in a database. In our method, various kinds of hash tables are generated by combination of principal components of a database for clustering neighbors. In the retrieval phase, the candidates of the nearest neighbor of a query are collected from every hash table and the nearest neighbor is selected from the candidates by distance computation.

The rest of this paper is organized as follows: Section 2 discusses the related works about nearest neighbor searching problems. Section 3 presents our approximate nearest neighbor searching method based on combination of principal component hashing. Section 4 presents Photomosaic method allowing rotation and overlap of images. In Section 5, our methods are evaluated for proving the effectiveness and Section 6 concludes this paper with discussions and possible future works.

## 2  Nearest Neighor Searching

In nearest neighbor searching problem, we divided the solutions into two categories, tree based approach [9,10] and hash based approach [11,12,13,14].

### 2.1  Approximate Nearest Neighbor

In tree based approach, Approximate Nearest Neighbor (ANN) is a method using a binary tree [9]. Each node of the tree represents a cell generated by subdividing space. Each leaf is associated with a single point lying within the bounding rectangle for the cell. In the searching, ANN gets candidates from tree search first. Then, the nearest data of the query is selected from the candidates by computing the distances between a query and each candidate.

In ANN, there is an important parameter $\epsilon$ for representing degree of approximation. $\epsilon = 0$ means the nearest neighbor searching. The larger $\epsilon$ provides smaller computation cost. However, the nearest neighbor may not be found instead of reducing the computation cost.

### 2.2  Locality Sensitive Hashing

Locality Sensitive Hashing (LSH) is one of approximate nearest neighbor searching methods using a hash [12,13].

In the registration phase, a $d$-dimensional input vector is converted into $L$ sets of $k$-dimensional vector by $L$ transform matrices. $L$ is the number of hash tables. Each $k$-dimensional vector is registered in a list of each hash tables by computing a hash value from $k$-dimensional vector. In the retrieval phase, a $d$-dimensional query vector is converted in the same way of the registration phase. Candidates of nearest neighbor vectors are selected from $L$ hash tables. Then, the nearest data of the query is selected from the candidates by computing the distances between a query and each candidate.

In LSH, $L$ transform matrices should be prepared such as $g_1(\boldsymbol{v}), \ldots, g_L(\boldsymbol{v})$. $g_i(\boldsymbol{v})$ has $k$ transform matrices for converting a $d$-dimensional vector into a natural number such as $g_i(\boldsymbol{v}) = (h_1(\boldsymbol{v}), \ldots, h_k(\boldsymbol{v}))$. $h_j(\boldsymbol{v}))$ is

$$h_{a,b}(\boldsymbol{v}) = \left\lfloor \frac{\boldsymbol{a} \cdot \boldsymbol{v} + b}{w} \right\rfloor \tag{1}$$

where $\boldsymbol{a}$ is a $d$-dimensional vector, $b$ adjusts bias in $[0, w]$ and $\lfloor \cdot \rfloor$ is a floor function. Each element of $\boldsymbol{a}$ is determined from normal random number.

The relationship between the relative error ratio and complexity of calculation is clearly defined in LSH. However, the searching of the nearest neighbor may not work because the transform matrices are prepared without considering the distribution of data in a database.

## 2.3   Principal Component Hashing

Principal Component Hashing (PCH) is inspired from LSH [14]. Compared with LSH, $a$ in Eq.2 is an eigenvector of a database in PCH. Each eigenvector is segmented into several buckets by making the density of each bucket be equivalent for clustering neighbors. The candidates are selected by sum of bucket sets on several eigenvectors. In the distance computation, the approximated nearest neighbor can be selected by cutting off the candidates effectively from first eigenvector's bucket.

In PCH, the nearest neighbor searching of a query starts from the buckets of the first eigenvector by computing a hash value of the query. The query is searched on a range of buckets on each eigenvector. However, the size of the range influence the accuracy of the nearest neighbor.

# 3   Combination of Principal Component Hashing

In Photomosaic, the selection of tiled images from a database should be addressed. A tiled image may be more than thousand dimension vector. In addition, the database may have more than ten thousand images. For this reason, we propose a quick searching method.

Our method is inspired by PCH and LSH. Our hash function is extended from that of PCH. This means that we adapt principal component analysis for converting a input space into lower dimensional space. The registration data by a hash and data retrieval are close to those of LSH. The transform matrices in Section 2.2 is composed of eigenvectors by PCA.

### 3.1   Registration

In LSH, a data is transformed into a hash key by using a uniform discretization step $w$ in Eq.2. On the other hand, $a \cdot v$ is discretized based on distribution of data in PCH. We adopt the method of PCH.

In Figure 1, discretized value $h_i(v)$ from a data $v$ on $i$-th eigenvector is shown. First, a discretization level $d$ is determined beforehand (in this case, $d = 3, 0 \leq h_i(v) \leq 2$). Thresholds for segmenting the eigenvector into several buckets are determined by making the number of elements in each bucket be same. In retrieval phase, a query is discretized by using the same thresholds. This process is done for the selected number of eigenvectors.

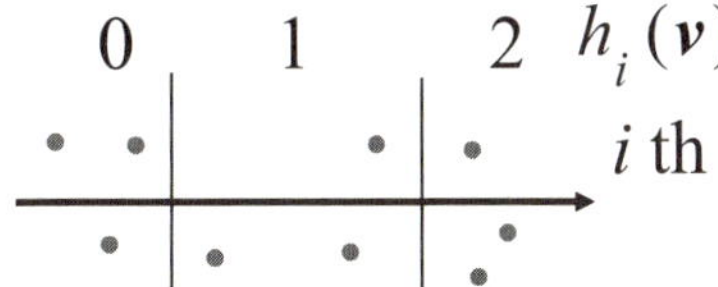


**Fig. 1.** Discretization

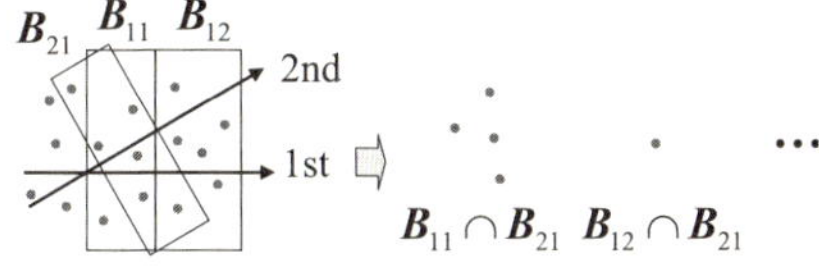


**Fig. 2.** Product Sets of Buckets

In PCH, an eigenvector corresponds to a hash table as $h_i(\boldsymbol{v})$ is a hash value. Candidates for the nearest neighbors of a query are collected from union of buckets on each eigenvector. The union sometimes provides the huge number of the candidates. Distance computation between a query and the candidates takes most time in approximated nearest neighbor searching. To reduce the number of the candidates, our method generates new buckets by product sets of buckets on several eigenvectors.

Figure 2 briefly shows our method in 2 dimension, where $\boldsymbol{B}_{ij}$ is a bucket of discretized value $j$ on $i$-th eigenvector. New buckets are generated by every product set of 2 buckets such as $\boldsymbol{B}_{11} \cap \boldsymbol{B}_{21}$. In PCH, one bucket is put on an eigenvector. On the other hand, one bucket is composed of several eigenvectors by product set.

Next, we explain the details in $n$ dimension. Important parameters in our method are as follows: $n$ is the number of selected eigenvectors, $m$ is the number of eigenvectors for computing a product set (less than $n$) and $d$ is a discretization level on each eigenvector. $n$ and $m$ define the number of hash tables because the number is a combination of $m$ out of $n$ $({}_nC_m)$. The case of 2 dimension as mentioned above has one hash table because of $n = 2$ and $m = 2$. In the hash table, a bucket is inserted into a list by computing a hash value from discretized values on each eigenvector. The number of lists in each hash table is $d^m$.

Figure 3 explains the case of $n = 4$ and $m = 3$. The number of generated hash tables is 4. A product set by each bucket of $m$ eigenvectors is stored in a list. A data $\boldsymbol{v}$ is registered in $x$-th hash table by computing a hash value $H_x$:

$$H_x = \sum_{y=0}^{m-1} h_{c_{xy}}(\boldsymbol{v})d^y \tag{2}$$

where $c_{xy}$ represents the eigenvector number in Figure 4. One data is registerd in ${}_nC_m$ hash tables by computing each hash value.

Our method is merged with PCH and LSH. The discretized value $h_i(\boldsymbol{v})$ comes from PCH. $L$ and $k$ in LSH correspond to ${}_nC_m$ and $m$ of our method respectively. Our main contribution is the way of making hash tables based on combination of principal components. Therefore, we call our method Combination of Principal Component Hashing (CPCH). In Section 5, the influence by the sizes of $n$, $m$ and $d$ for searching results is evaluated.

## 3.2   Retrieval

In retrieval phase, the candidates of a query $\boldsymbol{q}$ are collected from hash tables generated in Section 3.2. The nearest neighbor is selected from the candidates by distance computation.

First, a query $\boldsymbol{q}$ is transformed into ${}_nC_m$ hash values by using Eq.2. Data in each list are collected by the hash values as candidates. Each data may be counted several times because the date is stored in several lists. After candidates are collected, the candidates are sorted depending on the counts. Since the best count's candidate is not always the nearest neighbor of a query, the distance

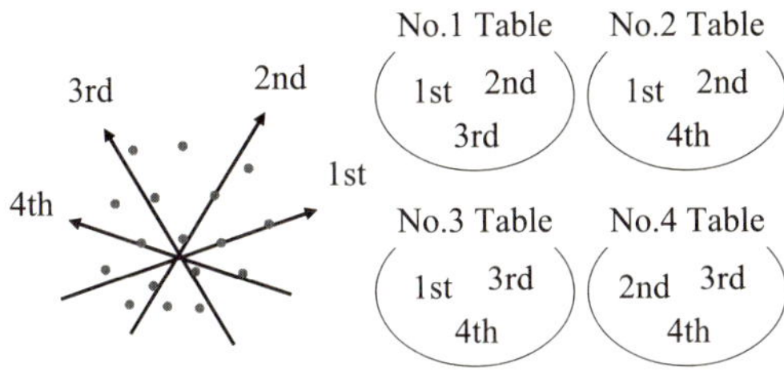



**Fig. 3.** Generation of Hash Tables

| Table Number \ Vector Number | $y$ = 0 | 1 | 2 |
|---|---|---|---|
| $x$ = 0 | 1 | 2 | 3 |
| 1 | 1 | 2 | 4 |
| 2 | 1 | 3 | 4 |
| 3 | 2 | 3 | 4 |

**Fig. 4.** Combination Patterns ($c_{xy}$ in Eq.2)

computation is done against several candidates. We use top $b$ % in the distance computation as PCH used for reducing the number of candidates. The number of candidates and the influence of $b$ are discussed in Section 5.

Next, we explain the details of collecting the candidates in Figure 5. In $t$-th list of $s$-th hash table, the new bucket $B'_{st}$ generated by a product set of several buckets $B_{ij}$ is stored. In our retrieval phase, the candidates of the nearest neighbors of a query $C(q)$ are collected by

$$C = \bigcup_{s=0}^{{}_nC_m-1} B'_{sH_s} \tag{3}$$

The equation represents that the candidates are collected from union of product sets of buckets. On the other hand, the candidates are collected from union of buckets in PCH.

After collection of the candidates, the distance computation between a query and each candidate is done by

$$D = \sqrt{\sum_{i=1}^{d}(x_i - y_i)} \tag{4}$$

where $x_i$ and $y_i$ are $d$-dimensional vector and $D$ is a distance. Finally, the approximate nearest neighbor of a query is found.

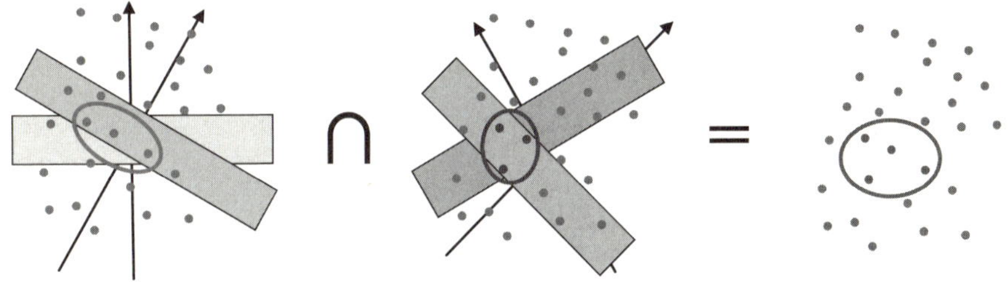

**Fig. 5.** Collection of Candidates

## 4  Photomosaic with Rotated Images

In previous Photomosaics, a tile corresponds to a pixel or a small square region. Our method can treat a rotated square region as a tile. In a database, square images are stored, which are collected from the Internet. Their size is transformed into same size in Figure 6(a).

In Photomosaic processing, a square region represented in Figure 6(c) are extracted at a target pixel as shown in Figure 6(b). Our method has several templates including rotated regions for making rotated squares be a tile. By preparing many templates, the range of the rotation is changeable. In addition, many sizes of images can be tiled by preparing their templates.

In our method, selection of a tiled image at each pixel is done first. At each pixel, the regions corresponding to each template are extracted. The similarities between the regions and images in a database are computed for determining the best matched template. After the similarity computation at each pixel finished, the tiling starts from the least similarity image.

For the region extracted by each template in a reference image, the nearest image is searched from a database by using CPCH described in Figure 3. In Figure 6(c), the number of templates is 4 and 4 images are searched at each pixel. For selecting one nearest image from 4 images, the similarities $R_{SSD}$ between the regions of each template $T$ and searched images $I$ are computed from

$$R_{SSD} = \sum_i \sum_j \sum_c (T(i,j,c) - I(i,j,c))^2 \tag{5}$$

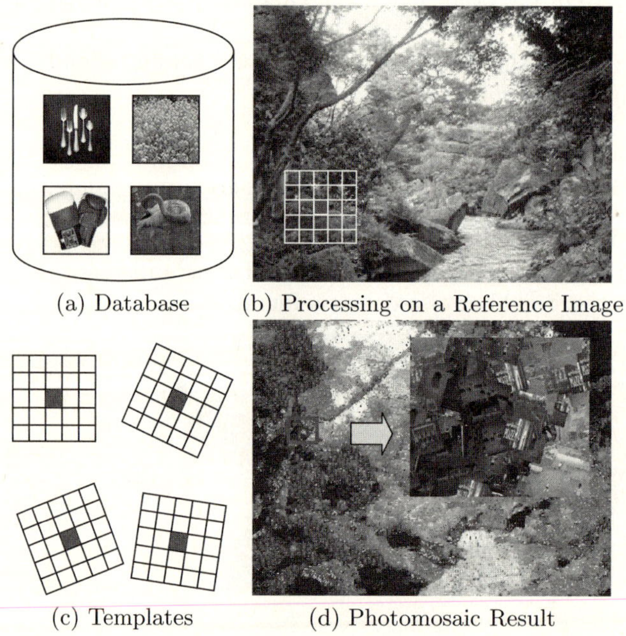

(a) Database     (b) Processing on a Reference Image

(c) Templates     (d) Photomosaic Result

**Fig. 6.** Tiling Overview

where $(i, j)$ is a pixel and $c$ is color channel. As a result, best similarity image is selected at each pixel.

This process is not performed in every pixel because many overlaps are occurred. For reducing the overlaps, we empirically set the interval of target pixels for this process. In case that the size of a square image in a database is M ×M and the maximum degree of the rotation is $\theta$, the interval is M × sin $\theta$.

In the previous process, one best similarity's image is selected from several templates at each target pixel. The order of tiling images starts from the least similarity's image. This causes less possibilities of higher similarity's image to be overlapped by another image.

Usually, a Photomosaic image has higher resolution than the reference image because the larger size of the square image in a database is tiled. The size of Figure 6(d) is five times larger than that of Figure 6(b).

## 5   Experimental Results

All parts of our algorithm are implemented in C++ and following experiments are carried out on Intel Core 2 Duo 2.2 GHz and 3GB RAM with Windows XP.

### 5.1   Perfomance Evaluation of CPCH

Our method has four parameters as $n$, $m$, $d$ and $b$. We report the influence of these parameters for the searching results.

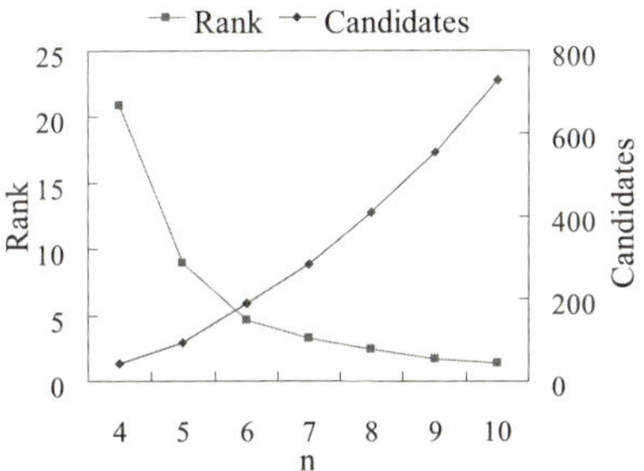

**Fig. 7.** n vs rank and candidates

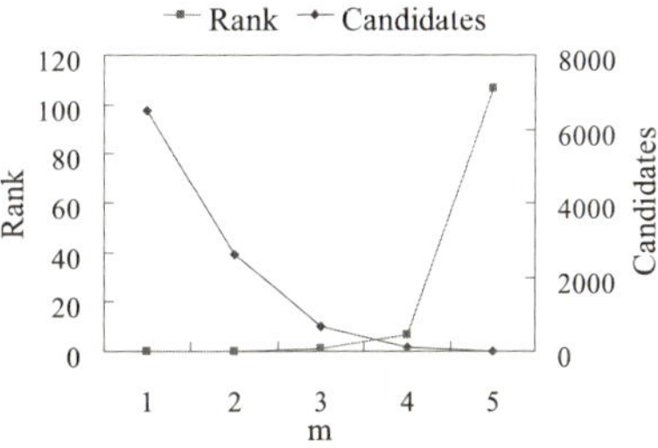

**Fig. 8.** m vs rank and candidates

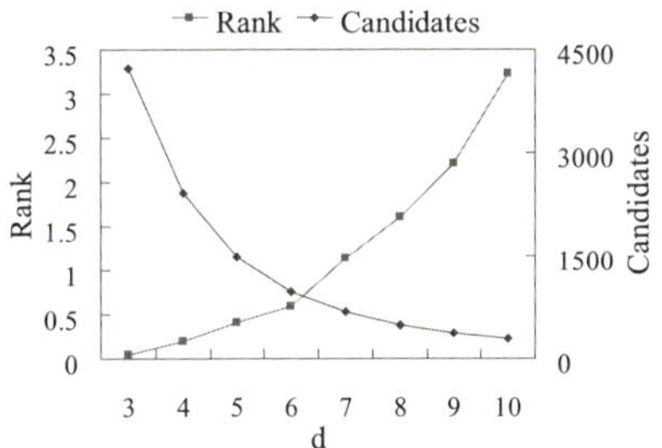

**Fig. 9.** d vs rank and candidates

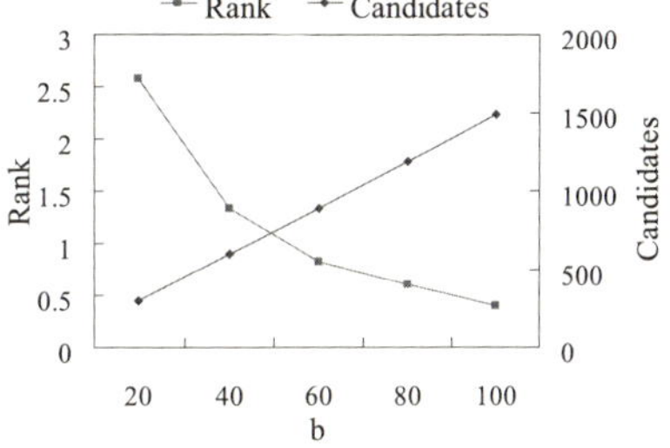

**Fig. 10.** b vs rank and candidates

(a) Lenna          (b) Mandrill

**Fig. 11.** Reference Images

**Table 1.** Averages of absolute difference

|          | b  | g  | r  |
|----------|----|----|----|
| Fig.12(a) | 27 | 35 | 35 |
| Fig.13(a) | 24 | 31 | 31 |
| Fig.12(b) | 34 | 35 | 34 |
| Fig.13(b) | 32 | 32 | 31 |

In a database, 10000 color images which size is $20 \times 20$ are stored. We handle an image as a 1200 dimensional vector. 500 images which are not included in the database are prepared as queries. In each query image, the distances with 10000 images are computed for making the rank order of the nearest as a ground truth beforehand.

In this experiment, the nearest neighbor image of each query image is searched from 10000 images by our method. For evaluating the accuracy of the searched image, the rank of the image is drawn out from the pre-computed rank order. If the rank is 0, the searched image is the nearest neighbor image. After the searching is done for every query image, the average rank is computed (Rank in Figure.7-10). In addition, the average number of candidates described in Section 3.2 is evaluated (Candidates in Figure.7-10) because the number influence computation time. The parameter in Figure.7-10 are as follows: $m = 3$, $d = 10$, $b = 100$ (in Figure 7). $n = 7$, $d = 7$, $b = 100$ (in Figure 8). $n = 7$, $m = 3$, $b = 100$ (in Figure 9). $n = 7$, $m = 3$, $d = 5$ (in Figure 10).

Since the number of hash tables is $_nC_m$, the number of candidates increases when $n$ increases and $m$ decreases in Figure 7 and 8. $n$, $m$ should be determined

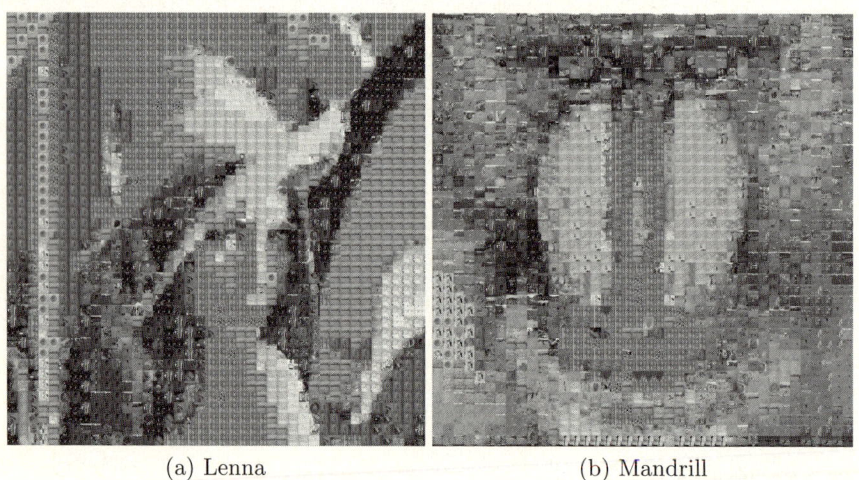

(a) Lenna                                    (b) Mandrill

**Fig. 12.** Tiling without rotated images

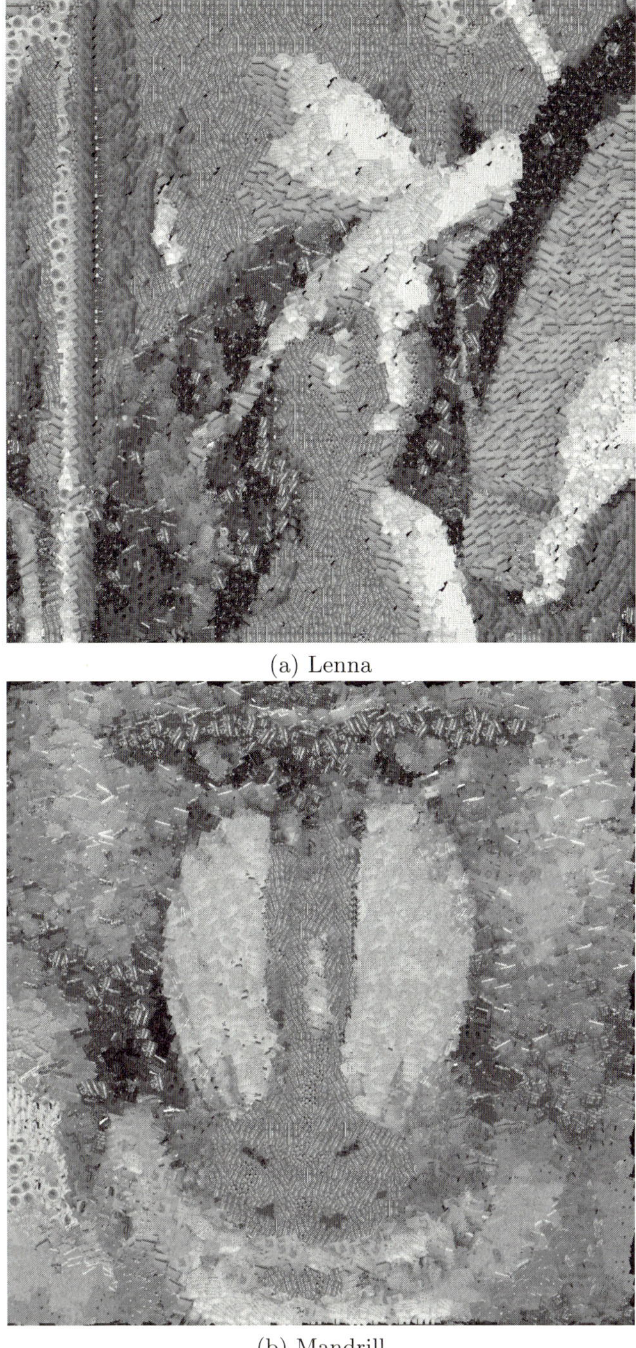

(a) Lenna

(b) Mandrill

**Fig. 13.** Tiling with rotated images

by considering $_nC_m$ for reducing the candidates. $d$ influences the number of lists and the number of elements in each list of a hash table. In Figure 9, the average number of candidates is 284 and the average rank is 3.2 at $d = 10$. In this case, the searched image can be the approximate nearest neighbor image because the average rank is still 3. From this result, larger $d$ may provide better approximate nearest neighbor searching. In Figure 10, the average rank is still 2.5 even if the top 20% candidates are used for the nearest neighbor searching. This represents that neighbor images of a query get more counts. $d$ can be small for reducing the candidates.

By determining $n$, $m$, $d$ and $b$ appropriately, the candidates are reduced with keeping the better searching results. The way of determining $n$, $m$, $d$ and $b$ automatically will be a next research topic.

### 5.2   Tiling Results

We report comparisons between a method with rotated images and without rotated images. 3500 square images in our database are collected by using Google Image Search and their size is transformed into $10 \times 10$. Two images ($200 \times 200$) are prepared as shown in Figure 11. We set the parameters of CPCH as $n = 10$, $m = 3$, $d = 5$ and $b = 100$.

In our tiling method, shapes of tiled images depend on prepared templates as described in Section 4. Our method can be applied to the previous method with no rotated image as shown in Figure 12. Figure 13 is generated by using 5 templates which rotation degrees are $-30°$, $-15°$, $0°$, $15°$, $30°$. When searched images are tiled, their size is converted from $10 \times 10$ to $40 \times 40$ for making the result be $800 \times 800$.

For comparing the result of two methods, average of absolute difference between a reference image and a generated image is computed. The size of the generated images is converted into $200 \times 200$ to be matched with that of the reference images. Table 1 represents that the result of rotated images provided less average of absolute difference in each reference image. From this result, the use of rotated images provides a better visual result.

## 6   Conclusions and Future Works

This paper presents Photomosaic method with rotated images and approximate nearest neighbor searching method called combination of principal component hashing. In our Photomosaic method, the templates for rotated images are prepared. At each pixel, the best template is selected. The order of the tiling starts from the least similarity images. The experimental results represent that Photomosaic with rotated images provides better visual result than that without rotated images. In our nearest neighbor searching, a hashing by combination of principal component is proposed. By clustering neighbors with a product set of eigenvectors, various hash tables are generated. In our retrieval, the candidates are collected from the hash tables. In the experimental results, the influence of $n$, $m$, $d$ and $b$ for searching result is presented.

In our tiling method, we didn't consider salient area in a tiled image and the area was sometimes overlapped by another image. For remaining the salient area steadily, the salient area is extracted using visual attention model [15] and the method for avoiding the overlap should be considered. In searching method, we will discuss how to determine appropriate $n$, $m$, $d$ and $b$ automatically in the next research topic. After that, comparison between CPCH and other nearest neighbor searching method should be done on the same environment.

# References


1. Hausner, A.: Simulating decorative mosaics. In: Proc. ACM SIGGRAPH, pp. 573–580 (2001)
2. Elber, G., Wolberg, G.: Rendering traditional mosaics. The Visual Computer 19, 67–78 (2003)
3. Blasi, G.D., Petralia, M.: Fast photomosaic. In: Proc. ACM Winter School on Computer Graphics (2005)
4. Andreamosaic, `http://www.andreaplanet.com/andreamosaic/`
5. Easy photo mosaic maker, `http://www.wyy2001.50megs.com/epmm/index.htm`
6. Klein, A.W., et al.: Video mosaics. In: Proc. NPAR, pp. 21–28 (2002)
7. Kim, J., Pellacini, F.: Jigsaw image mosaics. In: Proc. ACM SIGGRAPH, pp. 657–664 (2002)
8. Di Blasi, G., Gallo, G., Petralia, M.: Puzzle image mosaic. In: Proc. VIIP (2005)
9. Arya, S., et al.: An optimal algorithm for approximate nearest neighbor searching fixed dimensions. Journal of the ACM 45, 891–923 (1998)
10. Nister, D., Stewenius, H.: Scalable recognition with a vocabulary tree. In: Proc. CVPR, pp. 2161–2168 (2006)
11. Gionis, A., Indyk, P., Motwani, R.: Similarity search in high dimensions via hashing. In: Proc. VLDB, pp. 518–529 (1999)
12. Datar, M., et al.: Locality-sensitive hashing scheme based on p-stable distributions. In: Proc. SCG, pp. 253–262 (2004)
13. Andoni, A., Indyk, P.: Near-optimal hashing algorithms for approximate nearest neighbor in high dimensions. Communications of the ACM 51, 117–122 (2008)
14. Matsushita, Y., Wada, T.: Principal component hashing for general distributions. In: Proc. IPSJ SIG Technical Report, 283–288 (2008) (in Japanese)
15. Itti, L., Koch, C., Niebur, E.: A model of saliency-based visual attention for rapid scene analysis. IEEE Trans. PAMI 20, 1254–1259 (1998)

# A Stereo Self-adjustment Methodology for Resuming Active Camera Operation


Masafumi Nakagawa, Yoshihiro Kawai, and Fumiaki Tomita

National Institute of Advanced Industrial Science and Technology, Japan
m.nakagawa@aist.go.jp, y.kawai@aist.go.jp, f.tomita@aist.go.jp



**Abstract.** A stereo system for vehicles, Unmanned Aerial Vehicles (UAVs), and hand eye systems must tolerate vibration of its cameras and be robust against disturbances. We propose a stereo self-adjustment methodology for resuming autonomous stereo system operations. The methodology aims to achieve autonomous recovery of camera directions, even if the cameras rotate after a weak impact. In autonomous recovery, the self-adjustment procedure calculates the rotation values of rotated cameras. The camera directions of the stereo system then recover their initial directions using the rotation parameters. Moreover, we have verified the validity of our approach through experiments using an active stereo camera in which three cameras can rotate independently.

**Keywords:** Self-adjustment, Maintenance free stereo system, Active camera resume operation.


## 1 Introduction

A stereo vision system for vehicles and Unmanned Aerial Vehicles (UAVs) must tolerate vibration of its cameras. Stereo systems and hand eye systems in an intelligent factory also require high robustness against camera parameter changes during long-term operation.

In general, accurate 3D measurements using the stereo system require accurate camera parameter values, as calculated via camera calibration, which is normally conducted with a known test pattern board before the 3D measurements begin. However, shock or vibration to the stereo system may cause loss of the camera parameters, preventing accurate 3D measurements.

Tolerance to vibration in the stereo system can be considerably improved by mounting it on a stabilizer, which can reduce the influence of vibration on the cameras [1]. However, an expensive hardware system is required. If the camera parameters are lost during long term operation of the stereo system, they can be recovered via camera calibration using a test pattern board. However, frequent camera calibration is not practical for stereo systems in general environments. Alternatively, self-calibration, which autonomously estimates the current camera parameters using unknown observation data, can achieve calibration with unknown targets [2, 3, 4, 5, 6]. Accordingly, we believe that self-calibration has the potential to develop stereo systems that are vibration tolerant. Therefore, self-calibration is an essential technique


T. Wada, F. Huang, and S. Lin (Eds.): PSIVT 2009, LNCS 5414, pp. 680–691, 2009.

for use with vehicles, UAVs, and hand eye systems. The self-calibration methodology is characterized as follows.

'Self-calibration':
- A process of camera parameter estimation after a strong impact to the stereo camera
- Internal and external camera parameters are unknown.

In general, self-calibration is a flexible technique with few limitations. However, in theory, there are anomalous camera arrangements for which unique parameter estimation is impossible, and self-calibration becomes unstable in the neighborhood of these anomalous camera arrangements. Moreover, independence between parameters can be insufficient, because the available restriction parameters are fewer than the parameters being estimated. Accordingly, self-calibration processing is often unstable from the viewpoint of numerical evaluation, even if the camera arrangement is far from an anomalous camera arrangement [7]. Therefore, we have added some restrictions on using internal and external parameters. The self-adjustment methodology that we have developed is characterized as follows.

'Self-adjustment':
- The process of camera parameter modification after a weak impact to the stereo camera
- Internal and external camera parameters are available using camera calibration data as initial values
- Camera calibration processing is required as a preprocessing operation.

We propose a stereo self-adjustment methodology for stereo system resume operation. This aims to achieve an autonomous recovery of camera directions, even if cameras rotate after a weak impact. In the autonomous recovery, the self-adjustment procedure calculates rotation values for the rotated cameras. The camera directions of the stereo system are then returned to their initial values using the rotation parameters. Moreover, we have verified the validity of our approach through experiments using an active stereo camera in which three cameras can rotate independently.


## 2  Methodology

The cameras in the stereo system recover their initial directions via a self-adjustment procedure, as shown in Fig. 1. First, the stereo camera rotation parameters are acquired via a calibration using a known test pattern. In this state, the stereo system can measure objects correctly. However, after an impact to the stereo camera, the convergence angle of the stereo system changes. In this state, the stereo camera cannot measure objects correctly because stereo camera rotation parameters such as roll, pitch, and yaw are lost.

In that state, corresponding points are obtained from stereo images. In this approach, the corresponding points do not require 3D coordinate values. The camera rotation parameters are then recovered to their initial state via the self-adjustment procedure described in the next section. Using these camera rotation parameters, the stereo system obtains modified stereo rotation parameters, and the stereo system can measure objects again.

Moreover, relative rotation values of camera directions are obtained by calculating a difference between the stereo camera rotation parameters after camera calibration and after the self-adjustment procedure. The cameras can recover the initial directions physically after these relative rotation values are input to the active stereo camera.

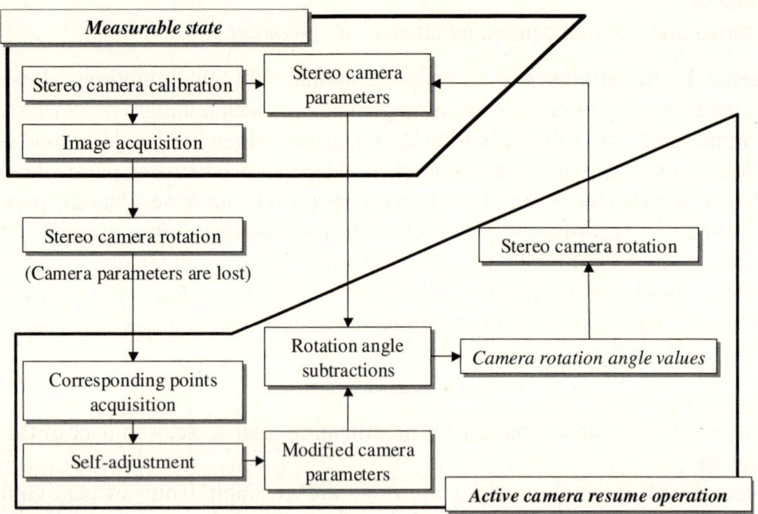


**Fig. 1.** Processing flow in the actual active camera resume operation

## 2.1  Self-adjustment

We now define the standard camera model as three cameras arranged in a triangle, as shown in Fig. 2. A point in the standard camera image is defined as $(x, y)$. A point changed by camera rotation in a standard camera image is defined as $(X, Y)$. In addition, the rotation parameters for the triplet camera directions are as shown in Fig. 3.

The sum of the position error between $P_l$ and $P_c$, a position error between $P_l$ and $P_c$, and a position error between $P_r$ and $P_c$ is minimized in triplet processing. These position errors are obtained as distances from the corresponding point $P_l$ to the

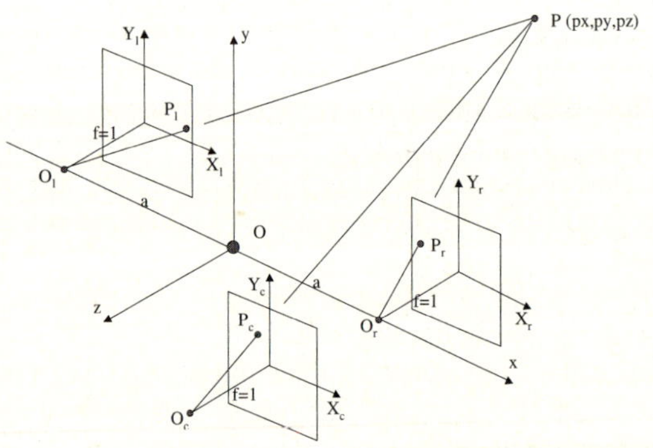


**Fig. 2.** Standard camera model (triplet)

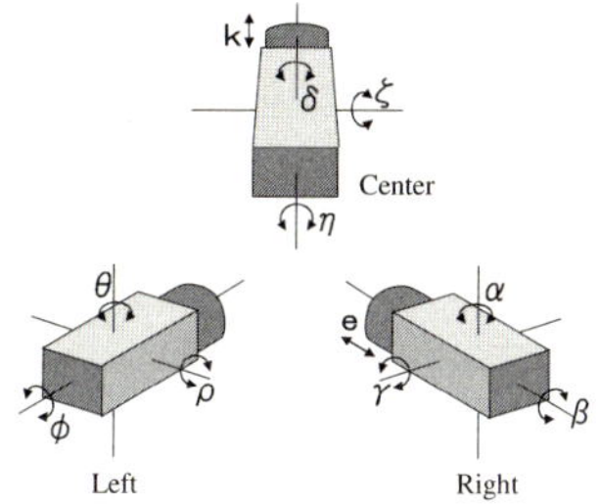


**Fig. 3.** Rotation parameters (triplet)

epipolar line in the left standard camera image and from the corresponding point $P_r$ to the epipolar line in the right standard camera image. Therefore, two points on the epipolar line in the left image are acquired.

As shown in Fig. 4, a straight line that connects the focal points of the left and right camera is defined as the x-axis. The center of the two points is defined as the starting point O. Moreover, the values of the focal points of the left camera $O_l$ and center camera $O_c$ are described as $(-a, 0, 0)$ and $(x_c, y_c, 0)$, When the image coordinate values of $P_l$ and $P_c$ are described as $(X_l, Y_l)$ and $(X_c, Y_c)$, a straight line connecting $P_c$ and $O_c$ is expressed as $(kX_c + x_c, kY_c + y_c, -k)$. Moreover, the focal lengths of the left and right cameras are defined as f. When the straight line is projected into the left image, the track on which the plane $z = -f$ intersects with a line that connects $(kX_c + x_c, kY_c + y_c, -k)$ and $(-a, 0, 0)$, is expressed as an epipolar line.

$$\frac{x+a}{kx_c - x_c + a} = \frac{y}{kY_c + y_c} = \frac{z}{-k} \tag{1}$$

That is, when the value of z is $-f$ in the preceding equation, the coordinate values on the epipolar line are expressed as follows.

$$x = fX_c - a + \frac{f}{k}(x_c + a) \qquad y = fY_c + \frac{f}{k}y_c \tag{2}$$

Here, points in $k = f$ and $k = \infty$ are defined as $(x_1, y_1, z_1)$ and $(x_2, y_2, z_2)$. These points are expressed as follows.

$$\begin{aligned}
x_1 &= fX_c + x_c & y_1 &= fY_c + y_c & z_1 &= -f \\
x_2 &= fX_c - a & y_2 &= fY_c & z_2 &= -f
\end{aligned} \tag{3}$$

The point Pl $(x_0, y_0, z_0)$ and the line that connects $(x_1, y_1, z_1)$ and $(x_2, y_2, z_2)$ exist in the same plane orthogonalized to the z-axis, because the coordinate values of point $P_l$ are $x_0 = fX_l - a$, $y0 = fY_l$, and $z0 = -f_l$. Thus, a quadratic of the position error or the distance value from the point to the line is expressed as follows.

$$\begin{aligned}
d_l{}^2 &= \frac{\{(x_2 - x_1)(y_1 - y_0) - (y_2 - y_1)(x_1 - x_0)\}^2}{(x_2 - x_1)^2 + (y_2 - y_1)^2} \\
&= \frac{f^2\{y_c(X_l - X_c) - (x_c + a)(Y_l - Y_c)\}^2}{\{(x_c + a)^2 + y_c{}^2\}}
\end{aligned} \tag{4}$$

When the focal position $O_R$ of the right camera is expressed as (a, 0, 0), a quadratic of the position error $d_r$ in the right camera is expressed as follows.

$$d_r^{\ 2} = \frac{f^2\{y_c(X_r - X_c)-(x_c - a)(Y_r - Y_c)\}^2}{\{(x_c - a)^2 + y_c^{\ 2}\}} \tag{5}$$

Therefore, the corresponding points in the three standard camera images after the self-adjustment procedure are expressed in the following equations.

$$X_l = \frac{x_l(\cos\theta\cos\varphi + \sin\theta\sin\varphi\sin\rho) - y_l(\cos\theta\sin\varphi - \sin\theta\cos\varphi\sin\rho) - \sin\theta\cos\rho}{x_l(\sin\theta\cos\varphi - \cos\theta\sin\varphi\sin\rho) - y_l(\sin\theta\sin\varphi + \cos\theta\cos\varphi\sin\rho) + \cos\theta\cos\rho}$$

$$Y_l = \frac{x_l\sin\varphi\cos\rho + y_l\cos\varphi\cos\rho + \sin\rho}{x_l(\sin\theta\cos\varphi - \cos\theta\sin\varphi\sin\rho) - y_l(\sin\theta\sin\varphi + \cos\theta\cos\varphi\sin\rho) + \cos\theta\cos\rho}$$

$$X_r = \frac{(e+1)\{x_r(\cos\alpha\cos\beta + \sin\alpha\sin\beta\sin\gamma) - y_r(\cos\alpha\sin\beta - \sin\alpha\cos\beta\sin\gamma) - \sin\alpha\cos\gamma\}}{x_r(\sin\alpha\cos\beta - \cos\alpha\sin\beta\sin\gamma) - y_r(\sin\alpha\sin\beta + \cos\alpha\cos\beta\sin\gamma) + \cos\alpha\cos\gamma}$$

$$Y_r = \frac{(e+1)(x_r\sin\beta\cos\gamma + y_r\cos\beta\cos\gamma + \sin\gamma)}{x_r(\sin\alpha\cos\beta - \cos\alpha\sin\beta\sin\gamma) - y_r(\sin\alpha\sin\beta + \cos\alpha\cos\beta\sin\gamma) + \cos\alpha\cos\gamma} \tag{6}$$

$$X_c = \frac{(k+1)\{x_c(\cos\delta\cos\varepsilon + \sin\delta\sin\varepsilon\sin\zeta) - y_c(\cos\delta\sin\varepsilon - \sin\delta\cos\varepsilon\sin\zeta) - \sin\delta\cos\zeta\}}{x_c(\sin\delta\cos\varepsilon - \cos\delta\sin\varepsilon\sin\zeta) - y_c(\sin\delta\sin\varepsilon + \cos\delta\cos\varepsilon\sin\zeta) + \cos\delta\cos\zeta}$$

$$Y_c = \frac{(k+1)(x_c\sin\varepsilon\cos\zeta + y_c\cos\varepsilon\cos\zeta + \sin\zeta)}{x_c(\sin\delta\cos\varepsilon - \cos\delta\sin\varepsilon\sin\zeta) - y_c(\sin\delta\sin\varepsilon + \cos\delta\cos\varepsilon\sin\zeta) + \cos\delta\cos\zeta}$$

Vertical motion is added to the left camera, in addition to the motions when there are two cameras. Moreover, the center or verifying camera has the same degree of freedom as the right camera.

Here, $\sin\theta$ and $\cos\theta$ in the denominators and the numerators in the equations are simplified as $\sin\theta \to \theta$ and $\cos\theta \to 1$ to stabilize the solution as follows.

$$X_l = \frac{x_l(1 + \theta\varphi\rho) - y_l(\varphi - \theta\rho) - \theta}{x_l(\theta - \varphi\rho) - y_l(\theta\varphi + \rho) + 1} \qquad Y_l = \frac{x_l\varphi + y_l + \rho}{x_l(\theta - \varphi\rho) - y_l(\theta\varphi + \rho) + 1}$$

$$X_r = \frac{(e+1)\{x_r(1 + \alpha\beta\gamma) - y_r(\beta - \alpha\gamma) - \alpha\}}{x_r(\alpha - \beta\gamma) - y_r(\alpha\beta + \gamma) + 1} \qquad Y_r = \frac{(e+1)(x_r\beta + y_r + \gamma)}{x_r(\alpha - \beta\gamma) - y_r(\alpha\beta + \gamma) + 1} \tag{7}$$

$$X_c = \frac{(k+1)\{x_c(1 + \delta\varepsilon\zeta) - y_c(\varepsilon - \delta\zeta) - \delta\}}{x_c(\delta - \varepsilon\zeta) - y_c(\delta\varepsilon + \zeta) + 1} \qquad Y_c = \frac{(k+1)(x_c\varepsilon + y_c + \zeta)}{x_c(\delta - \varepsilon\zeta) - y_c(\delta\varepsilon + \zeta) + 1}$$

Moreover, the values of X and Y in the preceding equations are assigned to a quadratic of the position error equation. Then, the following equation is minimized with f = 1.

$$S = \sum\{(Y_l - Y_r)^2 + d_l^{\ 2} + d_r^{\ 2}\} \tag{8}$$

Then, the simultaneous equations are solved with matrix N, which has the partial derivatives of S, and matrix M, which has the second-order partial derivatives of S. These equations give $N_0$ and $M_0$ when $\theta = \phi = \alpha = \beta = \gamma = e = 0$. Moreover, approximate values of $\theta$, $\phi$, $\alpha$, $\beta$, $\gamma$, and $e$ are calculated using the following equation.

$$M_0 \begin{pmatrix} \theta \\ \phi \\ \rho \\ \alpha \\ \beta \\ \gamma \\ e \\ \delta \\ \eta \\ \varsigma \\ \kappa \end{pmatrix} + N_0 = 0 \tag{9}$$

Values of $(X_l, Y_l)$, $(X_r, Y_r)$, and $(X_c, Y_c)$ are calculated using values obtained from the preceding equation. Then, the values $(X_l, Y_l)$, $(X_r, Y_r)$, and $(X_c, Y_c)$ are replaced by $(x_l, y_l)$, $(x_r, y_r)$, and $(x_c, y_c)$ to generate $M_0$ and $N_0$. The calculation is then repeated. The final rotation angles and zoom magnifications are accumulated as the product of the rotation and zoom matrices in the all the calculations. Thus, the adjustment matrix is obtained after some repetitions of the calculation.

## 3  Experiments

We conducted an experiment to validate our approach that cameras in a stereo system can recover their initial directions. The procedure of the experiment based on our approach shown in Fig. 1 is described as follows.

(1)  Stereo camera rotation parameters are obtained via stereo camera calibration.
(2)  Camera rotation directions are set as the initial camera directions after acquisition of initial images.
(3)  Cameras are rotated independently at the set angle values. That is, we prepare a state that cannot measure objects correctly because stereo camera rotation parameters are lost because of convergence angle changes in the stereo system. In this experiment, each camera rotation value is $1°$.
(4)  Camera rotation angle values, which are obtained via the self-adjustment procedure, are input into the active camera.
(5)  Steps (3) and (4) are repeated, five or 10 times in this experiment.

We prepared a triplet camera for this experiment, comprising a left camera, a right camera, and a verifying camera. The system was mounted on a turn stand with ultrasonic motors, as shown in Fig. 4. The resolution of the ultrasonic motors is $0.015°$. The specification of this stereo system is given in Table 1.

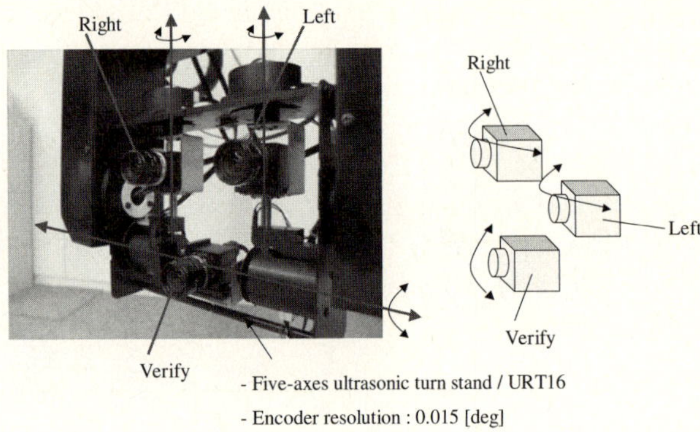



- Five-axes ultrasonic turn stand / URT16
- Encoder resolution : 0.015 [deg]

**Fig. 4.** Triplet camera

**Table 1.** Specification of stereo system

| Camera | Flea (Point Grey Research Inc.) | | |
|---|---|---|---|
| Lens | f = 16mm | | |
| Image size | VGA | | |
| | Gray scale | | |
| Camera position | Left | Right | Verify |
| Rotation axis | Horizontal | Horizontal | Vertical |
| Baseline | 10cm | | |
| Object distance | 130cm | | |

In this self-adjustment experiment, 27 targets were prepared on three boards, with nine targets per board. Images of these boards were captured and general edge detection processing acquired 27 corresponding points automatically. The following camera rotation patterns were prepared to verify the validity of our approach.

- Pattern 1: Left camera rotation
- Pattern 2: Right camera rotation
- Pattern 3: Verify camera rotation
- Pattern 4: Left and right camera rotations
- Pattern 5: Left and verify camera rotations
- Pattern 6: Right and verify camera rotations
- Pattern 7: Right, left, and verify camera rotations.

## 4   Results and Discussion

Results of camera rotation value transitions from patterns 1-7 are shown in Figs 5-11. The vertical axis shows the camera rotation value. Angle value 0° indicates the initial direction of a camera. The horizontal axis shows a camera rotation event as 'ID'. ID = 0 indicates the angle value to which the camera is first rotated physically to create a state that cannot measure objects correctly because the stereo camera rotation parameters are lost because of convergence angle changes in the stereo system. ID values greater than 1 indicate relative rotation values to which the camera rotates physically close to the initial direction via the self-adjustment procedure. Here, rotations leftward or upward are defined as positive values.

The results in all patterns show that camera directions recover the angle values of $0.000 \pm 0.015°$, usually within five iterations. The resolution of the active camera rotations is $0.015°$ in these experiments, so that the cameras recover the initial directions within the resolution value. Therefore, we can conclude that the results satisfy the required accuracy.

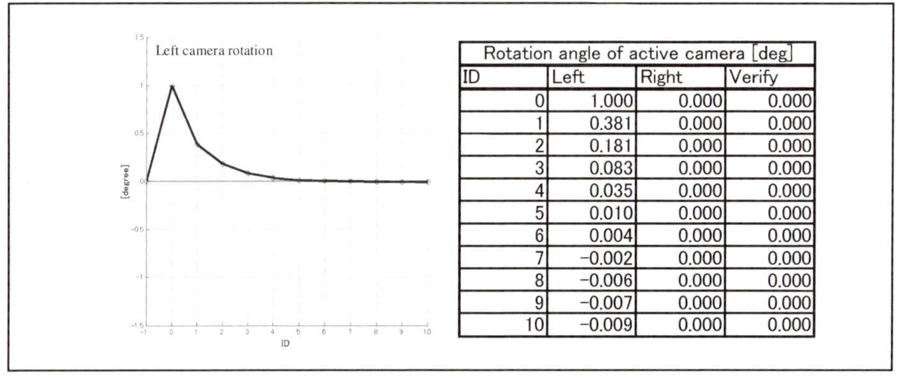

Fig. 5. Pattern 1: left camera rotation

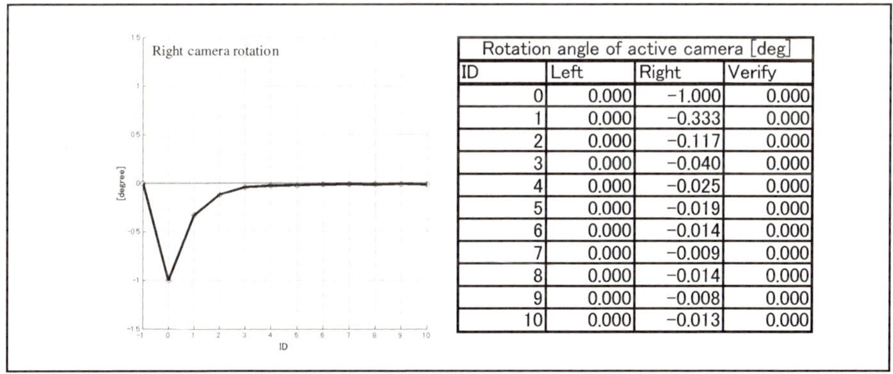

Fig. 6. Pattern 2: right camera rotation

In pattern 7, in which all cameras rotate, the self-adjustment procedure failed to recover the initial camera directions because the base directions of all cameras change. However, the stereo system can still measure objects correctly because the epipolar line is recovered in the self-adjustment procedure. Therefore, an epipolar line recovery, which is a state allowing objects to be measured correctly, is confirmed in pattern 7.

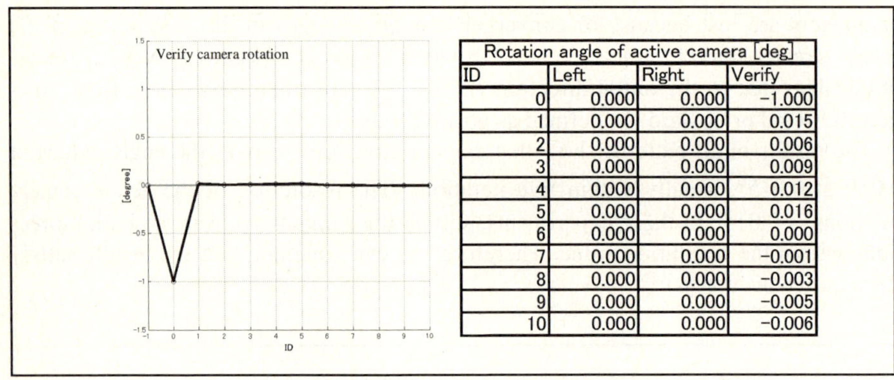

| Rotation angle of active camera [deg] | | | |
|---|---|---|---|
| ID | Left | Right | Verify |
| 0 | 0.000 | 0.000 | −1.000 |
| 1 | 0.000 | 0.000 | 0.015 |
| 2 | 0.000 | 0.000 | 0.006 |
| 3 | 0.000 | 0.000 | 0.009 |
| 4 | 0.000 | 0.000 | 0.012 |
| 5 | 0.000 | 0.000 | 0.016 |
| 6 | 0.000 | 0.000 | 0.000 |
| 7 | 0.000 | 0.000 | −0.001 |
| 8 | 0.000 | 0.000 | −0.003 |
| 9 | 0.000 | 0.000 | −0.005 |
| 10 | 0.000 | 0.000 | −0.006 |

**Fig. 7.** Pattern 3: verify camera rotation

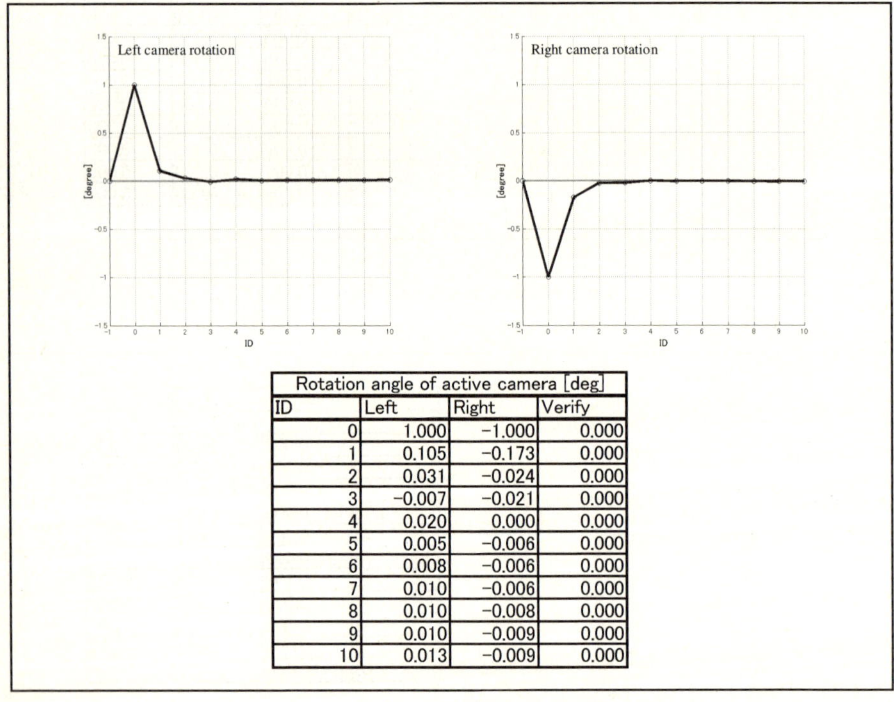

| Rotation angle of active camera [deg] | | | |
|---|---|---|---|
| ID | Left | Right | Verify |
| 0 | 1.000 | −1.000 | 0.000 |
| 1 | 0.105 | −0.173 | 0.000 |
| 2 | 0.031 | −0.024 | 0.000 |
| 3 | −0.007 | −0.021 | 0.000 |
| 4 | 0.020 | 0.000 | 0.000 |
| 5 | 0.005 | −0.006 | 0.000 |
| 6 | 0.008 | −0.006 | 0.000 |
| 7 | 0.010 | −0.006 | 0.000 |
| 8 | 0.010 | −0.008 | 0.000 |
| 9 | 0.010 | −0.009 | 0.000 |
| 10 | 0.013 | −0.009 | 0.000 |

**Fig. 8.** Pattern 4: left and right camera rotations

Figure 12 shows an epipolar line modification result via the self-adjustment procedure in pattern 7 in which all cameras rotate. The result is transformed based on the standard camera model as shown in Fig. 2.

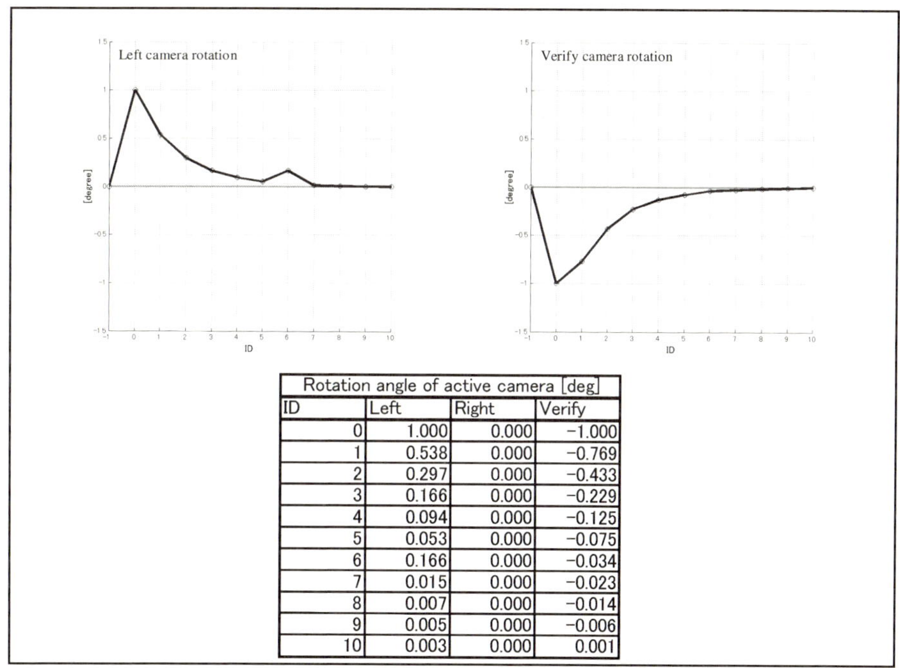

| Rotation angle of active camera [deg] | | | |
|---|---|---|---|
| ID | Left | Right | Verify |
| 0 | 1.000 | 0.000 | −1.000 |
| 1 | 0.538 | 0.000 | −0.769 |
| 2 | 0.297 | 0.000 | −0.433 |
| 3 | 0.166 | 0.000 | −0.229 |
| 4 | 0.094 | 0.000 | −0.125 |
| 5 | 0.053 | 0.000 | −0.075 |
| 6 | 0.166 | 0.000 | −0.034 |
| 7 | 0.015 | 0.000 | −0.023 |
| 8 | 0.007 | 0.000 | −0.014 |
| 9 | 0.005 | 0.000 | −0.006 |
| 10 | 0.003 | 0.000 | 0.001 |

**Fig. 9.** Pattern 5: left and verify camera rotations

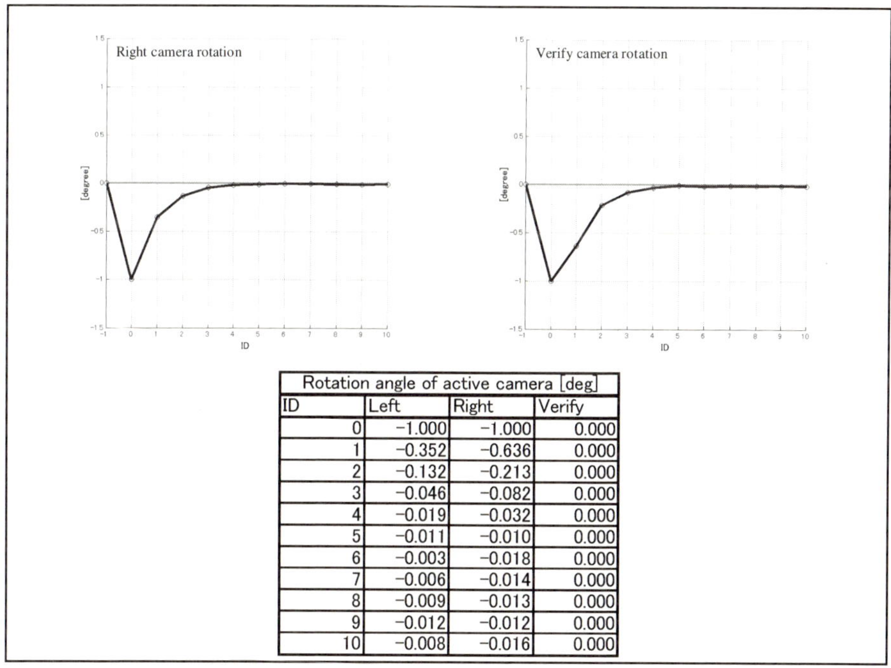

| Rotation angle of active camera [deg] | | | |
|---|---|---|---|
| ID | Left | Right | Verify |
| 0 | −1.000 | −1.000 | 0.000 |
| 1 | −0.352 | −0.636 | 0.000 |
| 2 | −0.132 | −0.213 | 0.000 |
| 3 | −0.046 | −0.082 | 0.000 |
| 4 | −0.019 | −0.032 | 0.000 |
| 5 | −0.011 | −0.010 | 0.000 |
| 6 | −0.003 | −0.018 | 0.000 |
| 7 | −0.006 | −0.014 | 0.000 |
| 8 | −0.009 | −0.013 | 0.000 |
| 9 | −0.012 | −0.012 | 0.000 |
| 10 | −0.008 | −0.016 | 0.000 |

**Fig. 10.** Pattern 6: right and verify camera rotations

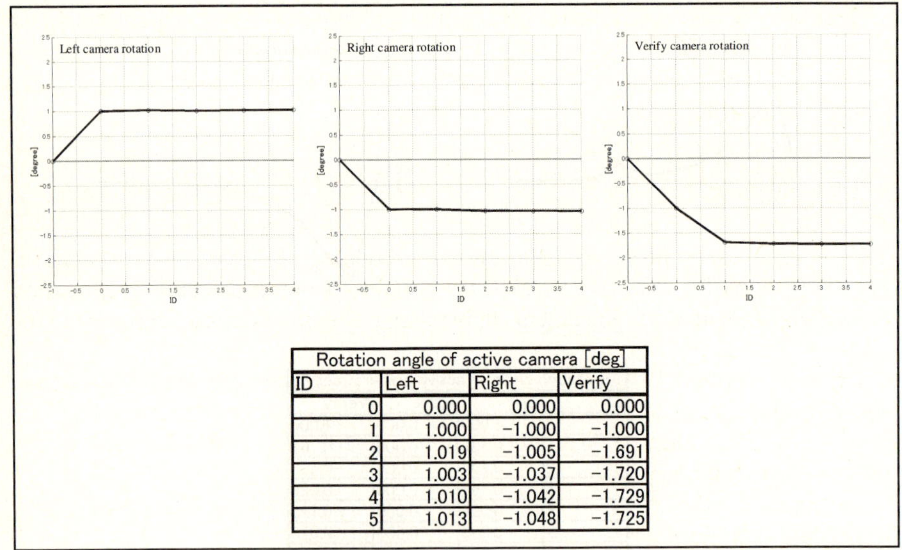

Fig. 11. Pattern 7: all camera rotations

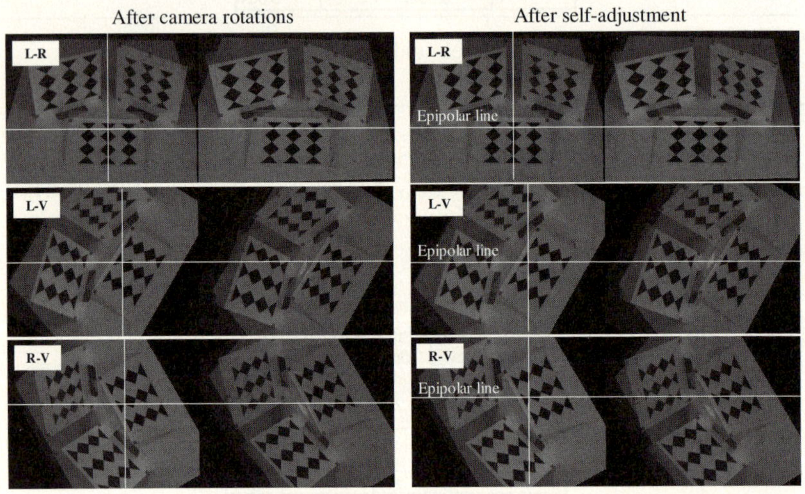

Fig. 12. Epipolar line modification result via the self-adjustment procedure

The epipolar line in a combination of the left and right images after the initial camera rotation, almost passes through corresponding points because the left and right cameras rotate in parallel to the epipolar line. On the other hand, the result shows that the epipolar line in a combination of the left and verify images and the epipolar line in a combination of the right and verify images, do not pass through corresponding points.

However, the result shows that epipolar lines in all combinations pass through corresponding points. We can thus conclude that the camera rotation directions recover their initial state because the camera rotation parameters are modified via the self-adjustment procedure.

## 5  Conclusion

We have proposed a stereo self-adjustment methodology for resuming stereo system operation. Moreover, we have verified the validity of our approach through experiments using an active stereo camera, showing that the three cameras can rotate independently.

We have confirmed that the self-adjustment procedure calculates the rotation values of rotated cameras. Moreover, the cameras in the stereo system recover their initial directions using the rotation parameters. Camera directions in some camera rotation patterns usually recover the required camera directions within five iterations. Moreover, even when all cameras rotate, the self-adjustment procedure can recover the initial state. From these results, we can conclude that we have successfully achieved the autonomous recovery of camera directions to improve the tolerance or robustness to vibration of stereo system for vehicles, UAVs, and hand eye systems.

## References


1. Gruen, A., Zhang, L.: Sensor modelling for aerial mobile mapping with Three-line Scanner (TLS) imagery Symposium of Commission II, Integrated System for Spatial Data Production, Custodian and Decision Support", Xian, China, 20-23 (August 2002)
2. Hemayed, E.E.: A survey of camera self-calibration. In: Proceedings. IEEE Conference on Advanced Video and Signal Based Surveillance, pp. 351–357 (2003)
3. Armstrong, M., Zisserman, A., Hartley, R.I.: Self-Calibration from Image Triplets. In: ECCV 1996, pp. I:1–I:16 (1996)
4. Kim, H., Hong, K.S.: Practical self-calibration of pan-tilt cameras. IEEE Proceedings on Vision, Image and Signal Processing 148(5), 349–355 (2001)
5. Oliensis, J.: Fast and accurate self-calibration, NEC Res. Inst. In: ICCV 1999, Princeton, NJ, pp. 745–752 (1999)
6. Faugeras, O., Luong, T., Maybank, S.: Camera self-calibration: theory and experiments. In: Sandini, G. (ed.) ECCV 1992. LNCS, vol. 588, pp. 321–334. Springer, Heidelberg (1992)
7. Ueshiba, T., Tomita, F.: National Inst. Advanced Industrial Sci. and Technol., Calibration of Multi - camera Systems Using Planar Patterns. In: CVIM, vol. 2002(102) (CVIM-135), pp. 47–54 (2002)

# Combining Invariant and Corner-Like Features to Optimize Image Matching

Jimmy Addison Lee and Kin-Choong Yow

School of Computer Engineering, Nanyang Technological University,
50 Nanyang Avenue, Singapore 639798
{jimm0002,kcyow}@ntu.edu.sg

**Abstract.** Significance and usefulness of local invariant features and traditional corner-like features have been widely proven in the literature. In this paper, we novelly combine the two types of features to select salient keypoints with the invariant and corner-like properties, which are highly distinctive and improving match performance. We use moment-derived complex image patterns (e.g., corner, T-junction, sectional cut, and chess-cross) to find corner-like features. We further optimize the matching results by finding corner-like patterns in the invariant matched point correspondences; and rebuff point correspondences that have dissimilar pattern responses which are most likely false matches.

**Keywords:** Keypoint extraction, salient keypoints, distinctive keypoints, corner-like patterns.

## 1   Introduction

The use of salient features, also known as keypoints or interest points, to find correspondences across multiple images is a key step in many image processing and computer vision applications. Some of the most notable examples are panorama stitching [1,4,5], wide baseline matching [2,8,10], image retrieval [12,22], object recognition [3,7,13], and object class recognition [14,16,17]. These salient features are landmarks in an image which are often intuitively palpable to humans. They include corners of buildings, edges of objects, features (e.g., eyes) on human faces, etc. The traditional salient features such as edges and corners have been significantly useful and applied to many problems including tracking. We use complex image patterns (e.g., predefined shapes, contour junctions, etc.) in this paper to detect corner-like features.

In recent years, there has been an increased interest within the content-based image retrieval community in finding new types of salient features (e.g., SIFT features [13]) which provide properties robust to changes in scale and/or affine transformations. Such invariant features have proven useful in the context of image registration and object recognition. In this paper, we novelly combine these invariant features with the traditional ones (corner-like features). This combination can be used to select salient keypoints which comprise of the invariant and corner-like properties. These keypoints are highly distinctive points so that

T. Wada, F. Huang, and S. Lin (Eds.): PSIVT 2009, LNCS 5414, pp. 692–701, 2009.

they can be easily distinguished from other similarly extracted points in the same or another image, and therefore improving match performance. This will be discussed in Section 3.1.

In additional, after matching the invariant keypoints, we further improve the matching results by finding corner-like patterns in the matched invariant point correspondences; and rebuff point correspondences that have dissimilar pattern responses which are most likely false matches. This will be discussed in Section 3.2.

## 2   Related Work

Many different keypoint detectors have been proposed with a wide range of definitions for what points in an image are interesting. Some detectors find points of high local symmetry, some find areas of highly varying texture, while others locate corner points. Corner points are interesting as they are formed from two or more edges and edges usually define the boundary between two different objects or parts of the same object. The earlier work on corner detectors can be traced back to the work of Moravec [18] used for stereo matching. It was then further improved by Harris and Stephens [9] to make it more repeatable under small image variations and near edges. While these detectors are called corner detectors, they are not selecting just corners, but rather any image location that has large gradients in all directions at a predetermined scale.

Complex image patterns, which also include corners and other predefined shapes, are informative as they are infrequent and provide rich description of images. In medical imaging, there is a tendency of replacing the traditional two-step object recognition (i.e. segmentation followed by shape identification) by methods directly extracting predefined objects from grey-level images (e.g., active contours [11,21]). Similarly, over the past years there has been considerable attention directed toward the detection of more complex contour features in raw-data images (e.g., [6,19]).

Recently, there has been impressive body of work on invariant local features which have been shown to be rather robust with respect to changes in scale and/or affine transformations (e.g., [2,13,15]). Lowe's Scale Invariant Feature Transform (SIFT) [13] is one of the well-known ones which looks promising for tracking applications. However the vast numbers of detected keypoints for matching at times can be rather time-consuming. There are also existence of false matches on occasion.

## 3   Combining Invariant and Corner-Like Features

In this paper, we demonstrate the combination of SIFT features (invarient features) and complex image patterns (corner-like features) for keypoint extraction and matching, which will be discussed in the following sub-sections (3.1 and 3.2). Complex image patterns will be discussed in sub-section 3.3.

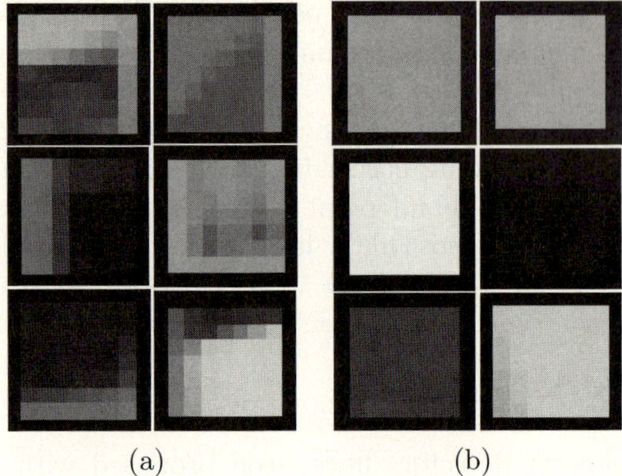

Fig. 1. Some invariant samples from SIFT. Some comprise of corner-like patterns as shown in (a), or no corner-like patterns as shown in (b).

## 3.1   Keypoint Extraction

SIFT uses Difference of Gaussian (DOG) Extrema detector [13] to detect keypoints which are invariant to scale change. However due to the large numbers of extrema, there could be up to thousands of detected keypoints in an image. Each of these keypoints after sampled to a $15 \times 15$ square window, may comprise of some corner-like patterns (as shown in Figure 1(a)), or no corner-like patterns (as shown in Figure 1(b)).

Subsequently, each of the samples is computed against the complex image patterns (e.g., corner and T-junction, discuss in sub-section 3.3) to ascertain that the sampled patch comprises at least one of these corner-like patterns. If it does not, it will be eradicated. Figure 2 illustrates this, which the two samples are tested for any corner-like patterns. We can see from the response results that the sample in Figure 2(a) has some responses from the complex image patterns detection while the sample in Figure 2(b) does not. Sample in Figure 2(a) is more distinctive in this case, which we know is apparently better for matching.

## 3.2   Matching

The matching is done through an Euclidean-distance based nearest neighbor approach. To increase robustness, matches are rejected for those keypoints for

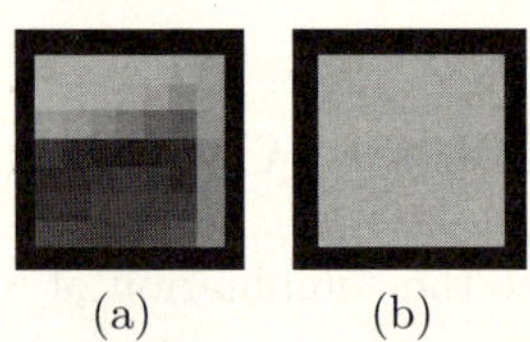

Fig. 2. Two invariant samples from SIFT. Complex image response for sample (a): Corner: 0.2218; T-junction: 0.5413, and Complex image response for sample (b): Corner: 0; T-junction: 0. Sample (b) does not comprise any corner-like patterns.

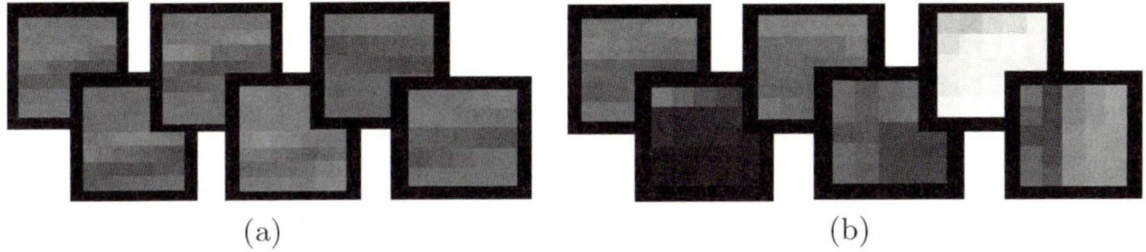

(a)           (b)

**Fig. 3.** Example of sample group in (a) with small pattern response differences. Example of sample group in (b) with huge pattern response differences.

which the ratio of the nearest neighbor distance to the second nearest neighbor distance is greater than some threshold $\tau_r$; or the other way round, a pair of keypoints is considered a match if the distance ratio between the nearest neighbor distance and a second nearest neighbor distance is below $\tau_r$:

$$\frac{d^2(f, f_{1st})}{d^2(f, f_{2nd})} < \tau_r^2, \tag{1}$$

where $f \in \Re^n$ is the descriptor to be matched and $f_{1st}$ and $f_{2nd}$ are the nearest and the second nearest descriptors respectively, with $d$ denoting the Euclidean distance between two descriptors. The threshold $\tau_r = 0.8$ suggested in [13] was found effective for general object recognition.

In additional, while SIFT provides invariant matched pairs, we scrutinize the difference in the responses of each pair of good distance match with complex image patterns. This can be done by sampling pixels within a 15 x 15 square window around the pair of point correspondences. If the difference in their pattern responses is huge (above a threshold of 0.5), it is very likely that this pair of point correspondences is a false match, and thus it will be eradicated. Figure 3 gives an example of two sample groups with similar and dissimilar patterns. The differences in the pattern responses of the group in Figure 3(a) (with similar pattern) are small, while the differences in the pattern responses of the group in Figure 3(b) (with dissimilar pattern) are huge.

### 3.3   Complex Image Patterns

Our work was inspired by moment-derived patterns [20] and we use them to find the pattern approximations of circular patches around keypoints. Corners and corner-like patterns (e.g., junctions) are predominantly significant as they generally preserve their geometry over a wide range of radii of circular patches. Thus, in this paper we demonstrated on four corner-like patterns which are commonly found in building images, i.e., proper corner, T-junction, sectional cut, and chess-cross. Two of them (corner and T-junction) will be discussed. The concept is identical for the rests. The model configuration of a corner over a circle of radius $R$ is defined by two angles and two intensities (or colors) as illustrated in Figure 4(a). Similarly, the model configuration of a T-junction consists of two angles and three intensities (or colors) is illustrated in Figure 4(b).

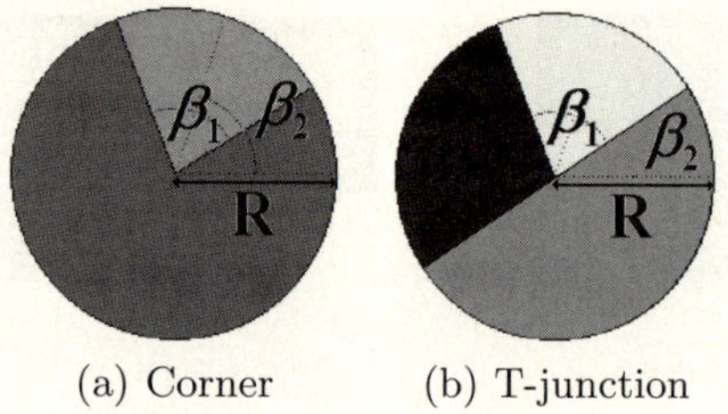


(a) Corner          (b) T-junction

**Fig. 4.** Model configurations of a corner (a) and a T-junction (b)

**Corner Model.** Given any circular image window of radius $R$, the parameters of its optimum corner approximation can be found from moment-based expression specified in [20]. The orientation angle $\beta_2$ in Figure 4(a) is extracted using

$$\beta_2 = \arctan 2(\pm m_{01}, \pm m_{10}) \tag{2}$$

while the angular width $\beta_1$ is computed from

$$\beta_1 = 2\arcsin\sqrt{1 - \frac{16[(m_{20} - m_{02})^2 + 4m_{11}^2]}{9R^2(m_{10}^2 + m_{01}^2)}} \tag{3}$$

or

$$2\arccos\frac{4}{3}\sqrt{\frac{(m_{20} - m_{02})^2 + 4m_{11}^2}{R^2(m_10^2 + m_{01}^2)}}. \tag{4}$$

The intensities $A_1$ (corner) and $A_2$ (background) are found using

$$A_1 = \frac{m_{00}}{\pi R^2} + \frac{3(2\pi - \beta_1)(m_{10}\cos\beta_2 + m_{01}\sin\beta_2)}{4\pi R^3 \sin 0.5\beta_1} \tag{5}$$

and

$$A_2 = \frac{m_{00}}{\pi R^2} - \frac{3\beta_1(m_{10}\cos\beta_2 + m_{01}\sin\beta_2)}{4\pi R^3 \sin 0.5\beta_1}. \tag{6}$$

**T-junction Model.** For T-junction in Figure 4(b), $\beta_1$ angular width and $\beta_2$ orientation angle can be computed using

$$\frac{\pi}{2} - \beta_2 - \frac{\beta_1}{2} = \frac{\arctan 2(\pm m_{02} \mp m_{20}, \pm 2m_{11})}{2} \tag{7}$$

and

$$m_{01}\cos\beta_2 - m_{10}\sin\beta_2 = \pm\frac{4}{3R}\sqrt{(m_{20} - m_{02})^2 + 4m_{11}^2} \tag{8}$$

respectively. The intensities are found as solutions of the following system of linear equations

$$\begin{cases} \frac{2m_{00}}{R^2} = A_1\pi + A_2\beta_1 + A_3(\pi - \beta_1) \\ \frac{3m_{10}}{R^3} = -2A_1c_2 + A_2(c_2 - c_{2-1}) + A_3(c_2 + c_{2-1} - 2s_2) \\ \frac{3m_{01}}{R^3} = -2A_1s_2 + A_2(s_2 - s_{2-1}) + A_3(s_2 + s_{2-1} + 2c_2) \end{cases} \tag{9}$$

where $c_x$ and $s_x$ indicate cos and sin functions of the corresponding arguments. Simple calculations can prove that results produced by Equations (2-4) and (7-8) are invariant to linear illumination changes and the angular width $\beta_1$ is invariant under any similarity transformation. Extensive experiments have also attested that the results are stable under both high and low frequency noise, image texturization and partial over and under saturation of image intensities.

The method is applicable to color images as well. In fact, it may be even more flexible since moments of color images are 3-dimensional vectors ($R$, $G$ and $B$ components) instead of scalars. Thus, the approximation equations for color patterns would be modified correspondingly. If scalar moments can be directly replaced by moment vectors, the gray-level solutions remain basically unchanged. For example, equation 3 is converted into

$$\beta_1 = 2\arcsin\sqrt{1 - \frac{16\left(\|\overrightarrow{m_{20}} - \overrightarrow{m_{02}}\|^2 + 4\|m_{11}\|^2\right)}{9R^2\left(\|m_{10}\|^2 + \|m_{01}\|^2\right)}}. \tag{10}$$

If the direct replacement of scalars by vectors is not straightforwardly possible (e.g., equation 8), the scalar moments would be replaced by the largest components of vector-moments. Subsequently, equation 8 would be replaced by

$$m_{01}(Z)\cos\beta_2 - m_{10}(Z)\sin\beta_2 \tag{11}$$

$$= \pm\frac{4}{3R}\sqrt{\|\overrightarrow{m_{20}} - \overrightarrow{m_{02}}\|^2 + 4\|m_{11}\|^2}$$

where $Z$ could be $R$, $G$ or $B$, depending for which color the value of $|m_{10}(Z)| + |m_{01}(Z)|$ is the largest. Colors of the approximations are calculated identically. We just apply equations 5, 6 and 9 separately to $R$, $G$ and $B$ colors, using the moments of the corresponding color.

## 4  Experimental Results

We have done experiments with images taken within the campus. As explained in Section 3.1, distinctive keypoints are found by selecting only those that comprise

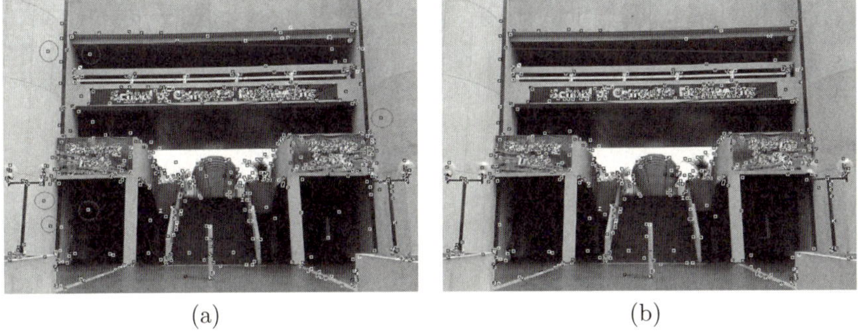

(a)           (b)

**Fig. 5.** In (a), 1326 invariant keypoints are detected from SIFT. Some of the keypoints without any corner-like patterns are circled in red. In (b), 1008 keypoints remain after selecting only those that comprise some corner-like patterns.

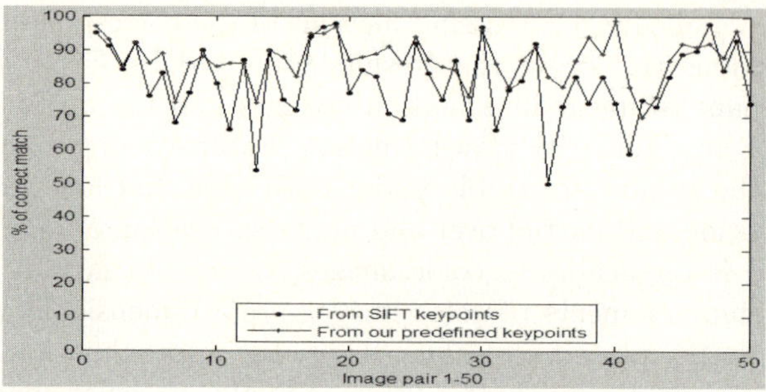


**Fig. 6.** Graph shows the percentage of correct match in 50 pairs of images with SIFT keypoints and predefined keypoints. Predefined keypoints improved matching results.

(a) 102 corresponding matches, with 11 false matches.

(b) 83 corresponding matches remain after eradicating those with dissimilar pattern responses. All false matches are being eradicated.

**Fig. 7.** Complex image patterns used to scrutinize the difference in responses of point correspondences in two images. Correspondences with dissimilar pattern responses are being eradicated in (b).

of the invariant and corner-like properties. This is illustrated in Figure 5. We can see that those keypoints that do not comprise any of the corner-like patterns are usually those that are rather homogeneous (circled in red in Figure 5(a)).

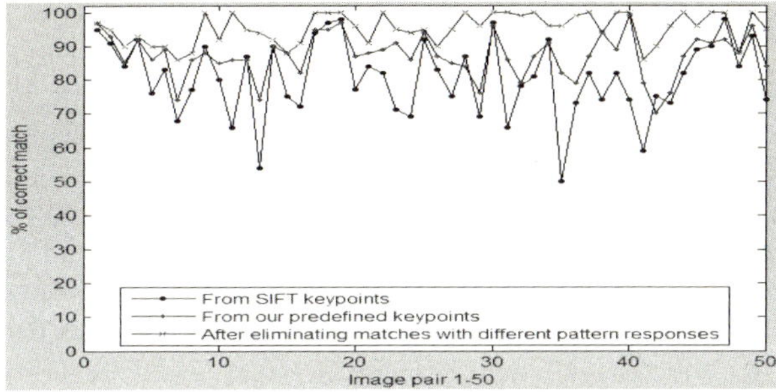


**Fig. 8.** Graph shows the percentage of correct match in 50 pairs of images. The matching results are further improved after eliminating matches/point correspondences that have different pattern responses.

These more distinctive keypoints can improve the match performance. For experiment, we took 51 images of similar campus scenes for matching. 1 image was taken as the main image while the rest of the 50 images were matched against it. The scenes were similar with some adjustments on the camera position at each shot, giving certain viewpoint and scale differences. Figure 6 displays a graph of the matching results from the 50 pairs of images. Most of the matchings were improved with the predefined keypoints.

Subsequently, the invariant keypoints were matched as described in Section 3.2. While SIFT gave invariant match, we scrutinized the difference in the pattern or corner-like responses of each pair of point correspondences. If the point correspondences were true match, the responses on the corner, T-junction, sectional cut, and chess-cross patterns would be similar. Figure 7 illustrates an example and we can see that some or most of the false matches (with dissimilar pattern responses) were eradicated as shown in Figure 7(b).

Figure 8 displays a graph of the matching results from the 50 pairs of images. As shown, the matching results have been further improved after eliminating matches/point correspondences with different pattern responses.

## 5   Conclusions

We have novelly combined the local invariant features (SIFT features in this paper) with the more traditional corner-like features for selecting salient keypoints. These keypoints were usually more distinctive and have shown to significantly improve on the match performance. The corner-like features were detected using moment-derived complex image patterns (i.e., proper corner, T-junction, sectional cut, and chess-cross).

While SIFT has provided invariant matched pairs of point correspondences, we further scrutinized the differences in the pattern or corner-like responses of each pair. Those pairs of point correspondences with dissimilar pattern responses which were most likely false matches have been eradicated. Through experimental results, we perceive the effectiveness of the approach which the matching results have been very much optimized.

# References


1. Agarwala, A., Agrawala, M., Cohen, M., Salesin, D., Szeliski, R.: Photographing long scenes with multi-viewpoint panoramas. In: Proceedings of the 33rd Internationl Conference and Exhibition on Computer Graphics and Interactive Techniques (SIGGRAPH 2006), Boston, Massachusetts, USA, vol. 25, pp. 853–861 (2006)
2. Baumberg, A.: Reliable feature matching across widely separated views. In: IEEE Computer Society International Conference on Computer Vision and Pattern Recognition (CVPR 2000), Hilton Head Island, South Carolina, USA, vol. 1, pp. 774–781 (2000)
3. Belongie, S., Malik, J., Puzicha, J.: Shape matching and object recognition using shape contexts. IEEE Transactions on Pattern Analysis and Machine Intelligence (PAMI 2002), 509–522 (2002)
4. Brown, M., Lowe, D.G.: Recognising panoramas. In: Proceedings of the 9th IEEE International Conference on Computer Vision (ICCV 2003), Nice, France, vol. 2, pp. 1218–1225 (2003)
5. Brown, M., Lowe, D.G.: Automatic panoramic image stitching using invariant features. International Journal of Computer Vision (IJCV 2007), 59–73 (2007)
6. Deriche, R., Giraudon, G.: A computation approach for corner and vertex detection. International Journal of Computer Vision (IJCV 1993), 101–124 (1993)
7. Frome, A., Huber, D., Kolluri, R., Bulow, T., Malik, J.: Recognizing objects in range data using regional point descriptors. In: Pajdla, T., Matas, J(G.) (eds.) ECCV 2004. LNCS, vol. 3023, pp. 224–237. Springer, Heidelberg (2004)
8. Goedeme, T., Tuytelaars, T., Van-Gool, L.: Fast Wide Baseline Matching for Visual Navigation. In: IEEE Computer Society International Conference on Computer Vision and Pattern Recognition (CVPR 2004), Washington, DC, vol. 1, pp. 24–29 (2004)
9. Harris, C., Stephens, M.: A combined corner and edge detector. In: 4th Alvey Vision Conference (AVC 1988), Manchester, UK, pp. 147–151 (1988)
10. Kannala, J., Brandt, S.S.: Quasi-dense wide baseline matching using match propagation. In: IEEE Computer Society International Conference on Computer Vision and Pattern Recognition (CVPR 2007), Minneapolis, Minnesota, USA, pp. 1–8 (2007)
11. Kass, M., Witkin, A., Terzopoulos, D.: Snakes: Active contour models. International Journal of Computer Vision (IJCV 1988), 321–331 (1988)
12. Katare, A., Mitra, S.K., Banerjee, A.: Content based image retrieval system for multi object images using combined features. In: Proceedings of the 17th International Conference on Computer Theory and Applications (ICCTA 2007), Alexandria, Egypt, pp. 595–599 (2007)
13. Lowe, D.G.: Distinctive Image Features from Scale-Invariant Keypoints. International Journal of Computer Vision (IJCV 2004) 60(2), 91–110 (2004)
14. Leordeanu, M., Hebert, M., Sukthankar, R.: Beyond local appearance: Category recognition from pairwise interactions of simple features. In: IEEE Computer Society International Conference on Computer Vision and Pattern Recognition (CVPR 2007), Minneapolis, Minnesota, USA (2007)
15. Mikolajczyk, K., Schmid, C.: An affine invariant interest point detector. In: Heyden, A., Sparr, G., Nielsen, M., Johansen, P. (eds.) ECCV 2002. LNCS, vol. 2350, pp. 128–142. Springer, Heidelberg (2002)
16. Mikolajczyk, K., Leibe, B., Schiele, B.: Multiple object class detection with a generative model. In: IEEE Computer Society International Conference on Computer Vision and Pattern Recognition (CVPR 2006), New York, USA, pp. 26–36 (2006)

17. Mutch, J., Lowe, D.G.: Multiclass object recognition with sparse, localized features. In: IEEE Computer Society International Conference on Computer Vision and Pattern Recognition, New York, USA, vol. 1, pp. 11–18 (2006)
18. Moravec, H.: Rover visual obstacle avoidance. In: Proceedings of the 7th International Joint Conference on Artificial Intelligence (IJCAI 1981), Vancouver, Canada, pp. 785–790 (1981)
19. Ruzon, M.A., Tomasi, C.: Edge, junction, and corner detection using color distributions. IEEE Transactions on Pattern Analysis and Machine Intelligence (PAMI 2001), 1281–1295 (2001)
20. Sluzek, A.: On moments-based local operators for detecting image patterns. IVC 23, 287–298 (2005)
21. Staib, L.H., Duncan, J.S.: Boundary fitting with parametrically deformable models. IEEE Transactions on Pattern Analysis and Machine Intelligence (PAMI 1992), 1061–1075 (1992)
22. Wang, J., Zha, H., Cipolla, R.: Combining interest points and edges for content-based image retrieval. In: Proceedings of the 12th International Conference on Image Processing (ICIP 2005), Genova, Italy, vol. III, pp. 1256–1259 (2005)

# Integrated Expression-Invariant Face Recognition with Constrained Optical Flow

Chao-Kuei Hsieh[1], Shang-Hong Lai[2], and Yung-Chang Chen[1]

[1] Department of Electrical Engineering, National Tsing Hua University, Taiwan
[2] Department of Computer Science, National Tsing Hua University, Taiwan
d903915@oz.nthu.edu.tw, lai@cs.nthu.edu.tw,
ycchen@ee.nthu.edu.tw

**Abstract.** Face recognition is one of the most intensively studied topics in computer vision and pattern recognition. A constrained optical flow algorithm, which combines the advantages of the unambiguous correspondence of feature point labeling and the flexible representation of optical flow computation, has been proposed in our pervious work for face recognition from expressional face images. In this paper, we propose an integrated face recognition system that is robust against facial expressions by combining information from the computed intra-person optical flow and the synthesized face image in a probabilistic framework. Our experimental results show that the proposed system improves the accuracy of face recognition from expressional face images.

**Keywords:** Face recognition, expression recognition, constrained optical flow, expression normalization.

## 1 Introduction

Face recognition has been studied for the past few decades. Even though the 2D face recognition methods have been actively studied in the past, there are still inherent disadvantages and drawbacks. It was shown that the recognition rate can drop dramatically when the head pose and illumination variations are too large, or when there is expression on the face image. Pose, illumination, and expression variations are three essential issues to be dealt with in the research of face recognition.

Some authors have proposed different approaches to deal with such expression variations. One way [1] is to compute the optical flow between the testing and training face image. Another way [2] used a mask or a morphable model for the image registration in a face recognition system. In our previous work, we combined the advantages of the above two approaches: the unambiguous correspondence of feature point labeling and the flexible representation of optical flow computation. A constrained optical flow algorithm was proposed, which can deal with position movements and intensity changes at the same time when handling the corresponding feature points. We have then applied the algorithm not only to the application of face recognition from expression normalization [3], but also on the inter- and intra-person

T. Wada, F. Huang, and S. Lin (Eds.): PSIVT 2009, LNCS 5414, pp. 702–713, 2009.

optical flow analysis [4], which can be used for further face and expression recognition. Both methods can improve the accuracy of the face recognition from expressional face images, even though different information is utilized in these two algorithms. In this paper, we propose to exploit two different types of information, i.e. the computed optical flow and the synthesized image, to improve the accuracy of face recognition. Experimental validation is given to show the improved performance of the proposed face recognition system.

The remaining of this paper is organized as follows. We briefly review the constrained optical flow computational technique and our previous works on expression normalization and expression optical flow analysis in section 2 and 3, respectively. The proposed face recognition system is presented in section 4. Section 5 gives some experimental results and section 6 concludes this paper.

## 2  Constrained Optical Flow Computation

The computational algorithms of traditional optical flow cannot guarantee that the computed optical flow corresponds to the exact pixels in different images, since the intensity variations due to expression may mislead the computation of optical flow. Teng et al. [5] proposed to minimize the following discrete energy function to compute the optical flow, which used an adaptive smoothness adjustment scheme considered both flow components ($u_i$ and $v_i$) and all the brightness variation multiplier and offset factors ($m_i$ and $c_i$)

$$
\begin{aligned}
f\left(\mathbf{u}\right) = \sum_{i \in D} w_i & \left( \frac{I_{x,i} u_i + I_{y,i} v_i + I_{t,i} + m_i I_i + c_i}{\sqrt{I_{x,i}^2 + I_{y,i}^2 + I_i^2 + 1}} \right)^2 \\
& + \lambda \sum_{i \in D} \left( \alpha_{x,i} u_{x,i}^2 + \alpha_{y,i} u_{y,i}^2 + \beta_{x,i} v_{x,i}^2 + \beta_{y,i} v_{y,i}^2 \right) \\
& + \mu \sum_{i \in D} \left( \gamma_{x,i} m_{x,i}^2 + \gamma_{y,i} m_{y,i}^2 + \delta_{x,i} c_{x,i}^2 + \delta_{y,i} c_{y,i}^2 \right),
\end{aligned}
\tag{1}
$$

Furthermore, it can be rewritten in a matrix-vector form and efficiently solved by the incomplete Cholesky preconditioned conjugate gradient (ICPCG) algorithm [5].

In order to guarantee the computed optical flow to be consistent to the motion vectors at these corresponding feature points, we modify the unconstrained optimization problem in the original formulation of the optical flow estimation to a constrained optimization problem [3] given as follows:

$$
minimize\ f\left(\mathbf{u}\right) = \mathbf{u}^T K \mathbf{u} - 2 \mathbf{u}^T \mathbf{b} + \mathbf{c},
$$

$$
subject\ to\ u\left(x_i, y_i\right) = \overline{u}_i,\ and\ v\left(x_i, y_i\right) = \overline{v}_i, \forall \left(x_i, y_i\right) \in S
$$

where $S$ is the set of feature points and $\left(\overline{u}_i, \overline{v}_i\right)$ is the specified optical flow vector at the $i^{th}$ feature point. We applied a modified ICPCG procedure to solve this constrained optimization problem and the details are referred to [3].

# 3  Previous Works

In this section, we briefly review expression normalization [3] and inter- and intra-person optical flow analysis [4] in our previous works.

## 3.1  Expression Normalization

The face recognition problem can be considered as to determine the class $c$ that minimizes the difference between the reference image $R_c$ and the synthesized neutral image from the testing facial expression image $T$ by using $R_c$ as the reference. After the image alignment and normalization of the input testing image $T$ and reference image $R_c$, where $c = 1,2,...,C$, and $C$ is the total number of subjects in the face database, we can formulate the face recognition problem as follows:

$$\arg\min_c \left\| R_c - Syn\left(T;OF\left(T;R_c\right)\right) \right\| \tag{2}$$

To further improve the computational efficiency, we modify the face recognition problem as follows:

$$\arg\min_c \left\| Syn\left(R_c;OF\left(R_c;NE_0\right)\right) - Syn\left(T;OF\left(T;NE_0\right)\right) \right\| \tag{3}$$

where $NE_0$ is a universal neutral face image. To be more specific, instead of transforming the input image to the neutral image for each class, we now transform all images to a universal coordinate as $NE_0$.

We define the operation, $Syn\left(T;OF\left(T;R_c\right)\right)$, as the *OF-Syn* operator. The modified system flow chart is shown in Fig. 1. Although there are $C+1$ OF-Syn operators in total, the $C$ OF-Syn operations among them can be performed in advance, thus only one such operation is needed in the testing or recognition phase.

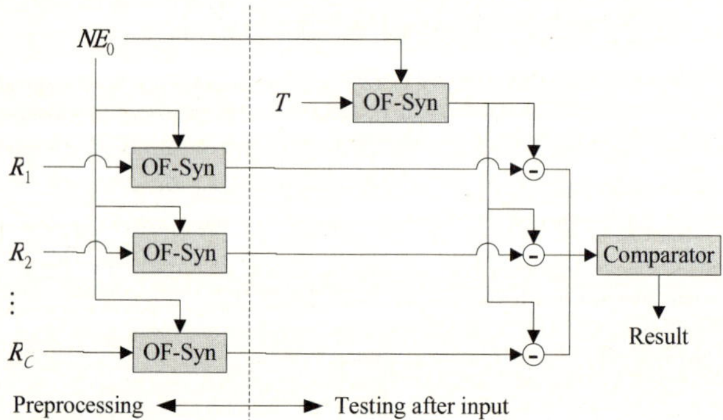


**Fig. 1.** The proposed expression-invariant face recognition flow chart according to Eq. (3)

## 3.2  Expression Optical Flow Analysis

The traditional expressive optical flow is computed from a neutral face image $NE_i$ of person $i$ to an expression image $EX_{i,k}$ with expression k of the same subject. However, the computed optical flows are generally not in the same coordinate, since the geometry of neutral faces is different for different persons. Some research only considered motion vectors at certain feature points to overcome this problem, but only limited information about facial movement is used in this case.

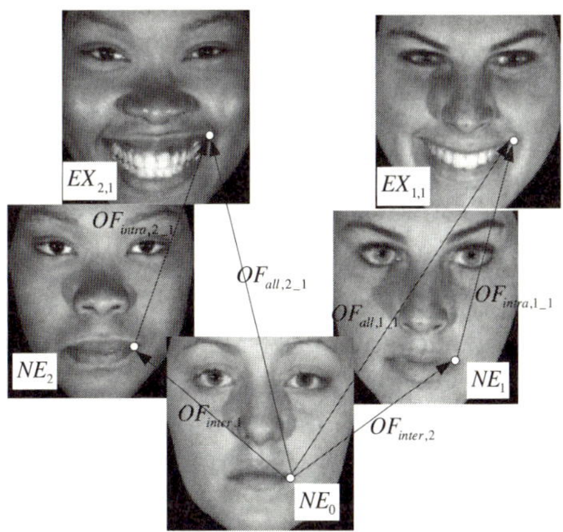


**Fig. 2.** Illustration of decomposing input optical flow ($OF_{all}$) to inter-person ($OF_{inter}$) and intra-person ($OF_{intra}$) parts

We proposed a different solution for optical flow normalization, as shown in Fig. 3. Instead of computing the intra-person optical flow $OF_{intra,i_k}$ directly from the neutral face to an expressive face image for each person, we start from a global neutral face $NE_0$ to obtain the inter-person optical flow $OF_{inter,i} = OF(NE_0; NE_i)$ and overall optical $OF_{all,i_k} = OF(NE_0; EX_{i,k})$. The intra-person optical flow can then be generated by pixel-wise differencing as follows:

$$OF_{intra,i_k} = OF_{all,i_k} - OF_{inter,i}. \tag{4}$$

There are two advantages of doing it this way: (1) all expressive face images of every subject have the same number of motion vectors; (2) all optical flows are computed on the same geometry of $NE_0$.

After obtaining the normalized optical flows from different expressions, we consider it as a problem of subspace modeling. In other words, we can extract $K$ optical flow bases $OB_{intra,k}$ to describe intra-person optical flows. Moreover, when there is an input image, we can recognize the face by determining the person $i$, whose inter-person optical flow $OF_{inter,i}$ makes the intra-person optical flow be best spanned by the trained optical flow bases. This can be formulated as the following optimization problem:

$$\arg\min_{i,\,b_{k,k=1,\ldots,K}} \left\| \left( OF_{input} - OF_{inter,i} \right) - \sum_{k=1}^{K} b_k OB_{intra,k} \right\| \tag{5}$$

Furthermore, the spanning coefficients $b_k$ of each basis $OB_{intra,k}$ may be used for expression recognition. A negative coefficient does not make sense in physical expression motion, thus we proposed a modified eigenvector algorithm to enforce non-negative projection coefficients.

## 4  Proposed Face Recognition System

There are two types of information generated by the constrained optical flow algorithm: the optical flow and the synthesized neural face image by image warping with the computed optical flow. As discussed in the previous section, the two face recognition methods based on the expression normalized images and the computed optical flow are described in section 3.1 and 3.2, respectively. In the first method, the optical flows for the input expression-variant images are different from different subjects in terms of geometry and dimensionality, thus the optical flow information was not used for comparison in the first method. On the other hand, in the second method, we compute the optical flow in the opposite direction, i.e. from the global neutral face to an input expression variant face, to preserve the same geometry for the computed optical flow, but it cannot be used directly to synthesize the corresponding neutral image for comparison. Only partial information was exploited in each of these two methods.

In this paper, we intend to integrate these two methods into the proposed expression-invariant face recognition system to fully exploit the information of the optical flow and the synthesized neutral image for face recognition. To do this, we formulate the problem as follows:

$$\max_{\mathbf{N}_i,E} P(\mathbf{N}_i,E \mid \mathbf{I}), i=1,2,...,N \tag{6}$$

where $\mathbf{I}$ is the input image, $\mathbf{N}_i$ is a neutral face image in training data set, and $E$ denotes the expression optical flow vector between $\mathbf{I}$ and $\mathbf{N}_i$. Based on the posterior probability, equation (6) can be rewritten as

$$\max_{\mathbf{N}_i,E} P(\mathbf{N}_i)P(E)P(\mathbf{I} \mid \mathbf{N}_i,E). \tag{7}$$

Furthermore, the occurrence probability of each candidate is assumed equally probable, i.e. $P(\mathbf{N}_i)$ is a constant for all $i$. The formulation can be simplified as

$$\max_{\mathbf{N}_i,E} P(E)P(\mathbf{I} \mid \mathbf{N}_i,E). \tag{8}$$

There are two parts in equation (8), i.e. the probability of the expression movement $P(E)$, and the probability of the input image under the condition of the subject $\mathbf{N}_i$ with the expression $E$. As discussed before, a single type of optical flow cannot keep the uniformity of dimensionality and geometry in both circumstances. Thus. we define $P(E)$ and $P(\mathbf{I} \mid \mathbf{N}_i, E)$ separately.

To further define $P(E)$ with preservation of identical geometry and dimensionality for each $\mathbf{N}_i$, we use the same strategy in method 2, i.e. the intra-person optical flow. With equation (4), the motion information $E$ in $P(E)$ is defined as

$$\boldsymbol{u}(x,y)_{@NE_0} = \boldsymbol{v}(x,y)_{@NE_0} - \boldsymbol{w}(x,y)_{@NE_0}, \tag{9}$$

where $v(x, y)$ is the overall optical flow from global neutral face $NE_0$ to input image $\mathbf{I}$, $w(x, y)$ is the inter-person optical flow from $NE_0$ to the guessed neutral face N, and $u(x, y)$ is the intra-person optical flow from $\mathbf{N}_i$ to $\mathbf{I}$. Moreover, and the symbol '$@NE_0$' denotes the optical flow represented with the geometry of $NE_0$, even though the intra-person optical flow is defined as the pixel-wised movement from $\mathbf{N}_i$ to $\mathbf{I}$.

The probability of $P(\mathbf{I} \mid \mathbf{N}_i, E)$ is then defined as the similarity between input image $\mathbf{I}$ and the synthesized image from neutral face $\mathbf{N}_i$ and the computed optical flow movement, i.e.

$$P(\mathbf{I} \mid \mathbf{N}_i, E) \propto \exp\left\{-\left\|I - Syn\left(N_i; \boldsymbol{u}_{@N_i}\right)\right\|^2 \Big/ \sigma^2\right\}. \tag{10}$$

Since the optical flow used for synthesizing neutral face $\mathbf{N}_i$ to a certain expression must be represented with the same geometry of $\mathbf{N}_i$, the intra-person optical flow $\boldsymbol{u}(x, y)_{@NE_0}$ in equation (9) is not appropriate in this circumstance. An estimated intra-person optical flow under the geometry of $\mathbf{N}_i$ is needed in equation (10). The MAP optimization problem is now rewritten as

$$\max_{\mathbf{N}_i, E} P(E) P(\mathbf{I} \mid \mathbf{N}_i, E) = \max_{\mathbf{N}_i, E} P\left(\boldsymbol{u}_{@NE_0}\right) \exp\left\{-\left\|I - Syn\left(N_i; \boldsymbol{u}_{@N_i}\right)\right\|^2 \Big/ \sigma^2\right\}, \tag{11}$$

Thus two components are needed to compute in the above formulation: one is the intra-person optical flow at the geometry of $NE_0$ ($Intra@NE_0$), and the other is the intra-person optical flow at the geometry of $NE_i$ ($Intra@\mathbf{N}_i$). We can first compute the optical flow $Intra@NE_0$ directly and warp it to obtain $Intra@NE_i$ (Fig. 1, defined as procedure 1), or oppositely, we can compute $Intra@NE_i$ first and then warp to $Intra@NE_0$ (Fig. 1, defined as procedure 2). In the first flow, we compute $Intra@NE_0$ as the diagram shown in Fig. 3, i.e.

$$\begin{aligned} Intra\,@\, NE_0 &\triangleq Input\,@\, NE_0 - Inter\,@\, NE_0 \\ &= OF\left(NE_0; Input\right) - OF\left(NE_0; NE_i\right). \end{aligned} \tag{12}$$

The optical flow $Intra@NE_i$ can be simply obtained by computing $OF(NE_i; Input)$. After collecting one type of intra-person optical flow, we can further obtain the other one by nonlinear warping with the inter-person optical flow as shown in Fig. 4. Take $Intra@NE_i$ to $Intra@NE_0$ for example. The movement of each pixel has been obtained in $Intra@NE_i$ calculation. The corresponding position in $NE_0$ of each pixel in $NE_i$ can be determined easily through inter-person optical flow $Inter@NE_i$. In most cases, the corresponding position is not on integer grid. We can estimate the motion of each non-integer pixel by bilinear interpolation.

The overall system flowcharts of procedure 1 and 2 are depicted in Fig. 5 and Fig. 6, respectively. In procedure 1, since the $OF$ block of $OF(NE_0; NE_i)$ can be pre-computed in the training process, only one optical flow calculation, the $Input@NE_0$ is needed in the testing process. However, the optical flow used for synthesis, which requires more precision, is obtained through a long computational procedure. This may damage the

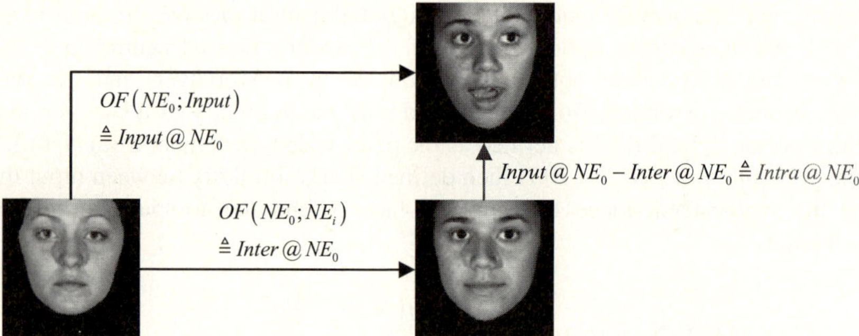



**Fig. 3.** Intra-person optical flow, $Intra @ NE_0$ calculation in procedure 1

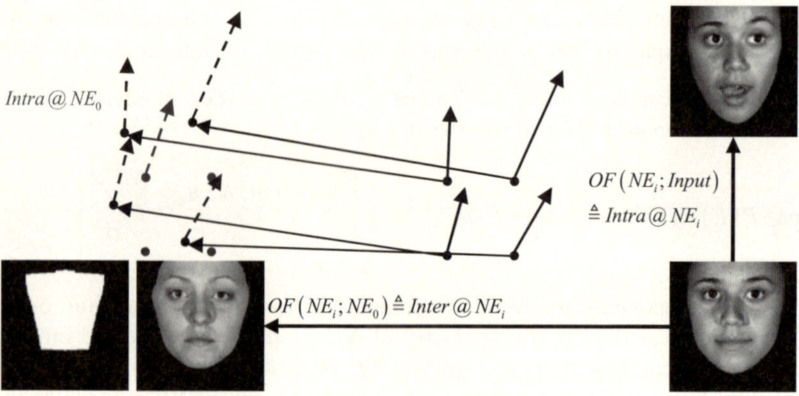



**Fig. 4.** Diagram of intra-person optical flow mapping from one person to another

quality of the synthesized result if any non-negligible inaccuracy is involved during the flow.

In procedure 2, on the other hand, even though the operation $OF(NE_0; NE_i)$ can be pre-computed in the training process as well, the *OF* block $OF(NE_i; Input)$ is required to compute for each guess. There are totally $C$ times of *OF* computations in the testing procedure, which are directly followed by image synthesis block.

The objective function can be computed after the two types of intra-person optical flow are calculated. We considered the probability of intra-person optical flow as a mixture of Gaussian probability distribution with centers corresponding to the samples in the training optical flow dataset, that is,

$$P\left(u_{@NE_0}\right) = \sum_{i=1}^{T} f_i(y) \propto \sum_{i=1}^{T} \exp\left\{-\frac{1}{2}(y - \bar{y}_i)^T \Sigma^{-1}(y - \bar{y}_i)\right\}, \tag{13}$$

where $\bar{y}_i$ is the intra-person optical flow in the training data, $i$ is the index and $T$ is the number of training sample, and $y$ denotes $u_{@NE_0}$. As for the similarity between the input image and the synthesized images, we directly calculate the reciprocal of the

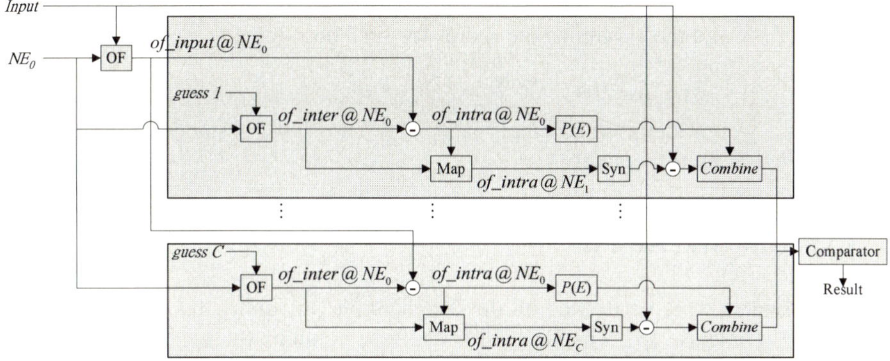

**Fig. 5.** System flowchart of procedure 1

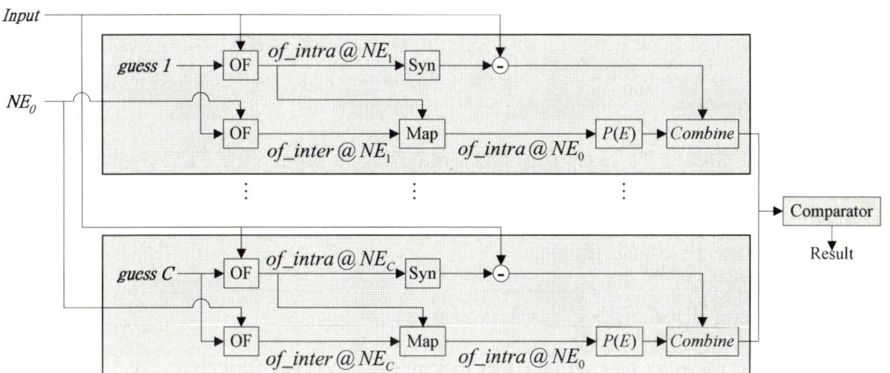

**Fig. 6.** System flowchart of procedure 2

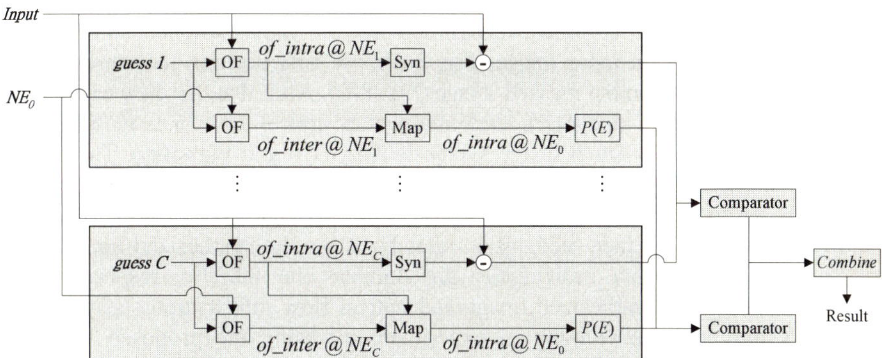

**Fig. 7.** Modified system flowchart of procedure 2

average of pixel-wise difference between them. According to the original definition, since the two values are under different scales, one will dominate the result of final probability. Instead of comparing the final result after combining the two values as shown in Fig. 6, we modify the flow to Fig. 7. We compare and score the two values separately first, and then combine the scores for final decision as

$$S_{Final} = r \times S_{P(E)} + S_{P(I| N, E)}, \tag{14}$$

where $r$ is a weight determined empirically. $S_{P(E)}$ and $S_{P(I| N, E)}$ stand for the score of $P(E)$ and $P(I| N, E)$ respectively.

## 5   Experimental Results

Our experiments were performed on the Binghamton University 3D Face Expression (BU-3DFE) Database [6]. The BU-3DFE database contains the face images and 3D face models of 100 subjects (56 females and 44 males) each with a neutral face and 6 different expressions (angry, disgust, fear, happy, sad, and surprised) at different levels (from level 1 (weakest) to 4 (strongest)). Note that only the 2D face images were used in our experiments. Among them, 34 subjects are randomly selected for intra-person optical flow training, and the others are used as the testing set.

### 5.1   Pre-processing

We manually labeled 21 feature points, including 3 points for each eyebrow and 4 points for each eye, one at the nose tip and the other 6 around the mouth region. With the labeled points, the distance between the outer corners of both eyes is used as the reference to normalize face images.

### 5.2   Face Recognition with Proposed System

As described in the previous section, we follow the modified flowchart shown in Fig. 8. We apply a mask (Fig. 8(b)) defined from the global neutral face $NE_0$ (Fig. 8(a)) to extract the region of interest. Moreover, the region inside the mouth is discarded, as illustrated in Fig. 8(e). Both the optical flow and the grayscales of the synthesized image within the mask will be used in face recognition process. Some experimental images are shown in Fig. 8. For an input image (Fig. 8(d)), we first position the corresponding mask (Fig. 8(e)) to obtain the masked image (Fig. 8(f)). After that, for each candidate in the database (Fig. 8(g) and 8(j)), the intra-person optical flow, i.e. $intra@NE_i$, is computed and used for virtual image synthesis (Fig. 8(h) and Fig. 8(k)). The masked images (Fig. 8(i) and 8(l)) can finally be applied for similarity comparison.

Expression-invariant face recognition results are listed in Table 1-3. According to the results, the average face recognition rates based on the synthesized image or the intra-person optical flow individually are 85.86% and 82.39%, respectively. In addition to using the synthesized image and optical flow information separately, we also carry out the face recognition experiment by using the proposed integrated solution, i.e. based on Equ. (14). In this experiment, 10 to 1 points are given to the top ten candidates in each comparison, and we equally weight the information of synthesized image and intra-person optical flow, i.e. $r = 1$. The recognition rate is improved to 90.28% as shown in Table 3.

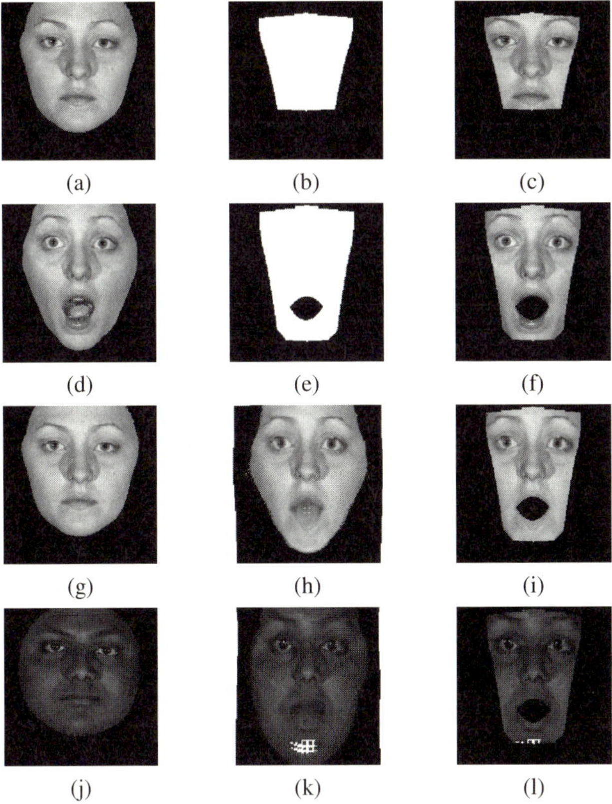

**Fig. 8.** Illustration of experimental images: (a) global neutral face, (b) mask image, (c) masked image of (a), (d) input image, (e) warped mask image, (f) masked input image, (g) guessed subject 1, (h) synthesized face from (g) to (d), (i) masked synthesized image (g) using mask image (e), (j) guessed subject 2, (k) synthesized face from (g) to (d), and (l) masked synthesized image (k) using mask image (e)

**Table 1.** Recognition result using the synthesized face images only

| Expression | Level 1(%) | Level 2(%) | Level 3(%) | Level 4(%) | Average |
|:---:|:---:|:---:|:---:|:---:|:---:|
| AN | 93.94 | 86.36 | 89.39 | 83.33 | |
| DI | 90.91 | 86.36 | 81.82 | 77.27 | |
| FE | 84.85 | 83.33 | 83.33 | 83.33 | |
| HA | 89.39 | 92.42 | 86.36 | 80.30 | |
| SA | 92.42 | 93.94 | 90.91 | 86.36 | |
| SU | 84.85 | 86.36 | 80.30 | 72.73 | 85.86% |

The impact of different weighting is also discussed in our experiment. We try different weightings ranging from 0.5 to 2 and the face recognition accuracies are depicted in Fig. 9. We can see that the proposed system can achieve the best accuracy at 93% when $r = 0.7$, which means the synthesized image is of higher significance.

**Table 2.** Recognition result using intra-person optical flow only

| Expression | Level 1(%) | Level 2(%) | Level 3(%) | Level 4(%) | Average |
|---|---|---|---|---|---|
| AN | 87.88 | 87.88 | 81.82 | 66.67 | |
| DI | 83.33 | 75.76 | 68.18 | 60.61 | |
| FE | 84.85 | 81.82 | 77.27 | 75.76 | |
| HA | 93.94 | 92.42 | 83.33 | 74.24 | |
| SA | 96.97 | 93.94 | 90.91 | 87.88 | |
| SU | 90.91 | 86.36 | 81.82 | 72.73 | 82.39% |

**Table 3.** Recognition result using the integrated information, including the synthesized images and intra-person optical flow

| Expression | Level 1 (%) | Level 2(%) | Level 3(%) | Level 4(%) | Average |
|---|---|---|---|---|---|
| AN | 98.48 | 92.42 | 87.88 | 84.85 | |
| DI | 87.88 | 86.36 | 80.30 | 81.82 | |
| FE | 90.91 | 90.91 | 87.88 | 87.88 | |
| HA | 96.97 | 93.94 | 95.45 | 87.88 | |
| SA | 98.48 | 96.97 | 93.94 | 90.91 | |
| SU | 93.94 | 90.91 | 90.91 | 78.79 | 90.28% |

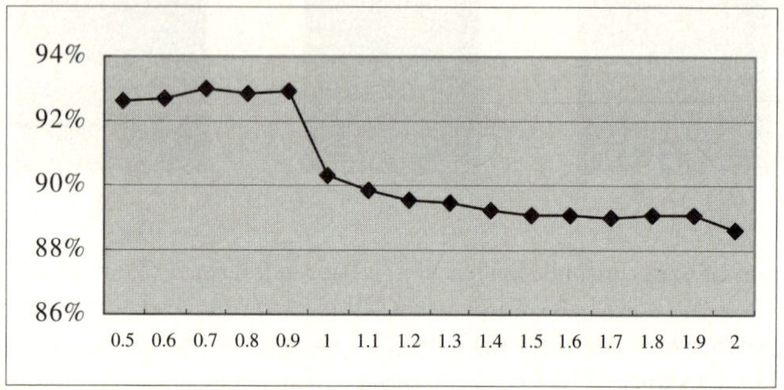

**Fig. 9.** Recognition result on the test data with different weighting parameters in eq.(14)

## 6   Conclusion

In this paper, we proposed an integrated expression-invariant face recognition system based on the constrained optical flow. In the previous works on optical flow based face recognition, either the synthesized face image or the intra-person flow is used individually for face and expression recognition. In this work, we proposed to integrate the information of synthesized images and the intra-person optical flow distribution probability to improve the face recognition accuracy. As the experimental results shows, the proposed system improves the accuracy of face and expression recognition on expressional face images. However, the proposed integrated system is more computationally costly compared to the previous works, since the optical flow computation, intra-person optical flow mapping and image synthesis are needed for all candidates in the database. This is the main research topic in our future study.

# References


1. Li, X., Mori, G., Zhang, H.: Expression-invariant face recognition with expression classification. In: Proc. 3rd Canadian Conf. on Computer and Robot Vision (June 2006)
2. Martinez, A.M.: Recognizing expression variant faces from a single sample image per class. In: Proc. IEEE Conf. Computer Vision Pattern Recognition (June 2003)
3. Hsieh, C.-K., Lai, S.-H., Chen, Y.-C.: Expression-invariant face recognition with accurate optical flow. In: Ip, H.H.-S., Au, O.C., Leung, H., Sun, M.-T., Ma, W.-Y., Hu, S.-M. (eds.) PCM 2007. LNCS, vol. 4810, pp. 78–87. Springer, Heidelberg (2007)
4. Hsieh, C.-K., Lai, S.-H., Chen, Y.-C.: Expressional face image analysis with constrained optical flow. In: Proc. of ICME, Hannover, Germany, June 23-26 (2008)
5. Teng, C.-H., Lai, S.-H., Chen, Y.-S., Hsu, W.-H.: Accurate optical flow computation under non-uniform brightness variations. In: Computer Vision and Image Understanding, vol. 97, pp. 315–346 (2005)
6. Yin, L., Wei, X., Sun, Y., Wang, J., Rosato, M.J.: A 3D facial expression database for facial behavior research. In: Proc. Intern. Conf. on Automatic Face and Gesture Recognition, pp. 211–216 (April 2006)

# Automatic Eigentemplate Learning
## for Sparse Template Tracker


Keiji Sakabe, Tomoyuki Taguchi, and Takeshi Shakunaga

Okayama University, 3-1-1, Tsushima-naka, Okayama, Japan
{sakabe,taguchi,shaku}@chino.cs.okayama-u.ac.jp



**Abstract.** Automatic eigentemplate learning is discussed for a sparse
template tracker. It is known that a sparse template tracker can effectively track a moving target using an eigentemplate when it is appropriately prepared for a motion class or for an illumination class. However,
it has not been easy to prepare an eigentemplate automatically for any
image sequences. This paper provides a feasible solution to this problem
in the framework of sparse template tracking. In the learning phase, the
sparse template tracker adaptively tracks a target object in a given image sequence when the first template is provided in the first image. By
selecting a small number of representative and effective images, we can
make up an eigentemplate by the principal component analysis. Once
the eigentemplate learning is accomplished, the sparse template tracker
can work with the eigentemplate instead of an adaptive template. Since
the sparse eigentemplate tracker doesn't require any adaptive tracking, it
can work more efficiently and effectively for image sequences in the class
of learned appearance changes. Experimental results are provided for
real-time face tracking when eigentemplates are learned for pose changes
and for illumination changes, respectively.


## 1   Introduction

Object tracking is one of the most significant problems in computer vision. Considerable work has already been proposed for unknown objects and for known
objects in a lot of applications. Among them, some robust algorithms were proposed for the tracking based on the eigenspace techniques [1] with combining
iterative projections and outlier detection. The iterative projection approaches,
however, often suffer from time-consuming implementation and the "breakdown
point" problem. In order to solve these problems, a sparse eigentemplate tracker
was proposed by Shakunaga et al. [2]. In their tracker, a particle filter is utilized for avoiding any iterative calculations. Shakunaga and Noguchi [3] showed
the tracker could be converted to an adaptive tracker by combining their sparse
template tracking and an on-line learning technique of Black and Jepson [4].

Although these two types of sparse template trackers work independently as
adaptive trackers, they sometimes fail to work in complex situations. In order to
cover complex situations, more adaptive processings are required in the adaptive trackers. This paper shows an approach to this problem by the cooperation


T. Wada, F. Huang, and S. Lin (Eds.): PSIVT 2009, LNCS 5414, pp. 714–725, 2009.

between the eigen and the adaptive trackers. In this approach, the adaptive tracker is utilized for automatic learning of eigentemplate for the eigentemplate tracker. Once a learning set of images are selected appropriately from the exemplar image sequence by the adaptive tracker, an eigen-template can be efficiently constructed and utilized by the eigen tracker. Since the two trackers are built in a common framework of sparse template tracker, the cooperation can be easily and widely utilized in a lot of applications.

## 2    Framework of Sparse Template Tracker

### 2.1    Formulations of Sparse Template Matching

Template matching is one of the most fundamental techniques in image processing and computer vision. A lot of variations have been developed for many applications  [5,1,6,2]. Among them, this paper basically utilizes sparse template matching formulated in [2], where the sparse template matching is also generalized to the sparse eigentemplate matching. Since the formulation is required for the following discussion in this paper, we summarize it at first as follows:

**(1) Template matching**
Let an $n$-vector $\mathbf{X}$ denote an original template with $n$ pixels, and $\mathbf{1}$ denote an $n$-vector of which every element is 1. Then, the normalized template $\mathbf{x}$ of an original template $\mathbf{X}$ is defined as $\mathbf{x} = \mathbf{X}/(\mathbf{1}^\top \mathbf{X})$.

Let $T$ denote any possible transformation from a given image $\mathbf{Y}$ into template image space. Then, $T\mathbf{Y}$ denotes an $n$-vector transformed by $T$ from an original image $\mathbf{Y}$. When an input image denoted by $\mathbf{Y}$ is given, template matching in a set of possible transformations $\{T\}$ is formulated as minimization of a dissimilarity measure.

An $n \times n$ diagonal matrix, $P$, called a part indicator matrix, is utilized in  [2] for discussing partial template matching, where each diagonal element of $P$ is 1 or 0. If the $j$th diagonal element, $p_{jj}$, is $1(0)$, the $j$th pixel is effective(ineffective) for partial template matching.

When $P$ is given, a partial template matching is formulated as a minimization problem,

$$\arg \min_{T \in \{T\}} \epsilon = \arg \min_{T \in \{T\}} \widehat{\rho}(P[\mathbf{x} - \frac{1}{\beta}T\mathbf{Y}]), \tag{1}$$

where $\widehat{\rho}(\mathbf{x})$ indicates a summation of Geman-McClure function, $\rho(x_i) = x_i^2/(c^2 + x_i^2)$, when $x_i$ indicates each vector element and $c = 0.4/n$. In this problem, $\beta$ is a normalization parameter calculated for each $T$ as

$$\beta = \frac{\mathbf{x}^\top PT\mathbf{Y}}{\mathbf{x}^\top P\mathbf{x}}. \tag{2}$$

When a partial template is specified by a set of sparse pixels, the partial template is called a sparse template. Partial template matching is called sparse template matching when $P\mathbf{x}$ represents a sparse template.

## (2) Eigentemplate matching

When an eigenspace is constructed from a set of normalized template images, it is called an eigentemplate. The formulation of sparse template matching can be generalized to eigentemplate matching as follows:

Let $\overline{\mathbf{x}}$ and $\Phi$ denote the mean vector and a matrix composed of most significant $m$ eigenvectors. Let $\tilde{\Phi}$ denote $[\Phi \ \ \overline{\mathbf{x}}]$. Then, the eigentemplate matching problem is formulated as

$$\arg\min_{T \in \{T\}} \epsilon = \arg\min_{T \in \{T\}} \hat{\rho}(\frac{1}{\beta}P[\tilde{\Phi}\tilde{\mathbf{y}}^* - T\mathbf{Y}]), \tag{3}$$

where $\tilde{\mathbf{y}}^*$ is an $(m+1)$-vector calculated for each $T$ as

$$\tilde{\mathbf{y}}^* = (P\tilde{\Phi})^+T\mathbf{Y}, \tag{4}$$

when $A^+ = (A^\top A)^{-1}A^\top$ and $\beta$ is the last element of $\tilde{\mathbf{y}}^*$. Note that the simple template matching is a special case of the eigentemplate matching where $\tilde{\Phi} = \overline{\mathbf{x}}$.

## 2.2   Sparse (Eigen)Template Tracking by Particle Filter

Sparse (eigen)template matching is implemented with a particle filter [7]. In the particle filter, a lot of particles are generated and propagated in a given pose space. Since a transformation matrix $T$ is specified by each particle in pose space, the minimization of $\epsilon$ in Eqs.(1) or (3) is implemented with the particle filter framework in a probabilistic manner.

While the tracker works even when $P$ is readily fixed, a selection of $P$ can be included in the parameter space as well as pose parameters, when a set of $P$ denoted by $\{P_i\}$ are provided for parameter estimation in Eqs.(2) or (4). The random selection of $P_i$ often results in more robust tracking against partial occlusions if a common $P$ is utilized in Eqs.(1) or (3). Here, $\{P_i\}$ are made up by the regional maximum/minimum criterion given in [2].

– Regional maximum/minimum criterion: The template image $\mathbf{x}$ is partitioned into $s$ rectangle subregions, and two pixels are selected in each subregion as they provide the maximum and minimum intensities in the subregion. The simple method provides a $2s$-point sparse template.

Figure 1 shows an example of the sparse template set. Five sparse templates, $P_1$-$P_5$, consist of 16 points, respectively, while $P$ consists of 64 points. Out of 2025 pixels in the entire template, only 16 or 64 pixels indicated by "x" are selected by the above criterion. In $P_1$, eight maximum/minimum pairs are selected in each octant subregion. In $P_2$-$P_5$, eight maximum/minimum pairs are selected in each octant subregion of each quadrant region.

Let $\{\mathbf{s}_t^{(k)}, k = 1, \cdots, K\}$ denote a time-stamped particle set in pose space, and $\pi_t^{(k)}$ is a weight associated with a particle $\mathbf{s}_t^{(k)}$, where $\pi_t^{(k)}$ approximately represents the conditional state-density at time $t$.

In the first frame, a particle set $\{\mathbf{s}_1^{(k)}, k = 1, \cdots, K\}$ is generated from a prior density and then an index $k$ is chosen with probability $\pi_1^{(k)} = 1/K$.

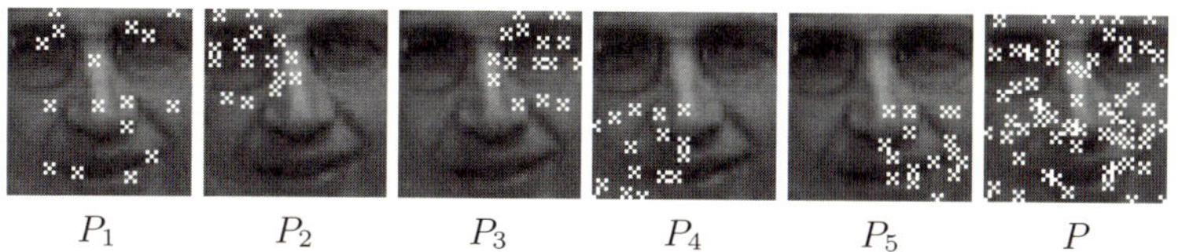


**Fig. 1.** Sparse templates for sparse template selection

When a weighted particle set $\{(\mathbf{s}_{t-1}^{(k)}, \pi_{t-1}^{(k)}), k = 1, \cdots, L\}$ is provided from time-step $t - 1$, two types of assumptions are evenly applied for generating the particle set: a half of particles are generated from no-move assumption and the other half particles are generated from constant-move assumption in the pose space.

$K(> 2L)$ particles are generated from $2L$ particles by selecting a given particle $\mathbf{s}_{t-1}^{(k)}$ with probability $\pi_{t-1}^{(k)}$. By adding a white Gaussian noise to each selected particle, a new particle $\mathbf{s}_t^{(k)}$ is generated.

The sparse template matching provides a measure for each particle $\mathbf{s}_t^{(k)}$, where a transformation matrix $T$ is generated from $\mathbf{s}_t^{(k)}$, and a sparse template indicator $P_i$ is selected at random. Let $\epsilon^{(k)}$ denote the $\epsilon$ value for $\mathbf{s}_t^{(k)}$.

After selecting most similar $L(< K)$ particles from $K$ particles, a weight for a particle $\mathbf{s}_t^{(k)}$ is calculated by

$$\pi_t^{(k)} = \frac{1/\epsilon^{(k)}}{\sum_{j=1}^{L} 1/\epsilon^{(j)}}. \tag{5}$$

Thus, a pose of the object is estimated at time-step $t$ by

$$\bar{\mathbf{s}}_t = \sum_{k=1}^{L} \pi_t^{(k)} \mathbf{s}_t^{(k)}. \tag{6}$$

## 2.3 Adaptive Tracking by WSL Template

The WSL appearance model [4] consists of stable, lost and wandering components, and an online EM algorithm updates five parameters of the model. Shakunaga and Noguchi [3] combined the sparse template tracker and the WSL model for implementing an adaptive real-time tracker. In their formulation, the WSL model is applied for each pixel value, and an adaptive template, called the WSL template, is updated by the on-line EM algorithm. Only the stable component of the WSL template, called the S-template, is utilized for the sparse template tracker, where the sparse template is made up from the S-template frame by frame. Thus, the adaptive real-time tracker can be made up in the same framework of sparse eigentemplate tracking.

Figure 2 shows how the dense and sparse S-templates are updated during a real tracking. The dense S-template changes due to appearance change, and the change of S-template affects the sparse S-template.

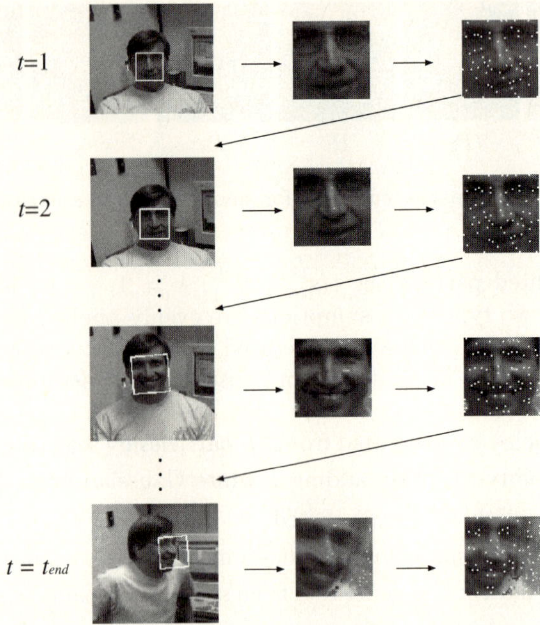

**Fig. 2.** Update process of sparse S-template: sparse S-template (shown by white dots in the right column) is created from S-template(shown in the center) at each frame

## 2.4   Comparison of Adaptive and Eigen Trackers

Both the eigentemplate tracker and the WSL-based adaptive tracker can adaptively track a target template in frame rate in different manners. The eigentemplate tracker can track a target very efficiently whenever the eigentemplate covers the changes of the target appearances. However, the eigentemplate learning is an open problem for complex appearance changes.

On the other hand, the WSL-based adaptive tracker can track a target more adaptively and flexibly without using any off-line learning. However, the adaptive tracking often results in inaccurate tracking because of gradual modification of the template.

While the two trackers have weak points, they can collaborate with each other as follows: If the eigentemplate can be learned by the results of adaptive tracking of a target, the open problem of eigentemplate learning is solved and the weak point of the adaptive tracker may be considerably compensated.

## 3   Automatic Eigentemplate Learning

### 3.1   Our Approach

This paper proposes an approach to automatic learning of eigentemplate for the sparse template tracker, where the learning is implemented in the adaptive tracker and the eigentemplate made up through the learning is utilized for more efficient and more stable tracking.

As described in the previous section, both the adaptive tracker and the eigentemplate tracker are implemented in the framework of sparse template tracker. Therefore, they seem to easily collaborate with each other in the sparse template tracker. For example, they can consist in dual CPU system as parallel processes. This consistence enables us to make a real-time improvement of tracking since a trial-and-error process can be safely implemented for eigentemplate learning. For this purpose, it is very important to select a learning image set from the result of automatic tracking by the adaptive tracker.

## 3.2 Automatic Tracking by Adaptive Tracker

The adaptive S-template tracker can track a target appearance even when it gradually changes. This means that a tracking result such as a sequence of S-templates seems to be utilized for the eigentemplate learning.

However, two requirements should be satisfied for successful eigentemplate learning. At first, a given image sequence should be carefully selected for effective learning. While the selection had better be accomplished autonomously by the tracking system, the selection is accomplished by a human operator in this paper. That is, a finite length of image sequence is assumed to be provided by a human operator. The initial position of a target object is also provided in the first image of the sequence.

The next problem concerns stability of the adaptive tracking. Since the adaptive tracking aims at eigentemplate learning in this paper, the accuracy requirement is more severe than when tracking itself is the objective. For the learning purpose, the two parameters $\alpha$ and $\sigma_w$ of the WSL model was tuned to $\alpha = 0.1$ and $\sigma_w = 100$ by preliminary experiments. We have also confirmed that the tracking stability is not so sensitive around the optimum values.

## 3.3 Reduction of Learning Set

Once a sequence of S-templates is extracted stably, the next problem is how to select the leaning set from the sequence. Appropriate selection is very useful for the efficient eigentemplate construction.

Let us use an input image instead of S-template for the learning set since S-templates are often deformed by the adaptation and the deformation is inappropriate for the eigentemplate learning. While PCA can be directly applied to all the input images, sufficient reduction of the learning set is required for efficient computation of PCA. The reduction of learning set is also effective for dimensionality reduction of the eigentemplate.

For discussing how to select the learning set from an image sequence, some notations should be defined as follows. Let $\mathbf{Y}_t$ and $\tilde{\Phi} = [\Phi \ \bar{\mathbf{x}}]$ denote an input image and the eigentemplate at time $t$, respectively. Let $Q_i(i = 1, 2, 3, 4)$ denote part indicator matrices which correspond to four quadrant regions of the whole template, respectively, and $Q_0 = Q_1 + Q_2 + Q_3 + Q_4 = I$ holds. Then, for

$i = 0, 1, 2, 3, 4$, a projection of (partial) image $Q_i\mathbf{Y}_t$ onto the (homogeneous) eigentemplate, $\tilde{\Phi}$, is represented as

$$\mathbf{Y}'_{ti} = \tilde{\Phi}(Q_i\tilde{\Phi})^+\mathbf{Y}_t. \tag{7}$$

Thus, a correlation, $C_i(\mathbf{Y}_t, \mathbf{Y}'_{ti})$, is calculated between $Q_i\mathbf{Y}_t$ and $Q_i\mathbf{Y}'_{ti}$, where $C_i(\mathbf{X}, \mathbf{Y})$ is defined as

$$C_i(\mathbf{X}, \mathbf{Y}) = \frac{(\mathbf{X} - \mathbf{1}^\top\mathbf{X}\mathbf{1}/tr(Q_i))^\top Q_i(\mathbf{Y} - \mathbf{1}^\top\mathbf{Y}\mathbf{1}/tr(Q_i))}{||Q_i\mathbf{X} - \mathbf{1}^\top Q_i\mathbf{X}\mathbf{1}/tr(Q_i)||\,||Q_i\mathbf{Y} - \mathbf{1}^\top Q_i\mathbf{Y}\mathbf{1}/tr(Q_i)||}. \tag{8}$$

In our current implementation, when all the following conditions are satisfied, the current input image $\mathbf{Y}_t$ is appended to the learning set. Otherwise, the current image is not appended to the learning set.

$$\begin{aligned}
(i) &\quad C_0(\mathbf{Y}_t, \mathbf{Y}'_{t0}) > 0.5, \\
(ii) &\quad 0.60 < \min_{i=1,2,3,4} C_i(\mathbf{Y}_t, \mathbf{Y}'_{ti}) < 0.68, \\
(iii) &\quad C_0(\mathbf{Y}_t, \mathbf{Y}_0) > 0
\end{aligned} \tag{9}$$

In the three requirements, the first requirement checks whether the full image is considerably correlated to the current eigentemplate. The second requirement checks whether the least correlated quadrant region is not very different but moderately different from the current eigentemplate. The third requirement is utilized for excluding drastic change of the template. In the three requirements, four parameters were roughly tuned over an example set in the current implementation. Although the parameters might be tuned carefully for some problems, the rough tuning works well for our experiments.

### 3.4  Eigentemplate Construction

When the learning set is updated, an eigentemplate is reconstructed by PCA. That is, the mean vector $\overline{\mathbf{x}}$ and a matrix $\Phi$ is composed from most significant $m$ eigenvectors, where $m$ is determined as the smallest number of vectors whose cumulative contribution rate gets over 95%.

## 4  Experimental Results in Face Tracking

### 4.1  Learning and Test Sequences

Let us conduct the eigentemplate learning on the image sequences of Cascia et al. [8]. In this database, we select 3 sequences for the eigentemplate learning. Let us call them **Jal7**, **Jam7** and **Jal5**, respectively, after the original file names.

Other sequences, named **Jal9**, **Jam5** and **Jal6**, are used for the test of the sparse eigentemplate tracking, where the eigentemplates are constructed from **Jal7**, **Jam7** and **Jal5**, respectively. The three learning sequences have different types of appearance changes; **Jal7** is characterized by illumination changes, **Jam7** is characterized by pose changes, and **Jal5** includes both the illumination and pose changes.

The target person is common in all the image sequences, and all the sequences consist of 199 images, respectively.

**Table 1.** Effect of learning set reduction

| Learning sequence | Selected images (from 199 images) | dimensionality ($m$) selected | dimensionality ($m$) all images |
|---|---|---|---|
| Jal7 | 5 | 3 | 7 |
| Jam7 | 6 | 5 | 65 |
| Jal5 | 9 | 5 | 38 |

## 4.2  Comparison

For fair comparison, an initial template of $57 \times 57$ pixel is provided by an human operator for each image sequence. Other parameters are commonly utilized for the three sequences as follows: $tr(P_i) = 16$ and $tr(P) = 64$ for the sparse template matching, respectively, and the two parameters of WSL model are set to $\alpha = 0.1$ and $\sigma_w = 100$.

Table 1 shows the effect of the reduction of the learning set. The proposed image selection method selected only 5, 6 and 9 images for the learning set from **Jal7**, **Jam7** and **Jal5**, respectively.

The learning set reduction resulted in dimensionality reduction as shown in the table, where the third column shows the minimum dimensionality of which the cumulative contribution rate reaches 95 %. The table shows that the eigentemplate is constructed more efficiently from the selected images than when it is constructed from all images.

## 4.3  Illumination Changes

For illumination changes, the proposed method can select only 5 images as shown in Fig. 3(a). The eigentemplate constructed from them is as shown in (b) while the eigentemplate constructed from all 199 images is as shown in (c). Since (b) and (c) look very similar, it is found that the proposed method works well for the illumination changes.

Once the eigentemplate is constructed, it can be utilized for more efficient tracking by the sparse eigentemplate tracker, as shown in Fig. 4. Although the test sequence **Jal9** includes pose changes as well as illumination changes, the sparse eigentracker can track the target very well. In 100 trials of the tracking, the tracking is very stable.

## 4.4  Pose Changes

For pose changes, the proposed method selected 6 images for the learning set as shown in Fig. 5(a). The eigentemplate constructed from them is as shown in (b) while the eigentemplate constructed from all 199 images is as shown in (c). Although the two eigentemplates, (b) and (c), look less similar than those extracted for the illumination changes, the proposed method is still effective enough for the pose changes.

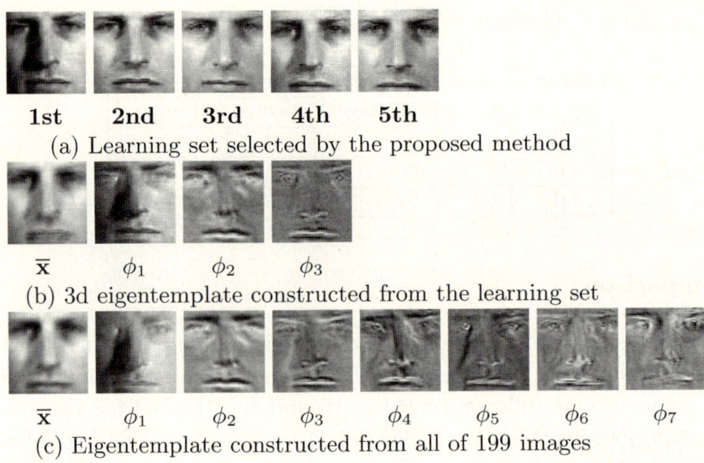



**Fig. 3.** Learning image set and constructed eigentemplates for **Jal7**

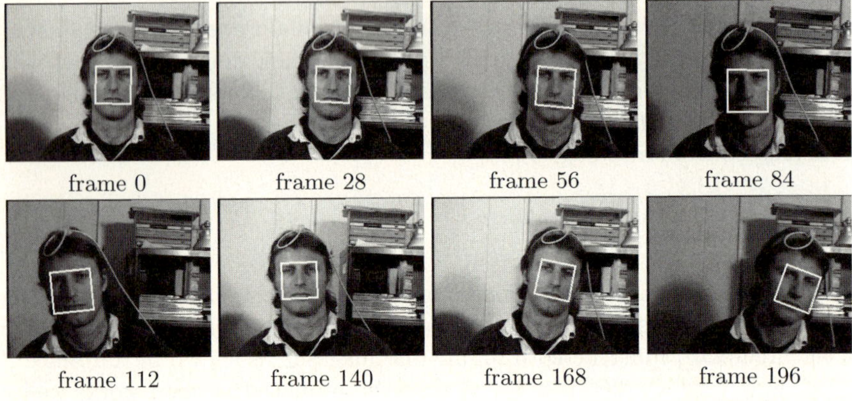



**Fig. 4.** Result of sparse eigentemplate tracking of **Jal9**

Once the eigentemplate is constructed, it can be utilized for sparse eigentemplate tracker, as shown in Fig. 6. Although the test sequence **Jam5** includes different pose changes from the learning sequence, the sparse eigentracker can track the target very well. In 100 trials of the tracking, the tracking is very stable in this case, too.

## 4.5    Illumination and Pose Changes

When the learning sequence includes both the illumination and pose changes, 9 images are selected for the learning set as shown in Fig. 7(a). The eigentemplate constructed from them is as shown in (b) while the eigentemplate constructed from all 199 images is as shown in (c). Although the two eigentemplates, (b) and (c), look less similar than those for **Jal7** and **Jam7**, the proposed method can

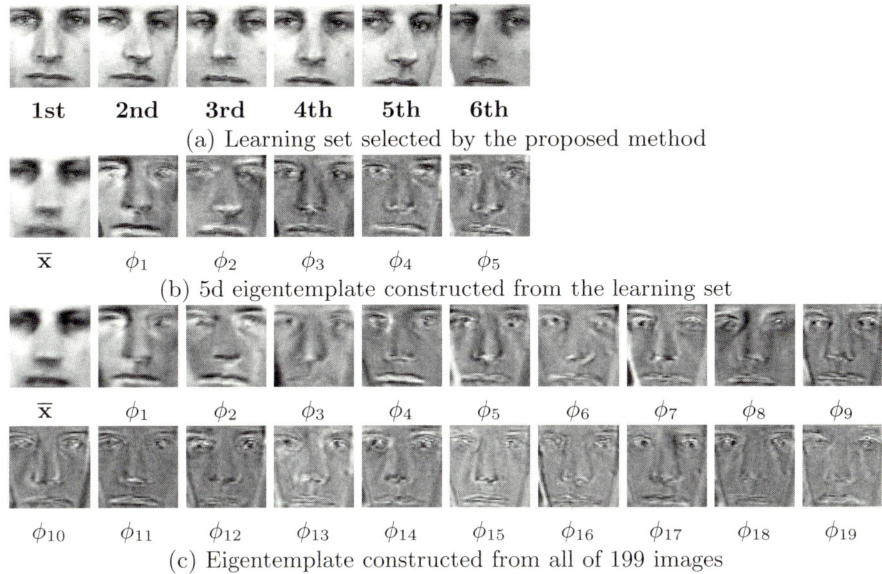



(a) Learning set selected by the proposed method



(b) 5d eigentemplate constructed from the learning set



(c) Eigentemplate constructed from all of 199 images

**Fig. 5.** Learning image set and constructed eigentemplates for **Jam7**

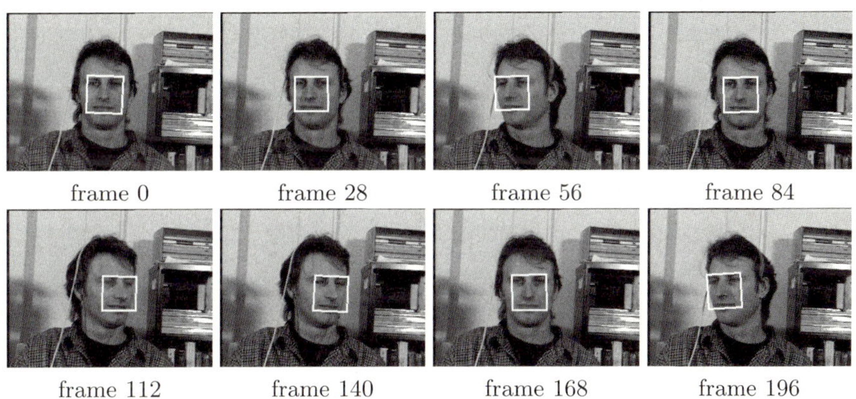



**Fig. 6.** Result of sparse eigentemplate tracking of **Jam5**

construct the eigentemplate. However, the constructed eigentemplate could not work always. Figure 8 shows that the eigentemplate learned from **Jal5** could not work with **Jal6** effectively since the two sequences include different combinations of illumination and pose changes. The eigen-tracking got unstable when a different combination appeared. Whole the combinations of illumination and pose changes could not be covered by the eigentemplate generated by the proposed method. This example shows a current limitation of the proposed method. The stability was checked with changing random number generation in the adaptive tracking in all the three experiments. In the results, the proposed method

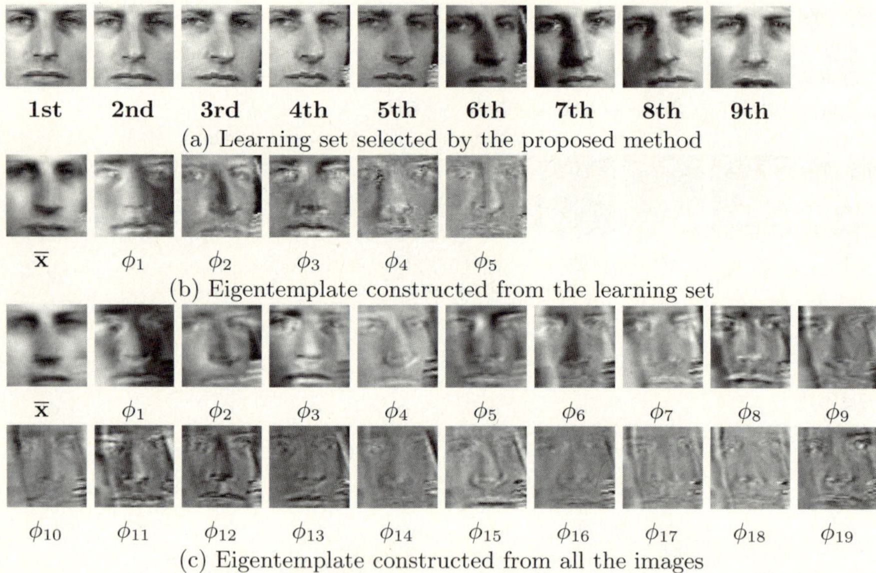

(a) Learning set selected by the proposed method

(b) Eigentemplate constructed from the learning set

(c) Eigentemplate constructed from all the images

**Fig. 7.** Learning image set and constructed eigentemplates for **Jal5**

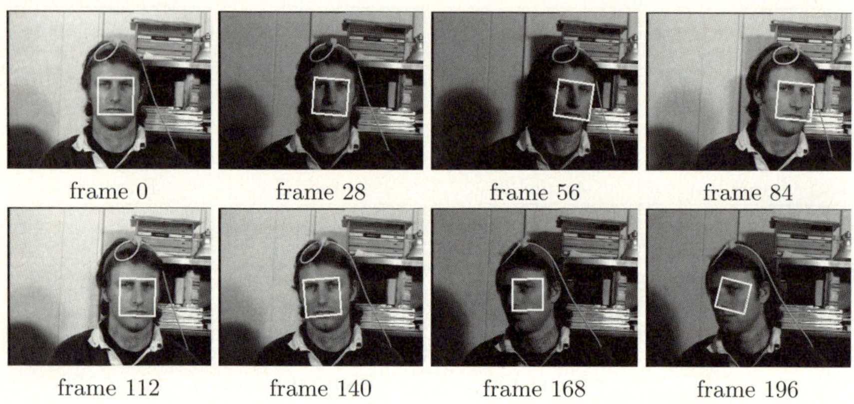

frame 0     frame 28     frame 56     frame 84

frame 112     frame 140     frame 168     frame 196

**Fig. 8.** Result of sparse eigentemplate tracking for **Jal6**

generated the effective eigentemplates very stably for **Jal7** and **Jam7**, respectively. Although the proposed method could still work for **Jal5**, it sometimes selected some redundant images.

## 5   Conclusions

Automatic eigentemplate learning is discussed for the sparse template tracker. In the learning phase, the adaptive tracker adaptively tracks a target for the eigentemplate learning. Once an eigentemplate learning is accomplished, the sparse template tracker can work with the eigentemplate instead of an adaptive template. Since the sparse eigentemplate tracker doesn't require any adaptive tracking, it can work more efficiently and effectively for image sequences in the class of learned appearance changes.

Experimental results show that the proposed method works well for illumination changes and for pose changes, respectively. Although the last example shows a current limitation, it should be noted that **Jal6** can be tracked by the adaptive tracker in frame rate. This fact suggests that parallel and consistent implementation of the adaptive and the eigentemplate trackers may provide a feasible answer for more automatic learning in future.

This work has been supported in part by a Grant-In-Aid for Scientific Research (No.20300067) from the Ministry of Education, Science, Sports, and Culture of Japan.

# References


1. Black, M., Jepson, A.: Eigentracking: Robust matching and tracking of articulated objects using a view-based representation. International Journal of Computer Vision 26(1), 63–84 (1998)
2. Shakunaga, T., Matsubara, Y., Noguchi, K.: Appearance tracker based on sparse eigentemplate. In: Proc. Int'l Conf. on Machine Vision & Applications, pp. 13–17 (2005)
3. Shakunaga, T., Noguchi, K.: Robust tracking of appearance by sparse template adaptation. In: Proc. 8th IASTED Int'l Conf. on Signal and Image Processing, pp. 85–90 (2006)
4. Jepson, A.D., Fleet, D.J., El-Maraghi, T.F.: Robust online appearance models for visual tracking. IEEE Trans. Pattern Analysis and Machine Intelligence 25(10), 1296–1311 (2003)
5. Moghaddam, B., Pentland, A.: Probabilistic visual learning for object representation. IEEE Trans. Pattern Analysis and Machine Intelligence 19(7), 696–710 (1997)
6. Hager, G.D., Belhumeur, P.N.: Efficient region tracking with parametric models of geometry and illumination. IEEE Trans. Pattern Analysis and Machine Intelligence 20(10), 1025–1039 (1998)
7. Isard, M., Blake, A.: Condensation – conditional density propagation for visual tracking. International Journal of Computer Vision 29(1), 5–28 (1998)
8. Cascia, M.L., Sclaroff, S., Athitsos, V.: Fast,reliable head tracking under varying illumination: An approach based on robust registration of texture-mapped 3d models. IEEE Trans. Pattern Analysis and Machine Intelligence 22(4), 322–336 (2000)

# Tracking without Background Model for Time-of-Flight Cameras

Luca Bianchi, Riccardo Gatti, Luca Lombardi, and Paolo Lombardi

University of Pavia, Dept. of Computer Engineering and Systems Science,
Via Ferrata 1, 27100 Pavia Italy
{luca.bianchi,riccardo.gatti,luca.lombardi}@unipv.it,
paolo.lombardi.vision@gmail.com

**Abstract.** Time-of-flight (TOF) cameras are relatively new sensors that provide a 3D measurement of a scene. By means of the distance signal, objects can be separated from the background on the basis of their distance from the sensor. For virtual studios applications, this feature can represent a revolution as virtual videos can be produced without a studio. When TOF cameras become available to the consumer market, everybody may come to be a virtual studio director. We study real-time fast algorithms to enable unprofessional virtual studio applications by TOF cameras. In this paper we present our approach to foreground segmentation, based on smart-seeded region growing and Kalman tracking. With respect to other published work, this method allows for working with a non-stationary camera and with multiple actors or moving objects in the foreground providing high accuracy for real-time computation.

**Keywords:** Time-of-flight cameras, region growing, tracking, virtual studio.

## 1   Introduction

Virtual studios allow blending real elements, usually actors or anchormen, with a computer graphics world and virtual objects in videos and TV shows. Actors play in indoor environments where walls and floors are shaded in uniform color, sometimes called blue or green rooms. Lighting plays a crucial role to achieve realistic blending: it must be carefully arranged so that shadows along wall-floor corners disappear and those projected by actors and objects are neat and clear. The background color is then subtracted, with a technique called chroma-keying [1], and substituted with virtual background. Special equipment, either electromechanical or optical, tracks the position of the recording camera and its movement is reproduced in the virtual world, so as to coordinate the shifts of actors and background along the image plane. Interaction between actors and virtual objects can be programmed, but remains often limited to occlusion management unless the actor's movement are somehow tracked [2].

Even though of less complicated realization than a real studio of comparable visual impact, virtual studios require a high expertise and ad-hoc recording conditions. Apart from the mentioned accuracy in lighting, unnatural acting in a blue room, unnatural acoustics and echo, time-consuming video processing in post-production, background

T. Wada, F. Huang, and S. Lin (Eds.): PSIVT 2009, LNCS 5414, pp. 726–737, 2009.

color contamination on foreground objects, and two-plane only segmentation are known limitations of this technique. Furthermore, many of these techniques are of difficult access for unprofessional users, such as content producers of modern Web 2.0 social networks.

The appearance of time-of-flight (TOF) scanner-less sensors in recent years seems to be about to bring a revolution in this field (see [3] for a very recent introduction, just come to our attention). When compared to laser-scanners or active illumination stereo devices, TOF cameras are able to deliver an entire depth image at video rate without employing any moving mechanical part. As costs rapidly descend, TOF cameras will become available also to local TV networks and eventually to semi-professional users like bloggers. Other than for video production, gaming and net-conferencing are obvious applications. Figure 1 shows two examples of TOF cameras currently on the market.

Fig. 1. Two time-of-flight cameras on the market: SR3000 by MESA (left) and Canesta (right)

TOF cameras allow substituting chroma-keying with depth keying [4]. Objects are separated from the background on the basis of their distance from the sensor, independently of the background appearance and clutter. Virtuality can be added at any plane in the image and interactivity with virtual 3D objects can be fully experienced.

However, TOF cameras are far from being traditional imaging devices augmented with a third dimension. TOF distance measurements are subject to specific characteristics and noise, and algorithms developed for traditional computer vision need to be tested and recalibrated on those characteristics. For the unprofessional virtual studio application, the first step is to segment foreground objects (actors) by means of depth data. In this application, two aspects of prominent importance are i) the quality of boundaries of extracted regions and ii) a low computational load so as to operate real-time.

Our complete system consists of a segmentation module complemented by tracking of image objects, a mapping module that remaps and refines TOF cluster boundaries to a TV-standard camera, and visual/TOF-based egomotion compensation.

In this paper we present our work on foreground segmentation for TOF images and on tracking of segmented clusters. For segmentation, we propose an approach that exploits the characteristic intensity signal produced by TOF sensors to drive segmentation of the distance signal. It proceeds by region growing from signal-dependent, smartly placed seeds. Our method does not use the classical background modeling typical of traditional cameras, and so it is less sensible to camera movements. For tracking, we experiment a typical Kalman tracker with very good results. Issues of data association for tracking and occlusion management will be discussed. Herein we do not discuss camera egomotion compensation, hence tracking results pertain only the stationary-camera configuration.

Section 2 presents an analysis of TOF camera signals and of some previous works related to people detection. Section 3 describes our foreground segmentation. Section 4 presents the Kalman tracker. Section 5 illustrates the experimental results, and Section 6 concludes the paper.

## 2   Problem Analysis

Time-of-flight cameras are active imaging sensors using laser light to measure distances from sensor to scene objects. TOF cameras are based either on pulsed light or modulated light. The first approach consists in producing a coherent wavefront and employing high frequency photon gating to measure the return time-of-flight. The ZCam by 3DV uses this technology [4]. This approach allows a relatively long range (10m) with a minimum range of 1m and a resolution of 0.5cm.

The second approach consists in a modulated carrier typically in the range of 20-50MHz and time-of-flight is measured by phase delay detection. The phase signal is limited by phase non-ambiguity so that 20MHz constrains the maximum range to 7.5m. An example of this implementation is SR3000 distributed by MESA [5].

### 2.1   Characteristics of TOF Signals

We employ the SR3000 in our project (Figure 1 left). SR3000 is a modulated-light camera. It produces two images per frame; one contains distance information and the other contains the amount of reflected light. Figure 2 shows a typical frame taken by the SR3000 device. The left image is the distance signal, the right image is the intensity signal, both at 16bit.

Active sources emit in the near infrared (around 850nm) so that no interference is perceivable in the visible spectrum. Interaction with other illumination sources varies in impact: neons and low-consumption lamps do not interact, whereas sunlight and traditional bulbs emit in the same bandwidth and can introduce high level of noise in distance measurements. In Figure 2 this effect is apparent in the central region of the distance signal (in dark blue), corresponding to a window in the real scene. Incoming sunlight makes those pixels appear at a range shorter than the person occluding the window, which is not the case in reality.

Opposite to what is reported in some papers for other cameras, the SR3000 does not provide a grey-level image, not at least in the classical sense. The intensity image depicts the intensity of light reflected by objects in the near infrared. Almost all of this intensity comes from the internal light sources. Even in image regions corresponding to windows the intensity signal is very low (see Figure 2, right). Thus, the TOF intensity image cannot be processed as if it were a traditional color-related intensity image. Instead, it may be used for other purposes, as we will discuss later on.

**Fig. 2.** A typical frame: distance image (left) and intensity image (right). Blue = low.

Typically, objects near the sensor get more illuminated, while faraway objects receive less light. Hence peaks in the intensity image tend to correspond to nearby objects. However, surface roughness and color alter the reflectance characteristics of objects also in the near infrared, and so intensity on dark objects is lower than on white objects standing at the same distance. For what concerns persons, this effect is particularly remarkable obviously on dark garments and – less obviously – on dark hair, curly hair, beard and moustaches.

The distance signal can be highly noisy. Causes of noise include scattering and multi-path reflection [6]. In our experiments, SNR for faraway pixels that receive little laser illumination is of the order of 3-6dB, and always less than 10dB. Conversely, in well illuminated image regions the SNR for range measurements reaches over 8dB, up to 15-18dB. As a consequence, the intensity of a pixel is correlated with noise in that pixel.

## 2.2 Related Works on Segmentation

Most TOF-based systems for foreground segmentation up to date have focused on two techniques, namely distance thresholds and background subtraction. The first method sets a "cube of interest" by defining minimum and maximum distances for foreground [4]. All objects falling within the cube are labeled as foreground. If the minimum threshold is set to 0 (camera sensor), the second threshold can be dynamically set after the first object. This latter approach works fine if the actor is the first object in the scene and if it is fairly isolated from its surroundings in 3D, however it detects only one actor at a time. Threshold techniques suffer particularly from noisy range measurements because they lack an inherent noise rejection criterion. Furthermore, additional processing is needed because selected pixels are to be clustered into objects.

The second method is inherited by motion detection techniques used in computer vision, notably in video surveillance applications. It consists in creating a model of the object-free scene by means of statistical analysis. The background model is most often pixel-based and only rarely region-based. Then, frame by frame, newly acquired images are compared to the model and pixels which differ significantly are marked as foreground. This technique provides aggregated foreground clusters of objects in motion, and so it is well suited for virtual studio application. Also, it includes a noise rejection criterion implicitly in its statistical nature. To our knowledge, it is the most popular approach implemented to date for TOF cameras [6], [7], [8], [9], sometimes using both depth and intensity values to build the model.

However, background subtraction requires a stationary camera and it suffers from other known problems like ghosts appearing when background objects leave the scene, absorption of immobile persons, bootstrapping requiring a few frames, insufficient modeling in presence of high frequency changes in background pixels (e.g. waving trees), and so on.

# 3   Foreground Segmentation

For virtual studios, working with a non-stationary camera gives wider choice to the creative inventiveness of directors. Thus we have established to study segmentation without background subtraction.

Foreground objects may potentially have any shape (human actors, animal actors, robots, etc), thus segmentation and tracking must be shape-free. Also, in our application the quality of boundaries is important. The earlier aspect excludes silhouette/rigid template tracking, detection based on PCA shape representation, etc. Considering both the previous aspects, we have elected to experiment with seeded region growing techniques. Our tests on simple thresholding techniques and histogram-based methods confirmed that such methods do not cope well with noise or blurring at boundaries because they neglect spatial connections of pixels. With respect to edge detection (e.g. Canny), region growing guarantees closed regions with clear boundaries and do not require further processing to connect/disconnect spurious edges.

Region growing is based on aggregation of pixels displaying similar characteristics. The process starts from some pixels called seeds that initialize the reference for region building. A similarity measure decides if a new pixel is absorbed if a feature associated with it is close enough to the reference [10]. Advantages are: i) no need to know in advance the number of clusters, ii) no constraint on cluster shape, iii) some resistance to noise.

By smart planting of seeds we manage to segment foreground objects with very little processing. Each foreground pixel is visited only once and background pixels are never visited, save for pixels along borders of foreground clusters. To achieve this, we carefully designed the growing strategy and the seed-planting strategy.

## 3.1   Growing Strategy

From what observed in Section 2.1, we may infer that distance segmentation has relevant reliability only when restricted to highly illuminated objects. In our experiments this condition is verified for objects close to the TOF camera, approximately up to 3-4m away.

Distance data on well illuminated objects (or persons) are homogeneous or smoothly changing, thus region growing on distance data brings correct results. Conversely, growing on the intensity map can be unreliable because its variations are sensible and uncorrelated with object distinctions. For example, folds of clothes in Figure 2 (right) reflect light at very different shades.

Given these considerations, we opt for growing solely on the distance map D. After experimenting with centroid region growing [10], DBSCAN [11] and other approaches, we have obtained satisfying results with a customized similarity measure. A similarity S between a cluster pixel x and a neighboring pixel y is defined as:

$$S(x, y) = |\mu_x - D_y| \qquad (1)$$

In (1), $D_y$ is the distance value of pixel y and $\mu_x$ is a local parameter related to the mean distance value around x, to be explained soon. The lower is S, the more similar the pixels. In our experiments we use 4-connected neighborhoods of radius 1, i.e. the 4 pixels north west south east.

Defining with $I_y$ the intensity value of pixel y and given two constant thresholds $\theta$ and $\lambda$, a pixel x belonging to a cluster C absorbs a neighbor y according to the following predicate:

$$\{ x \in C, S(x, y) < \theta, I_y > \lambda \} \rightarrow \{ y \in C \} \qquad (2)$$

When a seed is planted, $\mu_x$ in (1) is initialized to $D_x$. When a neighbor y of seed x is absorbed, $\mu_y$ is computed as follows:

$$\mu_y = (\mu_x \cdot n + D_y) / (n + 1) \qquad (3)$$

Parameter n is called *neighborhood size*, and actually it works as a smoothing or learning factor of the local mean of D. The rationale for the name is that, if pixel y has exactly n neighbors in the cluster, and if the mean of D in these neighbors is exactly $\mu_x$, then $\mu_y$ becomes the mean of D when y is added to the cluster.

Note that relation S in (1) is asymmetric, i.e. $S(y, x) \neq S(x, y)$, and also note that $\mu_y$ depends upon the pixel x that absorbed y. Hence the direction of the growing front has a significant influence on final segmentation. To minimize growing errors, we sort all similarities S of pixels that are along the cluster boundary and absorb the pixels with lower S first. This strategy propagates the $\mu$ of pixels closest to the father's D value. See Figure 3.

When compared to methods that use global region statistics, like e.g. in centroid region growing, our approach is faster: $\mu_y$ depends only on the history of pixel absorptions until y is first reached by a growing front, and not from later steps. Thus, as soon as a pixel y is reached by the cluster boundary, it can be tested for absorption.

Conversely, in centroid region growing, the addition of a pixel alters the global cluster mean and so the order in which boundary pixels are tested is significant.

The locality of growing used in our approach aggregates regions with more pronounced variations with respect to methods using global statistics, because it produces transitive closures of similarity. Figure 4 compares the performance of our cumulative approach with centroid region growing [10].


## 3.2  Seed Planting

As noted in Sections 2.1 and 3.1, high intensity pixels usually belong to close objects as well as objects with reliable distance values. It makes sense to plant seeds on these pixels.

An intensity threshold based on the Otsu method selects a first set of seeds. Also, we add seeds taken from the clusters being tracked by the Kalman filter (see Section 4).

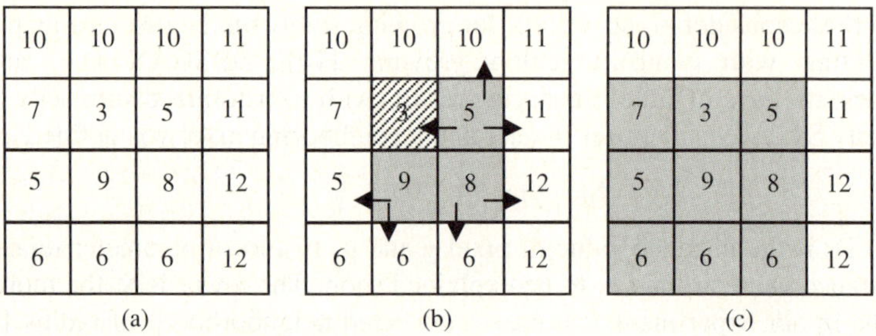

**Fig. 3.** Starting from the pixel value distribution in (a), suppose we have seeded the grey region in (b). The arrows show which new pixels are tested by each of the cluster pixels. Specifically the shaded pixel with value 3 is tested by the cluster pixel with value 5 because of the sorted-similarity rule. The tester propagates its $\mu$. The final growing with $\theta = 3$ is shown in (c).

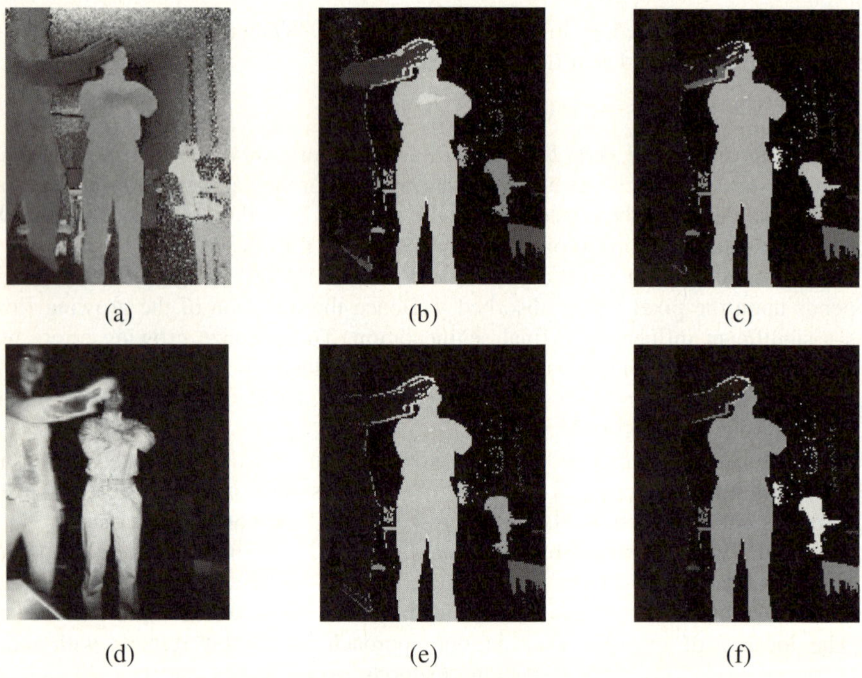

**Fig. 4.** Given the distance image (a) and intensity image (d), compare the results of centroid region growing (first line) with our method (second line), for $\theta = 7$ (b), (d), and $\theta = 11$ (c), (f). In (e) the extended arm is correctly taken with $\theta = 7$, whereas $\theta = 11$ in (c) is not yet enough. In these pictures we have seeded all regions with sufficient intensity, to show what happens without smart seeding.

Starting from the pixel with highest intensity, we grow a region and then set cluster pixels to $I < \lambda$ so as to exclude them from successive growths. We proceed this way for all seeds in order of descending intensity.

This strategy brings a few advantages. First, it automatically eliminates low-intensity, noisy regions without any global visit of the intensity image. Yet a low-intensity region may still be absorbed if it is connected through coherent distance data to a high intensity seed. Second, the seeds bear the most reliable distance measurements and so the growing is less subject to errors. Third, it selects foreground objects near the sensor to initialize new tracking. If on one side this feature imposes that actors enter the scene in a range 0-4m from the sensor, on the other side it guarantees that their regions have a sufficient SNR to be tracked. The overall effect is that reliability increases and the necessity of scene repetitions is possibly reduced. As a fourth advantage, there is no limitation to the number of persons being tracked or to the number of new clusters being initialized per frame.

A known drawback is that partial occlusions of a person may make a minor segment of its cluster disappear if the intensity on that part is too low to generate seeds itself. For example, consider a person waving an arm in front of a second one. If the arm separates a low-intensity part of the second person's cluster from its main body, none of our two sources of seeds will trigger region growing on that part. We intend to address this problem by seeding the entire cluster, which is planned as future work.

## 4 Tracking

We have experimented with a traditional Kalman filter to track the clusters. The Kalman state has six dimensions referring to centroid coordinates, i.e. $(x\ y\ z\ v_x\ v_y\ v_z)$, which respectively represents x,y,z position of centroid and velocity vector coordinates – all expressed in image coordinates, as the SR3000 provides output data already organized in cubic Cartesian coordinates. The transition matrix is a simple increment matrix (4).

After segmenting an image by region growing, we compare the detected clusters and those being tracked. The association between measured clusters and Kalman clusters is by minimum distance between their centroids.

We have observed that assigning a low value to the similarity threshold $\theta$ avoids the necessity of splitting without introducing irrecoverable segmentation errors. Also, single-step merging without splitting speeds up computation. We compute a Gaussian representation of Kalman cluster at time t-1 and use its updated centroid position at time t to delineate the image region where the cluster should appear in frame t. Then every unassigned cluster i is tested for merging with assigned clusters j as in (5).

$$
\begin{pmatrix}
1 & 0 & 0 & 1 & 0 & 0 \\
0 & 1 & 0 & 0 & 1 & 0 \\
0 & 0 & 1 & 0 & 0 & 1 \\
0 & 0 & 0 & 1 & 0 & 0 \\
0 & 0 & 0 & 0 & 1 & 0 \\
0 & 0 & 0 & 0 & 0 & 1
\end{pmatrix}
\tag{4}
$$

$$
\{\, d_M((x_i\ y_i\ z_i), (x_j\ y_j\ z_j)) < \delta \,\} \rightarrow \{\, \text{merge } C_i \text{ into } C_j \,\}
\tag{5}
$$

We use a Mahalanobis distance $d_M$ between centroids $(x_i\ y_i\ z_i)$ and $(x_j\ y_j\ z_j)$, where the covariance matrix is given by fitting a multivariate Gaussian over cluster j. If, after merging, a Kalman tracker i has not been assigned to any cluster yet, it is tested for occlusion by any of the assigned clusters j:

$$\{\ d_M((x_i\ y_i),(x_j\ y_j)) < \delta',\ z_i > z_j\ \} \rightarrow \{\ C_i \text{ is occluded by } C_j\ \} \qquad (6)$$

Clusters that are still unassigned after test (6) are used to initialize new Kalman trackers. If a Kalman tracker is not occluded according to (6), it is tested for leaving the field of view, and if so deleted.

In (5) and (6), $\delta$ and $\delta'$ are two thresholds manually set so as to optimize the tracking performance on training sequences.

The information stored in Kalman trackers is actively used during the segmentation step to plant seeds. Kalman trackers go through the 'predict step' of Kalman filtering. We seed in all pixels inside an area proportional to the x and y covariance of the multivariate Gaussian fitted at time t-1 around the predicted centroid at time t.

## 5   Experimental Results

Our system currently uses a SR3000 TOF camera. Images are 144x172 pixels and the aperture is 47.5x39.6 degrees. We have observed an acquisition rate between 18 and 20 fps when the camera is in pure acquisition mode, without any further elaboration. When our algorithms are run on a 2.0 GHz Intel Xeon PC, the rate still remains high, at 15 fps. A higher speed can be envisioned in the future by optimizing the code for real-time operations. To assess the performance of our region growing approach, we have manually labeled 30 static images portraying very different conditions: one actor alone, two well-separated actors, two actors close to each other, three actors, etc. The rationale for using static images is that we assess the pure performance without the help of Kalman trackers. We use smart seeding on pixels with an intensity value surpassing the threshold computed by the Otsu method. As our approach depends upon two parameters, i.e. the similarity threshold $\theta$ and the intensity threshold $\lambda$, we compute the performance on the same image set for various values of $\{\theta, \lambda\}$. Specifically, we vary $\theta$ in the range $[2, 12]*2^{\wedge}8$ and lambda in the range $[0, 2]*2^{\wedge}8$, with step $0.5*2^{\wedge}8$ and $0.1*2^{\wedge}8$ respectively. In this way, we obtain sufficient points to trace a ROC-like curve for the segmentation algorithm.

The output of the segmentation algorithm is compared with real objects data and some standard quality measures are computed. We use a comparison method similar to the one presented in [12], given a certain image, its objects O, and the algorithm output detected objects A, let us define TP (true positive) as the number of pixels in A that are also in O; FP (false positive) as the number of pixels in A that are not in O, FN (false negative) as the number of pixels in O that are not in A. Now we can define the following quality measures:

- *completeness* = **TP** / (**TP** + **FN**); the completeness is the percentage of the reference data that is explained by the extracted data. The optimum value is 1.
- *correctness* = **TP** / (**TP** + **FP**); the correctness represents the percentage of correctly extracted road data. The optimum value is 1
- *quality* = **TP** / (**TP** + **FP** + **FN**); the. quality is a more general measure accounting both completeness and correctness. The optimum value is 1.

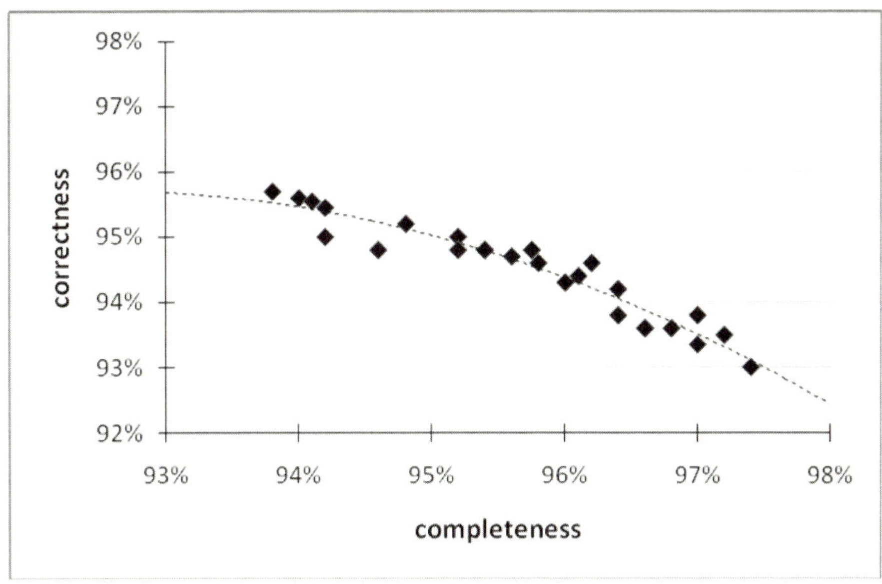


**Fig. 4.** Correctness/completeness plot. Every point represents a run of the algorithm with a different parameter set Every run is computed throughout the entire sequence.

These measures are intended to compare the results of different algorithms, rather than to evaluate our solution in an absolute way. We compute their values on individual frames, and thcn we take the averages throughout the test sequences. Fig. 4 presents the correctness/completeness plot (which is directly related to the precision / recall plot) of the experimental data. Specifically, the graph can be interpreted as the scatterplot of the upper part of the typical precision / recall plot. It shows that the trade-off between average completeness and average correctness of results almost reaches 95% along the diagonal - a fairly good value. A quantitative measure of goodness for this value is provided by quality. The average quality factor computed over the sequences we used, varies between 90% and 85%. Given the parameter values used in the experiments the scatterplot of Fig, 4 suggests that the algorithm is robust enough to parameter  changes. This consideration comes from the fact that neither completeness nor correctness ever dropped below 80%. As a consequence of such robustness, we cannot draw the whole completeness / correctness plot in the 0% - 100% interval with the experiments performed so far. The presented results are of course biased on the test sequences. A direct comparison with algorithms by other authors would be possible if tests on the same sequences are provided. Tracking accuracy has been measured in test sequences. The Kalman Filter provides good results only if detected clusters to Kalman clusters association is correctly achieved. This means that tacking results are good if only an object is on the stage and tend to get worse if we consider two or more objects moving nearly. Issues concerned to tracking ad cluster association will be addressed in future works.

# 6  Conclusions

Envisioning the development of low-cost time-of-flight cameras and their diffusion in the near future, we are studying the application of TOF cameras to unprofessional virtual video production. In this paper, we have presented an approach to foreground segmentation and tracking of objects that addresses two aspects specific to virtual studio applications: a non-stationary camera and multiple foreground objects.

Our approach exploits the intrinsic characteristic of the intensity and distance signals generated by modulated-light TOF to seed a region growing algorithm. Kalman tracking supports persistent seeding of identified objects. We use a region growing based on cumulative differences rather than on global statistics. Cumulative differences are smoothed by a parameter called neighborhood size, which, for high values, makes the approach similar to a global-statistics approach.

The proposed region growing method has a few advantages: i) pixels are visited only once, ii) only pixels with sufficient SNR are visited, and iii) grows in smoothly changing regions even with a low threshold, which reduces the need of merging operations. As with all region growing approaches, its main drawbacks reside in the sensitivity to the similarity threshold $\theta$ and in the sensitivity to seeds. Future work includes the mapping of the segmentation results onto color images coming from webcams and TV-standard cameras, as well as egomotion detection and compensation in TOF sensor cameras.

## Acknowledgements

This work has been partially supported by FIRB project: "Infrastrutture e piattaforme real-time per ambienti di ricerca e e-learning collaborativo".

## References


1. Shimoda, S., Hayashi, M., Kantsugu, Y.: New chroma-key imaging technique. IEEE Trans. On Broadcasting 35(4), 110–234 (1989)
2. Gibbs, S., Arapis, C., Breiteneder, C., Lalioti, V., Mostafawy, S., Speier, J.: Virtual Studios: an overview. IEEE Multimedia 5(1), 18–35 (1998)
3. Kolb, A., Barth, E., Koch, R.: ToF-Sensors: New Dimensions for Realism and Interactivity. In: CVPR 2008 Workshop On Time of Flight Camera based Computer Vision (TOF-CV) (accessed on July 23rd), http://www-video.eecs.berkeley.edu/Proceedings/CVPR_WS2008/data/workshops16.htm
4. Gvili, R., Kaplan, A., Ofek, E., Yahav, G.: Depth Key. In: SPIE Electronic Imaging 2003 Conference, Santa Clara, CA (2003)
5. Oggier, T., Lehmann, M., Kaufmann, R., Schweizer, M., Richter, M., Metzler, P., Lang, G., Lustenberger, F., Blanc, N.: An all-solid-state optical range camera for 3D real-time imaging with sub-centimeter depth resolution (SwissRanger). In: Mazuray, L., Rogers, P.J., Wartmann, R. (eds.) Optical Design and Engineering, Proceedings of the SPIE, vol. 5249, pp. 534–545 (2004)
6. Felder, J., Weiss, S.: Time-of-Flight Imaging for Industrial Applications, Master Thesis, ETH Swiss Federal Institute of Technology Zurich (2007)

7. Witzner, D., Mads, H., Hansen, S., Kirschmeyer, M., Larsen, R., Silvestre, D.: Cluster Tracking with Time-of-Flight Cameras. In: CVPR 2008 Workshop On Time of Flight Camera based Computer Vision (TOF-CV), `http://www-video.eecs.berkeley.edu/Proceedings/CVPR_WS2008/data/workshops16.htm`

8. Guðmundsson, S.A., Larsen, R., Aanæs, H., Pardàs, M., Casas, J.R.: TOF Imaging in Smart Room Environments towards Improved People Tracking. In: CVPR 2008 Workshop On Time of Flight Camera based Computer Vision (accessed 23/7/2008), `http://www-video.eecs.berkeley.edu/Proceedings/CVPR_WS2008/workshops16.htm`

9. Bevilacqua, A., Di Stefano, L., Azzari, P.: People tracking using a time-of-flight depth sensor. In: IEEE Int. Conference on Video and Signal Based Surveillance, p. 89 (2006)

10. Adams, R., Bischof, L.: Seeded Region Growing. IEEE Transactions on Pattern Analysis and Machine Intelligence 16(6), 641–647 (1994)

11. Ester, M., Kriegel, H.P., Sander, J., Xu, X.: A density-based algorithm for discovering clusters in large spatial databases with noise, pp. 226–231. AAAI Press, Menlo Park (1996)

# X-Ray Image Classification and Retrieval Using Ensemble Combination of Visual Descriptors


JeongHee Shim, KiHee Park, ByoungChul Ko, and JaeYeal Nam

Dept of Computer Engineering, Keimyung University
1000 Shindangdong, Dalseo-Gu, Daegu, 704-701, Korea
{sjh0229,khp5500,niceko,jynam}@kmu.ac.kr



**Abstract.** In this paper, we propose a novel algorithm for the efficient classification and retrieval of medical images, especially X-ray images. Since medical images have bright foreground against dark background, we extract MPEG-7 visual descriptor from only salient parts of foreground. For color descriptor, Color Structure Descriptor (H-CSD) is extracted from salient points, which are detected by Harris corner detector. For texture descriptor, Edge Histogram Descriptor (EHD) is extracted from global and local parts of images. Then extracted feature vector is applied to multi-class Support Vector Machine (SVM) to give membership scores for each image. From the membership scores of H-CSD and EHD, two membership scores are combined as one ensemble feature and it is used for similarity matching of our retrieval system, MISS (Medical Information Searching System). The experimental results using CLEF-Med2007 images show that our system can indeed improve retrieval performance compared to other global property-based or other classification-based retrieval methods.

**Keywords:** H-CSD, EHD, SVM, ensemble vector, MISS.


## 1 Introduction

With the increase the digitalized medical images, various medical assistance systems, such as the Picture Archiving Communication System (PACS), have also been introduced that integrate information communication, computer networking, database management, and a user interface [1]. Therefore, the classification and retrieval of the medical images are important issue and the related studies are going on. The medical images have different meaning according to observer's viewpoints and consist of some interesting foreground regions and meaningless background. Therefore different classification and retrieval methods are required for medical images. Traditionally, medical images have been classified by experts and retrieved using just text. Yet, traditional classification and retrieval can produce irrecoverable mismatches according to the subjectivity and viewpoint of the experts. Furthermore, this kind of retrieval is costly and time consuming. Thus, to overcome these problems, various types of classification and Retrieval methods [2-4] have been proposed over the last few decades.


T. Wada, F. Huang, and S. Lin (Eds.): PSIVT 2009, LNCS 5414, pp. 738–747, 2009.

Mojsilovic et al. [2] proposed a method for semantic description, classification and retrieval of medical images. In this method, they used a semantic set of visual features, their relevance and organization for capturing the semantics of different image modalities. The Greenspan [3] represented images as some blobs with the Gaussian Mixture Model and estimated the matching scores between images using the KL (Kullback-Leibler). The Bhattacharya et al. [4] extracted the feature vectors using a color layer descriptor and a histogram descriptor of MPEG-7 standard descriptors. The extracted feature vectors were applied to SVM and FCM, which used to classify the medical images.

In this paper, we propose a novel algorithm for the classification and retrieval of the medical images. To classify medical images, we propose a Color Structure Descriptor (H-CSD) based on Harris corner detector for color feature and Edge Histogram Descriptor (EHD) for texture feature in the medical images. Then each extracted feature vector is applied to multiclass-SVM to give membership scores to each image. From membership scores of H-CSD and EHD, we combine two vectors into one ensemble vector and apply it to K-NI (K-Nearest Images) for image retrieval. Consequently, we can improve problems of the previous related works and provide the efficient method of the higher performance than the previous researches in classification and retrieval fields.

Rest of this paper is organized as follows: In Section 2, the algorithms for feature extraction using visual descriptors are described. The proposed classification and retrieval for medical image is introduced in Section 3. Section 4 evaluates the accuracy and applicability of the proposed classification method based on experiments, and some final conclusions and areas for future work are presented in Section 5.


## 2   Extraction of the Feature Values Using Visual Descriptors

To efficiently classify a lot of medical images into pre-defined categories, we first extract the feature vectors from images stored in database. In this paper, we use a CSD for color and an EHD for texture defined in MEPG-7 standard, respectively. Especially, CSD is modified to be extracted from only salient foreground regions using Harris corner detector and we named it H-CSD.


### 2.1   Color Structure Descriptor (CSD) Using Harris Corner Detector

Color is one of the most widely used visual features in image retrieval since it is relatively robust to viewing angle, translation and rotation of image. In this paper, we use the Color Structure Descriptor (CSD) to extract color vector because it aims at identifying localized color distributions using a small window. Furthermore it supports not only better the retrieval performance but also ease implementation than other color descriptors. The CSD is a descriptor represents an image by both the color histogram of the image and the local spatial structure of the color [5]. The elements of CSD are decided flexibly its size and the number of sub-sampling by the size of an image.

First, an image is quantized with 128 gray levels because X-ray image has only dark background and bright foreground. Then, image is divided into N x N sub-blocks. The size of sub-block is 8 x 8 pixels because MPEG-7 standard defines the scale of structuring element to be 8 x 8. In this paper, sub-block performs the same function as a structuring element. As we can see from Fig. 1, since our X-ray images contain useless background regions, we need to remove it before generating CS Histogram. Therefore we first detect Harris corner [6] from quantized image and only select sub-blocks containing one or more Harris points. The Harris corner detector is a popular point detector due to its strong invariance and stability against variation of viewpoint, illumination direction, scale and noise. From selected sub-blocks, 128-bin CS Histogram is extracted from an image represented in the 128-quantized gray color space. The CSD is a 1-D array of m bit-quantized values.

$$CSD = \bar{h}_s(m), \quad m \in \{1,...,M\} \tag{1}$$

where $M$ is chosen from the set {256, 128, 64, 32} and where $s$ is the scale of the associated structuring element (sub-block). At each position of sub-blocks, the CS Histogram is updated (accumulated) on the basis of the color present within the sub-block. For examples, if the eight gray levels and eight CS Histogram in 8 x 8 sub-block is created, the number of relevant bin increases 1 when the position of the CSD's sub-block on the image is corresponded to the pre-divided CS Histogram. In this way, the feature values of the image are the distribution of the number of the CSD's sub-blocks corresponding to each color histogram by the recorded color histogram. At final step, extracted 128-bin CSD is normalized to the range 0~1 for training of Support Vector Machine.

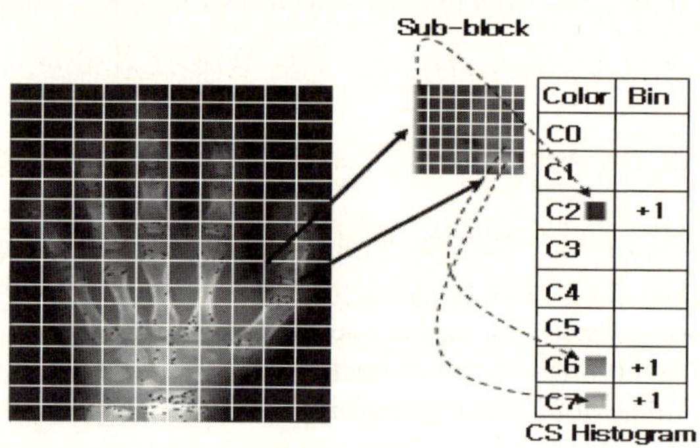


**Fig. 1.** Feature extraction process of H-CSD using Harris corner detector

## 2.2  Edge Histogram Descriptor (EHD)

EHD [7] is a descriptor that can represent the distribution of the regional edges of an image. Specially, dividing the image space into 4x4 non-overlapped sub-images and then each sub-image is further divided into non-overlapping square image blocks as shown in Fig. 2-(a). The local–edge distribution for each sub-image can be represented by a histogram. To generate the histogram, edges in the sub-images are categorized into five types; vertical, horizontal, 45 diagonal, 135 diagonal and non directional edges as shown in Fig. 2-(b). The size of the image block is decided by using equation (2) to divide input images into the same sized sub-images.

$$ x = \sqrt{\frac{width \times height}{desired\ Num\ block}}, \qquad blocksize = \left\lfloor \frac{x}{2} \right\rfloor \times 2 \tag{2} $$

where the *desired Num block* is the whole number of the image blocks in the image. We decided default value as 1100 through experiments. Each of the image-blocks is then classified into one of the five edge categories mentioned above or as a non-edge block. If feature values are extracted by applying each filter, the edge detector with the maximum edge value is then identified. If the edge value is above a given threshold, then the corresponding edge orientation is associated with the image-block. Since there are 16 sub-images, a total of 5x16=80 histogram bins are generated.

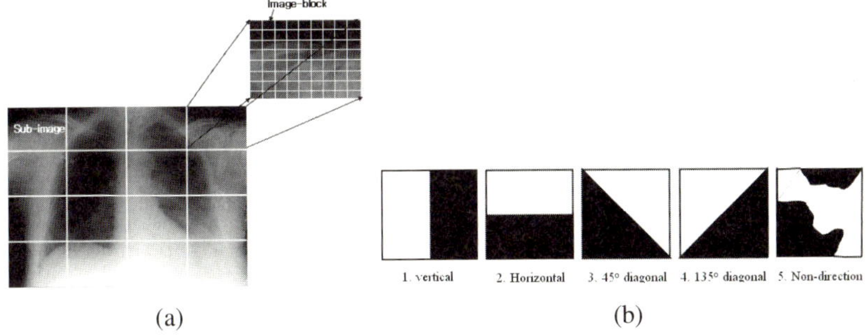


**Fig. 2.** (a) Definition of sub-image and image-blocks (b) five edge types for edge extraction

In classification and retrieval of medical images, especially, X-ray image, edge is the critical feature to improve the accuracy. Therefore we also extract five global edge histogram has 5 bins. Similarly, for semi-global edge histograms, we group 13 different subsets and generate edge distributions for five different edge types [7]. Finally, we use totally 150 edge histogram feature values by combining 80 regional edge histograms, 5 global edge histograms, and 65 (5 x 13) semi-local edge histograms.

## 3   Classification and Retrieval for Medical Images

After feature extraction, images are classified as one of predefined classes. To do this, we use multi-class Support Vector Machines (SVM) and two feature vector, H-CSE and EHD. By using training results, each image has membership scores on all 20 categories. These membership scores are estimated from H-CSD and EHD respectively and combined as one feature vector, *ensemble*. This ensemble feature vector is finally used for our content-based medical image retrieval system, MISS (Medical Information Searching System).

### 3.1  SVM Classification Using H-CSD and EHD Feature Vectors

An SVM can provide a good generalization performance for pattern classification problems without incorporating problem domain knowledge. Furthermore, an SVM does not require heuristic feature parameters for determining image classification.

Given training data $(\mathbf{x_1},...,\mathbf{x_N})$ that are vectors in space $\mathbf{x}_i \in \Re^d$ and their labels $(\mathbf{y_1},...,\mathbf{y_N})$ where $\mathbf{y}_i \in (+1,-1)^N$, the general form of the binary linear classification function is

$$g(\mathbf{x}) = \mathbf{w} \cdot \mathbf{x} + b \tag{3}$$

which corresponds to a separating hyperplane

$$\mathbf{w} \cdot \mathbf{x} + b = \mathbf{0} \tag{4}$$

where $\mathbf{x}$ is an input vector, $\mathbf{w}$ is a weight vector, and $b$ is a bias. The main goal of SVM classifier is to find the parameter w and b for the optimal hyperplane that correctly separates the largest fraction of data points while maximizing the distance of either class from the hyperplane.

The SVM classification function is defined by [8]:

$$f(x) = sign(\sum_{i=1}^{l} v_i \cdot k(\mathbf{x},\mathbf{x}_i) + b) \tag{5}$$

where $k(\cdot,\cdot)$ is a kernel function, $vi$ is weights for outputs of each kernel, $b$ is a bias term and the sign of $f(x)$ determine the class membership of $x$ such as $+1$ class and $-1$ class. The decision function $f(x)$ from the hyperplane determined by the support vectors can be used to measure how much an image belonging to the one category (+1) is different from the other categories (-1). Intuitively, the farther away a point is from the hyperplane, i.e. a larger positive $f(x)$, the more reliable the classification result.

For a linear SVM, the kernel function is just a simple dot product in the input space. However, in a non-linear SVM, the kernel function effectively projects the samples to a feature space of higher dimension $\mathbf{F}$ and constructs a hyperplane in $\mathbf{F}$ [8]. The SVM training algorithm then estimates a hyperplane that separates the data in $\mathbf{F}$ into two classes using the largest margin.

In this paper, we use multi-class SVM with RBF (Radial-Basis Function) Kernel instead of binary SVM because our x-ray images should be classified 20 classes according to regions of body. There are several commonly used methods, such as one-against-all, one-against-one, and directed acyclic graph [9]. Here we adapt the one-against-all method, which constructs $n$ SVM classifiers where $n$ is the number of classes. The $i$-$th$ SVM is trained using all of the examples in the $i$-$th$ class with positive labels (+1) and all others with negative labels (-1).

To perform the training, 1,754 images were randomly selected from 20 image categories as shown in Table 1. We used X-Ray images of IRMA (Image Retrieval in Medical Applications) which were used for Image CLEF med2007 [10].

In this paper, since we use two feature vectors respectively for performing training, $2n$ SVM classifiers are generated.

**Table 1.** Training classes and images per one class for SVM

| Category | Body Part | #of training data | Category | Body Part | #of training data |
|---|---|---|---|---|---|
| 1 | Breast | 100 | 11 | Finger | 100 |
| 2 | Pelvis | 100 | 12 | Wrist | 100 |
| 3 | Front head | 100 | 13 | Kneepan | 100 |
| 4 | Side head | 100 | 14 | Shoulder | 100 |
| 5 | Throat | 100 | 15 | Vertebrae | 100 |
| 6 | Knee | 100 | 16 | Front breast | 100 |
| 7 | Toe | 48 | 17 | Side breast | 100 |
| 8 | Front ankle | 100 | 18 | Fleshy | 47 |
| 9 | Side ankle | 100 | 19 | Elbow | 21 |
| 10 | Hand | 100 | 20 | Foot | 38 |

## 3.2 Ensemble Feature Vector Combination and Similarity Matching

After SVM training, all database images having feature vectors of H-CSD and EHD are fed to the corresponding SVM classifiers and category membership scores are obtained at the output. In Figure 7, extracted feature vectors, $F_c$ and $F_E$ ( $F_c$: feature vector of H-CSD, $F_E$: feature vector of EHD) of one image are fed to 2n SVM(2x20) classifiers respectively. Then SVM classifiers output 20 membership scores, $\vec{S}_c$ and $\vec{S}_E$, for each feature vector. Finally, the ensemble vector, $\vec{E} = [s_{c1}, s_{c2}, ... s_{c20}, s_{e1}, s_{e2}, ..., s_{e20}]$ is obtained by appending all category membership scores.

Originally, the test example $x$ is fed into these $i$-th SVM classifiers and the one with the highest output score ($dj$) is selected as the final class.

$$d_j(x) = \max_{i=1,...,n} d_i(x) \tag{6}$$

where $di$ is the output score about $i$-th class for input $x$ images. However, we combine output scores of 2n SVM classifiers as one ensemble vector. This ensemble vector is fed to final K-Nearest Neighbor cluster to predict the most likely top $k$ categories for the given image. To retrieve most similar top k images from top k categories, the final distance is estimated by (7) and the top nearest images are displayed in ascending order of the final distance.

$$S(q,t) = \sum_{i=1}^{2n} | s_i^q - s_i^t | \tag{7}$$

where $q$ and $t$ denote query and target image.

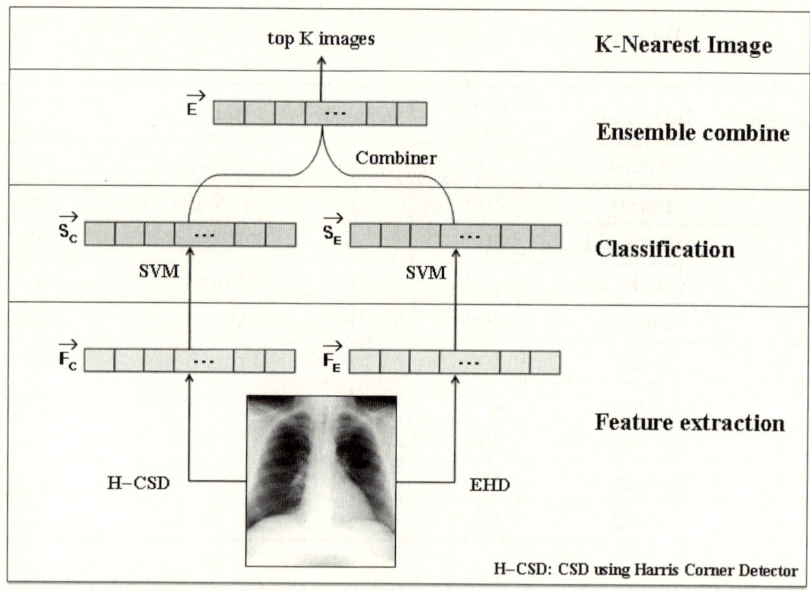


**Fig. 3.** Flow diagram of the classification and retrieval process

# 4   Experimental Results

The proposed system was developed using Visual C++ 6.0 language for off-line training and test system is developed based on ASP.NET 2.0 using C# language. For the test, we also use 1,000 images (20 categories) in IRMA (Image Retrieval in Medical Applications) [10]. Table 2 shows 20 categories for test and the number of test images for experiment. You can demonstrate our MISS system at our web-site, http://cvpr.kmu.ac.kr

**Table 2.** The titles of twenty categories and number of images for Test

| Category | Body Part | #of test data | Category | Body Part | #of test data |
|---|---|---|---|---|---|
| 1 | Breast | 60 | 11 | Finger | 50 |
| 2 | Pelvis | 60 | 12 | Wrist | 50 |
| 3 | Front head | 50 | 13 | Kneepan | 60 |
| 4 | Side head | 50 | 14 | Shoulder | 50 |
| 5 | Throat | 50 | 15 | Vertebrae | 60 |
| 6 | Knee | 50 | 16 | Front breast | 60 |
| 7 | Toe | 45 | 17 | Side breast | 50 |
| 8 | Front ankle | 50 | 18 | Fleshy | 40 |
| 9 | Side ankle | 50 | 19 | Elbow | 20 |
| 10 | Hand | 60 | 20 | Foot | 35 |

To complete a query, the user pushes the 'default' button and selects one retrieval method among eight methods. After that, the user clicks any image that he/she wants to retrieve and the top 20 nearest neighbors are returned. Figure 4 shows the retrieval interface of MISS.

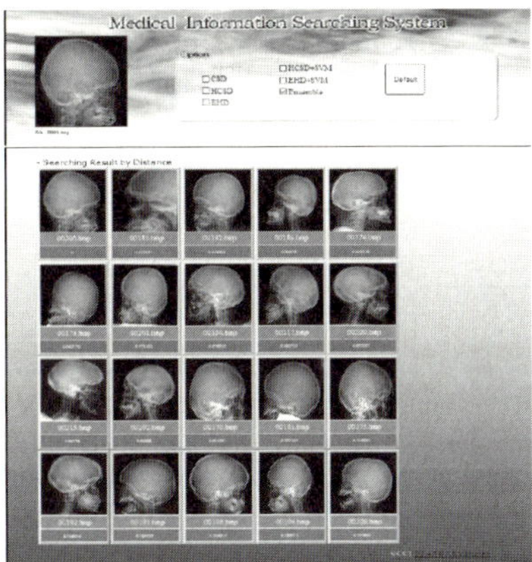

**Fig. 4.** Retrieval interface of MISS

To validate the effectiveness of our approach, we first compare the retrieval precision of our system with three methods which using only individual feature vector with SVM and similarity matching method.

The test is performed on 20 categories and 5 query images from each category. In all experiments, performance is measured using average retrieval precision. As shown in Table 3, the overall performance of our approach outperforms the other three methods as by percentages of 42.2%, 69.8%, 77.3%, and 96.5%. Especially, the retrieval performance of the proposed feature H-CSD showed a 27.6% improvement over the original CSD.

**Table 3.** The experimental results using descriptors independently

|  | Top = 5 | Top = 10 | Top = 20 | Average Precision |
|---|---|---|---|---|
| **CSD+SVM** | 0.52 | 0.426 | 0.32 | 0.422 |
| **H-CSD+SVM** | 0.744 | 0.693 | 0.658 | 0.698 |
| **EHD+SVM** | 0.81 | 0.77 | 0.7415 | 0.773 |
| **Ensemble** | 0.976 | 0.968 | 0.952 | 0.965 |

We also compared the retrieval performance with Bhattacharya et al. [4]'s algorithm. The Bhattacharya et al. [4] combined a color layer descriptor and EHD of MPEG-7 standard descriptors as one feature vector and applied it to SVM and FCM (Fuzzy C-mean Clustering). After that, the output scores of SVM and membership scores of FCM are linearly combined for classifing and retrieval the medical images. As we can see from Table 4, Bhattacharya's method shows the retrieval performance of an average 58.8%. In contrast, our proposed method showed a 37.7% improved retrieval performance. Figure 5 shows retrieval results of the MISS system.

**Table 4.** The experimental results using combination descripotrs

|  | Top = 5 | Top = 10 | Top = 20 | Average Precision |
|---|---|---|---|---|
| **Bhattacharya's method [SVM+FCM]** | 0.63 | 0.605 | 0.53 | 0.588 |
| **Ensemble vector** | 0.976 | 0.968 | 0.952 | 0.965 |

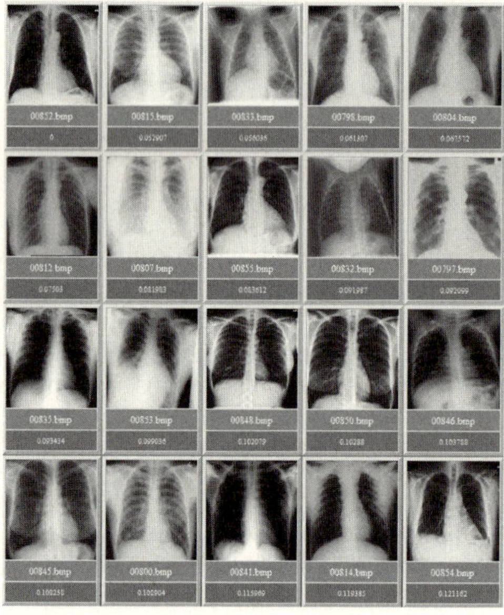

**Fig. 5.** Retrieval results using the proposed method about 'Front breast' category

## 5  Conclusion

In this paper, we proposed a novel algorithm for the efficient classification and retrieval of medical images, especially X-ray images. To classify medical images, we first extracted proposed Color Structure Descriptor (H-CSD) based on Harris corner detector for color feature. For texture descriptor, Edge Histogram Descriptor (EHD) was extracted from global and local parts of images. Then extracted feature vector was applied to multi-class Support Vector Machine (SVM) to give membership scores for each image. From the membership scores of H-CSD and EHD, ensemble one feature vector was generated and it was used for similarity matching of our retrieval system, MISS (Medical Information Searching System).The experimental results using CLEF-Med2007 images showed that our system could indeed improve retrieval performance compared to other global property-based or other classification-based retrieval methods.

In future works, improved algorithms for category classification and automatic annotation based on image classification are needed. Especially, we need to develop new feature to improve the classification performance on similar categories such as throat against vertebrae and finger against toe.

**Acknowledgments.** This work was supported by grant RTI04-01-01 from the Regional Technology Innovation Program of the Korean Ministry of Commerce, Industry, and Energy (MOCIE).

# References


1. Qi, H., Snyder, W.E.: Content-based image retrieval in PACS. Journal of Digital Imaging 2, 81–83 (1999)
2. Mojsilovc, A., Gomes, J.: Semantic based categorization, browsing and retrieval in medical image databases. Int.Conf. on Image Processing 3, 145–148 (2002)
3. Greenspan, H.: Medical Image Categorization and Retrieval for PACS Using the GMM-KL Framework. IEEE Transactions on Information Technology in BioMedicine 11, 190–202 (2007)
4. Bhattacharya, P., Rahman, M.M.: Image Representation and Retrieval Using Support Vector Machine and Fuzzy C-means Clustering Based Semantical Spaces. In: International Conference on Pattern Recognition, vol. 2, pp. 1162–1168 (2006)
5. Manjunath, B.S., Salembier, P., Sikora, T.: Introduction to MPEG-7. John Willy & Sons, LTD. (2002)
6. Harris, C., Stephens, M.J.: A combined corner and edge detector. In: Alvey Vision Conference, pp. 147–152 (1998)
7. Won, C.S., Park, D.K.: Efficient Use of MPEG-7 Edge Histogram Descriptor. ETRI Journal 24, 23–30 (2002)
8. Vapnik, V.: The Nature of Statistical Learning Theory. Springer, Heidelberg (1999)
9. Chen, S.-C., Murphy, R.F.: A graphical model approach to automated classification of protein subcellular location patterns in multi-cell images. BMC Bioinformatics 7, 1–13 (2006)
10. Deselaers, T.: The CLEF 2005 Automatic Medical Image Annotation Task. International Journal of Computer Vision 74, 55–58 (2007)

# Video-Based Motion Capturing for Skeleton-Based 3D Models

Liang-Yu Shih, Bing-Yu Chen, and Ja-Ling Wu

National Taiwan University
xdd@cmlab.csie.ntu.edu.tw, robin@ntu.edu.tw, wjl@csie.ntu.edu.tw

**Abstract.** In this paper, a semi-automatic method to capture motion data from a single-camera video is proposed. The input video is first segmented and analyzed, and a 3D character model with skeleton rigged is used as a reference model. Then, the reference model is modified to fit the subject's contour in the starting frame, and the body's and limbs' contours of the subject are also specified by the user. Our system then extracts the motion from the video by estimating the reference model's poses automatically in each video frame forwardly. Finally, the user can help to refine the result through a friendly user interface.

**Keywords:** Video-based motion capture, user-aid, reference model.

## 1  Introduction

With the booming popularity of 3D animations and video games, how to create or obtain the character motion becomes more and more important than before. Motion capture is a good solution for obtaining fantastic motions. Traditional motion capture methods require cooperation from the capturing subject, such as wearing markers, moving in a reduced space, and sometimes even needing to stay on a treadmill, and then the subject's motions are captured through the markers. However, it is impossible to ask for animals' cooperation like these. Therefore, some markerless methods are proposed, named as video-based motion capture, but as addressed in computer vision, automatic reconstruction of subject motion from a single-camera video is still very difficult.

In this paper, we develop a video-based system that extracts animal motions from an unrestricted monocular video with user's aid. In order to break the limitation of pure automatic method, a reference 3D model and user's intervention are used in the system. The concept is to estimate the reference model's pose in each video frame according to the difference between the reference model's and animal's contours, and the error and ambiguity correction is relied on the user's intervention. Beside these, our system uses an automatic method to estimate camera parameters and relationship between the camera and scene, and integrates some interactive techniques in order to provide the user a friendly and efficient interface. Fig. 1 shows the overview of our system, which uses a single-camera

T. Wada, F. Huang, and S. Lin (Eds.): PSIVT 2009, LNCS 5414, pp. 748–758, 2009.

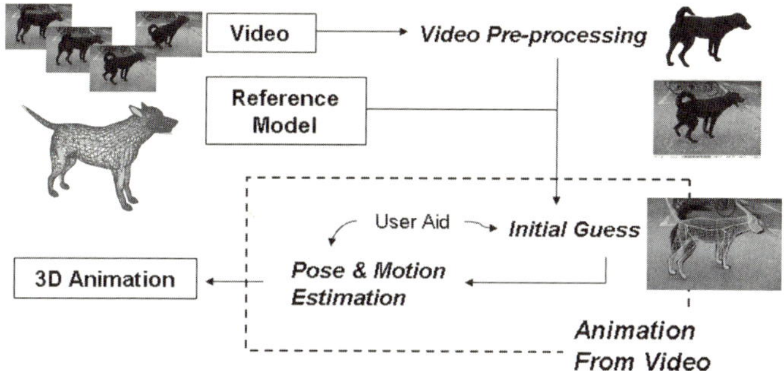


**Fig. 1.** Overview of our system

video and a reference 3D model as the input and extracts the motion for the model from the video.

## 2   Related Work

Video-based motion capture is a popular and difficult topic in computer vision. By relying on prior knowledge about human motion, Howe *et al.* [1] reconstructed the motion of human and resolve the ambiguity. On the other hand, Sidenbladh *et al.* [2] used a probabilistic method tracking 3D articulated human figures. Both of them are widely adopted for automatic character motion reconstruction from a single-camera video. However, Gleicher and Ferrier [3] showed that these techniques for the automatic video processing fail to provide reliable 3D information, such as stable joint angles over time. They conclude that using these methods is current not feasible. Recently, capturing motion from multi-view videos [4] [5] performs good results, even for reconstructing the character's mesh details like clothes. However, it requires complicated equipments and environment for making the multi-view videos, which is expensive and time consuming.

To reconstruct animal motion from a video, Wilhelms and Van Gelder [6] presented a method to extract the horse motion from a video by using deformable contour - active snake. The features on the snake contour anchor are used to specify the bones. When the features change in frames, the bones are pulled into the right positions. However, since active contour is very sensitive to noise and parameter tuning is also difficult, it usually needs user's interaction to adjust the contours that are failing to track. Examples-based approaches have recently been recognized as good alternatives to traditional shape modeling and animation methods. The basic idea is to interpolate between a given set of 3D poses or motion examples. Favreau *et al.* [7] apply Principal Component Analysis (PCA) to automatically select key-images from a live video. Then, the artist is asked to provide 3D pose examples of the key-images and the system interpolates the examples with Radial Basis Function (RBF). Finally, they generate high quality cyclic motions of animals from the video.

## 3   Video Pre-processing

### 3.1   Segmentation

In order to obtain character motion from a video, it is needed to cut out the contour of the character in the video. In our system, we provide an intuitive method - GrabCut [8] to help the user to do this. Since the contour of the target animal only lightly changes between two consecutive frames, we use the GrabCut's result of the previous frame as the initial guess of current frame's segmentation. With this modification, the user can cut out the contours easily and efficiently from the video.

### 3.2   Camera Calibration

Pollefeys *et al.* [9] provided a structure and motion analysis method to automatically reconstruct a sparse set of 3D scene points from a video. It also decides the camera parameters which describe the relationship between the camera and scene. In our system, we use this method by using Voodoo Camera Tracker[1] to obtain the camera parameters and estimates the projection matrix of each frame.

## 4   The Reference Model

To extract the animal motion from the video, a 3D model is used as the reference. Besides the mesh information, the reference model also provides the following information:

ASF File - This file defines a skeleton in terms of the model's shape, hierarchy, and properties of its joints and bones. The file format is used by the Acclaim Motion Capture System.
WGT File - This file defines how the skeleton affects the skin. Each vertex is influenced by several joints, and the total influence weights are 1.

There are two constraints for the skeleton although they are not recorded in the ASF File.

1. Limited Rotation - Some bones cannot be rotated such as pelvis and sacral.
2. Symmetric Bones - Animals have symmetric components, such as right foreleg is symmetric with the left. As a result, scaling one bone will have the same effect on the other symmetric bone.

## 5   Motion Extraction from a Video

Our approach automatically estimates the reference model's pose to fit the subject's contour in each frame. Wilhelms and Van Gelder [6] mentioned that when

---

[1] http://www.digilab.uni-hannover.de/

motion is not parallel to the image plane, extracting 3D positions at the joints is an extremely under-constrained problem. In this paper, we allow the subject to be at an angle to the image plane, instead of only limited to a parallel plane. However, the subject's motion is required to move along the subject plane, i.e. the $x - y$ plane of the subject's coordinate. The motion reconstruction process is as follow:

1. As a preliminary step, the user is asked to adjust the reference model to fit the subject in the video, which can be done interactively by choosing a best frame that can illustrate several parts of the subject.
2. The system estimates the pose of the reference model automatically in each frame forwardly.
3. The user can tune the estimated poses in an arbitrary frame, and the system will propagate the correction forwardly and backwardly.

### 5.1   Initial Fitting

By rotating and scaling the bones under the constraints mentioned in Sec. 4, the reference model is modified for the initial fitting. Because the target animals have different shapes and sizes, in order to reduce the differences between the target animal and the reference model, the user can adjust the reference model by scaling the components proportionately. Fig. 2 (d) indicates that the dog model's hind legs are modified to fit the target animal shown in Fig. 2 (b). A hint for the fitting is to make the model's contour lightly smaller than the subject's contour in the frame. Fig. 2 (c) shows the initial fitting of the reference model in Fig. 2 (a) to the reference frame shown in Fig. 2 (b).

**Scene Estimation.** Since our input video is a free-move single-camera video, we cannot simply put the reference model onto the image plane by using orthogonal projection. Instead, we must reconstruct the 3D virtual scene to simulate the real scene and put the reference model into it. The virtual scene is reconstructed by the result mentioned in Sec. 3.2. The user is asked to modify the subject's coordinate to align the ground and subject's orientation in the real scene. Fig. 3 (b) shows the result of the scene estimation process. The grey plane is subject's $x - z$ plane aligned with the ground in the virtual scene, and the camera is set at the origin in the first frame.

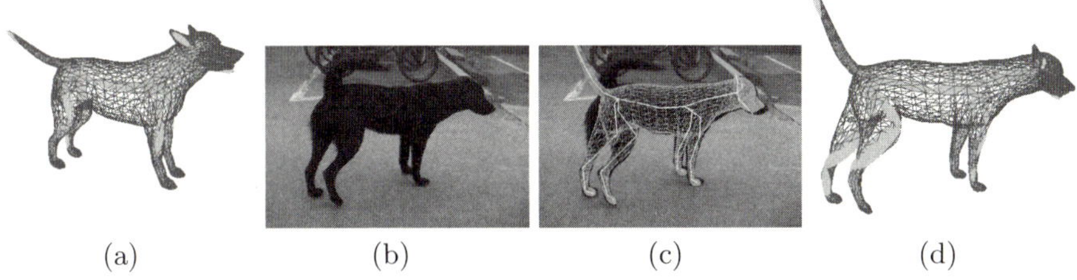

(a)         (b)         (c)         (d)

**Fig. 2.** Initial fitting. (a) The original reference model with skeleton. (b) The reference frame used for initial fitting. (c) The reference model is modified to fit the target animal in the reference frame (b). (d) The reference model after the initial fitting process.

(a)                              (b)

**Fig. 3.** Scene estimation. (a) 3D scene features project onto the image plane. (b) The reference model in the reconstructed virtual scene.

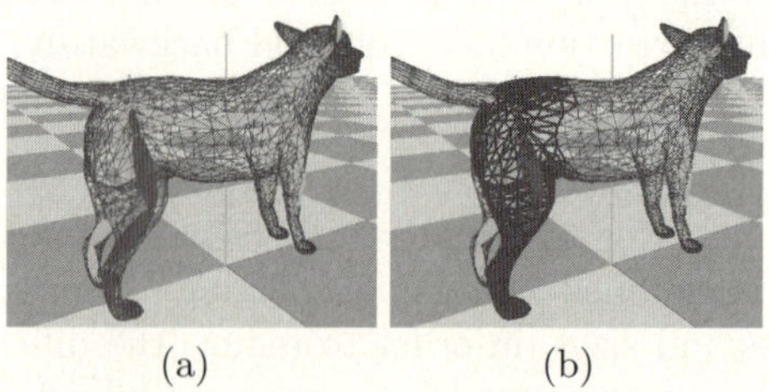

(a)                         (b)

**Fig. 4.** Component assignment. (a) The user specifies the red bones for right hind leg. (b) The purple triangles are influenced by the selected bones.

## 5.2   Pose Estimation

General animals have 7 components - head, torso, left and right forelegs, left and right hind-legs, and tail. Hence, the user is asked to specify the bones in each component of the reference model (Fig. 4 (a)). We define our bone as a joint pair $B = (j_1, j_2)$, which $j_1$ is $j_2$'s parent. After component specification, we need to find the edges $e = (v_1, v_2)$ which mainly influenced by each component's bones. With the weighting information in the WGT File described in Sec. 4, we can generate a map of edges and bones. A vertex $v$ is mainly influenced by the joint which has the maximum weighting, so that we can find a joint pair $(j_1, j_2)$ which mainly influence an edge. Since an edge often mainly influenced by a joint $(j_1 = j_2)$, we find the second large weight with a threshold $(w_i > 0.1)$ and put the higher hierarchy in $j_1$. Then, we can find the involved edges of each component from the map.

With the projection matrix obtained in Sec. 3.2 and the component specification, our system projects the involved edges of different components of the reference model onto the image plane, then identifies the contour points of each component. Fig. 5 (a) shows the right hind-leg's bones (green lines) specified by the user and the projected contour (blue strokes) on the image plane. Although we have the subject's contour in each frame, we still need to specify each component's contour as the reference in the pose estimation process. Agrawala *et al.* [10] presented an interactive contour tracking method, but it cannot be used when occlusion occurs. Hence, the user is asked to simply assign the subject's

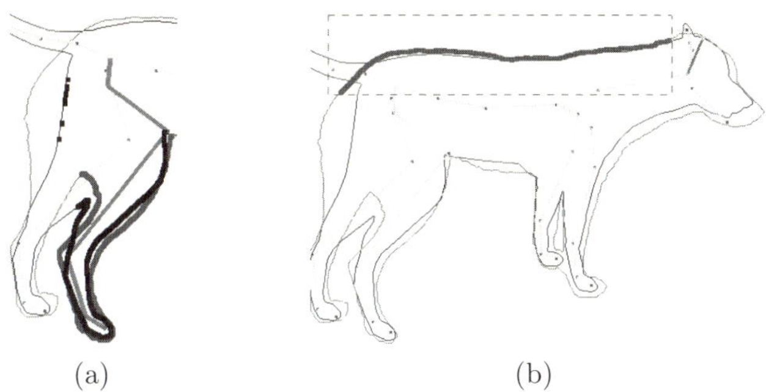

(a)                                    (b)

**Fig. 5.** (a) A partial projected frame, the model's contour overlaps the subject's one. (b) A square selection mechanism.

contour of different components in each frame via a square selection mechanism (Fig. 5 (b)).

After the pre-processing is done, the pose estimation is performed automatically by modifying the reference model while referring the information in the previous frame to fit the subject's contour in current frame. The pose estimation contains two processes - limbs rotation and body translation.

**Component Rotation Estimation.** Each bone $B$ in each component has two error items $E = \{e, e_d\}$. To record the difference between the subject's contour of this component and the model's contour which bone $B$ involved, bone $B$ forms a line on the image plane, and we denote the error on the right (positive) side of the line as $E_p$ and the left (negative) side as $E_n$.

Fig. 6 (a) shows an example about how we calculate the error $E$. Assume the model's contour $C$ is influenced by the bone $B$. Then, a point $c \in C$ can be projected onto $\overline{j_1 j_2}$ at point $o$ to form a line $L$ which is pedicular to $B$, and $L$ intersects the subject's contour $S$ at point $s$. Hence, $E_p$ is calculated by all $c$ lie

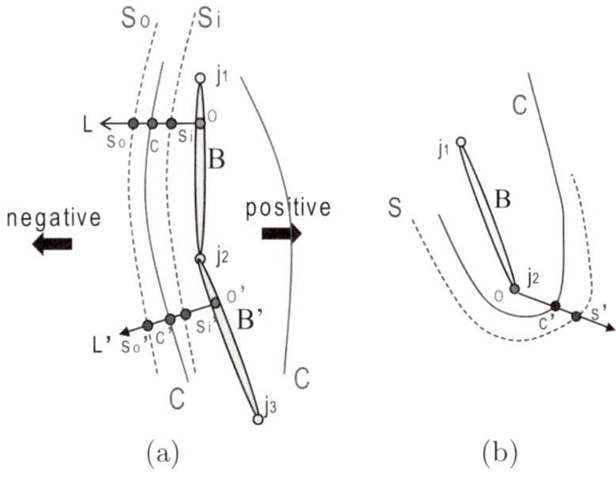


(a)                                    (b)

**Fig. 6.** Calculation of error data $E$

on the right side of $B$ with Eq. (1) and $E_n$ is calculated in the same way with all $c$ lie on the left side of $B$.

$$e = \frac{1}{n} \sum_{1}^{n} (\|\overline{so}\| - \|\overline{co}\|)$$
$$e_d = \frac{1}{n} \sum_{1}^{n} |(\|\overline{so}\| - \|\overline{co}\|)| \tag{1}$$

The model's contour of $B$ sometimes cannot be projected on line $\overline{j_1 j_2}$, like $c'$ in Fig. 6 (b). Hence, we try to project it onto $B$'s child bone $B'$ first (Fig. 6 (a)). If it still cannot be projected, we choose $j_1$ or $j_2$ as $o$ determined by smaller distance to $c'$ (Fig. 6 (b)).

Due to the occlusion or user's input, there are few or even no intersect point at the subject's contour of some components. Hence, we treat their $E$ as invalid. Algorithm 1 shows our method to estimate the component rotation, the system automatically rotates the bones by steps in hierarchy order until no rotation occurs. The goal of our algorithm is to minimize $D(E_p)$ and $D(E_n)$ calculated by Eq. (2) of each bone. Our system sets the weighting variable $w = 2$. After estimation, the difference of the contours between the model and the subject is similar to the that in the previous frame.

---

**Algorithm 1.** Component Rotation Algorithm

---

**Require:** Bones sort by hierarchy from high to low
 1: **repeat**
 2:     **for** $i = 1$ **to** $n$ **do**
 3:         **repeat**
 4:             choose valid $E$ between $E_p$ and $E_n$ as reduce goal
 5:             determine rotate direction to reduce $D(E)$
 6:             rotate $B_i$ with one *step* parallel to subject's $x - y$ plane
 7:             recompute error data $E_p$ and $E_n$
 8:         **until** reduction fails or *total_rotate* > *max_rotate*
 9:     **end for**
10: **until** no rotation occurs in all bones

---

$$D(E) = (d_1, d_2) = \|E_{frame} - E_{frame-1}\| = w^k (|e - e'|, |e_d - e_d'|),$$

where $(e, e_d) \in E_{frame}$, $(e', e_d') \in E_{frame-1}$, and $k = 1$ if $ee' < 0$ else $k = 0$.

$$\tag{2}$$

To rotate a bone, the system chooses the valid error data between $E_p$ and $E_n$ which has smaller distance $\|e_d - |e|\|$ of $E$ first. Then, the system determines the rotation direction by Algorithm 2, and the direction will be opposite when $E = E_n$. The bone is rotated by one step at a time, and then the reduction failure and total rotation steps are checked. The rotation will be stopped if the reduction failure occurs or total rotation steps are larger than a threshold. The reduction fails when $D(E)$ is larger than the previous step or both $E_p$ and $E_n$ are invalid.

**Algorithm 2.** Rotation Direction Determination Algorithm

1: **if** $E = E_p$ **then**
2:    **if** $e > e'$ **then** {$e'$ is error in previous frame}
3:       direction = positive
4:    **else**
5:       direction = negative
6:    **end if**
7: **end if**

(a)          (b)          (c)          (d)

**Fig. 7.** Translation estimation. (a) The green triangles are specified for the translation estimation. (b) The projection of triangles which are specified for translation estimation. (c) Overlap between the reference model's contour and the subject image (pink region). (d) The model's and subject's contours of the torso component. Notice that there is one side of the subject's contour.

**Translation Estimation.** Only the root joint of the model is translated. We use the region of translation the user specified to estimate the $x$ direction, and estimate the $y$ direction by minimizing $T(E)$ defined in Eq. (3).

$$T(E) = \sum_B (\|D(E_p)\| + \|D(E_n)\|), B \in Torso$$
$$\|D(E)\| = d_1 + d_2 \tag{3}$$

Fig. 7 (a) shows the triangles specified by the bones to estimate the translation of $x$, and Fig. 7 (b) shows the projected region of these triangles. The system translates $x$ to minimize the non-overlay region as shown as the green region of Fig. 7 (c) between the subject image and the projected triangles. The subject's tail often makes occlusion with the torso, so we eliminate the tail in segmentation process mentioned in Sec. 3.1 in order to make a better estimation. In $y$ direction, similar to estimate $x$, the system translates $y$ to minimize $T(E)$ which is the difference of the torso between the current and previous frames. In order to prevent the errors occur by large change of translation or rotation, we modify the reference model by a step at a time. Algorithm 3 shows our method of the pose estimation.

### 5.3   Refinement

The user can specify the amount of frames which the system makes estimation forwardly. There may be some incorrect estimation, and the incorrect result will propagate to the next frame by using our method. Hence, the user can refine the automatic estimated result and propagate the correction backwardly and forwardly. Fig. 8 shows the automatic estimation of the reference model poses in

**Algorithm 3.** Pose Estimation Algorithm

```
1: repeat
2:     translate x with one step to reduce non-overlay region of translation
3:     repeat
4:         translate y with one step and rotate torso to reduce T(E)
5:         rotate all components excluding torso
6:     until T(E) cannot be reduced
7: until non-overlay region of translation cannot be reduced
```

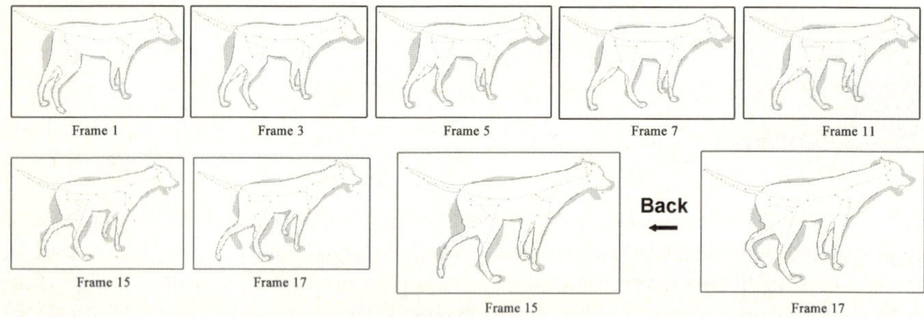


**Fig. 8.** Refinement. *Top:* The automatically estimated dog's pose in numbers of frame forwardly. *Bottom-Right:* The correction provided by the user is propagated to the backward frame.

**Fig. 9.** Result: sit

17 frames, and the bottom-right row shows the correction propagation of dog's left front leg from user's modification in Frame 17.

## 6  Results

Our system is implemented in C++ with OpenGL. The video source is captured by using SONY DCR TRV 900 video camera with frame rate 30 frames/$s$ and interlace mode. Fig. 9 shows our result of a dog's sitting motion and another motion – a dog's walking motion is shown in Fig. 10. We ignore the tail's motion because it moves too frequently to make estimation.

**Fig. 10.** Result: walk

## 7  Conclusions and Future Work

The main advantages of our method are as following:

- **UI:** Our system provides an intuitive and friendly user interface for users to make specifications and modifications. By using the reference model with rigged skeleton, the user can easily make the adjustment and instantly preview the change of model's contour in the initial fitting and refinement processes.
- **Animation:** With our system, it is easy to get a lively unrestricted in-plane motion even for the users who are not professional artists or do not have enough knowledge of the subject character.

There are two limitations of our method. Due to lack of depth information, our system cannot make estimation of out-subject-plane motion. Although we remain the manual modification of out-subject-plane motion for users, it is still difficult to make accurate estimation. Another limitation is that the unavoidable differences between the reference model and the subject character make our system not robust enough for all scenarios. For the future work, we would like to take into account prior knowledge and example motion data of the subject character in order to reduce the ambiguities and user's interventions.

## Acknowledgments

This work was partially supported by the National Science Council of Taiwan under NSC97-2221-E-002-224.

## References


1. Howe, N.R., Leventon, M.E., Freeman, W.T.: Bayesian reconstruction of 3d human motion from single-camera video. In: Proceedings of 1999 Neural Information Processing Systems, pp. 820–826 (1999)
2. Sidenbladh, H., Black, M.J., Fleet, D.J.: Stochastic tracking of 3d human figures using 2d image motion. In: Vernon, D. (ed.) ECCV 2000. LNCS, vol. 1843, pp. 702–718. Springer, Heidelberg (2000)
3. Gleicher, M., Ferrier, N.: Evaluating video-based motion capture. In: Proceedings of 2002 Computer Animation, pp. 75–80 (2002)
4. de Aguiar, E., Stoll, C., Theobalt, C., Ahmed, N., Seidel, H.P., Thrun, S.: Performance capture from sparse multi-view video. ACM Transactions on Graphics 27(3) (2008) (SIGGRAPH 2008 Conference Proceedings)
5. Vlasic, D., Baran, I., Matusik, W., Popovič, J.: Articulated mesh animation from multi-view silhouettes. ACM Transactions on Graphics 27(3) (2008)(SIGGRAPH 2008 Conference Proceedings)
6. Wilhelms, J., Gelder, A.V.: Combining vision and computer graphics for video motion capture. The Visual Computer 19(6), 360–376 (2003)
7. Favreau, L., Reveret, L., Depraz, C., Cani, M.P.: Animal gaits from video. In: Proceedings of 2004 ACM SIGGRAPH/Eurographics Symposium on Computer animation, pp. 277–286 (2004)
8. Rother, C., Kolmogorov, V., Blake, A.: "grabcut": interactive foreground extraction using iterated graph cuts. ACM Transactions on Graphics 23(3), 309–314 (2004) (SIGGRAPH 2004 Conference Proceedings)
9. Pollefeys, M., Van Gool, L., Vergauwen, M., Verbiest, F., Cornelis, K., Tops, J., Koch, R.: Visual modeling with a hand-held camera. International Journal of Computer Vision 59(3), 207–232 (2004)
10. Agarwala, A., Hertzmann, A., Salesin, D.H., Seitz, S.M.: Keyframe-based tracking for rotoscoping and animation. ACM Transactions on Graphics 23(3), 584–591 (2004) (SIGGRAPH 2004 Conference Proceedings)
11. Huang, J., Shi, X., Liu, X., Zhou, K., Wei, L.Y., Teng, S.H., Bao, H., Guo, B., Shum, H.Y.: Subspace gradient domain mesh deformation. ACM Transactions on Graphics 25(3), 1126–1134 (2006) (SIGGRAPH 2006 Conference Proceedings)

# Player Detection and Tracking in Broadcast Tennis Video

Yao-Chuan Jiang[1], Kuan-Ting Lai[2], Chaur-Heh Hsieh[3], and Mau-Fu Lai[4]

[1] I-Shou University, Kaohsiung County, Taiwan, R.O.C.
`m9503023@stmail.isu.edu.tw`
[2] Quanta Research Institute, Taoyuan, Taiwan, R.O.C.
`kuantinglai@gmail.com`
[3] Ming-Chuan University, Taoyuan, Taiwan, R.O.C.
`hsiehch@mail.mcu.edu.tw`
[4] Tungnan University, Taipei County, Taiwan, R.O.C.
`lai@mail.tnu.edu.tw`

**Abstract.** In this paper, we propose a novel algorithm for player detection and tracking in tennis games. The algorithm utilizes court knowledge as well as player color and edge information to extract deformable player figures. Several new techniques are presented in our algorithm: initially, the court lines are detected and reconstructed. Based on the court model, an adaptive search window is designed for locating the minimum region containing a player figure. After retrieving the region of interest, pixel data are processed by non-dominant color extraction and edge detection filters, respectively. Finally, the non-dominant color map and edge map are refined and combined, and a novel shadow removal method is then applied to isolate the player figure. The algorithm was tested on numerous videos with different courts and light condition. Experiments reveal promising results against various environmental factors.

## 1 Introduction

In recent years, sport video automatic annotation has attracted many research interests. Among numerous research domains, player detection and tracking is a fundamental but also most challenging area. A robust detection and tracking algorithm is required for many high-level operations such as player action recognition or content classification. Many relevant works of player detection have been published in past years [1-3, 5-11]. Early works explore temporal information of frame difference and then perform morphology operations [3, 10, 11] to extract player figure. Those methods are simple and fast, but easily affected by spectator movement or camera view change. Another approach is background subtraction, which constructs a background model to separate players [1, 2, 5, 6, 7, 9]. Major background models include empty court image, mean of continuous frames, and mean of dominant color. The empty court image is hard to retrieve and thus unrealistic. Using continuous frames to set up the statistical background model

T. Wada, F. Huang, and S. Lin (Eds.): PSIVT 2009, LNCS 5414, pp. 759–770, 2009.

shows great performance at fixed camera view, but not suitable for circumstance of frequently changed perspectives. The dominant color method has merits of computation simplicity and robustness under different perspectives. However, dominant color selection and range determination are still open problems requiring more effort. Furthermore, in tracking of players, the existing algorithms often employ a search window or bounding box that do not provide a close fit to a player's body. Although it makes no difference in tracking players, high level operations, like action recognition, still demand a best fit window and a complete body. In this paper, we propose a new player detection method which associates non-dominant color extraction and edge detection to effectively separate players from background. Moreover, an adaptive search window and varying bounding box are designed to make the extraction of player body more complete and the tracking more efficient and reliable.

The essential elements of our algorithm can be summarized as three blocks: adaptive search window, non-dominant color extraction and edge detection filter, and player refinement. The adaptive search window based on court knowledge is applied for locating the minimum region that contains a player figure. The region of interest is taken as input for non-dominant color extraction and edge detection filters. The two output maps are then combined to achieve the final detection result. The paper is organized as follows: Section 2 introduces the fundamental algorithms of the proposed system, including adaptive search window, non-dominant color extraction, edge detection and player refinement flow; Section 3 demonstrates experimental results of different tennis games, and the conclusion is given in Section 4.

## 2   Player Detection and Tracking System

The proposed player detection and tracking flow is illustrated in Fig. 1. For each input frame, we need to detect court lines and build the court model by using the work presented in [12], which is briefly described as follows. Court lines are white and can be detected by extracting white pixels. Nevertheless, the intensities of white pixels are changed by the weather, camera angle, different courts, etc. An adaptive threshold scheme is presented for adjusting color value of court lines. Moreover, some court lines often disappear during the zooming and panning of video camera. For missed lines, an algorithm is derived to efficiently reconstruct the court. The reconstructed court model is used to determine a search window that contains the player figure. The search window determines the region of interest (ROI) to be processed. The initial search window is fixed, whereas the search windows in the subsequent frames are adaptive (varying). The data in ROI are fed into the player detection unit which combines non-dominant color extraction with edge detection to extract player information. The detected result is further refined to achieve a complete player figure. The details are described in the following subsections.

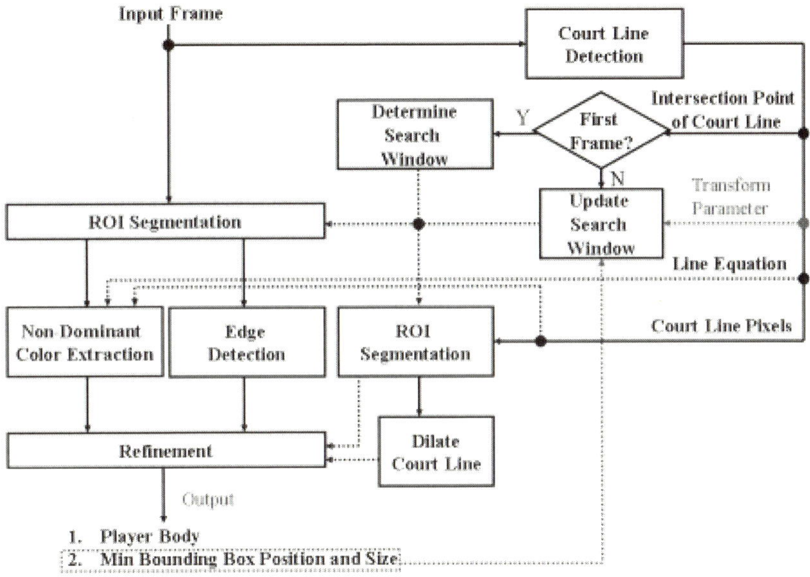


**Fig. 1.** Flow chart of player detection and tracking

## 2.1  Adaptive Search Window

At the first frame, the player position is unknown. By referring to the court model shown in Fig. 2, we define initial search areas around the court, where $(X_{Pi}, Y_{Pi})$ denotes the coordinate of a point Pi. The search areas contain upper court and lower court, as defined by the following equations.

$UpperCourt$

$$Left : \left[ X_{P4} - \frac{1}{2} * (X_{P4} - X_{P1}) \right] or(zero)$$

$$Right : \left[ X_{P20} + \frac{1}{2} * (X_{17} - X_{P20}) \right] or(image_width)$$

$$Top : \left[ max(Y_{P4}, Y_{P20}) - \frac{2}{3} * max(Y_{P4}, Y_{P20}) \right]$$

$$Bottom : [Y_{PC}]$$

$LowerCourt$

$$Left : \left[ X_{P1} - \frac{2}{3} * X_{P1} \right] or(zero)$$

$$Right : \left[ X_{P17} - \frac{2}{3} * (image_width - X_{P17}) \right] or(image_width)$$

$$Top : [Y_{PC}]$$

$$Bottom : \left[ max(Y_{P1}, Y_{P17}) - \frac{2}{3} * (image_height - max(Y_{P1}, Y_{P17})) \right]$$

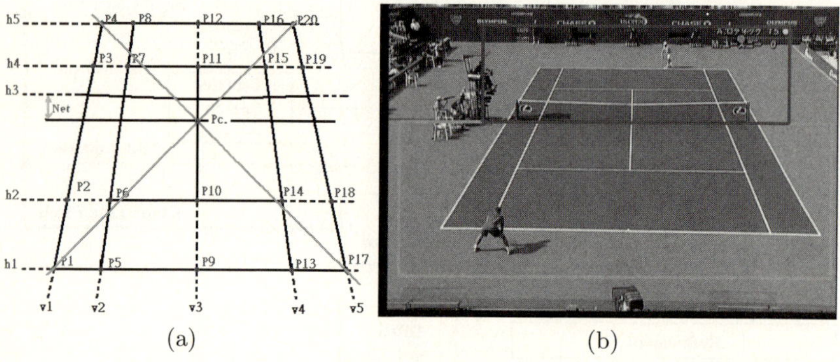

Fig. 2. (a) Court line model and (b) Initial search window

The initial search window can be used to locate the player in a video. Since a player is not a rigid object, we propose an adaptive search window to efficiently track the deformable player figure. According to [5], the speed of a player is around 2 - 7 meters per second. As a result, we use the maximum speed of 7 meters divided by the frame rate as the definition of the search window. Since the speed is only true in the real court, we apply the perspective transform to relate the coordinate in image space to that in real world. The generated adaptive search window is illustrated in Fig. 3 and the procedures are described below:

1. In image space, detect a player and calculate its centroid $(c_x, c_y)$
2. Map the centroid back into real court model $(r_x, r_y)$ by perspective transform
3. Calculate the maximal possible displaced locations in 4 directions (left, right, up, down), as the arrows shown in Fig. 3 (a)
4. Map the four locations in real court model into image space using perspective transform, as shown the arrows in Fig. 3 (b). The resulting locations indicate the possible centroids of a player in image space
5. Each possible centroid corresponds to a minimum bounding box. Using the minimum bounding boxes, we obtain a new search window, which is highlighted by the rectangle of dotted lines

## 2.2  Non-dominant Color Extraction and Edge Detection

After deciding the region of interest, we can start to extract the player figure. Major detection methods in literatures include dominant color detection [2, 5, 10] and background subtraction [9]. Due to the reason that background subtraction

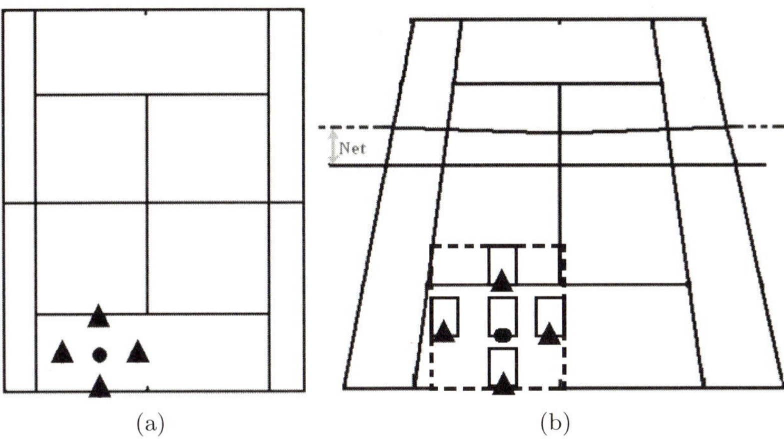

(a)                                                    (b)

**Fig. 3.** (a) Possible player locations in real court and (b) Possible player locations in image space, where the circle denotes the current location, and triangles denote possible locations

cannot handle camera viewpoint change, non-dominant color detection is employed in our system. J. Han et al presented a non-dominant color detection method in RGB color space [5]. Nevertheless, they selected the average color of full court as dominant color, which may have large deviation with the color in players neighbor. In addition, colors of different parts of the court are affected by light, shadow or camera viewpoint. To get more accurate value, we can take advantage of court knowledge and use average color of the field where player belongs to. According to the model of Fig. 2, we distinguish the court into four areas: inner field of upper court, outer field of upper court, inner field of lower court, and outer field of lower court. The court is split horizontally by net line, while inner and outer fields are defined by court lines. Figure 4 demonstrates the inner and outer fields of lower court.

$$Upper\ court\ inner\ field : [z \in (h5_{down} \cap v1_{right} \cap v5_{left}) \mid y\ of\ z > P_c]$$

$$Upper\ court\ outer\ field : [z \in h4_{up} \mid z \notin (h4_{up} \cap h5_{down} \cap v1_{right} \cap v5_{left})]$$

$$Lower\ court\ inner\ field : [z \in (h1_{up} \cap v1_{left} \cap v5_{right}) \mid y\ of\ z < P_c]$$

$$Lower\ court\ outer\ field : [z \in h2_{down} \mid z \notin (h2_{down} \cap h1_{up} \cap v1_{right} \cap v5_{left})]$$

In contrast to RGB color space [5], we select hue and value channels from HSV color space to detect non-dominant color pixels. First we calculate the mean $\mu$ and variance $\sigma^2$ of each channel in the selected region of court, then use (1) to determine the non-dominant color pixels. Parameter $\alpha$ is an adjustable parameter which is varied with the court conditions such as different courts or different lights of the same court. The experimental results indicate that the novel approach is robust against the varying court colors, which is demonstrated by the examples shown in Fig. 4.

$$NDC(x,y) = \begin{cases} 1, & if\,\|P_H - \mu_H\| > \alpha\sigma_H^2\,or\,\|P_V - \mu_V\| > \alpha\sigma_V^2 \\ 0, & otherwise \end{cases} \tag{1}$$

$$\alpha = \frac{0.5 * \beta + \sigma_H^2}{\sigma_H^2}$$

where $P_H$ and $P_V$ denote a pixel value of H and V channels, respectively. The $\beta$ is the quantization step size of H channel. Here we quantize H into 6 dominant colors, so $\beta$ is $0.5 * 1/6 = 1/12$.

During the fierce competition of a game, players perform various actions, such as swing or serve, which may cause false detection between player body and background. In order to enhance detection reliability, we add edge detection and utilize the result to compensate non-dominant color detection. Two examples are shown in Fig. 5, where images in second column are non-dominant color extraction results, and in third column are edge detection results. As we can see, some parts of player body are lost in non-dominant color extraction but preserved in edge map, and vice versa. A well-designed combination method is capable of producing a correct and complete player body.

In terms of the edge detection flow, the data are processed by Sobel filter and generate horizontal and vertical edge images. Each image is binarized by using $\mu \pm \sigma$ as threshold. Since smoothing causes edge expansion, we need to do 1/2

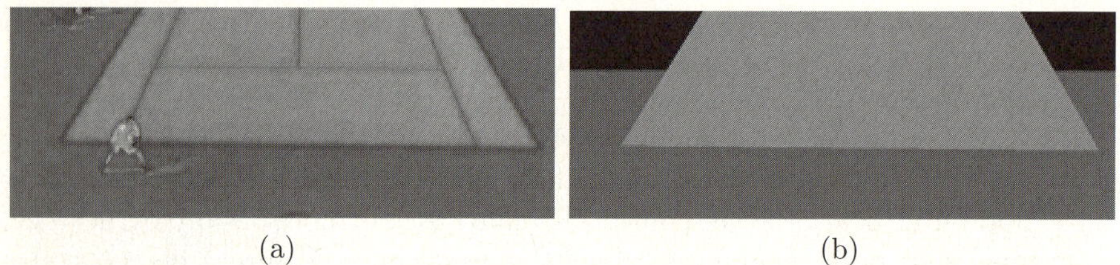

(a)                                        (b)

**Fig. 4.** (a) H channel image of lower court, (b) Dominant colors of inner field (purple) and outer field (blue)

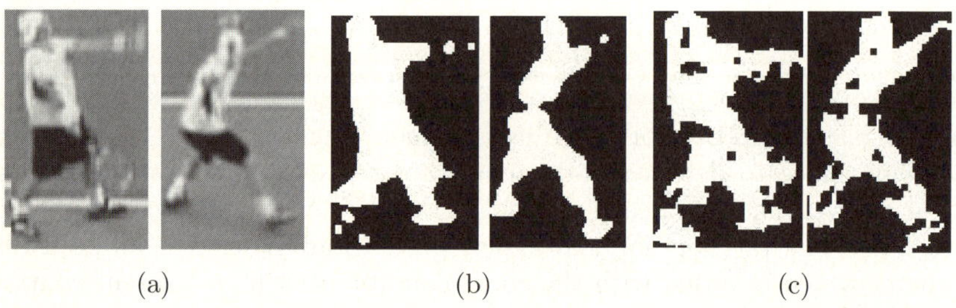

(a)                          (b)                          (c)

**Fig. 5.** Non-dominant color extraction and edge detection results. (a) Original image, (b) Non-dominant color extraction result, (c) Edge detection result.

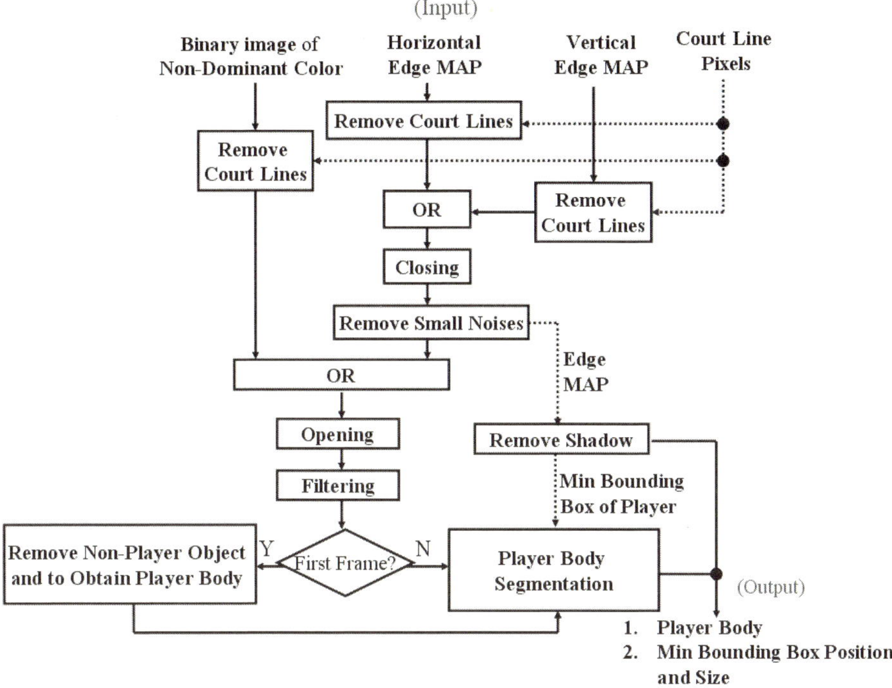


**Fig. 6.** Flowchart of player refinement

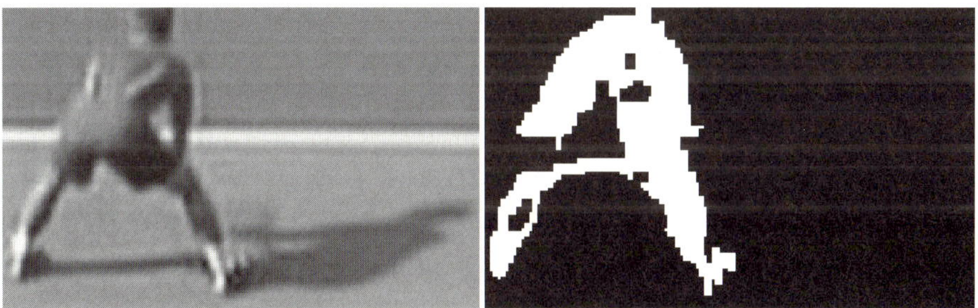

**Fig. 7.** Example of player shadows removal

sub-sampling to decrease edge width. Eventually we will get two output results, horizontal edge map and vertical edge map.

## 2.3 Refinement of Player Figure

The final step, refinement, is to remove undesired information and refine the player body. Figure 6 shows the flowchart of the refinement algorithm. The major steps include:

1. Remove court lines
2. Combine horizontal and vertical edge maps
3. Combine non-dominant color image and the new edge map
4. Remove cast shadow

At first, court lines must be removed from the three images. The previous developed work [12] is used to execute the job effectively. At second, we combine horizontal and vertical edge maps by performing OR and Closing operation of morphology, and use label connected components to remove noises. At third, the binary image of non-dominant color and the new edge map are merged by OR operation.

The merged result may contain shadows, thus we propose a new shadow removal technique. The shadows can be roughly classified into self shadows and cast shadows [13]. Removing self shadow is error prone and frequently eliminates parts of player body as well. Since our goal is to maintain the integrity of player figure, we concentrate on dealing with cast shadows. The color of shadow is gray or black, which has high saturation (S), and low value (V) in HSV color space. In addition, the hue (H) value is greater than that of the court color. We apply the following formulas to the edge pixels (corresponding to edge map), and the result is subtracted from the edge map, then we obtain the player figure without shadow, as illustrated in Fig. 7.

$$
\begin{aligned}
-\alpha\sigma_H^2 &\leq p_H - \mu_H < \tfrac{1}{6} \\
p_S - \mu_S &\geq -\alpha\sigma_S^2 \\
p_V - \mu_V &\leq -\alpha\sigma_V^2
\end{aligned}
\tag{2}
$$

## 3   Experimental Result

In this section, we provide experimental results of adaptive search window, player trajectory and player segmentation, respectively. The experimental data are selected from 12 videos of US Open, Wimbledon Open and French Open. The proposed algorithms are proved being robust and effective in different courts and under varying light conditions.

### 3.1   Adaptive Search Window

Figure 8 shows the adaptive search window (marked in black) and player window(marked in red) during the tracking period. It can be seen that both windows are changing frame by frame, which is adaptive according to the deformable player.

The results of other search algorithms [5, 8, 10] are shown in Fig. 9. The search windows are either too small or too large. Although those extraction results are sufficient for most tracking applications, they are not qualified for high level applications. Smaller search windows lead to lose parts of player body, and incur false judgment of player actions. Lager search windows contain too much noise and redundant information, make the tracking process inefficient. Due to the reasons above, the proposed adaptive window method is more suitable for high level automatic annotation system.

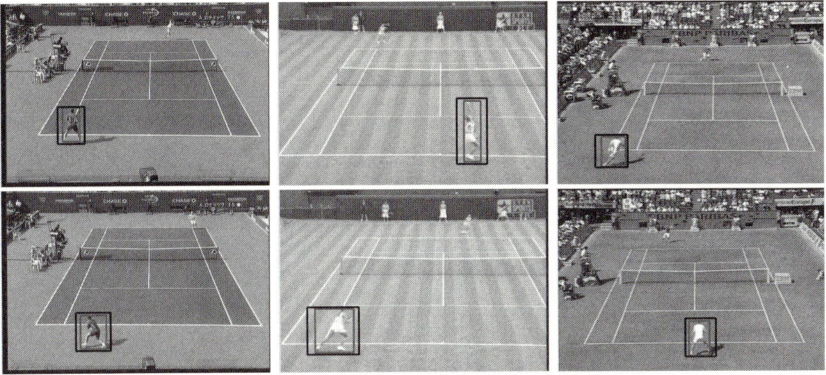

**Fig. 8.** Experimental results of proposed adaptive search window

**Fig. 9.** Search window of other algorithms [5, 8, 10]

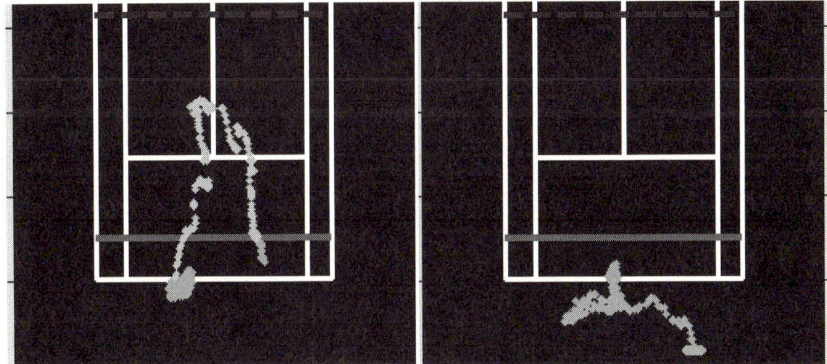

**Fig. 10.** Player trajectory of approach volley and ground stroke event

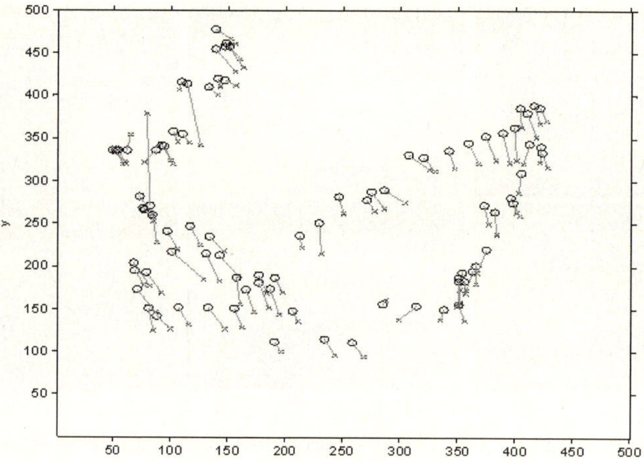

**Fig. 11.** o: manual tracking result, x: automatic tracking result, the connection line shows the difference between manual and automatic results

**Fig. 12.** Player figure extraction results

## 3.2   Player Trajectory

In terms of tracking players, we need to find the centroid of refined player figure for representing player position. The tracking results are shown in Fig. 10. The historic movement of approach volley event is in first image, while movement of event ground stroke is in the second. The comparison of manual and automatic tracking is shown in Fig. 11. Generally the automatic tracking results are close to manual results. Nevertheless, there are still a few mismatch errors. It is because that players white clothes, sometimes mixing with court lines, are incorrectly removed and lead to misjudge of players centroid.

### 3.3   Player Segmentation

The factors affecting accuracy of player segmentation are player window and segmentation algorithm. The proposed adaptive window and player body extraction algorithm are robust and effective, so we achieve excellent segmentation results, as shown in Fig. 12.

## 4   Conclusions

In this paper, a detection and tracking algorithm focusing on complete player figure extraction is proposed. Three schemes including adaptive search window, non-dominant color extraction filter, and edge detection filter, are developed to overcome problems of deformable player figure, various light conditions, camera viewpoint change, and different tennis courts. A novel shadow removal method is also presented to refine the player figure. Regarding with adaptive search window, we employ court knowledge and using perspective transform to calculate the search window; for non-dominant color extraction, hue and value are used as parameters and the region of interest is deliberate selected; for edge detection, a Sobel filter is applied for retrieving horizontal and vertical edge maps, which are associated with non-dominant color extraction result to refine the player figure. Around 50 video segments from 12 tennis games are used to test the algorithm. Experimental results demonstrate the new approach achieves robust player figure extraction as well as accurate movement tracking.

## References


1. Zhong, D., Chang, S.-F.: Long-term moving object segmentation and tracking using spatiotemporal consistency. In: IEEE International Conference on Image Processing, Thessaloniki, Greece (October 2001)
2. Zhong, D., Chang, S.-F.: Real-time view recognition and event detection for sports video. Journal of Visual Communication and Image Representation 15, 330–347 (2004)
3. Miyamori, H., Iisaku, S.I.: Video Annotation for Content-based Retrieval using Human Behavior Analysis and Domain Knowledge. In: Proceedings of the Fourth IEEE International Conference on Automatic Face and Gesture Recognition, pp. 320–325 (2000)
4. Huang, C.-L., Shih, H.-C., Chao, C.-Y.: Semantic Analysis of Soccer Video using Dynamic Bayesian Network. IEEE Trans. on Multimedia 8(4), 749–760 (2006)
5. Han, J., Farin, D., de With, P.H.N.: Multi-level analysis of Sports Video Sequences. In: SPIE Conference on Multimedia Content Analysis, Management, and Retrieval, San Jose, USA, vol. 1 (January 2006)
6. Han, J., de With, P.H.N.: A unified and Efficient framework for Court-Net Sports Videos Analysis Using 3-D Camera Modeling. In: SPIE Electronic Imaging, San Jose, USA, vol. 1, pp. 6506–6515 (January 2007)

7. Bertini, M., Cucchiara, R., Del Bimbo, A., Prati, A.: Semantic Adaptation of Sports Video with User-centred Performance Analysis. IEEE Transactions on Multimedia 8(3), 433–443 (2006)
8. Rea, N., Dahyot, R., Kokaram, A.: Classification and Representation of Semantic Content in Broadcast Tennis Videos. In: IEEE International Conference on Image Processing, 11-14, September, 2005, vol. 3, pp. III:1204–III:1207 (2005)
9. Zivkovic, Z., Petkovic, M., van Mierlo, R.J., van Keulen, M., van der Heijden, F., Jonker, W., Rijnierse, E.: Two Video Analysis Applications Using Foreground/Background Segmentation. In: Proceedings of the VIE- 2003 Conference on Visual Information Engineering, Surrey, Guildford, pp. 310–313 (July 2003)
10. Zhu, G., Huang, Q., Xu, C., Xing, L., Gao, W., Yao, H.: Human Behavior Analysis for Highlight Ranking in Broadcast Racket Sports Video. IEEE Transactions on Multimedia 09(06), 1167–1182 (2007)
11. Sudhir, G., Lee, J.C.M., Jain, A.K.: Automatic classification of tennis video for high-level content-based retrieval. In: Proc. Int. Workshop on Content-Based Access of Image and Video Databases, Bombay, pp. 81–90 (1998)
12. Jiang, Y.C., Hsieh, C.H., Kuo, C.M., Hung, M.H.: Court Line Detection and Reconstruction for Broadcast Tennis Videos. In: IPPR Conference on Computer Vision, Graphics and Image Processing (2008)
13. Andrea Prati, I.M., Mohan, M.T., Rita, C.: Detecting Moving Shadows: Formulation, Algorithms and Evaluation. IEEE Transactions on Pattern Analysis and Machine Intelligence 25(7) (July 2003)

# Unsupervised Pedestrian Re-identification
## for Loitering Detection

Chung-Hsien Huang, Yi-Ta Wu, and Ming-Yu Shih

Advanced Technology Center, Information & Communications Research Laboratories,
Industrial Technology Research Institute, Hsinchiu, Taiwan
`{davidchhuang,yitawu,myshih}@itri.org.tw`

**Abstract.** This paper presents a framework of detecting loitering pedestrians in a video surveillance system. First, to represent pedestrians an appearance feature which contains geometric information and color structure is proposed. After feature extraction, pedestrians are tracked by a proposed Bayesian-based appearance tracker. The tracker takes the advantage of Bayesian decision to associate the detected pedestrians according to their color appearances and spatial location among consecutive frames. The pedestrian's appearance is modeled as a multivariate normal distribution and recorded in a pedestrian database. The database also records time stamps when the pedestrian appears as an appearing history. Therefore, even though the pedestrian leaves and returns to the scene, he/she can still be re-identified as a loitering suspect. However, a critical threshold which determines whether two appearances are associated or not is needed to be set. Thus we propose a method to learn the associating threshold by observing two specific events from on-line video. A 10-minute video about three loitering pedestrians is used to test the proposed system. They are successfully detected and recognized from other passing-by pedestrians.

**Keywords:** Video surveillance, loitering detection, pedestrian re-identification, Bayesian decision, tracking.

## 1   Introduction

With the progress of computer vision, intelligent video surveillance systems have not only been widely investigated as research topics, but also been commercialized, such as ObjectVideo [1], ioimage [2], etc. To date, fundamental research issues of intelligent video surveillance include background subtraction, object detection and tracking, shadow removal, and even object recognition have been discussed extensively. Meanwhile, the researchers draws much attention in recent years to the high-level event detection [3], such as behavior analysis [4], abandon object detection and crowd density analysis. In this study, we focus on analyzing the behavior of loitering and propose a framework to detect loitering pedestrians, even though they leave and return to the area under monitoring.

Loitering refers to the sustained presence of one or more people over a given time period in an area. For example, graffiti offenders spend couple minutes in front of a wall to make their "art", prostitutes or baggers wander in the street corners, drug

T. Wada, F. Huang, and S. Lin (Eds.): PSIVT 2009, LNCS 5414, pp. 771–783, 2009.

dealers meet clients at bus stations, and people with suicide tendency hesitate at the end of platforms. In [5,6] and most of commercial products, the event of loitering is alarmed by locating and tracking an individual when he/she stays in the field of view (FOV) of the monitoring camera under temporal constrains. In [7], an appearance-based loitering method is developed to re-identify pedestrians and has been applied to detect drug dealers in public transportation areas when considering the leave-and-return problem.

In this study, a new appearance feature which contains geometric information and color structure is developed to present pedestrians. We also propose a Bayesian-based Appearance Tracker (BAT) to track pedestrians. BAT learns a short-term appearance model to represent a pedestrian via several consecutive frames and then associates the model in the coming frame. The association is performed by Bayesian decision [11] under the consideration of appearances and spatial locations. Meanwhile, the system also maintains a pedestrian database to integrate short-term appearance models as a long-term appearance model. Time stamps of each pedestrian who has visited the scene are also recorded. As a result, the event of loitering can be detected by comparing the time stamps with predefined rules. However, a critical threshold which determines whether two appearances are associated or not is needed to be selected. We thus propose a method to learn this associating threshold by observing specific events from on-line video.

The rest of the paper is organized as follows. Section 2 describes the loitering detection framework. Section 3 reveals the experimental results with a 10-minute testing video and discusses. Section 4 presents the conclusions and future works.

## 2  System Description

Figure 1 shows the flowchart of the proposed loitering detection algorithm. Several preprocessing procedures, such as background subtraction, shadow removal and connected-component labeling, are first performed to an input frame to extract image patches of pedestrian. Color and spatial features to represent the pedestrian are then extracted from each image patch. A proposed Bayesian-based appearance tracker (BAT) algorithm will evaluate those features, called candidates of pedestrian (COP) afterwards in this paper, in the adjacent frames to identify a pedestrian if the COP is stably appeared in the consecutive frames. Once a pedestrian is identified, a time stamp will be recorded into a pedestrian database by either updating the database if the pedestrian has already recorded, or adding a new record if it is a new pedestrian. Last, the event of loitering can be detected by comparing the time stamps of the pedestrian. The details of each module are presented in the following subsections.

### 2.1  Preprocessing

The Gaussian mixture model (GMM)-based background subtraction approach presented by Stauffer and Grimson [8] is a commonly used tool for extracting the moving objects. Basically, it uses couples of Gaussian to model the reasonable variation of the background pixels. Therefore, a pixel will be considered as foreground/moving object if the variation is larger than a threshold. In order to not only differentiate proper foreground (moving objects) from static background area, but also remove the casting shadows, the GMSM (Gaussian Mixture Shadow Model) approach proposed by Martel-Brisson and Zaccarin [9] is then applied. GMSM uses the GMM learning ability to build statistical models describing the moving cast shadows and can deal with complex and time-varying illumination.

In order to represent the spatial information of the extracted pedestrain candidates, a blob structure, $\mathbf{b} = \{r_{left}, r_{top}, r_{right}, r_{bottom}\}$, is used to record the smallest bounding box containing all the connected foreground pixels in which $r_{left}$, $r_{top}$, $r_{right}$ and $r_{bottom}$ indicate the left, top, right and bottom sides of the blob, respectively. Figure 2 (a) and (b) show a pedestrian and its corresponding foreground blob, respectively.

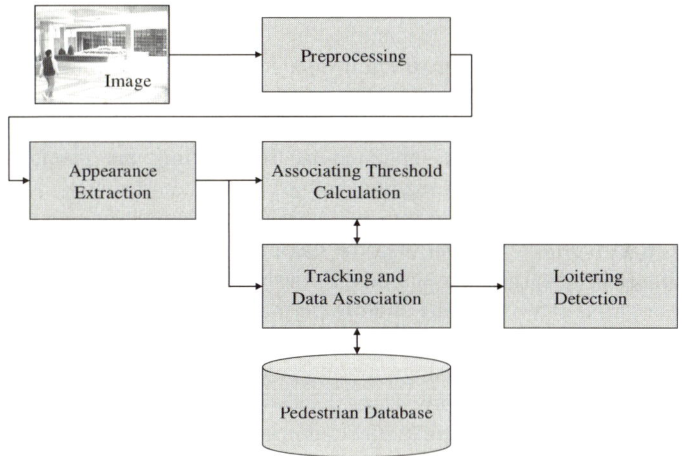


**Fig. 1.** Flowchart of the proposed loitering detection algorithm

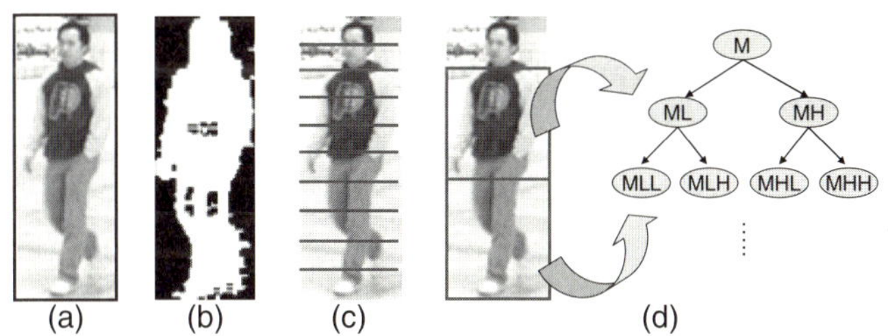


**Fig. 2.** Preprocessing and feature extraction of a pedestrian (a) the pedestrian candidate, (b) the GMM-foreground object, (c) Bird et al's approach [7] for feature extraction, and (d) our newly approach for feature extraction

## 2.2  Appearance Feature Extraction

In [7], Bird et al proposed a pedestrian representation method by using color features, as shown in Figure 2(c). They divided a pedestrian candidate into 10 equally spaced horizontal stripes as shown in Figure 2(c), and separately sorted the foreground pixels of each strip in R, G, and B channels according to the color intensity. The median in each sorting sequence is then selected as one of the color features of the stripe.

However, Bird et al.'s color feature will have following two problems. First, some strips of the 10 horizontal ones will be sensitive to the noises. For example, the features extracted from the top two strips containing the head portion are not stable since the color feature varies between the skin and hair colors. Second, 10 stripe segmentation is too fine to achieve re-identification if the image size of the pedestrian candidate is small. Therefore, we develop a new feature based on Bird et al.'s approach by adopting the loose segmentation strategy and considering the color structure as shown in Figure 2(d).

For the loose segmentation strategy, we segment a pedestrian candidate into three parts with height ratios of 2:4:4, and the features are extracted from the lower two parts by ignoring the head (top) part. The idea of our newly defined color structure is basically a sampling procedure to sample the histogram. That is, we iteratively segment a parent histogram into two child histograms by a medium intensity of the parent histogram, and collect those medium intensities to form a feature vector. Figure 2(d) shows an example of the color structure. The node of the tree structure contains a medium intensity, $M$, obtained by first sorting the pixels of original histogram, and then selecting the medium value from the sorted list. Obviously, the parent histogram will be separated into two child histograms in which the values in one child histogram will be smaller than the medium value, and the values in another child histogram will be larger than the medium value. We further segment each of the two child histograms into two parts and obtain the medium intensities, $ML$ and $MH$, from the two child histograms, respectively. In this way, we can iteratively segment a parent histogram into two child histograms and collect all the medium intensities from the tree structure to form our feature vector.

As shown in Fig. 2, the feature vector comprises two parts, body and legs. Each part has $3 \times 2^{l-1}$ scalars where 3 represents the R, G, and B channels and $l$ is the layer of the tree structure. We set $l = 3$. Thus, the feature vector $\mathbf{f}$ of a pedestrian candidate is composed by 24 color scalars as $\mathbf{f} = [R_{MLL}^{body}, G_{MLL}^{body}, B_{MLL}^{body}, R_{MLH}^{body}, ..., R_{MHH}^{legs}, G_{MHH}^{legs}, B_{MHH}^{legs}]$.

## 2.3 Bayesian-Based Appearance Tracker (BAT)

After the preprocessing at time $t$, a list of pedestrian candidates $\mathbf{C} = \{\mathbf{P}_j^t \mid j = 1, 2, ..., n\}$ is obtained for the tracking procedure, where $n$ is the number of candidates in this frame. Obviously, appearance and spatial relationship are important cues to associate candidates between two consecutive frames. We present a Bayesian-based appearance tracker to continuously track a moving object from image sequences. BAT considers the appearance features and spatial locations of two candidates from two adjacent image frames and the association between two candidates will be determined by a Bayesian decision. A sequence of consecutive candidates which have been associated is called a pedestrian's hypothesis $\mathbf{H} = \{\mathbf{P}^1, \mathbf{P}^2, ..., \mathbf{P}^t, \rho\}$ where $\mathbf{P}^1$ is the candidate of a pedestrian which appears but associate to none of existing hypotheses, $\mathbf{P}^2$ to $\mathbf{P}^t$ are consecutively associated candidates, and $\rho$ is called confidence level which indicates whether the hypothesis is reliable or not. Our BAT will maintain a list of hypotheses $\mathbf{M} = \{\mathbf{H}_i^t \mid i = 1,2,...,m\}$ by adding a new candidate if it is not existed in the $\mathbf{M}$ or updating the candidate information if it has already existed in the $\mathbf{M}$. Figure 3 illustrates the flowchart of BAT and the details are described below.

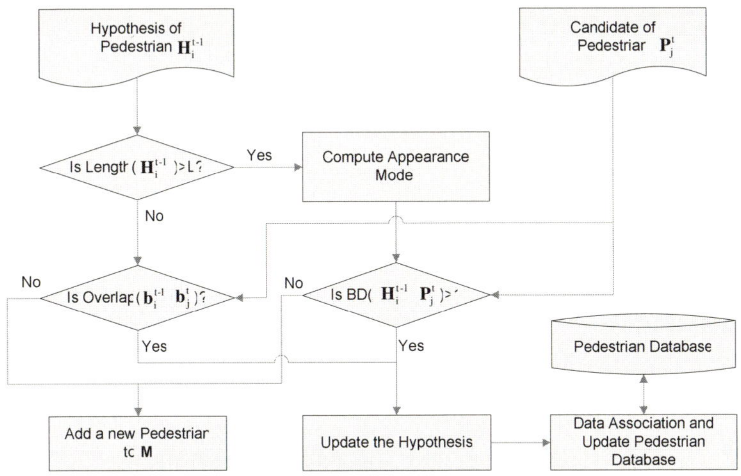


**Fig. 3.** Flowchart of our BAT

## I. Association by spatial overlap

For each hypothesis $\mathbf{H}_i^{t-1}$ in $\mathbf{M}$, if its trajectory length is shorter than $L$, the hypothesis is at its learning stage. At this stage, the spatial relationship is the only evidence to associate two candidates in different frames. If the blob $\mathbf{b}_j^t$ and the blob $\mathbf{b}_i^{t-1}$ have a large spatial overlapping in image, the candidate $\mathbf{P}_j^t$ is associated to the hypothesis $\mathbf{H}_i^{t-1}$ and then $\mathbf{H}_i^t$ will be formed by adding $\mathbf{P}_j^t$ to $\mathbf{H}_i^{t-1}$. Note that, $\mathbf{b}_j^t$ stands for the $j$-th blob in $\mathbf{P}_j^t$, and $\mathbf{b}_i^{t-1}$ stands for the last blob in $\mathbf{P}^{t-1}$ of $\mathbf{H}_i^{t-1}$.

## II. Association by appearance and spatial informaiton

On the other hand, if the trajectory length of $\mathbf{H}_i^{t-1}$ is larger than $L$, it means that $\mathbf{H}_i^{t-1}$ has been tracked at least $L$ frames, and $\mathbf{H}_i^{t-1}$ is already existed in $\mathbf{M}$. Therefore, in this stage, we will merely check whether a candidate $\mathbf{P}_j^t$ should be associated to $\mathbf{H}_i^{t-1}$ by Bayesian decision. The discriminant function is given by Eq. (1):

$$BD(\mathbf{H}_i^{t-1}, \mathbf{P}_j^t) = P(C_\mathbf{H} \mid \mathbf{P}_j^t) / P(\overline{C_\mathbf{H}} \mid \mathbf{P}_j^t)$$
$$= p(C_\mathbf{H})p(\mathbf{P}_j^t \mid C_\mathbf{H}) / p(\overline{C_\mathbf{H}})p(\mathbf{P}_j^t \mid \overline{C_\mathbf{H}}) \tag{1}$$

where $C_\mathbf{H}$ stands for $\mathbf{P}_j^t$ is associated to $\mathbf{H}_i^{t-1}$, and $\overline{C_\mathbf{H}}$ is the complement of $C_\mathbf{H}$, i.e. $\mathbf{P}_j^t$ is not associated to $\mathbf{H}_i^{t-1}$. Obviously, if $BD$ is larger than one, there is an association between $\mathbf{P}_j^t$ and $\mathbf{H}_i^{t-1}$.

The likelihood function $p(\mathbf{P}_j^t \mid C_\mathbf{H})$ of class $C_\mathbf{H}$ is modeled as a multivariate normal distribution $N(\mathbf{\mu}, \Sigma^2)$ as shown in Eq. (2) where $\mathbf{\mu}$ and $\Sigma$ stand for the mean vector and covariance matrix measured by the past $L$ observations (from $\mathbf{f}_i^{t-L_1}$ to $\mathbf{f}_i^{t-1}$), respectively.

$$p(\mathbf{P}_j^t \mid C_\mathbf{H}) = \frac{1}{\sqrt{\det \Sigma (2\pi^d)}} \exp(-\frac{1}{2}(\mathbf{f}_j^t - \mathbf{\mu})^T \Sigma^{-1}(\mathbf{f}_j^t - \mathbf{\mu})) \tag{2}$$

Meanwhile, the likelihood function $p(\mathbf{P}_j^t \mid \overline{C_\mathbf{H}})$ of class $\overline{C_\mathbf{H}}$ is simply modeled as a uniform distribution. Since the prior probabilities should reflect the prior knowledge of $C_\mathbf{H}$ and $\overline{C_\mathbf{H}}$, the prior probability $p(C_\mathbf{H})$ is modeled as a similarity metric which inversely proportions to the Euclidian distance between $\mathbf{b}_j^t$ and $\mathbf{b}_i^{t-1}$. Note that, $p(\overline{C_\mathbf{H}})$ is complement of $p(C_\mathbf{H})$, i.e. $p(\overline{C_\mathbf{H}}) = 1 - p(C_\mathbf{H})$. The measurement of $p(C_\mathbf{H})$ is shown in Eq. (3).

$$p(C_\mathbf{H}) = \exp(-\frac{D(\mathbf{b}_j^t, \mathbf{b}_i^{t-1})}{\sigma^2}) \tag{3}$$

where $\sigma$ can be tuned according to the frame rate or the average velocity of walking pedestrian in the scene. As a result, if $BD(\mathbf{H}_i^{t-1}, \mathbf{P}_j^t) \geq 1$, it shows the strong evidence that the observation $\mathbf{P}_j^t$ and the hypothesis $\mathbf{H}_i^{t-1}$ should be associated; otherwise $\mathbf{P}_j^t$ and $\mathbf{H}_i^{t-1}$ are belonged to different pedestrians.

### III. Hypothesis update

If $\mathbf{P}_j^t$ and $\mathbf{H}_i^{t-1}$ are associated, $\mathbf{H}_i^t = \{\mathbf{P}_i^1, \mathbf{P}_i^2, ..., \mathbf{P}_i^{t-1}, \mathbf{P}_j^t\}$ is derived by adding $\mathbf{P}_j^t$ to $\mathbf{H}_i^{t-1}$. Meanwhile, the confidence level $\rho_i$ is increased by adding a fragment $\Delta\rho$ until it reaches a maximum $\rho_{\max}$. If $\mathbf{H}_i^{t-1}$ has not been associated to any candidate of pedestrian $\mathbf{P}^t$ at frame $t$, $\rho_i$ is decreased by subtracting $\Delta\rho$. When $\rho_i$ is smaller than 0, we remove $\mathbf{H}_i^{t-1}$ from $\mathbf{M}$, the Hypothesis list, since $\mathbf{H}_i^{t-1}$ has not been observed for a long time. Any other situation is that if a candidate of pedestrian $\mathbf{P}^t$ can not be associated to any hypothesis in $\mathbf{M}$, we add a new hypothesis $\mathbf{H}_{m+1}^t = \{\mathbf{P}^t\}$ to $\mathbf{M}$ and set its confidence level $\rho_{m+1} = 0$.

### IV. Association to pedestrian database

Taking the advantage of Bayesian decision, each pedestrian is tracked and modeled as a multivariate normal distribution. The distribution is called a short-term appearance model since it is established by observing only $L$ frames. A long-term appearance model, established by integrating short-term appearance models, is utilized to represent each pedestrian and recorded into a pedestrian database. Therefore, even though a visitor left, he/she can be recognized and re-identified when he/she re-enter to the scene.

If the length of a hypothesis $\mathbf{H}_i^t$ is a multiple of $L$, a short-term appearance model $V = \{N(\boldsymbol{\mu}, \Sigma), \{s\}\}$ is established by measuring the mean vector $\boldsymbol{\mu}$ and the covariance matrix $\Sigma$ among the past $L$ observations. Note that, $\{s\}$ is a scalar sequence recording the time stamp when the model is established. As a result, each visitor is represented by his/her appearance model with a time-stamp sequence.

After that, the quotient by dividing the length a hypothesis $\mathbf{H}_i^t$ by $L$ can be derived, and there exists two situations for the quotient. First, when the quotient is equal to one, i.e. the pedestrian has been tracked in only $L$ frames, two circumstances may be happened. The first circumstance is that the pedestrian $V_i$ is a new comer and has not been observed in the past, while the second circumstance is that the $V_i$ is returning to the scene. In order to distinguish the two circumstances, $V_i$ is compared to all pedestrians listed in the pedestrian database $\{V_k \mid k = 1,2,...,r\}$ with their appearances. If the appearance distances between $V_i$ and some pedestrians are lower than an associating threshold $T$, then we associate he/she to the closest $V_k$. The appearance model is then updated by Eqs. (4)-(6). Otherwise, the pedestrian is regarded as a new comer and added to the database.

$$\tilde{V}_k = \{N(\tilde{\boldsymbol{\mu}}_k, \tilde{\Sigma}_k), \{s_k^1, s_k^2, ..., s_k^u, s_i^1, s_i^2, ..., s_i^v\}\} \tag{4}$$

$$\tilde{\boldsymbol{\mu}}_k = \frac{u \cdot \boldsymbol{\mu}_k + v \cdot \boldsymbol{\mu}_i}{u + v} \tag{5}$$

$$\tilde{\sigma}_k^2(x, y) = \frac{u \cdot \sigma_k^2(x, y) + v \cdot \sigma_i^2(x, y)}{u + v} \tag{6}$$

where $\sigma^2(x, y)$ stands for the element $(x,y)$ in the covariance matrix $\Sigma$, and $u$ and $v$ are the size of the time-stamp sequences of $V_k$ and $V_i$, respectively. In this case, $v = 1$ because the time-stamp sequence of $V_i$ only records a frame index $t$.

Second, when the quotient does not equal one, it means that the pedestrian $V_i$ has been tracked more than twice. Since a new pedestrian will be added to the database when he/she appears, definitely there is a pedestrian $V_k$ in databased associated to $V_i$. $V_k$ is then updated by adding $V_i$ as given in Eq. (4). Note that, the appearance distance, the distance between two normal distributions, is measured by computing the Kullback-Leibler (KL) divergence [10].

To define a proper associating threshold value $T$ is a critical issue since the threshold is used to determine whether two appearances are associated. Two appearances are marked as "same pedestrian" if the distance is smaller than $T$ and as "different pedestrians" otherwise. We propose a method to learn the associating threshold from the on-line video. This method will be discussed in the next subsection.

### 2.4  Associating Threshold Calculation

As mentioned in the previous subsection, the threshold to distinguish appearances is the most critical parameter for the problem of pedestrian re-identification. In [7], the threshold value is learnt off-line by Fisher Linear Discriminants (FLD) [11]. However, this approach requires lots of training images to build the FLD classifier and the threshold value can not be used in some conditions such as different lighting conditions. Therefore, we propose a method by considering two specific events to learn the threshold value to handle various conditions. Figure 4 illustrates the examples of these two events and the way to compute the associating threshold.

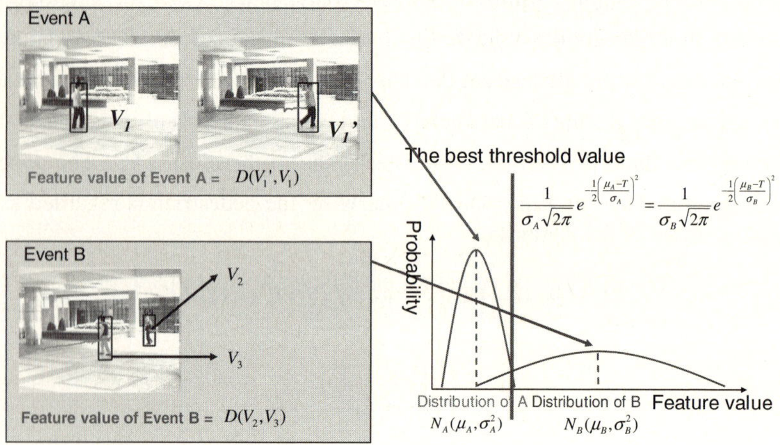


**Fig. 4.** Examples of two events for calculating the associating threshold

Consider the following two events. In event A, suppose a pedestrian $i$ is stably tracked for $2L$ frames starting from frame $t$, we can derive two appearances, $V_1'=AM(\mathbf{P}^t,\mathbf{P}^{t-1},...,\mathbf{P}^{t-L+1})$ and $V_1=AM(\mathbf{P}^{t-L},\mathbf{P}^{t-L-1},...,\mathbf{P}^{t-2L+1})$ , from the pedestrian's hypothesis $\mathbf{H}_i^t$ . The feature of event A is obtained by measuring the appearance distance between $V_1$ and $V_1'$. In event B, suppose there are two visitors $V_2$ and $V_3$ tracked in the same frame, the feature of event B can be derived by calculating the distance $V_2$ and $V_3$. After collecting a set of event A and B, the distributions of their features $N_A(\mu_A,\sigma_A^2)$ and $N_B(\mu_B,\sigma_B^2)$ thus obtained. As a result, the associating threshold $T$ can be determined by solving the following equation.

$$\frac{1}{\sigma_A\sqrt{2\pi}}e^{-\frac{1}{2}\left(\frac{\mu_A-T}{\sigma_A}\right)^2}=\frac{1}{\sigma_B\sqrt{2\pi}}e^{-\frac{1}{2}\left(\frac{\mu_B-T}{\sigma_B}\right)^2} \tag{7}$$

### 2.5  Loitering Detection

The definition of loitering is the fundamental of detecting loitering pedestrians. We categorize the loitering events into two class, local loitering and global loitering. The local loitering means that the pedestrian keeps loitering in the scene or may just leave for a while. Behaviors of graffiti offenders, street hookers or beggars can be classified into this category. Therefore, if a pedestrian's time stamp sequence is $\{s_1, s_2, ..., s_t\}$, he/she is classified as a locally loitering pedestrian when the following criterion is satisfied:

$$\frac{s_t - s_j}{t - j} > \alpha \tag{8}$$

where

$$j = \arg \max_{i=1,2,...,i-1} (s_t - s_i) \leq t_i \tag{9}$$

The global loitering means that the pedestrian loiters in an area but the camera only covers few part of this area. Therefore, the loitering pedestrian only appears in the video once in a while. Behaviors of drug dealer or pickpocket can be classified into this category. The global loitering is defined when the following criteria are satisfied.

$$s_t - s_1 > \beta \tag{10}$$

$$s_i - s_{i-1} < \gamma, \quad 1 < i \leq t \tag{11}$$

## 3  Experimental Results

To test the proposed system, a 10-min video was captured using Sony DCR-PC 110 DV Handycam camcorder with 320 × 240 resolution. The image sequences are obtained with frame rate at 25 frames/sec. For the 10-min video, 16246 frames were captured in which 1685 images of pedestrians have been segmented, accounting for 66 tracking instances tracked BAT. Three of the pedestrians appearing in the video are our colleagues and pretend to be loitering. They left and returned to the scene several times. Other pedestrians are passers who randomly pass by the scene.

### 3.1  Discriminability of Color Features

Figure 5 (a) shows the four pedestrians appearing in our testing video. In order to demonstrate the discriminability in the feature space, we collect 90 patches for each visitor, and display the feature vector in a 3-D Principle Component (PC) space as shown in Fig. 5 (b) by selecting three eigenvectors according to the first three largest eigenvalues after performing the Principle Component Analysis (PCA). Obviously, the clusters of four visitors are well separated at PC space, i.e. the color features are suitable for further high-level pattern analysis.

The comparison of our and Bird's appearance features are provided in Table.1. We generate three independent training and test sets by randomly selecting 15, 25 and 35 patches from the 90 patches for each visitor, and build 3 classifiers in the training set. The classification error rates of three classifiers are (9%, 0.77%, 2.27%) and (1.3%, 0%, 0%) for Bird's and our approaches. It is clear that our appearance feature outperform Bird's one by reducing the classification error rates.

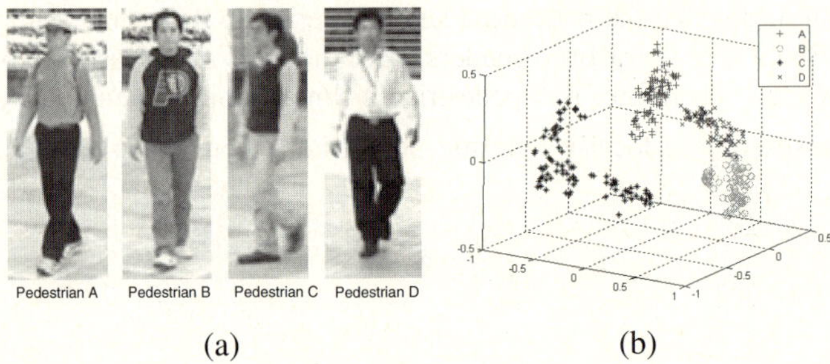


(a)                                                      (b)

**Fig. 5.** Discriminability of the proposed appearance features. (a) Image patches of four visitors (b) Map the color features to a 3-D Principle Component space.

**Table 1.** Comparison between Bird's appearance feature [7] and the proposed appearance feature

| Error Rate (%) | L = 15 | L = 25 | L = 35 |
|---|---|---|---|
| Bird's appearance feature [7] | 9.00 % | 0.77 % | 2.27 % |
| Proposed appearance feature | 1.30 % | 0.00 % | 0.00 % |

## 3.2  Threshold Selection

Figure 6 shows an example that the adaptively updated threshold will be converged through the 10-min video. It can be found the threshold varied in the first 3000 frames due to the limited number of positive and negative evidences. After collecting a certain number of evidences, it is not surprised that the threshold is converged.

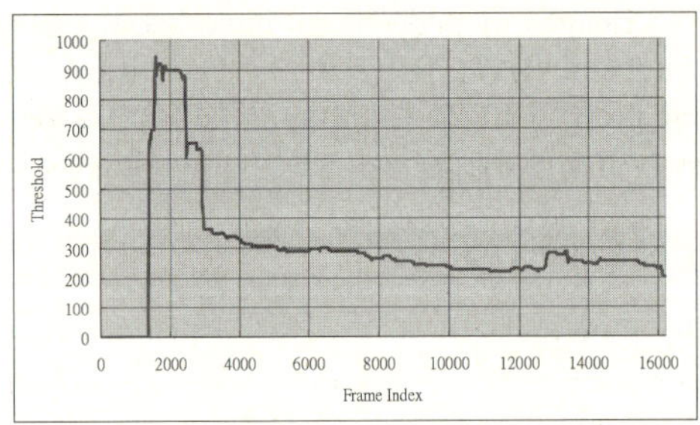


**Fig. 6.** An example shows the convergence of the updated threshold in the 10-min video

## 3.3  Pedestrian Re-identification

Figure 7 shows the history diagram of LV for the testing video when the threshold $T$ is set to 203.71. Note that the same color spots corresponding to the "same" pedestrian, which were judged by comparing appearance models. The pedestrians A, B, and C, who pretend to be loitering, are tracked and recognized successfully during the video. However, some pedestrians are misclassified as the same person such as (D, D', D'' and D'''), and (E, E' and E''). Since only color features are utilized, it is

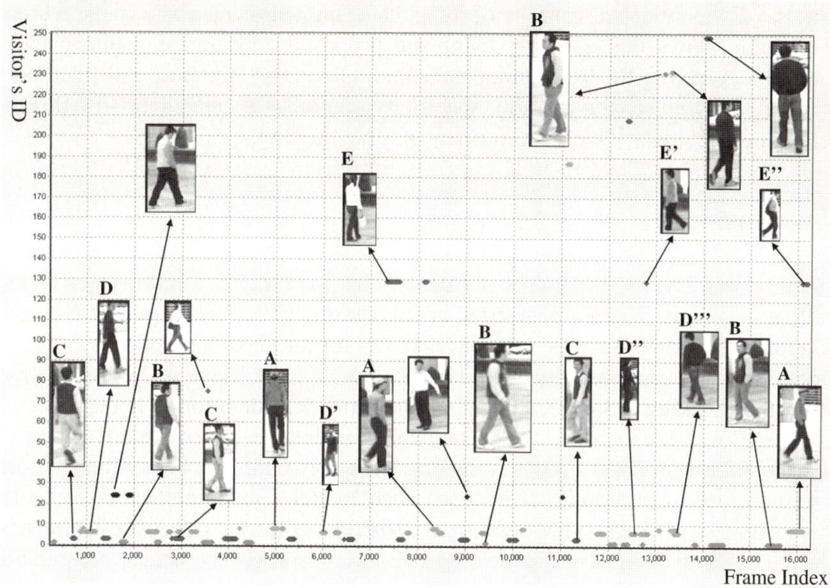

**Fig. 7.** History diagram of the detected pedestrians of the testing video

**Table 2.** Sensitivity and specificity of pedestrian re-identification with different approaches

| Method | Bird's appearance features [7] | | | The proposed method | | |
|---|---|---|---|---|---|---|
| Pedestrian | A | B | C | A | B | C |
| True positives | 18 | 61 | 50 | 32 | 66 | 63 |
| True negatives | 222 | 170 | 202 | 256 | 222 | 231 |
| False positives | 0 | 20 | 0 | 0 | 0 | 0 |
| False negatives | 13 | 2 | 1 | 6 | 6 | 0 |
| Sensitivity | 0.58 | 0.97 | 0.98 | 0.84 | 0.92 | 1 |
| Specificity | 1 | 0.89 | 1 | 1 | 1 | 1 |

not surprised that different pedestrians may not be distinguished when they dress similar color clothes.

Accuracy of the classification is then further analyzed. Consider the circumstance of associating the pedestrian A in the database. Suppose the testing pedestrian is A. A true positive (TP) means the testing pedestrian is correctly associated to A. A false negative (FN) occurs when the testing pedestrian is determined as a new pedestrian or associated to others. In contrast, suppose the testing pedestrian is not A. A false positive (FP) occurs when the testing pedestrian is incorrectly associated to A in the database. A true negative (TN) means the testing pedestrian is associated to other pedestrians or determined as a new pedestrian in the database. The accuracy is evaluated by sensitivity (=TP/(TP+FN)) and specificity (=TN/(FP+TN)). Table 2 shows the sensitivity and specificity of the loitering pedestrians in the testing video. In the left column, the appearance features were extracted by Bird's method [7] and the threshold was selected from the best results of numerous heuristic trials; while the right column shows the result by using the proposed appearance features and the method of calculating the associating threshold. Obviously, the proposed method not only improves the sensitivity and specificity but also avoids heuristic threshold selection, i.e. it can work well without any off-line training.

## 4  Conclusion

This study presents a framework to detect the loitering pedestrian in the video surveillance system. When a pedestrian appears in the FOV, he/she is first tracked by our Bayesian-based appearance tracker (BAT) to form a short-term appearance model of a pedestrian by associate the candidates in the adjacent frames. The association is performed by making a Bayesian decision under the consideration of appearances and spatial locations. Meanwhile, the system also maintains a pedestrian database to record the appearance and time stamps of each pedestrian. The pedestrians recorded can be considered as a long-term appearance model that combines all short-term appearance models of the same pedestrian. When a pedestrian candidate is identified, he/she is then compared to all pedestrians in the database. The pedestrian candidate will be identified as one of the pedestrian in the database and the time stamp will be updated if the difference between two objects are smaller than or equal to a pre-defined associating threshold. Otherwise, the pedestrian candidate will be added into the database as a new pedestrian. As a result, the behavior of loitering can be detected by comparing the time stamps with user-defined loitering rules. In addition, we propose a method to learn an associating threshold automatically for pedestrian association by observing two specific events from on-line video.

## References


1. ObjectVideo, Inc., `http://www.objectvideo.com/`
2. ioimage Ltd., `http://www.ioimage.com/`
3. Adam, A., Rivlin, E., Shimshoni, I., Reinitz, D.: Robust Real-Time Unusual Event Detection Using Multiple Fixed-Location Monitors. IEEE Trans. Pattern Analysis and Machine Intelligence 30(3), 555–560 (2008)
4. Hsieh, J.-W., Hsu, Y.-T., Liao, H.-Y., Chen, C.-C.: Video-Based Human Movement Analysis and Its Application to Surveillance Systems. IEEE Trans. Multimedia 10(3), 372–384 (2008)
5. Siebel, N.T., Maybank, S.: Fusion of multiple tracking algorithms for robust people tracking. In: Heyden, A., Sparr, G., Nielsen, M., Johansen, P. (eds.) ECCV 2002. LNCS, vol. 2353, pp. 373–387. Springer, Heidelberg (2002)
6. Black, J., Velastin, S., Boghossian, B.: A Real Time Surveillance System for Metropolitan Railways. In: Proceedings of IEEE Conference on Advanced Video and Signal Based Surveillance, pp. 189–194 (2005)
7. Bird, N.D., Masoud, O., Paapnikolopoulos, P.P., Isaacs, A.: Detection of Loitering Individuals in Public Transportation Areas. IEEE Trans. Intelligent Transportation Systems 6(2), 167–177 (2005)

8. Stauffer, C., Grimson, W.E.L.: Adaptive Background Mixture Models for Real-time Tracking. Proc. IEEE Comput. Vision Pattern Recognit. 2, 246–252 (1999)
9. Martel-Brisson, N., Zaccarin, A.: Learning and Removing Cast Shadows through a Multidistribution Apprach. IEEE Trans. Pattern Analysis and Machine Intelligence 29(7), 1133–1146 (2007)
10. Kullback, S.: Information Theory and Statistics. Dover Publications, New York (1968)
11. Duda, O.R., Hart, P.E., Stork, D.G.: Pattern Classification. A Wiley-Interscience Publication, Hoboken (2000)

# A Fast Macroblock Mode Decision Algorithm for the Baseline Profile in the H.264 Video Coding Standard

Chang-Hsing Lee, Cheng-Chang Lien, Jau-Ling Shih, and Ping-Yu Lin

Department of Computer Science and Information Engineering
Chung Hua University, Hsinchu, 300 Taiwan
{chlee,cclien,sjl,m09302036}@chu.edu.tw

**Abstract.** A fast macroblock (MB) mode decision algorithm is proposed to reduce the computational complexity of H.264 video coding. First, a SKIP mode detection algorithm is developed to detect as many "skipped" MB as possible. As a result, the encoding functions associated with all inter modes and all intra modes can be omitted. In addition, an early inter mode termination mechanism is developed to disable some inter modes and all intra modes during the motion estimation process. Compared with JM_FFS, the proposed algorithm can reduce 71.35% of the encoding time with a negligible degradation in video quality and compression ratio.

**Keywords:** H.264, Mode decision, SKIP mode detection.

## 1   Introduction

H.264 is the newest video coding standard, which was developed jointly by the ITU-T Video Coding Experts Group (VCEG) and the ISO-IEC Motion Picture Experts Group (MPEG) [1]. H.264 can achieve significant rate distortion (RD) improvements as compared with previous video coding standards such as MPEG-2, MPEG-4, H.263, etc. The key features responsible for the improved coding efficiency include variable block-size motion estimation (ME), multiple reference frames, quarter-pixel motion accuracy, context-adaptive variable length coding (CAVLC), in-loop de-blocking filter, multiple spatial prediction modes for intra prediction, etc. However, the improvement in RD performance is achieved at the expense of increased computational burden [2].

For inter coding of each $16 \times 16$ macroblock (MB), the H.264 encoder employs variable block-size ME to effectively remove temporal correlation between neighboring video frames. H.264 supports four inter coding modes, including $INTER16 \times 16$, $INTER16 \times 8$, $INTER8 \times 16$, and $P8 \times 8$, where a MB is partitioned into $16 \times 16$, $16 \times 8$, $8 \times 16$, or $8 \times 8$ blocks. For the $P8 \times 8$ mode, each $8 \times 8$ block can be further independently partitioned into $8 \times 8$, $8 \times 4$, $4 \times 8$, or $4 \times 4$ blocks.

To exploit the spatial correlation between pixels in the same video frame, H.264 supports two intra coding modes: $INTRA4 \times 4$ and $INTRA16 \times 16$. The

T. Wada, F. Huang, and S. Lin (Eds.): PSIVT 2009, LNCS 5414, pp. 784–795, 2009.

$INTRA4 \times 4$ mode allows nine prediction modes for each $4 \times 4$ block whereas the $INTRA16 \times 16$ mode allows four prediction modes for each $16 \times 16$ MB. In addition to the inter coding modes and intra coding modes, the H.264 baseline profile supports the $SKIP$ mode for P slices to improve the RD performance of video sequences in which neighboring MBs move in identical direction. The $SKIP$ mode implies that no motion information and residual signal have to be encoded. That is, only the mode indicator is actually transmitted for the $SKIP$ mode.

The H.264 reference software [3] incorporates an optional rate-distortion optimization (RDO) mode selection mechanism to select the best coding mode among the set of coding modes. For each coding mode, the RD cost ($RDcost$) is computed by a distortion model using a Lagrangian coefficient given as [4]:

$$J_{mode}(M) = D_{mode}(M) + \lambda_{mode} R(M), \tag{1}$$

where $M$ is the coding mode, $M \in CODING_MODES = \{SKIP, INTER16 \times 16, INTER16 \times 8, INTER8 \times 16, P8 \times 8, INTRA4 \times 4, INTRA16 \times 16\}$, $D_{mode}(M)$ is the distortion measured as the sum of squared difference (SSD) between the original MB and the reconstructed MB associated with the coding mode $M$, $R_{mode}(M)$ is the overall bit rate required for the encoding of the motion vector, reference frames, residual signals, etc., $\lambda_{mode}$ is the Lagrangian parameter for mode decision and is a function related to the quantization parameter (QP):

$$\lambda_{mode} = 0.85 \times 2^{(QP-12)/3}. \tag{2}$$

All coding modes will be exhaustively examined and the one with the minimum $RDcost$ is selected as the best coding mode, denoted $M^*$:

$$M^* = \arg \min_{M} J_{mode}(M), M \in CODING_MODES. \tag{3}$$

Since each MB is encoded multiple times (one for each coding mode), the computational cost of the RDO mechanism is too high and must be reduced. To reduce the computation time, Yin et al. [5] proposed a fast mode decision algorithm based on the assumption that the error surface versus block-size is probably monotonic. Tu et al. [6] used a merging procedure to determine the encoding block size. A small block-size ME is first performed. An adaptive threshold is then employed to determine whether two neighboring blocks can be merged into a larger block based on the difference between the MVs of these two blocks. A merging and splitting procedure based on the correlation of the MVs of different block-size modes is further employed for fast variable block-size ME [7].

Several studies extracted properties from a MB to predict its possible coding modes and thus omit the other coding modes. The prediction mechanisms can be based on the spatial correlation [8], homogeneous region detection [9], spatial homogeneity and the temporal stationary properties [10], both spatial correlation and temporal correlation [11][12], etc.

The SKIP mode prediction approach has been employed to reduce the motion search in H.263 video coding [13][14] in which the ME process will be stopped if the sum of absolute difference (SAD) at motion vector (0, 0) is less than a pre-defined threshold. This idea has been extended to reduce the computational complexity of H.264 video coding [15][16][17][18]. The SKIP mode is detected by checking whether all the quantized coefficients are all zeros [15][16], by comparing the *RDcost* with a predefined threshold [17], or by comparing the *RDcost* with an estimated *RDcost* computed from local sequence statistics [18]. The computation time is reduced by avoiding ME and subsequent encoding functions for those MBs being identified as "skipped" MBs.

In this study, a fast MB mode decision algorithm will be proposed to reduce the computational complexity of the H.264 encoding process. In the following section, we will describe the proposed fast MB mode decision algorithm. Simulation results are shown in Section 3 to show the efficiency of the proposed method. Finally, a conclusion is given in Section 4.

## 2    Proposed Fast Macroblock Mode Decision Algorithm

The proposed fast MB mode decision algorithm consists of two stages: early *SKIP* mode decision and early inter mode termination. First, a *SKIP* mode detection algorithm is developed to detect as many "skipped" MB as possible compared with the previous approaches. By early identifying a "skipped" MB, the encoding functions related to all inter modes and all intra modes can be omitted. During ME process, the early inter mode termination mechanism tries to disable some inter modes and all intra modes when the coding result of an inter mode is good enough in terms of *RDcost*.

### 2.1    Early SKIP Mode Decision

The *SKIP* mode refers to the coding mode where no ME or motion compensation (MC) is performed and no residual signal has to be encoded. Thus, if we can determine at early stage that the best coding mode of the current MB is the *SKIP* mode, all inter modes and all intra modes can be excluded from the mode decision process. Thus, the encoding functions associated with ME/MC, spatial prediction, and mode decision can be omitted. In general, the *SKIP* mode dominates among other coding modes, particularly for video sequences with slow or uniform motions (for example, *Akiyo*, *Hall*, and *Mother&Daughter*), as shown in Table 1. From this table, we can see that for every video sequence the larger the QP values, the more the number of "skipped" MBs. Therefore, early detection of the *SKIP* mode will save a significant amount of encoding time, particularly for slow motion video sequences or at low bit rates.

In H.264 reference software, when *RDO* mode selection mechanism is enabled, the *RDcost* of the *SKIP* mode is evaluated together with other coding modes. When *RDO* mode selection mechanism is disabled, the best coding mode of a MB is regarded as the *SKIP* mode if the following conditions are satisfied: (1) the best MC block size is $16 \times 16$; (2) the reference frame is just the previous one; (3) the MV is the same as its predictive motion vector (*PMV*); (4) all quantized

**Table 1.** Percentage of "skipped" MBs (%)

| Sequence | QP=28 | QP=32 | QP=36 | QP=40 |
|---|---|---|---|---|
| *Akiyo* | 87.17 | 90.82 | 93.70 | 95.78 |
| *Hall* | 69.86 | 89.58 | 94.86 | 97.17 |
| *Mother&Daughter* | 83.87 | 89.33 | 93.32 | 97.08 |
| *Silent* | 75.86 | 81.08 | 85.64 | 89.75 |
| *News* | 80.62 | 85.20 | 88.90 | 92.35 |
| *Foreman* | 34.45 | 47.96 | 59.92 | 68.86 |
| *Coastguard* | 14.83 | 29.86 | 50.58 | 70.18 |
| *Stefan* | 23.54 | 30.28 | 39.65 | 52.18 |
| *Table_Tennis* | 30.12 | 43.60 | 56.66 | 67.11 |
| *Mobile&Calendar* | 4.22 | 7.55 | 14.66 | 30.15 |

transformation coefficients are all zeros. Let $MB_o$ and $MB_{PMV}$ denote respectively the original MB and the MB located in the reference frame with MV being $PMV$. Let $RMB_{PMV}$ denote the residual MB obtained by taking the difference between $MB_o$ and $MB_{PMV}$, that is,

$$RMB_{PMV}(x, y) = MB_o(x, y) - MB_{PMV}(x, y), 0 \leq x, y \leq 15. \qquad (4)$$

In this study, we presume that $MB_o$ is highly probable to be a "skipped" MB if $RMB_{PMV}$ is an all-zero coefficients MB (AZCMB). A MB is referred to as an AZCMB if it is decomposed into a number of non-overlapping $4 \times 4$ blocks and every block is an all-zero coefficients block (AZCB) in which all quantized coefficients become zero. Table 2 shows the probability that the best coding mode is the $SKIP$ mode when $RMB_{PMV}$ is an AZCMB. It can be seen that it is highly probable that a MB will be "skipped" if its residual MB is an AZCMB.

The proposed early $SKIP$ mode decision algorithm tries to disable the other coding modes based on the early identification of an AZCMB. To determine whether a $4 \times 4$ block is an AZCB, a direct way is to perform integer transformation and quantization on this block. To save the computation time, several fast approaches have been proposed to detect AZCB without performing transformation

**Table 2.** Probability of a MB being encoded as the SKIP mode when it is an AZCMB

| Sequence | QP=28 | QP=32 | QP=36 | QP=40 |
|---|---|---|---|---|
| *Akiyo* | 0.9978 | 0.9963 | 0.9958 | 0.9946 |
| *Hall* | 0.8559 | 0.9637 | 0.9851 | 0.9950 |
| *Mother&Daughter* | 0.9920 | 0.9840 | 0.9808 | 0.9815 |
| *Silent* | 0.9917 | 0.9873 | 0.9846 | 0.9789 |
| *News* | 0.9934 | 0.9938 | 0.9921 | 0.9908 |
| *Foreman* | 0.9323 | 0.9310 | 0.9423 | 0.9371 |
| *Coastguard* | 0.9134 | 0.9374 | 0.9261 | 0.9351 |
| *Stefan* | 0.9388 | 0.9600 | 0.9737 | 0.9682 |
| *Table_Tennis* | 0.8591 | 0.8579 | 0.9140 | 0.9449 |
| *Mobile&Calendar* | 0.9257 | 0.9238 | 0.9331 | 0.9352 |

**Table 3.** Detection rate of AZCBs by Su's algorithm and the modified algorithm (%)

| Sequence | Su's algorithm | | | | Modified algorithm | | | |
|---|---|---|---|---|---|---|---|---|
| | QP=28 | QP=32 | QP=36 | QP=40 | QP=28 | QP=32 | QP=36 | QP=40 |
| *Akiyo* | 75.21 | 78.78 | 81.63 | 84.48 | 99.997 | 99.999 | 100.00 | 100.00 |
| *Hall* | 37.86 | 65.72 | 66.01 | 72.31 | 99.995 | 99.999 | 100.00 | 100.00 |
| *Mother&Daughter* | 65.02 | 65.83 | 72.11 | 83.13 | 99.999 | 100.00 | 100.00 | 100.00 |
| *Silent* | 18.17 | 25.00 | 36.94 | 59.03 | 99.992 | 99.997 | 100.00 | 100.00 |
| *News* | 49.76 | 61.56 | 64.41 | 69.83 | 99.991 | 99.998 | 99.999 | 100.00 |
| *Foreman* | 34.72 | 41.29 | 60.82 | 69.71 | 99.989 | 99.999 | 99.999 | 100.00 |
| *Coastguard* | 13.94 | 8.98 | 30.47 | 52.22 | 99.924 | 99.990 | 99.997 | 100.00 |
| *Stefan* | 82.87 | 85.09 | 79.89 | 75.49 | 99.954 | 99.980 | 99.979 | 99.999 |
| *Table_Tennis* | 52.29 | 48.76 | 57.05 | 68.75 | 99.955 | 99.995 | 99.999 | 99.999 |
| *Mobile&Calendar* | 69.96 | 65.19 | 63.61 | 45.93 | 99.939 | 99.949 | 99.938 | 99.990 |

**Table 4.** Percentage of non-AZCBs with $S < 2T_2$ (%)

| Sequence | QP=28 | QP=32 | QP=36 | QP=40 |
|---|---|---|---|---|
| *Akiyo* | 4.95 | 3.49 | 2.21 | 1.35 |
| *Hall* | 8.57 | 4.53 | 2.33 | 1.44 |
| *Mother&Daughter* | 9.71 | 5.91 | 3.28 | 1.60 |
| *Silent* | 9.16 | 6.94 | 4.96 | 3.12 |
| *News* | 6.27 | 4.78 | 3.56 | 2.66 |
| *Foreman* | 15.61 | 12.20 | 9.02 | 6.10 |
| *Coastguard* | 27.44 | 28.76 | 20.42 | 12.07 |
| *Stefan* | 11.41 | 15.80 | 16.48 | 14.81 |
| *Table_Tennis* | 20.91 | 13.81 | 7.65 | 5.36 |
| *Mobile&Calendar* | 10.77 | 15.04 | 16.91 | 17.72 |

## 2.2 Early Inter Mode Termination in ME Process

If $MB_o$ is not skipped, the inter modes are examined successively in the order of mode $INTER16 \times 16$, $INTER16 \times 8$, $INTER8 \times 16$, and $P8 \times 8$. For each inter mode $M$, ME is performed to find the corresponding MV, $\mathbf{mv}_M$, which minimizes the $RD$ function, $J_{motion}(MB_o, M)$. In fact, if the present examined inter mode is good enough, it is unnecessary to perform ME for subsequent inter modes. Let $J^*_{motion}(MB_o, M)$ denote the minimum $RDcost$ obtained in the ME process for inter mode $M$. If $J^*_{motion}(MB_o, M)$ is less than a pre-calculated threshold, $TH(M)$, it is presumed that the current coding mode is good enough and thus the other coding modes can be omitted. The major problem is how to determine the threshold. Since there exits high correlation between neighboring video frames, the threshold can be derived by the $RDcost$ of the MBs in the reference frame. Let $S(M)$ denote in the reference frame the set of MBs whose best coding mode is mode $M$, and $\overline{J}_{motion}(M)$ denote the average $RDcost$ of these MBs, that is,

$$\overline{J}_{motion}(M) = \frac{1}{|S(M)|} \sum_{B \in S(M)} J^*_{motion}(B, M^*(B)), \tag{16}$$

where $|\bullet|$ is the cardinality of a set, $M^*(B)$ is the best coding mode of a MB $B$. Similarly, let $S(INTER)$ denote the set of inter coded MBs in the reference frame, that is,

$$S(INTER) = S(INTER16 \times 16) \cup S(INTER16 \times 8) \cup (INTER8 \times 16) \cup S(P8 \times 8). \tag{17}$$

The average $RDcost$ of these inter coded MBs, $\overline{J}_{motion}(INTER)$, is then defined as follows:

$$\overline{J}_{motion}(INTER) = \frac{1}{|S(INTER)|} \sum_{B \in S(INTER)} J^*_{motion}(B, M^*(B)). \tag{18}$$

For each mode $M$, the adaptive threshold, $TH(M)$, is then defined as:

$$TH(M) = min\{\overline{J}_{motion}(M), \overline{J}_{motion}(INTER)\}. \tag{19}$$

If $J^*_{motion}(MB_o, M) < TH(M)$, the other inter modes as well as all intra modes will be disabled. Note that this early inter mode termination approach is performed during the ME process. As a result, the reduction of computation time is achieved by avoiding unnecessary ME(s), spatial predictions, and mode decisions of those disabled coding modes. In addition to the threshold-based mode termination approach, an additional early inter mode method based on the assumption that the error surface versus block-size is probably monotonic is developed before examining the time intensive $P8 \times 8$ mode. Since MEs on block sizes of $16 \times 16$, $16 \times 8$, and $8 \times 16$ have been examined before performing ME on each $8 \times 8$ block, if $INTER16 \times 16$ achieves the minimum $RDcost$, the $P8 \times 8$ mode can be omitted. That is, $P8 \times 8$ will be disabled if

$$J^*_{motion}(MB_o, INTER16 \times 16) < J^*_{motion}(MB_o, INTER16 \times 8) \tag{20}$$

and

$$J^*_{motion}(MB_o, INTER16 \times 16) < J^*_{motion}(MB_o, INTER8 \times 16) \tag{21}$$

During mode decision process, the best encoding mode is determined among the SKIP mode, enabled inter modes, and two spatially predictive intra modes, $INTRA16 \times 16$ and $INTRA4 \times 4$ if they are enabled. The selection of the best encoding mode is measured in terms of $RDcost$ defined in Eq. (1). The detailed steps of the proposed algorithm are given as follows.

**Step 1:** Let $MB_o$ denote the current MB being encoded. If $MB_o$ is an AZCMB, set the best coding mode of $MB_o$ the $SKIP$ mode and go to Step 8.

**Step 2:** Perform ME for the $INTER16 \times 16$ mode and get the corresponding minimum $RDcost$, $J^*_{motion}(MB_o, INTER16 \times 16)$. If $J^*_{motion}(MB_o, INTER16 \times 16) < TH(INTER16 \times 16)$, disable $INTER16 \times 8$, $INTER8 \times 16$, $P8 \times 8$, $INTRA16 \times 16$, and $INTRA4 \times 4$, go to Step 7.

**Step 3:** Perform ME for the $INTER16 \times 8$ mode and get the corresponding minimum $RDcost$, $J^*_{motion}(MB_o, INTER16 \times 8)$. If $J^*_{motion}(MB_o, INTER16 \times 8) < TH(INTER16 \times 8)$, disable $INTER8 \times 16$, $P8 \times 8$, $INTRA16 \times 16$, and $INTRA4 \times 4$, go to Step 7.

**Step 4:** Perform ME for the $INTER8 \times 16$ mode and get the corresponding minimum $RDcost$, $J^*_{motion}(MB_o, INTER8 \times 16)$. If $J^*_{motion}(MB_o, INTER8 \times 16) < TH(INTER8 \times 16)$, disable $P8 \times 8$, $INTRA16 \times 16$, and $INTRA4 \times 4$, go to Step 7.

**Step 5:** If $J^*_{motion}(MB_o, INTER16 \times 16) < J^*_{motion}(MB_o, INTER16 \times 8)$ and $J^*_{motion}(MB_o, INTER16 \times 16) < J^*_{motion}(MB_o, INTER8 \times 16)$, disable $P8 \times 8$ and go to Step 7.

**Step 6:** Perform ME for the $P8 \times 8$ mode.

**Step 7:** In the mode decision process, calculate the $RDcosts$ of the $SKIP$ mode, all enabled inter modes, and all enabled intra modes. Determine the best coding mode, $M^*$, which achieves the minimum $RDcost$ among the $SKIP$ mode and all enabled modes.

**Step 8:** Proceed with next MB, go to Step 1.


## 3   Experimental Results

The experiments were implemented by using the H.264 reference software JM-10.1 provided by the Joint Video Team (JVT). We compared the proposed fast mode decision algorithm with the fast algorithms proposed by Yang et al. [17] and Kannangara et al. [18]. The fast full search (JM_FFS) algorithm was tested for comparison. We have tested ten video sequences with different motion activities, including *Akiyo*, *Hall*, *Mother&Daughter*, *Silent*, *News*, *Foreman*, *Coastguard*, *Stefan*, *Table_Tennis*, and *Mobile&Calendar*. Each of them has 100 frames of the CIF format ($352 \times 288$). The length of a GOP is 10 and all frames within a GOP except the first frame (encoded as I frame) are encoded as P frames. The motion search range is 16 and the number of reference frame is 1. RDO and CAVLC are enabled in our experiments. The main encoding parameters are listed in Table 5.

To examine the performance at different bit rates, four QP values, 28, 32, 36, 40, are tested in our experiments. The comparison of average speed-up factors compared with JM_FFS algorithm is shown in Table 6. It can be seen that the proposed method outperforms Yang's and Kannangara's methods and the average speed-up factors is 71.35%. Table 7 shows the average number of mode searches during ME. This table also indicates that the proposed method requires

**Table 5.** Encoding parameters for JM-10.1 reference software

| Configuration | Parameters |
| --- | --- |
| Length of video frames for the simulation | 100 |
| Number of reference frames | 1 |
| Search range for the motion estimation | 16 |
| Hadamard transform for encoding DC components | ON |
| Rate-distortion optimization | ON |
| CAVLC entropy coding | ON |
| Length of GOP | 10 |
| Number of test video sequences (CIF format) | 10 |

**Table 6.** Comparison of computation time reduction compared with JM_FFS (S1: our SKIP mode decision method; S2: our early inter mode termination method)

| Sequence | Yang | Kannangara | S1 | S1+S2 |
|---|---|---|---|---|
| Akiyo | 38.30 | 62.37 | 69.31 | 83.46 |
| Hall | 33.29 | 47.97 | 63.26 | 81.03 |
| Mother&Daughter | 34.82 | 52.02 | 59.95 | 79.16 |
| Silent | 23.73 | 49.07 | 57.45 | 77.84 |
| News | 31.11 | 55.13 | 63.16 | 80.97 |
| Foreman | 21.43 | 32.43 | 34.31 | 67.17 |
| Coastguard | 8.60 | 15.91 | 18.43 | 61.54 |
| Stefan | 11.82 | 19.03 | 20.38 | 60.66 |
| Table_Tennis | 18.06 | 28.94 | 32.57 | 66.90 |
| Mobile&Calendar | 3.53 | 4.38 | 7.20 | 54.79 |
| Average | 22.47 | 36.73 | 42.60 | 71.35 |

**Table 7.** Comparison of the average number of mode operations

| Mode | Yang | Kannangara | S1 | S1+S2 |
|---|---|---|---|---|
| $SKIP$ | 35640 | 35640 | 35640 | 35640 |
| $INTER16 \times 16$ | 24682 | 20349 | 17956 | 18007 |
| $INTER16 \times 8$ | 24682 | 20349 | 17956 | 8754 |
| $INTER8 \times 16$ | 24682 | 20349 | 17956 | 5293 |
| $P8 \times 8$ | 24682 | 20349 | 17956 | 2088 |
| $INTRA16 \times 16$ | 24682 | 20349 | 17956 | 1547 |
| $INTRA4 \times 4$ | 24682 | 20349 | 17956 | 1547 |

**Table 8.** Average objective performance gains (avsnr)

| Sequence | Yang | | Kannangara | | S1 | | S1+S2 | |
|---|---|---|---|---|---|---|---|---|
| | PSNR | Rate(%) | PSNR | Rate(%) | PSNR | Rate(%) | PSNR | Rate(%) |
| Akiyo | -0.34 | 7.33 | 0.01 | -0.22 | -0.01 | 0.14 | -0.06 | 1.22 |
| Hall | -0.02 | 0.53 | 0.02 | -0.44 | 0.05 | -1.15 | -0.07 | 1.37 |
| Mother&Daughter | -0.73 | 21.54 | 0.01 | -0.03 | -0.01 | 0.41 | -0.08 | 2.05 |
| Silent | -0.22 | 5.49 | 0.00 | -0.02 | -0.01 | 0.30 | -0.14 | 3.56 |
| News | -0.29 | 5.30 | 0.00 | -0.05 | -0.02 | 0.37 | -0.18 | 3.16 |
| Foreman | -0.71 | 20.33 | -0.05 | 1.21 | -0.07 | 1.82 | -0.25 | 6.44 |
| Coastguard | -0.11 | 3.26 | -0.02 | 0.64 | -0.06 | 1.68 | -0.19 | 5.70 |
| Stefan | -0.12 | 2.38 | -0.01 | 0.18 | -0.03 | 0.56 | -0.17 | 3.46 |
| Table_Tennis | -0.37 | 11.14 | -0.05 | 1.31 | -0.07 | 2.07 | -0.24 | 7.19 |
| Mobile&Calendar | -0.08 | 1.50 | 0.00 | 0.06 | -0.05 | 1.08 | -0.23 | 4.38 |
| Average | -0.30 | 7.88 | -0.01 | 0.27 | -0.03 | 0.73 | -0.16 | 3.85 |

less number of mode operations than the other two methods. Table 8 gives the average rate and PSNR differences between the RD curves for each fast method and JM_FFS as calculated using the Bjontegaard measurement method [21]. From Table 8, we can see that Kannangara's approach yields the best RD performance but the reduction in computation time of our proposed approach is much better than Kannangara's approach (71.35% vs. 36.73%), as shown in Table 6.

## 4  Conclusion

A fast MB mode decision algorithm is proposed to reduce the computation time of H.264 video coding. Before ME, those MBs that are likely to be "skipped" are first identified. Computational saving is achieved without performing variable block-size ME and mode decisions. Further, an early inter mode termination approach is employed to disable some inter modes and all intra modes if the coding result of the current examined inter mode is good enough in terms of RD measure. Compared with JM_FFS, the proposed algorithm can reduce 71.35% of the encoding time with a negligible degradation in video quality and compression ratio.

## Acknowledgements

This research was supported in part by the National Science Council of R.O.C. under contract NSC-96-2221-E-216-043.

## References

[1] ITU-T: Recommendation H.264: Advanced Video Coding for Generic Audiovisual Services (2003)
[2] Ostermann, J., Bormans, J., List, P., Marpe, D., Narroschke, M., Pereira, F., Stockhammer, T., Wede, T.: Video coding with H.264/AVC: tools, performance and complexity. IEEE Circuits and Systems Magazine 4, 7–28 (2004)
[3] Joint Video Team (JVT) Reference software JM-10.1,
http://iphome.hhi.de/suehring/tml/
[4] Sullivan, G.J., Wiegand, T.: Rate-distortion optimization for video compression. IEEE Signal Processing Magazine 15, 74–90 (1998)
[5] Yin, P., Tourapis, H.Y.C., Tourapis, A.M., Boyce, J.: Fast mode decision and motion estimation for JVT/H.264. In: Int. Conf. on Image Processing, vol. 3, pp. 853–856 (2003)
[6] Tu, Y.K., Yang, J.F., Sun, M.T., Tsai, Y.T.: Fast variable-size block motion estimation for efficient H. 264/AVC encoding. Signal Processing: Image Communication 20, 595–623 (2005)
[7] Zhou, Z., Xin, J., Sun, M.T.: Fast motion estimation and inter-mode decision for H. 264/MPEG-4 AVC encoding. Journal of Visual Communication and Image Representation 17, 243–263 (2006)
[8] Li, G.L., Chen, M.J., Li, H.J., Hsu, C.T.: Efficient search and mode prediction algorithms for motion estimation in H.264/AVC. In: IEEE Int. Symp. on Circuits and Systems, vol. 6, pp. 5481–5484 (2005)
[9] Jing, X., Chau, L.P.: Fast approach for H. 264 inter mode decision. Electronics Letters 40, 1050–1051 (2004)

[10] Wu, D., Pan, F., Lim, K.P., Wu, S., Li, Z.G., Lin, X., Rahardja, S., Ko, C.C.: Fast intermode decision in H. 264/AVC video coding. IEEE Trans. on Circuits and Systems for Video Technology 15, 953–958 (2005)

[11] Yin, M., Wang, H.Y.: An improvement fast INTER mode selection for H.264 joint with spatio-temporal correlation. In: Int. Conf. on Wireless Communications, Networking and Mobile Computing, pp. 1237–1240 (2005)

[12] Khan, N.A., Masud, S., Ahmad, A.: A variable block size motion estimation algorithm for real-time H. 264 video encoding. Signal Processing: Image Communication 21, 306–315 (2006)

[13] Yang, J.F., Chang, S.C., Chen, C.Y.: Computation reduction for motion search in low rate video coders. IEEE Trans. on Circuits and Systems for Video Technology 12, 948–951 (2002)

[14] Zhao, Y., Richardson, I.: Macroblock classification for video encoder complexity management. In: Int. Picture Coding Symposium, pp. 371–376 (2003)

[15] Lee, J., Jeon, B.: Fast mode decision for H.264. In: IEEE Int. Conf.on Multimedia and Expo., pp. 1131–1134 (2004)

[16] Kim, Y., Choe, Y., Choi, Y.: Fast mode decision algorithm for H.264 using AZCB prediction. In: IEEE Int. Conf. on Consumer Electronics, pp. 33–34 (2006)

[17] Yang, L., Yu, K., Li, J., Li, S.: An effective variable block-size early termination algorithm for H. IEEE Trans. on Circuits and Systems for Video Technology 15, 784–788 (2005)

[18] Kannangara, C.S., Richardson, I.E.G., Bystrom, M., Solera, J.R., Zhao, Y., MacLennan, A., Cooney, R.: Low-complexity skip prediction for H. 264 through Lagrangian cost estimation. IEEE Trans. on Circuits and Systems for Video Technology 16, 202–208 (2006)

[19] Su, C.Y.: An enhanced detection algorithm for all-zero blocks in H. 264 video coding. IEEE Trans. on Consumer Electronics 52, 598–605 (2006)

[20] Malvar, H.S., Hallapuro, A., Karczewicz, M., Kerofsky, L.: Low-complexity transform and quantization in H. 264/AVC. IEEE Trans. on Circuits and Systems for Video Technology 13, 598–603 (2003)

[21] Bjontegaard, G.: Calculation of average PSNR differences between RD-curves. In: 13th VCEG-M33 Meeting (2001)

# Video Coding Using Spatially Varying Transform


Cixun Zhang[1], Kemal Ugur[2], Jani Lainema[2], and Moncef Gabbouj[1]

[1] Tampere University of Technology, Tampere, Finland
{cixun.zhang,moncef.gabbouj}@tut.fi
[2] Nokia Research Center, Tampere, Finland
{kemal.ugur,jani.lainema}@nokia.com



**Abstract.** In this paper, we propose a novel algorithm, named as Spatially Varying Transform (SVT). The basic idea of SVT is that we do not restrict the transform coding inside normal block boundary but adjust it to the characteristics of the prediction error. With this flexibility, we are able to achieve coding efficiency improvement by selecting and coding the best portion of the prediction error in terms of rate distortion tradeoff. The proposed algorithm is implemented and studied in the H.264/AVC framework. We show that the proposed algorithm achieves 2.64% bit-rate reduction compared to H.264/AVC on average over a wide range of test set. Gains become more significant at high bit-rates and the bit-rate reduction can be up to 10.22%, which makes the proposed algorithm very suitable for future video coding solutions focusing on high fidelity applications. The decoding complexity is expected to be decreased because only a portion of the prediction error needs to be decoded.

**Keywords:** H.264/AVC, video coding, transform, spatially varying transform (SVT).


## 1 Introduction

H.264/AVC (H.264 for short hereafter) is the latest international video coding standard and it provides up to 50% gain in coding efficiency compared to previous standards. However, this is achieved at the cost of both increased encoding and decoding complexity. It is estimated in [1] that the encoder complexity increases with more than one order of magnitude between MPEG-4 Part 2 (Simple Profile) and H.264 (Main Profile) and with a factor of 2 for the decoder. For mobile video services (video telephony, mobile TV etc.) and handheld consumer electronics (digital still cameras, camcorders etc), additional complexity of H.264 becomes an issue due to the limited resources of these devices. On the other hand, as display resolutions and available bandwidth/storage increases rapidly, High-Definition (HD) video is becoming more popular and commonly used, making the implementation of video codecs even more challenging.

To better satisfy the requirements of increased usage of HD video in resource constrained applications, two key issues should be addressed: coding efficiency and implementation complexity. In this paper, we propose a novel algorithm, named as Spatially Varying Transform (SVT), which provides coding efficiency gains over


T. Wada, F. Huang, and S. Lin (Eds.): PSIVT 2009, LNCS 5414, pp. 796–806, 2009.

H.264 and is expected to lower the decoding complexity. The technique is developed and studied mainly for coding HD resolution video, but it could be extended also for other resolutions. The motivations leading to design of SVT are two-fold:

1.  The block based transform design in most existing video coding standards does not align the underlying transform with the possible edge location. In this case, the coding efficiency decreases. In [2], directional discrete cosine transforms is proposed to improve the efficiency of transform coding for directional edges. However, efficient coding of horizontal/vertical edges inside the blocks and non-directional edges was not addressed.

2.  Coding the entire prediction error signal may not be the best in terms of rate distortion tradeoff. An example is the SKIP mode in H.264 [3], which does not code the prediction error at all.

The basic idea of SVT is that we do not restrict the transform coding inside normal block boundary but adjust it to the characteristics of the prediction error. With this flexibility, we are able to achieve coding efficiency improvement by selecting and coding the best portion of the prediction error in terms of rate distortion tradeoff. This is done by searching inside a certain residual region after intra prediction or motion compensation, for a sub-region and only coding this sub-region. The location parameter of the sub-region inside the region is coded into the bitstream if there are non-zero coefficients.

The proposed algorithm is implemented and studied in H.264 framework. Extensive experimental results show that it can improve the coding efficiency of H.264. In addition decoding complexity is expected to be lowered a little mainly because only a portion of the prediction error needs to be decoded. Encoding complexity of the proposed technique is higher mainly due to the brute force search process. Fast encoding algorithms are being studied to alleviate this aspect of the proposed technique.

The paper is organized as follows: The proposed algorithm is introduced in section 2 and its integration into H.264 framework is described in section 3. Experimental results are given in section 4. Section 5 concludes the paper and also presents future research directions.

## 2  Spatially Varying Transform

The basic idea of SVT is that the transform coding is not restricted inside normal block boundary but applied to a portion of the prediction error according to the characteristics of the prediction error. We only code a sub-region in a certain residual region after intra prediction or motion compensation. The sub-region is found by searching inside the region according to a certain criterion. Information of the location of the selected sub-region inside the region is coded into the bitstream, if there are non-zero coefficients. Fig. 1 shows an illustrative example of the idea: one 8x8 block inside a 16x16 macroblock is selected and only this 8x8 block is coded. In this paper, we focus our discussion on this particular configuration, which turns out to be promising, as we will see later. However, we note that there is no restriction of the "sub-region" and "region", for example, on their size, shape, etc when using the idea in a general sense. Other possible configurations of the idea to achieve further gain in coding efficiency are under study.

In the following, we further discuss two key issues of SVT in more detail: selection of location parameter candidates and filtering of block boundaries.

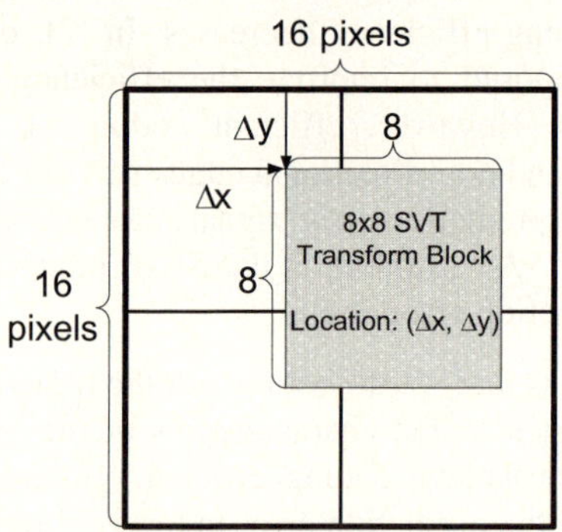


**Fig. 1.** Illustration of spatially varying transform

## 2.1 Selection of Location Parameter Candidates

When there are non-zero coefficients of the selected 8x8 block, its location inside the macroblock needs to be coded and transmitted to the decoder. As shown in Fig. 1, the location of the selected 8x8 block inside the current macroblock is denoted by ($\Delta$x, $\Delta$y) where $\Delta$x and $\Delta$y each can take integer value from 0 to 8, if the selected block is restricted to have the same size (which facilitates the transform design) for all locations. There are in total 81 possible combinations and we need to select the best one according to a certain criterion. In this paper, Rate-Distortion Optimization (RDO) is used to select the best ($\Delta$x, $\Delta$y) in terms of RD tradeoff by minimizing the following:

$$J = D + \lambda \cdot R .\qquad(1)$$

where J is the RD cost of the selected combination, D is the distortion, R is the bit rate and $\lambda$ is the Lagrangian multiplier. The reconstruction residue for the remaining part of the 16x16 residual macroblock is simply set to be 0 in our implementation, but different values can be used and might be beneficial in certain cases (luminance change, etc). Similarly, RDO can also be used to decide if SVT should be used for a macroblock.

Selection of location parameter candidates is important since it directly affects the encoding complexity and the performance of SVT. We study the frequency distribution of ($\Delta$x, $\Delta$y) and it is observed that the most frequently selected ($\Delta$x, $\Delta$y), are (0..8,0), (0..8,8), (0,1..7), (8,1..7)[1], which takes up a percentage around 60% of all 81 combinations. According to extensive experiments, this is generally true for

---

[1] In this paper, notation x..y is used to specify a range of integer values starting from x to y inclusive, with x, y being integer numbers.

different sequences, macroblock partitions and Quantization Parameters (QP). Fig. 2 below shows the distributions of ($\Delta x$, $\Delta y$) for different macroblock partitions of BigShips sequence when QP equal to 23. As we will see in section 4, using this subset of location parameters turns out to be an efficient configuration of the proposed algorithm.

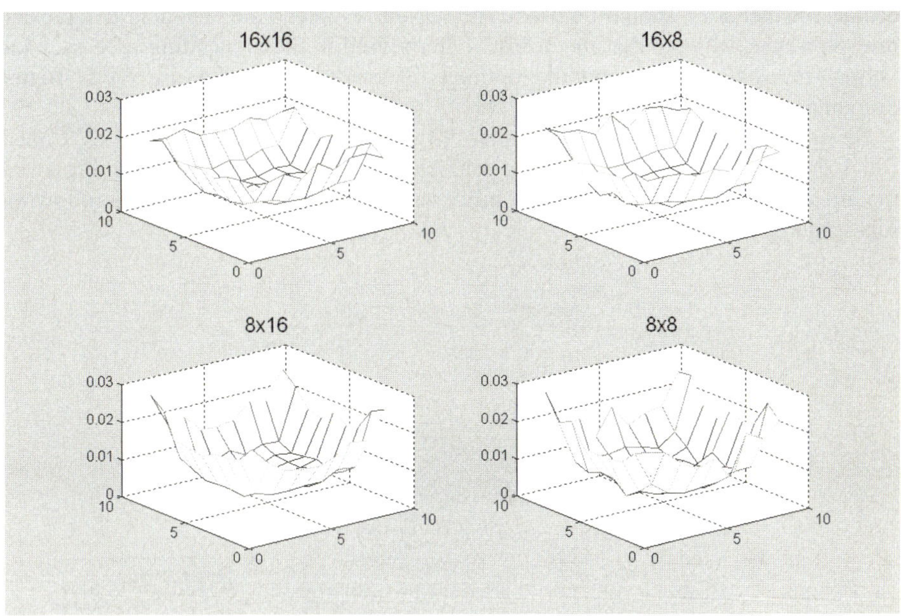

**Fig. 2.** Frequency distribution of ($\Delta x$, $\Delta y$) for different macroblock partitions of BigShips sequence, at QP=23 (Z axis denotes the frequency)

## 2.2   Filtering of Block Boundaries

Due to the coding (transform and quantization) of the selected 8x8 block, blocking artifacts may appear around its boundary with the remaining non-coded part of the macroblock. A deblocking filter can be applied to improve the subjective quality and possibly also the objective quality. An example in the framework of H.264 will be described in detail later in section 3.4.

## 3   Integration of Spatially Varying Transform into H.264 Framework

In this paper, we study the proposed technique in H.264 framework. Fig. 3 below is the block diagram of extended H.264 encoder with SVT. As shown in Fig. 3, encoder needs to search the best 8x8 block inside macroblocks that use SVT, which is marked as "SVT Search" in the diagram. Then encoder decides whether to use SVT for the current macroblock, using RDO in our implementation. The location parameter is coded and transmitted in the bitstream. A corresponding decoder needs to decode the location parameter for macroblocks that use SVT, which is marked as "SVT L.P. Decoding" in the diagram. One thing that is worth mentioning here is, in this paper and also the experimental results in section 4, we do not change the motion estimation, sub-macroblock partition decision process, even for the macroblocks that use SVT. After the residual macroblock is generated as normal, RDO is used to decide whether SVT should be used. The reason is to keep the encoding complexity low. However, we note that the normal criteria used in these encoding processes for normal macroblocks may not be optimal for macroblocks that use SVT. Better encoding algorithms are under study.

Several key parts of the H.264 standard [3], for example, macroblock types, Coded Block Pattern (CBP), entropy coding, deblocking, also need to be adjusted. Proposed modifications aiming at good compatibility with H.264 are described in the following sub-sections.

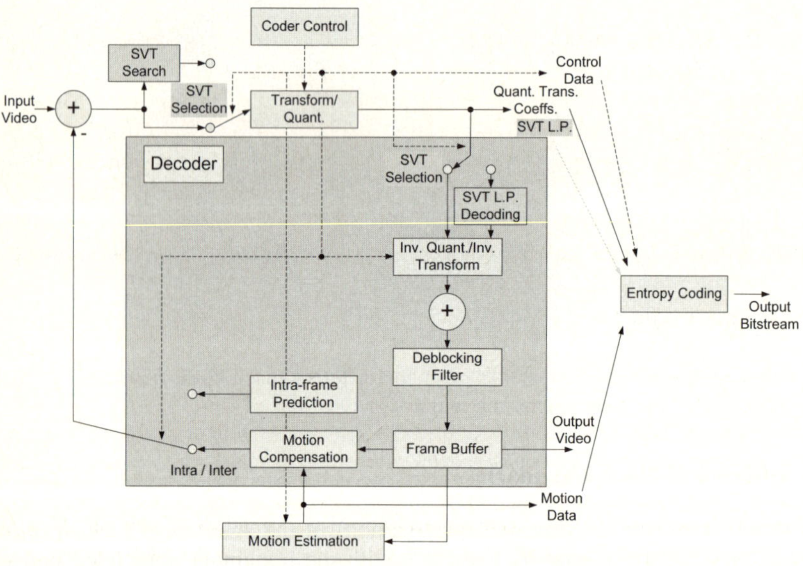


**Fig. 3.** Block diagram of extended H.264 encoder with spatially varying transform

## 3.1  Macroblock Types

In this work, we focus our study of SVT on coding inter prediction error in P slices although the idea can be easily extended to be also used in I and B slices. Table 1 below shows the extended macroblock types for P slices in H.264 [3] (original intra macroblock types in H.264 are not included), with the name of new macroblock types that use SVT in italics. The macroblock type index is coded using Exp-Golomb codes in the same way as H.264. The sub-macroblock types are kept unchanged and therefore not shown in the table.

**Table 1.** Extended macroblock types for P slices in H.264 with spatially varying transform

| mb_type | Name of mb_type |
|---------|-----------------|
| 0 | P_16x16 |
| 1 | *P_16x16_SVT* |
| 2 | P_16x8 |
| 3 | *P_16x8_SVT* |
| 4 | P_8x16 |
| 5 | *P_8x16_SVT* |
| 6 | P_8x8 |
| 7 | *P_8x8_SVT* |
| 8 | P_8x8ref0 |
| 9 | *P_8x8ref0_SVT* |
| Inferred | P_Skip |

### 3.2  Coded Block Pattern

In this work, we only use SVT for luma component coding. As shown in Fig. 1, since only one 8x8 block is selected and coded in macroblocks that use SVT, we can use 1 bit for luma CBP or jointly code it with chroma CBP as H.264 does [3]. However, in our experiments with many test sequences, we found that luma CBP is probably 1 when QP is low (and probably 0 when the QP is high) where most gain of SVT comes from, so we restrict the new macroblock modes to have luma CBP equal to 1 and there is no need to code this information. Chroma CBP is represented in the same way as H.264 [3]. An alternative way would be to infer the luma CBP according to QP.

### 3.3  Entropy Coding

In H.264 [3], when Context Adaptive Variable Length Coding (CAVLC) is used as the entropy coding, different coding table for total number of non-zero transform coefficients and trailing ones of current block is selected depending on the characteristics (the number of non-zero transform coefficients) of the neighboring blocks. For macroblocks that use SVT, for simplicity, a fixed coding table is used. Besides, we may also need to derive the information about the number of non-zero transform coefficients every luma 4x4 block has. When the selected 8x8 block aligns with the normal block boundaries, no special scheme is needed. Otherwise, the following scheme is used in our implementation:

1.  A luma 4x4 block is marked to have non-zero coefficients if it overlaps with a coded block that has non-zero coefficients in the selected 8x8 block, and marked not to have non-zero coefficients otherwise. This information may also be used in other processes, e.g., deblocking.
2.  The number of non-zero transform coefficients for each 4x4 block that is marked to have non-zero coefficients, is empirically set to the same to

$$(nC+nB/2)/nB .  \qquad (2)$$

where nC is the total number of non-zero transform coefficients in the current macroblock and nB is the number of blocks marked to have non-zero coefficients. Operator "/" is integer division with truncation of the result toward zero.

We note that due to the truncation in (2), a 4x4 block may be marked to have non-zero coefficients according to step 1 but has no non-zero coefficients according to (2) in step 2 at the same time. In our implementation, when only the information about whether a block has non-zero transform coefficients or not is, we use the result of step 1; while when the information about how many non-zero transform coefficients a block has is needed, we use the result of step 2.

### 3.4  Deblocking

As shown in Fig. 4 below, for macroblocks that use SVT, the deblocking process in H.264 [3] needs to be adjusted because the selected 8x8 block may not align with the normal block boundaries. The following scheme is used in our implementation:

1.  First, the boundary edges of the selected 8x8 block and the remaining part of the macroblock are filtered. The filtering criteria and process of these edges are similar to those used in H.264, with minor modifications based on empirical tests to produce visually pleasing results for a variety of content.
2.  Second, the normal internal edges and macroblock boundary edges are filtered except those which are inside the selected 8x8 block or overlap with the boundary edges which have already been filtered in the first step. The filtering criteria and process of these edges are kept unchanged as in H.264.

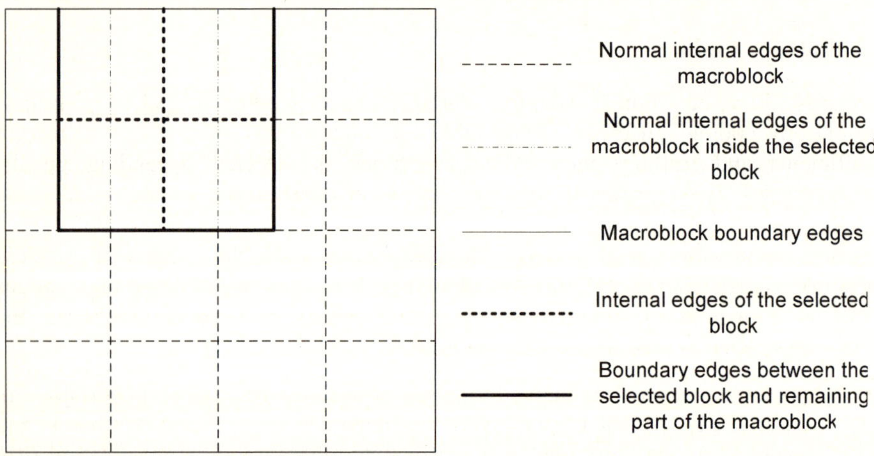


**Fig. 4.** Illustration of different edges of macroblocks that use spatially varying transform

## 4  Experimental Results

We implemented SVT on KTA1.8 reference software [4] in order to evaluate its effectiveness. Important coding parameters used in our experiments are listed as follows:

- High Profile
- QPI=22, 27, 32, 37, QPP=QPI+1
- CAVLC is used as the entropy coding
- Frame structure is IPPP, 4 reference frames
- Motion vector search range ±64 pels, resolution ¼-pel
- RDO in the "High Complexity Mode"
- Two configurations are tested. 1) Low complexity configuration: motion compensation block size are 16x16, 16x8, 8x16, 8x8, only 8x8 transform is used. In this case, also only 8x8 transform is used for macroblocks that use SVT. This represents a low complexity codec with most effective tools for HD video coding; 2) High complexity configuration: motion compensation block size are 16x16, 16x8, 8x16, 8x8, 8x4, 4x8, 4x4, both 4x4 and 8x8 transform are used. In this case, either 4x4 or 8x8 transform is selected for macroblocks that use SVT. This represents a high complexity codec with full usage of the tools provided in the standard.

We test three configurations of the proposed algorithm in our experiments:

1. SVT32: The location parameter $(\Delta x, \Delta y)$ is selected in the set: $\Phi_{32}=\{(0..8,0), (0..8,8), (0,1..7), (8,1..7)\}$ which has 32 candidates. The index is coded using 5-bit fixed length code. As we will see, this turns out to be an efficient configuration of SVT.

2. SVT4: The location parameter $(\Delta x, \Delta y)$ is selected in the set: $\Phi_4=\{(0,0), (0,8), (8,0), (8,8)\}$ which has 4 candidates. The index is coded using 2-bit fixed length code. This serves as a comparison to show the effectiveness and necessity of the searching process of SVT.

3. SVT81: The location parameter $(\Delta x, \Delta y)$ is selected in the set: $\Phi_{81}=\{(0..8,0..8)\}$ which has 81 candidates. The index is coded using 7-bit fixed length code. Although this overhead may be reduced a little by using variable length code, SVT81 serves as a meaningful comparison to show the performance of a configuration of the proposed algorithm with a selected subset of location parameters, which is SVT32 in our case.

**Table 2.** Experimental results (Low complexity configuration)

| Sequence | ΔBD-RATE | | |
|---|---|---|---|
| (1280x720/60p) | SVT32 | SVT4 | SVT81 |
| BigShips | -2.87% | -0.92% | -2.41% |
| ShuttleStart | -2.51% | -1.76% | -2.18% |
| City | -3.30% | -1.77% | -2.97% |
| Night | -2.33% | -0.55% | -1.95% |
| Optis | -2.65% | -0.12% | -2.04% |
| Spincalendar | -2.07% | -0.84% | -1.84% |
| Cyclists | -2.14% | -1.41% | -1.48% |
| Preakness | -2.34% | -0.17% | -2.26% |
| Panslow | -4.59% | -2.17% | -4.14% |
| Sheriff | -2.18% | -0.68% | -1.77% |
| Sailormen | -2.11% | -0.60% | -1.81% |
| Average | -2.64% | -1.00% | -2.26% |

this flexibility, we are able to achieve coding efficiency improvement by selecting and coding the best portion of the prediction error in terms of rate distortion tradeoff. The proposed algorithm is implemented and studied in H.264/AVC framework. Two key issues of SVT: selection of location parameter candidates and filtering of block boundaries, are addressed in detail. It is shown that a configuration of the proposed algorithm achieves on average 2.64% bit-rate reduction in low complexity configuration which represents a low complexity codec with most effective tools for HD video coding and on average 1.42% bit-rate reduction in high complexity configuration which represents a high complexity codec with full usage of the tools provided in the standard, respectively, compared to H.264/AVC. Gains become more significant at high bit-rates and the bit-rate reduction can be up to 10.22%, which makes the proposed algorithm very suitable for future video coding solutions focusing on high fidelity applications. The decoding complexity is expected to be decreased because only a portion of the prediction error needs to be decoded.

Future studies include: 1) Better configuration of the proposed algorithm to achieve better performance, e.g., by selecting different portions inside a macroblock. 2) Better encoding algorithms especially in motion estimation and macroblock partition decision to generate residuals more suitable to code for the proposed algorithm. 3) Encoding algorithms to reduce the encoding complexity.

# References


1. Ostermann, J., Bormans, J., List, P., Marpe, D., et al.: Video Coding with H.264 / AVC: Tools, Performance, and Complexity. IEEE Circuits and Systems Magazine 4(1), 7–28 (2004)
2. Zeng, B., Fu, J.: Directional discrete cosine transforms – A new framework for image coding. IEEE Trans. Circuits Syst. Video Technol. 18(3), 305–313 (2008)
3. Advanced video coding for generic audiovisual services, ITU-T Recommendation H.264 (March 2005)
4. KTA reference model 1.8m, `http://iphome.hhi.de/suehring/tml/download/KTA/jm11.0kta1.8.zip`
5. Bjontegaard, G.: Calculation of average PSNR differences between RD-curves, VCEG Doc. VCEG-M33 (March 2001)
6. Pateux, S., Jung, J.: An excel add-in for computing Bjontegaard metric and its evolution, VCEG Doc. VCEG-AE 2007 (January 2007)

# Comparison of Visible, Thermal Infra-Red and Range Images for Face Recognition

Ajmal Mian

School of Computer Science and Software Engineering
The University of Western Australia
35 Stirling Highway, Crawley, WA 6009, Australia
ajmal@csse.uwa.edu.au

**Abstract.** Existing literature compares various biometric modalities of the face for human identification. The common criterion used for comparison is the recognition rate of different face modalities using the same recognition algorithms. Such comparisons are not completely unbiased as the same recognition algorithm or features may not be suitable for every modality of the face. Moreover, an important aspect which is overlooked in these comparisons is the amount of variation present in each modality which will ultimately effect the database size each modality can handle. This paper presents such a comparison between the most common biometric modalities of the face namely visible, thermal infrared and range images. Experiments are performed on the Equinox and the FRGC databases with results indicating that visible images capture more interpersonal variations of the human face compared to thermal IR and range images. We conclude that under controlled conditions, visible face images have a greater potential of accommodating large databases compared to long-wave IR and range images.

## 1   Introduction

Face recognition is an important and challenging computer vision problem. It has many potential applications in security, surveillance and access control. One of the main challenges in face recognition is the fact that intra-class variations caused by changes in illumination, pose and facial expressions sometimes exceed inter-class variations. For example, different people tend to appear more similar from the same pose compared to the same person viewed from different poses. Likewise, different people in the same illumination condition sometimes appear more similar than the same person viewed in different illumination conditions. This is one of the main reasons why simple algorithms like Principal Component Analysis (PCA) [1] do not perform well under changing illumination, pose and facial expressions. A comprehensive survey of face recognition algorithms is given by Zhao et al. [2].

One way of dealing with the above challenges is to train the recognition system with multiple instances of each face under different conditions of illumination, expressions and pose. The training data are projected to a space which minimizes

T. Wada, F. Huang, and S. Lin (Eds.): PSIVT 2009, LNCS 5414, pp. 807–816, 2009.

the intra-class variation while maximizing the inter-class variation. This is the basic idea behind LDA (Linear Discriminant Analysis) based face recognition [3]. One assumption in LDA is that the data are linearly separable which is not always true about faces. Quadratic Discriminant Analysis (QDA) [4] relaxes this assumption and defines a quadratic surface to separate the classes. However, a common problem in LDA and QDA is that sufficient training samples covering all possible illuminations, expressions and poses of every individual are not always available. This is known as the small sample size problem [5].

In a hope to find invariant facial biometrics, researchers have investigated biometric modalities of the face other than the visible spectrum images. These modalities include the appearance of the face in the infra-red (IR) spectrum and the geometric shape of the face represented as range images or 3D polygonal models. 3D models of the face are completely invariant to illumination as they represent the facial geometry rather than the reflective properties of the face which are a function of the incident light, the facial pose, the face albedo and the facial geometry. However, the acquisition of 3D faces is not a completely illumination invariant process as it relies on controlled active illumination of the face (e.g. with laser stripes) in order to triangulate the facial geometry [6]. On the positive side, once the 3D face is acquired along with its coregistered texture (visible image), an infinite number of training samples (visible images) under different illuminations and poses can be synthesized to overcome the small sample size problem. Blanz and Vetter [7] fitted a 3D morphable model to single face images and generated many training samples to represent the same face in different illuminations and poses. 3D face models can also be used to handle expression variations. For example, Bronstein et al. [8] used isometric deformations on textured 3D faces to alleviate the effects of expressions on the face.

The infra-red spectrum can be roughly divided into four different bandwidths namely, Near-IR (NIR), Short-wave-IR (SWIR), Medium-wave-IR (MWIR) and Long-wave-IR (referred to as thermal IR in this paper). Out of the four, only the first and the last modalities have been investigated in existing literature. Two arguments are generally presented in favor of NIR images. The first one is that off-the-shelf CCD sensors are sensitive to this bandwidth and normal cameras can be modified to acquire NIR images. The second argument is that NIR is not visible to the human eye and active controlled NIR illumination can be used to acquire facial images while the system is still imperceptible to humans [9]. It is not surprising that by controlling illumination conditions good face recognition results can be achieved. However, this still does not solve the pose problem as the appearance of NIR images of the same face will change with pose.

It would not be incorrect to say that thermal IR is truly invariant to illumination conditions. Unlike 3D face and NIR face images, thermal IR images do not require the active controlled illumination of faces. In fact, thermal IR can be captured in complete darkness [10] as it is radiated by the human face due to internal heat. Thermal IR captures subsurface features believed to be unique to individuals [11]. On the downside, thermal IR imagery needs to be radio-metrically calibrated for each photo session as the calibration has a limited life span [12] i.e. the characteristics of FPA (Focal Plane Array) changes over time, no two FPAs have the same response, and the response changes with ambient conditions. Moreover, glasses are completely opaque to thermal IR [12].

The availability of many different biometric modalities of the face raises an important question. Which modality is the best for face recognition? Currently there is no agreement on what is the correct answer to this question. While the quest for the best biometric modality of the face for recognition is likely to remain an active research area, at least for some time, many researchers have attempted to perform an unbiased comparison of some of these modalities. Socolinsky and Selinger [13] performed a comparison of thermal IR and visible image based face recognition using PCA, LDA, LFA (Local Feature Analysis) [14] and ICA (Independent Component Analysis) [15]. Their results show that all four algorithms give higher recognition performance on the thermal IR images compared to the visible light images. The database used by Socolinsky and Selinger [13] contained illumination and expression variations.

Chen et al. [11] also compared thermal IR and visible image based face recognition but on a larger database and with greater time lapse between the acquisition of training and test images compared to [13]. They reported that in the case of no time-lapse in the acquisition sessions, there is negligible difference between thermal IR and visible image based recognition using PCA. In time-lapse recognition, the recognition rate of both visible and thermal IR images dropped; however PCA-based recognition performed better on visible light images.

Li et al. [9] compared the performance of visible and NIR image-based face recognition under weak illumination and reported that NIR performs better than visible images as the former produced better inter-class separation between different identities using an LBP-based (Linear Binary Patterns) [16] AdaBoost classifier. Chang et al. [17] performed a comparison of visible image and 3D face recognition using PCA and reported that both modalities give equal performance.

In almost all existing comparisons, the common criterion is the recognition rate of different face modalities using the same recognition algorithms. Such comparisons are not completely unbiased as the same recognition algorithm or features may not be suitable for every modality of the face. Moreover, an important aspect overlooked in these comparisons is the amount of variation present in each modality which will ultimately effect the maximum database size each modality can handle. To the best of our knowledge, existing literature does not compare different biometric modalities of the face using the amount of captured variation as a criterion. This paper attempts to cover these gaps and presents a comparison between the most common biometric modalities of the face using captured variation as a criterion. Experiments are performed on the Equinox [12] and the FRGC [18] databases and comparisons are presented for visible versus thermal IR and range images. Our results indicate that visible images capture more interpersonal variations compared to thermal IR and range images.

The rest of the paper is organized as follows. Section 2 gives justification of the criterion used in this paper to compared different biometric modalities of the face. Section 3 describes the databases used and the database normalization procedures used in our experiments. Section 4 describes the experimental setup and the results. Section 5 gives conclusions and some analysis of our results.

## 2   Justification of Comparison Criterion

The recognition performance of any biometric modality is a function of the following factors. (1) The accuracy of measurement. (2) Invariance of the biometric and the measurement process to extrinsic factors e.g. ambient conditions, temperature, illumination. (3) Invariance of the biometric to intrinsic properties e.g. facial expression, pose etc. (4) The feature extraction and classification algorithms. (5) Variance in the biometric modality. By in large, existing literature has focused on the first four factors for comparing different biometric modalities of the face. Socolinsky and Selinger [13] compared visible and thermal IR images for face recognition using different classifiers. However, they did not control illumination making their experiments a test of robustness of the modalities to illumination. Robustness of facial biometrics to extrinsic and intrinsic factors is important however, it is not the focus of this paper as these factors can be controlled in some applications e.g. when the subject is cooperative.

In this paper, we mainly focus on the last factor because we believe that variance in a biometric modality is an important indicator of its ability to perform well in large databases. As a crude example, imagine we were to identify people based on their heights or fingerprints. If we validate our classifiers using a small database of less than 20 individuals, both biometrics are likely to give similar performance. However, if we increase the database size from 20 to 2000, the fingerprints based classifier will give far better performance than the height based classifier. This is mainly because the variance in fingerprints of different individuals is more compared to their heights.

Ideally, the number of individuals enrolled using the biometric modalities under comparison must be increased to an extent that the gap between their recognition performances starts increasing. Moreover, the enrollment must be done under controlled conditions as the test is not of their robustness to extrinsic and intrinsic factors. This is a very difficult task and we argue that in the absence of such data, the variance in the biometric modalities is a good indicator of its ability to accommodate large databases. Statistically, the PDFs (Probability Distribution Functions) can be estimated from a small sample taken randomly from the population.

We give a more intuitive example using PDFs. Imagine two biometric modalities whose PDFs can be approximated by normal distributions as shown in Fig. 1. However, one biometric modality has higher variance than the other. As more and more measurements are taken, they are likely to fall within the same bins of the distribution and the more the variance in the distribution, the more will be the separation between these bins. In person identification, each bin corresponds to a unique individual and it is desirable to have as much separation between the bins as possible so that a person is correctly classified to the correct bin even in the presence of noise.

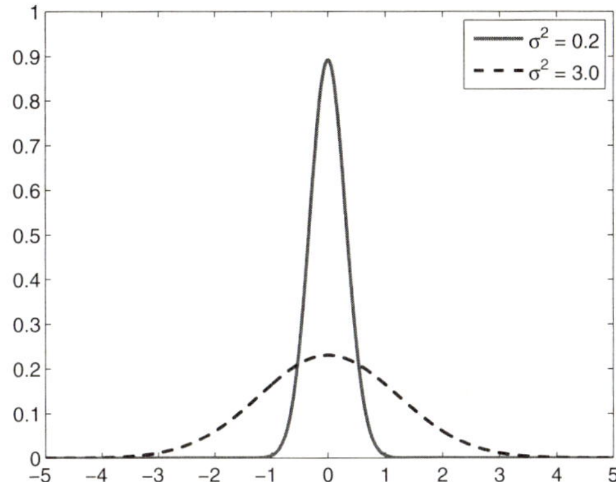


**Fig. 1.** Probability Distribution Functions with different variances

Variance in the biometric modalities could be measured in the raw data however, biometrics acquired through imaging have very high dimensionality and contains noise. Therefore, it is advantageous to consider only the most significant eigenvectors of the data by performing Principal Component Analysis. Recall that we are assuming controlled condition which means no intra-class variation in the data. Therefore, only a single sample per individual per modality is sufficient.

## 3   Data Normalization

We used the Equinox database [12] for comparing visible images with thermal IR images. For comparison of visible images with range images (3D data), we used the FRGC (Face Recognition Grand Challenge) database [18]. While performing the comparison between two biometric modalities of the face, every possible effort was made to make all other variables constant i.e. a constant frontal illumination was chosen and coregistered images belonging to the same acquisition session were chosen. In the case of the Equinox database, the same frame number was chosen for all individuals so that every individual has the same facial expression across different modalities and there is a one-to-one correspondence between the pixels of different modalities. Note that this paper compares the amount of interpersonal variation captured by different biometric modalities of the face as opposed to the invariance of the modalities to external variations such as illumination.

The corresponding visible and thermal IR images of the Equinox database were already coregistered. However, there were some scale and pose variations between the images of different individuals. Scale and pose were normalized across all the images by manual identification of four landmarks on the visible images and transforming both the visible and thermal IR images to the same coordinates. Note that the same transformation can be used for the corresponding thermal IR and visible images as they were already coregistered. A mask

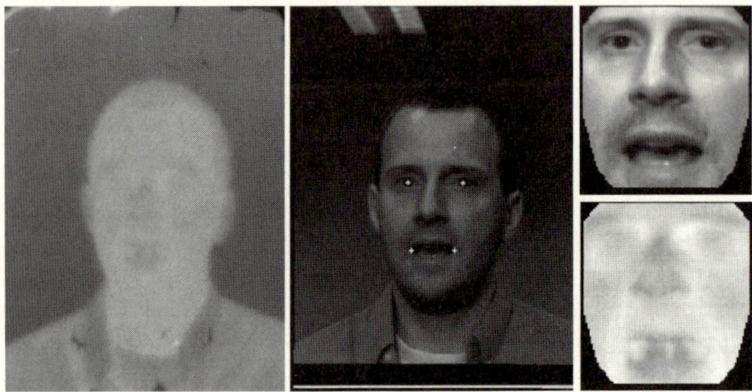

**Fig. 2.** Thermal IR image (left) and its coregistered visible light image (center) are normalized and cropped (right) using four landmarks selected on the visible image

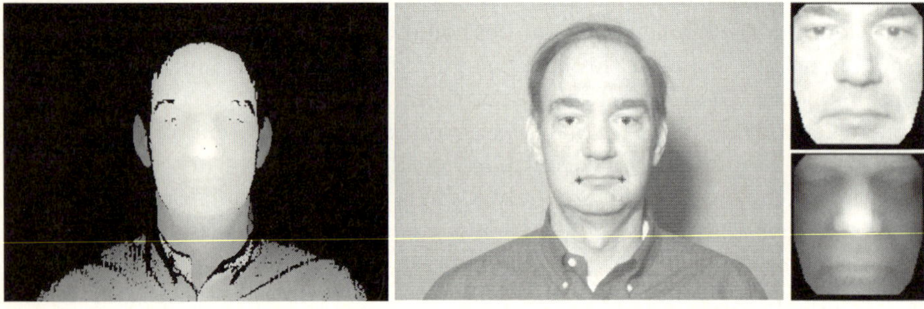

**Fig. 3.** Range image (left) and its coregistered visible image (center) are normalized and cropped (right) by manually identifying four landmarks. The range image is also preprocessed to remove holes and spikes.

was used to remove the background. Fig. 2 shows a sample pair of coregistered thermal IR and visible images before and after normalization.

For comparison between visible and range (3D) images, we used the FRGC database. The range images were preprocessed to remove spikes using a neighborhood distance constraint and fill holes using cubic interpolation. The visible and range image pairs where then normalized in a similar way to the thermal IR images i.e. by identifying four landmarks on the visible image and using the same transformation to normalize the visible and range images. Fig. 3 shows a sample pair of visible and range image before and after normalization.

## 4   Experiments and Results

Ideally, if a single database of coregistered images in the visible, thermal IR range and 3D data were available for a significant number of subjects, we would have performed a single experiment to compare the three modalities. However, there is no public database which offers simultaneously acquired and coregistered images in all the three modalities. Therefore, we performed two experiments. The first one to compare visible and thermal IR using the Equinox database and the second one to compare visible and range images using the FRGC database.

## 4.1 Experiment 1

The first experiment compares visible and thermal IR images. There were 89 subjects for which both modalities were available in the Equinox database. A single pair of visible and its coregistered thermal IR image was chosen for each subject. The images were normalized as discussed in the previous section and then projected to the PCA space. Each image in a given modality was converted to a column vector and placed in a matrix $\mathbf{I} = [I_1, I_2, \ldots I_n]$, where $I_1$ is the column vector of the first image and $n$ is the total number of images. Next, the covariance matrix of $\mathbf{I}$ is calculated.

$$ m = \frac{1}{n} \sum_{i=1}^{n} I_i \ , \tag{1} $$

$$ C = \frac{1}{n} \sum_{i=1}^{n} I_i I_i^T - mm^T \ , \tag{2} $$

where $m$ is the mean image and $C$ is the covariance matrix. The eigenvalues of the covariance matrix are calculated as follows:

$$ CV - DV \ , \tag{3} $$

where $V$ is the matrix of eigenvectors and $D$ is the diagonal matrix of eigenvalues $\lambda$. The eigenvalues are sorted in decreasing order ($\lambda_1$ being the highest eigenvalue) and the ratio $\psi_k$ of the sum of the first $k$ eigenvalues to the sum of all the eigenvalues is calculated

$$ \psi_k = \frac{\sum_{i=1}^{k} \lambda_i}{\sum_{i=1}^{n} \lambda_i} \ . \tag{4} $$

The ratio $\psi_k$ shows the fidelity of reconstruction of the original image from its highest $k$ eigenvalues. The higher the value of $\psi_k$ for a given $k$, the smaller is the variation in the images. In all our experiments $\psi_k$ is used as a metric to compare the variation between different modalities. Higher values of $\psi_k$ for a given modality mean that there is less variation in the modality. Fig. 4-a compares the $\psi_k$ curves of visible and thermal IR images. The figure clearly shows that visible images capture more variation in the human faces compared to thermal IR images.

## 4.2 Experiment 2

This experiment compares visible and range (3D) images. We picked a single pair of visible and range images for 89 subjects from the training set of the

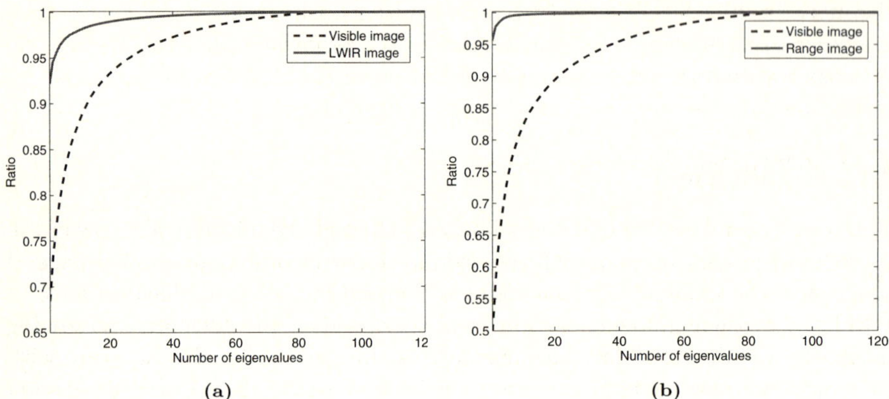


**Fig. 4.** The ratio $\psi_k$ (vertical axis) versus the number of eigenvalues $k$ (horizontal axis). (a) Results of experiment 1. Visible images capture more interpersonal variation in human faces compared to thermal IR images. (b) Results of experiment 2. Interpersonal variation in facial range images is significantly lower than visible images.

**Table 1.** Number of eigenvectors required to preserve 95% variance in facial images of different modalities. Higher values correspond to greater variation in the images.

| Database | Equinox | | FRGC | |
|---|---|---|---|---|
| Subjects | 89 | | 89 | |
| Modality | Visible Image | Thermal IR Image | Visible Image | Range Image |
| Eigenvalues | 27 | 3 | 38 | 1 |

FRGC data (Spring2003range [18]) as these images were acquired in controlled illumination with neutral facial expressions. The reason for choosing 89 images was to make the number of subjects compatible with experiment 1. Moreover, the 89 images were hand picked to avoid image pairs with poor coregistration, excessive number of holes (missing data) in the range image and other types of corrupted imagery. Note that hand picking good images does not bias our experiment as we are not performing recognition. In fact, this ensures that the data are not biased towards the range images which would otherwise show more variation due to sensor problems i.e. holes and spikes. The visible and range images were normalized as discussed in the previous section and then projected to the PCA space as described in Section 4.1. Fig. 4-b shows the $\psi_k$ curves for the two modalities. Notice that visible images capture more interpersonal variation compared to range images. In fact the difference is more significant in this case.

In Principal Component Analysis based compression techniques, the number of significant eigenvectors is usually chosen such that 95% of the total variance is preserved in the data (in our case images). Therefore, we chose 95% variance as a benchmark and compared the number of significant eigenvectors required by each modality to achieve this benchmark. The results of both experiments are compiled in Table 1.

## 5   Conclusion and Analysis

This paper presented a comparison of three different biometric modalities of the face. Unlike previous studies, which used face recognition rate as a criterion, this paper used the amount of variation as a comparison criterion. This criterion is significant as it will influence the performance of a given modality with increasing database size. Practical face recognition systems are expected to operate with very large databases, which are hard to generate for the purpose of experimental analysis. Our results conclude that visible images capture more interpersonal variation in the human faces compared to thermal IR and range images.

The outcomes of our experiments are not surprising. One can intuitively perceive that visible light is likely to capture more variation in human faces because under constant illumination, pose and facial expressions, the visible image is a function of two intrinsic properties of the face. These intrinsic properties are the face albedo (facial texture) and the 3D shape of the face. Even though visible image based face recognition algorithms are sometimes referred to as 2D face recognition algorithms, this is not entirely true as visible images also carry shape information which is exploited in shape from shading algorithms. Compared to the visible image, the thermal IR and range image each captures only a single intrinsic property of the face namely the radiated heat and the facial geometry. Human faces have the same topological shape and there is less variation in it compared to the facial texture.

## Acknowledgments

The author would like to thank Equinox Corporation for providing the thermal IR data and the FRGC organizers [18] for providing the range data. This research is supported by ARC grant DP0881813.

## References

1. Turk, M., Pentland, A.: Eigenfaces for Recognition. Journal of Cognitive Neuroscience 3, 71–86 (1991)
2. Zhao, W., Chellappa, R., Phillips, P.J., Rosenfeld, A.: Face Recognition: A Literature Survey. ACM Computing Survey, 399–458 (2003)
3. Belhumeur, P., Hespanha, J., Kriegman, D.: Eigenfaces vs. Fisherfaces: Recognition Using Class Specific Linear Projection. IEEE Transactions on Pattern Analysis and Machine Intelligence 19, 711–720 (1997)
4. Srivastava, S., Gupta, M., Frigyik, B.: Bayesian Quadratic Discriminant Analysis. The Journal of Machine Learning Research 8(3), 1277–1305 (2007)

5. Lu, J., Plataniotis, K., Venetsanopoulos, A.: Regularized discriminant analysis for the small sample size problem in face recognition. Pattern Recognition Letters 24(16), 3079–3087 (2003)
6. Bowyer, K.W., Chang, K., Flynn, P.: A Survey Of Approaches and Challenges in 3D and Multi-modal 3D + 2D Face Recognition. Computer Vision and Image Understanding 101(1), 1–15 (2006)
7. Blanz, V., Vetter, T.: Face Recognition Based on Fitting a 3D Morphable Model. IEEE Transactions on Pattern Analysis and Machine Intelligence 25, 1063–1074 (2003)
8. Bronstein, A.M., Bronstein, M.M., Kimmel, R.: Three-dimensional face recognition. International Journal of Computer Vision 64(1), 5–30 (2005)
9. Li, S.Z., Chu, R., Liao, S., Zhang, L.: Illumination invariant face recognition using near-infrared images. IEEE Transactions on Pattern Analysis and Machine Intelligence 29(4), 627–639 (2007)
10. Jain, A., Bolle, R., Pankanti, S.: Biometrics: Personal Identification in Networked Society. Kluwer Academic Publishers, Dordrecht (1999)
11. Chen, X., Flynn, P., Bowyer, K.: Ir and visible light face recognition. Computer Vision and Image Understanding 99(3), 332–358 (2005)
12. Socolinsky, D., Wolff, L., Neuheisel, J., Eveland, C.: Illumination invariant face recognition using thermal infrared imagery. In: IEEE Conference on Computer Vision and Pattern Recognition, vol. 1, pp. 527–534 (2001)
13. Socolinsky, D., Selinger, A.: A comparative analysis of face recognition performance with visible and thermal infrared imagery. In: International Conference on Pattern Recognition, vol. 4, pp. 217–222 (2002)
14. Penev, P., Attick, J.: Local Feature Analysis: A general statistical theory for object representation. Network: Computation in Neural Systems 7(3), 477–500 (1996)
15. Bartlett, M.S., Lades, H.M., Sejnowski, T.: Independent Component Representation for Face Recognition. In: SPIE, pp. 528–539 (1998)
16. Ahonen, T., Hadid, A., Pietikainen, M.: Face Recognition with Local Binary Patterns. In: Pajdla, T., Matas, J(G.) (eds.) ECCV 2004. LNCS, vol. 3021, pp. 469–481. Springer, Heidelberg (2004)
17. Chang, K., Bowyer, K., Flynn, P.: Multi-Modal 2D and 3D Biometrics for Face Recognition. In: IEEE Analysis and Modeling of Faces and Gestures, pp. 187–194 (2003)
18. Phillips, P.J., Flynn, P.J., Scruggs, T., Bowyer, K.W., Chang, J., Hoffman, K., Marques, J., Min, J., Worek, W.: Overview of the Face Recognition Grand Challenge. In: IEEE Computer Vision and Pattern Recognition, pp. 947–954 (2005)

# Enhanced Sports Image Annotation and Retrieval Based Upon Semantic Analysis of Multimodal Cues


Kraisak Kesorn and Stefan Poslad

School of Electronic Engineering and Computer Science,
Queen Mary University of London, Mile End Rd, London, E1 4NS, United Kingdom
{kraisak.kesorn,stefan.poslad}@elec.qmul.ac.uk



**Abstract.** This paper presents a framework for semi-automatic annotation and semantic image retrieval, applied to the sports domain, based upon semantic analysis of both image text captions and visual features of the image. Unstructured text captions of images are analysed in order to extract the concepts and restructure them into a semantic model. SVM classification of the multi-dominant colours and edge ratio information of the images are used to classify the sport genre. The novelty of the proposed semantic framework is that it can find both the indirectly relevant concepts (concepts not directly referred to) in the visual information and can represent the semantic of images at a higher level by combining image captions and visual feature information. In addition, integrating LSI into the semantic framework enables the proposed system to tolerate ontology imperfections. Experimental results show that the use of the semantic approach significantly enhances image retrieval. Semantic visual information classification and retrieval based upon multimodal cues.

**Keywords:** Ontology, Semantic Model, Image Classification, Knowledge base, Image Retrieval.


## 1 Introduction

Image understanding is one of the most difficult tasks and fastest-growing research areas in the field of computer vision. A huge research effort focuses on the automatic annotation and extraction of visual features which are able to represent semantic of images at the human perception level. The emerging approaches of this task are categorised into two groups [1], data-driven and knowledge-driven. The data-driven approach works on the basis of extracting low-level features and deriving the corresponding high-level content representations without any prior knowledge. While the knowledge-driven approach utilises high-level domain knowledge to extract appropriate content descriptions by guiding features extraction, analysis, and reasoning.

It has been argued that the low-level visual features are not sufficient for depicting the semantic level of the images. This information bears no semantic connection to the actual scene content because it is a simply output of some image processing algorithms. Text and image are two distinct types of information from different modalities [2], as they represent the 'thing' in a quite different way. However, there are some unbreakable and implicit connections between textual and visual information. In the image retrieval


T. Wada, F. Huang, and S. Lin (Eds.): PSIVT 2009, LNCS 5414, pp. 817–828, 2009.

research area, they can be used to enhance image retrieval by supplementing image content with textual information associated with the image.

In this paper, we propose a novel framework to exploit both low-level features and the associative textual information to perform semantic-based image annotation, indexing, and retrieval. A key feature is that the framework restructures the text captions into the semantic model and tries to predict sport genres using the extracted multi-dominant colours and edge ratio information. These textual and visual cues are combined together in order to narrow the semantic gap and aid the retrieval mechanism. In addition, the hybrid combination of natural language and semantic restructuring degrades nicely when ontology is incomplete as this is compensated by the LSI for natural language processing.

The remainder of this paper is organized as follows: Section 2 analyses state of the art frameworks. Section 3 describes the proposed framework infrastructure. Section 4 describes the implementation and evaluation. Section 5 concludes the strengths, weaknesses, and significance of our approach and, finally, our future work.

## 2   Related Work

There is a vast amount of sport images and videos being produced every day for news, sport, entertainment, and education by media companies and publishers etc. However, sport photograph classification and retrieval using only low-level visual descriptions has proven to be an extremely difficult task to obtain accurate results. Consequently, several techniques were proposed in order to classify and retrieve images at semantic level. Assfalg et al [3] classified sports video by using the playfield colour histogram of the keyframes. However, the keyframes may not contain significant parts of the playfield and the only colour feature is not sufficient to classify different types of sports. Hence, colour, texture, and shape features were deployed to classify sport genres [4]. However, system was limited to distinguishing some sport kinds which have visual similarity e.g., tennis and track events. Multi-coloured features of the playing surface and the team uniforms were used to classify sports video in [5, 6]. In some cases, however, uniform colours are not consistent. Therefore, using uniform colours is unreliable. Edge information was used to classify the sport genres by Yuan [7]. The K-NN algorithm was employed to classify the different sport genres. However, the combination of edge feature with other important visual features is needed in order to achieve more precision and recall.

In fact, even when content-based techniques are applied, textual information surrounding images should not be disregarded since it often includes some form of human generated descriptions of the images which often remain at a higher level to depict the properties that are very difficult to infer by visual features e.g., name of person, time, and place. Visual features, in turn, are useful to classify images into different categories when the associative textual information is not supplied. Therefore, neither textual nor visual information alone can suffice the users' requests. The combination of textual information with image features information has been suggested to improve image search relevance and precision [8], [9], [10]. Wang [11] proposed a data-driven approach for image retrieval using Web images and their textual annotations. By using the data-driven method, the framework is not able to search semantically. From the analysis above, we can draw the limitations of the surveyed state-of-the-art frameworks as follows:

*1) Image Classification*

1.1) Classification using K-NN technique has some drawbacks. For instance, the computation cost is high because it needs to compute the distance of each query instance to all training samples. In addition, the symmetry problem [12] raises other problems in image classification and automatic annotation.

1.2) Textual information is discarded. Whereas visual information represents content (low-level features) of an image, text captions are useful to describe the context of an image.

1.3) Only green, yellow, and white dominant colours, in some cases, are insufficient to distinguish some sport genres which have similar colour information.

*2) Image Retrieval*

2.1) The major weakness of the data-driven approach is that it fails to interact meaningfully with users since the built in associations between image semantic and its low-level features quantitative descriptions are not apparent to users. Therefore, the knowledge-driven approach is an alternative approach to solve this problem.

2.2) An image is subjective. A single picture can be interpreted differently by different people. Only visual information cannot support the different views from users.

## 3   Proposed Framework

The framework presented here addresses above limitations and represents the main novelty and contribution of this paper. This section presents a high-level architecture (Fig. 1.) for performing semantics extraction from images based on a predefined semantic model and semantic rules.

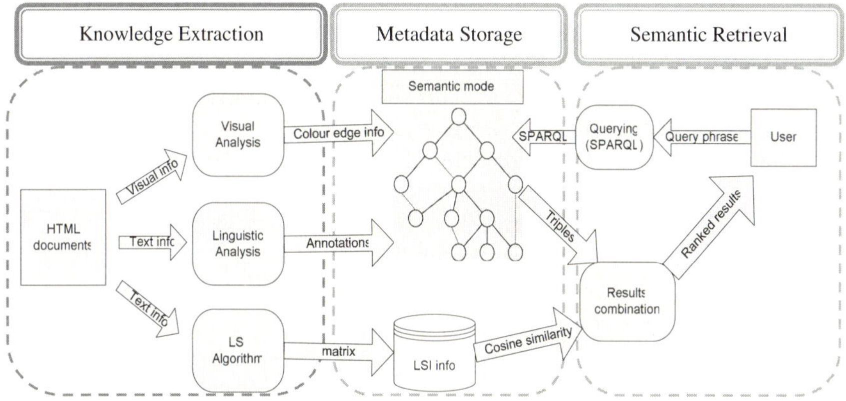


**Fig. 1.** High-level architecture of the knowledge-based search

### 3.1  Semantic Model

Among the several knowledge representation formalisms, ontology presents a number of advantages. It provides ways to define well structured concepts and their relationships and subsequently to ease the task of annotation and retrieval. In our framework, two main classes of ontology are defined [13], Domain and Photo annotation ontology. The *Domain ontology* describes the vocabulary and background knowledge of the photo's subject domain. It comprises two subclasses. The *Subject_matter* and the *Photo_features* are created in order to correspond to four main aspects such as what sport type does the photo depict? Who is an athlete in the picture? When and where was the photo made? What is the format of photo?  The *Photo Annotation Ontology* is designed to store the annotations of images in the sport domain.  This ontology provides the description template for annotation construction. Fig. 2 depicts the semantic model of the proposed framework.

### 3.2  Semantic Linguistic Analysis

First, the image captions are parsed from HTML documents and, then, a NLP framework, ESpotter [14], processes those text captions. The ESpotter generates an initial version of the annotated documents in the form of XML format. These annotated documents will then be extracted to form the *initial metadata* and will then be stored in a relational database.

In many cases, an initial metadata entity could match with several ontology entities e.g., the sentence *"Kumi Araki from Japan"*. For computer system, it is difficult to distinguish between 'Japan' which is the *'hostCountry'* and 'Japan' which is the *'Nationality'* of athletes; therefore, the *disambiguation step* is required to find the most suitable ontology entity for each metadata. Having been disambiguated, the *knowledge discovery step* finds any implicit relationship among ontology entities. To do this, *semantic rules* are applied to this task. Consequently, new metadata may be associated with an image. For instance, if date in the photograph is detected as "10 February 1998", this picture might have a relationship with the Nagano Olympic Games which took place in year 1998 in Nagano (the host city), and Japan (the host country) and it relates to Winter sport. This solves the data-driven approach limitation in the state of the art frameworks.

The ultimate goal is all semantic metadata will be added to suitable ontology entities. However, some metadata cannot be matched with any particular ontology entities because there is no predefined ontology entity to contain that metadata but it might be important to represent the meaning of an image. Therefore, our system does not discard these non-ontological named entities. They are assigned to the *'otherDetails'* ontology entity. On the other hands, some ontology entities might be incomplete by missing the necessary information because that information is not supplied in the text captions. The semantic rules also try to handle the missing information by interlinking the previous relevant semantic metadata and fulfilling any missing ontology information. The following is an example of a simple semantic rule used in our framework.

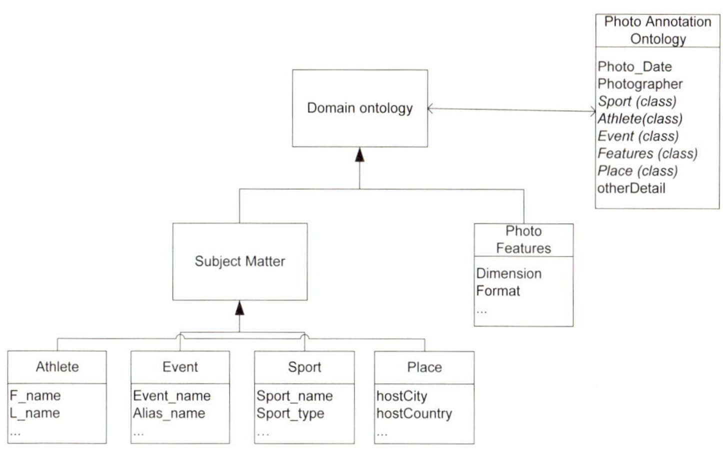

**Fig. 2.** The semantic model

Add x to M (metadata) if all of the following conditions hold:

$$\forall x \exists y \mid Photo(x) \wedge PhotoDate(x) \wedge happensDuring(x) \Rightarrow Event(y) \wedge$$
$$hostCity(y) \wedge hostCountry(y)$$

Nevertheless, it cannot be expected that the quality of the generated metadata reaches the same quality of manually created metadata. Therefore, manual correction and annotation of metadata are supported. Latent Semantic Indexing (LSI) is also exploited in this framework to solve the ontology imperfection problem. After textual information is parsed from image captions, LSI [15] creates a term-image matrix which contains the numbers of terms (frequency) that appeared with the image. This frequency is used to determine the degree of importance of those terms to the image. Each term will be assigned a weight to show the importance of that term to the image.

### 3.3 Semantic Visual Analysis

Linguistic analysis cannot take place when text captions are not available. To deal with this added uncertainty, the image signature e.g., colour and edge are essential cues to distinguish images. We exploit these features to classify images into different categories of sport types using the Support Vector Machine (SVM) approach.

The HSV (Hue, Saturation, and Value) colour model is intimately related to the way human eye perceives colour. Unlike the previous works, we utilise multi-dominant colours to classify images rather than using a single dominant colour of playfield [5, 6, 7]. In addition, our framework focuses on the close-up images. It is therefore more challenging to distinguish the sport types in sport images. In order to extract dominant colours, an image will be converted from RGB colour space to HSV colour space using Eq.1 [16].

$$H = \cos^{-1}\left\{ \frac{\frac{1}{2}\left[(R-G)+(R-B)\right]}{\sqrt{(R-G)^2 + (R-B)(G-B)}_-} \right\} \qquad (1)$$

Usually, the Hue varies from 0 to 1.0 and is divided into six corresponding colours vary from red through yellow, green, cyan, blue, and magenta. After RGB conversion, every image is normalised and only top three dominant colours which have smallest standard deviation (SD) are selected. As some different sport types have the same dominant colours, edge information is utilised to aid the image classification task. Every image acquires its edge information using the *"Canny edge detector"* approach. Next, every pixel of an image is examined. The *'edge pixel'* is the pixel which has value 1 and non-edge pixel is 0. The edge ratio is calculated by Eq. 2 [7].

$$edge\ ratio = \frac{sum\ of\ edge\ pixels}{sum\ of\ all\ pixels} \qquad (2)$$

To consider how good the edge information represent images in different categories, two statistical measures, SD and mean, are exploited to consider the edge information. Mean is an indicator of centre and the SD measures variability. In order to consistently represent the images, the SD should be as small as possible whereas the greater the spread of the mean of image categories, the easier to classify them. Table 1 shows the example of the dominant colours and edge ratio with SD.

In order to achieve fully automatic classification, the SVM is applied for supervised classification. The established SVM [17] is deployed for sport genre classification. The radial basis function (RBF) is used as a kernel function for classification as shown in the following formula:

$$K(x_i, x_j) = \exp(-\gamma \| x_i - x_j \|^2), \gamma > 0 \qquad (3)$$

Where $\gamma$ is a kernel parameter, $x_i$ and $x_j$ are training vectors. We select the RBF kernel because it can handle the case when the relationship between class labels and attributes is nonlinear. Furthermore, the RBF kernel has less numerical difficulties.

**Table 1.** Example of dominant colours, mean, and SD value in different sport categories

| Sport Categories | Dominant Colours | Average Edge Ratio* | SD of Edge |
|---|---|---|---|
| **Badminton** | Y, B, M | 0.071 | 0.6% |
| **Basketball** | Y, B, M | 0.093 | 0.5% |
| **Equestrian** | G, B, M | 0.097 | 1.87% |
| **Fencing** | G, B, M | 0.067 | 2.20% |
| **Football** | R, Y, C | 0.071 | 0.09% |
| **Sailing** | R, Y, M | 0.107 | 1.80% |

where R= Red, Y=Yellow, G=Green, C=Cyan, B=Blue, and M= Magenta

After images are classified, their annotations (sport genre) are stored in a relational database (RDBMS) and will be processed to find the indirect relationship to other classes in the semantic model using the semantic rules. The methodology for mapping from RDBMS to the semantic model is described in the next section.

### 3.4  Semantic Metadata Storage

The initial semantic metadata generated by the *Semantic Linguistic Analysis* and the *Semantic Visual Analysis* is stored in the RDBMS (MySQL). Later, this metadata will be restructured to the semantic model from which data is given a well defined meaning. This enables applications to use data in different contexts. To expose relational database in the semantic model (RDF format), the mapping process [18] is shown in Fig. 3.

1) The initial metadata is retrieved using the SQL select command and the record sets returned from the query are grouped by columns.
2) The Jena API [19] is deployed to create ontology instances and their properties. Jena is a Java class library, and is composed mainly of API and SPI (System Programming Interface).
3) The grouped record set metadata are assigned to the ontology instances created in step 2).

### 3.5  Semantic Image Retrieval

To retreieve images, the query keyword from user will be examined and stop words are eliminated. Then, *SPARQL querie* is performed. The SPARQL [20] query is executed against the knowledge base, which returns a list of instances that satisfy the query. The *cosine similarity* algorithm [24] is deployed to compute the similarity between query and image. As shown in Fig. 1, the result of LSI will be used instead of the result from the ontology when the knowledge-based search fails in order to support *Ontology imperfection*. In other words, the performance of the framework will degrade nicely when the domain ontology is incomplete by compensating using the LSI results.

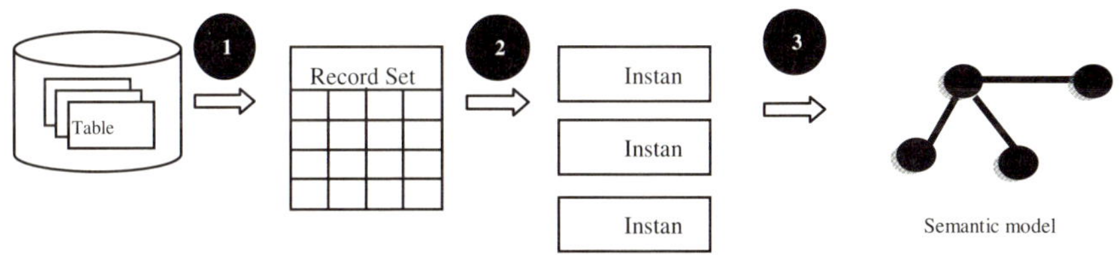


**Fig. 3.** The RDBMS to RDF mapping

## 4  Implementation and Evaluation

In this experiment, a collection of sport photographs from the Olympic organization website [21] was assembled.  To evaluate the retrieval performance, three retrieval methods were tested by selected sample queries, and compared the retrieval performance based on the precision and recall values. MTLAB v.7.5 is deployed for visual features extraction and SVM for the classification task.

### 4.1  Hypotheses to Evaluate the Retrieval Performance

Before proceeding to evaluate the classification and image retrieval performance, some hypotheses were established against the limitations of the existing solutions addressed in section 2.

*Hypothesis 1 (H1):* the extracted visual information such as dominant colours and edge information are able to distinguish the different types of sport efficiently.

*Hypothesis 2 (H2):* using the collateral textual information (image captions) and visual information together are able to improve the retrieval performance compared to the text-based and visual-based retrievals.

*Hypothesis 3 (H3):* the knowledge-driven approach can find implicit relationship among concepts which are not mentioned directly in the text captions but they might be semantically relevant.

*Hypothesis 4 (H4):* the proposed framework is able to support subjectivity of image by utilising the semantic model.

*Hypothesis 5 (H5):* the ontology-based search provides good results even though it is imperfect.

**Table 2.** The confusion matrix of sports classification using SVM approaches

| | Bm | Bb | Bk | Et | Fn | Fb | Sl | Sw | Tn | Rn | Ih | Sk | Total images |
|---|---|---|---|---|---|---|---|---|---|---|---|---|---|
| **Bm** | 8 | | | | | | | | 2 | | | | 10 |
| **Bb** | | 10 | | | | | | | | | | | 10 |
| **Bk** | | | 10 | | | | | | | | | | 10 |
| **Et** | | | | 8 | 1 | | | | 1 | | | | 10 |
| **Fn** | | | | 2 | 8 | | | | | | | | 10 |
| **Fb** | | | | | | 8 | 1 | | | 1 | | | 10 |
| **Sl** | | | 2 | | | | 8 | | | | | | 10 |
| **Sw** | | | | | | | | 10 | | | | | 10 |
| **Tn** | | | | | | | | | 10 | | | | 10 |
| **Rn** | | | | | | | 2 | | | 8 | | | 10 |
| **Ih** | | | | | 1 | | 1 | | | | 8 | | 10 |
| **Sk** | | | | | | | | | | | | 10 | 10 |
| **Accuracy** | 8 | 10 | 10 | 8 | 8 | 8 | 8 | 10 | 10 | 8 | 8 | 10 | 106/120 (88.33%) |

Bm=Batmiton, Bb=Baseball, Bk=Basketball, Et=Equestrian, Fn=Fencing, Fb=Football, Sl=Sailing
Sw=Swimming, Tn=Tennis, Rn=Running, Ih=Ice Hockey, Sk=Skating

### 4.2  Classification Performance

To distinguish the sports genres in images, 120 images were used for training purpose and creating a model by using LIBSVM [17] and another 120 images were used for testing. The classification results are shown in Table 2. It is evident that using multi-dominant colours and the edge ratio information can classify sports efficiently. The overall accuracy the classification model using SVM technique is 88.33%. This statistical information shows that the H1 hypothesis is clearly verified.

### 4.3  Retrieval Performance Measurement

To evaluate the rest of hypotheses, some sample queries have been selected. Three searching approaches, the keyword-based search (Lucene [22]), the content-based search (LIRe [23]), and the knowledge-based search (the proposed approach), are tested and compared the results. For the content-based search, an image is used as a query instead of keywords. The selected queries are listed as follows:

*Query 1 (Q1): Find all photographs of a specific sport type* e.g. swimming, football, or basketball. This query is used for the H2 hypothesis testing. Good image retrieval system should recognise all photographs which both syntactically and semantically related to the query keyword.

*Query 2 (Q2): Find all photographs which are semantically relevant to something.* For instance, swimming, sailing, and diving are semantically relevant to water. This aims to test the H3 hypothesis. By using the knowledge-driven approach, therefore, the new system should recognize this indirect relevance.

*Query 3 (Q3): Find all photographs about specific athlete name.* This is a simple query aiming for testing H4. This is because one might be interested in sport genre in an image whereas other might be interested in an athlete appeared in the picture. Therefore, if same images are returned by using different query keywords, this could imply that the proposed system is able to support the subjective issue.

*Query 4 (Q4): Find all photographs of a specific type of sport at specific location* e.g., swimming sport in the Sydney (host city). This query aims to test H5 hypothesis. Although a collection does not contain photos about swimming in the Sydney Games, the system should suggest some photographs for the user rather than return nothing to user.

### 4.4  Empirical Results and Evaluation

The framework was tested by 250 photographs. The ontology was created during the knowledge extraction step with more than 2300 instances stored in a RDF file. The experimental results were reported in the 11-point Interpolated Average Precision graphs which are shown in Figure 4 (a) and (b). As Figure 4a shows, in Q1, the knowledge-based search is superior to the other retrieval approaches. This is because the semantic search supports the expression of more precise information, leading to more accurate answers. Using string matching technique, the keyword-based search has difficulty recognising an image if query keyword is not addressed directly in the image captions. Consequently, it obtains a lower precision and recall. For the content-based search, only visual information cannot represent the meaning of an image precisely. Therefore, it obtains very poor results compared to others. To summarize, using both textual and visual information as the knowledge base there are dramatic improvements in precision and recall. Thus, the H2 hypothesis could be successfully evaluated.

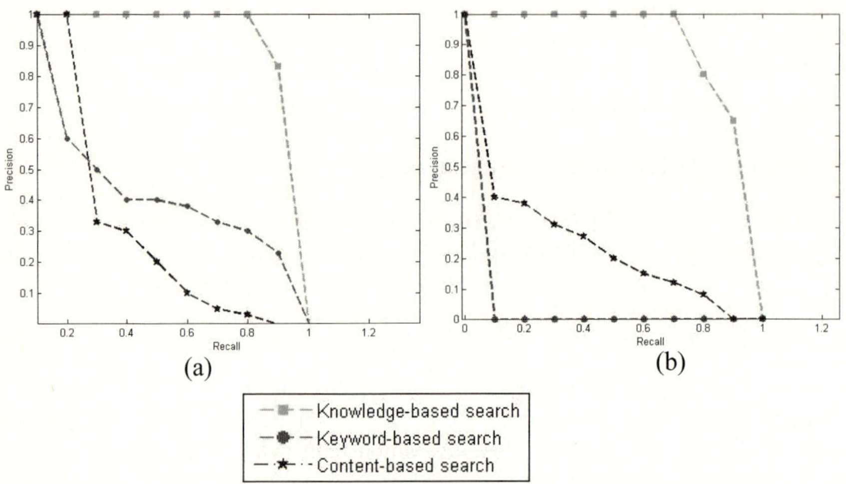



**Fig. 4.** The precision-recall graph for the three retrieval approaches

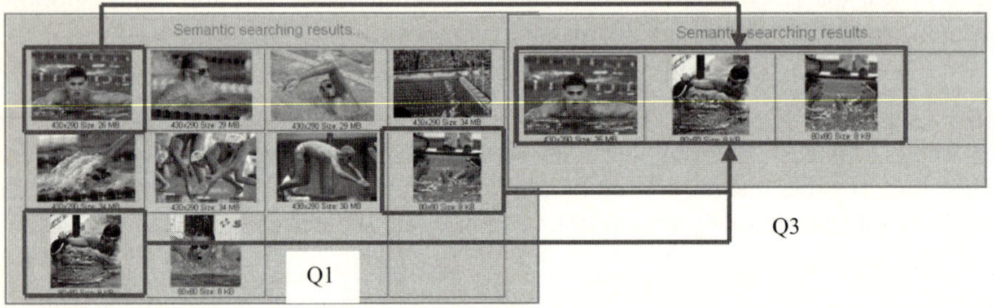



**Fig. 5.** The result from Q3 shows the overlapping images with Q1

To analyse the H3 hypothesis, the Q2 uses a query keyword which does not appear directly in the text captions. As shown in Fig. 4b, the keyword-based search fails because string matching is unsuccessful. The content-based search retrieves all photographs which have similar low-level features which, in many cases, are not semantically relevant to the query image whereas the knowledge-based search performs semantic search by retrieving all photographs which are relevant to a given concept e.g., water. This leads to the knowledge-base search obtaining higher precision and recall. In summary, the knowledge-driven approach improves the retrieval performance significantly and hence confirms the H3 hypothesis.

The Q3 aims to test the H4 hypothesis. If we analyse the return results shown in Fig. 5, there are some overlapping images between two result sets. Q1 retrieves images for those who are interested in a specific sport genre whereas Q3 searches images in which a particular athlete appeared. It is evident that the proposed system is able to deal with the image subjective issue. Hence, the H4 hypothesis is clearly validated. Finally, we need a query which fails our search mechanism. I deleted some

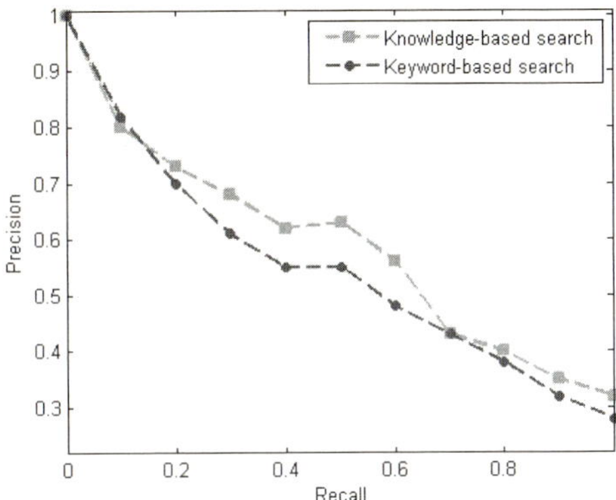


**Fig. 6.** The result of Q4 comparison for the two approaches

information about swimming in Sydney 2000. We selected the Q4 in order to test H5 hypothesis. Fig. 6 shows that the performance of the knowledge-based search and the keyword-based search are not different. This is because the knowledge-based search alone could not find any photographs which matched to the query. Although the proposed method fails from searching, LSI can find some images which are semantically relevant to the query using its indexing matrix. As a result, the proposed framework obtains higher precision-recall than the keyword search.

## 5   Conclusion and Future Work

This paper has proposed a framework in order to fulfil the limitations of the existing systems analysed in section 2. We utilised the NLP technique to extract and store knowledge in the semantic model. The main innovation is to combine an ontology-based model to restructure the semantic concepts in the natural language captions and visual features. The proposed framework can predict sport genre of an image efficiently when text captions are not supplied. In addition, the knowledge-based search degrades nicely when ontology is incomplete and is compensated by LSI. It is evident from the experimental results that the proposed framework can fulfil the limitations in the state-of-the-art frameworks. We conclude that the main hypotheses of the work, that the (Ontological) knowledge-driven technique can significantly enhance the image retrieval system effectiveness, have been validated.

In the future, several challenges need to be addressed. An appropriate ontology knowledge management technique needs to be investigated so that efficient and effective access and retrieval of the involved knowledge is ensured.

## References


1. Dasiopoulou, S., Spyrou, E., Avrithis, Y., Kompatsiaris, Y., Strintzis, M.G.: Color Image Processing: Methods and Applications. CRC Press / Taylor & Francis (October 2006)
2. Smeulder, A.W.M., Worring, M., Anntini, S., Gupta, A., Jain, R.: Content-based Image Retrieval at the End of the Early Years. IEEE Trans. Pattern Analysis and Machine Intelligence 22, 1349–1380 (2000)

3. Assfalg, J., Bertini, M., Colombo, C., Bimbo, A.D.: Semantic Annotation of Sports Video. IEEE Trans. Multimedia 9, 52–60 (2002)
4. Messer, K., Christmas, W., Kittler, J.: Automatic Sports Classification. In: 16th International Conference on Pattern Recognition, vol. 2, pp. 1005–1008 (August 2002)
5. Wang, L., Zeng, B., Lin, S., Xu, G., Shun, H.-Y.: Automatic Extraction of Semantic Colours in Sport Video. In: The International Conference on Acoustics, Speech, and Signal Processing, vol. 3, pp. 617–620 (May 2004)
6. Jang, S., Song, M., Cho, H.: Semantic Classification of Sports News Video Using Colour and Motion Features. In: The 2006 International Conference on Hybrid Information Technology, vol. 2, pp. 745–750 (November 2006)
7. Yuan, Y., Wan, C.: The Application of Edge Feature in Automatic Sport Genre Classification. In: The International Conference on Cybernetic and Intelligent System, vol. 2, pp. 1133–1136 (December 2004)
8. Frankel, C., Swain, M.J., Athitsos, V.: WebSeer: An Image Search Engine for the World Wide Web, Technical Report, The University of Chicago, Illinois (August 1996)
9. Hu, J., Bagga, A.: Categorizing Images in Web documents. IEEE Multimedia 11, 22–30 (2004)
10. Song, X., Ching-Yung, L., Ming-Ting, S.: Autonomous Visual Model Building based on Image Crawling through Internet Search Engines. In: 6th ACM SIGMM international workshop on Multimedia information retrieval (MIR 2004), pp. 315–322 (October 2004)
11. Wang, X., Ma, W., Li, X.: Data-Driven Approach for Bridging the Cognitive Gap in Image Retrieval. In: IEEE International Conference on Multimedia and Expo. (ICME 2004), vol. 3, pp. 2231–2234 (June 2004)
12. Hacid, H., Zighed, A.D.: Semantic-Based Visual Information Retrieval, ch. X. IRM Press, London (2007)
13. Schreiber, A., Dubbeldam, B., Wielemaker, J., Wielinga, B.J.: Ontology-based photo annotation. IEEE Intelligent Systems 16, 66–74 (2001)
14. Zhu, J., ESpotter- Adaptive Named Entity Recognition for Web Browsing,
`http://kmi.open.ac.uk/people/jianhan/ESpotter`
15. Chisholm, E., Kolda, T.G.: New Term Weighting Formulas for The Space Method in Information Retrieval. Computer Science and Mathematics Division (March 1999)
16. Histogram-Based Color Image Retrieval,
`http://scien.stanford.edu/class/psych221/projects/`
17. LIBSVM: A library for support vector machines,
`http://www.csie.ntu.edu.tw/~cjlin/libsvm`
18. D2R Map,
`http://www4.wiwiss.fu-berlin.de/bizer/d2rmap/ D2Rmap.htm`
19. Jena Semantic Web Framework, `http://jena.sourceforge.net`
20. SPARQL, `http://www.w3.org/TR/rdf-sparql-query`
21. Olympic organization, `http://www.olympic.org`
22. Apache Lucene, `http://lucene.apache.org`
23. Lucene Image Retrieval,
`http://www.semanticmetadata.net/wiki/doku.php?id=lire:lire`
24. Cosine Similarity and Term Weight Tutorial,
`http://www.miislita.com/information-retrieval-tutorial/ cosine-similarity-tutorial.html`

# Memory Efficient VLSI Architecture for QCIF to VGA Resolution Conversion

Asmar A. Khan and Shahid Masud

Department of Computer Science and Engineering
Lahore University of Management Sciences
Opp. Sector-U, D.H.A. Lahore 54792, Pakistan
{asmara,smasud}@lums.edu.pk

**Abstract.** This paper presents the design of an FPGA based real time video display size resolution conversion for QCIF to VGA. The architecture is based on a pre-computed memory mapping that facilitates reduction in memory size and latency. The scheme has been realized for real time resolution conversion of a QCIF video at 30 fps. The memory requirement has been reduced to 400 KB which is significantly lower than an earlier hardware based scheme [2] where memory used was nearly 5 MB. The results have been validated on Xilinx Spartan-2E FPGA running at 100MHz. The area of complete design is around 66K gates including input and output memory.

**Keywords:** Display resolution conversion, Image-scaling, VLSI architecture, FPGA, QCIF, VGA.

## 1   Introduction

In recent years, many hardware based designs have been proposed for different image resolution and resizing operations. Due to advancements in network and communication technologies, more and more multimedia applications and compatible devices are frequently coming in use. As a consequence, image scaling has become an important research problem. Growing demands on interoperability of emerging devices necessitate the use of image scaling and resolution conversion operations as well. Many devices connected to CDMA or GPRS network have different spatial resolutions. The data-broadcast by mobile switching centre (MSC) implies that each receiving device has its own transcoder making the image compatible to its spatial display resolution. The transcoder's operations include spatial resolution conversion for which image scaling is an important component. This paper focuses on the image scaling part of a video transcoding procedure. Most image resolution conversion techniques found in literature are software based [5] and [6] and meant for off-line processing. There is thus a need for dedicated hardware architecture that can achieve real time performance. Recently, some hardware based image scaling designs have been proposed in [2] and [3]. These schemes target only a fixed image size for which the ratio of size conversion is either an integer or a fraction close to a whole number. A large

T. Wada, F. Huang, and S. Lin (Eds.): PSIVT 2009, LNCS 5414, pp. 829–838, 2009.

memory would be needed in these existing schemes to support a non-integer image scaling ratio. Important objective of the work presented in this paper is to develop memory efficient techniques for image resizing in non-integer conversion ratios. The design presented here achieves QCIF (176x144) to VGA (640x480) resolution conversion while requiring far less memory than the previous architecture in [2] and it is capable of achieving real time performance. The design is modular and scalable and can be conveniently converted for other size resolutions. The rest of the paper is organized as follows. Section II presents a background on image scaling operation as well as interpolation techniques with specific examples of QCIF to VGA. Section III describes the proposed Controller Based design and its memory requirements. Results and analysis are included in section IV followed by the conclusions.

## 2     Image Scaling and Interpolation

Image scaling is the process of resizing an image. The focus in this paper is on upsizing operation that involves (a) signal processing operations to maintain subjective quality and (b) interpolation operations to construct the additional (missing) data. An image looses information when reduced in size and requires smoothing operation in order to maintain the subjective quality. When an image is increased in size, extra data (missing pixels) is inserted through interpolation to form the new image. Nearest Neighbor, Bi-cubic, Quadratic and Spline are some of the well known interpolation techniques [4],[5]. An important issue in image interpolation is that it is not possible to discover any more information in the image than what already exists and the image quality inevitably suffers. The methods that are used in improving the perceptual quality of scaled image are intensive in terms of computations and memory requirements. It is because of these reasons that the image scaling operation has traditionally been performed in software. Some recent works [9], [10] have proposed image scaling hardware but this QCIF to VGA conversion has not been targeted yet. Most software based implementations are serial in nature and less parallelism can be exploited; whereas the proposed dedicated hardware design can target resolution conversions more efficiently. A typical process of image scaling is shown in figure 1.

Some important issues encountered in peculiar QCIF to VGA size conversion are summarized below:

### 2.1     Image Interpolation Procedure and Techniques

The complete operation of image resizing is illustrated in figure 1. The process comprises three main steps, namely (i) Up-sampling, (ii) Interpolation and finally (iii) down-sampling. Up-sampling step introduces blank pixels interspersed between existing pixels depending on the resizing desired. This inevitably leads to blocking artifacts and blurring in the image. Block and edge distortions usually occur when an image is up-sampled to an extent where the pixels become visible enough and discrete nature of image becomes more evident. To improve

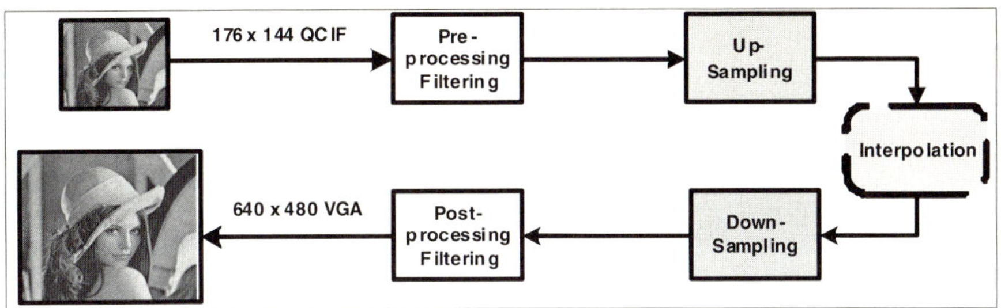


**Fig. 1.** Image scaling procedure for QCIF to VGA conversion

the perceptual quality, a post-processing operation is necessary. Here, the high frequency aberrations due to edges or scene changes are removed through the application of a low pass filter. Interpolation techniques approximate the blank pixels that have been introduced by up-sampling. An ideal interpolator has a frequency response which passes all frequency components in the original image and stops the remaining [1]. This is non-trivial operation in terms of computational complexity. Some advanced and complex interpolation techniques like Bi-cubic [4], Quadratic and Spline [5] are commonly used in software based transcoders [6], [8]. Hardware approaches discussed in [2], [3] and [4] require large amount of memory. The Bi-cubic interpolation proposed in [4] uses zoom processors to zoom a VGA resolution image. Although the proposed HABI design targets a real time scenario however, it consumes a large amount of Block-RAMs which is 44 in case of 8 zoom processors. The design is not scalable, as with high speed processing the required memory increases tremendously. A new memory mapped interpolation approach has been proposed in this paper that reduces not only the computational cost but also reduces the required memory for QCIF to VGA conversion. Any image which is down-sampled also suffers from aliasing. To avoid this artifact, the image is filtered through a low pass filter and then interpolated accordingly. This is shown as 'Pre-processing Filtering' in figure 1.

## 2.2 QCIF to VGA Memory Requirement

When a QCIF (176x144) image is converted to VGA (640x480), the conversion ratio for horizontal and vertical pixels is 40/11 and 10/3 respectively. Therefore, while converting 176 pixels to 640, an up-sampling by 40 is required followed by down-sampling by 11. Similarly, for converting 144 pixels to 480, an up-sampling by 10 and down-sampling by 3 is required. The intermediate storage of up-sampled rows and columns (by factors of 40 and 10) necessitate a huge memory requirement. Figure 2 compares this memory demand for some of the common conversions used in multimedia applications using up-sampling and down-sampling approach. Major problem in QCIF to VGA conversion is its non integer conversion factor. Most of the work in the past has been done on evenly divisible images [2], [3]. Although the schemes proposed in [4], [9] and [10] present scaling for non integer factors but estimated memory requirement

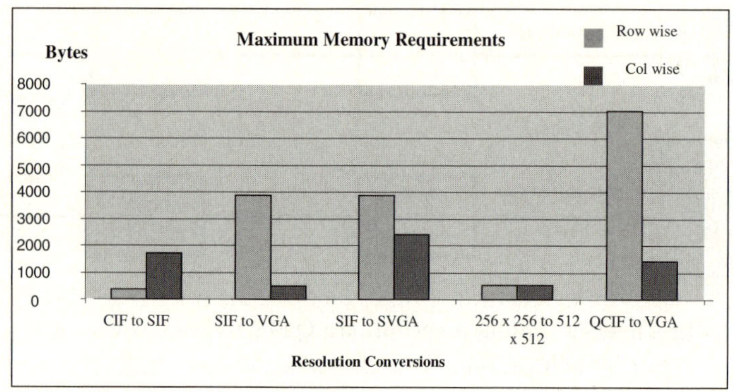



**Fig. 2.** Memory Requirements for Different Conversions

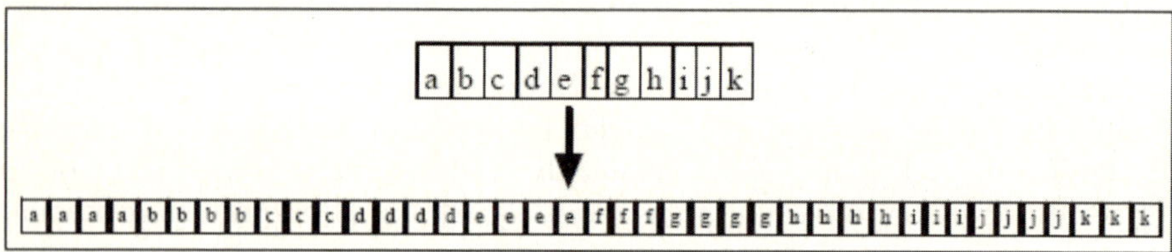



**Fig. 3.** Memory Mapping of 11 to 40 Samples

for QCIF to VGA is far greater than the ones proposed earlier. Furthermore, in case of complex schemes like Quadratic and Spline interpolation, the results are based only on software simulations using MATLAB or C-language and results have not been validated on any hardware platform [3].

A pre-computed memory mapping has been developed in this work that directly maps each pixel to its respective position in up-scaled image based on the calculations previously done off-line. Figure 3 shows the mapping of 11 samples to 40 samples. This scheme has been derived from the process of up-sampling 176 pixels to 7040 and then down-sampling them to 640. A routine in MATLAB was written to calculate this mapping. A QCIF image was up-sampled to 7040 in horizontal direction and then down-sampled to 640 to actually calculate the position of each pixel. The scheme maps a pixel at every 0.275 index value which is in fact the factor 11/40. As perceptual quality is usually measured in PSNR, it is assumed that PSNR best reflects the perceptual quality. Different QCIF images like 'cameraman' and 'lena', when scaled to VGA using the traditional software based up-sampling and down-sampling operations, were compared to the proposed technique with comparable PSNR values. This shows that the quality of images is not affected while memory mapping approach is applied. The technique is based on the Nearest Neighbor kernel provided in equation 1. The use of nearest neighbor interpolation has been used for being computationally cheapest. Another advantage of using nearest neighbor is to preserve edges [9].

$$h(x) = \begin{cases} 1 & 0 < |x| < 0.5 \\ 0 & \text{elsewhere} \end{cases} \tag{1}$$

# 3  Proposed Design

The proposed design is based on a controller based state machine which uses the memory map presented earlier and reduces the required memory by having a shared memory architecture. The architectural design of memory module is the key to meeting stringent timing requirements, memory latencies and delays. The proposed technique and its VLSI design is elaborated below. A comparison with slice based approach presented in [2] has also been made.

## 3.1  Controller Based Approach

A controller based approach is proposed in this work which reduces the memory required for QCIF to VGA scaling by utilizing the pre-computed memory map scheme. The design is based on a state machine which reads the data from external memory and then maps it to the memory with pre-calculated mapping. In this paper, the hardware has been designed for a specific conversion; however a generic formulation of mapping is possible. In this scheme, the input image is scaled in two stages; first stage is horizontal scaling factor calculation where rows to be interpolated are calculated and the map is used by state machine. This map is used to repeat (being the nearest neighbor) the columns which are interpolated in stage II. Second stage is the vertical scaling where each column is interpolated and scaled to the desired level. As a result, a complete image is scaled to the desired resolution. The proposed memory mapping technique obviates the need for pre-processing step as aliasing cannot occur for the sizes involved in this particular conversion. A state machine based controller reads the contents of a pre-computed memory map shown in figure 3. This mapping is used to repeat each column in order to write the data to new locations. This processing is done column-wise which is then repeated by pre-computed memory map. This process will interpolate the rows to the desired factor. The column-wise interpolation converts the 144 pixels to 480 using a similar map shown in figure 3. Completion of column-wise conversion implies that each column of 144 pixels will now be repeated by its count as per figure 3 and ultimately 176 rows will be scaled to 640 pixels. The scaling operation of a processing element is explained by the state diagram shown in figure 4. An input memory of 144 bytes and output memory of 480 bytes is needed to convert each column of 144 to 480 pixels. A register counts 3 input samples from the memory and then maps them to 10 locations, thus mapping every sample at 0.3 index value similar to figure 3. These 10 samples are convolved to the post-processing seven-tap filter. The filter coefficients, shown in equation 2 , are same as previously reported for SIF to CCIR-601 conversion [7].

$$[-12\ 0\ 140\ 256\ 140\ 0\ -12] \times \frac{1}{256} \tag{2}$$

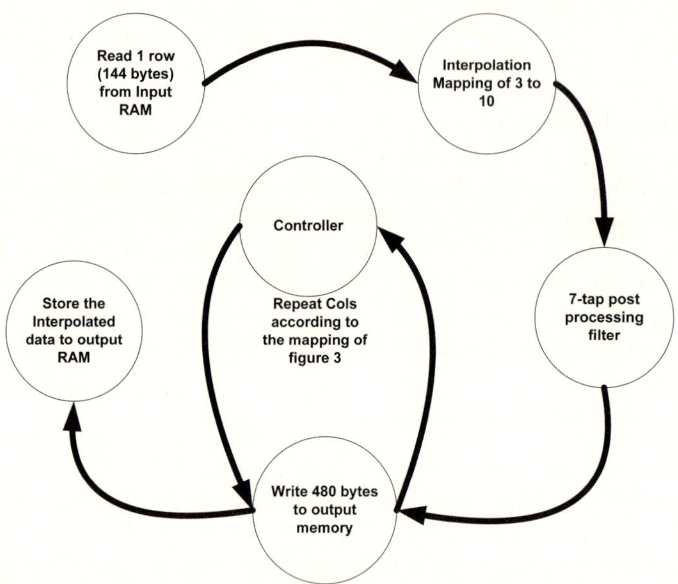

**Fig. 4.** State Diagram for Processing Element

These samples are then stored to the output memory which is 480 bytes wide. For an image with 144 columns, the requirement is of 144 parallel processing elements (PEs). Where each PE performs this particular operation on one complete column of 144 pixels. It must be mentioned that these 144 operations could be spread over multiple cycles if smaller segments from a column are processed in one go. However, this would slow down the processing accordingly and the conversion may not complete within the real-time constraints. The distributed memory architecture described later mitigates the timing delays encountered while performing this operation in serial fashion. The horizontal and vertical scaling is performed separately to reduce the computational complexity. After the scaling of column to 480 pixels, each column is repeated for horizontal scaling. For example, the first column must be repeated four times like pixel 'a' in figure 3. Similarly the index of each succeeding column will be repeated according to the map that is pre-calculated by the controller itself. The controller monitors the count for column index and repeats the pixel value of each column accordingly. The output of this operation is the desired VGA size image. This controller can be provided with desired scaling factor and can work as a generic image scaler as well. The controller circuitry is equipped to automatically read column index.

## 3.2   Distributed Memory Architecture

A distributed memory architecture has been developed in which each PE has its own memory module. The original image is distributed to these memory

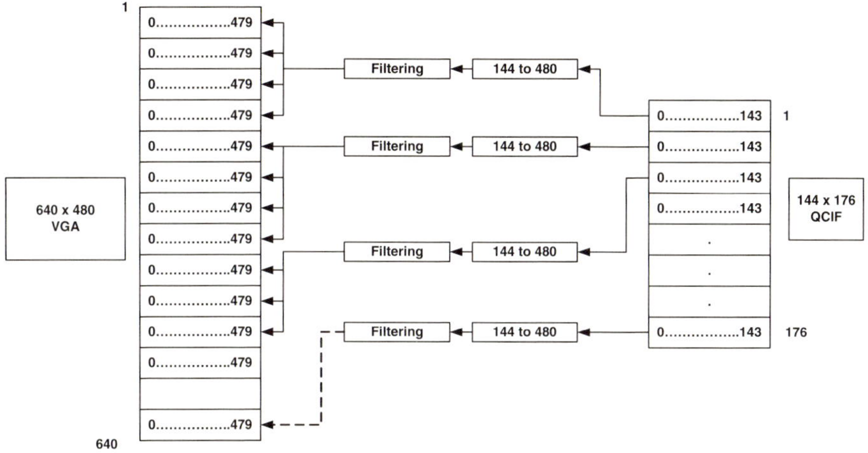

**Fig. 5.** Distributed Architecture for Controller Based Approach

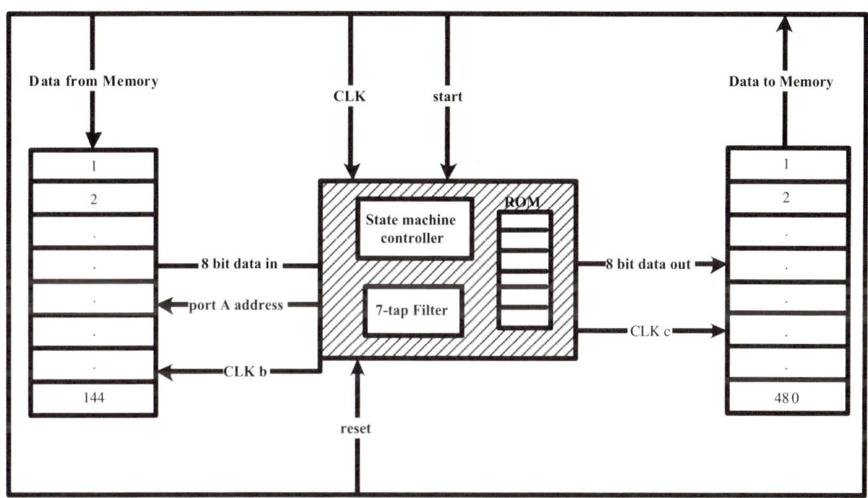


**Fig. 6.** Block Diagram of Processing Element

modules as column-wise input of 144x1 pixels. The pixels in the block boundaries have been processed by zero-padding the affected pixels. The processing
elements described above scale one column to the required resolution. A complete image conversion requires all columns and rows to be scaled; therefore, a
parallel hardware with distributed memory architecture has been developed to
meet stringent delay constraints. Figure 5 shows the block diagram of system
organization. The image is read column-wise and fed into 144 parallel processing
units which produce the complete VGA image. Figure 6 depicts the architecture
of a processing element and its operation. Each PE needs to have memory modules of 144 bytes and 480 bytes. The shaded area represents the state machine

based controller with post processing filter and registers for temporary storage required in memory mapping.

### 3.3  Memory Count

The system's memory requirement compared to the slice based approach presented in [2] is considerably reduced. Table 1 describes the proposed controller based system's memory requirements. The memory was calculated as per method presented in [2].

**Table 1.** Memory required for controller based approach

| Proposed Approach | Memory in (bytes) | Memory out (bytes) |
| --- | --- | --- |
| Col wise | 144 x 144 | 144 x 480 |
| Row wise | - | 640 x 480 |

The design was simulated on Modelsim and was mapped on Xilinx Spartan-II FPGA running at 100 MHz clock frequency. The processing time required for a single PE is 4.5 clock cycles which is sufficient to support a frame rate of 30 fps for QCIF frame size.

## 4  Analysis and Discussion

This section presents the analysis of the proposed design in comparison with the slice based approach presented in [2]. Although the design presented in [2] did not address this specific conversion (QCIF to VGA) but the technique claimed to be effective for evenly divisible images. The image is divided into equal size slices and all the slices are parallel scaled to the desired level. It uses the Nearest Neighbor interpolation method. Table 2 describes the memory requirement for slice based approach where 768 slices (each of 11x3 bytes of image) were up-scaled to 768 slices (each of 40x10 bytes). The actual calculations for this particular conversion were made using Table 2 provided in [2]. Some hardware based architectures like [4] proposed interpolation hardware which uses dual port Block-RAMs to store the image. In our proposed design, no extra memory is required to store the intermediate resultant image. In [4], there are 44 dual port Block-RAMs of 16Kb each required to achieve real time video processing frame rate. However, the memory requirement can not be reduced by using faster memory. Secondly the design proposed in [4] is valid for interpolation purposes only. The complete resolution conversion procedure was not presented.

Our proposed design is for luminance component only and chrominance has not been considered. The design is a proof of concept which can easily be extended to the chrominance as well. Nevertheless, this would influence the cost of design in terms of memory and time.

**Table 2.** Memory required for slice based approach

| Slice Based Approach | Memory in (bytes) | Memory out (bytes) |
|---|---|---|
| Col wise | 768 x 3 | 768 x 10 |
| Row wise | 768 x 176 x 3 | 768 x 640 x 10 |

### 4.1  Memory Requirement for Controller Based Approach

The QCIF to VGA conversion requires non-integer scaling. The memory requirements exceed tremendously while performing up-sampling and down-sampling
of pixels. Our work has reduced the required memory and hardware to a significant level. There are 144 + 480 units of memory for vertical scaling requiring
90KB of memory. The resultant image requires a memory of 640 x 480 which
makes the total required memory to be 397KB. This is more than 10 times less
than the design proposed in [2] where the memory requirement for this specific
conversion is estimated to be 5.33 MB.

### 4.2  Gate Count

The gate count for a single PE unit is 460 gates. There are 144 units. Thus the
total gate count for the complete resolution conversion hardware is 144 x 460
= 66K gates. This design is fully parallel however gate count could be further
reduced by using LUTs instead of ROM. As discussed earlier, our mapping uses
ROM and that is a big reason of large gate count [10].

### 4.3  Timing Constraints

A single PE unit, which converts a row of 144 to 480 pixels, takes 4.5 clock cycles at 100 MHz clock rate. The non integer clock cycle is due to the presence of
different clocks inside the state processing element. The controller takes another
4 clock cycles. This corresponds a time of 0.045 msec. The total time required
for conversion of one frame from QCIF to VGA consumes 144 x (45+40) =
12240 nsec = 12.24 msec. This corresponds to a frame rate of 80fps, which is far
greater than the one proposed in [10] for 16VGA to SXGA. The proposed architecture is scalable and modular where the controller can be provided with scaling
factor and can be used as a generic converter for real time video streaming. The
area occupied could be reduced through parallelism exploiting the redundancy
in multimedia data. Use of pipelining architecture can also contribute to further
reduction in area. However this will increase the computational complexity and
put stringent constraints on processing time. The throughput of the design can
be improved using high speed FPGA like Virtex-4 or Virtex-5 running at more
than 500 MHz.

## 5  Conclusion

The work proposes a specific resolution conversion with reduced resources yet
it targets a real time application [8]. This scheme is valid for decoded data and

does not require any compatibility for encoding scheme. The hardware can be used in small devices like mobile phone and PDAs due to its low complexity and reduced memory. The PE is building block of the design which interpolates and decimates the pixels by using a memory map causing the required memory to be reduced. The distributed memory architecture enables the design to meet the stringent real time processing requirements. The proposed design is a scalable and modular and capable of performing generic image scaling operations for any given conversion ratio.

## Acknowledgements

The authors acknowledge the support of Higher Education Commission Pakistan and Computer Science Department at Lahore University of Management Sciences, Pakistan.

## References


1. Lehmann, T.M.: Survey: Interpolation Methods in Medical Image Processing. IEEE transactions on medical imaging 18(11) (November 1999)
2. Aho, E., Vanne, J., Hämäläinen, T.D., Kuusilinna, K.: Block-Level Parallel Processing for Scaling Evenly Divisible Images. IEEE Transactions on circuits and systems 52(12), 2717–2725 (2005)
3. Ramachanran, S., Srinivasan, S.: Design and FPGA implementation of an MPEG based video scalar with reduced on-chip memory utilization. Journal of Systems Architecture 51, 435–450 (2005)
4. Aurelio, M., Arias-Estrada, M.O.: Real Time FPGA Based Architecture for Bicubic Interpolation: An Application for Digital Image Scaling. In: Proceedings of International Conference on Reconfigurable Computing and FPGAs, September 28-30 (2005)
5. Lin, T.-C., Truong, T.-K.: DCT-Based Image Codec Embedded Cubic Spline Interpolation with Optimal Quantization. In: Proceedings of IEEE international Symposium on Multimedia, pp. 2746–2749 (September 2006)
6. Wang, L., Wang, Q.: A fast Intra Mode Decision Algorithm for MPEG-2 to H.264 Video Transcoding. In: Proceedings of IEEE 10th International Symposium on Consumer Electronic, pp. 1–5 (December 2006)
7. Standards documents MPEG-1: Coding of moving pictures and associated audio for digital storage media at up to 1.5 Mbps. ISO/IEC 11172-2: video (November 1991)
8. Wanrong, L., Bushmitch, D.: Design and implementation of a high quality DV50-MPEG2 software transcoder. In: International Conference on Consumer Electronics, pp. 142–143 (June 2002)
9. Kim, C.-H., Seong, S.-M., Lee, J.-A., Kim, L.-S.: Winscale: An Image-Scaling Algorithm Using an Area Pixel Model. IEEE Transactions on Circuits and Systems for Video Technology 13(6), 549–553 (2003)
10. Aho, E., Vanne, J., Hämäläinen, T.D., Kuusilinna, K.: Configurable Implementation of Parallel Memory Based Real-time Video Downscaler. Microprocessors and Microsystems 31(5), 283–292 (2007)

# Towards an Interpretation of Intestinal Motility Using Capsule Endoscopy Image Sequences


Hai Vu[1], Tomio Echigo[2], Ryusuke Sagawa[1], Keiko Yagi[3], Masatsugu Shiba[4],
Kazuhide Higuchi[4], Tetsuo Arakawa[4], and Yasushi Yagi[1]

[1] The Institute of Scientific and Industrial Research, Osaka University
{vhai,sagawa,yagi}@am.sanken.osaka-u.ac.jp
[2] Osaka Electro-Communication University
echigo@isc.osakac.ac.jp
[3] Kobe Pharmaceutical University
k-yagi@kobepharma-u.ac.jp
[4] Graduate School of Medicine, Osaka City University
{shiba,khiguchi,arakawat}@med.osaka-cu.ac.jp



**Abstract.** Human intestinal motility is presented by the propagation of peristaltic waves with their frequencies gradually decreasing along the length of the small bowel. This paper describes a heuristic method, which can be used towards interpreting intestinal motility through recognizing their frequency characteristics from capsule endoscopy image sequences. First, image features that reflect peristaltic activities are extracted to build a functional signal. Then, a Multi-Resolution Analysis technique in the wavelet domain is used to decompose the functional signal taking into account the non-stationary nature of intestinal motility. For peristaltic waveform recognition, the method relies on the principle of peak detections from the decomposed signals. Each waveform is detected when it exceeds a baseline level. The frequency characteristics are interpreted through analysis of the waveform appearance and their velocity propagation. Three healthy sequences were tested in experiments. The estimated trends of the peristaltic wave propagation from the experimental results show a frequency gradient, which follows the well-recognized characteristics of intestinal motility propagation. Therefore, this study is the first demonstration of a detailed interpretation of intestinal motility, and we suggest that further research focuses on intestinal motility dysfunctions.


## 1   Introduction

Interpretation of human intestinal motility has been the subject of exhaustive research over many decades by physiologists. The intestinal motility consists of peristaltic waves (slow waves) [1,2], in which the propagation of waveforms along the length of the small bowel has also been well recognized and confirmed in the literature, e.g. [1,2,3]. There is a gradient in the propagation velocity of the peristaltic waves, where the frequency of appearance of waveforms is highest in the proximal regions and lowest in the distal regions; for example, in man the maximal frequency is 12 cycles/min in the duodenum and 3-5 cycles/min in


T. Wada, F. Huang, and S. Lin (Eds.): PSIVT 2009, LNCS 5414, pp. 839–850, 2009.

the terminal ileum [1,2,3]. Although the intestinal motility characteristics can be affected by disorders such as bacterial overgrowth, intestine obstruction or paralysis [1,2], the clinical applications of these findings are still limited because it is necessary to take many recordings along the entire length of the small bowel. The recent recording technique [4] is still an invasive measurement because of the long distance and loop configuration of the small bowel.

Capsule Endoscopy (CE) [5] was recently introduced as a non-invasive and effective means of inspecting bleeding regions, Crohn's disease and suspected tumors in the small bowel [6,7]. The CE utilizes a swallowable endoscopic device that is ingested and propelled by peristaltic waves through the GastroIntestinal (GI) tract. Although this technique was not originally designed for assessment of intestinal motility, CE image sequences present a useful source of information for investigating intestinal motility (e.g. works in [8,9,10,11]). Thus the aim of this study was to use a functional signal extracted from the CE image sequences to interpret intestinal motility. This is a promising method for overcoming the limitations of the current techniques because of its non-invasive nature and minimal demands on physicians' time. To investigate intestinal motility using CE image sequences, works in [9,10,11] proposed methods to detect intestinal contractions. They used the same approaches that utilized the learning schemes to recognize the contractions. The contractile patterns can be represented by star-wise patterns [9], linear radial patterns [10] or as a directional histogram of edge intestinal folds [11]. Although the results of these studies show successful recognition rates, it is still unclear what information can be derived from results of the detected contractions to understand intestinal motility. On the other hand, from the viewpoint of GI physiology [1,2], locating only the positions of the contractions does not seem to provide enough information to interpret intestinal motility. Thus, in contrast with the earlier approaches, we attempted to use a heuristic method, which measured the propagation of the peristaltic waves instead of identifying the contractile patterns.

We first considered the disparity of consecutive frames in a CE image sequence such as color dissimilarity, motion displacement, and changes in edges of the intestinal folds. This step can be considered a series of intestinal motility observations. Based on the high correlation of these features, a functional signal is built by averaging multiple observations to reduce artifacts or other influencing factors. Then, the signal is decomposed into its components at different scales by wavelet transformation taking into account the non-stationary characteristics of intestinal motility. The attractive properties of decomposition signals are that they reflect the noise level and baseline level, which form the waveforms of the peristaltic waves. For waveform recognition, the method relies on the principle of peak detection of the decomposed signal where each waveform exceeds a baseline level. The propagation of slow waves are influenced by the frequency appearance of the peaks and their velocity. The method was tested on sequences obtained from three healthy volunteers. Estimated trends of slow wave propagation along the CE and transit time determined from the experimental results matched the well-known frequency gradient of intestinal motility. This study was the first to provide a detailed interpretation of intestinal motility and that the results can be used to identify motility dysfunctions in patients.

## 2   Developing a Functional Signal of Intestinal Motility from CE Image Features

### 2.1   Intestinal Motility and Its Characteristics

Intestinal motility is manifested by electrical activity, that constitutes electrical oscillations called slow waves [2]. Schematic views of the waveforms (convex and concave waveforms) are shown in Fig. 1a. With intermittent bursts of rapid electrical oscillations, spike bursts occur and are superimposed on the slow waves signal (Fig. 1b). The spike bursts are associated with muscular contractions that produce the segmentary contractions (Fig. 1c). The characteristics of slow waves include the appearance or propagation velocity of these waveforms. As stated by [1,2], the propagation velocity decreases in a series of steps from proximal to distal regions of the small bowel, as shown in Fig. 1d. For further detail, please refer to Chapter 7 in [1] or Chapter 6 in [2].

It can be noted that the concave and/or convex waveforms are always present, even in the absence of contractions. For recognition of the contractile patterns from the CE image sequences, the contractions in Fig. 1c are well described in

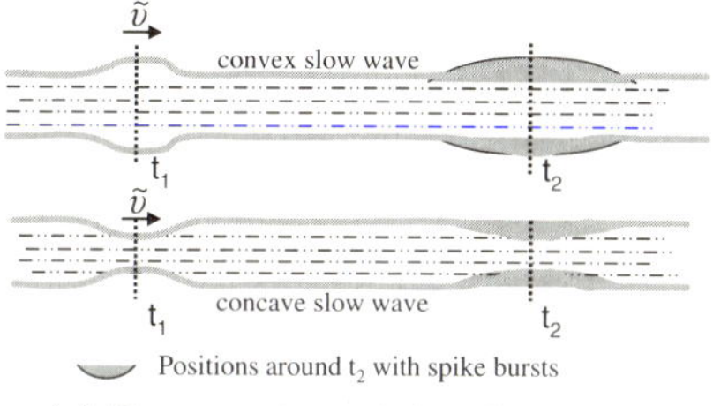


(a) Propagation of the slow wave

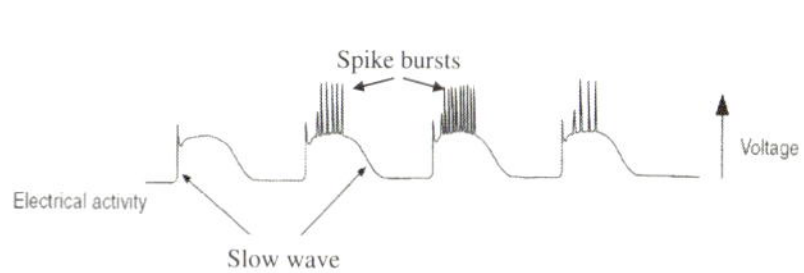


(b) Spike bursts superimposed on the slow wave signal

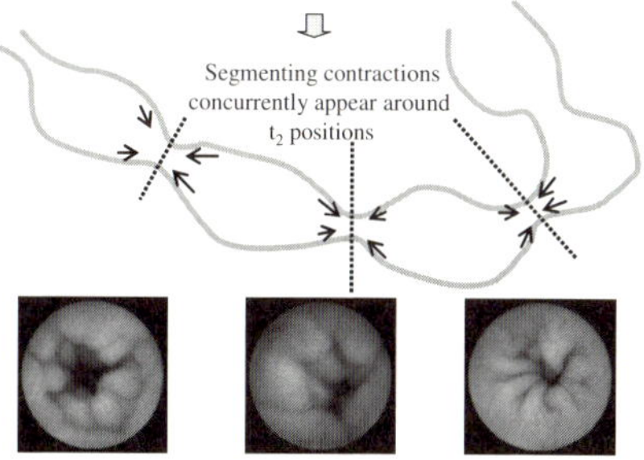


(c) Segmenting contractions

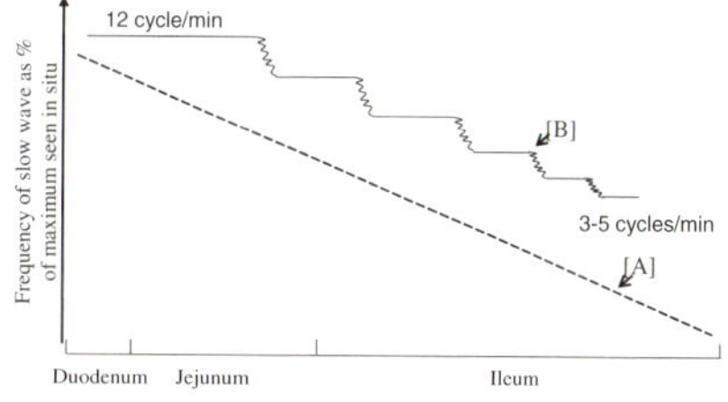


(d) A gradient frequency for slow wave propagation

**Fig. 1.** Organization and frequency characteristics of intestinal motility

the earlier studies [9,10,11], whereas the concave/convex patterns are ambiguously described. In fact, the propagation of slow waves propel the CE through the small bowel and, therefore, this represents the main factor responsible for the changes between the acquired images. These changes can be measured by identifying the disparity between consecutive frames. Although this measurement can be affected by other factors such as human activities during examinations or imminent movements (or non-rigidity) of the small intestine. From the view of signal processing, an ensemble averaging technique has advances as it eliminates undesirable noise through multiple observations. To develop a functional signal of intestinal motility from CE image sequences, these observations can be derived from image features that are high correlated.

## 2.2   Developing the Functional Signal from Image Features

In a typical examination, CE takes approximately 7-8 hours to pass through the GI tract and captures images at a rate of 2 fps. Therefore, an image sequence has around 57,000 frames, including 20,000 to 30,000 frames that belong to the small bowel regions, which can be used to investigate intestinal motility. To measure the disparity between adjacent frames, we considered a series of image features that were successfully used in previous studies. These features include the edges of intestinal folds (in [8,9,10,11] for recognizing the segmentary contractions), color dissimilarity and motion displacements (in [12] for evaluating image disparity).

The CE image features include a standard size of 256x256 pixels, 8 bit per channel in RGB color space [13]. To determine color dissimilarity between frames $\langle n, n+1 \rangle$ ($Dissim(n)$), we used the color local histogram method in [14]. The image is divided into blocks, with the number of blocks $N_{blocks} = 64$. The color histogram is applied to each block by dividing RGB components into $N_{bins} = 16$. The distance of local histograms is calculated by $L1$ distance. $Dissim(n)$ is obtained by accumulating the different blocks. The motion displacement ($Motion(n)$) is evaluated as the length of the maximum motion vector, in which the motion fields of frames $\langle n, n+1 \rangle$ are detected and tracked using the Kanade-Lucas-Tomasi (KLT) algorithm [15,16,17]. The Canny operator techniques [18] was used to identify the edges of intestinal folds. Edge pixels were counted in a region where most of the edges appear. $Edge(n)$ is calculated by subtracting the edge pixels detected in frames $\langle n, n+1 \rangle$. Feature extractions of a typical sequence including 50 frames are shown in Fig. 2.

The extracted signals are normalized into [0,1], with the maximum value indicating the most different and the minimum value indicating the best match of two consecutive frames. To evaluate the correlation of these signals, we calculated their energy in a duration $\Delta T$. Figure 3 shows the energy of the extracted signals with $\Delta T = 1$ min. of a full sequence. This figure shows the high correlations of the selected features. Therefore, the functional signal of intestinal motility was calculated by:

$$S(n) = \frac{Dissim(n) + Motion(n) + Edge(n)}{3} \tag{1}$$

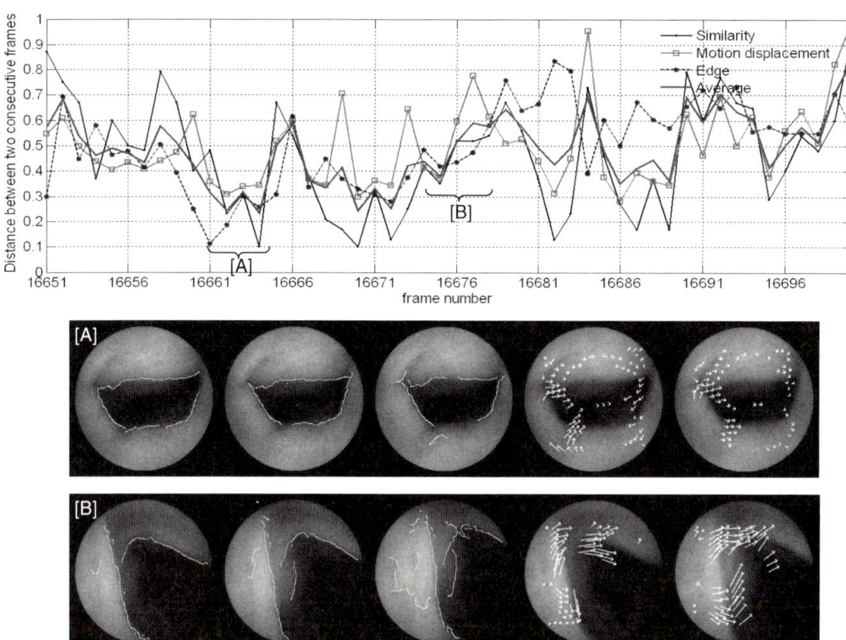

**Fig. 2.** The feature extractions of a typical sequence including 50 frames. Each bottom panel shows image features around the corresponding positions; the first three images show the edge detections. Results are superimposed on the original images. The next two images show the motion displacements between them.

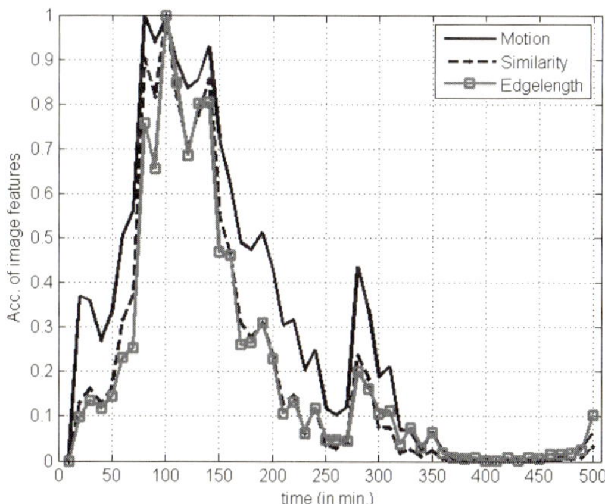

**Fig. 3.** Accumulating energy of the extracted signals within 1 minute of a full sequence

## 3 Multi-resolution Analysis and Waveform Detection from Decomposition Signals

### 3.1 Multi-resolution Analysis Technique

Similar to other non-stationary biosignals such as ECG and EGG, the functional signal $S(n)$ is affected by different conditions such as the subject's health condition, natural characteristics of intestinal motility. To exploit their properties such as frequency-time, Multi-Resolution Analysis (MRA) techniques are commonly used because the scale-based nature of the MRA effectively separates the components of the signal into pieces that can be subjected to further analysis. In this study, it is meaningful if the contents of the $S(n)$ signal such as noise and the waveforms of slow waves can be determined from the decomposed signals.

Of the available MRA methods, wavelet transformation is a common used technique. The signal was decomposed using a wavelet orthonormal function (for the details, please refer to Chapter 4 in [19]). Hereafter, we discuss two practical considerations that are the choice of mother wavelets and the decomposition level. Irrespective of the mathematical properties of the mother wavelet, a basic requirement is that it looks similar to the patterns we want to localize in the signal. As is well described in studies [1,2,3,20,21], the waveforms have an approximately triangular shape with some harmonics. Therefore, the Daubechies wavelet $db3$ configuration was selected. The decomposition level ($J$) is selected so that the center frequency at each scale can cover the frequency appearance of waveforms. As described in Sec.2, the predetermined value $J = 6$ is considered a reasonable value because at the capturing rate at 2 fps (or a sampling period $T = 0.5(s)$), the frequency at each scale can drop in a range from 2.5 cycles/min at level 6, 10 cycles/min at level 3 to 20 cycles/min at level 1. The MRA decomposes the signal $S(n)$ into the detail $D_j$ and smoothing $A_j$ components, with $j$ is a level from 1 to $J = 6$. Figure 4 shows the decomposed signals of an original signal including 1200 frames (in 10 minutes). The properties of MRA analysis ensure the energy preserving condition:

$$\|E\|^2 = \sum_{j=1}^{J=6} D_j^2 + S_6^2 \tag{2}$$

where $\|E\|^2$ is the energy of the signal, $\sum D_j^2$ is the energy of the detail signals and $S_6^2$ is the energy of the smoothing component at level 6.

### 3.2 Recognizing the Waveforms from the Decomposed Signals

In studies [20,21], intestinal motility was measured by electrical devices, such as strain gauge transducers. The local contractions are denoted by a triangular shape on the output signals with several criteria. For example, there is a baseline level where the threshold voltage is exceeded so that the beginning of the contraction can be recognized; or the duration of these contractions exceed a predetermined value. Based on these observations, we considered that a smoothing

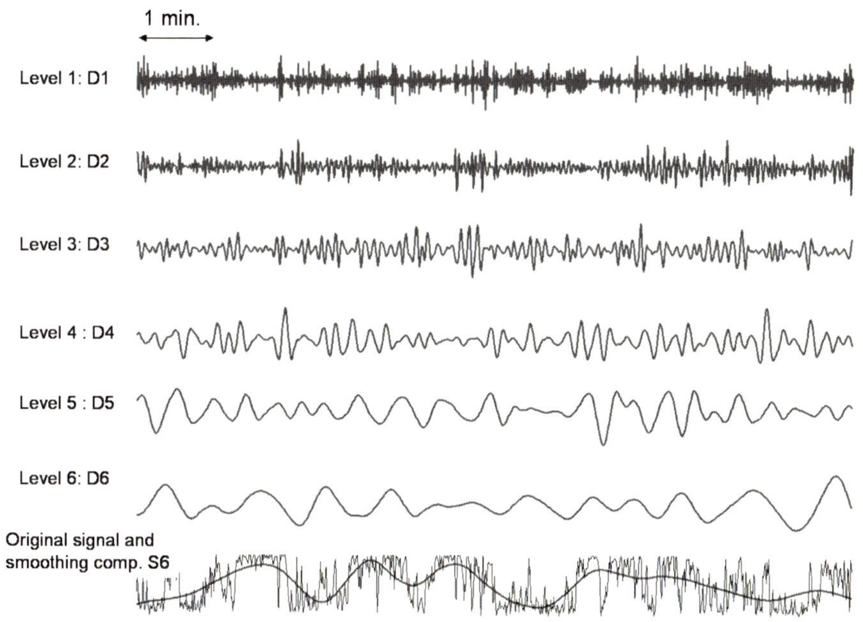


**Fig. 4.** Results of MRA decompositions with a signal length of 10 minutes. The bottom panel shows the original signal and smooth $A_6$ component.

component from the decomposed signals defines the baseline level, whereas the detailed components reveal the activities of the slow waves. On the other hand, artifacts and undesirable signals due to disturbing factors involve high frequencies, or are represented by detailed components at low scale levels. Therefore, in term of the energy preservation, (2) can be rewritten as:

$$\|E\|^2 = \sum_{j=1}^{k} D_j^2 + \sum_{j=k+1}^{J} D_j^2 + S_J^2 \tag{3}$$

where $\sum_{j=1}^{k} D_j^2$ can be filtered out from the original signal. When amount $\sum_{j=k+1}^{J} D_j^2$ is large enough, the signal after noise elimination is superimposed on the baseline level $S_J^2$. Therefore, it denotes a peak that can be considered as a waveform of the slow waves. For example, in Fig. 5a with $k = 2$ defined noise levels, the peaks within a duration of $\Delta T = 1$ min. exceeded the smoothing component at level 6. Results of the peak detection along a CE transit time of 1 hour are plotted in Fig. 5b.

## 3.3   Evaluating the Propagation of Slow Waves

Intuitively, the appearance of the waveforms at adjacent locations indicates the propagation of slow waves. The results in Sec. 3.2 allow for us to count the

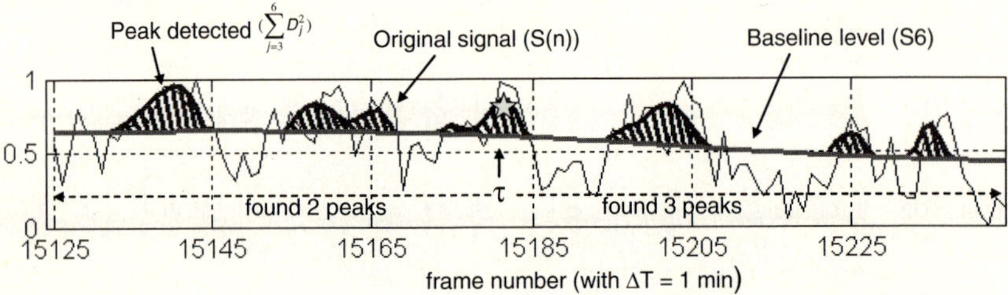


(a) Waveform detection at 1 min. around [A] (with detail components of scales 1 and 2 denoting noise and smoothing component at level 6 denoting a baseline)

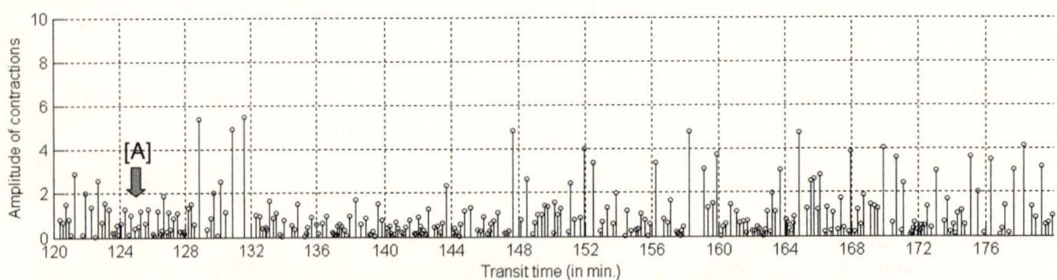


(b) Results of the waveform detection at 1 hour

**Fig. 5.** Waveform detection by the decomposed signals

appearance of waveforms around their neighbors. For example, the number of waveforms around the indicated peak (marked by yellow-star) in Fig. 5a is 6 (before 30 sec. and after 30 sec.). This means that the frequency of the slow waves at the selected position $\tau$ is $f_{sw} = 6$ cycles/min. In fact, within a certain period of time $\Delta T$, there are several values of $f_{sw}$ because it yields from various waveforms within $\Delta T$. Therefore, a probability of waveform appearances relying on the number of observations at a certain $f_{sw}$ is calculated by:

$$P_{f_{sw}^i} = \frac{C(f_{sw}^i)}{\sum (\text{peaks detected})}, \qquad (4)$$

with C(.) counting waveform appearances at $f_{sw}$ and $i = 1$ to $max(f_{sw})$ within time $\Delta T$.

The propagation of slow waves can also be measured by the velocity of each waveform along the CE transit time. If a waveform length is spread across $\delta t$ sec., and the accumulation of the CE displacements within $\delta t$ is denoted by $\Delta d$, then the velocity of the slow waves is defined by:

$$v_t = \frac{\Delta d}{\delta t} \ (\text{pixel/sec}) \qquad (5)$$

$Motion(n)$ is a reasonable feature to calculate $\Delta d$. Figure 6a and Fig. 6b show the propagation of the waveforms estimated by (5) within 1 minute in the proximal and distal regions, respectively. While Fig. 6a shows high propagation because of the short time in each waveform, Fig. 6b shows slower propagation.

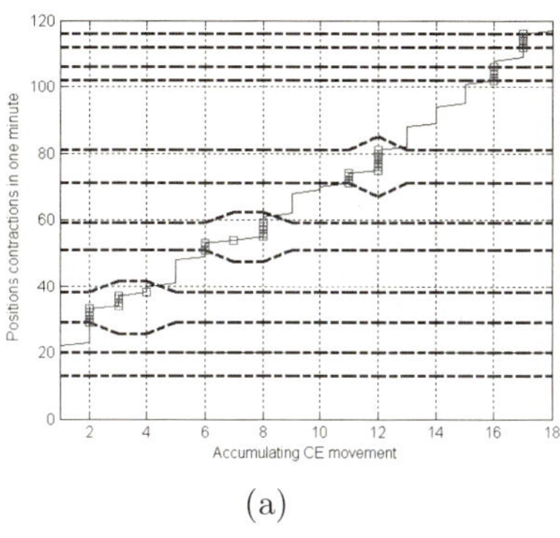

(a)

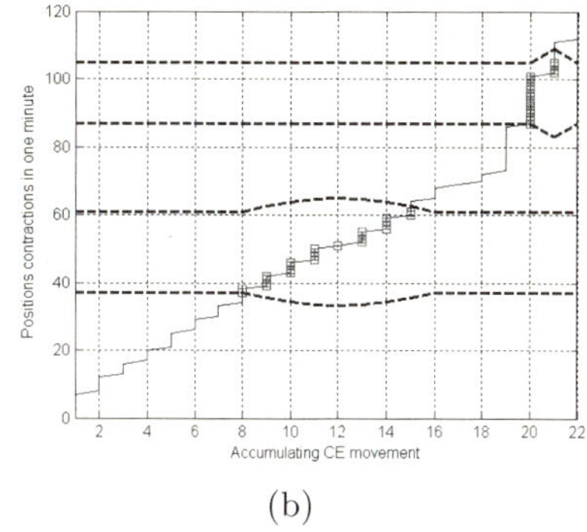

(b)

**Fig. 6.** Propagation of the waveforms within 1 min. in the proximal (a) and distal (b) regions. The solid lines show the accumulation of CE displacements. The dashed lines indicate the position of waveforms. Squares mark CE movement within a waveform.

## 4   Experimental Results

To test the proposed method, sequences were obtained from three healthy volunteers, which was supported by the Graduate School of Medicine, Osaka City University. These sequences were examined and the frames showing the digestive organs such as the first gastric, the first duodenum and the first ileum were marked by the endoscopist experts. Table 1 shows data used in the experiments. The procedures used to extract the image features in Sec .2.2 were implemented by a C++ program on a PC Pentium 3.2 GHz, 1 GB Ram. Wavelet Packet Toolbox in MatLab was used to implement the MRA technique in Sec. 3.1.

**Table 1.** The material in experiments

| Seq. | Total frames | The first frame of duodenum | The first frame of ileum | Total time | Time in Small bowel (in min.) |
|---|---|---|---|---|---|
| Seq_1 | 60392 | 3161 | 31798 | 8:23:16 | 238 |
| Seq_2 | 62350 | 7095 | 32863 | 8:39:35 | 214 |
| Seq_3 | 45020 | 3200 | 29037 | 6:15:10 | 215 |

Figure 7 shows the results of Seq_1. The left panel plots ribbons that shows frequency components $(f_{sw})$ along the CE transit time with predetermined configurations as described in Sec.3.2. Examining the ribbons of $f_{sw}$, we can see high probability at the end of the small bowel for low frequencies and with the contrasting observations for high frequencies. More clearly, Fig. 7b shows the probability (calculated by (4)) of low $f_{sw}$ values $(freq_1 \leq f_{sw} \leq freq_2)$ in the upper panel and high $f_{sw}$ values in the lower panel. The right panel in Fig. 7a plots the velocities of slow waves, as calculated by (5). A simple fitting model was used to estimate the trends of velocities. The trend shows that the velocity of slow wave propagation gradually reduces along the CE transit time. Similar

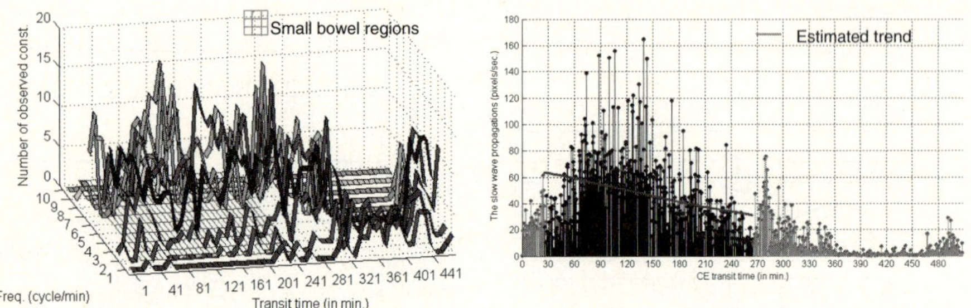

(a) Left panel: Ribbons of $f_{sw}$ components along the CE transit time. Right panel: The velocities calculated by (5). The slant line represents an estimated trend of the velocity in the small bowel regions (marked by stems) using a least square fitting model.

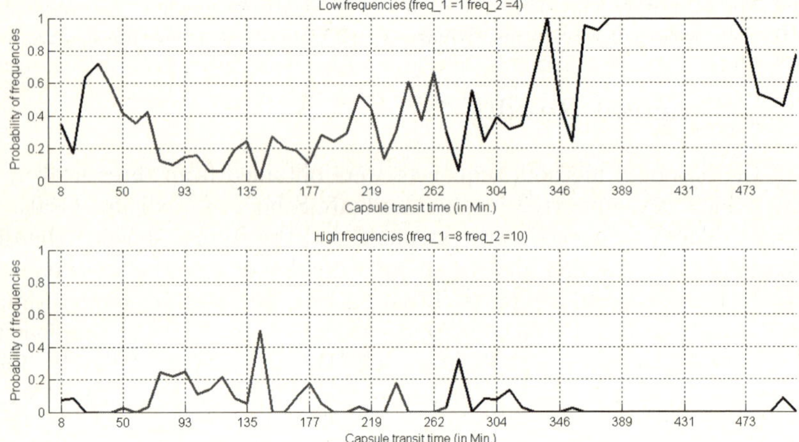

(b) Upper panel with $freq_1 = 1$ cycle/min $\leq f_{sw} \leq freq_2 = 4$ cycles/min . Lower panel with $freq_1 = 8$ cycles/min $\leq f_{sw} \leq freq_2 = 10$ cycles/min

**Fig. 7.** Slow wave propagation of Seq_1

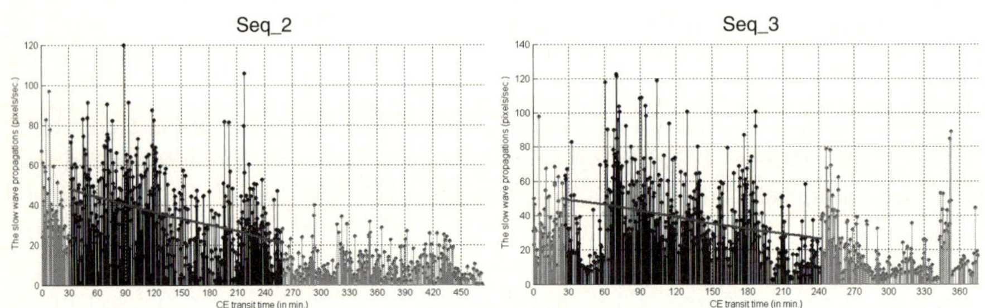

**Fig. 8.** Slow wave propagation of Seq_2 and Seq_3

results are also shown in Fig. 8 for Seq_2 and Seq_3. By examining the three sequences, the propagation of slow waves interpreted by the proposed method is a good match with well-known characteristics of slow waves, as stated in [1,2,3].

## 5   Discussions and Conclusions

This study was to investigate of the small intestinal motility using CE image sequences. In fact interest in small intestinal motility had also measured by other techniques such as in [4] or in [20,21]. The proposed method thus needs to be confirmed by these measurements using same healthy control data. On the other hand, the proposed method still lacks evidence and suffers ambiguous explanations for noise and other factors for separation from the decomposed signals. The relationship between the segmentary contractions and smoothing components can support the definition of the baseline level as well as verifying the waveform detection results. In terms of experimental data, the frequency patterns estimated from patient data, which represent dysfunctional motility can offer more valuable evaluation.

In summary, this paper proposed a heuristic method using functional signals extracted from CE image sequences to study intestinal motility. The functional signal was averaged from multiple image features, by observing the high correlations between them. To exploit the information content of the functional signal, a MRA technique in wavelet domain was used. MRA results allowed us to separate the noise and the slow wave signal. The slow wave waveforms were detected when their energy exceeded the baseline level. Some analyses relied on the frequency appearance of the waveforms and their velocity along CE transit time were evaluated to estimate the propagation of slow wave. The experimental results shown provide the first results of a detailed interpretation of intestinal motility from CE image sequences. Therefore, we believe that this provides a promising method with which to develop clinical applications.

## References


1. Grundy, D.: GastroIntestinal Motility - The Integration of Physiological Mechanisms. MTP Press Limited, Lancaster (1985)
2. Bronzino, J.D.: The Biomedical Engineering Handbook, 3rd edn. CRC Press, Boca Raton (2006)
3. Dunn, R.B., Linkens, D.A.: A mathematical model of the slow-wave electrical activity of the human small intestine. Medical and Biological Engineering 12, 750–758 (1974)
4. Hansen, M.B.: Small intestinal manometry. Physiological Research 51, 541–556 (2002)
5. Iddan, G., Meron, G., Glukovsky, A., Swain, P.: Wireless capsule endoscope. Nature 405, 417 (2000)
6. Adler, D.G., Gostout, C.J.: Wireless capsule endoscopy - state of art. Hospital Physician, 14–22 (2003)

7. Swain, P., Fritscher-Ravens, A.: Role of video endoscopy in managing small bowel disease. GUT 53, 1866–1875 (2004)
8. Spyridonos, P., Vilarino, F., Vitria, J., Azpiroz, F., Radeva, P.: Identification of intestinal motility events of capsule endoscopy video analysis. In: Blanc-Talon, J., Philips, W., Popescu, D.C., Scheunders, P. (eds.) ACIVS 2005. LNCS, vol. 3708, pp. 531–537. Springer, Heidelberg (2005)
9. Spyridonos, P., Vilarino, F., Vitria, J., Azpiroz, F., Radeva, P.: Anisotropic feature extraction from endoluminal images for detection of intestinal contractions. In: Larsen, R., Nielsen, M., Sporring, J. (eds.) MICCAI 2006. LNCS, vol. 4191, pp. 161–168. Springer, Heidelberg (2006)
10. Vilarino, F., Spyridonos, P., Vitria, J., Azpiroz, F., Radeva, P.: Linear radial patterns characterization for automatic detection of tonic intestinal contractions. In: Martínez-Trinidad, J.F., Carrasco Ochoa, J.A., Kittler, J. (eds.) CIARP 2006. LNCS, vol. 4225, pp. 178–187. Springer, Heidelberg (2006)
11. Vu, H., Echigo, T., Sagawa, R., Yagi, K., Shiba, M., Higuchi, K., Arakawa, T., Yagi, Y.: Contraction detection in small bowel from an image sequence of wireless capsule endoscopy. In: Ayache, N., Ourselin, S., Maeder, A. (eds.) MICCAI 2007, Part I. LNCS, vol. 4791, pp. 775–783. Springer, Heidelberg (2007)
12. Vu, H., Echigo, T., Sagawa, R., Yagi, K., Shiba, M., Higuchi, K., Arakawa, T., Yagi, Y.: Adaptive control of video display for diagnostic assistance by analysis of capsule endoscopic images. In: Proc. of the 18th ICPR, pp. 980–983 (2006)
13. American Society for Gastrointestinal Endoscopy - ASGE: Technology status evaluation report wireless capsule endoscopy. Gastrointestinal Endoscopy 56, 1866–1875 (2002)
14. Swain, M., Ballard, D.: Color indexing. International Journal of Computer Vision 7, 11–32 (1991)
15. Lucas, B.D., Kanade, T.: An iterative image registration technique with an application to stereo vision. In: Proc. of the Intl. Joint Conf. on Artificial Intelligence, pp. 674–679 (1981)
16. Tomasi, C., Kanade, T.: Detection and tracking of point features. Technical report (1991)
17. Birchfield, S.: KLT: Kanade-Lucas-Tomasi Feature Tracker (2006), http://www.ces.clemson.edu/~stb/klt/
18. Canny, J.: A computational approach to edge detection. IEEE T-PAMI 8, 679–698 (1986)
19. Percival, B.D., Walden, T.A.: Wavelet Methods for Time Series Analysis. Cambridge University Press, Cambridge (2000)
20. Schemann, M., Ehrlein, H.-J.: Computerised method for pattern recognition of intestinal motility: functional significance of the spread of contractions. Medical and Biological Engineering 23, 143–149 (1985)
21. De Ridder, W.J.E., Voeten, J.J., Rombouts, J.A.C.A., Van Nueten, J.M., Schuurkes, J.A.J.: Computer-assisted method for analysis of postprandial gastrointestinal motility in conscious dogs. Medical and Biological Engineering 27, 470–476 (1989)

# On JPEG2000 Error Concealment Attacks

Thomas Stütz and Andreas Uhl*

University of Salzburg, Department of Computer Sciences, Jakob-Haringerstr. 2,
Salzburg, Austria
{tstuetz,uhl}@cosy.sbg.ac.at

**Abstract.** In this work, JPEG2000 error resilience options and error
concealment strategies are discussed and evaluated. Error resilience options and error concealment strategies have been employed to mimic
attacks against selective / partial JPEG2000 encryption schemes. Thus
the security evaluation of these selective / partial encryption schemes
relies on the proper working of the JPEG2000 error concealment. Rec-
ommendations for JPEG2000 encryption given in previous work have to
be reassessed on the basis of our results. Improvements to the error concealment code of the JPEG2000 reference software JJ2000 are presented.

## 1   Introduction

Today visual data are predominantly present in digital form. Current threats
to these data are on the one hand transmission and storage errors that may
render the entire data useless and the illegitimate distribution of these data
on the other. In order to protect the visual data and fulfill application requirements specifically tailored encryption approaches are necessary [1,2,3]. Especially
JPEG2000 encryption has been the subject of a considerable amount of research
[4,5,6,7,8,9,10,11,12]. Many of the proposed encryption schemes can be applied
in a selective / partial way. There is a close connection between selective / partial encryption and an error-prone communication channel or storage device, as
in all these cases compressed visual data is damaged. An overview of the involved processes is given in figure 1. In [2, pp.107–114] selective encryption of
the JPEG2000 codestream is discussed and analyzed in terms of security. It is
proposed to employ the JPEG2000 built-in error resilience tools to mimic attacks
against selective encryption (therefore this attack is called error concealment attack). The main idea is that an attacker can identify the encrypted portions in
the codestream and reconstruct the image on the basis of the unencrypted data.
This idea of a distinct cryptanalytic model for selective encryption has later
been formulated more explicitly [13]. If parts of the JPEG2000 codestream are
encrypted, these parts introduce noise into the reconstructed image. An attacker
is interested in increasing the image quality and therefore needs to identify and
conceal the encrypted parts (thereby exploiting all available information). These

---

* This work has been partially supported by the Austrian Science Fund, project no.
15170.

T. Wada, F. Huang, and S. Lin (Eds.): PSIVT 2009, LNCS 5414, pp. 851–861, 2009.

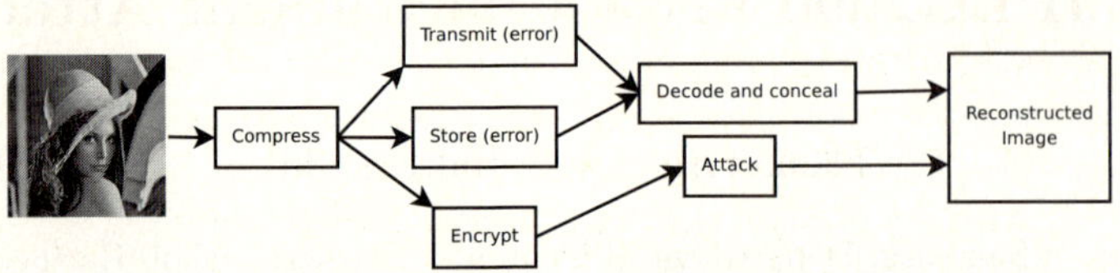


**Fig. 1.** Overview of the processes

attacks can be mimicked by JPEG2000 compression of the image with error resilience options enabled, which enable the JPEG2000 decoder to perform the appropriate error concealment. In [2] the authors conclude that on the basis of their experimental evaluations, it is sufficient to encrypt the leading 20% of the codestream in order to confidentially hide all image information. In this paper, we will show that this rule of thumb does not hold if the JPEG2000 reference software's error concealment is improved. In the technology examples of [3], confidentiality is claimed if only 1% of the JPEG2000 codestream is encrypted – a claim that that will have to be reconsidered. Additionally, several concealment strategies are evaluated.

The focus of previous contributions to JPEG2000 error resilience [14,15] has been the comparison of JPEG2000 with MPEG-4, which has revealed that JPEG2000 offers superior error resilience tools compared to MPEG-4. Apart from the reference software [16], namely JJ2000 (http://jj2000.epfl.ch) and JasPer, only few implementations are available, e.g., Taubman's Kakadu and an implementation distributed by the company Luratech. However, those implementations and their source codes are not publicly available and therefore of limited interest to the research community. JasPer does not conceal detected bitstream errors (in fact, only the error detection mechanism is standardized, not the concealment), but JJ2000 offers error concealment.

JPEG2000 will be briefly reviewed in section 2. In section 2.1 the JPEG2000 error resilience options and error concealment strategies are discussed in more detail. Improvements to the JJ2000 error concealment code are discussed in section 3. Experimental results for the different error resilience and concealment strategies are presented in section 4. Furthermore we will show that selective JPEG2000 encryption preserves considerable amount of visual information. Finally we conclude in section 5.

## 2    An Overview of the JPEG2000 Compression Pipeline

JPEG2000 [17] employs a wavelet transform; Part I of the standard [18] specifies an irreversible 9/7 and a reversible integer 5/3 wavelet transform. An image may consist of several components, which may be subject to an optional multiple component transform. The components are further subdivided into tiles, which are independently wavelet transformed. After the wavelet transform the coefficients are quantized and encoded using the EBCOT scheme, which renders distortion scalability possible. Thereby the coefficients are grouped into codeblocks and these are encoded bitplane by bitplane. The first non-zero bitplane is only coded with a cleanup pass, while every other bitplane is coded with three coding passes, namely significance propagation, magnitude refinement and cleanup pass. The JPEG2000 codestream – the standard's term for a JPEG2000 coded image – consists of headers (main header, tile headers, tile part headers) and packets, which are further subdivided into a packet header and a packet body. The packet header contains vital information for the decoding process, such as the number of leading zero bitplanes of a codeblock (all coefficients of the codeblock have a zero bit in these MSB bitplanes and only the remaining bitplanes are entropy coded). The packet bodies contain the entropy coded coefficient data of the codeblocks (also denoted the codeblock's bitstream). The codeblock's bitstream is partitioned such that each partition corresponds to the contribution of the codeblock to a certain quality layer. A packet body consists of the CCPs (codeblock contribution to a packet) of a certain resolution, quality layer and precinct (a spatial inter-subband partitioning structure that contains one to several codeblocks) of a tile of a component. The ordering of the packets defines the progression order of the JPEG2000 codestream.

## 2.1  JPEG2000 Error Resilience Options

There are several options of strengthening robustness of JPEG2000 against transmission errors, e.g., the insertion of start of packet (SOP) and end of packet header (EPH) marker sequences, the resetting of the contexts after each coding pass, the insertion of a segmentation marker after each cleanup pass and the predictable termination of each coding pass. Only the segmentation symbol and predictable termination are capable of the detection of bitstream errors, i.e., of errors in the entropy coded coefficient data.

The coding of an additional segmentation symbol at the end of the cleanup pass protects the bitstream on a bitplane basis. Thereby the four bit sequence "1010" is coded in uniform context at the end of each cleanup pass (the last pass of each bitplane). If we assume that errors randomly generate a "1010" sequence at the end of a cleanup pass (approximately following a uniform distribution), the occurrence of an error is detected with a probability of $15/16 = 0.9375$. This strategy is very well-performing in terms of compression efficiency (only a very slight compression overhead is introduced, as shown in figure 6). However, it is only capable of detecting errors on a bitplane basis and hence undamaged coding passes may also be discarded.

The employment of predictable termination of each coding pass is an improvement in the following sense: Every erroneous coding pass can be separately identified and concealed. Any bit error is likely to result in an arithmetic decoder state that is not consistent with the predictable termination policy. A detailed description of the detection of termination inconsistencies can be found in [17]. About 3.5 bit of error resilience information are left on the spare least significant bits of a coding pass (according to the JJ2000 documentation and backed up by own experiments). Thus every error in a coding pass is detected with a probability of $1 - 1/2^{3.5} \approx 0.91$. Both methods can be combined to improve error detection. Figures 2(a) and 2(b) illustrate these two error resilience options; "FNZBP" denotes the first non zero MSB bitplane, which is only coded with a cleanup pass ("CP"). "BP" denotes the consecutive bitplanes, "SP" the significance propagation pass, "MP" the magnitude refinement pass, and "ER" the error resilience information.

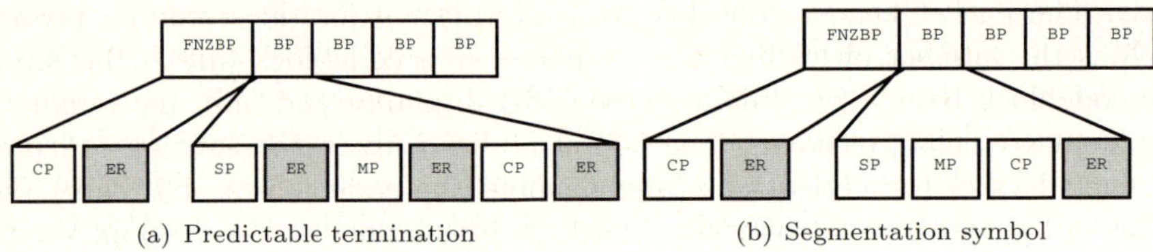


(a) Predictable termination        (b) Segmentation symbol

**Fig. 2.** JPEG2000 error resilience options

[17, p.509] remarks on the propagation of bitstream errors: "Since code-blocks are coded independently, errors may not propagate beyond the code-block whose bit-stream is corrupted." The remaining codeblock data after an error generally is useless. In [17] it is pointed out that this is not only the case for arithmetically coded data, but may also occur for raw codeword segments, as a single symbol error in the significance propagation pass may corrupt the state array, thus rendering the remainder of the bitstream unusable. Further dependencies are introduced by the wavelet transform, e.g., an error in the lowest resolution LL subband will propagate to several pixels in the spatial domain.

## 2.2  JPEG2000 Error Concealment

Note that only the detection of an error is standardized, the actual error concealment of the corrupted parts is a decoder choice.

A decoder has several possibilities when an error is detected:

1. truncate the JPEG2000 file at the position where the error has occurred (stop decoding immediately after the error),
2. set the corrupted coefficients to zero (as done in [14]), or
3. reset the coefficients to the last value before the detection of the error.

For the third strategy and predictable termination of each coding pass, the coefficient values can be saved before the decoding of a coding pass and can be reset to that values if an error is detected (reset on a coding pass basis). If the segmentation symbol is employed, the coefficients have to be saved after each successfully decoded cleanup pass (reset on a bitplane basis). It is a good idea to set all coefficient bits to the value before the detection of an error, and the bit (in the bitplane in which the error was detected) to one. If we assume that for all the remaining bits (which have not been decoded) every value is equally probable, this solution minimizes the average distortion.

It is not certain which strategy performs best. In section 4.3 empirical results are presented.

# 3 Improving the JJ2000 Error Concealment Code

The JJ2000 decoder resets the coefficients on a bitplane basis, regardless of which error resilience options are enabled. We have modified the decoder in order to enable the reset on a coding pass basis.

Apart from that we noticed two bugs in the JJ2000 decoder that severely degrade the error concealment performance. The first one is rather subtle. A coefficient is only reset if non-zero bits have already been decoded. To test for the decoding of non-zero bits, a bitwise AND is applied to the coefficient and a resetmask. The resetmask is computed incorrectly, such that the bit of the erroneous bitplane is taken into account. This subtle difference is decisive, especially if the previously decoded bits are all zero, which is the case for the first non-zero bitplane of a codeblock. As wavelet coefficients tend to be distributed around zero, the majority of the coefficients will have a zero bit in the erroneous bitplane. Hence the probability that this coefficient (that is reset by JJ2000) actually has a one bit in this bitplane is very low. In the file StdEntropyDecoder.java line 2475 (4.1 unix release) it is therefore advisable to set: "resetmask = (-1)<<(bp+1);" instead of "resetmask = (-1)<<(bp);". The JJ2000 comparison value is illustrated in figure 3(c); the corrected comparison value does not take the corrupted bit into account. A coefficient from an erroneous codeblock (an error has been detected in bitplane "bp") is illustrated in figure 3(a), the value to which it is reset to is illustrated in figure 3(b).

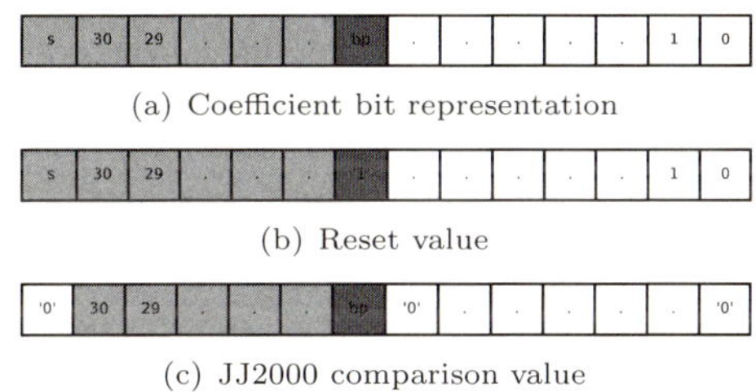

(a) Coefficient bit representation

(b) Reset value

(c) JJ2000 comparison value

Fig. 3. Improvements for JJ2000

The second bug occurs when the segmentation symbol and predictable termination are employed together. A correct termination of a coding pass overrides a previously detected error in the decoding of the segmentation symbol. Thus employing both strategies leads to the same results as using only predictable termination of each coding pass. The bug can be corrected by changing the line 2439 in the file StdEntropyDecoder.java (4.1 unix release) from "error = mq.checkPredTerm();" to "error = error || mq.checkPredTerm();".

As we will see in section 4 these modifications dramatically increases the performance of the error concealment. An improved version of JJ2000 can be found at `www.wavelab.at/sources`

# 4    Experimental Results

First we will present visual examples that reveal that visual information is preserved for selective JPEG2000 encryption. Then the influence on the compression performance of JPEG2000 is evaluated in order to show that the error resilience options are applicable. In section 4.3 error resilience options and concealment strategies are evaluated in a realistic scenario.

We assume that all headers (including packet headers) are well protected. The packet headers can be moved to the main header with the packed packet headers option, which may be treated with special care.

If not stated otherwise, JJ2000's default compression parameters have been employed, which include layer progression and 32 quality layers. The test sets have been derived from the freely available VQEG (video quality experts group) HDTV test set.

## 4.1    Visual Examples

Figures 4(a) and 4(b) illustrate that no concealment (decoding as if no error had been detected) and the JJ2000 concealment do not reveal any image information if the first 20% of the file (excluding headers) are encrypted or otherwise damaged. Additionally to the well-known PSNR (peak signal to noise ratio) the ESS (edge similarity score) as proposed in [19] is given in the figures. In the case of encryption one could assume that the image content is safely protected [2]. If the corrected concealment is applied, the image content (the Lena image) is clearly visible, as figure 5 reveals. Predictive termination and the segmentation symbol and error concealment on a coding pass basis have been applied. Decreasing the encryption percentage to 1% of the image data, as proposed in the technology examples of [3], will reveal even more visual information. From the encrypter's point of view, these results indicate that almost all of the JPEG2000 bitstream data has to be encrypted.

For partial encryption of the entire JPEG2000 codestream, i.e., including all headers, decoding the partially encrypted data may be hard, but the partial plaintext contains enough information to reconstruct the image obtained via the error concealment attack.

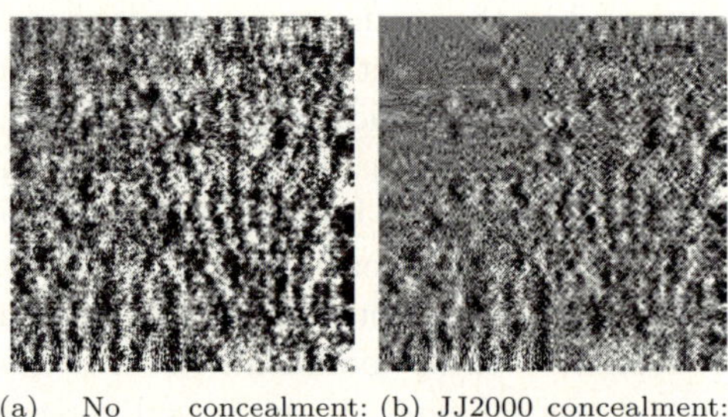

(a) No concealment: PSNR 8.4dB, ESS 0.23    (b) JJ2000 concealment: PSNR 9.7dB, ESS 0.23

**Fig. 4.** First 20% encrypted, 2bpp

**Fig. 5.** First 20% encrypted, 2bpp, corrected concealment: PSNR 14.5dB, ESS 0.0

If the last 80% of the codestream (coded with 2bpp) are corrupted, the JJ2000 concealment, which achieves a PSNR of 23.77dB, performs better than no concealment (19.47dB), while the corrected error concealment increases the image quality dramatically to a PSNR of 32.17dB. The corrected error concealment achieves 12.7dB more than no concealment and 8.4dB more than the default JJ2000 concealment, which is an enormous gain in image quality.

## 4.2   Compression Performance

The bitstream error resilience options in JPEG2000 are efficient in terms of compression performance (c.f. figure 6). These results were obtained by averaging a test set of 250 images with a resolution of 1024 times 576. Error resilience by means of the additional coding of the segmentation symbol (labeled "Seg avg." in figure 6) is most efficient in terms of compression performance, while predictable termination (labeled "Pterm avg.") is slightly more demanding at the cost of about 0.1dB for all bitrates.

Combining both methods (labeled "Combined avg.") adds the nearly negligible overhead of the coding of the segmentation symbol to the overhead of predictable termination.

In general, the bitstream error resilience options can be said to almost preserve JPEG2000's compression performance.

## 4.3   Resilience Options and Concealment Strategies

The location where an error has occurred is the predominant influence on the visual quality of the decoded image. Hence we present an evaluation where each combination of error resilience options and error concealment strategy is evaluated for an error in a certain location in the file.

The analysis on the basis of network error simulations with a bit error rate in the range of $10^{-2}$ to $10^{-4}$ [14,15,20] is too coarse grain to show the subtle differences between the error concealment strategies. Commonly, errors occur

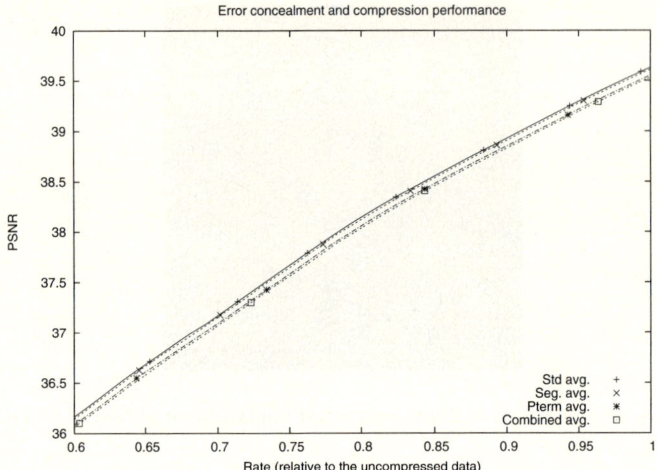



**Fig. 6.** Compression performance and error concealment strategies

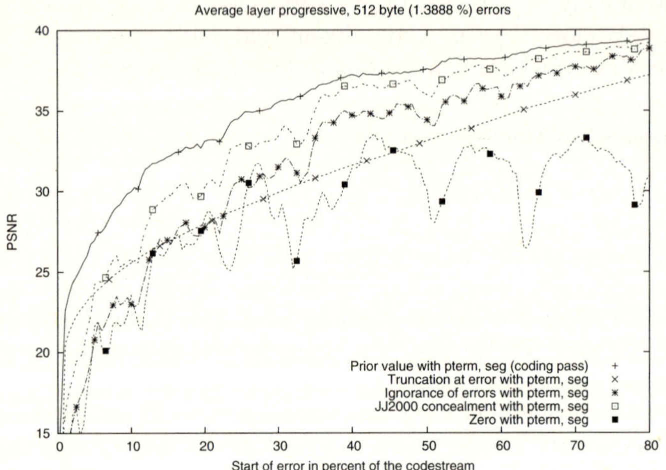



**Fig. 7.** Concealment strategies for combined bitstream resilience options

due to hardware damage of disks; for magnetic disks, sectors of 512 bytes are damaged. Selective encryption is similar to the occurrence of random errors. The results of figures 7 and 8 show the averaged results for a test set of 100 images with a resolution of 512 times 288 each compressed with JJ2000 default parameters and a bitrate of 2bpp. The error location is given in percentage of the codestream length. One damaged sector with 512 byte is assumed (which are 1.39% of the JPEG2000 file).

Figure 7 evaluates the different concealment strategies for both bitstream error resilience options enabled (segmentation symbol and predictable termination).

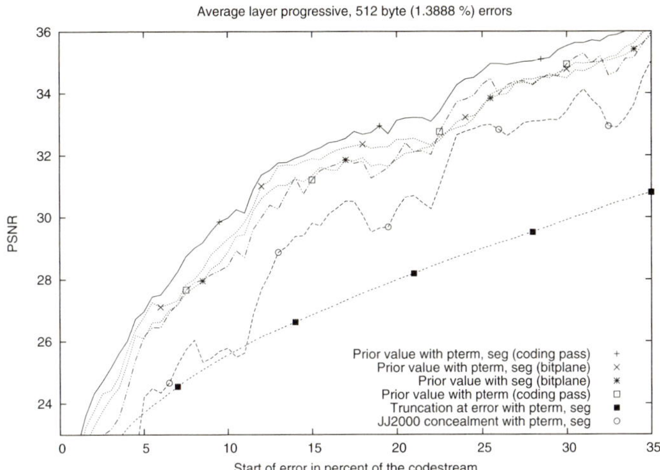


**Fig. 8.** Resilience options and concealment strategies

The best results in terms of PSNR are obtained by resetting the coefficients to their last value (before the detection of an error) on a coding pass basis and by employing both predictable termination and the segmentation symbol (labeled "Prior value with pterm, seg (coding pass)"). Interestingly, the JJ2000 concealment strategy (labeled "JJ2000 concealment with pterm, seg"), though obviously inaccurate, performs better than the other strategies, namely the ignorance of errors (labeled "Ignorance of errors with pterm, seg"), the truncation before the error (labeled "Truncation at error with pterm, seg") and setting the corrupted coefficients to zero (labeled "Zero with pterm, seg"). Compared to previously presented results (see section 4.1), where improvements up to 8.4dB could be reported, these results are surprising. As only a smaller portion of the codestream is affected, fewer CCPs are corrupted (in [10] an average CCP length of 83 bytes is reported for JJ2000 default compression parameters and a test set of 1035 images). Hence, several codeblocks after the error will not be affected and contribute to the image quality (these are not taken into account if the codestream is truncated before the error). Another aspect is the probability of the corruption of the first contribution of a codeblock (the first contributions of codeblock are especially harmful for JJ2000 error concealment code), which decreases if the length of the corrupted segment is reduced, as well as with the position of the error. Furthermore, the affected codeblocks will likely not cover the same spatial area in different subbands (due to the order of the CCPs in the packets). Thus errors of different codeblocks will not accumulate in the wavelet transform.

The worst performance is achieved by resetting the corrupted coefficients to zero. With layer progression, less influential portions of a codeblock's compressed coefficient data are located at the end of the file. However, if an error occurs in these portions, the entire coefficients are set to zero.

In figure 8 error resilience options and concealment strategies are evaluated in more detail. Only errors in the first 35% of the codestream are examined, as errors in this part of the codestream introduce severe distortion. For predictable termination and the segmentation symbol enabled, resetting the coefficients on a coding pass basis is superior to the reset on a bitplane basis (labeled "Prior value with pterm, seg (bitplane)"). Employing the segmentation symbol and predictable termination separately leads to a slightly worse PSNR (labeled "Prior value with seg (bitplane)" and "Prior value with pterm (coding pass)"), but both perform better than the JJ2000 error concealment. It is notable that the image quality is significantly improved by working on a coding pass basis.

## 5    Conclusion

In this paper improvements for JPEG2000 reference software JJ2000 error concealment code have been presented, which increase the image quality dramatically (up to 8.4 dB in our evaluation). These improvements directly influence the applicability of selective JPEG2000 encryption for confidentiality: It can no longer be considered applicable. Empirical results for the influence on the compression performance of the bitstream error resilience options are presented. Additionally, different JPEG2000 resilience options and error concealment strategies have been evaluated. Our results show that the best results are achieved by resetting the coefficients on a coding pass basis.

## References


1. Furht, B., Muharemagic, E., Socek, D.: Multimedia Encryption and Watermarking. Multimedia Systems and Applications, vol. 28. Springer, Heidelberg (2005)
2. Uhl, A., Pommer, A.: Image and Video Encryption. From Digital Rights Management to Secured Personal Communication. Advances in Information Security, vol. 15. Springer, Heidelberg (2005)
3. ISO/IEC 15444-8: Information technology – JPEG2000 image coding system, Part 8: Secure JPEG2000 (April 2007)
4. Grosbois, R., Gerbelot, P., Ebrahimi, T.: Authentication and access control in the JPEG2000 compressed domain. In: Tescher, A. (ed.) Applications of Digital Image Processing XXIV, San Diego, CA, USA. Proceedings of SPIE, vol. 4472, pp. 95–104 (July 2001)
5. Kiya, H., Imaizumi, D., Watanabe, O.: Partial-scrambling of image encoded using JPEG2000 without generating marker codes. In: Proceedings of the IEEE International Conference on Image Processing (ICIP 2003), Barcelona, Spain, September 2003, vol. III, pp. 205–208 (2003)
6. Wu, Y., Deng, R.H.: Compliant encryption of JPEG2000 codestreams. In: Proceedings of the IEEE International Conference on Image Processing (ICIP 2004), Singapore, October 2004, IEEE Computer Society Press, Los Alamitos (2004)
7. Wu, H., Ma, D.: Efficient and secure encryption schemes for JPEG2000. In: Proceedings of the 2004 International Conference on Acoustics, Speech and Signal Processing (ICASSP 2004), pp. 869–872 (May 2004)

8. Zhu, B., Yang, Y., Li, S.: JPEG2000 syntax-compliant encryption preserving full scalability. In: Proceedings of the IEEE International Conference on Image Processing (ICIP 2005), vol. 3 (September 2005)

9. Fang, J., Sun, J.: Compliant encryption scheme for JPEG2000 image code streams. Journal of Electronic Imaging 15(4) (2006)

10. Stütz, T., Uhl, A.: On format-compliant iterative encryption of JPEG2000. In: Proceedings of the Eighth IEEE International Symposium on Multimedia (ISM 2006), pp. 985–990. IEEE Computer Society, Los Alamitos (2006)

11. Engel, D., Stütz, T., Uhl, A.: Format-compliant JPEG2000 encryption in JPSEC: Security, applicability and the impact of compression parameters. EURASIP Journal on Information Security (Article ID 94565), 20 pages (2007), doi:10.1155/2007/94565

12. Yang, Y., Zhu, B.B., Yang, Y., Li, S., Yu, N.: Efficient and syntax-compliant JPEG2000 encryption preserving original fine granularity of scalability. EURASIP Journal on Information Security (2007)

13. Said, A.: Measuring the strength of partial encryption schemes. In: Proceedings of the IEEE International Conference on Image Processing (ICIP 2005), vol. 2 (September 2005)

14. Moccagatta, I., Soudagar, S., Liang, J., Chen, H.: Error resilient coding in JPEG2000 and MPEG-4. IEEE Journals of Selected Areas in Communications 18(6) (June 2000)

15. Dufaux, F., Ebrahimi, T.: Error-Resilient Video Coding Performance Analysis of Motion JPEG2000 and MPEG-4. In: Proceedings of Visual Communications and Image Processing, VCIP 2004. Motion analysis and image sequence processing, SPIE (2004)

16. ISO/IEC 15444-5: Information technology – JPEG2000 image coding system, Part 5: Reference software (November 2003)

17. Taubman, D., Marcellin, M.: JPEG2000 — Image Compression Fundamentals, Standards and Practice. Kluwer Academic Publishers, Dordrecht (2002)

18. ISO/IEC 15444-1: Information technology – JPEG2000 image coding system, Part 1: Core coding system (December 2000)

19. Mao, Y., Wu, M.: Security evaluation for communication-friendly encryption of multimedia. In: Proceedings of the IEEE International Conference on Image Processing (ICIP 2004), Singapore. IEEE Signal Processing Society, Los Alamitos (October 2004)

20. Dufaux, F., Baruffa, G., Frescura, F., Nicholson, D.: JPWL - an Extension of JPEG2000 for Wireless Imaging. In: Proceedings of IEEE Int. Symp. on Circuits and Systems, ISCAS 2006. IEEE, Los Alamitos (2006)

# Upper-Body Contour Extraction Using Face and Body Shape Variance Information


Kazuki Hoshiai[1], Shinya Fujie[2], and Tetsunori Kobayashi[1]

[1] Department of Computer Science and Engineering, Waseda University,
Okubo 3–4–1, Shinjuku–ku, Tokyo 169–8555, Japan
hoshiai@pcl.cs.waseda.jp, koba@waseda.jp
[2] Waseda Institute for Advanced Study, Waseda University,
Nishiwaseda 1–6–1, Shinjuku-ku, Tokyo 169–8050, Japan
fujie@pcl.cs.waseda.jp



**Abstract.** We propose a fitting method using a model that integrates face and body shape variance information for upper-body contour extraction. Accurate body-contour extraction is necessary for various applications, such as pose estimation, gesture recognition, and so on. In this study, we regard it as the shape model fitting problem. A model including shape variance information can fit to the contour robustly even in the noisy case. AAMs are one of these models and can fit to a face successfully. It needs appearance information for effective fitting, but it can not be used in our case because appearance of upper-body easily changes by clothes. Instead of intensity image, proposed method uses edge image as appearance information. However, discrimination between a true contour edge of upper-body and other edges is difficult. To solve this problem, we integrate shapes of upper-body and face. It is expected that this integrated model is more robust to edges in clutter background and various locations of the body than a body shape model using only body shape information. We conduct experiments and confirm improvement in accuracy by integration of face and body variance information.

**Keywords:** Contour extraction, Active Appearance Models, Active Body Shape Models, Active Integrated Shape Models.


## 1   Introduction

We propose a contour shape model integrating body shape variance information and face model of Active Appearance Models (AAMs) [1,2], and achieve accuracy improvement of upper-body contour extraction.

Extracting human contour with high accuracy is important to estimate positions of physical parts such as arm, head and so on. The most common approach to extract human contour is background subtraction [3]. A system such as a robot with active cameras can not utilize this approach which assumes fixed camera. There is "Snakes" [4] as another contour extraction method. It does not use prior knowledge about the contour shape. Owing to this, the model instance tends to converge on a wrong shape.

In this study, we regard body extraction problem as shape model fitting to a contour. We propose a new model and a novel fitting method using Inverse Compositional Image Alignment (ICIA) algorithm [2,5] of AAMs.


T. Wada, F. Huang, and S. Lin (Eds.): PSIVT 2009, LNCS 5414, pp. 862–873, 2009.

## 2   Integration of Face and Body Shape Model

We regard human contour extraction as shape model fitting to a body contour. In this study, we try to improve a model fitting accuracy, using the integrated model of face and body shape variance information.

This section describes fitting systems of face and body, and later describes a fitting system of integrated their systems.

### 2.1   Face Model

Active Shape Models (ASMs) [6] are a method of searching object contour using shape model. It has a habit of robustness to noise for learning the average shape and nonrigid deformation pattern using a set of training images preliminarily given the coordinates of feature points. For enormous amount of calculation, ASMs are extended to apply hierarchical approach using low-resolution images and motion prediction using Kalman filter for reducing iteration count of fitting [7]. One of the successful object detection and searching methods is AAMs. It has models constructed from both shape and appearance, and performs matching a normalized input image and a template image. AAMs allow real time tracking using ICIA algorithm as a model fitting algorithm.

ASMs and AAMs constrain deformation of the object shape which consists of a number of feature points by Principal Component Analysis (PCA). Their fitting algorithms have considerably difference between their models. After transferring each feature point, ASMs arrange the all points in accordance with PCA. On the other hand, AAMs transfer the general shape while maintaining consistency of the relation between the points, for solving the optimization problem of shape parameter based on eigen vector for fitting the object. As a result, AAMs can fit more accurately than ASMs. Furthermore, AAMs outperform ASMs about the convergence speed of fitting by ICIA algorithm.

The fitting process of AAMs is as follows. Firstly input images are transformed to template space using shape parameters. Secondly, the error of the translated image and the template image is calculated. Finally, the shape parameters, minimizing the error, are calculated using a face model. Model fitting to the face is performed using the shape parameters based on the calculation result. The fitting system of AAMs to face region is illustrated in Fig. 1 (a).

### 2.2   Body Model

We apply AAMs to upper-body contour for fitting. When we use AAMs to face, a template image is a face image. A face includes universal information that does not depend on individual, so it can use intensity values as appearance information directly. On the other hand, it is difficult for upper-body model to use only intensity values inside its contour, because upper-body vision changes by clothes easily. Using the edge detected in boundary of human region and background region, we regard an edge image as appearance information to solve this problem.

The flow of fitting system is similar to a system of face except for regarding an edge image as an input image. The fitting system to upper-body contour is illustrated in Fig. 1 (b).

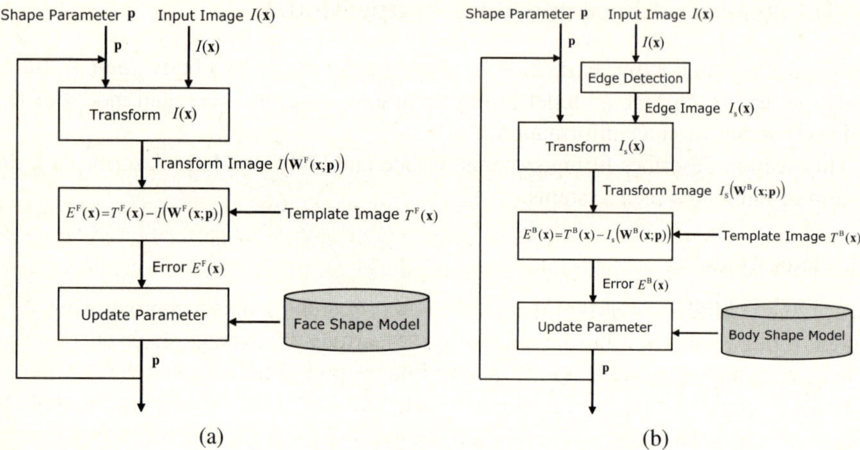



**Fig. 1.** Fitting algorithms for face shape model and upper-body shape model. (a) Fitting algorithm for face shape model, (b) Fitting algorithm for upper-body shape model.

## 2.3   Integrated Model

An edge image includes not only an upper-body contour edge of target person but also other edges. To distinguish an upper-body contour edge from other edges is difficult. Even in noisy environment, face model can be fitted because it does not depend on background. In this study, we integrate two models described in previous sections and

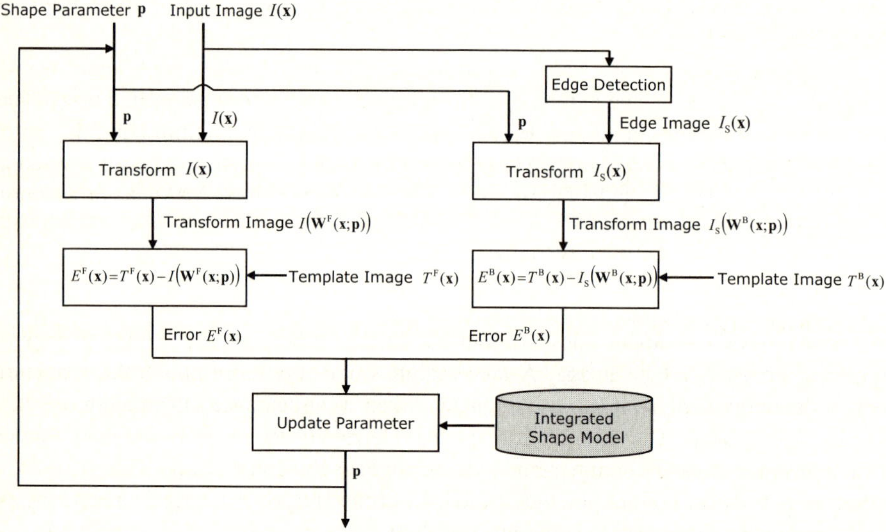



**Fig. 2.** Fitting algorithm for integrated model

limit the search space for upper-body contour based on the position, direction and scale of face.

Procedure of fitting the model which is constructed from both face and body shape variance information is as follows. Firstly we perform transforming input image in face region, and edge image in upper-body contour, using integrated shape parameters of face and body shape variance. Secondly, the errors are calculated for face and body, separately. Finally, the shape parameters minimizing that errors are calculated by the integrated model. Model fitting to a face and a body contour is performed based on the shape parameters obtained by calculation result. The fitting system of integrated model is illustrated in Fig. 2.

## 3  Active Appearance Models

We briefly overview the AAMs and their efficient fitting algorithm [1,2]. Then, we summarize the conditions which a model must satisfy, in order to apply that algorithm.

### 3.1  Shape Model

AAMs consist of two "active" models. First one is the shape model. A shape is defined as a set of $v$ vertices and lines connecting them, as shown in Fig. 3 (a). The shape vector $\mathbf{s}$ is represented as

$$\mathbf{s} = [\, x_1, y_1, x_2, y_2, \cdots, x_v, y_v \,]^T \tag{1}$$

where $x_i$ and $y_i$ represent $x$ and $y$ coordinate of $i$th vertex respectively. PCA is applied to training data which are face images with hand-labeled feature points, then a shape is represented by linear sum of the average shape and the difference shapes,

$$\mathbf{s} = \mathbf{s}_0 + \sum_{i=1}^{n} p_i \mathbf{s}_i \tag{2}$$

where $\mathbf{s}_0$ is the average shape and $\mathbf{s}_i$ is $i$th principal component as a difference shape. Shape parameters are represented as the vector $\mathbf{p} = [\, p_1, p_2, \cdots, p_n \,]^T$. The shape of model instance is determined by the $\mathbf{p}$.

### 3.2  Appearance Model

Second model is an appearance model. Appearance model represents the variance of grayscale image in template space. Template space is defined as 2-D space constructed by the average shape. Applying PCA to the face images of training data represented in template space, an average appearance $A_0(\mathbf{x})$ and $m$ principal components $A_i(\mathbf{x})$ are calculated. $\mathbf{x}$ then describes pixels in template space. We regard the average appearance as the averaged face image, and the principal components as difference face image.

$$A(\mathbf{x}) = A_0(\mathbf{x}) + \sum_{i=1}^{m} \lambda_i A_i(\mathbf{x}) \tag{3}$$

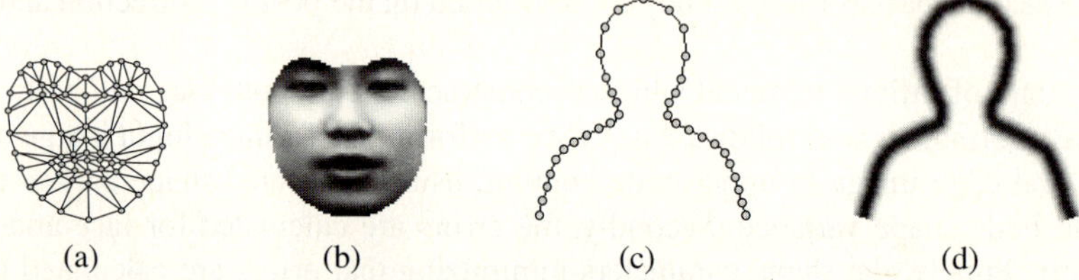

      (a)           (b)           (c)           (d)

**Fig. 3.** Active Appearance Models and Active Body Shape Models. (a) Basic shape of AAMs $s_0$, (b) Template image of AAMs $T(\mathbf{x})$, (c) Basic shape of ABSMs $s_0^{\mathrm{B}}$, (d) Template image of ABSMs $T^{\mathrm{B}}(\mathbf{x})$.

Appearance parameters are represented as the vector $\boldsymbol{\lambda} = [\ \lambda_1, \lambda_2, \cdots, \lambda_m\ ]^T$. The appearance of the model instance with respect to the face region is determined by the $\boldsymbol{\lambda}$. The averaged face image $A_0(\mathbf{x})$ is regarded as the template image $T(\mathbf{x})$ shown in Fig. 3 (b).

### 3.3   Fitting Algorithm

Fitting AAMs is regarded as minimizing the error between an input image and model instance. The error function is defined as

$$E(\mathbf{x}) = A_0(\mathbf{x}) + \sum_{i=1}^{m} \lambda_i A_i(\mathbf{x}) - I\big(W(\mathbf{x}; \mathbf{p})\big) \qquad (4)$$

where $I(\mathbf{x})$ is an input image and $W(\mathbf{x}; \mathbf{p})$ is a warp function warping points in template space to relative points in input image space. Note this warping function is determined by a shape parameter $\mathbf{p}$. For simplicity, we ignore appearance variation. Then, the target is to find a parameter $\mathbf{p}$ that minimizes the sum of square error function, that is

$$\underset{\mathbf{p}}{\mathrm{argmin}} \sum_{\mathbf{x} \in s_0} \left[ T(\mathbf{x}) - I\big(W(\mathbf{x}; \mathbf{p})\big) \right]^2 . \qquad (5)$$

Because, $I(\mathbf{x})$ is usually a non-linear function, it is difficult to calculate $\mathbf{p}$ directly. Then, AAMs use fitting algorithm named "Inverse Compositional Image Alignment (ICIA)." Small warp represented by $\Delta\mathbf{p}$ is introduced to template space,

$$\underset{\Delta\mathbf{p}}{\mathrm{argmin}} \sum_{\mathbf{x} \in s_0} \left[ T\big(W(\mathbf{x}; \Delta\mathbf{p})\big) - I\big(W(\mathbf{x}; \mathbf{p})\big) \right]^2 . \qquad (6)$$

$\Delta\mathbf{p}$ that minimizes the error function in context of given $\mathbf{p}$ is calculated.

## 4   Active Body Shape Models

We propose a fitting method of shape model using prior knowledge of contour variance information. We apply the framework of AAMs to body contour model in order to use prior knowledge. We call this model "Active Body Shape Models (ABSMs)."

## 4.1  Body Shape Model

A body shape model is represented by the vector of arranged $x$,$y$ coordinate value of $u$ feature points.

$$\mathbf{s}^{\mathrm{B}} = [\, x_1, y_1, x_2, y_2, \cdots, x_u, y_u \,]^T \tag{7}$$

An average shape $\mathbf{s}^{\mathrm{B}}$ and $l$ principal components $\mathbf{s}_i^{\mathrm{B}}$ are calculated by PCA for all training data, which are similar to Eq. (2).

$$\mathbf{s}^{\mathrm{B}} = \mathbf{s}_0^{\mathrm{B}} + \sum_{i=1}^{l} p_i^{\mathrm{B}} \mathbf{s}_i^{\mathrm{B}} \tag{8}$$

Here, $p_i^{\mathrm{B}}$ describes the size of shape variance in terms of upper-body contour. In addition, shape parameters are represented as the vector $\mathbf{p}^{\mathrm{B}} = [\, p_1^{\mathrm{B}}, p_2^{\mathrm{B}}, \cdots, p_l^{\mathrm{B}} \,]^T$. The shape of the model instance with respect to the upper-body contour is determined by $\mathbf{p}^{\mathrm{B}}$.

## 4.2  Applying ICIA Algorithm to ABSMs

The differences of ABSMs from normal AAMs are (1) input and template images are edge images, and (2) shape is just a line not closed polygons. Former means that the gradient of template image cannot be calculated because edge image is a set of shape lines. It also causes a problem for the error function calculation, because edge image is very sparse, so the error value has low reliability. Latter means the piece-wise Affine transform cannot be used as the warp function directly. Against these problems, we redefine template image, input image, and warp function.

1) Template image: $T^{\mathrm{B}}(\mathbf{x})$
A line is constructed by connecting vertices in basic shape sequentially. We smooth this line to a constant distance and treat it as a template image. We show examples of a basic shape and a template image in Fig. 3 (c),(d). We fixed the extraction range above elbows, and defined the number of feature points was 35, in this study.

2) Input image: $I_{\mathrm{s}}(\mathbf{x})$
The edge image is extracted by applying canny edge detector to original input image. Then this image is smoothed and the pixel values are normalized from 0 to 255 for the matching. We regard this image as new input image for ABSMs. An example of generation of an edge image is shown in Fig. 4.

3) Warp function: $W^{\mathrm{B}}(\mathbf{x}; \mathbf{p}^{\mathrm{B}})$
Template space is regarded as belt-like space around a line linking the feature points. This belt-like space is constructed by the set of quadrangular area. We can transform each quadrangular area in template space to input image space. The dividing boundaries are bisectors of angles between two lines through an objective point and two points next to that point. The warp function mapping from input image space to template space is piecewise bilinear warp using bilinear transform [8] for each quadrangle area. We consider a case of projection about four vertices of a certain quadrangle area in template

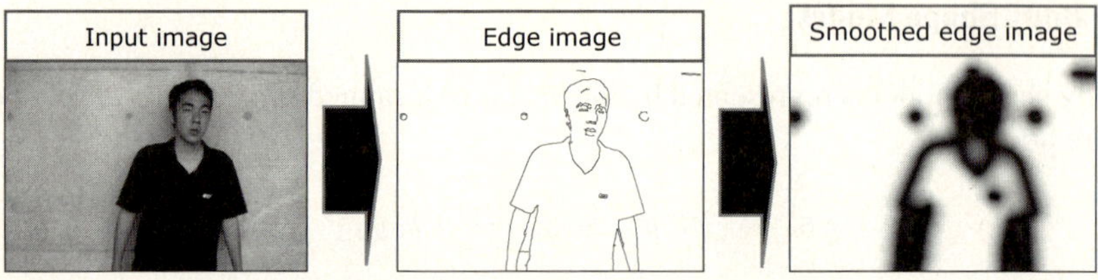


**Fig. 4.** Process of forming the smoothed edge image used for matching with the template image

space to $(x_{00}, y_{00}),(x_{10}, y_{10}),(x_{01}, y_{01}),(x_{11}, y_{11})$ with the shape parameter $\mathbf{p}^B$. When each pixel is denoted by $\mathbf{x} = [\, x, y\,]^T$, the warp function is described as follows.

$$W^B(\mathbf{x}; \mathbf{p}^B) = (1 - \alpha)(1 - \beta)[\, x_{00}, y_{00}\,]^T + \alpha(1 - \beta)[\, x_{10}, y_{10}\,]^T$$
$$+ (1 - \alpha)\beta[\, x_{01}, y_{01}\,]^T + \alpha\beta[\, x_{11}, y_{11}\,]^T \tag{9}$$

$\alpha$ and $\beta$ are transform coefficients of bilinear transform from template space to square space.

## 5   Integration of ABSMs and AFAMs

The upper-body extraction using only edge information is difficult, when there are many edges in background as well as the upper-body contour. In this section, we describe how we integrate two models to tackle this problem.

In following part, we call normal AAMs for face as "Active Face Appearance Models (AFAMs)," and attach F as superscript to parameters and model specific functions for AFAMs.

### 5.1   Integration of Shape Models

The new shape model is a model obtained by integrating two models, the body shape model of ABSMs and the face shape model of AFAMs. We call this model "integrated shape model."

$$\mathbf{s} = [\, x_1, y_1, x_2, y_2, \cdots, x_{v+u}, y_{v+u}\,]^T \tag{10}$$

An average shape $\mathbf{s}_0$ and $k$ principal components $\mathbf{s}_i$ are calculated by PCA for all training data.

$$\mathbf{s} = \mathbf{s}_0 + \sum_{i=1}^{k} p_i \mathbf{s}_i \tag{11}$$

In addition, shape parameters are represented as the vector $\mathbf{p} = [\, p_1, p_2, \cdots, p_k\,]^T$. The shape of the model instance with respect to both the upper-body contour and the face region is specified by the $\mathbf{p}$. An appearance model is constructed for only face appearance model of AFAMs. We call the model consisting of integrated shape model and face shape model and the fitting algorithm of it "Active Integrated Shape Models (AISMs)."

## 5.2  Fitting Algorithm

The evaluation function of fitting AISMs is defined as weighted sum of error for upper-body and error of face.

$$\underset{\Delta \mathbf{p}}{\operatorname{argmin}}\left((1-w)\sum_{\mathbf{x}\in \mathbf{s}_0^{\mathrm{B}}}\left[T^{\mathrm{B}}\left(W^{\mathrm{B}}(\mathbf{x};\Delta\mathbf{p})\right)-I_{\mathrm{s}}\left(W^{\mathrm{B}}(\mathbf{x};\mathbf{p})\right)\right]^2\right.$$

$$\left.+w\sum_{\mathbf{x}\in \mathbf{s}_0^{\mathrm{F}}}\left[T^{\mathrm{F}}\left(W^{\mathrm{F}}(\mathbf{x};\Delta\mathbf{p})\right)-I\left(W^{\mathrm{F}}(\mathbf{x};\mathbf{p})\right)\right]^2\right) \quad (12)$$

The range of weight is $0 < w < 1$. This weight represents ratio of influence by face information and body information. In this study, we empirically determined $w = 0.4$. We take the Taylor series expansion of $T^{\mathrm{B}}\left(W^{\mathrm{B}}(\mathbf{x};\Delta\mathbf{p})\right)$ and $T^{\mathrm{F}}\left(W^{\mathrm{F}}(\mathbf{x};\Delta\mathbf{p})\right)$ in Eq.(12).

$$(1-w)\sum_{\mathbf{x}\in \mathbf{s}_0^{\mathrm{B}}}\left[T^{\mathrm{B}}(\mathbf{x})+\nabla T^{\mathrm{B}}(\mathbf{x})\frac{\partial W^{\mathrm{B}}}{\partial \mathbf{p}}\Delta\mathbf{p}-I_{\mathrm{s}}\left(W^{\mathrm{B}}(\mathbf{x};\mathbf{p})\right)\right]^2$$

$$+w\sum_{\mathbf{x}\in \mathbf{s}_0^{\mathrm{F}}}\left[T^{\mathrm{F}}(\mathbf{x})+\nabla T^{\mathrm{F}}(\mathbf{x})\frac{\partial W^{\mathrm{F}}}{\partial \mathbf{p}}\Delta\mathbf{p}-I\left(W^{\mathrm{F}}(\mathbf{x};\mathbf{p})\right)\right]^2 \quad (13)$$

$\Delta\mathbf{p}$ minimizing Eq. (13) is computed.

$$\Delta\mathbf{p}=\mathbf{H}^{-1}\left((1-w)\sum_{\mathbf{x}\in \mathbf{s}_0^{\mathrm{B}}}\left[\nabla T^{\mathrm{B}}(\mathbf{x})\frac{\partial W^{\mathrm{B}}}{\partial \mathbf{p}}\right]\left[I_{\mathrm{s}}\left(W^{\mathrm{B}}(\mathbf{x};\mathbf{p})\right)-T^{\mathrm{B}}(\mathbf{x})\right]\right.$$

$$\left.+w\sum_{\mathbf{x}\in \mathbf{s}_0^{\mathrm{F}}}\left[\nabla T^{\mathrm{F}}(\mathbf{x})\frac{\partial W^{\mathrm{F}}}{\partial \mathbf{p}}\right]\left[I\left(W^{\mathrm{F}}(\mathbf{x};\mathbf{p})\right)-T^{\mathrm{F}}(\mathbf{x})\right]\right) \quad (14)$$

Then, we denote hessian matrix $\mathbf{H}$ as follows.

$$\mathbf{H}=(1-w)\sum_{\mathbf{x}\in \mathbf{s}_0^{\mathrm{B}}}\left[\nabla T^{\mathrm{B}}(\mathbf{x})\frac{\partial W^{\mathrm{B}}}{\partial \mathbf{p}}\right]^T\left[\nabla T^{\mathrm{B}}(\mathbf{x})\frac{\partial W^{\mathrm{B}}}{\partial \mathbf{p}}\right]$$

$$+w\sum_{\mathbf{x}\in \mathbf{s}_0^{\mathrm{F}}}\left[\nabla T^{\mathrm{F}}(\mathbf{x})\frac{\partial W^{\mathrm{F}}}{\partial \mathbf{p}}\right]^T\left[\nabla T^{\mathrm{F}}(\mathbf{x})\frac{\partial W^{\mathrm{F}}}{\partial \mathbf{p}}\right] \quad (15)$$

$\Delta\mathbf{p}$ minimizing Eq.(12) is calculated analytically by Eq.(14). $\mathbf{p}$ can be updated sequentially from obtained $\Delta\mathbf{p}$ and current $\mathbf{p}$. The optimal shape parameter is provided by $\Delta\mathbf{p}$ sequentially, and fitting to the body contour and the face is performed simultaneously.

## 6  Experiments

### 6.1  ABSMs Experiment

We evaluated the fitting to upper-body contour. We conducted comparative experiments for evaluating accuracy with proposed ABSMs of the modeling method described in 4 and ICIA algorithm described in 4.2.

**Setup.** We performed data collection to prepare test data for the evaluation and learning data to construct the body shape model. Subjects were 15 students in our laboratory. The collected data included four kinds of patterns.

1. facing on the front
2. facing sideways a little
3. inclining to front and back
4. inclining to right and left

The subjects performed the indicated movement of each pattern. We collected 200 image data, capturing the video corresponding to each pattern. The examples of experiment data are shown in Fig. 5.

We computed the error between fitting result and labeled data. We regarded the distance from the correct feature point to a nearest pixel on the fitting result as the error. The image data for experiment were 200 images described in 6.2. The data were divided into four sets, and then one set consists of 50 images. Three sets including 150 images were learning data, and one set was test data. We performed experiments with four combinations. We utilized Snakes which is widely used for the contour extraction as comparison method of ABSMs. Drawing a line by connecting the start point and the end point of feature points, we generated the edge, and artificially made closed region. We performed the model fitting to the closed region of upper-body contour. We set the same shape of initial model instance. These initial model instances were randomly determined as slightly larger than hand labeled correct shapes. We set the distance $d$, of which there are ten kinds from 1 to 10, from the model instances. We prepared one hundred combinations of the points which draw apart from the three correct feature points, and measure the error for each combination.

**Results and discussion.** We calculated the error per one data of Snakes and proposed ABSMs. Note that the unconverged data were eliminated for this evaluation. We calculated the mean of the errors of all test data. They are 475.0 for Snakes and 378.5 for ABSMs. This result shows that ABSMs is more accurate than the traditional method.

The model instance of Snakes converged inside the closed region consisting of the upper-body contour, when the closed region was broken by lacking the edge over the upper-body contour. In contrast, ABSMs fitted the contour successfully even in such a case, because the model instance keeps the shape consistency for the body shape model.

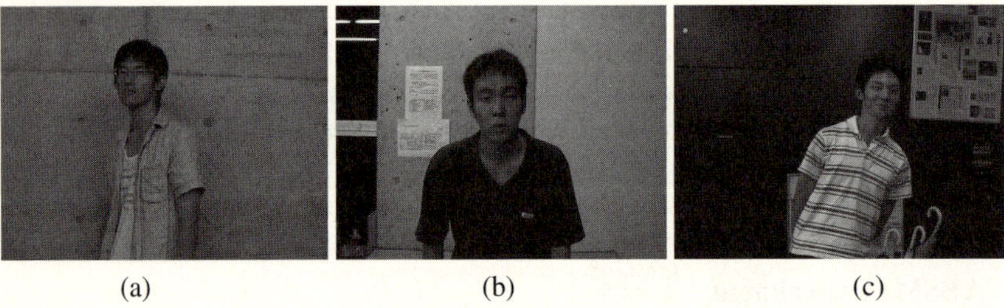

(a)     (b)     (c)

**Fig. 5.** The example of experiment data: (a) facing sideway, (b) inclining to front, (c) inclining to left

## 6.2   AISMs Experiment

We conducted an experiment with ABSMs and AISMs to measure the model fitting accuracy to upper-body contour.

**Setup.**  We performed data collection to prepare test data for the evaluation and learning data to construct the models. Subjects were 5 students in our laboratory. The collecting data included three kinds of pattern.

1. facing on the front
2. facing sideway a little
3. inclining to right

We gave instruction to the subjects to pose each pattern. We captured the image at random from the video and collected in total 500 images which includes 100 images per subject. We labeled feature points by hand to a face and a body contour on the captured images, and these points coordinate were used as correct label representing shape.

In this study, we used total 103 of the feature points which consist of 68 face points and 35 upper-body contour points. We show an labeled image and the feature point location in Fig. 6.

We used 100 images of one subject as test data and the other data as learning data, and performed 5-fold cross validation. We used the images of training data sets and flipped images of them to construct the models. 481 images succeeded in face detection. The shape parameter of ABSMs converged for 440 images. The shape parameter of AISMs converged for 399 images. The shape parameter of both ABSMs and AISMs converged for 393 image. The face position was determined automatically by the face detector [9], and the position of initial model instance was determined by the face position around the body. We updated the shape parameter until it converges. When the parameter converges, we measured the distance error per point between the model instance of feature points and the hand-labeled correct feature points. We counted the error of the data which converge both of ABSMs and AISMs, and then we calculated the averaged error per feature point.

**Results and discussion.**  The averaged errors per feature point for ABSMs and AISMs were 9.9 and 8.7 respectively. Fig. 7 shows the cumulative frequency distribution of

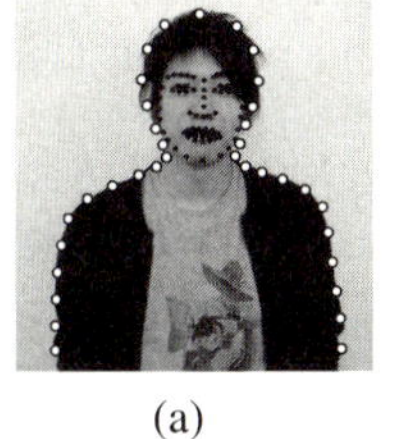
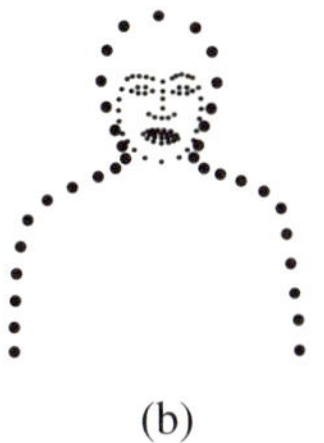

(a)              (b)

**Fig. 6.** The example of labeled image: big points are feature points of upper-body, and small points are feature points of face region, (a) Labeled image, (b) Feature points location

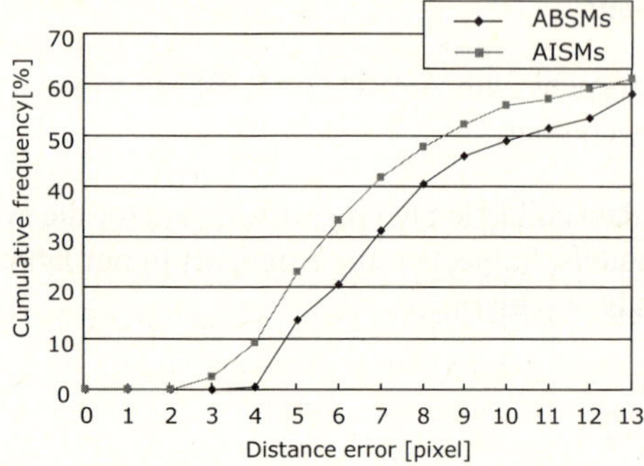


**Fig. 7.** Cumulative frequency distribution of the distance error per feature point for ABSMs and AISMs

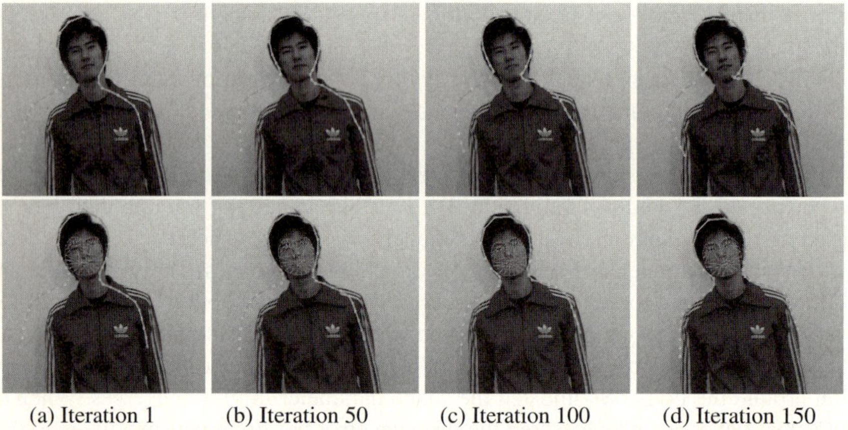

(a) Iteration 1          (b) Iteration 50          (c) Iteration 100          (d) Iteration 150

**Fig. 8.** Process of fitting convergence, the upper row:ABSMs, and the lower row:AISMs (Iteration count 1,50,100,150)

the distance error per feature point. This result concludes that AISMs often converge nearer than ABSMs. We confirmed that the integration of the face information made the error reduced. The precision of the model fitting are improved by the integration of ABSMs and AFAMs. The fitting process of the model instance is shown in Fig. 8. The round points show feature points, and the line of the model instance shows the result of upper-body extraction.

We discuss the experiment result of Fig. 8. The position of the initial model instance was determined by the face region. Thereby, the upper-body was considerably away from correct position with respect to this sample. In consequence, the model instance did not fit to the contour by ABSMs. However, AISMs succeeded in the body part of the model fitting to the contour while the face part of the model instance turned around to the correct position by using face information. The upper-body contour and face shape variance constrained each other by integration of body and face shape, while fitting to the face using the input image, the model instance fits to the contour along the position, direction, and scale of face. Therefore the model instance fitted the upper-body contour.

## 7  Conclusions

For upper-body contour extraction, we proposed ABSMs as the fitting method using ICIA algorithm. ABSMs has an upper-body contour shape model that represents shape variance information. We confirmed that fitting precision of ABSMs was high in comparison with the traditional method to the upper-body extraction by the experiment. Furthermore, we proposed AISMs as the fitting method that integrated AFAMs and ABSMs. We introduced weight for a face and physical error function in AISMs and defined new evaluation function. Proposed method can estimate the most suitable shape parameter using ICIA algorithm for this evaluation function. We evaluated the fitting precision for ABSMs and AISMs. As a result, high fitting precision of AISMs was achieved in comparison with ABSMs and we showed the effectiveness of using face information for the issue of upper-body contour extraction.

In this study, we used a fixed weight for the error function of face and the upper-body contour extraction. In future, we are going to use a dynamic weight obeying a reliability with an upper-body contour extraction and a face information. This reliability can be calculated with the complexity of the edge by the background. Moreover we aim at precision improvement by taking in the appearance information of clothes and using much appearance information.

## Acknowledgment

This work was partly supported by New Energy and Industrial Technology Development ment Organization (NEDO), Japan.

## References

1. Cootes, T.F., Edwards, G.J., Taylor, C.J.: Active appearance models. IEEE Trans. on Pattern Analysis and Machine Intelligence 23(6), 681–685 (2001)
2. Matthews, I., Baker, S.: Active appearance models revisited. International Journal of Computer Vision 60(2), 1405–1573 (2004)
3. Li, L., Huang, W., Gu, I.Y., Tian, Q.: Statistical modeling of complex backgrounds for foreground object detection. IEEE Trans. on Image Processing 13(11), 1495–1472 (2004)
4. Kass, M., Witkin, A., Terzopoulos, D.: Snakes: Active contour models. International Journal of Computer Vision 1(4), 321–331 (1988)
5. Baker, S., Matthews, I.: Lucas-kanade 20 years on: A unifying framework. International Journal of Computer Vision 56(3), 221–255 (2004)
6. Cootes, T.F., Taylor, C.J., Cooper, D.H., Graham, J.: Active shape models–their training and application. Computer Vision and Image Understanding 61(1), 38–59 (1995)
7. Lee, S.W., Kang, J., Shin, J., Paik, J.: Hierarchical active shape model with motion prediction for real-time tracking of non-rigid objects. IET Computer Vision 1(1), 17–24 (2007)
8. Heckbert, P.S.: Fundamentals of texture mapping and image warping. Master's thesis, University of California (1989)
9. Viola, P., Jones, M.J.: Rapid object detection using a boosted cascade of simple features. International Journal of Computer Vision 57(2), 137–154 (2004)

# Approximated Ground Truth
# for Stereo and Motion Analysis
# on Real-World Sequences


Zhifeng Liu and Reinhard Klette

The *.enpeda..* Project, The University of Auckland
Auckland, New Zealand
`carlos.zf.liu@gmail.com`



**Abstract.** This paper approximates ground truth for real-world stereo sequences and demonstrates its use for the performance analysis of a few selected stereo matching and optical flow techniques. Basically we assume zero roll and constant tilt of an ego-vehicle (for about 10 seconds) driving on a planar road.

**Keywords:** Performance evaluation, stereo analysis, motion analysis, real-world sequences, driver assistance.


## 1   Introduction

Stereo matching and motion analysis are two very active research areas in computer vision. The quantitative evaluation of algorithms, as offered by the Middlebury stereo website[1] and their optical flow website[2] are often cited today as the state-of-the art of current performance evaluation of stereo or optical flow algorithms. Those evaluations have contributed considerably to significant advances in algorithm performance. However, evaluations on those Middlebury websites are based on high quality and high resolution color images, which are also only short sequences (of only a few frames) that are recorded in a lab environment, typically carefully designed to test for particular features. The challenges for stereo and optical flow algorithm in today's real world applications surpass such designed datasets and evaluation methods.

This paper deals with real-world stereo sequences. We refer to Set 1 (provided by Daimler AG) of the *.enpeda..* sequences[3], as described in [4]. These seven stereo sequences are taken with two Bosch (12-bit, gray-value) night vision cameras. Each sequence contains 250 or 300 frames ($640{\times}481$), and features different driving environments, including highway (see Figure 1), urban road and rural area. Camera calibration is used for geometric rectification, such that image pairs are characterized by standard epipolar geometry as specified in [3].

---

[1] `http://vision.middlebury.edu/stereo/`
[2] `http://vision.middlebury.edu/flow/`
[3] `http://www.mi.auckland.ac.nz/` and follow the *EISATS* link


T. Wada, F. Huang, and S. Lin (Eds.): PSIVT 2009, LNCS 5414, pp. 874–885, 2009.

**Fig. 1.** Sample of a stereo pair (of Sequence 1)

Intrinsic camera parameters and extrinsic calibration parameters for left and right camera (also in relation to the car) are provided. The vehicle's movement status is also given for each frame. We discuss a way to extract ground truth from these sequences.

## 2  Quality Metrics

To evaluate the performance of a stereo or optical flow algorithm and understand how their parameters affect results, we need a quantitative way to measure the quality of calculated stereo correspondences or motion vectors.

### 2.1  Stereo

The general approach of stereo evaluation is to compute error statistics based on given ground truth. (Note that any ground truth comes with some measurement error; ground truth is not truth.) We use the same error measurements as on the Middlebury stereo website, namely the *root mean squared error* between the disparity map $d(x, y)$ and the ground truth map $d_T(x, y)$, defined as follows:

$$E_R = (\frac{1}{n} \sum |d(x, y) - d_T(x, y)|^2)^{\frac{1}{2}} \tag{1}$$

where $n$ is the total number of pixels, and the percentage of *bad matching pixels*, defined as follows:

$$E_B = \frac{1}{n} \sum (|d(x, y) - d_T(x, y)| > \delta_d) \tag{2}$$

where $\delta_d$ is the threshold of disparity tolerance.

### 2.2  Optical Flow

Quality metrics for optical flow evaluation have to measure the result in a 2D space. We use the common *angular error* defined as the average angle between estimated optical flow vector $\mathbf{u}$ and the true flow vector $\mathbf{u}_T$,

$$E_{AE} = \frac{1}{n} \sum \arccos \left( \frac{\mathbf{u} \cdot \mathbf{u}_T}{|\mathbf{u}||\mathbf{u}_T|} \right) \tag{3}$$

where $|\mathbf{u}|$ denotes the length (magnitude) of a vector, and the *end point error* which measures the absolute distance between end points of vectors $\mathbf{u}$ and $\mathbf{u}_T$,

$$E_{EP} = \sqrt{(u - u_T)^2 + (v - v_T)^2} \tag{4}$$

# 3   Approximate Ground Truth

We approximate ground truth with respect to an assumed (!) planar road surface, using known parameters of ego-vehicle and cameras (as saved in the *camera.dat* file and in the file header of every frame; see [4]).

## 3.1   Disparities on Road Surface

We consider the test sequences to be ego-motion compensated, which means that the horizon is always parallel with the row direction in the images. We conclude that pixels on the same image row have the same depth value if a projection of the planar road surface.

A side-view of the camera setting is shown in Figure 2, where $\theta$ is the known tilt angle, $P$ is a road surface point which is projected into $p = (x_p, y_p)$ on the image plane, $H$ is the height of the camera. It follows that

$$Z = d_e(OP_c) = d_e(OP)\cos\psi = \frac{H}{\sin(\theta + \psi)}\cos\psi \tag{5}$$

According to the stereo projection equations, the disparity $d$ can be written as

$$d = \frac{b \cdot f}{Z} = \frac{b \cdot f}{\frac{H}{\sin(\theta+\psi)}\cos\psi} \tag{6}$$

where angle $\psi$ can be calculated as follows, using focal length $f$ and pixel coordinate $y_p$ in the image:

$$\psi = \arctan\left(\frac{(y_p - y_0)s_y}{f}\right) \tag{7}$$

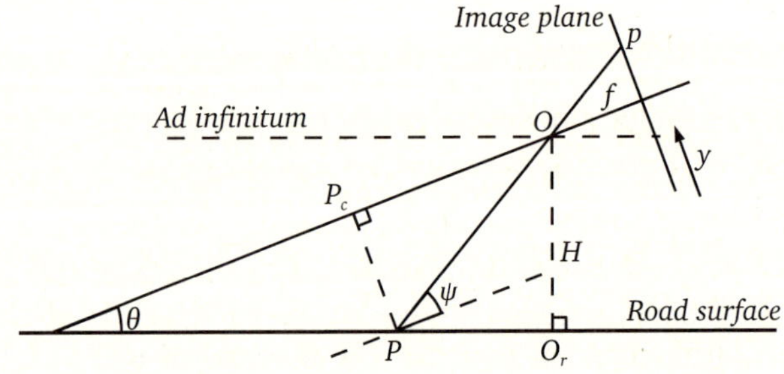


**Fig. 2.** Projection of a point $P$ of the road surface

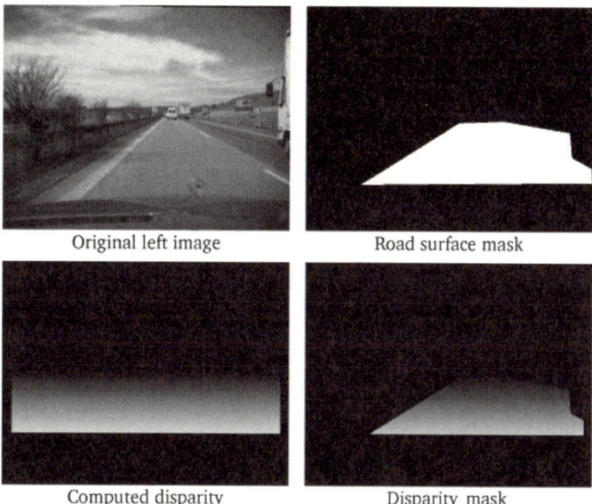

<table>
<tr><td>Original left image</td><td>Road surface mask</td></tr>
<tr><td>Computed disparity</td><td>Disparity mask</td></tr>
</table>

**Fig. 3.** Generation of a disparity mask: input image, manually generated mask, depth map of a planar road, and resulting disparity mask

Here, $y_0$ is the $y$-coordinate of the principal point, and $s_y$ is the pixel size in $y$-direction. We can also compute the $y$-coordinate of a line that projects to infinity

$$y_{inf} = \frac{y_0 - f \cdot \tan \theta}{s_y}$$

This is the upper limit of the road surface, and points on it should have zero disparity (if no objects block the view).

Figure 3 illustrates the process of generating an approximated disparity map on road surface areas, also using manual input for a conservative outline of the road area in a given image. In the given camera setting (of the seven sequences), there is a yaw angle (0.01 radian) which makes the cameras looking a little bit to the left. This angle can be ignored because it only defines the right camera to be about 3 mm behind the left camera.

### 3.2 Local Displacements of Road Surface

Speed and direction (yaw rate) of the ego-vehicle are given for all frames of those seven sequences. The road is, obviously, static, what makes the calculation of relative movement of road surface points (with respect to the camera) straight forward.

Given a pixel $p$ on the image plane at time $t$, which is projected to a road surface point $P$. Let $P$ move to a new position $P'$ at time $t + \delta t$, where $\delta t$ is the time interval between two consecutive frames (called `CycleTime` in the seven sequences, either equals 0.04 s or 0.08 s). Then, $P'$ is projected back to the image plane at $p'$; see Figure 4. The approximation of local displacement at a pixel can then proceed as follows:

First, assume that the vehicle speed equals $\mathbf{v}$ at time $t$, and $\mathbf{v}'$ at time $t + \delta t$; the average speed during this time interval equals $\delta t$ is $\overline{\mathbf{v}} = \frac{\mathbf{v}+\mathbf{v}'}{2}$, having $\delta t$ very

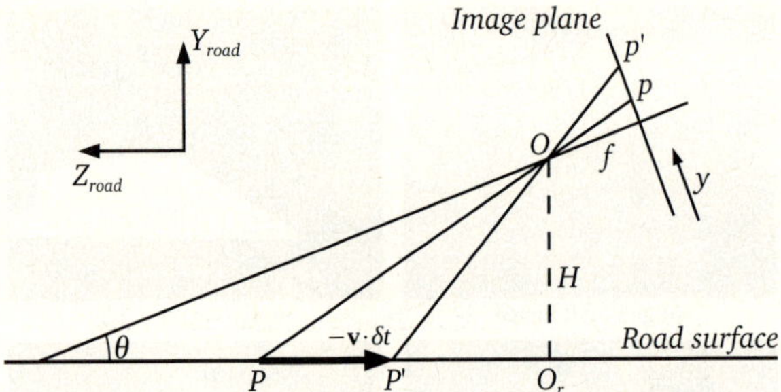


**Fig. 4.** Approximation of local displacement in $y$-direction: $P$ and $P'$ is the same road surface point, just in two consecutive frames. $P$ is projected into $p = (x, y)$ in the image plane, $P'$ is projected into $p' = (x', y')$.

small in the sequences. Distances (in $Z_{road}$ coordinates) of moving points are defined as follows:

$$d_Z(P, P') = |\overline{\mathbf{v}}| \cos(\overline{\varphi} + \varphi_c)\delta t = \frac{|\mathbf{v_1}| + |\mathbf{v_2}|}{2} \cos(\frac{\varphi_1 + \varphi_2}{2} + \varphi_c)\delta t$$

where $\varphi_1$ and $\varphi_2$ are the yaw angles of the ego-vehicle at $t$ and $t + 1$, and $\varphi_c$ is the yaw angle of the camera installation (see Figure 5). Therefore, the distance between the point $P$ and the host vehicle becomes

$$Z_{P'} = d_Z(O_r, P') = d_Z(O_r, P) - d_Z(PP') = \frac{H}{\tan(\theta + \psi)} - d_Z(PP')$$

Then, the angle between the projection ray $OP'$ and the optical axis of the camera may be determined as follows:

$$\psi' = \arctan\left(\frac{H}{d_Z(O_r, P')}\right) - \theta = \arctan\left(\frac{H}{d_Z(O_r, P) - d_Z(P, P')}\right) - \theta$$

where $d_Z(O_r, P) = \frac{H}{\tan(\theta + \psi)}$.

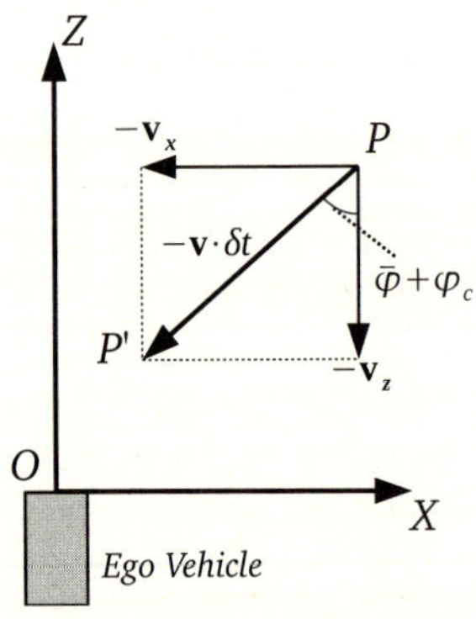


**Fig. 5.** Change in relative position between road surface point $P$ and ego-vehicle

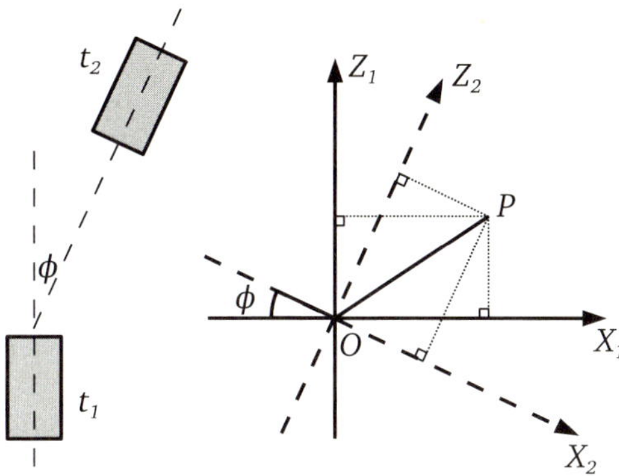

**Fig. 6.** A rotation of the ego-vehicle

Therefore, according to Equation (7), the $y$-coordinate of the local displacement $\mathbf{u}$ at point $P'$ can be written as

$$v = \Big(\frac{f \cdot \tan(\psi')}{s_y} + y_0\Big) - y_p$$

Thus, we are also able to specify the position of point $P$ in $x$-direction as follows

$$X_P = \frac{Z_P \cdot x_p}{f}$$

with $Z_P = \frac{H}{\sin(\theta + \psi)} \cos\psi$, which is actually already a known value from the previous stereo ground truth approximation.

The position of $P'$ (for the next frame) can then be calculated by using speed $\mathbf{v}$ and time interval $\delta t$,

$$X_{P'} = X_P - |\mathbf{v}| \sin(\overline{\varphi} + \varphi_c)\delta t$$

Now we have the new relative position between the road surface point and the vehicle at time $t + \delta t$. - In a next step, we need to rotate the vehicle coordinate system by an angle according to the yaw rate given in the vehicle movement parameters; see Figure 6. Therefore, the final (relative) position is given as follows:

$$\begin{bmatrix} X_{P'}^{\phi} \\ Z_{P'}^{\phi} \end{bmatrix} = \begin{bmatrix} \cos(\phi) & -\sin(\phi) \\ \sin(\phi) & \cos(\phi) \end{bmatrix} \begin{bmatrix} X_{P'} \\ Z_{P'} \end{bmatrix}$$

In a final step, point $P$ is projected back to a pixel $p'$ on the camera's image plane. Then, the local displacement is obtained by comparing locations of $p$ and $p'$, as follows:

$$\psi' = \arctan\Big(\frac{H}{Z_{P'}^{\phi}}\Big) - \theta$$

$$v = y_p' - y_p = \Big(\frac{f \cdot \tan(\psi')}{s_y} + y_0\Big) - y_p \quad \text{and} \quad u = x_{p'} - x_p = \frac{f \cdot X_{P'}^{\phi}}{\frac{H}{\sin(\theta + \psi')} \cos(\psi')} - x_p$$

## 4    Recalibration of Tilt Angle

Although a camera tilt angle is already given for these sequences, we noticed
that the angle is not always true when verifying the data. This problem might be
caused by several reasons, for example, the road surface is changing (downhill,
uphill), the car coordinate system is not parallel to the road surface in some
situations (acceleration, braking), drivers of different weight, or driving with flat
tires, or the installation of cameras may change for some reasons. (Actually,
changes are easy to detect by reading the position of the Mercedes star in the
given images.)

The outlined process for obtaining approximate stereo ground truth identified
the importance of the tilt angle for the estimated values. We propose a method
to estimate the average tilt angle for a given sequence of frames. This method
is similar to the road surface stereo approximation, just in a reverse order. We
estimate the tilt angle based on given depth at some feature points (i.e., with
known disparities) which can be measured or identified manually.

See Figure 3 and assume a given pair of corresponding points, with disparity
$d$. By Equation (6) we have that the tilt angle can be written as follows:

$$\theta = \arcsin\left(\frac{H\cos\psi \cdot d}{b \cdot f}\right) - \psi \tag{8}$$

where $\psi$ is as given in Equation (7).

Altogether, at first, we randomly select five or six frames from a sequence of
frames, then, we calculate or choose pairs of corresponding pixels on the road
surface area, and obtain disparities between those. Each disparity (of one pixel

**Table 1.** Results of tilt angle estimation for the given seven sequences

| Sequence name | Tilt angle (radian) |
|---|---|
| 1: 2007-03-06_121807 | 0.01608 |
| 2: 2007-03-07_144703 | 0.01312 |
| 3: 2007-03-15_182043 | 0.02050 |
| 4: 2007-04-20_083101 | 0.06126 |
| 5: 2007-04-27_145842 | 0.06223 |
| 6: 2007-04-27_155554 | 0.06944 |
| 7: 2007-05-08_132636 | 0.05961 |

**Table 2.** Results of tilt angle estimation for short frame periods (first pair of frames
and the following 19 pairs of frames) of sequence 2007-04-27_155554

| First pair of frames | 1 | 11 | 21 | 31 | 41 | 51 | 61 | 71 | 81 | 91 | 101 | 111 |
|---|---|---|---|---|---|---|---|---|---|---|---|---|
| Tilt angle ($10^{-3}$ of a radian) | 80 | 71 | 60 | 60 | 62 | 63 | 65 | 70 | 77 | 71 | 63 | 66 |
| First pair of frames | 121 | 131 | 141 | 151 | 161 | 171 | 181 | 191 | 201 | 211 | 221 | 231 |
| Tilt angle ($10^{-3}$ of a radian) | 60 | 50 | 50 | 59 | 58 | 54 | 55 | 56 | 58 | 53 | 53 | 42 |

pair) can be used to calculate a tilt angle using Equation (8), and a mean of those provides a tilt angle estimation; see Table 1 for results for the seven sequences. A more refined estimation is illustrated by Table 2; here, overlapping intervals of 20 frames are used to estimate tilt in each interval, and the table illustrates the actual variations.

## 5  Results for Selected Techniques

We illustrate the proposed ground truth estimation by providing resulting evaluation data for a few stereo and optical flow techniques, as available on [5], or re-implementing published methods.

### 5.1  Stereo

For stereo, we run a standard stereo dynamic programming (DP) approach (e.g., see [3]), also modified by using some spatial propagation of disparities (from previous row to the current row, with a weight of 20%) or some temporal propagation of disparities (from the same row in the previous pair of frames, again with a weight of 20%).

Furthermore, we run Birchfield-Tomasi (BT, designed to be an improvement of standard stereo DP), and also implemented a semi-global matching technique using mutual information (SGM-MI) as a cost function (with three pyramid levels and 16 paths). See the Middlebury website for related references. (The experiment on Sequence 7 is only performed on the first 220 frames, instead of the total number of 250, because the road surface is reduced to a very small area after the ego-vehicle makes a large turn to the left.)

Regarding the standard DP algorithm, sequence 1 returns smallest RMS errors and bad matching percentages. In contrast, Sequence 6 returns the largest error values out of the seven sequences.

In spatial propagation (DPs), the method takes 20% of the disparity value from the previous scanline into the final result. In other words, we apply

$$d'_{y,t} = (1 - \lambda_1)d_{y,t} + \lambda_1 d_{y-1,t} \quad \text{where} \quad \lambda_1 = 0.2$$

Temporal propagation (DPt) uses

$$d'_{y,t} = (1 - \lambda_2)d_{y,t} + \lambda_2 d_{y,t-1} \quad \text{where} \quad \lambda_2 = 0.2$$

and temporal and spatial propagation combined (DPts) uses

$$d'_{y,t} = (1 - \lambda_1 - \lambda_2)d_{y,t} + \lambda_1 d_{y-1,t} + \lambda_2 d_{y,t-1}$$

where $\lambda_1 = 0.1$ and $\lambda_2 = 0.1$.

Figure 7 shows a comparison between DP and DPt for all the frames of Sequence 1. Time propagation shows here (and for the other sequences) an obvious improvement by keeping the RMS error about at the local minimum of the standard DP. Of course, driving on a plane means that disparity values should remain

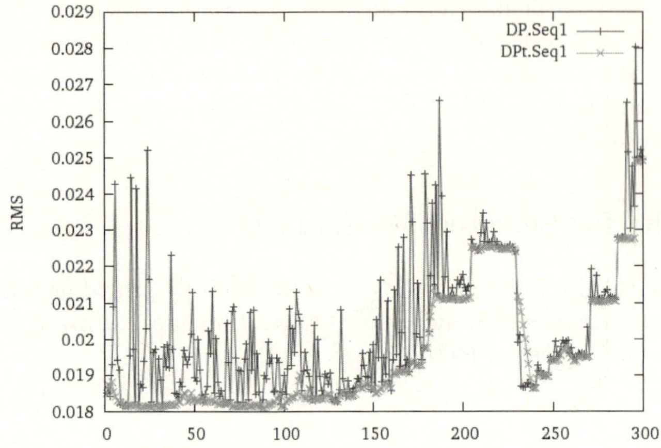

**Fig. 7.** Comparing RMS error results between DP and DPt

constant, and any deviation from this may be used to detect a change, such as a 'bumpy' road.

A comparison with respect to the second quality metric (percentage of bad matches) is shown in Figure 8. Similar to RMS errors, DPt shows best results. (Note that this evaluation is only restricted to the road surface area.)

Now we discuss the Birchfield-Tomasi algorithm (BT). Surprisingly (?), compared with DP techniques, the disparity maps and the quality metrics indicate bad results for BT; disparity values are typically incorrect on the road surface.

This bad performance may be due to the following two reasons. First, the BT algorithm is developed on the concept of the existence of depth discontinuities. However, depth discontinuities may not exist in many real world situations, such as on the road. Second, the BT algorithm uses a disparity propagation method to fill in untextured areas, both in horizontal and vertical directions. However, within the road surface area, the true disparities only change very smoothly in vertical direction.

We also run the BT algorithm (as implemented) on Middlebury stereo data. The same problem, as widely visible in the road scenes, occurs in the untextured area in the upper right corner.

The third stereo algorithm, to be discussed here for the provided approximated ground truth, is SGM-MI algorithm (16 directions for cost aggregation, three pyramid levels to calculate mutual information iteratively). Again, this experiment does not follow performance evaluations results as published on the Middlebury stereo page, this time for SGM: Calculated disparity maps are quite sparse in untextured road surface areas, but more dense in other areas, like vehicles, buildings or trees. Possibly we simply did not use a sufficient number of iterations for mutual information calculations. Because SGM shows more reasonable results on objects or textured areas, it might be recommended to have DPt in lower regions of the image sequence, and an SGM technique (probably not MI) in upper parts of the images.

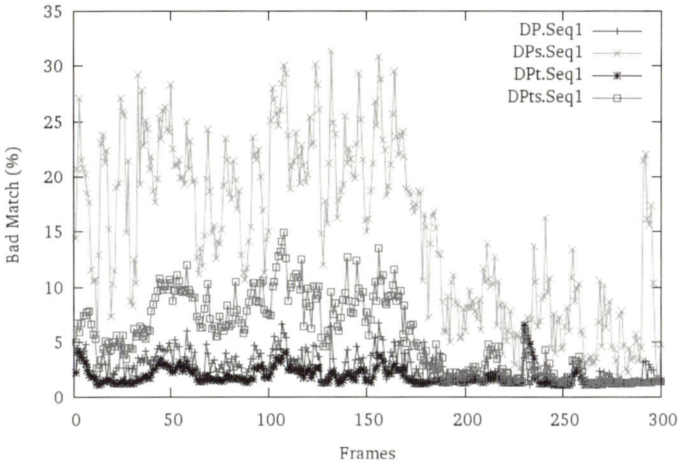

**Fig. 8.** Percentages of bad matches for DP and its variants

## 5.2   Optical Flow

This section reports about experimental results for three 'classical' optical flow algorithms (Horn-Schunck, Lucas-Kanade, and Pyramid Lucas Kanade) on those seven real-world sequences, using the evaluation metrics as given in Section 2.2.

At first we discuss the original Horn-Schunck (HS) and the Lucas-Kanade (LK) algorithm. Results obtained for HS and LK are meaningless and unsuitable for comparison, certainly because of the given 'structureless' images (Sobel preprocessing improves the results, similar to [2], where this was noticed for stereo belief propagation on those seven sequences). There might be two reasons for this problem. First, these seven real-world sequences are captured by night-vision cameras which produce somehow blurry and low contrast images, with large non-textured areas on road surfaces. Second, these two classic algorithms may only handle small displacements properly (say, magnitudes of 3-5 pixels), but most pixels in the road mask have actually much larger local displacements than that.

| Sequence name | Number of frames | Angular error (degrees) | End point error (pixels) |
|---|---|---|---|
| 1: 2007-03-06_121807 | 300 | 73 | 20.7 |
| 2: 2007-03-07_144703 | 300 | 97 | 8.9 |
| 3: 2007-03-15_182043 | 300 | 64 | 9.5 |
| 4: 2007-04-20_083101 | 250 | 45 | 14.4 |
| 5: 2007-04-27_145842 | 250 | 66 | 13.4 |
| 6: 2007-04-27_155554 | 250 | 32 | 20.9 |
| 7: 2007-05-08_132636 | 220 | 32 | 6.5 |

**Fig. 9.** Mean angular errors and end point errors for the PyrLK optical flow algorithm

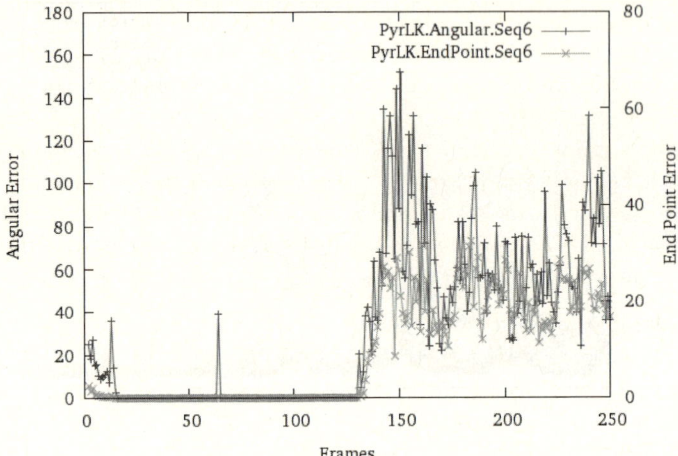

**Fig. 10.** Angular errors and endpoint errors for PyrLK on Sequence 6

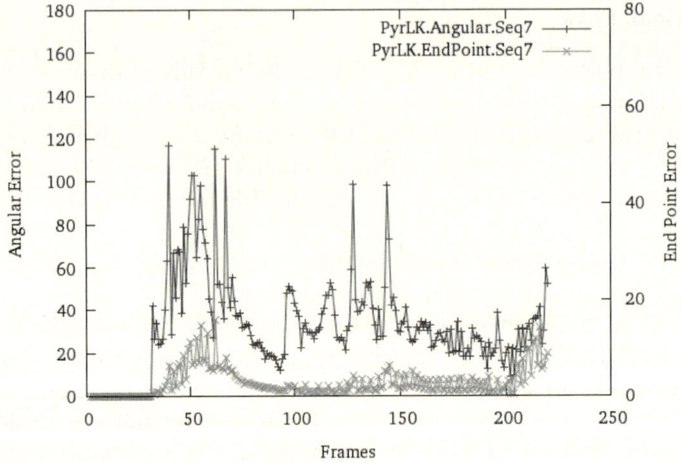

**Fig. 11.** Angular errors and endpoint errors for PyrLK on Sequence 7

The third algorithm is the pyramid Lucas-Kanade (PyrLK) algorithm. This algorithm runs at first a Canny edge detector on the input images, and uses then edge points as feature points. Finally. it uses five pyramid levels and a $3 \times 3$ window to compute optical flow vectors for those feature points (only). Figure 9 shows the evaluation results of the PyrLK algorithm on each sequence. Average angular errors range from about 30 to 100. This is because many of the computed optical flow vectors are actually normal flow, which is perpendicular to the local edge.

Figure 10 shows the quality metrics for PyrLK results on Sequence 6. In the first 135 frames, the ego vehicle stops, and both errors are close to zero. After that, the vehicle starts doing 'snake-like' movements, and causes that the quality of optical flow result drops significantly. Figure 11 shows the quality metrics for Sequence 7. In the first 30 frames, the ego-vehicle is parked besides the road, then, in the next 70 frames, the ego-vehicle turns to the right. During this period, the quality also drops, because the road surface is bumpy. After that the vehicle starts moving straight on a flat road surface, and the errors reduce smoothly.

By comparing quality metrics with vehicle data (see image headers), we notice that the occurrence of a local maximum in errors is most likely to match with a change in the `CycleTime`, normally equals 0.04, but occasionally 0.08.

## 6   Conclusions

The difficulty for the evaluation of stereo and motion techniques on real-world sequences is the lack of ground truth. This problem is partially solved in this paper by approximating the 3D geometry of the road.

Algorithms (and parameters for those) have mainly be selected for illustrating the proposed evaluation methodology. Further approximate ground truth (such as estimated poses of simple objects, such as rectangular faces in the scene) might be accumulated, to go, step by step, towards a 3D modeling of the actually recorded real scene. Of course, some objects or features are not of interest with respect to applications such as driver assistance or traffic monitoring.

The order of the algorithms' performance is clearly inconsistent to that reported on the Middlebury stereo or optical flow website. This difference shows the necessity for establishing performance evaluation methods also (!) on various real-world sequences.

## References


1. .enpeda.. Image Sequence Analysis Test Site. Link EISATS on
   `http://www.citr.auckland.ac.nz/6D/`
2. Guan, S., Klette, R., Woo, Y.K.: Belief-propagation for stereo analysis of image sequences. In: Wada, T., Huang, F., Lin, S. (eds.) PSIVT 2009. LNCS, vol. 5414, pp. 932–943. Springer, Heidelberg (2009)
3. Klette, R., Schlüns, K., Koschan, A.: Computer Vision. Springer, Singapore (1998)
4. Liu, Z., Klette, R.: Performance evaluation of stereo and motion analysis on rectified image sequences. Technical report, Computer Science Department, The University of Auckland (2007)
5. Intel Open Source Computer Vision Library,
   `http://www.intel.com/research/mrl/research/opencv/`

# Cooperative Surveillance System with Fixed Camera Object Localization and Mobile Robot Target Tracking


Chih-Chun Chia, Wei-Kai Chan, and Shao-Yi Chien

Media IC and System Lab
Graduate Institute of Electronics Engineering and Department of Electrical
Engineering, National Taiwan University, Taipei 106, Taiwan
b93901158@ntu.edu.tw, r3943041@ee.ntu.edu.tw, sychien@cc.ee.ntu.edu.tw



**Abstract.** This paper presents a cooperative surveillance system. It presents a cooperation scheme between fixed cameras and a mobile robot. The fixed cameras detect the objects with background subtraction and locate the objects on a map with homography transform. At the same time, the information of the target to track, including the position and the appearance, is transmitted to the mobile robot. After Breadth First Search in a map of boolean array, the mobile robot finds the target in its view by use of a stochastic scheme with the information given, then the mobile robot will track the target and keep it in the robot's view wherever he or she goes. By proposing this system, the dead spot problem in typical surveillance systems with only fixed cameras is considered and resolved.


## 1   Introduction

Recent approaches in surveillance systems typically include the use of static cameras along with the content analysis algorithm [1] [2]. The drawback is that dead spot can not be covered and intruders can try to avoid the fixed camera's sight, which results in less robustness for the surveillance system. Systems employing PTZ cameras or omni-directional camera system can increase the covering range [3] [4] [5]. However, there may still be dead spots and the covering area still depends on the cameras' positions decided in the deployment phase. Besides, several object tracking algorithms that are capable of tracking targets with a mobile camera are developed in recent years [6] [7]. The critical issue in the use of these algorithms is the initialization of the track, which is usually manually selected without automatic initialization scheme.

We now propose and construct a cooperative prototype system which consists of fixed cameras and a mobile robot as shown in Fig. 1. In this system, we propose a cooperation scheme between fixed cameras and a mobile robot. The fixed cameras can do object detection [8] [9] and feature extraction automatically. Then, the object localization in the environment is achieved with homographic relations [10], which is constructed in the camera calibration phase, between the


T. Wada, F. Huang, and S. Lin (Eds.): PSIVT 2009, LNCS 5414, pp. 886–897, 2009.

fixed cameras and a global map. After these fixed camera operations, the information of the object's location in the map and its appearance is provided to the mobile robot, in which a target finding algorithm and a target tracking algorithm are implemented. The target finding is done robustly with a stochastic scheme presented in this paper. After finding the target, we use a particle filter based method to track the target and the robot will follow the target throughout the entire environment and keep it in the center of the robot's view. Note that, by proposing this system, the restriction of dead spots in typical surveillance systems is resolved with a mobile robot and the intruders will be tracked wherever he or she goes.

The remaining sections are organized as follows. Section 2 describes the process of intruder detection and localization. Section 3 presents the algorithm on target finding and tracking with mobile robot. Section 4 presents the implementation of our prototype system and gives the experimental results. Finally, Section 5 concludes this paper.

## 2  Target Detection and Localization

In this section, we introduce the *Target Detection and Localization* subsystem in Fig. 1 (b). In this subsystem, two localization mechanisms, Zigbee Localization and Vision Localization, are presented and integrated.

### 2.1  Zigbee Localization

Zigbee is a specification for a suite of high level communication protocols using small, low-power digital radios based on the IEEE 802.15.4 standard for wireless personal area networks (WPANs). It is generally targeted at radio-frequency applications that require a low data rate, long battery life, and secure networking.

Being widely deployed in wireless monitoring applications with high-reliability and larger range, Zigbee transmitters spread around the environment. We assume that all in-comers who are authorized to come in should be wearing a Zigbee receiver so that their locations can always be monitored. The control center can receive information about the number of authorized visitors and their rough locations [11].

### 2.2  Vision Localization

Our vision Localization is based on homography transform [10]. After background subtraction, which is a technique widely employed in surveillance applications [2] [8] [9], and appropriate denoising, the segmentation result can be used to detect and localize the objects in the view of each fixed camera. Here, we use the bottom-centroid of segmented object blob as the object's location in the view of each fixed camera. In order to localize the object in a global coordinate system with map, a homography transform [10] is employed to build the correspondences between fixed camera views and a global map. Homography

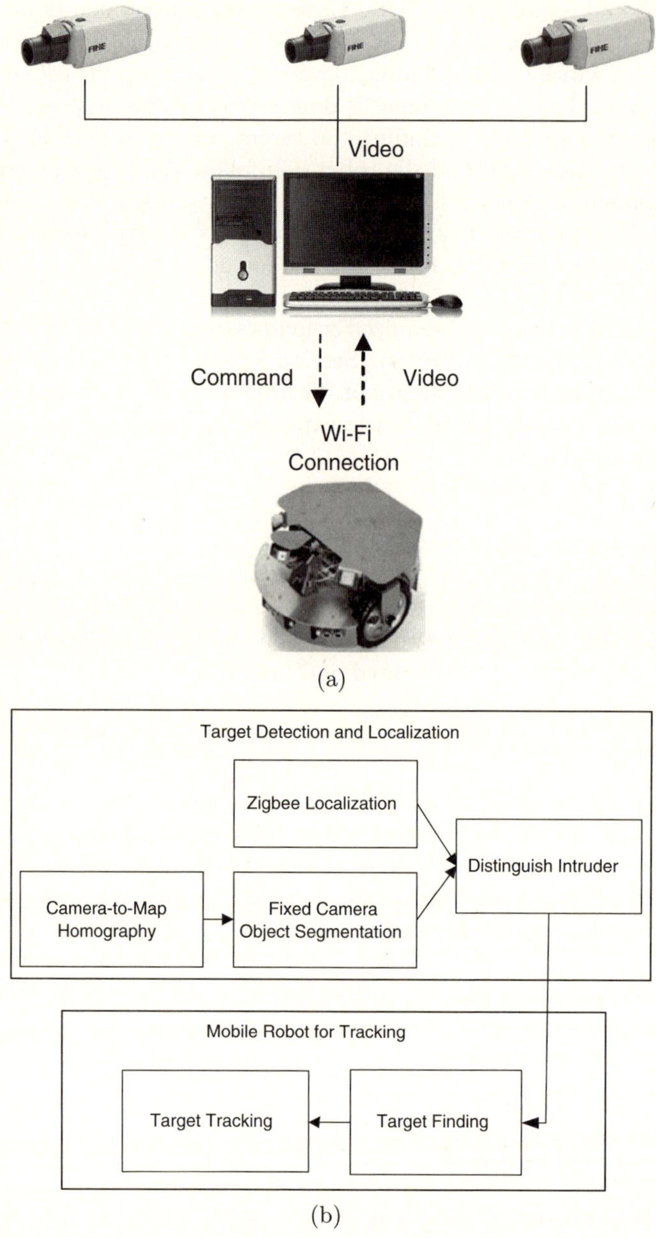



**Fig. 1.** (a) The proposed cooperative system; (b) the proposed cooperation scheme

is defined as a mapping between a point on a ground plane as seen from one camera, to the same point on the ground plane as seen from the second camera. Here, we extent it to build the point correspondence between fixed camera views and a global map. As shown in Fig. 2(a), two views $O_l$ and $O_r$ are viewing the

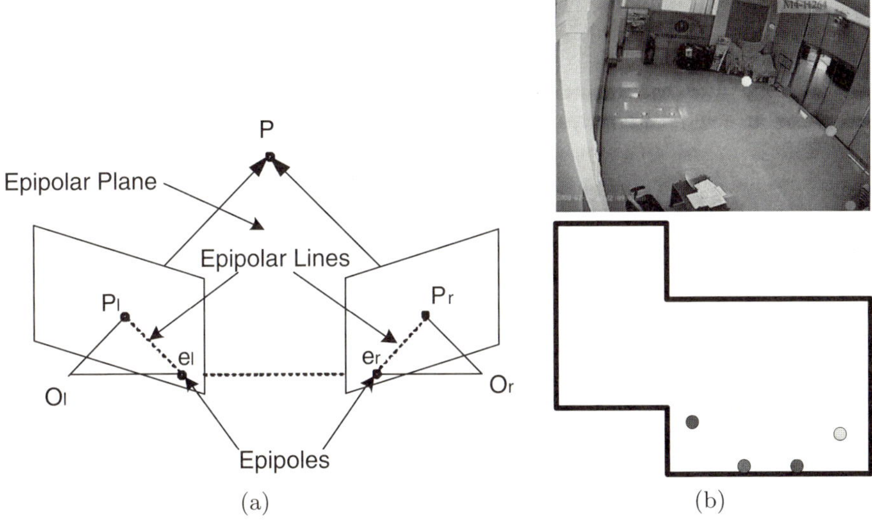

**Fig. 2.** (a) Two views viewing the same point; (b) shot of the test environment taken by one of the fixed cameras and a simple global map. The colored points are the four corresponding pairs of points chosen.

same point $P$. The coordinate of $P$ in the left view's ground plane is denoted as $P_l$, while $P_r$ represents that of the right view. Through the mathematical definition of homography, which is given by

$$P_l = \begin{pmatrix} X_l \\ Y_l \\ 1 \end{pmatrix}, P_r = \begin{pmatrix} X_r \\ Y_r \\ 1 \end{pmatrix}, H_{lr} = \begin{pmatrix} H_{11} & H_{12} & H_{13} \\ H_{21} & H_{22} & H_{23} \\ H_{31} & H_{32} & H_{33} \end{pmatrix} \tag{1}$$

Then, we will have :

$$\omega * P_r = H_{lr} P_l \tag{2}$$

In the above equation, $\omega$ is a scaling factor [10]. According to [10], if we have four pairs of corresponding points with coordinates denoted by $(X_{lc}, Y_{lc})$ and $(X_{rc}, Y_{rc})$ (where $1 \leq c \leq 4$, l and r stands for the two views), we can obtain a system of eight equations with eight unknowns while letting $H_{33}$ constant as 1. The matrix $H_{lr}$ can be solved by:

$$\begin{pmatrix} X_{l1} & Y_{l1} & 1 & 0 & 0 & 0 & -X_{l1}*X_{r1} & -Y_{l1}*X_{r1} \\ X_{l2} & Y_{l2} & 1 & 0 & 0 & 0 & -X_{l2}*X_{r2} & -Y_{l2}*X_{r2} \\ X_{l3} & Y_{l3} & 1 & 0 & 0 & 0 & -X_{l3}*X_{r3} & -Y_{l3}*X_{r3} \\ X_{l4} & Y_{l4} & 1 & 0 & 0 & 0 & -X_{l4}*X_{r4} & -Y_{l4}*X_{r4} \\ 0 & 0 & 0 & X_{l1} & Y_{l1} & 1 & -X_{l1}*Y_{r1} & -Y_{l1}*Y_{r1} \\ 0 & 0 & 0 & X_{l2} & Y_{l2} & 1 & -X_{l2}*Y_{r2} & -Y_{l2}*Y_{r2} \\ 0 & 0 & 0 & X_{l3} & Y_{l3} & 1 & -X_{l3}*Y_{r3} & -Y_{l3}*Y_{r3} \\ 0 & 0 & 0 & X_{l4} & Y_{l4} & 1 & -X_{l4}*Y_{r4} & -Y_{l4}*Y_{r4} \end{pmatrix} \begin{pmatrix} H_{11} \\ H_{12} \\ H_{13} \\ H_{21} \\ H_{22} \\ H_{23} \\ H_{31} \\ H_{32} \end{pmatrix} = \begin{pmatrix} X_{r1} \\ X_{r2} \\ X_{r3} \\ X_{r4} \\ Y_{r1} \\ Y_{r2} \\ Y_{r3} \\ Y_{r4} \end{pmatrix} \tag{3}$$

Note that we use the global map as one view in the homography transform and a fixed camera's view as the other view. One example of four-points correspondence to solve matrix $H_{lr}$ is shown in Fig. 2(b) After solving the matrix in the camera calibration phase, the object localized in each fixed camera's view can be given a global coordinate on the map. The vision localization gives information about all objects, including authorized and unauthorized, when they are detected with background subtraction.

## 2.3   Integration for Identification

Identification (Intruder detection) can be easily done by comparing the results from Zigbee Localization in Subsection 2.1 and those from Vision Localization in Subsection 2.2. From the Zigbee Localization, the system may receive information about the number of authorized visitors and their rough locations. At the same time, fixed cameras can find the objects(people), including authorized and unauthorized, and locate them in terms of global coordinates. Intruders who have no authority to come in can be detected by comparing the object information from the fixed cameras with those from the Zigbee.

# 3   Mobile Robot for Tracking

From section 2, the coordinate of the intruder can be inferred. A template of the intruder can also be obtained from segmentation. Information about object's location and appearance will then be transmitted immediately to the mobile robot to start tracking. In this section, we will introduce our *Mobile Robot for Tracking* subsystem in Fig. 1 (b).

## 3.1   Target Model and Similarity Measure

Since the camera on the robot may be different from the fixed cameras, specific camera calibration techniques, including those for cameras with different lighting conditions and orientations, can be useful for the processing and analysis [12]. In this paper, the template of the intruder will be analyzed into a color histogram. The object, or model image, is represented by an ellipse. The sample points of the model image are denoted by $x_i$ and $h(x_i)$, where $x_i$ is the 2D coordinates and $h(x_i)$ is the corresponding color index of the histogram. The number of color indexes used denoted as $\beta$. As long as we have segmented out the suspected intruder's image, we can construct the p.d.f of the object's color distribution as follows [7]:

$$p(u_j) = \sum_{i=1}^{I} k(\|\frac{x_i - c}{\sigma}\|)\delta[h(x_i) - u_j], 0 \le j \le \beta \tag{4}$$

where I is the number of pixels in the region, $u_j$ is the color index. $\sigma$ is the bandwidth in the spatial space and c is the center of this space. $\delta$ is the well-known Kronecker delta function(1 if $h(x_i) = u_j$, 0 otherwise). To increase the reliability of the color distribution, smaller weights are assigned to pixels farther away from the center (denoted as c), which are more likely to belong to the background. The weighting function we use is the well-known Epanechnikov kernel : $k(u) = \frac{3}{4}(1 - u^2)$, $|u| \leq 1$.

Here we adopt the commonly used similarity measure called Bhattacharyya coefficient. We can estimate the p.d.f. of the model image and that of the candidate image(denoted by $p_x$ and $p_y$, respectively), then measure the dissimilarity between these two distributions as below [7]:

$$B(I_x, I_y) = \sqrt{1 - \rho(p_x p_y)} \tag{5}$$

where function $\rho$ is defined as

$$\rho(p_x, p_y) = \int \sqrt{p_x(u)p_y(u)}du \tag{6}$$

## 3.2  Target Finding with Mobile Robot

The mobile robot will receive information about the intruder, including its coordinate and appearance (color distribution). We assume that the robot stays at a fixed location when no event occurs. With the target coordinate given, the mobile robot may go to an initial location that is convenient to find the target. The initial location and the initial direction of the robot's view can be decided according to different environments in advance with respect to any target location. The mobile robot can go to any location, including the initial location, by Breadth First Search with a 2D boolean array, in which the array element stores 1 or 0 indicating whether reachable or not [13].

After arriving at the initial location and turning to the initial direction with the help of a compass module on the robot, the robot have to find the target within its view. In order to do so, we employ a stochastic scheme here. First, we randomly choose different regions to make hypotheses about the target's location and size. Regions are again represented by an ellipse, with randomly chosen center. However, the ratio of the two axis is fixed into 3.5:1 (which approximately stands for a person's ratio in height and width).

The number of regions chosen is denoted by $N_r$. Every region is analyzed into color histogram, and we estimate the Bhattacharyya distance (denoted as $B_i$, $1 \leq i \leq N_r$) between those hypothetical regions and the model image.

With the Bhattacharyya distance for every hypothetical regions, we can further calculate the mean $\mu_r$ and standard deviation $\sigma_r$ of $B_i$ ($1 \leq i \leq N_r$). Thus we can select the regions with their Bhattacharyya distance less than $\mu_r - 2\sigma_r$. That is to say, if we assume that the distances between hypothetical regions and the model image is approximately Gaussian distributed, this would indicate 95% confidence level that the selected region is almost our target. Finally, we estimate the target's location and size by averaging the chosen regions' location and size.

## 3.3  Target Tracking with Mobile Robot

We use particle filter with color-based features to do target tracking with mobile robot. Particle filter, also known as Sequence Monte Carlo method or Sampling-Importance-Resampling (SIR) filter, is a state estimation technique based on simulation [14] [15]. Here, the state of target is described by the center of the ellipse and a scale factor representing the length of axis, since the ratio of the two axes is fixed.

The idea of particle filter is to evaluate the probability of all the particles and thus estimate the location of our target. We use a particle sample set $S = \{s^{(n)} | n = 1 \ldots N\}$, each sample s is a hypothetical state of the target.

After successfully locating the target according to Section 3.2, we can construct a sample set with all the samples equivalent to the target just found and then start evolution. Evolution of the particles is described by propagating each particle according to a Gaussian noise added to its center.

Many previous approaches may have propagated the particles according to a system model including moving direction and speed in order to model a person who may move in the same way and constant speed most of the time. However, we do not consider moving direction and speed here, since in our case, the tracker robot is also moving.

After the particles have finished propagation, weighting of the sample set can be computed by estimating the Bhattacharyya coefficient. Obviously, we would give larger weight to samples whose color distributions are more similar to the model. The weighting of each sample is given as follows:

$$\pi'^{(n)} = \frac{1}{\sqrt{2\pi}\sigma} e^{-\frac{1-\rho(p_{(n)}, q)}{2\sigma^2}} \tag{7}$$

Normalizing $\pi'^{(n)}$ with the following equation, we obtain $\pi^{(n)}$.

$$\pi^{(n)} = \pi'^{(n)} / \sum \pi'^{(n)} \tag{8}$$

We can then estimate the location of our target as:

$$E[S] = \sum_{n=1}^{N} \pi^{(n)} s^{(n)} \tag{9}$$

We determine the scale of the target by testing scales between 0.9 and 1.1 of the original size, since a person obviously have speed limit. Between 0.9 and 1.1, $\beta$ scales are chosen and their weighting are evaluated from Bhattacharyya distance. A weighted average of these scales is calculated to obtain the final size of the target.

In the last step, i.e. resampling, samples with higher weights will be reproduced more times than the samples with lower weights [14]. When the next frame comes, the whole process can be repeated again to continue tracking.

Note that using mobile robot is a big difference in our tracking job from others. After locating the target in each frame, the robot will judge if the target

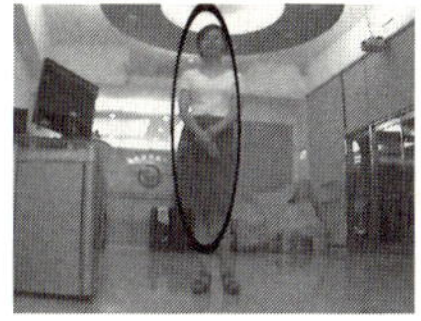

**Fig. 3.** Some key shots from a tracking test sequence

is in the left-side or the right-side of its view in order to decide which way it should turn. At the same time, it makes decision on going forward or backward according to the change in target's scale.

Here, we also present a way to make the mobile robot move more smoothly by using threshold. Since video frames may be taken at times when the robot is turning or when the person is moving irregularly, so make moving judgment every frame rather diminished its tracking ability. Action-threshold is set so that only if there are consecutive $\alpha$ frames making the same judgment will the robot actually move or turn.

Fig. 3 shows some key shots from a tracking result. The tracked target is bounded by a thick black ellipse. We see that no matter the target moved right or left, the robot turns with it to keep the target in the center of its view.

## 4   System Implementation and Experiment

### 4.1   System Implementation

All of the processing tasks are implemented on a Core 2 Quad 2.4GHz PC (1066MHz FSB) with C♯ in Visual Studio 2005. The mobile robot we used is Dr.Robot X80, which offers full WiFi (802.11g) wireless multimedia transmission. Due to the low data rate transmission limit in the robot, we abandoned the use of camera built inside Dr.Robot X80. Instead, Vivotek Network Camera IP 7137, a wireless camera with video streaming function, provides the video for analysis. The IP 7137 Network Camera is placed on the robot and the captured video is transmitted to the PC to analysis. After the video is analyzed, the command to control robot movement is transmitted from the PC to robot. The robot and camera is shown in Fig. 4. The overall system can track the target with the robot at 3-5 fps while the code is not optimized.

Our test environment is the technology exhibition center at Ming-Da building $1^{st}$ floor of Electrical Engineering Department of National Taiwan University with three fixed camera. The individual views of these three cameras are shown in Fig. 5. The videos captured with these fixed cameras are also transmitted to the PC for analysis with our algorithms.

### 4.2   Experimental Result

In this section, we present some results of this cooperative surveillance system. In the first place, we setup two different scenarios for testing this system. The

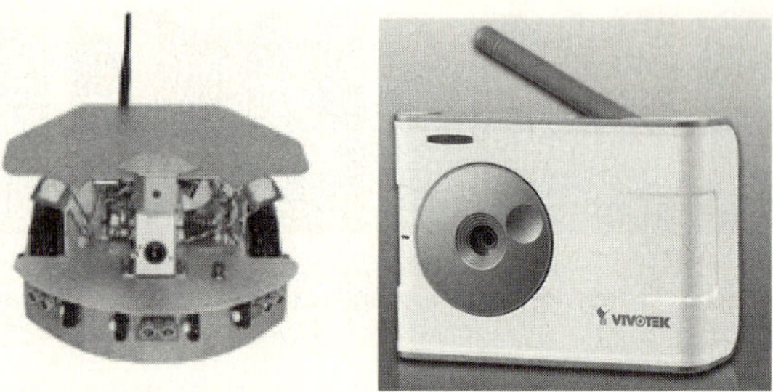

**Fig. 4.** (a) Dr.Robot X80; (b) Vivotek WLAN Network Camera IP7137

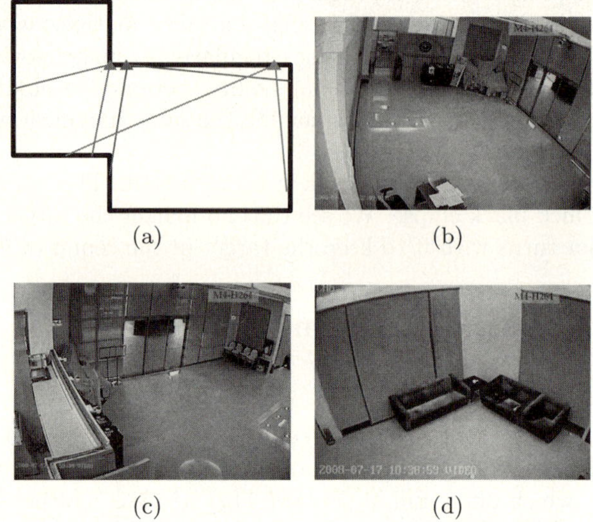

(a)          (b)

(c)          (d)

**Fig. 5.** The environment of Ming-Da Building: (a) A simple map of the environment with the three fixed cameras and their view range marked; (b) the image of camera colored in red; (c) the image of camera colored in blue; (d) the image of camera colored in green

first one(Fig. 6) is that an intruder comes in and goes to dead spots that fixed cameras can not cover. The second scenario(Fig. 7) is that an intruder is going out of the building, which the fixed camera obviously cannot cover. In these two scenarios, our system have shown great robustness in successfully locating and tracking the intruder.

Each figure contains one map with four sequential images. The map shows the intruder and the robot's route, where the small black man represents the intruder and a mark (viewpoint) represents the robot and its viewing direction. The four sequential images are taken from the moving camera (i.e. the robot's view), and in each image, the target being tracked is shown with an ellipse surrounding it. In the map, the position of the green mark(robot) and the green-framed small man(target) shows where the first image is taken, while blue for the second

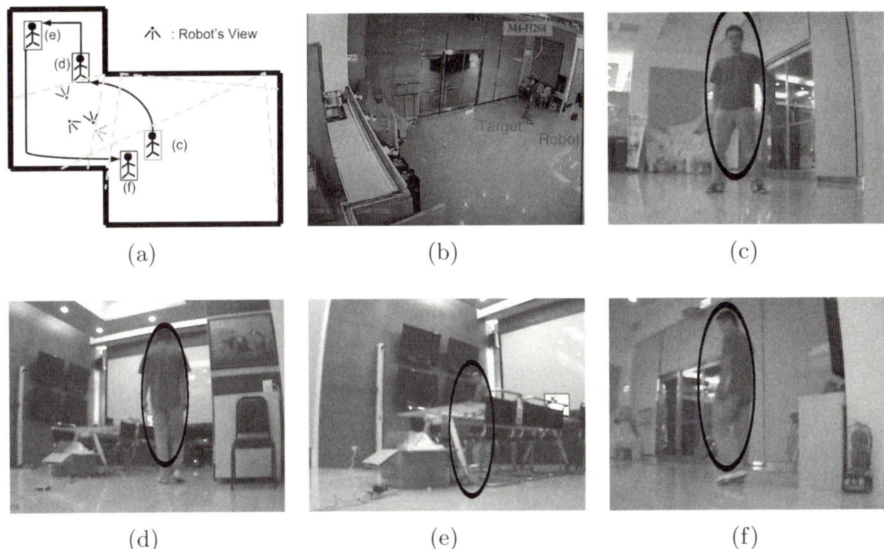

Fig. 6. Scenario one - Dead Spot Experiment, in image (d) and (e), the intruder goes into a dead spot where the fixed cameras cannot see

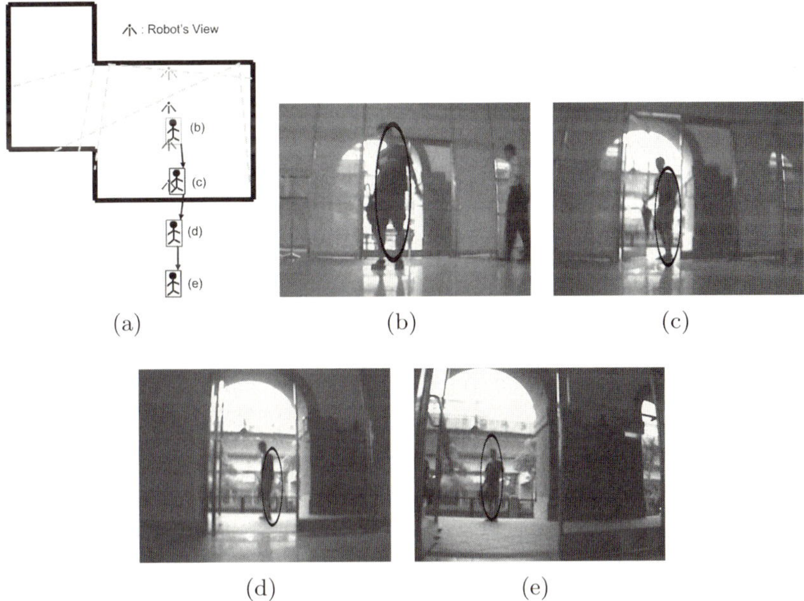

Fig. 7. Scenario two - Out of Building Experiment, in image (d) and (e), the intruder escaped out of the door where the fixed camera cannot continue tracking

image, red for the third image, and purple for the last image. In scenario 1, we also show the moment that the robot found the target by including Fig. 6(b) taken with the fixed camera.

## 5   Conclusions

This paper presents a cooperative surveillance system with fixed camera target localization and mobile robot target tracking. Vision localization is based on fixed camera's segmentation combined with the concept of homography. After locating the intruder, the robot will receive the commands, then start target finding and tracking by a stochastic scheme and a particle filter based tracking algorithm. In this system, the dead spot problem in typical surveillance systems with only fixed cameras is overcome with mobile robot target finding and tracking.

## References


1. Regazzoni, C., Ramesh, V., Foresti, G.L.: Special issue on video communications, processing, and understanding for third generation surveillance systems. Proc. IEEE 89(10), 1355–1367 (2001)
2. Stauffer, C., Grimson, W.E.L.: Adaptive background mixture models for real-time tracking. In: IEEE Computer Society Conference on Computer Vision and Pattern Recognition, pp. 246–252 (July 1999)
3. Micheloni, C., Foresti, G.L., Snidaro, L.: A Network of Cooperative Cameras for Visual-Surveillance. IEE Proc. on Visual, Image and Signal Processing, 152(2), 205–212 (2005)
4. Foresti, G.L., Micheloni, C., Snidaro, L., Remagnino, P., Ellis, T.: Active Video-based Surveillance Systems: the low-level image and video processing techniques needed for implementation. IEEE Signal Processing Magazine 22(2), 25–37 (2005)
5. Iwata, K., Satoh, Y., Yoda, I., Sakaue, K.: Hybrid Camera Surveillance System by Using Stereo Omni-directional System and Robust Human Detection. In: Chang, L.-W., Lie, W.-N. (eds.) PSIVT 2006. LNCS, vol. 4319, pp. 611–620. Springer, Heidelberg (2006)
6. Maggio, E., Smerladi, F., Cavallaro, A.: Adaptive Multifeature Tracking in a Particle Filtering Framework. IEEE Trans. Circuits Syst. Video Technol. 17(10), 1348–1359 (2007)
7. Comaniciu, D., Ramesh, V., Meer, P.: Kernel-based object tracking. IEEE Trans. Pattern Anal. Machine Intell. 25(5), 564–577 (2003)
8. Chien, S.-Y., Ma, S.-Y., Chen, L.-G.: Efficient Moving Object Segmentation Algorithm Using Background Registration Technique. IEEE Trans. Circuits Syst. Video Technol. 12(7) (July 2002)
9. Chan, W.-K., Chien, S.-Y.: Real-time memory-efficient video object segmentation in dynamic background with multi-background registration technique. In: Proc. IEEE Multimedia Signal Processing Workshop (October 2007)
10. Bradshaw, K.J., Reid, I.D., Murray, D.W.: The active recovery of 3D motion trajectories and their use in prediction. IEEE Transactions on Pattern Analysis and Machine Intelligence 19(3), 219–234 (1997)

11. Lorincz, K., Welsh, M.: MoteTrack: A Robust, Decentralized Approach to RF-Based Location Tracking. In: Strang, T., Linnhoff-Popien, C. (eds.) LoCA 2005. LNCS, vol. 3479, pp. 63–82. Springer, Heidelberg (2005)
12. Haralick, R.M., Shapiro, L.G.: Computer and Robot Vision. Addison Wesley, Reading (1992)
13. Cormen, T.H., Leiserson, C.E., Rivest, R.L., Stein, C.: Introduction to Algorithms, 2nd edn. McGraw Hill/The MIT Press (2001)
14. Ristic, B., Arulampalam, S., Gordon, N.: Beyond the Kalman Filter: Particle Filters for Tracking Applications. Artech House (Copyright 2004)
15. Nummiaro, K., Koller-Meier, E., Gool, L.V.: An Adaptive Color-Based Particle Filter. Image and Vision Computing 21(1, 10), 99–110 (2003)
16. Chang, C., Ansari, R.: Kernel Particle Filter for Visual Tracking. IEEE Signal Processing Letters 12(3) (March 2005)

# On the Security of an MPEG-Video Encryption Scheme Based on Secret Huffman Tables


Shujun Li[1,*], Guanrong Chen[2], Albert Cheung[3], Kwok-Tung Lo[4],
and Mohan Kankanhalli[5]

[1] Fachbereich Informatik und Informationswissenschaft, Universität Konstanz,
Fach M697, Universitätsstraße 10, 78457 Konstanz, Germany
[2] Department of Electronic Engineering, City University of Hong Kong, Kowloon,
Hong Kong, China
[3] Department of Building and Construction and Shenzhen Applied R&D Centres,
City University of Hong Kong, Kowloon, Hong Kong SAR, China
[4] Department of Electronic and Information Engineering, The Hong Kong
Polytechnic University, Hung Hom, Kowloon, Hong Kong SAR, China
[5] School of Computing, National University of Singapore, 117590 Singapore
`Shujun.Li@uni-konstanz.de`, `{EEGCHEN,clacc}@cityu.edu.hk`,
`enktlo@polyu.edu.hk`, `mohan@comp.nus.edu.sg`



**Abstract.** This paper re-studies the security of an MPEG-video encryption scheme based on secret Huffman tables. The present cryptanalysis shows that: 1) the key space of the encryption scheme is not sufficiently large against divide-and-conquer (DAC) ciphertext-only attack; 2) its security against the chosen-plaintext attack is very weak. The insecurity is mainly due to the separated use of different Huffman tables for different sets of syntax elements. A brief discussion on how to improve this MPEG-video encryption scheme is also given.


## 1  Introduction

The extensive use of digital images and videos in today's digital world makes the security and privacy issues become more important. To fulfill such an increasing demand, various encryption algorithms have been proposed in recent years as possible solutions to content protection of digital images and videos [1, 2, 3, 4, 5, 6, 7, 8, 9, 10], among which MPEG videos attract special attention due to its prominent prevalence in consumer electronic markets [11, 12, 13]. As an important way of designing MPEG-video encryption schemes, secret Huffman tables have been suggested in some designs [2, 7, 14, 15, 16, 17, 18].

The MPEG-video encryption scheme proposed in [14] (i.e., Algorithm 1 in [2]) is a light-weight scheme, which encrypts the plain-video by shuffling VLC (variable-length coding) entries of same size in each Huffman table. However, because the bit length of each VLC codeword does not change, the position of each VLC codeword in the video stream does not change either. Thus, an attacker can uniquely locate (and thus determine) all VLC codewords contained

---


[*] The corresponding author, personal web site: http://www.hooklee.com



T. Wada, F. Huang, and S. Lin (Eds.): PSIVT 2009, LNCS 5414, pp. 898–909, 2009.
© Springer-Verlag Berlin Heidelberg 2009

in the cipher-video stream, if the plain-video stream or an independent part (such as a picture or a slice) is known. Once all distinct VLC codewords are obtained, the whole secret Huffman table is uniquely reconstructed and the encryption scheme is broken. That is, this light-weight scheme is not secure against known/chosen-plaintext attacks. In addition, as pointed out in [2], the key space of this encryption scheme is very limited (especially for Huffman tables with a small number of VLC entries), so even a brute-force attack may be feasible.

The MPEG-video encryption scheme proposed in [15] can be considered as an enhanced version of that in [14]. In this scheme, five different Huffman tables are shuffled separatedly and the shuffling operations are generalized to work on VLC entries with different sizes, in the hope that the key space can be enlarged and the security against plaintext attacks can be improved. Furthermore, as a second guard on the security, random bit flipping operations are also introduced to further encrypt each secret Huffman table.

In [7, 16, 17, 18], multiple Huffman tables (MHT) are introduced, from which one table is secretly chosen for the encryption of each VLC codeword. A so-called "Huffman tree mutation process" is also proposed in [7, 16, 17] to derive more candidate Huffman tables from several original tables. Some cryptanalysis results about known-plaintext attacks have been reported recently [19, 20].

This paper mainly focuses on some security problems with the MPEG-video encryption scheme proposed in [15]. Our cryptanalysis shows that this scheme is not sufficiently secure against DAC (divide-and-conquer) ciphertext-only attack and very weak against chosen-plaintext attack.

The rest of this paper is organized as follows. In the next section, a brief introduction to the MPEG-video encryption scheme under study is given. Then, the cryptanalysis results are presented in detail in Sec. 3. Finally, Section 4 gives a brief discussion on how to improve the security of the MPEG-video encryption scheme, and the last section concludes this paper.

## 2  MPEG-Video Encryption Scheme Under Study

In MPEG-1/2 standards, Huffman coding is used to realize lossless compression of quantized DCT coefficients. Each Huffman tree is represented as a 1-D Huffman table, which transforms an input value into a VLC codeword. There are in total 15 Huffman tables used in MPEG-2 standard [12] (less in MPEG-1 standard [11]), among which 10 ones (Tables B-1 to B-9) are used for coding syntax elements in various headers and the following six ones are for visual information – DCT coefficients in each block and motion vectors in each macroblock:

- Table B-10: for encoding motion vectors;
- Table B-11 (not used in MPEG-1 standard): for encoding the differential motion vectors of the dual prime prediction;

– Table B-12: for encoding the bit size of the differential values of DC coefficients in intra luminance blocks;
– Table B-13: for encoding the bit size of the differential values of DC coefficients in intra chrominance blocks;
– Table B-14: for encoding all DCT coefficients of non-intra blocks and AC coefficients of intra blocks with $intra_vlc_format = 0$, where $intra_vlc_format$ is a picture-specific flag defined in MPEG-2 standard (which does not exist for MPEG-1 videos and the value shall be taken as 0);
– Table B-15 (not used in MPEG-1 standard): for encoding all AC coefficients of intra blocks with $intra_vlc_format = 1$.

The encryption scheme proposed in [15] is designed by concealing the original Huffman tables, i.e., using different (secret) Huffman tables to replace the original ones. Five Huffman tables used for coding visual information, B-10, B-12, B-13, B-14 and B-15, are chosen to be kept secret. Table B-11 is not selected, since it is only a very small Huffman table with three entries. The five secret Huffman tables are derived from the original ones by performing the following two encryption operations.

– *Shuffling VLC codewords:* grouping all VLC codewords into several subsets according to their bit sizes, and then randomly shuffling these VLC codewords within each sub-set.
– *Random bit flipping:* randomly flipping the last bit of each VLC codeword, and adjusting (if needed) other VLC codewords to keep the prefix rule valid.

After encrypting all the five Huffman tables, the bit sizes of some (at least one) VLC codewords should be slightly changed to resist known-plaintext attacks (as discussed in Sec. 1 of this paper), but the change should not be too much to avoid a large influence on compression efficiency.

In [15], the key space was estimated by enumerating all "good" encryption methods[1] of shuffling and random bit flipping operations carried out on some selected significant (not all) VLC codewords, as shown in Table 2. As a result of the large key space, the scheme was considered sufficiently secure.

In [15], an additional measure is suggested to further enhance the security against plaintext attacks – reshuffling the Huffman tables after a certain number

**Table 1.** Number of good encryption methods of each Huffman table (Table 3.6 of [15])

| Huffman table | Number of good encryption methods |
|:---:|:---:|
| B-10 | $3!$ |
| B-12 | $7! \times 2^6$ |
| B-13 | $6! \times 2^8$ |
| B-14 | $6!$ |
| B-15 | $16!$ |
| Total | $(3!) \times \left(7! \times 2^6\right) \times \left(6! \times 2^8\right) \times (6!) \times (16!) \approx 2^{92}$ |

---

[1] An encryption method is "good" if it can produce unintelligible images.

of frames. In the following, we will mainly consider the basic scheme without the reshuffling mechanism. The effect of the reshuffling mechanism will be discussed later in Sec. 4.

# 3   Cryptanalysis

In this section, the security of the aforementioned MPEG-video encryption scheme based on secret Huffman tables is reconsidered, and it is found that the scheme is not so secure as evaluated in [15]. In this section, the terms and notations in MPEG-2 standard [12] will be used, except those only existing in MPEG-1 videos. The following terms are used throughout this section to facilitate the description: 1) the term "picture" is used instead of "frame", since the encryption scheme is independent of the syntactic differences between a picture and a frame; 2) macroblock is abbreviated as "MB"; 3) the term "MB header" is used to denote the set of all syntax elements occurring before the first encoded block in an MB (if none of the blocks is coded, the MB header is the MB itself).

## 3.1   Ciphertext-Only Attack

The ciphertext-only attack is the most common attack in practice, since in general the communication channels are open to the public, which means that an attacker can observe as many ciphertexts as possible and then use them to break an encryption scheme [21]. There are two different goals in a ciphertext-only attack: recovering the plaintexts and recovering the secret key. This paper mainly focuses on the recovery of the secret key, i.e., the secret Huffman tables in the MPEG-video encryption scheme under study.

The simplest ciphertext-only attack is to exhaustively search all possible keys to find the unique correct one (or an equivalent key), which is called brute-force attack [21]. Here, a criterion is needed to verify each searched key. For the MPEG-video encryption scheme under study, the occurrence of syntax errors can serve as such a criterion for detecting wrong keys. When a wrong Huffman table is used to decode a cipher-picture, syntax errors may occur in the decoding procedure due to (but not limited to) the following reasons.

- As mentioned in Sec. 1, to ensure the security against plaintext attacks, there should be at least two distinct bit sizes for each input value in a Huffman table. However, once the bit size of a VLC codeword is wrong, all the following syntax elements in the current slice cannot be correctly located and decoded.
- For each Huffman table, not all FLC codewords of a specific bit size are valid VLC codewords.
- All stuffing bits at the end of a slice should be zero bits.
- There may exist some marker bits (must be "1" to avoid "start code emulation", i.e., the occurrence of fake start codes) in the bit stream:
    - (for MPEG-2 videos only) when $concealment_motion_vectors = 1$ in an intra-block, there exists a marker bit in the MB header;

- (for MPEG-1 videos only) in D-picture, the last bit of each MB must be a marker bit named *end_of_macroblock*.
  - There exist some constraints on the decoded syntax elements:
    - each decoded DCT coefficient should not be out of the range $[-2048, +2047]$;
    - each decoded motion vector should not be out of the range defined in Table 7-8 of the MPEG-2 standard [12], and must be within the reference picture after adding the coordinates of the predicted MB.
  - There must be an EOB VLC codeword at the end of each block, before which the total number of decoded DCT coefficients must not be greater than 64.
  - The number of MBs within each picture should not be greater than a maximal value.
  - Some slice headers may be skipped when the video is decoded with wrong Huffman tables, which is forbidden for most videos (for example, an MPEG-1/2 video stream with a restricted slice structure).

By detecting syntax errors occurring in the decoding procedure, one can distinguish most wrong Huffman tables. In addition, there exist a lot of information redundancies in decoded video. Therefore, even when no syntax error is detected, one can still distinguish a wrong Huffman table if there exist too many abrupt changes around the borders of adjacent blocks. Finally, note that if no syntax error is found for a wrong key, then this wrong key tends to be an equivalent key to decrypt the cipher-video (or some part of the cipher-video), which happens when some VLC codewords are not involved in the encoding process of the plain-video or part of it.

Because the five Huffman tables are used for different sets of syntax elements of the whole video bit-stream, it is possible to separatedly guess them one by one. This means that one can use the so-called divide-and-conquer (DAC) attack [21] to break the MPEG-video encryption scheme. In other words, the key space of the encryption scheme will be the **sum**, not the **product**, of the sub-key-spaces of the five tables. Next, let us see how to separatedly break the five Huffman tables by detecting syntax errors in the video decoding procedure.

**Reconstructing Table B-10.** Following the MPEG-2 standard, Tables B-12/13/14/15 are all independent of the decoding of the first MB header in a slice[2], which makes the separated reconstruction of Table B-10 possible. When a wrong Table B-10 is used, the following syntax errors may occur when the first MB header of a slice is decoded.

  - Some decoded motion vectors may be invalid, especially for those MBs near the picture edge.
  - When *concealment_motion_vectors* $= 1$ in an intra-block, the marker bit in the MB will be wrong (i.e., equal to 0) with a probability of 0.5 (under the assumption that each bit in the video stream is distributed uniformly) and then a fake start code might also occur.

---

[2] All other MBs cannot be located without knowing Tables B-12/13/14/15.

– When $macroblock_pattern = 1$, "0000 0000 0" never occurs in $coded_block_$
$pattern$ encoded by Table B-9.

Since in each slice only the first MB header can be used to detect syntax errors
about Table B-10, the average number of involved syntax elements may be too
small, especially for pictures with a small number of slices and/or slow motion.
Under such a condition, one has to exhaustively search for Table B-10 and Table
B-14 together such that all motion vectors can be used.

**Reconstructing Table B-14.** Since all DCT coefficients in a non-intra MB
are encoded with Table B-14, syntax errors may occur when a wrong Table B-14
is used to decoded a non-intra MB. Considering most MBs in a P/B-picture are
non-intra MBs, the occurrence probability of such errors will be relatively high.

To test how frequently syntax errors of this kind occur in real attacks, we
observed the decoding process by exchanging the following two VLC codewords
in Table B-14 – "00101" and "000110", which represent RLE codewords (0,3)
and (1,2), respectively[3]. For a large number of test MPEG-1/2 videos, syntax
errors all occurred in the first P-picture (i.e., the 2nd picture of the whole video).
Figure 1 shows the results for an MPEG-1 video "Carphone" (of size $176 \times 144$)
and an MPEG-2 video "Tennis" (of size $704 \times 576$), where the pink areas (light
grey areas on the printed version of the paper) in the decoded pictures denote
decoding failures caused by syntax errors (the same hereinafter). Note that all
the pictures are displayed as raw data (i.e., the differential pictures) since the
reference I-pictures are still unknown at this stage of attack. If the whole Huffman
table is heavily shuffled, syntax errors will definitely occur more frequently.

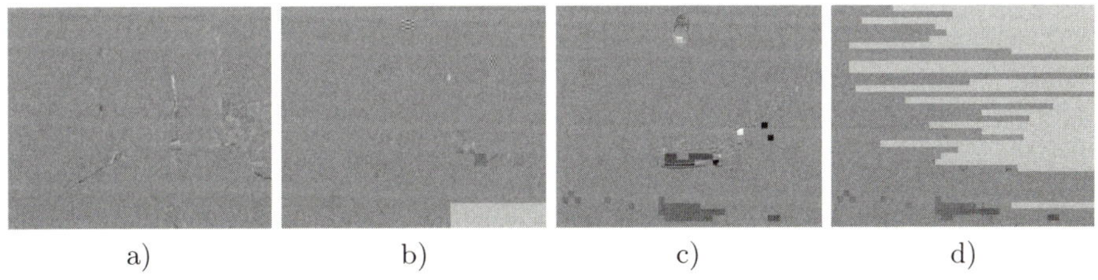

a)                  b)                  c)                  d)

**Fig. 1.** The decoded results of an MPEG-1 video "Carphone" and an MPEG-2 video
"Tennis", when only two VLC codewords were exchanged in Table B-14: a) the 2nd
picture of "Carphone"; b) the decoded 2nd picture of "Carphone"; c) the 2nd picture
of "Tennis"; d) the decoded 2nd picture of "Tennis"

**Reconstructing Table B-12.** Once Table B-14 is reconstructed, Table B-12
can be further exhaustively searched for in intra MBs with $intra_vlc_format = 0$.
If all intra MBs in all known plain-videos are encoded with $intra_vlc_format = 1$,
Table B-12 has to be exhaustively searched for together with Table B-15 (see

---

[3] These two VLC codewords were taken from the "good" VLC codewords selected by
the authors of [15] to shuffle the corresponding Huffman table. The same rule also
applies to other experiments in this paper.

904     S. Li et al.

below), which is generally a rare event when an attacker can collect a number
of cipher-pictures to carry out the ciphertext-only attack.

In the case that only two VLC codewords, "00" and "01", in Table B-12 were
swapped, we tested the decoding results for some MPEG-1/2 videos. Two results
are shown in Fig. 2. Note that the swapped VLC codewords have the same bit
size, so a stronger shuffling shall cause much more syntax errors.

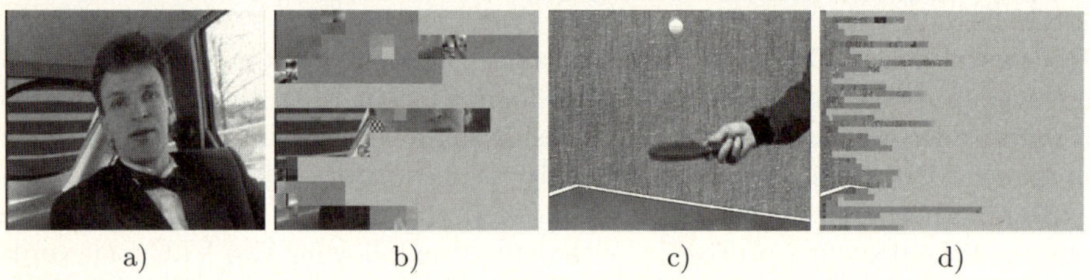

a)      b)      c)      d)

**Fig. 2.** The decoded results of the MPEG-1 video "Carphone" and the MPEG-2 video
"Tennis", when only two VLC codewords were exchanged in Table B-12: a) the 1st
picture of "Carphone"; b) the decoded 1st picture of "Carphone"; c) the 1st picture of
"Tennis"; d) the decoded 1st picture of "Tennis"

**Reconstructing Table B-15.** If Table B-12 has been successfully guessed,
Table B-15 can be exhaustively searched for in luminance blocks of intra MBs
with $intra_vlc_format = 1$, just like the case of reconstructing Table B-14. If
Table B-12 cannot be separatedly broken, Tables B-12 and B-15 have to be
exhaustively searched for together.

By swapping two VLC codewords "00101" and "000110", which represent
RLE codewords (2,1) and (4,1), respectively, in Table B-15, we tested the de-
coding results of some MPEG-2 videos (note that this table is not used in the
MPEG-1 standard). Figure 3 gives one result for the MPEG-2 video "Tennis".

**Reconstructing Table B-13.** After Tables B-12, 14 and 15 are broken, Table
B-13 can be exhaustively searched for in chrominance blocks of intra MBs. If
there are intra MBs with $intra_vlc_format = 0$, Table B-13 can be exhaustively
broken immediately after Table B-14 is broken, without knowing Table B-15.

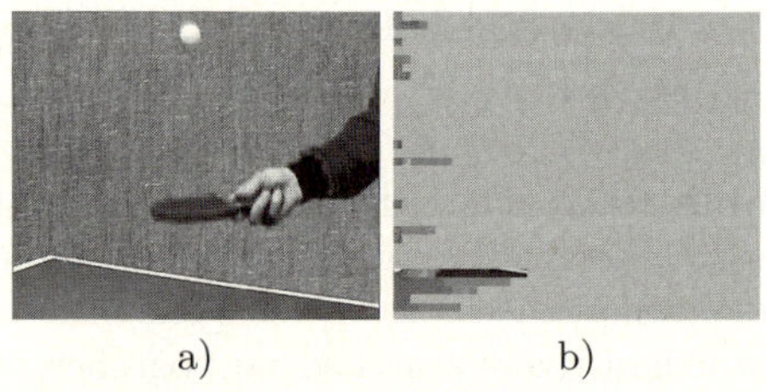

a)          b)

**Fig. 3.** The decoded result of the MPEG-2 video "Tennis", when only two VLC codewords were exchanged in Table B-15: a) the 1st picture of the original video; b) the
decoded 1st picture

By exchanging two VLC codewords, "01" and "10", in Table B-13, we tested the decoding results of some MPEG-1/2 videos. The results corresponding to the MPEG-1 video "Carphone" and the MPEG-2 video "Tennis" are shown in Fig. 4. Once again, many syntax errors can be observed.

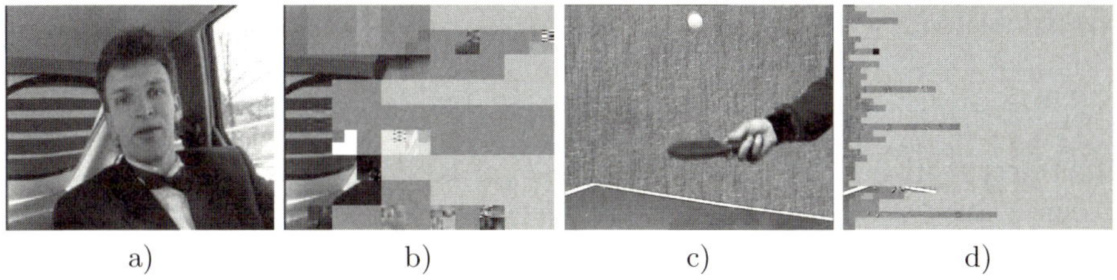

a)          b)          c)          d)

**Fig. 4.** The decoded results of the MPEG-1 video "Carphone" and the MPEG-2 video "Tennis", when only two VLC codewords were exchanged in Table B-13: a) the 1st picture of "Carphone"; b) the decoded 1st picture of "Carphone"; c) the 1st picture of "Tennis"; d) the decoded 1st picture of "Tennis"

Finally, based on the above analysis, we can estimate the complexity of the DAC attack under four different conditions as follows:

- *when Table B-10 is separatedly searched for*:
  - *when Table B-12 is separatedly searched for*: $(3!) + (7! \times 2^6) + (6! \times 2^8) + (6!) + (16!) \approx 2^{44.3}$;
  - *when Table B-12 is searched for together with Table B-15*: $(3!) + (7! \times 2^6) \times (16!) + (6! \times 2^8) + (6!) \approx 2^{62.5}$;
- *when Table B-10 is not separatedly searched for*:
  - *when Table B-12 is separatedly searched for*: $(3!) \times (6!) + (7! \times 2^6) + (6! \times 2^8) + (16!) \approx 2^{44.3}$;
  - *when Table B-12 is searched for together with Table B-15*: $(3!) \times (6!) + (7! \times 2^6) \times (16!) + (6! \times 2^8) \approx 2^{62.5}$.

One can see that in all cases the complexity is much smaller than the one estimated in [15]: $(3!) \times (7! \times 2^6) \times (6! \times 2^8) \times (6!) \times (16!) \approx 2^{92}$.

As long as a VLC codeword appears frequently, syntax errors caused by encrypting it will occur with a high probability, which means that this VLC codeword will be reconstructed easily (i.e., wrong guesses of the VLC codeword can always be recognized). On the other hand, if a VLC codeword does not appear very frequently such that syntax errors do not occur for a given MPEG-video, the performance of encrypting this VLC codeword will not be "good" enough, so it should not be included in the key. In other words, a "good" key for encryption performance actually means a "bad" key that can be easily guessed with the DAC brute-force attack. Therefore, the efficiency of the DAC attack is ensured in a natural way. In addition, as shown in our experiments, only a single cipher-picture (or even several slices in a single cipher-picture) would be enough to carry out the above DAC attack effectively.

## 3.2   Chosen-Plaintext Attack

The chosen-plaintext attack is a very strong attack, in which one can (intentionally) choose some plaintexts and observe the corresponding ciphertexts to break an encryption scheme [21]. With the help of some chosen plaintexts and ciphertexts, it is possible to directly determine the secret Huffman tables without exhaustively guessing them in all possible candidates. In the following, we show how to choose a few number of plain-MBs to carry out a successful chosen-plaintext attack.

**Reconstructing Table B-10.** Choose a P-picture, in which there are a number of consecutive slices that contains only one "Not Coded" non-intra MB. In this case, there will be only one slice header and one MB header in each slice. Then, one can easily locate the only MB header in each slice, and extract a bit segment composed of two motion vectors from the MB header. In the extracted bit segment, the values of *motion_residuals*, *dmvectors*, and the sign bits of the motion vectors can be chosen to uniquely distinguish each *motion_code*, i.e., each VLC codeword encoded with the secret Table B-10. If necessary, $f_code[r][s]$ can also be intentionally chosen to help the extraction of the VLC encoded *motion_codes*. By choosing the values of $n$ consecutive *motion_codes* to be the $n$ values corresponding to unknown VLC codewords, the whole secret Table B-10 can be reconstructed. Since $n = 3$ for the secret Table B-10 under study and each MB in a P-picture has two motion vectors, only 2 MBs (in 2 slices) are needed for this purpose. If a B-picture is chosen, then 1 MB is enough since there can be four motion vectors.

**Reconstructing Table B-14.** After reconstructing Table B-10, one can continue to break Table B-14 by choosing a block in a non-intra MB with the following pattern: "$(run_1, level_1)$, $(run_e, level_e)$, $\cdots$, $(run_i, level_i)$, $(run_e, level_e)$, $\cdots$, EOB" where $(run_i, level_i)$ is the $i$-th entry in the secret Table B-14 and $(run_e, level_e)$ is an Escape RLE codeword. By choosing $(run_e, level_e)$ properly, one can easily recognize each VLC codeword corresponding to the RLE codeword $(run_i, level_i)$. If a single block cannot contain all the encrypted VLC codewords, one more block can be chosen. For the encryption scheme under study, all the 6 encrypted VLC codewords in Table B-14 can be put in the same block, so only one chosen-block in a single non-intra MB is enough. Note that this table can also be broken in a similar way by choosing one intra blocks, after Tables B-12 and B-13 are firstly recovered as described in next paragraph.

**Reconstructing Tables B-12/13.** Since AC coefficients of intra-blocks are encoded in a similar way to the motion vectors, the method of reconstructing Table B-10 can also be used to break Tables B-12 and B-13. To break the entry corresponding to $dct_dc_size = s$, choose an intra-block as follows: "*level*, EOB", where the DC coefficient *level* has $s$ significant bits. Then, the video bitstream corresponding to this block will be "*dct_dc_size*, *dc_dct_differential*, EOB". Since EOB and *dc_dct_differential* are both known, it is easy to determine the VLC encoded *dct_dc_size*. Given 7 luminance blocks with different values of $s$, all the

7 encrypted VLC codewords in Table B-12 can be reconstructed. Similarly, given 6 chrominance blocks, Table B-13 can be completely reconstructed. According to the value of *chroma_format*, the maximal numbers of required chosen intra MBs for reconstructing Tables B-12 and 13 are 2 and 3, respectively. Since an MB can include both luminance and chrominance blocks, at most 3 intra MBs are needed to break the two secret Huffman tables.

**Reconstructing Table B-15.** After reconstructing Tables B-12 and B-13, one can break Table B-15 by choosing some intra-blocks, in the same way of reconstructing Table B-14. The 16 encrypted VLC codewords in Table B-15 and the RLE codewords used as locators can not be included in a single block, but two blocks in one intra MB are enough to reconstruct all the encrypted VLC codewords.

As a whole, to completely reconstruct all the secret Huffman table, at most 4 intra MBs in an I-picture and 3 non-intra MBs in a P-picture (or 2 non-intra MBs in a B-picture) are needed. While two chosen pictures are needed to break all the secret Huffman tables, note that not all the five Huffman tables are used for a single picture. For example, for an I-picture, Table B-10 is not used, and for a P- or B-picture, most blocks are non-intra coded without Tables B-12 and B-13. This implies that only one chosen picture is enough to recover all secret Huffman tables needed for decoding the same type of pictures (and part of other types of pictures). So the MPEG-video encryption scheme is very weak against chosen-plaintext attack.

## 4   More Discussions

In this section, a brief discussion is given on how to improve the security of the MPEG video encryption scheme under study. A simple measure is to change the secret Huffman tables frequently. In [15], it was suggested to reshuffle them after certain number of frames. Generally speaking, these reshuffling operations might be enough to provide an acceptable resistance against ciphertext-only attack. However, even reshuffling these Huffman tables frame by frame is generally not sufficient for the security against the above chosen-plaintext attack, since a few number of MBs may be enough to break the secret Huffman tables. From the most conservative point of view, one has to reshuffle the Huffman tables for each VLC codeword. Such a heavy reshuffling process will dramatically reduce the speed of the whole system and become impractical in many real applications.

Another possible solution is to use multiple Huffman tables (MHT) as suggested in [7, 16, 17, 18]. While some configurations of MHT encryption have been known insecure [19, 20], the following one remains secure: a stream cipher (or a secure PRNG) is adopted to determine the secret Huffman table from multiple candidate tables for each VLC codeword. However, as is well known in cryptology, a stream cipher is not secure against plaintext attacks if the key is reused to encrypt more than two plain messages. Thus, in real applications, to guarantee the security against plaintext attacks, some practical measures must be adopted to avoid reuse of the same key for different plaintexts, such as using a key-management system to assign a different key for different encryption session.

Though using a stream cipher with MHT might be able to ensure the security against plaintext attack in practice, its performance could be worse than simply using the same stream cipher to mask the video bitstream. Assume that the number of different Huffman tables is 256 and the output of the stream cipher is a sequence of 8-bit integers. In this case, because the average bit size of VLC codewords is less than 8, more than one iterations of the stream cipher are required for encryption of each plain-byte. As a comparison, if the stream cipher's output is directly used to mask the video bitstream, only one iteration of the stream cipher is needed for each plain-byte. It needs more further research to see if there exist some other possibilities to enhance the performance of MHT-based secure Huffman coding algorithms.

## 5    Conclusions

This paper has re-analyzed the security of an MPEG-video encryption scheme based on secret Huffman tables. It is found that the scheme is not sufficiently secure against divide-and-conquer ciphertext-only attack, and is very weak against the chosen-plaintext attack. A brief discussion has also been given on how to improve the security of the MPEG-video encryption scheme.

## Acknowledgments

Shujun Li was supported by a fellowship from the Zukunftskolleg, Universität Konstanz under the support of the "Exzellentinitiative" program of the German Research Foundation (Deutsche Forschungsgemeinschaft – DFG), and also by a research fellowship from the Alexander von Humboldt Foundation, Germany. K.-T. Lo was supported by the Research Grants Council of the Hong Kong SAR Government under Project no. 523206 (PolyU 5232/06E).

## References

1. Qiao, L., Nahrsted, K.: Comparison of MPEG encryption algorithms. Comput. Graph. 22(4), 437–448 (1998)
2. Bhargava, B., Shi, C., Wang, S.Y.: MPEG video encryption algorithms. Multimedia Tools Appl. 24(1), 57–79 (2004)
3. Furht, B., Kirovski, D. (eds.): Multimedia Security Handbook. CRC Press, LLC (2004)
4. Furht, B., Muharemagic, E., Socek, D. (eds.): Multimedia Encryption and Watermarking. Springer, Heidelberg (2005)
5. Uhl, A., Pommer, A.: Image and Video Encryption: From Digital Rights Management to Secured Personal Communication. Springer, Heidelberg (2005)
6. Zeng, W., Yu, H., Lin, C.Y. (eds.): Multimedia Security Technologies for Digital Rights Management. Academic Press, London (2006)

7. Wu, C.P., Kuo, C.C.J.: Design of integrated multimedia compression and encryption systems. IEEE Trans. Multimedia 7(5), 828–839 (2005)
8. Wen, J., Severa, M., Zeng, W., Luttrell, M.H., Jin, W.: A format-compliant configurable encryption framework for access control of video. IEEE Trans. Circuits and Systems for Video Technology 12(6), 545–557 (2002)
9. Zeng, W., Lei, S.: Efficient frequency domain selective scrambling of digital video. IEEE Trans. Multimedia 5(1), 118–129 (2003)
10. Mao, Y., Wu, M.: A joint signal processing and cryptographic approach to multimedia encryption. IEEE Trans. Image Processing 15(7), 2061–2075 (2006)
11. ISO/IEC: Information technology – coding of moving pictures and associated audio for digital storage media at up to about 1,5 Mbit/s – Part 2: Video. MPEG-1 standard: ISO/IEC 11172-2 (1993)
12. ISO/IEC, ITU-T: Information technology – generic coding of moving pictures and associated audio information: Video. MPEG-2 standard: ISO/IEC 13818-2 and ITU-T Rec. H.262 (2000)
13. ISO/IEC: Information technology – coding of audio-visual objects – Part 2: Visual. ISO/IEC 14496-2, MPEG-4 (2004)
14. Shi, C., Bhargava, B.: Light-weight MPEG video encryption algorithm. In: Shaping the Future: Proc. Int. Conference on Multimedia (Multimedia 1998), pp. 55–61 (1998)
15. Kankanhalli, M.S., Guan, T.T.: Compressed-domain scrambler/descrambler for digital video. IEEE Trans. Consumer Electronics 48(2), 356–365 (2002)
16. Wu, C.P., Kuo, C.C.J.: Fast encryption methods for audiovisual data confidentiality. In: Multimedia Systems and Applications III. Proc. SPIE, vol. 4209, pp. 284–295 (2001)
17. Wu, C.P., Kuo, C.C.J.: Efficient multimedia encryption via entropy codec design. In: Security and Watermarking of Multimedia Contents III. Proc. SPIE, vol. 4314, pp. 128–138 (2001)
18. Xie, D., Kuo, C.C.J.: An enhanced MHT encryption scheme for chosen plaintext attack. In: Internet Multimedia Management Systems IV. Proc. SPIE, vol. 5242, pp. 175–183 (2003)
19. Zhou, J., Liang, Z., Chen, Y., Au, O.C.: Security analysis of multimedia encryption schemes based on multiple Huffman table. IEEE Signal Processing Letters 14(3), 201–204 (2007)
20. Jakimoski, G., Subbalakshmi, K.P.: Cryptanalysis of some multimedia encryption schemes. IEEE Trans. Multimedia 10(3), 330–338 (2008)
21. Schneier, B.: Applied Cryptography – Protocols, Algorithms, and Souce Code in C, 2nd edn. John Wiley & Sons, Inc., New York (1996)

# H.264/AVC Video Encoder Realization and Acceleration on TI DM642 DSP*

Daw-Tung Lin and Chung-Yu Yang

Department of Computer Science and Information Engineering
National Taipei University
151, University Rd., San-Shia, Taipei, 237 Taiwan
dalton@mail.ntpu.edu.tw

**Abstract.** This work develops and optimizes H.264/AVC video encoder on the TM320DM642 DSP platform. In order to transplant x264 source program onto the DSP and to accelerate the coding speed, a series of optimization methods have been proposed in this paper, including 2-D fast mode decision, sub-pixel optimization for motion estimation, and weighted matrix quantization. Furthermore, based on the architectural features of TM320DM642, various system level optimization techniques have been utilized. This paper focuses on the reduction of algorithm complexity. Experimental results reveal that the optimized H.264 video encoder retains satisfactory quality with very low degradation. The implemented codec can achieve the coding speed of 22.6fps and more than 40fps for VGA (640×480) and CIF (352×288) resolution, respectively. The proposed H.264 codec can be employed in many real-time applications.

**Keywords:** H.264/AVC encoder, TM320DM642 DSP, mode decision, motion estimation, quantization, optimization.

## 1   Introduction

H.264/AVC video coding technology provides better bit rate saving and high flexibility of use in a broad variety of domains video compression standards. However, the computational complexity of H.264 is much higher. It is important to optimize and realize an H.264 encoder for real time applications. Special purpose H.264 IC and embedded system are common solutions. Besides, the embedded software approach possesses the advantage of flexibility in updating and adding new functions. The embedded system has more potential.

In the recent years, a large amount of works have been focused on the development and optimization of H.264 algorithms. However, rare literatures disclosed the impact of implementing H.264 on the embedded system. We believe that creating H.264 video encoding/decoding application with good performance will

---

* This work was supported in part by the National Science Council, Taiwan, R.O.C. grants NSC96-2622-E-305-001-CC3 and Ministry of Economics grant: Construction of Vision-Based Intelligent Environment (II).

T. Wada, F. Huang, and S. Lin (Eds.): PSIVT 2009, LNCS 5414, pp. 910–920, 2009.

amplify the value of H.264. Recently, the improvement and implementation of H.264 codec on embedded system is getting more and more important. K. Goto *et al.* ported H.264 algorithm on a low-power DSP which achieves 15fps for QVGA (320×240) resolution [1]. T.-C. Chen *et al.* proposed a low power integer motion estimation algorithm and implemented it on a VLSI architecture with good performance [2]. The encoding speed achieves 30fps for CIF (352×288) resolution. L. Zhuo and Z. Li also optimized the motion estimation algorithm and implemented on DM642 DSP platform with encoding speed of 24fps for CIF format video chips [3,4]. Z. Wei adopted advance assembly instruction and re-wrote kernel function and encoded the QCIF video in real-time speed [5]. Experiments of the limited storage resources on chip was also studied in detail to accelerate encoding speed. H.-J. Wang *et al.* and I. Werda *et al.* employed memory space allocation optimization to speed up the system which were realized on TMS320DM642 and TMS320C6416 DSP, respectively [6,7].

The remainder of this paper is organized as follows. Section 2 gives an overview of the H.264 video encoder and the TI DM642 DSP. Section 3 then presents the proposed algorithm optimization approaches and the implementation. Section 4 analyzes the experimental results, and compares them with those of other encoding schemes implemented on DM642 DSP. Conclusions are finally drawn in Section 5.

## 2   Overview of H.264 and DM642 DSP

H.264/AVC is an advanced video compression standard. It is also known as MPEG-4 Part 10. The main objective of the H.264/AVC is to create a standard capable of providing good video quality at substantially lower bit rates than the previous standards. H.264 has some features including low bit-rate, high quality, wide application, and robust video transmission (error resilient). In order to achieve the above features, H.264 employs many innovative techniques such as intra prediction, variable block size for inter coding, motion estimation with multiple reference frames, quarter pixel interpolation, 4×4 integer DCT, in-loop de-blocking filter, and advanced entropy coding (CAVLC and CABAC). By taking the advantages of these techniques, H.264 achieves a better performance than previous video coding standards like MPEG2 and MPEG4. Although these techniques improve the coding performance, they increase the complexity of the codec at the same time. Some literatures show that the complexity of H.264 is about 5 to 8 times that of H.263 [8]. Therefore, it is very difficult to implement the H.264 codec in real time on the embedded system. How to optimize and implement H.264 codec is a very important research issue.

Texas Instruments TMS320DM642 digital signal processor is a general purpose processor with video in/out peripheral [9]. The clock rate of DM642 is 720MHz. DM642 is one of the C6000 series with very long instruction word (VLIW) architecture which is able to issue a fixed number of instructions in parallel. In additional to the capability of high speed com-2 computation (720MHz,

5760MIPS) and SIMD, the DM642 process can execute eight 32 bits instructions in each clock cycle. In other words, it is able to fetch a 256 bits long instruction from program memory in each clock cycle. There are two register banks in DM642 CPU core, four ALU units on each side, totally eight ALU units can execute instructions simultaneously. There are 16k bytes L1 data cache, 16k bytes L1 code cache, 256k bytes programmable L2 SRAM. There is a DMA controller on chip for data movement. Its EMDA offers 2GB per second I/O bandwidth in 64 independent channels [9].

## 3   The Proposed Optimization Approach

The objective of this work is to implement and optimize H.264 video encoding system on TI DM642EVM board based on x264 open source library. The x264 is one of the major open source encoder developed in 2004 licensed under the GPL [10]. It performs the best in term of time complexity compared with most of the H.264-based algorithms. The coding speed of x264 is about 40-50 times faster than that of reference encoder JM (Joint Model) based on our simulations with video clips Foreman, Football, Akiyo and Water fall. As the major open-source H.264 encoder, x264 plays the role of a near-complete monopoly of H.264 encoder in the industry and has been used by many major corporations including Google Video, MobileASL, Speed Demos Archive, and TASvideos.

Before doing optimization, we analyze the complexity of each x264 function including the the kernel function clock cycle, execution time and code size. Figure 1 shows the run time percentage of each function. Apparently, motion estimation (ME) and macroblock size mode decision are the most time consuming functions. In order to transplant x264 source program onto the DSP and to accelerate the coding speed, a series of optimization methods have been proposed including 2-D fast mode decision, sub-pixel optimization for motion estimation, and weighted matrix quantization. For the other operations such as x264_clip, abs, sad, satd, etc., we rewrote these functions with assembly code and rearrange the instruction utilizing the features of hardware architecture.

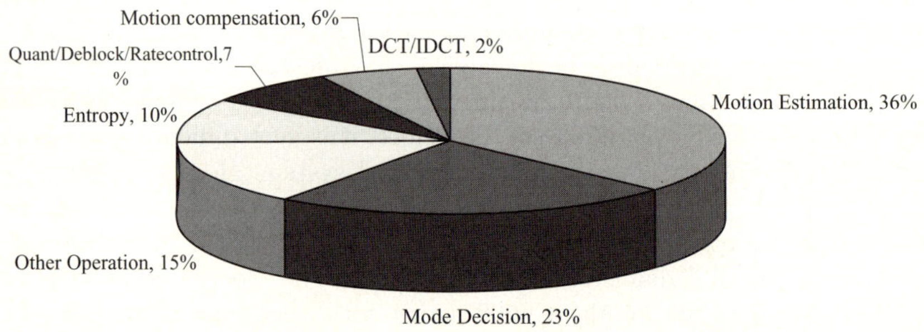


**Fig. 1.** Runtime percentage analysis of x264 kernel functions

### 3.1   Macroblock Coding 2-D Fast Mode Decision

According to the analysis of the H.264 block modes distribution of many video sequences, the skip mode and 16×16 mode hold more than 50% of the block modes. When the macroblock is resided in the background or in the smooth region, the 16×16 or skip mode will be chosen, and the same mode will be clustered together. Chang *et al.* proposed a fast mode decision for P-frames in H.264 using the average rate-distortion (RD) cost threshold for the decision of early skip [11]. We utilized this early skip method and further proposed a new mode decision algorithm which adapts to the hardware structure feature of DM642. The proposed 2-D fast mode decision is based on the mode status in time domain and spatial domain, taking advantage of those block information to reduce the complexity of mode decision. The detail analysis is referred to [11]. We define three statuses of block mode as shown in Fig. 2. Gray block in Fig. 2 represents the current frame block to be decided. $A_n, B_n$ and $C_n$ denote the neighborhood block mode of the current frame. $D_{n-1}$ and $E_{n-1}$ are the block modes of the lower and right blocks, respectively, in previous frame. We further set $T_1$ as an integer threshold used to decided skip mode. Moment $T_2$ is firstly defined as the average R-D cost of $A_n, B_n$ and $C_n$. When more than two block modes of $A_n, B_n$ and $C_n$ are the same, $Cost(Mode_n)$ will be defined as the R-D cost of the current block using this mode. Otherwise, the moment $T_2$ is set as the average R-D cost of $D_{n-1}$ and $E_{n-1}$. When the block modes of $D_{n-1}$ and $E_{n-1}$ are the same, $Cost(Mode_{n-1})$ is define as the R-D cost of the current block using this mode. Then, the mode decision is based on the parameters of $T_1, T_2, Cost(Mode_n)$ and $Cost(Mode_{n-1})$. The main procedure of the proposed method is described as follows.

**Step1:** Check the skip mode, if R-D cost is small than $T_1$, choose skip mode and go to Step6.

**Step2:** If the MB is in the first row or first column, test all mode and select the best one, go to Step6.

**Step3:** Set $T_2$ equals to the average R-D cost of $A_n, B_n$ and $C_n$. Check MB $A_n, B_n$ and $C_n$, if more than two MB types are the same and $Cost(Mode_n) < T_2$, then use this mode, go to Step6.

**Step4:** Set $T_2$ equals to the average R-D cost of $D_{n-1}$ and $E_{n-1}$. Check MB $D_{n-1}$ and $E_{n-1}$, if the MB types are the same and $Cost(Mode_{n-1}) < T_2$, then use this mode, go to Step6.

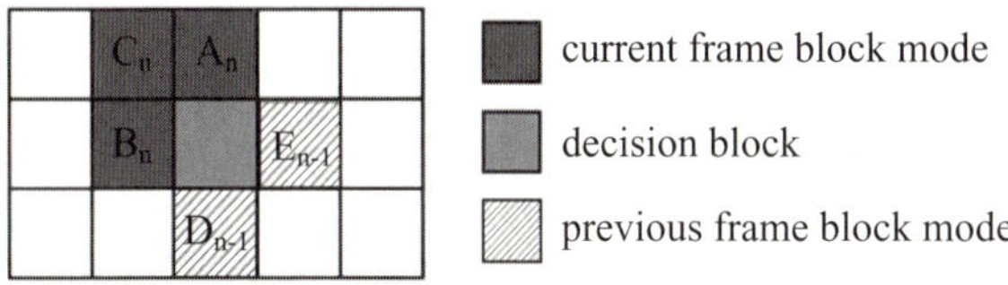


**Fig. 2.** Three types of block modes

**Step5:** Check the remaining modes.
**Step6:** Stop.

## 3.2  Sub-pixel Motion Estimation Optimization

One of the important motion estimation optimization issues is sub-pixel motion estimation. Sub-pixel motion estimation usually finds a better position than full-pixel motion estimation and therefore leads to a smaller SAD and bit rate. For sub-pixel motion estimation, half-pixel search is frequently used in H.263, MPEG-1, MPEG-2 and MPEG-4. Quarter-pixel search is adopted in MPEG-4 and H.264/AVC to achieve more accurate motion description and higher compression efficiency. In our system, sub-pixel ME needs sub-pixel interpolation for the whole search area before performing diamond search. However, it costs a lot of computation complexity. After finding the best position in full-pixel precision, it searches only eight neighboring half-pixel positions (denoted as square block in Fig. 3). When the motion vector moves from position "1" to position "3" (shown in Fig. 3), the integer search starts from point "1", then the half-pixel search will find point "2". Finally point "3" will be found by quarter-pixel search. Due to high complexity of the sub-pixel search algorithm, we use integer-pixel search to engage the first sub-pixel search, then use quarter-pixel search to finish the sub-pixel motion estimation. This search method improves the sub-pixel searching speed avoiding complicated computation and is useful for our DSP platform.

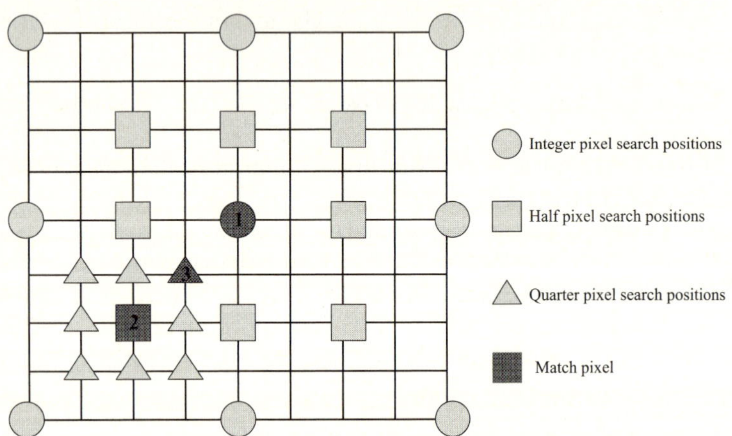


**Fig. 3.** Sub-pixel motion estimation

## 3.3  Quantization and DCT Optimization

The weighting quantization method of H.264 has been introduced from high profile. Different quantization steps will be applied for various coefficients and regions with a scalar quantizer. The quantization method of H.264 is combined with transformation and quantization, thus the design of weighting quantization differs from the prior quantization matrix. The weighting quantization $C_{ij}$ at position $(i,j)$ is introduced as:

$$C_{ij} = D_{ij} \times LevelScale(QP\%6, i, j) >> (15 + floor(\frac{QP}{6})), \qquad (1)$$

where $LevelScale(QP\%6, i, j) = (\frac{MF_{ij} \times 16}{Scale_{ij}})$ in which $MF_{ij}$ denotes the multiplication factor (see Table 1 [12]), $Scale_{ij}$ represents the value of the corresponding scaling table (illustrated in below), "%" denotes the modular operation and $>>$ indicates a binary shift right operation.

The de-quantization factor $D_{ij}$ is computed as:

$$D_{ij} = C_{ij} \times DeLevelScale(QP\%6, i, j) << (QP/6 - 4), \qquad (2)$$

where $DeLevelScale(QP\%6, i, j) = V_{ij} \times Scale_{ij}$ in which $V_{ij}$ is defined in Table 2 for $0 \leq QP \leq 5$, and $<<$ denotes the binary shift left operation. We can observe from the quantization function that after introducing quantization table, both forward and inverse quantization between $MF$ and $V_{ij}$ are scaled by a factor of $Scale_{ij}$. From our simulation results, after weighting quantization is applied, the video quality (PSNR) will be increased and the coding speed is also improved.

**Table 1.** Multiplication factor MF [12]

| QP | Positions<br>(0,0), (2,0), (2,2), (0,2) | Positions<br>(1,1), (1,3), (3,1), (3,3) | Other positions |
|----|------|------|------|
| 0 | 13107 | 5243 | 8066 |
| 1 | 11916 | 4660 | 7490 |
| 2 | 10082 | 4194 | 6554 |
| 3 | 9362 | 3647 | 5825 |
| 4 | 8192 | 3355 | 5243 |
| 5 | 7282 | 2893 | 4559 |

**Table 2.** Scaling factor V [12]

| QP | Positions<br>(0,0), (2,0), (2,2), (0,2) | Positions<br>(1,1), (1,3), (3,1), (3,3) | Other positions |
|----|------|------|------|
| 0 | 10 | 16 | 13 |
| 1 | 11 | 18 | 14 |
| 2 | 13 | 20 | 16 |
| 3 | 14 | 23 | 18 |
| 4 | 16 | 25 | 20 |
| 5 | 18 | 29 | 23 |

Eight scaling tables are defined in below: including intra luma 8×8, intra chroma U4×4, intra chroma V4×4, inter luma 4×4, inter chroma U4×4, inter chroma V4×4, intra luma 8×8 and inter luma 8×8. The coefficients of the above mentioned equations are suggested by JVT [13].

$$Intra4 \times 4_Luma = Intra4 \times 4_ChromaU$$

$$= Intra4 \times 4_ChromaV = \begin{bmatrix} 0 & 12 & 19 & 26 \\ 12 & 19 & 26 & 31 \\ 19 & 26 & 31 & 35 \\ 26 & 31 & 35 & 39 \end{bmatrix}, \tag{3}$$

$$Inter4 \times 4_Luma = Inter4 \times 4_ChromaU$$

$$= Inter4 \times 4_ChromaV = \begin{bmatrix} 0 & 13 & 18 & 21 \\ 13 & 18 & 21 & 24 \\ 18 & 21 & 24 & 27 \\ 21 & 24 & 27 & 30 \end{bmatrix}, \tag{4}$$

$$Intra8 \times 8_Luma = \begin{bmatrix} 0 & 10 & 13 & 16 & 19 & 24 & 26 & 28 \\ 10 & 12 & 16 & 19 & 24 & 26 & 28 & 31 \\ 13 & 16 & 19 & 24 & 26 & 28 & 31 & 33 \\ 16 & 19 & 24 & 26 & 28 & 31 & 33 & 35 \\ 19 & 24 & 26 & 28 & 31 & 33 & 35 & 37 \\ 24 & 26 & 28 & 31 & 33 & 35 & 37 & 39 \\ 26 & 28 & 31 & 33 & 35 & 37 & 39 & 42 \\ 28 & 31 & 33 & 35 & 37 & 39 & 42 & 44 \end{bmatrix}, \tag{5}$$

$$Inter8 \times 8_Luma = \begin{bmatrix} 0 & 12 & 14 & 16 & 18 & 19 & 21 & 22 \\ 12 & 13 & 16 & 18 & 19 & 21 & 22 & 24 \\ 14 & 16 & 18 & 19 & 21 & 22 & 24 & 25 \\ 16 & 18 & 19 & 21 & 22 & 24 & 25 & 27 \\ 18 & 19 & 21 & 22 & 24 & 25 & 27 & 28 \\ 19 & 21 & 22 & 24 & 25 & 27 & 28 & 30 \\ 21 & 22 & 24 & 25 & 27 & 28 & 30 & 31 \\ 22 & 24 & 25 & 27 & 28 & 30 & 31 & 33 \end{bmatrix}, \tag{6}$$

$$Y = C_f \times C_f^T \otimes E_f = \begin{bmatrix} 1 & 1 & 1 & 1 \\ 2 & 1 & -1 & -2 \\ 1 & -1 & -1 & 1 \\ 1 & -2 & 2 & -1 \end{bmatrix} \times \begin{bmatrix} 1 & 2 & 1 & 1 \\ 1 & 1 & -1 & -2 \\ 1 & -1 & -1 & 2 \\ 1 & -2 & 1 & -1 \end{bmatrix} \otimes \begin{bmatrix} a^2 & \frac{ab}{2} & a^2 & \frac{ab}{2} \\ \frac{ab}{2} & \frac{b^2}{4} & \frac{ab}{2} & \frac{b^2}{4} \\ a^2 & \frac{ab}{2} & a^2 & \frac{ab}{2} \\ \frac{ab}{2} & \frac{b^2}{4} & \frac{ab}{2} & \frac{b^2}{4} \end{bmatrix}, \tag{7}$$

To simplify the implementation of the DCT transform and reduce multiplications by half in the transform of $CXC^T$ which could result in loss of accuracy using integer arithmetics on the DSP platform. The final forward transform is reformed as Eq. (7). We adopt a low-complexity transform proposed by Henrique S.Malvar [14], and lead to a new set of coefficients, which is shown in Fig. 4. There only consists of shift operations for FDCT and IDCT functions, which can benefit for the assembly code re-arrangement.

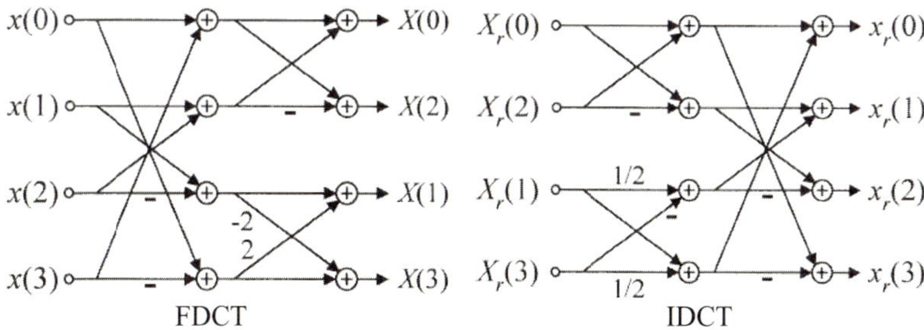


Fig. 4. Fast implementation of the H.264 direct transform [14]

## 4   Experimental Results

To evaluate the effectiveness of the proposed optimization algorithm, the optimized H.264 video encoder was implemented on the DM642 DSP platform. We set up a TI DM642EVM development environment including a target board, Code Composer Studio (CCS) profile tools, an input device (camera) and an output device (monitor) as shown in Fig. 5. Note that the rate control algorithm was not changed. Furthermore, system level optimization skills were also studied according to TI technical documents [15,16,17,18,19,20]. The x264 encoder was

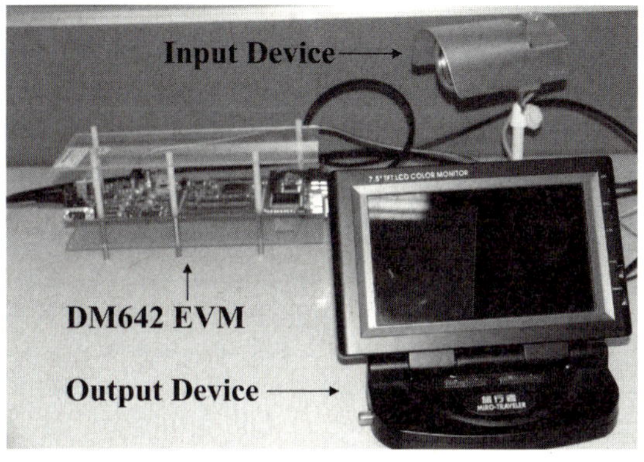


Fig. 5. Loopback system peripheral

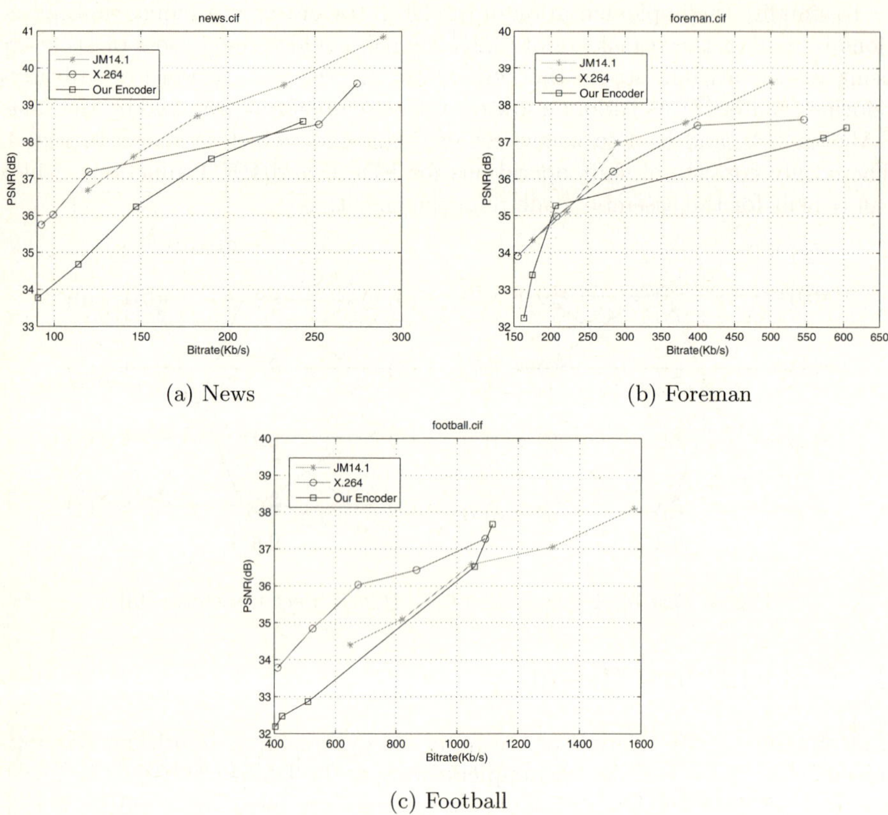

(a) News

(b) Foreman

(c) Football

**Fig. 6.** The RD-curves of three codecs tested on three video clips: (a) News, (b) Foreman, and (c) Football

optimized and transplanted to DM642, and achieved the coding speed of 22.6fps for VGA (640x480) size video. The performance indices bitrate (Kbs), PSNR (db) and FPS of each optimization approach has been measured on three benchmark video clips: news, football and foreman. Table 3 reveals and compares the progress of all optimization steps, including (a) direct porting of baseline x264 encoder, (b) quantization and DCT optimization, (c) sub-pixel motion estimation optimization, and (d) 2-D fast mode decision optimization. The overall performances with DSP implementation and optimization are listed in the most right column in Table 3.

In order to evaluate the PSNR and bitrate of the optimized encoder, we compare our encoder with JM14.1 and x264 on Intel CPU T2250 @ 1.73GHz platform with 1GB DDR RAM. Figures 6(a), (b) and (c) demonstrate the RD-curves of these three codecs with different QP values 26, 28, 30, 32 and 34 for CIF video clips News, Foreman and Football, respectively. Although our encoder results in less PSNR (all less than 2db), the proposed encoding speed is increased up to 30-50 fps which is faster than the orignal X.264.

**Table 3.** The performance indices bitrate (Kbs), PSNR (db) and FPS of the implemented codec on DM642 with different optimization step: (a) direct porting of baseline x264 encoder, (b) quantization and DCT optimization, (c) sub-pixel motion estimation optimization, and (d) 2-D fast mode decision optimization, and overall results

| Video clips | | Optimization Step | | | | |
|---|---|---|---|---|---|---|
| | | (a) | (a)+(b) | (a)+(b) +(c) | (a)+(b) +(c)+(d) | Overall result |
| | BitRate | 307.42 | 294.877 | 254.825 | 203.305 | 252.46 |
| News | PSNR | 40.823 | 40.274 | 39.647 | 38.68 | 38.533 |
| | FPS | 15.30 | 15.59 | 29.22 | 32.94 | 42.50 |
| | BitRate | 1971.71 | 1983.12 | 1454.13 | 1132.42 | 1058.47 |
| Football | PSNR | 40.589 | 41.764 | 38.324 | 38.208 | 37.669 |
| | FPS | 7.09 | 7.61 | 15.97 | 21.45 | 31.95 |
| | BitRate | 1003.43 | 1014.67 | 908.95 | 869.77 | 872.76 |
| Foreman | PSNR | 40.103 | 40.928 | 38.427 | 37.692 | 37.399 |
| | FPS | 10.49 | 11.77 | 22.69 | 29.35 | 36.64 |

# 5   Conclusion

In this paper, we optimize the H.264/AVC baseline video encoder based on x264 codec and implement the optimized codec on TI DM642 DSP platform. A series of optimization methods have been proposed, including 2-D fast mode decision, sub-pixel optimization for motion estimation, and weighted matrix quantization. Both code level and system level optimization principals are adopted. Experimental results reveal that the optimized H.264 video encoder retains satisfactory quality with very low degradation. The implemented codec can achieve the coding speed of 22.6fps and more than 40fps for VGA (640×480) and CIF (352×288) resolution, respectively. The proposed H.264 codec can be employed in many real-time applications. Compared to the special purpose IC solution of H.264 codec, the embedded DSP system has advantages of high flexibility and re-configuration.

# References


1. Goto, K., Hatabu, A., Nishizuka, H., Matsunaga, K., Nakamura, R., Mochizuki, Y., Miyazaki, T.: H.264 video encoder implementation on a low-power DSP with low and stable computational complexity. In: IEEE Workshop on Signal Processing Systems Design and Implementation, SIPS 2006, pp. 101–106 (2006)
2. Chen, T.-C., Chen, Y.-H., Tsai, S.-F., Chien, S.-Y., Chen, L.-G.: Fast algorithm and architecture design of low-power integer motion estimation for H.264/AVC. IEEE Transactions on Circuits and Systems for Video Technology 17(5), 568–577 (2007)

3. Zhuo, L., Wang, Q., Feng, D.-D., Shen, L.: Optimization and implementation of H.264 encoder on DSP platform. In: IEEE International Conference on Multimedia and Expo., 232–235 (2007)
4. Li, Z., Xing, Q., Zhu, X.: H.264 video encoder implementation and optimization based on DM642 DSP. In: IEEE International Conference on Networking, Sensing and Control, ICNSC 2008, pp. 891–894 (2008)
5. Wei, Z., Cai, C.: Realization and optimization of DSP based H.264 encoder. In: Proceedings. 2006 IEEE International Symposium on Circuits and Systems, ISCAS 2006, p. 4 (2006)
6. Wang, H.-J., Hou, Y.-Y., Li, H.: H.264/AVC video encoder algorithm optimization based on TI TMS320DM642. In: Third International Conference on Intelligent Information Hiding and Multimedia Signal Processing, IIHMSP 2007, vol. 1 (2007)
7. Werda, I., Chaouch, H., Samet, A., Ayed, M.A.B., Masmoudi, N., Akbal, E., Ergen, B., Muljadi, H., Takeda, H., Ando, K., et al.: Optimal DSP-based motion estimation tools implementation for H.264/AVC baseline encoder. IJCSNS 7(5), 141 (2007)
8. Wiegand, T., Sullivan, G.J., Bjntegaard, G., Luthra, A.: Overview of the H.264/AVC video coding standard. IEEE Transactions on Circuits and Systems for Video Technology 13(7), 560–576 (2003)
9. Texas Instrument. TMS320C64x DSP Video Port/VCXO Interpolated Control Port (2006)
10. LFree Software Foundation. GNU operating system, http://www.gnu.org/
11. Chang, C.-Y., Pan, C.-H., Chen, H.: Fast mode decision for P-frames in H. 264. In: Picture Coding Symposium (PCS) (2004)
12. Richardson, I.E.G.: H. 264 and MPEG-4 video compression. Wiley, Chichester (2003)
13. J.V. Team. Draft ITU-T recommendaation and final draft international standard of joint video specification (March 2003)
14. Malvar, H., Hallapuro, A., Karczewicz, M., Kerofsky, L.: Low-complexity transform and quantization in H.264/AVC. IEEE Transactions on Circuits and Systems for Video Technology 13(7), 598–603 (2003)
15. Texas Instrument. TMS320C6000 Assembly Language Tools v6.0 Beta (2005)
16. Texas Instrument. Code Composer Studio User's Guide (2000)
17. Texas Instrument. TMS320C6000 DSP/BIOS User's Guide (2000)
18. Texas Instrument. TMS320C64x/C64x+ DSP CPU and instruction set reference guide
19. Texas Instrument. Video Encoding Optimization on TMS320DM64x/C64x (2004)
20. Texas Instrument. TMS320C64x DSP Two-Level Internsl Memory Rfference Guide (2006)

# Improved Two-Level Model Averaging Techniques in Drosophila Brain Modeling


Cheng-Chi Wu[1], Chao-Yu Chen[1], Hsiu-Ming Chang[2], Ann-Shyn Chiang[2],
and Yung-Chang Chen[1]

[1] Department of Electrical Engineering
[2] Department of Life Science
National Tsing Hua University,
101, Section 2, Kuang-Fu Road, Hsinchu, Taiwan, R.O.C.
{dennis,ordnance,ycchen}@benz.ee.nthu.edu.tw,
{hmchang,aschiang}@life.nthu.edu.tw



**Abstract.** Two-level model averaging techniques have been proposed to construct the 3D reference template for the Drosophila brain. The surface-based reference template is suitable for integration of experimental data from different laboratories. The 3D distance transform is the most memory and time consuming part in the model averaging algorithm. With the improvement of microscopic scanning technology, images of higher resolution can be acquired. Thus, the memories required for 3D distance transform become critical. In this paper, improved two-level model averaging techniques are proposed with three improvements. A two-scale distance map creation algorithm is introduced to reduce the memory cost in the distance transform. The computational time is reduced by a reduction of computation points in the distance map creation. The third improvement is an outlier rejection module to improve the robustness of the resulting average model.

**Keywords:** Model averaging, Drosophila, surface-based.


## 1 Introduction

In the field of neuroscience, atlas of the specific structure is pursued in many applications. Especially in the brain research, brain atlases are needed for studies of laboratory animals and human brain. The brain atlas could be either a representative individual brain [1] or an average model generated from a number of datasets [2]. Since the individual variability exists in all species, the average model is preferred.

Methods for averaging multiple image datasets can be categorized into two groups: the voxel-based averaging algorithms and the surface-based averaging algorithms. The voxel-based averaging algorithms are typically based on local decision fusion schemes. Voxel-based probabilistic atlases [3,4] have been proposed for the honeybee brain and the Drosophila brain. A probability atlas provides only a boundary for statistical confidence instead of an absolute anatomic shape and position. It is suitable for distinguishing normal brains from disease specific ones.


T. Wada, F. Huang, and S. Lin (Eds.): PSIVT 2009, LNCS 5414, pp. 921–931, 2009.

For serving as a reference template for data integration, a surface-based atlas is preferred. In the Drosophila brain atlas, data from different laboratories can be integrated via a surface warping with specific landmarks, such as the brain cortex or specific neuropils. Two-level model averaging techniques [5] are introduced to construct the average shape model for the cortex and neuropils of the Drosophila brain. The first step is coarse-level model averaging. Global characteristics of different individual models are averaged in this step. After coarse-level model averaging, each individual model is transformed into a corresponding pseudo-average model.

In the fine-level model averaging step, the average model can be obtained by determining the shape average of the globally-registered pseudo-average models. A 3D distance field [6] is utilized to generate the signed distance map for each pseudo-average model.

Many efforts have been made on building a signed distance map of a triangular mesh. The procedure can be separated into two parts: sign determination and distance transformation. In the first half, a famous method is to count the intersection of a ray going from the given point to infinity. The point is determined to be within the model if the intersection number is odd and vice versa [7]. Another well known method utilizes the normal of the closest feature on mesh of the given point. Angle weighted pseudo normal method [8] computes the normal of all faces, edges, and points on the triangular mesh. In the distance transformation part, brute force algorithm directly computes all of the distance from the given point to the mesh points. Many methods have been proposed to improve the computational efficiency [9].

In the two-level model averaging algorithm, a linear time algorithm for distance transformation is applied. With the improvement of microscopic scanning technology, images of higher resolution can be acquired. The memories required for computing the distance transformation become the bottleneck of the system when the source images are of high resolution. In the mean while, the increase of time consumption for the algorithm is in proportion to the number of points needed for distance transformation.

In this paper, improved two-level model averaging techniques are proposed to generate the average model from a set of triangular mesh models. Three improvements are made in the proposed algorithm. First, a two-scale distance map creation is introduced to reduce the memory cost. Second, the computational time consumption is reduced by a point-reduction scheme in the distance transformation. Third, an outlier rejection procedure is implemented to improve the robustness of the proposed algorithm.

The paper is organized as follows. Section 2 overviews the proposed algorithms. Section 3 and 4 describe the coarse-level and the fine-level model averaging accordingly. The outlier rejection procedure is presented in Section 5. Section 6 contains experimental results and conclusions are made in Section 7.

## 2 System Overview

Original datasets used in this study are confocal microscopic image slices. An experienced expert helps to label the object to be averaged from the image slices. The object boundary in each image is assumed to be composed of several non-crossing simple closed contours. 3D surface models of the objects are constructed from these labeled sequential parallel 2D sections by the algorithm describes in [10]. The proposed algorithm is trying to build an average 3D surface model from a group of individual datasets.

The system flowchart of the two-level model averaging algorithm is shown in Fig. 1. The goal of the coarse-level model averaging is to register the global characteristic of different individual models, such as orientations and positions. The candidate of the reference model is chosen to be the individual model which has the volume size closest to the average volume size. Each individual model is transformed into a corresponding pseudo-average model after coarse-level model averaging.

The next step is the fine-level model averaging. A signed distance map is built for each pseudo-average model. After cumulating the signed distance maps of all pseudo-average models, the surface of a pro forma average model can be extracted by zero-crossing detection of the cumulative distance field.

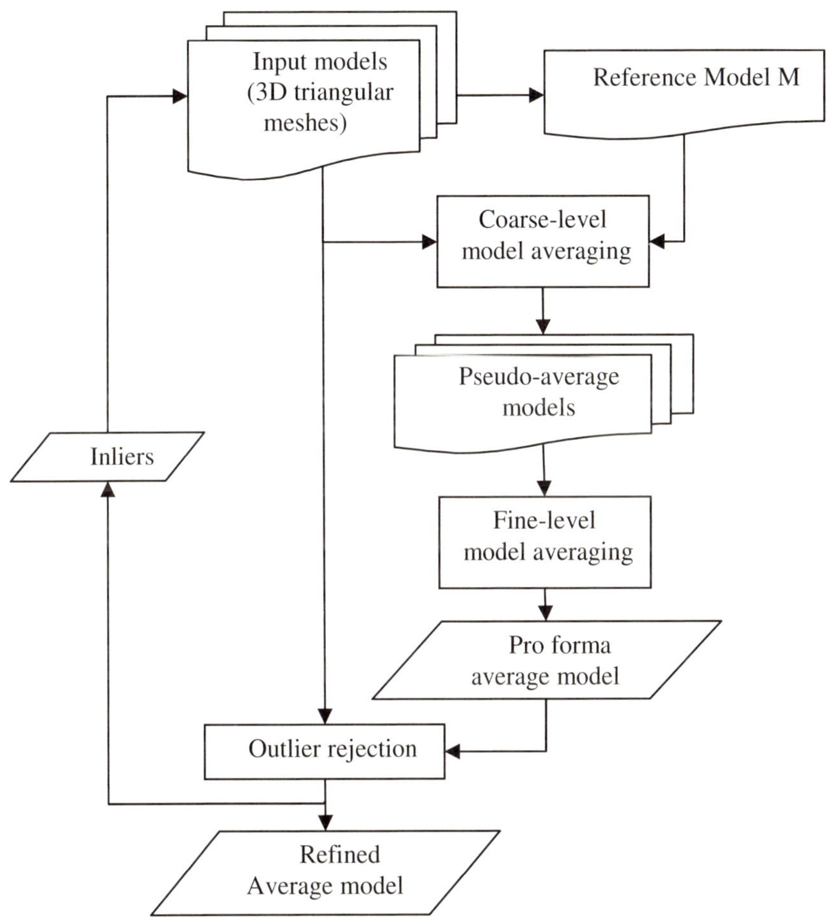


**Fig. 1.** System flowchart of the improved two-level model averaging algorithm

The final step is an outlier rejection to improve the robustness of the average model. Outliers can be picked out by an outlier rejection procedure. A refined average model can be obtained by performing the improved two-level model averaging algorithm with the remaining inliers.

## 3 Coarse-Level Model Averaging

The coarse-level model averaging is implemented by a rigid registration. In general, the affine registration can achieve better alignments than that of the rigid registration. However, the shearing and scaling are two unwanted properties in the coarse-level model averaging. The affine registration is easily biased by an improper reference model. If the reference model is a tilted model, all other individual models will be tilted after transformation.

Instead, the rigid registration allows only translation and rotation of the target model. The geometry of the model is preserved under rigid transformation. For globally registering the individual models, the rigid registration is a reliable choice.

A rigid transformation is define as:

$$\mathbf{x}' = \mathbf{R}(\mathbf{x} - \mathbf{C}) + \mathbf{C} + \mathbf{T} . \tag{1}$$

where $\mathbf{x}$ is the position vector of the original point on the target model. $\mathbf{x}'$ is the position vector of the transformed point. $\mathbf{C} = [C_x, C_y, C_z]^T$ is the center of rotation. $\mathbf{T} = [T_x, T_y, T_z]^T$ is the translation matrix. $\mathbf{R}$ is the rotation matrix, which is represented by the product of three elementary rotation matrices

$$\mathbf{R} = \mathbf{R}_x \mathbf{R}_y \mathbf{R}_z . \tag{2}$$

where $\mathbf{R}_x$, $\mathbf{R}_y$, and $\mathbf{R}_z$ are defined by

$$\mathbf{R}_x = \begin{bmatrix} 1 & 0 & 0 \\ 0 & \cos\theta_x & \sin\theta_x \\ 0 & -\sin\theta_x & \cos\theta_x \end{bmatrix}, \ \mathbf{R}_y = \begin{bmatrix} \cos\theta_y & 0 & \sin\theta_y \\ 0 & 1 & 0 \\ -\sin\theta_y & 0 & \cos\theta_y \end{bmatrix}, \ \mathbf{R}_z = \begin{bmatrix} \cos\theta_z & \sin\theta_z & 0 \\ -\sin\theta_z & \cos\theta_z & 0 \\ 0 & 0 & 1 \end{bmatrix} . \tag{3}$$

The average distance between target and reference model is defined as:

$$D = \frac{1}{N} \sum_{i=1}^{N} d^2(\mathbf{x}') . \tag{4}$$

where $d^2(\mathbf{x}')$ is the distance between $\mathbf{x}'$ and the reference model and $N$ is the number of points on the target model.

Let $\mathbf{p} = (T_x, T_y, T_z, \theta_x, \theta_y, \theta_z)$ denotes the parameters of the rigid transformation. Since $D$ is a function of $\mathbf{p}$, the parameters of the rigid transformation can be solved by minimizing the average distance $D(\mathbf{p})$ via the following iteration:

$$\mathbf{p}' = \mathbf{p} - \delta \cdot \nabla D(\mathbf{p}) . \tag{5}$$

where $\delta$ is the step size of iteration and

$$\nabla D(\mathbf{p}) = \left[ \frac{\partial D(\mathbf{p})}{\partial \theta_x}, \frac{\partial D(\mathbf{p})}{\partial \theta_y}, \frac{\partial D(\mathbf{p})}{\partial \theta_z}, \frac{\partial D(\mathbf{p})}{\partial T_x}, \frac{\partial D(\mathbf{p})}{\partial T_y}, \frac{\partial D(\mathbf{p})}{\partial T_z} \right]. \tag{6}$$

An individual model is transformed into a corresponding pseudo-average model by applying a rigid transformation with the parameters solved in (5).

## 4  Fine-Level Model Averaging

The final average model can be obtained by fine-level model averaging of the pseudo-average models. The shape-based averaging method [11] is implemented on the triangular meshes. A signed distance map $SDM\left(\bar{x}\right)_i$ is built for each pseudo-average model $M_i$. $SDM\left(\bar{x}\right)_i$ is defined as:

$$SDM\left(\bar{x}\right)_i = \begin{cases} + \min_{\bar{x}_i \in surface} d\left(\bar{x},\bar{x}_i\right), & \text{if } \bar{x} \text{ is outside the model .} \\[2mm] - \min_{\bar{x}_i \in surface} d\left(\bar{x},\bar{x}_i\right), & \text{if } \bar{x} \text{ is inside the model .} \end{cases} \tag{7}$$

where $d\left(\bar{x},\bar{x}_i\right)$ is the Euclidean distance between $\bar{x}$ and $\bar{x}_i$ . Therefore, $SDM\left(\bar{x}\right)_i$ contains the information that either $\bar{x}$ is inside or outside the model $M_i$ , and how far it is from the surface boundary. $\bar{x}$ is on the surface if $SDM\left(\bar{x}\right)_i = 0$ .

The cumulative signed distance map $R\left(\bar{x}\right)$ is defined as:

$$R\left(\bar{x}\right) = \sum_{i=1}^{K} SDM\left(\bar{x}\right)_i \tag{8}$$

where $K$ is the number of pseudo-average models. The surface of the final average model can be extracted by zero-crossing detection of $R\left(\bar{x}\right)$ .

A 2D example is shown is Fig. 2. The inputs are two ellipses (Fig. 2(a) and 2(b)). The signed distance maps is computed for both ellipses and drawn in 3D(Fig. 2(c) and 2(d)). The cumulative signed distance map is shown in Fig. 2(e). The averaging result of the inputs is a flattened ellipse (Fig. 2(f)).

In [6], a linear time algorithm is proposed for computing the Euclidean distance transform. The algorithm has a serial computational complexity linear in the number of image pixels. However, memories required for storing the signed distance map depend on the voxel number of the model. The memory cost becomes the bottleneck of the system when the source images are of high resolution. A two-scale distance map creation algorithm is proposed to reduce the memory cost.

A point-reduction scheme is introduced to reduce the time expense for computing the distance transform. This is achieved by computing the distance transform only on the necessary voxels.

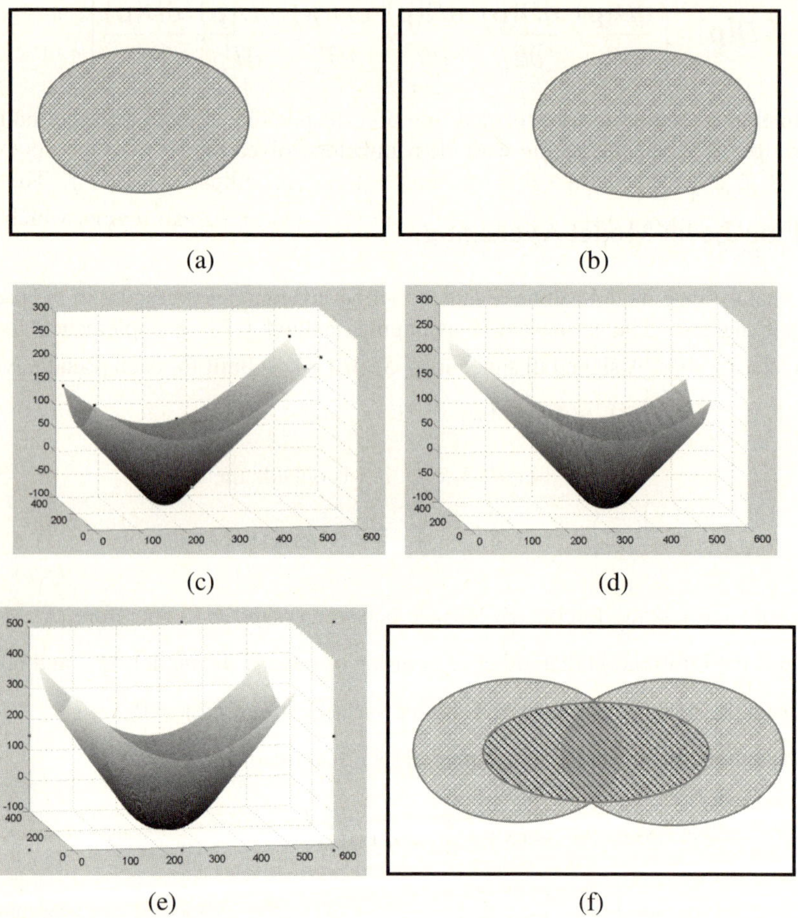

**Fig. 2.** A 2D example of model averaging. (a) and (b): two input ellipses. (c) and (d): the corresponding signed distance map of (a) and (b). (e): the cumulative signed distance map. (f): the averaging result (ellipse with oblique lines) of two ellipses.

## 4.1  Two-Scale Distance Map Creation

A two-scale distance map creation algorithm is proposed to reduce the memory cost by a factor of $\beta^3$. The idea is to compute the distance transform in two steps. Denote $O(v)$ as the voxel space of the object $O$. In the first step, $O(v)$ is down-sampled by a factor of $\beta$ in each axis. The down-sampled voxel space of the object is denoted as

$O_\beta(v)$. The distance map of $O_\beta(v)$ can be generated as $DM_\beta$. The exact distance transform of the voxel on the original scale can be computed only in a small region.

A 2D example is shown in Fig. 3. The object $O$ is the ellipse. The hollow circles around the ellipse are the down-sampled object $O_\beta(v)$. The distance map of $O_\beta(v)$ is calculated on the grid points. Assuming the exact distance transform of a certain voxel, point $G$, on the original scale is to be computed. The rough distance map of the down-sampled space is generated.

In the down-sampled space, the neighborhood of $G$ is the point set $\{A, B, C$ and $D\}$. Closest feature point set on the ellipse is $\{E, F\}$. The exact distance transform on the original scale can be found in a small region, which is the up-sampled space encloses $ACEFDB$.

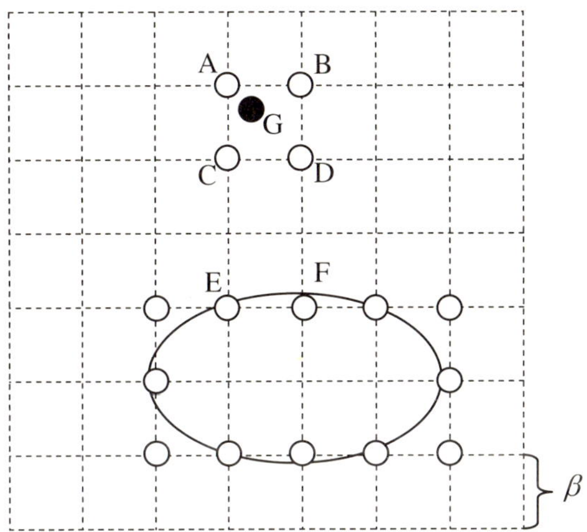


**Fig. 3.** An ellipse down-sampled by a factor of $\beta$. $E$ and $F$ are the closest feature points of $\{A, B, C$ and $D\}$.

### 4.2  Point-Reduction Scheme in the Distance Transform

The computational time consumption is reduced by a point-reduction scheme in the distance transformation. Recall that the surface of the final average model is extracted by zero-crossing detection of the cumulative signed distance map. After coarse-level model averaging, the pseudo-average models are aligned to the same coordinate space. Voxels in this coordinate spaces can be classified into three groups: 1) voxels inside every models; 2) voxels outside every models; 3) the remaining voxels.

For the first group of voxels, the value of the signed distance map of the same voxel is negative for all pseudo-average models. For the second group of voxels, the value of the signed distance map of the same voxel is positive for all pseudo-average models. Thus, the cumulative distance map of such voxels will never be zero. In other words, the first and second group of voxels well not be on the surface boundary of the average model. These voxels can be assigned to be inside or outside of the average model directly.

Only the third group of voxels need to compute distance transform. The two-scale distance map creation method is applied on these voxels for each pseudo-average model.

## 5  Outlier Rejection

The rejection of outliers is based on the distance information. Let $I_i$ be the $i$th individual model and $K$ be the number of individual models. The average model, $M_{avg}$, can be generated by the proposed improved two-level model averaging techniques. A corresponding distance map for $M_{avg}$ can be built subsequently. To determine whether model $I_i$ is an outlier, $I_i$ is first rigidly registered to $M_{avg}$. For every point on $I_i$, the minimum distance from it to $M_{avg}$ can be computed. The mean distance between $I_i$ and $M_{avg}$ can be calculated by the following equation:

$$\overline{x}_i = \frac{1}{N} \sum_{i=1}^{N} D(x_i)$$

(9)

where $x_i$ is the point on $I_i$ and $N$ is the number of points in $I_i$. $\overline{x}_i$ is the mean distance between $I_i$ and $M_{avg}$.

The mean distance of all individual models can be computed serially. The mean distance of all individual models can be defined as:

$$\overline{X} = \frac{1}{K} \sum_{i=1}^{K} \overline{x}_i \ .$$

(10)

The standard deviation of all individual models can be computed by the following equation:

$$\sigma = \sqrt{\frac{1}{K} \sum_{i=1}^{K} (\overline{x}_i - \overline{X})^2} \ .$$

(11)

Finally, the model is regarded as an outlier if the following inequality is satisfied:

$$\begin{cases} \overline{x}_i > \overline{X} + \sigma, & \text{if } \sigma \geq T_H. \\ \overline{x}_i > \overline{X} + T_H, & \text{if } \sigma < T_H. \end{cases}$$

(12)

where $T_H$ is a pre-defined threshold.

## 6  Experimental Results

There are 34 datasets of female Drosophila used in this study. Fig. 4 shows the results for model averaging of the brain cortex. The superposition of 34 pseudo-average models after coarse-level averaging is shown in Fig. 4(a). The average model and the superposition of 34 pseudo-average models are depicted in Fig. 4(b).

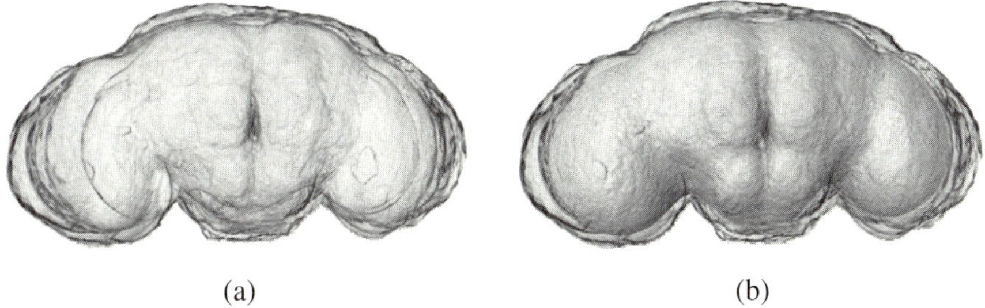

(a)                                        (b)

**Fig. 4.** The results for model averaging of the brain cortex. (a): 34 pseudo-average models after coarse-level model averaging. (b): The average model (opaque) and the superposition of 34 pseudo-average models (transparent).

Fig. 5 illustrates the point-reduction scheme and the two-scale hierarchy in the distance transform. Given pseudo-average models, Fig. 5(a) shows the points needed to compute the distance transform in a slice. The corresponding region for the two-scale distance map creation is depicted in Fig. 5(b).

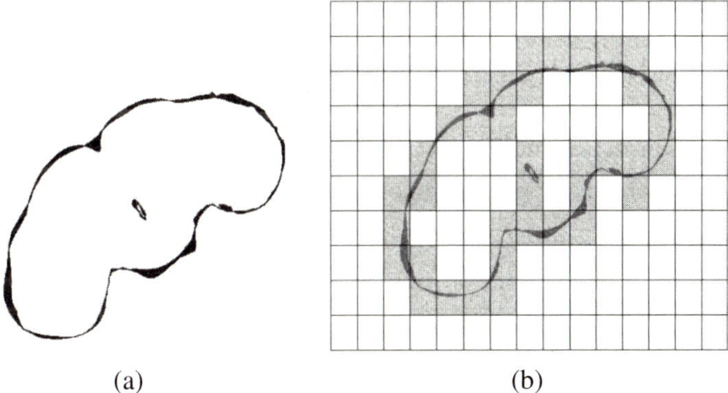

(a)                                        (b)

**Fig. 5.** Example of the point-reduction scheme and the two-scale hierarchy in the distance transform. (a) The points needed to compute the distance transform. (b) The corresponding region for the two-scale distance map creation.

The performance improvement in the distance transform is shown in Table 1. Measurements were obtained using a workstation with Intel dual Xeon 2.0GHz CPU. This workstation was equipped with 4 GBytes of memory. The linear time distance transform algorithm will be out of memory for images constructed from the high

**Table 1.** The performance improvement of distance transform

| Voxel number | The linear time distance transform algorithm | Two-scale and point-reduction in distance transform |
|---|---|---|
| $320 \times 327 \times 139$ | 13343 (milliseconds) | 10032 (milliseconds) |
| $600 \times 614 \times 206$ | Out of memory | 34735 (milliseconds) |
| $900 \times 880 \times 289$ | Out of memory | 43157 (milliseconds) |

resolution confocal microscopy. With the improvements in distance transform, both memory and time consumption can be reduced.

The results of outlier rejection is shown in Fig. 6. Four outliers are detected by the outlier rejection algorithm.

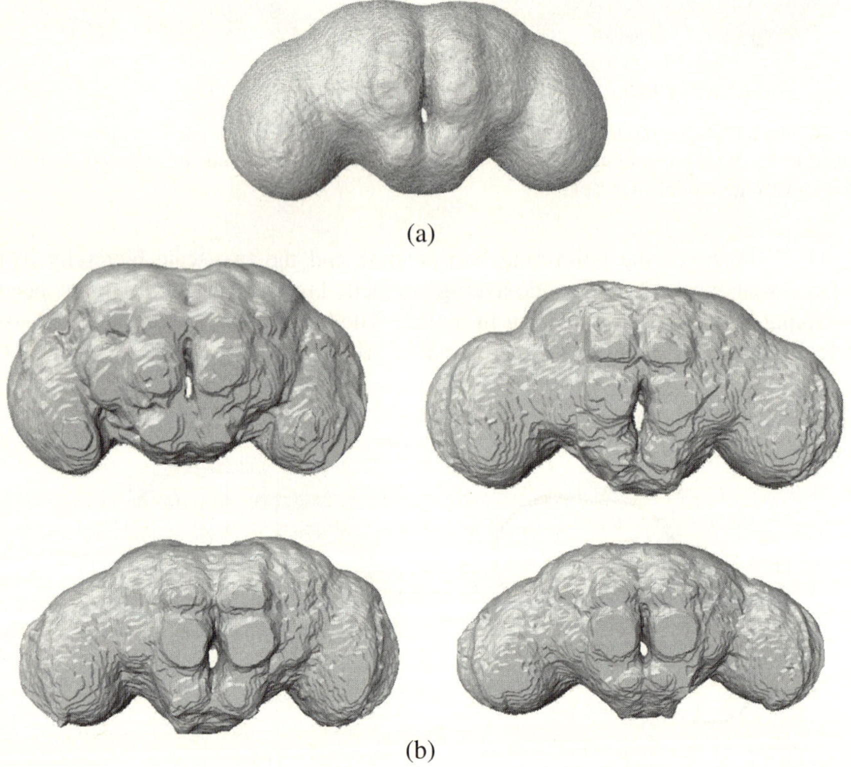

(a)

(b)

**Fig. 6.** (a) The average model of the 34 datasets. (b) The outliers: no. 12, no. 29, no. 30, and no. 31.

## 7  Conclusions

In this paper, an improved two-level model averaging algorithm is proposed for the Drosophila brain modeling. Two improvements are made in the fine-level model averaging. A two-scale distance map creation is introduced to reduce the memory cost. The computational time consumption is reduced by a point-reduction scheme in the distance transform. With these two improvements, average model can be constructed from high resolution confocal microscopic images.

An outlier rejection procedure is implemented to improve the robustness of the model averaging algorithm. A refined average model can be obtained by performing the improved two-level model averaging algorithm with the remaining inliers.

# References


1. Talairach, J., Tournoux, P.: Coplanar Stereotaxic Atlas of the Human Brain. Thieme Medical, New York (1988)
2. Friston, K.J., Holmes, A.P., Worsley, K.J., Poline, J.P., Frith, C.D., Frackowiak, R.S.J.: Statistical Parametric Maps in Functional Imaging: A general Linear Approach. Human Brain Mapping 2, 189–210 (1995)
3. Brandt, R., Rohlfing, T., Rybak, J., Krofczik, S., Maye, A., Westerhoff, M., Hege, H.-C., Menzel, R.: Three-Dimensional Average-Shape Atlas of the Honeybee Brain and its Applications. J. Comp. Neurol. 492, 1–19 (2005)
4. Rein, K., Zockler, M., Mader, M.T., Grubel, C., Heisenberg, M.: The Drosophila Standard Brain. Current Biology 12, 227–231 (2002)
5. Chen, Y.C., Chen, Y.C., Chiang, A.S.: Two-Level Model Averaging Techniques in Dorsophila Brain Imaging. In: Proceedings of 2002 IEEE International Conference on Image Processing, vol. 2, pp. 941–944. Rochester, New York (2002)
6. Maurer, C.R., Qi, R., Raghavan, V.: A linear time algorithm for computing exact Euclidean distance transforms of binary images in arbitrary dimensions. IEEE Trans. on Pattern Analysis and Machine Intelligence 25, 265–270 (2003)
7. Dachille, F., Kaufman, A.: Incremental Triangle Voxelization. In: Proc. Graphics Interface, pp. 205–212 (2000)
8. Baerentzen, J.A., Aanaes, H.: Signed Distance Computation Using the Angle Weighted Pseudonormal. IEEE Trans. on Visualization and Computer Graphics 11(3), 243–253 (2005)
9. Gue'ziec, A.: Meshsweeper: Dynamic Point-to-Polygonal Mesh Distance and Applications. IEEE Trans. on Visualization and Computer Graphics 7(1), 47–60 (2001)
10. Chen, Y.C., Chen, Y.C., Chiang, A.S., Hsieh, K.S.: A Reliable Surface Reconstruction System in Biomedicine. Computer Methods and Programs in Biomedicine 86(2), 141–152 (2007)
11. Rohlfing, T., Maurer, C.R.: Shape-Based Averaging. IEEE Trans. on Image Proc. 16(1), 153–161 (2007)

# Belief Propagation for Stereo Analysis of Night-Vision Sequences

Shushi Guan[1], Reinhard Klette[1], and Young W. Woo[2]

[1] The *.enpeda..* Project, The University of Auckland, New Zealand
[2] Dept. of Multimedia Eng., Dong-Eui University, Busan, Korea

**Abstract.** This paper studies different specifications of belief propagation for stereo analysis of seven rectified stereo night-vision sequences (provided by Daimler AG). As shown in [4], Sobel preprocessing of images has obvious impacts on improving disparity calculations. This paper considers other options of preprocessing (Canny and Kovesi-Owens edge operators), and concludes with a recommended setting for belief propagation on those sequences.

**Keywords:** Performance evaluation, stereo analysis, motion analysis, real-world sequences, driver assistance.

## 1 Introduction

Coarse-to fine belief propagation (see, e.g., [6]) is a possible technique for stereo analysis, and it receives good rankings for engineered indoor high-contrast stereo pairs, see [9]. The question arises how this technique behaves on real-world stereo sequences, such as the seven night-vision sequences provided on [2] in Set 1, and described in [8]. See Figure 1 for examples for these sequences. Each sequence contains between 250 and 300 stereo pairs, each image $680 \times 350$ in 12-bit resolution.

**Fig. 1.** Examples of stereo pairs of Set 1 on the *enpeda..* test sequence website (from Sequences 5, 6, and 7, recorded with 12-bit Bosch night vision cameras)

T. Wada, F. Huang, and S. Lin (Eds.): PSIVT 2009, LNCS 5414, pp. 932–943, 2009.
© Springer-Verlag Berlin Heidelberg 2009

## 2    Belief Propagation for Stereo Analysis

Felzenszwalb and Huttenlocher [3] provide a detailed guide for implementing coarse-to-fine belief propagation (BP); see also `people.cs.uchicago.edu/~pff/bp/` for free sources. In our implementation, we decided for max-product, 4-adjacency, truncated quadratic cost function (in difference to [4] where only the simple Potts model was used; the lower envelope calculation may follow [5]), the red-black speed-up method, and coarse-to-fine processing, for more reliable (and also time-efficient) matching. Below we provide further specifications of the recommended BP implementation; those specifications resulted from experimental optimizations with respect to the given seven test stereo sequences. (So far, we have not used any initialization of belief values in message boards by those obtained at time $t - 1$, for $t > 0$; initialization is always by the data term using intensity differences at time $t$.)

Following [3], we also state two 'typical' features of belief propagation. (*Asymmetry*) The strength of message passing from low-difference (homogeneous) areas to high-difference (busy) areas is smaller than the strength of message passing from high-difference areas to low-difference areas. (*Influence of Discontinuities*) Message passing is blocked by discontinuities (such as edges in images).

Due to these observed features, it is not surprising that [4] suggests Sobel pre-processing [12] prior to BP for those real-world sequences. Figure 2 illustrates the

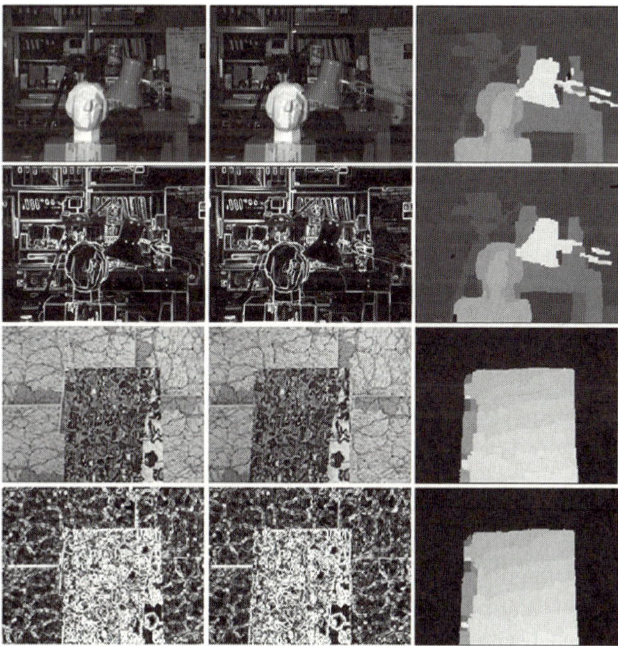

**Fig. 2.** Upper row: original *Tsukuba* images and BP result. Second row: their Sobel images and BP result. Third row: original *Map* images and BP result. Bottom row: their Sobel images and BP result.

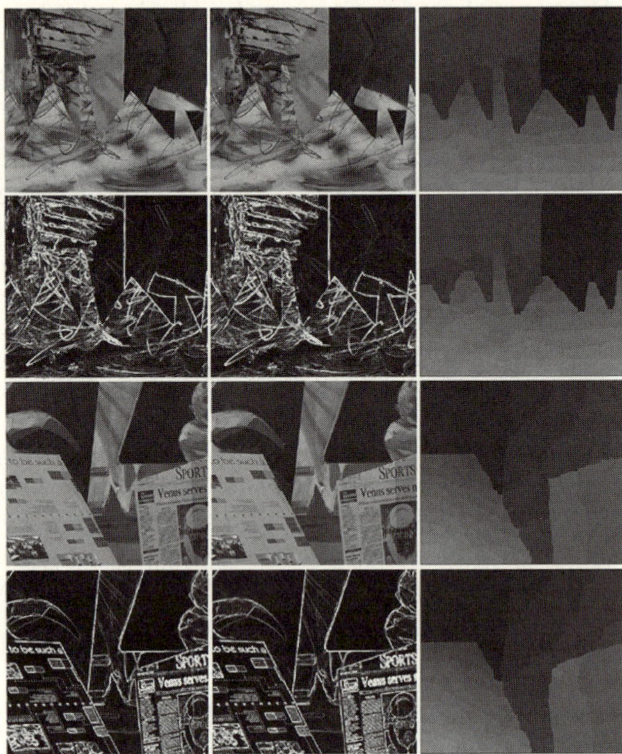

**Fig. 3.** Upper row: original *Sawtooth* images and BP result. Second row: their Sobel images and BP result. Third row: original *Venus* images and BP result. Bottom row: their Sobel images and BP result.

**Table 1.** Percentage of bad matches of our BP algorithm on Middlebury stereo pairs, without or with Sobel preprocessing

| Pair | Tsukuba | with S. | Map | with S. | Sawtooth | with S. | Venus | with S. |
|---|---|---|---|---|---|---|---|---|
| Error | 1.75 | 1.81 | 0.31 | 0.33 | 0.94 | 0.95 | 0.99 | 1.02 |

'tuned' BP algorithm on Middlebury stereo examples, without and with Sobel preprocessing. There is actually a slight increase in errors for those engineered images.

As shown in [4], the situation is totally different for the studied real-world sequences; see Figure 4 for an example for Sequence 1. There are (at least) two obvious problems for original images for Sequence 1, namely bad matches due to lack of texture (e.g., middle of the road), and mismatches due to 'fuzzy depth discontinuities' (such as in the sky or in trees). Sobel preprocessing contributes towards solutions of both problems.

This experience can be made for all the seven sequences. Figure 5 shows samples of depth maps, one for each sequence, without using any edge preprocessing.

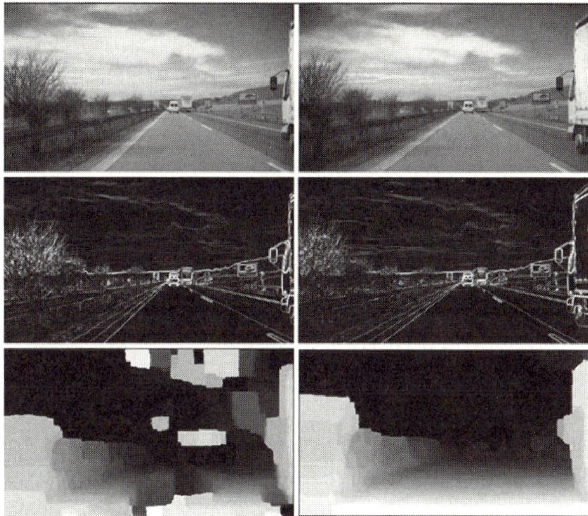

**Fig. 4.** Sample of left and right image for Sequence 1 (upper row), Sobel images of both (middle row), and BP results (lower row) for original images (left) and Sobel images (right)

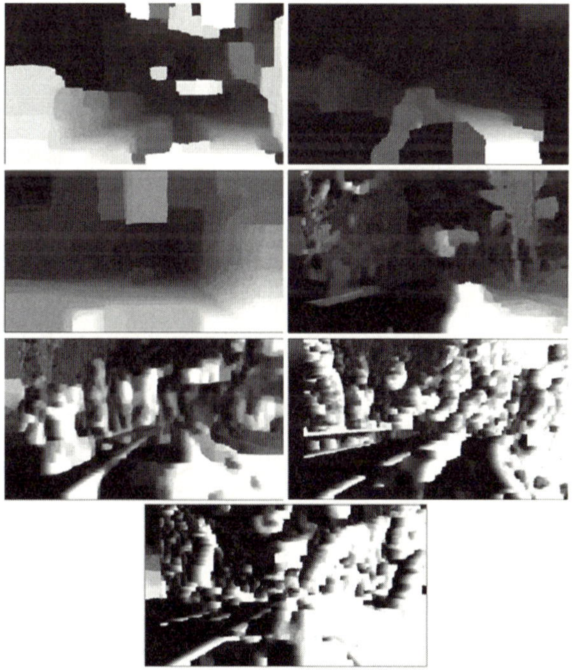

**Fig. 5.** Samples of depth maps, one for each of the seven sequences (without any edge preprocessing)

For example, Sequences 5 to 7 show many trees along the road side, and trunks, branches and leaves of the trees cause serious stereo mismatching.

## 3    Comparing Three Edge Detectors

A Sobel edge image is certainly 'noisy', but provides this way features or details of original images which allow that the message passing mechanism proceeds more 'in accordance' with the actual data. Figure 6 shows typical depth maps obtained for those seven sequences, for the same pairs of frames as already illustrated in Figure 5.

In general, compared to BP on original image pairs, major discontinuities are now, in general, correctly detected. For example, the visual border of a tree may be recovered despite of an obvious fuzziness of image intensities along its visual border. In particular, road and sky are now often accurately located. In most cases, another car is also detected if at a reasonable distance. However, there are still remaining problems. For example, depth maps of first image pairs of Sequence 6 show that the traffic light is not matched correctly (there are 'two traffic lights' in the depth maps).

In some images, we cannot identify many depth details, especially in images with lots of trees. Refer to Sequence 6 again for an example. Vertical edges disappear in depth maps. The reason might be that we have chosen a small

**Fig. 6.** BP results based on Sobel edge images

discontinuity penalty (see next section) based on an attempt to identify one uniform 'best' set of parameters. Using a higher discontinuity penalty in BP produces more edges or details in depth maps, but also more noise or matching errors. Automatic adaptation might be a possibility. In Sequence 5, the road in the generated depth map is not a smooth, even-leveled surface; this is caused by the shadows of the trees on the road which result in horizontal stripes in depth maps. Approximately constant intensity within an epipolar line shows negative impacts, despite the 2D belief propagation mechanism.

We compare effects obtained by using Sobel preprocessing with those possible if using the popular Canny operator [1]. We briefly recall: a Canny edge algorithm blurs the image by using a Gaussian mask; it produces a binary image; it adopts hysteresis between two threshold values to remove edge pixels caused by noise. We use 5 as lower threshold, and 12 as upper threshold. Resulting Canny edge images are certainly not 'noisy' (compared to Sobel images). The Canny edge operator 'aims' at clear edges in the original images. Figure 7 shows BP stereo results on Canny edge images, for the same stereo pairs as already illustrated in Figure 5.

Obviously, results are worse compared to BP results based on Sobel edge images. For example, depth maps for Sequence 1 show mismatches in the sky (top right), and the road is not a smooth, even surface. Similar problems occur in the depth maps of Sequence 2. However, the truck on the right hand side, and the cars in front of the ego-vehicle may still be recovered. Depth maps of

**Fig. 7.** BP results based on Canny edge images

Sequences 3, 4 and 7 show that the road is not correctly located. Moreover, cars in these images remain undetected. In Sequence 4, we cannot identify trees along the roadside, the road is often mismatched, and a safety fence in the left lane is not present in the depth map at all. Canny preprocessing was best for depth maps of Sequence 5 (the road is smooth, the safety fence is apparent, and cars at reasonable distances are also detected).

In general we conclude that Canny edge images are filtering out to many details from images. (This was further verified by varying the used thresholds.)

Finally, we selected the Kovesi-Owens operator [7,10,11] due to its accuracy in general (for image analysis processes depending on detecting actual edge locations). The Canny edge detector often fails in low contrast regions. However, the Kovesi-Owens method has a good response for detecting features in low contrast regions. Compared to the Sobel edge image, edges and corners seem to be brighter, thicker, and larger in Kovesi-Owens edge images.

The Kovesi-Owens edge algorithm is unaffected by changes in image contrast or brightness; it uses phase congruency values, which a range potentially between 0 and 1. We decided to use 0.4 as the phase congruency value. Figure 8 shows BP stereo results on Kovesi-Owens edge images, for the same stereo pairs as already illustrated in Figure 5. Compared with BP on original image pairs of the seven sequences, most objects of interest (e.g., cars, safety fences, trees) in the image are now correctly recovered.

**Fig. 8.** BP results based on Kovesi-Owens edge images

**Fig. 9.** An example from Sequence 5: this image pair (with histograms) shows significant brightness differences between left and right image

However, the Kovesi-Owens depth map results are in general slightly worse compared to Sobel-based results. For example, the road is often not an even surface. The reason might be that the Kovesi-Owens algorithm is here 'too sensitive'.

Figure 9 illustrates brightness differences between left and right image, which occur from time to time in these sequences. In any of the tested cases, such brightness differences create obvious problems for the tested BP techniques, and Kovesi-Owens seems to adapt best to those cases.

## 4   Tuning of the Algorithm

The selection of 'best values' was based on visual (subjective) evaluation and also on selected quantitative performance evaluations. For the latter ones we defined manually rectangular regions in images (such as a face of a truck, or a rectangular approximation of a car driving in front of the ego-vehicle; see Figure 10) and identified their 3D location (by specifying manually disparities of all four corners). This way we also had some approximate ground truth for those sequences available for a more objective performance evaluation.

Figure 11 illustrates the need of large numbers of iterations if no coarse-to-fine technique is applied, and Table 2 shows numbers of iterations for different num-

**Table 2.** About equivalent performance of BP with Sobel preprocessing for different pyramid levels (coarse-to-fine strategy) and numbers of iterations

| Pyramid levels | Seq. 1 | Seq. 2 | Seq. 3 | Seq. 4 | Seq. 5 | Seq. 6 | Seq. 7 |
|---|---|---|---|---|---|---|---|
| 1 | 410 | 1210 | 1120 | 100 | 265 | 150 | 310 |
| 2 | 100 | 290 | 310 | 35 | 70 | 45 | 100 |
| 3 | 26 | 120 | 60 | 10 | 25 | 20 | 30 |
| 4 | 13 | 75 | 20 | 5 | 10 | 10 | 9 |
| 5 | 5 | 35 | 9 | 3 | 4 | 5 | 5 |
| 6 | 5 | 15 | 7 | 3 | 3 | 4 | 4 |

**Fig. 10.** Examples of manually specified rectangular regions for approximated ground truth: in original sequences (left) and in Sobel-based BP results (right)

bers of levels of the used pyramid, always aiming at about the same performance of Sobel-based BP on the given sequence.

For example, Sequence 2 shows a need for a larger number of levels, to ensure a reasonable reduction of numbers of iterations. Figure 12 illustrates the data in Table 2 by means of function graphs.

Table 3 shows the actually used numbers of iterations for 5 to 7 levels of the used pyramid (note: using the fine to coarse strategy!) for the seven sequences together with used maximum disparity values (defining the number of used mes-

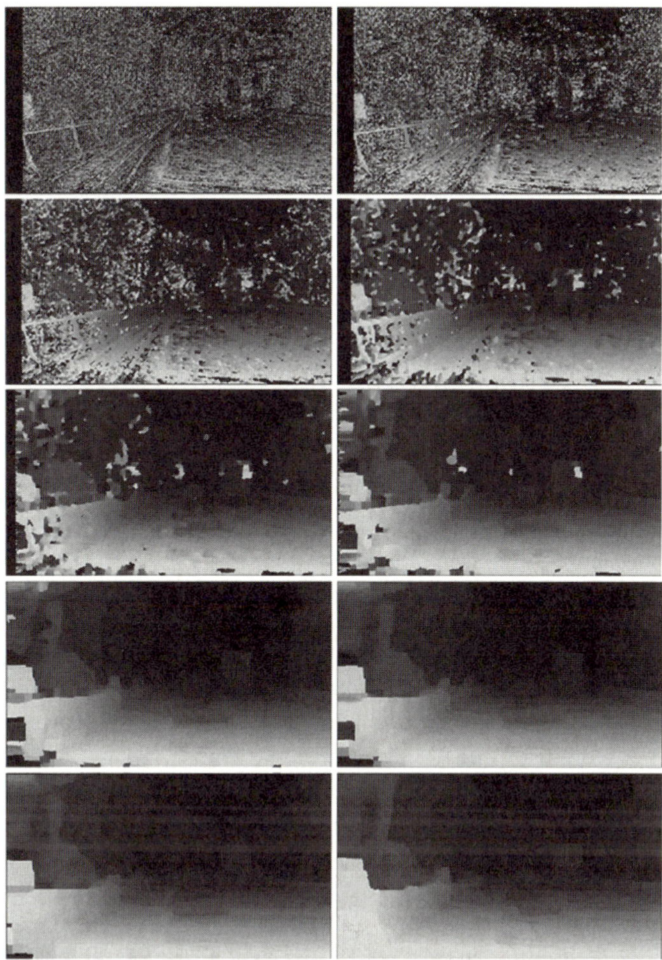

**Fig. 11.** BP stereo results without using a coarse-to-fine method: BP results (using Sobel preprocessing) after 1 (top left), 2 (top right), 4, 8, 16, 32, 64, 128, 256 (bottom, left), and 300 (bottom right) iterations

sage boards) and truncation thresholds used for discontinuity and data terms. Running time is the mean per image pair per sequences, including Sobel preprocessing (as our final choice) for each pair of frames (Intel Quad Core 2.4 GHz, 2 Gigabyte memory, NVIDIA Geforce 8800GT video card, WinXP operation system).

Note that constant parameter settings cannot handle variations in the input data, such as different brightness in left and right image. Some type of adaptation needs to be designed.

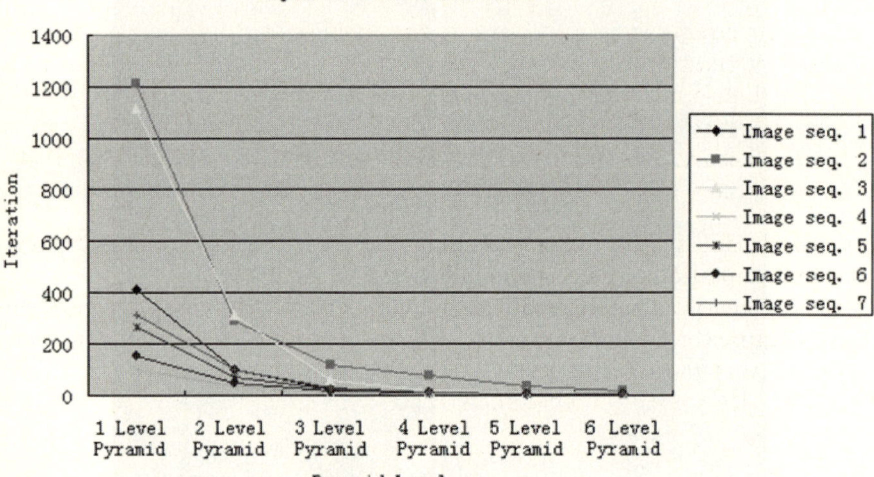


**Fig. 12.** Performance comparison of BP algorithm with pyramid level and its iteration number for our stereo image pairs

**Table 3.** Parameters of the used coarse-to-fine BP algorithm for the given seven sequences (number of message boards, truncation thresholds for discontinuity and for data term), with mean run time for a single stereo pair of one sequence

| Sequence | Max-disparity | Iterations | T (discontinuity) | T (data) | Run time |
|---|---|---|---|---|---|
| 1 | 30 *pixel* | 7 | 11 | 30 | 2.9 *s* |
| 2 | 35 *pixel* | 7 | 11 | 25 | 3.1 *s* |
| 3 | 40 *pixel* | 5 | 23 | 20 | 2.9 *s* |
| 4 | 30 *pixel* | 7 | 20 | 60 | 2.9 *s* |
| 5 | 30 *pixel* | 5 | 11 | 30 | 2.7 *s* |
| 6 | 35 *pixel* | 6 | 10 | 30 | 3.1 *s* |
| 7 | 40 *pixel* | 5 | 11 | 30 | 2.9 *s* |

In general we conclude from our experiments with those seven sequences that a coarse-to-fine strategy not only reduces computation time but also improves accuracy and robustness of stereo results.

## 5   Conclusions

In general, edge preprocessing leads to more accurate stereo correspondence results when using BP. This result, already indicated in [4], was further verified in more extensive research reported in this paper.

BP stereo results based on Sobel edge images appear to be better in general (for those seven sequences!) than those based on Kovesi-Owens or Canny preprocessing.

At a very general level, we conclude from our studies:

- The edge detector used for preprocessing should reflect and highlight important structural features of the original images.
- It should also not filter any depth-related information or features from the original images.
- It should not add any information or features, by overemphasizing some edge information.

Future work should also cover changes in brightness between left and right image, and some adaptation of parameters in general.

BP has potentials to match real-time requirements in driver assistance systems (DAS), because the BP message updating mechanism at each iteration is actually in parallel, that means multi-CPU hardware is able to reduce run time. Thus, BP is definitely a good candidate for further DAS related studies.

# References


1. Canny, J.: A computational approach to edge detection. IEEE Trans. Pattern Analysis Machine Intelligence 8, 679–714 (1986)
2. .enpeda.. Image Sequence Analysis Test Site (follow the data link), `www.mi.auckland.ac.nz/`
3. Felzenszwalb, P.F., Huttenlocher, D.P.: Efficient belief propagation for early vision. Int. J. Computer Vision 70, 41–54 (2006)
4. Guan, S., Klette, R.: Belief-propagation on edge images for stereo analysis of image sequences. In: Sommer, G., Klette, R. (eds.) RobVis 2008. LNCS, vol. 4931, pp. 291–302. Springer, Heidelberg (2008)
5. Klette, G.: Euclidean distance transform (August 2006), `http://www.cs.auckland.ac.nz/ rklette/TeachAuckland.html/mm/ MI30slides.pdf`
6. Klette, R.: Lecture notes about belief propagation, `http://www.cs.auckland.ac.nz/ rklette/TeachAuckland.html/mm/ MI66slides.pdf`
7. Kovesi, P.: Phase congruency detects corners and edges. In: The Australian Pattern Recognition Society Conference: DICTA 2003, pp. 309–318 (2003)
8. Liu, Z., Klette, R.: Performance evaluation of stereo and motion analysis on rectified image sequences. Technical report, Computer Science Department, The University of Auckland (2007)
9. Middlebury Stereo Website, `http://vision.middlebury.edu/stereo/`
10. Morrone, M.C., Owens, R.A.: Feature detection from local energy. Pattern Recognition Letters 6, 303–313 (1987)
11. Robbins, B., Owens, R.A.: 2D feature detection via local energy. Image and Vision Computing 15, 353–368 (1997)
12. Sobel, I., Feldman, G.: A $3 \times 3$ isotropic gradient operator for image processing. Presented at a talk at the Stanford Artificial Project in 1968 (unpublished)

# Region-Based Super Resolution for Video Sequences Considering Registration Error


Osama A. Omer* and Toshihisa Tanaka

Department of Electrical and Electronic Engineering, Tokyo University of Agriculture and Technology, 2-24-16, Nakacho, Koganei-shi, Tokyo 184-8588, Japan
`osama@sip.tuat.ac.jp, tanakat@cc.tuat.ac.jp`



**Abstract.** Super-resolution (SR) for video sequences is a technique to obtain a higher resolution image by fusing multiple low-resolution (LR) frames of the same scene. In a typical super-resolution algorithm, image registration is one of the most affective steps. The difficulty of this step results in the fact that most of the existing SR algorithms can not cope with local motions because they assume global motion. In this paper, we propose a SR algorithm that takes into account inaccurate estimates of the registration parameters and the point spread function. When frames obey the assumed global motion model, these inaccurate estimates, along with the additive Gaussian noise in the low-resolution image sequence, result in different noise level for each frame. However, in case of existence of local motion and/or occlusion, regions that have local motion and/or occlusion have different noise level. To cope with this problem, we propose to adaptively weight each segment according to its reliability. The segments are generated by segmenting the reference frame using watershed segmentation. The experimental results using real video sequences show the effectiveness of the proposed algorithm compared to three state-of-the-art SR algorithms.

**Keywords:** Super-resolution, affine model, image registration, resolution enhancement, region-based global weight.


## 1   Introduction

In many applications such as remote sensing, video surveillance, and medical diagnostics, the demand for high-resolution images is gradually increasing since high resolution images offer more details that provide to the viewer. One way to obtain high-resolution images is to physically reduce the pixel size and therefore increase the number of pixels per unit area. However, since a reduction of pixel size causes a decrease in the amount of light, shot noise is generated that severely degrades the image quality. Instead of altering the sensor manufacturing technology, digital image processing methods to obtain a high resolution image from low-resolution observations have been investigated by many researchers [3, 4, 5, 6, 7, 8, 9, 10, 11, 12, 13, 14, 15, 16, 17, 18, 19].

Super-resolution (SR) is an approach to obtain HR image(s) from a set of low-resolution (LR) images. The most important steps of SR algorithms are image registration and data fusion. Image registration process has been paid more attention for


---

* Part of this work has been done while the first author with Nokia R&D Tokyo-Japan center. This work is supported in part by Egyptian Ministry of High Education.

T. Wada, F. Huang, and S. Lin (Eds.): PSIVT 2009, LNCS 5414, pp. 944–954, 2009.
© Springer-Verlag Berlin Heidelberg 2009

the last two decades [1, 2]. However, image registration of images containing locally moving parts is still a challenging task. Data fusion is the process which fuses the registered images to construct the HR image. In most recently proposed SR algorithms [3, 4, 5, 6, 7, 8, 9, 10] the SR results depend on fusion step. As a cost function, the $L_2$- or $L_1$-norm is used to fuse LR images [3, 4, 5]. Also, the weighted $L_2$-norm is used measure function in [6, 7, 8, 9, 10]. The main problems of the previous SR algorithms are as follows. Even if $L_2$-norm is suitable for Gaussian noise, it is implicitly assumed that the extra resolution content is equally distributed among all LR images [3]. Therefore the result is obtained by averaging the contributions from all LR images. The averaging process leads to propagation of the outlier pixels from any of the LR images into the HR image which means that it fails with local motion. In spite of the fact that $L_1$-norm is suitable for Laplacian noise and robust against outliers[4, 5], it can not cope with errors resulting from occlusion that happens in video sequences containing local motions. The failure of this algorithm in case of occlusion is due to that, the model converges to the median over the measured data without pre-weighting the LR images, which may lead to failure in case of existence of locally moving parts in the scene.

To overcome the problems of registration error in locally moving parts, three techniques are appeared in the literature. The first is to use different global (or local) weight for different registration error level [6, 7, 8, 9, 10, 11]. The main idea behind this technique is to weight the frames (or pixels) that have high registration error with small weight or even discard them. The second is to use local motion (or multi-motion) estimation to improve the accuracy of registration in the locally moving parts [12, 13, 14]. The main idea behind this technique is to incorporate information from different frames as much as possible. The third is a combination of the previous categories.

The idea of using different weight for different registration error levels is used in the super resolution literature [6, 7, 8, 9, 10]. This idea is based on rejecting pixels or even whole frames that have high registration error. Two categories are used in the literature, the first is the global weighting [6, 7, 8], where each frame is weighted with certain weight based on the error in the whole frame. The second is the local weighting [9, 10], where each pixel has its individual weight. In [6], for each frame the weight is chosen so that it decreases as the error increases and increases as the smoothness of the HR image increases. Three weighting functions are presented in [6], namely, linear, square root and logarithmic functions. The main problem of this method is that it globally weights each frame, then in case of existence of occlusion and/or local motion the whole frame will be weighted with small weight even if only the parts that have occlusion and/or local motion parts are inaccurately registered then they should be penalized by small weight. Moreover, assuming affine motion model can result in different error level for different region if the actual motion is projective motion. A similar algorithm is proposed in [7]. In this algorithm, the authors proposed to use a global weight for each frame and also have different regularization parameter so that as the error increases the weight decreases and the regularization parameter increases. This algorithm suggests different regularization for different frame, however it is still have the same problem as that in [6] in case of existence of occlusion and/or local motion. In [8], the global weighting function is used as exponential function of the registration error. This algorithm is a modified version of [6], where the convexity of weighting function is taken into consideration.

On the other hand, the use of local weights has been proposed [9, 10, 11, 12, 13]. However, in [9], the weights are not adaptive to the registration error and then it can not cope with the error resulting from inaccurate image registration. In [13], weights are determined based on the information about the corrupting noise which is not known in practical. In [11], a pixel-level selection strategy for outlier rejection is proposed. In this algorithm, a similarity measure is used to determine the reliability of each LR pixel in the SR estimation process. Pixel is discarded from the estimation process if the measure evaluated at this pixel location is greater than certain threshold. The performance of this algorithm highly depends on the selection of the threshold. In [10], local weights have been selected for each pixel using an exponential function. The registration error (the absolute difference between the reference frame and the warped frames) has been used as exponent. The main problem of this algorithms is that the local weights are sensitive to noise because they are determined pixel by pixel.

In addition, region segmentation has been used before to enhance resolution [15, 16, 17, 18]. In [15, 16], a region-based super-resolution algorithm is proposed in which different filters are used according to the type of region. But in this method the segmentation information is not fully used where it is used only to classify regions into homogeneous and inhomogeneous regions. In [17], the image is segmented into different types of regions according to the local higher order statistics (HOS). The weight function of the regularization term is determined by the segmentation label. This method achieves anisotropic diffusion for edge pixel and isotropic diffusion for pixel in smooth region. In [18], the image is segmented into background and different objects and each of these are super-resolved separately using traditional technique [19] and then the super-resolved regions are merged to construct the HR image.

The motivation of this paper is therefore to develop a robust algorithm that can cope with the local registration errors even by using global motion estimation technique. To do that, we propose to segment the reference frame into arbitrary shaped regions and to use a global weight for each region. For each region, the weight is adjusted so that region with high registration error (due to local motion in this region) will be considered with small weight or even discarded depending on the amount of error. This technique can achieve better results than both global and local weighting techniques because it combines the advantages of both techniques, where weights are less sensitive to noise and also regions which don't suffer from registration error will not be affected by weights.

## 2  Problem Description and Error Modeling

### 2.1  Observation Model

Assume that $K$ LR frames of the same scene in Lexicographical order denoted by $\underline{Y}_k(1 \le k \le K)$, each containing $M^2$ pixels, are observed, and they are generated from the HR frame denoted by $\underline{X}$, containing $L^2$ pixels, where $L \ge M$. We use the underscore notation to indicate a vector. The observation of $K$ LR frames are modeled by the following degradation process:

$$\underline{Y}_k = D_k H_k F_k \underline{X} + \underline{V}_k, \tag{1}$$

where $F_k$, $H_k$ and $D_k$ are the motion operator, the blurring operator (due to camera), and the down-sampling operator respectively, $\underline{X}$ is the unknown HR frame, $\underline{Y}_k$ is the $k^{th}$ observed LR frame, and $\underline{V}_k$ is an additive random noise for the $k^{th}$ frame. We assume that $H_k$ are constant for all the $K$ frames ($H_k = H$ for all $1 \leq k \leq K$), and $D_k$ are constant for all the $K$ frames ($D_k = D$ for all $1 \leq k \leq K$). Then the degradation model is simplified as

$$\underline{Y}_k = DHF_k\underline{X} + \underline{V}_k. \tag{2}$$

Throughout the paper, we assume that $D$ and $H$ are known and the additive noise is Gaussian with zero mean. Therefore the problem here in this paper is to find the original image $\underline{X}$.

## 2.2  Iterative Super-Resolution

To avoid matrixes inversion, super-resolution problem is usually solved iteratively. In order to minimize the error function in (3), the method of iterative gradient descent is commonly employed [9].

$$J(\underline{X}) = \sum_{k=1}^{K} \rho\left(DHF_k\underline{X} - \underline{Y}_k\right) + \lambda Z(\underline{X}) \tag{3}$$

where $\rho$ is a general data fidelity function, $Z$ is the property function and $\lambda$ is the regularization parameter. This optimization technique seeks to converge towards a local minimum following the trajectory defined by the negative gradient. That is, at iteration $n$, the high-resolution image according to observation $\underline{Y}^k$, is updated as

$$\underline{X}^{n+1} = \underline{X}^n + \beta \sum_{k=1}^{K} \underline{R}_k^n \tag{4}$$

where $\underline{R}_k^n$ is the residual gradient at for frame $k$ at iteration $n$. It is computed as

$$\underline{R}_k^n = F_k^T H^T D^T \psi\left(DHF_k\underline{X}^n - \underline{Y}_k\right) + \lambda \Phi(\underline{X}^n) \tag{5}$$

where $\psi$ is the gradient of the data fidelity term, and $\Phi$ is the gradient of the regularization term. This equation reveals that the iterative super-resolution method is in fact an iterative fusion of the gradients of the cost function. Using this idea, Mejdi et. al proposed to use LMS-based adaptive weight for gradient at each pixel. Also, the global weighting method can be seen as globally weighting the gradient at each frame.

## 3  Region-Based Weight for Super-Resolution

In this paper we propose to use exponential function to globally weight each region rather than the whole frame. It is assumed that each region have the same motion and

---

**Algorithm 1.** The proposed algorithm.

Pre-compute:

1. register low-resolution frames with respect to the reference frame using Lucas-Kanade affine motion model [2],
2. segment the reference frame into sub-regions using watershed segmentation.

Iterate until convergence:

1. determine weights for each region using Eqs. 6 to 8,
2. update HR image using steepest decent using Eq. 4.

---

then have the same error level. Therefore, weighting each region with same weight is a reasonable choice. The weight for region $\Re_i$ in frame $k$ is weighted as follows: let the error vector at frame $k$ be

$$\underline{E}^k = DHF^k\underline{X} - \underline{Y}^k, \tag{6}$$

we define the error value at each region as

$$E^k_{\Re_i} = \frac{1}{N_\Re} \sum_{j \in \Re_i} |\underline{E}^k(j)| \tag{7}$$

and $N_{\Re_i}$ is the number of pixels in region $\Re_i$. To spread the range of $E^k_{\Re_i}$ between 0 and 1, the values $E^k_{\Re_i}$ for all regions are divided by the maximum value for the same region among the frames $P_{\Re_i}$. Then the weight at each region is used as

$$W^k_{\Re_i} = \exp\left(-\frac{E^k_{\Re_i}}{P_{\Re_i}}\right), \tag{8}$$

The weights are normalized so that the summation of the weights for the same region equals the number of frames. The whole algorithm is described in 1. The data fidelity term in the error function is used as the weighted $L_1$-norm. While the regularization term is used as bilateral total variation [4, 5]. The updating equation can be described as:

$$\underline{X}^{n+1} = \underline{X}^n + \beta \left\{ \sum_{k=1}^{K} F^{k^T} H^T D^T W^k sign\left(DHF^k\underline{X}^n - \underline{Y}^k\right) \right.$$

$$\left. + \lambda \sum_{l=-P}^{P} \sum_{m=-P}^{P} \alpha^{|l|+|m|}\left(\mathcal{I} - S_x^{-l}S_y^{-m}\right) sign\left(\underline{X}^n - S_x^l S_y^m \underline{X}^n\right) \right\} \tag{9}$$

where $S_x^l$ and $S_y^m$ are the shifting operators in $x$ and $y$ by $l$ and $m$ respectively, $S_x^{-l}$ and $S_y^{-m}$ are the inverse operator for $S_x^l$ and $S_y^m$ respectively, $sign$ is the signum function, and $0 < \alpha < 1$, $\beta$ is a scalar representing the step size in the direction of the gradient.

# 4   Simulation Results and Discussion

## 4.1   Data Set

For test, two different video sequences including Table Tennis and Mobile sequence are tested. Both of the two sequences are in SIF format ($240 \times 352$). Color images are commonly represented by the RGB channels. However, humans are more sensitive to changes in luminance than to changes in color. Thus, instead of using the RGB color model, we use the YCbCr color space where the Y channel represents luminance and the Cb and Cr channels represent chromaticity. In our method, the chromaticity components from the Cb and Cr channels are simply interpolated using bicubic interpolation from the low-resolution image to the target high-resolution image. Hence, only the luminance values from the Y channel are used in the resolution enhancement process. Moreover, we assumed that the sequence is already demosaicked or captured by three CCD sensors.

## 4.2   Experiment Setup

To test the efficiency of the proposed region-based weight, we compared the proposed algorithm with three state-of-the-art SR algorithms, namely $L_2$-norm [3], $L_1$-norm [4] and frame-based weighted $L_2$-norm [8]. In the simulation, we used 20 steepest decent iterations for all the algorithms.

In the simulation, two scenarios are used to evaluate the efficiency of the proposed algorithm. In the first scenario, we assumed that the available sequence is HR sequence then the LR frames were generated from the original HR video sequences according to the model as in (2), where the frames were blurred by Gaussian operator ($5 \times 5$ with variance equal 1), down-sampled by a decimation factor of 2 in the horizontal and vertical directions, and distorted by an additive white Gaussian noise with 30 dB signal-to-noise ratio. Then we used different SR algorithm to reverse these operations. This enables us to compare the resulting HR frames with the original HR frame. In the second scenario, we directly applied SR algorithms to enhance the resolution for a given sequence where the original HR frames are unknown. In the following results, we applied the first scenario to the Table Tennis sequence, and we applied the second scenario to the Mobile sequence.

## 4.3   Results and Discussion

Figure 1 shows the first LR frame and the segmented regions of each of Table Tennis and Mobile sequences. For their importance, the locally moving objects are marked with ellipses or rectangles.

To show the efficiency of the proposed algorithm, zoomed part containing moving objects is shown in Fig. 2. In this figure, zoomed parts of the resulting HR image using different SR algorithms are shown. Obviously shown in this figure that using L2-norm is sensitive to registration error which is obvious at the locally moving parts as ball and train in this example (see Fig. 2a) where the projection of the registration error of each LR frame appears. Also, although it is robust to registration error, L1-norm cannot cope

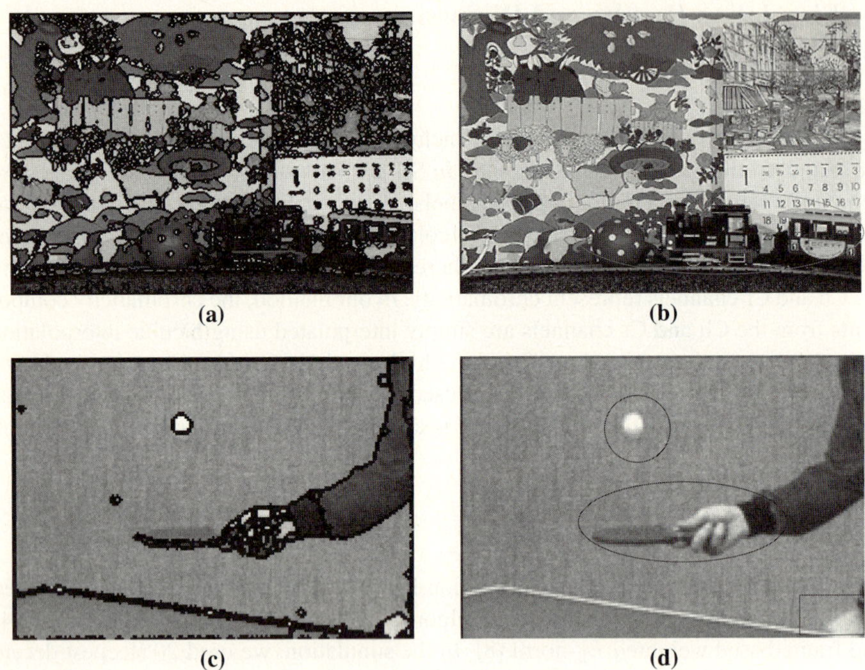

**Fig. 1.** Mobile sequence: (a) Segmented regions, (b) LR frame, and Table Tennis sequence: (c) Segmented regions, (d) LR frame

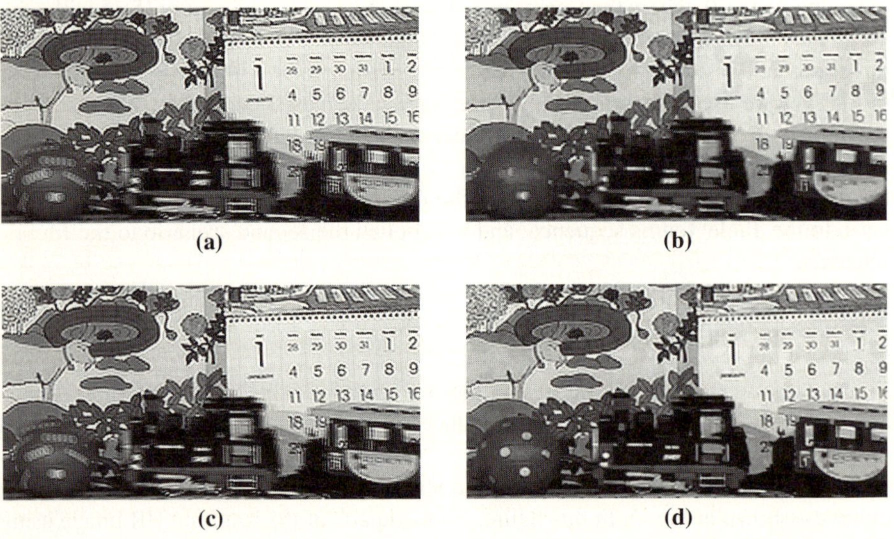

**Fig. 2.** Mobile sequence: HR frame using; (a) L2-norm [3], (b) L1-norm [4], (c) Global weighted L2-norm [8], and (d) proposed algorithm

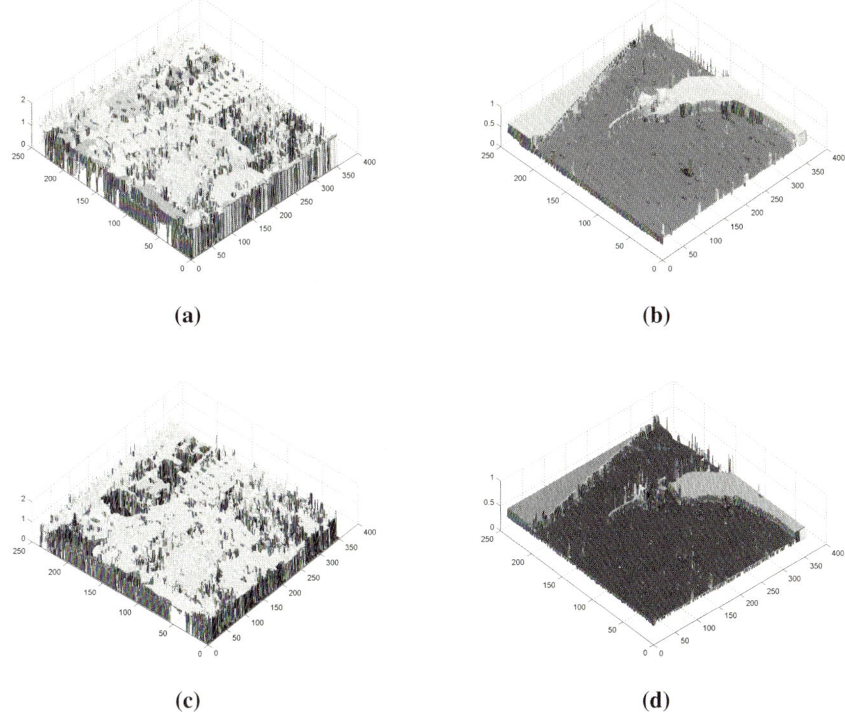

(a)              (b)

(c)              (d)

**Fig. 3.** Local weights for the second frame using proposed method for: (a) mobile sequence, and (b) Tennis sequence, Local weights for the fourth frame for: (c) mobile sequence, and (d) Tennis sequence

with the local registration error. Instead of projecting the registration error of all LR frames, L1-norm select the median over the LR frames which is not suitable for local registration error as shown in Fig. 2b. In addition, using frame-based weight is suitable in case of global registration error and when the area of local errors is big so that global weight can be dominated by these local errors and then frames containing this error can be discarded. However, in case of small moving objects the global weight (frame-based weight) is not suitable as shown in Fig. 2c. On the other hand, using region-based weighting function can overcome the problem of local motion and/or occlusion as shown in Fig. 2d.

Another example to demonstrate the effectiveness of the proposed algorithm is shown in Fig. 4. In this example, the LR frames are generated from known HR frames using the model in Eq. 2. The original HR frame is shown in Fig. 4a. This sequence contains three locally moving objects as marked in Fig. 1d. Due to averaging over the LR frames, L2-norm deforms the moving objects as shown in Fig. 4b where the upper hand and ball are repeated and the lower hand partially disappeared. Also, using L1-norm and frame-based weight still have the same problems with locally moving objects as lower hand and ball. On the other hand, using region-based weight overcame the problem of local motion in most of regions as ball, upper and lower hand. However, a small

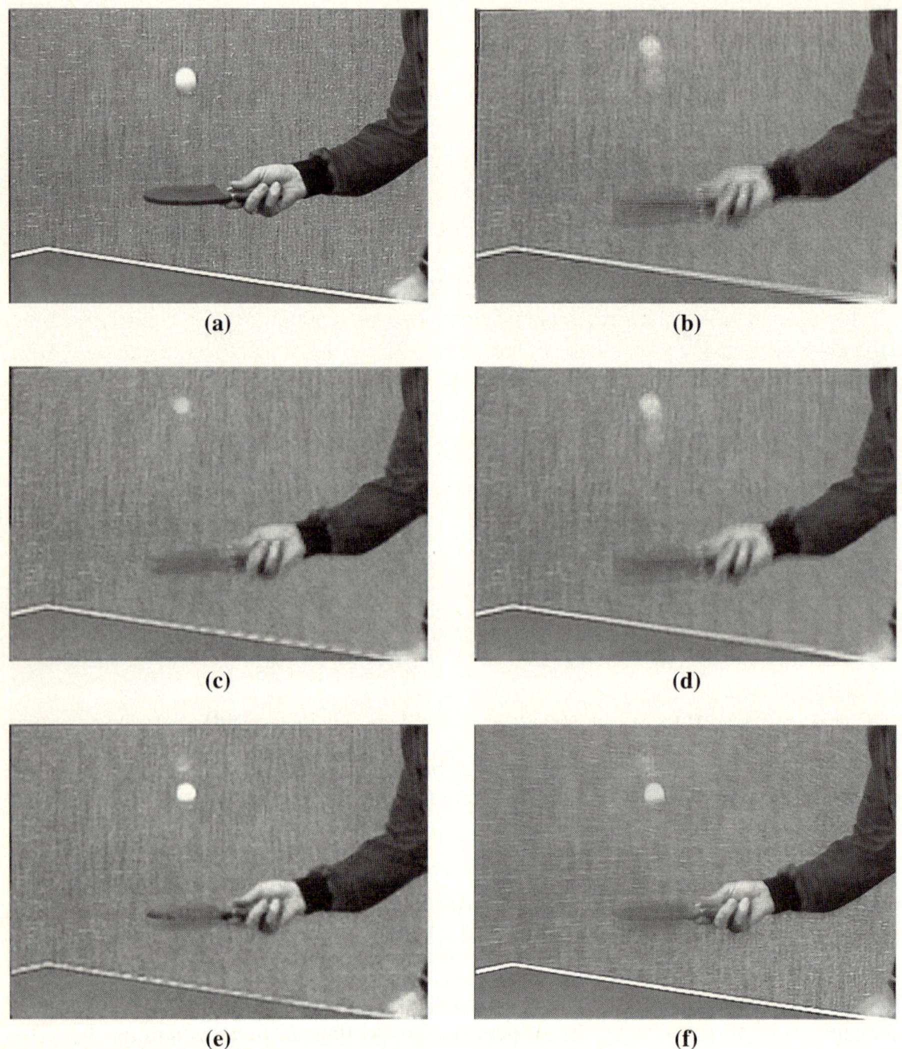

**Fig. 4.** Table Tennis sequence, (a) Original HR frame, HR frame using; (b) L2-norm [3], (c) L1-norm [4], (d) Global weighted L2-norm [8], (e) proposed algorithm, and the HR frame beyond the available resolution using proposed algorithm

deformation in the background at the occluded part appears. This deformation is due to that the weights of some inaccurately registered regions are very small but not zero so small error still appears in the HR frame as shown in Fig. 4e. Moreover, to show the efficiency of the proposed algorithm, the resolution is increased beyond the available resolution (the resolution of the original frames) as shown in Fig. 4f.

The weights for two different frames (second and fourth frames) for the tested sequences are plotted in three dimensions in Fig. 3. This figure shows how the proposed weighting function penalizes the local registration error for each region.

# 5   Conclusion

In this paper, we presented an algorithm for image and video resolution enhancement. The proposed algorithm takes into account inaccurate estimates of the registration parameters and the point spread function. These inaccurate estimates, along with the additive Gaussian noise in the low-resolution image sequence, result in different noise level for each frame. However, in case of existence of local motion and/or occlusion, regions that have local motion and/or occlusion have different noise level. The proposed algorithm is based on global weighting for each region. The weights are determined globally for each region. The regions are determined by segmenting the reference frame into sub-regions using watershed segmentation. The proposed algorithm can cope with the local motion and occlusion problems. Affine motion model is assumed. For color video sequences, only the luminance is processed with the super-resolution algorithm while the chrominance is interpolated using bicubic interpolation. Also, the sequences are assumed to be demosaicked or being captured by three CCD sensors.

# References


1. Bergen, J.R., Anandan, P., Hanna, K.J., Hingorani, R.: Hierarchical model-based motion estimation. In: Sandini, G. (ed.) ECCV 1992. LNCS, vol. 588, pp. 237–252. Springer, Heidelberg (1992)
2. Lucas, B., Kanade, T.: An iterative image registration technique with an application to stereo vision. In: Proceedings of the International Joint Conference on Artificial Intelligence (1981)
3. Elad, M., Hel-Or, Y.: A fast super-resolution reconstruction algorithm for pure transnational motion and common space invariant blur. IEEE Trans. on Image Processing 10(8), 1187–1193 (2001)
4. Farsiu, S., Robinson, D., Elad, M., Milanfar, P.: Fast and robust multi-frame super-resolution. IEEE Trans. on Image Processing 13(10), 1327–1344 (2004)
5. Farsiu, S., Robinson, D., Elad, M., Milanfar, P.: Robust shift-and-add approach to super-resolution. In: Proc. of the 2003 SPIE Conf. on Applications of Digital Signal and Image Processing, San Diego, California (August 2003)
6. Lee, E.S., Kang, M.G.: Regularized adaptive high-resolution image reconstruction considering inaccurate subpixel registration. IEEE Trans. on Image Processing 12(7) (July 2003)
7. He, H., Kondi, L.P.: An image super-resolution algorithm for different error levels per frame. IEEE Trans. on Image Processing 15(3), 592–603 (2006)
8. Park, M.K., Kang, M.G., Katsaggelos, A.K.: Regularized Super-Resolution Image Reconstruction Considering Inaccurate Motion Information. SPIE Optical Engineering 46(11), 117004-1–117004-12 (2007)
9. Trimeche, M., Ciprian Bilcu, R., Yrjanainen, J.: Adaptive outlier rejection in image super-resolution. EURASIP Journal on Applied Signal Processing 2006, Article ID 38052 (2006)
10. Omer, O.A., Tanaka, T.: Multiframe image and video super-resolution algorithm with inaccurate motion registration errors rejection. In: Proc. of the 2008 SPIE Conf. on Visual Communication and Image Processing, San Jose, California (January 2008)
11. Ivanovski, Z.A., Panovski, L., Karam, L.J.: Robust super-resolution based on pixel-level selectivity. In: Proceedings of SPIE, vol. 6077 (2006)
12. Schultz, R.R., Stevenson, R.t.L.: Extraction of high-resolution frames from video sequences. IEEE Trans. on Image Processing 5(6) (June 1996)

13. Zhao, W.Y., Sawhney, S.: Is super-resolution with optical flow feasible? In: Heyden, A., Sparr, G., Nielsen, M., Johansen, P. (eds.) ECCV 2002. LNCS, vol. 2350, pp. 599–613. Springer, Heidelberg (2002)
14. Andrew, J., Patti, M.I.: Robust methods for high-quality stills from interlaced video in the presence of dominant motion. IEEE Trans. on Circuits and Systems for Video Technology 7(2) (April 1997)
15. Choi, B., Ra, J.B.: Region-based super-resolution using multiple blurred and noisy undersampled images. In: IEEE International Conference on Acoustics, Speech, and Signal Processing, vol. 2, pp. 609–612 (2006)
16. Choi, B., Kim, S.D., Ra, J.B.: Region-based super-resolution using adaptive diffusion regularization. Optical Engineering 47(2), 027006 (February 2008)
17. Qiao, J., Liu, J.: HOS-based image super-resolution reconstruction. In: Sebe, N., Liu, Y., Zhuang, Y.-t., Huang, T.S. (eds.) MCAM 2007. LNCS, vol. 4577, pp. 213–222. Springer, Heidelberg (2007)
18. van Eekeren, A., Schutte, K., Dijk, J., de Lange, D.J.J., van Vliet, L.J.: Super-resolution on moving objects and background. In: Proc. Int. Conf. Image Processing (ICIP 2006), vol. 2, pp. 2709–2712 (2006)
19. Hardie, R.C., Barnard, K.J., Bognar, J.G., Armstrong, E., Watson, E.A.: High-resolution image reconstruction from a sequence of rotated and translated frames and its application to an infrared imaging system. Optical Engineering 37(1), 247–260 (1998)
20. De Smet, P., De Vleschauwer, D.: Performance and scalability of highly optimized rainfalling watershed algorithm. In: Proc. Int. Conf. on Imaging Science, Systems and Technology, CISST 1998, Las Vegas, NV, USA, pp. 266–273 (July 1998)

# A High Performance H.264 Deblocking Filter

Vagner Rosa, Altamiro Susin, and Sergio Bampi

Federal University of Rio Grande do Sul – Informatics Institute
Av. Bento Gonçalves, 9500 - Campus do Vale - Bloco IV
Bairro Agronomia - Porto Alegre - RS -Brasil
CEP 91501-970 Caixa Postal: 15064
vsrosa@inf.ufrgs.br, Altamiro.Susin@ufrgs.br, bampi@inf.ufrgs.br

**Abstract.** Although the H.264 Deblocking Filter process is a relatively small piece of code in a software implementation, profile results shows it cost about a third of the total CPU time in the decoder. This work presents a high performance architecture for implementing a H.264 Deblocking Filter IP that can be used either in the decoder or in the encoder as a hardware accelerator for a processor or embedded in a full-hardware codec. A developed IP using the proposed architecture support multiple high definition processing flows in real-time.

## 1 Introduction

The standard developed by the ISO/IEC MPEG-4 Advanced Video Coding (AVC) and ITU-T H.264 experts set new levels of video quality for a given bit-rate. In fact, H.264 (from this point the standard will be referred only by its ITU-T denomination) outperforms previous standards in bit-rate reduction. In H.264 an Adaptative Deblocking Filter is included in the standard to reduce blocking artifacts, very common in very high compressed video streams. In fact, most video codecs use some filtering as a pre/post-processing task. The main goal of the inclusion of this kind of filter as a part of the standard was to put it inside the feedback loop in the encoding process. As a consequence, a standardized, well tuned, and inside the encoding loop filter could be designed, achieving better objective and subjective image quality for the same bit-rate. The H.264 Deblocking Filter is located in the DPCM loop as shown in Figure 1 for the decoder (it is also called Loop Filter by this reason). Exactly the same filter is used in the encoder and the decoder. The Deblocking Filter in the H.264 standard is not only a single low pass filter, but a complex decision algorithm and filtering process with 5 different filter strengths. Its objective is to maintain the sharpness of the real images while eliminating the artifacts introduced by intra-frame and inter-frame predictions at low bit-rates, while mitigating the characteristic "blurring" effect of the filter at high bit-rates.

The filter itself is very optimized, with very small kernels of simple coefficients, but the complexity of the decision logic and filtering process makes the H.264 Deblocking Filter responsible for about one third [4] of the processing power needed in the decoder process.

T. Wada, F. Huang, and S. Lin (Eds.): PSIVT 2009, LNCS 5414, pp. 955–964, 2009.

In this paper an architecture for the H.264 deblocking filter is proposed. The architecture was developed focusing FPGA, aiming making a balanced use of the resources (logic, registers, and memory) available in FPGA architectures, although it can be synthesized using an ASIC flow. The performance goal was to exceed 1080p requirements when synthesized to a XILINX Virtex II FPGA. A Xilinx Virtex II pro FPGA was used to validate the developed IP.

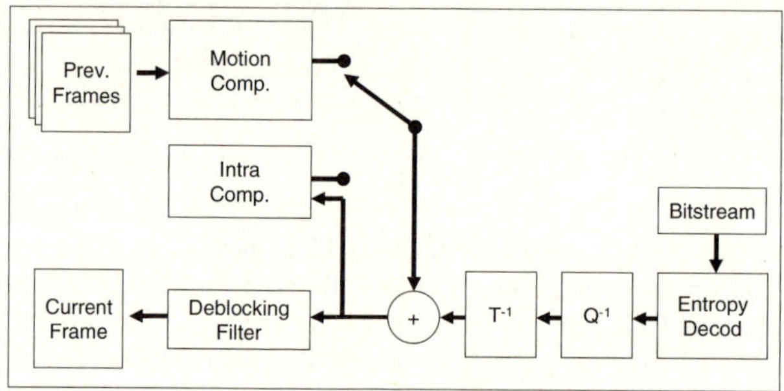


**Fig. 1.** H.264 Decoder

The rest of this paper is organized as follows. The section 2 describes the standardized algorithm for the H.264 deblocking filter. Section 3 presents the proposed architecture and section 4 the results obtained. Finally the section 5 presents the conclusions and future work.

## 2  Deblocking Filter Algorithm

In the H.264 standard the image is divided in small units called blocks. Each block is 4x4 pixels. The color format is YCbCr 4:2:0 (main profile), meaning the crominance (croma) components being sub-sampled to half the sample rate of the luminance (luma) in both directions. The blocks are then grouped in macroblocks which is a 4x4 block matrix for luma and 2x2 matrix for each croma component. Each block edge has to be filtered. The Deblocking Filter is applied to each decoded block of a given macroblock for luma and croma samples in raster scan order. For each block, four different edges are filtered separately, in the sequence presented in Figure 2.

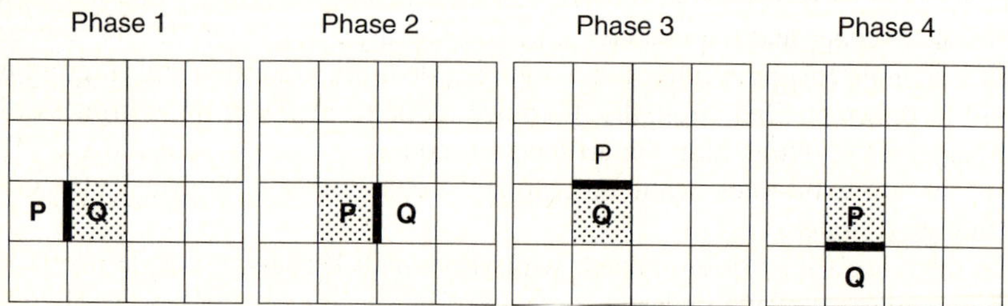


**Fig. 2.** Edge positions for a given 4x4 block inside a 16x16 macroblock

For each block edge, the filter is applied to the pixel component values perpendicular to that edge. The naming conventions for the pixels around the edge are showed in figure 3. Pixel components in both the current (Q) and the previews (P) block can have values changed. Pixels already modified during a filter stage can be modified again in a subsequent filter operation (this causes some data dependencies). The filtering algorithm is adaptive, so that the pixel values, the position of a block inside the macroblock, the type of prediction employed (inter or intra), the motion vectors (inter prediction) and the quantization parameter are taken into account for the boundary strength calculation.

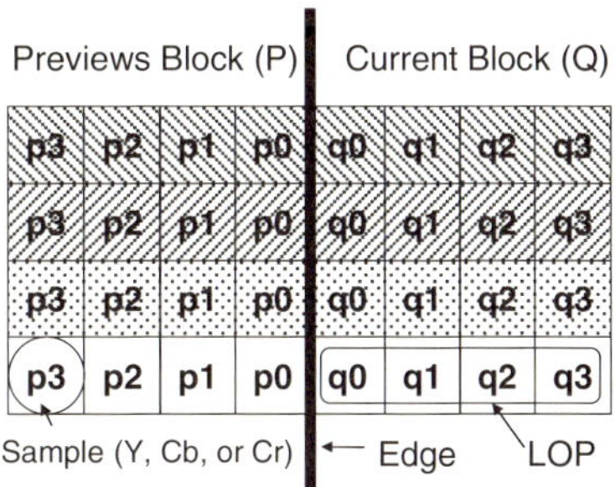


**Fig. 3.** Filter conventions

The boundary strength (BS) can assume five different values from 0 (no filtering) to 4 (strongest filtering) and is defined as follows.

• If the edge is not a slice edge (the filter is not applied across slice edges) then the filter can be applied, else BS=0. Based on pixel values, it can be found that a edge can contain a natural discontinuity in the values, making the BS to be set to 0.

• If the block is intra coded, then BS=3 if it is an internal edge or BS=4 if it is a external edge. Internal edges are those involving two blocks of the same macroblock, while external edges are those involving two blocks from different macoblocks.

• If neither blocks are intra-coded and at least one contain coded coefficients (non zero transform residues) then BS=2

• BS=1 is used when none of the above conditions are satisfied and the reference frames of two blocks are different or when the reference frames are the same but any component of the two motion vectors has difference more than 4 (1 pixel sample).

The Boundary Strength for croma is the same as for the corresponding luma block, but the filters employed for luma and croma are different. The quantization parameter (QP) and the pixel values are taken into account. The parameters α and β are QP dependent and set thresholds for filtering to be applied. Saturation functions (clip and clip3) need do be used in some steps of the calculations. This makes the BS decision logic a complex set of sequential calculations. The BS calculation needs to be done for every LOP (Line Of Pixels – figure 3) pair. More details on Deblocking Filter process can be obtained in [1] and a complete flowchart in [3].

# 3  Proposed Architecture

The proposed architecture was developed to exceed HDTV 1080p resolution requirements (1920x1080x30) in the H.264 Main Profile. The initial architectural concept was initially based on the work developed by [4], but was evolved to be a datapath block, different from the coprocessor block proposed by [4]. The primary differences from this work related to others found in the literature ([4], [5] and their references) are the use of local memory for the whole process, instead of accessing the main memory. The use of FPGAs as a primary implementation device also leaded to some architectural decisions that leaded to a more efficient resources usage and higher speed. In this scenario, the development of high-depth pipeline architecture was straightforward: each Logic Element in current FPGA can behave as a look-up-table (LUT), a single bit flip-flop (register), and a carry logic at the same time. The unneeded parts of the logic elements (ex. Flip-flops in combinational logic block) are bypassed and can not be used in other blocks due to routing limitations in typical FPGA architectures.

## 3.1  Numbering and Color Conventions

Figure 4 illustrates the block numbering and macroblock color convention adopted from this point.

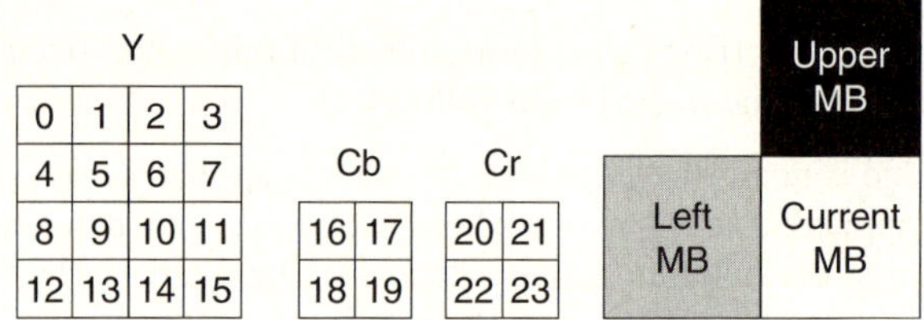

**Fig. 4.** Luma and Croma block enumeration; Macroblock color diagram

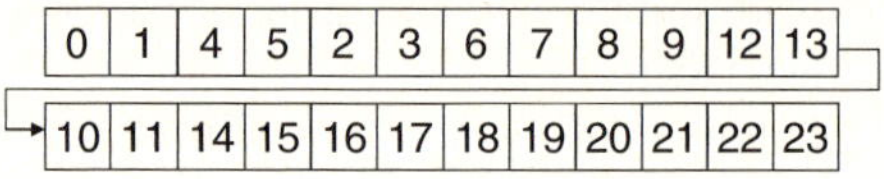

**Fig. 5.** Input block sequence in the input buffer of the Deblocking Filter

The input data for a given luma/croma macroblock arrives in the sequence presented in Figure 5: Y first, then Cb and Cr; double Z scan for luma.

## 3.2  Proposed Filter Architecture

In the Deblocking Filter process, the edge filter is the heart of the process. It is responsible for all filter functionality, including the thresholds and BS calculation and filtering itself. The remaining of the process is only sequence control and memory for block ordering.

The Edge Filter architecture can accept one LOP per cycle for Q and P blocks and produce the filtered Q' and P' LOP. This process is illustrated in Figure 6 (parameter lines are omitted for simplicity). Using this scheme, an entire block border will enter in the Edge Filter each four cycles (one block border is four LOPs tall, as illustrated in Figure 3).

**Fig. 6.** Edge Filter

Based on the diagram presented in Figure 6, a pipelined architecture for the Edge Filter was designed. As stated before, the procedure for calculation of all parameters needed to decide whether to filter or not and what BS to use requires a lot of sequential calculations (data dependencies). The pipelined architecture was designed so that only one arithmetic or logic operation is to be done every stage of the pipeline. This lead to an 11-stage pipeline only to calculate the BS, used to select the correct filter. All the filters could be done in parallel to BS calculation, so a 12 stage pipeline would be enough to achieve the maximum possible operation frequency. However, if an entire column of luma blocks (for vertical edges) that consist of four blocks stacked are processed before the next one, the first LOP of the first Q block (the uppermost) will be the first LOP of the first P block after 16 LOP cycles. If an Edge Filter architecture with a 16 stage pipeline can be designed, the output P' could be connected directly to the input Q. The croma Cb and Cr, wich are half the height (only 2 blocks tall), can be stacked so they can be processed as a luma block. This approach makes the implementation of the control logic much simpler. A 16-stage pipelined Edge Filter, presented in Figure 7, was then designed to meet the above criteria.

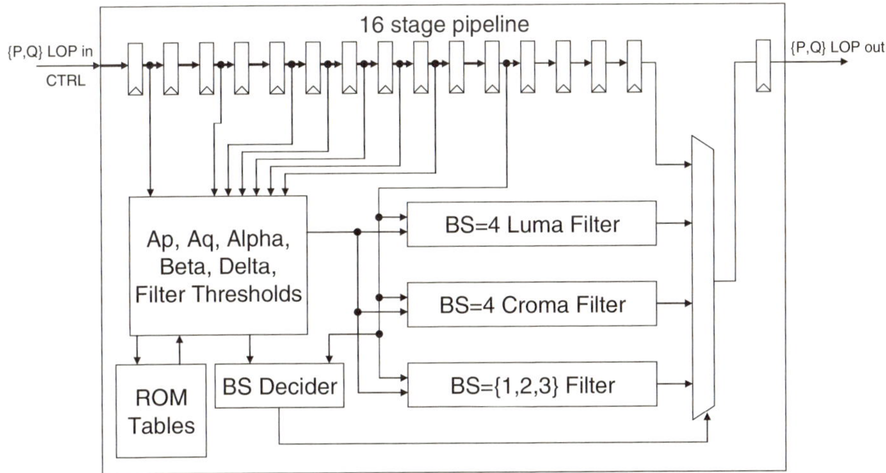


**Fig. 7.** Edge Filter

The architecture presented in figure 7 consumes two LOPs (one for Q and other for P blocks) and their respective parameters (QP, offsets, prediction type and neighborhood information) every clock cycle, producing two filtered LOPs (Q' and P') 16 clock cycles later.

This pipelined edge filter can be then encapsulated in such way only the Q input and P' outputs are visible, as illustrated in Figure 8.

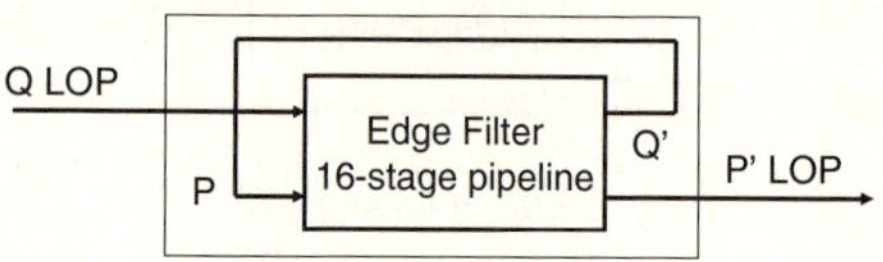


**Fig. 8.** Filter encapsulation

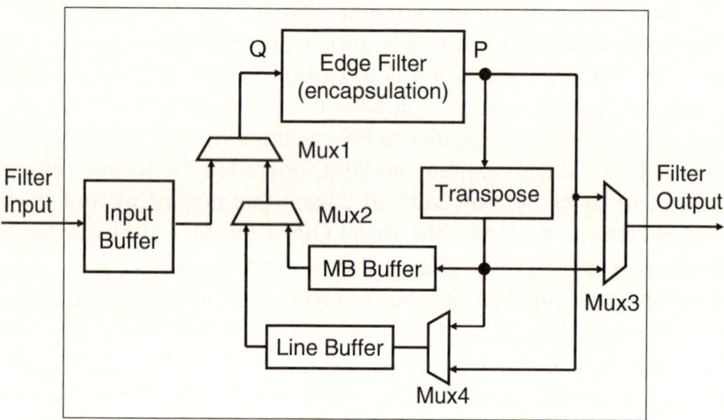


**Fig. 9.** Proposed Deblocking Filter architecture

Using this encapsulation turns the control logic simpler, but at a cost of a small overhead: P data can only be fed by the Q input, so the first P data need to be fed 16 cycles before the filtering process can start. During this 16 cycles, the BS should be forced to 0, so that no filtering is applied to P data while they passes through the Q datapath. After finishing the processing of a macroblock, the Edge filter must be emptied, so another 16 cycle have to be spent. Fortunately, the empting and filling phases stages can be overlapped, so the overhead is much lower.

Finally, the architecture of the proposed deblocking filter is presented in Figure 9. As stated in section 2, the filter has to be applied to both vertical and horizontal edges. In the proposed architecture, a single Edge Filter filters both horizontal and vertical edges. A transpose block is employed to convert vertically aligned samples in the block into horizontally aligned ones, so that horizontal edges can be filtered by the same Edge Filter.

The input buffer is needed only for data reordering, as input blocks arrive in a different order they are consumed in the deblocking process.

The MB and Line buffers are used to store blocks and block information data (QP, type, filter offset, state) which are not completely filtered (horizontal or vertical filtering is missing). The size of MB buffer is 32 blocks (512 samples plus 32 block information data) and the line buffer depends on the maximum frame size the filter is supposed to process (7680 samples, plus 480 block information data for a 1080p HDTV frame).

## 3.3  Filter Operation

The filter data flow description follows. First, pixel and control data are fed to the filter toward the Input Buffer. This buffer is needed because data is read from input buffer in a different order it comes in. Also this buffer provides some burst capability, as it accept one LOP per clock cycle. Once a complete luma/croma macroblock is available in the input buffer, the filtering process can be started.

The Encapsulated Edge Filter entity contains a 16 stage pipeline edge filter where the input P is connected to the output Q. The mux1 and mux2 are set so that MB buffer data is fed to the input Q of the Encapsulated Edge Filter. The data read from the MB buffer is the blocks 3, 7, 11, and 15 from the left macroblock. As the data is read one LOP at a time, it takes four clock cycles to read an entire block into the Encapsulated Edge Filter.

Exactly 16 cycles are needed to read four 4x4 blocks. During this phase the filter is set to bypass (BS=0), so pixel data fed are not filtered. As stated before, the Q output of the Edge Filter is connected to the P input in the encapsulated edge filter. The next clock cycle after the load of the aforementioned blocks will put then into the edge filter again, but in the P input. At this point, the mux1 is switched so the Encapsulated Edge Filter can receive data from the Input Buffer. The blocks 0, 4, 8, and 12 is read from input buffer, a LOP at a time.

The Edge Filter Process now is being fed with the data needed for the filtering process for the external vertical edge to start. Immediately after the block 12 the blocks 1, 5, 9, and 13 can be fed and then the blocks 2, 6, 10, 14 and 3, 7, 11, 15. 32 cycles after the block 3 from the left MB started being read from the MB buffer, the filtered block 3 will appear at the P output of the Encapsulated Edge Filter.

The data can take 3 different destinations: the MB Buffer, The Line Buffer or the output of the filter. In the case of the blocks 3, 7 and 11, there is no other processing to be done for these blocks, and the mux3 is selected to output directly from the output P of the Encapsulated Edge Filter. The block 15 from the left macroblock is fed to the Line Buffer toward the Transpose process to be used latter in the horizontal filtering process. The blocks 0 to 15 are sent to the MB buffer toward the Transpose to be filtered horizontally. The Transpose takes for cycles for reading the entire block and makes it available in the transposed form.

After filtering the vertical edge of all luma blocks the job for the horizontal edge can be done. In order to obtain the maximum throughput, the croma vertical filtering is done immediately after the luma. Then, blocks 17, 19, 21, and 23 from the left Cb and Cr macroblock are read from the MB Buffer. Notice that the Cb and Cr blocks are stacked in order to achieve the 16 LOPs needed to fill the Edge Filter pipeline. As with the luma blocks, this initial operation only loads the Edge Filter with the P blocks and then the filter is deactivated. Then the croma blocks 16, 18, 20, and 22 are read from Input Buffer and then the blocks 17, 19, 21, and 23. The blocks 17 and 21 from the left Cb and Cr macroblocks, respectively are completely filtered and then can be sent to the output. The blocks 19 and 23 from the left Cb and Cr macroblocks respectively are send to the Line Buffer toward the Transposer in order to be used in the horizontal external edge filtering. The blocks from the current Cb and Cr macroblocks are stored transposed in the MB Buffer for the horizontal filtering process.

At this moment, the horizontal edge filtering for luma and croma can take place. The luma data dependency was solved by the luma/croma interleaving and the blocks 12, 13, 14, and 15 from the upper macroblock stored in the Line Buffer are fed to the Encapsulated Edge Filter, followed by the blocks 0, 1, 2 and 3 from the current macroblock stored in the MB Buffer. The process follows by reading the blocks 4, 5, 6, and 7 and then 8, 9, 10, 11 and finally, 12, 13, 14 and 15. The output of the Encapsulated Edge Filter has different destinations. The blocks 12, 13, 14, and 15 from the upper macroblock are completely filtered and can be output from the filter, as well as the blocks 0, 1, 2, 4, 5, 6, 8, 9, 10. The remaining blocks takes two destinations: The blocks 3, 7, 11, 15 goes to the MB Buffer toward the Transpose for the next external vertical edge filtering; The blocks 12, 13, 15 goes to the Line Buffer, without being transposed (they are actually transposed and will be used as upper blocks in the filtering process for the macroblock below them).

The last phase of the filtering is the application of horizontal edge filtering to the croma blocks. As in the vertical edge filtering, the croma macroblocks need to be aligned and filtered together in order to fit in the 16 stage pipeline edge filter. The horizontal edges filtering for croma samples starts by reading the blocks 18, 19, 22, and 23 from the upper macroblocks stored in Line Buffer followed by reading the blocks 16, 17, 20, and 21 from the current macroblock stored in the MB Buffer, and finally the blocks 18, 19, 22, and 23. The blocks 16 and 20 are completely filtered and can be output from the filter. The blocks 17, 19, 21, and 23 are stored in the MB Buffer toward the Transpose and the blocks 18 and 22 are stored in the Line Buffer.

A total of 256 clock cycles are needed to process an entire 4:2:0 macroblock (24 blocks). If data is not available at the beginning of a 256 cycle operation, a bubble is inserted in the pipeline. All pipelines are emptied and the filter operation stops until there is data available in the input buffer. The stop cycle is also a 256 cycle operation.

Figure 10 illustrates the output sequence of blocks (as enumerated in figure 4) for the implemented filter architecture. Observe that for the 24 blocks output corresponding to an entire luma/croma macroblock processing cycle, the output have blocks belonging to three different macroblocks interleaved. The destination of that data is the reference frames (or the output video, when a frame is ready to display). A simple look-up-table can be implemented to ease the reference frame memory address.

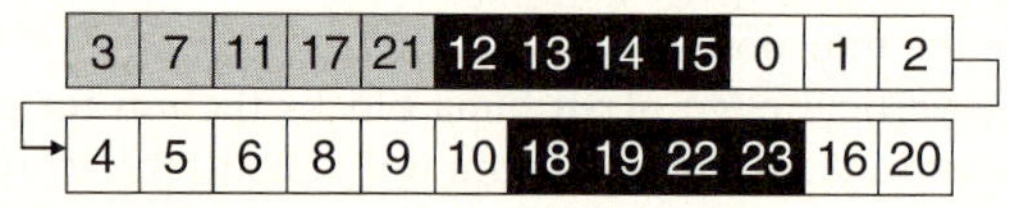

**Fig. 10.** Filter Output block sequence

# 4   Implementation and Results

The architecture presented in Section 3 was described in VHDL. About 3,500 lines of code were written. The design behavior was validated by simulation using some testbench files and data extracted from the JVT reference software using some public domain video sequences. The validated behavioral design was then synthesized, the post place and route was validated and performance results were obtained for a Xilinx Virtex2-pro FPGA.

Using the reference software CODEC, extracted data before and after the Deblocking Filter process was used to ensure the correctness of the implemented architecture. Table 1 presents the number of Xilinx LUTs and BRAMs used to synthesize the developed Deblocking Filter. Observe the balance between the amount of logic (LUTs) and memory employed, related to the total amount available in the target device.

**Table 1.** Synthesis results

| Device | XC2VP30 | XC5VLX30 |
| --- | --- | --- |
| LUTs | 4008/27392 (14%) | 4275/19200 (21%) |
| BRAMs | 20/136 (14%) | 7/32 (21%) |
| Fmax (MHz) | 148 | 197 |
| FPS@1080p | 71 | 95 |

Running at 148MHz in the Virtex II Pro device, this implementation is 2.36 times faster than the requirement for HDTV (1080p). For the Virtex-5, running at 197MHz, it is 3.14 times the requirement for HDTV. This IP can be used to build an encoder or decoder for a systems with the following characteristics:

- Ultra-high definition (4K x 2K pixel @ 24fps);
- High definition stereo video (two HDTV streams);
- Multi stream surveillance (up to 2K CIF streams);
- Scalable high definition;
- Low-power HDTV, where the device can operate at lower frequency, lower voltages and still achieve HDTV requirements.

Table 2 presents some performance comparison. The IP implemented with the developed architecture only loses to [5], but [5] do not include the external memory access penalty needed to obtain the upper MB data.

**Table 2.** Literature comparison

| | Cycles/MB | Memory type | fps@1080p |
| --- | --- | --- | --- |
| our | 256 | Dual-port | 95 |
| [4] | variable | Two-port | 45 |
| [5] | 96 | Two-port | 100 |
| [6] | 192 | Dual-port | 30 |

The maximum resolution achievable by the proposed architecture is only limited to the size of the line buffer (Figure 9) implemented. This buffer represents a significant amount of the total memory employed by this design and impacts the number of Block RAM (BRAM) used by the IP. The results presented in Table 1 is for a 2048 pixel wide frame, including the memory necessary to store block parameters, needed by the BS decision process. The maximum picture width is determined by a parameter in the synthesizable code and the height is unlimited.

## 5   Conclusion

This work presented a high performance architecture for H.264 Deblocking Filter IP targeted to exceed HDTV requirements in FPGA. The primary contribution of this work was the high performance deep pipeline architecture employed to improve the speed in the Boundary Strength decision and at the same time reducing the control logic. The proposed architecture stores all intermediate information in its own memory, differently from most works in literature that rely on external memory to store some blocks not completely filtered in a line of macroblocks. The developed IP based on the proposed architecture was synthesized to a Virtex II Pro and for a Virtex 5 device and prototyped in a XUP-V2Pro (Virtex II-Pro XC2VP30 device). Results showed its capability to exceed the processing rate for HDTV, reaching 71 frames per second in the Virtex II Pro device and 95 frames per second in the Virtex 5 device at 1080p (1920x1080) resolution.

Future work will address the support for high profiles, scalability and multi-view amendments of the H.264 standard, which require small modification in the BS decision logic and in the data width for pixel values.

## References


1. Draft ITU-T Recommendation and Final Draft international Standard of Joint Video Specification (ITU-T Rec. H.264/ISO/IEC 14496-10 AVC) (March 2003)
2. List, P., Joch, A., Lainema, J., Bjotergaard, G., Karczewicz, M.: Adaptative deblocking filter. IEE trans. Circuits Syst. Video Technol. 13, 614–619 (2003)
3. Puri, A., Chen, X., Luthra, A.: Video coding using the H.264/MPEG-4 AVC compression standard. Signal Processing: Image Communication 19, 793–849 (2004)
4. Sima, M., Zhou, Y., Zhang, W.: An Efficient Architecture for Adaptative Deblocking Filter of H.264/AVC Video Coding. IEEE Trans. On Consumer Electronics 50(1), 292–296 (2004)
5. Lin, H.-Y., Yang, J.-J., Liu, B.-D., Yang, J.-F.: Efficient deblocking filter architecture for H.264 video coders. In: 2006 IEEE International Symposium on Circuits and Systems, IS-CAS 2006, May 21–24 (2006)
6. Khurana, G., Kassim, A.A., Chua, T.-P.: M.B.A Mi Pipelined hardware implementation of in-loop deblocking filter in H.264/AVC. IEEE Transactions on Consumer Electronics 52(I.2), 536–540 (2006)

# Steganalysis of JPEG Images with Joint Transform Features

Zohaib Khan and Atif Bin Mansoor

College of Aeronautical Engineering,
National University of Sciences & Technology, Pakistan
zohaibkh_27@yahoo.com, atif-cae@nust.edu.pk

**Abstract.** In this paper, a universal steganalysis scheme for JPEG images based upon joint transform features is presented. We first analyzed two different transform domains (Discrete Cosine Transform and Discrete Wavelet Transform) separately, to extract features for steganalysis. Then a combination of these two feature sets is constructed and employed for steganalysis. A Fisher Linear Discriminant classifier is trained on features from both clean and steganographic images using all three feature sets and subsequently used for classification. Experiments performed on images embedded with two variants of F5 and Model based steganographic techniques reveal the effectiveness of proposed steganalysis approach by demonstrating improved detection for joint features.

**Keywords:** Steganography, Steganalysis, Information Hiding, Feature Extraction, Classification.

## 1   Introduction

The word steganography comes from the Greek words *steganos* and *graphia*, which together mean 'hidden writing'. Steganography is the art of hiding a message in plain sight. In the digital sense, it involves embedding a secret message file into an inconspicuous cover file, such as an image [1].

Steganography is an ancient subject, with its roots lying in ancient Greece and China, where it was already in use thousands of years ago. However, the modern formulation of steganography is often given in terms of the prisoners' problem [2], where Alice and Bob are two accomplices in a jail who wish to communicate in order to hatch an escape plan. However, all communication between them is examined by the warden, Wendy, who will put them in a high security prison at the slightest suspicion of covert communication. Specifically, in the general terms of a steganography model shown in Figure 1, we have Alice wishing to send a secret message $m$ to Bob. In order to do so, she 'embeds' secret message $m$ into a cover-object $c$ according to a shared secret key $k$ to obtain the stego-object $s$. The stego-object $s$ is then sent by Alice through the public channel to Bob, $m$ unnoticed by Wendy. Once Bob receives the stego-object $s$, he is able to recover the secret message $m$ using the shared secret key $k$.

T. Wada, F. Huang, and S. Lin (Eds.): PSIVT 2009, LNCS 5414, pp. 965–975, 2009.

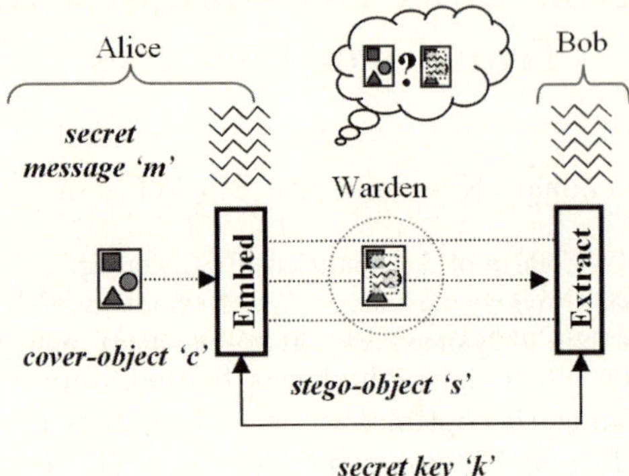


**Fig. 1.** A general steganography model

Steganography and cryptography are closely related data hiding methods. The purpose of cryptography is to scramble a message so that it cannot be understood, while that of steganography is to hide the message so that it cannot be seen. In general a message in cipher text might arouse suspicion on an observer while an 'invisible' message created with steganographic methods will not. Sometimes, steganography and cryptography are combined in a way that the message may be encrypted before hiding to provide additional security. Those who conceal communications through steganography are countered by those who wish to unveil such communications. The field devoted to counter steganography is known as *steganalysis*. The first and foremost goal of a steganalyst is to detect the presence of steganography so that the secret message may be stopped before it is received. Then the second goal is to identify the steganography tool so that the secret message may be spoofed and/or corrupted or even extracted from the stego file.

Generally, two approaches are followed for steganalysis; one is to come up with a steganalysis method specific to a particular steganographic algorithm. The other is to develop universal steganalysis techniques which are independent of the steganographic algorithm. Both approaches have their own strengths and weaknesses. A steganalysis technique specific to an embedding method would give very good results when tested only on that embedding method; but might fail on all other steganographic algorithms as in [4], [5], [6] and [7]. On the other hand, a steganalysis technique which is independent of the embedding algorithm might perform less accurately overall but still shows its effectiveness against new and unseen embedding algorithms as in [8], [9], [10] and [11]. Our research work is concentrated on the second approach due to its wide applicability.

In this paper, we propose a steganalysis technique by extracting features from two transform domains; the discrete wavelet transform and the discrete cosine transform. The features are investigated individually and combinatorially. The rest of the paper is organized as follows: In Section 2, we discuss the previous research work related to steganalysis. In Section 3, we present our proposed approach. Experimental results are presented in Section 4. Finally, the paper is concluded in Section 5.

## 2  Related Work

Due to the increasing availability of new steganography tools over the internet, there has been an increasing interest in the research for new and improved steganalysis techniques which are able to detect both previously seen and unseen embedding algorithms. A good survey of benchmarking of steganography and steganalysis techniques is given by Kharrazi et al. [3].

Fridrich et al. presented a steganalysis method which can reliably detect messages hidden in JPEG images using the steganography algorithm F5, and also estimate their lengths [4]. This method was further improved by Aboalsamh et al. [5] by determining the optimal value of the message length estimation parameter $\beta$. Westfeld and Pfitzmann presented visual and statistical attacks on various steganographic systems including EzStego v2.0b3, Jsteg v4, Steganos v1.5 and S-Tools v4.0, by using an embedding filter and the $\chi^2$ statistic [6]. A steganalysis scheme specific to the embedding algorithm Outguess is proposed in [7], by making use of the assumption that the embedding of a message in a stego image will be different than embedding the same into a cover image.

Avcibas et al. proposed that the correlation between the bit planes as well as the binary texture characteristics within the bit planes will differ between a stego image and a cover image, thus facilitating steganalysis [8]. Farid suggested that embedding of a message alters the higher order statistics calculated from a multi-scale wavelet decomposition [9]. Particularly, he calculated the first four statistical moments (mean, variance, skewness and kurtosis) of the distribution of wavelet coefficients at different scales and subbands. These features (moments), calculated from both cover and stego images were then used to train a linear classifier which could distinguish them with a certain success rate. Fridrich showed that a functional obtained from marginal and joint statistics of DCT coefficients will vary between stego and cover images. In particular, a functional such as the global DCT coefficient histogram was calculated for an image and its decompressed, cropped and recompressed versions. Finally the resulting features were obtained as the $L_1$ norm of the difference between the two. The classifier built with features extracted from both cover and stego images could reliably detect F5, Outguess and Model based steganography techniques [10]. Avcibas et al. used various image quality metrics to compute the distance between a test image and its lowpass filtered versions. Then a classifier built using linear regression showed detection of LSB steganography and various watermarking techniques with a reasonable accuracy [11].

## 3  Proposed Approach

### 3.1  Feature Extraction

Since the dimensionality of image data is huge, it is not feasible to use the complete image data directly for steganalysis. A better option is to extract a certain amount of useful data and use it to represent the image instead of the image itself for steganalysis. This useful set of data points are called features.

The addition of a message to a cover image does not affect the visual appearance of the image but may affect some statistics. The features required for the task of steganalysis should be able to catch these minor statistical disorders that are created during the data hiding process.

In our approach, we first extract features in the discrete wavelet transform domain, followed by the discrete cosine transform domain and finally combine both extracted features to make a joint feature set.

**DWT Based Features.** For extraction of features in the Discrete Wavelet Transform domain, we chose three scale decomposition as proposed by Wang and Moulin [12]. Figure 2 shows the levels and selection of subbands for this decomposition. Using *'Haar'* wavelet filter we obtained nine detail subbands (Horizontal $\mathbf{H}_i$, Vertical $\mathbf{V}_i$ and Diagonal $\mathbf{D}_i, i = 1, 2, 3$) and three approximation subbands (Lowpass $\mathbf{L}_i, i = 1, 2, 3$). We further decomposed the first scale diagonal subband $\mathbf{D}_1$ to improve the performance of the features [12]. As $\mathbf{D}_1$ is the finest detail subband and each of its coefficients involves diagonal differences in a four pixel block. So, $\mathbf{\acute{H}}_1$, $\mathbf{\acute{V}}_1$ and $\mathbf{\acute{D}}_1$ will contain more information about the difference of differences between neighboring pixels.

Various statistical measures are used in our analysis. Particularly, the first three normalized moments of the characteristic function are computed. The K-point discrete Characteristic Function (CF) is defined as

$$\Phi(k) = \sum_{m=0}^{M-1} h(m)e^{\left\{\frac{j2\pi mk}{K}\right\}} . \tag{1}$$

where $\{h(m)\}_{m=0}^{M-1}$ is the $M$ bin histogram which is an estimate of the PDF, $p(x)$ of the wavelet coefficients distribution. The $n^{th}$ absolute moment of discrete CF is defined as

$$M_n^A = \sum_{k=0}^{K-1} \Phi(k) \sin^n \left(\frac{\pi k}{K}\right) . \tag{2}$$

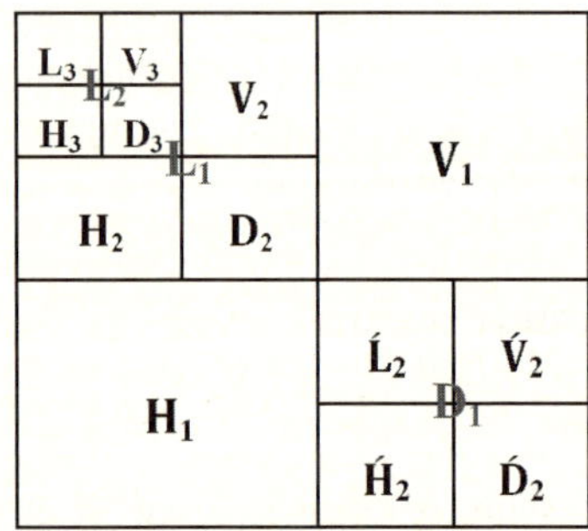

**Fig. 2.** A three scale wavelet decomposition

Finally, the normalized CF moment is defined as

$$\hat{M}_n^A = \frac{M_n^A}{M_0^A} \, .$$

(3)

where $M_0^A$ is the zeroth order moment. We calculated the first three normalized CF moments for each of the 16 subbands, giving a **48-D** feature vector.

**DCT Based Features.** The DCT based feature set is constructed following the approach of Fridrich [10]. A vector functional $\boldsymbol{F}$ is applied to the JPEG image $J_1$. This image is then decompressed to the spatial domain, cropped by 4 pixels in each direction and recompressed with the same quantization table as $J_1$ to obtain $J_2$. The vector functional $\boldsymbol{F}$ is then applied to $J_2$. The final feature $f$ is obtained as the $L_1$ norm of the difference of the functional applied to $J_1$ and $J_2$.

$$f = \|\boldsymbol{F}(J_1) - \boldsymbol{F}(J_2)\|_{L_1} \, .$$

(4)

The rational behind this procedure is that the recompression after cropping by 4 pixels does not see the previous JPEG compression's $8 \times 8$ block boundary and thus it is not affected by the previous quantization and hence embedding in the DCT domain. So, $J_2$ can be thought of as an approximation to its cover image.

We calculated the global, individual and dual histograms of the DCT coefficient array $d_{(k)}(i,j)$ as the first order functionals. The symbol $d_{(k)}(i,j)$ denotes the $(i,j)^{th}$ quantized DCT coefficient $(i,j = 1,2,...,8)$ in the $k$-$th$ block, $(k = 1,2,...,B)$. The global histogram of all $64B$ DCT coefficients is given as, $H(m)_{m=L}^{R}$, where $L = min_{k,i,j} d_{(k)}(i,j)$ and $R = max_{k,i,j} d_{(k)}(i,j)$. We computed $H/\|H\|_{L_1}$, the normalized global histogram of DCT coefficients as the first functional.

Steganographic techniques that preserve global DCT coefficients histogram may not necessarily preserve the histogram of individual DCT modes. So, we calculated $h^{ij}/\|h^{ij}\|_{L_1}$, the normalized individual histograms $h(m)_{m=L}^{R}$ of 5 low frequency DCT modes, $(i,j) = (2,1), (3,1), (1,2), (2,2), (1,3)$ as the next five functionals.

The dual histogram is an $8 \times 8$ matrix which indicates the number of how many times the value '$d$' occurs as the $(i,j)^{th}$ DCT coefficient over all blocks $B$ in the image. We computed $g_{ij}^d/\|g_{ij}^d\|_{L_1}$, the normalized dual histograms where

$$g_{ij}^d = \sum_{k=1}^{B} \delta(d, d_{(k)}(i,j)) \text{ for 11 values of } d = -5, -4, ..., 4, 5.$$

Inter block dependency is captured by the second order features *variation* and *blockiness*. Most steganographic techniques add entropy to the DCT coefficients which is captured by the *variation* $(V)$

$$V = \frac{\sum_{i,j=1}^{8} \sum_{k=1}^{|I_r|-1} |d_{I_r(k)}(i,j) - d_{I_r(k+1)}(i,j)| + \sum_{i,j=1}^{8} \sum_{k=1}^{|I_c|-1} |d_{I_c(k)}(i,j) - d_{I_c(k+1)}(i,j)|}{|Ir| + |Ic|} \, .$$

(5)

where $I_r$ and $I_c$ denote the vectors of block indices while scanning the image 'by rows' and 'by columns' respectively.

*Blockiness* is calculated from the decompressed JPEG image and is a measure of discontinuity along the block boundaries over all DCT modes over the whole image. The $L_1$ and $L_2$ *blockiness* $(B_\alpha, \alpha = 1, 2)$ is defined as

$$B_\alpha = \frac{\sum\limits_{i=1}^{\lfloor (M-1)/8 \rfloor} \sum\limits_{j=1}^{N} |x_{8i,j} - x_{8i+1,j}|^\alpha + \sum\limits_{j=1}^{\lfloor (N-1)/8 \rfloor} \sum\limits_{i=1}^{M} |x_{i,8j} - x_{i,8j+1}|^\alpha}{N \lfloor (M-1)/8 \rfloor + M \lfloor (N-1)/8 \rfloor} \tag{6}$$

where $x_{i,j}$ are the grayscale intensity values of an image with dimensions $M \times N$.

The final DCT based feature vector is **20-D** (Histograms: 1 global, 5 individual, 11 dual. *Variation*: 1. *Blockiness*: 2).

**Joint Features.** After extracting the features in the discrete cosine transform and the discrete wavelet transform domain, we finally combine the extracted feature sets into one joint feature set, giving a **68-D** feature vector, (48 DWT + 20 DCT).

## 3.2 Classifier

We used the two class Fisher Linear Discriminant (FLD) classifier [19]. Let $x_i, i = 1, \ldots, N_x$ and $y_j, j = 1, \ldots, N_y$ represent the samples from each of the two classes of the training set. The within class means are given by

$$m_x = \frac{1}{N_x} \sum_{i=1}^{N_x} x_i, m_y = \frac{1}{N_y} \sum_{j=1}^{N_y} y_j. \tag{7}$$

The between class mean is

$$m = \frac{1}{N_x + N_y} \left( \sum_{i=1}^{N_x} x_i + \sum_{j=1}^{N_y} y_j \right). \tag{8}$$

The within class scatter matrix is

$$S_w = M_x M_x^T + M_y M_y^T . \tag{9}$$

where $M_x = x_i - m_x, M_y = y_j - m_y$ are the matrices containing the zero-meaned $i^{th}$ and $j^{th}$ samples respectively. The between class scatter matrix is

$$S_b = N_x (m_x - m)(m_x - m)^T + N_y (m_y - m)(m_y - m)^T . \tag{10}$$

The maximal generalized eigenvalue eigenvector $e$ is related to $S_b$ and $S_w$ by

$$S_b e = \lambda S_w e \tag{11}$$

By projecting the training samples $x_i$ and $y_j$ onto one dimensional linear subspace $e$ ($x_p = x_i^T e, y_p = y_j^T e$), the within class scatter is minimized and the between class scatter is maximized. In any classification problem, this effect is highly desirable as it maintains the discriminability while simultaneously reduces the dimensions of data. An unknown sample $z$ can now be tested for its class by projecting it onto the same subspace $e$ ($z_p = z^T e$) and its class determined on the basis of a threshold $T_h$.

## 4   Experimental Results

### 4.1   Image Datasets

**Cover Image Dataset.** For our experiments, we used 1338 grayscale images of size 512x384 obtained from the Uncompressed Colour Image Database (UCID) constructed by Schaefer and Stich [13], available at [14]. These images contain a wide range of indoor/outdoor, daylight/night scenes, providing a real and challenging environment for a steganalysis problem. All images were converted to JPEG at 80% quality for our experiments.

**F5 Stego Image Dataset.** Our first stego image dataset is generated by the steganography software F5 [15], proposed by Andreas Westfeld. F5 steganography algorithm embeds information bits by incrementing and decrementing the values of quantized DCT coefficients from compressed JPEG images [16]. F5 also uses an operation known as 'matrix embedding' in which it minimizes the amount of changes made to the DCT coefficients necessary to embed a message of certain length. Matrix embedding has three parameters $(c, n, k)$, where $c$ is the number of changes per group of $n$ coefficients, and $k$ is the number of embedded bits. These parameter values are determined by the embedding algorithm.

F5 algorithm first compresses the input image with a user defined quality factor before embedding the message. We chose a quality factor of 80 for stego images. Messages were successfully embedded at rates of 0.05, 0.10, 0.20, 0.3, 0.40 and 0.60 bpc (bits per non-zero DCT coefficients). We chose F5 because recent results in [8], [9], [12] have shown that F5 is harder to detect than other commercially available steganography algorithms.

**MB Stego Image Dataset.** Our second stego image dataset is generated by the Model Based steganography method [17], proposed by Phil Sallee [18]. The algorithm first breaks down the quantized DCT coefficients of a JPEG image into two parts and then replaces the perceptually insignificant component with the coded message signal. The algorithm has two types; MB1 is normal steganography and MB2 is steganography with deblocking. The deblocking algorithm adjusts the unused coefficients to reduce the blockiness of the resulting image to the original blockiness. Unlike F5, the Model Based steganography algorithm does not recompress the cover image before embedding. We embed at rates of 0.05, 0.10, 0.20, 0.3, 0.40 0.60 and 0.80 bpc. The model based steganography algorithm has also shown high resistance against steganalysis techniques in [3], [10].

**Table 1.** The number of images in the stego image datasets given the message length. F5 with matrix embedding turned off $(1, 1, 1)$ and turned on $(c, n, k)$. Model based steganography without deblocking (MB1) and with deblocking (MB2). (U = unachievable rate).

| Embedding Rate (bpc) | F5 $(1, 1, 1)$ | F5 $(c, n, k)$ | MB1 | MB2 |
|---|---|---|---|---|
| 0.05 | 1338 | 1338 | 1338 | 1338 |
| 0.10 | 1338 | 1338 | 1338 | 1338 |
| 0.20 | 1338 | 1337 | 1338 | 1334 |
| 0.30 | 1337 | 1295 | 1338 | 1320 |
| 0.40 | 1332 | 5 | 1338 | 1119 |
| 0.60 | 5 | U | 1332 | 117 |
| 0.80 | U | U | 60 | U |

The reason for choosing the message length proportional to the number of non-zero DCT coefficients was to create a stego image database for which the steganalysis is roughly of the same level of difficulty. We further carried out embedding at different rates to observe the steganalysis performance for messages of varying length. It can be seen in Table 1 that the Model based steganography is more efficient in embedding as compared to F5; since longer messages can be accommodated in images using Model based steganography.

## 4.2    Evaluation of Results

The Fisher Linear Discriminant classifier described in Section 3.2 was utilized for our experiments. Each steganographic algorithm was analyzed separately for the evaluation of the steganalytic classifier. For a fixed relative message length, we created a database of training images comprising 669 cover and 669 stego images. Both DWT based features (DWT) and DCT based features (DCT) were extracted from the training set and were combined to form a Joint feature set (JNT), according to the procedure explained in Section 3.1. The FLD classifier was then tested on the features extracted from a different database of test images comprising 669 cover and 669 stego images. The Receiver Operating Characteristics (ROC) curves, which give the variation of the Detection Probability ($P_d$, the fraction of correctly classified stego images) with the False Alarm Probability ($P_f$, the fraction of stego images wrongly classified as cover image), were computed for each steganographic algorithm and embedding rate. The area under the ROC curve (AUC) was measured to determine the overall classification accuracy.

Figures 3-5 give the obtained ROC curves for the steganographic techniques under test for different embedding rates. Note that due to the space limitation, these figures are displayed in small size. However, readers are encouraged to take a look by using zoom to 400%. We observe that the DCT based features outperform the DWT based features for all embedding rates. As could be expected, the detection of F5 without matrix embedding is better than F5 with matrix

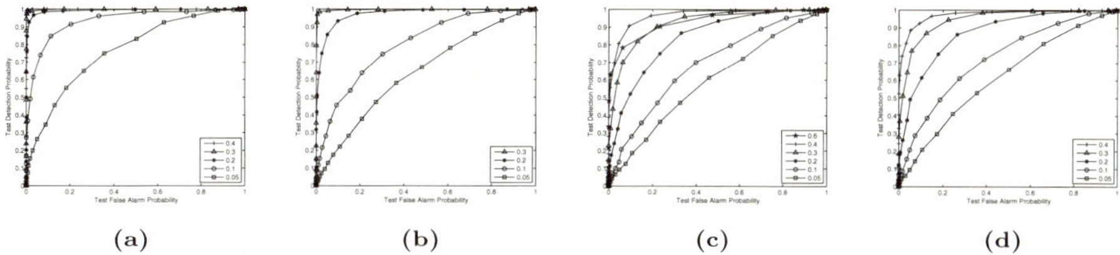

**Fig. 3.** ROC curves using DCT based features. (a) F5 (without matrix embedding) (b) F5 (with matrix embedding) (c) MB1 (without deblocking) (d) MB2 (with deblocking).

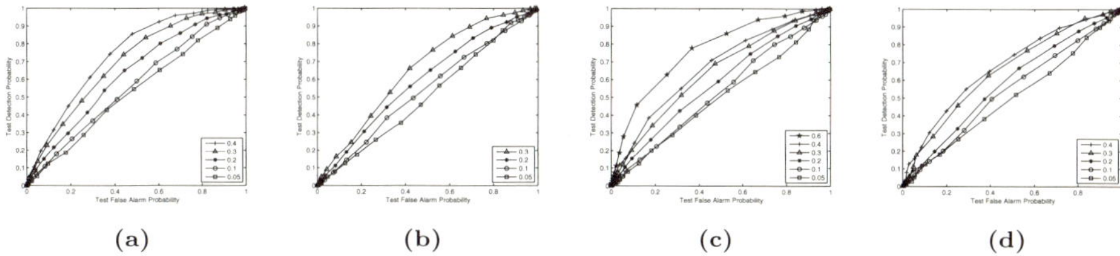

**Fig. 4.** ROC curves using DWT based features. (a) F5 (without matrix embedding) (b) F5 (with matrix embedding) (c) MB1 (without deblocking) (d) MB2 (with deblocking).

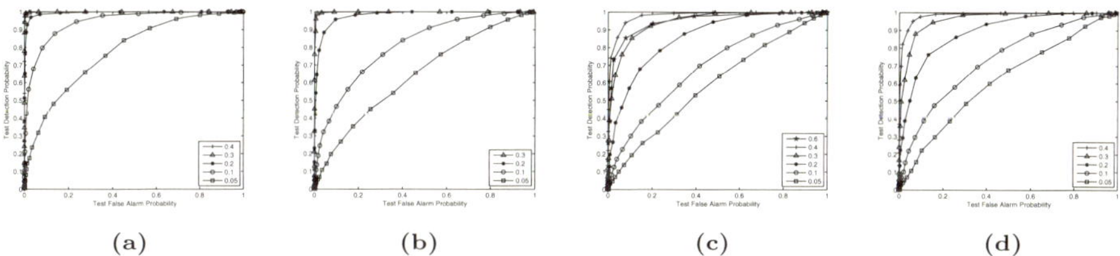

**Fig. 5.** ROC curves using Joint features. (a) F5 (without matrix embedding) (b) F5 (with matrix embedding) (c) MB1 (without deblocking) (d) MB2 (with deblocking).

embedding as the matrix embedding operation significantly reduces detectability at the expense of message capacity.

Table 2 summarizes the classification results. For F5 without matrix embedding, the proposed Joint transform features dominate both DCT and DWT based features for embedding rates till 0.20 bpc. For higher embedding rates the DCT based features perform better. For F5 with matrix embedding, both the proposed joint features and the DCT based features are close competitors.

For MB1 algorithm (without deblocking), the proposed joint features outperform both the DCT and DWT based features for all embedding rates. For MB2 algorithm (with deblocking), the joint features perform close to the DCT based features. It is observed that the detection of MB1 is better than MB2, as the deblocking algorithm in MB2 reduces the blockiness of the stego image to match the original image.

**Table 2.** Classification results (AUC) using FLD for all embedding rates. F5 with matrix embedding turned off $(1, 1, 1)$ and turned on $(c, n, k)$. Model based steganography without deblocking (MB1) and with deblocking (MB2). (U = unachievable rate).

| Embedding Rate (bpc) | F5 $(1, 1, 1)$ | F5 $(c, n, k)$ | MB1 | MB2 | |
|---|---|---|---|---|---|
| 0.05 | 0.767 | 0.640 | 0.622 | 0.598 | DCT |
| 0.05 | 0.531 | 0.491 | 0.498 | 0.492 | DWT |
| 0.05 | 0.770 | 0.636 | 0.614 | 0.588 | JNT |
| 0.10 | 0.932 | 0.794 | 0.732 | 0.692 | DCT |
| 0.10 | 0.562 | 0.528 | 0.535 | 0.520 | DWT |
| 0.10 | 0.943 | 0.796 | 0.729 | 0.686 | JNT |
| 0.20 | 0.993 | 0.971 | 0.872 | 0.841 | DCT |
| 0.20 | 0.624 | 0.592 | 0.581 | 0.580 | DWT |
| 0.20 | 0.993 | 0.966 | 0.890 | 0.849 | JNT |
| 0.30 | 0.998 | 0.998 | 0.942 | 0.924 | DCT |
| 0.30 | 0.689 | 0.653 | 0.654 | 0.639 | DWT |
| 0.30 | 0.993 | 0.996 | 0.954 | 0.931 | JNT |
| 0.40 | 0.999 | U | 0.972 | 0.965 | DCT |
| 0.40 | 0.735 | U | 0.667 | 0.666 | DWT |
| 0.40 | 0.997 | U | 0.980 | 0.978 | JNT |
| 0.60 | U | U | 0.984 | U | DCT |
| 0.60 | U | U | 0.693 | U | DWT |
| 0.60 | U | U | 0.991 | U | JNT |

# 5   Conclusion

This paper presents a new DCT and DWT based joint features approach for universal steganalysis. DCT and DWT based statistical features are investigated individually, followed by research on combined features. The Fisher Linear Discriminant classifier is employed for classification. The experiments were performed on image datasets with different embedding rates for F5 and Model based steganography algorithms. Experiments revealed that for JPEG images the DCT is a better choice for extraction of features as compared to the DWT. The experiments with joint transform features reveal that the extraction of features in more than one transform domain improves the steganalysis performance.

**Acknowledgments.** The work on this paper was supported by the National University of Sciences and Technology, Pakistan.

# References

1. Johnson, N.F., Jajodia, S.: Exploring Steganography: Seeing the Unseen. IEEE Computer 31(2), 26–34 (1998)
2. Simmons, G.J.: 'Prisoners' Problem and the Subliminal Channel. In: CRYPTO 1983-Advances in Cryptology, pp. 51–67 (1999)

3. Kharrazi, M., Sencar, T.H., Memon, N.: Benchmarking Steganographic and Steganalysis Techniques. In: Proc. of SPIE Electronic Imaging, Security, Steganography and Watermarking of Multimedia Contents VII, San Jose, California, USA (2005)

4. Fridrich, J., Goljan, M., Hogea, D.: Steganalysis of JPEG images: Breaking the F5 Algorithm. In: Proc. 5th International Workshop on Information Hiding, Noordwijkerhout, The Netherlands, pp. 310–323 (October 2002)

5. Aboalsamh, H.A., Dokheekh, S.A., Mathkour, H.I., Assassa, G.M.: Breaking the F5 Algorithm: An Improved Approach. Egyptian Computer Science Journal 29(1), 1–9 (2007)

6. Westfeld, A., Pfitzmann, A.: Attacks on Steganographic Systems. In: Proc. 3rd Information Hiding Workshop, Dresden, Germany, pp. 61–76 (1999)

7. Fridrich, J., Goljan, M., Hogea, D.: Attacking the OutGuess. In: Proc. ACM Workshop on Multimedia and Security 2002. ACM Press, Juan-les-Pins (December 2002)

8. Avcibas, I., Memon, N., Sankur, B.: Image Steganalysis with Binary Similarity Measures. In: Proc. of the IEEE International Conference on Image Processing, Rochester, New York (September 2002)

9. Farid, H.: Detecting Hidden Messages Using Higher-order Statistical Models. In: Proc. of the IEEE International Conference on Image Processing, vol. 2, pp. 905–908 (2002)

10. Fridrich, J.: Feature-Based Steganalysis for JPEG Images and its Implications for Future Design of Steganographic Schemes. In: Moskowitz, I.S. (ed.) Information Hiding 2004. LNCS, vol. 2137, pp. 67–81. Springer, Heidelberg (2005)

11. Avcibas, I., Memon, N., Sankur, B.: Steganalysis Using Image Quality Metrics. IEEE Transactions on Image Processing 12(2), 221–229 (2003)

12. Wang, Y., Moulin, P.: Optimized Feature Extraction for Learning-Based Image Steganalysis. IEEE Transactions on Information Forensics and Security 2(1) (2007)

13. Schaefer, G., Stich, M.: UCID - An Uncompressed Colour Image Database. In: Proc. SPIE, Storage and Retrieval Methods and Applications for Multimedia, San Jose, USA, pp. 472–480 (2004)

14. UCID – Uncompressed Colour Image Database (visited on 02/08/08),
    `http://vision.cs.aston.ac.uk/datasets/UCID/ucid.html`

15. Steganography Software F5 (visited on 02/08/08),
    `http://wwwrn.inf.tu-dresden.de/~westfeld/f5.html`

16. Westfeld, A.: F5 – A Steganographic Algorithm: High capacity despite better steganalysis. In: Moskowitz, I.S. (ed.) 4th International Workshop Information Hiding. LNCS, pp. 289–302. Springer, Heidelberg (April 2001)

17. Model Based JPEG Steganography Demo (visited on 02/08/08),
    `http://www.philsallee.com/mbsteg/index.html`

18. Sallee, P.: Model Based Steganography. In: International Workshop on Digital Watermarking, Seoul, Korea, pp. 174–188 (October 2003)

19. Duda, R.O., Hart, P.E., Stork, D.G.: Pattern Classification, 2nd edn. John Wiley & Sons, New York (2001)

# Hardware Design of Shape-Preserving Contour Tracing for Object of Segmented Images

Roy Chaoming Hsu*, Yaw-Yu Lee, Bin-Wen Kao, and Din-Yuen Chan

Department of Computer Science and Information Engineering
National Chiayi University
300 University Road, East District Chiayi City, Chiayi, Taiwan
{rchsu,s0960412,dychan}@mail.ncyu.edu.tw,
goodmorning7337@yahoo.com.tw

**Abstract.** A hardware design of shape-preserving contour tracing for objects in a segmented image for robot vision and pattern recognition applications is presented in this paper. The proposed contour tracing consists of two processes, namely progressive boundary linking (PBL) and synchronous redundancy pruning (SRP). The proposed method is realized on a System on Chip (SoC) with open-source processor IP core, LEON3, utilizing AMBA bus. Implementation results show that the proposed design achieves better results in terms of accuracy and hardware efficiency comparing with other existing boundary extraction methods such as morphological boundary extraction.

**Keywords:** Boundary Extraction, Contour Tracing, SOC, AMBA bus.

## 1 Introduction

Boundary extraction is a technique for accurately extracting the boundary of an object from a digitally-processed image. Such techniques are widely applied for preprocessing purposes in many image/video multimedia applications, including pattern recognition based on shape features, target tracking using object gestures, shape coding, and so forth. Hardware realization of boundary extraction enables extraction of important object features of an image in real-time such that it is of important practice in industrial and medical applications such as vision-based robot and medical imaging. Modern multimedia applications commonly involve the use of image/video segmentation, compression and even simple digitization routines, which inevitably introduce noise and distortion into the original images. As a result, the quality of subsequent image/video automatic recognition and shape-coding applications, in which the object boundary information is of fundamental importance, is inevitably degraded. When applying common contour extraction methods to noisy object boundaries, it is generally found that morphology-based methods provide more accurate results than those obtained using edge-detection schemes. However, visible distortion of the object profile is often apparent when morphology methods based on nonlinear filters (conventionally referred to as structuring elements (SE's)) are applied. Such methods not only suppress

---

* Corresponding author.

T. Wada, F. Huang, and S. Lin (Eds.): PSIVT 2009, LNCS 5414, pp. 976–987, 2009.
© Springer-Verlag Berlin Heidelberg 2009

undesirable noise within the image, but also inadvertently eliminate nontrivial details such as textural branches, cracks, shape contour features, and so forth. Therefore, there is a practical need to develop robust contour tracing schemes which effectively suppress the noise content of an image, while simultaneously retaining the fine details of the object contours. In this paper, a hardware design of shape-preserving contour tracing for objects in a segmented image for vision-based robot and pattern recognition applications is presented. The proposed contour tracing consists of two processes, namely progressive boundary linking (PBL) and synchronous redundancy pruning (SRP). The proposed method is realized on FPGA and the simulation result is compared with that of a morphological method.

## 2   Related Work

FPGA technology [9] for digital design is much more efficient in fast realization of multimedia applications not only in computational cost but also in fast prototyping toward a complete IC. To improve computational efficiency, in [10] a hardware arithmetic ability of ALU is presented utilizing FPGA to realize the complex algorithm and to reduce hardware cost. Hardware realization of noise/redundancy removal is often found in recent literatures of image processing [1, 2]. A FPGA implementation of median filter is presented in [1], where the median filter finds the median value by sorting the image pixels within a 3×3 mask and replaces the value of the center pixel with the median one. By using vertical-horizontal-diagonal sorting [1], hardware space in the realization is hence reduced. In [2], by adding parallelism into the architecture of vertical-horizontal-diagonal sorting, better performance within each clock cycle for the noise removal is achieved. Edge detection is a simple method for extraction of object's boundary of an image. The SUSAN algorithm is developed by parallel modules in order to improve its performance for real-time edge and corner detection process. FPGA architecture of edge and corner detection based on the SUSAN algorithm is presented in [3] to achieve real-time processing of boundary extraction. Mathematical morphology has been an important methodology on image processing [14]. By using basic morphological operations, such as dilation or erosion, and utilizing structuring element as processing unit, noise cleaned and boundary extracted images are produced [5-7]. Morphological cleaning is a process to remove noise of image, by using erosion following by dilation, and then dilation following by erosion to produce a noise-cleaned image. Owing to its simplicity, the morphological operations are often implemented using hardware. In [8], the authors aim at optimizing performances of morphological algorithms with respect to high throughput real-time execution on FPGA. The implemented morphological algorithms were then integrated for complex applications such as vision-based robots or real-time processing and displaying of video flows. It is commonly acknowledged that hardware architecture design is an important factor for improving algorithm complexity. Parallelism of well-pipelined architecture can accelerate the computing time of algorithm and reach real-time requests for most applications [11-13]. In this paper, we focus on the hardware design of a shape-preserving contour tracing [15] for robot vision and pattern recognition applications. The proposed method, hardware design architecture, and simulation result using a development board are described in the following.

## 3   Shape-Preserving Contour Tracing

The proposed shape-preserving contour tracing consists of two processes, namely progressive boundary linking (PBL) and synchronous redundancy pruning (SRP) [15].

### 3.1   Progressive Boundary Linking (PBL)

Process of PBL consists of the following steps.

1. Determining a boundary point of object from either vertical or horizontal direction in a segmented image. The determined boundary point is the initial contour point for starting with the contour tracing.
2. Adding the coordinate of the detected contour point to a contour array to construct the contour image.
3. Moving the mask onto the current detected contour point as the center point, using policy of maximum priority selection, whose function will be described later, to decide the next contour point, and adding the decided next contour point to the contour array.
4. If no new contour point can be decided in Step 3, PBL is finished, otherwise Synchronous Redundancy Pruning (SRP) will be executed, as will be described next, along the contour tracing to determine and remove any redundant points, the contour tracing goes back to step 3 for next iteration to find the next contour point.

### 3.2   Synchronous Redundancy Pruning (SRP)

Whenever a point is determined as a contour point, SRP will start to execute the following two phases to improve the definition of the countor.

1. Whether previous points have crack in between or not is checked in the first phase. Herein, the previous points are defined as the previous three points of the new contour points. If there is crack, the crack is filled with the same bi-level value of the nearby contour point and the contour array is updated. If no cracks exist between previous points, SRP continues in executing phase 2.
2. If SRP determines there is branch formed by previous points, SRP will remove the redundancy by pruning the branch and updates the contour array. Hence a redundancy-free contour path can be constructed by the SRP process.

The contour tracing then goes back to PBL to find next contour point, and redundancy, if exists, will be checked and removed by SRP to finally obtain a shape-preserving contour image.

## 4   Hardware Architecture

Fig. 1. shows the proposed hardware design of the shape-preserving contour tracing. The architecture is composed of main controller, and PBL and SRP modules.

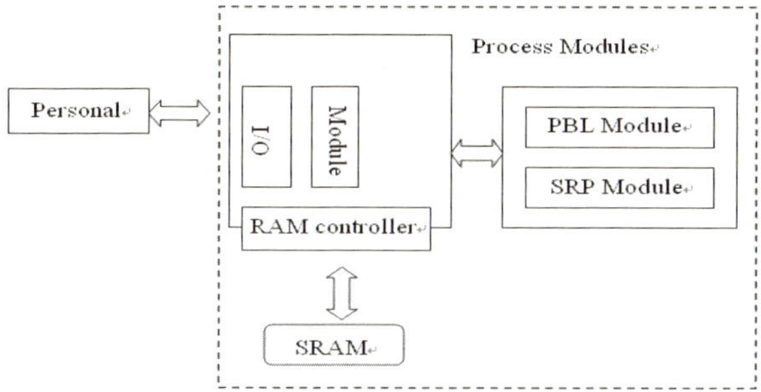


**Fig. 1.** Hardware architecture of the proposed method

## 4.1  Main Controller

Main controller's function is to control timing of access to memory and loading and storing of data input and output for processing. The main controller reads input image pixels as an array of $M \times N$ in the main SRAM memory and initializes the contour tracing by utilizing a finite state machine (FSM) as shown in Fig. 2.

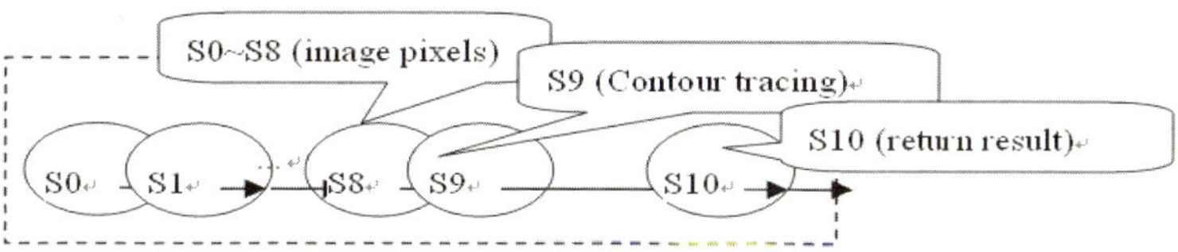


**Fig. 2.** Finite state machine of the main controller

In state S0 to S8, image pixels in a 3×3 mask is accessed sequentially and the process modules will start to process the contour tracing at state S9. After the contour point is found, the main controller stores the result to a contour array of the SRAM at state S10 and resumes contour tracing for next boundary point. The main controller will continue tracing contour until a closed contour is constructed.

## 4.2  PBL Module

PBL module is composed of two sub-modules, priority calculation and decision module and selection of maximum priority point module. The PBL first calculates the surrounding points priorities of the central boundary point by priority calculation and decision module, then the priorities between the surrounding points are compared to decide which point is selected as the next contour point by selection of maximum priority point module.

*Priority calculation and decision module*
This module calculates priority of 8 candidate contour pixels surrounding the current contour points within the 3x3 mask. The rule of priority calculation and decision consists of three steps. First, if any one of 8 neighboring point of the current boundary

point is 1, it will be considered as a candidate point of the next contour point. Second, the two neighboring points of the candidate point are checked whether they have only one pixel equals to 0 [15]. If it is, the output value is set as 0 (first priority). If the value of both the neighboring pixels equal to 0, the output is set as 1 (second priority), otherwise the candidate point is considered as "don't care" and will not be candidate anymore. To better explain how the priority calculation module functions, the relationship between candidate point and its two neighboring points and how the output is decided are shown in Fig. 3. In Fig. 3(a), only one of the two neighboring points of the underlined point is 0, and the output will be set to 0, while in Fig. 3(b) and 3(c) the output is set to 1 and "don't care", respectively. Third, the output value of the candidate points are added with it's occurrence times (OT) value, the number of times the candidate is decided as a boundary point and is stored in memory previously, using an adder to obtain the final priority vale as below

$$Priority = OT + output \tag{1}$$

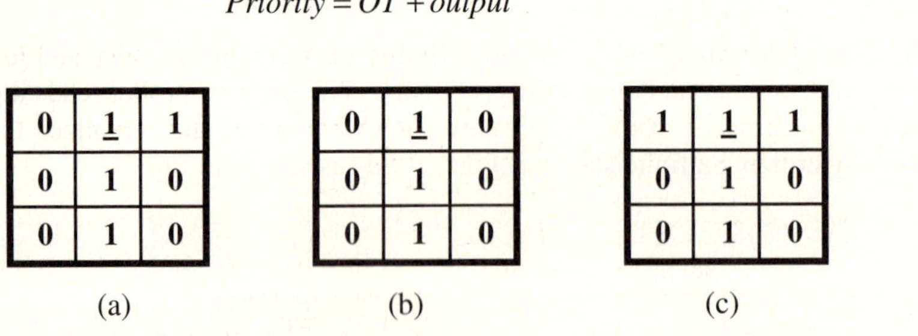

Fig. 3. Second step of the rule of priority calculation. (a) Output of Underlined point is 0, (b) Output of Underlined point is 1, (c) Output of Underlined point is "don't care".

In this study, the value of OT is 0 and 1, with lower value represents larger priority, which represents for not being decided as boundary and already being decided as boundary point once, respectively. The combination of priority output with OT will constitute with two bits in (OT,output) form, (OT,output)= (0,0) means output priority is 0 and the candidate point is not yet decided as boundary such that this candidate point has the maximum priority for next boundary point. Fig. 4. show the hardware design of the priority calculation module, where In1 and In2 represent the value of two neighboring points of the candidate point and there are eight modules constructed in parallel for the 8 neighboring points of the current boundary point. The enable bit is from the candidate boundary point.

*Selection of maximum priority module*
This module will select the point with maximum priority as output. The priority comparison is done by using 2-input comparator sequentially, and the point with the maximum priority is selected as next contour point and stored in the contour array.

## 4.3  SRP Module

Whenever PBL determines a new contour point, SRP will start to check whether the previous contour points are cracks or branches and the cracks and branches are subsequently be filled or removed, respectively, to improve the definition of contour

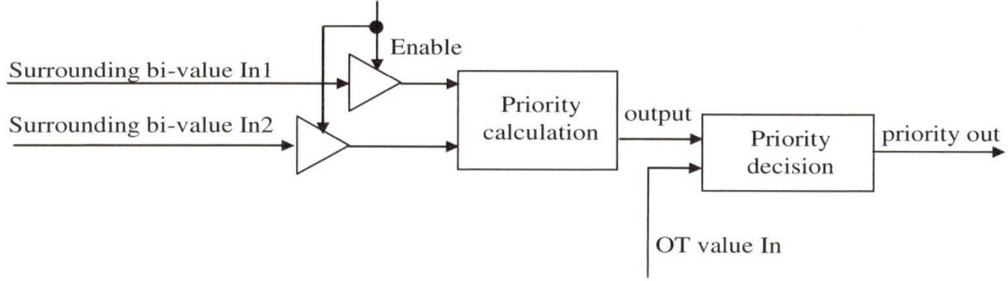


**Fig. 4.** Hardware design of single priority calculation and decision module

along the contour tracing. Fig. 5 shows how SRP module works on redundancy pruning by crack filling and branch removing, where Pi is the current contour point, Pi-1,Pi-2,Pi-3 are previous contour points in order before Pi, with each point accessed from the contour array in the memory. Fig. 5(a) is the original image where distance between Pi and Pi-3 is 2. In Fig. 5(b) SRP executes Phase 1, the crack is filled by replacing 1 with 0. Distance between Pi and Pi-3 is 1 now and a branch exists. Fig. 5(c) shows that SRP executing Phase 2 to remove branch by replacing 1's , i.e., Pi-1, Pi-2, with 0's. In executing the SRP module, the distance of $P_i$ and $P_{i-3}$, needs to be realized with the distance are defined as below.

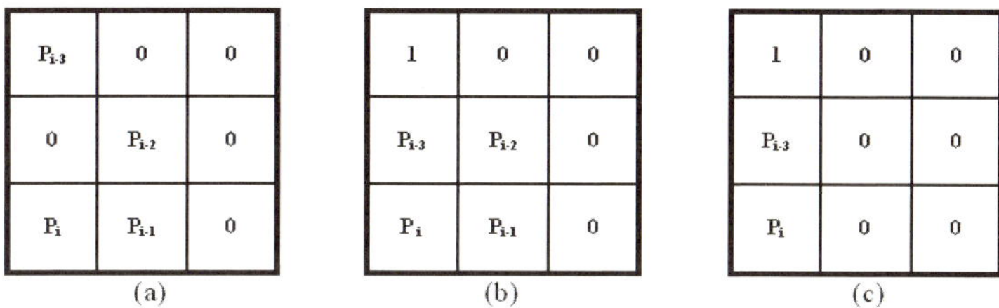

| $P_{i-3}$ | 0 | 0 |
|---|---|---|
| 0 | $P_{i-2}$ | 0 |
| $P_i$ | $P_{i-1}$ | 0 |

(a)

| 1 | 0 | 0 |
|---|---|---|
| $P_{i-3}$ | $P_{i-2}$ | 0 |
| $P_i$ | $P_{i-1}$ | 0 |

(b)

| 1 | 0 | 0 |
|---|---|---|
| $P_{i-3}$ | 0 | 0 |
| $P_i$ | 0 | 0 |

(c)

**Fig. 5.** SRP Execution examples (a) Original image with Distance (Pi,Pi-3)=2, a crack is exists. (b) the result after executing SRP Phase 1, Distance(Pi,Pi-3)=1 (c) SRP executes Phase 2 by removing the branches to obtain the final result.

$$Distance(P_i , P_{i-3}) = max(|x_i - x_{i-3}|, |y_i - y_{i-3}|) \qquad (2)$$

If the distance equals to 2, SRP decides that crack exists and execute phase 1 to fill the crack by storing a 1 to the positions between Pi and Pi-3 of the contour array. If there is no crack, SRP goes to phase 2. In Phase 2, if the distance between Pi and Pi-3 equals to 0 or 1, branch exists and the branch is then removed and SRP ends. Fig. 6 shows the hardware design of SRP module. In executing SRP, the redundancy is pruned by filling the crack or removing the branch and the contour array in the memory is updated. The contour tracing goes back to PBL and SRP for next contour point.

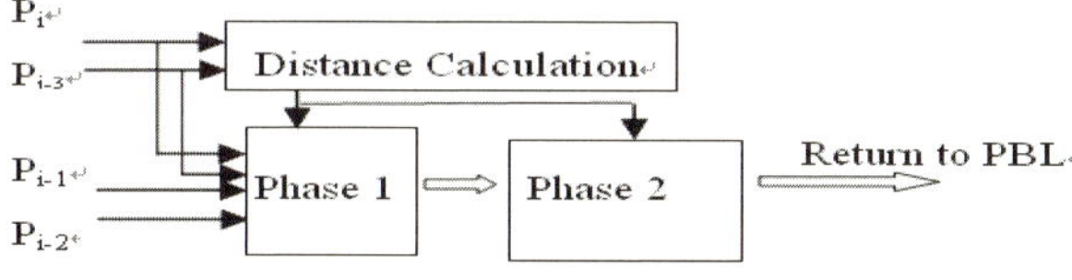


**Fig. 6.** Hardware design of SRP module

## 5  Simulation Results

The proposed FPGA design for contour tracing is realized on a System on Chip (SoC) with open-source processor IP core, LEON3, and AMBA bus, using Verilog hardware description language and the performances are compared with an existing morphological noise cleaning and contour extraction method. The LEON3 is a synthesizable VHDL model of a 32-bit processor compliant with the SPARC V8 architecture, which is highly configurable, and particularly suitable for system-on-a-chip (SOC) designs. GR-XC3S-1500 development board, from Gaisler Research and Pender Electronic Design [17], is used in realization of the contour tracing. The board incorporates a Xilinx Spartan3-1500 FPGA, and is capable of operating stand-alone from a single +5V power supply.

The existing morphological method is composed of morphological cleaning and boundary extraction. The morphological cleaning is performed by a closing following an opening using a cross-shaped SE, while the morphological boundary extraction is performed by taking the difference between the eroded and original noise-cleaned image. In realization of the morphological method, a low complexity architecture for binary image erosion and dilation is used [16] by decomposing a 3×3 symmetric structuring element into structuring elements of 1×3 (SE1) and 3×1 (SE2). The equation for erosion and dilation is shown in (3) and (4), respectively.

$$Erosion(A, SE) = (Erosion((Erosion(A, SE_1), SE_2)) \tag{3}$$

$$Dilation(A, SE) = {\sim} (Erosion((Erosion({\sim} A, SE_1), SE_2)) \tag{4}$$

In low complexity architecture, only erosion hardware is required to be designed, while the dilation's structure will be designed by utilizing the erosion hardware with two additional NOT gate (inverse) to reduce the hardware cost per (4). Fig. 7 shows the 1-D erosion of the low complexity architecture by the 1×3 structuring element.

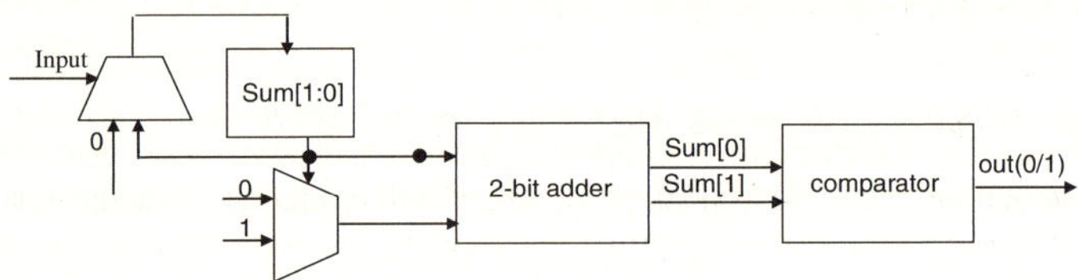


**Fig. 7.** Hardware structure of 1-D erosion

In Fig. 7, the variable Sum is initialized with 0, and the image pixel is fed in sequentially and is decided whether it is 0 or not. If input is zero, Sum will be reset to 0, otherwise it will be incremented by the adder and the result will be compared with 3. The output will be 1 if the sum equals to 3, otherwise the output will be zero. The 1-D erosion can be realized using two XORs, two ANDs, and two multiplexers. A 2-D erosion or dilation is then realized by utilizing by a 1-D erosion along the x-axis following a 1-D y-axis erosion. The morphological contour extraction is produced by the XOR gate of noise-cleaned image and the eroded morphological noise-cleaned image. The contour extraction equation is the following

$$EdgeExtract(A) = XOR(A, erosion(A)) \tag{5}$$

where A is the morphological noise-cleaned image. The performances of the proposed shape-preserving contour tracing and mathematical morphology method are evaluated using three 352×288 test images shown in Fig. 8(a), namely "Dog", "Hammer" and "Vase". To demonstrate the capabilities of the proposed contour tracing in shape preservation and redundancy suppression, random noises with bit error rate of 1% are inserted in the test images as shown in Fig. 8(b). Fig. 8(c) and Fig. 8(d) show the experiment result obtained by the morphological method and the shape-preserving contour tracing, respectively.

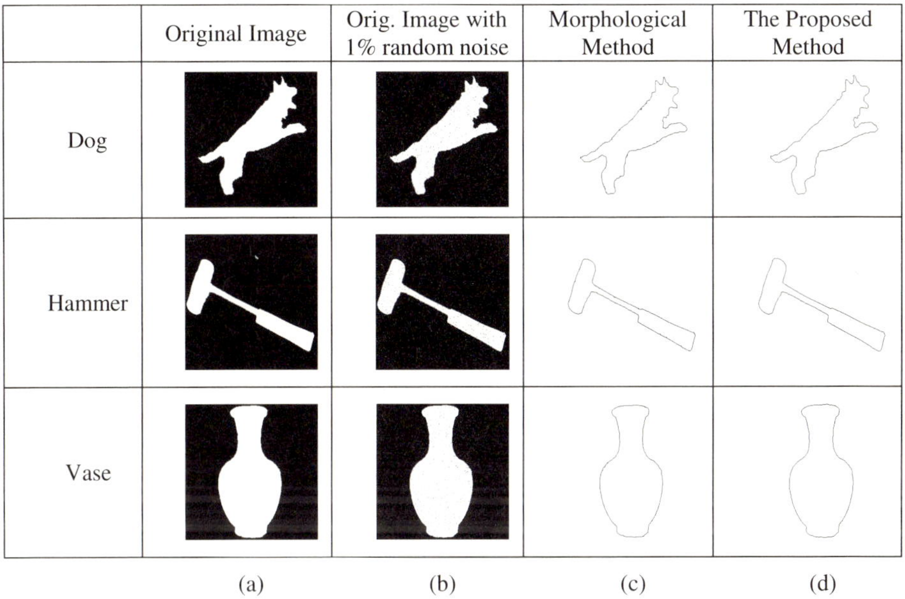

| | Original Image | Orig. Image with 1% random noise | Morphological Method | The Proposed Method |
|---|---|---|---|---|
| Dog | | | | |
| Hammer | | | | |
| Vase | | | | |
| | (a) | (b) | (c) | (d) |

**Fig. 8.** (a) Original image. (b) Noisy image by adding random noise with bit error rate of 1% to the original image. (c) Experiment result obtained by the morphological method. (d) Experiment result obtained by the shape-preserving contour tracing.

In the performance evaluation, three evaluation metrics are adopted for comparing experimental results of the proposed method and morphological method, which are accuracy, total execution time, and memory requirement. *Accuracy measurement:* The baseline-based mean absolute difference (BMAD) [15], as given below, is used for accuracy measurement,

$$BMAD = \frac{1}{N_p}\sum_{j=1}^{N_p}\left|\hat{d}_j - \overline{d}_j\right| \text{ for } \hat{d}_j \neq \infty \wedge \overline{d}_j \neq \infty \tag{6}$$

where $\hat{d}_j$ and $\overline{d}_j$ are the orthogonal distances measured from the $j^{th}$ sampling point of the reference baseline axis to the traced contour and the accurate contour, respectively. According to Eq. (6), the overall quality of the extracted contour is evaluated by computing the mean of individual baseline-based absolute difference obtained for each of the $N_p$ measurements. When the *BMAD* is lower, it means that the traced contour and the accurate contour will have lower mean distance error, and the accuracy between the traced and accurate is relatively higher.

Without lose of generality, the accuracy is defined as (1- *BMAD*)×100%. Table 1 shows the accuracy of the results obtained by morphological method and the proposed method. From inspection, the accuracy for Fig.8(d) is saliently larger than that obtained for Fig. 8(c), which exhibits that the proposed method outperforms the morphological boundary extraction following morphological cleaning process in precisely delineating object's contour under the environment with random noises.

**Table 1.** Accuracy comparison between morphological method and the proposed method

|  | Morphological Method | The Proposed Method |
|---|---|---|
| Dog | 25% | 98% |
| Hammer | 30% | 99% |
| Vase | 33% | 99% |

In the morphological method, the boundary extracted image is given by taking the difference image between the eroded image and the original morphological cleaned image [14], and consequently, this technique tends to "shrunk" the object's shape and boundary when a 3×3 square SE is used. As a result, the extracted boundary pixels are "eroded" with respect to the actual contour pixels. Moreover, the morphological cleaning operations lead to noticeable distortions on semantic object's significant details and concavities such as that occurring at "Dog" ears areas in Fig. 9(a), "Hammer" neck in Fig. 9(b), and "Vase" top in Fig. 9(c).

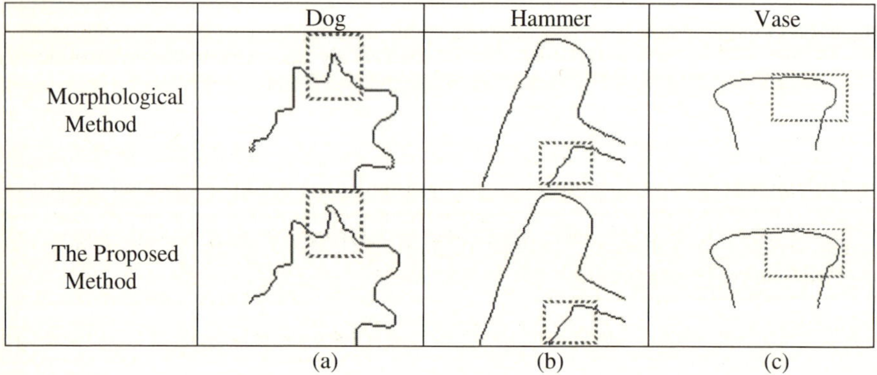


**Fig. 9.** Magnified portions of boundary extraction results. (a) Dog's ear, (b) Hammer's neck, (c) Vase top.

*Total Execution Time Measurement*

Assuming that $P$ boundary points are extracted in our proposed method, which means that PBL and SRP executes $P$ times. According to PBL and SRP, it takes 7 and 1 clock cycles, respectively, for PBL and SRP to decide a boundary point such that the total execution of the proposed method is 8P, which is proportional to the number of P as below.

$$T_{proposed} = 8P \propto P \tag{7}$$

In realization of the mathematical morphological method using low complexity architecture, the total execution time can be reduced which is proportional to $M{\times}N$, size of the image, for a single erosion operation as below

$$T_{low-complexity} \propto M \times N \tag{8}$$

It requires two erosions and two dilations in realization for a single morphological cleaning and one erosions and one XOR operations in realization for morphological boundary extraction such that the total execution time of the low complexity morphological method is about $6{\times}M{\times}N$, which is proportional to the size of the image. Table 2 shows the total execution time measured from the main controller using a software timer. From inspection, it is apparent that our proposed method obtains fast execution result for boundary extraction (i.e. lower total execution time) than the morphological method in every case. Based upon the evidence provided in Table 2, it seems reasonable to verify that the longer execution time of the morphological method is the result primarily of processing the whole image.

*Memory Requirement*

Memory utilization, such as logic and storage utilization, is commonly acknowledged metric in measuring the hardware realization of an algorithm. The flip-flop and latch are the basic storage unit, while 4-input look-up table (LUT) is the logic component for calculation. Besides, gate count is also a good measurement for space cost of a hardware realization. Hence, flip-flop, latch, 4-input LUT, and gate count are used in comparing the realization of the proposed method and the morphological method. Table 3 shows the metrics generated by running ISE Foundation, a FPGA design tool from Xilinx. From inspection, the 4 measuring metrics of the proposed method are in comparable of the morphological method, which means the hardware cost of the two methods are almost the same. This comparison exhibits that under the same hardware cost the proposed method outperforms the morphological method in accuracy and execution time. Significantly, it is precisely the fast execution time and accuracy of boundary extraction which are of most importance in realizing the contour extraction of the automatic robot vision and pattern-recognition applications used to analyze medical images, remote sensing images, and so forth. Hence, the present results suggest that the proposed method is in practical use as a preprocessing technique for such applications.

**Table 2.** Total execution time measurement of morphological method and the proposed method

| | Morphological Method | The Proposed Method | | |
|---|---|---|---|---|
| Total Execution time (in 0.1 ns) | 4,159,301 | Dog | Hammer | Vase |
| | | 32,480 | 33,768 | 29,841 |

**Table 3.** Memory requirement comparison of morphological method the proposed method

| Number of | Morphological Method | | The Proposed Method | |
|---|---|---|---|---|
| Slice registers | Flip-flips | Latches | Flip-flips | Latches |
| | 4,382 | 4 | 4,409 | 4 |
| 4-input LUTs | 14,143 | | 14,177 | |
| Gate count | 1,458,474 | | 1,458,879 | |

# 6  Conclusions

In this paper, a hardware design of shape-preserving contour tracing for object in a segmented image for robot vision and pattern recognition applications is presented. The proposed contour tracing consists of progressive boundary linking and synchronous redundancy pruning processes. Simulation results by realizing the proposed method on SoC shows that the proposed design achieves better results in terms of accuracy and hardware efficiency comparing with morphological boundary extraction. The present results suggest that the proposed method is in practical use as a preprocessing technique for automatic robot vision and pattern-recognition applications used to analyze medical images, remote sensing images, and so forth.

# References


1. Bates, G.L., Nooshabadi, S.: FPGA Implementation of a Median Filter. In: Proc. of IEEE on Speech and Image Technologies for Computing and Telecommunications, pp. 437–440 (1997)
2. Hazra, A., Bhattacharyya, J., Banerjee, S.: Real Time Noise Cleaning of Ultrasound Images. In: Proc. of IEEE Symposium on Computer-Based Medical Systems, pp. 379–384 (2004)
3. Torres-Huitzil, C., Arias-Estrada, M.: An FPGA Architecture for High Speed Edge and Corner Detection. In: Proc. of IEEE International Workshop on Computer Architectures for Machine Perception, pp. 112–116 (2000)
4. Hussmann, S., Ho, T.H.: A High-speed Subpixel Edge Detector Implementation Inside a FPGA. Real-Time Imaging 9(5), 361–368 (2003)
5. Jun, Y., Li, X.: Boundary Detection Using Mathematical Morphology. Pattern Recognition Letters 16(12), 1277–1286 (1995)
6. Shih Frank, Y., Shouxian, C.: Adaptive Mathematical Morphology for Edge Linking. Information Sciences 167(1), 9–21 (2004)

7. Dong, P.: Implementation of Mathematical Morphological Operations for Spatial Data Processing. Computers & Geosciences 23(1), 103–107 (1997)
8. Baumann, D., Tinembart, J.: Designing Mathematical Morphology Algorithms on FPGAs: An Application to Image Processing. In: Gagalowicz, A., Philips, W. (eds.) CAIP 2005. LNCS, vol. 3691, pp. 562–569. Springer, Heidelberg (2005)
9. Ali, K.S.: Digital Circuit Design using FPGAS. Computers & Industrial Engineering 31(1), 127–129 (1996)
10. Gustin, V.: An FPGA Extension to ALU Functions. Microprocessors and Microsystem 22(9), 501–508 (1999)
11. Iakovidis, D.K., Maroulis, D.E., Bariamis, D.G.: FPGA Architecture for Fast Parallel Computation of Co-occurrence Matrices. Microprocessors and Microsystems 31(2), 160–165 (2007)
12. Batlle, J., Marti, J., Ridao, P., Amat, J.: A New FPGA/DSP-Based Parallel Architecture for Real-Time Image Processing. Real-Time Imaging 8(5), 345–356 (2002)
13. Oswaldo, C., Graham, M.: A Clocking Technique for FPGA Pipelined Designs. Journal of Systems Architecture 50(11), 687–696 (2004)
14. Gonzalez, R.C., Woods, R.E.: Digital Image Processing 2/e. Prentice-Hall. Inc., New Jersey (2002)
15. Chan, D.-Y., Hsu, R.C.: Robust Shape-Preserving Contour Tracing with Synchronous Redundancy Pruning. Pattern Recognition Letters (29), 569–579 (2008)
16. Hedberg, H., Kristensen, F., Nilsson, P., Owall, V.: A low complexity architecture for binary image erosion and dilation using structuring element decomposition. In: IEEE International Symposium on Circuits and Systems, vol. 4, pp. 3431–3434 (2005)
17. Gaisler Research, http://www.gaisler.com

# Weighted Threshold Secret Image Sharing[*]

Shyong Jian Shyu[1,**], Chun-Chieh Chuang[2], Ying-Ru Chen[1], and Ah-Fur Lai[2]

[1] Department of Computer Science and Information Engineering, Ming Chuan University,
No. 5, De-Ming Road, Guei-Shan, Taoyuan 33348, Taiwan
Tel.: 886-3-3507001 Ext.3404; Fax: 886-3-3593874
[2] Department of Computer Science, Taipei Municipal University of Education,
No. 1, Ai-Guo West Road, Taipei 10048, Taiwan
`sjshyu@mail.mcu.edu.tw, {hellion0724,cindyooxx}@gmail.com,`
`lai@tmue.edu.tw`

**Abstract.** Given a secret image $I$, a threshold $r$, and a set of $n$ ($\geq r$) participants $\mathcal{P} = \{1, 2, \dots, n\}$ with a set of weights $\mathcal{W} = \{w_1, w_2, \dots, w_n\}$ where $w_i$ is the weight (which indicates the degree/rank of importance) of participant $i$ and we assume that $w_1 \leq w_2 \leq \dots \leq w_n$. The idea of weighted threshold secret image sharing encodes $I$ into $n$ shadows $S_1, S_2, \dots, S_n$ with sizes $|S_1| \leq |S_2| \leq \dots \leq |S_n|$ in which $S_i$ is distributed to participant $i$ such that only when a group of $r$ participants can reconstruct $I$ by using their shadows, while any group of less than $r$ participants cannot. We propose a novel weighted threshold secret image sharing scheme based upon Chinese remainder theorem in this paper. As compared to the conventional Shamir's and recent Thien-Lin's schemes, which produce shadows with the same size, our scheme is more flexible due to the reason that the dealer is able to distribute various-sized shadows to participants with different degrees/ranks of importance in terms of practical concerns.

**Keywords:** Threshold secret sharing, Secret image sharing, Weighted shadow size, Chinese remainder theorem.

## 1 Introduction

The concept of *threshold secret sharing* aims at sharing a secret value among several participants where each participant owns a part of the secret called *shadow* and only when a certain number (called *threshold*) of participants utilize their shadows can the secret be reconstructed, while less than the threshold number of participants cannot. Consider a secret $s$ and a set of participants $P = \{1, 2, \dots, n\}$ sharing $s$. Any approach that achieves the requirements of secret sharing for $s$ with a threshold $r$ among the $n$ participants in $P$ is called an $r$ out of $n$ (or $(r, n)$) secret sharing scheme.

Shamir [14] and Blakley [2] independently proposed the threshold secret sharing schemes in 1979. Shamir's approach is based upon the *polynomial interpolation* in a

---

[*] This research was partly supported by National Science Council of the Republic of China under contract NSC-97-2221-E-130-022-MY3.
[**] Corresponding author.

T. Wada, F. Huang, and S. Lin (Eds.): PSIVT 2009, LNCS 5414, pp. 988–998, 2008.

two-dimensional space, while Blakley's scheme originates from the intersections of some high-dimensional planes in a high-dimensional space. Shamir's scheme is simple and easy to implement so that it has attracted many researchers' attention [3, 4, 9, 11, 16]. Consider an $r-1$ degree polynomial:

$$f(x) = a_0 + a_1 x^1 + a_2 x^2 + \ldots + a_{r-1} x^{r-1} \tag{1}$$

where all computations are perform in $GF(p)$ in which $p$ is a prime (or a power of 2 or a prime), $1 \le a_{r-1} < p$, $0 \le a_w < p$ for $0 \le w \le r-2$, and $1 \le x < p$. Shamir's $(r, n)$ scheme utilizes this polynomial to share a secret $s$ as follows. The dealer sets $s$ to be $a_0$ and randomly chooses $a_1, a_2, \ldots , a_{r-1}$ to form $f(x)$. Then, he/she chooses $x_1, x_2, \ldots , x_n$ as *keys* based upon which $f(x_1), f(x_2), \ldots , f(x_n)$ are computed as *shadows*. The $n$ pairs of $(f(x_i), x_i)$'s, $1 \le i \le n$, are distributed to the $n$ participants one by one. Since any group of $r$ (or more) $(f(x_i), x_i)$'s is able to compute $(a_0, a_1, \ldots , a_{r-1})$ by solving the $r$ equations by polynomial interpolation, $s$ $(= a_0)$ is thus recovered. None of any group of less than $r$ participants can solve the $r$ equations completely. We say that $s$ is shared by $n$ participants in an $(r, n)$ threshold structure.

Thien and Lin [17] in 2002 extended Shamir's scheme so that the idea can be apply to share a secret image. Consider an image $P$ with $N$ pixels in total to be shared in an $(r, n)$ threshold structure. Thien-Lin's scheme first diffuses all $N$ pixels in $P$ and organizes them into $N/r$ segments with $r$ pixels each. Let the $r$ pixels in segment $t$ be denoted as $(a_0, a_1, \ldots , a_{r-1})_t$, $1 \le t \le N/r$. The values of these $r$ pixels of segment $t$ are assigned to be the $r$ coefficients of the above formula to form $f_t(x)$. Then, the dealer determines $n$ keys $x_1, x_2, \ldots , x_n$, and computes $f_t(x_1), f_t(x_2), \ldots , f_t(x_n)$ for $1 \le t \le N/r$. After that, $f_1(x_i), f_2(x_i), \ldots , f_{N/r}(x_i)$ are merged into a *shadow image* $D_i$ for $1 \le i \le n$. The dealer gives $(D_i, x_i)$ to participant $i$ for $1 \le i \le n$. It is not hard to see that only $r$ (or more) participants can recover $(a_0, a_1, \ldots , a_{r-1})_t$ by using their $r$ pairs of keys and shadows in polynomial interpolation for all equations $f_t(x)$'s, $1 \le t \le N/r$. $(a_0, a_1, \ldots , a_{r-1})_1, (a_0, a_1, \ldots , a_{r-1})_2, \ldots , (a_0, a_1, \ldots , a_{r-1})_{N/r}$ are indeed the $N$ pixels in $P$ which have been diffused before. After re-order all of the pixels, we reconstruct $P$. The shadow size of Thien-Lin's approach is $N/r$, that is, $D_i$ contains $N/r$ pixels for $1 \le i \le n$. If the original Shamir's approach is directly applied to share an image, the size of each shadow is $N$. Therefore, Thien-Lin's scheme reduces the size of the shadows as compared to Shamir's.

However, the sizes of all shadow images are the same in either Thien-Lin's or Shamir's approach. In real-world applications, this might not always be an advantage. For instance, a particular participant (the boss, a secret agent, etc.) would like to carry a shadow with a smaller (or larger) size for reducing the burden, cost (or increasing the secrecy) or other reasons. Our interest in this paper is thus to design a threshold secret image sharing scheme which produces shadows with various sizes. Since the dealer could define the weights of the participants and distribute the different-sized shadows to the participants according to their weights, we call our design the *weighted threshold secret image sharing scheme*. Essentially, the proposed scheme is based upon the *Chinese remainder theorem*.

The rest of the paper is organized as follows. We introduce Chinese remainder theorem and how to apply CRT to accomplish secret sharing in Section 2. Our design for a weighted threshold secret image sharing scheme is proposed in Section 3. Some experiments results are reported in Section 4. The secrecy analysis of our scheme is discussed in Section 5. Section 6 gives some concluding remarks.

## 2  Previous Studies

### 2.1  Chinese Reminder Theorem

Consider a secret value $x$ and $m \geq 2$ positive relatively prime moduli, namely $q_1, q_2, \ldots, q_m$. Let $Q = q_1 \times q_2 \times \ldots \times q_m$ and $s_i$ be the remainder of $x$ modulo $q_i$ for $1 \leq i \leq m$. The Chinese remainder theorem (CRT) asserts that the following system has a unique solution $x$ in $Z_Q$ [6]:

$$x \equiv s_1 \ (\text{mod } q_1)$$
$$x \equiv s_2 \ (\text{mod } q_2)$$
$$\ldots$$
$$x \equiv s_m \ (\text{mod } q_m) \ . \tag{2}$$

Give a number $x$ and $m$ positive relatively prime moduli $q_1, q_2, \ldots, q_m$ where $x \in Z_Q$, the above system is described as:

$$(s_1, s_2, \ldots, s_m) = CRT_remainders(x, m, q_1, q_2, \ldots, q_m). \tag{3}$$

The solution $x$ in $Z_Q$ can be obtained by many ways. One of the popular approaches is to compute $M_i$ and its multiple inverse $c_i$ (under modulus $q_i$) for all moduli $q_i$, $1 \leq i \leq m$ [15] first as follows:

$$M_i = Q / q_i \ , \tag{4}$$

$$c_i M_i \equiv 1 \ \text{mod } q_i \ . \tag{5}$$

Then $x$ can be obtained by

$$x = ( \sum_{i=1}^{m} s_i c_i M_i \ ) \ \text{mod } Q \ . \tag{6}$$

To ease the following applications of finding a solution based upon CRT, we organize these operations a procedure:

$$x = CRT_solution(m, q_1, q_2, \ldots, q_m, s_1, s_2, \ldots, s_m) \tag{7}$$

where $x \equiv s_i \ (\text{mod } q_i)$ for $1 \leq i \leq m$.

### 2.2  Threshold Secret Sharing by CRT

Let $x$ be a secret value and $q_1, q_2, \ldots, q_m$ be $m$ positive relatively prime moduli where $Q = q_1 \times q_2 \times \ldots \times q_m$ and $x \in Z_Q$. Since $(s_1, s_2, \ldots, s_m) = CRT_remainder(x, m, q_1, q_2, \ldots, q_m)$, a naïve idea for applying CRT for sharing $x$ among $m$ participants may be using $s_i$ as the shadow for participant $i$, $1 \leq i \leq m$. (This was adopted by Mcher and Patra [12] in their secret image sharing scheme in 2006.) For instance, assume that $m = 3$ and $(q_1, q_2,$

$q_3$) = (3, 5, 7). Consider a secret $x = 97$ sharing by 3 (= $m$) participants. Since ($s_1$, $s_2$, $s_3$) = (1, 2, 6) (= *CRT_remainder*(97, 3, 3, 5, 7)), i.e.

$$97 \equiv 1 \bmod 3$$
$$97 \equiv 2 \bmod 5$$
$$97 \equiv 6 \bmod 7 \, ,$$

($s_i$, $q_i$) might be distributed to participant $i$ for $i = 1, 2, 3$. Then, only when all three participants utilize their information, they can compute $x = 97$; while any group of less than two participants cannot.

Yet, we give an example to illustrate that such naïve application is incorrect in some cases. Consider the same scenario except for $x = 18$. We have ($s_1$, $s_2$, $s_3$) = (0, 3, 4) (= *CRT_remainder*(18, 3, 3, 5, 7)):

$$18 \equiv 0 \bmod 3$$
$$18 \equiv 3 \bmod 5$$
$$18 \equiv 4 \bmod 7 \, .$$

Indeed, all three participants can obtain 18 (18 = *CRT_solution*(3, 3, 5, 7, 0, 3, 4). However, participants 1 and 3 (or 2 and 3) can do so by using their (0, 3) and (4, 7) (or (3, 5) and (4, 7)) (18 = *CRT_solution*(2, 3, 7, 0, 4) = *CRT_solution*(2, 5, 7, 3, 4)) too. Thus, it is not a (3, 3) scheme. This naïve application of CRT cannot construct a threshold secret sharing scheme.

To share a secret by using CRT is not a new topic, Mignotte [13] and Asmuth-Bloom [1] proposed ($r$, $n$) threshold secret sharing schemes in 1983 individually. Some following studies can be found in [5, 7, 8, 10]. Our scheme is based upon Mignotte's idea that is introduced as follows.

Consider $n$ relatively positive prime moduli $q_1 < q_2 < \ldots < q_n$. Let $\alpha = q_{n-r+2} \times q_{n-r+3} \times \ldots \times q_n$ (the product of maximal $r-1$ moduli) and $\beta = q_1 \times q_2 \times \ldots \times q_r$ (the product of the minimal $r$ moduli). Let secret $x$ satisfy $\alpha < x < \beta$. The dealer distributes ($s_i$, $q_i$) to participant $i$ for $1 \leq i \leq n$ where ($s_1$, $s_2$, $\ldots$, $s_n$) = *CRT_remainder*($x$, $n$, $q_1$, $q_2$, $\ldots$, $q_n$) so as to accomplish sharing $x$ among the $n$ participants in an ($r$, $n$) structure. Assume that any group of $r-1$ participants, say $\{i_1, i_2, \ldots, i_{r-1}\}$, compute as follows with their shadows and moduli:

$$y = CRT_solution(r-1, q_{i_1}, q_{i_2}, \ldots, q_{i_{r-1}}, s_{i_1}, s_{i_2}, \ldots, s_{i_{r-1}}) \, .$$

They can only retain a solution $y$ in $Z_{Q'}$ where $Q' = q_{i_1} \times q_{i_2} \times \ldots \times q_{i_{r-1}} \leq \alpha \, (= q_{n-r+2} \times q_{n-r+3} \times \ldots \times q_n)$ according to CRT. Since $y < \alpha < x$, $y \neq x$. On the other hand, when $r$ participants, say $i_1, i_2, \ldots, i_r$, compute as follows with all their shadows and moduli, they can recover $x$:

$$x = CRT_solution(r, q_{i_1}, q_{i_2}, \ldots, q_{i_r}, s_{i_1}, s_{i_2}, \ldots, s_{i_r}) \, .$$

Therefore, the ($r$, $n$) threshold property holds.

## 3  The Proposed Scheme

Consider an $h \times w$ secret image $I$ with $M$ bits in total and a set of $n$ participants sharing $I$. Our encoding process first chooses $n$ relatively prime moduli $q_1 < q_2 < \ldots < q_n$, and compute $\alpha = q_{n-r+2} \times q_{n-r+3} \times \ldots \times q_n$ and $\beta = q_1 \times q_2 \times \ldots \times q_r$. We regard secret image $I$ as a series of $l$ blocks with $d$-bit each (i.e. $d \times l = M$) block where each block, say $I_k$, as an encoding unit where $0 \leq x_k = value(I_k) \leq 2^d - 1$ for $1 \leq k \leq l$ where $value(I_k)$ denotes the $d$-bit value of $I_k$. To cope with cases like natural images which contains similar colors (values of pixels), we simply introduce a series of random numbers in range $[0, 2^d - 1]$ with an initial seed $e$ and perform "xor" operation to all values of all blocks in order to diffuse those similar colors.

To maintain the $(r, n)$ threshold property, we adjust the value of $x_k$ to be $x_k'$ such that the constraint $\alpha < x_k' < \beta$ is met. This is done by adding the diffused value $x_k'$ with a pre-determined offset $p$ where $\alpha < p < \beta - 2^d$. Formally, we set $e$ as the seed of the random sequence, i.e.

$$random_ seed(e) \tag{8}$$

and set the range of the random numbers, i.e. $[0, 2^d - 1]$, by

$$random_range(0:2^d - 1) ; \tag{9}$$

then perform

$$x_k' = (x_k \oplus random()) + p \tag{10}$$

for all $I_k$'s, $1 \leq k \leq l$ where $random()$ returns a random number which is a member of a random sequence in $[0, 2^d - 1]$ seeded by $e$. Note that we deliberately set $p$ as the seed $e$, i.e. $e = p$ in our implementation. Then, $x_k'$ is shared among the $n$ participants in an $(r, n)$ structure by using CRT for all $I_k$'s:

$$(s_{k,1}, s_{k,2}, \ldots , s_{k,n}) = CRT_remainder(x_k', n, q_1, q_2, \ldots , q_n). \tag{11}$$

where $0 \leq s_{k,i} < q_i$. We take $z_i = \lceil \log_2 q_i \rceil$ bits to store $s_{k,i}$ for $1 \leq k \leq l$ and $1 \leq i \leq n$. All $z_i$-bit remainders distributed to participant $i$ are merged $z_i$-bit by $z_i$-bits to form shadow $S_i$:

$$S_i = s_{1,i} \| s_{2,i} \| \ldots \| s_{l,i} \tag{12}$$

where $\|$ denotes the concatenation operation. Thus, the bit-length of $S_i$ is $| S_i | = z_i \times l (= \lceil \log_2 q_i \rceil \times M/d)$.

Further, $p$ is shared among the $n$ participants in the $(r, n)$ structure by using CRT, too. That is

$$(a_1, a_2, \ldots , a_n) = CRT_remainder(p, n, q_1, q_2, \ldots , q_n) . \tag{13}$$

The dealer thus distributes $(S_i, a_i, q_i)$ to participant $i$ for $1 \leq i \leq n$. Since $q_1 < q_2 < \ldots < q_n$, we have $(\lceil \log_2 q_1 \rceil \times M/d) \leq (\lceil \log_2 q_2 \rceil \times M/d) \leq \ldots \leq (\lceil \log_2 q_n \rceil \times M/d)$ and consequently $| S_1 | \leq | S_2 | \leq \ldots \leq | S_n |$. That means the sizes of the shadows are weighted in terms of those of the moduli. Or, each participant receives a part of information whose size is related to his/her weight.

The encoding algorithm is formally illustrated as follows.

---

**Encoding algorithm**

Input: a secret image $I$ with $M$ bits in total, a set of participants $P = \{1, 2, \ldots, n\}$ with a set of weights $W = \{w_1, w_2, \ldots, w_n \mid w_1 \leq w_2 \leq \ldots \leq w_n\}$, threshold $r$ ($2 \leq r \leq n$), and parameter $d$.

Output: shadows $S_i$ and $a_i$, and modulus $q_i$ for $1 \leq i \leq n$.

1. Choose $\{q_1, q_2, \ldots, q_n \mid (q_i, q_j) = 1, 2 < q_1 < q_2 < \ldots < q_n < 2^d\}$ according to $W$ and $d$

2. $\alpha = q_{n-r+2} \times q_{n-r+3} \times \ldots \times q_n$; $\beta = q_1 \times q_2 \times \ldots \times q_r$ // $\alpha < \beta < 2^d$

3. Choose seed $p$ randomly with $\alpha < p < \beta - 2^d$

4. $random_seed(p)$; $random_range(0{:}2^d - 1)$
  // set $p$ as the seed of the random sequence ranging from 0 to $2^d$

5. Partition $I$ into $l$ ($= M/d$) segments: $I_1, I_2, \ldots, I_l$ // $I_k$ is with $d$ bits, $1 \leq k \leq l$

6. for (each $I_k$, $1 \leq k \leq l$) do

6.1 { $x_k = value(I_k)$

6.2   $x_k' = (x_k \oplus random()) + p$

6.3   for (each $i$, $1 \leq i \leq n$) do $s_{k,i} = x_k' \bmod q_i$ // $\mid s_{k,i} \mid = \lceil \log_2 q_i \rceil$

  }

7. for (each $i$, $1 \leq i \leq n$) do

7.1 { $S_i = \varnothing$

7.2   for (each $k$, $1 \leq k \leq l$) do $S_i = S_i \cup \{s_{k,i}\}$
    // Append $s_{k,i}$ ($\mid s_{k,i} \mid = \lceil \log_2 q_i \rceil$) after $S_i$: $S_i = S_i \parallel s_{k,i}$

  }

8. for (each $i$, $1 \leq i \leq n$) do $a_i = p \bmod q_i$

9. Output($S_1, S_2, \ldots, S_n, a_1, a_2, \ldots, a_n, q_1, q_2, \ldots, q_n$)
  // the dealer distributes ($S_i, a_i, q_i$) to participant $i$

---

Participant $i$ would get ($S_i, a_i, q_i$) from the dealer for $1 \leq i \leq n$. It is noticed that the size of shadow $S_i$ is $\lceil \log_2 q_i \rceil \times M/d$ for $1 \leq i \leq n$. Thus the sizes of $S_1, S_2, \ldots, S_n$ are determined by those of $q_1, q_2, \ldots, q_n$ which are based upon the weights $w_1, w_2, \ldots, w_n$ accordingly. This offers a flexible decision for the dealer about which participant is more/less important at his/her convenience.

The decoding algorithm is shown in the following.

---

**Decoding algorithm**

Input: $r$ participants $i_1, i_2, \ldots, i_r \in P$ and the corresponding moduli $q_{i_1} < q_{i_2} < \cdots < q_{i_r}$, shadows $S_{i_1}, S_{i_2}, \ldots, S_{i_r}$, and $a_{i_1}, a_{i_2}, \ldots, a_{i_r}$, and parameter $d$.

Output: the secret image $I$.

1. $p = CRT_solution(r, a_{i_1}, a_{i_2}, \ldots, a_{i_r}, q_{i_1}, q_{i_2}, \ldots, q_{i_r})$

2. for ($1 \leq j \leq r$) $z_j = \lceil \log_2 q_{i_j} \rceil$

3. $random_seed(p)$; $random_range(0{:}2^d - 1)$

4. $I = \varnothing$

5. $l = \mid S_{i_1} \mid / z_1$  // $l$ is the number of blocks; each shadow has the same $l$

---

6.      for (each $k$, $1 \leq k \leq l$) do
6.1     {     for (each $S_{i_j}$, $1 \leq j \leq r$) do
              {     $s_{k,j}$ = the first $z_j$ bits of $S_{i_j}$
                    $S_{i_j} = S_{i_j} - \{s_{k,j}\}$          // delete the first $z_j$ bits from $S_{i_j}$
              }
6.2           $y_k = CRT_solution(r, s_{k,1}, s_{k,2}, \ldots, s_{k,r}, q_{i_1}, q_{i_2}, \ldots, q_{i_r})$
6.3           $x_k = (y_k - p) \oplus random()$
6.4           make $x_k$ to be $d$-bit long
6.5           $I = I \cup \{x_k\}$    // Append $x_k$ after $I$ by $d$-bit concatenation ($I = I \parallel x_k$)
        }
7.      Output($I$)

## 4  Experimental Results

We report the implementation results of our scheme for testing a simple (3, 4) case in this section. The program was coded in Microsoft C# and tested in a PC with Windows. A 256×256 color Mandrill image was tested the secret image $I$ as shown in Fig. 1 which is shared by four participants: 1, 2, 3 and 4 with weights $w_1 \leq w_2 \leq w_3 \leq w_4$. We assume that the dealer would like to produce four shadows $S_1$, $S_2$, $S_3$ and $S_4$ for participants 1, 2, 3 and 4 respectively with $|S_1| \leq |S_2| \leq |S_3| \leq |S_4|$.

In our implementation, we set $d$ as 29 and $(q_1, q_2, q_3, q_4) = (1009, 2026, 5095, 31651)$; thus, $\alpha = 5095 \times 31651 = 161261845$ and $\beta = 1009 \times 2026 \times 5095 = 10415372230$. The secret image is treated as a one dimensional array with 256×256×24 bit (since one color pixel takes 24 bits specifying the R, G, B colors in a Windows environment). The number of blocks in our experiment is $l = \lceil M/d \rceil = 54237$. Note that we simply append white pixels in the last block to make the number of pixels in it to be 29.

**Fig. 1.** Secret image to be shared

Fig. 2 shows the four shares $S_1$, $S_2$, $S_3$ and $S_4$ produced by our encoding algorithm with sizes 89×256, 98×256, 115×256 and 133×256 respectively which meet the requirement of $|S_1| \leq |S_2| \leq |S_3| \leq |S_4|$. Let us explain why the size (or pixels) of $S_1$ is 89×256. Each remainder of the value corresponding to a 29-bit block in $I$ under modulus $q_1$ (= 1009) is less than 1009 and is stored by using $\lceil \log_2 q_1 \rceil = \lceil \log_2 1009 \rceil = 10$ bits.

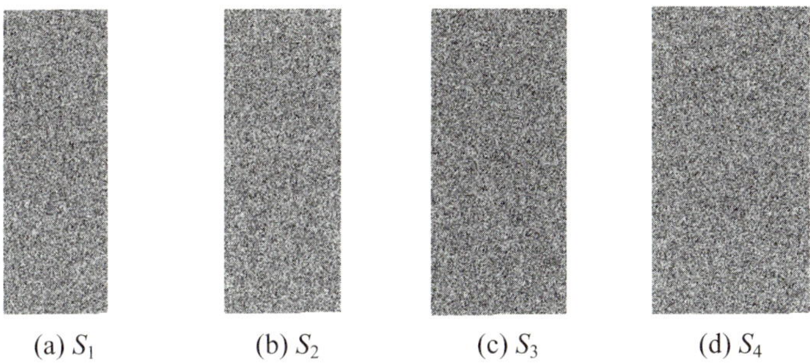

(a) $S_1$     (b) $S_2$     (c) $S_3$     (d) $S_4$

**Fig. 2.** Shadows produced by the encoding algorithm

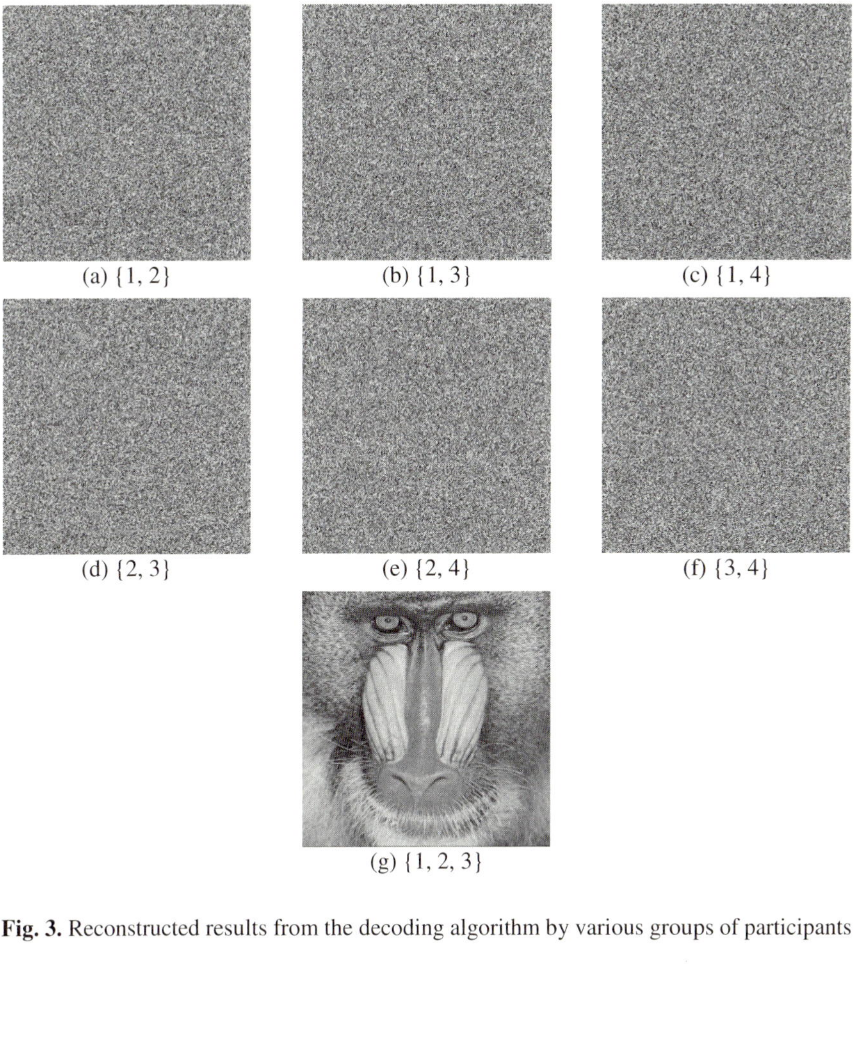

(a) $\{1, 2\}$     (b) $\{1, 3\}$     (c) $\{1, 4\}$

(d) $\{2, 3\}$     (e) $\{2, 4\}$     (f) $\{3, 4\}$

(g) $\{1, 2, 3\}$

**Fig. 3.** Reconstructed results from the decoding algorithm by various groups of participants

Thus, after encoding all $l$ blocks, there are $54237 \times 10 = 542370$ encoded bits which constitute $S_1$. The bit-lengths of the other shadows are determined in the same way. For the display and comparison purposes, we regarded these consecutive bits as a serious of 24-bit color pixels which constitute a color image with a height of 256. Since $\lceil (542370/24)/256 \rceil = 89$, thus the size of $S_1$ becomes $89 \times 256$.

Fig. 3 illustrates the reconstructed images from our decoding algorithm by various groups of participants where (a)-(g) are by $\{1, 2\}$, $\{1, 3\}$, $\{1, 4\}$, $\{2, 3\}$, $\{2, 4\}$, $\{3, 4\}$, $\{1, 2, 3\}$ respectively. Note that the results obtained by $\{1, 2, 4\}$, $\{1, 3, 4\}$. $\{2, 3, 4\}$ and $\{1, 2, 3, 4\}$ are exactly the same as Fig. 3 (g), which is the same as the original baboon image, so that we just omit them here. Besides, the sizes (or pixels) of these resultant images are all $256 \times 256$. This is due to our assumption that the groups of more than one participant knew $d$ (the block size), $l$ (the number of blocks) and the decoding algorithm so that they applied CRT to recover the 29-bit secret blocks by using their information and displayed their result as a 24-bit based color image.

It is easily seen from Fig. 3 that any group of less than three participants cannot recover $I$, while any group of three or more participants can. The attractive feature is that $|S_1| \le |S_2| \le |S_3| \le |S_4|$ whose sizes are determined by the values of the chosen moduli which define the degree/rank of importance of the participants. These results demonstrated the feasibility and applicability of our scheme.

## 5  Secrecy Analysis

Since $p$ is shared in an $(r, n)$ manner, thus, only when $r$ participants can recover them correctly. Assume that a group of $r-1$ participants, say $\{i_1, i_2, \ldots, i_{r-1}\}$ with $w_{i_1} < w_{i_2} < \ldots < w_{i_{r-1}}$, tries to recover $I$ by using information what they have. The best case for them is to guess $i_0$'s information $(S_{i_0}, a_{i_0}, q_{i_0})$ where $i_0 < i_1$ (or $q_{i_0} < q_{i_1}$) (since it would be harder to guess $i_j$'s $(> i_{r-1})$ information, $j > r-1$). Due to the reason that the number of blocks $l$ is the same among all participants, we have $l = |S_{i_j}| / \lceil \log_2 q_{i_j} \rceil$ for each $j$, $1 \le j \le r-1$. That is, we know the number of blocks in $S_{i_0}$. Still, $a_{i_0}$, $q_{i_0}$ and the content of $S_{i_0}$ are unknown by now. Since $a_{i_0}$ is a certain remainder under modulus $q_{i_0}$, thus $a_{i_0} < q_{i_0}$. The probability for blindly guessing $a_{i_0}$ and $q_{i_0}$ right is $1/(a_{i_0}) \times 1/(q_{i_0})$ ($< 1/(q_{i_1})^2$ because of $a_{i_0} < q_{i_0} < q_{i_1}$). Once $a_{i_0}$ and $q_{i_0}$ are correctly obtained, $p$ can be obtained by computing

$$p = CRT_solution(r, a_{i_0}, a_{i_1}, \ldots, a_{i_{r-1}}, q_{i_0}, q_{i_1}, \ldots, q_{i_{r-1}}) .$$

By guessing the value $s_{k,0}$ in block $k$ of $\lceil \log_2 q_{i_0} \rceil$ bits in $S_{i_0}$ (i.e. a remainder under modulus $q_{i_0}$), we compute:

$$x_k' = CRT_solution(r, s_{k,0}, s_{k,1}, \ldots, s_{k,r-1}, q_{i_0}, q_{i_1}, \ldots, q_{i_{r-1}})$$

where $s_{k,j}$ is the value of block $k$ in $S_{i_j}$ for $0 \le j \le r-1$ and $1 \le k \le l$. By using

$$x_k = (x_k' - p) \oplus random() ,$$

we get $x_k$, which is the value of block $I_k$ with $d$ bits in $I$ where *random*() returns a random number seeded initially at $p$ with a range of $[0, 2^d-1]$. If all $x_k$'s are found and merged ($d$-bit by $d$-bit) for $1 \le k \le l$, we obtain $I$. That is $I = x_1 \parallel x_2 \parallel \dots \parallel x_l$.

The probability of guessing $s_{k,0}$ right (and subsequently finding out $x_k$) is $1/q_{i_0}$ ($< 1/q_{i_1}$) and a bound of that of guessing all $l$ blocks' $s_{k,0}$'s ($1 \le k \le l$) right (and subsequently finding out $I$) is $(1/q_{i_1})^l$. Thus an upper bound of the probability for this group of $r-1$ participants to decode $(S_{i_0}, a_{i_0}, q_{i_0})$ is

$$(1/(q_{i_1})^2) \times (1/q_{i_1})^l = (1/q_{i_1})^{l+2} \; (= (1/q_{i_1})^{M/d+2}) \, . \tag{14}$$

As mentioned earlier, once $(S_{i_0}, a_{i_0}, q_{i_0})$ is found, the secret image $I$ can be reconstructed by this group of the $r-1$ participants.


## 6  Concluding Remarks

We propose, analyze and implement a novel weighted threshold secret image sharing scheme by using CRT in this paper. The shadow sizes produced by our scheme are correlated with the weights of the participants which imply the degrees/ranks of importance of the participants. As compared to the conventional Shamir's and the recent Thien-Lin's approaches which produce shadows with the same size, our scheme is more flexible so that it can be applied to some practical situations that the parts of information given to different participants are with different sizes in terms of their degrees/ranks of importance.

In the decoding and encoding algorithms, $d$ is designed to be an input parameter and the seed $e$ is the same as $p$. To increase the level of secrecy, $d$ and $e$ might be shared as well among the $n$ participants in an $(r, n)$ structure. For a certain parameter $d$, how to determine the $n$ relative prime moduli (all less than $2^d$) is a critical concern in our scheme, especially, to enhance the level of secrecy (as discussed in Section 5). It is an interesting topic to go on. The authors are also interested in how to find the $n$ relative prime moduli which are proportional to the values of the weights efficiently.


## References


1. Asmuth, C., Bloom, J.: A modular approach to key safeguarding. IEEE Transactions on Information Theory IT-29(2), 208–210 (1983)
2. Blakley, G.R.: Safeguarding cryptographic keys. In: AFIPS Conf. Proc., vol. 48, pp. 313–317 (1979)
3. Brickell, E.F.: Some ideal secret sharing schemes. Journal of Combinatorial Mathematics and Combinatorial Computing 6, 105–113 (1989)
4. Chang, C.-C., Hwang, R.-J.: Sharing secret images using shadow codebooks. Information Sciences 111(1-4), 335–345 (1998)
5. Galibus, T., Matveev, G.: Generalized mignotte's sequences over polynomial rings. Electr. Notes Theor. Comput. Sci. 186, 43–48 (2007)
6. Hardy, D.W., Walker, C.L.: Applied Algebra: codes, ciphers, and discrete algorithms. Prentice Hall, Englewood Cliffs (2003)

7. Iftene, S.: Compartmented secret sharing based on the Chinese remainder theorem. Cryptology ePrint Archive (2005)
8. Iftene, S.: General secret sharing based on the Chinese remainder theorem. Cryptology ePrint Archive, Report 2006/166 (2006)
9. Ito, M., Saito, A., Nishizeki, T.: Secret sharing scheme realizing general access structure. In: Proceedings of IEEE, Globecom 1987, pp. 99–102 (1987)
10. Li, H.-X., Pang, L.-J., Cai, W.-D.: An efficient threshold multi-group-secret sharing scheme. Advances in Soft Computing 40, 911–918 (2007)
11. Lin, C.-C., Tsai, W.-H.: Secret image sharing with steganography and authentication. Journal of Systems and Software 73(3), 405–414 (2004)
12. Meher, P.K., Patra, J.C.: A new approach to secure distributed storage, sharing and dissemination of digital image. In: Proceedings of the IEEE International Symposium on Circuits and Systems, pp. 373–376 (2006)
13. Mignotte, M.: How to share a secret. In: Beth, T. (ed.) EUROCRYPT 1982. LNCS, vol. 149, pp. 371–375. Springer, Heidelberg (1983)
14. Shamir, A.: How to share a secret. Communications of the ACM 22(11), 612–613 (1979)
15. Stallings, W.: Cryptography and Network Security Principles and Practices, 4th edn. Prentice Hall, Englewood Cliffs (2005)
16. Tan, K.J., Zhu, H.W.: General secret sharing scheme. Computer Communications 22, 755–757 (1999)
17. Thien, C.-C., Lin, J.-C.: Secret image sharing. Computers and Graphics 26, 765–770 (2002)

# Removal of Specular Reflection Component Using Multi-view Images and 3D Object Model

Shu-Kam Chow and Kwok-Leung Chan

Department of Electronic Engineering, City University of Hong Kong,
83 Tat Chee Avenue, Kowloon, Hong Kong
{shukchow,itklchan}@cityu.edu.hk

**Abstract.** Image-based 3D model reconstruction method can use the same multi-view image sequence of the object for the generation of both the geometry model and texture map. Texture is very critical for virtual exhibition of 3D model and should be of high quality comparable to the geometry data. One problem is that the object surface may exhibit specular reflection of illuminated light. The texture extracted directly from the images can be unnatural. We propose a method for the removal of specular reflection component in each image. Each camera view is calibrated and a 3D mesh model of the object is generated. For each triangle patch, the projected colors on all visible views are found. The specular chromaticity is replaced by the corresponding diffuse chromaticity. We test the method on image sequences of synthetic and real objects. The diffuse image sequence can be used to generate the texture map.

**Keywords:** specularity removal, dichromatic reflection model, 3D model reconstruction, texture mapping.

## 1 Introduction

To create photorealistic three-dimensional (3D) model of real scenes and objects is an old and challenging computer vision problem. We intend to develop a system for the reconstruction and interactive exhibition of 3D object models on the web. Real object models can be reconstructed automatically using active and passive methods [1]. Object range scanning by laser and structured light are typical examples of the active methods. One of the most significant advantages of laser scanners is their high accuracy in geometry measurements. The passive methods exploit images of the object acquired by digital cameras locating at different viewpoints and reconstruct the 3D model using photogrammetry. They are of low cost and useful when direct access to the object is prohibited. While there are methods for 3D digitization of objects with high geometric resolution, there are still limitations in generating high quality texture for virtual exhibition. Texture is very critical for virtual exhibition of objects such as cultural artefacts and often should be of high resolution comparable to the range data [2]. One problem is that the object surface exhibits specular reflection of illuminated light during the acquisition of surface texture. The texture reconstructed from the multi-view image sequence, such as by texture stitching, can be unnatural. Also, the lighting during texture capturing of one object may not be the same as that of other objects. This is certainly undesirable for a virtual scene with many objects.

T. Wada, F. Huang, and S. Lin (Eds.): PSIVT 2009, LNCS 5414, pp. 999–1009, 2009.

To solve the problem, we need to remove the specular reflection and relight the texture mapped 3D model. We propose a method for the removal of specular reflection component in each image. Each camera view is calibrated and a 3D mesh model of the object is generated. With the availability of the 3D model and multi-view images, the correspondence of the image pixels is established. For each triangle patch, the projected colors on all visible views are found. The specular chromaticity is replaced by the corresponding diffuse chromaticity. No assumptions on the light source characteristics are made.

A review of previous work on specularity removal is presented in the following section. Section 3 presents the steps involved in the reconstruction of 3D object from a multi-view image sequence. Section 4 explains our proposed technique for the removal of specularity reflection component in each image. We test our method on image sequences of synthetic and real objects. Finally we conclude the paper and suggest some future work.


## 2    Related Work

Many methods for the identification and removal of specular reflection component demand polarizer filter, light source arrangement or rely on information obtained in one or more images. Due to page limit, we only present a review on the latter approach in here.

Klinker *et al.* [3] first introduce the single-image approach for specularity removal. Based on the dichromatic reflection model (most applicable to dielectrics) [4], diffuse and specular pixels form linear clusters of skewed-T in the color histogram. The limitations are that surfaces should be homogeneous (non-textured, locally valid if pre-segmentation is performed) with negligible image noise, specular lobe is sufficiently narrow, and diffuse (object) and specular (illuminant) colors are different. Tan *et al.* [5] introduce an inpainting technique for specularities removal. Information for determining the diffuse reflection of specular pixel is obtained based on the dichromatic reflection model and the assumption of a uniform illuminant color in the highlight. The method can preserve the diffuse shading in the highlight region which has been delineated manually. Problems may arise from discontinuities in surface colors. Later, they [6] extend the method by examining higher-order color data in the form of spatial color distributions. This data, which can be obtained outside the highlight region, can provide valuable information in determining diffuse colors within the highlight region. Tan and Ikeuchi [7] propose an iterative method to separate diffuse and specular reflection components. The image is normalized by the illumination chromaticity. This image is then transformed to a specular-free image by shifting the intensity and maximum chromaticity of the pixels nonlinearly while retaining their hue. Diffuse pixels are identified by using intensity logarithmic differentiation on both the normalized image and its specular-free image. The restrictions are that diffuse reflection component always exists in each pixel, and the surface color is chromatic.

Lin and Shum [8] propose a method to perform decomposition of diffuse and specular reflection using two photometric images. Surface reflection is modeled as a linear function of three basis functions. Specular reflection is assumed to have the same spectral composition as the incident illumination. Corresponding pixels in two images are assumed to be known. Specular highlights do not saturate and do not spatially overlap between the images. Lin *et al.* [9] propose a method based on color analysis and multi-baseline stereo that simultaneously separates the diffuse and specular reflections and estimates the true depth. Specular pixels are identified by a voting-based multiple tri-view color histogram differencing. Disparity of specular pixels is estimated based on neighboring diffuse pixels according to continuity constraint. The corresponding diffuse pixels are found based on the disparity of specular pixel. The method is applicable on grey-scale image. The method is sensitive to color saturation, image noise, and changes of specular color among the viewpoints.

Mallick *et al.* [10] present a unified framework for separating diffuse and specular reflection components in images and videos. Using a known illumination color, each image is transformed into SUV space, and three functions are computed. Specular/diffuse separation is achieved locally by numerically evolving the appropriate multi-scale erosion PDE on one function. Yu *et al.* [11] propose an algorithm to reconstruct the triangulated 3D model and the View Independent Reflectance Map (VIRM) from multiple calibrated images of an object. VIRM represent the joint effect of the linearly related diffuse and specular reflections, and illumination. The reflectance model is designed for objects with the same material and is illuminated by distant lighting with no self-shadowing and inter-reflections. Criminisi *et al.* [12] describe a new approach for analyzing the epipolar-plane-image (EPI) volume generated by the image sequence captured from a linearly translating camera. The EPI volume can be segmented into EPI strips and EPI tubes. Based on the geometric and photometric behavior of specularities in the EPI volume, the static scene can be decomposed into its diffuse and specular components.

## 3  3D Model Reconstruction

The camera calibration is to obtain the intrinsic and extrinsic parameters defining the internal camera properties and the viewpoint orientation with respect to the object. A box is fabricated which has calibration patterns posted on 5 viewable planes. During image acquisition, the target object is placed onto the top plane of the box (see Figure 1). Both the object and the calibration patterns are captured simultaneously in each image. Therefore, the camera can be placed anywhere and each view can be calibrated independently. Each calibration pattern consists of groups of red and blue lines. Each intersection of a red line and a blue line is a calibration point. We adopt Tsai's method [13] for camera calibration. Depending on the viewpoint, coplanar or non-planar algorithm can be employed.

The volumetric modeling is an important step in the reconstruction of 3D object model from a multi-view image sequence. It represents a world coordinate frame and the volume space in which the object occupies, and makes decision about whether a volumetric primitive (voxel) contains the object. The contour of the object is simply extracted from each of the input images, e.g. by the blue-screen technique with the use of a monochromatic background. We adopt the voting-based shape-from-silhouette method [14] for volumetric modeling.

**Fig. 1.** Picture of target object and calibration box

It is more favorable to represent the 3D object model in piecewise-planar surfaces. Majority of rendering techniques such as shading and hidden surface removal are performed on geometrically defined surfaces. Moreover, the polygon is easy to process, and so the rendering and display of object can be speed up. Therefore, in our system, the volumetric model is converted into polygonal surface model using the marching cubes algorithm [15]. The number of triangles generated by the marching cubes algorithm is as much as the number of voxels in the volumetric model. However, such a lot of triangles are not only useless to improve the visual quality of the model, but also burden the overall reconstruction process and even increase the computational time. Therefore, polygon simplification is implemented to simplify the model. When the model is simplified, neighboring polygons sometimes form a sharp transition. This defect is easily observed in the curved surface of the object. To overcome this problem, surface smoothing is performed in order to provide the visually pleasing surface model.

## 4  Specularity Removal

With the calibrated multi-view images, the correspondence of the image pixels is established. But for real objects, the shape can be complex. Therefore, visibility of the model must be checked. For each triangle patch, the projected colors on all visible views are found. The diffuse chromaticity is determined by searching for the maximum chromaticity. Special care is taken when performing the specularity removal on texture boundary. The specularity removal algorithm is shown below.

*For each camera view*
        *Find triangle patches that are facing backward*
        *Find triangle patches that are occluded*
        *Create a list of visible surface for that camera view*
*End For*
*For each image*
        *For each visible triangle patch*
                *Get the projected colors in the current camera view*
                *Get the corresponding projected colors in other camera views*
                *Determine the diffuse colors*
        *End For*
        *Replace the specular colors by the corresponding diffuse colors*
*End For*

## 4.1  Visibility of Triangle Patch

Here, we want to find out those triangle patches that are invisible (e.g. facing backward or occluded by other triangle patches) in a particular camera viewpoint. This is very important to eliminate all the impossible projections and make our multi-view specular-to diffuse color transformation reliable.

A back face triangle is invisible in a particular camera view and hence does not provide true projected colors. Basically, our algorithm compares the orientation of the triangles with the camera viewpoint and determines those triangles that cannot be seen. The visibility test is best carried out in the view space. We examine the dot product of the triangle's outward normal vector $\hat{N}_t$ and the vector from the camera's centre of projection $\hat{N}$ as shown in Figure 2. The triangle is visible only if the value of the dot product is larger than the pre-defined threshold (i.e. $\hat{N}_t \bullet \hat{N} > threshold$ ).

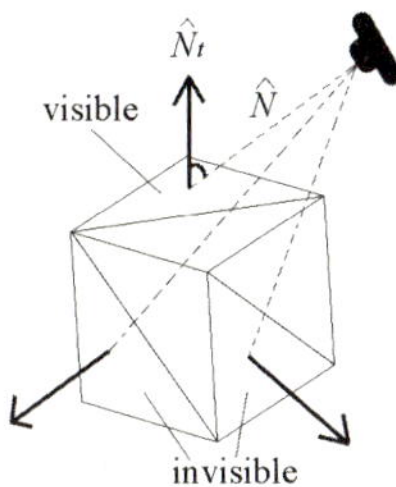


**Fig. 2.** Identification of back face triangle ( $\hat{N}_t$ is the unit normal vector of triangle, $\hat{N}$ is the 'line of sight' unit vector)

For concave or self-occluded object, some triangles may be occluded by other surfaces in a particular camera view. Occluded triangles should be removed from the list of visible surface $V$ for that viewpoint. We identify the occluded triangles by counting the number of non-occluded pixels projected on the camera view $C$. We assign the triangle ID as a label to each projected pixel of a target triangle $T_1$. If another triangle $T_2$ projects to a region that overlaps with the triangle $T_1$, and $T_2$ is closer to the camera than $T_1$, we update the label with the $T_2$'s triangle ID. If all the labels of $T_1$ are being overwritten, $T_1$ will be removed from the list of visible surface $V$ for camera view $C$.

## 4.2  Specular-to-Diffuse Transformation

To remove the specular reflection component, we first estimate the illumination color which is used for normalizing and renormalizing the whole set of multi-view images. Various methods exist for illumination color estimation. Here, we adopt the single-image based illumination color estimation method proposed by Tan et al. [16].

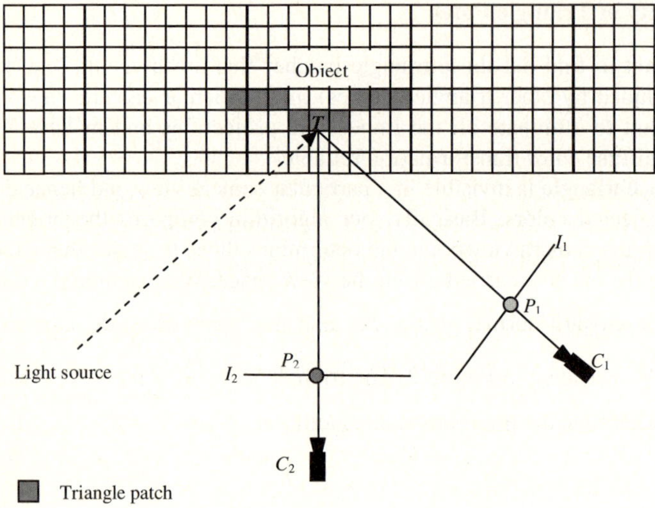


**Fig. 3.** Projection of specular surface on multi-view images

Assume the image to be corrected is $I_1$ for camera view $C_1$ as shown in Figure 3. For a visible triangle patch $T$, the projected color is $P_1$. If the object surface is specular and for this orientation of the triangle patch with respect to the light source direction and camera viewpoint, the projected color appears brighter than the actual color of the object. Assume $T$ is also visible in camera view $C_2$. The corresponding projected color is $P_2$ on image $I_2$. As $C_2$ is away from the ideal specular reflection orientation, the projected color is close to the actual color of the object. After checking all the visible views, we obtain a list of projected colors for $T$ which can help us to obtain the diffuse color. Lastly, we replace the specular color by the diffuse color.

We adopt the dichromatic reflection model. Illumination at any point comes from a single light source plus ambient light which is in equal amounts in all directions. Therefore, light reflected from a dielectric object $P$ is a linear combination of diffuse $P_d$ and specular $P_s$ reflections:

$$P = m_d P_d + m_s P_s \qquad (1)$$

where $m_d$ and $m_s$ (varying from point to point) are the magnitudes of diffuse and specular reflections respectively. It is assumed that the spectral power distribution of the specular reflection is similar to the spectral power distribution of the incident light. Therefore, $P_s$ can be considered as the illumination color. When the image is normalized by the estimated illumination color, the reflection model is changed to:

$$P' = m_d P'_d + m_s \qquad (2)$$

where $P' = \dfrac{P}{P_s}$ is the normalized observed color, and $P'_d = \dfrac{P_d}{P_s}$ is the normalized

diffuse color. Assume we obtain $M$ projected colors in $M$ visible views of the triangle patch $T$. They all share the same $m_d P'_d$ with varying $m_s$. As the camera is made rotating around the object, it is very likely that the $M$ projected colors contain the diffuse color. Purely diffuse pixel has the maximum chromaticity. Therefore, to solve for $m_d P'_d$, we search for the maximum chromaticity in the list of visible projected colors.

As the mesh model is simplified, the projection of a triangle patch on the image is a region rather than a single pixel. The projected region may contain different colors due to texture or shading of the object. Therefore, we segment the region into different sub-regions. Each sub-region will only contain one color. We avoid using the original colors since specular highlight may occur within the region. Therefore, we group the colors into sub-regions by using the specular-free color. The chromaticity $\kappa$ is defined as:

$$\kappa = \frac{P'}{\sum\limits_{R,G,B} P'} = \frac{m_d P'_d + m_s}{m_d \sum\limits_{R,G,B} P'_d + 3 m_s} \tag{3}$$

This equation can be reformulated to produce the definition of $m_s$:

$$m_s = \frac{m_d \left\{ \left[ \kappa \sum\limits_{R,G,B} P'_d \right] - P'_d \right\}}{1 - 3\kappa} \tag{4}$$

By substituting Equation (4) into Equation (2):

$$P' = \frac{\kappa m_d \left[ 3 P'_d - \sum\limits_{R,G,B} P'_d \right]}{3\kappa - 1} \tag{5}$$

In normalized image, we can set $\sum\limits_{R,G,B} P'_d = 1$ without loss of generality. When the pixel is converted to purely diffuse (when specular reflection component is eliminated, $P' = m_d P'_d$), $\kappa = P'_d$ and $m_d = \sum\limits_{R,G,B} P'$. Therefore, Equation (5) can be reformulated as:

$$m_d = \frac{P'[3\kappa - 1]}{\kappa[3 P'_d - 1]} \tag{6}$$

Purely diffuse pixel has the maximum chromaticity. Referring to Equation (3), $P'$ and $P'_d$ are at their maximum $\overline{P'}$ and $\overline{P'_d}$ respectively. The color of the pixel is specular-free, that is, $m_d = \sum_{R,G,B} P' = \sum_{R,G,B} P'_{sf}$. Therefore,

$$\sum_{R,G,B} P'_{sf} = \frac{\overline{P'}\left|3\overline{\kappa}-1\right|}{\overline{\kappa}\left[3\overline{P'_d}-1\right]} \tag{7}$$

where $\overline{\kappa} = \dfrac{\overline{P'}}{\sum_{R,G,B} P'}$. While $\overline{P'}$ and $\overline{\kappa}$ can be obtained from the normalized image, $\overline{P'_d}$ is unknown. By setting $\overline{P'_d}$ to a sufficiently large value (e.g. 0.5) for all pixels, we can obtain the sum of color intensities of the corresponding specular-free image using Equation (7). For non-diffuse pixels:

$$m_s = \frac{\sum_{R,G,B} P' - \sum_{R,G,B} P'_{sf}}{3} \tag{8}$$

$$P'_{sf} = P' - m_s \tag{9}$$

Although the specular-free color may not equal to the original color, it is very consistent on different views. If the difference of the specular-free colors of two pixels is less than a pre-defined threshold, we group the two pixels into one sub-region. For each sub-region, we search for the existence of similar sub-regions in all visible views. Using similar idea, we check the specular-free color of sub-regions in other visible views. If the color difference of two sub-regions is less than the sub-region difference threshold, we save the sub-region color into a color list. In order to preserve the texture or pattern on the object surface, we applied an adaptive threshold in this checking. We set a low sub-region difference threshold value initially. Then we increase the threshold if the checking fails to find a sub-region. In case the checking fails after a certain number of iterations, we ignore this view and proceed to the next view.

In real situation, it is common to encounter saturated highlights which violate the assumption of the dichromatic reflection model. While the transformation method mentioned so far can only handle non-saturated specular reflections, we need a special procedure to cater for saturated specular reflections. Before the image is normalised, we detect the existence of grey scale colors by checking the maximum chromaticity of the pixels. The pixel is identified as grey scale if its maximum chromaticity is less than the grey scale detector threshold. We cannot use the specular-free color to find the corresponding pixels since the specular-free color of grey scale pixels are almost black. Instead, we simply get the colors directly from other corresponding and visible views and search for the diffuse color.

# 5  Results

First, we test our method on a synthetic object. The first row of Figure 4 shows different views of the synthetic teapot model which is illuminated by some light sources. The corresponding diffuse images are obtained as ground truth (second row of Figure 4). The third row of Figure 4 shows the diffuse images obtained by our method. The estimated illuminant color is (R=0.27, G=0.34, B=0.39). The sub-region color difference threshold is initially set as 5 and the increment in each iteration is 5. For better judgment of the specularity removal capability, the difference between the ground truth and the diffuse images obtained by our method are shown in the last row of Figure 4. It can be seen that most of the highlights are removed.

Then, we test our method on a real object. The left column of Figure 5 shows different views of the plastic toy object. The middle column of Figure 5 shows the diffuse images obtained by our method. Each image is interactively segmented into 2 parts and processed separately. The right column of Figure 5 shows the mask of one part. The illuminant color estimated in the region of the mask is (R=0.3, G=0.46, B=0.46). The illuminant color estimated in the remaining region is (R=0.32, G=0.27, B=0.39). The sub-region color difference threshold is initially set as 2 and the increment in each iteration is 2. The grey scale detector threshold is 0.35. Figure 6 shows the zoom in views of the results of specularity removal. It can be seen that most of the highlights are removed and replaced by the correct colors.

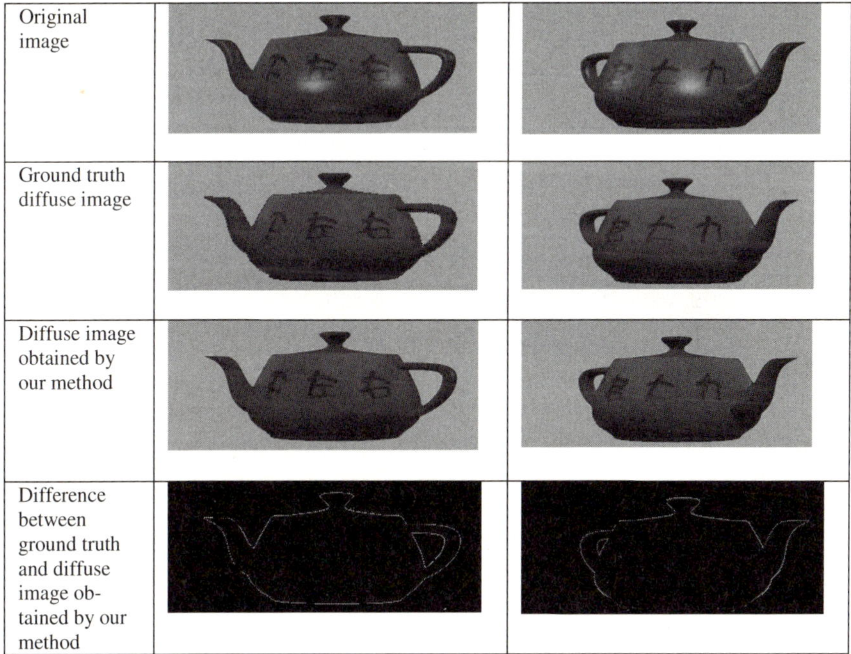

**Fig. 4.** Results of specularity removal on synthetic object

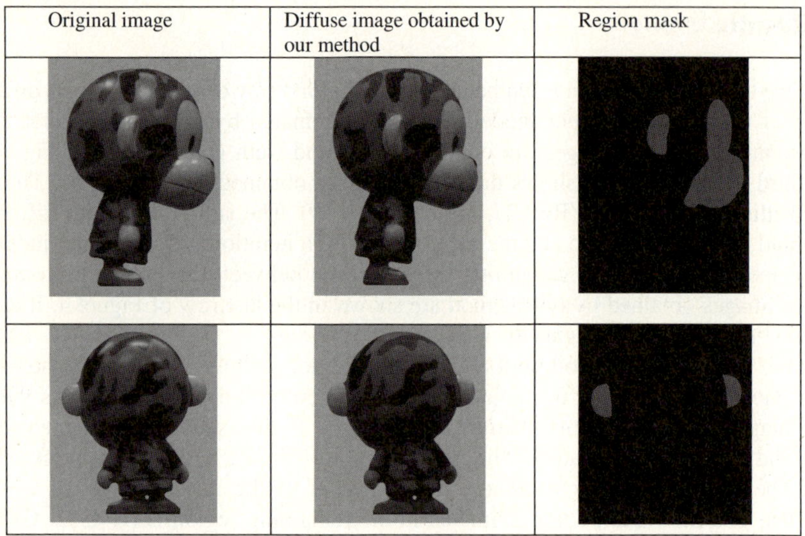

Original image | Diffuse image obtained by our method | Region mask

**Fig. 5.** Results of specularity removal on real object

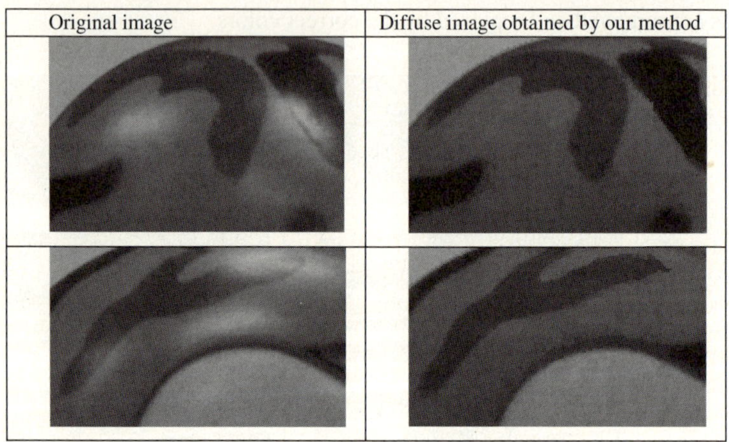

Original image | Diffuse image obtained by our method

**Fig. 6.** Zoom in views of the results of specularity removal

## 6  Conclusion

We propose a method for the removal of specular reflection component on multi-view images. Each camera view is calibrated and a 3D mesh model of the object is generated. For each triangle patch, the projected colors on all visible views are found. The specular chromaticity is replaced by the corresponding diffuse chromaticity based on the fact that a purely diffuse pixel has maximum chromaticity. We test the method on image sequences of synthetic and real objects. In the future, we intend to speed up the method by parallelizing the algorithm. We also want to investigate how good our method performs on other kinds of object.

## Acknowledgement

The work described in this paper was fully supported by a grant from the Research Grant Council of Hong Kong Special Administrative Region, China [Project No. CityU 110807].

## References


1. Pavlidis, G., Koutsoudis, A., Arnaoutoglou, F., Tsioukas, V., Chamzas, C.: Methods for 3D digitization of cultural heritage. Journal of Cultural Heritage 8, 93–98 (2007)
2. Blais, F., Beraldin, J.-A.: Recent developments in 3D multi-modal laser imaging applied to cultural heritage. Machine Vision and Applications 17, 395–409 (2006)
3. Klinker, G.J., Shafer, S.A., Kanade, T.: The measurement of highlights in color images. International Journal of Computer Vision 2(1), 7–32 (1990)
4. Shafer, S.: Using color to separate reflection components. Color Research and Applications 10, 210–218 (1985)
5. Tan, P., Lin, S., Quan, L., Shum, H.-Y.: Highlight removal by illuminant-constrained inpainting. In: Proceedings of IEEE International Conference on Computer Vision, pp. 164–169 (2003)
6. Tan, P., Lin, S., Quan, L.: Separation of highlight reflections on textured surfaces. In: Proceedings of IEEE Conference on Computer Vision and Pattern Recognition, vol. 2, pp. 1855–1860 (2006)
7. Tan, R.T., Ikeuchi, K.: Separating reflection components of textured surfaces using a single image. IEEE Transactions on Pattern Analysis and Machine Intelligence 27(2), 178–193 (2005)
8. Lin, S., Shum, H.-Y.: Separation of diffuse and specular reflection in color images. In: Proceedings of IEEE Conference on Computer Vision and Pattern Recognition, vol. 1, pp. 341–346 (2001)
9. Lin, S., Li, Y., Kang, S.B., Tong, X., Shum, H.-Y.: Diffuse-specular separation and depth recovery from image sequences. In: Proceedings of European Conference on Computer Vision, pp. 210–224 (2002)
10. Mallick, S.P., Zickler, T., Belhumeur, P.N., Kriegman, D.J.: Specularity removal in images and videos: a pde approach. In: Proceedings of European Conference on Computer Vision, Part I, pp. 550–563 (2006)
11. Yu, T., Xu, N., Ahuja, N.: Shape and view independent reflectance map from multiple views. International Journal of Computer Vision 73(2), 123–138 (2007)
12. Criminisi, A., Kang, S.B., Swaminathan, R., Szeliski, R., Anandan, P.: Extracting layers and analyzing their specular properties using epipolar-plane-image analysis. Computer Vision and Image Understanding 97, 51–85 (2005)
13. Tsai, R.Y.: A versatile camera calibration technique for high-accuracy 3D machine vision metrology using off-the-shelf TV cameras and lenses. Journal of Robotics and Automation RA-3(4), 323–344 (1987)
14. Matsumoto, Y., Fujimura, K., Kitamura, T.: Shape-from-silhouette/stereo and its application to 3-D digitizer. In: Proceedings of Discrete Geometry for Computing Imagery, pp. 177–188 (1999)
15. Lorensen, W.E., Cline, H.E.: Marching cubes: a high resolution 3D surface construction algorithm. Computer Graphics 21(4), 163–169 (1987)
16. Tan, R.T., Nishino, K., Ikeuchi, K.: Color constancy through inverse-intensity chromaticity space. Journal of Optical Society of America A 21(3), 321–334 (2004)

# An ROI/xROI Based Rate Control Algorithm in H.264|AVC for Video Telephony Applications

Changhee Kim[1], Taeyoung Na[1], Jeongyeon Lim[2], Youngho Joo[2], Kimun Kim[2], Jaewoan Byun[2], and Munchurl Kim[1]

[1] School of Engineering, Information and Communications University
119 Munjiro, Yuseong-gu, Daejeon, 305-732, Korea
{changhee21c,tyna,mkim}@icu.ac.kr
[2] Core Network Development Team, Institute of Network Technology, SK Telecom
Soonae-dong, Bundang-gu, Sungnam, Kyunggido, 463-784, Korea
{jylim,yhzoo,kmkim,jbyun}@sktelecom.com

**Abstract.** Channel bandwidth in 3G communication networks is very much limited for video telephony services. Therefore, it is worthwhile to enhance a subjective quality of video contents via ROI based coding. In this paper, An ROI/xROI based rate-control method is proposed, which considers the coding of both the ROI and the extended ROIs (xROI's) in non-ROI to meet given target bitrates. In the proposed method, the QP values are increasingly assigned in MB wide inside the non-ROI away from ROI. This reduces the abrupt change in visual quality and the amounts of residual signals along the border between ROI and non-ROI. In this regard, the subjective visual quality is enhanced as well as the proposed rate control has flexibility to control the amounts of the output bitstreams. Experimental results show that the proposed scheme can more effectively achieve the average target bitrates with the better subjective quality than the existing rate control algorithm in H.264|AVC by reducing the variation of the output bitstream amounts.

**Keywords:** ROI, xROI, rate control, H.264|AVC, video telephony.

## 1  Introduction

The H.264|AVC standard has been developed by the Joint Video Team (JVT), which was jointly established by ISO/IEC MPEG and ITU-T VCEG [1]. The H.264|AVC enhances coding efficiency by adopting some innovative features such as 4x4 integer transform, multiple reference frames, various block types for MC, deblocking filters, and a rate-distortion optimization (RDO) based mode decision [2].

The *Baseline* profile of H.264|AVC is largely intended for mobile video telephony and mobile TV applications which require real-time transmission via limited channel bandwidths. Constant bit-rate channels can not deal with variable bitrates data stream of H.264|AVC in real-time unless an appropriate rate control mechanism is incorporated. Rate control algorithms adaptively adjust quantization parameter (QP) values to accomplish required target bitrates [3].

T. Wada, F. Huang, and S. Lin (Eds.): PSIVT 2009, LNCS 5414, pp. 1010–1021, 2009.

H.264|AVC utilizes RDO to select an optimal mode for each MB, which causes the rate control to be more complicated. In H.264|AVC, the RDO based coding requires QP assignment *a priori*, and QP is determined by using Mean Absolute Differences (MAD). However, the MAD of the current MB is available only after RDO based coding is completed. This problem is called '*Chicken and Egg Dilemma*'. In order to solve this dilemma, the rate control algorithm for H.264|AVC uses a linear model to estimate MAD of each MB in the current frame from that of co-located MB in the previous frame, and adopts a quadratic Rate-Distortion (R-D) model to predict QP. This predicted QP may not be accurate because the estimated information is not completely associated with the current frame [4]. Therefore, the fluctuation of output bitrates is high, and QP dependency of RDO causes the rate control algorithm of H.264|AVC to be computationally expensive. To solve these problems, a lot of studies have been accomplished by using other models in [5]-[7].

Recently, the demands for video telephony services on mobile devices are increasing in the 3rd Generation (3G) communication networks. The channel bandwidth for each user is 64kbps at maximum. For video transmission, approximately 48kbps is used at most in circuit-switched channels. H.263 is currently adopted for video telephony services, but the video quality is not good enough to satisfy user's needs. To overcome this situation, substituting H.263 with H.264|AVC has been tried, yet it is difficult to directly employ the existing H.264|AVC. Especially, the current rate control algorithm for H.264|AVC should be improved because of the large fluctuation of bitrates and high complexity. Furthermore, Region-Of-Interest (ROI) based coding is a good means to maintain the visual quality of important parts in video at somewhat satisfactory levels under such a low bit-rate environment [8]. In [9]-[10], ROI based rate control algorithms have been proposed. However, these papers focused on the improvement of subjective visual quality by utilizing the ROI based coding which divides a frame only into two regions: ROI and non-ROI.

In this paper, an effective ROI/xROI based rate control algorithm compatible with H.264|AVC is introduced for video telephony applications. The xROI stands for extended ROI and non-ROI is divided into multiple xROI's in MB wide around ROI. The proposed scheme incorporates a simple update rule for assigning QP values to reduce the fluctuation of output bitrates in GOP. The QP values to be applied for the xROI's inside the non-ROI are increasingly assigned away from ROI so that the visual quality is smoothly degraded. The rest of this paper is organized as follows: In Section 2, the ROI/xROI based coding is introduced. The proposed rate control algorithm is addressed in Section 3, and experimental results are given in Section 4. Finally, we conclude this paper in Section 5.


## 2   ROI/xROI Based Coding

The existing ROI based coding splits a frame into two regions including ROI and non-ROI [8]. On the other hand, a large difference in visual quality between ROI and non-ROI can make the reconstructed frames unpleasant. To solve this drawback, the QP values are increasingly assigned for the xROI's (in MB-wide strip regions) in non-ROI away from ROI. This also reduces the amounts of residual signals along the border between ROI and non-ROI so that coding efficiency is increased.

We improve subjective visual quality using the ROI/xROI based coding. When xROI is applied into non-ROI, non-ROI is split into more than two areas. Fig. 1 shows an example of partitioning a frame into ROI (marked as ①) and non-ROI which is further divided into multiple xROI's, that is, $xROI_1$, $xROI_2$ and $xROI_3$, marked as ②, ③ and ④, respectively.

| ① | ROI |
|---|---|
| ② | $xROI_1$ |
| ③ | $xROI_2$ |
| ④ | $xROI_3$ |

**Fig. 1.** Example of a frame in which the ROI/xROI based coding is employed for *Car phone* sequence / QCIF, ROI Size: 30MBs

In this scheme, the lowest QP value is assigned to ROI ($QP_1$) and QP is increasingly assigned to the regions, $xROI_1$ ($QP_2$), $xROI_2$ ($QP_3$) and $xROI_3$ ($QP_4$), respectively.

$$QP_1 \leq QP_2 \leq QP_3 \leq QP_4 \tag{1}$$

So, the visual quality of the reconstructed frame is gracefully degraded away from the ROI. Then, QP of each xROI is increased by a constant value (QP-Step) depending on the distance from the ROI. So, ROI has the best quality and the area closer to ROI gets the better quality. This can enhance both the subjective and the objective video quality in comparison with the existing ROI based coding.

## 3  Proposed Rate Control Algorithm

### 3.1  Overall Algorithm

The proposed ROI/xROI based rate control algorithm performs a frame-level adjustment on the QP values (QP values for ROI and xROI's in non-ROI) to reduce the difference between the amounts of target bit and output bit and the bit fluctuation per a Group of Pictures (GOP) as well as the computational complexity, compared to the existing rate control algorithm in H.264|AVC. Fig. 2 illustrates the flow chart of the proposed ROI/xROI based rate control method.

**Stage 1:** Allocate a target bits for I- and P-pictures at frame-level.
**Stage 2:** Compute the remaining bit amount (=target bits-output bits of the previous frame) for the current frame and accumulate these remaining bits within the GOP.

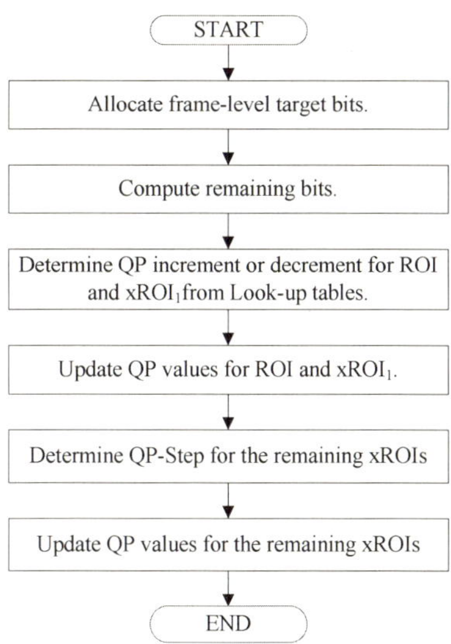



**Fig. 2.** Flow Chart of the Proposed ROI/xROI based Rate Control Algorithm

**Stage 3:** Determine QP increment or decrement for ROI and $xROI_1$ from Look-up tables by taking into account the remaining bits of the previous frame and the accumulated remaining bits in the current GOP.

**Stage 4:** Update QP values for ROI and $xROI_1$ using the QP increment or decrement in Stage 3.

**Stage 5:** Determine QP-Step for the remaining xROI's by taking into account the QP value for $xROI_1$.

**Stage 6:** Update QP values for the remaining xROI's using QP-Step in Stage 5.

## 3.2   Frame-Level Update of the QP Values for I- and P-Pictures

As explained in the previous section, we need to adjust the QP values to be applied for coding ROI and xROI's in non-ROI to meet the target bit rates. Video telephony may require video transmission of QCIF size in average of 10 fps via the circuit-switched channel of 42kbps for satisfactory services. In this case, we may have each GOP with 10 frames including one I-frame and 9 P-frames. Our goal is to meet the target bitrates per GOP with the output bitrates. The QP values are renewed on a frame-level to meet the average target bitrates. An encoding target bit amount is assigned for the I-picture in the first GOP. The excess or remnant bit amount for each I-picture is computed for a given target bitrates (42kbps in our case) after I-picture encoding, which is also taken into account when the OP values for ROI and xROI's in the next I-picture are to be adjusted. The remaining bits after the I-picture encoding is equally divided and distributed for the following P-pictures as their target bitrates in the current GOP. For each P-picture, adjustment of QP values for ROI and xROI's is done depending on the excess or remnant bit for the P-picture encoding as well as the accumulated amount of the excess and remnant bits until the previous P-pictures in GOP. The adjustment of QP increments and decrements is made by a look-up table based on the amounts of the remaining bit amount in the previous P-picture and the accumulated bit amount until the previous in each GOP, which is experimentally determined by various training sequences with slow and fast motion.

We assume that the ROI is already selected. The ROI includes a face, consisting of 30 MBs. For this, we set an appropriate ROI in the first frame of each sequence and fix its position during encoding. Automatic segmentation of ROI is outside the scope of this paper. A detailed explanation of the ROI/xROI based rate control algorithm is given as follows:

**Stage 1: *Frame-level Target Bits Allocation***

**If** (The current frame == I-frame) {
The target bit amount for an I-frame in a GOP is computed as

$$R_{GOP,t\arg et} = R_{t\arg et} , \; R_{I,t\arg et} = \alpha_I \cdot R_{GOP,t\arg et} \tag{2}$$

where $R_{GOP,t\arg et}$, $R_{t\arg et}$ are the target bitrates for a GOP and a sequence, respectively. $\alpha_I$ is selected experimentally from various video sequences with $\alpha_I = 0.35$.

}
**Else{**
**If** (The previous frame == I-frame)
The amount of the target bits for P-frame in $i$-th GOP is derived as

$$R^i{}_{P,t\arg et} = (R_{GOP,t\arg et} - R^i{}_{I,output}) / N^{GOP}_{P,frame} \tag{3}$$

where $R^i_{I,output}$ is the number of the output bits of I-frame in $i$-th GOP, $N^{GOP}_{P,frame}$ is the number of P-frames in a GOP and is set to 9 in our case.

}

**Stage 2: *Computation of Remaining Bits***

**If** (The current frame == I-frame)
The remaining bits of I-frame in $i$-th GOP, $G^i_{I,frame}$ are calculated as

$$G^i_{I,frame} = R_{I,t\arg et} - R^{i-1}_{I,output} \tag{4}$$

**Else{**
**If** (The current frame == The first P-frame in sequence)

$$G^{1,1}_{P,GOP} = 0 \tag{5}$$

where $G^{1,1}_{P,GOP}$ is the initial accumulated remaining bits for the first P-frame in the 1$^{st}$ GOP.

**Else if** (The previous frame == I-frame)

$$G^{i,1}_{P,GOP} = G^{i-1,N^{GOP}_{P,frame}}_{P,GOP} \tag{6}$$

**Else{**

The remaining bits of $(n\text{-}1)$-th P-frame in $i$-th GOP are provided by

$$G_{P,frame}^{i,n-1} = R_{P,t\arg et}^{i} - R_{P,output}^{i,n-1} \; (n\text{>=}2) \tag{7}$$

where $R_{P,output}^{i,n-1}$ is the amount of the output bits after encoding the $(n\text{-}1)$-th P-frame in $i$-th GOP. Then, we accumulate the remaining bits from the first P-frame to $(n\text{-}1)$-th P-frame in $i$-th GOP. The accumulated remaining bits for $n$-th P-frame in $i$-th GOP are given by

$$G_{P,GOP}^{i,n} = \sum_{k=1}^{n-1} G_{P,frame}^{i,k} \; (n\text{>=}2) \tag{8}$$

    }
}

**Stage 3:** *Determination of QP increment or decrement amount from Look-up tables*

**If** (The current frame == P-frame && The Previous frame != I-frame){
The amounts of QP increment/decrement for ROI and xROI$_1$ are decided as follows:

**If** ( $PSNR_{P,ROI}^{i,n-1} < PSNR_{P,xROI_1}^{i,n-1}$ && $PSNR_{P,ROI}^{i,n-1} > PSNR_Th_1$ )

$$\Delta QP_{p,ROI}^{i,n} = Qp_{ROI}^{1}, \; \Delta QP_{p,xROI_1}^{i,n} = Qp_{xROI_1}^{1}$$

where $PSNR_{P,ROI}^{i,n-1}$ and $PSNR_{P,xROI_1}^{i,n-1}$ are the PSNR values of $(n\text{-}1)$-th P-frame in $i$-th GOP for ROI and xROI$_1$, respectively. Accordingly, $\Delta QP_{p,ROI}^{i,n}$ and $\Delta QP_{p,xROI_1}^{i,n}$ arc the QP changes for $n$-th P-frame in $i$-th GOP for ROI and xROI$_1$, respectively. $Qp_{ROI}^{1}$ and $Qp_{xROI_1}^{1}$ are the QP changes defined in Table 1 for ROI and xROI$_1$, respectively. $PSNR_Th_1$ is a PSNR threshold for ROI. $PSNR_Th_1$ is set to 35dB in our case.

**Else if** ( $PSNR_{P,ROI}^{i,n-1} < PSNR_Th_2$ && $G_{P,GOP}^{i,n} > \beta_1$ )

$$\Delta QP_{p,ROI}^{i,n} = Qp_{ROI}^{2}, \; \Delta QP_{p,xROI_1}^{i,n} = Qp_{xROI_1}^{2}$$

where $PSNR_Th_2$ is a PSNR threshold for ROI. $PSNR_Th_2$ is set to 33dB in our case. $\beta_1$ is a threshold for the accumulated remaining bits in GOP and is determined by experiments with $\beta_1 = \text{-}500$. $Qp_{ROI}^{2}$ and $Qp_{xROI_1}^{2}$ are the QP changes defined in Table 1 for ROI and xROI$_1$, respectively.

**Else**

    **If** ( $G_{P,GOP}^{i,n} < 0$ ) { $\Delta QP_{p,ROI}^{i,n} = Qp_{ROI}^{3}, \; \Delta QP_{p,xROI_1}^{i,n} = Qp_{xROI_1}^{3}$ , Go to **Step 1** }

    **Else**     { $\Delta QP_{p,ROI}^{i,n} = Qp_{ROI}^{4}, \; \Delta QP_{p,xROI_1}^{i,n} = Qp_{xROI_1}^{4}$ , Go to **Step 2** }

    where $Qp_{ROI}^{3}$, $Qp_{ROI}^{4}$ and $Qp_{xROI_1}^{3}$, $Qp_{xROI_1}^{4}$ are the QP changes defined in Table 1 for ROI and xROI$_1$, respectively.

}

Table 1 gives the values of $Qp_{\mathrm{ROI}}$, $Qp_{\mathrm{xROI_1}}$ depending on $G_{P,GOP}^{i,n}$, $G_{P,frame}^{i,n-1}$. $QP_{\mathrm{x}}$ is the QP value for xROI$_1$ in the previous frame. $\max QP$ is set to 51 in H.264|AVC.

**Table 1.** QP Adjustment Table for P-frames

$$( G_{GOP} = G_{P,GOP}^{i,n},\ G_{frame} = G_{P,frame}^{i,n-1},\ QP_{\mathrm{x}} = QP_{P,\mathrm{xROI_1}}^{i,n-1} )$$

| Condition | $Qp_{\mathrm{ROI}}^{1}$ | $Qp_{\mathrm{xROI_1}}^{1}$ |
|---|---|---|
| · | -5 | +10 |
| **Condition** | $Qp_{\mathrm{ROI}}^{2}$ | $Qp_{\mathrm{xROI_1}}^{2}$ |
| $if\,(G_{GOP} > 5000)$ | -5 | -7 |
| $else_if\,(G_{GOP} > 3000)$ | -4 | -5 |
| $else_if\,(G_{GOP} > 1000)$ | -3 | -4 |
| else | -3 | +5 |
| **Condition** | $Qp_{\mathrm{ROI}}^{3}$ | $Qp_{\mathrm{xROI_1}}^{3}$ |
| $if\,(G_{GOP} < -2000)$ | +4 | +6 |
| $else_if\,(G_{GOP} < -500)$ | +2 | +4 |
| $else_if\,(G_{GOP} < -100)$ | +1 | +3 |
| else | 0 | +2 |
| **Condition** | $Qp_{\mathrm{ROI}}^{3a}$ | $Qp_{\mathrm{xROI_1}}^{3a}$ |
| $if\,(G_{GOP} < -2000)$ | +1 | $\max QP - QP_{\mathrm{x}}$ |
| $else_if\,(G_{GOP} < -1000)$ | +2 | $\max QP - QP_{\mathrm{x}}$ |
| $else_if\,(G_{GOP} < -500)$ | +1 | +6 |
| $else_if\,(G_{GOP} < -300)$ | +1 | +2 |
| else | +1 | +1 |
| **Condition** | $Qp_{\mathrm{ROI}}^{3b}$ | $Qp_{\mathrm{xROI_1}}^{3b}$ |
| · | +1 | $\max QP - QP_{\mathrm{x}}$ |

| Condition | $Qp_{\mathrm{ROI}}^{4}$ | $Qp_{\mathrm{xROI_1}}^{4}$ |
|---|---|---|
| $if\,(G_{GOP} > 3000)$ | -2 | -5 |
| $else_if\,(G_{GOP} > 2000)$ | -1 | -3 |
| $else_if\,(G_{GOP} > 1000)$ | 0 | -3 |
| **Condition** | $Qp_{\mathrm{ROI}}^{4a}$ | $Qp_{\mathrm{xROI_1}}^{4a}$ |
| $if\,(G_{GOP} > 3000)$ | -3 | 0 |
| $else_if\,(G_{GOP} > 2000)$ | -1 | -2 |
| $else_if\,(G_{GOP} > 1000)$ | -1 | -2 |
| **Condition** | $Qp_{\mathrm{ROI}}^{4b}$ | $Qp_{\mathrm{xROI_1}}^{4b}$ |
| $if\,(G_{GOP} > 4000)$ | -3 | -3 |
| $else_if\,(G_{GOP} > 3000)$ | -2 | -1 |
| $else_if\,(G_{GOP} > 2000)$ | -1 | +1 |
| $else_if\,(G_{GOP} > 1500)$ | -2 | +1 |
| $else_if\,(G_{GOP} > 1000)$ | -1 | +3 |
| Else | 0 | -1 |
| **Condition** | $Qp_{\mathrm{ROI}}^{4c}$ | $Qp_{\mathrm{xROI_1}}^{4c}$ |
| $if\,(G_{GOP} > 3000)$ | -1 | -2 |
| $else_if\,(G_{GOP} > 2000)$ | -1 | -2 |
| $else_if\,(G_{GOP} > 1000$ $\&\& G_{frame} > 0)$ | -1 | -2 |
| $else_if\,(G_{GOP} > 1000)$ | 0 | -2 |
| $else_if$ $(G_{frame} < -2000)$ | +1 | +2 |

**Step 1:** Fine-tuning of QP changes when the accumulated remaining bits in GOP are negative

**If** $(n == N_{P,frame}^{GOP}\ \&\&\ G_{P,frame}^{i,n-1} < \beta_2)\ \Delta QP_{p,\mathrm{ROI}}^{i,n}\ {+}{=}\ Qp_{\mathrm{ROI}}^{3a},\ \Delta QP_{p,\mathrm{xROI_1}}^{i,n}\ {+}{=}\ Qp_{\mathrm{xROI_1}}^{3a}$

where $n$ is the index of the current frame, and $\beta_2$ is a threshold for the remaining bits of the previous P-frame in $i$-th GOP and is experimentally determined with $\beta_2 = 1500$. $Qp_{\mathrm{ROI}}^{3a}$ and $Qp_{\mathrm{xROI_1}}^{3a}$ are the QP changes defined in Table 1 for ROI and xROI$_1$, respectively.

**Else{  If** $(n== N^{GOP}_{P,frame} - 1$ && $G^{i,n}_{P,GOP} < \beta_3)$

$$\Delta QP^{i,n}_{p,\text{ROI}} += Qp^{3b}_{\text{ROI}}, \ \Delta QP^{i,n}_{p,\text{xROI}_1} += Qp^{3b}_{\text{xROI}_1} \ \}$$

where $\beta_3$ is a threshold for the accumulated remaining bits for the current frame in $i$-th GOP and is experimentally determined with $\beta_3 = -2000$. $Qp^{3b}_{\text{ROI}}$ and $Qp^{3b}_{\text{xROI}_1}$ are the QP changes defined in Table 1 for ROI and xROI$_1$, respectively.

**Step 2:** Fine-tuning of QP changes when the accumulated remaining bits in GOP are positive

**If** $(G^{i,n}_{P,GOP} > \beta_4$ && $G^{i,n-1}_{P,frame} > \beta_5)$

    **If** $(n == N^{GOP}_{P,frame})$  $\Delta QP^{i,n}_{p,\text{ROI}} += Qp^{4a}_{\text{ROI}}, \ \Delta QP^{i,n}_{p,\text{xROI}_1} += Qp^{4a}_{\text{xROI}_1}$

    **Else** $\quad\quad\quad \Delta QP^{i,n}_{p,\text{ROI}} += Qp^{4b}_{\text{ROI}}, \ \Delta QP^{i,n}_{p,\text{xROI}_1} += Qp^{4b}_{\text{xROI}_1}$

where $\beta_4$ and $\beta_5$ are the threshold values for the accumulated remaining bits until the previous frame, and for the remaining bits of the previous frame after encoding in $i$-th GOP, respectively. They are experimentally determined with $\beta_4 = 4,000$ and $\beta_5 = 300$. $Qp^{4a}_{\text{ROI}}$, $Qp^{4b}_{\text{ROI}}$ and $Qp^{4a}_{\text{xROI}_1}$, $Qp^{4b}_{\text{xROI}_1}$ are the QP changes defined in Table 1 for ROI and xROI$_1$, respectively.

**Else {** If $(n == N^{GOP}_{P,frame})$  $\Delta QP^{i,n}_{p,\text{ROI}} += Qp^{4c}_{\text{ROI}}, \ \Delta QP^{i,n}_{p,\text{xROI}_1} += Qp^{4c}_{\text{xROI}_1} \ \}$

**Stage 4:** *Update of QP values for ROI and xROI$_1$*

  **If** (The current frame == I-frame) {

    **If** (The current frame == The first I-frame in the sequence)

$$QP^1_{I,\text{ROI}} = QP^{init}_{\text{ROI}}, \ QP^1_{I,\text{xROI}_1} = QP^{init}_{\text{xROI}_1}$$

where $QP^{init}_{\text{ROI}}$ and $QP^{init}_{\text{xROI}_1}$ are the initial QP values for ROI and xROI$_1$ in the first I-frame of the sequence. $QP^{init}_{\text{ROI}}$ and $QP^{init}_{\text{xROI}_1}$ are set to 30 and 35, respectively, in our experiments.

  **Else {**

    **If(** $|G^{i-1}_{I,frame}| > \alpha_G \cdot R_{I,target}$ )

$$QP^i_{I,\text{ROI}} = (\sum_{n=1}^{N^{GOP}_{P,frame}} QP^{i-1,n}_{P,\text{ROI}})/N^{GOP}_{P,frame}, \ QP^i_{I,\text{xROI}_1} = (\sum_{n=1}^{N^{GOP}_{P,frame}} QP^{i-1,n}_{P,\text{xROI}_1})/N^{GOP}_{P,frame}$$

    **Else** $\quad QP^i_{I,\text{ROI}} = QP^{i-1}_{I,\text{ROI}}, \ QP^i_{I,\text{xROI}_1} = QP^{i-1}_{I,\text{xROI}_1} \ (i>=2)$          (9)

where $\alpha_G$ is a threshold determined by experiments with $\alpha_G = 0.4$. $QP^{i-1,n}_{P,\text{ROI}}$, $QP^{i-1,n}_{P,\text{xROI}_1}$ are the QP values for ROI and xROI$_1$ of $n$-th P-frame in $(i-1)$-th GOP.

    }

  }

**Else {**

    **If** (The previous frame == I-frame)

$$QP_{P,\mathrm{ROI}}^{i,1} = QP_{I,\mathrm{ROI}}^{i}, \quad QP_{P,\mathrm{xROI}_1}^{i,1} = QP_{I,\mathrm{xROI}_1}^{i}$$

    **Else**      $QP_{P,\mathrm{ROI}}^{i,n} = QP_{P,\mathrm{ROI}}^{i,n-1} + \Delta QP_{p,\mathrm{ROI}}^{i,n}$

$$QP_{P,\mathrm{xROI}_1}^{i,n} = QP_{P,\mathrm{xROI}_1}^{i,n-1} + \Delta QP_{p,\mathrm{xROI}_1}^{i,n} \tag{10}$$

**}**

**Stage 5: *Determination QP-Step for the remaining xROI's***
The QP-Step of n-th P-frame in i-th GOP is computed by

$$S_{\mathrm{xROI}}^{i,n} = (\max QP - QP_{\mathrm{xROI}_1}^{i,n}) / (N_{region}^{\mathrm{xROI}} - 1) \tag{11}$$

where $N_{region}^{\mathrm{xROI}}$ is the number of divided xROI regions in a frame. The QP-Step is
bounded by the maximum value set to 5.

**Stage 6: *Update of QP values for the remaining xROI's***
    **For**($m=2$; $m < N_{region}^{\mathrm{xROI}}$ ; $m$++)

$$QP_{\mathrm{xROI}_m}^{i,n} = QP_{\mathrm{xROI}_1}^{i,n} + S_{\mathrm{xROI}}^{i,n} \cdot (m-1) \tag{12}$$

# 4  Experimental Results

We implement the proposed ROI/xROI based rate control algorithm in the reference
software, JM 11.0 [12]. The experiments are performed based on the *Baseline* profile
of H.264/AVC with RDO ON, search range ±16, intra period 10, the Hadamard transform ON, and FMO type 2. The five sequences were used in the experiments, including *Carphone* (*C*), *Foreman* (*F*), *Silent* (*S*), *Salesman* (*M*), and *Grandma* (*G*) with
QCIF, 100 frames and 10fps. The PC for the simulation has Pentium4 3.0GHz CPU
and 2.0Gbyte RAM.

**Table 2.** Comparison of the bitrates (kbps) and PSNR values (dB) in Each Region Between JM
11.0 and the Proposed Algorithm

| Seq. | values | Original JM 11.0 | | | | Proposed method | | | |
|---|---|---|---|---|---|---|---|---|---|
| | | ROI | xROI$_1$ | xROI$_2$ | xROI$_3$ | ROI | xROI$_1$ | xROI$_2$ | xROI$_3$ |
| *C* | Y-PSNR | 32.54 | 34.05 | 34.61 | 33.3 | 34.81 | 31.80 | 30.17 | 26.66 |
| | bitrates | 45.78 | | | | 41.51 | | | |
| *F* | Y-PSNR | 30.43 | 30.62 | 31.22 | 30.41 | 33.74 | 28.67 | 27.59 | 25.18 |
| | bitrates | 42.1 | | | | 41.34 | | | |
| *S* | Y-PSNR | 32.04 | 33.18 | 33.33 | 33.80 | 34.48 | 31.05 | 29.24 | 26.32 |
| | bitrates | 42.06 | | | | 41.24 | | | |
| *M* | Y-PSNR | 32.41 | 34.72 | 35.39 | 34.16 | 34.156 | 31.86 | 29.89 | 26.14 |
| | bitrates | 42.57 | | | | 41.59 | | | |
| *G* | Y-PSNR | 34.75 | 38.3 | 38.65 | 38.99 | 35.32 | 34.39 | 32.75 | 30.66 |
| | bitrates | 43.19 | | | | 41.96 | | | |

(QCIF, 100frames, 10fps, GOP 10frames, Target Bitrates 42kbps, ROI Size: 30MBs).

In order to evaluate the proposed algorithm, we compare the performance of our scheme with that of in the original JM 11.0. Table 2 gives the comparisons of the bitrates, and Y-PSNR values in each region between the original JM 11.0 and the proposed algorithm. In the proposed algorithm, it is shown that the video quality of ROI is the best and the region nearer to ROI obtains the better quality. This effect can elevate the overall perceptual quality. Since the bit amounts spent on ROI have been more increased for ROI with higher motion, the amounts of output bits for xROI's have been reduced accordingly to compensate them. Moreover, the Y-PSNR value of non-ROI (xROI's) is more sensitive than that of ROI because non-ROI usually has less motion than ROI. This is taken into account for QP adjustments in xROI's.

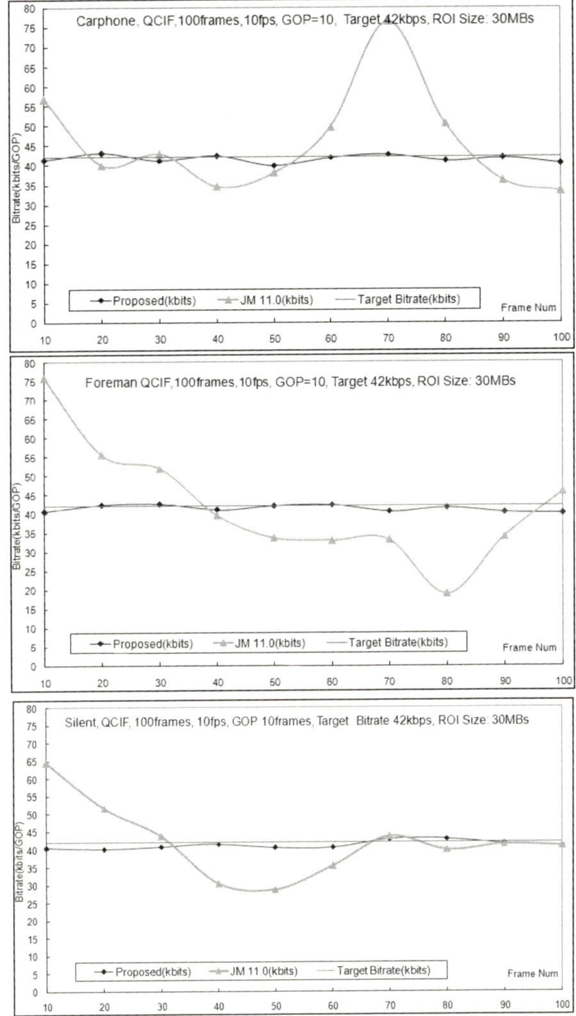



**Fig. 3.** Comparisons of the bitrates fluctuation per GOP between JM 11.0 and the proposed rate control algorithm for *C*, *F* and *S* sequences

Fig. 3 shows the comparison of the bitrates per GOP on both methods for the sequences ($C$, $F$ and $S$). As shown in Fig. 3 the proposed rate control algorithm yields output bitrates very close to the target bitrates per GOP and reduces the variation of output bitrates compared with the original rate control in JM 11.0.

Fig. 4 shows the comparison of the subjective quality between JM 11.0 and the proposed scheme. As shown in Fig. 4, it is demonstrated that the proposed algorithm outperforms the existing scheme of JM 11.0 in the perceived visual quality.

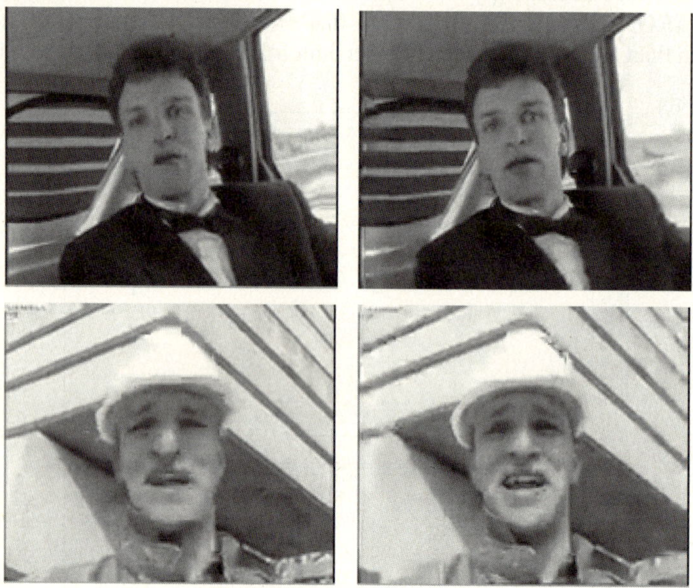

**Fig. 4.** Comparisons of the subjective quality between JM 11.0 (left) and the proposed rate control algorithm (right) in each sequence for $C$ (top) and $F$ (bottom) sequences

The additional experimental results are shown in Table 3. Table 3 tabulates the times taken for encoding, the standard deviations of PSNR values and the bitrates per GOP. The standard deviation implies the extent of the fluctuation. It is observed that the proposed algorithm can lower the temporal quality change with the significantly decreased fluctuation of output bitrates in comparison with the existing scheme in JM 11.0. Furthermore, the total encoding time can be saved up to approximately 5% of the encoding time in JM 11.0.

**Table 3.** Additional Results between JM 11.0 and the Proposed Algorithm

| Sequence | Std. of PSNR (dB) | | Std. of Bitrates (kbits) | | Encoding Times (sec) | |
|---|---|---|---|---|---|---|
|  | JM 11.0 | Proposed | JM 11.0 | Proposed | JM 11.0 | Proposed |
| $C$ | 2.52 | 1.92 | 13.24 | 1.0 | 58.87 | 57.69 |
| $F$ | 2.74 | 1.25 | 15.92 | 0.93 | 59.77 | 59.12 |
| $S$ | 1.69 | 0.44 | 10.35 | 0.97 | 60.02 | 58.69 |
| $M$ | 1.49 | 0.45 | 13.12 | 1.33 | 59.7 | 58.19 |
| $G$ | 1.16 | 0.56 | 7.2 | 0.99 | 59.21 | 56.29 |

# 5  Conclusion

The proposed algorithm enhances the subjective spatial quality by increasingly assigning QP values in xROI's away from ROI, thus making it more visually appealing. Also, it allows for more flexibility in controlling the output bitrates with such QP assignments in ROI and xROI's. The experimental results exhibit that the proposed algorithm is more applicable for video telephony than the original JM 11.0 of H.264|AVC for mobile communication networks with limited transmission bandwidth.

# References


1. ISO/IEC 14496-10, Information Technology-Coding of Audio Visual Objects-part 10: Advanced Video Coding (December 2003)
2. Wiegand, T., Sullivan, G.J., Bjontegard, G., Luthra, A.: Overview of the H.264/AVC Video Coding Standard. IEEE Trans. Circuit System. Video Technology 13, 560–576 (2003)
3. Richardson, I.E.G.: H.264 and MPEG-4 Video Compression, pp. 256–262. Wiley, Chichester (2003)
4. Li, Z.G., Gao, W., Pan, F.: Adaptive rate control for H.264. Visual Communication & Image Representation, 376–406 (August 2005)
5. He, Z., Kim, Y.K., Mitra, S.K.: Low-Delay Rate Control for DCT Video Coding via $\rho$-domain Source Modeling. IEEE Trans. Circuit System. Video Technology 11, 928–940 (2001)
6. He, Z., Mitra, S.K.: A Unified Rate-Distortion Analysis Framework for Transform coding. IEEE Trans. Circuit System. Video Technology 11, 1221–1236 (2001)
7. He, Z., Chen, T.: Linear rate control for JVT video coding. In: International Conference on Information Technology. Research and Education, Newark (2003)
8. Leuven, S.V., Schevensteen, K.V., Dams Peter, T.: Implementation of Multiple Region-Of-Interest Models in H.264/AVC. In: SITIS, pp. 502–511 (2006)
9. Li, H., Wang, Z., Cui, H., Tang, K.: An Improved ROI-Based Rate Control Algorithm for H.264/AVC. In: IEEE International Conference on Signal Processing 2006 (2006)
10. Liu, Y., Li, Z.G., Soh, Y.C.: Region-of-Interest Based Resource Allocation for Conversational Video Communication of H.264/AVC. IEEE Trans. Circuit System. Video Technology 18, 134–139 (2008)
11. Joint Model – H.264/AVC Reference Software,
    http://iphome.hhi.de/suehring/download

# Simplifying the Rate Control Scheme for Distributed Video Coding by Flexible Slepian-Wolf Decoding


Ralph Hänsel and Erika Müller

University of Rostock – Institute of Communications Engineering
Richard-Wagner-Strasse 31, 18119 Rostock, Germany
{ralph.haensel,erika.mueller}@uni-rostock.de
http://www.int.uni-rostock.de



**Abstract.** Distributed video coding (DVC) is an important topic for emerging applications, for example visual sensor networks and mobile video streaming. However, the major handicap applying DVC for real world applications is still the mandatory feedback channel. In previous approaches, the rate allocation algorithm was relying on feedback channel data. Commonly bit plane by bit plane decoding is done in a turbo code-based Slepian-Wolf decoder. In this paper inter bit plane decoding replaces the conventional method. The proposed inter bit plane decoding facilitates the rate control, whereas only the sum data rate has to be estimated/requested but not the data rate for each bit plane. This is one step forward to distributed video coding systems free of feedback channels.


## 1   Introduction

Distributed video coding (DVC) gained much interest in recent years. There is great potential for important application fields, such as low complexity encoders for mobile video streaming, multi-view video coding in visual sensor networks and error robust video transmission. This paper is focused on the low power scenario, although the presented algorithm is not bound to it.

The key idea of distributed video coding is the disjoint encoding and joint decoding of video sources. For example, disjoined encoding is performed for the frames of a video sequence whereas the decoding is done jointly, by exploiting the temporal correlation. This is the basic principle of a low complexity encoder. The computational expensive motion estimation is shifted from the encoder to the decoder. The principle of separate encoding is applied for example on frame level, on camera level (multi-view coding) or on pixel level.

The "intelligent" component of this encoder/decoder structure is the decoder. Because it holds most of the tools for data compression and control. It is the contrary interpretation as for a conventional video coding system (e.g. Mpeg2, Mpeg4, H.264/AVC). In a conventional encoder/decoder structure the encoder is the "intelligent" component, which controls the decoder.


T. Wada, F. Huang, and S. Lin (Eds.): PSIVT 2009, LNCS 5414, pp. 1022–1033, 2009.
© Springer-Verlag Berlin Heidelberg 2009

Typically, the "intelligent" component controls the encoder/decoder system. This leads to a problem for the distributed video coding, because the decoder (as the "intelligent" component) needs to control the encoder. For this reason, a feedback channel from decoder to encoder is used. A bidirectional communication between the encoder and decoder is therefore mandatory.

Up to now, the major handicap for distributed video coding is the mandatory bidirectional communication, to become applicable in many real world scenarios with unidirectional communication. (e.g. video storage, unidirectional video streaming). The efficient storage of a DVC bit stream and subsequent decoding is not possible by now, due to the unavailable feedback channel.

In the next section, a brief description of the related work on distributed video coding is given, as well as a detailed description of the Slepian-Wolf decoding. The new algorithm is presented in section 3, which helps to avoid the feedback channel and makes the distributed video coding scheme more practical. The proposed decoding scheme is called "Flexible Slepian-Wolf Decoding", because it gives the decoder the opportunity to use the data received from the encoder in a more flexible way. The simulation results are presented in section 4 and the conclusions are given at the end of this paper (section 5).

## 2    Distributed Video Coding – Related Work

A distributed video coding system is based on the theories of D. Slepian, J. Wolf [1] and A. D. Wyner, J. Ziv [2], describing lossless and lossy distributed source coding.

### 2.1    Low Complexity Wyner-Ziv CoDec

One major benefit of distributed video coding is the possibility to design low complexity encoders by a disjoint encoding and joint decoding of the frames of a video sequence. Hence, the complex motion estimation is not needed on the encoder side, as in conventional video coding. Therefore, the decoder exploit the temporal correlation by motion estimation.

The basic structure of a common distributed video coding system with low encoder complexity ([3], [4]) is shown in figure 1. The input video sequence is split up into two types of frames. One type of frame called key frame ($K$) is encoded by a conventional intra encoder ( H.264intra, JPEG2000 ). Every second frame is typically encoded as a key frame. The other frames are encoded as Wyner-Ziv frames ($X$) by distributed video coding techniques. A Wyner-Ziv frame is encoded separately (without the knowledge of other frames), whereas the decoding is done jointly with knowledge of the neighboring key and Wyner-Ziv frames. The key frames are temporally interpolated to calculate the side information ($Y$). The side information is a lossy version of the original Wyner-Ziv frame ($X$). The decoded key frames ($\hat{K}$) and Wyner-Ziv frames ($\hat{X}$) are finally combined to form the reconstructed video sequence (fig. 1).

As mentioned, the side information is a lossy (corrupted) version of the original Wyner-Ziv frame. Thus, the side information needs to be corrected to get the original frame. Which is commonly obtained using channel coding techniques

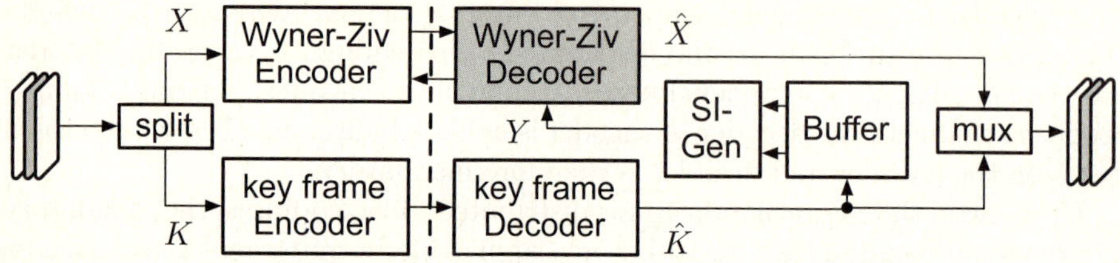

**Fig. 1.** DVC CoDec scheme with low encoder complexity

(e.g. [5], [6]). Typically, the Wyner-Ziv encoder generates some parity bits by a channel encoder (convolution code, LDPC - Low Density Parity Check) and transmits them to the decoder. The decoder itself decodes the Wyner-Ziv frames by correcting the side information with the help of the parity bits. The required number of parity bits highly depends on the correlation between the side information and the original Wyner-Ziv frame. For that reason, the decoder must request more and more bits until successful decoding. This method is called decoder rate control. It needs a feedback channel for operation. On the other hand, the encoder can also estimate the necessary data rate and send a fixed number of parity bits (encoder rate control scheme, [7]). Therefore, no feedback channel is needed, but it is not guaranteed that decoding will be successful.

## 2.2 Slepian-Wolf Encoding and Decoding

A key component of the Wyner-Ziv encoder/decoder is the Slepian-Wolf (SW) encoder/decoder. It is responsible for lossless distributed source coding. The lossy source coding is achieved by introducing a quantizer on the encoder side and a reconstruction on the decoder side. The Wyner-Ziv encoder and decoder as well as the Slepian-Wolf CoDec are shown in figure 2.

A more detailed description of the Wyner-Ziv pixel domain encoder/decoder and the purpose of the SW CoDec is provided in this section. At first, each pixel $x_i$ of the frame $X$ is quantized and consequently transformed to a quantizer symbol $q_i$. Each quantizer symbol is split up into its bit planes ($q_i^{(1)}$ - most significant bit (MSB), $q_i^{(M)}$ - least significant bit (LSB)). Whereas each bit plane

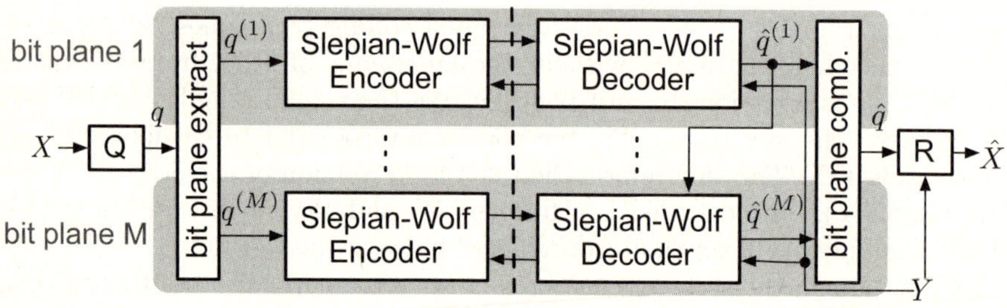

**Fig. 2.** Wyner-Ziv encoder/decoder

is fed to a separate Slepian-Wolf (SW) encoder, which generates some parity bits and sends them on request. The bit plane extraction is necessary for coding, due to the fact, that the Slepian-Wolf encoder/decoder is implemented using binary channel codes. For example, turbo codes or LDPC codes are used for Slepian-Wolf coding.

The decoding process is more complex. At first, bit plane 1 is decoded. The side information ($Y$) and some parity bits are used for decoding. If the decoding is not successful, the decoder requests more bits until it is able to successfully decode the bit plane. In the next step bit plane 2 is decoded in the same way. But the already decoded bit plane is used to improve the decoding performance. Thus, all bit planes are decoded in a sequential way. It is called bit plane by bit plane decoding. Typically, it starts with the MSB and ends with the LSB, but it's not fixed to this order. An inverse bit plane order decoding is proposed in [8].

After successful decoding of all bit planes, the bit planes $\hat{q}_i^{(b)}$ are combined to form the decoded quantization symbol $\hat{q}_i$. The reconstructed frame $\hat{X}$ is calculated based on the quantizer symbols $\hat{q}$ and the side information $Y$.

The decoder has to request more and more parity bits until successful decoding, which is a problem in this scheme. The requests need to be done for every bit plane in a decoder rate control scheme. On the other hand, the encoder must estimate the data rate for each bit plane $b$ accurately ($R^{(b)}$) rather than only the sum data rate ($R_{sum} = R^{(1)} + R^{(2)} + \ldots$) in an encoder rate control scheme. Each bit planes has a fixed data rate as shown in figure 3(a).

The aim of the proposed flexible decoding is a non-fixed data rate for each bit plane, which would greatly facilitate the encoder and decoder rate control.


## 3    Proposed Inter Bit Plane Decoding


This section points out the proposed inter bit plane decoding algorithm. Furthermore, a model for the quantizer operation, the correlation noise and LLR value calculation are given, which are necessary for flexible inter bit plane decoding.

The aim of the inter bit plane decoding algorithm proposed in this paper is to facilitate the rate control. As mentioned in the related work section, two kinds of rate control schemes are available. A decoder rate control, which needs a feedback channel and an encoder rate control which estimates the necessary data rate at the encoder. In the second case, the rate control has to estimate the data rate for each bit plane accurately, if a bit plane by bit plane decoding scheme is used. Hence, the potential benefit of our inter bit plane decoding is that the encoder rate control has only to estimate the sum data rate. The exact data rate for each bit plane has not to be estimated because the inter bit plane decoding can exchange information between the bit planes. The only constraint is that the data rate for each bit plane is within a specific range, as shown in figure 3(b). The data rate for the first bit plane $R^{(1)}$ can vary between a minimum $R_{min}^{(1)}$ and maximum data rate $R_{max}^{(1)}$, whereas the sum data rate $R_{sum}$ must remain constant. The minimum data rate for the MSB $R_{min}^{(1)}$ and the maximum data

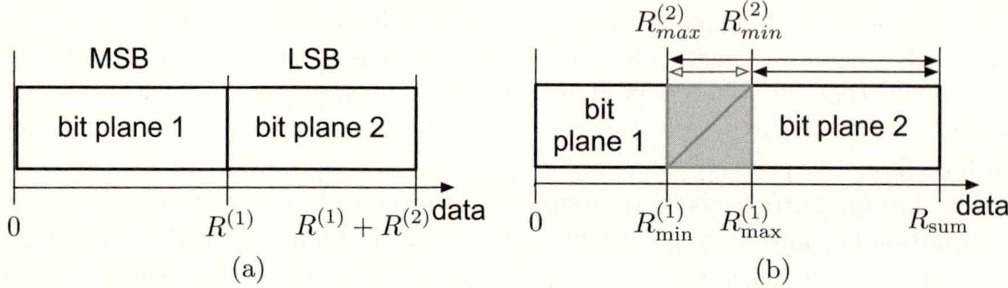

**Fig. 3.** (a) Fixed and (b) Flexible data rate for each bit plane

rate for the MSB $R_{max}^{(1)}$ are given by the bit plane by bit plane decoding. On the one hand, if the MSB is decoded at first than the data rate is at its maximum. On the other hand if the MSB is decoded at last the data rate will be minimum.

The proposed inter bit plane decoding algorithm performs joint decoding of all bit planes. At first, the soft information (LLR value, $L_c(\hat{q}_i^{(b)})$) for every bit plane of the quantization symbol is calculated using the correlation noise model and side information, but independent of the other bit planes. The decoder requests some parity bits from the encoder and performs turbo decoding for every bit plane. The first decoding iteration is typically not successful, because of the not yet performed information exchange. For this reason the soft information is exchanged between the bit planes to reduce the bit rate required for each bit plane. The process of soft information exchange is described below in more detail. Now, turbo decoding and soft information exchange is done again until successful decoding or stopped after 10 iterations. If the decoding is successful the decoder starts over with the reconstruction process. If the decoding was not successful the decoder requests more data from the encoder in a decoder rate control scheme. Inter bit plane decoding is started again with increased amount of data. The decoding fails in case of a encoder rate control scheme, because there is no chance to request more data.

### 3.1   LLR Calculation and Modeling

The calculation of the soft information (LLR generation, fig. 5) is the key component of our inter bit plane SW decoder. For this reason we present a detailed description of the LLR calculation below.

At the encoder the values of $X$ are scaled to the range $0\ldots1$ and quantized before Slepian-Wolf coding. This operation is described by the following formula,

$$q_i = \lfloor x_i \cdot 2^M \rfloor = Q(x_i) \tag{1}$$

where $x_i$ is a scaled value of $X_i$ (pixel of input frame), $M$ is the quantization parameter and $Q$ is the quantization operation.

The Slepian-Wolf decoder uses the received parity bits to correct the side information $Y$. The turbo decoder needs the LLR value $L_c(\hat{q}_i^{(b)})$ for every bit plane $b$ of a quantization symbol $\hat{q}_i$, therefore it is calculated beforehand (eq. 2).

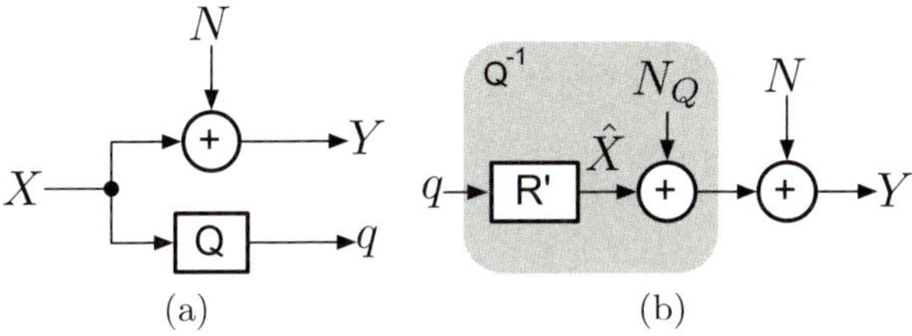

**Fig. 4.** (a) Relation between $q$ and $Y$, (b) Inverse quantizer to compute $p(y_i|q_i)$

$$L_c(\hat{q}_i^{(b)}) = \ln \frac{p(y_i|q_i^{(b)} = 0, \hat{q}_i^{(k)})}{p(y_i|q_i^{(b)} = 1, \hat{q}_i^{(k)})} \quad \forall k, k \in [1 \ldots M], k \neq b \tag{2}$$

The conditional pdf $p(y_i|q_i^{(b)} = 0, \hat{q}_i^{(k)})$ (probability density function) is needed to calculate the LLR value. For this reason a statistical description of the dependency between $q_i$ and $y_i$ is needed. The known relation between the original frame $X$, the side information $Y$ and the quantizer symbol $q$ is shown in figure 4(a). The side information $Y$ is a noisy version of $X$ and the quantization symbol $q$ the quantised version of $X$. This setup is transformed into the one shown in figure 4(b) to calculate the dependence between $q$ and $Y$. The quantizer Q is replaced by its inverse process (grey highlighted).

The quantizer noise $N_Q$ is modeled as equal distribution $p_q(n_{qi})$ (eq. 3) because it is assumed that the original values $X_i$ are equal distributed, too. Furthermore, the correlation noise $p_N(n_i)$ is modeled as Laplacian distributed (eq. 4).

$$p_q(n_{qi}) = \begin{cases} \frac{1}{\Delta} & : & |n_{qi}| < \frac{\Delta}{2} \\ 0 & : & else \end{cases} \tag{3}$$

$$p_N(n_i) = \frac{1}{2}\lambda e^{-\lambda|n_i|} \tag{4}$$

A mathematical description of the reconstruction process ( R' - inverse quantizer model) is given in equation 5 ( rescaling is not included ). The quantization step size is given by $\Delta = 2^{-M}$. The reconstruction is split up for every bit plane of $q$ in equation 6.

This process can be also described statistically. The corresponding probability density function (pdf) is given in equation 7 and is split up into one pdf for every bit plane $b$ of $q_i$ (see eq. 8), where $\delta(x)$ is the delta function. The pdf $p_R(\hat{x}_i|q_i)$ characterizes the reconstruction of $q_i$ and is calculated by convolution of all pdfs for each bit plane (eq. 9). This is possible due to the fact that the reconstruction of $q_i$ is split up into a sum of separate reconstruction for each bit plane ($q_i^{(b)}$, eq. 6).

Furthermore, equation 10 (adaption of eq. 8) allows inter bit plane decoding. It takes the probabilities for the bit plane $b$ into account which are calculated from the LLR output values. This allows transfer of information between the decoders of each bit plane. The information transfer is possible before the plane is fully decoded, because the probability for a bit plane $q_i^{(b)}$ is sufficient to calculate the LLR value for the other bit planes.

$$\hat{x}_i = q_i \cdot 2^{-M} + \frac{\Delta}{2} \tag{5}$$

$$\hat{x}_i = q_i^{(1)} \cdot 2^{-1} + \ldots + q_i^{(M)} \cdot 2^{-M} + \frac{\Delta}{2} \tag{6}$$

$$p_R(\hat{x}_i|q_i) = 1 \cdot \delta(\hat{x} - (q_i 2^{-M} + \frac{\Delta}{2})) \tag{7}$$

$$p_{R,b}(\hat{x}_i|q_i^{(b)}) = 1 \cdot \delta(\hat{x} - (q_i^{(b)} 2^{-b})) \tag{8}$$

$$p_R(\hat{x}_i|q_i) = p_{R,1}(\hat{x}_i|q_i^{(1)}) * p_{R,M}(\hat{x}_i|q_i^{(M)}) * \delta(\hat{x}_i - \frac{\Delta}{2}) \tag{9}$$

$$p_{R,b}(\hat{x}_i|q_i^{(b)}) = Pr(q_i^{(b)} = 0) \cdot \delta(\hat{x}) + Pr(q_i^{(b)} = 1) \cdot \delta(\hat{x} - (q_i 2^{-b})) \tag{10}$$

At least, the dependency between $y_i$ and $q_i$ is given in the following equation. The LLR value is calculated by equation 2 and 12.

$$y_i = \mathrm{R}'(q_i) + n_{qi} + n_i \tag{11}$$

$$p(y_i|q_i^{(b)} = 0, \hat{q}_i^{(k)}) = p_R(\hat{x}_i|q_i, q_i^{(b)} = 0) * p_q(n_{qi}) * p_N(n_i) \tag{12}$$

Our proposed LLR value calculation has the advantage that the decoder can do bit plane by bit plane decoding in a non-fixed order as well as inter bit plane decoding. Hence, a bit plane must not be fully decoded to start over with another bit plane. It's possible to switch from one bit plane to another and back (with improved information) before the successful decoding of the bit plane is performed. This one of the main advantages of the proposed inter bit plane decoding.

Our Slepian-Wolf decoder with inter bit plane decoding is shown in figure 5. The LLR values are calculated by equation 2 using the side information $Y$ and the correlation noise parameter $\lambda$. The LLR values are passed to a separate decoder (figure 5) for every bit plane $b = 1 \ldots M$. Each decoder also obtains the punctured LLR values $L_c(p^{(b)})$ of the transmitted parity bits. Then the turbo decoder starts decoding and provides the a-posteriori LLR value to the LLR value calculation for the next decoding step. In that way, the decoders for the different bit planes can exchange information.

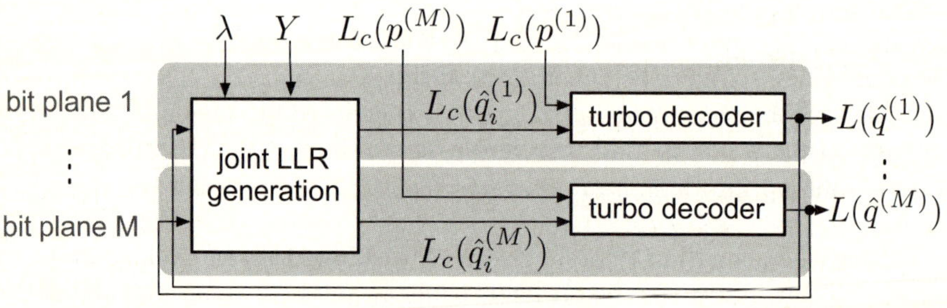


**Fig. 5.** Slepian-Wolf decoder

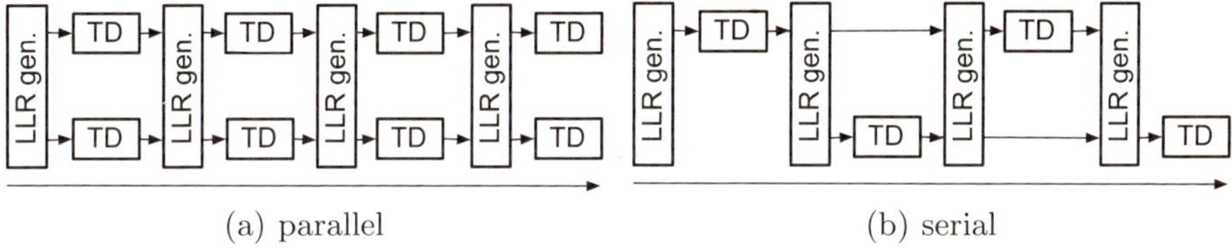

(a) parallel             (b) serial

**Fig. 6.** Joint Slepian-Wolf decoding of the bit planes (TD - turbo decoder)

## 3.2   Scheduling

The scheduling of the joint decoding for two bit planes is done in a serial or parallel way. In parallel joint decoding (figure 6(a)), the LLR values for each bit plane are calculated and turbo decoding is done before calculating the LLR values again. The serial joint decoding (figure 6(b)) does LLR calculation and afterwards only decodes one bit plane. Before decoding the next bit plane the LLR values are calculated again. The serial decoding is more complex but performs better and is thus used for the proposed joint bit plane decoding.

## 4   Simulation Results

The key component of our flexible Slepian-Wolf decoding is the inter bit plane decoding. It enables the flexible distribution of the data between the bit planes at the decoder side. The range for the data rate $R^{(b)}$ of a bit plane $b$ is given by $R^{(b)}_{min} \ldots R^{(b)}_{max}$. We focus on the 2 bit plane coding here (only MSB and LSB), because the scheduling for more than two bit planes is not solved by now.

The sequences `foreman`, `coastguard`, `hall`, and `mother_daughter` are used for simulation (QCIF, 30fps). A key frame distance of two frames is used (KWK...), where lossless coded key frames are assumed. An uniform quantizer is applied in the Wyner-Ziv CoDec. Furthermore, the Slepian-Wolf encoder is implemented by two parallel concatenated recursive convolutional codes ($G = [1, 33/31]_8$) and a random interleaver. The Slepian-Wolf decoder is implemented by a binary turbo decoder. The data rate is adapted by random puncturing (puncturing period $L_p = 128$) and side information is obtained by temporal interpolation of the neighboring loss less key frames.

### 4.1   Inter Bit Plane Decoding

The number of parity bits for the MSB and LSB bit planes and the accumulated sum bit rate is shown in figure 7. The data rate for the MSB is linearly increased. Also the data rate for the LSB is determined for successful decoding. This is done for each data rate of the MSB. As shown in figure 7, the necessary data rate for the LSB is decreased while increasing the data rate for the MSB. The sum data rate is a slight increased between 7% and 16%, which results in a performance loss.

The point for the highest MSB data rate is the same as the bit plane by bit plane (MSB to LSB) decoding in conventional state-of-the-art DVC CoDecs, where the

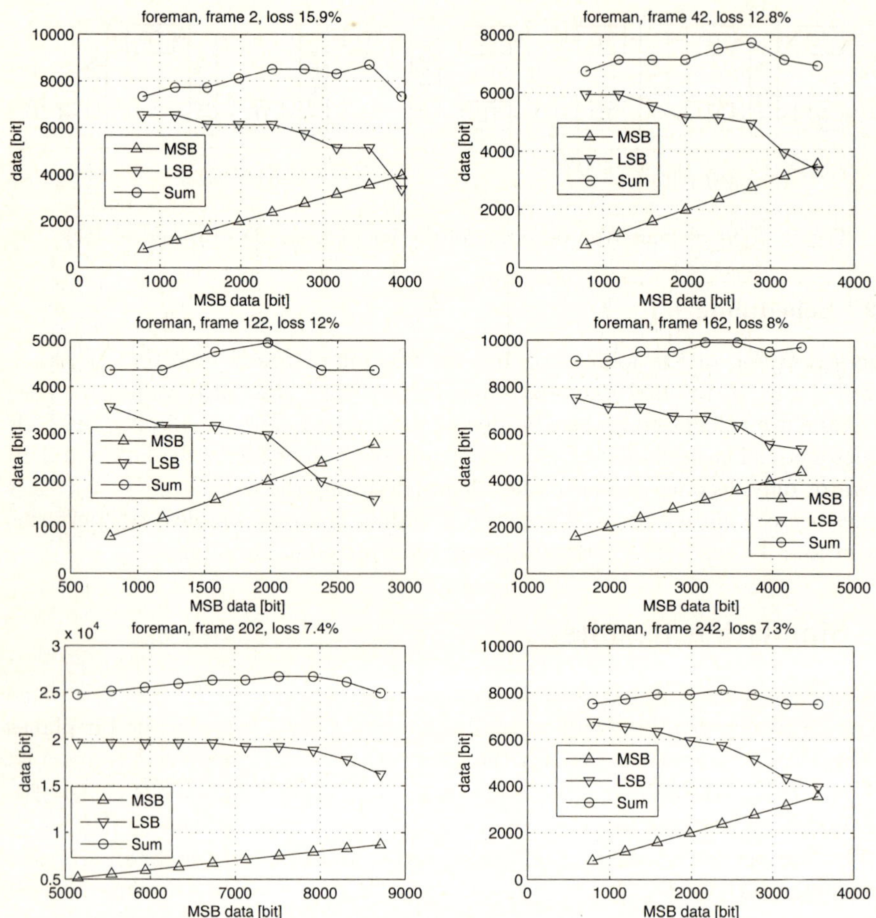

**Fig. 7.** Inter bit plane decoding: data rate for LSB, MSB, and Sum, including performance loss (`foreman`, QCIF)

MSB is decoded first. Furthermore, the point for the lowest MSB data rate is equivalent to the bit plane by bit plane decoding in LSB to MSB order, where the LSB is decoded first (fig. 7, frame 42). The data rate point between this borders are only accessible by inter bit plane decoding. For example the data rate distribution at 2000bit MSB data rate (frame 2) cannot be decoded by the conventional bit plane by bit plane decoding, because neither the amount of data for MSB nor for the amount of data for LSB is sufficient to decode this bit plane at first.

The inter bit plane decoding does not influence the reconstruction quality, since the quality remains constant for the same quantization symbol $q$ and identical side information $Y$. Therefore, the inter bit plane decoding only influences the necessary data rate for decoding (sum data rate).

## 4.2   Fixed Rate Ratio Coding

The motivation for the "Flexible Slepian-Wolf Decoding" is, that the encoder has not to adjust the data rate for each bit plane, but only the sum data rate.

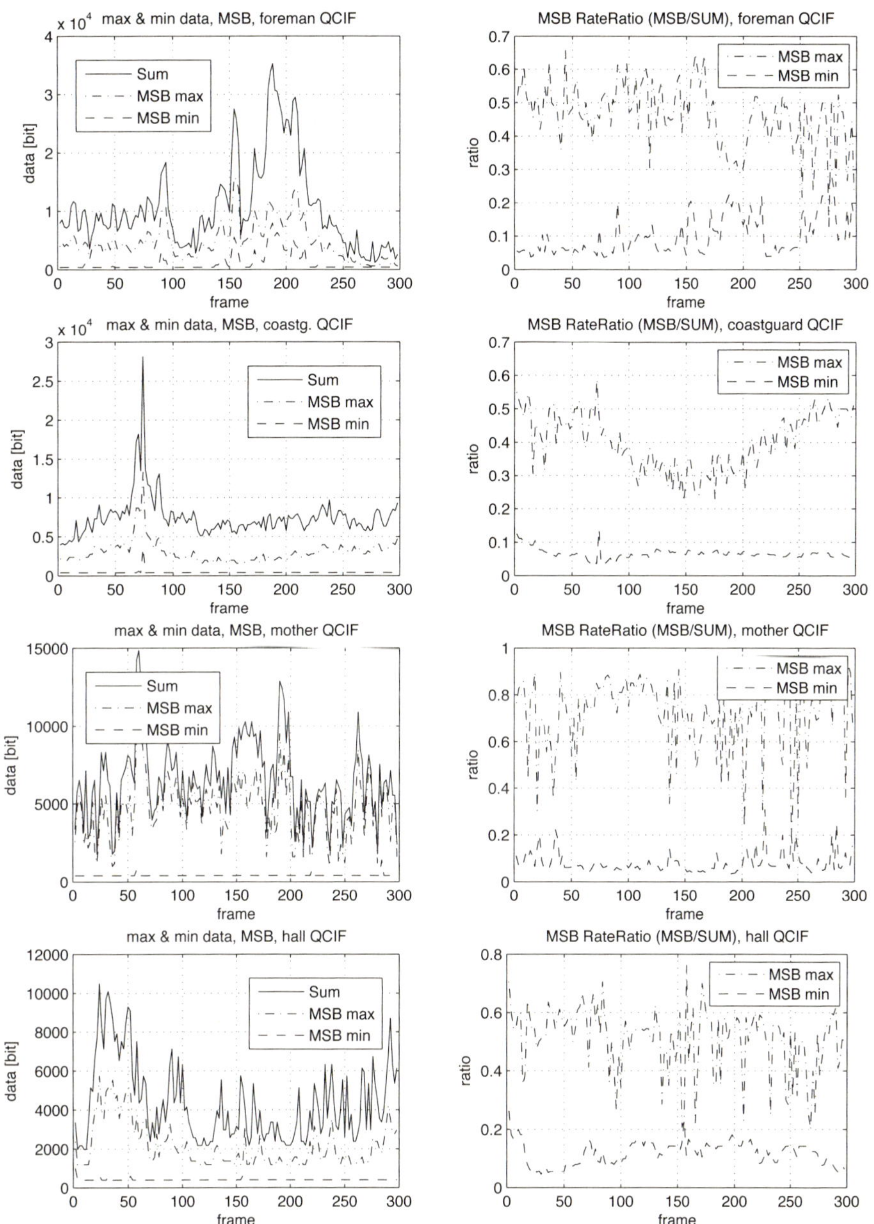

**Fig. 8.** (left) Bits per bit plane, (right) $ratio^{(1)}_{(min)} \ldots ratio^{(1)}_{(max)}$ for sequences `foreman`, `coastguard`, `mother and daughter`, and `hall`

In figure 8 the amount of data needed for successfully decoding of the MSB is shown for both MSB to LSB (max) and LSB to MSB (min) decoding order. This two cases mark the range within the inter bit plane coding can work. The upper and lower borders for the data rate are $R_{min}$ and $R_{max}$, see figure 3(b). Thus, the needed data for the MSB ($R^{(1)}$) can only be adapted within the range $R_{min}^{(1)} \leq R^{(1)} \leq R_{max}^{(1)}$.

The rate ratio for the MSB ($ratio^{(1)} = R^{(1)}/R_{sum}$) can vary in a given range ($ratio_{min}^{(1)} \ldots ratio_{max}^{(1)}$). A rate ratio of $ratio^{(1)} = 0.25$ is in the majority of frames within the range (fig.8). Consequently, for a fixed ratio of 0.25 the transmitted data can be decoded in nearly all cases.

The rate control has thus only to control the sum data rate precisely. On the one hand a encoder rate control only has to estimate the sum data rate, and on the other hand a decoder rate control only hast to request more sum rate and not data for a specific plane. This greatly facilitates both rate control schemes.

## 5    Conclusion

In this paper, we presented a flexible Slepian-Wolf decoding scheme facilitating the rate control scheme for distributed video coding. Thus, it is a step toward a feedback channel-free distributed video coding system, which transmits data over an unidirectional communication channel (e.g. video storage, unidirectional mobile video streaming).

The encoder has not to control the data rate for each bit plane precisely, because nearly all frames can be decoded at a rate ratio of 0.25 (25% of data for MSB and 75% for LSB). In this way, the encoder has only to estimate the sum data rate precisely.

The fixed rate ratio coding is only possible by the use of the proposed inter bit plane decoding (Flexible Slepian-Wolf Decoding). It does data exchange between the bit planes at the decoder side. Furthermore, the inter bit plane decoding will preserve the reconstruction quality of the video, while the data rate is slightly increased.

Further work will include investigation on the case of sub sum rate decoding, when the amount of data is lower than necessary for successful decoding.

## Acknowledgment

Special thanks to my colleagues for some inspiring discussions and also for some helpful editorial remarks.

## References

1. Slepian, D., Wolf, J.: Noiseless coding of correlated information sources. IEEE Transactions on Information Theory 19(4), 471–480 (1973)
2. Wyner, A.D., Ziv, J.: The rate-distortion function for source coding with side information at the decoder. IEEE Transactions on Information Theory 22(1), 1–10 (1976)

3. Aaron, A., Zhang, R., Girod, B.: Wyner-Ziv Coding of Motion Video. In: Proc. Asilomar Conference on Signals, Systems, and Computers, Pacific Grove, CA (November 2002)
4. Pereira, F., Ascenso, J., Brites, C.: Studying the GOP Size Impact on the Performance of a Feedback Channel-Based Wyner-Ziv Video Codec. In: Proc. Pacific-Rim Symposium on Image and Video Technology, pp. 801–815 (December 2007)
5. Aaron, A., Girod, B.: Wyner-Ziv Video Coding with Low Encoder Complexity. In: Proc. Picture Coding Symposium (PCS), SF/USA, December 15-17 (2004)
6. Artigas, X., Ascenso, J., Dalai, M., Klomp, S., Kubasov, D., Ouaret, M.: The DISCOVER Codec: Architecture, Techniques and Evaluation. In: Proc. Picture Coding Symposium (PCS), Lisboa (November 2007)
7. Brites, C., Pereira, F.: Encoder Rate Control for Transform Domain Wyner-Ziv Video Coding. In: Proc. IEEE International Conference on Image Processing (ICIP) (September 2007)
8. Vatis, Y., Klomp, S., Ostermann, J.: Inverse Bit Plane Decoding Order for Turbo Code Based Distributed Video Coding. In: Proc. IEEE International Conference on Image Processing (ICIP) (September 2007)

# Glass Patterns and Artistic Imaging

Giuseppe Papari and Nicolai Petkov

Institute of Mathematics and Computing Science, University of Groningen
`g.papari@rug.nl, n.petkov@rug.nl`

**Abstract.** The theory of Glass patterns naturally combines three essential aspects of painterly artworks: perception, randomness, and geometric structure. Therefore, it seems a suitable framework for the development of mathematical models of the visual properties that distinguish paintings from photographic images. With this contribution, we introduce a simple mathematical operator which transfers the microstructure of a Glass pattern to an input image, and we show that its output is perceptually similar to a painting. An efficient implementation is presented. Unlike most of the existing techniques for unsupervised painterly rendering, the proposed approach does not introduce 'magic numbers' and has a nice and compact mathematical description, which makes it suitable for further theoretical analysis. Experimental results on a broad range of input images validate the effectiveness of the proposed method in terms of lack of undesired artifacts, which are present with other existing methods, and easy interpretability of the input parameters.

## 1   Introduction

Computer aided generation of painting-like images is an interesting subfield of image processing and non-photorealistic rendering (NPR). The classic approach consists in generating a set of possibly overlapping brush strokes, which are rendered in a certain order on a white or canvas-textured background. There is a large variety of available painterly rendering algorithms (PRA), both unsupervised [1, 2, 3] and interactive [4, 5, 6]. Much effort has been made in order to model different painting styles [7, 8, 9] and to design efficient interactive user interfaces [5, 10], some of which deploy special-purpose hardware [10]. For a survey of these techniques we refer to [11].

One limitation of the aforementioned PRA is that they are not derived from general principles [9], due to the lack of a universally accepted mathematical model of the visual properties that distinguish paintings from photographic images. Consequently, many 'ad hoc' computational steps are deployed, and several 'magic numbers' need to be introduced (such as, for instance, the threshold of the Sobel edge detector deployed in [1] or the mixture parameter introduced in [12]). Moreover, as admitted in [6], these PRA may fail as soon as one of the intermediate operations does not perform well for some particular input image.

In contrast, considerable improvement can be gained if one abstracts from the imitation of classical tools and focuses on the visual properties of the desired

T. Wada, F. Huang, and S. Lin (Eds.): PSIVT 2009, LNCS 5414, pp. 1034–1045, 2009.
© Springer-Verlag Berlin Heidelberg 2009

output. In this paper we consider three important aspects of painterly artworks: perception, randomness and geometric structure. The former stems from the fact that artists put in their paintings their personal interpretation of a given natural scene [13, 14]. Randomness is important because artists never make two identical paintings of the same scene. Geometric structure plays a central role in visual arts because people perceive geometric dispositions of objects in the space [15]. Moreover, artists may deliberately align brush strokes according to the principle of good continuation in order to enhance the perception of forms and to make their paintings more vibrant.

A mathematical framework on which these concepts meet each other naturally is the theory of Glass Patterns (GP). A GP is defined as the superposition of two random point sets, one of which is obtained from the other by means of a small geometric transformation. Examples of such patterns are shown in Fig. 1.

GP have drawn the attention of many researchers from different disciplines. Direct measurement of the neural activity in the V1 and V2 areas of the brain of primates indicates that, when GP are presented, neurons of the visual cortex strongly respond to the local orientation of dot pairs [16, 17]. Such responses are then processed by means of association fields, thus extracting long chains of collinear segments [18, 19]; such chains determine the geometrical structure perceived in GP. Circular and spiral structures in GP are the most salient geometries [20, 21, 22], indicating that the contour integration process that is performed by the visual system is more sensitive to closed structures [23]. This might be the basis of the gestalt principles of closure and praegnanz [23, 24]. Several computational models of the perception of GP have been proposed [23, 25, 26].

GP have also been studied from a purely mathematical point of view in terms of their macro and microstructure. The former concerns local dot density, which turns out to be lower in the center of the pattern. The related phenomenology has been exhaustively studied [27, 28], and it can be explained by the general theory of moiré effects [29]. On the other hand, microstructure concerns the orientation field that is induced by the strong correlation between the two superposed point sets that compose a GP. Microstructural properties of GP can be studied naturally in the framework of the dynamical systems theory [30, 31] and algorithms able to synthesize any microstructure have been provided [31].

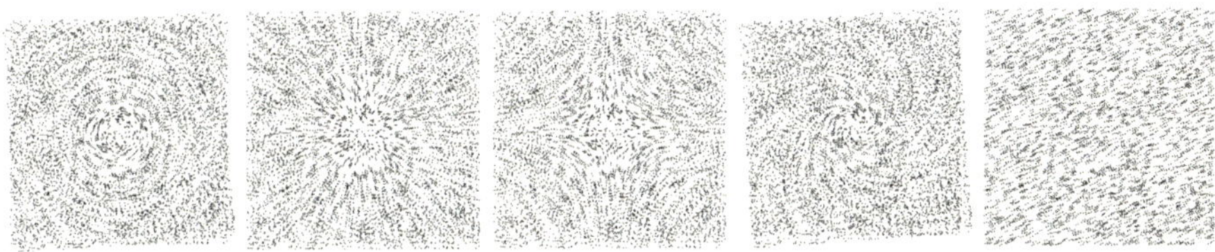

**Fig. 1.** Glass patterns obtained by several geometric transformations. From left to right: rotation, isotropic scaling, expansion and compression in the horizontal and vertical directions respectively, combination of rotation and isotropic scaling, and translation. Note that translational GP are the least salient.

In this paper, we propose a simple mathematical operator which transfers the microstructure of a GP to a natural image, thus resulting in a nice artistic effect. The method is validated by a wide range of experimental results and comparisons with well-estabilished PRA.

## 2    Mathematical Formalism

In this section we review the mathematical formalism related to classic discrete GP (Section 2.1), then we extend it to the continuous case (Section 2.2), and we show how to transfer their microstructure to a photographical image (Section 2.3).

### 2.1    Discrete Glass Patterns

Let $\mathbf{v}(\mathbf{r})$ be a vector field defined on $\mathbb{R}^2$ and let us consider the following differential equation:

$$\frac{d\mathbf{r}}{dt} = \mathbf{v}(\mathbf{r}) \tag{1}$$

We indicate the solution of (1), with the initial condition $\mathbf{r}(0) = \mathbf{r}_0$, by $\mathbf{r}(t) = \boldsymbol{\Phi}_\mathbf{v}(\mathbf{r}_0, t)$. For a fixed value of $t$, $\boldsymbol{\Phi}_\mathbf{v}$ is a map from $\mathbb{R}^2$ to $\mathbb{R}^2$, which satisfies the condition $\boldsymbol{\Phi}_\mathbf{v}(\mathbf{r}, 0) = \mathbf{r}$.

Let $S = \{\mathbf{r}_1, ..., \mathbf{r}_N\}$ be a random point set and let be $\boldsymbol{\Phi}_\mathbf{v}(S, t) \triangleq \{\boldsymbol{\Phi}_\mathbf{v}(\mathbf{r}, t) | \mathbf{r} \in S\}$. Using this notation, we define the Glass pattern $G_{\mathbf{v},t}(S)$ associated with $S$, $\mathbf{v}$, and $t$ as follows:

$$G_{\mathbf{v},t}(S) \triangleq S \bigcup \boldsymbol{\Phi}_\mathbf{v}(S, t) \tag{2}$$

Examples of GP generated by linear differential equations are shown in Fig. 1. More general vector fields give rise to more sophisticated geometries, which are related to the streamlines of $\mathbf{v}(\mathbf{r})$ (Fig. 2).

### 2.2    Continuous Glass Patterns (CGP)

In order to extend the GP formalism to the continuous case, we first represent a point sets $S$ with a binary fields $b_S(\mathbf{r})$ which, by definition, takes the value 1

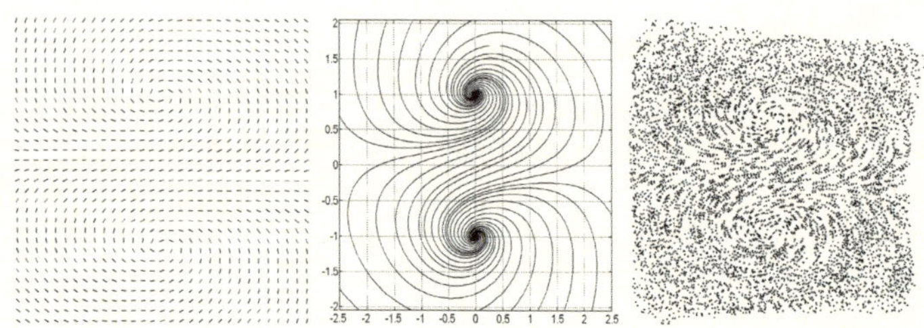

**Fig. 2.** From left to right: vector field $\mathbf{v}(x, y) = [y^2 - 1 + \frac{1}{3}xy, \frac{1}{3}(y^2 - 1) - xy]^\mathsf{T}$, the trajectories which solve the corresponding differential equation $\dot{\mathbf{r}} = \mathbf{v}(\mathbf{r})$, and a corresponding GP

for $\mathbf{r} \in S$ and is equal to 0 for $\mathbf{r} \notin S$. It is straightforward to see that the binary field associated with the superposition of two point sets $S_1$ and $S_2$ is equal to the maximum of $b_{S_1}(\mathbf{r})$ and $b_{S_2}(\mathbf{r})$. Therefore, from (2), we see that the binary field associated with a GP is equal to:

$$b_{G_{\mathbf{v},t}(S)}(\mathbf{r}) = \max\{b_S(\mathbf{r}), b_S[\boldsymbol{\Phi}_{\mathbf{v}}(\mathbf{r}, t)]\} \tag{3}$$

The generalization of (3) to the continuous case is straightforward: first, a continuous set of patterns $b_S[\boldsymbol{\Phi}(\mathbf{r}, \tau)]$, with $\tau \in [0, 1]$ is considered, instead of only two as in (3); second, any real valued random image $z(\mathbf{r})$ can be used instead of a Poisson process $b_S(\mathbf{r})$. Specifically, a *continuous Glass pattern* (CGP) $\mathcal{G}_{\mathbf{v},z}(\mathbf{r})$ is defined as follows:

$$\mathcal{G}_{\mathbf{v},z}(\mathbf{r}) \triangleq \max_{\tau \in [0,1]} \{z[\boldsymbol{\Phi}_{\mathbf{v}}(\mathbf{r}, \tau)]\} \tag{4}$$

We indicate by $A_{\mathbf{v}}(\mathbf{r})$ the arc of streamline $\mathbf{r}(t) = \boldsymbol{\Phi}_{\mathbf{v}}(\mathbf{r}, t)$ with $t \in [0, 1]$, i.e. $A_{\mathbf{v}}(\mathbf{r}) \triangleq \{\boldsymbol{\Phi}_{\mathbf{v}}(\mathbf{r}, t) | t \in [0, 1]\}$, and rewrite (4) more compactly as:

$$\mathcal{G}_{\mathbf{v},z}(\mathbf{r}) = \max_{\boldsymbol{\rho} \in A_{\mathbf{v}}(\mathbf{r})} \{z(\boldsymbol{\rho})\} \tag{5}$$

Examples of CGP are shown in Fig. 3, first row, where $z(\mathbf{r})$ is random noise, in which the histograms of all images have been equalized for visualization purposes. These patterns are related to the vector fields $\mathbf{v}(\mathbf{r}) = [y, -x]^{\mathsf{T}}$ (rotation) and $\mathbf{v}(\mathbf{r}) = [x, y]^{\mathsf{T}}$ (isotropic scaling) and, as we see, CGP exhibit similar geometric structures to the corresponding discrete GP.

## 2.3  Cross-CGP

Finally, in order to transfer the structure of a CGP to a color image $\mathbf{I}(\mathbf{r})$, we define the *cross-CGP* $C_{\mathbf{v}}\{z(\mathbf{r}), \mathbf{I}(\mathbf{r})\}$ as follows:

$$C_{\mathbf{v}}\{z(\mathbf{r}), \mathbf{I}(\mathbf{r})\} \triangleq \mathbf{I}\{\boldsymbol{\rho}_0(\mathbf{r})\}, \qquad \boldsymbol{\rho}_0(\mathbf{r}) \triangleq \arg \max_{\boldsymbol{\rho} \in A_{\mathbf{v}}(\mathbf{r})} \{z(\boldsymbol{\rho})\} \tag{6}$$

In other words, instead of directly considering the maximum of $z(\mathbf{r})$ over $A_{\mathbf{v}}(\mathbf{r})$, we first identify the point $\boldsymbol{\rho}_0(\mathbf{r})$ which maximize $z(\boldsymbol{\rho})$, and we take the value of $\mathbf{I}(\mathbf{r})$ at that point. It is easy to see that if the input image $\mathbf{I}(\mathbf{r})$ coincides with $z(\mathbf{r})$, cross-CGP coincide with CGP:

$$C_{\mathbf{v}}\{z(\mathbf{r}), z(\mathbf{r})\} = \mathcal{G}_{\mathbf{v},z}(\mathbf{r}) \tag{7}$$

Examples of cross-CGP are shown in Fig. 3, second row, for a natural image $\mathbf{I}(\mathbf{r})$. As we see, both randomness and the geometric structure of a GP are present in a cross-CGP.

Given $\mathbf{v}(\mathbf{r})$, $z(\mathbf{r})$, and $\mathbf{I}(\mathbf{r})$, cross-CGP can be computed in a straightforward way by integrating (1) numerically, and by taking the maximum of $z(\mathbf{r})$ over $A_{\mathbf{v}}(\mathbf{r})$, as indicated in (5). We implemented (5) by means of an optimized version of the Euler algorithm whose pseudo-code is shown in Fig. 4. Our algorithm starts with a cross-CGP computed over a 1-pixel-long arc $A_{\mathbf{v}}(\mathbf{r})$, and doubles the length of $A_{\mathbf{v}}(\mathbf{r})$ at each iteration. Therefore, the computation time is logarithmic with the length of $A_{\mathbf{v}}(\mathbf{r})$.

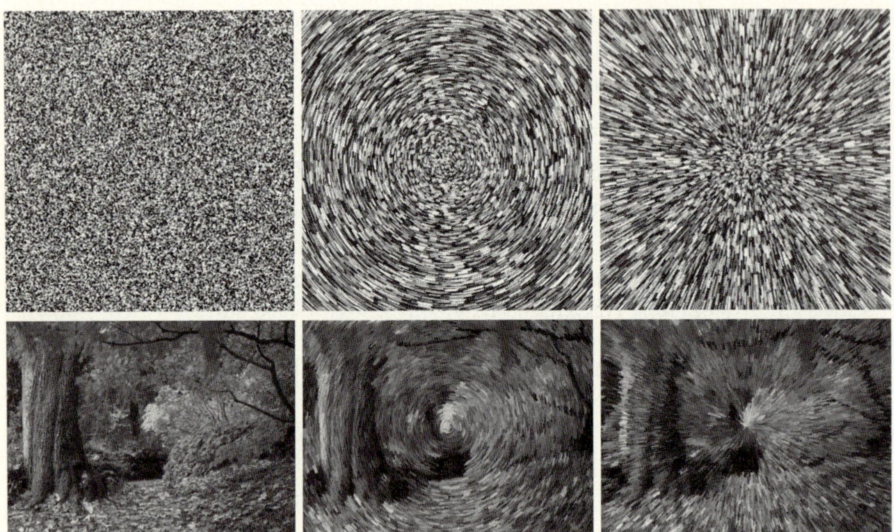

**Fig. 3.** Examples of CGP and cross-CGP. First row: random image $z(\mathbf{r})$ and CGP obtained from it, by means of the vector fields $\mathbf{v}(\mathbf{r}) = [y, -x]^\mathsf{T}$ and $\mathbf{v}(\mathbf{r}) = [x, y]^\mathsf{T}$ respectively. Their geometrical structure is analogous to the discrete case. Second row: an input image and cross-CGP related to the same random image $z(\mathbf{r})$ and the same vector fields $\mathbf{v}(\mathbf{r})$. Cross-CGP succeeds in transferring randomness and geometric structure of a GP to an image.

## 3  Proposed PRA

In this section, we describe a simple approach to add artistic effects to a photographic image $\mathbf{I}(\mathbf{r})$, as depicted in Fig. 5. The idea is to compute the cross-CGP $C_\mathbf{v}(z, \mathbf{I})$ of $\mathbf{I}(\mathbf{r})$, where $z(\mathbf{r})$ is random noise and $\mathbf{v}(\mathbf{r})$ is a vector field extracted from the input image.

In order to determine $\mathbf{v}(\mathbf{r})$, we first compute the orientation $\theta_\sigma(\mathbf{r})$ of the color gradient of $\mathbf{I}(\mathbf{r})$. Following [32], we define $\theta_\sigma(\mathbf{r})$ as the direction of the eigenvector associated with the maximum eigenvalue of the following matrix:

$$K_\sigma(\mathbf{r}) = \sum_{i=1}^{3} \left[ \nabla_\sigma I^{(i)}(\mathbf{r}) \right] \left[ \nabla_\sigma I^{(i)}(\mathbf{r}) \right]^\mathsf{T} \tag{8}$$

where $I^{(i)}(\mathbf{r})$ is the $i-th$ color component of $\mathbf{I}(\mathbf{r})$ and $\nabla_\sigma I^{(i)}(\mathbf{r})$ is the result of the convolution of $I^{(i)}(\mathbf{r})$ with the gradient of a Gaussian function with standard deviation $\sigma$. Then, the vector field $\mathbf{v}(\mathbf{r})$ is chosen to have constant length $a$ and to form a constant angle $\theta_0$ with the direction $\theta_\sigma(\mathbf{r})$ of $\nabla_\sigma I$, where $a$ and $\theta_0$ are input parameters:

$$\mathbf{v}(\mathbf{r}) = a[\cos(\theta_\sigma(\mathbf{r}) + \theta_0), \ \sin(\theta_\sigma(\mathbf{r}) + \theta_0)]^\mathsf{T} \tag{9}$$

```
SubRoutine FastCrossCGP(I, z, Vx, Vy, N_iter, h)
    % I        = Input image I(r)
    % z        = Random noise z(r)
    % Vx, Vy   = x and y components of v(r)
    % N_iter   = Number of iterations
    % h        = Step size of the Euler algorithm
    For i = 1 : N_iter {
        I1 = evaluate(I, Vx, Vy, h);
        z1 = evaluate(z, Vx, Vy, h);
        For each (x,y) {
            if z(x,y) ≤ z1(x,y)
                I(x,y) = I1(x,y);
        }
        z = max(z, z1);
        Wx = evaluate(Vx, Vx, Vy, h);
        Wy = evaluate(Vy, Vx, Vy, h);
        Vx = Vx + Wx;
        Vy = Vy + Wy;
    }
    Return I;
```

**Fig. 4.** Pseudo-code of the proposed implementation of cross-CGP. The subroutine 'evaluate', which is not detailed here, takes in input three real valued functions $I(x,y)$, $V_x(x,y)$, and $V_y(x,y)$, with $(x,y) \in \mathbb{Z}^2$, and a scalar $h$, and returns the function $U(x,y) \triangleq I[x + h \cdot V_x(x,y), y + h \cdot V_y(x,y)]$, which is computed by means of bilinear interpolation.

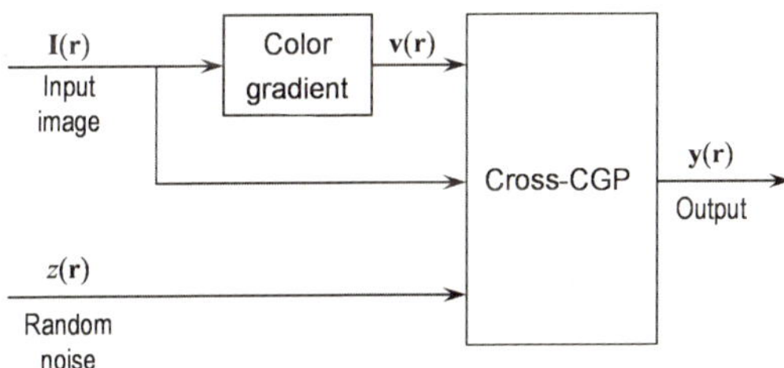


**Fig. 5.** Scheme of the proposed PRA

The value of $\theta_\sigma(\mathbf{r})$ is undefined on points $\mathbf{r}$ for which the eigenvalues of $K_\sigma(\mathbf{r})$ are equal. For such points we take by definition $\mathbf{v}(\mathbf{r}) = \mathbf{0}$.

Finally, the output $\mathbf{y}(\mathbf{r})$ of the proposed operator is simply the cross-CGP associated with the input image $\mathbf{I}(\mathbf{r})$, the vector field $\mathbf{v}(\mathbf{r})$ defined in (9), and a random noise $z(\mathbf{r})$:

$$\mathbf{y}(\mathbf{r}) = C_\mathbf{v}\{z(\mathbf{r}), \mathbf{I}(\mathbf{r})\} \tag{10}$$

An example of the output of the proposed operator is shown in Fig. 6 for the input image of Fig. 3, second row ($921 \times 660$ pixel), for $\sigma = 6$, $a = 18$ and $\theta_0 = \pi/2$. As we see, the output presents curved brush strokes oriented along

**Fig. 6.** Output of the proposed operator for the input image of Fig. 3, second row

(a)        (b)

(c)        (d)

**Fig. 7.** (a) Input image, (b) output of the proposed operator, (c) noisy input image and (d) output of the proposed operator. Adding a small noise to the input image makes impressionist whirls visible on texture-less area too.

**Table 1.** Values of the parameters used for the studied approaches, with each color component of the input image ranging between 0 and 1

| Algorithm | Parameter values |
|---|---|
| Proposed approach | $a = 16$, $\sigma = 6$, $\lambda = 0.3$, $\theta_0 = \pi/2$ |
| IR [1] | $l = 5$, $w = 1$, $\Delta r = \Delta g = \Delta b = 0.06$, $\Delta I = 0.15$ |
| AV [6] | Segm. levs. = 48, Enh. levs. = 96, Brush. Art. lev. = 40, $\alpha = 50\%$ |

the object contours. It is easy to prove that for $\theta_0 = \pi/2$ the streamlines of $\mathbf{v}(\mathbf{r})$ are closed curves, thus, the brush strokes tend to form whirls which are typical of some impressionist paintings.

The proposed operator does not introduce new colors to the input image. Consequently, brush strokes are not visible on non-textured areas (Fig 7b). However, this problem is solved by simply adding a small monochromatic random noise to the input image before computing the cross-CGP (Fig. 7c-d).

Concerning the input parameters, $a$ determines the length of the brush strokes, $\sigma$ influences the smoothness of the lines traced out by the brush strokes and the

Fig. 8. (a) An input image and outputs of (b) the proposed algorithm, (c) AV [6], and (d) IR [1]

size of the impressionist whirls, and $\theta_0$ controls the angle between each brush stroke and the nearest edge.

## 4   Results and Comparison

In this section, some experimental results are presented and commented. Our approach is compared with two of the most popular PRA, namely the impressionist rendering (IR) proposed in [1] and the NPR technique called *artistic vision* (AV) presented in [6]. IR consists in rendering overlapping rectangular brush strokes of a given size and orientation. In AV, curved brush strokes of different sizes

**Fig. 9.** (a) An input image and outputs of (b) the proposed algorithm, (c) AV [6], and (d) IR [1]

(a)         (b)

(c)         (d)

**Fig. 10.** Illustration of the influence of the parameter $\theta_0$. (a) Input image and outputs of the proposed operator for (b) $\theta_0 = \pi/2$, (c) $\theta_0 = \pi/4$, and (d) $\theta_0 = 0$.

are rendered by means of a more sophisticated segmentation approach. We show some results in Figs. 8-10; a larger set of examples is available online[1]. Unless differently specified, we use the parameter values according to Table 1.

The output of the proposed operator for the input images of Figs. (8-9)a is shown in Figs. (8-9)b. As we see, our operator effectively mimics curved brush strokes oriented along object contours, and the whirls that are present in contourless areas resemble some impressionist paintings. In Figs (8-9)c, the outputs of AV are shown for the same input images; though simulation of curved brush strokes is attempted, several artifacts are clearly visible, especially on flat areas. IR (Figs. (8-9)d) does not produce artifacts, but it tends to produce blurry contours and fails in rendering impressionist whirls.

In Fig. 10, the output of the proposed operator is shown for different values of the parameter $\theta_0$ ($\theta_0 = \frac{\pi}{2}, \frac{\pi}{4}, 0$), which controls the angle between the brush strokes and the nearest object contour. As we see, different artistic effects can be achieved by varying the value of $\theta_0$. Specifically, for $\theta = \pi/2$, the strokes follow the object contours and form whirls in flat areas, while for $\theta = 0$, the strokes are orthogonal to the contours and build star-like formations in flat regions.

---

[1] http://www.cs.rug.nl/~imaging/PSIVT2009

# 5   Summary and Conclusions

We use the theory of GP for unsupervised automatic painterly rendering. Specifically, we show that transferring the microstructure of a GP to a photographical image results in a nice artistic effect. The proposed algorithm is simple, can be implemented very efficiently, does not introduce 'magic numbers' and, unlike many other methods, is expressed by a compact mathematical expression, which makes it suitable for further theoretical analysis. Due to its simplicity, input parameters are easily interpretable, and undesired artifacts that affect some existing algorithms are avoided. Moreover, the possibility to achieve considerably different artistic effects by simply changing the values of certain input parameters (such as $\theta_0$, see Fig. 10) makes the method versatile and promising. This work improves a previous work of us presented in [33] in terms of a smaller amount of computational steps and input parameters. Experimental results on a broad range of input images validate the effectiveness of the proposed method.

# References


[1] Litwinowicz, P.: Processing images and video for an impressionist effect. In: Siggraph, pp. 407–414 (1997)

[2] Shiraishi, M., Yamaguchi, Y.: An algorithm for automatic painterly rendering based on local source image approximation. In: NPAR, pp. 53–58 (2000)

[3] Li, N., Huang, Z.: Zhiyong Huang. Feature-guided painterly image rendering. In: ICIP, pp. 653–656 (2002)

[4] Haeberli, P.: Paint by numbers: Abstract image representations. Computer Graphics 24(4), 207–214 (1990)

[5] De Carlo, D., Santella, A.: Stylization and abstraction of photographs. ACM Transactions on Graphics (TOG) 21(3), 769–776 (2002)

[6] Gooch, B., Coombe, G., Shirley, P.: Artistic vision: painterly rendering using computer vision techniques. In: NPAR, pp. 83–90 (2002)

[7] Hertzmann, A.: Painterly rendering with curved brush strokes of multiple sizes. In: Siggraph, pp. 453–460 (1998)

[8] Kasao, A., Miyata, K.: Algorithmic painter: a NPR method to generate various styles of painting. The Visual Computer 22(1), 14–27 (2006)

[9] Collomosse, J.P., Hall, P.M.: Salience-adaptive painterly rendering using genetic search. International Journal on Artificial Intelligence Tools 15(4), 551–575 (2006)

[10] Santella, A., DeCarlo, D.: Abstracted painterly renderings using eye-tracking data. In: Spencer, S.N. (ed.) NPAR, pp. 75–82. ACM Press, New York (2002)

[11] Hertzmann, A.: A survey of stroke-based rendering. IEEE Computer Graphics and Applications 23(4), 70–81 (2003)

[12] Olsen, S.C., Maxwell, B.A., Gooch, B.: Interactive vector fields for painterly rendering. In: Proceedings of Graphics Interface 2005, pp. 241–247 (2005)

[13] Arnheim, R.: Art and Visual Perception: A Psychology of the Creative Eye. University of California Press (1974)

[14] Arnheim, R.: Toward a psychology of art. University of California Press, Berkeley (1966)

[15] Ogden, R.M.: Naive geometry in the psychology of art. American Journal of Psychology 49(2), 198–216 (1937)

[16] Smith, M.A., Bair, W., Movshon, J.A.: Signals in macaque striate cortical neurons that support the perception of Glass patterns. Journal of Neuroscience 22(18), 8334–8345 (2002)

[17] Smith, M.A., Kohn, A., Movshon, J.A.: Glass pattern responses in macaque V2 neurons. Journal of Vision 7(3), 5 (2007)

[18] Yen, S.C., Finkel, L.H.: Extraction of perceptually salient contours by striate cortical networks. Vis. Res. 38(5), 719–741 (1998)

[19] Li, Z.: A neural model of contour integration in the primary visual cortex. Neur. Comp. 10(4), 903–940 (1998)

[20] Maloney, R.K., Mitchison, G.J., Barlow, H.B.: Limit to the detection of Glass patterns in the presence of noise. J. Opt. Soc. Am. A 4(12), 2336–2341 (1987)

[21] Wilson, H.R., Wilkinson, F.: Detection of global structure in Glass patterns: implications for form vision. Vision Research 38(19), 2933–2947 (1998)

[22] Seu, L., Ferrera, V.P.: Detection thresholds for spiral Glass patterns. Vision Research 41(28), 3785–3790 (2001)

[23] Dakin, S.C.: The detection of structure in Glass patterns: Psychophysics and computational models. Vision Research 37(16), 2227–2246 (1997)

[24] Prazdny, K.: Psychophysical and computational studies of random-dot moire patterns. Spatial Vision 1(3), 231–242 (1986)

[25] Phillips, T.H., Rosenfeld, A.: A simplified method of detecting structure in Glass patterns. Pattern Recognition Letters 4(3), 213–217 (1986)

[26] Wilson, J.A., Switkes, E., De Valois, R.L.: Glass pattern studies of local and global processing of contrast variations. Vision Research 44(22), 2629–2641 (2004)

[27] Amidror, I.: Unified approach for the explanation of stochastic and periodic moirés. Journal of Electronic Imaging 12(4), 669–681 (2003)

[28] Amidror, I.: Glass patterns as moiré effects: new surprising results. Optics Letters 28(1), 7–9 (2003)

[29] Amidror, I.: The theory of the Moiré phenomenon, volume 1: periodic layers. Springer, Heidelberg (2000)

[30] Glass, L.: Looking at dots. Math. Intell. 24(4), 37–43 (2002)

[31] Amidror, I.: Dot trajectories in the superposition of random screens: analysis and synthesis. Journal of the Optical Society of America A 21(8), 1472–1487 (2004)

[32] Cumani, A.: Edge detection in multispectral images. CVGIP 53(1), 40–51 (1991)

[33] Papari, G., Petkov, N.: Continous glass patterns for painterly rendering. IEEE Transactions on Image Processing (to appear)

# Classification of Similar 3D Objects with Different Types of Features from Multi-view Images
## – An Approach to Classify 100 Apples –


Hitoshi Niigaki and Kazuhiro Fukui

University of Tsukuba, Graduate School of Systems and Information Engineering,
1-1-1 Tennoudai, Tsukuba, Ibaraki, Japan
niigaki@cvlab.cs.tsukuba.ac.jp, kfukui@cs.tsukuba.ac.jp



**Abstract.** This paper proposes a method for classifying 3D objects with similar appearances using different types of features from multi-view images. We can find this type of task in various practical applications, such as flaw inspection of industrial components, quality checking, ans screening of fruits and vegetables. In this paper, as an example such a concrete task, we will deal with the problem of classifying apples, a task that is difficult even for human vision. To tackle this task, we will introduce the mutual subspace method (MSM)-based methods as a weak classifiers in an ensemble learning framework. In addition, we will consider three types of features: shape, texture and color in the terms of invariants of position and scale, as input vectors of each MSM-based classifier. The effectiveness of the proposed method will be demonstrated through the results of evaluation experiments using 100 apples.


## 1 Introduction

Many view-based methods have been proposed for 3D object recognition, which is one of active research areas in computer vision[1]. Several investigations into the issue suggest the effectiveness of utilizing rich information obtained from multi-view images to achieve high-performance[2]-[6].

The mutual subspace method (MSM) has the ability to handle multiple images, including sequential images or multi-view images, and so is suitable and efficient for recognizing 3D objects. Let an $n \times n$ pixel pattern be treated as a vector $\mathbf{x}$ in $n^2$-dimensional space. In MSM, the set of patterns of each class is represented by a low-dimensional linear subspace using Karhunen-Loève(KL) expansion, also known as principal component analysis (PCA). The classification of a set of patterns is executed based on the canonical angles $\theta$ between subspaces, $\mathcal{P}$ and $\mathcal{Q}$, where smaller angles indicate higher similarity between the two subspaces as shown in Fig. 1.

MSM and its extensions, CMSM[4] and OMSM[5], have been successfully applied to various practical applications, such as face recognition[6], ISAR image analysis[7], and lip reading[8]. The successes in face recognition are especially


T. Wada, F. Huang, and S. Lin (Eds.): PSIVT 2009, LNCS 5414, pp. 1046–1057, 2009.

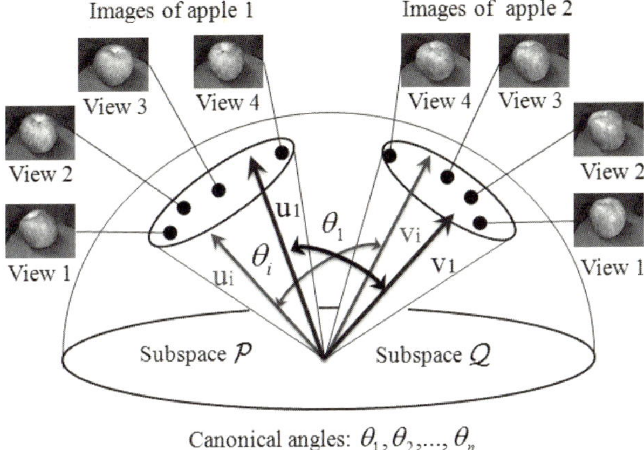


**Fig. 1.** Similarity between two distributions of multi-view image patterns

noteworthy. However, face recognition may be a relatively easy classification problem, considering that it can be easily executed by human vision. This leads us to the question, how well the MSM-based methods perform in classifying 3D objects with appearances so similar that even human vision has difficulty classifying them? There are many types of 3D objects with such characteristics in various practical applications; flaw inspection of industrial component, quality checking, and screening of fruits and vegetables[9][10].

In this paper, we consider the challenging problem of classifying 100 apples as a representative task. As shown in Fig. 2, even human vision has trouble classifying them as the number of apples increases. If MSM-based methods achieve high performance in this task, it should indicate a potential applicability to the classification of other objects with very similar appearances.

**Fig. 2.** Multi-view image patterns of apples

Face recognition systems based on MSM-based methods have achieved high performance by using only single appearance feature. However, to perform more difficult tasks such as those described above, it is necessary to use multiple feature types obtained from multi-view images, and use them by considering their characteristics. We consider three types of features: shape-type(P-type Fourier Transform descriptor[11]), texture-type(2D FFT power spectrum, view, HOG[12], HLAC[13]) and color-type(color histogram) in the terms of invariants of position and scale. These are used as input vectors for each MSM-based methods. Then the multiple classification results from all the MSM-based methods are combined in a ensemble learning framework.

The rest of the paper is organized as follows. Section 2 outlines an our method, including the algorithms of the MSM-based methods. Section 3 demonstrates the effectiveness of our method through evaluation experiments using 100 apples. Section 4 presents our conclusions.

## 2    The Proposed Method

In this section, we first describe the algorithm of the MSM-based methods, MSM, CMSM and OMSM before discussing various feature types extracted from multi-view images in the term of invariant of position and scale. Then, we combine the results of all the MSM-based classifiers using different feature types in the framework of the ensemble learning.

### 2.1    Mutual Subspace Method (MSM)

As mentioned in Sec. 1, MSM measures the similarity between the distributions of reference patterns and input patterns by using canonical angles between two subspaces. These canonical angles can be calculated by the following procedure.

Given an $m$-dimensional subspace $\mathcal{P}$ and an $n$-dimensional subspace $\mathcal{Q}$ (as a matter of convenience $m \geq n$), the $n$ canonical angles $\{0 \leq \theta_1, \theta_2, .., \theta_n \leq \pi/2\}$ are determined as shown in Fig. 1. The first canonical angle is the smallest angle between the two subspaces and the second canonical angle is the smallest angle along the direction orthogonal to the first canonical angle. $cos^2\theta_i$ for $i = 3, \ldots, n$ are calculated similarly. The canonical angles $\theta_i$ between $\mathcal{P}$ and $\mathcal{Q}$ are uniquely defined as :

$$\cos^2 \theta_i = \max_{\substack{u_i \perp u_j (j = 1, 2, ..., i-1) \\ v_i \perp v_j (j = 1, 2, ..., i-1)}} \frac{(\mathbf{u}_i \cdot \mathbf{v}_i)^2}{\| \mathbf{u}_i \|^2 \| \mathbf{v}_i \|^2} , \tag{1}$$

where $\mathbf{u}_i \in \mathcal{P}, \mathbf{v}_i \in \mathcal{Q}$.

Let $\mathbf{\Phi}_i$ and $\mathbf{\Psi}_i$ denote the $i$-th $n$-dimensional orthonormal basis vectors of the subspaces $\mathcal{P}$ and $\mathcal{Q}$, respectively. These orthonormal basis vectors can be obtained as the eigenvectors of the autocorrelation matrix $\sum_{i=1}^{l} \mathbf{x}_i \mathbf{x}_i^T$ calculated from the $l$ learning patterns $\{\mathbf{x}\}$ of each class.

A practical method of finding the canonical angles is by computing the matrix $\mathbf{X}=\mathbf{A}^T\mathbf{B}$, where $\mathbf{A} = [\mathbf{\Phi}_1, \ldots, \mathbf{\Phi}_m]$ and $\mathbf{B}=[\mathbf{\Psi}_1, \ldots, \mathbf{\Psi}_n]$. Let $\{\kappa_1, \ldots, \kappa_n\}$

$(\kappa_1 \geq, \ldots, \geq \kappa_n)$ be the singular values of the matrix $\mathbf{X}$. The canonical angles $\{\theta_1, \ldots, \theta_n\}$ can be obtained as $\{cos^{-1}(\kappa_1), \ldots, cos^{-1}(\kappa_n)\}$.

## 2.2   Definition of Similarity

The similarity between two subspaces is defined as

$$S[n'] = \frac{1}{n'} \sum_{i=1}^{n'} \cos^2 \theta_i \ , \tag{2}$$

where $n'$ is the number of canonical angles used for calculating the similarity. The value $S[n']$ reflects the structural similarity between two subspaces. In cases in which two subspaces coincide completely with each other, $S[n']$ is 1.0, since all canonical angles are zero. The similarity $S[n']$ becomes smaller as the two subspaces separate. The similarity $S[n']$ is zero, only when the two subspaces are orthogonal to each other.

## 2.3   Extensions of MSM: CMSM and OMSM

In order to improve the performance of MSM, it has been extended to the constrained mutual subspace method (CMSM[4]) and the Orthogonal Mutual Subspace Method (OMSM[5]).

In CMSM, each class subspace is projected onto a discriminant space referred to as the constraint subspace $\mathcal{D}$. This projection extracts a common subspace of all the class subspaces from each class subspace, such that the canonical angles between class subspaces are enlarged to approach orthogonal relation. Given the projection matrices $\mathbf{P}_i(i = 1, 2, ..., k)$ of $k$ classes, the constraint subspace $\mathcal{D}$ is spanned by the eigenvectors corresponding to the $N_d$-th smallest eigenvalue of the following matrix:

$$\mathbf{G} = \sum_{i=1}^{k} \mathbf{P}_i \ . \tag{3}$$

The dimension $N_d$ is set experimentally.

OMSM also realizes the orthogonalization by Fukunaga and Koontz's method [14], so that it improves the performance of MSM. In their method, orthogonalization is achieved by applying the whitening transformation matrix $\mathbf{O}$ to the training patterns or orthonormal basis vectors of each class subspace. The whitening matrix $\mathbf{O}$ is defined as

$$\mathbf{O} = \mathbf{\Lambda}^{-1/2} \mathbf{B}^T \ , \tag{4}$$

where $\mathbf{\Lambda}^{-1/2}$ is the diagonal matrix whose $i$-th component is the reciprocal of the square root of the $i$-th highest eigenvalue of $\mathbf{G}$. $\mathbf{B}$ is the matrix whose $i$-th column vector is the eigenvector of the matrix $\mathbf{G}$ corresponding to the $i$-th highest eigenvalue.

## 2.4    Valid Features Extracted from Multi-view Images

The conventional MSM-based methods have mainly used the "view (appearance) feature" that is obtained by raster scan of an image. However, the view feature varies largely depending on the position and scale of an object. Thus, we can predict that using only view feature is inadequate to classify similar 3D objects with a high degree of accuracy. There are numerous features that we can extract from multi-view images.

- **Shape-type**: P-type Fourier Transform descriptor(P-FT)
  P-FT is based on the boundary-based shape descriptor, which is position and scale invariant feature. However, it is not so robust with regards to variations caused by shadows and illumination. When the number of objects is large, its classification ability may decrease.
- **Texture-type**: HOG, HLAC, 2D-DFT descriptor(2D-DFT), view feature
  HOG is based on the magnitude information of edges in local region. HLAC is based on the autocorrelation between pixels in a local region. 2D-DFT is obtained as low-frequency Fourier components of an image. HLAC and 2D-DFT are invariant to position. In contrast, HOG and view feature are not invariant.
- **Color-type**: Color histogram
  This type is widely used in image retrieval, as it is position and scale invariant. However, when the number of apples increases, its classification ability may drop.

As shown in Table 1, these features are classified into three types: shape, texture and color. From this table, we can see that these characteristics are mutually complementary. Therefore, it should be effective to utilize multiple different feature types obtained from multi-view images in order to realize the classification of many apples that have very similar appearances.

## 2.5    Ensemble Learning

In this section, we construct the ensemble classification based on multiple MSM-based classifiers with different kinds of features. Fig. 3 shows the flow chart of

**Table 1.** Characteristics of each feature

| | Shape type | Texture type | Color type | Position invariant | Scale invariant |
|---|---|---|---|---|---|
| View | | o | | x | x |
| HOG | | o | | x | x |
| P-FT | o | | | o | o |
| 2D-DFT | | o | | o | x |
| HLAC | | o | | o | x |
| Color histogram | | | o | o | o |

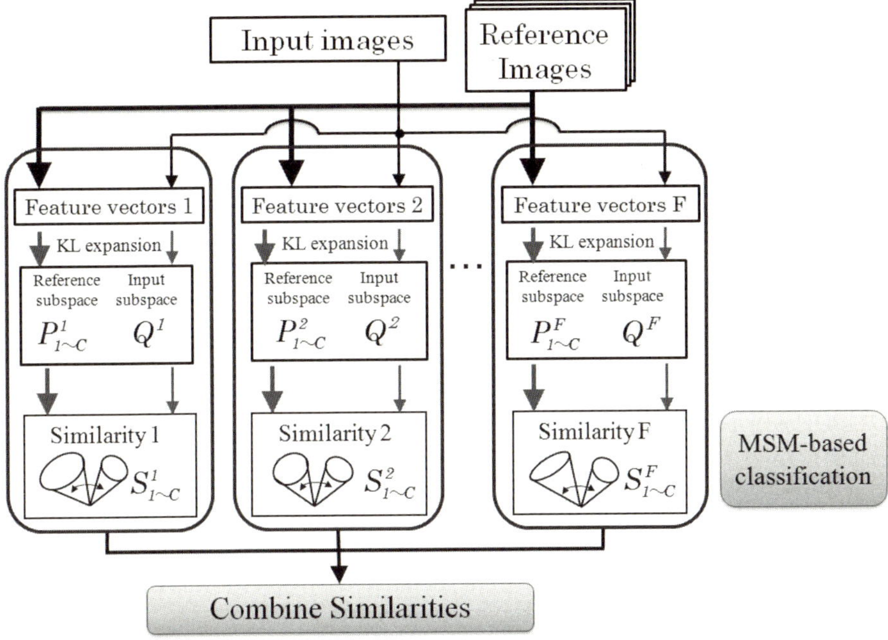


**Fig. 3.** Ensemble classification

the ensemble classification, which consists of a learning stage and a classification stage.

### Learning stage

1. The multiple kinds of feature vectors $\{\mathbf{x}^f_i\}(i = 1,\ldots,C, f = 1,\ldots,F)$ are extracted from learning multi-view images, where $F$ is the number of feature types and $C$ is the number of classes.
2. The reference subspaces $P^f_i$ are generated from learning set $\{\mathbf{x}^f_i\}$ using KL expansion.
3. The above operations are executed for all the $C$ classes.

### Classification stage

1. An input subspace $Q^f$ is generated from feature vectors extracted from input multi-view images using KL expansion.
2. The similarity $S^f_i$ between an input subspace $Q^f$ and reference subspace $P^f_i$ is measured using MSM-based method.
3. The similarity $S^f_i$ from feature $f$ is normalized to $S^{f'}_i$ by dividing it by the max similarity among $\{S^f_1,\ldots,S^f_C\}$.
4. The normalized similarities $\{S^{1'}_i,\ldots,S^{F'}_i\}$ are combined by using $\frac{1}{F}\sum^F_{f'=1} S^{f'}_i$. This operation is executed for all the $C$ classes.
5. The input set is classified as the class with the highest similarity.

# 3    Experiments

In this section, we first describe the details of each feature extraction. Next, we execute a preliminary experiment to evaluate the effectiveness of several features. We then show the results of classification of 100 apples using a single feature are shown. Finally, we demonstrate the effectiveness of using multiple different types of features.

## 3.1    Details of Each Feature Extraction

- **P-type Fourier Transform descriptor (P-FT)**[11]
  The P-type Fourier descriptor is a representation of the object boundary. In this experiment, we used 40 low-frequency components extracted from two images, which were an original $320 \times 240$ pixel image and a half size $160 \times 120$ pixel image. The dimension of feature vector was set to $80 (= 40 \times 2)$.
- **Color histogram feature**
  Color histogram was made by partitioning the red, green and blue axes into 16 regions. Histogram elements were divided by the number of pixels in the object for normalization. A 96-dimensional feature vector was extracted from the two images described in the explanation of P-FT.
- **View base feature**
  A 768-dimensional feature vector was extracted from the $32 \times 24$ pixels monochrome image converted from an input image.
- **2D Discrete Fourier Transform descriptor (2D-DFT)**
  The feature vector was obtained as the low-frequency components by applying the Fourier transform to an input image. A 198-dimensional feature vector was extracted from the two images described in P-FT.
- **Histograms of Oriented Gradients descriptor (HOG)**[12]
  A $32 \times 24$ pixel image converted from an input image was divided into cells of $8 \times 8$ pixels, and each group of $2 \times 2$ cells was integrated into a block. Each cell consisted of an 8-bin histogram of oriented gradients and each block consisted of a vector of combined histograms of its cells.
  The vector was normalized with respect to each block, and its dimension was $32 (= 8 \times 4)$. The dimension of HOG was set to $192 (= 32 \times 6)$, as an image had 6 blocks,
- **Higher-order Local Auto-Correlation feature (HLAC)**[13]
  HLAC is defined as :

$$X(a_1, ...a_n) = \int I(r)I(r + a_1)....I(r + a_n)dr \ , \tag{5}$$

where the $n$th-order autocorrelation functions with $n$ displacements $\{a_1, ..., a_n\}$. $I(r)$ denotes the pixel value of the image. Here, we restrict the order $n$ up to the second and restrict the range of displacements within a local $3 \times 3$ window.
The feature vectors (HLAC1) were extracted from the two images described in P-FT. The feature vectors (HLAC2) were extracted from an $x$-orient

differential image and a $y$-orient differential image, and the image size was $320 \times 240$. The dimensions of HLAC1 and HLAC2 feature were set to 70.

## 3.2   Preliminary Experiment Using Five Apples

**Experimental conditions**

We collected multi-view images of apples by using a gathering system with an IEEE1394 camera and a turntable as shown in Fig. 4. We captured multiple images of an apple while rotating the turntable. This operation was repeated three times for each apple. Note that the positions of the apples were different for the three gatherings.

In the first gathering, two hundred images were captured at 1.8 degree intervals around the entire circumference. These images were used as training data. The reference subspaces were generated from these 200 images. In the second and third gatherings, the multi-view images were captured at the 3.6 degree intervals, while changing the range $\theta$ of the view angles from 36 degrees to 360 degrees, as in Fig. 4. We thus obtained the six test sets. The numbers of images in the sets were 10, 13, 20, 25, 50, and 100. These images were used as testing data. The dimensions of all the reference subspace were set to 10. The dimension of the input subspace was set to 3.

**Experimental Results and Discussion**

Fig. 5 shows the changes of the recognition rate against the range $\theta$ of the view angles. We can see that the recognition rate increases as the range of view angle widens. When the range $\theta$ was set to more than 90 degrees, the classification rates of P-FT, 2D-DFT, color histogram and HLAC2 were over 90%. The rate of HLAC2 was higher than that of HLAC1 when the range $\theta$ was small. On the other hand, the rates of view feature and HOG were not particularly high even when the range $\theta$ was set to 360 degrees. This difference indicates that position invariant features are effective for MSM-based method in classification of 3D objects. From these results, for the next experiment using a large data set

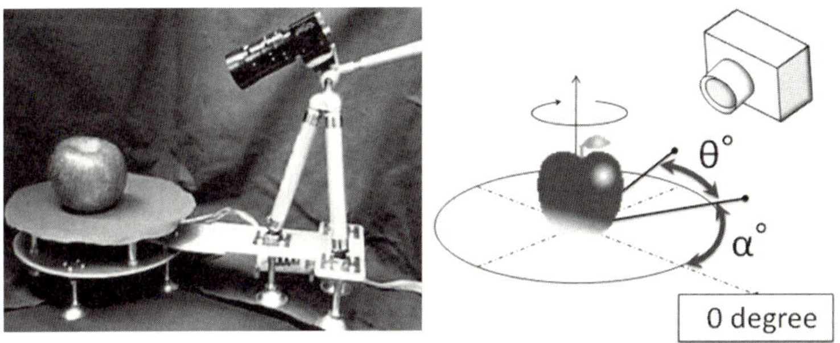


**Fig. 4.** Gathering system of multi-view images of apples

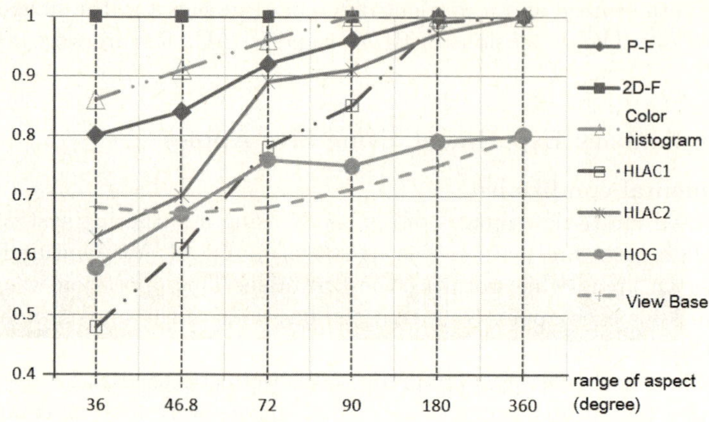


**Fig. 5.** Recognition rate against the range $\theta$ of view angles

we chose some position invariant features: P-FT, 2D-DFT, color histogram and HLAC2 and the range $\theta$ of the view angles to 90 degrees.

### 3.3   Classification of 100 Apples Using a Single Feature

**Experimental conditions**

We used the MSM-based methods (MSM, CMSM, OMSM) and $k$-NN method as classifiers and compared their performances. An input subspace was generated from 25 images obtained in the range $\theta$ from $\alpha$ to $\alpha+90$ degrees. We changed the start angle $\alpha$ at steps of 36 degrees. Such image gathering was executed twice, and so the total number of the evaluation trials was 2000 (=10(=360/36) × 2 (two rotations) × 100 (number of apples)).

The reference subspaces were generated from 200 learning images. The dimensions of reference subspaces were set to 10. The dimension of the input subspace varied from 1 to 5. The constraint subspace $\mathcal{D}$ and the whitening matrix $\mathbf{O}$ were generated from learning data obtained from 20 apples that were different from the 100 apples used in the above learning phase.

In $k$-NN method, we registered 10 vectors created by clustering of 200 training data for each class. Given $m$ input patterns, the output is determined by the $k \times m$ voting result.

**Results and Discussion**

Table 2 and Table 3 show the experimental results. In the tables, the best recognition rates are shown when the number of canonical angles, $n'$, in Equation 2, varied from 1 to 5. The notation between brackets () indicates the value of $n$. In the "classifier" column, the figures for "CMSM " item indicate the dimension of the principal component subspace $\mathcal{M}$ [4].

We compared the performances of all the classifiers. The performance of $k$-NN was worst among them. We can see that the recognition rates of CMSM and

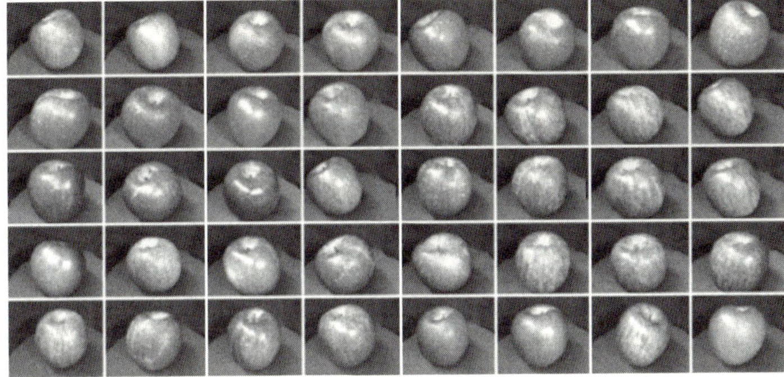

**Fig. 6.** 40 of all the apples used in the experiments

**Table 2.** Recognition rate of each classifier (%)

| Classifier | P-FT | 2D-FT | Color histogram | HLAC |
|---|---|---|---|---|
| MSM | 76.9(3) | 89.75(4) | 89.6(3) | 54.9(5) |
| CMSM-1 | 85.6(3) | 92.2(4) | 94.55(1) | 76.95(4) |
| CMSM-2 | 88.25(3) | 93.4(4) | 94.25(1) | 94.9(2) |
| CMSM-5 | 88.25(2) | 92.15(4) | 94(1) | 98.75(1) |
| CMSM-10 | 80.3(1) | 90.65(4) | 93(1) | 99(1) |
| OMSM | 82.2(5) | 86.2(4) | 98.45(1) | 94.45(1) |
| NN | 87.75 | 72.7 | 91.95 | 34.9 |
| 3-NN | 79.4 | 69.35 | 83.4 | 28.85 |
| 5-NN | 70.1 | 61.75 | 72.95 | 23.8 |

OMSM were largely improved in comparison with that of MSM. For example, the performance of MSM using HLAC was extremely low, whereas even when HLAC was used, the performance of CMSM and OMSM were extremely superior. This result suggests that MSM lacks in the classification ability as compared with CMSM and OMSM. None of the classifiers using P-FT achieved the rate of 90%. The reason may be that the stable extraction of the contour of the apples was affected by shadows. Color histogram feature had better performance for all the methods in comparison with the other types of features. From the above results, we can confirm that these four kinds of features have different characters for classification of apples.

## 3.4   Classification of 100 Apples Using Ensemble Learning

We evaluated the effectiveness of the ensemble classification using four kinds of features. In this experiment, we used MSM,CMSM and OMSM. The experimental conditions were as described above.

**Table 3.** Equal error rate of each classifier (%)

| Classifier | P-FT | 2D-FT | Color histogram | HLAC |
|---|---|---|---|---|
| MSM | 11.7(3) | 6.2(4) | 5.8(3) | 21.7(5) |
| CMSM-1 | 8.4(3) | 4.5(4) | 4.1(1) | 15.4(4) |
| CMSM-2 | 7.3(3) | 3.9(4) | 4.1(1) | 17.9(2) |
| CMSM-5 | 7.7(2) | 4.0(4) | 5.1(1) | 2.8(1) |
| CMSM-10 | 9.7(1) | 4.4(4) | 6.6(1) | 1.6(1) |
| OMSM | 10.8(5) | 6.4(4) | 8.9(1) | 24.4(1) |

**Table 4.** Recognition performance(%). Similarity $S[n']$ is defined in Sec. 2.2.

| Classifier | S[1] | S[2] | S[3] | S[4] | S[5] |
|---|---|---|---|---|---|
| MSM | 94.3 | 90.75 | 97.9 | 98.75 | 98.9 |
| CMSM-1 | 88.5 | 96.1 | 98.7 | 99.25 | 99.1 |
| CMSM-2 | 91.5 | 98.05 | 99.1 | 99.4 | 99.25 |
| CMSM-5 | 92.4 | 98.05 | 99.15 | 99.2 | 99.05 |
| CMSM-10 | 91.95 | 97.95 | 99.1 | 99.05 | 98.75 |
| OMSM | 94.9 | 96.35 | 98.85 | 99.15 | 99.35 |

**Table 5.** Equal Error Rate (%)

| Classifier | S[1] | S[2] | S[3] | S[4] | S[5] |
|---|---|---|---|---|---|
| MSM | 45.9 | 2.8 | 0.8 | 0.3 | 0.4 |
| CMSM-1 | 4.5 | 1.1 | 0.3 | 0.1 | 0.1 |
| CMSM-2 | 3.2 | 0.7 | 0.2 | 0.2 | 0.2 |
| CMSM-5 | 2.9 | 0.6 | 0.3 | 0.2 | 0.3 |
| CMSM-10 | 3.1 | 0.6 | 0.3 | 0.3 | 0.4 |
| OMSM | 2.1 | 1.1 | 0.4 | 0.3 | 0.3 |

**Results and Discussion**

Table 4 and Table 5 show the performances of all the methods. In the ensemble classification framework, all the performances were largely improved in comparison with using only a single feature. The best recognition rates were 98.9% by MSM, 99.4% by CMSM and 99.35% by OMSM. Especially the improvements of EER were particularly notable.

In addition, the performances were better as the number $n$ of the canonical angles increases. This tendency is not seen in the experiment using a single feature. This implies that the ensemble classification well derived the effectiveness of using multiple canonical angles.

## 4    Conclusion

In this paper we have proposed a method to classify 3D objects with similar appearances. We considered the classification of one hundred apples as a concrete task. To tackle this challenging task, we used three types of feature of shape, texture and color type as input vectors for each of the MSM-based classifiers. The results of classification from all the MSM-based methods were combined in the the ensemble learning framework. The effectiveness of the proposed method was demonstrated through the results of the evaluation experiments using 100 apples. In future works, we will evaluate the performance of our method by using larger data sets to estimate the limitations of classification ability of MSM-based methods.

# References


1. Murase, H., Nayar, S.K.: Visual Learning and Recognition of 3-D Objects from Appearance. International Journal of Computer Vision 14, 5–24 (1995)
2. Li, Y., Gong, S., Liddell, H.: Video-Based Online Face Recognition Using Identity Surfaces. In: ICCV Workshop on Recognition, Analysis, and Tracking of Faces and Gestures in Real-Time Systems (2001)
3. Satoh, S., Katayama, N.: An Efficient Implementation and Evaluation of Robust Face Sequence Matching. In: International Conference on Image Analysis and Processing, pp. 266–271 (1999)
4. Fukui, K., Yamaguchi, O.: Face Recognition Using Multi-viewpoint Patterns for Robot Vision. In: International Symposium of Robotics Research, pp. 192–201 (2003)
5. Kawahara, T., Nishiyama, M., Kozakaya, T., Yamaguchi, O.: Face Recognition based on Whitening Transformation of Distribution of Subspaces. In: Workshop on ACCV 2007, Subspace 2007, pp. 97–103 (2007)
6. Maeda, K., Yamaguchi, O., Fukui, K.: Towards 3-Dimensional Pattern Recognition. In: SSPR 2004 & SPR 2004, pp. 1061–1068 (2004)
7. Maki, A., Fukui, K.: Ship identification in sequential ISAR imagery. Machine Vision and Applications 15, 149–155 (2004)
8. Ichino, M., Sakano, H., Komatsu, N.: Speaker recognition using Kernel Mutual Subspace Method. In: Proc. of International Conference on Control, Automation, Robotics and Vision, vol. 1, pp. 397–402 (2004)
9. Diaz, R., Gil, L., Serrano, C., Blasco, M., Moltó, E., Blasco, J.: Comparison of three algorithms in the classification of table olives by means of computer vision. Journal of Food Engineering 61, 101–107 (2004)
10. Rocha, A., Hauagge, D.C., Wainer, J., Goldenstein, S.: Automatic produce classification from images using color, texture and appearance cues. In: Proc. of the Brazilian Symposium of Computer Graphics and Image Processing (2008)
11. Zheng, Z., Iwata, I., Hirata, Y., Tamura, Y.: Quantitative evaluation of the degree of sprout leaf bending of rice cultivars using P-type Fourier descriptors and principal component analysis. Euphytica 163(2), 259–266 (2008)
12. Dalal, N., Triggs, B.: Histograms of Oriented Gradients for Human Detection. In: CVPR, pp. 886–893 (2005)
13. Otsu, N., Kurita, T.: A New Scheme for Practical Flexible and Intelligent Vision Systems. In: Proc. of IAPR Workshop on Computer Vision, pp. 431–435 (1988)
14. Fukunaga, K., Koontz, W.L.G.: Application of the Karhunen-Loève Expansion to Feature Selection and Ordering. IEEE Trans. on Computers C-19(4), 311–318 (1970)

# Recovery Rate of Clustering Algorithms

Fajie Li[1] and Reinhard Klette[2]

[1] Institute for Mathematics and Computing Science, University of Groningen
P.O. Box 800, 9700 AV Groningen, The Netherlands
F.Li@rug.nl
[2] Computer Science Department, The University of Auckland
Private Bag 92019, Auckland 1142, New Zealand
r.klette@auckland.ac.nz

**Abstract.** This article provides a simple and general way for defining the recovery rate of clustering algorithms using a given family of old clusters for evaluating the performance of the algorithm when calculating a family of new clusters.

Under the assumption of dealing with simulated data (i.e., known old clusters), the recovery rate is calculated using one proposed exact (but slow) algorithm, or one proposed approximate algorithm (with feasible run time).

## 1 Introduction

Clustering has many applications in image or video analysis, such as segmentation (e.g., see [14]), learning (e.g, see [23]), bags-of-features representations of images (e.g., see [5]), or video retrieval (e.g., see [20]) - just to cite (by random selection) four examples within a large diversity of clustering applications in this area.

In general, there are hundreds of clustering algorithms proposed in the literature, often applicable in a wide diversity of areas such as computer networks, data mining, image or video analysis, and so forth. For estimating the total number of clustering algorithms, see page 5 in [13], page 13 in [17] or page 130 in [22]. This all illustrates that clustering problems are very important, and often also difficult to solve. Clustering describes unsupervised learning in its most general form.

Clustering not only interests computing scientists but also, for example, astronomers [9,11,15]: Given is an observed set of stars (considered to be a set of points); how to find (*recover*) clusters which are the contributing galaxies to the observed union of those clusters? White dwarfs and red giants were one of the great discoveries in astronomy [12].

This paper focuses on a general evaluation of clustering algorithms. Previous methods, such as [1,3,4,6,8,18,25], all restrict on evaluating a very small subset of clustering algorithms, while the approaches of [2] (Section 7.2.2, pages 221–222) and [21] are more complicated. Since there is a huge number of clustering algorithms, it is very important to design a simple evaluation method in order to choose a suitable clustering algorithm for a given data set. This paper proposes a sound, general and simple method to evaluate the performance of an arbitrary clustering algorithm.

T. Wada, F. Huang, and S. Lin (Eds.): PSIVT 2009, LNCS 5414, pp. 1058–1069, 2009.
© Springer-Verlag Berlin Heidelberg 2009

For example, if a given image segmentation task may be described by simulated data, then the provided method can be used for comparing various clustering techniques designed for solving this image segmentation task.

The rest of this paper is organized as follows: Section 2 gives our definition of recovery rate. Section 3 describes algorithms for computing recovery rate of a clustering algorithm with respect to simulated input data. Section 4 gives some examples to illustrate the computation of recovery rate. Section 5 shows the experimental results. Section 6 concludes the paper.

## 2   Definitions

A definition of recovery rate is needed for having a sound measure when comparing clustering techniques.

Let $d$, $n$, and $n_i$ be positive integers, for $i = 1, 2, \ldots, n$. Let $x_{i_j} \in \mathbb{R}^d$, where $i = 1, 2, \ldots, n$ (the index of a cluster) and $j = 1, 2, \ldots, n_i$ (the subindex of a point in cluster $i$ which contains $n_i$ points). $x_{i_j}$ is called a *dD data point*.[1]

Let $C_i = \{x_{i_j} : j = 1, 2, \ldots, n_i\}$, for $i = 1, 2, \ldots, n$. $C_i$ is called a *cluster* of $dD$ data points. Each cluster $C_i$ is uniquely identified by its *cluster ID*. Here we simply take index $i$ to be the cluster ID of cluster $C_i$. Clusters are always assumed to be pairwise disjoint. (We do not address fuzzy clustering in this paper.)

**Definition 1.** *A* clustering algorithm, *denoted by* $\mathcal{A}$, *is an algorithm which maps a finite set of points of* $\mathbb{R}^d$ *into a family of clusters.*

We consider the case where the union

$$C = \cup_{i=1}^{n} C_i, \text{ with } N = \operatorname{card} C,$$

of the given family of *old clusters* defines the input of a clustering algorithm, without having any further information about points in this set, such as their cluster ID. The output is a partition of this union $C$ into a finite number of *new clusters* $G_k$, where $k = 1, 2, \ldots, m$:

$$\cup_{k=1}^{m} G_k = C$$

A new cluster $G_k$ may contain data points from different old clusters, and we partition $G_k$ into subsets based on the cluster ID of the old clusters:

$$G_k = \cup_{t_k=1}^{s_k} G_{k t_k}$$

where $G_{k t_k}$ is a subset of an old cluster, for $t_k = 1, 2, \ldots, s_k$.

Obviously, indices $i$ and $k$ are in some permutation (old cluster $C_i$ is not necessarily 'more related' to new cluster $G_i$ than to any other new cluster $G_k$), and we may even have that $n \neq m$.

---

[1] We prefer to write $x_{i_j}$ rather than $x_{ij}$, for indicating that $j$ is a subindex in the cluster identified by index $i$.

For defining the recovery rate, we assume that each old cluster can only be represented by one new cluster, defining a mapping $i \to k$, and for this $k$ we then have the defined subset $G_{k_{i_k}}$ which should have maximum cardinality compared to all the other $G_{k_{t_k}}$ of new cluster $G_k$. However, for defining the recovery rate we have to detect the maximum of all possible global mappings $i \to k$; just a value for one particular $i$ will not do.

**Definition 2.** *Assume that* $G_{1_{t_1'}}, G_{2_{t_2'}}, \ldots, G_{m_{t_m'}}$ *satisfy*

(i) *For* $i, j \in \{1_{t_1'}, 2_{t_2'}, \ldots, m_{t_m'}\}$, *there exist two old clusters* $C_i$ *and* $C_j$ *such that* $G_{i_{t_i'}} \subseteq C_i$ *and* $G_{j_{t_j'}} \subseteq C_j$; *and*

(ii) $\sum_{k=1}^{m} \frac{cardG_{k_{t_k'}}}{cardC_k} = \max\{\sum_{k=1}^{m} \frac{cardG_{k_{t_k}}}{cardC_k} : t_k = 1, 2, \ldots, s_k\}$

*The value*

$$\frac{\sum_{k=1}^{m} \frac{cardG_{k_{t_k'}}}{cardC_k}}{m} \times 100\%$$

*is called the* recovery rate *of the clustering algorithm* $\mathcal{A}$ *with respect to the input* $\cup_{i=1}^{n} C_i$.

Definition 2 assumes that we have $m \leq n$; the number of new clusters is upper bounded by the the number of old ones. We do not consider this as a crucial restriction of generality.

It is obvious that if all $cardC_i$ are identical, where $i = 1, 2, \ldots, n$, then item (ii) in Definition 2 can be simplified as follows:

$$\sum_{k=1}^{m} cardG_{k_{t_k'}} = \max\{\sum_{k=1}^{m} cardG_{k_{t_k}} : t_k = 1, 2, \ldots, s_k\}$$

And the recovery rate of the clustering algorithm with respect to the input is the value below:

$$\frac{\sum_{k=1}^{m} cardG_{k_{t_k'}}}{\sum_{i=1}^{n} cardC_i} \times 100\%$$

Obviously, there can be further options of defining a recovery rate, for example by enforcing $m = n$ and always comparing $G_i$ with $C_i$, but we consider the above definition as the least restrictive. We only mention one more option here for (possibly) defining a recovery rate:

**Definition 3.** *Assume that* $G_{1_{t_1}}, G_{2_{t_2}}, \ldots, G_{m_{t_m}}$ *satisfy*

(i) *For* $i, j \in \{1_{t_1}, 2_{t_2}, \ldots, m_{t_m}\}$, *there exist two old clusters* $C_i$ *and* $C_j$ *such that* $G_{i_{t_i}} \subseteq C_i$ *and* $G_{j_{t_j}} \subseteq C_j$;

(ii) $G_{i_{t_i}} \neq \emptyset$, *where* $i \in \{1, 2, \ldots, m\}$; *and*

(iii) $m$ *is maximal.*

*The value*

$$\frac{m}{n} \times 100\%$$

*is called the* pseudo recovery rate *of the clustering algorithm* $\mathcal{A}$ *with respect to the input* $\cup_{i=1}^{n} C_i$.

Our definitions are very intuitive (and certainly easy to understand). Our method does not need to introduce other functions such as an $F$-function as in [16], or entropy as in [2] or [4].

In the next section we will illustrate that the pseudo recovery rate is actually not a reasonable choice, and we will then only apply recovery rate as defined in Definition 2 afterwards.


## 3    Algorithms

This section assumes simulated data, such that both the old and new clusters are known.

We propose two different algorithms and discuss their properties afterwards, also for the purpose of comparing both with one-another. The first algorithm is straightforward, but computationally expensive:

**Algorithm 1: Exact Recovery Rate**

Input: Old clusters $C_i$, where $i = 1, 2, \ldots, n$; and new clusters $G_j$, where $j = 1, 2, \ldots, m$, obtained from a clustering algorithm $\mathcal{A}$.

Output: The recovery rate of $\mathcal{A}$ with respect to $C_i$, where $i = 1, 2, \ldots, n$.

1. Let $M$ be an $m \times n$ matrix, initially with zeros in all of its elements.

2. For each $j \in \{1, 2, \ldots, m\}$ and for each $x \in G_j$, if there exists an $i \in \{1, 2, \ldots, n\}$ such that $x \in C_i$, then update $M$ as follows: $M(j, i) = M(j, i) + 1$, where $M(j, i)$ is the $(j, i)$-th entry of $M$.

3. Find $m$ different integers (i.e., column indices) $i_k \in \{1, 2, \ldots, n\}$ such that

$$\sum_{k=1}^{m} \frac{M(k, i_k)}{cardC_{i_k}} = \max\{\sum_{j=1}^{m} \frac{M(j, i_j)}{cardC_{i_j}} : i_j \in \{1, 2, \ldots, n\}\}$$

4. Output the recovery rate as being the value

$$\frac{\sum_{k=1}^{m} \frac{M(k, i_k)}{cardC_{i_k}}}{m} \times 100\%$$

The main computations of Algorithm 1 occur in Step 3, and its time complexity (note: $m \leq n$) equals

$$O(n(n-1) \cdots (n - m + 2)(n - m + 1)) \geq O(m!) \geq O(2^m)$$

Obviously, this exponential time algorithm calculates the correct recovery rate.

The following is only an approximate algorithm for computing the recovery rate, but with feasible running time.

**Algorithm 2: Approximate Recovery Rate**

Input and Steps 1 and 2 are the same as in Algorithm 1.

Output: The approximate recovery rate of $\mathcal{A}$ with respect to $C_i$, where $i = 1$, 2, ..., $n$.

3.0. For each entry $M(i, j)$ of $M$, let $M(i, j) = \frac{M(i,j)}{card C_j}$, where $i = 1, 2, \ldots, m$; $j = 1, 2, \ldots, n$.

3.1. For each $j \in \{1, 2, \ldots, m\}$, find the maximum entry of $M$, denoted by $m_j = M(i, k)$.

3.2. Update $M$ by removing the $i$-th row and $k$-th column of $M$ and go to Step 3.1.

4. Output the approximate recovery rate as the value

$$\frac{\sum_{j=1}^{m} m_j}{m} \times 100\%$$

It follows that the approximate recovery rate, obtained from Algorithm 2, is less than or equal to the exact recovery rate obtained from Algorithm 1. The time complexity of Algorithm 2 is in $\mathcal{O}(mn)$.

Both of our algorithms are very simple to implement. We only use a single matrix, while [2] uses several matrices.

## 4    Examples

The first two examples are on purpose easy to follow such that the reader may follow the proposed definitions and algorithms. Let

$$C_1 = \{(1, 5, 5), (5, 9, 3), (6, 9, 6), (7, 6, 4), (9, 6, 0)\}$$

and

$$C_2 = \{(7, 14, 13), (10, 15, 12), (14, 16, 7), (15, 7, 16), (16, 7, 12)\}$$

be two clusters of 3D data points (see Figure 1, left).

$$C_1 \cup C_2 = \{(1, 5, 5), (5, 9, 3), (6, 9, 6), (7, 6, 4), (7, 14, 13), (9, 6, 0), (10, 15, 12),$$
$$(14, 16, 7), (15, 7, 16), (16, 7, 12)\}$$

is the union of $C_1$ and $C_2$ (see Figure 1, middle).

Let $\mathcal{A}$ be the algorithm for clustering data in MATLAB$^{TM}$, called *cluster-data*. The obtained output is $G_1 = \{(5, 9, 3), (7, 6, 4), (6, 9, 6), (9, 6, 0), (1, 5, 5), (10, 15, 12), (14, 16, 7), (7, 14, 13)\}$, and $G_2 = \{(15, 7, 16), (16, 7, 12)\}$ (see Figure 1, right).

Let $G_1 = G_{1_1} \cup G_{1_2}$, where $G_{1_1} = \{(5, 9, 3), (7, 6, 4), (6, 9, 6), (9, 6, 0), (1, 5, 5)\}$, $G_{1_2} = \{(10, 15, 12), (14, 16, 7), (7, 14, 13), \}$; $G_1 = G_{2_1}$, where $G_{2_1} = \{(15, 7, 16), (16, 7, 12)\}$.

 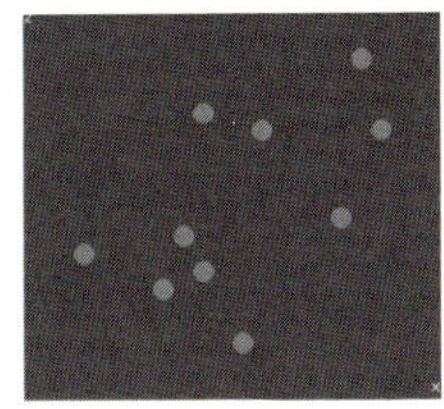 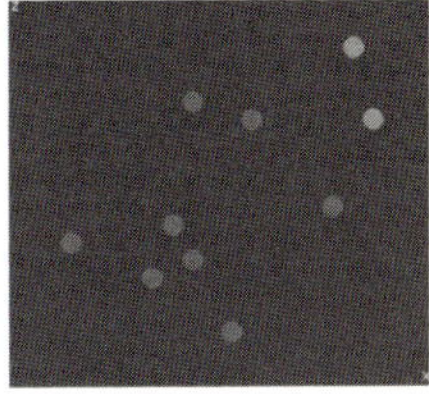

**Fig. 1.** Left: red points belong to $C_1$; green points belong to $C_2$. middle: the union of $C_1$ and $C_2$. right: red points belong to $G_1$; green points belong to $G_2$.

*Example 1.* By Algorithm 1, we have that

$$M = \begin{pmatrix} 5 & 3 \\ 0 & 2 \end{pmatrix}$$

In Step 3 of Algorithm 1, there are only two cases to select different column indices: $i_1 = 1$ and $i_2 = 2$ or $i_1 = 2$ and $i_2 = 1$. Thus, the recovery rate of $\mathcal{A}$ with respect to $C_1 \cup C_2$ is equal to

$$(M(1,1) + M(2,2))/|G_1 \cup G_2| \times 100\% = (5+2)/10 \times 100\% = 70\%$$

*Example 2.* By Algorithm 2, we have the same matrix $M$ as in Algorithm 1. We obtain that $m_1 = 5$ and $m_2 = 2$ in Step 3 of Algorithm 2. Thus, the approximate recovery rate of $\mathcal{A}$ with respect to $C_1 \cup C_2$ is equal to

$$(m_1 + m_2)/|G_1 \cup G_2| \times 100\% = (5+2)/10 \times 100\% = 70\%$$

So far about these simple two examples, where both algorithms actually produce the same result (i.e., recovery rate). The next two examples show that Algorithms 1 and 2 could produce different results.

We combine an adaptive mean shift based clustering algorithm (see [10]) with traditional clustering algorithm *kmeans* (another clustering algorithm in MAT-LAB) to obtain a variant of mean shift based clustering algorithm, denoted by $\mathcal{K}$.

We illustrate problems of clustering (for easier illustration) in the following two examples for a simulation of astronomical data (publicly available on [7]) rather than for some examples of image or video data. Clusters in those astronomical data (further illustrated in Section 5) are characterized by being highly overlapping. Obviously, the recovery of highly overlapping data is difficult, if not even (nearly) impossible. Even currently published cluster algorithms (see, for example, [24]) work neither efficiently nor correctly.

There are 10,000 3D data points in each cluster (which is stored in a text file named "en_angmom_f_000.i", where $i = 00, 01, 02, 04,$ and $05$). For example, Figure 2 shows the first 20 data points in cluster 0 (i.e., in the file en_angmom_f_000.00).

The union of these five old clusters is shown in Figure 3.

mean shift based clustering algorithm, denoted by $\mathcal{K}$ (or $\mathcal{C}$). We continue with the astronomical data as used in Examples 3 and 4.

## 5.1   The Input Data Set

There are 10,000 3D data points in each cluster of the data set on [7] (which is stored in a text file named "en_angmom_f_000.i", where $i = 00, 01, 02, \ldots, 09, 10, \ldots, 32$). For example, Figure 2 shows the first 20 data points in cluster 0 (i.e., in the file en_angmom_f_000.00). The union of the first 10 clusters is shown in Figure 4.

Input data used in experiment below refer to this data set, but after the following normalization (just for scale reduction): For each point $p = (x, y, z)$ in the data set, replace $p$ by $(x/20, y/11, z/11)$.

## 5.2   Some Results

Tables 1 and 2 show recovery rates, approximate recovery rates, and pseudo recovery rates of Algorithms $\mathcal{K}$ and $\mathcal{C}$. $n$ is the number of old clusters of the input data in Section 5.1 (i.e., the first $n$ old clusters of the 33 old clusters). We use either one (Table 1) or two (Table 2) iterations. $k_1$ ($c_1$) is the recovery rate of Algorithm $\mathcal{K}$ ($\mathcal{C}$), which is obtained by Algorithm 2. $k_2$ ($c_2$) is the approximate recovery rate of Algorithm $\mathcal{K}$ ($\mathcal{C}$), which is obtained by Algorithm 1. $p$ is short for pseudo recovery rate. $t_i$ is the running time for obtaining $k_i$ ($c_i$), where $i = 1, 2$.

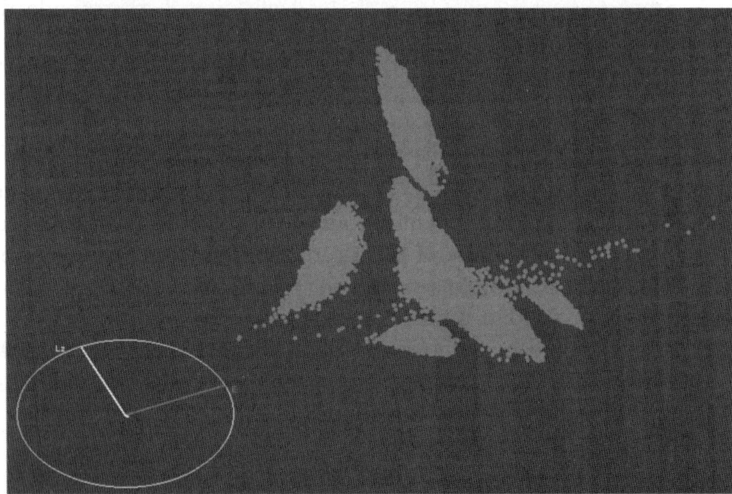

**Fig. 4.** An example of a very heavily overlapping data set: This shows a 2D projection of a union of 10 clusters, where each cluster contains 10,000 3D data points [11]

**Table 1.** This table shows the results of Iteration 1

| $n$ | $(k_1\%,\ t_1$ sec, $k_2\%,\ t_2$ sec, $p\%)$ | $(c_1\%,\ t_1$ sec, $c_2\%,\ t_2$ sec, $p\%)$ |
|---|---|---|
| 5 | (59.4, 6.2e-4, 59.4, 4.3e-3, 100) | (39.6, 8.8e-4, 39.6, 4.3e-3, 80) |
| 6 | (51.6, 7.2e-4, 56.0, 4.6e-2, 100) | (40.2, 7.0e-4, 40.2, 2.7e-2, 66.7) |
| 7 | (58.7, 8.4e-4, 58.7, 0.3, 100) | (28.9, 9.1e-4, 28.9, 0.3, 57.1) |
| 8 | (44.5, 0.01, 44.5, 2.3, 87.5) | (15.7, 9.9e-4, 15.7, 2.4, 50) |
| 9 | (47.6, 1e-3, 47.6, 23.2, 88.9) | (12.5, 0.3, 12.5, 23.3, 44.4) |
| 10 | (44.4, 0.4, 44.9, 285.1, 90) | (24.7, 1.2e-3, 24.7, 256.5, 40) |

**Table 2.** This table shows the results of Iteration 2

| $n$ | $(k_1\%,\ t_1$ sec, $k_2\%,\ t_2$ sec, $p\%)$ | $(c_1\%,\ t_1$ sec, $c_2\%,\ t_2$ sec, $p\%)$ |
|---|---|---|
| 5 | (51.8, 6.0e-4, 58.2, 4.3e-3, 100) | (36.8, 5.9e-4, 36.8, 5.0e-3, 60) |
| 6 | (66.2, 6.7e-4, 66.2, 2.9e-2, 100) | (46.6, 6.9e-4, 46.6, 3.4e-2, 83.3) |
| 7 | (57.4, 7.6e-4, 57.4, 0.3, 71.4) | (39.2 , 7.6e-4, 39.2, 0.3, 85.7) |
| 8 | (49.9, 8.6e-4, 49.9, 2.3, 87.5) | (42.8, 1.1e-3, 42.8, 2.4, 75) |
| 9 | (46.7, 3.3e-3, 46.7, 23.6, 77.8) | (26.3, 0.01, 26.3, 23.1, 66.7) |
| 10 | (53.4, 9.1e-3, 53.4, 303.1, 90) | (51.0, 1.7e-3, 51.0, 272.8, 80) |

Tables 1 and 2 show that Algorithm 2 is a good approximation to Algorithm 1 when $n \leq 10$. They also illustrate that the running time of Algorithm 1 is indeed significantly longer than that of Algorithm 2 when $n \geq 10$.

## 6   Conclusions

In conclusion, in this paper we defined a recovery rate of unconstrained clustering, and provided a time-efficient approximate algorithm for estimating this recovery rate. We are now ready to compare the performance of any two clustering algorithms by comparing their recovery rates for a simulated input (for example, assuming that a clustering task in image or video analysis allows to have quite realistic simulated input data). In particular we may analyze next lower bounds for recovery rates of clustering; see [19].

## Acknowledgement

The first author thanks Prof. A. Helmi for providing the url of the simulated astronomical data set (on the public web site [7]), and acknowledges that his research is part of the project "Astrovis", research program STARE (STAR E-Science), funded by the Dutch National Science Foundation (NWO), project no. 643.200.501.

# References


1. Allan, J., Feng, A., Bolivar, A.: Flexible Intrinsic Evaluation of Hierarchical Clustering for TDT. In: Proc. CIKM 2003, New Orleans, Louisiana, USA, November 3–8 (2003)
2. Borgelt, C.: Prototype-based Classification and Clustering. Ph.D. Thesis, University of Magdeburg, Germany (2006)
3. Brohee, S., van Helden, J.: Evaluation of clustering algorithms for protein-protein interaction networks. BMC Bioinformatics 7, 488 (2006)
4. Crabtree, D., Gao, X., Andreae, P.: Universal Evaluation Method for Web Clustering Results. Technical Report CS-IR-05-3, Department of Computer Science, Victoria University of Wellington, New Zealand (2005)
5. Csurka, G., Dance, C., Fan, L., Willamowski, J., Bray, C.: Visual categorization with bags of keypoints. In: Proc. ECCV Workshop Statistical Learning Computer Vision, pp. 59–74 (2004)
6. Datta, S.: Evaluation of clustering algorithms for gene expression data. BMC Bioinformatics 7(suppl. 4), 17 (2006)
7. Simulated astronomical data,
   http://www.astro.rug.nl/~ahelmi/simulations_gaia.tar.gz
8. Datta, S.: Methods for evaluating clustering algorithms for gene expression data using a reference set of functional classes. BMC Bioinformatics 7, 397 (2006)
9. Efstathiou, G., Frenk, C.S., White, S.D.M., Davis, M.: Gravitational clustering from scale-free initial conditions. Monthly Notices RAS 235, 715–748 (1988)
10. Georgescu, B., Shimshoni, I., Meer, P.: Mean Shift Based Clustering in High Dimensions: A Texture Classification Example. In: Proc. 9th IEEE International Conference on Computer Vision (ICCV) (2003)
11. Helmi, A., de Zeeuw, P.T.: Mapping the substructure in the Galactic halo with the next generation of astrometric satellites. Astron. Soc. 319, 657–665 (2000)
12. Hertzsprung-Russell, en.wikipedia.org/wiki/Hertzsprung-Russell_diagram
13. Jain, A.K., Murty, M.N., Flynn, P.J.: Data clustering: A review. ACM Computing Surveys 31(3), 264–323 (1999)
14. Kehtarnavaz, N., Monaco, J., Nimtschek, J., Weeks, A.: Color image segmentation using multi-scale clustering. In: Proc. IEEE Southwest Symp. Image Analysis Interpretation, pp. 142–147 (1998)
15. Knebe, A., Gill, S.P.D., Kawata, D., Gibson, B.K.: Mapping substructures in dark matter haloes. Astron. Soc. 357, 35–39 (2005)
16. Larsen, B., Aone, C.: Fast and Effective Text Mining Using Linear Time Document Clustering. In: Proc. 5th ACM SIGKDD Conference on Knowledge Discovery and Data Mining, pp. 16–22. ACM Press, San Diego (1999)
17. Law, H.C.: Clustering, Dimensionality Reduction, and Side Information. Ph.D. Thesis, Michigan State University, the United States (2006)
18. Leouski, A.V., Croft, W.B.: An Evaluation of Techniques for Clustering Search Results. Technical Report IR-76, Department of Computer Science, University of Massachusetts, Amherst (1996)
19. Li, F., Klette, R.: About the calculation of upper bounds for cluster recovery rates. Technical Report CITR-TR-224, Computer Science Department, The University of Auckland, Auckland, New Zealand (2008), www.citr.auckland.ac.nz
20. Lian, N.-X., Tan, Y.P., Chan, K.L.: Efficient video retrieval using shot clustering and alignment. In: Proc. ICICS-PCM, pp. 1801–1805 (2003)

21. Rand, W.M.: Objective criteria for the evaluation of clustering methods. Journal of the American Statistical Association 66, 846–850 (1971)
22. Silverman, B.W.: Density Estimation. Chapman & Hall, London (1986)
23. Wang, Z., Chen, S.C., Sun, T.: MultiK-MHKS: a novel multiple kernel learning algorithm. IEEE PAMI 30, 348–353 (2008)
24. Wu, K.L., Yang, M.S.: Mean shift-based clustering. Pattern Recognition 40, 3035–3052 (2007)
25. Zhao, Y., Karypis, G.: Evaluation of hierarchical clustering algorithms for document datasets. In: Proc. CIKM 2002, McLean, Virginia, USA, November 4–9 (2002)

# Multiple View Geometry of Projector-Camera Systems from Virtual Mutual Projection

Shuhei Kobayashi, Fumihiko Sakaue, and Jun Sato

Department of Computer Science and Engineering
Nagoya Institute of Technology
Nagoya 466-8555, Japan

**Abstract.** Recently, projector camera systems have been used actively for image synthesis and for 3D reconstruction. For using the projector camera systems in these applications, it is very important to compute the geometry between projectors and cameras accurately. Recently, it has been shown that by using the mutual projection of cameras, multiple cameras are calibrated quite accurately. However, this property cannot be used for projector camera systems, since projectors are light-emitting devices and the projection of cameras cannot be obtained in projector images. In this paper, we show that by using the shadow of cameras and the shadow of projectors generated by projector light, we can generate virtual mutual projections between projectors and cameras, and projectors and projectors. These virtual mutual projections can be used for calibrating projector-camera systems quite accurately. Furthermore, the calibration can be achieved without using any 3D points unlike the existing calibration methods. The accuracy of the proposed method is evaluated by using real and synthetic images.

## 1   Introduction

In recent years, projector-camera systems have been studied extensively and used actively as new information presenting systems[2,4,7,5]. For using the projector-camera systems, it is very important to calibrate cameras and projectors accurately. Since projectors can be considered as single viewpoint cameras, camera calibration methods such as the standard 8 point algorithm are often used for calibrating projector-camera systems. However, the existing methods require many 3D points for calibrating the systems accurately and stably [8,9]. To cope with this problem, Nishie et al.[3] proposed a useful calibration method, which uses the shadow information of objects generated by a projector light. The method enables us to calibrate projector-camera systems only from two 3D points. However, the method does not provide us good results, if these two points are close to the screen, or these two points are collinear with cameras and projectors.

On the other hand, Sato[6] showed that multiple cameras can be calibrated very accurately, if the cameras are projected to each other. It is called a mutual projection of cameras. Since projectors can be considered as single viewpoint cameras, we can expect that projector-camera systems can be calibrated accurately and reliably by using the mutual projection between projectors and

T. Wada, F. Huang, and S. Lin (Eds.): PSIVT 2009, LNCS 5414, pp. 1070–1081, 2009.
© Springer-Verlag Berlin Heidelberg 2009

cameras. Unfortunately, the mutual projection between projectors and cameras does not occur, since the projectors are light emitting devices and they cannot see the 3D world unlike cameras. Also, if we have multiple projectors, these projectors cannot see other projectors, and mutual projection between multiple projectors does not occur.

However, we in this paper show that by using the shadow of cameras and the shadow of projectors generated by the light of projectors, we can virtually generate the mutual projection between projectors and cameras, and projectors and projectors. Based on these properties, we propose a new method for calibrating projector-camera systems quite accurately from shadows of cameras and projectors. Unlike the existing calibration methods, the proposed method does not require any 3D point for calibrating projector-camera systems except the shadow information, and thus singular cases of the existing methods, e.g. coplanar 3D points, are no longer singular in the proposed method.

## 2   Shadow Projection in Projector-Camera Systems

The projector-camera systems consist of multiple cameras and multiple projectors. Since a projector has a single center of projection, it can be considered as a camera. Thus, the geometry between multiple projectors and multiple cameras can be analyzed by using the multiple view geometry of multiple cameras.

In general a projector projects light on a planar screen. Thus, we can consider a planar homography, $\mathbf{H}_{pc}$, between a projector and a camera with respect to the screen. The homography, $\mathbf{H}_{pc}$, can be obtained by projecting four or more than four points from the projector to the screen, and observing these points by the camera. In the following part of this paper, we assume that planar homographies between a camera and projectors are available.

Let us consider a 3D point, $\mathbf{X}$, a projector, $\mathbf{P}$, and a camera, $\mathbf{C}$, as shown in Fig. 1. Because of a light of the projector $\mathbf{P}$, a shadow $\mathbf{X}'$ of the point $\mathbf{X}$ is generated on a screen $\varPi$. Let $\mathbf{X}$ and $\mathbf{X}'$ be projected to $\mathbf{x}$ and $\mathbf{x}'$ in an image of the camera $\mathbf{C}$. Also, let $\mathbf{x}_p$ be a point in the projector image, which corresponds to the 3D point $\mathbf{X}$. Then, the relationship between $\mathbf{x}_p$ and $\mathbf{x}'$ can be described by using the planar homography $\mathbf{H}_{pc}$ as follows:

$$\mathbf{x}' \sim \mathbf{H}_{pc}\mathbf{x}_p \tag{1}$$

where, $\sim$ denotes an equality up to a scale, and point coordinates are represented by using homogeneous coordinates.

Now, if we consider a projection matrix $\mathbf{A}$ of the camera $\mathbf{C}$ and a projection matrix $\mathbf{A}^p$ of the projector $\mathbf{P}$, the 3D point $\mathbf{X}$ is projected to $\mathbf{x}$ and $\mathbf{x}_p$ as follows:

$$\mathbf{x} \sim \mathbf{A}\mathbf{X} \tag{2}$$

$$\mathbf{x}_p \sim \mathbf{A}^p\mathbf{X} \tag{3}$$

Thus, the 3D point $\mathbf{X}$ is projected to the projection, $\mathbf{x}'$, of the shadow point, $\mathbf{X}'$, as follows:

$$\mathbf{x}' \sim \mathbf{A}'\mathbf{X} \tag{4}$$

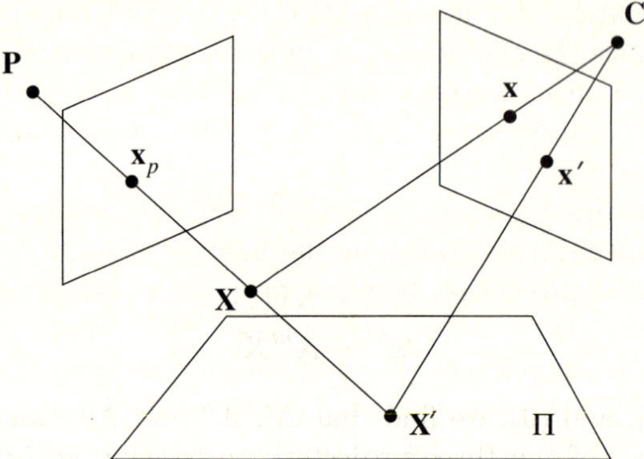

**Fig. 1.** The shadow projection in a projector-camera system which consists of a projector and a camera

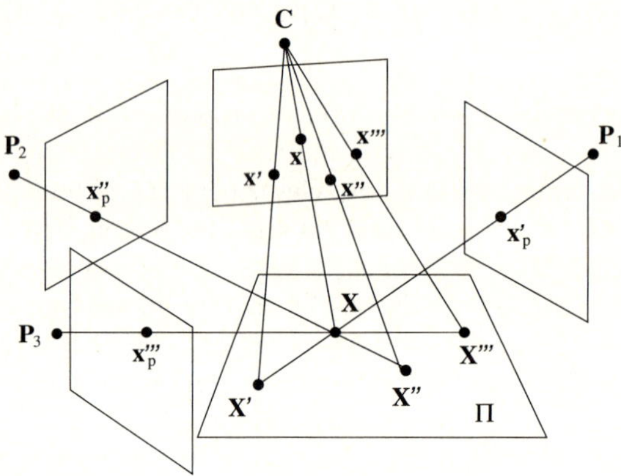

**Fig. 2.** The shadow projection in a projector-camera system which consists of three projectors and a camera

where, $\mathbf{A}'$ is the following projection matrix:

$$\mathbf{A}' = \mathbf{H}_{pc}\mathbf{A}^p \tag{5}$$

From (2) and (4), we find that the projection, $\mathbf{x}$, of $\mathbf{X}$ and the projection, $\mathbf{x}'$, of its shadow $\mathbf{X}'$ are considered as a pair of stereo camera images, and thus $\mathbf{A}$ and $\mathbf{A}'$ are projection matrices of a pair of stereo cameras. Since the relationship between $\mathbf{A}'$ and $\mathbf{A}^p$ can be described by using a planar homography $\mathbf{H}_{pc}$ as shown in (5), $\mathbf{A}'$ and $\mathbf{A}^p$ are projectively equivalent. Thus, $\mathbf{A}'$ is considered as a projection matrix of the projector $\mathbf{P}$ up to a projective ambiguity. Thus, two view geometry between $\mathbf{A}$ and $\mathbf{A}^p$ is equivalent to the two view geometry between $\mathbf{A}$ and $\mathbf{A}'$ up to a projective ambiguity.

The above discussions can be hold for projector camera systems with two or more than two projectors. Suppose we have a camera and three projectors as shown in Fig. 2, and three shadows $\mathbf{X}'$, $\mathbf{X}''$ and $\mathbf{X}'''$ of a 3D point $\mathbf{X}$ are generated by these three projectors. These shadows are observed as $\mathbf{x}'$, $\mathbf{x}''$ and $\mathbf{x}'''$ in the camera image. Then the relationships between the 3D point $\mathbf{X}$ and image points can be described by using projection matrices as follows:

$$\mathbf{x} \sim \mathbf{A}\mathbf{X} \tag{6}$$

$$\mathbf{x}' \sim \mathbf{A}'\mathbf{X} \tag{7}$$

$$\mathbf{x}'' \sim \mathbf{A}''\mathbf{X} \tag{8}$$

$$\mathbf{x}''' \sim \mathbf{A}'''\mathbf{X} \tag{9}$$

From (6), (7), (8), and (9), we find that $\mathbf{A}'$, $\mathbf{A}''$ and $\mathbf{A}'''$ can be considered as projection matrices of the three projectors up to a projective ambiguity, and thus we can consider the multiple view geometry of multiple projectors and a camera by using the projections of shadow points.

## 3   Virtual Mutual Projection of Projectors and Cameras

We next consider virtual mutual projections between projectors and cameras, and projectors and projectors. Sato [6] showed that if multiple cameras are projected to each other, then the multiple view geometry of these cameras can be computed more reliably from less corresponding points. The mutual projection occurs between two cameras. However, it does not occur between a projector and a camera, since the projector is a light emitting device, and it cannot observe the camera. Also, the mutual projection between a projector and another projector does not occur. However, if we use shadow information caused by the projector light, we can virtually generate mutual projection between a projector and a camera, and a projector and another projector.

Let us consider a camera $\mathbf{C}$ and three projectors $\mathbf{P}_1$, $\mathbf{P}_2$ and $\mathbf{P}_3$. Let $\mathbf{C}'$, $\mathbf{C}''$ and $\mathbf{C}'''$ be shadows of the camera $\mathbf{C}$ generated by the projector light of $\mathbf{P}_1$, $\mathbf{P}_2$ and $\mathbf{P}_3$ respectively. Also, let $\mathbf{X}_{ij}$ be a shadow of $\mathbf{P}_j$ generated by the projector light of $\mathbf{P}_i$. These shadows $\mathbf{C}'$, $\mathbf{C}''$, $\mathbf{C}'''$, $\mathbf{X}_{12}$, $\mathbf{X}_{13}$ and $\mathbf{X}_{23}$ are projected to the camera image as $\mathbf{e}'$, $\mathbf{e}''$, $\mathbf{e}'''$, $\mathbf{e}'_{12}$, $\mathbf{e}'_{13}$ and $\mathbf{e}'_{23}$ respectively, and are visible in the camera image.

Then, $\mathbf{C}$, $\mathbf{P}_1$ and $\mathbf{e}'$ are collinear as shown in Fig. 3. Therefore, $\mathbf{e}'$ is an epipole of $\mathbf{P}_1$ in the image of $\mathbf{C}$. Also, $\mathbf{e}''$ and $\mathbf{e}'''$ are epipoles of $\mathbf{P}_2$ and $\mathbf{P}_3$ in the image of $\mathbf{C}$. On the other hand, $\mathbf{e}'_{12}$ is the projection of $\mathbf{X}_{12}$ which is collinear with $\mathbf{P}_1$ and $\mathbf{P}_2$. This means $\mathbf{e}'_{12}$ is the indirect observation of an epipole $\mathbf{e}_{12}$ between $\mathbf{P}_1$ and $\mathbf{P}_2$. Also, $\mathbf{e}'_{13}$ and $\mathbf{e}'_{23}$ are the indirect observation of epipole $\mathbf{e}_{13}$ of $\mathbf{P}_1$ and $\mathbf{P}_3$, and epipole $\mathbf{e}_{23}$ of $\mathbf{P}_2$ and $\mathbf{P}_3$ respectively. The relationship between $\mathbf{e}_{ij}$ and $\mathbf{e}'_{ij}$ can be described by using planar homographies between the camera and projectors as follows:

$$\mathbf{e}_{12} \sim \mathbf{H}_{c1}\mathbf{e}'_{12} \tag{10}$$

$$\mathbf{e}_{13} \sim \mathbf{H}_{c1}\mathbf{e}'_{13} \tag{11}$$

$$\mathbf{e}_{23} \sim \mathbf{H}_{c2}\mathbf{e}'_{23} \tag{12}$$

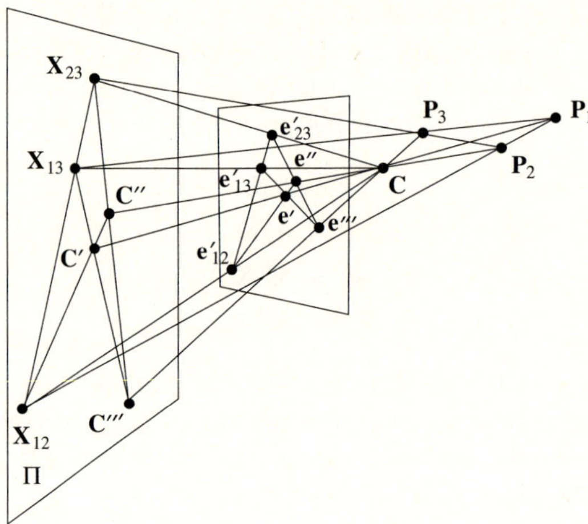

**Fig. 3.** Virtual Mutual Projection between cameras and projectors

where, $\mathbf{H}_{c1}$ and $\mathbf{H}_{c2}$ denote planar homographies between the camera and projector $\mathbf{P}_1$, and the camera and projector $\mathbf{P}_2$ respectively.

Thus, by observing the shadows of a camera, $\mathbf{e}'$, $\mathbf{e}''$, $\mathbf{e}''$, and the shadows of projectors, $\mathbf{e}'_{12}$, $\mathbf{e}'_{13}$, $\mathbf{e}'_{23}$, we can directly extract all the epipoles in the multiple view geometry of the projector-camera system. This means by observing the shadows of the camera and the projectors in the camera image, we can generate mutual projection between projectors and cameras virtually.

In the next section, we show a method for computing the multiple view geometry of projector-camera systems by using the virtual mutual projection.

## 4   Multiple View Geometry from Virtual Mutual Projection

### 4.1   2 View Geometry

Let us first consider the multiple view geometry of a projector-camera system which consists of a projector, $\mathbf{P}_1$, and a camera, $\mathbf{C}$, as shown in Fig. 4. The light of the projector $\mathbf{P}_1$ generates the shadow $\mathbf{X}'$ of a 3D point $\mathbf{X}$ and the shadow $\mathbf{C}'$ of the camera $\mathbf{C}$ on the screen. Then, $\mathbf{X}$, $\mathbf{X}'$ and $\mathbf{C}'$ are projected to $\mathbf{x} = [x^1, x^2, x^3]^\top$, $\mathbf{x}' = [x'^1, x'^2, x'^3]^\top$ and $\mathbf{e}' = [e'^1, e'^2, e'^3]^\top$ in the camera image. Since $\mathbf{x}$, $\mathbf{x}'$ and $\mathbf{e}'$ are collinear as shown in Fig. 4, the auto-epipolar holds and the relationship between $\mathbf{x}$ and $\mathbf{x}'$ can be described as follows:

$$x^i x'^j e'^k \epsilon_{ijk} = 0 \tag{13}$$

where, $\epsilon_{ijk}$ denotes a tensor whose value is 1 for even permutation, $-1$ for odd permutation and 0 for the other case. In this paper, the Einstein's summation convention is used for describing tensor equations.

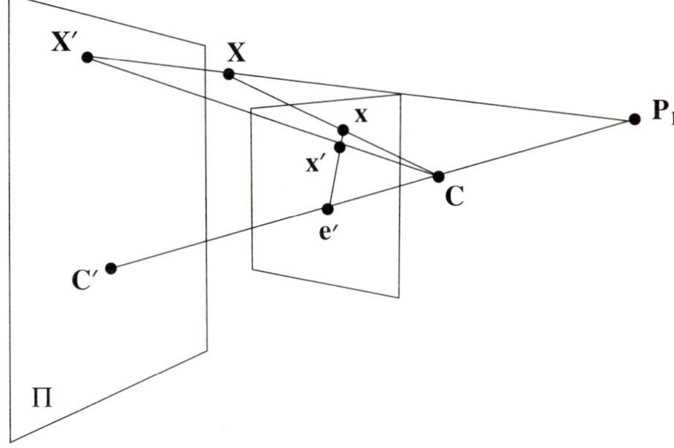

**Fig. 4.** Two view geometry of a projector-camera system

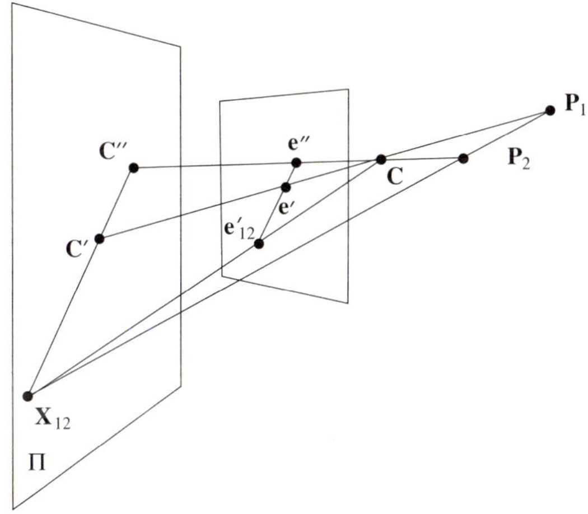

**Fig. 5.** Three view geometry of a projector-camera system

As shown in (13), the two view geometry of projector-camera systems can be described by using just an epipole, $\mathbf{e}'$, i.e. the projection of the shadow of camera $\mathbf{C}$ in its own image. Thus, we no longer need any corresponding points for computing the two view geometry of a projector-camera system except a shadow of the camera.

## 4.2   3 View Geometry

We next consider the three view geometry of a projector-camera system, which consists of two projectors, $\mathbf{P}_1$ and $\mathbf{P}_2$, and a camera, $\mathbf{C}$, as shown in Fig. 5.

Let $\mathbf{e}'$ and $\mathbf{e}''$ be the projections of shadow $\mathbf{C}'$ and shadow $\mathbf{C}''$, which are generated by the projector light of $\mathbf{P}_1$ and $\mathbf{P}_2$ respectively. The shadows $\mathbf{X}'$ and $\mathbf{X}''$

of a 3D point $\mathbf{X}$ are generated by the projector light of $\mathbf{P}_1$ and $\mathbf{P}_2$ respectively. Suppose $\mathbf{X}$, $\mathbf{X}'$ and $\mathbf{X}''$ are projected to $\mathbf{x}$, $\mathbf{x}'$ and $\mathbf{x}''$ in the camera image. Then, the auto-epipolar holds as two view geometry, and thus, the projection matrix $\mathbf{A}$ of camera $\mathbf{C}$, the projection matrix $\mathbf{A}'$ of projector $\mathbf{P}_1$ and the projection matrix $\mathbf{A}''$ of projector $\mathbf{P}_2$ can be described by using $\mathbf{e}'$ and $\mathbf{e}''$ as follows:

$$\mathbf{A} = \begin{bmatrix} \mathbf{I} \ 0 \end{bmatrix}, \ \mathbf{A}' = \begin{bmatrix} \mathbf{I} \ -\mathbf{e}' \end{bmatrix}, \ \mathbf{A}'' = \begin{bmatrix} \mathbf{I} \ -\alpha\mathbf{e}'' \end{bmatrix} \tag{14}$$

where, $\alpha$ denotes a relative distance of $\mathbf{P}_2$ with respect to the projective frame defined by $\mathbf{C}$ and $\mathbf{P}_1$. The relative scale $\alpha$ can be described by using an epipole, $\mathbf{e}'_{12}$, between projector $\mathbf{P}_1$ and projector $\mathbf{P}_2$ and epipoles $\mathbf{e}'$ and $\mathbf{e}''$ as follows:

$$e'^i_{12} = e'^i - \alpha e''^i \tag{15}$$

Thus, if we have $\mathbf{e}'$, $\mathbf{e}''$ and $\mathbf{e}_{12}$, then we can compute $\alpha$ from (15).

Since the projection matrices of the camera and the projectors are as shown in (14), the trilinear relationship between $\mathbf{x}$, $\mathbf{x}'$ and $\mathbf{x}''$ can be described as follows:

$$x^i x'^j x''^k \epsilon_{jqu}\epsilon_{kiv}e'^q - \alpha x^i x'^j x''^k \epsilon_{jiu}\epsilon_{krv}e''^r = 0_{uv} \tag{16}$$

This is the minimal representation of the three view geometry of a projector-camera system.

From (15) and (16), we find that the three view geometry of a projector-camera system can be derived just from the shadows of the camera, $\mathbf{e}'$ and $\mathbf{e}''$, and the shadow of the projector, $\mathbf{e}'_{12}$, in the camera image. We do not need any corresponding point except these shadows for computing the three view geometry of a projector-camera system.

### 4.3    4 View Geometry

We next consider a projector-camera system which consists of three projectors, $\mathbf{P}_1$, $\mathbf{P}_2$ and $\mathbf{P}_3$, and a camera, $\mathbf{C}$, as shown in Fig. 3.

Let $\mathbf{e}'$, $\mathbf{e}''$ and $\mathbf{e}'''$ be the projections of the shadows of camera $\mathbf{C}$, which are generated by the projector light of $\mathbf{P}_1$, $\mathbf{P}_2$ and $\mathbf{P}_3$. Also, let $\mathbf{e}'_{ij}$ be the projection of the shadow of $\mathbf{P}_j$ generated by the projector light of $\mathbf{P}_i$. Suppose the projector light of $\mathbf{P}_1$, $\mathbf{P}_2$ and $\mathbf{P}_3$ generate shadows $\mathbf{X}'$, $\mathbf{X}''$ and $\mathbf{X}'''$ of a 3D point $\mathbf{X}$, and these points are projected to $\mathbf{x}'$, $\mathbf{x}''$, $\mathbf{x}'''$ and $\mathbf{x}$ in the camera image. Then, because of the auto-epipolar, the projection matrix $\mathbf{A}$ of camera $\mathbf{C}$ and the projection matrices $\mathbf{A}'$, $\mathbf{A}''$ and $\mathbf{A}'''$ of projector $\mathbf{P}_1$, $\mathbf{P}_2$ and $\mathbf{P}_3$ can be described as follows:

$$\mathbf{A} = \begin{bmatrix} \mathbf{I} \ 0 \end{bmatrix}, \ \mathbf{A}' = \begin{bmatrix} \mathbf{I} \ -\mathbf{e}' \end{bmatrix}, \ \mathbf{A}'' = \begin{bmatrix} \mathbf{I} \ -\alpha\mathbf{e}'' \end{bmatrix}, \ \mathbf{A}''' = \begin{bmatrix} \mathbf{I} \ -\beta\mathbf{e}''' \end{bmatrix} \tag{17}$$

where, $\alpha$ and $\beta$ are relative distance of $\mathbf{P}_2$ and $\mathbf{P}_3$ with respect to the projective frame defined by $\mathbf{C}$ and $\mathbf{P}_1$, and can be computed from the following relationship between $\alpha$, $\beta$ and epipoles:

$$e'^i_{12} = e'^i - \alpha e'''^i \ , \ e'^i_{13} = \beta e''''^i - e'^i \ , \ e'^i_{23} = \alpha e''^i - \beta e''''^i \tag{18}$$

From (17) we find that the following quadrilinear relationship holds for $\mathbf{x}$, $\mathbf{x}'$, $\mathbf{x}''$ and $\mathbf{x}'''$:

$$x^i x'^j x''^k x'''^l \epsilon_{ipa}\epsilon_{jqb}\epsilon_{krc}\epsilon_{lsd}(-\epsilon^{rsp}e'^q + \alpha\epsilon^{spq}e''^r - \beta\epsilon^{pqr}e'''^s) = 0_{abcd} \qquad (19)$$

This is the minimal representation of the four view geometry of a projector-camera system. Since $\alpha$ and $\beta$ can be computed from epipoles, the four view geometry can be computed just from the shadows of the camera and the shadows of the projectors. We do not need any other corresponding point in the camera image except these shadows for calibrating the projector-camera systems. Thus, projector-camera systems can be calibrated without using any 3D points in the scene.

## 5    Experiments

### 5.1    Real Image Experiments

In this section, we show the results from real image experiments. In these experiments, we synthesized shadows which should be generated by the projector light of arbitrary projectors by using multilinear relationships computed from the shadow of cameras and projectors.

Fig. 6 shows a projector-camera system used in our experiments. It consists of three projectors and a camera. The shadows of arbitrary projectors are generated from the trilinear relationship and the quadrilinear relationship computed from shadow information. In the experiment of trilinear relationship, we used two of these three projectors. The projector 1, 2 and 3 project red, green and blue light respectively, and the shadows caused by these projectors are separated by using color information.

Fig. 7 (a) shows a camera image obtained in the experiment of three view geometry. The epipole 1 and 2 in this figure show the center of shadows of the camera generated by projector 1 and 2 respectively. These epipoles were

**Fig. 6.** Experimental set up of a projector-camera system

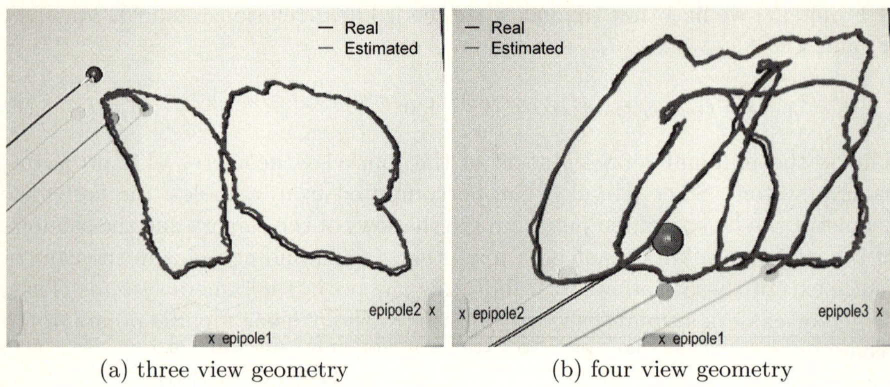


(a) three view geometry        (b) four view geometry

**Fig. 7.** The real shadows and the shadows generated by the proposed method

extracted manually. The shadows caused by projector 2 were generated by using the trilinear relationship computed from the proposed method. The red curve shows shadow generated from the proposed method, and the blue curve shows the real shadow. As shown in this figure, the shadow of an arbitrary projector is generated properly by using the proposed method. Fig. 7 (b) shows the result from the four view geometry extracted from the proposed method. Again, the shadow generated from the proposed method is accurate.

## 5.2   Stability Evaluations

We next evaluate the stability of the proposed method. In this evaluation, bi-focal, trifocal and quadrifocal tensors are computed from the proposed virtual mutual projection method, and image points are transferred from one view to another view by using the estimated multifocal tensors. The image noises with the standard deviation of 1.0 are added to all the image points. The RMS errors are computed between the estimated image points and the real image points. The results are compared with those from Nishie's method [3]. The Nishie's method requires at least two 3D points for computing multifocal tensors, while the proposed does not require any 3D point. If these 3D points are close to the screen, Nishie's method is close to singular, and it is unstable. Thus, we compare these two methods changing the distance between the screen and the 3D points. Since we cannot transfer image points by using bifocal tensors, we evaluated the epipolar distance, i.e. the distance between a transferred point and an epipolar line, for the two view case.

Fig. 8 shows the RMS errors derived from the estimated bifocal tensors. The horizontal axis shows the distance between the screen and the 3D points used in Nishie's method. The red line shows the result from the proposed method and the blue line shows that from Nishie's method. As shown in this graph, Nishie's method is unstable if the 3D points are close to the screen, while the proposed method does not require any 3D point and is stable all the time.

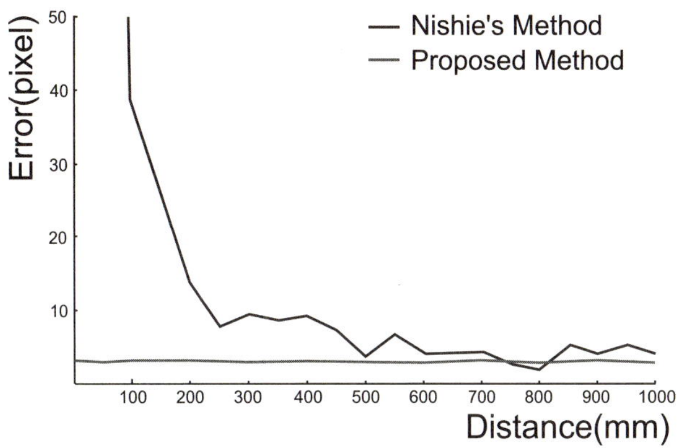

Fig. 8. Stability evaluation in the two view geometry

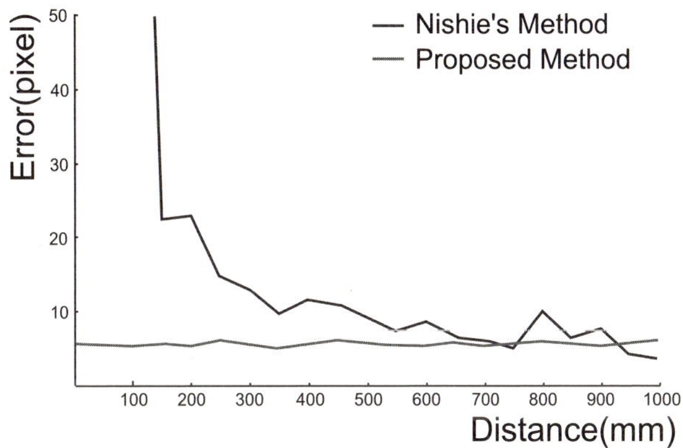

Fig. 9. Stability evaluation in the three view geometry

Fig. 9 and Fig. 10 show results from the three view case and the four view case respectively. As shown in these graphs, the stability of the proposed method is again better than Nishie's method. Since the stability of Nishie's method [3] is much better than that of traditional 8 point algorithm [1], the proposed method is quite stable and is useful for calibrating projector-camera systems.

## 5.3  Accuracy of Estimated Epipoles

We next evaluate the accuracy of epipoles estimated as the center of gravity of shadows. If the distance between the camera and the projector is large, the shadow of camera is small, and the epipole estimated from the shadow is close to the ground truth. Thus, we evaluated the relationship between the distance from the camera to the projector and the error of estimated epipoles of a camera. The result is shown in Fig. 11 (a). We also evaluated the error of epipoles of a

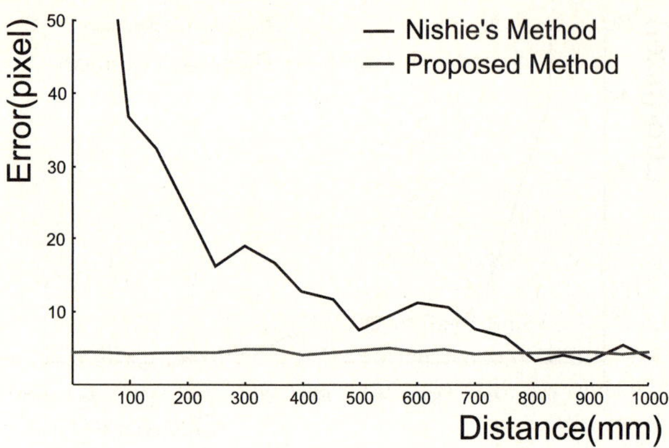



**Fig. 10.** Stability evaluation in the four view geometry

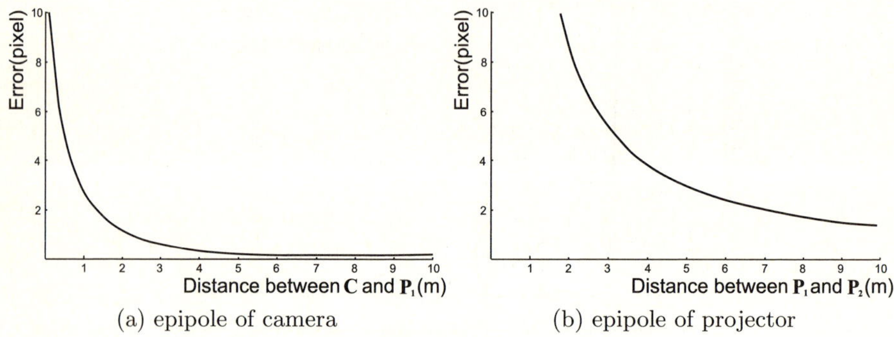



(a) epipole of camera          (b) epipole of projector

**Fig. 11.** Error of estimated epipoles

projector, changing the distance between two projectors. Fig. 11 (b) shows the result of the evaluation.

## 6   Conclusion

In this paper, we proposed a method for calibrating projector-camera systems by using mutual projections of projectors and cameras. In general mutual projections between projectors and cameras do not occur, since projectors are light emitting devices and they can not see the 3D world unlike cameras. However, we in this paper showed that by using the shadow of cameras and the shadow of projectors generated by projector lights, we can generate virtual mutual projections between projectors and cameras, and projectors and projectors. These virtual mutual projections enable us to compute the multiple view geometry of projector-camera systems and calibrate them quite accurately. Furthermore, the proposed method does not require any 3D points for calibrating projector-camera systems, while the traditional 8 point algorithm requires minimum of 8 points and Nishie's method requires minimum of 2 points.. The excellent stability of the proposed method was shown in the experiments.

# References

1. Hartley, R., Zisserman, A.: Mutiple View Geometry in Computer Vision. Cambridge University Press, Cambridge (2000)
2. Milgram, P., Kishino, F.: A taxonomy of mixed reality visual display. IEICE Transactions on Information and System E77-D(12), 1321–1329 (1994)
3. Nishie, K., Sato, J.: 3D reconstruction from uncalibrated cameras and uncalibrated projectors from shadows. In: Proc. International Conference on Pattern Recognition, vol. 1, pp. 15–18 (2006)
4. Oka, K., Sato, I., Nakanishi, Y., Sato, Y., Koike, H.: Interaction for entertainment contents based on direct manipulation with bare hands. In: Proc. IWEC, pp. 397–404 (2002)
5. Okatani, T., Deguchi, K.: Autocalibration of a projector-camera system. IEEE Trans. PAMI 27(12), 1845–1855 (2005)
6. Sato, J.: Recovering multiple view geometry from mutual projections of multiple cameras. International Journal of Computer Vision 66(2), 123–140 (2006)
7. Sukuthankar, R., Stockton, R., Mullin, M.: Smarter presentations: Exploiting homography in camera-projector systems. In: Proc. ICCV 2001 (2001)
8. Raskar, R., Beardsley, P.: A self-correcting projector. In: Proc. Computer Vision and Pattern Recognition (2001)
9. Griesser, A., Van Gool, L.: Automatic Interactive Calibration of Multi-Projector-Camera Systems. In: Proc. Conference on Computer Vision and Pattern Recognition Workshop (2006)

# Automatic Appropriate Segment Extraction from Shots
# Based on Learning from Example Videos


Yousuke Kurihara, Naoko Nitta, and Noboru Babaguchi

Graduate School of Engineering, Osaka University
2-1 Yamada-oka, Suita, Osaka, 565-0871 Japan
{kurihara,naoko,babaguchi}@nanase.comm.eng.osaka-u.ac.jp



**Abstract.** Videos are composed of shots, each of which is recorded continuously by a camera, and video editing can be considered as a process of re-sequencing shots selected from original videos. Shots usually include redundant intervals, which are often edited out by professional editors. Defining the intact interval which is used in the edited video as the appropriate segment and all other intervals of equal length as inappropriate segments, this paper proposes a method for automatically extracting appropriate segments from shots. Since what kinds of characteristics make an interval appropriate to be used in the edited video should be different among shots with different content, the proposed method firstly categorizes shots according to their content with Support Vector Machines. Then, the appropriate segments are extracted based on the temporal patterns of audio and visual features in appropriate and inappropriate segments learned with Hidden Markov Models for each shot category. The effectiveness of the proposed method is verified with experiments.

**Keywords:** video editing, segment extraction, shot categorization, example videos.


## 1 Introduction

Video editing is to create a new video content by combining segments selected from original videos. There are two purposes of video editing, 1)efficiently conveying information to viewers and 2)stimulating viewers' interests. As an example of automatic video editing techniques, video summarization has been realized by extracting only semantically important video shots based on metadata to achieve the former purpose [1], and by extracting important shots based on video tempo created by shot length, motion intensity, and audio energy to achieve the latter purpose [2]. Although the videos created by their methods have been verified to include similar content as manually edited videos, they are still inferior in quality to professionally edited videos in terms of stimulating viewers' interests. This is attributed to the fact that most existing methods consider shots, each of which is recorded continuously by a camera, as the minimum units of video segments. However, a shot often includes redundant intervals. Therefore,


T. Wada, F. Huang, and S. Lin (Eds.): PSIVT 2009, LNCS 5414, pp. 1082–1093, 2009.

extracting only the essential intervals from shots is necessary to create videos which more effectively stimulate viewer's interests. In what follows, the interval of a shot which is used in the edited video is referred as an *appropriate segment* and all other intervals of equal length as *inappropriate segments*.

There are some related work for extracting appropriate segments from shots. For example, a shot was shortened so that the motion intensity, direction, and speed are similar between adjacent cut-out segments [3]. Further, important sub-shots [4], which were divided based on the local maximum of frame difference, speech segments [5], clips with clearly audible sound [6], and clips without excessive camera motion or overexposure [7] have been extracted as the appropriate segments. However, since the rules to evaluate the appropriateness of segments are determined manually, questions still remain in their legitimacy.

We therefore propose a method for extracting appropriate segments from shots based on temporal audio-visual patterns automatically obtained from example videos. However, since the temporal audio-visual patterns can be different among shots with different content, shots firstly need to be categorized based on their content. Therefore, the proposed method starts with learning the audio and visual characteristics of each shot category with Support Vector Machines(SVMs). Then, for each shot category, given sets of appropriate and inappropriate segments as examples, the proposed method learns the temporal patterns of how frame-level audio and visual features change in each type of segment with Hidden Markov Models(HMMs). Finally, when an original shot is given, the method determines its shot category with the learned SVMs and extracts an appropriate segment from the shot based on its likelihood value to be observed in the learned HMMs.

## 2 Appropriate Segment Extraction

Fig. 1 shows the outline of the proposed method. The proposed method consists of two phases: Learning Phase and Segment Extraction Phase. We assume that audio and visual features change in a characteristic way in appropriate segments selected by professional editors. However, since the temporal patterns in appropriate segments can be different among shots with different content, shots need to be categorized first. Therefore, in Learning Phase, after extracting a set of audio and visual features from each shot, the characteristics of each shot category are learned with SVMs. Then, given sets of appropriate and inappropriate segments as examples for each shot category, the temporal patterns of how audio and visual features change in each type of segment are learned with HMMs. Each feature is discretized to represent frames with similar audio and visual features with a symbol. Then, symbol sequence patterns in appropriate segments and inappropriate segments are learned with HMMs, generating a HMM for appropriate segments and a HMM for inappropriate segments respectively.

In Segment Extraction Phase, when an original shot and the length of the segment to be extracted are given, the shot category is determined based on the learned SVMs. A symbol sequence of the original shot is obtained and the

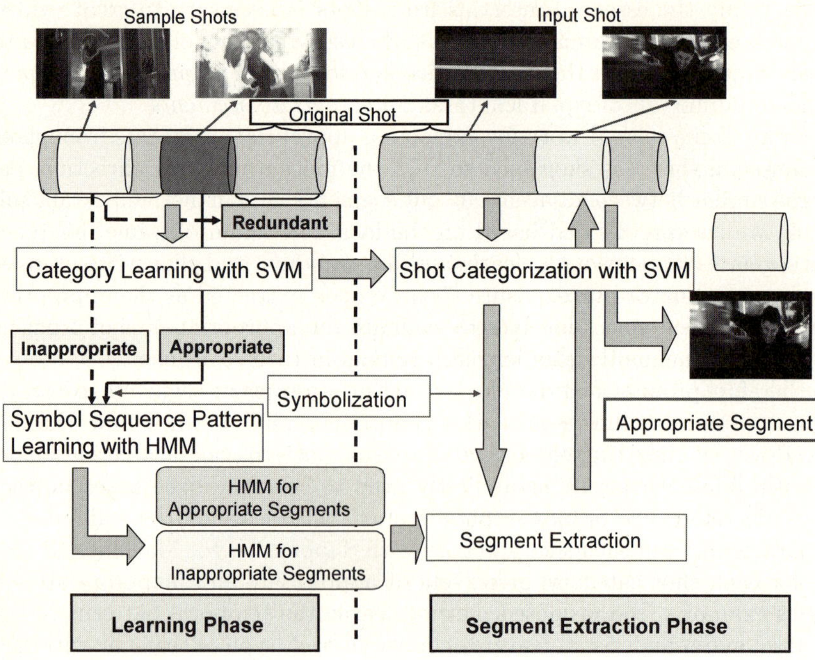


**Fig. 1.** Outline of the method

likelihoods for all segments of the specified length to be observed in each HMM
are calculated. The segment with the maximum ratio between the likelihood
values for the HMMs for appropriate segments and for inappropriate segments
is extracted as the most appropriate segment. The proposed method requires
the following four procedures.

1. Shot Categorization with SVMs
2. Symbolization
3. Symbol Sequence Pattern Learning with HMMs
4. Segment Extraction

## 2.1   Shot Categorization with SVMs

Audio and visual temporal patterns in appropriate segments should be different
among shots with different content. For example, in shots which include camera motion or fast moving objects, large visual changes tend to attract human
attention. In shots which include dialogue, human-voice intervals are considered
important. This paper especially focuses on these two types of shots and defines
the former shots as Action, the latter as Conversation, and the other shots as
Others.

In Learning Phase, after extracting audio or visual features which can describe the difference among three shot categories from sample shots, the proposed method firstly learns the audio-visual characteristics of each shot category.

The characteristic of each shot category is shown in Table 1. There can be large visual changes only in Action shots. Moreover, Conversation and Others differ in whether they include voice and human faces or not. We therefore use a hierarchical structure as shown in Fig. 2 to categorize shots. Shots are initially categorized into Action and Non-Action shots based on visual features. In the next step, Non-Action shots are categorized into Conversation and Others based on audio and visual features.

Since Action shots include large luminance change and their shot length is relatively short, we use the shot length, visual disturbance and average luminance difference as the visual features. Visual disturbance is computed based on the structural tensors of frames in each shot[8]. In addition, since the frequency spectrum are different between Conversation and Others shots and Zero Crossing Ratio(ZCR) varies widely in human-voice intervals, we use the mean and variance of ZCR, and Energy Ratio of SubBand at frequency band(ERSB[1/2/3]) as the audio features[9]. Furthermore, since Conversation shots usually include human faces, we compute the ratio of human face areas to the image size using the face detection algorithm in OpenCV library[10][11].

We use SVMs for shot categorization. SVM is one of the machine learning methods, which is easily adaptable to two-category problems. Since the shots are categorized into two categories in each hierarchy, SVM is adaptable to shot categorization in the proposed method.

Finally, given an original shot, Segment Extraction Phase categorizes it as one of the three categories based on its extracted features with SVMs learned in Learn

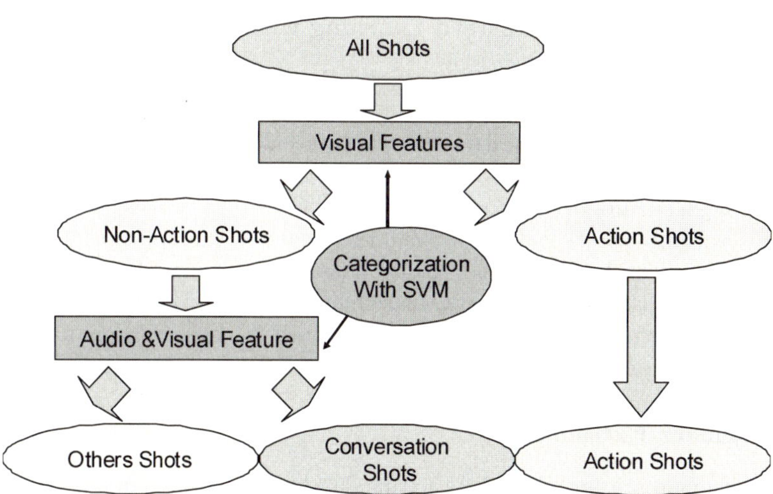


**Fig. 2.** Shot Categorization with SVM

**Table 1.** Characteristics of Shot Category

| Category | Visual Characteristic | Audio Characteristic |
| --- | --- | --- |
| Action | large change | none |
| Conversation | small change<br>human faces | voice |
| Others | small change | non-voice |

## 2.2  Symbolization

After categorization, temporal patterns in the appropriate segments need to be learned with HMMs. Which audio or visual features change characteristically in appropriate segments should depend on the shot categories. Therefore, the audio and visual features which suit for each shot category need to be extracted. In this paper, focusing especially on Conversation and Action shots, we extract features suitable for each shot category[12]. Table 2 summarizes the characteristics of appropriate segments for each shot category and audio and visual features determined to be used based on the characteristics. In this table, STE stands for Short-Time Energy, ESTD for STE Standard Deviation, and LSTER for Low Short-Time Energy Ratio[9], According to the table, we extract relevant features for each category from each frame in order to see how these features change over a sequence of frames.

We use Principal Component Analysis(PCA) to reduce the noise contained in features, and as a result, to reduce the dimension of features. After discretization of each component, all features in each discretized feature vector space is represented with a symbol. Consequently, a sequence of frames is transformed into a sequence of symbols.

## 2.3  Symbol Sequence Pattern Learning with HMMs

Hidden Markov Models(HMMs) are used to learn the temporal patterns of the symbol sequence of appropriate segments and inappropriate segments. HMM is one of the popular techniques to construct an efficient model which describes the temporal patterns of data sequence [13]. The main advantages over other methods, such as Support Vector Machines and Neural Networks, are their ability to model variable-length patterns. Since the length of the appropriate segments is varied for each shot, we need to use a recognition model which can learn variable-length patterns. The symbol sequences of appropriate segments and inappropriate segments for each shot category are fed into two separate HMMs. The parameters of HMM are learned with Baum-Welch algorithm[13].

## 2.4  Segment Extraction

Finally, when an original shot and the time length of the segment to be extracted are specified by a user, the proposed method extracts an appropriate segment of the specified length based on the learned HMMs. Fig. 3 shows the flow of

**Table 2.** Audio and Visual Features

| Shot Category | Characteristics of appropriate segments | audio and visual features |
| --- | --- | --- |
| | clearly audible voice | STE, ESTD, LSTER |
| Conversation | frequency spectrum which largely differs from that in non-voice segments | ERSB |
| | widely varied zero crossing ratio | ZCR |
| | large luminance change | Luminance |
| Action | widely varied zero crossing ratio | ZCR |
| | sharp loud sound effects | STE |

segment extraction. $k$ denotes the number of frames of the appropriate segment. First, a symbol sequence is extracted from the given original shot. $h_k(f)$, the log likelihood for a sequence of $k$ symbols centered at the $f$th symbol to be observed in the HMM for appropriate segments, and $g_k(f)$, the log likelihood for the same sequence to be observed in the HMM for inappropriate segments, are calculated with Forward algorithm[13]. Then, a segment centered at the $F$th frame, is extracted as the most appropriate segment as follows.

$$F = \arg\max_{f}(h_k(f) - g_k(f)) \qquad (1)$$

## 3   Experiments

We evaluated our proposed method using 26 action movies and their trailers. Movie trailers are one of the representative professionally edited videos, mainly designed to attract viewers' interests. Another benefit of using these videos are that both of the original videos and edited videos are easily available.

### 3.1   Shot Categorization

We categorized shots selected randomly from action movies into three categories, 1)Action, 2)Conversation, and 3)Others. The title of movies and the number of sample and test shots are shown in Table 3 and the result of shot categorization is shown in Table 4. 75.9%((43+39)/108) of shots were correctly categorized into Action and Non-Action shots, and 71.8%((16+12)/39) of Non-Action shots were correctly categorized into Conversation and Others. However, 34.3%((12+14+6+5)/108) of shots were incorrectly categorized.

Fig. 4 shows some examples of incorrectly categorized shots. For example, a Conversation shot (a) was incorrectly categorized as an Action due to its large visual change. Since Conversation shots tend to include close-up faces as shown in Fig. 5, small motions of characters largely increases luminance difference which makes them resemble to Action shots.

An Action shot (b) was incorrectly categorized as a Non-Action shot since the intervals of large visual change were relatively short against the shot length

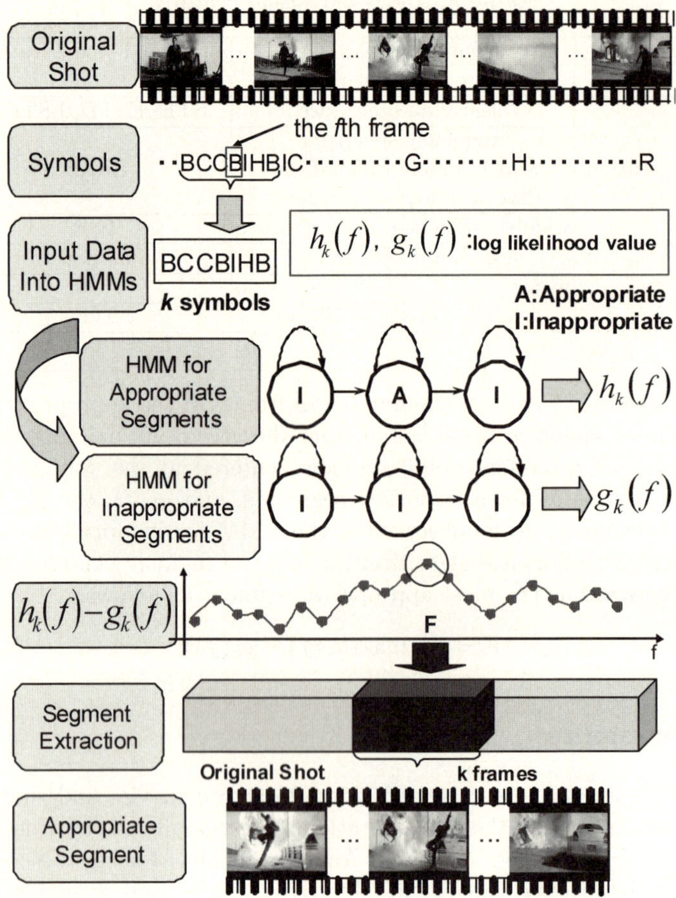



**Fig. 3.** Appropriate Segment Extraction

and the average luminance difference was low. Similarly, a Conversation shot (c) was incorrectly categorized as an Others shot since the length of dialogue was relatively short against the shot length and human face areas were small. In this paper, we extracted audio and visual features per frame which are influenced by the shot length as a visual feature. We therefore need to consider other features which are not influenced by the shot length, such as the max luminance difference.

Moreover, an Others shot (d) was incorrectly categorized as a Conversation since the moaning sound of the character yielded similar audio features to Conversation shots. However, since intervals which include moaning sound of the character could be essential, it could have an insignificant effect on appropriate segment extraction.

**Table 3.** Sample and Test Shots for Shot Categorization

| Movie Title | Action | | Conversation | | Others | |
|---|---|---|---|---|---|---|
| | Sample Shot | Test Shot | Sample Shot | Test Shot | Sample Shot | Test Shot |
| Back to the Future Part II | 9 | 0 | 10 | 0 | 7 | 0 |
| Butterfly Effect | 0 | 0 | 0 | 2 | 0 | 0 |
| Day After Tomorrow | 0 | 5 | 0 | 3 | 0 | 0 |
| Harry Potter II | 0 | 0 | 0 | 4 | 0 | 0 |
| Harry Potter III | 3 | 0 | 3 | 1 | 2 | 1 |
| Harry Potter IV | 0 | 2 | 0 | 0 | 7 | 3 |
| Harry Potter V | 0 | 1 | 0 | 0 | 0 | 8 |
| I, ROBOT | 0 | 9 | 0 | 0 | 0 | 0 |
| Live Free or Die Hard | 0 | 1 | 0 | 0 | 0 | 1 |
| MI:2 | 0 | 0 | 0 | 1 | 0 | 0 |
| MI:3 | 0 | 6 | 0 | 0 | 0 | 0 |
| Minority Report | 5 | 0 | 6 | 4 | 0 | 0 |
| Mr. and Mrs. Smith | 0 | 4 | 0 | 4 | 0 | 0 |
| New Police Story | 0 | 1 | 0 | 1 | 0 | 0 |
| Pirates of the Caribbean II | 0 | 7 | 0 | 3 | 0 | 0 |
| Star Wars I | 0 | 0 | 0 | 2 | 0 | 0 |
| Resident Evil: Apocalypse | 0 | 1 | 0 | 0 | 0 | 0 |
| Star Wars II | 0 | 13 | 0 | 2 | 0 | 0 |
| Star Wars III | 2 | 0 | 5 | 0 | 4 | 0 |
| The Lord of the Rings I | 8 | 0 | 2 | 0 | 2 | 3 |
| The Lord of the Rings II | 3 | 0 | 1 | 0 | 1 | 0 |
| The Lord of the Rings III | 0 | 3 | 0 | 3 | 0 | 4 |
| Transformers | 0 | 4 | 0 | 1 | 1 | 0 |
| Van Helsing | 3 | 0 | 8 | 0 | 2 | 0 |
| Total | 33 | 57 | 35 | 31 | 26 | 20 |

## 3.2 Appropriate Segment Extraction

We extracted shots from movie trailers as the appropriate segments, and the corresponding shots as the original shot. Then, the intervals excluding the appropriate segments are extracted from the original shot as the redundant intervals. Table 5 shows the titles and the number of sample and test original shots. Here, appropriate and inappropriate segments obtained from sample original shots are used as examples and an appropriate segment is extracted from the test original shot by the proposed method.

**Objective Evaluation.** As an objective evaluation, we compared the appropriate segments extracted by the proposed method with the segments used in movie trailers[12], In what follows, we call segments extracted by the proposed method *extracted segments*, and segments used in movie trailers *correct segments*. In evaluation, wc allowed the frame difference between the extracted segment and the correct segment up to $t$ frames. Table 6 shows the results of objective

**Table 4.** Result of Shot Categorization with SVMs

| | | Result of Categorization | |
|---|---|---|---|
| | | Action | Non-Action |
| | Action | 43 | 14 |
| Correct | Non-Action | 12 | 39 |
| Shot | | Conversation | Others |
| Category | Conversation | 16 | 5 |
| | Others | 6 | 12 |

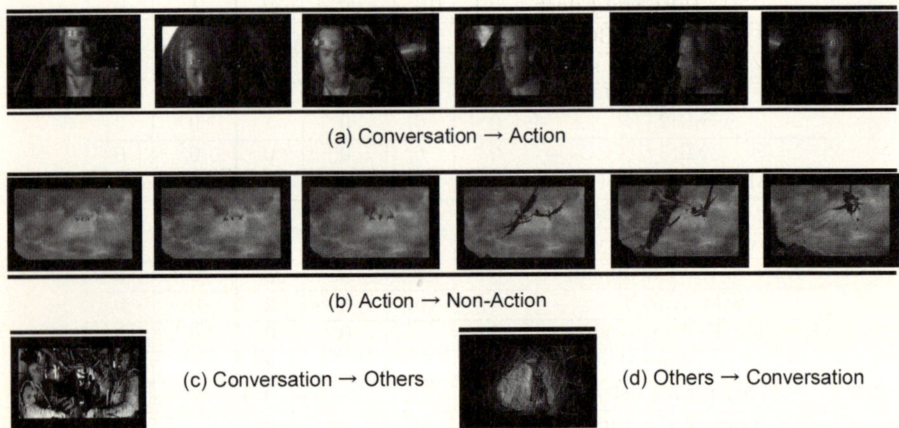

(a) Conversation → Action

(b) Action → Non-Action

(c) Conversation → Others

(d) Others → Conversation

**Fig. 4.** Examples of Incorrectly Categorized Shots

evaluation. When $t = 5$, the appropriate segments were correctly extracted from 72.5% of the original shots.

Fig. 6 shows an example of extracting an appropriate segment. The original shot includes a crash scene in which a truck nearly hits a character, which corresponds to the correct segment, and the proposed method was able to extract the same segment within 3-frame difference by the proposed method.

**Subjective Evaluation.** As a subjective evaluation, we also conducted a questionnaire to evaluate if users feel the extracted segments are appropriate to be used in edited videos. This questionnaire was administered to 14 people. First, we presented them the original shot and then three segments as the appropriate

**Fig. 5.** Conversation Shots

**Table 5.** Sample and Test Shots for Appropriate Segment Extraction

| Movie Title | Action | | Conversation | |
|---|---|---|---|---|
| | Sample Shot | Test Shot | Sample Shot | Test Shot |
| New Police Story | 1 | 0 | 1 | 1 |
| MI:2 | 0 | 0 | 1 | 0 |
| MI:3 | 2 | 4 | 0 | 0 |
| Mr. and Mrs. Smith | 3 | 2 | 4 | 2 |
| Day After Tomorrow | 1 | 3 | 2 | 1 |
| Minority Report | 0 | 0 | 3 | 1 |
| Butterfly Effect | 0 | 0 | 1 | 2 |
| I, ROBOT | 3 | 6 | 0 | 0 |
| Dead Man's Chest | 0 | 7 | 0 | 3 |
| Star Wars I | 0 | 1 | 0 | 3 |
| Star Wars II | 0 | 13 | 0 | 2 |
| Star Wars III | 0 | 4 | 0 | 2 |
| Resident Evil: Apocalypse | 0 | 1 | 0 | 0 |
| Harry Potter I | 0 | 0 | 0 | 1 |
| Harry Potter II | 0 | 5 | 0 | 2 |
| Harry Potter III | 0 | 1 | 0 | 2 |
| Total | 10 | 47 | 12 | 22 |

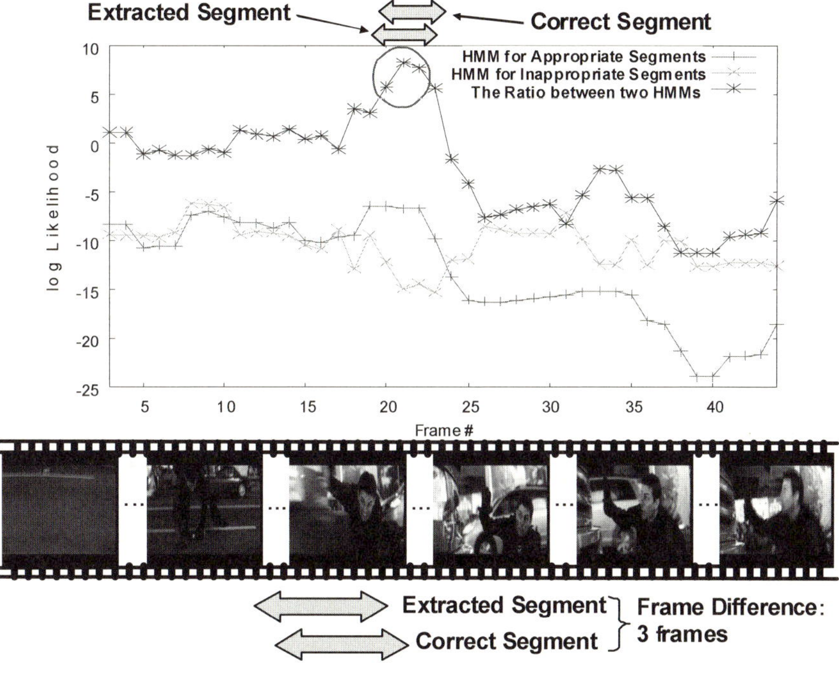


**Fig. 6.** An Example of Extracting an Appropriate Segment

**Table 6.** Results of Objective Evaluation

|      | Accuracy | |
|------|-----------|-------------|
|      | Action | Conversation |
| t=2 | 53%(25/47) | 60%(11/22) |
| t=3 | 60%(28/47) | 64%(14/22) |
| t=5 | 72%(34/47) | 73%(16/22) |

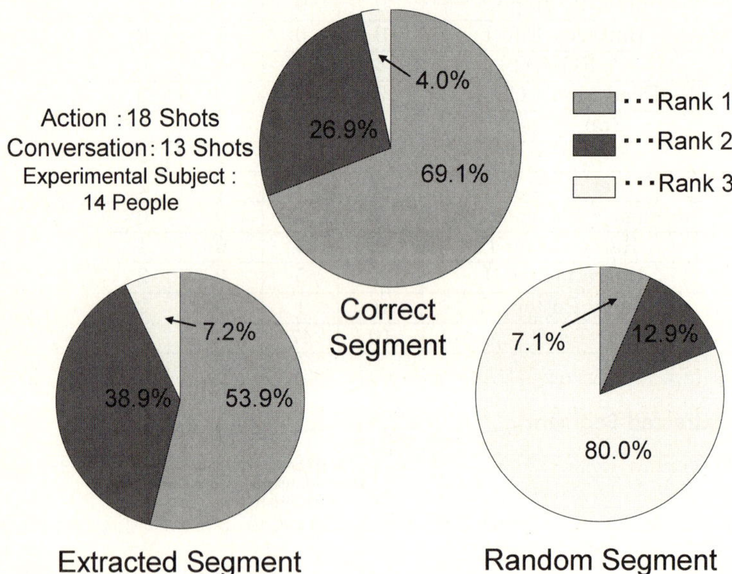


**Fig. 7.** Result of Subjective Evaluation

segment, 1)correct segment, 2)extracted segment, and 3)random segment, and
asked them to rank the three segments in terms of their adequacy[12]. In this
questionnaire, we allowed them to rank more than two segments in the same
rank. Fig. 7 shows the results of the subjective evaluation. These results have
verified that the proposed method was able to extract subjectively appropriate
segments.

## 4 Conclusion

In this paper, we proposed a method for automatically extracting an appropriate
segment from an original shot based on the temporal patterns of how the audio
and visual features change both in the appropriate and inappropriate segments,
which are automatically learned from examples. The proposed method is composed of shot categorization with SVMs and segment extraction with HMMs.

We experimented the proposed method using examples obtained from movies and their trailers. According to the experiments, 75.4% of shots were correctly categorized into Action and Non-Action shots, and 71.8% of Non-Action shots were correctly categorized into Conversation and Others. However there is still need for more argument about which audio and visual features should be used to categorize shots. Results of objective and subjective evaluation have verified the effectiveness of the proposed method in extracting appropriate segments. We need to consider how to automatically determine the number of frames of appropriate segments to be extracted.

# References


1. Takahashi, Y., Nitta, N., Babaguchi, N.: Video Summarization for Large Sports Video Archives. In: Proceedings of ICME 2005 (July 2005)
2. Chen, H.W., Kuo, J.H., Chu, W.T., Wu, J.L.: Action Movies Segmentation and Summarization Based on Tempo Analysis. In: Proceedings of MIR 2004, pp. 251–258 (October 2004)
3. Takemoto, R., Yoshitaka, A., Hirashima, T.: Hirashima: Video Editing based on Movie Effects by Shot Length Transition, Technical Report of IEICE PRMU 2005-149-183, pp.19–24 (January 2006)
4. Hua, X.S., Lu, L., Zhang, H.J.: Optimization-Based Automated Home Video Editing System. IEEE Transactions on TCSVT 2004 14(5) (May 2004)
5. Aoyanagi, S., Kourai, K., Sato, K., Takada, T., Sgawara, T.: Evaluation of New Video Skimming Method Using Audio and Video Information. In: Proceedings of DEWS 2003 2-A-01 (March 2003)
6. Lienhart, R.: Abstracting Home Video Automatically. In: Proceedings of ACMMM 1999, pp. 37–40 (1999)
7. Foote, J., Cooper, M., Girgenshon, A.: Creating Music Videos using Automatic Media Analysis. In: Proceedings of ACMMM 2002, pp. 553–560 (December 2002)
8. Rasheed, Z., Shah, M.: Video Categorization Using Semantics and Semiotics. In: VIDEO MINING, pp. 185–217. Kluwer Academic Publishers, Dordrecht (2003)
9. Wang, Y., Liu, Z., Huang, J.C.: Multimedia Content Analysis Using Both Audio and Visual Clues. IEEE Signal Processing Magagine, 12–36 (November 2000)
10. http://www.intel.com/research/mrl/research/opencv/ OpenCV library, Intel
11. Viola, P., Jones, M.: Rapid object detection using a boosted cascade of simple features. In: Proceedings of CVPR 2001, pp. 511–518 (December 2001)
12. Kurihara, Y., Nitta, N., Babaguchi, N.: Appropriate segment extraction from shots based on temporal patterns of example videos. In: Satoh, S., Nack, F., Etoh, M. (eds.) MMM 2008. LNCS, vol. 4903, pp. 253–264. Springer, Heidelberg (2008)
13. Rabiner, L.R.: A Tutorial on Hidden Markov Models and Selected Applications in Speech Recognition. Proceeding IEEE 77, 257–285 (1989)

# Localization of Lesions in Dermoscopy Images Using Ensembles of Thresholding Methods

M. Emre Celebi[1,*], Hitoshi Iyatomi[2], Gerald Schaefer[3], and William V. Stoecker[4]

[1] Department of Computer Science, Louisiana State University, Shreveport, LA, USA
`ecelebi@lsus.edu`
[2] Department of Electrical Informatics, Hosei University, Tokyo, Japan
[3] School of Engineering and Applied Science, Aston University, Birmingham, UK
[4] Stoecker & Associates, Rolla, MO, USA

**Abstract.** Dermoscopy is one of the major imaging modalities used in the diagnosis of melanoma and other pigmented skin lesions. Due to the difficulty and subjectivity of human interpretation, automated analysis of dermoscopy images has become an important research area. Border detection is often the first step in this analysis. In this article, we present an approximate lesion localization method that serves as a preprocessing step for detecting borders in dermoscopy images. In this method, first the black frame around the image is removed using an iterative algorithm. The approximate location of the lesion is then determined using an ensemble of thresholding algorithms. Experiments on a large set of images demonstrate that the presented method achieves both fast and accurate localization of lesions in dermoscopy images.

## 1   Introduction

Malignant melanoma, the most deadly form of skin cancer, is one of the most rapidly increasing cancers in the world, with an estimated incidence of 62,480 and an estimated total of 8,420 deaths in the United States in 2008 alone [1]. Early diagnosis is particularly important since melanoma can be cured with a simple excision if detected early.

Dermoscopy, also known as epiluminescence microscopy, has become one of the most important tools in the diagnosis of melanoma and other pigmented skin lesions. This non-invasive skin imaging technique involves optical magnification, which makes subsurface structures more easily visible when compared to conventional clinical images [2]. This in turn reduces screening errors and provides greater differentiation between difficult lesions such as pigmented Spitz nevi and small, clinically equivocal lesions [3]. However, it has also been demonstrated that dermoscopy may actually lower the diagnostic accuracy in the hands of

* This work was supported by grants from the Louisiana Board of Regents (LEQSF2008-11-RD-A-12) and the Ministry of Education, Culture, Science, and Technology of Japan (Grant-in-Aid for Scientific Research C, 20591461, 2008-2010).

T. Wada, F. Huang, and S. Lin (Eds.): PSIVT 2009, LNCS 5414, pp. 1094–1103, 2009.

inexperienced dermatologists [4]. Therefore, in order to minimize the diagnostic errors that result from the difficulty and subjectivity of visual interpretation, the development of computerized image analysis techniques is of paramount importance [5,6].

Automated border detection is often the first step in the automated analysis of dermoscopy images [7,8,9]. It is crucial for the image analysis for two main reasons. First, the border structure provides important information for accurate diagnosis, as many clinical features, such as asymmetry, border irregularity, and abrupt border cutoff, are calculated directly from the border. Second, the extraction of other important clinical features such as atypical pigment networks, globules, and blue-white areas, critically depends on the accuracy of border detection.

A number of methods have been developed for preprocessing dermoscopy images. Most of these focused on the removal of artifacts such as hairs and bubbles. Of the studies dealing with hair removal, Lee *et al.* [10] approached the problem using mathematical morphology. Fleming *et al.* [5] applied curvilinear structure detection with various constraints followed by gap filling. A method for bubble removal was introduced in [5], where the authors utilized a morphological top-hat operator followed by a radial search procedure.

## 2   Materials and Methods

### 2.1   Black Frame Removal

Dermoscopy images often contain black frames that are introduced during the digitization process. These need to be removed because they might interfere with the subsequent lesion localization procedure. In order to determine the darkness of a pixel with (R, G, B) coordinates, the lightness component of the HSL color space is utilized. A pixel is considered to be black if its lightness value is less than 20. Using this criterion, the image is scanned row-by-row starting from the top. A particular row is labeled as part of the black frame if it contains 60% black pixels. The top-to-bottom scan terminates when a row that contains less than the threshold percentage of pixels is encountered. The same scanning procedure is repeated for the other three main directions.

### 2.2   Approximate Lesion Localization

Although dermoscopy images can be quite large, the actual lesion often occupies a relatively small area. Therefore, if we can determine the approximate location of the lesion, the border detection algorithm can focus on this region rather than the whole image. An accurate bounding box (the smallest axis-aligned rectangular box that encloses the lesion) might be useful for various reasons: (i) it provides an estimate of the lesion size (certain image segmentation algorithms such as region growing and morphological flooding can use the size of the region as a termination criterion), (ii) it might improve the border detection accuracy since the procedure is focused on a region that is guaranteed to contain the lesion, (iii) it speeds up the border detection since the procedure is performed on a region that is often smaller than the whole image, (iv) its surrounding might be utilized in the estimation of the background skin color, which is useful for various operations including the elimination of spurious regions that are discovered during the border detection procedure [9] and the extraction of dermoscopic features such as blotches [11] and blue-white areas [12].

In many dermoscopic images, the lesion can be roughly separated from the background skin using a grayscale thresholding method applied to the blue channel [7,8]. While there are a number of thresholding methods that perform well in general, the effectiveness of a method strongly depends on the statistical characteristics of the image [13]. Fig. 1 illustrates this phenomenon[1]. Here, methods 1(d), 1(e), and 1(g) perform quite well. In contrast, methods 1(c) and 1(h) underestimate the optimal threshold, whereas method 1(f) overestimates the optimal threshold. Although method 1(c) is the most popular thresholding algorithm in the literature, for this particular image, it performs the second worst.

A possible approach to overcome this problem is to fuse the results provided by an ensemble of thresholding algorithms. In this way, it is possible to exploit the peculiarities of the participating thresholding algorithms synergistically, thus arriving at more robust final decisions than is possible with a single thresholding algorithm. We note that the goal of the fusion is not to outperform the individual thresholding algorithms, but to obtain accuracies comparable to that of the best thresholding algorithm independently of the image characteristics. In this study, we used the threshold fusion method proposed by Melgani [13], which we describe briefly in the following.

Let $X = \{x_{mn} : m = 0, 1, \ldots, M - 1, \ n = 0, 1, \ldots, N - 1\}$ be the original scalar $M \times N$ image with $L$ possible gray levels ($x_{mn} \in \{0, 1, \ldots, L - 1\}$) and $Y = \{y_{mn} : m = 0, 1, \ldots, M - 1, \ n = 0, 1, \ldots, N - 1\}$ be the binary output of the threshold fusion. Consider an ensemble of $P$ thresholding algorithms. Let $T_i$ and $A_i$ ($i = 1, 2, \ldots, P$) be the threshold value and the output binary image associated with the i-th algorithm of the ensemble, respectively. Within a Markov Random Field (MRF) framework the fusion problem can be formulated as an energy minimization task. Accordingly, the local energy function $U_{mn}$ to be minimized for the pixel $(m, n)$ can be written as follows:

$$U_{mn} = \beta_{SP} \cdot U_{SP}\left[y_{mn}, Y^S(m, n)\right] + \sum_{i=1}^{P} \beta_i \cdot U_{II}\left[y_{mn}, A_i^S(m, n)\right] \qquad (1)$$

where $S$ is a predefined neighborhood system associated with pixel $(m, n)$, $U_{SP}(\cdot)$ and $U_{II}(\cdot)$ refer to the spatial and inter-image energy functions, respectively, whereas $\beta_{SP}$ and $\beta_i$ ($i = 1, 2, \ldots, P$) represent the spatial and inter-image parameters, respectively. The spatial energy function can be expressed as:

$$U_{SP}\left[y_{mn}, Y^S(m, n)\right] = - \sum_{y_{pq} \in Y^S(m,n)} I\left(y_{mn}, y_{pq}\right) \qquad (2)$$

---

[1] The frame of this image is left intact for visualization purposes.

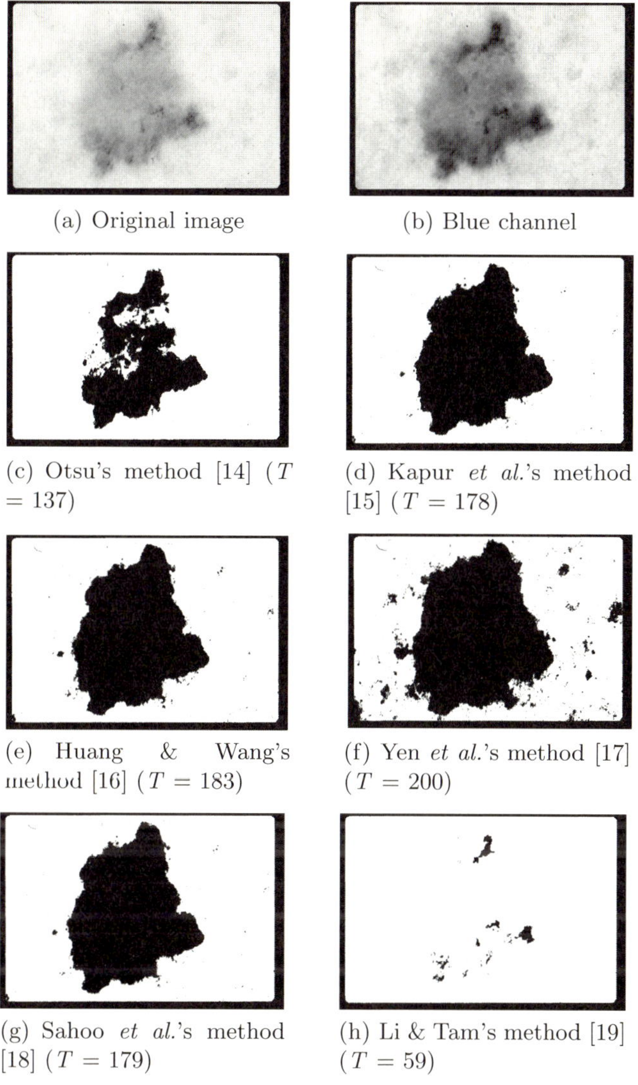

(a) Original image

(b) Blue channel

(c) Otsu's method [14] ($T = 137$)

(d) Kapur *et al.*'s method [15] ($T = 178$)

(e) Huang & Wang's method [16] ($T = 183$)

(f) Yen *et al.*'s method [17] ($T = 200$)

(g) Sahoo *et al.*'s method [18] ($T = 179$)

(h) Li & Tam's method [19] ($T = 59$)

**Fig. 1.** Comparison of various thresholding methods ($T$: threshold)

where $I(.,.)$ is the indicator function defined as:

$$I(y_{mn}, y_{pq}) = \begin{cases} 1 & \text{if } y_{mn} = y_{pq} \\ 0 & \text{otherwise} \end{cases} \tag{3}$$

The inter-image energy function is defined as:

$$U_{II}\left[y_{mn}, A_i^S(m,n)\right] = - \sum_{A_i(p,q) \in A_i^S(m,n)} \alpha^i(x_{pq}) \cdot I\left[y_{mn}, A_i(p,q)\right] \tag{4}$$

where $\alpha^i(\cdot)$ is a weight function given by:

$$\alpha^i(x_{mn}) = 1 - \exp\left(-\gamma\,|x_{mn} - T_i|\right) \tag{5}$$

This function controls the effect of unreliable decisions at the pixel level that can be incurred by the thresholding algorithms. At the global (image) level decisions are weighed by the inter-image parameters $\beta_i$ $(i = 1, 2, \ldots, P)$, which are computed as follows:

$$\beta_i = \exp\left(-\gamma\,|\bar{T} - T_i|\right) \tag{6}$$

where $\bar{T}$ is the average threshold value:

$$\bar{T} = \frac{1}{P}\sum_{i=1}^{P} T_i \tag{7}$$

The MRF fusion strategy proposed in [13] is as follows:

1. Apply each thresholding algorithm of the ensemble to the image $X$ to generate the set of thresholded images $A_i$ $(i = 1, 2, \ldots, P)$
2. Initialize $Y$ by minimizing for each pixel $(m, n)$ the local energy function $U_{mn}$ defined in Eq. 1 without the spatial energy term i.e., by setting $\beta_{SP} = 0$.
3. Update $Y$ by minimizing for each pixel $(m, n)$ the local energy function $U_{mn}$ defined in Eq. 1 including the spatial energy term i.e., by setting $\beta_{SP} \neq 0$.
4. Repeat step 3 $K_{max}$ times or until the number of different labels in $Y$ computed over the last two iterations becomes very small.

In our preliminary experiments, we observed that, besides being computationally demanding, the iterative part (step 3) of the fusion algorithm makes only marginal contribution to the quality of the results. Therefore, in this study, we considered only the first two steps. The $\gamma$ parameter was set to the recommended value of 0.1 [13]. For computational reasons, $\alpha$ (Eq. 5) and $\beta$ (Eq. 6) values were precalculated and the neighborhood system $S$ was chosen as a $3 \times 3$ square window.

The most important performance factor in the fusion algorithm seems to be the choice of the thresholding algorithms. We considered six popular thresholding algorithms to construct the ensemble: Otsu's [14], Kapur et al.'s [15], Huang & Wang's [16], Yen et al.'s [17] , Sahoo et al.'s [18], and Li & Tam's [19] methods. In order to determine the best combination, we evaluated ensembles with 3 (20 ensembles), 4 (15 ensembles), 5 (6 ensembles), and 6 (1 ensemble) methods.

Fig. 2 shows the output of two particular ensembles: Otsu-Kapur-Huang and Huang-Yen-Sahoo-Li. Note that both ensembles contain at least one method that either underestimates or overestimates the optimal threshold. It can be seen that both ensembles perform equally well, which demonstrates that failures in pathological cases might be prevented using a proper fusion strategy.

Fig. 3(a) shows the result of the ensemble Otsu-Kapur-Huang-Sahoo. Here, the blue bounding box encloses the dermatologist determined border (see

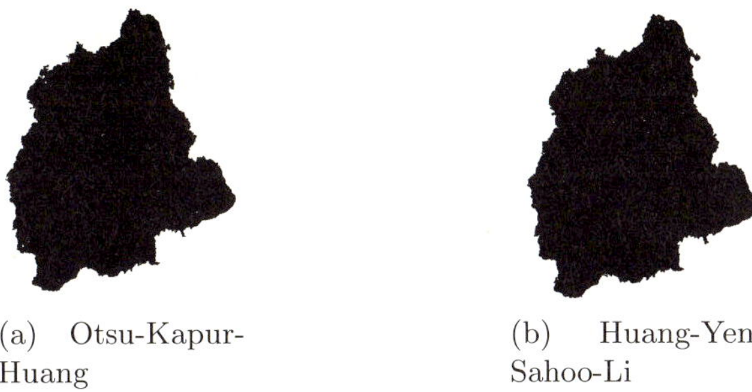

(a)   Otsu-Kapur-Huang

(b)   Huang-Yen-Sahoo-Li

**Fig. 2.** Comparison of two threshold ensembles

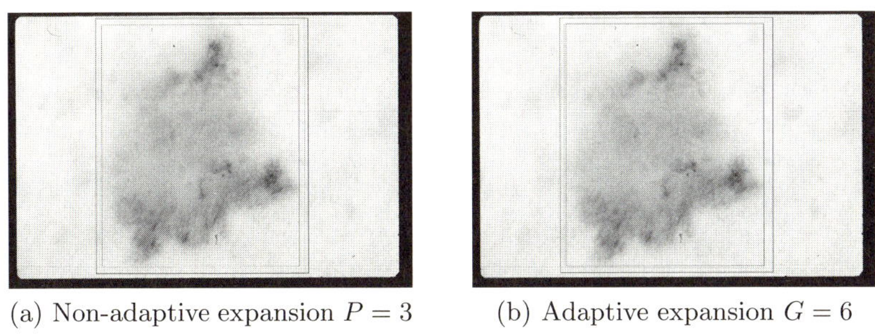

(a) Non-adaptive expansion $P = 3$

(b) Adaptive expansion $G = 6$

**Fig. 3.** Comparison of the bounding box expansion methods

Section 3), whereas the red one encloses the binary output of the threshold fusion. It can be seen that the red box is completely contained inside the blue box. This was observed in many cases because the automated thresholding methods tend to find the sharpest pigment change, whereas the dermatologists choose the outmost detectable pigment. We experimented with two different expansion methods to solve this problem. The first one involves expanding the automatic box by $P\%$ in four main directions. In other words, an automatic box of size $M_B \times N_B$ is expanded by $M_B \cdot P/100$ pixels in the West and East directions and $N_B \cdot P/100$ pixels in the North and South directions. The second one involves incrementing the threshold values obtained by each algorithm in the ensemble by $G$ gray levels. In the rest of this article, we will refer to these expansion methods as non-adaptive and adaptive, respectively. Figs. 3(a) and 3(b) show the results of these methods with the expanded box shown in green. In this particular example, the non-adaptive method performs better in bringing the automatic box closer to the manual one. In order to determine the optimal expansion amounts we evaluated $P \in \{2, 4, 6, 8\}$ and $G \in \{4, 6, 8, 10\}$.

## 3   Results and Discussion

The proposed method was tested on a set of 428 dermoscopy images obtained from the EDRA Interactive Atlas of Dermoscopy [2] and the Keio University

Hospital. An experienced dermatologist determined the manual borders. The bounding box error was quantified using the following formula [20]:

$$\varepsilon = \frac{\text{Area}(AutomaticBox \oplus ManualBox)}{\text{Area}(ManualBox)} \cdot 100 \tag{8}$$

where $AutomaticBox$ is the binary image obtained by filling the bounding box of the fusion output, $ManualBox$ is the binary image obtained by filling the bounding box of the dermatologist-determined border, $\oplus$ is the exclusive-OR operation, which essentially determines the pixels for which the $AutomaticBox$ and $ManualBox$ disagree, and Area($I$) denotes the number of pixels in the binary image $I$.

We determined the optimal parameter combination for the presented approximate bounding box computation method as follows. First, the black frame removal procedure described in Section 2.1 is performed on each image in the data set. The lesion bounding box is then computed using the fusion method described in Section 2.2 with one of the 42 ensembles. Finally, the approximate bounding box is expanded using either the non-adaptive method with $P \in \{2, 4, 6, 8\}$ or the adaptive method with $G \in \{4, 6, 8, 10\}$. Table 1 shows various statistics associated with the four most accurate ensembles for each expansion method. The last two columns refer to the mean and standard deviation values, respectively for the percentage image size reduction, i.e. $\frac{\text{Area}(AutomaticBox)}{M \cdot N} \cdot 100$, provided by the bounding box computation. The following observations are in order: (i) both expansion methods reduce the mean bounding box error, (ii) the lowest mean errors were obtained using the ensemble Otsu-Kapur-Huang-Sahoo, (iii) the non-adaptive expansion method was more effective than the adaptive one, (iv) the computation of the bounding box reduced the original image size by about 260%.

The adaptive method was less effective than the non-adaptive one probably because the former often expands the approximate box by unpredictable amounts: either too little (as in Fig. 3(b)) or too much depending on the shape of the histogram and the value of the $G$ parameter. In contrast, the latter always expands the approximate box by an amount specified by the $P$ parameter.

**Table 1.** Ensemble statistics ($\mu$: mean, $\sigma$: std. dev., $\varepsilon_i$: initial box error, $\varepsilon_x$: expanded box error)

| Ensemble | Expansion Method | $\mu_{\varepsilon_i}$ | $\sigma_{\varepsilon_i}$ | $\mu_{\varepsilon_x}$ | $\sigma_{\varepsilon_x}$ | $\mu_s$ | $\sigma_s$ |
|---|---|---|---|---|---|---|---|
| Otsu-Kapur-Huang-Sahoo | Non-adaptive ($P = 2$) | 10.25 | 8.10 | 7.58 | 8.13 | 268.31 | 185.64 |
| Otsu-Huang-Yen-Li | Non-adaptive ($P = 4$) | 11.92 | 7.59 | 7.89 | 6.30 | 260.55 | 183.85 |
| Otsu-Huang-Sahoo-Li | Non-adaptive ($P = 4$) | 11.98 | 7.62 | 7.90 | 6.20 | 260.95 | 184.14 |
| Otsu-Huang-Sahoo | Non-adaptive ($P = 2$) | 11.14 | 7.17 | 7.91 | 6.71 | 273.84 | 195.69 |
| Otsu-Kapur-Huang-Sahoo | Adaptive ($G = 6$) | 10.25 | 8.10 | 9.27 | 7.68 | 276.92 | 192.14 |
| Kapur-Huang-Sahoo-Li | Adaptive ($G = 8$) | 10.98 | 7.66 | 9.43 | 7.69 | 279.03 | 194.42 |
| Otsu-Kapur-Huang-Sahoo | Adaptive ($G = 4$) | 10.25 | 8.10 | 9.44 | 7.56 | 279.98 | 194.26 |
| Kapur-Huang-Sahoo-Li | Adaptive ($G = 6$) | 10.98 | 7.66 | 9.67 | 7.58 | 282.09 | 196.58 |

**Table 2.** Individual statistics ($\mu$: mean, $\sigma$: std. dev., $\varepsilon_i$: initial box error, $\varepsilon_x$: expanded box error)

| Thresholding Method | Expansion Method | $\mu_{\varepsilon_i}$ | $\sigma_{\varepsilon_i}$ | $\mu_{\varepsilon_x}$ | $\sigma_{\varepsilon_x}$ | $\mu_s$ | $\sigma_s$ |
|---|---|---|---|---|---|---|---|
| Otsu | Non-adaptive ($P = 2$) | 12.05 | 9.10 | 9.00 | 8.95 | 275.07 | 199.28 |
| Kapur | Non-adaptive ($P = 2$) | 12.87 | 16.86 | 12.68 | 17.56 | 261.95 | 197.94 |
| Huang | Non-adaptive ($P = 2$) | 20.31 | 67.97 | 17.17 | 69.76 | 269.59 | 190.09 |
| Yen | Non-adaptive ($P = 2$) | 14.98 | 27.12 | 15.74 | 27.74 | 255.61 | 250.53 |
| Sahoo | Non-adaptive ($P = 2$) | 13.43 | 24.60 | 13.37 | 25.19 | 254.43 | 184.36 |
| Li | Non-adaptive ($P = 2$) | 15.12 | 9.65 | 11.06 | 9.07 | 293.54 | 215.80 |
| Otsu | Non-adaptive ($P = 4$) | 12.05 | 9.10 | 9.10 | 9.14 | 256.86 | 182.82 |
| Kapur | Non-adaptive ($P = 4$) | 12.87 | 16.86 | 15.54 | 18.61 | 245.36 | 183.78 |
| Huang | Non-adaptive ($P = 4$) | 20.31 | 67.97 | 16.83 | 70.69 | 251.99 | 174.44 |
| Yen | Non-adaptive ($P = 4$) | 14.98 | 27.12 | 19.32 | 28.49 | 239.46 | 230.91 |
| Sahoo | Non-adaptive ($P = 4$) | 13.43 | 24.60 | 16.43 | 25.98 | 238.32 | 170.38 |
| Li | Non-adaptive ($P = 4$) | 15.12 | 9.65 | 9.41 | 7.99 | 273.93 | 198.61 |

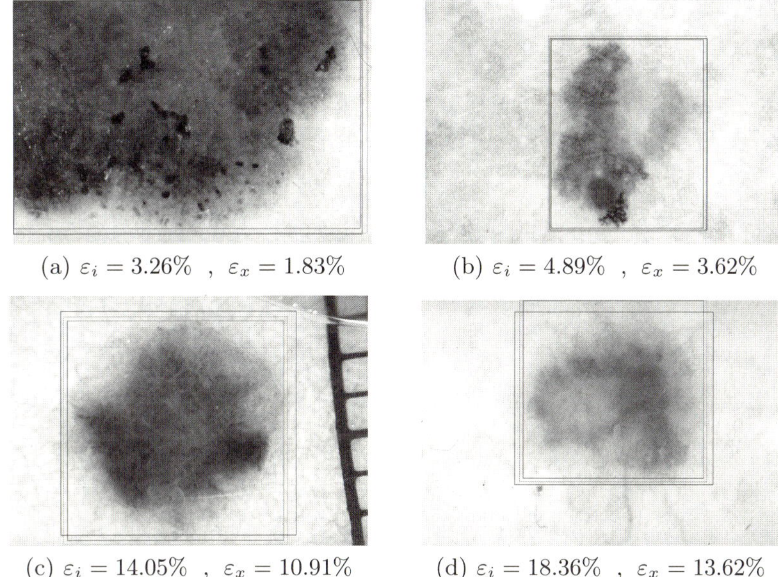

(a) $\varepsilon_i = 3.26\%$ , $\varepsilon_x = 1.83\%$    (b) $\varepsilon_i = 4.89\%$ , $\varepsilon_x = 3.62\%$

(c) $\varepsilon_i = 14.05\%$ , $\varepsilon_x = 10.91\%$    (d) $\varepsilon_i = 18.36\%$ , $\varepsilon_x = 13.62\%$

**Fig. 4.** Sample results ($\varepsilon_i$: initial box error, $\varepsilon_x$: expanded box error)

Table 2 shows the statistics for the individual thresholding methods. Note that, due to space limitations, we report only the results of the non-adaptive expansion method (as in the ensemble case, the adaptive method has inferior performance). It can be seen that, in most configurations, the individual methods obtain significantly higher mean errors than the best ensemble methods, i.e. the first four rows of Table 1. This is because, as explained in Section 2.2, the individual methods are more prone to catastrophic failures when given pathological input images. The high standard deviation values also support this explanation. Only the performance of Otsu (with $P = 2, 4$) and Li $et$ $al.$'s (with $P = 4$) methods is close to the performance of the ensembles. However, as mentioned in Section 2.2, the goal of fusion is not to outperform the individual thresholding algorithms, but to obtain accuracies comparable to that of the best thresholding algorithm independently of the image characteristics.

Fig. 4 shows sample bounding box computation results obtained using the ensemble Otsu-Kapur-Huang-Sahoo with $P = 2$. It can be seen that the presented method determines an accurate bounding box even for lesions with fuzzy borders.

## 4  Conclusions

In this paper, an automated method for approximate lesion localization in dermoscopy images is presented. The method is comprised of three main phases: black frame removal, initial bounding box computation using an ensemble of thresholding algorithms, and expansion of the initial bounding box. The execution time of the method is about $0.15$ seconds for a typical image of size $768 \times 512$ pixels on an Intel Pentium D 2.66Ghz computer.

The presented method may not perform well on images with significant amount of hair or bubbles since these elements alter the histogram, which in turn results in biased threshold computations. Future work will be directed towards testing the utility of this method in a border detection study. The implementation of the threshold fusion method will be made publicly available as part of the Fourier image processing and analysis library, which can be downloaded from http://sourceforge.net/projects/fourier-ipal

## References


1. Jemal, A., Siegel, R., Ward, E., et al.: Cancer Statistics. CA: A Cancer Journal for Clinicians 2008 58(2), 71–96 (2008)
2. Argenziano, G., Soyer, H.P., De Giorgi, V., et al.: Dermoscopy: A Tutorial. EDRA Medical Publishing & New Media, Milan (2002)
3. Steiner, K., Binder, M., Schemper, M., et al.: Statistical Evaluation of Epiluminescence Dermoscopy Criteria for Melanocytic Pigmented Lesions. Journal of American Academy of Dermatology 29(4), 581–588 (1993)
4. Binder, M., Schwarz, M., Winkler, A., et al.: Epiluminescence Microscopy. A Useful Tool for the Diagnosis of Pigmented Skin Lesions for Formally Trained Dermatologists. Archives of Dermatology 131(3), 286–291 (1995)
5. Fleming, M.G., Steger, C., Zhang, J., et al.: Techniques for a Structural Analysis of Dermatoscopic Imagery. Computerized Medical Imaging and Graphics 22(5), 375–389 (1998)
6. Celebi, M.E., Kingravi, H.A., Uddin, B., et al.: A Methodological Approach to the Classification of Dermoscopy Images. Computerized Medical Imaging and Graphics 31(6), 362–373 (2007)

7. Iyatomi, H., Oka, H., Saito, M., et al.: Quantitative Assessment of Tumor Extraction from Dermoscopy Images and Evaluation of Computer-based Extraction Methods for Automatic Melanoma Diagnostic System. Melanoma Research 16(2), 183–190 (2006)
8. Celebi, M.E., Aslandogan, Y.A., Stoecker, W.V., et al.: Unsupervised Border Detection in Dermoscopy Images. Skin Research and Technology 13(4), 454–462 (2007)
9. Celebi, M.E., Kingravi, H.A., Iyatomi, H., et al.: Border Detection in Dermoscopy Images Using Statistical Region Merging. Skin Research and Technology 14(3), 347–353 (2008)
10. Lee, T.K., Ng, V., Gallagher, R., et al.: Dullrazor: A Software Approach to Hair Removal from Images. Computers in Biology and Medicine 27(6), 533–543 (1997)
11. Stoecker, W.V., Gupta, K., Stanley, R.J., et al.: Detection of Asymmetric Blotches in Dermoscopy Images of Malignant Melanoma Using Relative Color. Skin Research and Technology 11(3), 179–184 (2005)
12. Celebi, M.E., Iyatomi, H., Stoecker, W.V., et al.: Automatic Detection of Blue-White Veil and Related Structures in Dermoscopy Images. Computerized Medical Imaging and Graphics 32(8) (to appear, 2008)
13. Melgani, F.: Robust Image Binarization with Ensembles of Thresholding Algorithms. Journal of Electronic Imaging 15(2), 023010, 11 pages (2006)
14. Otsu, N.: A Threshold Selection Method from Gray Level Histograms. IEEE Trans. on Systems, Man and Cybernetics 9(1), 62–66 (1979)
15. Kapur, J.N., Sahoo, P.K., Wong, A.K.C.: A New Method for Gray-Level Picture Thresholding Using the Entropy of the Histogram. Graphical Models and Image Processing 29(3), 273–285 (1985)
16. Huang, L.-K., Wang, M.-J.J.: Image Thresholding by Minimizing the Measures of Fuzziness. Pattern Recognition 28(1), 41–51 (1995)
17. Yen, J.C., Chang, F.J., Chang, S.: A New Criterion for Automatic Multilevel Thresholding. IEEE Trans. on Image Processing 4(3), 370–378 (1995)
18. Sahoo, P.K., Wilkins, C., Yeager, J.: Threshold Selection Using Renyi's Entropy. Pattern Recognition 30(1), 71–84 (1997)
19. Li, C.H., Tam, P.K.S.: An Iterative Algorithm for Minimum Cross Entropy Thresholding. Pattern Recognition Letters 18(8), 771–776 (1998)
20. Hance, G.A., Umbaugh, S.E., Moss, R.H., Stoecker, W.V.: Unsupervised Color Image Segmentation with Application to Skin Tumor Borders. IEEE Engineering in Medicine and Biology 15(1), 104–111 (1996)

# Active Contour Tracking of Moving Objects Using Edge Flows and Ant Colony Optimization in Video Sequences


Dong-Xian Lai[1], Yuan-Hsiang Chang[2], and Zhi-He Zhong[1]

[1,2] Dept.of Information & Computer Engineering, Chung Yuan Christian Univ., 200,Chung Pei Rd., Jhingli,32023 Taiwan, R.O.C.
`{egria7314,specr0000}@hotmail.com,`
`changyh@ice.cycu.edu.tw`



**Abstract.** Object segmentation and tracking are important techniques in video applications. In this paper, we present a novel system for active contour tracking of moving objects in video sequences. Our method includes preprocessing to identify an initial object contour, and object contour segmentation to refine the contour of the moving object. The edge flows and ant colony optimization are incorporated to improve the efficiency during system convergence. Experimental results demonstrated that our system has achieved the automatic segmentation accuracy of < 1 pixel on average as compared with manual segmentation results. In summary, our system is particularly useful in segmenting and tracking a moving object without constructing a background model for a video scene. Ultimately, our system could be used in object-based video coding or other analysis such as behavior analysis in video surveillance systems.

**Keywords:** Active contour model, Ant colony optimization, Edge flow, Object tracking.


## 1 Introduction

Object contour segmentation and tracking in video sequences are important parts of video applications and can be used in video compression, motion analysis, pose estimation, or behavior analysis, etc. [1-6] For examples, in object-based video coding, video object contour segmentation can be used to extract foreground objects while eliminating redundant background information for storage, thus achieving a high compression ratio. In video surveillance systems, video object tracking can be used as a preprocessing for pose estimation or behavior analysis in video sequences.

Among the past researches, techniques for the segmentation of object contours are necessary for further analysis [7-10]. Object contour segmentation is generally achieved using techniques of single image segmentation. For examples, Comaniciu and Meer [7] proposed a general nonparametric technique for the analysis of a complex multimodal feature space and the mean-shift clustering was used to extract object contours. Shi and Malik [8] treated object segmentation as a graph partitioning problem and proposed a normalized cut criterion to measure both the total dissimilarity


T. Wada, F. Huang, and S. Lin (Eds.): PSIVT 2009, LNCS 5414, pp. 1104–1116, 2009.

between the different groups as well as the total similarity within the group. Xu and Ahuja [9] presented a normalized cuts based algorithm to track object contour, and the algorithm did not require any priori global shape model for tracking objects with deformable shapes and appearances. Kass *et al.* [10] proposed the use of snakes, which are energy-minimizing splines guided by external constraint forces and influenced by image forces, for the object contour segmentation. In Kass's approach, the choice of initial contour is important. If gradient-based approach is used, the initial contour must be outside and shrunk to the object contour. If region-based approach is used, the initial contour can be inside or outside of the object contour, and expanded or shrunk to the object contour.

In recent years, various approaches to video object tracking have been proposed. A typical approach is to construct a background model such that the model can be used for foreground object extraction in a video scene. For examples, Stauffer and Grimson [11] proposed an approach to model each pixel as a mixture of Gaussians and to evaluate the adaptive Gaussian model which is most likely to be the background. They classified the pixel based on whether the Gaussian distribution is considered as part of the background model and updated the model on-line. Elgammal *et al.* [12] proposed a nonparametric kernel density estimation to construct statistical representations for scene background and foreground region. Although these approaches can be applied in video object tracking, they are generally limited for scenes with small foreground objects and the background model must be updated constantly.

The objective of this research is aimed to develop a novel system for active contour tracking of moving objects using edge flows and ant colony optimization in video sequences. Our approach is designed in an attempt to segment and track the foreground object in video sequences without constructing and updating a background model. In particular, this system is effective when tracking non-rigid objects (e.g. human) in a scene where the complete background can not be acquired from the whole video sequence.

Section 2 presents the system framework and related methodology. Our system module includes preprocessing and object contour segmentation. Section 3 explains our experimental environment, and results. Section 4 presents conclusion of our approach and discusses potential video applications.


## 2  Method

Our system is designed for the analysis of video sequences that are limited to the following constraints: (1) the surrounding background is static, therefore not a moving background; (2) the camera position is fixed and static (i.e., no panning, tilting, or zooming, etc.); and (3) the boundary between the foreground object and its background is well-defined.

Fig. 1 shows a simplified flow chart in our system framework for active contour tracking of moving objects in video sequences. The system framework can be divided into two parts: (1) preprocessing; and (2) object contour segmentation. The preprocessing includes: region growing, motion image detection, background edge removal, and motion boundary extraction (Fig. 2). The object contour segmentation includes: energy calculation, search space construction, pheromone definition, transition

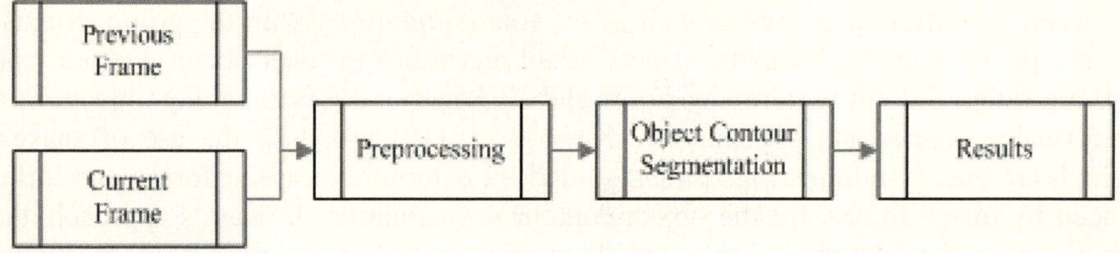

**Fig. 1.** A simplified flow chart in our system framework for active contour tracking of moving objects in video sequences

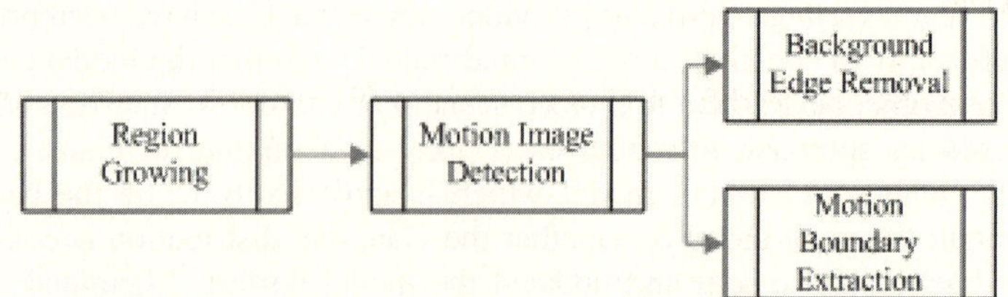

**Fig. 2.** A simplified flow chart of the preprocessing in our system

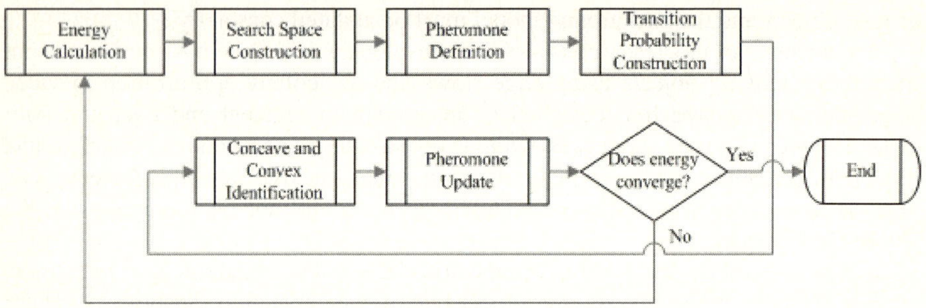

**Fig. 3.** A simplified flow chart of the object contour segmentation in our system

probability construction, concave and convex identification, pheromone update, and energy convergence criterion (Fig. 3).

## 2.1  Preprocessing

The objective of the preprocessing is to define an initial object contour outside the ideal contour of the moving object in the current frame. The initial object contour is obtained as a combination of the object contour in the previous frame and the region where the object motion occurs in the current frame.

### 2.1.1  Region Growing

In this step, our goal is to find a closed region as the location of the moving object, using the object contour from the previous frame. The processes include: (1) identify the geometric center of the object contour from the previous frame; and (2) use the

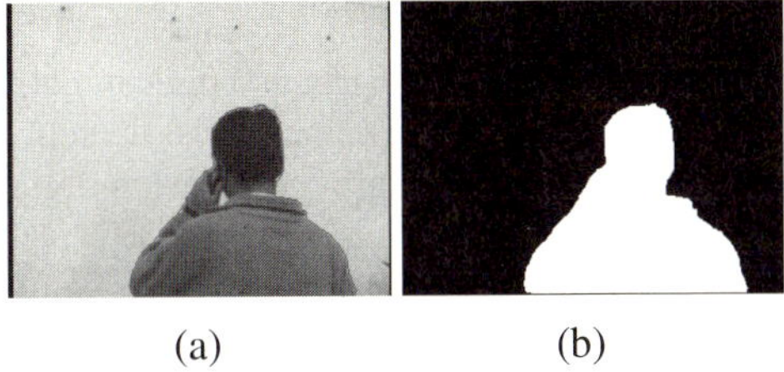

(a)                          (b)

**Fig. 4.** An example of the region growing, where (a) contains the contour and the geometric center in the 28$^{th}$ frame from Frank.avi shown in 'red'; and (b) is the resulting image after region growing

geometric center as the seed for region growing to fill inside the contour. An example of the region growing is shown in Fig. 4.

### 2.1.2 Motion Image Detection

In this step, our goal is to detect motion changes near the object contour and construct a motion image using the difference of the previous frame at time $t - 1$ and the current frame at time $t$.

Let $I(x, y, t)$ be the gray-level of the image coordinate $(x, y)$ in the frame at time $t$, $t = 1,\ldots, n$, where $n$ is the total number of frames in a video sequence. Then, the difference of frames can be defined by:

$$df(x, y, t) = \begin{cases} 1 & if \ |I(x, y, t) - I(x, y, t-1)| \geq T_d \\ 0 & otherwise \end{cases} \tag{1}$$

where $T_d$ is a threshold. Further, the motion image containing the moving object can be defined by:

$$M(x, y, t) = \begin{cases} 1 & if \ df(x, y, t) = 1 \cup gr(x, y, t-1) = 1 \\ 0 & otherwise \end{cases} \tag{2}$$

where $gr(x, y, t - 1)$ is the previous frame after region growing (1 means foreground, 0 means background). Fig. 5 shows an example of the motion image detection.

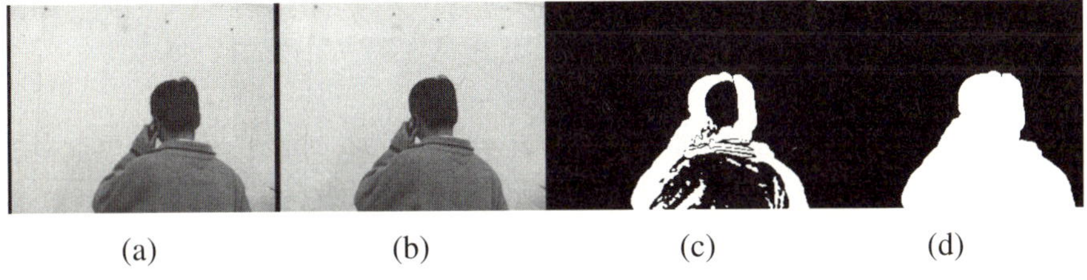

(a)                    (b)                    (c)                    (d)

**Fig. 5.** An example of the motion image detection, where (a) is the original 28$^{th}$ frame from Frank.avi; (b) is the original 29$^{th}$ frame from Frank.avi; (c) is frame difference between 28th and 29th frame after thresholding; and (d) is the resulting image containing the moving object

### 2.1.3  Background Edge Removal

In this step, our goal is to eliminate the background edges in current frame. Let $I_{edge}(x, y, t)$ be the resulting image of applying the Canny edge detection [13] to the original image $I(x, y, t)$. Then, we remove the background edges and generate the foreground edge image by:

$$\hat{I}_{edge}(x, y, t) = \begin{cases} I_{edge}(x, y, t) & \text{if } M(x, y, t) = 1 \\ 0 & \text{if } M(x, y, t) = 0 \end{cases} \tag{3}$$

where $M(x, y, t)$ is used as a mask. This resulting image is later used in the object contour segmentation as the ideal object contour. An example of the background edge removal is shown in Fig .6.

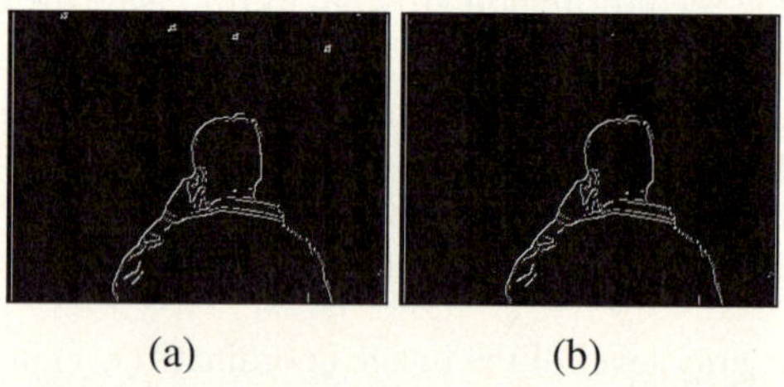

(a)                                    (b)

**Fig. 6.** An example of the background edge removal, where (a) is the resulting image edge after Canny edge detection in the $29^{th}$ frame in Frank.avi and (b) is the same image with background edges removed

### 2.1.4  Motion Boundary Extraction

This step attempts to extract a motion boundary of the moving object by:

$$\hat{I}(x, y, t) = M(x, y, t) - M(x, y, t) \ominus S. \tag{4}$$

where $S$ is a structuring element and $\ominus$ is the morphological erosion [14]. The resulting image after the motion boundary extraction contains the initial object contour that is slightly larger than the ideal object contour in the current frame. Fig.7 shows an example of the motion boundary extraction.

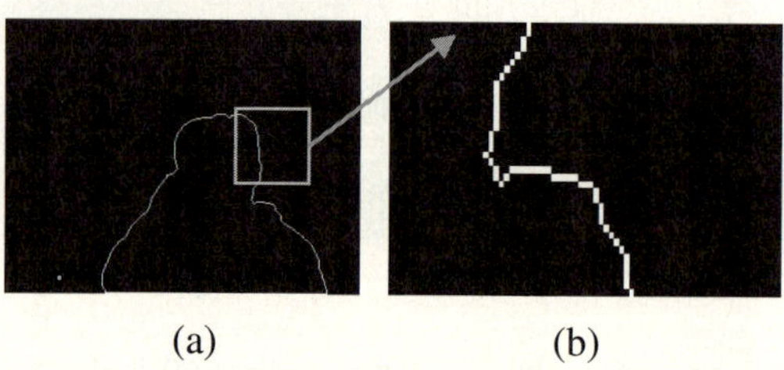

(a)                                    (b)

**Fig. 7.** An example of motion boundary extraction, where (a) is the motion boundary of $29^{th}$ frame in Frank.avi; and (b) shows part of the motion boundary in (a)

## 2.2  Object Contour Segmentation

The purpose of the object contour segmentation is to obtain a well-defined contour for the moving object in each frame. The processes start using the initial object contour in the image $\hat{I}(x, y, t)$ after preprocessing as an active contour model, and iteratively refine the model by the ant colony optimization (ACO) algorithm [15,16]. Our approaches incorporate not only the ACO algorithm but also the concept of edge flows [17], in an attempt to improve the efficiency during contour convergence.

### 2.2.1  Energy Calculation

The object contour is iteratively refined by minimizing an energy function. Using the active contour models, the contour curve is defined parametrically as

$$v(s) = \left[ x(s), y(s) \right].$$ (5)

where $x(s)$ and $y(s)$ are $x$, $y$ coordinates along object contour, and $s \in [0, 1]$. The energy of the object contour can be defined by:

$$E_{snake} = \int_0^1 E_{int}(v(s)) + E_{image}(v(s))ds.$$ (6)

where $E_{int}$ represents the internal energy of object contour due to bending, $E_{image}$ denotes image force. The internal object contour energy can be written as

$$E_{int} = w_{elas} \left| \frac{dv}{ds} \right|^2 + w_{stiff} \left| \frac{d^2 v}{ds^2} \right|^2.$$ (7)

where $w_{elas}$ and $w_{stiff}$ specify the elasticity and stiffness. In addition, the image force $E_{image}$ can defined by:

$$E_{image} = g(x, y) = 255 - \nabla I_{block}.$$ (8)

where $g$ is a function and attracts the object contour with large image gradients, and $\nabla I_{block}$ is obtained from the Canny gradient image and represent a maximum gradient value in a 3×3 block at current pixel $(x, y)$. Our goal is to search a contour $\Gamma$ that minimizes the energy function such that:

$$\Gamma = \arg \min_{s \in (0,1)} E_{snake}(v(s)).$$ (9)

### 2.2.2  Search Space Construction

In ACO algorithm, we construct a search space for the ant to find the next possible pixel on the object contour. To improve the efficiency of ACO algorithm, the concept of edge flows is incorporated in the selection of the search space and the processes can be described as follows:

Step 1:  Randomly place an ant on the current object contour.
Step 2:  Acquire the next contour pixel and compute its edge flow direction.

Step 3:  Select a number of candidate pixels along the edge flow direction as the search space for the ant to explore.

Step 4:  Check if the candidate pixels are close to the ideal object contour defined in $\hat{I}_{edge}(x, y, t)$.

Step 5:  If yes, the algorithm terminates. If not, search for all eight directions and re-select the candidate pixels along the direction closest to the ideal object contour.

The use of edge flow is originally proposed by Ma and Manjunath [17]. The direction of edge flow is computed by:

$$\theta(x, y, t) = \arg\max_{\theta} \left\{ \sum_{\theta \le \theta' < \theta + \pi} P(x, y, t, \theta') \right\}. \tag{10}$$

where $P(x, y, t, \theta')$ represents the probability of finding edge along orientation $\theta'$ at location $(x, y)$, and is defined by:

$$P(x, y, t, \theta) = \frac{Error(x, y, t, \theta)}{Error(x, y, t, \theta) + Error(x, y, t, \theta + \pi)}. \tag{11}$$

where $Error(x, y, t, \theta)$ represents the prediction error along orientation $\theta$, and is defined by:

$$Error(x, y, t, \theta) = \left| I_\sigma(x + d\cos\theta, y + d\sin\theta, t) - I_\sigma(x, y, t) \right|. \tag{12}$$

where $I_\sigma(x, y, t)$ represents the frame at time $t$ after Gaussian smoothing with $\sigma$ and $d$ is a distance of prediction and proportional of $\sigma$, in the system we assign $d = 4\sigma$.

### 2.2.3  Pheromone Definition

In ACO algorithm, pheromone is defined to help ants communicate with each other, and the concentration of pheromone can influence ants to explore in the next iteration. The initial concentration of pheromone is defined by:

$$\tau_{ij} = \frac{1}{E_{snake}(\Gamma_k)}. \tag{13}$$

where $i$ is the pixel in the image $I(x, y, t)$ and $j$ is its neighboring pixel, and $\Gamma_k$ represents object contour at the $k$-th iteration.

### 2.2.4  Transition Probability Construction

For the ant to explore the next pixel on the object contour, a transition probability is assigned to each candidate pixel in the search space as defined by:

$$P_{ij} = \begin{cases} \dfrac{\tau_{ij}^\alpha \cdot \eta_{ij}^\beta}{\sum\limits_{l \in candidate\ pixels} \tau_{il}^\alpha \cdot \eta_{il}^\beta} & if\ j \in candidate\ pixels \\ \\ 0 & otherwise \end{cases}. \tag{14}$$

where $i$ represents current pixel on object contour, and $j$ represents the next pixel to explore in the search space. $\tau_{ij}$ represents the concentration of pheromone between pixels $i$ and $j$. $\eta_{ij}$ represents the visibility and equal to reciprocal of distance between pixels $i$ and $j$. $\alpha$ represents the weight of pheromone concentration, and $\beta$ represents the weight of visibility.

### 2.2.5  Concave and Convex Processing

To insure that the ant will explore in the direction more closely to the ideal object contour, we incorporate a criterion for three consecutive pixels $v_{i-1}$, $v_i$, and $v_{i+1}$ in two difference situations, namely the concave and the convex cases. Fig. 8 shows the two different cases which can be described as follows:

(a)　Concave case: In this case, we check if the pixels on the straight-line from $v_i$ to $v_{i+1}$ are associated with opposite edge flow directions between two neighboring pixels. If yes, each pixel on the straight-line finds the closest point on the ideal contour and choose the closest one as the next pixel to explore; if not, the straight-line remains unchanged.

(b)　Convex case: In this case, we simply check whether $v_{i+1}$ is close to the ideal object contour. If yes, do nothing; if not, find the pixels close to the ideal object contour along eight possible directions and choose the closest one as the next pixel to explore.

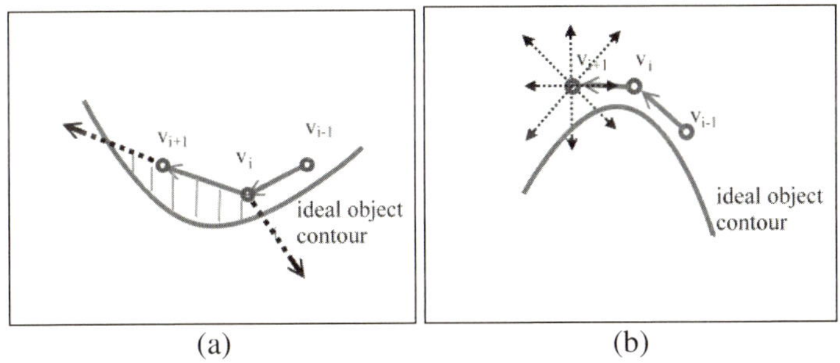

(a) concave case; (b) convex case.

**Fig. 8.** (a) concave case; (b) convex case. The ideal object contour is obtained by edge detection, and $v_{i-1}$, $v_i$, and $v_{i+1}$ are represent three consecutive pixels in the current object contour.

### 2.2.6  Pheromone Update

In this step, we update the concentration of pheromone on the object contour to make the best contour so far more probable to be selected in the next iteration. In our approach, the new object contour with smaller energy is used to replace old contour with larger energy at each iteration. In addition, pheromone on the contour is evaporated and the concentration is decreased. The algorithm can be simply described by:

$$
\begin{array}{l}
\text{For } k = 1 \text{ to } m \text{ do} \\
\quad \text{if } E_{snake}(\Gamma_k) < E_{snake}(\Gamma) \text{ then } \Gamma \leftarrow \Gamma_k \\
\text{For every } edge(i,j) \\
\quad \Delta\tau_{ij} = \begin{cases} \dfrac{1}{E_{snake}(\Gamma)} & if\ (i,j) \in \Gamma \\ 0 & otherwise \end{cases} \\
\quad \tau_{ij} = \tau_{ij} + \Delta\tau_{ij}
\end{array}
$$

where $k$ represents the iteration number, $\Gamma$ represents the best contour so far.

### 2.2.7  Energy Convergence

At each iteration, our system check if the following criterion satisfies:

$$
\frac{\left| E_{snake}(\Gamma_k) - E_{snake}(\Gamma) \right|}{E_{snake}(\Gamma)} < \varepsilon . \tag{15}
$$

where $\varepsilon$ is the convergence threshold. If yes, the system outputs the object contour segmentation result. Otherwise, the system repeats the processes again.

Fig. 9 shows an example of the object contour segmentation for the 29th frame of Frank.avi. The human object is moving from right to left.

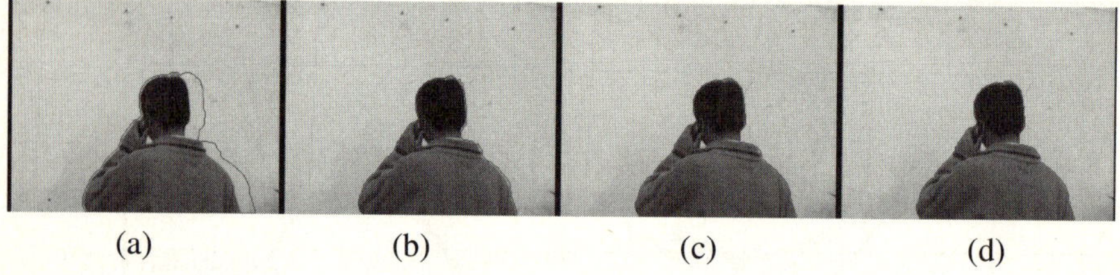

(a)    (b)    (c)    (d)

**Fig. 9.** An example of the object contour segmentation for the 29th frame of Frank.avi, after preprocessing; where (a) is initial object contour after preprocessing; (b) is the object contour after the 1st iteration; (c) is the object contour at the 2nd iteration; and (d) is the resulting object contour after convergence

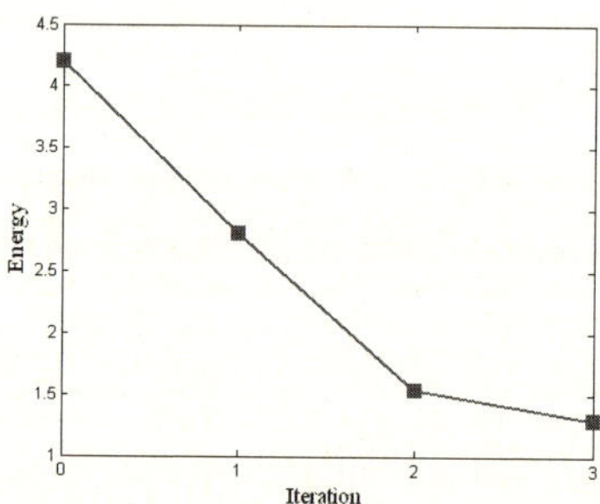


**Fig. 10.** The corresponding energy as computed during system convergence for the object contour segmentation shown in Fig. 9

## 2.3  System Evaluation

To evaluate our system, we quantitatively measure the similarity between two segmentation results, i.e., manually and automatically segmented results, using the root mean square (RMS) error by:

$$e_{RMS} = \sqrt{\frac{1}{N}\sum_{i=1}^{N} d\left(\hat{P}_i, P_i\right)^2}.$$  (16)

where $N$ represents the number of pixels on the manually segmented contour, $\hat{P}_i$ represents the $i$-th pixel on the manually segmented contour, and $P_i$ represents the pixel on the automatically segmented contour that is the closest pixel to the $i$-th pixel in manually segmented contour. $d\left(\hat{P}_i, P_i\right)$ means the Euclidean distance between the two pixels $\hat{P}_i$ and $P_i$. A small RMS error means the two segmented contour are closely matched.

## 3  Results

The video sequences used for our system evaluation are with the two kinds of resolutions: 320×240 pixels or 176×144 pixels in each video frame. All the original video sequences contain 24-bit color video frames, that have been previously processed to gray-level images prior to the object contour segmentation and tracking. Table 1 summaries the system parameters used in our system for active contour tracking of moving objects.

**Table 1.** System parameters used in the active contour tracking of moving object

| Preprocessing | | Object Contour Segmentation | |
|---|---|---|---|
| $T_d$ | 10 | $w_{elas}$ | 1.0 |
| | | $w_{stiff}$ | 1.0 |
| | | $\sigma$ | 1.0 |
| | | $\alpha$ | 1 |
| | | $\beta$ | 1 |
| | | $\varepsilon$ | 0.2 |

Experimental results of the object contour segmentation are shown in Fig. 11 (Frank.avi) and Fig. 12 (Akiyo.avi), respectively. The segmented object contour is highlighted in 'red'. To evaluate our system, the object contour as automatically segmented is compared with the object contour as extracted manually. Because manual segmentation is too tedious, we only compute the RMS error in selected frames. The contour of the moving object is manually extracted using commercially available software (i.e., PhotoImpact) by an observer. Table 2 and 3 show the RMS errors of selected frames between the manual and automatic segmentation results.

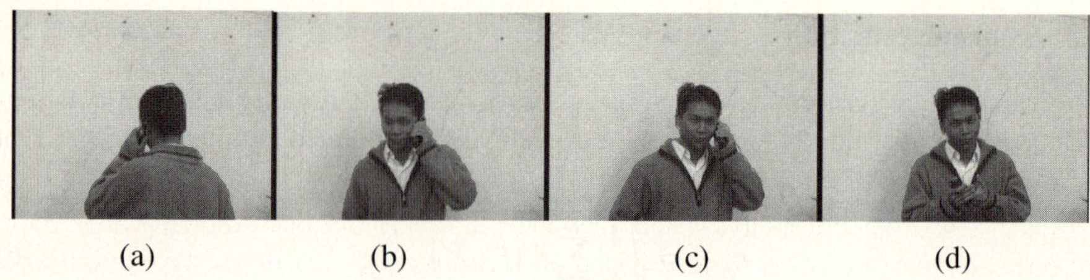

(a)          (b)          (c)          (d)

**Fig. 11.** Segmentation results of object contour in the (a) 29$^{th}$, (b) 39$^{th}$, (c) 49$^{th}$, and (d) 59$^{th}$ frame from Frank.avi, where the segmented object contour is highlighted in 'red'

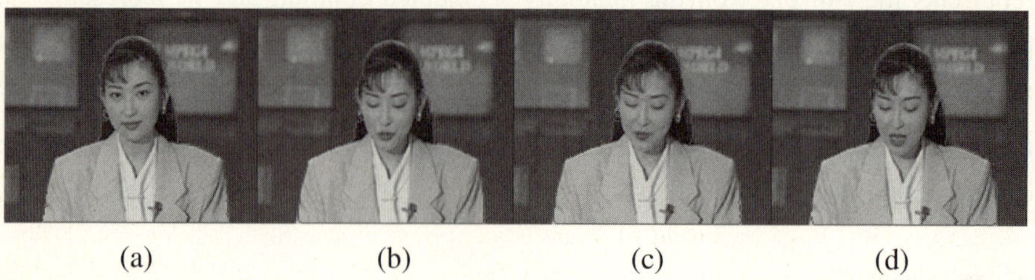

(a)          (b)          (c)          (d)

**Fig. 12.** Segmentation results of object contour in the (a) 2$^{nd}$, (b) 42$^{nd}$, (c) 82$^{nd}$ and (d) 122$^{nd}$ frame from Akiyo.avi, where the segmented object contour is highlighted in 'red'

**Table 2.** The RMS error of selected frames between the manual and automatic segmentation results in Frank.avi. The mean and standard deviation of the RMS error are also shown (Unit: pixels).

| | Frame No. of Frank.avi | | | | Mean | Standard Deviation |
|---|---|---|---|---|---|---|
| | 29$^{th}$ | 39$^{th}$ | 49$^{th}$ | 59$^{th}$ | | |
| $e_{RMS}$ | 1.12 | 0.96 | 0.95 | 0.78 | 0.95 | 0.12 |

**Table 3.** The RMS error of selected frames between the manual and automatic segmentation results in Akiyo.avi

| | Frame No. of Akiyo.avi | | | | Mean | Standard Deviation |
|---|---|---|---|---|---|---|
| | 2$^{th}$ | 42$^{th}$ | 82$^{th}$ | 122$^{th}$ | | |
| $e_{RMS}$ | 0.76 | 1.06 | 0.91 | 0.96 | 0.92 | 0.22 |

## 4   Conclusion

In this paper, we present a novel system for the active contour tracking of moving objects using edge flows and ant colony optimization in video sequences. Our system incorporates the use of edge flows in the ACO algorithm such that the efficiency could be improved. The method is particularly useful in segmenting and tracking a moving object (e.g., human) without constructing a background model for a video scene. Our experimental results demonstrated that our system has achieved the automatic segmentation accuracy of < 1 pixel on average as compared with the manual segmentation results. Ultimately, our system could be used to identify foreground objects from their background, leading to an effective object-based video coding (e.g., H.264/AVC). In addition, if the contour of the moving object can be extracted, further analysis (e.g., behavior analysis, video content retrieval, or object tracking and recognition) can therefore be performed based on the moving object in a video surveillance system. However, our system was designed assuming the camera is static, other techniques (e.g., video stabilization [18]) may be required before defining the object contour in real video scenes (e.g., video vibration induced by unwanted camera motion).

## References


1. Xiang, T., Gong, S.: Video behavior profiling for anomaly detection. IEEE Trans. Pattern Anal. Mach. Intell. 30, 893–908 (2008)
2. Gupta, A., Mittal, A., Davis, L.S.: Constraint integration for efficient multiview pose estimation with self-occlusions. IEEE Trans. Pattern Anal. Mach. Intell. 30, 493–506 (2008)
3. Sundaramoorthi, G., Yezzi, A., Mennucci, A.C.: Coarse-to-fine segmentation and tracking using sobolev active contours. IEEE Trans. Pattern Anal. Mach. Intell. 30, 851–864 (2008)
4. Zhao, T., Nevatia, R., Wu, B.: Segmentation and tracking of multiple humans in crowded environments. IEEE Trans. Pattern Anal. Mach. Intell. 30, 1198–1211 (2008)
5. Han, B., Comaniciu, D., Zhu, Y., Davis, L.S.: Sequential kernel density approximation and its application to real-time visual tracking. IEEE Trans. Pattern Anal. Mach. Intell. 30, 1186–1197 (2008)
6. Briassouli, A., Ahuja, N.: Extraction and Analysis of multiple periodic motions in video sequence. IEEE Trans. Pattern Anal. Mach. Intell. 29, 1244–1261 (2007)
7. Comaniciu, D., Meer, P.: Mean shift: A robust approach toward feature space analysis. IEEE Trans. Pattern Anal. Mach. Intell. 24, 603–619 (2002)
8. Shi, J., Malik, J.: Normalized cuts and image segmentation. IEEE Trans. Pattern Anal. Mach. Intell. 22, 888–905 (2000)
9. Xu, N., Ahuja, N.: Object contour tracking using graph cuts based active contours. In: IEEE Proceedings International Conference on Image Processing, vol. 3, pp. III-277–III-280 (2002)
10. Kass, M., Witkin, A., Terzopoulos, D.: Snakes: Active contour models. International Journal of Computer Vision 1, 321–331 (1988)
11. Stauffer, C., Grimson, W.: Adaptive background mixture models for real-time tracking. In: IEEE Computer Society Conference on Computer Vision and Pattern Recognition, vol. 2, p. 252 (1999)
12. Elgammal, A., Duraiswami, R., Hardwood, D., Davis, L.S.: Background and foreground modeling using nonparametric kernel density estimation for visual surveillance. IEEE Proceeding 90(7), 1151–1163 (2002)
13. Canny edge detection tutorial (2008), http://www.pages.drexel.edu/~weg22/can_tut.html
14. Gonzalez, R.C., Wood, R.E.: Digital Image Processing, 2nd edn. Prentice Hall, New Jersey (2002)
15. Dorigo, M., Maniezzo, V., Colorni, A.: The ant system: Optimazation by a colony of co-operating agents. IEEE Trans. Systems, Man, and Cybernetics 26, 29–41 (1996)

16. Wang, X.N., Feng, Y.J., Feng, Z.R.: Ant colony optimization for image segmentation. In: IEEE Proceeding International conference on Machine Learning and Cybernetics, vol. 9, pp. 5355–5360 (2005)
17. Ma, W.Y., Manjunath, B.S.: Edge flow: A framework of boundary detection and image segmentation. In: IEEE Proceedings. Computer Society Conference on Computer Vision and Pattern Recognition, pp. 744–749 (1997)
18. Litvin, A., Konrad, J., Karl, W.C.: Probabilistic video stabilization using kalman filtering and mosaicking. In: Proceedings of SPIE-IS&T Electronic Imaging, SPIE, vol. 5002, pp. 663–674 (2003)

Printing: Mercedes-Druck, Berlin
Binding: Stein+Lehmann, Berlin